YOUNG ADULT FICTION
CORE COLLECTION

CORE COLLECTION SERIES

**FORMERLY
STANDARD CATALOG SERIES**

SHAUNA GRIFFIN, MLIS, GENERAL EDITOR

**CHILDREN'S CORE COLLECTION
MIDDLE AND JUNIOR HIGH CORE COLLECTION
SENIOR HIGH CORE COLLECTION
PUBLIC LIBRARY CORE COLLECTION: NONFICTION
FICTION CORE COLLECTION
GRAPHIC NOVELS CORE COLLECTION**

YOUNG ADULT FICTION CORE COLLECTION

FOURTH EDITION

EDITED BY
KENDAL SPIRES
AND
JULIE CORSARO

H. W. Wilson
A Division of EBSCO Information Services, Inc.
Ipswich, Massachusetts
2021

GREY HOUSE PUBLISHING

ISBN 978-1-64265-743-2

The Dewey Decimal Classification is © 2003-2017 OCLC Online Computer Library Center, Inc. Used with Permission. DDC, Dewey, Dewey Decimal Classification and WebDewey are registered trademarks/service marks of OCLC Online Computer Library Center, Inc.

Young Adult Fiction Core Collection, Fourth Edition, published by Grey House Publishing, Inc., Amenia, NY, under exclusive license from EBSCO Information Services, Inc.

Publisher's Cataloging-In-Publication Data
(Prepared by The Donohue Group, Inc.)

Names: Spires, Kendal, editor. | Corsaro, Julie, editor.
Title: Young adult fiction core collection / edited by Kendal Spires and Julie Corsaro.
Other Titles: Core collection series.
Description: Fourth edition. | Ipswich, Massachusetts : H.W. Wilson, a division of EBSCO Information Services ; Amenia, NY : Grey House Publishing, 2021. | Includes bibliographical references and indexes.
Identifiers: ISBN 9781642657432
Subjects: LCSH: Young adult fiction—Bibliography. | Young adults—Books and reading—United States. | Best books.
Classification: LCC Z1037.A1 Y68 2021 | DDC 011.62/5—dc23

CONTENTS

PREFACE

YOUNG ADULT FICTION CORE COLLECTION is a curated list of classic and contemporary fiction for young adults. It may be used to develop a collection serving general young adult readers in any kind of library.

This Core Collection is derived from the MIDDLE AND JUNIOR HIGH CORE COLLECTION and the SENIOR HIGH CORE COLLECTION databases available from EBSCO Information Services. These databases have an additional two recommendation levels, Lexile measures, book reviews and articles, expanded metadata, and include nonfiction as well as fiction for the appropriate audiences. They are updated weekly. Contact your EBSCO or NoveList sales rep for a free trial, or visit https://www.ebscohost.com/novelist/our-products/core-collections for more information. EBSCO also invites feedback from Core Collections customers at novelist@ebsco.com.

What's in this Edition?

This edition continues to emphasize equity, diversity, and inclusion, representing and reflecting a varied community in which many voices can be heard. Significant weeding is undertaken to ensure that older, outdated books are removed in favor of more relevant recommendations.

This fourth print edition of YOUNG ADULT FICTION contains more than 2,500 novels appropriate for the age range and reading level; approximately 650 of those are *Essential* titles. Titles cover all fictional genres including science fiction, realistic fiction, mysteries, mythology, and more. Short story collections and graphic novels are not included.

Beginning with this volume, we are using more robust, complete, and consistently applied genre and subject headings across all titles. All entries for titles in series will also include the name of that series. Lists of Morris and Printz Award winners can be found at the back of the book.

As always, a star (★) at the start of an entry indicates that a book is an *Essential* title, our highest recommendation level. These titles are the essential books in a given category or on a given subject; while there are often a number of recommended titles, this designation helps users who want only a small selection. Non-starred entries represent *Recommended* titles, which provide a fuller list of recommended books.

History

Due to the growing popularity of young adult fiction—with readers at the middle, high school, and adult levels—and the ever-increasing availability of new titles, librarians need guidance now more than ever to select the highest quality works within limited budgets. YOUNG ADULT FICTION CORE COLLECTION gives librarians an easy-to-use resource to strengthen their YA fiction collections with the most highly recommended titles available, saving libraries time and money.

The first edition of YOUNG ADULT FICTION was envisioned in 2015 to provide librarians with a targeted resource to build up their YA fiction collections. It was and continues to be derived from the MIDDLE & JUNIOR HIGH CORE COLLECTION and the SENIOR HIGH CORE COLLECTION databases. This fourth edition, like the previous ones, was curated by librarians at EBSCO Information Services in partnership with Grey House Publishing to present users with a curated list of the *Essential* and *Recommended* titles in YA fiction. Our team of librarians comb through thousands of titles, selecting the highest quality works to provide librarians with thoughtful collection development recommendations for young adult fiction.

Scope

This Core Collection is intended to serve the needs of any library serving readers of YA fiction, at all age levels, regardless of library or patron type. Recommendations contained herein stand as a basic or "opening day" collection. The newer titles help in identifying areas in a collection that can be updated or strengthened, while the retention of materials from previous editions enables the librarian to make informed decisions about weeding a collection.

YOUNG ADULT FICTION excludes non-English-language materials (with the exception of bilingual titles); graphic novels; short story collections; and most works widely known as adult "classics." This was done as an effort to both save space and to concentrate on recommending titles that are perhaps less well-known. Additionally, extensive conversations with high school librarians indicated that the inclusion of classics in senior high libraries were based primarily on local curricula, not on recommendations from the Core Collections product line.

With its alphabetical-by-author-then title arrangement, complete bibliographic data, and descriptive and critical annotations, the YOUNG ADULT FICTION CORE COLLECTION provides useful information for teen librarians, public librarians, school media specialists, university librarians, and collection development directors.

Many books are listed with multiple ISBNs-those that offer only one are most frequently for a hardcover edition published in the United States, or published in Canada or the United Kingdom and distributed in the U.S. Out-of-print titles are retained in the belief that good books are not obsolete simply because they happen to go out of print.

Database

This Core Collection is derived from the SENIOR HIGH and MIDDLE & JUNIOR HIGH CORE COLLECTION databases available from EBSCO Information Services. Metadata for the titles in this volume is provided by the metadata librarians at NoveList, who manage and apply a controlled vocabulary that adapts as terms come in and out of style, or as events require new ones. There are additional, browsable access points, plus full-text book reviews and articles, full-color cover art, Lexile measures, and all of the *Supplemental* book recommendations and *Weeded* titles online. These databases are updated weekly. For more information or for a free trial, contact your EBSCO or NoveList sales rep, or visit https://www.ebscohost.com/novelist/our-products/core-collections. EBSCO also invites feedback from Core Collections customers at novelist@ebsco.com.

Preparation

Books included in Core Collections are selected by experienced librarians representing public library systems, school libraries, and academic libraries across the United States and Canada, as well as NoveList staff. These librarians also act as advisors on library policy, trends, and special projects. The names of participating librarians and their affiliations are listed in the Acknowledgements.

Core Collections Products

For recommendations for books for children and teens, librarians are encouraged to investigate the following databases and their associated print versions:

CHILDREN'S CORE COLLECTION
MIDDLE AND JUNIOR HIGH CORE COLLECTION
SENIOR HIGH CORE COLLECTION

For adult nonfiction for the general reader, try the database NONFICTION CORE COLLECTION or the associated print volume PUBLIC LIBRARY CORE COLLECTION: NONFICTION. For fiction, please use FICTION CORE COLLECTION, either as a database or the associated print version.

For Graphic Novels for all ages, try the GRAPHIC NOVELS CORE COLLECTION in print or database form, which includes both fiction and nonfiction recommendations.

PURPOSE AND ORGANIZATION

Purpose

CORE COLLECTIONS is designed to serve a number of purposes:

As an aid in purchasing. Core Collections is designed to assist in the selection and ordering of titles. Summaries and evaluative excerpts are provided for each title along with information regarding the publisher, ISBN, page count, and publication year. In evaluating the suitability of a work, each library will want to consider the needs of the unique patron base it serves.

As an aid in verification of information. For this purpose, bibliographical information is provided in the list of works. Entries also include recommended subject headings based on NoveList's proprietary subject vocabulary. Notes may describe editions available and other content; for the most up-to-date metadata, please consult the EBSCOhost database.

As an aid in curriculum or programming support. The classified approach, subject indexing, annotations, and evaluative excerpts are helpful in identifying materials appropriate for classroom support, for book discussions, and other programming.

As an aid in collection maintenance. Information about titles available on a subject facilitates decisions to rebind, replace, or discard items. If a book has been demoted to the Supplemental or Weeded recommendation levels and therefore no longer appears in the print abridgement of the database, that demotion is not intended as a sign that the book is no longer valuable or that it should necessarily be weeded from your library's collection.

As an aid in professional development or instruction. The Core Collection is useful in courses or professional training that deal with collection development and readers' advisory; it may also be used in course that deal with literature and book selection, especially in the creation of bibliographies and reading lists.

As an aid to readers' advisory. Every title in this Core Collection is a recommended work and can be given with confidence to a user who expresses a need based on topic, genre, etc. Readers' advisory and user service are further aided by series and awards information, by the descriptive summaries and evaluative excerpts from trusted review sources, and by the subject headings in the Title and Subject Index applied by professional metadata librarians at NoveList.

Organization

This Core Collection is organized into two parts: a List of Fictional Works and at Author, Title, and Subject Index. You will also find a list of Printz and Morris Award winners following the Index.

Part 1. List of Fictional Works

Part 1 lists works of fiction in alphabetical order by last name of the author or by title, if the title is the main entry.

Each listing consists of a bibliographical description. Entries include, where relevant, series names and publication history. Whenever possible, a summary and an evaluative excerpt from a quoted source are also included. The following is an example of a typical entry and a description of its components:

Chbosky, Stephen

★ The **perks** of being a wallflower. Stephen Chbosky. Pocket Books, 1999 213 p.

Grades: 9 10 11 12

1. High school students; 2. Teenage boys; 3. Teenagers—Sexuality; 4. Teenagers—Drug use; 5. Teenagers—Alcohol use; 6. Pennsylvania; 7. Epistolary novels; 8. Diary novels; 9. Coming-of-age stories; 10. Books for reluctant readers

9780671027346; 9781471100482, UK; 9781471180811, Paperback, UK; 9781471116148, print, UK; 9781847829702, large print, UK

YALSA Popular Paperbacks for Young Adults, 2014; YALSA Quick Picks for Reluctant Young Adult Readers, 2000; YALSA Best Books for Young Adults, 2000.

Charlie is shy, introspective, intelligent beyond his years yet socially awkward; he is a wallflower, caught between trying to live his life and trying to run from it. Charlie attempts to navigate his way through the uncharted territory of high school: the world of first dates and mix-tapes, family dramas and new friends. Standing on the fringes of life offers a unique perspective. But there comes a time to see what it looks like from the dance floor.

Grounded in a specific time (the 1991/92 academic year) and place (western Pennsylvania), Charlie, his friends, and family are palpably real... This report on his life will engage teen readers for years to come. —*School Library Journal*

Now a major motion picture.

The star at the start of the title indicates that this is an *Essential* title. The name of the author, Stephen Chbosky, is given in conformity with Library of Congress Authorities. The title of the book is The perks of being a wallflower. The book was published by Pocket Books in 1999.

The book has 213 pages. If it were part of a series, the series name would follow the page count. It is appropriate for readers in grades 9-12.

The numbered terms are subject headings and genres applied by NoveList metadata librarians.

ISBN (International Standard Book Numbers) are included to facilitate ordering; however, there will often be many editions and formats of a given title; due to space constraints these ISBNs are not all provided in the print edition. The Library of Congress control number is provided when available.

Next are the awards this title has won, as well as the international and national short lists and best lists the book has appeared on that are tracked by NoveList staff. These are followed by a brief summary and an evaluative excerpt from a critical reviewing source, in this case *School Library Journal.* Such summaries and excerpts are useful in evaluating books for selection and in determining which of several books on the same subject is best suited for the individual reader or purchasing library. Notes are also made to describe special features, such as publication history, film adaptations, or series order.

Part 2. Author, Title, and Subject Index

The Index is three separate alphabetical lists of all the books entered in the Core Collection. Each book is entered under author, title, and subject. The page number is the key to the location of the main entry for the book in the List of Works.

The following are examples of index entries for the book cited above:

Author   Chbosky, Stephen, 242
Title   The perks of being a wallflower, 242
Subject   **TEENAGE BOYS**
               Chbosky, Stephen. The perks of being a wallflower, 242

WAYS TO USE THE RECOMMENDATIONS
IN THIS CORE COLLECTION

As an aid in purchasing. The Core Collection is designed to assist in the selection and ordering of titles. Annotations are provided for each title along with information concerning the publisher, ISBN, price, and availability. In evaluating the suitability of a work each library will want to consider the special character of the school and/or community it serves.

As an aid to the reader's advisor. The work of the reader's advisor is furthered by the information about sequels and companion volumes and the descriptive and critical annotations in the List of Fictional Works, and by the subject access in the Index.

As an aid in veri.cation of information. For this purpose, full bibliographical data are provided in the List of Fictional Works. Entries also include recommended subject headings based upon *Sears List of Subject Headings*. Notes describe editions available, awards, publication history, and other titles in the series.

As an aid in curriculum support. Subject indexing, grade levels, and annotations are helpful in identifying materials appropriate for lesson planning and classroom use.

As an aid in collection maintenance. Information about titles available on a subject facilitates decisions to rebind, replace, or discard items. If a book has been deleted from the Core Collection in this edition because it is no longer in print, that deletion is not intended as a sign that the book is no longer valuable or that it should necessarily be weeded from the collection. "Weeded" titles since the last edition are still visible in the Core Collection databases as "Archival Materials."

As an instructional aid. The Core Collection is useful in courses that deal with literature and book selection for young adults.

The Core Collections are an essential resource to enhance and enrich library collections with the highest quality titles available.

ACKNOWLEDGMENTS

H.W. Wilson, NoveList, and EBSCO Information Services express special gratitude to the following librarians who both advised in editorial matters and assisted in the selection and weeding of titles for this Core Collection.

Stephen Ashley
Librarian
Carrboro, NC

Robin Brenner
Teen Librarian
Brookline Public Library
Brookline, MA

Heather Cover
Special Projects Librarian
Homewood Public Library
Homewood, AL

Marcela Peres
Director
Lewiston Public Library
Lewiston, ME

Jennie Stevens
Teen Librarian
Naperville Public Library
Naperville, IL

Sarah Bean Thompson
Youth Services Manager
Springfield-Green County
Springfield, MO

The editors would also like to thank NoveList Metadata Librarian Renee Young for her help in creating this collection, as well as Collection Development Coordinator Lisa Schimmer and Software Engineer Dwayne Nance.

YOUNG ADULT FICTION CORE COLLECTION

Fourth Edition

50 Cent

Playground. Razorbill, 2011 314 p.

Grades: 7 8 9 10

1. African American teenage boys; 2. Bullying and bullies; 3. Psychotherapy; 4. Overweight teenage boys; 5. Friendship; 6. Long Island, New York; 7. Realistic fiction; 8. African American fiction; 9. Books for reluctant readers

9781595144348

YALSA Quick Picks for Reluctant Young Adult Readers, 2012.

Readers who were ever confused about having a gay parent, or being overweight, or going through a parental breakup, or just wanting to fit in and be accepted by their peers, will relate to Butterball. 50 Cent's debut young adult novel is a quick read that will be great for discussions on a variety of important and timely topics. —*Voice of Youth Advocates*

Abawi, Atia

★ A **land** of permanent goodbyes. Atia Abawi. 2018 272 p.

Grades: 7 8 9 10 11 12

1. Refugees; 2. Bombings; 3. Muslims; 4. Terrorism; 5. War; 6. Syria; 7. Realistic fiction

9780399546839; 9780399546853; 9780399546846, ebook, US

LC 2017021847

Westchester Fiction Award, 2019.

After their home in Syria is bombed, Tareq, his father, and his younger sister seek refuge, first with extended family in Raqqa, a stronghold for the militant group, Daesh, and then abroad.

A heartbreaking, haunting, and necessary story that offers hope while laying bare the bleakness of the world Tareq leaves and the new one he seeks to join. —*Kirkus*

Abdel-Fattah, Randa

★ **Does** my head look big in this? Randa Abdel-Fattah. Orchard Books, 2007 368 p.

Grades: 7 8 9 10 11 12

1. Sixteen-year-old girls; 2. Teenage girls; 3. Teenage boys; 4. Muslims; 5. Identity (Psychology); 6. Melbourne, Victoria; 7. Australia; 8. Australian fiction; 9. Realistic fiction; 10. Teen chick lit

9780439919470

LC 2006029117

Australian Book Industry Awards, Book of the Year for Older Children, 2006; YALSA Popular Paperbacks for Young Adults, 2013.

Year Eleven at an exclusive prep school in the suburbs of Melbourne, Australia, would be tough enough, but it is further complicated for Amal when she decides to wear the hijab, the Muslim head scarf, full-time as a badge of her faith—without losing her identity or sense of style.

While the novel deals with a number of serious issues, it is extremely funny and entertaining. —*School Library Journal*

★ The **lines** we cross. Randa Abdel-Fattah. Scholastic Press, 2017 360 p.

Grades: 9 10 11 12

1. Refugees; 2. Muslim teenagers; 3. Teenage romance; 4. Private schools; 5. Schools; 6. Australia; 7. Realistic fiction; 8. Australian fiction; 9. Multiple perspectives

9781338118667; 9781743534977, Australia; 9781407173474, print, UK

Victorian Premier's Literary Awards, People's Choice Award, 2017; Victorian Premier's Literary Awards, Prize for Young Adult Fiction, 2017.

A story about the power of choosing tolerance by the award-winning author of Does My Head Look Big in This? finds basketball enthusiast Michael attending anti-immigration rallies with his parents until a friendship with a Muslim refugee newcomer from Afghanistan compels him to question his family's politics.

An engaging romance within a compelling exploration of the sharply opposing beliefs that tear people apart, and how those beliefs can be transformed through human relationships. —*Publishers Weekly*

Abrahams, Peter

Reality check. By Peter Abrahams. HarperTeen, 2009 330 p.

Grades: 7 8 9 10

1. Missing persons; 2. Teenage boy detectives; 3. High school football players; 4. Teenage boys; 5. Social classes; 6. Montana; 7. Vermont; 8. Mysteries

9780061227660

LC 2008022593

Edgar Allan Poe Award for Best Young Adult, 2010.

After a knee injury destroys sixteen-year-old Cody's college hopes, he drops out of high school and gets a job in his small Montana town, but when his ex-girlfriend disappears from her Vermont boarding school, Cody travels cross-country to join the search.

Abrahams writes a fine thriller that is pitched to attract everyone from reluctant readers to sports fans to romantic idealists. —*Voice of Youth Advocates*

Laura Geringer books.

Acevedo, Elizabeth

Clap when you land. Elizabeth Acevedo. HarperCollins, 2020 432 p.

Grades: 9 10 11 12

1. Half sisters; 2. Fathers — Death; 3. Family secrets; 4. Grief in teenage girls; 5. Airplane accidents; 6. New York City; 7. Dominican Republic; 8. Realistic fiction; 9. Novels in verse; 10. Multiple perspectives

9780062882769, hardback, US; 9781471409127, Paperback, UK

LC 2020933571

School Library Journal Best Books, 2020; Kirkus Prize for Young Readers' Literature finalist, 2020.

An evocative novel in verse follows the experiences of two grieving sisters who navigate the loss of their father and the impact of his death on their relationship.

The book is blunt about the financial disparity between the girls and its implications, but it's also tender as the two families, or what's left of them, come together in the Dominican Republic to bury the girls' father and, despite hurt and betrayal, find connections. —*Bulletin of the Center for Children's Books*

★ The **poet** X. Elizabeth Acevedo. HarperTeen, 2018 368 p.

Grades: 9 10 11 12

1. Teenage poets; 2. Poets; 3. Secrets; 4. Catholics; 5. Teenage girls; 6. Harlem, New York City; 7. Realistic fiction; 8. Novels in verse; 9. Coming-of-age stories; 10. Books for reluctant readers

9780062662804; 9780062662811

ALA Notable Children's Book, 2019; Amelia Bloomer List, 2019; Boston Globe-Horn Book Award for Fiction and Poetry, 2018; Carnegie Medal, 2019; Green Mountain Book Award (Vermont), 2020; Indies' Choice Book Awards, Young Adult, 2019; Los Angeles Times Book Prize for Young Adult Literature, 2018; Michael L. Printz Award, 2019; National Book Award for Young People's Literature, 2018; Pura Belpre Award for Narrative, 2019; School Library Journal Best Books, 2018; Walter Award, Teen, 2019; YALSA Best Fiction for Young Adults, 2019; YALSA Quick Picks for Reluctant Young Adult Readers, 2019; Golden Kite Honor Book for Fiction, 2019; Kirkus Prize for Young Readers' Literature finalist, 2018.

Xiomara Batista feels unheard and unable to hide in her Harlem neighborhood. Ever since her body grew into curves, she has learned to let her fists and her fierceness do the talking.

Themes as diverse as growing up first-generation American, Latinx culture, sizeism, music, burgeoning sexuality, and the power of the written and spoken word are all explored with nuance. Poignant and real, beautiful and intense, this story of a girl struggling to define herself is as powerful as Xiomara's name: 'one who is ready for war.' —*Kirkus*

★ **With** the fire on high. Elizabeth Acevedo. Harperteen, 2019 400 pages
Grades: 9 10 11 12
1. Teenage mothers; 2. Cooking; 3. Grandmother and granddaughter; 4. Teenage cooks; 5. High school students; 6. Philadelphia, Pennsylvania; 7. Spain; 8. First person narratives; 9. Realistic fiction; 10. Coming-of-age stories; 11. Books for reluctant readers
9780062662835; 9781760504922, Paperback, Australia
Notable Books for a Global Society, 2020; School Library Journal Best Books, 2019; YALSA Quick Picks for Reluctant Young Adult Readers, 2020; Golden Kite Honor Book for Fiction, 2020.

Navigating the challenges of finishing high school while caring for a daughter, talented cook Emoni Santiago struggles with a lack of time and money that complicate her dream of working in a professional kitchen.

Acevedo's second serving offers a much-needed nuanced exploration of teen parenting that belongs on all shelves. —*School Library Journal*

Aceves, Fred
The **closest** I've come. Fred Aceves. Harpercollins Childrens Books, 2017 256 p.
Grades: 9 10 11 12
1. Hispanic American teenagers; 2. Self-discovery in teenage boys; 3. Child-abuse victims; 4. Mothers and sons; 5. Abusive men; 6. Coming-of-age stories; 7. Realistic fiction
9780062488534
YALSA Best Fiction for Young Adults, 2018.

Marcos Rivas yearns for love, a working cell phone, and maybe a pair of sneakers that aren't falling apart. But more than anything, Marcos wants to get out of Maesta, his hood, away from his indifferent mom and her abusive boyfriend—which seems impossible.

It's a memorable, hard-hitting portrait of a teenager trying to shape his own destiny after being dealt a difficult hand. —*Publishers Weekly*

The **new** David Espinoza. Fred Aceves. 2020 336 p.
Grades: 9 10 11 12
1. Self-perception in teenage boys; 2. Body image; 3. Bodybuilding; 4. Teenage boys; 5. Body dysmorphic disorder; 6. Realistic fiction
9780062489883, (hardcover)
LC 2019026614
Obsessed with the idea that he is not muscular enough and tired of being bullied, David, age seventeen, begins using steroids, endangering his relationships with family and friends.

Toxic masculinity, which is cringingly part and parcel of the testosterone-filled world that Aceves portrays, is threaded through the narrative in a contextualized way. —*Kirkus*

Adams, Richard
Watership Down. Richard Adams. Macmillan, 1974 448 p. (Rabbit tales)
Grades: 6 7 8 9 10 11 12 Adult
1. Rabbits; 2. Survival; 3. Safety; 4. Peace; 5. Nature; 6. Fantasy fiction; 7. Books to movies; 8. Classics.
9780027000306; 9780684836058; 9780708980125; 9780141354965, print, UK; 9780141341934, UK; 9781780749662, print,UK; 9781780747316, ebook, UK; 9780141378947, Paperback, UK; 9781786070272, Hardback, UK; 97801411866
LC 73006044
California Young Reader Medal, Young Adult, 1977; Carnegie Medal, 1972.

In a constant struggle against oppression, a group of rabbits search for peaceful co-existence. Chronicles the adventures of a group of rabbits searching for a safe place to establish a new warren where they can live in peace.

Lapine glossary.

Adams, S. J.
Sparks: the epic, completely true blue, (almost) holy quest of Debbie. S.J. Adams. Flux, 2011 264 p.
Grades: 8 9 10 11 12
1. Lesbian teenagers; 2. Religion; 3. Secrets; 4. Best friends; 5. Crushes (Interpersonal relations); 6. Des Moines, Iowa; 7. Humorous stories; 8. Realistic fiction; 9. Coming-of-age stories
9780738726762
LC 2011022913
Rainbow List, 2013; YALSA Popular Paperbacks for Young Adults, 2014; Stonewall Children's & Young Adult Literature Honor Book, 2013.

A sixteen-year-old lesbian tries to get over a crush on her religious best friend by embarking on a "holy quest" with a couple of misfits who have invented a wacky, made-up faith called the Church of Blue.

Adams has an easy sense of humor...and Debbie and her offbeat cohorts are nuanced and authentic as they follow a circuitous path to greater self-awareness and self-reliance. —*Publishers Weekly*

Adeyemi, Tomi
★ **Children** of blood and bone. Tomi Adeyemi. Henry Holt & Co, 2018 448 p. (Legacy of Orisha, 1)
Grades: 9 10 11 12
1. Magic; 2. Imaginary kingdoms; 3. Princes; 4. Escapes; 5. Seventeen-year-old girls; 6. Afrofuturism and Afrofantasy; 7. Fantasy fiction; 8. African American fiction
9781250170972; 9781250294623; 9781529039245, Hardback, UK
ALA Notable Children's Book, 2019; Buckeye Teen Book Award (Ohio), Grades 9-12, 2019; Children's Africana Book Awards, Older Readers, 2019; Goodreads Choice Award, 2018; Nebula Awards: Andre Norton Award for YA Science Fiction and Fantasy, 2018; School Library Journal Best Books, 2018; Thumbs Up! Award (Michigan), 2019; Westchester Fiction Award, 2019; YALSA Best Fiction for Young Adults, 2019; Georgia Peach Honor Book for Teen Readers, 2019; Kirkus Prize for Young Readers' Literature finalist, 2018; William C. Morris Debut Award finalist, 2019.

Coming of age in a land where her magi mother was killed by the zealous king's guards along with other former wielders of magic, Zelie embarks on a journey alongside her brother and a fugitive princess to restore her people's magical abilities.

Well-drawn characters, an intense plot, and deft writing make this a strong story. That it is also a timely study on race, colorism, power, and injustice makes it great. —*Kirkus*

Children of virtue and vengeance. Tomi Adeyemi. Henry Holt & Co, 2019 448 p. (Legacy of Orisha, 2)
Grades: 9 10 11 12
1. Magic; 2. Imaginary kingdoms; 3. Resistance to government; 4. Teenage girls; 5. Inheritance and succession; 6. Afrofuturism and Afrofantasy; 7. Fantasy fiction; 8. Allegories.
9781250170996; 9781509899456, Paperback, UK; 9781529034790, Paperback, UK; 9781529034431, Hardback, UK
LC Bl2019000703
Loan Stars Favourites, 2019.

After Zelie and Amari bring magic back to the land of Orisha, the monarchy and military unite to keep control of Orisha, forcing Zelie to fight to secure Amari's right to the throne and protect the new maji from the monarchy's wrath.

While the first installment builds the narrating characters' foundations and familiarizes readers with the Yoruba orïshas, this follow-up gets into their psyches and unleashes the power of the deities and their respective maji as they fight for claim of Orïsha. —*Booklist*

Adlington, L. J.
★ The **diary** of Pelly D. By L.J. Adlington. Greenwillow Books, 2005 282 p.
Grades: 7 8 9 10
1. Construction workers; 2. Fourteen-year-old boys; 3. Fifteen-year-old girls; 4. Teenagers; 5. Diarists; 6. Dystopian fiction; 7. Science fiction; 8. First person narratives.
9780060766153; 9780060766160
LC 2004052258
YALSA Best Books for Young Adults, 2006; USBBY Outstanding International Book, 2006.

When Toni V, a construction worker on a futuristic colony, finds the diary of a teenage girl whose life has been turned upside-down by holocaust-like events, he begins to question his own beliefs.

Adlington has crafted an original and disturbing dystopian fantasy told in a smart and sympathetic teen voice. —*Booklist*

Agard, John
★ The **young** inferno. By John Agard; illustrated by Satoshi Kitamura. Frances Lincoln Children's, 2009 80 p.
Grades: 8 9 10 11 12
1. Hell; 2. Voyages and travels; 3. Sin; 4. Novels in verse; 5. Classics-inspired fiction; 6. Illustrated books.
9781845077693

The narrative poems in this short book are accessible and have important things to say about the state of the human race.... The hoodie-wearing protagonist...awakens in a strange and frightening forest. A dark man appears and introduces himself as the tale-teller Aesop: he is to be the teen's escort through Hell.... As the pair travels through the Circles of Hell, they see the sins of mankind.... The scribbled, heavy-lined black ink and watercolor illustrations convey exactly the right mood for a book about a modern-day expedition into Hell. This will be a great book to pair with a discussion about Dante's Inferno and/or poetic structure. —*School Library Journal*

Aguirre, Ann
Enclave. Ann Aguirre. Feiwel and Friends, 2011 272 p. (Razorland, 1)
Grades: 8 9 10
1. Hunters; 2. Zombies; 3. Dystopias; 4. Corruption; 5. Post-apocalypse; 6. Dystopian fiction; 7. Science fiction; 8. Books for reluctant readers
9780312650087
LC 2010031039
RITA Award for Best Young Adult Romance, 2012; YALSA Best Fiction for Young Adults, 2012; YALSA Quick Picks for Reluctant Young Adult Readers, 2012.

In the aftermath of war and plague, most of New York City's survivors have moved underground, establishing enclaves where they eke out an existence and hide from zombie-like Freaks. After 15-year-old Deuce, an enclave-dweller, earns the rank of Huntress, she is paired with a mysterious outsider named Fade...and the two of them discover a secret that could destroy their precarious society.

Aguirre has created a gritty and highly competent heroine, an equally deadly sidekick/love interest, and a fascinating if unpleasant civilization. —*Publishers Weekly*

Ahdieh, Renee
The **beautiful**. Renee Ahdieh. 2019 448 p. (Beautiful, 1)
Grades: 9 10 11 12
1. Seamstresses; 2. Vampires; 3. Murder investigation; 4. Supernatural; 5. Murder; 6. New Orleans, Louisiana; 7. 1870s; 8. 19th century; 9. Historical fantasy; 10. Fantasy mysteries; 11. Multiple perspectives.
9781524738174; 9781529368130, Hardback, UK; 9781529368154, Paperback, UK

In 19th century New Orleans, Celine, a dressmaker from Paris, becomes embroiled in a murder mystery that's connected to a glamorous supernatural cohort.

Vampires never stay dead for long, and best-selling Ahdieh's approach—part homage to the classics, part fresh-eyed revitalization—will intrigue all but the most committed skeptics. —*Booklist*

Flame in the mist. Renee Ahdieh. G.P. Putnam's Sons, an imprint of Penguin Random House LLC, 2017 392 p. (Flame in the mist, 1)
Grades: 7 8 9 10 11 12
1. Disguises; 2. Samurai; 3. Political intrigue; 4. Revenge; 5. Arranged marriage; 6. Japan; 7. Tokugawa period (1600-1868); 8. Historical fantasy; 9. Multiple perspectives; 10. Asian-influenced fantasy
9780399171635; 9780698185913, print, UK; 9781473664425, print, UK; 9781473657991, ebook

The daughter of a prominent samurai in feudal Japan is targeted by a dangerous gang of bandits who want to prevent her political marriage, a situation that compels her to disguise herself as a boy and infiltrate the gang's ranks in order to stop the individual behind the plot.

Ahdieh delivers an elaborate fantasy set in feudal Japan, where a resilient young woman defies class conventions and gender roles in a quest for vengeance and autonomy. —*Publishers Weekly*

The **rose** & the dagger. Renee Ahdieh. G.P. Putnam's Sons, an imprint of Penguin Group (USA), 2016 432 p. (Wrath & the dawn, 2)
Grades: 9 10 11 12
1. Curses; 2. Political intrigue; 3. Princes; 4. Love triangles; 5. Loyalty; 6. Fantasy fiction; 7. Fairy tale and folklore-inspired fiction; 8. Middle Eastern-influenced fantasy
9780399171628; 9781473657960, UK

Above all there is the shattering, triumphant catharsis of love—between man and woman, parent and child, teacher and student, sisters and cousins, friends old and new. In a story about stories, love is "the power to speak without words." Thrillingly full of feeling. —*Kirkus*

Smoke in the sun. Renee Ahdieh. G.P. Putnam's Sons, 2018 408 pages; (Flame in the mist, 2)
Grades: 7 8 9 10 11 12
1. Courts and courtiers; 2. Brothers and sisters; 3. Gender role; 4. Weddings; 5. Samurai; 6. Japan; 7. Tokugawa period (1600-1868); 8. Historical fantasy; 9. Asian-influenced fantasy
9781524738143, HRD, US; 9781524738150, ebook, US; 9781473664432, Hardback, Australia; 9781473658028, Paperback, UK

LC 2018007928

When Okami is captured, Mariko returns to Inako, where she pretends to be the dutiful bride-to-be to infiltrate the emperor's ranks.
Sequel to: *Flame in the mist.*

The **wrath** & the dawn. Renee Ahdieh. Putnam Juvenile, 2015 400 p. (Wrath & the dawn, 1)
Grades: 9 10 11 12
1. Revenge; 2. Curses; 3. Princes; 4. Love triangles; 5. Marriage; 6. Fantasy fiction; 7. Fairy tale and folklore-inspired fiction; 8. Middle Eastern-influenced fantasy
9780399171611; 9781473657939, UK

LC 2014046249

Westchester Fiction Award, 2016; YALSA Best Fiction for Young Adults, 2016.

In this reimagining of The Arabian Nights, Shahrzad plans to avenge the death of her dearest friend by volunteering to marry the murderous boy-king of Khorasan but discovers not all is as it seems within the palace.

It's not a completely faultless debut—the prose very occasionally turns purple, but that's a minor offense; the characters are redeemingly nuanced and well crafted. Even more impressive, Ahdieh is in complete control of her plot, tightly spooling out threads of the richly layered story just as surely as Shahrzad herself. The result is that the reader can't help but be absorbed by the time the crescendoing conclusion comes—and in true Arabian Nights fashion, it's a cliff-hanger. Like the caliph, we will just have to wait for the rest. —*Booklist*

Ahmadi, Arvin
★ **How** it all blew up. Arvin Ahmadi. Viking, 2020 304 p.
Grades: 9 10 11 12
1. Iranian Americans; 2. Closeted gay teenagers; 3. Outing (Sexual or gender identity); 4. Extortion; 5. Bullying and bullies; 6. Rome, Italy; 7. LGBTQIA fiction; 8. Realistic fiction; 9. Coming-of-age stories
9780593202876
School Library Journal Best Books, 2020.

Fleeing to Rome in the wake of coming out to his Muslim family, a failed relationship and blackmail, 18-year-old Amir Azadi embarks on a more authentic life with new friends and dates in the Sistine Chapel before an encounter with a U.S. Customs officer places his hard-won freedom at risk.

A funny and propulsive read, nuanced and full of heart. —*School Library Journal*

Ahmed, Samira
★ **Love,** hate & other filters. Samira Ahmed. 2018 288 p.
Grades: 8 9 10 11
1. Muslims; 2. East Indian Americans; 3. Terrorism; 4. Dating (Social customs); 5. Teenage boy/girl relations; 6. Chicago, Illinois; 7. Realistic fiction
9781616958473; 9781616959999; 9781616958480, ebook, US

LC 2017021616

School Library Journal Best Books, 2018.

Maya Aziz, seventeen, is caught between her India-born parents world of college and marrying a suitable Muslim boy and her dream world of film school and dating her classmate, Phil, when a terrorist attack changes her life forever.

A well-crafted plot with interesting revelations about living as a secular Muslim teen in today's climate. —*Kirkus*

Alban, Andrea
Anya's war. Andrea Alban. Feiwel and Friends, 2011 208 p.
Grades: 7 8 9 10
1. Jewish teenage girls; 2. Abandoned infants; 3. Immigration and emigration; 4. Immigrants, Russian; 5. Refugees; 6. Shanghai, China; 7. China; 8. 1930s; 9. Historical fiction.
9780312370930

LC 2010037089

Amelia Bloomer List, 2012.

In 1937, the privileged and relatively carefee life of a fourteen-year-old Jewish girl, whose family emigrated from Odessa, Ukraine, to Shanghai, China, comes to an end when she finds an abandoned baby, her hero, Amelia Earhart, goes missing, and war breaks out with Japan. Based on the author's family history.

Most moving are the scenes with the full cast of family characters, who are irritating, irritable, funny, surprising, mean, and prejudiced. Alban also explores the complexities of Anya's Jewish community.... An important addition to literature about WWII refugees. —*Booklist*

Albert, Melissa
★ The **Hazel** Wood. Melissa Albert. Flatiron Books, 2018 368 p. (Hazel Wood series, 1)
Grades: 10 11 12
1. Mothers and daughters; 2. Characters and characteristics in fairy tales; 3. Bad luck; 4. Kidnapping; 5. Rescues; 6. Fantasy fiction
9781250147905; 9781250147936
YALSA Best Fiction for Young Adults, 2019; RUSA Reading List Short List, 2019.

Seventeen-year-old Alice and her mother have spent most of Alice's life on the road, always a step ahead of the uncanny bad luck biting at their heels. But when Alice's grandmother, the reclusive author of a cult-classic book of pitch-dark fairy tales, dies alone on her estate, the Hazel Wood, Alice learns how bad her luck can really get: Her mother is stolen away—by a figure who claims to come from the Hinterland, the cruel supernatural world where her grandmother's stories are set.

Highly literary, occasionally surreal, and grounded by Alice's clipped, matter-of-fact voice, it's a dark story that readers will have trouble leaving behind. —*Booklist*

The **night** country: a Hazel Wood novel. Melissa Albert; illustrations by Jim Tierney. Flatiron Books, 2020 336 p. (Hazel Wood series, 2)
Grades: 10 11 12
1. Parallel universes; 2. Teenage girls; 3. Escapes; 4. Murder; 5. Doorways; 6. Fantasy fiction; 7. Urban fantasy; 8. Multiple perspectives
9781250246073, HRD, US; 9781250246080, ebook, US; 9780241370285, Paperback, UK

LC 2019044036

Finds Alice and her fellow survivors targeted by a dark adversary at the same time Finch seeks a way back home in a deteriorating Hinterland.

What Albert renders on the page is audacious: with resounding success, she keeps a firm grip on her characters and their stories, and her prose weaves a magic of its own, animating the ever-expanding fantastical premise through lyrical language, striking metaphor, and a mastery of tone that forces readers to feel the magic along with the underlying emotional stakes. —*Booklist*

Sequel to: *The Hazel Wood*.

Albertalli, Becky

Leah on the offbeat. By Becky Albertalli. 2018 368 p.
Grades: 9 10 11 12
1. Bisexual teenage girls; 2. High school seniors; 3. Identity (Psychology); 4. Quarreling; 5. Friendship; 6. LGBTQIA fiction; 7. Realistic fiction
9780062643803; 9780062643810
LC Bl2018052518

Goodreads Choice Award, 2018; YALSA Best Fiction for Young Adults, 2019.

With prom and graduation around the corner, senior Leah Burke struggles when her group of friends start fighting.

With complex characters, authentic dialogue, and messy-but- beautiful friendships, this sequel is more than capable of standing on its own. —*Kirkus*

★ **Simon** vs. the homo sapiens agenda. Becky Albertalli. Balzer + Bray, an imprint of HarperCollinsPublishers, 2018 303 p.
Grades: 9 10 11 12
1. Gay teenagers; 2. Extortion; 3. Secrets; 4. Coming out (Sexual or gender identity); 5. Gay teenagers; 6. LGBTQIA fiction; 7. Realistic fiction; 8. Coming-of-age stories.
9780062348678; 9780062839701; 9780141356099, print, Australia
LC 2014022536

Green Mountain Book Award (Vermont), 2017; Nutmeg Children's Book Award, High School category, 2018; Rainbow List, 2016; William C. Morris YA Debut Award, 2016; YALSA Best Fiction for Young Adults, 2016; YALSA Best Fiction for Young Adults: Top Ten, 2016; Georgia Peach Honor Book for Teen Readers, 2016.

Sixteen-year-old and not-so-openly gay Simon Spier prefers to save his drama for the school musical. But when an email falls into the wrong hands, his secret is at risk of being thrust into the spotlight. Now change-averse Simon has to find a way to step out of his comfort zone before he's pushed out—without alienating his friends, compromising himself, or fumbling a shot at happiness with the most confusing, adorable guy he's never met.

While Simon is focused on Blue, other characters go on journeys of their own, and the author is careful not only to wrap up Simon's story, but to draw attention to the stories the romance plot might overshadow in lesser hands. Funny, moving and emotionally wise. —*Kirkus*

Love, Simon

The **upside** of unrequited. Becky Albertalli. 2017 352 p.
Grades: 9 10 11 12
1. Crushes in teenage girls; 2. Lesbian teenagers; 3. First loves; 4. Children of LGBTQIA parents; 5. Body image; 6. Realistic fiction; 7. LGBTQIA fiction
9780062348708; 9780141356112, print, UK
LC 2016938957

YALSA Best Fiction for Young Adults, 2018; Rainbow List, 2018.

Avoiding relationships to protect her sensitive heart, plus-sized Molly supports her once-cynical twin, Cassie, when the latter has her own bout of lovesickness, a situation that is complicated by sibling dynamics and an unexpected romantic triangle.

Albertalli's keen ear for authentic teen voices will instantly make readers feel that they are a part of Cassie and Molly's world, filled with rich diversity.., love, support, and a little heartache. —*School Library Journal*

★ **What** if it's us. Becky Albertalli & Adam Silvera. HarperTeen, an imprint of HarperCollinsPublishers, 2018 384 p.
Grades: 9 10 11 12
1. Dating (Social customs); 2. Gay teenagers; 3. Self-discovery; 4. Summer; 5. High school students; 6. New York City; 7. Realistic fiction; 8. Parallel narratives
9780062795250; 9781471176395, Paperback, UK; 9780062795236
LC 2018013361

Great Lakes Great Books Award (Michigan), Grades 9-12, 2019; YALSA Best Fiction for Young Adults, 2019; Rhode Island Teen Honor Book, 2020.

Told in two voices, when Arthur, a summer intern from Georgia, and Ben, a native New Yorker, meet it seems like fate, but after three attempts at dating fail they wonder if the universe is pushing them together or apart.

In the coauthors' capable hands, Arthur and Ben are distinct, empathetic heroes: Broadway-loving Arthur, who has Ivy League aspirations, adapts to the ways his recent coming out changed his friendships, while Ben struggles in school but dreams of writing, and sometimes isn't sure how to connect with his Puerto Rican heritage when he passes as white. —*Booklist*

Yes no maybe so. Becky Albertalli & Aisha Saeed. Balzer + Bray, 2020 448 p.
Grades: 9 10 11 12
1. Political activists; 2. Jewish teenage boys; 3. Muslim teenagers; 4. Pakistani Americans; 5. Childhood friends; 6. Realistic fiction; 7. Multiple perspectives.
9780062937049; 9781471184666, Paperback, UK

Jamie Goldberg, who chokes when speaking to strangers, and Maya Rehman, who is having the worst Ramadan ever, are paired to knock on doors and ask for votes for the local state senate candidate.

With topical references to state and national issues—including hijab bans, bathroom bills, and the subtle politics of meme culture—this is a warm, beautiful story about relationships' beginnings, endings, and transitions; what it means to fight the good fight; and the transformative power of local activism. —*School Library Journal*

Aldredge, Betsy

Sasquatch, love, and other imaginary things. Betsy Aldredge and Carrie DuBois-Shaw. Merit Press, 2017 272 p.
Grades: 7 8 9 10
1. Reality television programs; 2. Competition; 3. Jewish teenage girls; 4. Social classes; 5. Sasquatch; 6. Realistic fiction; 7. First person narratives
9781507202807

Dragged around her whole life by her obsessed yeti-hunting parents, Samantha is humiliated when her parents participate in a reality show under the watch of a contemptuous prep-school crew, including a boy who scorns Samantha's humble Ohio roots.

Samantha's first-person narration is marked by her sarcastic, wry, and delightfully snarky humor. 'Squatching' doesn't get any funnier than this. —*Kirkus*

Alegria, Malin

Estrella's quinceanera. Malin Alegria. Simon & Schuster Books for Young Readers, 2006 272 p.
Grades: 7 8 9 10
1. Mexican Americans; 2. Mexican American women; 3. Mexican American teenage girls; 4. Fourteen-year-old girls; 5. Rich girls; 6. Realistic fiction.
9780689878091

LC 2005014540

Estrella's mother and aunt are planning a gaudy, traditional quinceanera for her, even though it is the last thing she wants.

Alegria writes about Mexican American culture, first love, family, and of moving between worlds with poignant, sharp-sighted humor and authentic dialogue. —*Booklist*

Alender, Katie
   The **dead** girls of Hysteria Hall. Katie Alender. Point, an imprint of Scholastic Inc, 2015 304 p.
Grades: 7 8 9 10 11 12
   1. Haunted houses; 2. Psychiatric hospitals; 3. Ghosts; 4. Families; 5. Secrets; 6. Horror; 7. Ghost stories; 8. Books for reluctant readers
9780545639996
                                        LC 2014046681
YALSA Quick Picks for Reluctant Young Adult Readers, 2016.
   Murdered by a spirit in her house, which was previously an insane asylum, sixteen-year-old Cordelia wanders the house, meeting other trapped ghosts and learning the houses dark secrets, searching for a way to save her family, and perhaps herself.

Alender creates a fascinating, eerie world that turns on a nicely original use of time and features constantly interesting characters. —*Kirkus*

Alexander, Jill
   ★ The **sweetheart** of Prosper County. Jill Alexander. Feiwel and Friends, 2009 224 p.
Grades: 7 8 9 10
   1. Teenage girls; 2. Self-confidence; 3. Mothers and daughters; 4. Fourteen-year-old girls; 5. Bullying and bullies; 6. Texas
9780312548568
                                        LC 2008034757
   In a small East Texas town largely ruled by prejudices and bullies, fourteen-year-old Austin sets out to win a ride in the next parade and, in the process, grows in her understanding of friendship and helps her widowed mother through her mourning.

This is a warm, humorous story.... A refreshing picture of teen angst, with realistic dialogue and memorable characters. —*School Library Journal*

Alexander, Kwame
   ★ **Booked**. Kwame Alexander. Houghton Mifflin Harcourt, 2016 320 p.
Grades: 5 6 7 8 9
   1. Children of divorced parents; 2. Boy soccer players; 3. Bullying and bullies; 4. Soccer; 5. Appendectomy; 6. Realistic fiction; 7. Novels in verse; 8. African American fiction.
9780544570986; 9781783444656, print, UK
ALA Notable Children's Book, 2017; Beehive Young Adult Book Award (Utah), 2018; Golden Archer Awards (Wisconsin): Middle/Jr. High, 2017; YALSA Best Fiction for Young Adults, 2017; YALSA Quick Picks for Reluctant Young Adult Readers, 2017.
   Twelve-year-old Nick loves soccer and hates books, but soon learns the power of words as he wrestles with problems at home, stands up to a bully, and tries to impress the girl of his dreams.

Alexander scores again with this sports-themed verse novel, a companion to his Newbery Medal-winning The Crossover.... Emotionally resonant and with a pace like a player on a breakaway. —*Publishers Weekly*

   ★ The **crossover**: a basketball novel. Kwame Alexander. Houghton Mifflin Harcourt, 2014 240 p. (Crossover (Kwame Alexander), 1)
Grades: 6 7 8 9 10

   1. Twin brothers; 2. Boy basketball players; 3. African Americans; 4. Coping; 5. Fathers and sons; 6. Sports fiction; 7. Realistic fiction; 8. Basketball stories; 9. Books for reluctant readers
9780544107717; 9780544935204; 9780358064732, paperback, US
ALA Notable Children's Book, 2015; Black-Eyed Susan Book Award (Maryland), Grades 6-9, 2016; Buckeye Children's Book Award (Ohio), Grades 6-8, 2016; Garden State Teen Book Award (New Jersey), Fiction (Grades 6-8), 2017; Indian Paintbrush Book Award (Wyoming), 2018; Iowa Teen Award, 2018; Kentucky Bluegrass Award for Grades 6-8, 2016; Lee Bennett Hopkins Poetry Award (Pennsylvania Center for the Book), 2015; Newbery Medal, 2015; Rebecca Caudill Young Reader's Book Award (Illinois), 2017; School Library Journal Best Books: Fiction, 2014; Sequoyah Book Awards (Oklahoma), Intermediate Books, 2017; Street Lit Book Award Medal: Emerging Classic, 2016; YALSA Best Fiction for Young Adults, 2015; YALSA Best Fiction for Young Adults: Top Ten, 2015; YALSA Quick Picks for Reluctant Young Adult Readers, 2015; YALSA Quick Picks for Reluctant Young Adult Readers: Top Ten, 2015; Coretta Scott King Honor Book for Authors, 2015.
   Fourteen-year-old twin basketball stars Josh and Jordan wrestle with highs and lows on and off the court as their father ignores his declining health.

Despite his immaturity, Josh is a likable, funny, and authentic character. Underscoring the sports and the fraternal tension is a portrait of a family that truly loves and supports one another. Alexander has crafted a story that vibrates with energy and heart and begs to be read aloud. —*School Library Journal*
   Prequel: *Rebound*.

   He said, she said. By Kwame Alexander. Harper, an imprint of HarperCollinsPublishers, 2013 256 p.
Grades: 9 10 11 12
   1. Protest movements; 2. High school football players; 3. African-American teenagers; 4. Teenage romance; 5. High schools; 6. Charleston, South Carolina; 7. Realistic fiction; 8. African American fiction; 9. Multiple perspectives
9780062118967
   Claudia Clarke—sharp, opinionated, and Harvard-bound—is the only girl who isn't impressed by quarterback Omar T-Diddy Smalls. Omar takes a bet that he can win Claudia over, and when his usual seduction tactics fail, he applies his social clout to Claudia's cause du jour. His burgeoning social awareness and transformation from carefree jock to true campus leader are satisfying and convincing. —*Horn Book Guide*

   Solo. Blink, 2017 458 p.
Grades: 7 8 9 10 11 12
   1. Family secrets; 2. Identity (Psychology); 3. Fathers and sons; 4. African American teenage boys; 5. Children of rock musicians; 6. Los Angeles, California; 7. Ghana; 8. Realistic fiction; 9. Novels in verse; 10. African American fiction
9780310761839
YALSA Quick Picks for Reluctant Young Adult Readers, 2018; Children's Africana Book Awards Honor Book, Older Readers, 2018.
   Seventeen-year-old Blade, who endeavors to resolve painful issues from his past to navigate the challenges of his former rockstar father's addictions, scathing tabloid rumors, and a protected secret that threatens his own identity.

A contemporary hero's journey, brilliantly told. —*Kirkus*

   Swing. Kwame Alexander with Mary Rand Hess. Blink, 2018 448 p.
Grades: 9 10 11 12
   1. Teenage artists; 2. African American teenage boys; 3. Creativity; 4. Best friends; 5. Prejudice; 6. Novels in verse; 7. Coming-of-age stories; 8. Realistic fiction; 9. Books for reluctant readers

9780310761914; 9780310761945; 9780310761938, Paperback, UK

LC 2018030417

YALSA Quick Picks for Reluctant Young Adult Readers, 2020.

Noah and his best friend Walt want to become cool, make the baseball team, and win over Sam, the girl Noah has loved for years. When Noah finds old love letters, Walt hatches a plan to woo Sam. But as Noah's love life and Walt's baseball career begin, the letters alter everything.—Provided by publisher.

This important and recommended contemporary YA will inspire young people to find their own voices and take a swing at life. A must-have. —*School Library Journal*

Alexie, Sherman

★ The **absolutely** true diary of a part-time Indian. By Sherman Alexie; art by Ellen Forney. Little, Brown, 2007 240 p.
Grades: 8 9 10
1. Native American teenage boys; 2. Identity (Psychology); 3. Teenage cartoonists; 4. Emotions in teenagers; 5. Spokane Indians; 6. Washington (State); 7. Diary novels; 8. Realistic fiction; 9. Coming-of-age stories.
9780316013680; 9781407450902, large print, UK

LC 2007022799

Boston Globe-Horn Book Award for Fiction and Poetry, 2008; California Young Reader Medal, Young Adult, 2010; Delaware Diamonds (book award), High School, 2009; Great Lakes Great Books Award (Michigan), Grades 9-12, 2009; National Book Award for Young People's Literature, 2007; New York Times Notable Children's Book, 2007; School Library Journal Best Books, 2007; YALSA Best Books for Young Adults, 2008; YALSA Popular Paperbacks for Young Adults, 2010.

Budding cartoonist Junior leaves his troubled school on the Spokane Indian Reservation to attend an all-white farm town school where the only other Indian is the school mascot.

The many characters, on and off the rez, with whom he has dealings are portrayed with compassion and verve.... Forney's simple pencil cartoons fit perfectly within the story and reflect the burgeoning artist within Junior. —*Booklist*

Ali, S. K.

Love from A to Z. S. K. Ali. Salaam Reads, 2019 352 p.
Grades: 8 9 10 11 12
1. Muslim teenagers; 2. Prejudice; 3. Grief; 4. Islamophobia; 5. Families; 6. Qatar; 7. Indiana; 8. Contemporary romances; 9. Epistolary novels; 10. Multiple perspectives; 11. Books for reluctant readers
9781534442726; 9781534442740

LC 2018056836

OLA Best Bets, 2019; School Library Journal Best Books, 2019; YALSA Quick Picks for Reluctant Young Adult Readers, 2020.

Eighteen-year-old Muslims Adam and Zayneb meet in Doha, Qatar, during spring break and fall in love as both struggle to find a way to live their own truths.

Heartfelt, honest, and featuring characters readers will fall in love with, this is sure to become a beloved book for many. —*School Library Journal*

★ **Saints** and misfits. S.K. Ali. Salaam Reads, 2017 352 p.
Grades: 9 10 11 12
1. Multiracial teenage girls; 2. Sexually abused teenage girls; 3. Muslims; 4. Identity (Psychology); 5. Muslim teenagers; 6. Realistic fiction; 7. Canadian fiction
9781481499248; 9781481499262, ebook, US

LC 2016041455

OLA Best Bets, 2017; YALSA Best Fiction for Young Adults, 2018; Amelia Bloomer List, 2018; William C. Morris Debut Award finalist, 2018; Middle East Book Award, Honorable Mention, 2017.

Fifteen-year-old Janna Yusuf, a Flannery O'Connor-obsessed book nerd and the daughter of the only divorced mother at their mosque, tries to make sense of the events that follow when her best friend's cousin—a holy star in the Muslim community—attempts to assault her at the end of sophomore year.

Ali pens a touching exposition of a girl's evolution from terrified victim to someone who knows she's worthy of support and is brave enough to get it. Set in a multicultural Muslim family, this book is long overdue, a delight for readers who will recognize the culture and essential for those unfamiliar with Muslim experiences. —*Booklist*

Almond, David

★ The **fire-eaters**. David Almond. Delacorte Press, 2004 224 p.
Grades: 7 8 9 10
1. Boys; 2. Sick fathers; 3. Hope; 4. Magicians; 5. Schools; 6. Great Britain
9780385731706; 9780385902076; 9780340773833, print, UK; 9781840329636, print, UK

LC 2003055709

ALA Notable Children's Book, 2005; Boston Globe-Horn Book Award for Fiction and Poetry, 2004; Nestle Children's Book Prize for Nine to Eleven Year Olds, 2003; Whitbread Book Award for Children's Book of the Year, 2003; YALSA Best Books for Young Adults, 2005.

In 1962 England, despite observing his father's illness and the suffering of the fire-eating Mr. McNulty, as well as enduring abuse at school and the stress of the Cuban Missile Crisis, Bobby Burns and his family and friends still find reasons to rejoice in their lives and to have hope for the future.

The author's trademark themes...are here in full, and resonate long after the last page is turned. —*School Library Journal*

Portions of this novel appeared in the magazines *Panurge, Stand,* and *A Kind of Heaven.*

Half a creature from the sea: a life in stories. David Almond; illustrated by Eleanor Taylor. Candlewick Press, 2015 222 p.
Grades: 7 8 9 10
1. England; 2. Magical realism; 3. Short stories; 4. Illustrated books
9780763678777; 9781406354348, Australia; 9781406365597, print, UK

Taylor's illustrations help add depth, as do the interstitial author's notes offering glimpses into each story's autobiographical roots and other inspirations. Likely to appeal to aspiring writers and fans of The Tightrope Walkers. —*Horn Book Guide*

★ **Kit's** wilderness. David Almond. Delacorte Press, 2000 229 p.
Grades: 6 7 8 9 10
1. Teenage boys; 2. Ghosts; 3. Coal mining towns; 4. Child ghosts; 5. Grandfather and child; 6. England; 7. Ghost stories.
9780385326650; 9780340727164, print, UK

LC 99034332

ALA Notable Children's Book, 2001; Booklist Editors' Choice: Books for Youth, 2000; Michael L. Printz Award, 2001; Nestle Children's Book Prize for Nine to Eleven Year Olds, 1999; School Library Journal Best Books, 2000; YALSA Best Books for Young Adults, 2001.

Thirteen-year-old Kit goes to live with his grandfather in the decaying coal mining town of Stoneygate, England, and finds both the old man and the town haunted by ghosts of the past.

The author explores the power of friendship and family, the importance of memory, and the role of magic in our lives. This is a highly satisfying literary experience. —*School Library Journal*

★ **Raven** summer. David Almond. Delacorte Press, 2009 198 p.
Grades: 7 8 9 10 11 12
1. Abandoned children; 2. Foster children; 3. Secrets; 4. War; 5. Fourteen-year-old boys; 6. England; 7. Northumberland, England; 8. Realistic fiction; 9. First person narratives.
9780385738064; 9780340881996, print, UK; 9781405663779, print, UK; 9780340881989, print, UK
USBBY Outstanding International Book, 2010.
The tension builds to a shocking and totally believable ending.... A haunting story, perfect for group discussion. —*Booklist*

★ **Skellig**. David Almond. Delacorte Press, 1998 182 p.
Grades: 5 6 7 8 9 10
1. Angels; 2. Sick children; 3. Moving, Household; 4. Strangers; 5. Families; 6. England; 7. Fantasy fiction; 8. Books to movies; 9. Classics.
9780385326537
LC 98-23121
Carnegie Medal, 1998; Booklist Editors' Choice: Books for Youth, 1999; Garden State Teen Book Award (New Jersey), Fiction (Grades 6-8), 2002; New York Times Notable Children's Book, 1999; Whitbread Book Award for Children's Book of the Year, 1998; School Library Journal Best Books, 1999; Michael L. Printz Honor Book, 2000.
Unhappy about his baby sister's illness and the chaos of moving into a dilapidated old house, Michael retreats to the garage and finds a mysterious stranger who is something like a bird and something like an angel.
The plot is beautifully paced and the characters are drawn with a graceful, careful hand.... A lovingly done, thought-provoking novel. —*School Library Journal*

★ A **song** for Ella Grey. David Almond. 2014 272 p.
Grades: 9 10 11 12
1. Love; 2. Friendship; 3. Loss (Psychology); 4. Death; 5. Mythology, Greek; 6. England; 7. Mythological fiction; 8. First person narratives; 9. Love stories
9780553533590; 9780553533606
LC 2014040181
YALSA Best Fiction for Young Adults, 2016.
Claire witnesses a love so dramatic it is as if Ella Grey has been captured and taken from her, but the loss of her best friend to the arms of Orpheus is nothing compared to the loss she feels when Ella is taken from the world in this modern take on the myth of Orpheus and Eurydice set in Northern England.
Patient readers will likely be transfixed by this rhapsodic modern retelling of a classic tragedy. —*Booklist*

The **true** tale of the monster Billy Dean, telt by hisself. David Almond. Candlewick Press, 2014 256 p.
Grades: 9 10 11 12
1. Healing; 2. Children of clergy; 3. Mediums; 4. Dystopias; 5. Thirteen-year-old boys; 6. Apocalyptic fiction
9780763663094
Booklist Editors' Choice: Books for Youth, 2014.
The opening scenes of this postapocalyptic, psychological novel describing the protagonist's confinement in a small, locked room is strongly reminiscent of Emma Donoghue's adult title *Room* (Little, Brown, 2010). ... The compelling story is told from Billy's point of view and with the language and phonetic spelling of a child whose development has been stunted by his lifelong imprisonment... This challenging title demands to

be read more than once, and even then it will leave questions unanswered. —*School Library Journal*

Alonzo, Sandra
★ **Riding** invisible: an adventure journal. . Disney Press, 2010 240 p.
Grades: 7 8 9 10
1. Runaway teenage boys; 2. Frustration in teenage boys; 3. Brothers and sisters of people with mental illnesses; 4. Teenage boys; 5. Fifteen-year-old boys; 6. Diary novels; 7. Adventure stories.
9781423118985
YALSA Best Fiction for Young Adults, 2011.
Written in a journal style and punctuated with sketches depicting Yancy's experiences, there's a lot here to engage readers. —*Horn Book Guide*

Alsaid, Adi
Come on in: 15 stories about immigration and finding home. Adi Alsaid. Harlequin Books 2020 256 p.
Grades: 9 10 11 12
1. Immigration and emigration; 2. Immigrants; 3. Home (Concept); 4. Teenagers; 5. Families; 6. Anthologies; 7. Short stories.
9781335146496
Moving and deeply relevant to our contemporary world. A must-have antidote to xenophobia and a much-needed, compassionate mirror for many. —*Kirkus*

Let's get lost. Adi Alsaid. Harlequin Books, 2014 304 p.
Grades: 9 10 11 12
1. Strangers; 2. Self-discovery in girls; 3. Voyages and travels; 4. Runaway teenage girls; 5. Teenage girl orphans; 6. Realistic fiction; 7. Multiple perspectives
9780373211241; 9781848453357, print, UK
With romantic interludes, witty banter, some exhilarating minor law breaking, occasional drinking, an empowering message, and satisfying conclusions for everyone involved, this will likely be a popular summer hit, especially for older teens about to embark on their own journeys of self-discovery. —*Booklist*

Never always sometimes. Adi Alsaid. Harlequin Teen, 2015 313 p.
Grades: 9 10 11 12
1. Best friends; 2. High school seniors; 3. Rules; 4. Teenage romance; 5. High schools; 6. Contemporary romances
9780373211548; 9781848453906, print, UK
There is a kernel of truth in every clich, and Alsaid cracks the teen-lit trope of friends becoming lovers wide open, exposing a beautiful truth inside. He also perfectly captures the golden glow of senioritis, a period when teens are bored and excited and wistful and nostalgic all at once. Everything is possible in this handful of weeks, including making up for squandered time. A good romance is hard to come by. This is a great one. —*Kirkus*

We didn't ask for this. Adi Alsaid. Inkyard Press, 2020 352 p.
Grades: 8 9 10 11 12
1. High school students; 2. Protests, demonstrations, vigils, etc; 3. Environmentalism; 4. Teenagers — Political activity; 5. High schools; 6. Realistic fiction; 7. Multiple perspectives.
9781335146762, HRD, Canada
Every year, lock-in night changes lives. This year, when a group of students stages an eco-protest, it might just change the world.
Central International School's annual lock-in is legendary. Bonds are made. Contests are fought. Stories are forged that will be passed down from student to student for years to come. This year's lock-in begins normally enough. But when a group of students led by Marisa Cuevas stage an ecoprotest and chain themselves to the doors, vowing to keep everyone

trapped inside until their list of demands is met, everything changes. Some students rally to their cause—but others are crushed to watch their own plans fall apart. Amira has trained all year to compete in the school decathlon her own way. Peejay wanted to honor his brother by throwing the greatest party CIS has ever seen. Kenji was ready to shine at his improv showcase. Omar hoped to spend some time with the boy he's been crushing on. Celeste, adrift in a new country, was hoping to connect with someone— anyone. And Marisa, once so certain of her goals, must now decide how far she'll go to attain them. Every year, lock-in night changes lives. This year, it might just change the world.

Through multiple points of view, Alsaid movingly examines characters' home lives, their dreams and crushes, and their changing attitudes, leaving readers to decide whether the protest is a success. —*Publishers Weekly*

Altebrando, Tara
The **Leaving**. Tara Altebrando. 2016 432 pages
Grades: 9 10 11 12
1. Memory; 2. Small towns; 3. Identity (Psychology); 4. Missing children; 5. Kidnapping; 6. Mysteries; 7. Multiple perspectives
9781619638037; 9781408877807, print, UK
LC 2015037730
Its engrossing, both as a thriller and a meditation on memory its limits, its loss, and the ways it deceives and constructs identity. —*Publishers Weekly*

Alvarez, Julia
★ **Before** we were free. Julia Alvarez. A. Knopf, 2002 167 p. : Illustration; Map
Grades: 7 8 9 10
1. Trujillo Molina, Rafael Leonidas, 1891-1961; 2. Political prisoners; 3. Separated friends, relatives, etc; 4. Attempted assassination; 5. Girls; 6. Families; 7. Dominican Republic; 8. 1960s; 9. Diary novels; 10. Historical fiction; 11. First person narratives
9780375815447; 9780375915444
LC 2001050520
Americas Book Award for Children's and Young Adult Literature, 2002; Pura Belpre Award for Narrative, 2004; ALA Notable Children's Book, 2003; YALSA Best Books for Young Adults, 2003.
In the Dominican Republic of 1960, Anita de la Torre is baffled when her "best-friend cousins" suddenly leave the country for the U.S. and the secret police show up at her extended family's compound. When her uncle disappears and her parents seem increasingly nervous and secretive, Anita begins keeping a diary to sort things out. This novel describes—from a young girl's perspective—the bloody rule of the dictator General Trujillo and the attempts to overthrow his regime.
This is a realistic and compelling account of a girl growing up too quickly while coming to terms with the cost of freedom. —*Horn Book Guide*
Companion to: *How the Garcia girls lost their accents*.

Amateau, Gigi
A **certain** strain of peculiar. Gigi Amateau. Candlewick Press, 2009 272 p.
Grades: 6 7 8 9
1. Runaway teenage girls; 2. Grandmother and granddaughter; 3. Self-acceptance in teenage girls; 4. Grandmothers; 5. Thirteen-year-old girls; 6. Alabama; 7. Realistic fiction; 8. First person narratives
9780763630096
LC 2008935295

Tired of the miserable life she lives, Mary Harold leaves her mother behind and moves back to Alabama and her grandmother, where she receives support and love and starts to gain confidence in herself and her abilities.
Mary Harold is a wonderfully complex and honest character.... [Her] narrative is heartfelt and poignant, and the message that being different is nothing to be ashamed of will resonate with readers. —*Voice of Youth Advocates*

Amato, Mary
Invisible lines. By Mary Amato; illustrations by Antonio Caparo. Egmont USA, 2009 336 p.
Grades: 6 7 8 9
1. Classism; 2. Poor teenage boys; 3. Self-fulfillment in teenage boys; 4. Social classes; 5. Self-fulfillment; 6. Washington, D.C.
9781606840436
LC 2009014639
Coming from a poor, single-parent family, seventh-grader Trevor must rely on his intelligence, artistic ability, quick wit, and soccer prowess to win friends at his new Washington, D.C. school, but popular and rich Xander seems determined to cause him trouble.
The author's subtle sense of humor is at work here.... This fresh story is enhanced by notes and drawings from Trevor's fungi notebook. With its short chapters, snappy dialogue, and scientific extras, the novel should find a wide audience. —*School Library Journal*

Anderson, Jodi Lynn
★ **Midnight** at the Electric. Jodi Lynn Anderson. HarperTeen, an imprint of HarperCollinsPublishers, 2017 257 p.
Grades: 9 10 11 12
1. Near future; 2. Teenage girl orphans; 3. Hispanic American teenage girls; 4. Resilience (Personal quality); 5. Letters; 6. Kansas; 7. Wichita, Kansas; 8. Science fiction; 9. Parallel narratives
9780062393548
YALSA Best Fiction for Young Adults, 2018.
In the months before her one-way trip to Mars, Adri Ortiz is sent to Wichita to live with a elderly cousin and finds herself fixating on where she came from and the stories of two women who lived more than a hundred years earlier.
Anderson deftly tackles love, friendship, and grief in this touching exploration of resilience and hope. —*School Library Journal*

★ **Tiger** Lily. Jodi Lynn Anderson. HarperTeen, 2012 256 p.
Grades: 8 9 10 11
1. Unrequited love; 2. Native American teenage girls; 3. Fairies; 4. Magic; 5. Peter Pan (Fictitious character); 6. Fantasy fiction; 7. Classics-inspired fiction.
9780062003256
LC 2011032659
School Library Journal Best Books, 2012; YALSA Best Fiction for Young Adults, 2013.
Fifteen-year-old Tiger Lily receives special protections from the spiritual forces of Neverland, but then she meets her tribe's most dangerous enemy—Peter Pan—and falls in love with him.

The **vanishing** season. Jodi Lynn Anderson. HarperTeen, 2014 247 p.
Grades: 7 8 9 10 11 12
1. Serial murders; 2. Crimes against teenage girls; 3. Self-discovery; 4. Friendship; 5. Murder; 6. Wisconsin; 7. Thrillers and suspense
9780062003270
For all the mythic overtones of Maggie and Paulines friendship, Anderson still manages to give her characters authentic teen voices, striking an uneasy balance between navet and worldliness. The pace might be slow

for some, but readers who like their romances tragic and dreamy should dive in. —*Booklist*

Anderson, Katie D.

Kiss & make up. Katie D. Anderson. Amazon Children's Publishing, 2012 307 pages

Grades: 7 8 9 10

1. Telepathy; 2. Kissing; 3. Supernatural; 4. Teenage boy/girl relations; 5. Guilt in teenage girls; 6. Paranormal romances; 7. Teen chick lit

9780761463160

Emerson Taylor can read the mind of any person whom she kisses on the lips, and when she decides to use this power to steal secrets and test answers, Emerson does not envision her plot being complicated by feelings of love.

Anderson, Laurie Halse

★ **Ashes**. Laurie Halse Anderson. Atheneum Books for Young Readers, 2016 304 p. (Seeds of America trilogy, 3)

Grades: 6 7 8 9 10

1. Teenage slaves; 2. Teenage soldiers; 3. Runaways; 4. Teenagers and war; 5. Slavery; 6. United States; 7. Revolutionary America (1775-1783); 8. 18th century; 9. Historical fiction; 10. First person narratives

9781416961468

School Library Journal Best Books, 2016; YALSA Best Fiction for Young Adults, 2017.

Its a gripping finish to an epic journey that speaks resoundingly to the human capacity to persevere. —*Publishers Weekly*

★ **Chains**. Laurie Halse Anderson. Simon & Schuster Books for Young Readers, 2008 304 p. (Seeds of America trilogy, 1)

Grades: 6 7 8 9 10

1. Slavery; 2. Teenage slaves; 3. Spies; 4. Loyalists (United States history); 5. Sisters; 6. New York City; 7. United States; 8. Revolutionary America (1775-1783); 9. 18th century; 10. Historical fiction; 11. First person narratives

9781416905851

LC 2007052139

Scott O'Dell Historical Fiction Award, 2009; YALSA Popular Paperbacks for Young Adults, 2014; ALA Notable Children's Book, 2009; Booklist Editors' Choice: Books for Youth, 2008; YALSA Best Books for Young Adults, 2009; National Book Award for Young People's Literature finalist, 2008.

After being sold to a cruel couple in New York City, a slave named Isabel spies for the rebels during the Revolutionary War.

This gripping novel offers readers a startlingly provocative view of the Revolutionary War.... [Anderson's] solidly researched exploration of British and Patriot treatment of slaves during a war for freedom is nuanced and evenhanded, presented in service of a fast-moving, emotionally involving plot. —*Publishers Weekly*

Sequel to: *Forge*.

★ **Fever,** 1793. Laurie Halse Anderson. Simon & Schuster Books for Young Readers, 2000 251 p.

Grades: 5 6 7 8 9

1. Survival; 2. Epidemics; 3. Yellow fever; 4. Teenage girls; 5. Sixteen-year-old girls; 6. Pennsylvania; 7. Philadelphia, Pennsylvania; 8. Early America (1784-1819); 9. 1790s; 10. Historical fiction; 11. Classics.

9780689838583

LC 32238

Great Lakes Great Books Award (Michigan), Grades 4-5, 2003; Rebecca Caudill Young Reader's Book Award (Illinois), 2003; YALSA Best Books for Young Adults, 2001.

In 1793 Philadelphia, sixteen-year-old Matilda Cook, separated from her sick mother, learns about perseverance and self-reliance when she is forced to cope with the horrors of a yellow fever epidemic.

A vivid work, rich with well-drawn and believable characters. Unexpected events pepper the top-flight novel that combines accurate historical detail with a spellbinding story line. —*Voice of Youth Advocates*

★ **Forge**. Laurie Halse Anderson. Atheneum Books for Young Readers, 2010 272 p. (Seeds of America trilogy, 2)

Grades: 6 7 8 9 10

1. Teenage slaves; 2. Teenage soldiers; 3. Teenagers and war; 4. Slavery; 5. African American teenage boys; 6. Pennsylvania; 7. Valley Forge, Pennsylvania; 8. Revolutionary America (1775-1783); 9. 18th century; 10. Historical fiction; 11. First person narratives

9781416961444

LC 2010015971

YALSA Best Fiction for Young Adults, 2011.

Separated from his friend Isabel after their daring escape from slavery, fifteen-year-old Curzon serves as a free man in the Continental Army at Valley Forge until he and Isabel are thrown together again, as slaves once more.

Weaving a huge amount of historical detail seamlessly into the story, Anderson creates a vivid setting, believable characters both good and despicable and a clear portrayal of the moral ambiguity of the Revolutionary age. Not only can this sequel stand alone, for many readers it will be one of the best novels they have ever read. —*Kirkus*

Sequel to: *Chains*.

★ The **impossible** knife of memory. Laurie Halse Anderson. 2014 40 pages

Grades: 9 10 11 12

1. Children of military personnel; 2. Fathers and daughters; 3. Post-traumatic stress disorder; 4. Family problems; 5. Single-parent families; 6. New York (State); 7. Realistic fiction; 8. Multiple perspectives

9780670012091; 9781407147666, print, UK; 9781922182227, print, Australia

LC 2013031267

Booklist Editors' Choice: Books for Youth, 2014; School Library Journal Best Books: Fiction, 2014; YALSA Best Fiction for Young Adults, 2015.

Hayley Kincaid and her father move back to their hometown to try a "normal" life, but the horrors he saw in the war threaten to destroy their lives.

With powerful themes of loyalty and forgiveness, this tightly woven story is a forthright examination of the realities of war and its aftermath on soldiers and their families. —*School Library Journal*

★ **Speak**. Laurie Halse Anderson. Farrar Straus Giroux, 1999 197 p.

Grades: 7 8 9 10

1. Misfits (Persons); 2. High school students; 3. Teenage rape victims; 4. Teenage girls; 5. Emotional problems; 6. Realistic fiction; 7. Books to movies; 8. Classics; 9. Books for reluctant readers

9780374371524

Booklist Editors' Choice: Books for Youth, 1999; Garden State Teen Book Award (New Jersey), Fiction (Grades 9-12), 2002; Carolyn W. Field Award (Pennsylvania), 2000; Golden Kite Award for Fiction, 1999; Heartland Award, 2001; Kentucky Bluegrass Award for Grades 9-12, 2001; School Library Journal Best Books, 1999; Sequoyah Book Awards (Oklahoma), Young Adult Books, 2002; South Carolina Book Award, Young Adult Books, 2002; YALSA Best Books for

Young Adults, 2000; YALSA Popular Paperbacks for Young Adults, 2015; YALSA Quick Picks for Reluctant Young Adult Readers, 2000; Michael L. Printz Honor Book, 2000; National Book Award for Young People's Literature finalist, 1999.

A traumatic event in the summer has a devastating effect on Melinda's freshman year of high school.

The novel is keenly aware of the corrosive details of outsiderhood and the gap between home and daily life at high school; kids whose exclusion may have less concrete cause than Melinda's will nonetheless find the picture recognizable. This is a gripping account of personal wounding and recovery. —*Bulletin of the Center for Children's Books*

Twisted. Laurie Halse Anderson. Viking, 2007 256 p.
Grades: 9 10 11 12
1. Seventeen-year-old boys; 2. Popularity; 3. Family problems; 4. High schools; 5. Teenage boy/girl relations; 6. Ohio; 7. Realistic fiction; 8. Coming-of-age stories; 9. Books for reluctant readers
9780670061013; 9781407138602, print, UK
LC 2006031297
Eliot Rosewater Indiana High School Book Award (Rosie Award), 2009; YALSA Popular Paperbacks for Young Adults, 2012; YALSA Quick Picks for Reluctant Young Adult Readers, 2008; YALSA Best Books for Young Adults, 2008.

After finally getting noticed by someone other than school bullies and his ever-angry father, seventeen-year-old Tyler enjoys his tough new reputation and the attentions of a popular girl, but when life starts to go bad again, he must choose between transforming himself or giving in to his destructive thoughts.

This is a gripping exploration of what it takes to grow up, really grow up, against the wishes of people and circumstances conspiring to keep you the victim they need you to be. —*Bulletin of the Center for Children's Books*

★ **Wintergirls**. By Laurie Halse Anderson. Viking, 2009 288 p.
Grades: 8 9 10 11 12
1. Anorexia nervosa; 2. Best friends — Death; 3. Eating disorders; 4. Teenage girls with eating disorders; 5. Self-harm; 6. Realistic fiction; 7. First person narratives; 8. Books for reluctant readers
9780670011100; 9781407171067, print, UK; 9781407117485, print, UK
LC 2008037452
YALSA Popular Paperbacks for Young Adults, 2016; Amelia Bloomer List, 2010; YALSA Quick Picks for Reluctant Young Adult Readers, 2010; Booklist Editors' Choice: Books for Youth, 2009; YALSA Best Books for Young Adults, 2010.

Eighteen-year-old Lia comes to terms with her best friend's death from anorexia as she struggles with the same disorder.

As events play out, Lia's guilt, her need to be thin, and her fight for acceptance unravel in an almost poetic stream of consciousness in this startlingly crisp and pitch-perfect first-person narrative. —*School Library Journal*

Anderson, M. T.

★ The **astonishing** life of Octavian Nothing, traitor to the nation: the pox party. Taken from accounts by [Octavius Nothing's] own hand and other sundry sources; collected by Mr. M.T. Anderson of Boston. Candlewick Press, 2006 368 p. (Astonishing life of Octavian Nothing, traitor to the nation, 1)
Grades: 9 10 11 12
1. African American boys; 2. Human experimentation in medicine; 3. Slavery; 4. Freedom; 5. Octavian (Fictitious character); 6. Massachusetts; 7. United States; 8. Revolutionary America (1775-1783); 9. Historical fiction; 10. Diary novels; 11. Multiple perspectives

9780763624026
LC 2006043170
Boston Globe-Horn Book Award for Fiction and Poetry, 2007; National Book Award for Young People's Literature, 2006; New York Times Notable Children's Book, 2006; Booklist Editors' Choice: Books for Youth, 2006; YALSA Best Books for Young Adults, 2007; School Library Journal Best Books, 2006; Michael L. Printz Honor Book, 2007.

At the dawn of the Revolutionary War, young Octavian is raised in highly unusual circumstances at the Novanglian College of Lucidity. Though the scholars give him a first-rate education, they also monitor him closely?too closely. As he grows older, Octavian learns the horrifying truth of his situation, and that truth leads him to question his understanding of himself and the Revolution: if the Patriots can fight for their freedom, why can't he fight for his?

Teens looking for a challenge will find plenty to sink into here. The questions raised about race and freedom are well developed and leave a different perspective on the Revolutionary War than most novels. —*Voice of Youth Advocates*

★ The **astonishing** life of Octavian Nothing, traitor to the nation, volume II: the kingdom on the waves. M.T. Anderson. Candlewick Press, 2008 592 p. (Astonishing life of Octavian Nothing, traitor to the nation, 2)
Grades: 9 10 11 12
1. Escapes; 2. African American teenage boys; 3. Teenage slaves; 4. Loyalists (United States history); 5. African American boys; 6. Massachusetts; 7. Boston, Massachusetts; 8. Revolutionary America (1775-1783); 9. Diary novels; 10. Historical fiction; 11. First person narratives.
9780763629502, HRD, US
Booklist Editors' Choice: Books for Youth, 2008; New York Times Notable Children's Book, 2008; YALSA Best Books for Young Adults, 2009; Michael L. Printz Honor Book, 2009.

When he and his tutor escape to British-occupied Boston, Octavian learns of Lord Dunmore's proclamation offering freedom to slaves who join the counterrevolutionary forces.

Burger Wuss. M.T. Anderson. Candlewick Press, 1999 192 p.
Grades: 7 8 9 10 11 12
1. Fast food restaurants, chains, etc; 2. Self-acceptance in teenage boys; 3. Bullying and bullies; 4. Teenage boys; 5. Conformity; 6. Humorous stories; 7. Realistic fiction.
9780763606800
LC 99014257
YALSA Popular Paperbacks for Young Adults, 2011.

Hoping to lose his loser image, Anthony plans revenge on a bully which results in a war between two competing fast food restaurants, Burger Queen and O'Dermott's.

★ **Feed**. M.T. Anderson. Candlewick Press, 2002 237 p.
Grades: 8 9 10 11 12
1. Computers and civilization; 2. Consumerism; 3. Environmental degradation; 4. Consumers; 5. Teenagers; 6. Science fiction; 7. Dystopian fiction.
9780763617264; 9780744590852, print, UK
LC 2002023738
Booklist Editors' Choice: Books for Youth, 2002; Golden Duck Awards: Hal Clement Award for Young Adult; Los Angeles Times Book Prize for Young Adult Fiction, 2002; New York Times Notable Children's Book, 2002; YALSA Best Books for Young Adults, 2003; YALSA Popular Paperbacks for Young Adults, 2010; National Book Award for Young People's Literature finalist, 2002.

In a future where most people have computer implants in their heads to control their environment, a boy meets an unusual girl who is in serious trouble.

An ingenious satire of corporate America and our present-day value system. —*Horn Book Guide*

★ **Landscape** with invisible hand. M.T. Anderson. Candlewick Press, 2017 160 p.
Grades: 9 10 11 12
1. Poverty; 2. Aliens; 3. Teenage artists; 4. Near future; 5. Television programs; 6. Science fiction.
9780763687892
Booklist Editors' Choice: Books for Youth, 2017; School Library Journal Best Books, 2017; YALSA Best Fiction for Young Adults, 2018.

Anderson takes issues of colonialism, ethnocentrism, inequality, and poverty and explodes them on a global, even galactic, scale. A remarkable exploration of economic and power structures in which virtually all of humanity winds up the losers. —*Publishers Weekly*

Anderson, Natalie C.

★ **City** of saints & thieves. Natalie C. Anderson. G.P. Putnam's Sons, 2017 432 p.
Grades: 7 8 9 10
1. Refugees; 2. Revenge; 3. Gangs; 4. Thieves; 5. Sisters; 6. Congo (Democratic Republic); 7. Kenya; 8. Thrillers and suspense
9780399547584; 9781786072290, print, UK; 9781786072306, ebook
YALSA Best Fiction for Young Adults, 2018.

Sixteen-year-old Tina and two friends leave Kenya and slip into the Congo, from where she and her mother fled years before, seeking revenge for her mother's murder but uncovering startling secrets.

The novel is peppered with Swahili words and phrases, and Anderson makes an effort to paint a picture of the country. A story full of twists and turns, proving nothing is ever as black and white as it may seem. —*Kirkus*

Andrews, Jesse

Me and Earl and the dying girl. By Jesse Andrews. Amulet Books, 2012 288 p.
Grades: 8 9 10
1. Jewish teenagers; 2. Teenage girls with leukemia; 3. Teenage filmmakers; 4. Alienation (Social psychology); 5. Leukemia; 6. Pittsburgh, Pennsylvania; 7. Pennsylvania; 8. Books to movies; 9. Realistic fiction; 10. Books for reluctant readers
9781419701764; 9781760290443, print, UK
LC 2011031796
Westchester Fiction Award, 2013; YALSA Best Fiction for Young Adults, 2013; YALSA Popular Paperbacks for Young Adults, 2014; YALSA Quick Picks for Reluctant Young Adult Readers, 2013.

Seventeen-year-old Greg has managed to become part of every social group at his Pittsburgh high school without having any friends, but his life changes when his mother forces him to befriend Rachel, a girl he once knew in Hebrew school who has leukemia.

Munmun. By Jesse Andrews. 2018 416 p.
Grades: 7 8 9 10 11 12
1. Size; 2. Social classes; 3. Dystopias; 4. Wealth; 5. Money; 6. Science fiction
9781419728716; 9781525275142, Paperback, Australia; 9781419734786; 9781911630128, Paperback, UK
LC 2017043773
In a society where a person's size is directly proportional to his or her wealth, littlepoor Warner, thirteen, and Prayer, fifteen, struggle to improve their lot in a world built against them.

Brilliant, savage, hilarious, a riveting journey through a harsh world that mirrors our own. —*Kirkus*

Anstey, Cindy

Carols and chaos. Cindy Anstey. Swoon Reads, 2018 328 pages;
Grades: 7 8 9 10
1. Household employees; 2. Counterfeits and counterfeiting; 3. Flirtation; 4. Christmas; 5. Romantic love; 6. Great Britain; 7. Kent, England; 8. 1810s; 9. Holiday romances; 10. Historical romances
9781250174871; 9781250174864, ebook, US
LC 2018003012
Kate Darby, a lady's maid, and Matt Harlow, a valet, get involved in a devious counterfeiting scheme at Christmas time, 1817, as they try to stave off their feelings for each other.
Sequel to: *Suitors and sabotage.*

Anthony, Jessica

Chopsticks. Jessica Anthony and Rodrigo Corral. Penguin/Razorbill, 2012 304 p.
Grades: 9 10 11 12
1. Missing persons; 2. Teenagers with mental illnesses; 3. Teenage prodigies; 4. Teenage pianists; 5. Teenage romance; 6. Mysteries; 7. Illustrated books.
9781595144355
YALSA Popular Paperbacks for Young Adults, 2013.

In a love story told in photographs and drawings, Glory, a brilliant piano prodigy, is drawn to Frank, an artistic new boy, and the farther she falls, the deeper she spirals into madness until the only song she is able to play is "Chopsticks."

Antieau, Kim

Ruby's imagine. Written by Kim Antieau. Houghton Mifflin Co, 2008 201 p;
Grades: 6 7 8 9
1. Hurricane Katrina, 2005; 2. Grandmother and granddaughter; 3. Memories; 4. African American girls; 5. Secrets; 6. New Orleans, Louisiana; 7. Coming-of-age stories; 8. Realistic fiction.
9780618997671
LC 2007047736
Tells the story of Hurricane Katrina from the point of view of Ruby, an unusually intuitive girl who lives with her grandmother in New Orleans but has powerful memories of an earlier life in the swamps.

Antieau offers a complex, personal account of Katrina and its aftermath.... Ruby's atmospheric narrative is as dense and pungent as the bayou. —*Booklist*

Arbuthnott, Gill

The **Keepers'** tattoo. Gill Arbuthnott. Chicken House, 2010 425 p.
Grades: 6 7 8 9
1. Twin brothers and sisters; 2. Tattooing; 3. Courage in teenage girls; 4. Despotism in men; 5. Despotism; 6. Fantasy fiction.
9780545171663
LC 2009026327
Months before her fifteenth birthday, Nyssa learns that she is a special member of a legendary clan, the Keepers of Knowledge, as she and her uncle try to escape from Alaric, the White Wolf, who wants to use lines tattooed on her to destroy the rest of her people.

Arbuthnott writes with restraint and thoughtfulness, never condescending to her readers. Nyssa is a convincing mixture of ignorance, courage, and resourcefulness. —*Publishers Weekly*

Archer, E.
    Geek: fantasy novel. E. Archer. Scholastic Press, 2011 110 p.
Grades: 7 8 9 10
    1. Geeks (Computer enthusiasts); 2. Wishing and wishes; 3. Fairy
godmothers; 4. Americans in Great Britain; 5. Summer; 6. Fantasy
fiction.
9780545160407
    Ralph Stevens, a geek through-and-through, travels to England to
spend a summer with his cousins and set up their family's wireless network. When his strange aunt Chessie unexpectedly visits, Ralph learns
why his parents have never allowed him to make wishes: if he performs a
fantasy quest, then Chessie can make his wish come true. As the novel's
constantly interfering narrator relates, Ralph and his cousins soon set off
on some highly unusual adventures, where they encounter everything
from evil queens and oppressed fairies to killer bunny rabbits and
homicidal unicorns.
    This is a stunning, often befuddling, and wildly amusing novel that
will likely confound and enchant sci-fi and fantasy fans alike. —*Bulletin
of the Center for Children's Books*

Arcos, Carrie
    ★ **Out** of reach. Carrie Arcos. Simon Pulse, 2012 250 p;
Grades: 9 10 11 12
    1. Drug addicts; 2. Runaways; 3. Brothers and sisters; 4.
Methamphetamine; 5. Drug abuse; 6. Southern California; 7. Realistic
fiction; 8. First person narratives.
9781442440531
                                                 LC 2011044501
National Book Award for Young People's Literature finalist, 2012.
    Accompanied by her brother's friend, Tyler, sixteen-year-old Rachel
ventures through San Diego and nearby areas seeking her brother, eighteen-year-old Micah, a methamphetamine addict who ran away from
home.

    There will come a time. Carrie Arcos. Simon Pulse, 2014 315 pages;
Grades: 9 10 11 12
    1. Grief; 2. Twin brothers and sisters; 3. Filipino Americans; 4. Sisters
— Death; 5. Families; 6. Los Angeles, California; 7. Realistic fiction;
8. First person narratives
9781442495852
                                               LC 2014002771
    Overwhelmed by grief and guilt after his twin sister Grace's acciden-
tal death, seventeen-year-old Mark Santos is persuaded by her best friend
to complete the "bucket list" from Grace's journal.
    This nuanced story presents a close study on how different people re-
act to loss while posing many thorny questions about relationships.
—*Booklist*

Armistead, Cal
    Being Henry David. By Cal Armistead. Albert Whitman, 2013 304 p.
Grades: 8 9 10 11 12
    1. Thoreau, Henry David, 1817-1862; 2. Teenage boys with amnesia;
3. Redemption; 4. Identity (Psychology); 5. Amnesia; 6. Guilt; 7.
Concord, Massachusetts; 8. New York City; 9. Realistic fiction; 10.
First person narratives.
9780807506158
                                               LC 2012017377
    Seventeen-year-old "Hank," who can't remember his identity, finds
himself in Penn Station with a copy of Thoreau's *Walden* as his only possession and must figure out where he's from and why he ran away.

Armstrong, Kelley
    Aftermath. Kelley Armstrong. Random House Childrens Books,
2018 384 p.
Grades: 7 8 9 10
    1. Murder; 2. School shootings; 3. Families of murderers; 4. Secrets;
5. Muslims; 6. Mysteries; 7. First person narratives; 8. Multiple
perspectives.
9780399550362; 9780385686457, print, Canada
Willow Awards, Snow Willow category, 2019.
    In the aftermath of a school shooting, best friends Skye and Jesse un-
cover evidence that could clear Skye's brother's name, but someone wants
the truth to stay buried.

    The **summoning**. Kelley Armstrong. HarperCollins Publishers, 2008
400 p. (Darkest powers, 1)
Grades: 7 8 9 10
    1. Children with emotional illnesses; 2. Magic (Occultism); 3. Ghosts;
4. Puberty; 5. Supernatural; 6. Ghost stories; 7. Horror; 8. First person
narratives.
9780061662720; 9780385667494
                                               LC 2008014221
Stellar Awards (British Columbia), 2011; OLA Best Bets, 2008.
    When Chloe Saunders sees a terrifying and grotesque ghost she has a
breakdown and is sent to Lyle House, a group home. But soon bizarre situations start occurring at the house, not only to her, but also to the other residents.
    Suspenseful, well-written, and engaging, this page- turning...[novel]
will be a hit. —*Voice of Youth Advocates*

Armstrong, William H.
    ★ **Sounder**. Illustrations by James Barkley. Harper, 1969 116 p.
Grades: 5 6 7 8
    1. Dogs; 2. African American sharecroppers; 3. African American
families; 4. Depressions; 5. Poor families; 6. Coming-of-age stories;
7. Books to movies; 8. Classics.
9780060201432
                                               LC 70085030
Mark Twain Award (Missouri), 1972; Nene Award (Hawaii), 1973;
Newbery Medal, 1970.
    Angry and humiliated when his sharecropper father is jailed for steal-
ing food for his family, a young black boy grows in courage and understanding by learning to read and with the help of his devoted dog Sounder.
    Set in the South in the era of sharecropping and segregation, this suc-
cinctly told tale poignantly describes the courage of a father who steals a
ham in order to feed his undernourished family; the determination of the
eldest son, who searches for his father despite the apathy of prison authorities; and the devotion of a coon dog named Sounder. —*Fiction for Youth,
3rd edition*

Arnold, David
    ★ **Mosquitoland**. David Arnold. 2015 352 pages
Grades: 9 10 11 12
    1. Runaway teenage girls; 2. Mental illness; 3. Voyages and travels; 4.
Mothers and daughters; 5. Blended families; 6. Mississippi; 7.
Cleveland, Ohio; 8. Realistic fiction.
9780451470775
                                               LC 2014009137
Booklist Editors' Choice: Books for Youth, 2015.
    When she learns that her mother is sick in Ohio, Mim confronts her
demons on a thousand-mile odyssey from Mississippi that redefines her
notions of love, loyalty, and what it means to be sane.

There is no shortage of humor in Mim's musings, interspersed with tender scenes and a few heart-pounding surprises. Mim's triumphant evolution is well worth the journey. —*Publishers Weekly*

Arnold, Elana K.
Damsel. Elana K. Arnold. 2018 320 p.
Grades: 9 10 11 12
1. Women with amnesia; 2. Transformations, Personal; 3. Misogyny; 4. Dragons; 5. Princes; 6. Fantasy fiction; 7. Allegories
9780062742322

LC 2017057175
Amelia Bloomer List, 2019; Booklist Editors' Choice: Books for Youth, 2018; Michael L. Printz Honor Book, 2019.

Required to slay a dragon and rescue a damsel to be his bride in order to inherit, a crown prince astonishes the girl of his choice, who has no memory of her capture by a dragon and who discovers unsettling truths about the legends shaping their lives.

Arnold's...pitch-black fairy tale is not subtle in its delivery, but, as its volcanic ending attests, this is not a tale that requires subtlety. It's not an easy read: physical, sexual, and psychological violence all come into play, and adults may want to be on hand for discussions. But for teens, especially girls, learning to transform sadness and fear into active, productive fury, it's an essential allegory. —*Booklist*

Infandous. By Elana K. Arnold. Carolrhoda Lab, 2015 200 p.
Grades: 9 10 11 12
1. Mothers and daughters; 2. Teenage girl artists; 3. Secrets; 4. Teenage surfers; 5. Single-parent families; 6. Los Angeles, California; 7. Venice (Los Angeles, Calif.); 8. Realistic fiction; 9. Coming-of-age stories; 10. Parallel narratives
9781467738491

LC 2014008998
Amelia Bloomer List, 2016; Westchester Fiction Award, 2016.

Seventeen-year-old Sephora, a surfer and artist who loves fairy tales and mythology, struggles with a secret so horrible she cannot speak it aloud, especially not to her beautiful, single mother, although they have always been unusually close.

Clocking in at just 200 pages, this is a story that packs no less of a punch for its brevity. Sephoras grim reimaginings of fairy tales are anti-Disney in the extreme (making this best suited for more mature readers). The strands are worked so surely into the narrative that they feel powerful instead of tired. Sephora herself is a narrator who defies convention, and her story, harsh and spare, is unforgettable. —*Booklist*

★ **Red** hood. Elana K. Arnold. Balzer & Bray, 2020 368 p.
Grades: 9 10 11 12
1. Wolves; 2. Hunters; 3. Teenage girls; 4. Grandmothers; 5. Menstruation; 6. Fairy tale and folklore-inspired fiction; 7. Magical realism; 8. Second person narratives
9780062742353

Since her grandmother became her caretaker when she was four years old, Bisou Martel has lived a quiet life in a little house in Seattle. She's kept mostly to herself. She's been good. But then comes the night of homecoming, when she finds herself running for her life over roots and between trees, a fury of claws and teeth behind her. A wolf attacks. Bisou fights back. A new moon rises. And with it, questions.

A fantastic novel in the #MeToo era, empowering women to share their stories by reaching out, speaking up, and demanding a change. —*School Library Journal*

What girls are made of. By Elana K. Arnold. Carolrhoda Lab, 2016 208 p.
Grades: 9 10 11 12

1. Dating (Social customs); 2. Family problems; 3. Teenage volunteers; 4. Animal shelters; 5. Sixteen year-old girls; 6. Realistic fiction; 7. First person narratives
9781512410242; 9781783447718, Paperback, UK

LC 2016006372
Golden Kite Award for Fiction, 2018; School Library Journal Best Books, 2017; YALSA Best Fiction for Young Adults, 2018; Amelia Bloomer List, 2018; National Book Award for Young People's Literature finalist, 2017.

Sixteen-year-old Nina Faye navigates the difficult world of teenage relationships and dysfunctional family dynamics.

Smart, true, and devastating, this is brutally, necessarily forthcoming about the crags of teen courtship. —*Booklist*

Ashby, Amanda
Zombie queen of Newbury High. By Amanda Ashby. Speak, 2009 199 p.
Grades: 7 8 9 10
1. Zombies; 2. Proms; 3. Spells (Magic); 4. Supernatural; 5. Best friends; 6. Teen chick lit; 7. Australian fiction
9780142412565

LC 2008041035
While trying to cast a love spell on her date on the eve of the senior prom, Mia inadvertently infects her entire high school class with a virus that will turn them all into zombies.

Zombie Queen is light, fast-paced, and...will quench the thirst of the Christopher Pike and R. L. Stine set. —*School Library Journal*

Asher, Jay
★ The **future** of us. Jay Asher and Carolyn Mackler. Razorbill, 2011 368 p.
Grades: 8 9 10 11 12
1. Internet; 2. Consequences; 3. Computers; 4. Friendship; 5. Teenage boy/girl relations; 6. 1990s; 7. Multiple perspectives
9781595144911

It's 1996, and Emma Nelson has just received her first computer.... When Emma powers up the computer, she discovers her own Facebook page (even though Facebook doesn't exist yet) and herself in an unhappy marriage15 years in the future. Alternating chapters from Josh and Emma over the course of five days propel this riveting read, as Emma discovers she can alter her future by adjusting her present actions and intentions. —*Booklist*

Thirteen reasons why: a novel. By Jay Asher. Razorbill, 2008 288 p.
Grades: 8 9 10 11 12
1. Suicide victims; 2. Rape; 3. Emotions in teenagers; 4. Guilt; 5. Suicide; 6. Realistic fiction; 7. Multiple perspectives; 8. First person narratives; 9. Books for reluctant readers
9781595141712; 9780141328294, UK; 9780141387772, UK film tie in

LC 2007003097
Abraham Lincoln Illinois High School Book Award, 2013; Delaware Diamonds (book award), High School, 2011; Garden State Teen Book Award (New Jersey), Fiction (Grades 9-12), 2010; Gateway Readers Award (Missouri), 2010; Heartland Award, 2009; Iowa High School Book Award, 2012; Kentucky Bluegrass Award for Grades 9-12, 2009; Sequoyah Book Awards (Oklahoma), High School Books, 2010; South Carolina Book Award, Young Adult Books, 2010; YALSA Popular Paperbacks for Young Adults, 2012; YALSA Quick Picks for Reluctant Young Adult Readers, 2008; YALSA Best Books for Young Adults, 2008.

When high school student Clay Jenkins receives a box in the mail containing thirteen cassette tapes recorded by his classmate Hannah, who committed suicide, he spends a bewildering and heartbreaking night criss-crossing their town, listening to Hannah's voice recounting the events leading up to her death.

Clay's pain is palpable and exquisitely drawn in gripping casually poetic prose. The complex and soulful characters expose astoundingly rich and singularly teenage inner lives. —*School Library Journal*

Adapted into a web television series for Netflix in 2017 entitled: Th1rteen R3asons Why.

Aspin, Diana
Ordinary miracles. Diana Aspin. Red Deer Press, 2003 168 p;
Grades: 7 8 9 10
1. Orphans; 2. Teenagers; 3. Foster children; 4. British in Canada; 5. Undertakers; 6. Ontario; 7. Short stories; 8. Canadian fiction.
9780889952775
LC BL2003017639

Interconnected stories trace the lives of English immigrant Arthur Pinner, who is rescued by a "girl from the future" while escaping an abusive foster home and goes on to become a small-town Canadian mortician, and his family.

This is a riveting collection.... The author has created a work that leaves readers awash with feelings of empathy for each young protagonist. —*School Library Journal*

Atkins, Jeannine
★ **Stone** mirrors: the sculpture and silence of Edmonia Lewis. Jeannine Atkins. Atheneum Books for Young Readers, 2017 192 p.
Grades: 9 10 11 12
1. Lewis, Edmonia; 2. Sculptors; 3. Multiracial persons; 4. Artists; 5. Women sculptors; 6. Scandals; 7. 1860s; 8. Historical fiction; 9. Biographical fiction; 10. Novels in verse
9781481459051; 9781481459075, ebook, US
LC 2016003598

A biographical novel in verse of a half Native American, half African American female sculptor, Edmonia Lewis, working in the years right after the Civil War.

How this brave, driven young woman overcame prejudice and trauma to pursue her artistic calling to the highest level—her work, once dismissed as démodé for its neoclassicism, now resides in top museums—is a story that warrants such artful retelling. —*Booklist*

Includes bibliographical references and index.

Atta, Dean
★ The **black** flamingo. Dean Atta. Balzer + Bray, 2020 416 p.
Grades: 9 10 11 12
1. Gay teenagers — Identity; 2. Drag queens; 3. Self-acceptance; 4. Multiracial persons — Identity; 5. Multiracial teenage boys; 6. London, England; 7. England; 8. Coming-of-age stories; 9. LGBTQIA fiction; 10. Novels in verse
9780062990297; 9781444948585, Hardback, UK; 9781444948608, Paperback, UK
School Library Journal Best Books, 2020; Stonewall Book Award for Children's and Young Adult Literature, 2020.

A boy comes to terms with his identity as a mixed-race gay teen—then at university he finds his wings as a drag artist, The Black Flamingo. A bold story about the power of embracing your uniqueness. Sometimes, we need to take charge, to stand up wearing pink feathers—to show ourselves to the world in bold colour.

[O]ffers a welcome exploration of the intersections of race, gender, and sexuality. —*Horn Book Guide*

Atwater-Rhodes, Amelia
Persistence of memory. By Amelia Atwater-Rhodes. Delacorte Press, 2008 212 p.
Grades: 8 9 10 11 12
1. Sixteen-year-old girls; 2. Vampires; 3. Mental illness; 4. Schizophrenia; 5. Supernatural; 6. Horror
9780385734370
LC 2008016062

Diagnosed with schizophrenia as a child, sixteen-year- old Erin has spent half of her life in therapy and on drugs, but now must face the possibility of weird things in the real world, including shapeshifting friends and her "alter," a centuries-old vampire.

What sets this novel apart...are the two narrators—Erin, grown used to, and even comfortable with, the idea that she is mentally ill; and Shevaun, willing to do anything to protect the family she's cobbled together. Secondary characters are equally compelling, and the world that Atwater-Rhodes has created is believable and intriguing. —*School Library Journal*

Auch, Mary Jane
Guitar boy. MJ Auch. Henry Holt, 2010 272 p.
Grades: 6 7 8 9
1. Parent-separated teenagers; 2. Guitar; 3. Kindness; 4. Musicians; 5. Brain injury; 6. New York (State); 7. Adirondack Mountains, New York; 8. Realistic fiction.
9780805091120
LC 2009050782

After his mother is severely injured in an accident and his father kicks him out of the house, thirteen-year-old Travis attempts to survive on his own until he meets a guitar maker and some musicians who take him in and help him regain his confidence so that he can try to patch his family back together.

Budding musicians will be fascinated by the details, but all readers will find their heartstrings plucked by this story. —*Booklist*

Christy Ottaviano books.

Avasthi, Swati
Chasing shadows. Swati Avasthi; illustrated by Craig Phillips. Alfred Knopf, 2013 320 p.
Grades: 9 10 11 12
1. Grief; 2. Visions; 3. Friendship; 4. Children of police; 5. Twin brothers and sisters; 6. Chicago, Illinois; 7. Realistic fiction; 8. Graphic novel hybrids.
9780375863424
LC Bl2013032709

YALSA Best Fiction for Young Adults, 2014.

Acting out superhero fantasies on the streets and rooftops of Chicago, best friends Corey, Holly, and Savitri are shattered by a murderous act of violence that leaves two of them disillusioned and unable to move on.

Savitri's boyfriend Corey is killed and her best friend, Holly (Corey's sister), is injured by a seemingly senseless shooting. With the killer at large, Holly teeters on the brink of sanity. The narrative alternates among Savitri's voice; a second-person narrator; and Holly's perspective, told through first-person text and dramatic graphic novel style interludes. Avasthi delves deeply into the pysche of both girls. —*Horn Book Guide*

Split. Swati Avasthi. Random House Childrens Books 2010 240 p.
Grades: 10 11 12
1. Teenage abuse victims; 2. Emotions in teenagers; 3. Sixteen-year-old boys; 4. Teenage boys; 5. Violence in men.
9780375963407
International Reading Association Children's Book Award for Young Adult Fiction, 2011; YALSA Best Fiction for Young Adults, 2011.

Moving in with his estranged brother after being abused by their father, 16-year-old Jace Witherspoon struggles to move on in a new school while remembering the people he left behind and protecting a haunting secret.

Readers seeking sensational violence should look elsewhere; this taut, complex family drama depicts abuse unflinchingly but focuses on healing, growth and learning to take responsibility for one's own anger. —*Kirkus*

Avery, Lara

The **memory** book. Lara Avery. Little, Brown and Company, 2016 368 p.
Grades: 9 10 11 12
1. Teenagers with terminal illnesses; 2. Memory; 3. Medical genetics; 4. Debates and debating; 5. Teenage romance; 6. Vermont; 7. Realistic fiction
9780316283748; 9780316283779; 9780316283762
LC 2015029157
Minnesota Book Award for Young People's Literature, 2017.

When a rare genetic disorder steals away her memories and then her health, teenaged Sammie records notes in a journal to her future self, documenting moments great and small.

When Sammie gets the diagnosis her senior year—that a genetic condition will rob her of her mind, the one thing she valued over everything else—its just one more thing for her to overcome, with the help of her memory book, a diary that will remind her future self of the Sammie she once was. But as the realities of her condition become more glaring, Sammie has to reevaluate everything she thought made her who she is.... Though there are moments recorded in Sammie's book that seem like they were captured at a very unlikely time to journal, each entry adds to a story of self-discovery thats hard to put down. —*Booklist*

Aveyard, Victoria

King's cage. Victoria Aveyard. HarperTeen, an imprint of HarperCollinsPublishers, 2017 512 p. (Red queen (Victoria Aveyard), 3)
Grades: 7 8 9 10
1. Prisoners; 2. Superhuman abilities; 3. Princesses; 4. Resistance to government; 5. Blood; 6. Fantasy fiction; 7. Dystopian fiction
9780062310699; 9781409151197; 9781409150763, print, UK

With Mare powerless as a prisoner of Maven Calore, the boy she once loved, her rebel Reds continue to organize and train as they prepare for war, while exiled prince Cal sets out to rescue Maven from captivity.

Red queen. Victoria Aveyard. HarperTeen, 2015 416 p. (Red queen (Victoria Aveyard), 1)
Grades: 8 9 10 11
1. Thieves; 2. Revolutions; 3. Superhuman abilities; 4. Princesses; 5. Blood; 6. Fantasy fiction; 7. Dystopian fiction; 8. Books for reluctant readers
9780062310637; 9781409150725, UK
Abraham Lincoln Illinois High School Book Award, 2017; California Young Reader Medal, Young Adult, 2017; Golden Sower Award (Nebraska), Young Adult, 2017; Grand Canyon Reader Award (Arizona), Teen Book Category, 2017; Kentucky Bluegrass Award for Grades 9-12, 2017; South Carolina Book Award, Young Adult Books, 2017; Truman Readers Award (Missouri), 2018; YALSA Quick Picks for Reluctant Young Adult Readers, 2016; YALSA Quick Picks for Reluctant Young Adult Readers: Top Ten, 2016; Young Reader's Choice Award (Pacific Northwest), Senior, 2018.

When her latent supernatural powers manifest in front of a noble court, Mare, a thief in a world divided between commoners and superhumans, is forced to assume the role of lost princess before risking everything to help a growing rebellion.

First-time author Aveyard has created a volatile world with a dynamic heroine, and while there are moments of romance, they refreshingly take a backseat to the action. Anticipation is already high for this debut, and with the movie rights already acquired and two sequels to come, it will likely only grow. —*Booklist*

Avi

The **button** war: a tale of the Great War. Avi. Candlewick Press, 2018 240 p.
Grades: 5 6 7 8
1. Soldiers; 2. Stealing; 3. Competition in boys; 4. Twelve-year-old boys; 5. Friendship; 6. Poland; 7. 1910s; 8. Historical fiction
9780763690533; 9781406380835, Paperback, UK

Running with friends who entertain themselves by coming up with risky dares, Patryk watches as their village is occupied by hostile nations throughout the Great War, before his friends begin looting the dead soldiers as part of their competition.

★ **City** of orphans. Avi; illustrated by Greg Ruth. Atheneum Books for Young Readers, 2011 288 p.
Grades: 5 6 7 8
1. Newspaper vendors; 2. Malicious accusation; 3. Homeless girls; 4. Lawyers; 5. Gangs; 6. New York City; 7. 1890s; 8. Historical fiction.
9781416971023
LC 2010049229
Land of Enchantment Book Award (New Mexico), Young Adult category, 2014.

In 1893 New York, thirteen-year-old Maks, a newsboy, teams up with Willa, a homeless girl, to clear his older sister, Emma, from charges that she stole from the brand new Waldorf Hotel, where she works. Includes historical notes.

Avi's vivid recreation of the sights and sounds of that time and place is spot on, masterfully weaving accurate historical details with Maks' experiences. —*Kirkus*

A Richard Jackson Book.

★ **Crispin**: the cross of lead. Avi. Hyperion Books for Children, 2002 256 p. (Crispin, 1)
Grades: 5 6 7 8
1. Malicious accusation; 2. Orphans; 3. Secrets; 4. Boys; 5. Identity (Psychology); 6. Great Britain; 7. Medieval period (476-1492); 8. Plantagenet period (1154-1485); 9. Historical fiction.
9780786808281
LC 2001051829
ALA Notable Children's Book, 2003; Newbery Medal, 2003.

Falsely accused of theft and murder, an orphaned peasant boy in fourteenth-century England flees his village and meets a larger-than-life juggler who holds a dangerous secret.

This book is a page-turner from beginning to end.... A meticulously crafted story, full of adventure, mystery, and action. —*School Library Journal*

Sequel: *Crispin: at the edge of the world.*

Nothing but the truth: a documentary novel. Avi. Orchard Books, 1991 177 p.
Grades: 6 7 8 9 10
1. Journalism; 2. Student suspension; 3. Patriotism; 4. Teacher-student relationships; 5. Women high school principals
9780545174152, paperback, US; 9780439327305, hardback, US; 9780030546662, hardback, US; 9780380719075, paperback, US
LC 91009200
ALA Notable Children's Book, 1992; Charlotte Award (New York), Young Adult, 1994; Garden State Teen Book Award (New Jersey),

Fiction (Grades 6-8), 1995; Grand Canyon Reader Award (Arizona), Teen Book Category, 1994; Newbery Honor Book, 1992.

A ninth-grader's suspension for singing "The Star-Spangled Banner" during homeroom becomes a national news story.

Ayres, Katherine

North by night: a story of the Underground Railroad. Delacorte Press, 1998 176 p.
Grades: 6 7 8 9
1. Underground Railroad; 2. Fugitive slaves; 3. Sixteen-year-old girls; 4. Teenage girls; 5. Ohio; 6. Diary novels; 7. Historical fiction
9780385325646

LC 98-10039

Presents the journal of a sixteen-year-old girl whose family operates a stop on the Underground Railroad.

This is an absorbing tale. Ayres slips in a lot of evocative detail about the hard work of running a farm and a household before the Civil War, as well as some rather charming musing about kissing and its myriad effects on the psyche. —*Booklist*

Azad, Nafiza

The **candle** and the flame. Nafiza Azad. Scholastic Press, 2019 391 p.
Grades: 8 9 10 11
1. Genies; 2. Transformations (Magic); 3. Political intrigue; 4. Civil war; 5. Magic; 6. Silk Road; 7. Middle East; 8. Middle Eastern-influenced fantasy; 9. Mythological fiction; 10. Fantasy fiction.
9781338306040; 9781338306057

LC 2018041274

Loan Stars Favourites, 2019; William C. Morris Debut Award finalist, 2020.

Fatima lives in the city of Noor, on the Silk Road, which is currently protected by the Ifrit, djinn of order and reason, from attacks by the violent and ruthless Shayateen djinn—but Fatima was infused with the fire of the Ifrit who died saving her when she was four years old, and when one of the most important Ifrit dies she finds herself drawn into the intrigues of the court, the affairs of the djinn, and the very real dangers of a magical battlefield.

...Azad combines Islamic concepts and Middle Eastern mythology with a variety of other traditions to create a magical treatise on identity, community, friendship, and love. Readers will identify with female characters who struggle against limiting societal expectations. The themes of trauma and grief are treated with care. Azad's vivid depiction of the details of Noor's sights and sounds make the city come alive. —*School Library Journal*

Bacigalupi, Paolo

The **doubt** factory: a novel. Paolo Bacigalupi. 2014 496 p.
Grades: 9 10 11 12
1. Whistle blowing; 2. Corporations; 3. Corruption; 4. Social action; 5. Corporate greed; 6. Connecticut; 7. Thrillers and suspense
9780316220750; 9780316220743, ebook, US; 9780316364836, ebook, US

LC 2014002543

When a radical band of teen activists claim that Alix's powerful father covers up corporate wrongdoing that knowingly allows innocent victims to die in order to make enormous profits from unsafe products, she must decide if she will blow the whistle on his misdeeds.

This openly didactic novel asks challenging questions about the immorality of the profit motive and capitalism, but does so within the context of a highly believable plot...and well-developed, multifaceted characters. —*Publishers Weekly*

★ The **Drowned** Cities. By Paolo Bacigalupi. Little, Brown and Co, 2012 448 p.
Grades: 9 10 11 12
1. Dystopias; 2. Post-apocalypse; 3. Orphans; 4. Genetic engineering; 5. Rescues; 6. Science fiction; 7. Multiple perspectives.
9780316056243; 9781907411113, UK

LC 2011031762

YALSA Best Fiction for Young Adults, 2013.

In a dark future America that has devolved into unending civil wars, orphans Mahlia and Mouse barely escape the war-torn lands of the Drowned Cities, but their fragile safety is soon threatened and Mahlia will have to risk everything if she is to save Mouse, as he once saved her.

Companion to: *Ship breaker* and *Tool of war.*

★ **Ship** breaker: a novel. By Paolo Bacigalupi. Little, Brown and Co, 2010 326 p.
Grades: 8 9 10 11 12
1. Post-apocalypse; 2. Shipwreck survivors; 3. Dystopias; 4. Scavenging; 5. Clipper-ships; 6. Gulf Coast (United States); 7. Dystopian fiction; 8. Science fiction.
9780316056212

LC 2009034424

Great Lakes Great Books Award (Michigan), Grades 9-12, 2011; Locus Young Adult Book Award, 2011; Michael L. Printz Award, 2011; YALSA Popular Paperbacks for Young Adults, 2016; ALA Notable Children's Book, 2011; YALSA Best Fiction for Young Adults, 2011; National Book Award for Young People's Literature finalist, 2010.

Bacigalupi's cast is ethnically and morally diverse, and the book's message never overshadows the storytelling, action-packed pacing, or intricate world-building. At its core, the novel is an exploration of Nailer's discovery of the nature of the world around him and his ability to transcend that world's expectations. —*Publishers Weekly*

Companion novels: *The Drowned Cities* and *Tool of war.*

Tool of war. Paolo Bacigalupi. 2017 384 p.
Grades: 8 9 10 11 12
1. Genetically engineered men; 2. Resistance to government; 3. Revenge; 4. Dystopias; 5. Soldiers; 6. Science fiction; 7. Multiple perspectives
9780316220835; 9780316220828, ebook, US; 9780316364775, ebook, US

LC 2016051846

In a future beset with rising seas, corporate government, and constant civil war, a bioengineered half-man/half-beast super-soldier who calls himself Tool breaks his conditioning to overcome his genetically enhanced sense of loyalty to the corporation that created him and seeks revenge against his old masters.

Tool is at center stage at last as readers move through Bacigalupi's exploration of the intricate relationships connecting hunter and prey, master and enslaved, human and monster. Masterful. —*Kirkus*

Companion to: Ship breaker and The Drowned Cities.

Badger, Darcie Little

★ **Elatsoe**. Levine Querido, 2020 368 p.
Grades: 9 10 11 12
1. Native American women; 2. Ghosts; 3. Murder; 4. Magic; 5. Teenage girls; 6. Fantasy fiction
9781646140053

Elatsoe lives in this slightly stranger America. She can raise the ghosts of dead animals, a skill passed down through generations of her

Lipan Apache family. Her beloved cousin has just been murdered, in a town that wants no prying eyes. But she is going to do more than pry. The picture-perfect facade of Willowbee masks gruesome secrets, and she will rely on her wits, skills, and friends to tear off the mask and protect her family.

Indigenous myths, modern-day technology, and the supernatural successfully blend to build a fast-paced murder mystery in Little Badger's intriguing solo debut Publishers Weekly

Badoe, Adwoa

Between sisters. Adwoa Badoe. Groundwood Books/House of Anansi Press, 2010 205 p;
Grades: 9 10 11 12
1. Sixteen-year-old girls; 2. Ghanaians; 3. Family problems; 4. Nannies; 5. Interpersonal relations; 6. Ghana; 7. First person narratives; 8. Canadian fiction.
9780888999962; 9780888999979

This honest glimpse of one adolescent is as particular to the well-detailed West African setting as it is universal in subject and theme. —*Horn Book Guide*

Bailey, Kristin

Legacy of the clockwork key. By Kristin Bailey. Simon Pulse, 2013 403 p. (Secret order, 1)
Grades: 7 8 9 10
1. Secret societies; 2. Teenage girl orphans; 3. Teenage household employees; 4. Inventors; 5. Time machines; 6. London, England; 7. Great Britain; 8. Victorian era (1837-1901); 9. Steampunk
9781442440265

LC 2011049871

A orphaned sixteen-year-old servant in Victorian England finds love while unraveling the secrets of a mysterious society of inventors and their most dangerous creation.

Bannen, Megan

The bird and the blade. Megan Bannen. Balzer + Bray, 2018 432 p.
Grades: 7 8 9 10 11 12
1. Women slaves; 2. Exiles; 3. Princes; 4. Rulers; 5. Marriage; 6. Mongol Empire; 7. 13th century; 8. Historical fiction
9780062674159

A slave with a secret past is forced to serve the exiled prince she loves as he risks his life in a desperate effort to forge a political marriage with a powerful and deadly princess.

Barakiva, Michael

One man guy. Michael Barakiva. Farrar Straus Giroux, 2014 256 pages (One man guy, 1)
Grades: 9 10 11 12
1. Gay teenagers; 2. Armenian Americans; 3. Summer schools; 4. Coming out (Sexual or gender identity); 5. Teenage same-sex romance; 6. New Jersey; 7. New York City; 8. LGBTQIA fiction; 9. Realistic fiction
9780374356453; 9780374356460, ebook, US

LC 2013033518

Rainbow List, 2015.

When Alek's high-achieving, Armenian-American parents send him to summer school, he thinks his summer is ruined. But then he meets Ethan, who opens his world in a series of truly unexpected ways.

Barakiva avoids stereotypes and clichs to create a sweet portrait of nascent adolescent love between two boys growing up and finding themselves (with some help from nearby New York City). —*Publishers Weekly*

Baratz-Logsted, Lauren

Crazy beautiful. By Lauren Baratz-Logsted. Houghton Mifflin Harcourt, 2009 208 p.
Grades: 7 8 9 10
1. People who have had amputations; 2. Teenage boys with disabilities; 3. Friendship; 4. Interpersonal relations; 5. High school students; 6. Multiple perspectives; 7. Realistic fiction; 8. Fairy tale and folklore-inspired fiction; 9. Books for reluctant readers
9780547223070

LC 2008040463

YALSA Quick Picks for Reluctant Young Adult Readers, 2010.

In this contemporary retelling of "Beauty and the Beast," a teenaged boy whose hands were amputated in an explosion and a gorgeous girl whose mother has recently died form an instant connection when they meet on their first day as new students.

This romance transcends all of its potential pitfalls to create a powerful story about recovery and friendship. —*Kirkus*

The **twin's** daughter. By Lauren Baratz-Logsted. Bloomsbury Children's Books, 2011 304 p.
Grades: 7 8 9 10
1. Identical twins; 2. Separated friends, relatives, etc; 3. Aunts; 4. Murder; 5. Families; 6. London, England; 7. Great Britain; 8. Victorian era (1837-1901); 9. 19th century; 10. Historical mysteries; 11. Gothic fiction; 12. Mysteries
9781599905136

LC 2010008234

In Victorian London, thirteen-year-old Lucy's comfortable world with her loving parents begins slowly to unravel the day that a bedraggled woman who looks exactly like her mother appears at their door.

Baratz-Logsted's gothic murder mystery is rife with twists and moves swiftly and elegantly.... The ending will intrigue and delight readers. —*Booklist*

Bardugo, Leigh

★ **Crooked** kingdom. Leigh Bardugo. 2016 546 pages (Six of crows, 2)
Grades: 9 10 11 12
1. Revenge; 2. Criminals; 3. Rescues; 4. Friendship; 5. Teenage boys; 6. High fantasy; 7. Fantasy fiction.
9781627792134; 9781250076977; 9781627797917; 9781780622316, print, UK; 9781510107038, Hardback, UK

LC 2016945089

This is dark and violent... but gut-wrenchingly genuine. Astonishingly, Bardugo keeps all these balls in the air over the 500-plus pages of narrative. How can such a hefty tome be un-put-down-able excitement from beginning to end? —*Kirkus*

★ **King** of scars. Leigh Bardugo. Imprint, a part of Macmillan Publishing Group, LLC, 2019 527 p. (King of Scars duology, 1)
Grades: 8 9 10 11 12
1. Rulers; 2. Transformations (Magic); 3. Imaginary kingdoms; 4. Demonic possession; 5. Demons; 6. High fantasy; 7. Fantasy fiction
9781250142283; 9781510105669, Paperback, UK; 9781510104457, Hardback, UK; 9781250231079; 9781250225047; 9781250225061; 9781250225795; 9781250231185

When the dark magical force within him challenges his effort to forge new alliances and build a defense against a new threat, Nikolai Lantsov, the young king of Ravka, embarks on a journey to his country's most magical places to vanquish it.

Deadly clever political intrigue, heart-stopping adventure, memorable characters, and several understated, hinted-at romances (how will we wait?!) come together in one glorious, Slavic-folklore-infused package. —*Booklist*

The **language** of thorns: midnight tales and dangerous magic. Leigh Bardugo; illustrated by Sara Kipin. Imprint, 2017 224 p.
Grades: 9 10 11 12
1. Good and evil; 2. Magic; 3. Characters and characteristics in fairy tales; 4. Fairy tale and folklore-inspired fiction; 5. Short stories
9781250122520; 9781510104518, print, UK; 9781510104419, Hardback, UK
YALSA Best Fiction for Young Adults, 2018.
Travel to a world of dark bargains struck by moonlight, of haunted towns and hungry woods, of talking beasts and gingerbread golems, where a young mermaid's voice can summon deadly storms and where a river might do a lovestruck boy's bidding but only for a terrible price.
Bardugo may be best known for her exemplary world building, but here more than anything, it is her language, lovely and unsettling, that is on display, as well as the accompanying characters who, like the stories themselves, are never what they seem. —*Booklist*

Ruin and rising. Leigh Bardugo. 2014 448 p. (Grisha trilogy, 3)
Grades: 8 9 10 11 12
1. Quests; 2. Orphans; 3. Power (Social sciences); 4. Firebird (Mythical bird); 5. Good and evil; 6. High fantasy; 7. Fantasy fiction.
9780805094619; 9781780621166, print, UK; 9781780621845, print, UK; 9781510105256, Paperback, UK
LC 2013049306
The Darkling rules Ravka from his shadow throne. Alina forges new alliances as she and Mal search for Morozova's last amplifier. But as she begins to unravel the Darkling's secrets, she reveals a past that alters her understanding of the bond they share and the power she wields
Alina and company have only one hope: if they can kill the Firebird, its magical bones can be used to break the Darkling's chokehold on Ravka. In this concluding volume, Alina must rely on her childhood friend Mal's preternatural tracking ability. Bardugo's longstanding theme of power corrupts is developed organically; the magic she invents will surprise and delight readers. —*Horn Book Guide*

Shadow and bone. Leigh Bardugo. Henry Holt, 2012 368 p. (Grisha trilogy, 1)
Grades: 8 9 10 11
1. Orphans; 2. Power (Social sciences); 3. Monsters; 4. Good and evil; 5. Elite (Social sciences); 6. High fantasy; 7. Fantasy fiction.
9780805094596; 9781510105249, Paperback, UK
LC 2011034012
YALSA Best Fiction for Young Adults, 2013; Romantic Times Reviewer's Choice Award, 2012.
Orphaned by the Border Wars, Alina Starkov is taken from obscurity and her only friend, Mal, to become the protege of the mysterious Darkling, who trains her to join the magical elite in the belief that she is the Sun Summoner, who can destroy the monsters of the Fold.

Siege and storm. Leigh Bardugo. Henry Holt and Company, 2013 384 p. (Grisha trilogy, 2)
Grades: 8 9 10 11 12
1. Orphans; 2. Power (Social sciences); 3. Monsters; 4. Visions; 5. Magic; 6. High fantasy; 7. Fantasy fiction; 8. First person narratives.
9780805094602; 9781780621708, print, UK; 9781510105263, Paperback, UK; 9780805097115, ebook, US
LC 2012046361
Hunted across the True Sea and haunted by the lives she took on the Fold, Alina must try to make a life with Mal in an unfamiliar land, all while keeping her identity as the Sun Summoner a secret.

★ **Six** of crows. Leigh Bardugo. 2015 480 pages (Six of crows, 1)

Grades: 9 10 11 12
1. Criminals; 2. Misfits (Persons); 3. Prisons; 4. Rescues; 5. Spies; 6. High fantasy; 7. Fantasy fiction.
9781627792127; 9781627795098; 9781250076960; 9781510106284, Hardback, UK
LC 2015005469
Colorado Blue Spruce YA Book Award, 2017; Abraham Lincoln Illinois High School Book Award, 2018; Georgia Peach Book Award for Teen Readers, 2017; YALSA Best Fiction for Young Adults: Top Ten, 2015; YALSA Best Fiction for Young Adults, 2016; Romantic Times Reviewer's Choice Award, 2015.
Six dangerous outcasts must learn to work together after they are offered an impossible heist that can save the world from destruction.
Cracking page-turner with a multiethnic band of misfits with differing sexual orientations who satisfyingly, believably jell into a family. —*Kirkus*

Wonder Woman: Warbringer. Leigh Bardugo. Random House, 2017 304 p. (DC icons, 1)
Grades: 6 7 8 9 10
1. Superheroines; 2. Women warriors; 3. Teenage girl orphans; 4. Wonder Woman (Fictitious character); 5. Rescues; 6. Superhero stories; 7. Multiple perspectives; 8. Franchise books
9780399549731; 9780399549748; 9780399549762; 9780141387376, print, UK; 9780399549755, ebook, US
LC 2016044698
Diana, Princess of the Amazons, journeys to the World of Man in this coming-of-age young adult story.
Bardugo breathes zippy new life into the story with a twisty plot, whip-smart characters, and her trademark masterful writing. —*Booklist*

Barker, Michelle
The **house** of one thousand eyes. Michelle Barker. Annick Press, 2018. 2018 354 p.
Grades: 10 11 12
1. Communism; 2. Teenage girls; 3. Disappeared persons; 4. Orphans; 5. Aunts and uncles; 6. East Berlin, Germany; 7. East Germany; 8. 1980s; 9. Thrillers and suspense; 10. Historical fiction; 11. Canadian fiction
9781773210711; 9781773210704; 9781773210728; 9781773210735
Amy Mathers Teen Book Award, 2019; YALSA Best Fiction for Young Adults, 2019.
Life in East Germany in the early 1980's is very hard for Lena following the death of her parents and the sudden disappearance and consequent erasure of her uncle's existence by the secret service police, the Stasi. Lena is determined to unearth what happened to her beloved uncle. —Provided by publisher.
The rich historical details plunge readers into a chillingly realistic world where it is impossible for citizens to trust each other and in which Lena struggles with mental illness, sexual assault, and grief. A stunning and compassionate portrait of a young woman fighting to retain her sense of self under a repressive regime. —*Kirkus*

Barkley, Brad
Jars of glass: a novel. By Brad Barkley & Heather Hepler. Dutton Childrens Books, 2008 208 p.
Grades: 7 8 9 10 11 12
1. Family problems; 2. Mental illness; 3. Emotional problems; 4. Brothers and sisters; 5. Adoption; 6. Realistic fiction.
9780525479116
LC 2007052657
Two sisters, aged fourteen and fifteen, offer their views of events that occur during the year after their mother is diagnosed with schizophrenia

and their family, including a recently adopted Russian orphan, begins to disintegrate.

Barkley and Hepler are the masters of alternating narration, with Chloe's and Shana's voices both believable, clearly different, and usefully complementary.... This is an affecting story about families struggling to readjust in the face of one member's affliction. —*Bulletin of the Center for Children's Books*

Barnaby, Hannah Rodgers
Wonder show. Houghton Mifflin, 2012 288 p.
Grades: 7 8 9 10 11 12
1. Runaway girls; 2. Freaks (Entertainers); 3. Circus; 4. Missing persons; 5. Schools; 6. 1930s; 7. Historical fiction; 8. Multiple perspectives.
9780547599809
YALSA Best Fiction for Young Adults, 2013; William C. Morris Debut Award finalist, 2013.

Traveling with circus sideshow performers after fleeing a school for wayward girls, Portia Remini feels out of place among her companions while wondering about her missing father and fearing capture by the school's sinister headmaster.

Melodrama aside, this predominantly third-person narration is richly textured with psychological tension, complex characterization, a vivid setting, and a suspenseful plot. Information in context and an author's note provide insights about circus life. Dark themes, some steamy elements, and a generous dose of swearing suggest a mature audience, but one that will be spellbound by this intriguing reading experience. —*School Library Journal*

Barnard, Sara
Fragile like us. Sara Barnard. Simon Pulse, 2017 399 p.
Grades: 10 11 12
1. Self-destructive behavior; 2. Accidents; 3. Friendship; 4. Best friends; 5. Interpersonal relations; 6. England; 7. Brighton, England; 8. Realistic fiction; 9. First person narratives
9781481486101; 9781509803538, print, UK

Best friends Caddy and Rosie have always been close, but as Caddy turns sixteen, she longs to be more confident and interesting like Rosie and turns to Suzanne, an exciting new friend who has a mysterious past.

A beautiful, heartfelt appreciation of the importance of girls' friendships. —*Kirkus*

Barnes, Jennifer
Killer spirit. Jennifer Lynn Barnes. Laurel Leaf Books, 2008 324 p; (Squad, 2)
Grades: 7 8 9 10
1. Teenage spies; 2. Hackers; 3. Cheerleading; 4. Undercover operations; 5. Dating (Social customs); 6. Spy fiction; 7. Humorous stories; 8. Teenagers' writings
9780385734554
LC 2007017733

As if it were not bad enough that sophomore computer hacker Toby Klein has to be a cheerleader to be part of the elite group of government operatives called the Squad, now she is part of the Homecoming court and has agreed to attend the dance with the most popular boy in school.

Perfect cover. Jennifer Lynn Barnes. Delacorte Press, 2008 288 p. (Squad, 1)
Grades: 7 8 9 10
1. Teenage spies; 2. Cheerleading; 3. High schools; 4. Teenage girls; 5. Hackers; 6. Spy fiction; 7. Humorous stories; 8. Teenagers' writings

9780385734547; 9780385904773
LC 2007009352
YALSA Popular Paperbacks for Young Adults, 2009.

High school sophomore Toby Klein enjoys computer hacking and wearing combat boots, so she thinks it is a joke when she is invited to join the cheerleading squad but soon learns cheering is just a cover for an elite group of government operatives known as the Squad.

In addition to offering crafty plotting and time-honored, typical teen conflicts and rivalries, Barnes maintains a sharp sense of humor in this action-adventure series. —*Bulletin of the Center for Children's Books*

Barnes, Jennifer Lynn
The **inheritance** games. Jennifer Lynn Barnes. Little Brown & Co, 2020 384 p. (Inheritance games, 1)
Grades: 9 10 11 12
1. Inheritance and succession; 2. Billionaires; 3. Puzzles; 4. Teenage girls; 5. Families; 6. Mysteries
9781368052405

Avery Grambs has a plan for a better future: survive high school, win a scholarship, and get out. But her fortunes change in an instant when billionaire Tobias Hawthorne dies and leaves Avery virtually his entire fortune. The catch? Avery has no idea why—or even who Tobias Hawthorne is. To receive her inheritance, Avery must move into sprawling, secret passage-filled Hawthorne House, where every room bears the old man's touch—and his love of puzzles, riddles, and codes. Caught in a world of wealth and privilege, with danger around every turn, Avery will have to play the game herself just to survive.

Barnes's meticulously crafted novel is like the film *Knives Out* for the YA world, perfect for any reader seeking suspense, romance, and glamour. —*School Library Journal*

Barnes, John
★ **Tales** of the Madman Underground: an historical romance, 1973. John Barnes. Viking, 2009 480 p.
Grades: 10 11 12
1. Teenage boys; 2. Emotional problems of teenage boys; 3. Teenage children of alcoholics; 4. Friendship; 5. Mothers and sons; 6. Ohio; 7. 1970s; 8. Coming-of-age stories; 9. Realistic fiction.
9780670060818
LC 2009011072
YALSA Best Books for Young Adults, 2010; Michael L. Printz Honor Book, 2010.

In September 1973, as the school year begins in his depressed Ohio town, high-school senior Kurt Shoemaker determines to be "normal," despite his chaotic home life with his volatile, alcoholic mother and the deep loyalty and affection he has for his friends in the therapy group dubbed the Madman Underground.

Teens initially turned off by Barnes's liberal use of profanities and the book's length will be captured by the sharp, funny dialogue and crisp personalities of the Madmen. Even minor characters are distinctive.... [This] is an excellent selection for book clubs of older teens that like sinking their teeth into longer stories with substance. —*Voice of Youth Advocates*

Barnholdt, Lauren
Through to you. Lauren Barnholdt. Simon Pulse, 2014 256 pages
Grades: 9 10 11 12
1. Teenage baseball players; 2. Family problems; 3. Interpersonal attraction; 4. Dating (Social customs); 5. Teenage romance; 6. Contemporary romances; 7. Multiple perspectives
9781442434639; 9781442434653, ebook, US
LC 2013048226

When bad-boy Penn reaches out to cautious Harper, a tumultuous relationship blossoms, and the two learn that their bond may not be strong enough to overcome their obvious differences.

Chapters alternate between the two characters vantage points, providing an insightful and humorous look into the complex connections among feelings, actions and words and how easily they can be misconstrued. An absorbing, skillfully written depiction of two teens caught in a vortex of doubt, insecurity, and miscommunication. —*Kirkus*

Barratt, Mark

Joe Rat. By Mark Barratt. Eerdmans Books for Young Readers, 2009 307 p.
Grades: 7 8 9 10
1. Homeless children; 2. Sewers; 3. Crime; 4. Runaways; 5. Boy orphans; 6. London, England; 7. Great Britain; 8. Victorian era (1837-1901); 9. Historical fiction.
9780802853561, PAP, US; 9781862302181, PAP, UK
LC 2008055972

In the dark, dank sewers of Victorian London, a boy known as Joe Rat scrounges for valuables which he gives to "Mother," a criminal mastermind who considers him a favorite, but a chance meeting with a runaway girl and "the Madman" transforms all their lives.

The unraveling of the Madman's identity is but one of the pleasures of Barratt's leisurely and convincing historical fiction. —*Booklist*

The **wild** man. By Mark Barratt. Eerdmans Books for Young Readers, 2010 310 p.
Grades: 7 8 9 10
1. Homeless children; 2. Interclass friendship; 3. Jealousy in boys; 4. Impostors; 5. Boy orphans; 6. London, England; 7. Great Britain; 8. Victorian era (1837-1901); 9. Historical fiction.
9780802853776
LC 2010010937

In Victorian England, Joe Rat has escaped the clutches of the criminal mastermind, Mother, and is trying to make an honest living in a better part of London, but when a rich philanthropist tracks down a man claiming to be Joe's missing father—a British army deserter—he must determine where his loyalties lie.

Barratt writes as if he is keeping an adjacent berth to Dickens; here's hoping scrappy Joe has a few more tricks up his ratty sleeves. —*Booklist*
Sequel to: *Joe Rat.*

Barrett, Tracy

The **stepsister's** tale. Tracy Barrett. Harlequin Teen, 2014 304 pages
Grades: 7 8 9 10
1. Stepsisters; 2. Poverty; 3. Blended families; 4. Balls (Parties); 5. Poor families; 6. Fairy tale and folklore-inspired fiction
9780373211210
LC Bl2014023484

Jane cares for her mother and sister until her stepfather dies, leaving nothing but debts and Jane's spoiled stepsister behind, but a mysterious boy from the woods and an invitation to a royal ball are certain to change her fate.

Sometimes it feels like fairy-tale retellings are a dime a dozen, and this is certainly not the first or the last account of a misunderstood antagonist. But, Barrett's comparably quiet account of a household of women working to survive together as a family, sometimes in spite of one another, shines with soft, bucolic realism...Overall, this is an enjoyable read. The inclusion of discussion questions in the back makes it a solid choice for book clubs. —*Voice of Youth Advocates*

Barron, T. A.

The **book** of magic. T.A. Barron; illustrated by August Hall. Philomel Books, 2011 167 p. : Illustration; Map
Grades: 4 5 6 7
1. Wizards; 2. Magic; 3. Imaginary places; 4. Merlin (Legendary character); 5. Avalon (Legendary place); 6. Arthurian fantasy; 7. Historical fantasy
9780399247415
LC 2011013552

A compendium of maps, character descriptions, magical terms, timelines, and other tidbits from the author's Merlin saga.

Guides to long-running series have two important jobs. They should remind fans of all the things they particularly love about the books, and they should whet the appetites of newcomers, thus creating more fans. Barron's guide to his 12-book saga about Merlin succeeds in both objectives. —*School Library Journal*

Doomraga's revenge. T. A. Barron. Philomel Books, 2009 256 p. (Merlin's dragon trilogy, 2)
Grades: 6 7 8 9
1. Dragons; 2. Magic; 3. Fathers and sons; 4. Black magic; 5. Wizards; 6. Arthurian fantasy; 7. Historical fantasy
9780399252129
LC 2008055872

The dragon Basil, now grown mighty in strength, size, and courage, addresses and seeks the cause of a new series of crises that threaten the stability of Avalon, while his friend Merlin is distracted by problems with his son, Krystallus.

No one can compare to Barron when writing about Merlin or Avalon. Once again, he brings texture, color, and love to the seven realms. His many fans will gobble up this...offering. —*School Library Journal*

The **fires** of Merlin. T. A. Barron. Philomel Books, 1998 261 p. (Lost years of Merlin, 3)
Grades: 5 6 7 8
1. Wizards; 2. Fire; 3. Child wizards; 4. Magic; 5. Merlin (Legendary character); 6. Arthurian fantasy; 7. Historical fantasy
9780399230202
LC 9749561

Having voyaged to the Otherworld in his quest to find himself, the young wizard Merlin must face fire in many different forms and deal with the possibility of losing his own magical power.

This saga just keeps getting richer in characterization, ambience, and Celtic lore. —*Booklist*
Sequel to: *The seven songs of Merlin*; Sequel: *The mirror of Merlin.*

★ The **lost** years of Merlin. T.A. Barron. Philomel Books, 1996 326 p. (Lost years of Merlin, 1)
Grades: 5 6 7 8
1. Wizards; 2. Child wizards; 3. Magic; 4. Merlin (Legendary character); 5. Arthurian fantasy; 6. Historical fantasy
9780399230189
LC 96-33920
YALSA Best Books for Young Adults, 1997.

A young boy who has no identity nor memory of his past washes ashore on the coast of Wales and finds his true name after a series of fantastic adventures.

A boy, hurled on the rocks by the sea, regains consciousness unable to remember anything—not his parents, not his own name. He is sure that the secretive Branwen is not his mother, despite her claims, and that Emrys is not his real name. The two soon find themselves feared because of Branwen's healing abilities and Emrys' growing powers.... Barron has created not only a magical land populated by remarkable beings but also a completely magical tale, filled with ancient Celtic and Druidic lore, that will enchant readers. —*Booklist*

Sequel: *The seven songs of Merlin.*

Merlin's dragon. By T.A. Barron. Philomel Books, 2008 336 p. (Merlin's Dragon trilogy, 1)
Grades: 6 7 8 9
1. Dragons; 2. Wizards; 3. Magic; 4. Identity (Psychology); 5. Smell; 6. Arthurian fantasy; 7. Historical fantasy
9780399247507

LC 2008002469
Basil, a small, flying lizard who is searching for others like himself, discovers that there is more to him than he knows, as he becomes engaged in Avalon's great war between the evil Rhita Gawr and the forces of good.

Basil is an appealing, complex character.... This first book in a new series will captivate readers already familiar with the fantasist's Merlin chronicles. —*Booklist*

The **mirror** of Merlin. T. A. Barron. Philomel Books, 1999 245 p. (Lost years of Merlin, 4)
Grades: 5 6 7 8
1. Wizards; 2. Child wizards; 3. Magic; 4. Merlin (Legendary character); 5. Arthurian fantasy; 6. Historical fantasy
9780399234552

LC 99013043
Through adventures involving a haunted marsh, talking trees, and the creature called the ballymag, the young wizard Merlin continues to experience both his growing powers and his essential humanity.

With lots of surprises and some laugh-out-loud humor to leaven the palpable feeling of doom, this should be eagerly devoured by the saga's fans. —*Booklist*

Sequel to: *The fires of Merlin.*; Sequel: *The wings of Merlin*; Book four of The lost years of Merlin.

The **seven** songs of Merlin. T. A. Barron. Philomel Books, 1997 306 p. (Lost years of Merlin, 2)
Grades: 5 6 7 8
1. Wizards; 2. Child wizards; 3. Magic; 4. Merlin (Legendary character); 5. Arthurian fantasy; 6. Historical fantasy
9780399230196

LC 97-9619
Having stumbled upon his hidden powers, the young wizard Merlin voyages to the Otherworld in his quest to find himself and the way to the realm of the spirit.

The tale is spellbinding (pun intended), and readers will relish not only the action and the well-crafted setting but also Merlin's growth from a callow youth to a wiser, more caring wizard-in-training. —*Booklist*

Sequel to: *The lost years of Merlin*; Sequel: *The fires of Merlin.*

Ultimate magic. T.A. Barron. Philomel Books, 2010 223 p. : Map (Merlin's dragon trilogy, 3)
Grades: 6 7 8 9
1. Dragons; 2. Self-sacrifice; 3. Magic; 4. Wizards; 5. Merlin (Legendary character); 6. Arthurian fantasy; 7. Fantasy fiction
9780399252174

LC 2009041645
The dragon Basilgarrad leads the ultimate battle to save the land of Avalon, and finally must decide whether to obey his dear friend Merlin's request, even though it means giving up his powers as a warrior.

The many fans of Barron's various Merlin sagas will not be disappointed. —*Booklist*

The **wings** of Merlin. T. A. Barron. Philomel Books, 2000 352 p. (Lost years of Merlin, 5)
Grades: 5 6 7 8

1. Wizards; 2. Magic; 3. Warriors; 4. Escapes; 5. Merlin (Legendary character); 6. Arthurian fantasy; 7. Historical fantasy
9780399234569

LC 27553
Merlin's fragile home on the isle of Fincayra is threatened by the attack of a mysterious warrior with swords for arms and by the escape of Stangmar from his imprisonment, as Merlin continues to move toward his ultimate destiny.

Barron brings his Lost Years of Merlin saga to a resounding, satisfying close with this fifth volume. —*Booklist*

Sequel to: *The mirror of Merlin.*

Bartlett, Claire Eliza
★ **We** rule the night. Claire Eliza Bartlett. Little, Brown and Company, 2019 400 p.
Grades: 8 9 10 11 12
1. Fighter pilots; 2. Women soldiers; 3. War and society; 4. Magic; 5. Interpersonal conflict; 6. Historical fantasy.
9780316417273; 9780316417266; 9780316417280

LC 2018022805
Seventeen-year-olds Revna, the daughter of a traitor, and Linne, the daughter of a general, must use forbidden magic to fly planes in wartime despite their deep dislike of each other.

Rich characterizations and an enemy that, while it looms in the background, never feels quite as threatening as the country the girls are fighting for complete a story set against the bright, brutal backdrop of war. A breathless series starter from a new voice to watch. —*Booklist*

Bartoletti, Susan Campbell
★ The **boy** who dared. By Susan Campbell Bartoletti. Scholastic Press, 2008 202 p.
Grades: 5 6 7 8
1. Hubener, Helmuth; 2. Seventeen-year-old boys; 3. Courage in teenage boys; 4. Nazism; 5. Anti-Nazi movement; 6. Mormon teenage boys; 7. Germany; 8. 1940s; 9. Biographical fiction; 10. Historical fiction.
9780439680134

LC 2007014166
Carolyn W. Field Award (Pennsylvania), 2009; William Allen White Children's Book Award (Kansas) for Sixth-Eighth Grade, 2011; YALSA Popular Paperbacks for Young Adults, 2014; Booklist Editors' Choice: Books for Youth, 2008; YALSA Best Books for Young Adults, 2009.

In October, 1942, seventeen-year-old Helmuth Hubener, imprisoned for distributing anti-Nazi leaflets, recalls his past life and how he came to dedicate himself to bring the truth about Hitler and the war to the German people.

Bartoletti does and excellent job of conveying the political climate surrounding Hitler's ascent to power, seamlessly integrating a complex range of socioeconomic conditions into her absorbing drama. —*Publishers Weekly*

Barwin, Steven
Hardball. Steven Barwin. 2014 192 p.
Grades: 7 8 9 10
1. Baseball players; 2. Bullying and bullies; 3. Hazing; 4. Teenage baseball players; 5. High school seniors; 6. Baseball stories; 7. Canadian fiction; 8. High interest-low vocabulary books
9781459804418

LC 2014935389
Short, fast-paced chapters keep the narrative moving with a mix of baseball play-by-plays and sleuthing. A drug-dealing subplot adds a layer

of suspense and raises the stakes well beyond troubles on the ball field. Ideal for reluctant readers, this books gritty undertones will appeal to the intended high/low audience of sports fans. —*Booklist*

High interest story designed for reluctant readers or those reading below grade level.

Barzak, Christopher

The **gone** away place. Christopher Barzak. 2018 304 p.
Grades: 7 8 9 10
1. Tornadoes; 2. Survivor guilt; 3. Grief in teenage girls; 4. Friends' death; 5. Seventeen-year-old girls; 6. Ohio; 7. Middle West; 8. Ghost stories; 9. Multiple perspectives
9780399556098

LC 2017044047

After tornadoes demolish Newfoundland, Ohio, Ellie, seventeen, is haunted by ghosts of the dead, as well as survivors struggling to cope, but a chance encounter shows her how to free the lingering spirits.

★ **Wonders** of the invisible world. Christopher Barzak. Alfred A. Knopf, 2015 352 p.
Grades: 9 10 11 12
1. Family secrets; 2. Psychic ability; 3. Teenage boy/boy relations; 4. Memories; 5. Dreams; 6. Ohio; 7. Paranormal romances
9780385392792
Rainbow List, 2016; Stonewall Children's & Young Adult Literature Honor Book, 2016.

With leisurely pacing and simple, expressive language, Barzak expertly balances magical realism, historical flashbacks, and contemporary teen romance in Aidens journey of self-discovery. Give this to teen readers who want a quieter paranormal tale or a sincere love story between two boys. —*Booklist*

Bashardoust, Melissa

Girl, serpent, thorn. Melissa Bashardoust. Flatiron Books, 2020 336 p.
Grades: 9 10 11 12
1. Princesses; 2. Curses; 3. Transformations, Magic; 4. Demons; 5. Freedom; 6. Fairy tale and folklore-inspired fiction; 7. Middle Eastern-influenced fantasy; 8. Fantasy fiction.
9781250196149, HRD, US; 9781250196156, ebook, US; 9781529379075, Hardback, UK

LC 2019059176

Soraya, a princess cursed to be poisonous to the touch, has lived eighteen years in the shadows but as her twin brother's wedding approaches, she faces choices with unimaginable consequences.

Though weighty foreshadowing mars plot twists, Bashardoust's exceptional attention to folktale structure and Soraya's hard-won acceptance of herself make for a lyrical, inspiring read. —*Publishers Weekly*

Girls made of snow and glass. Melissa Bashardoust. Flatiron Books, 2017 400 p.
Grades: 7 8 9 10
1. Stepmothers; 2. Princesses; 3. Rulers; 4. Fathers; 5. Inheritance and succession; 6. Fairy tale and folklore-inspired fiction; 7. Fantasy fiction; 8. Multiple perspectives
9781250077738; 9781529381368
Amelia Bloomer List, 2018.

A feminist fantasy reimagining of "Snow White" relates the past and present experiences of a magician's daughter-turned-heartless queen and her beautiful rival stepdaughter.

Compellingly flawed characters, vivid world building, and pitch-perfect pacing make this utterly superb. —*Booklist*

Baskin, Nora Raleigh

All we know of love. Nora Raleigh Baskin. Candlewick Press, 2008 201 p;
Grades: 6 7 8 9 10
1. Mother-deserted children; 2. Bus travel; 3. Love; 4. Dating (Social customs); 5. Obsession; 6. Connecticut; 7. Florida; 8. Realistic fiction; 9. Coming-of-age stories.
9780763636234

LC 2007022396

Natalie, almost sixteen, sneaks away from her Connecticut home and takes the bus to Florida, looking for the mother who abandoned her father and her when she was ten years old.

Baskin takes a familiar story line and examines it in a new and interesting way that will engage readers. —*Voice of Youth Advocates*

Bass, Karen

Graffiti knight. Karen Bass. Pajama Press Inc, 2013 288 p. Map
Grades: 7 8 9 10
1. Anger in teenage boys; 2. Graffiti; 3. World War II — Post-war aspects; 4. Teenage boys; 5. Courage in teenage boys; 6. Germany; 7. Historical fiction; 8. Canadian fiction
9781927485538, paperback, Canada
Canadian Library Association Young Adult Book Award, 2014; Geoffrey Bilson Award for Historical Fiction, 2014; USBBY Outstanding International Book, 2015; OLA Best Bets, 2013.

In post-war Leipzig, teen Wilm feels justified in spray painting messages at night on police buildings in order to voice his displeasure, until one night his actions go too far.

Just as Ruta Sepetys revealed a different perspective of the Holocaust in Between Shades of Gray (2011), Bass introduces another view of history unknown to many American readers...This eye-opening story shows that war's end is never tidy. —*Booklist*

Bassoff, Leah

★ **Lost** girl found. Leah Bassoff and Laura DeLuca. Groundwood Books/House of Anansi Press, 2014 212 p.
Grades: 6 7 8 9 10
1. Girl refugees; 2. Refugee camps; 3. Survival; 4. Civil war; 5. Refugees, Sudanese; 6. Sudan; 7. Kenya
9781554984169; 9781773061955, Paperback, Canada
YALSA Best Fiction for Young Adults, 2015; USBBY Outstanding International Book, 2015.

For Poni, life in her small village in southern Sudan is simple and complicated at the same time. But then the war comes and there is only one thing for Poni to do. Run. Run for her life. Driven by the sheer will to survive and the hope that she can somehow make it to the Kakuma refugee camp in Kenya, Poni sets out on a long, dusty trek across the east African countryside with thousands of refugees.

After her southern Sudan village is bombed, Poni arrives at a Kenyan refugee camp, where conditions are brutal. Poni wants to finish her education, and she has a chance to do so when she escapes the refugee camp. Poni is a fully realized and sympathetic character. This fast-paced novel covers a lot of ground and incorporates a good deal of historical background. —*Horn Book Guide*

Bastedo, Jamie

Cut off. Jamie Bastedo. Midpoint Trade Books Inc, 2015 338 p.
Grades: 7 8 9 10
1. Teenage boy prodigies; 2. Addiction; 3. Bloggers; 4. Guitarists; 5. Attention-seeking; 6. Coming-of-age stories; 7. First person narratives; 8. Canadian fiction.
9780889955110

Indio's narration is completely believable throughout as he wrestles with identity and belonging. Bastedo gives readers who may be inclined to scoff at the addictive-cyberdevice premise the space to assess Indio's actions and reasoning and reach their own conclusions, all the while keeping the tension and pace high. A first-rate adventure with a powerful message. —*Kirkus*

On thin ice. Red Deer Press, 2006 348 p.
Grades: 8 9 10 11 12
1. Sixteen-year-old girls; 2. Teenage girls; 3. Teenagers; 4. Uncles; 5. Missing persons; 6. Arctic regions; 7. Canada; 8. First person narratives; 9. Thrillers and suspense; 10. Canadian fiction.
9780889953376

Set in Canada's far north, this book is a fascinating blend of both fact and fiction. Sixteen year old Ashley, who's from Inuit and French Canadian descent, is haunted by strange, ominous dreams. When a classmate's mangled body is found outside of her Arctic town, Ashley's dreams take on a frightening twist. Plunged into the mysterious underworld of ancient Inuit legends, Ashley strives to understand her changing world. Many of the problems, northern communities face today are touched upon in this fast paced novel for teens.

Set in the remote Arctic village of Nanurtalik, this novel follows Ashley as she journeys on the shaman path chosen for her through the Inuit line of her father. Disturbed by haunting —sometimes frightening—dreams of a gigantic polar bear that seems bent on destroying her, Ashley furiously draws her dreams onto paper, capturing the very essence of the bear within.... This novel is told with richness of language, culture, and emotion, but its sense of place sparkles brightest. —*Voice of Youth Advocates*

Bates, Marni
    Awkward. Marni Bates. KTeen, 2012 259 p; (Smith High, 1)
Grades: 7 8 9 10
1. Misfits (Persons); 2. Teenage girls; 3. Fame; 4. Internet videos; 5. Seventeen-year-old girls; 6. First person narratives; 7. Teen chick lit.
9780758269379
                                            LC Bl2011036321
When a humiliating accident at school is captured on video and posted on the Internet, clumsy Mackenzie is turned into an overnight Internet sensation, and is sucked into the world of rock stars, paparazzi, and worldwide popularity.

A brilliant but socially inept girl finds herself starring in a YouTube video gone viral when she knocks over a football player and tries to give him CPR.... Mackenzie tries to keep her head down as the entire nation laughs at her for her awkward video moves.... But her notoriety takes a positive turn when the hottest rock group around turns her film into a music video with a new hit song, boosting her fame even further.... Bates keeps her prose light, always focusing on the comedy as she lampoons high-school popularity, and gives narrator Mackenzie some good one-liners.... Very funny. Should please lots of readers, awkward or not. —*Kirkus*

Bauer, Joan
    ★ **Hope** was here. Joan Bauer. G. P. Putnam's Sons, 2000 192 p.
Grades: 7 8 9 10
1. Political corruption; 2. Aunt and niece; 3. Diners (Restaurants); 4. Moving to a new state; 5. People with leukemia; 6. Wisconsin; 7. Realistic fiction.
9780399231421
                                            LC 38232
ALA Notable Children's Book, 2001; Amelia Bloomer List, 2002; School Library Journal Best Books, 2000; Thumbs Up! Award (Michigan), 2001; YALSA Best Books for Young Adults, 2001; YALSA Popular Paperbacks for Young Adults, 2010; Young Reader's

Choice Award (Pacific Northwest), Senior, 2003; Newbery Honor Book, 2001.

When sixteen-year-old Hope and the aunt who has raised her move from Brooklyn to Mulhoney, Wisconsin, to work as waitress and cook in the Welcome Stairways diner, they become involved with the diner owner's political campaign to oust the town's corrupt mayor.

    ★ **Peeled**. Joan Bauer. G.P. Putnam's Sons, 2008 256 p.
Grades: 6 7 8 9 10
1. Teenage journalists; 2. Haunted houses; 3. Independence (Personal quality); 4. Supernatural; 5. Journalism; 6. New York (State); 7. Mysteries
9780399234750
                                            LC 2007042835
In an upstate New York farming community, high school reporter Hildy Biddle investigates a series of strange occurrences at a house rumored to be haunted.

This is a warm and funny story full of likable, offbeat characters led by a strongly voiced, independently minded female protagonist on her way to genuine, well-earned maturity. —*School Library Journal*

    ★ **Squashed**. Joan Bauer. Delacorte Press, 1992 194 p;
Grades: 6 7 8 9
1. Overweight teenage girls; 2. Self-perception; 3. Pumpkin; 4. Rural life; 5. Body image; 6. Iowa; 7. Romantic comedies; 8. Realistic fiction
9780385307932
                                            LC 91044905
As a sixteen-year-old pursues her two goals—growing the biggest pumpkin in Iowa and losing twenty pounds herself—she strengthens her relationship with her father and meets a young man with interests similar to her own.

Skillful plot development and strong characterization are real stengths here. Ellie's perspective, intelligent, and funny narrative keeps the story lively right up to its satisfying conclusion. —*School Library Journal*

Bauman, Beth Ann
    Rosie and Skate. Beth Ann Bauman. Wendy Lamb Books, 2009 217 p;
Grades: 9 10 11 12
1. Alcoholism; 2. Sisters; 3. Fathers and daughters; 4. Dating (Social customs); 5. Family problems; 6. New Jersey; 7. Realistic fiction; 8. Coming-of-age stories.
9780385737357
                                            LC 2009010575
Booklist Editors' Choice: Books for Youth, 2009.

New Jersey sisters Rosie, aged fifteen, and Skate, aged sixteen, cope differently with their father's alcoholism and incarceration, but manage to stay close to one another as they strive to lead normal lives and find hope for the future.

Bauman's prose is lovely and real. Vivid descriptions bring her characters to life, and the dialogue is both believable and funny.... The novel expertly captures the ever-hopeful ache of adolescents longing for love, stability and certainty. —*Kirkus*

Bayard, Louis
    ★ **Lucky** strikes. Louis Bayard. Henry Holt and Company, 2016 288 p.
Grades: 6 7 8 9
1. Orphans; 2. Poverty; 3. Service stations; 4. Brothers and sisters; 5. Drifters; 6. Virginia; 7. Depression era (1929-1941); 8. Historical fiction
9781627793902; 9781250115096; 9781627793919, ebook, US

LC 2015023829

Set in Depression Era Virginia, this is the story of orphaned Amelia and her struggle to keep her siblings together.

Her foible-ridden supporting cast features more adults than kids, and in an interesting twist, they give young readers insight into grown-up issues that transcend those usually found in youth books. Most of all, though, this is a darn good yarn with plenty of room for rooting and more than a few laughs. —*Booklist*

Bayerl, Katie
A **psalm** for lost girls. Katie Bayerl. 2017 368 p.
Grades: 8 9 10 11 12
1. Grief in teenage girls; 2. Kidnapping; 3. Sisters — Death; 4. Saints; 5. Death; 6. Massachusetts; 7. Mysteries; 8. Multiple perspectives
9780399545252

LC 2016027798

Determined to protect her sister Tess's memory, Callie da Costa sets out to prove Tess wasn't really a saint and finds herself pulled into a kidnapping investigation.

Bayron, Kalynn
Cinderella is dead. Kalynn Bayron. Bloomsbury YA, 2020 389 pages;
Grades: 9 10 11 12
1. Balls (Parties); 2. Lesbian teenagers; 3. Missing teenage girls; 4. Lesbians; 5. Patriarchy; 6. Fantasy fiction; 7. LGBTQIA fiction; 8. Fairy tale and folklore-inspired fiction
9781547603879; 9781526621979, Paperback, UK

LC 2019048162

It's 200 years since Cinderella found her prince, but the fairytale is over. Sophia knows the story though, off by heart. Because every girl has to recite it daily, from when she's tiny until the night she's sent to the royal ball for choosing. And every girl knows that she has only one chance. For the lives of those not chosen by a man at the ball are forfeit. But Sophia doesn't want to be chosen—she's in love with her best friend, Erin, and hates the idea of being traded like cattle. And when Sophia's night at the ball goes horribly wrong, she must run for her life. Alone and terrified, she finds herself hiding in Cinderella's tomb. And there she meets someone who will show her that she has the power to remake her world.

Bayron's deconstructive reimagining of the classic fairy tale is ambitious, replacing the happily-ever-after with a tragic legacy and a defiant, feminist tone. —*Publishers Weekly*

Beam, Cris
★ **I** am J. By Cris Beam. Little, Brown, 2011 352 p.
Grades: 9 10 11 12
1. Transgender teenagers; 2. Rejection (Psychology); 3. Emotional problems of teenagers; 4. Identity (Psychology); 5. Friendship; 6. Realistic fiction; 7. LGBTQIA fiction; 8. Books for reluctant readers
9780316053617

LC 2010008640

Rainbow List, 2012; YALSA Best Fiction for Young Adults, 2012; YALSA Popular Paperbacks for Young Adults, 2014; YALSA Quick Picks for Reluctant Young Adult Readers, 2012.

J, who feels like a boy mistakenly born as a girl, runs away from his best friend who has rejected him and the parents he thinks do not understand him when he finally decides that it is time to be who he really is.

The book is a gift to transgender teens and an affecting story of self-discovery for all readers. —*Horn Book Guide*

Beaudoin, Sean
Wise Young Fool. By Sean Beaudoin. Little, Brown and Company, 2013 448 p.
Grades: 10 11 12
1. Juvenile delinquents (Boys); 2. Teenage musicians; 3. Bands (Music); 4. Juvenile jails; 5. Teenage guitarists; 6. Realistic fiction; 7. First person narratives.
9780316203791

LC 2012032472

YALSA Best Fiction for Young Adults, 2014.

A teenaged guitarist in a rock band deals with loss and anger as he relates the events that landed him in a juvenile detention center.

This coming-of-age story is told in alternating story lines, leading up to Ritchie Sudden's arrest and his time in a juvenile detention center... There are a lot of messages about the importance of safe driving and staying away from drugs and alcohol without being preachy. This is not a typical rock band story; it is actually interesting. The author does a brilliant job getting into the head of a troubled teen and does not shy away from racy topics. —*School Library Journal*

Beaufrand, Mary Jane
Primavera. Little, Brown, 2009 256 p.
Grades: 6 7 8 9
1. Art, Renaissance (Europe); 2. Painting, Renaissance (Europe); 3. Power (Social sciences); 4. Girls; 5. European Renaissance; 6. Florence, Italy; 7. Italy; 8. Renaissance (1300-1600); 9. Coming-of-age stories; 10. Historical fiction.
9780316016452

Political, historical, and art historical details provide a canvas on which this tale of murder, intrigue, and young romance is played out, but are painted with a broad stroke. —*School Library Journal*

The **rise** and fall of the Gallivanters. M.J. Beaufrand. Amulet Books, 2015 304 p.
Grades: 9 10 11 12
1. Bands (Music); 2. Missing girls; 3. Friendship; 4. Punk rock musicians; 5. Friendship; 6. Portland, Oregon; 7. 1980s; 8. Historical fiction
9781419714955

LC 2014013556

In 1983, a band led by a David Bowie lookalike prepares to compete in a battle of the bands at a possibly evil brewery, and must also cope with the fact that bass player Evan is getting sicker and sicker, much like his best friend Noah's abusive father did before his death several years earlier.

Beaufrand's masterful pace compels readers toward the satisfying though heartbreaking conclusion, prodding them to question throughout whether Noah's story takes place in reality or in a dissociative hellscape. A chilling yet poignant story about the suffering in front of us that we can't bear to see. —*Kirkus*

★ **Useless** Bay. M. J. Beaufrand. Amulet Books, 2016 336 p.
Grades: 8 9 10 11
1. Quintuplets; 2. Missing children; 3. Family secrets; 4. Islands; 5. Brothers and sisters; 6. Washington (State); 7. Mysteries; 8. Pacific Northwest fiction; 9. Multiple perspectives
9781419721380

LC 2016007659

On Whidbey Island, north of Seattle, the Gray family's quintuplets join the search for a young boy gone missing and soon discover deep family secrets and that crimes have been committed.

Short in length but long on atmosphere, its a gripping mystery with a supernatural overlay that makes its setting all the more haunting. But its the irresistible Gray quints, subject to their own rumors and local mythos, who steal the show. —*Publishers Weekly*

Bechard, Margaret

Hanging on to Max. By Margaret Bechard. Roaring Brook Press, 2002 142 p.
Grades: 7 8 9 10
 1. Teenage parents; 2. Teenage fathers; 3. Fathers and sons; 4. Seventeen-year-old boys; 5. Single teenage fathers; 6. Portland, Oregon; 7. Oregon; 8. Pacific Northwest fiction; 9. Realistic fiction; 10. Books for reluctant readers
9780761315797; 9780340883709, print, UK

LC 2001048335

Black-Eyed Susan Book Award (Maryland), High School, 2005; YALSA Quick Picks for Reluctant Young Adult Readers, 2003; YALSA Best Books for Young Adults, 2003; School Library Journal Best Books, 2002.

When his girlfriend decides to give their baby away, seventeen-year-old Sam is determined to keep him and raise him alone.

Becker, Tom

Lifeblood. By Tom Becker. Orchard Books, 2008 288 p. (Darkside, 2)
Grades: 7 8 9 10
 1. Vampires; 2. Secret places; 3. Mothers and sons; 4. Murder; 5. Murderers; 6. London, England; 7. England; 8. Horror
9780545037426

LC 2007051180

As Jonathan searches London's Darkside for the same murderer that his mother was seeking when she disappeared twelve years earlier, it becomes clear that it is Jonathan who is being hunted.

Horror lovers will thrill to this gleeful gothic bloodbath. —*Horn Book Guide*

Bedford, Martyn

★ **Flip**. Martyn Bedford. Wendy Lamb Books, 2011 272 p.
Grades: 8 9 10 11 12
 1. Teenagers with asthma; 2. Identity (Psychology); 3. Soul; 4. Body swapping; 5. Supernatural; 6. England; 7. Psychological suspense; 8. Paranormal fiction.
9780385739900; 9780385670104

School Library Journal Best Books, 2011.

A teenager wakes up inside another boy's body and faces a life-or-death quest to return to his true self or be trapped forever in the wrong existence.

Bedford packs so much exhilarating action and cleanly cut characterizations into his teen debut that readers will be catapulted head-first into Alex's strange new world. —*Kirkus*

Bell, Cathleen Davitt

Slipping. By Cathleen Davitt Bell. Bloomsbury U.S.A. Children's Books : 2008 215 p.
Grades: 6 7 8 9
 1. Intergenerational relations; 2. Death; 3. Fathers and sons; 4. Ghosts; 5. Family relationships; 6. New York (State); 7. Ghost stories
9781599902586

LC 2008004420

Thirteen-year-old Michael and an unlikely group of allies journey to the river of the dead to help Michael's grandfather release his hold on a ghostly life and, in the process, heal wounds that have kept Michael's father distant.

The balance between the supernatural and genuine human feelings creates a compelling mix. —*Booklist*

Bell, Hilari

Fall of a kingdom. Hilari Bell. Simon Pulse, 2005 422 p; (Farsala trilogy, 1)
Grades: 7 8 9 10
 1. Teenage heroes and heroines; 2. Peddlers; 3. Prophecies; 4. Teenage girls; 5. Teenage boys; 6. High fantasy; 7. Fantasy fiction.
9780689854149

When the rulers mistakenly believe that they can destroy the evil force approaching Farsala, Jiaan, Soraya, and Kavi must find a way on their own to stop their town from being led into the Flames of Destruction.

Forging the sword. Hilari Bell. Simon & Schuster Books for Young Readers, 2006 512 p. (Farsala trilogy, 3)
Grades: 7 8 9 10
 1. Teenage heroes and heroines; 2. Magic; 3. Prophecies; 4. Teenage girls; 5. Teenage boys; 6. High fantasy; 7. Fantasy fiction.
9780689854163

LC 2005017730

Farsalans, including Lady Soraya and her half-brother, Jiaan, Kavi, and others, work relentlessly and often secretly in their shared strategies regarding the ultimate defeat of the Hrum.

Bell brings the Farsala Trilogy to a rousing conclusion.... The author maintains the complexity of her main characters and the intensity of the story line. —*Booklist*

★ The **last** knight. Hilari Bell. Eos, 2007 357 p; (Knight and rogue novels, 1)
Grades: 7 8 9 10
 1. Misadventures; 2. Knights and knighthood; 3. Former convicts; 4. Seventeen-year-old boys; 5. Rescues; 6. High fantasy; 7. Fantasy fiction; 8. Multiple perspectives
9780060825034; 9780060825041

YALSA Best Books for Young Adults, 2009.

Given the choice of going to jail for his mischievous ways or helping a knight on an errand to rescue a damsel in distress, the young con artist Fisk accepts the latter of the options and heads out on a mission with little intention of helping at all, especially when he discovers that the girl is a suspect in a murder case!

The novel is brimming with saved-by-a-hair escapades and fast-paced realistic action.... This well-created fantasy is a great read with worthwhile moral issues pertinent to its intended audience. —*School Library Journal*

Rise of a hero. Hilari Bell. Simon & Schuster Books for Young Readers, 2005 462 p. : Map (Farsala trilogy, 2)
Grades: 7 8 9 10
 1. Teenage heroes and heroines; 2. Magic; 3. Prophecies; 4. Teenage girls; 5. Teenage boys; 6. High fantasy; 7. Fantasy fiction.
9780689854156

LC 2003025164

Although the Hrum believe their war against Farsala is nearly over, Soraya has strategic information that will help if she can reach Jiaan and Kavi and their separate resistance movements, but discord and Time's Wheel seem destined to keep them apart.

With a palpable sense of danger and an ending that promises much to be revealed, this is a sequel that will fly off the shelf. —*Booklist*

Shield of stars. By Hilari Bell. Simon & Schuster Books For Young Readers, 2007 272 p. (Shield, sword, and the crown, 1)
Grades: 6 7 8 9 10
 1. Fourteen-year-old boys; 2. Pickpockets; 3. Treason; 4. Teenage boys; 5. Teenagers; 6. Fantasy fiction.
9781416905943

LC 2005035571

When the Justice he works for is condemned for treason, fourteen-year-old and semi-reformed pickpocket Weasel sets out to find a notorious bandit who may be able to help save his master's life.

Traitor's son. Hilari Bell. Houghton Mifflin, 2012 288 p. (Raven duet, 2)
Grades: 7 8 9 10 11 12
1. Native American teenage boys; 2. Shapeshifters; 3. Plague; 4. Family feuds; 5. Indians of North America; 6. Alaska; 7. Fantasy fiction.
9780547196213
In Alaska in the middle of the twenty-first century, Jase is drafted by a Native American trickster spirit to help stop a bio-plague caused by disruptions in the earth's flow of magic, and finds himself in the middle of a shapeshifter war.

The juxtaposition of magic with science is fascinating, and the waking dreams into the spirit world will keep readers riveted. It does help to have read *Trickster's Girl* first. —*School Library Journal*

Trickster's girl. By Hilari Bell. Houghton Mifflin, 2010 281 p; (Raven duet, 1)
Grades: 7 8 9 10
1. Shapeshifters; 2. Environmental degradation; 3. Grief in teenage girls; 4. Grief; 5. Fathers — Death; 6. Fantasy fiction.
9780547196206
LC 2010006785
In the year 2098, grieving her father and angry with her mother, fifteen-year-old Kelsa joins the magical Raven on an epic journey from Utah to Alaska to heal the earth by restoring the flow of magic that humans have disrupted.

The degree of nuance will sit especially well with readers who prefer their speculative fiction to be character-driven, and they'll appreciate the compelling exploration of the ways the hopeful can cope with uncertainty. —*Bulletin of the Center for Children's Books*

Bell, Joanne
Juggling fire. Joanne Bell. Orca Book Publishers, 2009 171 p;
Grades: 7 8 9 10
1. Sixteen-year-old girls; 2. Father-separated teenage girls; 3. Searching; 4. Father-deserted families; 5. Voyages and travels; 6. Yukon Territory; 7. First person narratives; 8. Coming-of-age stories; 9. Canadian fiction.
9781554690947
Rachel's dad left ten years ago to spend some "alone time" in the northern wilderness, but never returned. Haunted by this, Rachel vows to unravel the mystery of his sudden disappearance and embarks on a solo journey to retrace her dad's footsteps. Travelling through Canada's remote northern forests tests Rachel's survival skills to the max and it's through shear wit and tenacity that she is finally able to answer some of the questions that have plagued her for years.

Sixteen-year-old Rachel's father disappeared years earlier from her family's home in the Yukon wilderness.... The teen sets off on a trek through the tundra and forest with only her dog as a companion, hoping to find clues about her father's disappearance.... Bell beautifully captures the natural world through descriptions of the mountainous terrain as well as nail-biting encounters with bears and wolves. Rachel is a smart, resourceful narrator. —*School Library Journal*

Belleza, Rhoda
Empress of a thousand skies. Rhoda Belleza. Razorbill, an imprint of Penguin Random House, 2017 313 p.
Grades: 7 8 9 10 11 12
1. Princesses; 2. Revenge; 3. Frameups; 4. Refugees; 5. Memory; 6. Science fiction; 7. Multiple perspectives
9781101999103
Determined to reclaim her crown from a corrupt government and exact revenge for the deaths of her parents, Crown Princess Rhiannon narrowly escapes an assassination attempt and finds herself on the run in outer space alongside a refugee pilot who has been framed for the attack.

This is a multiplanet, multiculture, multitech world and a timely tale. An exceptionally satisfying series opener. —*Kirkus*

Bennardo, Charlotte
Blonde ops. . St. Martins Press, 2014 256 p.
Grades: 9 10 11 12
1. Teenage girls; 2. Americans in Italy; 3. Espionage; 4. SIxteen-year-old girls; 5. Teenage hackers; 6. Rome, Italy; 7. Spy fiction; 8. Thrillers and suspense
9781250030399
Sixteen-year-old Bec thinks she's in Rome for a boring internship at a fashion magazine. But it turns out her summer is anything but boring: Bec investigates—along with the CIA—a plot to kidnap the visiting First Lady, while juggling two cute guys. Bec's fashion-meets-espionage escapades are surprisingly tedious, but her computer skills (she's adept at hacking) add some hi-tech pizazz. —*Horn Book Guide*

Bennett, Holly
Shapeshifter. Holly Bennett. Orca Book Publishers, 2010 244 p. : Illustration; Map; Portrait
Grades: 7 8 9 10
1. Shapeshifters; 2. Warlocks; 3. Black magic; 4. Teenage girls; 5. Deer; 6. Ireland; 7. Historical fantasy; 8. Mythological fiction; 9. Canadian fiction.
9781554691586
This is a rich, slightly revisionist retelling of an ancient Irish legend. Basic human emotionsfear, love, greedmove the tale along, and short first-person narratives that personalize the action are interspersed throughout. —*Booklist*

Bennett, Jenn
Alex, approximately. By Jenn Bennett. 2017 400 p.
Grades: 9 10 11 12
1. Love-hate relationships; 2. Films; 3. Moving to a new state; 4. Teenage surfers; 5. Identity (Psychology); 6. California; 7. Contemporary romances
9781481478779; 9781471161049, print, UK; 9781471161056, eBook
LC 2016028663
YALSA Best Fiction for Young Adults, 2018.
Seventeen-year-old Bailey moves to California to live with her father and, perhaps, finally meet an online friend and fellow film buff, but soon finds herself attracted to an annoying co-worker.

There are a few mature references to sex, drugs, and drinking. Steamy romantic scenes capture the anticipation of young love and are carefully crafted to build to the inevitable and satisfying conclusion. —*School Library Journal*

Starry eyes. By Jenn Bennett. Simon Pulse, 2018 320 p.
Grades: 9 10 11 12
1. Misfits (Persons); 2. Former boyfriends; 3. Camping; 4. Survival; 5. Dating (Social customs); 6. California; 7. Realistic fiction; 8. Survival stories
9781481478809; 9781471161063, Paperback, UK; 9781481478816; 9781481478823, ebook, US
LC 2017025646

Rhode Island Teen Honor Book, 2020.

When teens Zorie and Lennon, a former couple, are stranded in the California wilderness together, they must put aside their differences, and come to terms with lingering romantic feelings, in order to survive.

A layered adventure-love story thats as much about the families we have and the families we make ourselves as it is about romance. —*Booklist*

Benoit, Charles

★ **You**. Charles Benoit. HarperTeen, 2010 208 p.
Grades: 8 9 10 11 12
1. Teenage boy misfits; 2. Consequences; 3. Crushes in teenage boys; 4. Crushes (Interpersonal relations); 5. Personal conduct; 6. Realistic fiction; 7. Second person narratives; 8. Books for reluctant readers
9780061947049
LC 2009043990
YALSA Quick Picks for Reluctant Young Adult Readers, 2011.

Fifteen-year-old Kyle discovers the shattering ramifications of the decisions he makes, and does not make, about school, the girl he likes, and his future.

The rapid pace is well suited to the narrative.... In the end, Benoit creates a fully realized world where choices have impact and the consequences of both action and inaction can be severe. —*School Library Journal*

Benway, Robin

Also known as. By Robin Benway. Walker Books For Young Readers, 2013 320 p. (Also known as novels, 1)
Grades: 7 8 9 10
1. Teenage spies; 2. Safecrackers; 3. High schools; 4. Sixteen-year-old girls; 5. Teenage girls; 6. New York City; 7. Spy fiction; 8. Books for reluctant readers
9780802733900
LC 2012026254
YALSA Quick Picks for Reluctant Young Adult Readers, 2014.

As the active-duty daughter of international spies, sixteen-year-old safecracker Maggie Silver never attended high school so when she and her parents are sent to New York for her first solo assignment, Maggie is introduced to cliques, school lunches, and maybe even a boyfriend.

While the framework requires more than a little suspension of disbelief, the absolutely delightful cast of characters and snappy dialogue transform this book into a huge success. —*School Library Journal*

★ **Far** from the tree. Robin Benway. HarperTeen, 2017 256 p.
Grades: 7 8 9 10 11 12
1. Adoption; 2. Brothers and sisters; 3. Families; 4. Teenage pregnancy; 5. Love; 6. Realistic fiction; 7. Multiple perspectives.
9780062330628; 9781471164330, paperback, UK
National Book Award for Young People's Literature, 2017; YALSA Best Fiction for Young Adults, 2018; Rainbow List, 2018.

Feeling incomplete as an adopted child after placing her own baby up for adoption, teen Grace tracks down her biological siblings and finds herself struggling with the dynamics of being a middle child between an embittered older brother and an outspoken younger sister.

Benway delves into the souls of these characters as they wrestle to overcome feelings of inadequacy, abandonment, and betrayal, gradually coming to understand themselves and each other. —*Publishers Weekly*

Benwell, Fox

★ The **last** leaves falling. Sarah Benwell. Simon & Schuster, 2015 352 p.
Grades: 7 8 9 10 11 12

1. Amyotrophic lateral sclerosis; 2. Teenagers with terminal illnesses; 3. Assisted suicide; 4. Internet; 5. Friendship; 6. Japan; 7. Realistic fiction
9781481430654; 9781909512322, Australia
USBBY Outstanding International Book, 2016.

References to samurai culture and snippets of poetry will leave readers at peace with the drifting ending. Benwell's gentle treatment of friendship and death with dignity will touch fans of John Green's The Fault in Our Stars (2012). —*Kirkus*

Berk, Ari

Death watch. Ari Berk. Simon & Schuster Books for Young Readers, 2011 496 p. (Undertaken trilogy, 1)
Grades: 7 8 9 10
1. Father-separated teenage boys; 2. Undertakers; 3. Clocks and watches; 4. Ghosts; 5. Seventeen-year-old boys; 6. Fantasy fiction; 7. Gothic fiction.
9781416991151
LC 2011006332
When seventeen-year-old Silas Umber's father disappears, Silas is sure it is connected to the powerful artifact he discovers, combined with his father's hidden hometown history, which compels Silas to pursue the path leading to his destiny and ultimately, to the discovery of his father, dead or alive.

Berk's setting is atmospheric and creepy, fleshed out with a wealth of funereal traditions and folklore. —*Publishers Weekly*

Berk, Josh

Guy Langman, crime scene procrastinator. Josh Berk. Alfred A. Knopf, 2012 240 p.
Grades: 7 8 9 10 11 12
1. Sixteen-year-old boys; 2. Grief in teenage boys; 3. Forensic sciences; 4. Criminal investigation; 5. Jewish teenage boys; 6. New Jersey; 7. Humorous stories; 8. Mysteries
9780375957017
LC 2011023864
Sixteen-year-old Guy Langman, his best friend Anoop, and other members of the school Forensics Club investigate a break-in and a possible murder, which could be connected to the mysterious past of Guy's recently-deceased father.

A Borzoi book.

Bernard, Romily

Find me. Romily Bernard. HarperTeen, an imprint of HarperCollinsPublishers, 2013 288 p. (Wick Tate series, 1)
Grades: 7 8 9 10 11 12
1. Teenage hackers; 2. Foster teenagers; 3. Children of criminals; 4. Sisters; 5. Teenage romance; 6. Thrillers and suspense; 7. Books for reluctant readers
9780062229038
LC 2013021519
YALSA Quick Picks for Reluctant Young Adult Readers, 2015.

When teen hacker and foster child Wick Tate finds a dead classmate's diary on her front step, with a note reading "Find me," she sets off on a perverse game of hide-and-seek to catch the killer.

Bernobich, Beth

Fox & Phoenix. Beth Bernobich. Viking, 2011 360 p. : Map (Long City series, 1)
Grades: 7 8 9 10
1. Teenage apprentices; 2. Sick persons; 3. Princesses; 4. Spirits; 5. Magic; 6. Fantasy fiction; 7. Asian-influenced fantasy

9780670012787

LC 2011009388

Sixteen-year-old Kai, a magician's apprentice and former street tough, must travel to the Phoenix Empire, where his friend Princess Lian is studying statecraft, and help her escape so she can return home before her father, the king, dies.

The characters and creatures in this book are interesting and believable; the plot is a compelling mixture of adventure, mystery, and fantasy. The most remarkable element, however, is the world Beth Bernobich has created. —*Voice of Youth Advocates*

Berry, Julie

All the truth that's in me. By Julie Berry. Viking, 2013 288 p.
Grades: 7 8 9 10 11 12

1. Teenage girls who are mute; 2. Teenage girl kidnapping victims; 3. Teenage girl misfits; 4. Crushes in teenage girls; 5. Community life; 6. Historical fiction; 7. First person narratives.
9780670786152; 9780732298067, Australia; 9781848771727, print, UK

LC 2012043218

Inky Awards (Australia): Silver Inky, 2014; School Library Journal Best Books, 2013; Westchester Fiction Award, 2014; YALSA Best Fiction for Young Adults, 2014; YALSA Best Fiction for Young Adults: Top Ten, 2014.

Rendered an outsider by a horrifying trauma that killed her best friend and left her unable to speak, Judith spends her days longing for the boy she loves until an attack on the community reveals long-buried secrets and compels Judith to reclaim her voice, even if it means changing her world, and the lives around her, forever.

Berry's novel is set in a claustrophobic village that seems to resemble an early American colonial settlement. Readers gradually learn all the truth from eighteen-year-old narrator Judith, who speaks directly (though only in her head) to her love, Lucas. Berry keeps readers on edge, tantalizing us with pieces of the puzzle right up until the gripping conclusion. —*Horn Book Guide*

★ **Lovely** war. Julie Berry. Viking, 2019 468 pages;
Grades: 9 10 11 12

1. Storytelling; 2. Love; 3. War; 4. Gods and goddesses, Greek; 5. World War I; 6. First World War era (1914-1918); 7. Second World War era (1939-1945); 8. Love stories; 9. War stories; 10. Historical fiction.
9780451469939, HRD, US; 9781984836236, paperback, US; 9780698157484, ebook, US

LC 2018289934

Booklist Editors' Choice: Books for Youth, 2019; Golden Kite Award for Fiction, 2020; Westchester Fiction Award, 2020.

Meeting in a World War II-era Manhattan hotel for a forbidden tryst, immortals Ares and Aphrodite are caught by the latter's jealous husband before she defends her actions by imparting the tale of four young humans who became connected during World War I.

An unforgettable romance so Olympian in scope, human at its core, and lyrical in its prose that it must be divinely inspired. —*Kirkus*
Includes bibliographical references (pages 465-466).

★ The **passion** of Dolssa. By Julie Berry. Penguin Group, 2016 480 p.
Grades: 7 8 9 10

1. Inquisition; 2. Faith; 3. Albigenses; 4. Christian heresies; 5. Teenage girls; 6. France; 7. Provence, France; 8. Medieval period (476-1492); 9. 13th century; 10. Historical fiction; 11. Magical realism; 12. Multiple perspectives
9780451469922

LC 2015020814

School Library Journal Best Books, 2016; Booklist Editors' Choice: Books for Youth, 2016; YALSA Best Fiction for Young Adults, 2017; Michael L. Printz Honor Book, 2017.

In mid-thirteenth century Provence, Dolssa de Stigata is a fervently religious girl who feels the call to preach, condemned by the Inquisition as an "unnatural woman," and hunted by the Dominican Friar Lucien who fears a resurgence of the Albigensian heresy; Botille is a matchmaker trying to protect her sisters from being branded as gypsies or witches—but when she finds the hunted Dolssa dying on a hillside, she feels compelled to protect her, a decision that may cost her everything.

A (fictional) Catholic mystic, Dolssa de Stigata, escapes being burned as a heretic in 1241 France; mostly, this is the story of Botille, an enterprising young matchmaker from a tiny fishing village who rescues Dolssa. Botille's spirited character, the heart-rending suspense of events, and the terrifying context of the Inquisition in medieval Europe all render the novel irresistibly compelling. —*Horn Book Guide*
Includes bibliographical references.

Berry, Nina

The **Notorious** Pagan Jones. Nina Berry. Harlequin Teen, 2015 394 p. (Pagan Jones, 1)
Grades: 9 10 11 12

1. Teenage actors and actresses; 2. Intrigue; 3. Espionage; 4. Cold War; 5. Guilt; 6. Berlin, Germany; 7. 1960s; 8. Historical fiction; 9. Thrillers and suspense; 10. Spy fiction
9780373211432; 9780373211906; 9781489210296, print, Australia
YALSA Popular Paperbacks for Young Adults, 2017.

Scary in all the right places, with a strong setup for the sequel. —*Kirkus*

Bertagna, Julie

★ **Exodus**. Julie Bertagna. Walker : 2008 352 p. (Exodus (Julie Bertagna), 1)
Grades: 6 7 8 9 10

1. Survival; 2. Global warming; 3. Near future; 4. Refugees; 5. Climate change; 6. 22nd century; 7. Apocalyptic fiction; 8. Science fiction
9780802797452; 9780330400961, print, UK

LC 2007023116

YALSA Popular Paperbacks for Young Adults, 2010.

In the year 2100, as the island of Wing is about to be covered by water, fifteen-year-old Mara discovers the existence of New World sky cities that are safe from the storms and rising waters, and convinces her people to travel to one of these cities in order to save themselves.

Astonishing in its scope and exhilarating in both its action and its philosophical inquiry. —*Booklist*
Originally published in the U.K. in 2002; Sequel: *Zenith*.

Zenith. Julie Bertagna. Walker Pub. Co. : 2008 340 p. (Exodus (Julie Bertagna), 2)
Grades: 6 7 8 9 10

1. Survival; 2. Global warming; 3. Near future; 4. Refugees; 5. Pirates; 6. 22nd century; 7. Apocalyptic fiction; 8. Science fiction
9780802798039

LC 2008007591

After finding that New Mungo is not the refuge they sought, Mara, leaving Fox behind, again sets out to sea with a ship full of refugees and, with the help of the "Gipsea" boy Tuck, tries to find land at the top of the world that will be safe from storms and rising water.

This is mostly Mara's story—a plucky, imperfect heroine leading the way to an uncertain future in a hostile world. —*Booklist*
Sequel to: *Exodus*.

Betts, A. J.

Zac and Mia. By A. J. Betts. Houghton Mifflin Harcourt, 2014 310 p.

Grades: 9 10 11 12

1. Teenagers with cancer; 2. Teenagers with leukemia; 3. Cancer; 4. Leukemia; 5. Friendship; 6. Realistic fiction; 7. Australian fiction.

9780544331648; 9781922147257, paperback, Australia; 9781443432658

NSW Premier's Literary Awards, Ethel Turner Prize for Young People's Literature, 2014.

The last person Zac expects in the room next door is a girl like Mia, angry and feisty with questionable taste in music. In the real world, he wouldn't—couldn't—be friends with her. In hospital different rules apply, and what begins as a knock on the wall leads to a note—then a friendship neither of them sees coming. —Provided by publisher

Above average in this burgeoning subgenre; it's the healing powers of friendship, love and family that make this funny-yet-philosophical tale of brutal teen illness stand out. —*Kirkus*

Beyer, Kat

The **demon** catchers of Milan. Kat Beyer. Egmont USA, 2012 288 p. (Demon catchers of Milan trilogy, 1)

Grades: 7 8 9 10 11

1. Demonic possession; 2. Exorcism; 3. Americans in Italy; 4. Demons; 5. Families; 6. Italy; 7. Milan, Italy; 8. Urban fantasy

9781606843147

LC 2011034348

After surviving being possessed by a demon, sixteen-year-old Mia leaves her family in New York to stay with cousins in Milan, Italy, where she must study her family's heritage of demon catching in order to stay alive.

Bick, Ilsa J.

The **Sin** eater's confession. By Ilsa J. Bick. Carolrhoda Lab, 2013 320 p.

Grades: 6 7 8 9 10 11 12

1. Hate crimes; 2. Farm life; 3. Photography; 4. Murder; 5. Homosexuality; 6. Wisconsin; 7. Realistic fiction; 8. LGBTQIA fiction

9780761356875

Westchester Fiction Award, 2014; YALSA Best Fiction for Young Adults, 2014.

While serving in Afghanistan, Ben writes about incidents from his senior year in a small-town Wisconsin high school, when a neighbor he was trying to help out becomes the victim of an apparent hate crime and Ben falls under suspicion.

Bickle, Laura

The **hallowed** ones. Laura Bickle. Graphia, 2012 304 p. (Hallowed ones, 1)

Grades: 7 8 9 10 11 12

1. Amish; 2. Survival; 3. Post-apocalypse; 4. Amish teenage girls; 5. Hiding; 6. Apocalyptic fiction.

9780547859262

LC 2012014800

Amelia Bloomer List, 2013.

Amish teen Katie smuggles a gravely injured young man, an outsider, into her family's barn despite the elders' ruling that no one can come in or out of the community while some mysterious and massive unrest is wreaking havoc in the "English" world.

Sequel: *The outside.*

The **outside**. Laura Bickle. Graphia, Houghton Mifflin Harcourt, 2013 320 p. (Hallowed ones, 2)

Grades: 7 8 9 10 11 12

1. Amish; 2. Survival; 3. Post-apocalypse; 4. Amish teenage girls; 5. Vampires; 6. Apocalyptic fiction.

9780544000131

Sequel to: *The hallowed ones.*

Bigelow, Lisa Jenn

Starting from here. Lisa Jenn Bigelow. Amazon Children's Pub, 2012 282 p. :

Grades: 8 9 10 11 12

1. Lesbian teenagers; 2. Teenagers and dogs; 3. Loneliness; 4. Dating (Social customs); 5. Dogs; 6. Realistic fiction; 7. LGBTQIA fiction

9780761462330

LC 2011040129

Rainbow List, 2013.

Sixteen-year-old Colby is barely hanging on with her mother dead, her long-haul trucker father often away, her almost-girlfriend dumping her for a boy, and her failing grades, when a stray dog appears and helps her find hope.

Bilen, Tracy

What she left behind. Tracy Bilen. Simon Pulse, 2012 256 p.

Grades: 9 10 11 12

1. Family violence; 2. Resilience in teenage girls; 3. Missing persons; 4. Resilience (Personal quality); 5. Fathers; 6. Realistic fiction.

9781442439511

LC 2011028989

Sixteen-year-old Sara's mother goes missing before she and Sara can move to a new town to escape Sara's physically abusive father.

Sharp prose and an increasingly tense plot make this debut a page-turner. —*Publishers Weekly*

Billingsley, Franny

★ **Chime**. By Franny Billingsley. Dial Books for Young Readers, 2011 320 p.

Grades: 7 8 9 10 11 12

1. Twin sisters; 2. Guilt in teenage girls; 3. Swamps; 4. Guilt; 5. Supernatural; 6. England; 7. Historical fantasy.

9780803735521; 9781408803844, print, UK

LC 2010012140

Booklist Editors' Choice: Books for Youth, 2011; YALSA Best Fiction for Young Adults, 2012; YALSA Popular Paperbacks for Young Adults, 2016; School Library Journal Best Books, 2011; National Book Award for Young People's Literature finalist, 2011.

Plagued by guilt for harm that she believes she brought on her family, 17-year-old Briony Larkin is convinced that she's a witch. But there are many dark secrets in Briony's village of Swampsea, and when a London engineer and his handsome son arrive to drain the marshes—causing the supernatural Old Ones who live in the swamp to retaliate—those secrets begin bubbling to the surface.

Filled with eccentric characters—self-hating Briony foremost—and oddly beautiful language, this is a darkly beguiling fantasy. —*Publishers Weekly*

Bingham, Kelly L.

★ **Shark** girl. Kelly Bingham. Candlewick Press, 2007 288 p.

Grades: 7 8 9 10

1. People who have had amputations; 2. Coping in teenage girls; 3. Teenage girl artists; 4. Artists; 5. Coping; 6. Realistic fiction; 7. Novels in verse.

9780763632076

LC 2006049120

Iowa Teen Award, 2011.

After a shark attack causes the amputation of her right arm, fifteen-year-old Jane, an aspiring artist, struggles to come to terms with her loss and the changes it imposes on her day-to-day life and her plans for the future.

In carefully constructed, sparsely crafted free verse, Bingham's debut novel offers a strong view of a teenager struggling to survive and learn to live again. —*Booklist*

Sequel: *Formerly shark girl.*

Birch, Carol

Jamrach's menagerie. Carol Birch. Doubleday, 2011 295 p.
Grades: 11 12 Adult

1. Poor boys; 2. Exotic animals; 3. Ocean travel — History; 4. Human behavior; 5. Seafaring life; 6. England; 7. Great Britain; 8. Victorian era (1837-1901); 9. Historical fiction; 10. Adventure stories; 11. Adult books for young adults.
9780385534406; 9781443405164; 9781921758454, Australia; 9781847676566, print, UK; 9781847676573, print, UK
Booklist Editors' Choice: Adult Books for Young Adults, 2011; School Library Journal Best Books: Best Adult Books 4 Teens, 2011; Shortlisted for the Man Booker Prize, 2011.

Recruited by a famed importer of exotic animals to capture a fabled dragon during a three-year whaling expedition, former street urchin Jaffy Brown and his friend and rival, Tim, successfully capture the beast only to find themselves targeted by superstitious sailors.

Jaffy's experience could well move the reader as profoundly as it changed the narrator. —*Kirkus*

Black, Holly

Black heart. Holly Black. Margaret K. McElderry Books, 2012 320 p. (Curse workers, 3)
Grades: 7 8 9 10

1. Teenage boys; 2. Civil service workers; 3. Love; 4. Crime; 5. Seventeen-year-old boys; 6. Urban fantasy
9781442403468

LC 2011028143

Cassel Sharpe, a powerful transformation worker, is torn between his decision to work for the federal government and his love for Lila, who has joined her father's criminal organization.

★ The **cruel** prince. Holly Black. Little Brown & Co, 2018 384 p. (Folk of the air, 1)
Grades: 9 10 11 12

1. Fairies; 2. Orphans; 3. Political intrigue; 4. Princes; 5. Courts and courtiers; 6. High fantasy; 7. Fantasy fiction
9780316310277; 9780316310314; 9781471407031, print, UK; 9781471406464, HB
ALA Notable Children's Book, 2019; Inky Awards (Australia): Silver Inky, 2019; YALSA Best Fiction for Young Adults, 2019.

Jude was seven years old when her parents were murdered and she and her two sisters were stolen away to live in the treacherous High Court of Faerie. Ten years later, Jude wants nothing more than to belong there, despite her mortality. But many of the fey despise humans. Especially Prince Cardan, the youngest and wickedest son of the High King.

This is a heady blend of Faerie lore, high fantasy, and high school drama, dripping with description that brings the dangerous but tempting world of Faerie to life. —*Kirkus*

Poison eaters: and other stories. Holly Black. Small Beer Press, 2010 256 p.

Grades: 9 10 11 12

1. Fairies; 2. Devil; 3. Magic; 4. Good and evil; 5. Fantasy fiction; 6. Short stories
9781931520638

For those with a penchant for dark, edgy, fantasy fiction, Holly Black...offers readers a collection of twelve stories. Ten tales have appeared in anthologies; two appear in print here for the first time.... Deftly blending both believable characters and realistic settings, Black serves up heady concoctions for those who like their fairy tales on the chilly side. The graphic nature of some of this collection's stories make it best suited for fantasy fans in senior high school. —*Voice of Youth Advocates*

★ The **queen** of nothing. Holly Black; illustrations by Kathleen Jennings. Little, Brown and Company, 2019 320 p. (Folk of the air, 3)
Grades: 9 10 11 12

1. Fairies; 2. Rulers; 3. Curses; 4. Twin sisters; 5. Courts and courtiers; 6. High fantasy; 7. Fantasy fiction
9780316310420, HRD, US; 9780316310376; 9780316310406, ebk, US; 9780316310390, library edition ebk, US; 9781471408502, Paperback, UK; 9781471407581, Hardback, UK

LC 2019021819

As the exiled Queen of Faerie, Jude must travel back to Elfhame to help her twin sister, Taryn, and uncover how to break a dark curse threatening the whole Faerie world—Provided by publisher.

Whether you came for the lore or the love, perfection. —*Kirkus*

Red glove. Holly Black. Margaret K. McElderry Books, 2011 320 p. (Curse workers, 2)
Grades: 7 8 9 10

1. Criminals; 2. Gangsters; 3. Curses; 4. Swindlers and swindling; 5. Magic; 6. Urban fantasy
9781442403390

LC 2010031884

YALSA Best Fiction for Young Adults, 2012.

When federal agents learn that seventeen-year-old Cassel Sharpe, a powerful transformation worker, may be of use to them, they offer him a deal to join them rather than the mobsters for whom his brothers work.

This offers a sleek a stylish blend of urban fantasy and crime noir. —*Booklist*

★ The **white** cat. Holly Black. Margaret K. McElderry Books, 2010 320 p. (Curse workers, 1)
Grades: 7 8 9 10

1. Dreams; 2. Brothers; 3. Swindlers and swindling; 4. Memory; 5. Sleep-walking; 6. Urban fantasy
9781416963967

LC 2009033979

YALSA Popular Paperbacks for Young Adults, 2015; YALSA Best Fiction for Young Adults, 2011.

Cassel Sharpe comes from a family of criminals and "curse workers," people who practice magic illegally and can alter others' luck or memories with a single touch. Cassel, who doesn't seem to have inherited his family's talents, tries very hard to convince his private-school classmates that he's just a regular guy. But he's haunted by a dirty secret from his past, and a white cat that keeps appearing in his nightmares.

This starts out with spine-tingling terror, and information is initially dispensed so sparingly, readers will be hooked. —*Booklist*

★ The **wicked** king. Holly Black. Little Brown & Co, 2019 336 p. (Folk of the air, 2)
Grades: 9 10 11 12

1. Fairies; 2. Inheritance and succession; 3. Rulers; 4. Brothers; 5. Betrayal; 6. High fantasy; 7. Fantasy fiction
9780316310352; 9780316310321; 9781471407352, Hardback, UK; 9781471407369, Paperback, UK

Goodreads Choice Award, 2019.

After the jaw-dropping revelation that Oak is the heir to Faerie, Jude must keep her younger brother safe. To do so, she has bound the wicked king, Cardan, to her, and made herself the power behind the throne. Navigating the constantly shifting political alliances of Faerie would be difficult enough if Cardan were easy to control. But he does everything in his power to humiliate and undermine her even as his fascination with her remains undiminished. When it becomes all too clear that someone close to Jude means to betray her, threatening her own life and the lives of everyone she loves, Jude must uncover the traitor and fight her own complicated feelings for Cardan to maintain control as a mortal in a Faerie world.

Black expands the reaches of her brutally beautiful world and the depths of her deadly, vulnerable characters, and the employ of yet another cliff-hanger ending will leave readers agonized. A sinister, singular thrill. High-demand Backstory: Black's practically a household name, the film rights to *The Cruel Prince* have been sold, and the six-figure marketing campaign for this installment means that the buzz is deafening. —*Booklist*

Blair, Jamie M.
Leap of Faith. Jamie Blair. Simon & Schuster Books for Young Readers, 2013 256 p.
Grades: 9 10 11 12
1. Children of drug abusers; 2. Kidnapping; 3. Runaway teenage girls; 4. Seventeen-year-old girls; 5. Teenage girls; 6. Ohio; 7. Florida; 8. Realistic fiction; 9. First person narratives
9781442447134

Seventeen-year-old Faith shepherds her neglectful, drug-addicted mother through her pregnancy and then kidnaps the baby, taking on the responsibility of being her baby sister's parent while hiding from the authorities.

While the novel's realism may suffer from the idyll Faith finds so suddenly in Florida, the poignancy of her plight and the desperate sincerity of her motives easily overcome any quibbles about plausibility. Just a marvelous debut, moving and suspenseful. —*Kirkus*

Blake, Ashley Herring
Girl made of stars. Ashley Herring Blake. 2018 304 p.
Grades: 9 10 11 12
1. Twin brothers and sisters; 2. Date rape; 3. Best friends; 4. Bisexual teenagers; 5. Secrets; 6. Realistic fiction
9781328778239
LC 2017015661

Amelia Bloomer List, 2019; YALSA Best Fiction for Young Adults, 2019.

When Mara's twin brother Owen is accused of rape by her friend Hannah, Mara is forced to confront her feelings about her family, her sense of right and wrong, a trauma from her past, and the future with her girlfriend, Charlie.

The book explores so many topics—consent, slut shaming, rape culture, what it means to move on from trauma— but the tone never veers into pedantic territory, and the pace moves remarkably quickly for such heavy and emotional content. —*School Library Journal*

Blake, Kendare
★ **Anna** dressed in blood. Kendare Blake. St. Martins Press, 2011 320 p. (Anna Korlov series, 1)
Grades: 8 9 10 11 12
1. Girl ghosts; 2. Ghosts; 3. Psychics; 4. Detectives; 5. Knives; 6. Horror; 7. Ghost stories; 8. Books for reluctant readers
9780765328656; 9780765328670; 9781408320723, print, UK

Westchester Fiction Award, 2011; YALSA Best Fiction for Young Adults, 2012; YALSA Quick Picks for Reluctant Young Adult Readers, 2012; YALSA Popular Paperbacks for Young Adults, 2017.

For three years, seventeen-year-old Cas Lowood has carried on his father's work of dispatching the murderous dead, traveling with his kitchen-witch mother and their spirit-sniffing cat, but everything changes when he meets Anna, a girl unlike any ghost he has faced before.

Blake populates the story with a nice mixture of personalities, including Anna, and spices it with plenty of gallows humor, all the while keeping the suspense pounding.... Abundantly original, marvelously inventive and enormous fun, this can stand alongside the best horror fiction out there. We demand sequels. —*Kirkus*
Sequel: *Girl of nightmares.*

Blankman, Anne
Conspiracy of blood and smoke. Anne Blankman. Balzer + Bray, an imprint of HarperCollinsPublishers, 2015 336 p. (Prisoner of night and fog, 2)
Grades: 9 10 11 12
1. Hitler, Adolf; 2. Nazis; 3. Dating (Social customs); 4. Jews; 5. Murder investigation; 6. Teenage girls; 7. Germany; 8. Between the Wars (1918-1939); 9. 1930s; 10. Historical fiction
9780062278845; 9781472207876, print, UK
LC 2014038687

In 1933, eighteen-year-old Gretchen, niece of Adolph Hitler, reunites with her Jewish boyfriend when she leaves the safety of England to return to Germany to investigate a murder and expose the evil of the Nazi regime.

Suspenseful and clever, intertwining historical truth with action-packed shootouts. —*Kirkus*
Sequel to: *Prisoner of night and fog;* Includes bibliographical references.

Prisoner of night and fog. Anne Blankman. Balzer + Bray, 2014 336 pages (Prisoner of night and fog, 1)
Grades: 7 8 9 10 11 12
1. Hitler, Adolf; 2. Nazis; 3. Journalists; 4. Jews; 5. Love; 6. Fathers — Death; 7. Germany; 8. Munich, Germany; 9. Between the Wars (1918-1939); 10. 1930s; 11. Historical fiction
9780062278814; 9781472207821, print, UK
LC 2013043071

In 1930s Munich, the favorite niece of rising political leader Adolph Hitler is torn between duty and love after meeting a fearless and handsome young Jewish reporter.

It takes moxie to feature Adolf Hitler as a lead character, but that's just what debut author Blankman does, rejecting the safer route of hiding him offstage. It's a winning gamble, providing a fictionalized portrait of a man both approachably normal and chillingly unknowable...There is much to like here: the realistic changing of Gretchen's ingrained beliefs, the icy fright of her psychotic Nazi brother, side roles for everyone from Rudolf Hess to Eva Braun, and Blankman's exhaustive research. If it feels incomplete, that's because (thankfully) more is coming. —*Booklist*

Bliss, Bryan
No parking at the end times. Bryan Bliss. Greenwillow Books, an imprint of HarperCollins Publishers, 2015 336 p.
Grades: 9 10 11 12
1. Twin brothers and sisters; 2. Faith; 3. Homeless persons; 4. Family problems; 5. Teenagers; 6. San Francisco, California; 7. Realistic fiction; 8. First person narratives
9780062275417
LC 2014037503

Abigail's parents, believing the end of the world is near, sell their house, give the money to an end-of-times preacher, and drive from North Carolina to San Francisco where they remain homeless and destitute, as Abigail fights to keep her parents, her twin brother, and herself united against all odds.

Bliss's depiction of a middle-class, suburban family's transition to life on the inhospitable San Francisco streets is nuanced and character-driven; the tightly focused first-person narration centers the story squarely on Abigail as she gathers the courage to choose between her family and her future. Bliss's debut explores family, sacrifice, and the power of everyday faith with a deft and sensitive hand. —*Horn Book Guide*

★ **We'll** fly away. Bryan Bliss. Harpercollins Childrens Books 2018 320 p.
Grades: 9 10 11 12
1. High school seniors; 2. Death row prisoners; 3. Best friends; 4. Dysfunctional families; 5. Abusive men; 6. Multiple perspectives; 7. Realistic fiction
9780062494276; 9780062494283
YALSA Best Fiction for Young Adults, 2019; Booklist Editors' Choice: Books for Youth, 2018.

Best friends Toby and Luke are bound together by the goal of leaving their hometown and family problems behind, but a series of choices each makes during their senior year threatens their bright future plans.

A powerful story of loyalty, betrayal, and crippling family dysfunction. —*Publishers Weekly*

Block, Francesca Lia
★ **Love** in the time of global warming. Francesca Lia Block. Henry Holt and Company, 2013 224 p.
Grades: 8 9 10 11 12
1. Survival; 2. Earthquakes; 3. Voyages and travels; 4. Teenage romance; 5. Post-apocalypse; 6. Los Angeles, California; 7. Magical realism; 8. Apocalyptic fiction
9780805096279; 9780805099027, ebook, US
LC 2012047808
Rainbow List, 2014.

After a devastating earthquake destroys the West Coast, causing seventeen-year-old Penelope to lose her home, her parents, and her ten-year-old brother, she navigates a dark world, holding hope and love in her hands and refusing to be defeated.

In this Odyssey-inspired story, after the devastating Earth Shaker, Penelope sets out into the brutal Los Angeles landscape in search of her family. She meets an intriguing boy named Hex who joins her on her journey. Block's imagery is remarkable in this sophisticated melding of post-apocalyptic setting, re-imagined classic, and her signature magical realism. —*Horn Book Guide*
Christy Ottaviano Books.

The **rose** and the beast: fairy tales retold. By Francesca Lia Block. HarperCollins, 2000 229 p.
Grades: 7 8 9 10
1. Teenage incest victims; 2. Teenage drug users; 3. Teenage fashion models; 4. Escapes; 5. Teenage girls; 6. Los Angeles, California; 7. Short stories; 8. Fairy tale and folklore-inspired fiction
9780060281298
LC 22444
YALSA Popular Paperbacks for Young Adults, 2016.
Nine fairy tales are turned "inside out".

The author's beautiful words turn modern-day Los Angeles into a fantastical world of fairies, angels, and charms. The context is very modern, with issues of drug addiction, rape, and suicide smoothly woven into the stories, which are infused with a palpable if not explicit eroticism. —*Booklist*

Weetzie Bat. Francesca Lia Block. Harper & Row, 1989 88 p. (Weetzie Bat, 1)
Grades: 9 10 11 12
1. Teenage girls; 2. Teenagers; 3. Punk culture; 4. Pregnant teenagers; 5. Gay teenagers; 6. Los Angeles, California; 7. Magical realism
9780060205348
LC 88006214
Phoenix Award, 2009.

Follows the wild adventures of Weetzie Bat and her Los Angeles punk friends, Dirk, Duck-Man, and Secret-Agent-Lover-Man.

A brief, off-beat tale that has great charm, poignancy, and touches of fantasy.... This creates the ambiance of Hollywood with no cynicism, from the viewpoint of denizens who treasure its unique qualities. —*School Library Journal*
A Charlotte Zolotow book.

Bloor, Edward
★ **Taken**. Edward Bloor. Alfred A. Knopf, 2007 256 p.
Grades: 6 7 8 9 10
1. Near future; 2. Kidnapping; 3. Kidnapping victims; 4. Social classes; 5. Gated communities; 6. Florida; 7. Science fiction
9780375836367; 9780375936364
LC 2006035561

In 2036 kidnapping rich children has become an industry, but when thirteen-year-old Charity Meyers is taken and held for ransom, she soon discovers that this particular kidnapping is not what it seems.

Deftly constructed, this is as riveting as it is thought-provoking. —*Publishers Weekly*

Blume, Judy
★ **Forever...**: a novel. Judy Blume. Bradbury Press, 1975 199 p.
Grades: 9 10 11 12
1. Teenage romance; 2. Sexuality; 3. Teenage girls; 4. Teenagers — Sexuality; 5. Eighteen-year-olds; 6. Love stories; 7. Classics.
9780027110302; 9780330397803, print, UK
LC 74022850
YALSA Popular Paperbacks for Young Adults, 2008.

Katherine and Michael, along with various friends and acquaintances in suburban New Jersey, discover the possibilities and limitations of love and personal commitment.

The story of a teenage senior-year love affair based primarily on physical attraction. Once Katherine Danziger and Michael Wagner meet at a party, they have eyes only for each other, and their romance progresses rapidly from kissing to heavy petting to lying together and finally to frequent sexual intercourse after Kath gets the Pill from a Planned Parenthood officer.... Characters—including adults and friends of the protagonists—are well developed, dialog is natural, and the story is convincing; however, the explicit sex scenes will limit this to the mature reader. —*Booklist*

Tiger eyes: a novel. Judy Blume. Bradbury Press, 1981 206 p.
Grades: 7 8 9 10
1. Teenagers and death; 2. Fathers — Death; 3. Grief in teenagers; 4. Anger in teenagers; 5. Fifteen-year-old girls; 6. Los Alamos, New Mexico; 7. Realistic fiction; 8. Books to movies
9780878881857
LC 81006152
Buckeye Children's Book Award (Ohio), Grades 3-5, 1983; California Young Reader Medal, Middle School, 1983; Colorado Blue Spruce

YA Book Award, 1985; Iowa Teen Award, 1985; YALSA Popular Paperbacks for Young Adults, 2015.

Resettled in Los Alamos, New Mexico with her mother and brother, Davey Wexler recovers from the shock of her father's death during a holdup of his 7-Eleven store in Atlantic City.

The plot is strong, interesting and believable.... The story though intense and complicated flows smoothly and easily. —*Voice of Youth Advocates*

Blumenthal, Deborah

Mafia girl. Deborah Blumenthal. Albert Whitman & Company, 2014 256 pages
Grades: 8 9 10 11
1. Mafia; 2. Private schools; 3. Identity (Psychology); 4. Police; 5. Schools; 6. Manhattan, New York City; 7. Realistic fiction
9780807549117
LC 2013028440

As the daughter of an infamous mob boss, seventeen-year-old Gia struggles to come out of the shadow of her family's notorious reputation and be her own person.

Gia, the prized daughter of a New York Mafia boss, enjoys the carefree lifestyle her father's money and connections afford her. When the feds begin to close in on the family business, Gia must find an identity outside of Don's Daughter. Gia's voice is an entertaining, effervescent stream-of-consciousness, but the book's frantic pace muddles too many competing plot lines. —*Horn Book Guide*

Blundell, Judy

Strings attached. Judy Blundell. Scholastic Press, 2011 320 p.
Grades: 7 8 9 10
1. Teenage girl dancers; 2. Mafia; 3. High school dropouts; 4. Former boyfriends; 5. Italian Americans; 6. New York City; 7. 1950s; 8. Historical fiction.
9780545221269
LC 2010041078
YALSA Best Fiction for Young Adults, 2012; YALSA Popular Paperbacks for Young Adults, 2015.

When she drops out of school and struggles to start a career on Broadway in the fall of 1950, seventeen-year-old Kit Corrigan accepts help from an old family friend, a lawyer said to have ties with the mob, who then asks her to do some favors for him.

Blundell successfully constructs a complex web of intrigue that connects characters in unexpected ways. History and theater buffs will especially appreciate her attention to detail—Blundell again demonstrates she can turn out first-rate historical fiction. —*Publishers Weekly*

★ **What** I saw and how I lied. Judy Blundell. Scholastic Press, 2008 288 p.
Grades: 8 9 10 11 12
1. Family problems; 2. Secrets; 3. Stepfathers; 4. Teenage girls — Relations with older men; 5. Fifteen-year-old girls; 6. Florida; 7. 1940s; 8. Historical fiction.
9780439903462; 9781407116150, print, UK
LC 2008008503
National Book Award for Young People's Literature, 2008; YALSA Popular Paperbacks for Young Adults, 2011; YALSA Best Books for Young Adults, 2009; School Library Journal Best Books, 2008.

In 1947, with her jovial stepfather Joe back from the war and family life returning to normal, teenage Evie, smitten by the handsome young ex-GI who seems to have a secret hold on Joe, finds herself caught in a complicated web of lies whose devastating outcome change her life and that of her family forever.

Using pitch-perfect dialogue and short sentences filled with meaning, Blundell has crafted a suspenseful, historical mystery. —*Booklist*

Bock, Caroline

★ **Lie**. Caroline Bock. St. Martin's Griffin, 2011 224 p.
Grades: 8 9 10 11 12
1. Hate crimes; 2. Right and wrong; 3. Racism; 4. Personal conduct; 5. Bullying and bullies; 6. Long Island, New York; 7. Psychological suspense; 8. Multiple perspectives; 9. First person narratives.
9780312668327
LC 2011019824
Told in several voices, a group of Long Island high school seniors conspire to protect eighteen-year-old Jimmy after he brutally assaults two Salvadoran immigrants, until they begin to see the moral implications of Jimmy's actions and the consequences of being loyal to a violent bully.

This effective, character-driven, episodic story examines the consequences of a hate crime on the teens involved in it.... Realistic and devastatingly insightful, this novel can serve as a springboard to classroom and family discussions. Unusual and important. —*Kirkus*

Bodeen, S. A.

The **compound**. S.A. Bodeen. Feiwel and Friends, 2008 248 p;
Grades: 7 8 9 10
1. Deception; 2. Psychopaths; 3. Fallout shelters; 4. Survival; 5. Fathers; 6. Thrillers and suspense; 7. Books for reluctant readers
9780312370152
LC 2007036148
Black-Eyed Susan Book Award (Maryland), Grades 6-9, 2011; Golden Sower Award (Nebraska), Young Adult, 2012; YALSA Popular Paperbacks for Young Adults, 2013; YALSA Quick Picks for Reluctant Young Adult Readers, 2009; Young Hoosier Book Award, Middle Books, 2011.

After his parents, two sisters, and he have spent six years in a vast underground compound built by his wealthy father to protect them from a nuclear holocaust, fifteen-year-old Eli, whose twin brother and grandmother were left behind, discovers that his father has perpetrated a monstrous hoax on them all.

The audience will feel the pressure closing in on them as they, like the characters, race through hairpin turns in the plot toward a breathless climax. —*Publishers Weekly*
Sequel: *The fallout*.

The **raft**. S. A. Bodeen. Feiwel & Friends, 2012 240 p.
Grades: 7 8 9 10
1. Airplane accidents; 2. Castaways; 3. Survival (after airplane accidents, shipwrecks, etc.); 4. Rafts; 5. FIfteen-year-old girls; 6. Survival stories; 7. Adventure stories; 8. Books for reluctant readers
9780312650100
Nutmeg Children's Book Award, Teen category, 2015; South Carolina Book Award, Junior Books, 2015; Truman Readers Award (Missouri), 2015; YALSA Quick Picks for Reluctant Young Adult Readers, 2013.

When her last-minute cargo flight to the Pacific Islands Midway Atoll is brought down by a catastrophic storm, lone passenger Robie finds herself drifting in the middle of the ocean on a raft with the co-pilot, Max, with whom she struggles to survive without supplies.

There is an odd lack of panic to much of the proceedings, but if you can get beyond that, this is tight, engaging, cleverly constructed fiction, with a late-in-the-game twist that makes perfect, if heartbreaking, sense. —*Booklist*

Bolden, Tonya
★ **Crossing** Ebenezer Creek. By Tonya Bolden. Bloomsbury, 2017 240 p. (Crossing Ebenezer Creek, 1)
Grades: 7 8 9 10 11 12
1. African Americans; 2. Freed slaves; 3. Resilience (Personal quality); 4. Sherman's March to the Sea; 5. Brothers and sisters; 6. Georgia; 7. United States; 8. American Civil War era (1861-1865); 9. Historical fiction; 10. African American fiction; 11. Multiple perspectives
9781599903194
LC 2016037742
School Library Journal Best Books, 2017; YALSA Best Fiction for Young Adults, 2018.
Freed from slavery, Mariah and her young brother Zeke join Sherman's march through Georgia, where Mariah meets a free black named Caleb and dares to imagine the possibility of true love, but hope can come at a cost.
A poetic, raw, and extraordinary imagining of a little-known, shameful chapter in American history. —*Kirkus*

Inventing Victoria. By Tonya Bolden. Bloomsbury, 2019 272 p. (Crossing Ebenezer Creek, 2)
Grades: 8 9 10 11 12
1. Social classes; 2. African American women; 3. Ambition; 4. Upward mobility; 5. Young women; 6. Savannah, Georgia; 7. Washington, D.C; 8. 1880s; 9. Gilded Age (1865-1898); 10. Historical fiction; 11. Coming-of-age stories; 12. African American fiction.
9781681198071; 9781681198088, ebook, US
LC 2018024642
Essie, a young black woman in 1880s Savannah, is offered the opportunity to leave her shameful past and be transformed into an educated, high-society woman in Washington, D.C.
Standalone follow-up to *Crossing Ebenezer Creek.*

Saving Savannah. By Tonya Bolden. Bloomsbury, 2020 240 p.
Grades: 8 9 10 11 12
1. African Americans; 2. Suffragists; 3. Social change; 4. Socialism; 5. Postwar life; 6. Washington (D.C.); 7. 1900s (Decade); 8. Historical fiction
9781681198040, HRD, US; 9781681198057, ebook, US
LC 2019019792
Savannah Riddle feels suffocated by her life as the daughter of an upper class African American family in Washington, D.C, until she meets a working-class girl named Nella who introduces her to the suffragette and socialist movements and to her politically active cousin Lloyd.
While Savannah's characterization lacks some nuance, the story is richly complex in its historical detail, and it builds to a revelatory climax. Enhanced by a comprehensive author's note, this is a valuable portrayal of affluent African-American society and of post-WWI life. —*Publishers Weekly*

Bond, Gwenda
Fallout. By Gwenda Bond. 2015 304 pages. (Lois Lane (Gwenda Bond), 1)
Grades: 7 8 9 10
1. Video gamers; 2. Virtual reality; 3. Bullying and bullies; 4. Mind control; 5. Superman (Fictitious character); 6. Mysteries; 7. Superhero stories; 8. Franchise books
9781630790059; 9781782023685, print, UK
LC 2014026793
Lois Lane is the new girl at East Metropolis High, and her instinct to ask questions brings her and her online friend, Smallville Guy, into con-flict with some bullying video gamers called the Warheads, who are being used in a dangerous virtual reality experiment.

Boone, Martina
Compulsion. Martina Boone. Simon & Schuster, 2014 320 p. (Heirs of Watson Island trilogy, 1)
Grades: 9 10 11 12
1. Plantations; 2. Supernatural; 3. Family secrets; 4. Spirits; 5. Compulsive behavior; 6. Paranormal fiction; 7. Gothic fiction.
9781481411226
Though the novel is grounded in the present day, theres an old-fashioned quality to Boones dialogue and characters; she skillfully blends rich magic and folklore with adventure, sweeping romance, and hidden treasure, all while exploring the island and its accompanying legends. An impressive start to the Heirs of Watson Island series. —*Publishers Weekly*

Booth, Coe
★ **Bronxwood.** Coe Booth. PUSH, 2011 320 p.
Grades: 10 11 12
1. Sixteen-year-old boys; 2. Children of former convicts; 3. Family problems; 4. Teenage boy/girl relations; 5. African American teenage boys; 6. Bronx, New York City; 7. Realistic fiction; 8. First person narratives; 9. African American fiction; 10. Books for reluctant readers
9780439925341, HRD, US; 9780439925358, paperback, US
YALSA Best Fiction for Young Adults, 2012; YALSA Quick Picks for Reluctant Young Adult Readers, 2012.
Tyrell's life is spinning out of control after his father is released from prison, his little brother is placed in foster care, and the drug dealers he's living with are pressuring him to start dealing.
Action scenes combine with interpersonal exchanges to keep the pace moving forward at a lightning speed, but Booth never sacrifices the street-infused dialogue and emotional authenticity that characterize her works. She has created a compelling tale of a teen still trying to make the right choices despite the painful consequences. —*School Library Journal*

Tyrell. Coe Booth. PUSH, 2006 320 p.
Grades: 9 10 11 12
1. African American teenage boys; 2. Homeless teenagers; 3. Children of prisoners; 4. Fifteen-year-old boys; 5. Teenage boys; 6. Bronx, New York City; 7. South Bronx, New York City; 8. Realistic fiction; 9. African American fiction; 10. Books for reluctant readers
9780439838795, hardback, US; 9780439838801, paperback, US
LC 2005037330
Los Angeles Times Book Prize for Young Adult Fiction; YALSA Best Books for Young Adults, 2007; YALSA Popular Paperbacks for Young Adults, 2010; YALSA Quick Picks for Reluctant Young Adult Readers, 2007.
Fifteen-year-old Tyrell, who is living in a Bronx homeless shelter with his spaced-out mother and his younger brother, tries to avoid temptation so he does not end up in jail like his father.
The immediate first-person narrative is pitch perfect: fast, funny, and anguished... Unlike many books reflecting the contemporary street scene, this one is more than just a pat situation with a glib resolution; it's filled with surprising twists and turns that continue to the end. —*Booklist*

Booth, Molly
Saving Hamlet. Molly Booth. 2016 352 p.
Grades: 7 8 9 10
1. Shakespeare, William, 1564-1616; 2. Theater; 3. Time travel (Past); 4. Actors and actresses; 5. Crushes in teenage girls; 6.

Fifteen-year-old girls; 7. England; 8. Elizabethan era (1558-1603); 9. Fantasy fiction.
9781484752746

LC 2015045426

Fifteen-year-old Emma is acting as stage manager for her school's production of *Hamlet* when she finds herself transported to the original staging of Hamlet in Shakespearean England.

Emma is an easy-to-root-for heroine whose struggles will resonate with teens, drama geeks or otherwise, and her forays into Shakespeare's London add insight into gender identity in the theater. A fun, imaginative debut. —*Booklist*

Bourne, Holly
It only happens in the movies. Holly Bourne. Houghton Mifflin Harcourt, 2020 368 p.
Grades: 9 10 11 12
1. Teenage girls; 2. Cynicism; 3. Love; 4. Children of divorced parents; 5. Divorce; 6. Romantic comedies
9780358172062

Turning cynical about love in the face of her parents' acrimonious divorce, her own shifting relationships and the fictional portrayals of love in movies, Audrey bonds with a flirtatious co-worker, Harry, who encourages her to take a chance in the real world.

Audrey and Harry's relationship sings with witty banter, electric heat, and feverish emotion, but Audrey's journey to self-discovery reaps even more rewards, leaving readers with a fresh, realistic look at first love. —*Kirkus*

Bow, Erin
★ The **scorpion** rules. Erin Bow. Margaret K. McElderry Books, 2015 374 p. (Prisoners of Peace, 1)
Grades: 9 10 11 12
1. Children of heads of state; 2. Hostages; 3. Artificial intelligence; 4. Political intrigue; 5. Insurgency; 6. Dystopian fiction; 7. Science fiction; 8. Books for reluctant readers
9781481442718
Canadian Library Association Young Adult Book Award, 2016; Monica Hughes Award for Science Fiction and Fantasy, 2016; Westchester Fiction Award, 2016; YALSA Quick Picks for Reluctant Young Adult Readers, 2016; OLA Best Bets, 2015.

In order to keep the peace, an artificial intelligence called Talis takes the children of world leaders hostage because if any leader starts a war their child will be killed. Things get shaken up when a new hostage named Elián doesn't accept the system and shows duchess and crown princess Greta the truth about the world they live in.

Bowman, Akemi Dawn
Starfish. Akemi Dawn Bowman. 2017 352 pages
Grades: 7 8 9 10
1. Multiracial teenage girls; 2. Artists; 3. Self-perception in teenage girls; 4. Self-perception; 5. Family problems; 6. Nebraska; 7. California; 8. Realistic fiction
9781481487726

LC 2016045829

William C. Morris Debut Award finalist, 2018.

Kiko Himura yearns to escape the toxic relationship with her mother by getting into her dream art school, but when things do not work out as she hoped Kiko jumps at the opportunity to tour art schools with her childhood friend, learning life-changing truths about herself and her past along the way.

The story will resonate deeply with readers who have experienced abuse of any kind, or who have been held back by social anxiety. This is a stunningly beautiful, highly nuanced debut. —*Booklist*

Summer bird blue. Akemi Dawn Bowman. Simon Pulse, 2018 384 p.
Grades: 7 8 9 10 11 12
1. Parent-separated teenage girls; 2. Survivor guilt; 3. Sisters — Death; 4. Intergenerational friendship; 5. Grief in teenagers; 6. Hawaii; 7. Coming-of-age stories; 8. Realistic fiction.
9781481487757; 9781785302275, Paperback, Australia

Rumi Seto plans to spend her life writing music with her younger sister, Lea. When Lea dies in a car accident, her mother sends Rumi to live with her aunt in Hawaii while she deals with her own grief. Struggling with the loss of her sister, abandoned by her mother, and without music in her life, Rumi turns to the friendship of a teenage surfer named Kai, and an eighty-year-old named George Watanabe. And Rumi is determined to write the song she and Lea never had the chance to finish.—adapted from jacket.

Bradbury, Jennifer
★ **Shift**. Jennifer Bradbury. Atheneum Books for Young Readers, 2008 245 p.
Grades: 7 8 9 10 11 12
1. Missing teenage boys; 2. Transcontinental journeys; 3. Children of rich people; 4. Family problems; 5. Bicycling; 6. Realistic fiction; 7. Coming-of-age stories.
9781416947325

LC 2007023558

YALSA Popular Paperbacks for Young Adults, 2015; YALSA Best Books for Young Adults, 2009.

After graduating from high school, best friends Win and Chris take a cross-country bicycle trek from West Virginia to Washington state, during which they discover amazingly beautiful places, meet fascinating people...and have a nasty fight. Win abandons Chris in Montana with no explanation, so Chris finishes the trip solo and returns home to start college...and until an FBI agent shows up to question him about the details of their trip, Chris has no idea that Win never made it back. Outdoor types, armchair travelers, and mystery fans won't be able to flip these pages fast enough.

Bradbury's keen details...add wonderful texture to this exciting [novel.]...Best of all is the friendship story. —*Booklist*

Brahmachari, Sita
Jasmine skies. Sita Brahmachari. Albert Whitman & Company, 2014 330 pages;
Grades: 6 7 8 9
1. East Indian British teenagers; 2. Family visits; 3. British in India; 4. Families; 5. Teenage boy/girl relations; 6. India; 7. London, England; 8. Realistic fiction
9780807537824; 9781509855353, print, UK

LC 2014013302

Fourteen-year-old Mira Levenson travels from London to Kolkata to meet her aunt and her cousin and to find out why the families haven't spoken in years..

Vivid descriptions of the exotic setting, an emotionally honest (if naive and stubborn) narrator, and a sweet romance should captivate readers. —*Booklist*
Sequel to: *Mira in the present tense*.

Brant, Wendy
★ **Zenn** diagram. Wendy Brant. KCP Loft, 2017 328 p.
Grades: 8 9 10 11 12

1. Genius; 2. Teenage artists; 3. Visions; 4. Teenage romance; 5. New students; 6. Paranormal romances; 7. First person narratives
9781771387927, hardback, Canada; 9781525300264, Paperback, Canada

A teen math genius who secretly possesses the ability to read the emotions, fears and dreams of anyone she touches is drawn to an artistic newcomer with a troubled home life only to discover their shattering common history.

Though the plot coincidences stretch belief at times, they are forgiven in light of the strengths of the story, which include a unique premise, natural dialogue, and complex characters. —*Booklist*

Brashares, Ann

The **sisterhood** of the traveling pants. Ann Brashares. Delacorte Press, 2001 294 p. (Sisterhood of the Traveling Pants series, 1)
Grades: 8 9 10
1. Best friends; 2. Blue jeans; 3. Teenage girls — Friendship; 4. Teenage girls — Personal conduct; 5. Teenagers; 6. Coming-of-age stories; 7. Realistic fiction; 8. Teen chick lit
9780385729338
Black-Eyed Susan Book Award (Maryland), High School, 2003; Book Sense Book of the Year for Children's Literature, 2002; Eliot Rosewater Indiana High School Book Award (Rosie Award), 2004; Garden State Teen Book Award (New Jersey), Fiction (Grades 9-12), 2004; Gateway Readers Award (Missouri), 2004; Heartland Award, 2003; Iowa Teen Award, 2004; Rhode Island Teen Book Award, 2002; Sequoyah Book Awards (Oklahoma), Young Adult Books, 2004; Young Hoosier Book Award, Middle Books, 2004; Young Reader's Choice Award (Pacific Northwest), Senior, 2004; Booklist Editors' Choice: Books for Youth, 2001; YALSA Popular Paperbacks for Young Adults, 2009; YALSA Best Books for Young Adults, 2002.

Four best girlfriends spend the biggest summer of their lives enchanted by a magical pair of pants.

Four lifelong high-school friends and a magical pair of jeans take summer journeys to discover love, disappointment, and self-realization. —*Booklist*

Brashear, Amy

The **incredible** true story of the making of the Eve of Destruction. Amy Brashear. Soho Teen, 2018 320 p.
Grades: 8 9 10 11 12
1. Cold War; 2. Filmmaking; 3. Nuclear weapons; 4. Stepbrothers and stepsisters; 5. Teenagers; 6. Arkansas; 7. 1980s; 8. Historical fiction.
9781616959036; 9781641290487; 9781616959043, ebook, US
LC 2018027722
In 1984, while grappling with her parents' divorce and her mother's remarriage to an African-American man, sixteen-year-old Laura wins a walk-on role in the nuclear holocaust movie being filmed in her Arkansas town.

Braxton-Smith, Ananda

★ **Merrow**. Ananda Braxton-Smith. Candlewick Press, 2016 240 p. (Secrets of Carrick, 1)
Grades: 9 10 11 12
1. Teenage girl orphans; 2. Missing women; 3. Civilization, Medieval; 4. Rumor; 5. Truth; 6. Historical fantasy; 7. Australian fiction
9780763679248; 9781742031361, Australia
Children's Book Council of Australia: Notable Australian Children's Book; YALSA Best Fiction for Young Adults, 2017.

A sparkling paean to the stories we tellplain and embroidered, fantastical, amazing, truethat get us through the night. —*Kirkus*

Bray, Libba

★ **Beauty** queens. Libba Bray. Scholastic Press, 2011 400 p.
Grades: 8 9 10 11 12
1. Castaways; 2. Beauty contestants; 3. Survival (after airplane accidents, shipwrecks, etc.); 4. Beauty contests; 5. Survival; 6. Humorous stories.
9780439895972
LC 2011002321
Amelia Bloomer List, 2012; Rainbow List, 2012; Romantic Times Reviewers' Choice Award, 2011; YALSA Best Fiction for Young Adults, 2012; YALSA Popular Paperbacks for Young Adults, 2014.

When a plane crash strands thirteen teen beauty contestants on a mysterious island, they struggle to survive, to get along with one another, to combat the island's other diabolical occupants, and to learn their dance numbers in case they are rescued in time for the competition.

A full-scale send-up of consumer culture, beauty pageants, and reality television:...it makes readers really examine their own values while they are laughing, and shaking their heads at the hyperbolic absurdity of those values gone seriously awry. —*Bulletin of the Center for Children's Books*

★ The **diviners**. By Libba Bray. Little, Brown, 2012 608 p. (Diviners, 1)
Grades: 9 10 11 12
1. Teenage girl psychics; 2. Occultism; 3. Museums; 4. Uncles; 5. Murder; 6. New York City; 7. 1920s; 8. Historical fantasy
9780316126113; 9781742375229, Australia; 9780316126106; 9781743319482, Australia; 9781907410390, print, UK
LC 2012022868
School Library Journal Best Books, 2012; YALSA Best Fiction for Young Adults, 2013; YALSA Popular Paperbacks for Young Adults, 2017.

After humiliating her parents with her unrestrained behavior at a party, privileged young Evie O'Neill is sent to live with her eccentric uncle in New York City—a "punishment" that utterly delights Evie, who can't wait to mix with Ziegfield girls and sneak into some big-city speakeasies (it's the Roaring Twenties). But when her Uncle Will, curator of the Museum of American Folklore, Superstition, and the Occult, is called on to help solve a rash of bizarre, other-worldly murders, Evie is drawn in to the investigations because of a special ability she's tried to keep secret.

★ **Going** bovine. Libba Bray. Delacorte Press, 2009 496 p.
Grades: 9 10 11 12
1. Sick persons; 2. Automobile travel; 3. Mad cow disease; 4. Quests; 5. Teenage boys; 6. Classics-inspired fiction.
9780385733977
LC 2008043774
Michael L. Printz Award, 2010; YALSA Popular Paperbacks for Young Adults, 2012; Booklist Editors' Choice: Books for Youth, 2009; YALSA Best Books for Young Adults, 2010.

Cameron Smith, a disaffected sixteen year-old who, after being diagnosed with Creutzfeld Jakob's (aka mad cow) disease, sets off on a road trip with a death-obsessed video gaming dwarf he meets in the hospital in an attempt to find a cure.

Bray's wildly imagined novel, narrated in Cameron's sardonic, believable voice, is wholly unique, ambitious, tender, thought-provoking, and often fall-off-the-chair funny, even as she writes with powerful lyricism about the nature of existence, love, and death. —*Booklist*

A **great** and terrible beauty. Libba Bray. Delacorte Press, 2004 416 p. (Gemma Doyle trilogy, 1)
Grades: 9 10 11 12

1. Sixteen-year-old girls; 2. Boarding schools; 3. Teenage girls; 4. Women — History; 5. Friendship; 6. Great Britain; 7. England; 8. Victorian era (1837-1901); 9. 19th century; 10. Historical fantasy
9780385730280; 9780385901611

LC 2003009472

Iowa High School Book Award, 2007; YALSA Best Books for Young Adults, 2004.

After the suspicious death of her mother in 1895, sixteen-year-old Gemma returns to England, after many years in India, to attend a finishing school where she becomes aware of her magical powers and ability to see into the spirit world.

The reader will race to the end to discover the mysterious and realistic challenges of an exciting teenage gothic mystery. —*Library Media Connection*

Sequel: *Rebel Angels*.

Lair of dreams: a Diviners novel. Libba Bray. Little, Brown and Company, 2015 608 p. (Diviners, 2)
Grades: 9 10 11 12

1. Teenage girl psychics; 2. Dreams; 3. Sleep; 4. Psychic ability; 5. Supernatural; 6. New York City; 7. 1920s; 8. Historical fantasy
9780316126045; 9781907410420, print, UK; 9781742375236, print, Australia

Rainbow List, 2016.

A multilayered, character-driven, and richly rewarding installment to the paranormal historical fiction series. —*School Library Journal*

Rebel angels. Libba Bray. Delacorte Press, 2005 560 p. (Gemma Doyle trilogy, 2)
Grades: 9 10 11 12

1. Sixteen-year-old girls; 2. Boarding schools; 3. Teenage girls; 4. Good and evil; 5. Magic; 6. London, England; 7. England; 8. Victorian era (1837-1901); 9. 19th century; 10. Historical fantasy
9780385730297; 9780385902571

LC 2005003805

YALSA Best Books for Young Adults, 2006.

Gemma and her friends from the Spence Academy return to the realms to defeat her foe, Circe, and to bind the magic that has been released.

The writing never falters, and the revelations (such as Felicity's childhood of abuse, discreetly revealed) only strengthen the characters. Clever foreshadowing abounds, and clues to the mystery of Circe may have readers thinking they have figured everything out; they will still be surprised. —*School Library Journal*

Sequel to: *A great and terrible beauty*; Sequel: *The sweet far thing*.

The **sweet** far thing. Libba Bray. Delacorte Press, 2007 560 p. (Gemma Doyle trilogy, 3)
Grades: 9 10 11 12

1. Sixteen-year-old girls; 2. Boarding schools; 3. Teenage girls; 4. Good and evil; 5. Visions; 6. London, England; 7. England; 8. Victorian era (1837-1901); 9. 19th century; 10. Historical fantasy
9780385730303; 9780385902953; 9780440237778; 9781847383259, print, UK

LC 2007031302

At Spence Academy, sixteen-year-old Gemma Doyle continues preparing for her London debut while struggling to determine how best to use magic to resolve a power struggle in the enchanted world of the realms, and to protect her own world and loved ones.

The novel's fast-paced and exciting ending and Bray's lyrical descriptions of the decaying realms are sure to enchant readers who loved Gemma's previous exploits. —*School Library Journal*

Sequel to: *Rebel angels*.

Brennan, Sarah Rees

The **demon's** lexicon. Sarah Rees Brennan. Margaret K. McElderry Books, 2009 322 p. (Demon's lexicon trilogy, 1)
Grades: 9 10 11 12

1. Demon slayers; 2. Magicians; 3. Demons; 4. Black magic; 5. Good and evil; 6. England; 7. Urban fantasy
9781416963790

YALSA Best Books for Young Adults, 2010.

Ever since their father was murdered, brothers Nick and Alan Ryves have been on the run from evil, power-crazed magicians who conjure demons to do their bidding. According to Alan, the magicians are after the protective charm that the boys' mother stole. But brooding, cold-hearted Nick is starting to suspect that his older brother, the only person he's ever trusted, is lying to him about...well, everything.

A fresh voice dancing between wicked humor and crepuscular sumptuousness invigorates this urban fantasy.... The narrative peels back layers of revelation, deftly ratcheting up the tension and horror to a series of shattering climaxes. —*Kirkus*

In other lands: a novel. Sarah Rees Brennan. Big Mouth House : 2017 432 p.
Grades: 8 9 10 11 12

1. Bisexual teenagers; 2. Schools; 3. Friendship; 4. Imaginary creatures; 5. Bisexual teenage boys; 6. Fantasy fiction; 7. Coming-of-age stories
9781618731203

LC 2016059543

Despite his aversion to war, work, and most people (human or otherwise), teenaged Elliott, a human transported to a fantasy world where he attends a school for warriors and diplomatic advisers, finds that two unlikely ideas, friendship and world peace, may actually be possbile.

Smart explorations of gender stereotypes, fluid sexuality, and awkward romance only add to the depth and delight of this glittering contemporary fantasy. —*Publishers Weekly*

Brewer, Zac

The **cemetery** boys. Heather Brewer. HarperTeen, 2015 288 p.
Grades: 9 10 11 12

1. Small towns; 2. Children of people with mental illnesses; 3. Twin brothers and sisters; 4. Supernatural; 5. Dating (Social customs); 6. Michigan; 7. Horror
9780062307880

LC 2014027404

When Stephen moves to the midwestern town where his father grew up, he quickly falls in with punk girl Cara and her charismatic twin brother, Devon, but the town has a dark secret, and the twins are caught in the middle of it.

The novel's final pages will surely shock readers: The author takes great glee in not just presenting a great reveal toward the end, but also twisting the knife. Keen-eyed readers may spot the twist, but few will predict just how far it goes. A slick, spooky, chilling mystery. —*Kirkus*

Brezenoff, Steven

Brooklyn, burning. By Steve Brezenoff. Carolrhoda Lab, 2011 202 p.
Grades: 8 9 10 11

1. Teenage musicians; 2. Drummers; 3. Crushes in teenagers; 4. Crushes (Interpersonal relations); 5. Interpersonal relations; 6. Brooklyn, New York City; 7. New York City; 8. Realistic fiction; 9. LGBTQIA fiction
9780761375265

LC 2010051447

Rainbow List, 2012; YALSA Best Fiction for Young Adults, 2012.

Sixteen-year-old Kid, who lives on the streets of Brooklyn, loves Felix, a guitarist and junkie who disappears, leaving Kid the prime suspect in an arson investigation, but a year later Scout arrives, giving Kid a second chance to be in a band and find true love.

Homelessness, queerness and the rougher sides of living on the street are handled without a whiff of sensationalism, and the moments between Kid, the first-person narrator, and Scout, addressed as you, are described in language so natural and vibrant that readers may not even notice that neither character's gender is ever specified.... Overall, the tone is as raw, down-to-earth and transcendent as the music Scout and Kid ultimately make together. —*Kirkus*

Brignull, Irena
★ The **hawkweed** prophecy. Irena Brignull. Weinstein Books, 2016 362 p. (Hawkweed prophecy, 1)
Grades: 7 8 9 10
    1. Witches; 2. Prophecies; 3. Love triangles; 4. Family secrets; 5. Identity (Psychology); 6. Paranormal fiction; 7. Coming-of-age stories; 8. Multiple perspectives
9781602863002
    The third-person narration switches focus from character to character as they make frustrating, heart-rending, totally believable choices. Fantasy and nonfantasy readers alike will appreciate this gritty and intriguing coming-of-age story. —*Kirkus*

Brockenbrough, Martha
The **game** of Love and Death. Martha Brockenbrough. Arthur A. Levine Books, an imprint of Scholastic Inc, 2015 352 p.
Grades: 9 10 11 12
    1. Adopted teenage boys; 2. African American teenage girls; 3. Teenage orphans; 4. Love; 5. Death (Personification); 6. Seattle, Washington; 7. Depression era (1929-1941); 8. 1930s; 9. Magical realism; 10. Love stories; 11. Multiple perspectives
9780545668347; 9781407159546, print, UK; 9780545668354, ebook, US
LC 2014033339
Booklist Editors' Choice: Books for Youth, 2015; Kirkus Prize for Young Readers' Literature finalist, 2015.
    In Seattle in 1937 two seventeen-year-olds, Henry, who is white, and Flora, who is African-American, become the unwitting pawns in a game played by two immortal figures, Love and Death, where they must choose each other at the end, or one of them will die.
    There is a deliberately archetypal quality to the story, but the fully realized setting and characters make this more than just a modern fairy tale. It's a poignant reminder of how far weve come since the 1930s in terms of race, class, and sexual orientation—and how far we still have to go. —*Horn Book Guide*

Brockmann, Suzanne
Night sky. Suzanne Brockmann and Melanie Brockmann. Sourcebooks Fire, 2014 480 p. (Night sky, 1)
Grades: 9 10 11 12
    1. Kidnapping; 2. Psychic ability; 3. Supernatural; 4. Rescues; 5. Criminals; 6. Paranormal fiction
9781492601449
LC 2014022430
Sixteen-year-old Skylar Reid joins her best friend Cal, Dana, a girl with supernatural abilities, and Dana's friend Milo on a quest to rescue young Sasha from the Organization that kidnapped her because, according to Dana, Sky and Sasha both have specialabilities, too.

With a little something for everyone and a hip sense of humor, dialogue and teen angst, this is a gripping page-turner from first to last. —*Kirkus*

Brooks, Bruce
The **moves** make the man: a novel. By Bruce Brooks. Harper & Row, 1984 280 p.
Grades: 7 8 9 10 11 12
    1. Interracial friendship; 2. Sports; 3. Teenagers with emotional illnesses; 4. Racism; 5. Basketball; 6. North Carolina; 7. Realistic fiction
9780060206987
LC 83049476
Boston Globe-Horn Book Award for Fiction, 1985; ALA Notable Children's Book, 1985; Newbery Honor Book, 1985.
A 13-year-old Black boy and an emotionally troubled white boy in North Carolina form a precarious friendship.
    This is an excellent novel about values and the way people relate to one another. —*New York Times Book Review*

Brooks, Kevin
The **bunker** diary. Kevin Brooks. 2015 246 pages : Illustration
Grades: 9 10 11 12
    1. Captives; 2. Strangers; 3. Psychological games; 4. Bunkers (Fortification); 5. Teenage boys; 6. Thrillers and suspense; 7. Diary novels.
9781467754200; 9780141326122
Booklist Editors' Choice: Books for Youth, 2015; YALSA Best Fiction for Young Adults: Top Ten, 2015; Carnegie Medal, 2014; YALSA Best Fiction for Young Adults, 2016.
    Brooks' latest is not an easy novel, but it's one that begs for rereading to suss the intricacies of its construction of plot, character development and insight into the human condition. Not for everyone, this heady novel is worthy of study alongside existentialist works of the 20th century. —*Kirkus*
First published in 2013 by Penguin Books Ltd, 80 Strand, London WC2R 0RL, England.

IBoy. Kevin Brooks. Chicken House, 2011 304 p.
Grades: 9 10 11 12
    1. Gangs; 2. Rape; 3. Revenge in teenage boys; 4. Revenge; 5. Violence; 6. London, England; 7. England; 8. Science fiction; 9. Books for reluctant readers
9780545317689
LC 2010054240
YALSA Quick Picks for Reluctant Young Adult Readers, 2012; USBBY Outstanding International Book, 2012.
    Sixteen-year-old Tom Harvey was an ordinary Londoner until an attack that caused fragments of an iPhone to be embedded in his brain, giving him incredible knowledge and power, but using that power against the gang that attacked him and a friend could have deadly consequences.
    This classic superhero plot, at once cutting-edge science fiction and moral fable, is guaranteed to keep even fiction-averse, reluctant readers on the edge of their seats. —*Kirkus*

Brothers, Meagan
Weird girl and what's his name. Meagan Brothers. Three Rooms Press, 2015 288 p.
Grades: 9 10 11 12
    1. Best friends; 2. Runaways; 3. Secrets; 4. Gay teenagers; 5. Loners; 6. North Carolina; 7. Realistic fiction
9781941110270

Rainbow List, 2017.

Recommended for fans of realistic fiction with relationship drama and an LGBTQ focus. —*School Library Journal*

Brouwer, Sigmund

Devil's pass. Sigmund Brouwer. Orca Book Pub, 2012 256 p. (Seven, 6)

Grades: 6 7 8 9 10

1. Seventeen-year-old boys; 2. Wills; 3. Grandfathers; 4. Wilderness areas; 5. Teenage boys; 6. Toronto, Ontario; 7. Canada; 8. Canadian fiction; 9. Realistic fiction.

9781554699384

Seventeen-year-old Webb, a street musician from Toronto, faces grizzly bears and a madman when he travels to the Canol Trail in Canada's Far North in order to fulfill a request made in his grandfather's will.

Brown, Echo

Black girl unlimited: the remarkable true story of a teenage wizard. Echo Brown. 2020 304 p.

Grades: 10 11 12

1. African American teenage girls; 2. Poverty; 3. Magic; 4. Racism; 5. Women wizards; 6. Cleveland, Ohio; 7. Magical realism; 8. Coming-of-age stories; 9. Autobiographical fiction

9781250309853

LC 2019018533

School Library Journal Best Books, 2020; William C. Morris Debut Award finalist, 2021.

A largely autobiographical story infused with magical realism follows the transcendent coming-of-age of a teen from the East Side who transitions from the world of her home to that of a privileged West Side school while navigating an ominous veil of depression.

Through Echo's lessons, readers learn what it's like to persist despite hopelessness, survive in a world propelled by oppressive and exploitative systems, and cope with feelings of connection and disconnection. A much-needed story. Just brilliant. —*Kirkus*

Brown, Jaye Robin

Georgia peaches and other forbidden fruit. Jaye Robin Brown. HarperTeen, 2016 288 p.

Grades: 9 10 11 12

1. Lesbian teenagers; 2. Promises; 3. Moving to a new city; 4. Secrets; 5. Secrecy; 6. LGBTQIA romances; 7. Contemporary romances; 8. LGBTQIA fiction

9780062270986

Rainbow List, 2017.

Joanna meets the perfect girl for her and must decide whether to break a promise that could change everything for her and her family or lose out on love.

Faith matters in this book, but so do family, friends, and being funny. The dialogue is snappy—Joanna is sharp tongued and sometimes bratty—and the characters arent types. Rather, theyre individuals navigating a complicated world, which makes for a rich and satisfying read. —*Publishers Weekly*

No place to fall. Jaye Robin Brown. HarperTeen, 2014 368 p.

Grades: 10 11 12

1. Teenage girl singers; 2. Family problems; 3. Teenage boy/girl relations; 4. Singers; 5. High schools; 6. North Carolina; 7. Realistic fiction

9780062270993, HRD, US

Sixteen-year-old Amber Vaughn dreams of attending the North Carolina School of the Arts to gain confidence in using her amazing singing voice, but her family is falling apart and she is torn between two boys.

Debut author Brown is off to a wonderful start with authentic characters who speak in true voices. Amber could be the best friend you had in high school—she's funny and moody and truthful and absolutely the real deal, and readers will clamor for another well-paced story featuring her and her friends. —*School Library Journal*

Brown, Jennifer

Bitter end. By Jennifer Brown. Little, Brown, 2011 368 p.

Grades: 10 11 12

1. Dating violence; 2. Jealousy in teenage boys; 3. Grief; 4. Best friends; 5. Friendship; 6. Realistic fiction.

9780316086950

LC 2010034258

YALSA Best Fiction for Young Adults, 2012.

When seventeen-year-old Alex starts dating Cole, a new boy at her high school, her two closest friends increasingly mistrust him as the relationship grows more serious.

Gritty and disturbing, this novel should be in all collections serving teens. It could be used in programs about abuse, as well as in psychology or sociology classes. —*School Library Journal*

Perfect escape. By Jennifer Brown. Little, Brown, 2012 368 p.

Grades: 9 10 11 12

1. Obsessive-compulsive disorder; 2. Cross-country automobile trips; 3. Brothers and sisters; 4. Automobile travel; 5. Seventeen-year-old girls; 6. Realistic fiction.

9780316185578

LC 2011027348

Seventeen-year-old Kendra, living in the shadow of her brother's obsessive-compulsive disorder, takes a life-changing road trip with him.

Though the book suffers from implausibility and too many moments of emotional drama that come to seem redundant, readers will nevertheless be fascinated by Brown's insightful treatment of the realities of OCD and how it controls a person's life. —*Booklist*

Brown, Skila

To stay alive: Mary Ann Graves and the tragic journey of the Donner Party. Skila Brown. Candlewick Press, 2016 275 p.

Grades: 6 7 8 9 10

1. Graves, Mary Ann; 2. Donner Party; 3. Overland journeys to the Pacific; 4. Survival; 5. Cannibalism; 6. Blizzards; 7. American Westward Expansion (1803-1899); 8. 1840s; 9. Historical fiction; 10. Novels in verse

9780763678111

ALA Notable Children's Book, 2017.

A young survivor of the tragic Donner Party of 1846 describes how her family and others became victims of freezing temperatures and starvation.

The strong novel in verse uses beautiful, descriptive words to depict the vastness of the landscape and the emotional and mental toll of perpetual suffering. This is a well-crafted narrative in which readers get to know and empathize with Mary Ann as her adventure shifts to survival. However, it might be difficult to stomach the travelers' desperate choices: the book does not shy away from the Donner Party's well-known resort to cannibalism. —*School Library Journal*

Bruchac, Joseph

★ **Code** Talker. Joseph Bruchac. Dial Books, 2005 240 p.

Grades: 6 7 8 9 10

1. Native American teenage boys; 2. Codes (Communication); 3. War; 4. Cryptography; 5. Sixteen-year-old boys; 6. Second World War era (1939-1945); 7. Historical fiction.
9780803729216

LC 2003022792

YALSA Popular Paperbacks for Young Adults, 2014; ALA Notable Children's Book, 2006; YALSA Best Books for Young Adults, 2006.

After being taught in a boarding school run by whites that Navajo is a useless language, Ned Begay and other Navajo men are recruited by the Marines to become Code Talkers, sending messages during World War II in their native tongue.

Bruchac's gentle prose presents a clear historical picture of young men in wartime.... Nonsensational and accurate, Bruchac's tale is quietly inspiring. —*School Library Journal*

Includes bibliographical references.

Found. Joseph Bruchac. Seventh Generation, 2020 120 p.
Grades: 7 8 9 10 11 12
1. Indigenous peoples; 2. Murder witnesses; 3. Survival; 4. Native American teenage boys; 5. Camp counselors; 6. Survival stories; 7. Thrillers and suspense; 8. High interest-low vocabulary books
9781939053237

Nick, a teenage Native American survival expert, needs to avoid being found by the outlaws in relentless pursuit of him. Can he stay safe until the odds are in his favor?

A fast and riveting read that puts an Indigenous spin on the classic crime tradition. —*Kirkus*

Killer of enemies. Joseph Bruchac. Tu Books, 2013 400 pages (Killer of enemies, 1)
Grades: 7 8 9 10 11 12
1. Native American teenage girls; 2. Dystopias; 3. Monsters; 4. Near future; 5. Genetic engineering; 6. Southwest (United States); 7. Science fiction; 8. Apocalyptic fiction; 9. Books for reluctant readers
9781620141434

LC 2013023567

American Indian Youth Literature Awards, Best Young Adult Book, 2014; YALSA Quick Picks for Reluctant Young Adult Readers, 2014.

In a world that has barely survived an apocalypse that leaves it with pre-twentieth century technology, Lozen is a monster hunter for four tyrants who are holding her family hostage.

A deadly assassin with extrasensory powers, Lozen (named for an Apache-Chiricahua warrior-woman forebear) takes out genetically modified superbeasts; her family is being held hostage to ensure her continued service. Bruchac devises ever-more-dangerous battles for his protagonist in the increasingly suspenseful story. What really makes the narrative vibrate is Lozen's sardonic voice, capturing both gallows humor and a very human vulnerability. —*Horn Book Guide*

Sacajawea: the story of Bird Woman and the Lewis and Clark Expedition. Silver Whistle, 2000 199 p.
Grades: 6 7 8 9 10
1. Sacagawea; 2. Shoshoni Indians; 3. Biographical fiction; 4. Historical fiction
9780152022341

LC 99047653

Sacajawea, a Shoshoni Indian interpreter, peacemaker, and guide, and William Clark alternate in describing their experiences on the Lewis and Clark Expedition to the Northwest.

This is an intelligent, elegantly written novel. —*School Library Journal*

Includes map.

Walking two worlds. Joseph Bruchac; illustrated by David Fadden. 7th Generation, 2015 120 p.

Grades: 5 6 7 8 9
1. Parker, Ely Samuel, 1828-1895; 2. Native American teenage boys; 3. Seneca Indians; 4. Prejudice; 5. Racism; 6. Boarding schools; 7. New York (State); 8. 1840s; 9. Historical fiction
9781939053107

Though the book lacks formal resources and references, and the time frame of events, including Ely's birth date, is occasionally unclear, Ely's challenges and successes are supportively portrayed, and may inspire readers to learn more about his life and times. An afterword provides some information on his later years. —*Booklist*

Bruton, Catherine
I predict a riot. Catherine Bruton. Electric Monkey, 2014 291 p.
Grades: 7 8 9 10
1. Gangs; 2. Riots; 3. Filmmakers; 4. Neighborhoods; 5. Children of politicians; 6. Realistic fiction
9781405267199

Maggie's video camera seems to represent all the stories that aren't told in the media, making this searing tale one that will get readers talking. —*Booklist*

Bryant, Jennifer
★ **Ringside,** 1925: views from the Scopes trial. Jen Bryant. Alfred A. Knopf, 2008 240 p.
Grades: 8 9 10 11 12
1. Scopes, John Thomas; 2. Scopes Trial, 1925; 3. Evolution — Study and teaching; 4. Community life; 5. Trials; 6. Small towns; 7. Dayton, Tennessee; 8. Tennessee; 9. 1920s; 10. Novels in verse; 11. Historical fiction.
9780375840470; 9780375940477

LC 2007007177

Visitors, spectators, and residents of Dayton, Tennessee, in 1925 describe, in a series of free-verse poems, the Scopes "monkey trial" and its effects on that small town and its citizens.

Bryant offers readers a ringside seat in this compelling and well-researched novel. It is fast-paced, interesting, and relevant to many current first-amendment challenges. —*School Library Journal*

Bryant, Megan E.
Glow. Megan E. Bryant. Albert Whitman and Company, 2017 248 p.
Grades: 9 10 11 12
1. Painting; 2. Artists; 3. Watch dial painters; 4. Radium paint — Toxicology; 5. Teenage romance; 6. Mysteries; 7. Parallel narratives
9780807529638

Discovering a series of antique paintings containing hidden glowing images, a young thrift-store aficionado investigates their origins and discovers the haunting true story of a group of young women artists, the Radium Girls, who used dangerous radioactive paint to create the world's first glow-in-the-dark products.

Bryant brilliantly lures readers into an engaging mystery, a page-turner that begins beneath layers revealed in both paintings and chapters. A riveting story of ambitious and self-sufficient women, both in the present and past. —*Kirkus*

Bryce, Celia
Anthem for Jackson Dawes. By Celia Bryce. Bloomsbury USA Childrens, 2013 272 p.
Grades: 7 8 9 10
1. Teenagers with cancer; 2. Teenage boy/girl relations; 3. Hospital patients; 4. Cancer; 5. Brain cancer; 6. Realistic fiction.
9781599909752; 9781408827116, UK

LC 2012024989

When Megan, thirteen, arrives for her first cancer treatment, she is frustrated to be on the pediatric unit where the only other teen is Jackson Dawes, who is as cute and charming as he is rebellious and annoying, and who helps when her friends are frightened away by her illness.

Sensitive and honest, this novel addresses meaningful questions concerning mortality and soul searching, and its content is appropriate for younger teens. —*School Library Journal*

Buckley-Archer, Linda

The **many** lives of John Stone. Linda Buckley-Archer. Simon & Schuster Books for Young Readers, 2015 464 p.

Grades: 8 9 10 11

1. Diaries; 2. Longevity; 3. Courts and courtiers; 4. Supernatural; 5. Summer employment; 6. England; 7. Paranormal fiction; 8. Parallel narratives

9781481426374

Sparks contemporary coming-of-age story is brilliantly heightened by the readers understanding of her secret connection to John Stone. Exceptionally well orchestrated and a simply magnificent story. —*Booklist*

Budhos, Marina Tamar

Ask me no questions. Marina Budhos. Atheneum Books for Young Readers, 2006 176 p.

Grades: 7 8 9 10

1. Muslim families; 2. Undocumented immigrants; 3. Teenage girls; 4. Fourteen-year-old girls; 5. Immigrants; 6. New York City; 7. Family sagas; 8. First person narratives

9781416903512

LC 2005001831

ALA Notable Children's Book, 2007; Booklist Editors' Choice: Books for Youth, 2006; James Cook Book Award (Ohio), 2007; YALSA Best Books for Young Adults, 2007; YALSA Popular Paperbacks for Young Adults, 2013.

Fourteen-year-old Nadira, her sister, and their parents leave Bangladesh for New York City, but the expiration of their visas and the events of September 11, 2001, bring frustration, sorrow, and terror for the whole family.

Nadira and Aisha's strategies for surviving and succeeding in high school offer sharp insight into the narrow margins between belonging and not belonging. —*Horn Book Guide*

Ginee Seo Books.

Tell us we're home. Marina Budhos. Atheneum Books for Young Readers, 2010 304 p.

Grades: 6 7 8 9 10

1. Teenage immigrants; 2. Interethnic friendship; 3. Interpersonal conflict; 4. Best friends; 5. Immigrants; 6. New Jersey; 7. Realistic fiction.

9781416903529

LC 2009027386

YALSA Popular Paperbacks for Young Adults, 2013.

Three immigrant girls from different parts of the world meet and become close friends in a small New Jersey town where their mothers have found domestic work, but their relationships are tested when one girl's mother is accused of stealing a precious heirloom.

These fully realized heroines are full of heart, and their passionate struggles against systemic injustice only make them more inspiring. Keenly necessary. —*Kirkus*

Watched. Marina Budhos. Wendy Lamb Books, 2016 272 p.

Grades: 9 10 11 12

1. Muslim teenagers; 2. Informers; 3. Police surveillance; 4. Ethnic identity; 5. Immigrants; 6. Queens, New York City; 7. Realistic fiction.

9780553534184

Notable Books for a Global Society, 2017; YALSA Best Fiction for Young Adults, 2017; YALSA Quick Picks for Reluctant Young Adult Readers, 2017; Asian Pacific American Asian Pacific American Award for Literature: Young Adult Literature Honor Book, 2017; Walter Honor Book, 2017.

Moving quickly throughout his Queens immigrant neighborhood to avoid the watchful eyes of his hardworking Bangladeshi parents, their gossipy neighbors and surveillance cameras mounted everywhere, charismatic but troubled youth Naeem is offered a deal by the cops to become a community protector in ways that challenge his sense of identity.

Action takes second place to a deeper message, and room is left for readers to speculate on the fates of certain characters. While the absence of certainty may frustrate some readers, it also speaks to the underlying takeaway: you can never be sure what others' intentions are, even if you have made it your job to study them. —*Kirkus*

Buffie, Margaret

Winter shadows. Margaret Buffie. Tundra Books, 2010 327 p.

Grades: 7 8 9 10

1. Metis teenage girls; 2. Stepmothers; 3. Ghosts; 4. Metis; 5. Mothers — Death; 6. Ghost stories; 7. Canadian fiction.

9780887769689; 9781770493582

In the winter of 1856, Beatrice Alexander returns from Upper Canada to her home on the Red River, in what is now Manitoba. Her father's new wife is threatened by Beatrice and drives a wedge into the family. Five generations later, in the same house, Christmas promises to be a miserable time. Cass's mother died of cancer and her father has remarried a woman with an attitude that's very hard to take. When Cass discovers the star brooch belonging to Beatrice, her visions lead her to Beatrice's diary. Is she really able to communicate with Beatrice across time, or is it all in her imagination?

Hatred for their wicked stepmothers bonds two girls living in a stone house in Manitoba, Canada, more than 150 years apart. Grieving for her dead mother, high-school senior Cass is furious that she has to share a room with the daughter of her dad's new, harsh-tempered wife. Then she finds the 1836 diary of Beatrice, who is part Cree and faces vicious racism as a half-breed in her mostly white community.... The alternating narratives are gripping, and the characters are drawn with rich complexity. —*Booklist*

Bullen, Alexandra

Wish: a novel. By Alexandra Bullen. Point, 2010 323 p. (Wish series (Alexandra Bullen), 1)

Grades: 8 9 10 11 12

1. Twin sisters; 2. Wishing and wishes; 3. Shyness in teenage girls; 4. Shyness; 5. Grief; 6. California; 7. San Francisco, California; 8. Fantasy fiction.

9780545139052

The detailed descriptions of San Francisco and above all the sisters' relationship provide solid grounding for a touching, enjoyable read. —*Kirkus*

Burd, Nick

★ The **vast** fields of ordinary. By Nick Burd. Dial Books, 2009 309 p.

Grades: 10 11 12

1. Coming out (Sexual or gender identity); 2. Family relationships; 3. Self-discovery in teenage boys; 4. Homosexuality; 5. Growing up; 6.

Iowa; 7. LGBTQIA romances; 8. Coming-of-age stories; 9. First person narratives.
9780803733404

LC 2008046256

Stonewall Book Award for Children's and Young Adult Literature, 2010; Rainbow List, 2010.

The summer after graduating from an Iowa high school, eighteen-year-old Dade Hamilton watches his parents' marriage disintegrate, ends his long-term, secret relationship, comes out of the closet, and savors first love.

A refreshingly honest, sometimes funny, and often tender novel. —*School Library Journal*

Burgess, Melvin

The **hit**. Melvin Burgess. Chicken House/Scholastic Inc, 2014 304 p.
Grades: 9 10 11 12
1. Drugs; 2. Near future; 3. Grief; 4. Death; 5. Designer drugs; 6. England; 7. Manchester, England; 8. Dystopian fiction; 9. Multiple perspectives
9780545556996

Burgess' dystopian novel posits a near-future world in which the gap between rich and poor has grown to an unbridgeable chasm. In their despair, many have-nots are taking a new drug called Death that offers seven days of euphoric bliss followed by the oblivion of death...the novel is viscerally exciting and emotionally engaging. Best of all, it is sure to excite both thoughtful analysis and heated discussion among its readers. A clear winner from Burgess. —*Booklist*

Smack. Melvin Burgess. H. Holt, 1998
Grades: 9 10 11 12
1. Teenage drug abusers; 2. Drug abuse; 3. Prostitution; 4. Teenagers; 5. Runaway teenagers; 6. 1980s; 7. Realistic fiction; 8. Multiple perspectives; 9. First person narratives.
9780805058017

LC 97040629

YALSA Best Books for Young Adults, 1999; School Library Journal Best Books, 1998.

In many different voices, from the addicts to the people around them, this book tells the story of a group of young people addicted to drugs.

Although the omnipresent British slang (most but not all of which is explained in a glossary) may put off some readers, lots of YAs will be drawn to this book because of the subject. Those who are will quickly find themselves absorbed in an honest, unpatronizing, unvarnished account of teen life on the skids. —*Booklist*

Originally published in 1996 under the title: *Junk*.

Busby, Cylin

The **stranger** game. Cylin Busby. Balzer + Bray, an imprint of HarperCollins Publishers, 2016 281 p.
Grades: 9 10 11 12
1. Teenage girls with amnesia; 2. Impersonation; 3. Sisters; 4. Teenage girls; 5. Mysteries; 6. Multiple perspectives; 7. First person narratives
9780062354600

With compelling, memorable storytelling, Busby...captures the complicated and often fraught relationship between siblings, especially in the aftermath of family trauma. —*Booklist*

Buzo, Laura

Love and other perishable items. Laura Buzo. Alfred A. Knopf, 2012 256 p.
Grades: 9 10 11 12

1. Crushes in teenage girls; 2. Unrequited love; 3. Supermarkets; 4. Crushes (Interpersonal relations); 5. College students; 6. Realistic fiction; 7. Teen chick lit; 8. Australian fiction
9780375870002, paperback ; 9780375970009, hardcover; 9780375986741, ebook; 9780307929747, paperback ; 9781741759976, Australia

Children's Book Council of Australia: Notable Australian Children's Book; YALSA Best Fiction for Young Adults, 2014; William C. Morris Debut Award finalist, 2013.

A fifteen-year-old Australian girl gets her first job and first crush on her unattainable university-aged co-worker, as both search for meaning in their lives.

Cabot, Meg

★ **All-American** girl. Meg Cabot. Harper Collins Publishers, 2002 247 p.
Grades: 7 8 9 10
1. Presidents — Assassination attempts; 2. Heroes and heroines; 3. Attempted assassination; 4. Teenage romance; 5. Interpersonal relations; 6. Washington, D.C; 7. Teen chick lit; 8. Books for reluctant readers
9780060294694; 9780060294700

LC 2002019049

Garden State Teen Book Award (New Jersey), Fiction (Grades 9-12), 2005; YALSA Quick Picks for Reluctant Young Adult Readers, 2003.

A sophomore girl stops a presidential assassination attempt, is appointed Teen Ambassador to the United Nations, and catches the eye of the very cute First Son.

There's surprising depth in the characters and plenty of authenticity in the cultural details and the teenage voicesparticularly in Sam's poignant, laugh-out-loud narration. —*Booklist*

Sequel: *Ready or Not*.

★ The **princess** diaries: Princess diaries, vol. I. Meg Cabot. 2020 238 p. (Princess diaries, 1)
Grades: 6 7 8 9
1. Princesses; 2. Identity (Psychology); 3. Fathers and daughters; 4. Fourteen-year-old girls; 5. Teenage girls — Identity; 6. New York City; 7. Diary novels; 8. Romantic comedies; 9. Teen chick lit; 10. Books for reluctant readers
9780062998453; 9780380978489; 9780060292102; 9781447280620, print, UK; 9781405034098, print, UK

LC 99046479

YALSA Popular Paperbacks for Young Adults, 2014; YALSA Quick Picks for Reluctant Young Adult Readers, 2001; YALSA Best Books for Young Adults, 2001.

Fourteen-year-old Mia, who is trying to lead a normal life as a teenage girl in New York City, is shocked to learn that her father is the Prince of Genovia, a small European principality, and that she is a princess and the heir to the throne.

Readers will relate to Mia's bubbly, chatty voice and enjoy the humor of this unlikely fairy tale. —*School Library Journal*

Caine, Rachel

Ash and quill. Rachel Caine. Berkley, 2017 368 p. (Great library, 3)
Grades: 10 11 12
1. Near future; 2. Libraries; 3. Dystopias; 4. Teenage boys; 5. Brightwell, Jess (Fictitious character); 6. Alternative histories; 7. Dystopian fiction; 8. Fantasy fiction.
9780451472410; 9780749017422

LC 2016058978

Imprisoned in Philadelphia after fleeing London, Jess and his band of exiles confront book-burning adversaries before striking a bargain to share their knowledge about a machine capable of breaking the Library's rule.

A strong ensemble adventure, grim, gritty, and genuinely enjoyable. —*Kirkus*

Ink and bone. Rachel Caine. New American Library, 2015 352 p. (Great library, 1)
Grades: 8 9 10 11 12
1. Near future; 2. Libraries; 3. Dystopias; 4. Smugglers; 5. Sixteen-year-old boys; 6. Alternative histories; 7. Dystopian fiction; 8. Fantasy fiction.
9780451472397

LC 2015001509
Caine has created a Dickensian future with an odd mix of technologies and elements of sorcery. A strong cast of characters and nail-biting intensity make for a promising start to this new series. —*School Library Journal*

Prince of Shadows: a novel of Romeo and Juliet. Rachel Caine. New American Library, 2014 354 pages
Grades: 7 8 9 10 11 12
1. Thieves; 2. Revenge; 3. Feuds; 4. Love; 5. Families; 6. Verona, Italy; 7. Italy; 8. 16th century; 9. Historical fiction; 10. Shakespeare-inspired fiction.
9780451414410; 9781921901881, print, Australia; 9780749015138, print, UK

LC 2013033482
The star-crossed tale of Romeo and Juliet, told through the eyes of Romeo's cousin, Benvolio, a thief known as the Prince of Shadows.

Choosing *Romeo and Juliet* as her base, Caine expands the story from the viewpoint of Benvolio, Romeo's Montague cousin. While Shakespeare's plot clearly anchors Caine's, the novel focuses on providing context for the well-known story rather than embellishing it.... Most impressive is the author's simulation of Shakespeare's language in her prose. Never too obscure for modern readers, it retains the flavor of Shakespearean dialogue throughout, lending an atmosphere of verisimilitude that's reinforced by the detailed city setting. Simply superb. —*Kirkus*

Cajoleas, Jimmy
The **good** demon. Jimmy Cajoleas. Amulet Books, 2018 320 p.
Grades: 9 10 11 12
1. Demonic possession; 2. Teenage girls; 3. Exorcism; 4. Demons; 5. Exorcists; 6. Southern states; 7. Gothic fiction; 8. Horror; 9. First person narratives
9781419731273
Clare, miserable since an exorcism took away the demon that was like a sister to her, discovers the occult roots of her small Southern town and must question the fine lines between good and evil, love and hate, and religion and free will.

Caletti, Deb
★ **Essential** maps for the lost. By Deb Caletti. Simon Pulse, 2016 320 p.
Grades: 9 10 11 12
1. Depression; 2. Survivors of suicide victims; 3. Mental illness; 4. Grief; 5. Teenage romance; 6. Seattle, Washington; 7. Realistic fiction; 8. Multiple perspectives
9781481415163; 9781481415194, ebook, US

LC 2015024672
When Mads discovers a dead body while she's swimming in the lake, she begins to obsess over who the woman was and what led her to commit suicide by jumping off a bridge. But when she starts to fall for Billy the woman's troubled son Mads isn't sure how much longer she can keep her obsession a secret.

A moving story about rescuing yourself as well as finally being found. —*Booklist*

The **fortunes** of Indigo Skye. Deb Caletti. Simon & Schuster Books for Young Readers, 2008 298 p;
Grades: 9 10 11 12
1. Waitresses; 2. Diners (Restaurants); 3. Wealth; 4. Eccentrics and eccentricities; 5. Values; 6. Seattle, Washington; 7. Realistic fiction; 8. Pacific Northwest fiction; 9. Coming-of-age stories.
9781416910077

LC 2007008744
YALSA Popular Paperbacks for Young Adults, 2011; YALSA Best Books for Young Adults, 2009.
Eighteen-year-old Indigo is looking forward to becoming a full-time waitress after high school graduation, but her life is turned upside down by a large check given to her by a customer who appreciates that she cares enough to scold him about smoking.

The author builds characters with so much depth that readers will be invested in her story.... Caletti spins a network of relationships that feels real and enriching. —*Publishers Weekly*

★ **Girl,** unframed. By Deb Caletti. Simon & Schuster 2020 368 p.
Grades: 9 10 11 12
1. Children of celebrities; 2. Beauty; 3. Abusive men; 4. Objectification (Social psychology); 5. Mothers and daughters; 6. San Francisco, California; 7. Thrillers and suspense; 8. Coming-of-age stories.
9781534426979; 9781534426993, ebook, US

LC 2018041558
While spending a summer with her famous mother and her criminal boyfriend, Sydney Reilly, age fifteen, finds love with Nicco but her premonition of something bad coming proves dreadfully accurate.

With a subtle, believable twist that encapsulates this particular mother/daughter relationship, Caletti delivers the near impossible: a page-turner grounded in thoughtful feminism. —*Booklist*

★ A **heart** in a body in the world. Deb Caletti. Simon Pulse, 2018 368 p.
Grades: 9 10 11 12
1. Teenage girls; 2. Sexual violence; 3. Teenage rape victims; 4. High school students; 5. Violence and guns; 6. Realistic fiction
9781481415200
Amelia Bloomer List, 2019; Josette Frank Award, 2019; YALSA Best Fiction for Young Adults, 2019.
Followed by Grandpa Ed in his RV and backed by her brother and friends, Annabelle, runs from Seattle to Washington, D.C, becoming a reluctant activist as people connect her journey to her recent trauma.

The joy and power of this story is in taking the physical and mental journey with Annabelle as she relinquishes her feelings of self-blame and inspires others to act. Calettis lyrical third-person, present-tense narration blends immediate detail with gut-wrenching flashbacks to great effect. —*Horn Book Guide*

★ The **last** forever. Deb Caletti. Simon Pulse, 2014 320 pages
Grades: 8 9 10 11 12
1. Grief in teenage girls; 2. Automobile travel; 3. Loss (Psychology); 4. Plants; 5. Fathers and daughters; 6. Realistic fiction; 7. First person narratives
9781442450004; 9781442450011, ebook, US

LC 2013031010
After her mother's death, it's all Tessa can do to keep her friends, her boyfriend, her happiness from slipping away. Even the rare plant her mother entrusted to her care starts to wilt. Then she meets Henry. Though

secrets stand between them, each has a chance at healing...if first, Tessa can find the courage to believe in forever.

Featuring sharp-witted first-person narration, some fascinating facts about plants and seeds, relatable characters, and evocative settings, Caletti's (*The Story of Us*) inspiring novel eloquently depicts the nature of mutability. As with her previous books, this love story reverberates with honesty and emotion. —*Publishers Weekly*

The **secret** life of Prince Charming. Deb Caletti. Simon & Schuster Books for Young Readers, 2009 322 p.
Grades: 8 9 10 11 12
1. Children of divorced parents; 2. Selfishness in men; 3. Stolen property recovery; 4. Automobile travel; 5. Fathers and daughters; 6. Realistic fiction.
9781416959403
LC 2008013014

Seventeen-year-old Quinn has heard all her life about how untrustworthy men are, so when she discovers that her charismatic but selfish father, with whom she has recently begun to have a tentative relationship, has stolen from the many women in his life, she decides she must avenge this wrong.

This is a thoughtful, funny, and empowering spin on the classic road novel.... Because of its strong language and the mature themes, this is best suited to older teens, who will appreciate what it has to say about love, relationships, and getting what you need. —*School Library Journal*

★ The **six** rules of maybe. By Deb Caletti. Simon Pulse, 2010 321 p.
Grades: 8 9 10 11 12
1. Self-perception in teenage girls; 2. Hope; 3. Pregnant women; 4. Sisters; 5. Interpersonal relations; 6. Oregon; 7. Realistic fiction; 8. Pacific Northwest fiction
9781416979692
LC 2009022232

Scarlet, an introverted high school junior surrounded by outcasts who find her a good listener, learns to break old patterns and reach for hope when her pregnant sister moves home with her new husband, with whom Scarlet feels an instant connection.

Reminiscent of the best of Sarah Dessen's work, this novel is beautifully written, deftly plotted, and movingly characterized. —*School Library Journal*

Stay. By Deb Caletti. Simon Pulse, 2011 320 p.
Grades: 8 9 10 11 12
1. Stalking victims; 2. Former boyfriends; 3. Children of authors; 4. Fathers and daughters; 5. Secrets; 6. Washington (State); 7. Realistic fiction; 8. First person narratives; 9. Pacific Northwest fiction
9781442403734
YALSA Best Fiction for Young Adults, 2012.

In a remote corner of Washington State where she and her father have gone to escape her obsessive boyfriend, Clara meets two brothers who captain a sailboat, a lighthouse keeper with a secret, and an old friend of her father who knows his secrets.

Fear tinges this summer romance and underscores the issue of abusive and claustrophobic relationships among teens. —*School Library Journal*

Callahan, Erin
The **art** of escaping. Erin Callahan. 2018 324 p.
Grades: 9 10 11
1. Escape artists; 2. Magic tricks; 3. Self-esteem in teenagers; 4. Friendship; 5. Recluses; 6. Rhode Island; 7. Realistic fiction; 8. Multiple perspectives
9781944995652
LC 2017057654

When Mattie, seventeen, seeks out the reclusive Miyu, daughter of a famed escapologist, to indulge her secret desire to learn the craft, it leads to a friendship with classmate Will, who bears a huge secret of his own.

Callender, Kacen
Felix ever after. Kacen Callender. 2020 368 p.
Grades: 9 10 11 12
1. Transgender teenagers; 2. Transphobia; 3. Revenge; 4. Gender identity; 5. Genderqueer; 6. LGBTQIA fiction; 7. Realistic fiction
9780062820259
LC 2020003451

Felix Love, a transgender seventeen-year-old, attempts to get revenge by catfishing his anonymous bully, but lands in a quasi-love triangle with his former enemy and his best friend.

Callender (*King and the Dragonflies*) excels, producing an exhilarating cast of queer characters, many of whom are people of color, who are as relatable as they are realistic, and a whodunit that will keep readers guessing to the last twist. —*Publishers Weekly*

Cameron, Janet E.
Cinnamon toast and the end of the world. Janet E. Cameron. Hachette Books Ireland, 2013 384 p.
Grades: 9 10 11 12
1. Teenage boys; 2. First loves; 3. Happiness in teenagers; 4. High school students; 5. Teenage boy/girl relations; 6. Nova Scotia; 7. 1980s; 8. Coming-of-age stories; 9. Canadian fiction.
9781444743968
Rainbow List, 2015.

Where this novel truly excels is in its ability to tackle several difficult subjects with clarity and conviction. From homophobia to bullying to parental abuse, Cameron doesn't shy away from the complexity of her material, and the effects are heart-wrenching. This stunning debut will surely appeal to both teenage readers and adults. —*Quill & Quire*

Cameron, Peter
★ **Someday** this pain will be useful to you. Peter Cameron. Farrar, Straus and Giroux, 2007 229 p;
Grades: 9 10 11 12
1. Teenage boys; 2. Alienation in teenagers; 3. Gay teenagers; 4. Personal conduct; 5. Anxiety in teenagers; 6. New York City; 7. Manhattan, New York City; 8. Realistic fiction; 9. Coming-of-age stories; 10. First person narratives
9780374309893
LC 2006043747
Rainbow List, 2008; YALSA Best Books for Young Adults, 2008.

Eighteen-year-old James living in New York City with his older sister and divorced mother struggles to find a direction for his life.

James makes a memorable protagonist, touching in his inability to connect with the world but always entertaining in his first-person account of his New York environment, his fractured family, his disastrous trip to the nation's capital, and his ongoing bouts with psychoanalysis. In the process he dramatizes the ambivalences and uncertainties of adolescence in ways that both teen and adult readers will savor and remember. —*Booklist*

Cameron, Sharon
The **dark** unwinding. By Sharon Cameron. Scholastic Press, 2012 352 p.
Grades: 6 7 8 9
1. Teenage girl orphans; 2. Inheritance and succession; 3. Eccentrics and eccentricities; 4. Uncles; 5. Inventions; 6. Great Britain; 7.

England; 8. Victorian era (1837-1901); 9. 1850s; 10. Historical fiction.
9780545327862

LC 2011044431

YALSA Best Fiction for Young Adults, 2013; YALSA Popular Paperbacks for Young Adults, 2015.

In 1852, when seventeen-year-old Katharine is sent to her family's estate to prove that her uncle is insane, she finds he is an inventor whose work creating ingenious clockwork figures supports hundreds of families, but strange occurences soon have her doubting her own sanity.

Sequel: *A spark unseen*.

The **Forgetting**. Sharon Cameron. 2016 416 pages (The Forgetting (Sharon Cameron), 1)
Grades: 8 9 10 11 12
1. Memory; 2. Amnesia; 3. Conspiracies; 4. Dystopias; 5. Books; 6. Dystopian fiction; 7. Science fiction.
9780545945219

LC 2016007978

Westchester Fiction Award, 2017.

Canaan is a quiet city on an idyllic world, hemmed in by high walls, but every twelve years the town breaks out in a chaos of bloody violence, after which all the people undergo the Forgetting, in which they are left without any trace of memory of themselves, their families, or their lives—but somehow seventeen-year-old Nadia has never forgotten, and she is determined to find out what causes it and how to put a stop to the Forgetting forever.

Effective worldbuilding and strong characterization (even minor players have emotional depth) add substance to the fast-paced plot. A cosmetic resemblance to blockbuster teen dystopias allows Cameron to toy slyly with readers' expectations, but this is no retread. —*Kirkus*

The **Knowing**. Sharon Cameron. 2017 448 pages (The Forgetting (Sharon Cameron), 2)
Grades: 8 9 10 11 12
1. Memory; 2. Amnesia; 3. Conspiracies; 4. Secrets; 5. Friendship; 6. Dystopian fiction; 7. Science fiction; 8. Multiple perspectives.
9780545945240; 9780545945257; 9781338281965

LC 2017022644

The underground city of New Canaan is safe from the Forgetting which afflicts Canaan above ground, but in her rigidly controlled and repressive city eighteen-year-old Samara, one of the Knowing, is plagued by her memory of the horrors she has seen, and determined to seek answers in the cursed city above—where she will find Beckett Rodriguez and his parents, on a mission from Earth to study the lost colony.

In this companion novel to The Forgetting, Cameron once again fashions an elaborate dystopian narrative that fairly prickles with suspense. —*School Library Journal*

The **light** in hidden places. Sharon Cameron. Scholastic 2020 400 p.
Grades: 8 9 10 11 12
1. Resistance to military occupation; 2. Holocaust (1933-1945); 3. Catholic girls; 4. Hiding; 5. Nazis; 6. Poland; 7. Second World War era (1939-1945); 8. Historical fiction; 9. Biographical fiction; 10. First-person narratives
9781338355932; 9781529106534, Paperback, UK

LC 2019025341

Sixteen-year-old Catholic Stefania Podgorska has worked in the Diamant family's grocery store for four years, even falling in love with one of their sons, Izio; but when the Nazis came to Przemyl, Poland, the Jewish Diamants are forced into the ghetto (and worse) but Izio's brother Max manages to escape, and Stefania embarks on a dangerous course—protecting thirteen Jews in her attic, caring for her younger sister, Helena, and keeping everything secret from the two Nazi officers who are living in her house.

Cameron, Sophie

Last bus to Everland. Sophie Cameron. Roaring Brook Press, 2019 336 p.
Grades: 7 8 9 10 11 12
1. Gay teenagers; 2. Alienation (Social psychology); 3. Parallel universes; 4. Misfits (Persons); 5. Options, alternatives, choices; 6. Gateway fantasy; 7. Magical realism; 8. Coming-of-age stories.
9781250149930; 9781509853182, Paperback, UK

Forging a bond with a compassionate artist, a youth in the projects joins a band of misfits and miscreants who meet weekly for adventures in a Narnia-inspired world, before dwindling magic forces him to choose between those he loves.

Everland is a lovely conceit amid beautifully realized worlds and wonderfully individual, empathetic characters. —*Booklist*

Out of the blue. Sophie Cameron. Roaring Brook Press, 2018 272 p.
Grades: 7 8 9 10 11
1. Mothers — Death; 2. Angels; 3. Grief; 4. Friendship; 5. Teenage romance; 6. Edinburgh, Scotland.
9781250149916

A strong infusion of magic and wonder distinguish this debut novel. —*Kirkus*

Cann, Kate

Possessed. By Kate Cann. Point, 2010 336 p.
Grades: 10 11 12
1. Fear in teenage girls; 2. Mansions; 3. Supernatural; 4. Historic buildings; 5. Independence in teenage girls; 6. England; 7. Horror
9780545128124; 9781407135465, print, UK

LC 2009020977

Sixteen-year-old Rayne escapes London, her mother, and boyfriend for a job in the country at Morton's Keep, where she is drawn to a mysterious clique and its leader, St. John, but puzzles over whether the growing evil she senses is from the manor house or her new friends.

This atmospheric and deliciously chilling British import gets off to a quick start, and readers will empathize with the very likable 16-year-old protagonist, who is clearly out of her element.... With a minimum of actual bloodshed, this supernatural delight can even be enjoyed by the faint of heart. —*Booklist*

Sequel: *Consumed*.

Capetta, Amy Rose

Once & future. Amy Rose Capetta and Cori McCarthy. 2019 336 p. (Once & future duology, 1)
Grades: 9 10 11 12
1. Arthur, King; 2. Rulers; 3. Battles; 4. Wizards; 5. Quests; 6. Despotism; 7. Science fiction; 8. Fairy tale and folklore-inspired fiction; 9. Arthurian fantasy.
9780316449274; 9781786076540, Paperback, UK

LC 2018059696

Resets the Arthurian legend in outer space, with King Arthur reincarnated as seventeen-year-old Ari, a female king whose quest is to stop a tyrranical corporate government, aided by a teenaged Merlin.
JIMMY Patterson Books.

Sword in the stars. Amy Rose Capetta and Cori McCarthy. JIMMY Patterson Books, 2020 368 p. (Once & future duology, 2)
Grades: 9 10 11 12

1. Arthur, King; 2. Knights and knighthood; 3. Time travel (Past); 4. Grail; 5. Wizards; 6. Rulers; 7. Science fiction; 8. Arthurian fantasy; 9. Fairy tale and folklore-inspired fiction.
9780316449298; 9781786077011, Paperback, UK

An epic conclusion to the story that began with Once & Future finds Ari, the cursed wizard Merlin and the Rainbow knights traveling thousands of years into the past to steal King Arthur's Grail without damaging history's timeline.

All hail this worthier-than-ever, fresh, and affirming reincarnation of the legendary king and her round table of knights which dazzles with heroic flair, humor, and suspense. —*Kirkus*

Capin, Hannah
The **dead** queens club. Hannah Capin. Ink Yard Press, 2019 464 p.
Grades: 9 10 11 12
1. High school seniors; 2. Dating (Social customs); 3. Death; 4. Moving to a new state; 5. Popularity; 6. Indiana; 7. Mysteries; 8. First person narratives
9781335542236

Moving from Cleveland to Lancaster, Indiana, Annie Marck transformed into teenage royalty by entering Lancaster High on the arm of Henry, the king of the school. He's the jock, the genius and the brooding bad boy all in one. Which sort of explains why he's on his sixth girlfriend in two years. What it doesn't explain is why two of them are dead. Annie is determined to find out what really happened to Lancaster's dead queens—ideally before history repeats itself.—adapted from jacket OCLC

A gripping, history-based mystery that finds its footing among a group of determined, very different girls. —*Booklist*

When Henry's king, being queen can be a killer.

Card, Orson Scott
★ **Ender's** game. Orson Scott Card. T. Doherty Associates, 1985 357 p. (Ender Wiggin, 1)
Grades: 7 8 9 10 11 12 Adult
1. Gifted children; 2. Space warfare; 3. Aliens (Humanoid); 4. Wiggin, Ender (Fictitious character); 5. Brothers and sisters; 6. Hard science fiction; 7. Science fiction classics; 8. Science fiction; 9. Adult books for young adults.
9780312932084; 9780765370624; 9780356501888, print, UK; 9780356500843, UK
Hugo Award for Best Novel, 1986; Nebula Award for Best Novel, 1985; YALSA Popular Paperbacks for Young Adults, 2015.

Six-year-old Ender Wiggin and his fellow students at Battle School are being tested and trained to determine whether they possess the abilities to remake the world—if the world survives an all-out war with an alien enemy.

The key, of course, is Ender Wiggin himself. Mr. Card never makes the mistake of patronizing or sentimentalizing his hero. Alternately likable and insufferable, he is a convincing little Napoleon in short pants. New York Times Book Review.

Part of this novel was published in Analog.

★ **Pathfinder**. Orson Scott Card. Simon Pulse, 2010 432 p. (Pathfinder (Orson Scott Card), 1)
Grades: 6 7 8 9 10
1. Teenage boy psychics; 2. Space and time; 3. Space colonies; 4. Psychic ability; 5. Time travel (Past); 6. Science fiction.
9781416991762
LC 2010023243
Booklist Editors' Choice: Books for Youth, 2010.

Thirteen-year-old Rigg has a secret ability to see the paths of others' pasts, but revelations after his father's death set him on a dangerous quest that brings new threats from those who would either control his destiny or kill him.

While Card delves deeply into his story's knotted twists and turns, readers should have no trouble following the philosophical and scientific mysteries, which the characters are parsing right along with them. An epic in the best sense, and not simply because the twin stories stretch across centuries. —*Publishers Weekly*

Cardi, Annie
The **chance** you won't return. Annie Cardi. Candlewick Press, 2014 352 p.
Grades: 9 10 11 12
1. Children of people with mental illnesses; 2. High school juniors; 3. Delusions; 4. Fear in teenagers; 5. Women pilots; 6. Realistic fiction; 7. First person narratives.
9780763662929

The author creates nuanced characters and presents them with their flaws and strengths intact, including a character with a mental disorder who never loses her humanity or becomes a caricature.... This novel delivers something far more rare: a well-written, first-person narrative about negotiating life's curve balls that has a realistic ending. An honest, uncompromising story. —*Kirkus*

Cardinal, Ann Davila
Five midnights. Ann Davila Cardinal. 2019 288 p. (Five midnights, 1)
Grades: 9 10 11 12
1. Puerto Ricans; 2. Mythical creatures; 3. Murder investigation; 4. Multiracial teenage girls; 5. Recovering addicts; 6. Puerto Rico; 7. Supernatural mysteries; 8. Horror; 9. Fairy tale and folklore-inspired fiction.
9781250296078

If Lupe Davila and Javier Utierre can survive each other's company, together they can solve a series of grisly murders sweeping though Puerto Rico. But the clues lead them out of the real world and into the realm of myths and legends. And if they want to catch the killer, they'll have to step into the shadows to see what's lurking there?murderer, or monster?—

Carey, Edward
Heap House. Written and illustrated by Edward Carey. The Overlook Press, 2014 416 p. : Illustration (Iremonger, 1)
Grades: 5 6 7 8 9 10
1. Mansions; 2. Family secrets; 3. Orphans; 4. Household employees; 5. Solid waste disposal; 6. London, England; 7. England; 8. Victorian era (1837-1901); 9. 1870s; 10. Historical fantasy; 11. Gothic fiction; 12. First person narratives
9781468309539; 9781443424226; 9781443424233

Young Clod, living in his family's mansion amongst a mass of shifting forgotten items, becomes aware of the items whispering to him and senses a growing storm ahead, needing the help of an orphan servant to unravel the mystery.

Living among sentient trash heaps, Clod Iremonger has always been able to hear the voices of the objects that his family members carry, but the arrival of serving girl Lucy imbues the objects with a new and dangerous energy. Descriptive prose and black-and-white portraits create a unique cast of characters in a bleak, dilapidated home. Fans of Joan Aiken will flock to this dark mystery. —*Horn Book Guide*

Carey, Janet Lee
★ **Dragon's** keep. Janet Lee Carey. Harcourt, 2007 320 p. (Wilde Island chronicles, 1)
Grades: 7 8 9 10

1. Dragons; 2. Prophecies; 3. Inheritance and succession; 4. Princesses; 5. Teenage girls; 6. British Isles; 7. 12th century; 8. Historical fantasy
9780152059262; 9781428739291; 9780571233113

LC 2006024669

YALSA Best Books for Young Adults, 2008; School Library Journal Best Books, 2007.

Long ago, it was prophesied that Princess Rosalind would restore glory to her dragon-infested home of Wilde Island. But Rosalind isn't sure how she's supposed to achieve her destiny when her hands are constantly hidden to conceal the dragon's talon that grows in place of her left ring finger. It isn't until she's kidnapped by the formidable dragon Lord Faul that Rosalind discovers the secret behind her dragon claw.

This is told in stunning, lyrical prose.... Carey smoothly blends many traditional fantasy tropes here, but her telling is fresh as well as thoroughly compelling. —*Booklist*

Carleson, J. C.

The **tyrant's** daughter. J.C. Carleson. Alfred A. Knopf, 2014 304 p.
Grades: 8 9 10 11 12

1. Exiles; 2. Political intrigue; 3. Dictators; 4. Culture shock; 5. Refugees; 6. Washington, D.C; 7. Realistic fiction
9780449809976

YALSA Best Fiction for Young Adults, 2015.

Removed from her unnamed Middle Eastern country after her father is murdered during a coup, 15-year-old Laila is now living near Washington D. C. with her mother and brother...This is more than just Laila's story; rather, it is a story of context, beautifully written (by a former undercover CIA agent), and stirring in its questions and eloquent observations about our society and that of the Middle East. —*Booklist*

Carriger, Gail

★ **Curtsies** & conspiracies. Gail Carriger. Little, Brown and Company, 2013 320 p. (Finishing school, 2)
Grades: 7 8 9 10 11 12

1. Boarding schools; 2. Espionage; 3. Schools; 4. Etiquette; 5. Robots; 6. Great Britain; 7. Victorian era (1837-1901); 8. 19th century; 9. Steampunk; 10. Historical fantasy
9780316190114; 9781907411601, print, UK

LC 2012048520

In her alternate England of 1851, fifteen-year-old Sophronia tries to uncover who is behind a plot to control a prototype that has the potential to alter human and supernatural travel, and to learn what role Mademoiselle Geraldine's academy for young spies plays in the affair.

With the school's dirigible heading toward London for a liaison with an inventor studying aetherospheric travel, Sophronia (*Etiquette & Espionage*) is convinced that her professors are Up To Something. Is the academy affiliated with vampire hives, werewolf packs, the anti-supernatural Picklemen, or the Crown—all of whom would benefit from controlling aether technology? A witty and suspenseful steampunk romp. —*Horn Book Guide*

★ **Etiquette** & espionage. By Gail Carriger. Little, Brown, 2013 320 p. (Finishing school, 1)
Grades: 7 8 9 10 11 12

1. Boarding schools; 2. Espionage; 3. Schools; 4. Etiquette; 5. Robots; 6. Great Britain; 7. Victorian era (1837-1901); 8. 19th century; 9. Steampunk; 10. Historical fantasy
9780316190084

LC 2012005498

ALA Notable Children's Book, 2014; YALSA Best Fiction for Young Adults, 2014; YALSA Popular Paperbacks for Young Adults, 2015.

In an alternate England of 1851, spirited fourteen-year-old Sophronia is enrolled in a finishing school where, she is suprised to learn, lessons include not only the fine arts of dance, dress, and etiquette, but also diversion, deceit, and espionage.

Waistcoats & weaponry. Gail Carriger. Little Brown & Co 2014 298 pages; (Finishing school, 3)
Grades: 6 7 8 9 10 11 12

1. Werewolves; 2. Espionage; 3. Boarding schools; 4. Schools; 5. Etiquette; 6. Great Britain; 7. Victorian era (1837-1901); 8. 19th century; 9. Steampunk; 10. Historical fantasy
9780316190275; 9780316279611, ebook, US; 9780316279628, ebook, US

LC 2014002829

In her alternate England of 1851, while taking her friend Sidheag by train to her werewolf pack in Scotland, sixteen-year-old Sophronia uncovers a plot that threatens to dissolve all of London into chaos and must decide where her loyalties lie once and for all.

Carson, Rae

★ The **bitter** kingdom. Rae Carson. Greenwillow Books, 2013 400 p. (Fire and thorns trilogy, 3)
Grades: 8 9 10 11 12

1. Teenage rulers; 2. Prophecies; 3. Rescues; 4. Civil war; 5. Magic; 6. High fantasy; 7. Fantasy fiction.
9780062026545

LC 2013011912

Elisa, a fugitive in her own kingdom, faces great challenges to rescue the man she loves from her enemies, prevent a civil war, and take back her throne but as her magic grows, Elisa discovers the shocking truth about her enemy's ultimate goal.

★ The **crown** of embers. By Rae Carson. Greenwillow Books, 2012 416 p. (Fire and thorns trilogy, 2)
Grades: 8 9 10 11 12

1. Teenage rulers; 2. Attempted assassination; 3. Crushes in teenage girls; 4. Magic; 5. Teenage romance; 6. High fantasy; 7. Fantasy fiction.
9780062026514

Elisa, struggling to master the power of the Godstone, takes a leap of faith and crosses an ocean accompanied by a one-eyed warrior, an enemy defector, and the man she is falling in love with in search of the source of its power.

Carson's world building and character development do not lag in this middle part of a trilogy, and the heat of the love story makes this accessible even for those who have yet to read the first volume (although they will then race for it). Both religion and politics play roles that invite discussion, and Elisa, not only brave but brilliant, tracks her own growing awareness with a self-consciousness credible for her age. —*Booklist*

★ The **girl** of fire and thorns. Rae Carson. Greenwillow Books, 2011 448 p. (Fire and thorns trilogy, 1)
Grades: 8 9 10 11 12

1. Princesses; 2. Self-hate in teenage girls; 3. Self-fulfillment in teenage girls; 4. Sixteen-year-old girls; 5. Overweight girls; 6. High fantasy; 7. Fantasy fiction.
9780062026484

YALSA Best Fiction for Young Adults, 2012; William C. Morris Debut Award finalist, 2012.

This fast-moving and exciting novel is rife with political conspiracies and machinations. —*School Library Journal*

Like a river glorious. Rae Carson. Greenwillow Books, an imprint of HarperCollinsPublishers, 2016 406 p. (Gold seer trilogy, 2)

Grades: 9 10 11 12

1. Gold mines and mining; 2. Superhuman abilities; 3. Gold Rush; 4. Teenage romance; 5. Uncles; 6. California; 7. American Westward Expansion (1803-1899); 8. Historical fantasy
9780062242945

Having arrived in California, Lee Westfall's magical power is growing and changing every day and may be enough, with help from her true friends, to stop her villainous Uncle Hiram when he kidnaps her and sends her deep into his gold mine.

Aside from Jefferson, the Native Americans mostly act as the stereotypical backdrop of decimated Indians. By keeping them largely naked and hidden, Carson diminishes the historical Native American resistance against Western expansion in the Sacramento area, and she adds insult to injury by ultimately making them collaborators in Leah's theft of their land. —*Kirkus*

Walk on Earth a stranger. Rae Carson. Harpercollins Childrens Books, 2015 432 p. (Gold seer trilogy, 1)
Grades: 7 8 9 10

1. Gold; 2. Superhuman abilities; 3. Gold Rush; 4. Magic; 5. Voyages and travels; 6. Georgia; 7. California; 8. American Westward Expansion (1803-1899); 9. Historical fantasy
9780062242914

Spur Award for Juvenile Fiction, 2016; YALSA Best Fiction for Young Adults, 2016.

Carson's story is simply terrific—tense and exciting, while gently and honestly addressing the brutal hardships of the westward migration. Even minor characters are fully three-dimensional, but it's Leah who rightfully takes center stage as a smart, resourceful, determined, and realistic heroine who embodies the age-old philosophy that it isn't what happens to you, but how you react to it that matters. —*Publishers Weekly*

Carter, Ally

All fall down. By Ally Carter. Scholastic, 2015 320 p. (Embassy Row novels, 1)
Grades: 7 8 9 10

1. Diplomatic and consular service; 2. Ambassadors; 3. Intrigue; 4. Murder; 5. Mothers — Death; 6. Thrillers and suspense
9780545654746; 9780545654807; 9781408334379, print, UK; 9781760153465, print, Australia

YALSA Popular Paperbacks for Young Adults, 2017.

This exciting first book in the Embassy Row series features sixteen-year-old Grace, who has moved into the United States Embassy on the coast of Adria with her ambassador grandfather. It is the first time in three years that she has been back to Adria, since her mothers tragic death in a fire... Her quest to find the truth is one that readers will love to follow, through the twists and turns of Embassy Row and with a diverse array of characters. Some help her, and some stand in her way...but Grace is a fighter, and she will stop at nothing to find out what happened to her mother. Readers will love this first book in what promises to be an exciting, thrilling mystery series from best-selling author Carter. —*Voice of Youth Advocates*

Don't judge a girl by her cover. By Ally Carter. Hyperion Books for Children, 2009 240 p. (Gallagher girls, 3)
Grades: 6 7 8 9

1. Teenage spies; 2. Kidnapping; 3. Boarding school students; 4. Boarding schools; 5. Fifteen-year-old girls; 6. Spy fiction.
9781423116387; 9780734417237, print, Australia; 9781408309537, print, UK

These girls remain the most awesome, kick-butt teens ever, but now readers are also getting a glimpse at what makes them vulnerable. —*Voice of Youth Advocates*

Sequel to: *Cross my heart and hope to spy.*

Heist society. Ally Carter. Disney/Hyperion, 2010 304 p. (Heist society novels, 1)
Grades: 7 8 9 10

1. Art thefts; 2. Thieves; 3. Revenge; 4. Families; 5. Friendship; 6. New York (State); 7. Europe; 8. Teen chick lit.
9781423116394; 9781408309551, print, UK
LC 2009040377

YALSA Popular Paperbacks for Young Adults, 2013.

A group of teenagers uses their combined talents to re-steal several priceless paintings and save fifteen-year-old Kat Bishop's father, himself an international art thief, from a vengeful collector.

Carter skillfully maintains suspense.... This is a thoroughly enjoyable, cinema-ready adventure. —*Booklist*

Not if I save you first. Ally Carter. 2018 304 p.
Grades: 8 9 10 11

1. Fathers and daughters; 2. Wilderness survival; 3. Rescues; 4. Forgiveness; 5. Best friends; 6. Alaska; 7. Thrillers and suspense; 8. Books for reluctant readers
9781338134148; 9781408349090
LC 2017049072

Beehive Young Adult Book Award (Utah), 2020; YALSA Quick Picks for Reluctant Young Adult Readers, 2019.

After six years of no word from her best friend, Logan, he shows up on the doorstep of the remote Alaskan cabin Maddie and her father live in with an assailant in pursuit.

A tightly plotted thriller helmed by a firecracker that never loses her spark. —*Kirkus*

Perfect scoundrels: a Heist society novel. Ally Carter. Disney Hyperion, 2013 304 p. (Heist society novels, 3)
Grades: 7 8 9 10

1. Thieves; 2. Swindlers and swindling; 3. Corporations; 4. Inheritance and succession; 5. Crime; 6. Teen chick lit; 7. Books for reluctant readers
9781423166009; 9781408326459, print, UK
LC 2012032405

YALSA Quick Picks for Reluctant Young Adult Readers, 2014.

When feisty teenaged thief Kat's on-again off-again boyfriend, Hale, suddenly inherits his family's billion dollar company, Kat gets a tip-off that the will is a fake.

Carter, Caela

Me, him, them, and it. By Caela Carter. Bloomsbury : 2013 272 p.
Grades: 9 10 11 12

1. Pregnant teenagers; 2. Emotions in teenage girls; 3. Family problems; 4. Teenage pregnancy; 5. Sixteen-year-old girls; 6. Realistic fiction.
9781599909585
LC 2012014331

Playing the "bad girl" at school to get back at her feuding parents, sixteen-year-old Evelyn becomes pregnant and faces a difficult decision.

Casella, Jody

Thin space. Jody Casella. Simon Pulse; 2014 256 p.
Grades: 9 10 11 12

1. Twin brothers; 2. Grief in teenage boys; 3. Fatal traffic accidents; 4. New neighbors; 5. Coping; 6. New England; 7. Thrillers and suspense; 8. Paranormal fiction; 9. First person narratives

9781582704357

Consumed by guilt and secrets about his twin brother's death, Marsh Windsor is looking for a thin space—a place where the barrier between this world and the next is thin enough for a person to cross over—in hopes of setting things right.

The final plot twist will catch most readers by surprise, making a second reading almost mandatory, to look for missed clues. The story is atmospheric and chilling, with a few four letter words, a bit of romance, and a satisfying ending. —*School Library Journal*

Cashore, Kristin

★ **Fire**. Kristin Cashore. Dial Books, 2009 461 p. (Graceling realm, 2)
Grades: 9 10 11 12

1. Teenage girl psychics; 2. Mind control; 3. Beauty; 4. Political corruption; 5. Monsters; 6. High fantasy; 7. Fantasy fiction.
9780803734616; 9781473233263, Paperback, UK

LC 2009005187

Garden State Teen Book Award (New Jersey), Fiction (Grades 9-12), 2012; YALSA Popular Paperbacks for Young Adults, 2013; Booklist Editors' Choice: Books for Youth, 2009; YALSA Best Books for Young Adults, 2010; School Library Journal Best Books, 2009.

In a kingdom called the Dells, Fire is the last human-shaped monster, with unimaginable beauty and the ability to control the minds of those around her, but even with these gifts she cannot escape the strife that overcomes her world.

Many twists propel the action...[and] Cashore's conclusion satisfies, but readers will clamor for a sequel to the prequela book bridging the gap between this one and Graceling. —*Publishers Weekly*

Map by Jeffery C. Mathison

★ **Graceling**. Kristin Cashore. Harcourt, 2008 480 p. (Graceling Realm, 1)
Grades: 8 9 10 11 12

1. Girl warriors; 2. Political corruption; 3. Princes; 4. Rulers; 5. Uncles; 6. High fantasy; 7. Fantasy fiction.
9780152063962; 9781473233256, Paperback, UK

LC 2007045436

California Young Reader Medal, Young Adult, 2012; Green Mountain Book Award (Vermont), 2011; Mythopoeic Award for Children's Literature, 2009; Rhode Island Teen Book Award, 2011; YALSA Popular Paperbacks for Young Adults, 2012; Amelia Bloomer List, 2009; Booklist Editors' Choice: Books for Youth, 2008; YALSA Best Books for Young Adults, 2009; School Library Journal Best Books, 2008.

In a world where some people are born with extreme and often-feared skills called Graces, Katsa struggles for redemption from her own horrifying Grace, and teams up with another young fighter to save their land from a corrupt king.

This is gorgeous storytelling: exciting, stirring, and accessible. Fantasy and romance readers will be thrilled. —*School Library Journal*

Prequel: *Fire*.

Jane, unlimited. Kristin Cashore. Kathy Dawson Books, 2017 464 p.
Grades: 8 9 10 11 12

1. Teenage girl orphans; 2. Bisexual teenage girls; 3. Mansions; 4. Rich people; 5. Teenage romance; 6. Fantasy fiction
9780803741492

LibraryReads Favorites, 2017; School Library Journal Best Books, 2017; YALSA Best Fiction for Young Adults, 2018.

Creation, compassion, and choice repeatedly emerge as themes in this ambitious, mind-expanding novel. —*Booklist*

Cast, P. C.

Moon chosen. P.C. Cast. St. Martin's Griffin, 2016 590 p. (Tales of a new world, 1)
Grades: 9 10 11 12

1. Post-apocalypse; 2. Healers; 3. Alliances; 4. Human/animal relationships; 5. Teenage romance; 6. Fantasy fiction.
9781250100726; 9781925483727, print, Australia

Cast's vivid and transcendent epic is sure to engross fantasy readers. —*Voice of Youth Advocates*

Castellucci, Cecil

Beige. Cecil Castellucci. Candlewick Press, 2007 320 p.
Grades: 7 8 9 10

1. Fathers and daughters; 2. Punk rock music; 3. French-Canadian teenagers; 4. French-Canadians; 5. French-Canadians in the United States; 6. Los Angeles, California; 7. California; 8. Coming-of-age stories; 9. Books for reluctant readers
9780763630669

LC 2006052458

YALSA Quick Picks for Reluctant Young Adult Readers, 2008; YALSA Best Books for Young Adults, 2008.

Katy, a quiet French-Canadian teenager, reluctantly leaves Montreal to spend time with her estranged father, an aging Los Angeles punk rock legend.

Boy proof. Cecil Castellucci. Candlewick Press, 2005 208 p.
Grades: 7 8 9 10

1. Teenage misfits; 2. New students; 3. Film industry and trade; 4. Teenage girls; 5. Teenagers; 6. Los Angeles, California; 7. First person narratives; 8. Realistic fiction; 9. Books for reluctant readers
9780763623333

LC 2004050256

YALSA Quick Picks for Reluctant Young Adult Readers, 2006; YALSA Best Books for Young Adults, 2006.

Feeling alienated from everyone around her, Los Angeles high school senior and cinephile Victoria Denton hides behind the identity of a favorite movie character until an interesting new boy arrives at school and helps her realize that there is more to life than just the movies.

This novel's clipped, funny, first-person, present-tense narrative will grab teens... with its romance and the screwball special effects, and with the story of an outsider's struggle both to belong and to be true to herself. —*Booklist*

Castle, Jennifer

You look different in real life. Jennifer Castle. HarperTeen, an imprint of HarperCollinsPublishers, 2013 432 p.
Grades: 7 8 9 10

1. Documentary films — Production and direction; 2. Identity (Psychology); 3. Reunions; 4. Interpersonal relations; 5. Families; 6. New York (State); 7. Realistic fiction
9780061985812

LC 2012051743

Five teens starring in a documentary film series about their ordinary lives must grapple with questions of change and identity under the scrutiny of the camera.

Castor, H. M.

VIII. H.M. Castor. Simon & Schuster Books for Young Readers, 2013 432 p.
Grades: 8 9 10 11 12

1. Henry VIII, King of England, 1491-1547; 2. Rulers; 3. Warriors; 4. Families; 5. Great Britain; 6. Tudor period (1485-1603); 7. 16th

century; 8. Historical fiction; 9. Biographical fiction; 10. First person narratives.
9781442474185; 9781442474208, ebook, US

LC 2012021550

Hal, a young man of extraordinary talents, skill on the battlefield, sharp intelligence, and virtue, believes he is destined for greatness but, haunted by his family's violent past, he embarks on a journey that leads to absolute power and brings him face to face with his demons as he grows to become Henry VIII.

Catmull, Katherine

The **radiant** road: a novel. By Katherine Catmull. Dutton Books, an imprint of Penguin Random House LLC, 2016 336 p.
Grades: 7 8 9 10
1. Fairies; 2. Half-human hybrids; 3. Parallel universes; 4. Magic; 5. Identity (Psychology); 6. Ireland; 7. Urban fantasy
9780525953470

LC 2015020678

After nine years Clare Macleod and her father are finally returning to their old home in Ireland, a house by the sea, with a yew tree growing inside it, a tree with its roots in both the human and fairy world—and soon Clare, who has always been able to sense the "Strange," meets the boy Finn, and discovers that she must battle against the forces of evil in to restore order to both worlds.

Catmull has created an eerily lovely story, writing with an old-fashioned style that at times sings like a lullaby. An excellent addition to either teen or juvenile collections of all sizes. —*Booklist*

Cavallaro, Brittany

A **study** in Charlotte. Brittany Cavallaro. Katherine Tegen Books, 2016 336 p. (Charlotte Holmes, 1)
Grades: 9 10 11 12
1. Prep schools; 2. Murder investigation; 3. Teenage detectives; 4. Teenagers; 5. Teenage romance; 6. Connecticut; 7. Mysteries; 8. Classics-inspired fiction
9780062398901
YALSA Best Fiction for Young Adults, 2017.

Sherlock Holmes and Dr. Watson descendants, Charlotte and Jamie, students at a Connecticut boarding school, team up to solve a murder mystery.

Less a mystery for readers to solve, Cavallaro's debut, yet another reimagining of the iconic detecting duo, is more of a joyous excuse to watch one of the literary world's most beloved pairings come together. Readers will delight in the romantic friction between Holmes and Watson, particularly when it comes to their long-awaited union. —*Booklist*

Chaltas, Thalia

Because I am furniture. By Thalia Chaltas. Viking, 2009 352 p.
Grades: 8 9 10 11
1. Child abuse; 2. Child sexual abuse; 3. Guilt in teenage girls; 4. Guilt; 5. Violence in men; 6. Novels in verse; 7. Realistic fiction; 8. First person narratives
9780670062980

LC 2008023235

Amelia Bloomer List, 2010; YALSA Best Books for Young Adults, 2010.

The youngest of three siblings, fourteen-year-old Anke feels both relieved and neglected that her father abuses her brother and sister but ignores her, but when she catches him with one of her friends, she finally becomes angry enough to take action.

Incendiary, devastating, yet—in total—offering empowerment and hope, Chaltas's poems leave an indelible mark. —*Publishers Weekly*

Chambers, Aidan

★ **Postcards** from no man's land: a novel. Aidan Chambers. Bodley Head, 1999 336 p.
Grades: 11 12
1. Soldiers; 2. World War II; 3. Identity (Psychology); 4. Euthanasia; 5. Extramarital affairs; 6. Amsterdam, Netherlands; 7. Classics.
9780370323763
Booklist Editors' Choice: Books for Youth, 2002; Carnegie Medal, 1999; Michael L. Printz Award, 2003; YALSA Best Books for Young Adults, 2003.

Visiting his grandfather's grave during the annual commemoration of the Battle of Arnhem, Jacob Todd finds his view of himself, his country and his place in the world are overturned when he starts chatting to a very special elderly Dutch woman.

This novel is beautifully written, emotionally touching, and intellectually challenging. —*Voice of Youth Advocates*

Chan, Crystal

★ **All** that I can fix. Crystal Chan. Simon Pulse, 2018 320 p.
Grades: 7 8 9 10 11
1. Multiracial teenage boys; 2. Small town life; 3. Responsibility in teenage boys; 4. Fifteen-year-old boys; 5. Children of people with depression; 6. Indiana; 7. Realistic fiction; 8. Coming-of-age stories
9781534408883; 9781534408890

LC 2017039196

School Library Journal Best Books, 2018.

When his world starts falling apart, Ronney, who people know as the kid from the mixed-race family with the dad who attempted suicide, the druggie mom, and the genius kid sister, struggles to hold it together.

A superbly entertaining read that weaves issues of mental health and gun control with adolescent angst. —*Kirkus*

Chan, Gillian

The **disappearance**. Gillian Chan. Annick Press, 2017 208 p.
Grades: 8 9 10 11 12
1. Missing teenage boys; 2. Group homes; 3. Psychic ability; 4. Supernatural; 5. Bullying and bullies; 6. Paranormal fiction
9781554519835; 9781554519828

Scarred physically and emotionally after the murder of his younger brother, Mike, a teenager, ends up in a group home, where he encounters Jacob, a strange young boy who seems to be from another place and time, and seems to know everything about Mike, including what happened to his brother.

Reluctant highly capable readers will be enticed, as will fans of R. L. Stine, Ripleys Believe It or Not, and ghost stories. —*Voice of Youth Advocates*

Chao, Gloria

Rent a boyfriend. Gloria Chao. Simon Pulse, 2020 320 p.
Grades: 9 10 11 12
1. Women college students; 2. Men/women relations; 3. Asian Americans; 4. Dating (Social customs); 5. Pretending; 6. Contemporary romances; 7. Romantic comedies
9781534462458

Chloe Wang is nervous to introduce her parents to her boyfriend, because the truth is, she hasn't met him yet either. She hired him from Rent for Your 'Rents, a company specializing in providing fake boyfriends trained to impress even the most traditional Asian parents. When Chloe rents Drew, the mission is simple: convince her parents fake Drew is worthy of their approval so they'll stop pressuring her to accept a proposal from Hongbo, the wealthiest (and slimiest) young bachelor in their tight-knit Asian American community. But when Chloe starts to fall for the real Drew—who, unlike his fake persona, is definitely not "rent-worthy"—her carefully curated life begins to unravel. Can she figure out what she wants before she loses everything?

This spirited novel is perfect for fans of Sandhya Menon, Jenny Han, and the fake-dating trope, as it entertainingly explores embracing life's challenges, navigating strict cultural viewpoints, and learning to be the person you know in your heart you should be. —*Booklist*

Chapman, Elsie
Caster. Elsie Chapman. Scholastic Press, 2019 336 p. (Caster (Elsie Chapman), 1)
Grades: 8 9 10 11 12
1. Superhuman abilities; 2. Tournaments; 3. Debt; 4. Magic; 5. Competition; 6. Asian-influenced fantasy; 7. Dystopian fiction; 8. Canadian fiction
9781338332629

LC 2018060381

Aza Wu knows that casting magic can kill—it killed her sister—but she needs money desperately to pay off Saint Willow, who controls her sector of Lotusland, and save the family teahouse, so she secretly enters an underground casting tournament—and finds herself competing against other castors with "full magic," and where even victory could cause her to lose her freedom, her magic, and her life.

Chapman ... has created compelling young adult novels before, but this is a cut above; the fully realized and atmospheric dystopia is crafted at a level not seen often. This stunning fantasy will fly off the shelves. —*Booklist*

Chapman, Erica M.
Teach me to forget. Erica M. Chapman. Merit Press, 2016 256 p.
Grades: 9 10 11 12
1. Accidents; 2. Grief in teenage girls; 3. Suicide; 4. Teenage romance; 5. Teenage boy/girl relations; 6. Realistic fiction
9781440594571

Ellery is heartbreakingly realistic, and readers will find themselves lost in her turmoil. This is contemporary realistic fiction at its best, as all of the characters are fully formed, with distinct and believable behaviors. —*Voice of Youth Advocates*

Charbonneau, Joelle
Graduation day. Joelle Charbonneau. 2014 320 p. (The Testing trilogy, 3)
Grades: 7 8 9 10 11 12
1. Dystopias; 2. Loyalty; 3. Resistance to government; 4. Survival; 5. Love; 6. Dystopian fiction; 7. Science fiction.
9780547959214; 9781783700226, print, UK; 9781471407024, print, UK

LC 2013034743

The United Commonwealth wants to eliminate the rebel alliance fighting to destroy The Testing for good. Cia is ready to lead the charge, but will her lethal classmates follow her into battle?

Charbonneau concludes her dystopian Testing trilogy with this action-packed finale, which sees Cia Vale secretly tasked by the President of the United Commonwealth to remove the officials behind the lethal Testing process that has claimed so many young lives...As in the previous books, Charbonneau remains focused on philosophical worries and moral tests over spectacle and bloodshed, with multiple layers and twists to keep readers forever guessing. Enough potential threads are left dangling to leave room for future stories. —*Publishers Weekly*

Independent study. By Joelle Charbonneau. 2014 320 pages (The Testing trilogy, 2)

Grades: 7 8 9 10 11 12
1. Dystopias; 2. Examinations; 3. Universities and colleges; 4. Survival; 5. Resistance to government; 6. Dystopian fiction; 7. Science fiction.
9780547959207; 9781848771680, print, UK; 9781471407017, print, UK

LC 2013004815

Now a freshman at the University in Tosu City with her hometown sweetheart, Tomas, Cia Vale attempts to expose the ugly truth behind the government's grueling and deadly Testing put her and her loved ones in great danger.

In this sequel to The Testing (Houghton Harcourt, 2013), Cia is drawn deeper into the political machinations of Tosu City as she enters the University...Fans of The Testing will be thrilled with this new installment and will be anxiously waiting for the story's conclusion. —*School Library Journal*

★ The **Testing**. By Joelle Charbonneau. Houghton Mifflin Harcourt, 2013 336 p. (The Testing trilogy, 1)
Grades: 7 8 9 10 11 12
1. Dystopias; 2. Examinations; 3. Survival; 4. Schools; 5. Universities and colleges; 6. Dystopian fiction; 7. Science fiction; 8. Books for reluctant readers
9780547959108; 9781471407000, print, UK

LC 2012018090

Anthony Award for Best Children's or Young Adult Novel, 2014; YALSA Quick Picks for Reluctant Young Adult Readers, 2014; YALSA Popular Paperbacks for Young Adults, 2016.

Sixteen-year-old Malencia (Cia) Vale is chosen to participate in The Testing to attend the University; however, Cia is fearful when she figures out her friends who do not pass The Testing are disappearing.

Charles, Tami
Becoming Beatriz. By Tami Charles. Charlesbridge, 2019 272 p.
Grades: 7 8 9 10
1. Teenage girl dancers; 2. Puerto Ricans; 3. Gangs; 4. Gang members; 5. Brothers — Death; 6. Newark, New Jersey; 7. 1980s; 8. Historical fiction; 9. First person narratives; 10. African American fiction.
9781580897785, hardback, US; 9781632896117, ebook, US

LC 2018031378

In 1984 Newark, Beatriz Mendez navigates romance, gang culture, and her family's past. After her gang-leader brother is killed, Beatriz gives up her dreams of dancing in order to run the gang. But her eyes are re-opened to her dream of a career in dance when the school brainiac asks her to compete in a dance competition with him—but will the gang let her go?

Readers with diverse backgrounds will feel at home with Beatriz's identities as Latina, Black, and American, and everyone will be cheering her on, right up until the satisfying, heartwarming end. —*Booklist*
Companion to: *Like Vanessa*.

Like Vanessa. Tami Charles. 2018 288 p.
Grades: 5 6 7 8
1. Williams, Vanessa; 2. African American teenage girls; 3. Beauty contests; 4. Self-acceptance; 5. Thirteen-year-old girls; 6. Inner city schools; 7. Newark, New Jersey; 8. 1980s; 9. Realistic fiction; 10. Historical fiction; 11. African American fiction
9781580897778

LC 2016053961

It is 1983 and Vanessa Martin, a thirteen-year-old African American girl in Newark's public housing, dreams of following in the footsteps of the first black Miss America, Vanessa Williams; but the odds are against her until a new teacher at school organizes a beauty pageant and encourages Vanessa to enter.

Companion: *Becoming Beatriz*

Charlton-Trujillo, E. E.

★ **Fat** Angie. E. E. Charlton-Trujillo. Candlewick Press, 2013 272 p. (Fat Angie, 1)

Grades: 9 10 11 12

1. Overweight teenage girls; 2. Bullying and bullies; 3. High school freshmen; 4. Interpersonal relations; 5. High schools; 6. Ohio; 7. Realistic fiction; 8. LGBTQIA fiction

9780763661199

Rainbow List, 2014; Stonewall Book Award for Children's and Young Adult Literature, 2014; Westchester Fiction Award, 2014.

Angie overeats to cope with the taunts of the ultra-mean girls, her attempted suicide in front of a packed gym, and the status of her captured war-hero sister, until KC Romance comes to town and sees Angie for who she really is.

Chayil, Eishes

Hush. Eishes Chayil. Walker, 2010 292 p.

Grades: 8 9 10 11 12

1. Jewish Americans; 2. Child sexual abuse; 3. Hasidim; 4. Culture conflict; 5. Rules; 6. Borough Park (New York City); 7. New York City; 8. Realistic fiction.

9780802720887

LC 2010010329

Amelia Bloomer List, 2012; YALSA Best Fiction for Young Adults, 2012; William C. Morris Debut Award finalist, 2011.

After remembering the cause of her best friend Devory's suicide at age nine, Gittel is determined to raise awareness of sexual abuse in her Borough Park, New York, community, despite the rules of Chassidim that require her to be silent.

The author balances outrage at the routine cover-up of criminal acts with genuine understanding of the community's fear of assault on their traditions by censorious gentiles. Moreover, she delivers her central message in an engaging coming-of-age story in which tragedy is only one element in a gossipy milieu of school and career decisions and arranged marriages, designer shoes and tasteful cosmetics, and sneak peaks out from a world of restraint and devotion into the world of Oprah. —*Bulletin of the Center for Children's Books*

Chbosky, Stephen

★ The **perks** of being a wallflower. Stephen Chbosky. Pocket Books, 1999 213 p.

Grades: 9 10 11 12

1. High school students; 2. Teenage boys; 3. Teenagers — Sexuality; 4. Teenagers — Drug use; 5. Teenagers — Alcohol use; 6. Pennsylvania; 7. Epistolary novels; 8. Diary novels; 9. Coming-of-age stories; 10. Books for reluctant readers

9780671027346; 9781471100482, UK; 9781471180811, Paperback, UK; 9781471116148, print, UK; 9781847829702, large print, UK

YALSA Popular Paperbacks for Young Adults, 2014; YALSA Quick Picks for Reluctant Young Adult Readers, 2000; YALSA Best Books for Young Adults, 2000.

Charlie is shy, introspective, intelligent beyond his years yet socially awkward; he is a wallflower, caught between trying to live his life and trying to run from it. Charlie attempts to navigate his way through the uncharted territory of high school: the world of first dates and mix-tapes, family dramas and new friends. Standing on the fringes of life offers a unique perspective. But there comes a time to see what it looks like from the dance floor.

Grounded in a specific time (the 1991/92 academic year) and place (western Pennsylvania), Charlie, his friends, and family are palpably real...This report on his life will engage teen readers for years to come. —*School Library Journal*

Film adaptation under same name (2012).

Chee, Traci

★ The **reader**. Traci Chee. 2016 464 pages (Sea of ink and gold, 1)

Grades: 8 9 10 11 12

1. Books; 2. Orphans; 3. Pirates; 4. Reading; 5. Kidnapping; 6. Fantasy fiction.

9780399176777

LC 2015039924

School Library Journal Best Books, 2016; YALSA Best Fiction for Young Adults, 2017; Kirkus Prize for Young Readers' Literature finalist, 2016.

Set in a world where reading is unheard-of, Sefia makes use of a mysterious object to track down who kidnapped her aunt Nin and what really happened the day her father was murdered.

This cleverly layered fantasy leaves more questions than it answers, but fortunately, it's only the first of what promises to be an enchanting series. —*Kirkus*

The **speaker**. Traci Chee; map and interior illustrations by Ian Schoenherr. G.P. Putnam's Sons, 2017 512 p. (Sea of ink and gold, 2)

Grades: 8 9 10 11 12

1. Books; 2. Orphans; 3. Pirates; 4. Reading; 5. Kidnapping; 6. Fantasy fiction.

9780399176784; 9780147518064, Paperback, UK

Filled with even more magic and intrigue than its predecessor, this is a gripping follow-up that will leave readers speculating and wanting more. —*Kirkus*

We are not free. Traci Chee. Houghton Mifflin Harcourt, 2020 400 p.

Grades: 7 8 9 10 11 12

1. Japanese in the United States — Mass internment, 1942-1945; 2. Japanese Americans — Forced removal and incarceration, 1942-1945; 3. World War II — Japanese Americans; 4. Teenagers; 5. Friendship; 6. Japantown, San Francisco, California; 7. San Francisco, California; 8. Historical fiction; 9. Multiple perspectives; 10. First person narratives

9780358131434, HRD, US; 9780358330004, ebook, US

LC 2019029407

School Library Journal Best Books, 2020; Michael L. Printz Honor Book, 2020; Walter Honor Book, Teen, 2020.

Growing up together in the community of Japantown, San Francisco, four second-generation Japanese American teens find their bond tested by widespread discrimination and the mass incarcerations of people of Japanese ancestry during World War II.

Ambitious in scope and complexity, this is an essential contribution to the understanding of the wide-ranging experiences impacting people of Japanese ancestry in the U.S. during WWII. —*Publishers Weekly*

Chen, Justina

Lovely, dark, and deep. Justina Chen. 2018 352 p.

Grades: 9 10 11 12

1. Asian American teenage girls; 2. Teenage romance; 3. Allergy; 4. Asian Americans; 5. Photosensitivity disorders; 6. Contemporary romances

9781338134063

LC 2017042553

Teenager Viola Li and her sister Roz are selling bean buns at a science fiction gathering in Seattle when she suddenly collapses—she wakes up in the hospital to find that somehow she has developed an extreme case of photosensitivity (so bad that even ordinary lights can cause blisters), and somehow, in her senior year of high school, she has to craft a new life that will still include journalism school, activism, and the new guy who caught her as she fell.

Chibbaro, Julie

Deadly. Julie Chibbaro; illustrated by Jean-Marc Superville Sovak. Atheneum Books for Young Readers, 2011 304 p.
Grades: 6 7 8 9 10
1. Typhoid Mary; 2. Epidemiology; 3. Epidemics; 4. Father-separated teenage girls; 5. Gender role; 6. Typhoid fever; 7. New York City; 8. 1900s (Decade); 9. Diary novels; 10. Historical fiction.
9780689857386

LC 2010002291
Amelia Bloomer List, 2012; National Jewish Book Award, 2011.

In the early 1900s, sixteen-year-old Prudence Galewski leaves school to take a job assisting the head epidemiologist at New York's Department of Health and Sanitation, investigating the intriguing case of "Typhoid Mary," a seemingly healthy woman who is infecting others with typhoid fever.

A deeply personal coming-of-age story set in an era of tumultuous social change, this is top-notch historical fiction that highlights the struggle between rational science and popular opinion as shaped by a sensational, reactionary press. —*School Library Journal*

Chim, Wai

★ The **surprising** power of a good dumpling. By Wai Chim. 2020 400 p;
Grades: 9 10 11 12
1. Children of people with mental illnesses; 2. Chinese in Australia; 3. Families; 4. Mental illness; 5. Familial love; 6. Australian fiction.
9781338656114; 9781760631581, Paperback, Australia

Anna Chiu has her hands pretty full looking after her brother and sister and helping out at her dad's restaurant, all while her mum stays in bed. Dad's new delivery boy, Rory, is a welcome distraction and even though she knows that things aren't right at home, she's starting to feel like she could just be a normal teen. But when Mum finally gets out of bed, things go from bad to worse. And as Mum's condition worsens, Anna and her family question everything they understand about themselves and each other. A nourishing tale about the crevices of culture, mental wellness and family, and the surprising power of a good dumpling.

Gritty details lend depth to this viscerally powerful tale of a teen struggling to help her troubled family. —*Kirkus*

Chima, Cinda Williams

★ The **Demon** King: a Seven Realms novel. Cinda Williams Chima. Disney/Hyperion Books, 2009 506 p. : Map (Seven Realms novels, 1)
Grades: 7 8 9 10 11 12
1. Princesses; 2. Former gang members; 3. Amulets; 4. Good and evil; 5. Wizards; 6. High fantasy; 7. Fantasy fiction; 8. Multiple perspectives
9781423118237

LC 2008046178
YALSA Popular Paperbacks for Young Adults, 2012; YALSA Best Fiction for Young Adults, 2011.

Relates the intertwining fates of former street gang leader Han Alister and headstrong Princess Raisa, as Han takes possession of an amulet that once belonged to an evil wizard and Raisa uncovers a conspiracy in the Grey Wolf Court.

With full-blooded, endearing heroes, a well-developed supporting cast and a detail-rich setting, Chima explores the lives of two young adults, one at the top of the world and the other at the bottom, struggling to find their place and protect those they love. —*Publishers Weekly*

Map on lining papers.

The **exiled** queen: a Seven Realms novel. Cinda Williams Chima. Disney/Hyperion, 2010 592 (Seven Realms novels, 2)
Grades: 7 8 9 10 11 12
1. Wizards; 2. Princesses; 3. Forced marriage; 4. Amulets; 5. Former gang members; 6. High fantasy; 7. Fantasy fiction; 8. Multiple perspectives
9781423118244

LC 2009047749
Teen Buckeye Book Award (Ohio), 2011.

Two teenagers, one fleeing from a forced marriage and the other from a dangerous family of wizards, cross paths and fall in love.

The pacing of the story is pitch-perfect, with the focus shifting back and forth from Han to Raisa until their paths merge, making this an excellent choice for reluctant readers. —*Voice of Youth Advocates*

★ The **warrior** heir. Cinda Williams Chima. Hyperion Books for Children, 2006 426 p. (Heir chronicles, 1)
Grades: 7 8 9 10 11 12
1. Warriors; 2. Magic swords; 3. Dueling; 4. Wizards; 5. Magic; 6. Ohio; 7. Great Britain; 8. Fantasy fiction.
9780786839162

LC 2005052720
YALSA Popular Paperbacks for Young Adults, 2008.

After learning about his magical ancestry and his own warrior powers, sixteen-year-old Jack embarks on a training program to fight enemy wizards.

Twists and turns abound in this remarkable, nearly flawless debut novel that mixes a young man's coming-of-age with fantasy and adventure. Fast paced and brilliantly plotted. —*Voice of Youth Advocates*

Choi, Mary H. K.

★ **Emergency** contact. Mary H. K. Choi. Simon & Schuster, 2018 240 p.
Grades: 9 10 11 12
1. Text messages; 2. Dating (Social customs); 3. Misfits (Persons); 4. Universities and colleges; 5. Secrets; 6. Contemporary romances.
9781534408968; 9781534408975; 9780349003467, Paperback, UK; 9781534408982, ebook, US

LC 2017048139
After a chance encounter, Penny and Sam become each other's emergency contacts and find themselves falling in love digitally, without the humiliating weirdness of having to see each other.

Chokshi, Roshani

★ The **gilded** wolves. Roshani Chokshi. 2019 400 p. (Gilded wolves, 1)
Grades: 9 10 11 12
1. Treasure hunters; 2. Quests; 3. Decadence (Concept); 4. Multiracial persons; 5. Secrets; 6. Paris, France; 7. 1880s; 8. Historical fantasy; 9. Multiple perspectives.
9781250144546

LC 2018031842
Keeping close secrets in the wake of the Exposition Universelle in 1889 Paris, a wealthy hotelier and treasure-hunter is tapped by a powerful order to lead an elite team on a quest to track down an ancient artifact of world-changing significance.

Chokshi creatively reimagines history, weaving fantastical elements with symbology and broadening the scope of her narrative by integrating multiethnic worldviews. An opulent heist adventure that will leave readers voracious for more. —*Kirkus*

The **star-touched** queen. Roshani Chokshi. Griffin, 2016 352 p. (Star-touched queen, 1)
Grades: 9 10 11 12
1. Fate and fatalism; 2. Teenage rulers; 3. Arranged marriage; 4. Characters and characteristics in mythology; 5. Prophecies; 6. High fantasy; 7. Fantasy fiction; 8. Mythological fiction
9781250085474
A unique fantasy that is epic myth and beautiful fairy tale combined. —*Booklist*

Chotjewitz, David
Daniel, half human: and the good Nazi. David Chotjewitz; translated from the German by Doris Orgel. Atheneum Books for Young Readers, 2004 291 p.
Grades: 7 8 9 10
1. Nazis; 2. Boys; 3. Best friends; 4. Antisemitism; 5. Ethics; 6. Germany; 7. 1930s; 8. Historical fiction; 9. Translations
9780689857478; 9783551580450
LC 2003025554
ALA Notable Children's Book, 2005; YALSA Best Books for Young Adults, 2005; Batchelder Honor Book, 2005.
In 1933, best friends Daniel and Armin admire Hitler, but as anti-Semitism buoys Hitler to power, Daniel learns he is half Jewish, threatening the friendship even as life in their beloved Hamburg, Germany, is becoming nightmarish. Also details Daniel and Armin's reunion in 1945 in interspersed chapters.
Orgel's translation reads smoothly and movingly. An outstanding addition to the large body of World War II/Holocaust fiction. —*School Library Journal*
A Richard Jackson Book.

Christopher, Lucy
The **killing** woods. Lucy Christopher. 2014 384 pages
Grades: 9 10 11 12
1. Games; 2. Post-traumatic stress disorder; 3. Children of military personnel; 4. Murder; 5. Drug use; 6. Mysteries; 7. Multiple perspectives; 8. First person narratives
9780545461009; 9780545461016; 9780545576710
LC 2013022566
When her father, an ex-soldier suffering from post-traumatic stress disorder or PTSD, is arrested for murder, Emily's efforts to exonerate him take her into the woods to play the Game, an extreme version of childhood games.
This taut, psychologically realistic murder mystery knits trauma, danger, tragedy and hope into one cohesive tale...Readers will be riveted by slow, potent reveals about the rough nature of the Game, Ashlee's insistence on danger and adrenaline, and what happened that night. The answers hurt, but they feel right and they make sense. A sprout of hope at the end is fragile and unforced. A gripping, heartbreaking, emotionally substantial look at war wounds and the allure of danger. —*Kirkus*

Chupeco, Rin
Wicked as you wish. Rin Chupeco. Sourcebooks Fire, 2020 432 p. (Hundred names for magic, 1)
Grades: 8 9 10 11 12
1. Filipino Americans; 2. Princes; 3. Characters and characteristics in fairy tales; 4. Imaginary kingdoms; 5. Magic; 6. Arizona; 7. Fairy tale and folklore-inspired fiction; 8. Urban fantasy; 9. Fantasy fiction.
9781492672661, HRD, US

LC 2019032045
Years after the evil Snow Queen desolated the magical kingdom of Avalon, Prince Alexei, his friend Tala, and a ragtag band, inspired by the appearance of the Firebird, try to reclaim their land.
Readers looking for a vibrant, Harry Potteresque fantasy full of secrets, spies, magic, monsters, and mayhem need look no further. —*Booklist*

Cisneros, Sandra
★ The **house** on Mango Street. Sandra Cisneros. Alfred A. Knopf, 1984 134 p.
Grades: 7 8 9 10 11 12 Adult
1. Home (Concept); 2. Mexican American girls; 3. Growing up; 4. Friendship; 5. Family relationships; 6. Chicago, Illinois; 7. Illinois; 8. Coming-of-age stories; 9. Novels in verse; 10. Classics.
9780679433354, hardback, US; 9780679734772, paperback, US
LC 93043564
For Esperanza, a young girl growing up in the Hispanic quarter of Chicago, life is an endless landscape of concrete and run-down tenements, and she tries to rise above the hopelessness.
This is a composite of evocative snapshots that manages to passionately recreate the milieu of the poor quarters of Chicago. Commonwealth.
Originally published, in somewhat different form, by Arte Publico Press in 1984. Reprinted by Vintage Books, a division of Random House, Inc, in 1991

Clare, Cassandra
Chain of gold. Cassandra Clare. Simon & Schuster 2020 624 p. (Last hours (Shadowhunters), 1)
Grades: 9 10 11 12
1. Secret societies; 2. Demons; 3. Quarantine; 4. Supernatural; 5. Teenage girls; 6. London, England; 7. Edwardian era (1901-1914); 8. Historical fantasy.
9781481431873; 9781406390766, Paperback, Australia; 9781406358094, Hardback, UK; 9781406390988, Paperback, UK
LC 2019032235
Cordelia Carstairs, a Shadowhunter trained to battle demons, travels with her brother to London where they reconnect with childhood friends but soon must face devastating demon attacks in the quarantined city.
YA fantasy powerhouse Clare returns with a new generation of Shadowhunters, once again taking on themes of love, friendship, and family to deliver a thrilling story that's nostalgic for longtime fans but accessible for new readers, with nearly 600 pages to get accustomed to the large cast of characters and immersive world. —*Booklist*

City of bones. Cassandra Clare. Margaret K. McElderry Books, 2007 485 p. (Mortal instruments, 1)
Grades: 9 10 11 12
1. Resourcefulness in teenage girls; 2. Demon slayers; 3. Monsters; 4. Demons; 5. Vampires; 6. New York City; 7. Urban fantasy; 8. Books to movies; 9. Books to TV
9781416914280; 9781406362169, UK; 9781406307627, UK; 9781406372533, print, UK; 9781406365061, print, UK; 9781406381320, print, UK
LC 2006008108
Abraham Lincoln Illinois High School Book Award, 2010; YALSA Popular Paperbacks for Young Adults, 2011; Young Reader's Choice Award (Pacific Northwest), Senior, 2010.
Suddenly able to see demons and the Darkhunters who are dedicated to returning them to their own dimension, fifteen-year-old Clary Fray is drawn into this bizarre world when her mother disappears and Clary herself is almost killed by a monster.

This version of New York, full of Buffyesque teens who are trying to save the world, is entertaining and will have fantasy readers anxiously awaiting the next book in the series. —*School Library Journal*

Sequel: *City of ashes.*; Adapted into a film in 2013 under the title: *The mortal instruments: city of bones.* Also adapted for television in 2016 under the title: *Shadowhunters.*

Clockwork angel. Cassandra Clare. Margaret K. McElderry Books, 2010 496 p. (Infernal devices, 1)

Grades: 9 10 11 12

1. Teenage girl orphans; 2. Shapeshifters; 3. Supernatural; 4. Missing persons; 5. Magic; 6. London, England; 7. Great Britain; 8. Victorian era (1837-1901); 9. Historical fantasy; 10. Steampunk
9781416975861; 9781406365269, print, UK; 9781406393279, Hardback, UK

LC 2010008616

Inky Awards (Australia): Silver Inky, 2011; Sequoyah Book Awards (Oklahoma), High School Books, 2013; Westchester Fiction Award, 2010.

When sixteen-year-old orphan Tessa Fell's older brother suddenly vanishes, her search for him leads her into Victorian-era London's dangerous supernatural underworld, and when she discovers that she herself is a Downworlder, she must learn to trust the demon-killing Shadowhunters if she ever wants to learn to control her powers and find her brother.

Mysteries, misdirection, and riddles abound, and while there are some gruesome moments, they never feel gratuitous. Fans of the Mortal Instruments series and newcomers alike won't be disappointed. —*Publishers Weekly*

Clark, Jay

Finding Mr. Brightside. Jay Clark. Christy Ottaviano Books, Henry Holt and Company, 2015 288 p.

Grades: 9 10 11 12

1. Loss (Psychology); 2. Coping in teenagers; 3. Fatal traffic accidents; 4. Coping; 5. Dating (Social customs); 6. Contemporary romances
9781250073655; 9780805092578; 9780805096385, ebook, US

LC 2014039994

Growing up unaware of each other until their parents have a torrid affair that culminates in a devastating car accident, Abram and Juliette meet again a year later and embark on a life-changing relationship.

Though the problems the teens face are myriad, the story never bogs down. Instead, the uncomfortable silences, the awkward conversations, and the slow but gradual trust that connects both the teens and their surviving parents ground the novel in the stark reality that sometimes life is full of genuine surprises. —*Booklist*

Clark, Kristin

★ **Freakboy**. Kristin Clark. 2013 448 pages

Grades: 8 9 10 11 12

1. Sexual orientation; 2. Gender identity; 3. Transgender persons; 4. High schools; 5. Schools; 6. LGBTQIA fiction; 7. Realistic fiction; 8. Novels in verse.
9780374324728

LC 2012050407

Rainbow List, 2014; YALSA Best Fiction for Young Adults, 2014; YALSA Best Fiction for Young Adults: Top Ten, 2014.

Told from three viewpoints, seventeen-year-old Brendan, a wrestler, struggles to come to terms with his place on the transgender spectrum while Vanessa, the girl he loves, and Angel, a transgender acquaintance, try to help.

High school wrestler Brendan likes girls too much, / and not in / the same / way / everyone / else / does. Brendan's story weaves together with his girlfriend Vanessa's and that of transgender woman Angel in three-part verse-harmony. Each individual has a unique personality all his or her own in this sincere, profound rendering of sexuality, queerness, and identity. —*Horn Book Guide*

Clarke, Hannah Abigail

The **scapegracers**. Hannah Abigail Clarke. Erewhon, 2020 400 p. (Scapegracers, 1)

Grades: 9 10 11 12

1. Teenage witches; 2. Lesbian teenagers; 3. Covens; 4. Female friendship; 5. Cliques; 6. Paranormal fiction.
9781645660002

Forging an unexpected coven with the three most popular girls in school, an outcast lesbian witch casts curses, searches for love and eludes fundamentalist witch hunters while privately struggling with the realities of human friendships and supernatural perils.

Unapologetically queer—many of the characters, including Sideways and her adoptive dads, fall under the LGBTQ umbrella—and seething with raw emotion, this fantasy opens strong while leaving much to be explored in future installments. —*Publishers Weekly*

Clarke, Judith

One whole and perfect day. Judith Clarke. Front Street, 2006 248 p.

Grades: 7 8 9 10

1. Eccentric families; 2. Birthday parties; 3. Grandparents; 4. Families; 5. Familial love; 6. Australia; 7. Realistic fiction; 8. Australian fiction; 9. Multiple perspectives
9781932425956

LC 2006020126

Queensland Premier's Literary Awards, Young Adult Book Award, 2007; USBBY Outstanding International Book, 2008; YALSA Best Books for Young Adults, 2008; Michael L. Printz Honor Book, 2008.

As her irritating family prepares to celebrate her grandfather's eightieth birthday, sixteen-year-old Lily yearns for just one whole perfect day together.

The author's sharp, poetic prose evokes each character's inner life with rich and often amusing vibrancy. —*Horn Book Guide*

Clayton, Dhonielle

The **Belles**. Dhonielle Clayton. Freeform, 2018 448 p. (Belles (Dhonielle Clayton), 1)

Grades: 9 10 11 12

1. Sisters; 2. Beauty; 3. Magic; 4. Secrets; 5. Ugliness; 6. Fantasy fiction
9781484728499; 9781473223967, UK; 9781473223974, Paperback, UK; 9781484732519
YALSA Best Fiction for Young Adults, 2019; Booklist Editors' Choice: Books for Youth, 2018.

Born one of the revered Belles in the opulent world of Orleans, where people are naturally born gray and seek the talented Belles to transform themselves with beauty, Camellia dreams of being declared the queen's favorite before her arrival at court exposes dark and dangerous realities within the palace walls.

With a refreshingly original concept, this substantial fantasy, the first in a duology, is an undeniable page-turner. —*Kirkus*

The **everlasting** rose. By Dhonielle Clayton. 2019 352 p. (Belles (Dhonielle Clayton), 2)

Grades: 9 10 11 12

1. Beauty; 2. Insurgency; 3. Social classes; 4. Sisters; 5. Magic; 6. Fantasy fiction.

9781484728482; 9781473223998, Paperback, UK; 9781473224001, Paperback, UK

LC 2018034809

Camille, Edel, and Remy, aided by The Iron Ladies and backed by alternative newspaper The Spider's Web, race to outwit Sophia, find Princess Charlotte, and return her to Orleans.

Clinton, Cathryn
★ A **stone** in my hand. Cathryn Clinton. Candlewick Press, 2002 208 p.
Grades: 8 9 10 11
1. Muslims; 2. Families; 3. Eleven-year-old girls; 4. Arab-Israeli relations; 5. Palestinian families; 6. Gaza Strip; 7. Middle East; 8. 1980s; 9. Coming-of-age stories.
9780763613884

LC 2001058423

Booklist Editors' Choice: Books for Youth, 2002.

Eleven-year-old Malaak and her family are touched by the violence in Gaza between Jews and Palestinians when first her father disappears and then her older brother is drawn to the Islamic Jihad.

With a sharp eye for nuances of culture and the political situation in the Middle East, Clinton has created a rich, colorful cast of characters and created an emotionally charged novel. —*School Library Journal*

Cluess, Jessica
A **poison** dark and drowning. Jessica Cluess. Random House, 2017 432 p. (Kingdom on fire, 2)
Grades: 7 8 9 10
1. Demons; 2. Teenage wizards; 3. Good and evil; 4. Magic; 5. Teenage romance; 6. London, England; 7. Great Britain; 8. Victorian era (1837-1901); 9. Historical fantasy.
9780553535952; 9780553535969, ebook, US

LC 2016043364

Even though she is not the chosen one—the sorcerer destined to defeat all seven Ancient demons terrorizing humanity in Victorian England—Henrietta Howel battles alongside the sorcerers in the war against the demons, journeying to find mystical weapons, gather allies, and uncover secrets about herself and her enemies.

As in the previous volume, Cluess keeps the action moving in the right direction. Fans will anxiously wait for the conclusion to this romantic and magical fantasy series. —*School Library Journal*

★ A **shadow** bright and burning. Jessica Cluess. Random House, 2016 416 p. (Kingdom on fire, 1)
Grades: 7 8 9 10
1. Prophecies; 2. Teenage wizards; 3. Magic; 4. Good and evil; 5. Sixteen-year-old girls; 6. London, England; 7. Great Britain; 8. Victorian era (1837-1901); 9. Historical fantasy.
9780553535907; 9780553535914; 9780553535921, ebook, US

LC 2015014593

When her unusual powers mark her as the one destined to lead the war against the seven Ancients, Henrietta trains to become the first female sorcerer in centuries—though the true nature of her ability threatens to be revealed.

Clues's clever prose employs Dickensian names and rolls along at a speedy and compelling clip. —*Booklist*

Coakley, Lena
★ **Witchlanders**. Lena Coakley. Atheneum Books for Young Readers, 2011 224 p.
Grades: 7 8 9 10 11 12

1. Witches; 2. Prophecies; 3. Assassins; 4. Quests; 5. Magic; 6. Fantasy fiction; 7. Multiple perspectives; 8. Canadian fiction.
9781442420045; 9781442420052

LC 2010051922

Westchester Fiction Award, 2013; OLA Best Bets, 2011.

After the prediction of Ryder's mother, once a great prophet and powerful witch, comes true and their village is destroyed by a deadly assassin, Ryder embarks on a quest that takes him into the mountains in search of the destroyer.

Plot twists unfold at a riveting pace, the boys' characters are compellingly sketched, and Coakley explores her subject matter masterfully without falling prey to safe plot choices. —*Publishers Weekly*

Coats, J. Anderson
The **wicked** and the just. By Jillian Anderson Coats. Harcourt, 2012 384 p.
Grades: 7 8 9 10 11 12
1. Teenage household employees; 2. Resentfulness in teenagers; 3. Civilization, Medieval; 4. Resentfulness; 5. Prejudice; 6. Wales; 7. Medieval period (476-1492); 8. 13th century; 9. Historical fiction; 10. First person narratives; 11. Multiple perspectives
9780547688374

LC 2011027315

School Library Journal Best Books, 2012; YALSA Best Fiction for Young Adults, 2013.

In medieval Wales, follows Cecily whose family is lured by cheap land and the duty of all Englishman to help keep down the "vicious" Welshmen, and Gwenhwyfar, a Welsh girl who must wait hand and foot on her new English mistress.

Coben, Harlan
Shelter: a Mickey Bolitar novel. Harlan Coben. G. P. Putnam's Sons, 2011 288 p. (Mickey Bolitar novels, 1)
Grades: 8 9 10 11 12
1. Parent-separated teenagers; 2. Missing teenage girls; 3. Conspiracies; 4. Uncles; 5. Dating (Social customs); 6. New York City; 7. Mysteries
9780399256509; 9781409150596, print, UK; 9781409124450, print, UK; 9781409135364, print, UK; 9781445892986, print, UK

LC 2011009004

After tragic events tear Mickey Bolitar away from his parents, he is forced to live with his estranged Uncle Myron and switch high schools, where he finds both friends and enemies, but when his new girlfriend, Ashley, vanishes, he follows her trail into a seedy underworld that reveals she is not what she seems to be.

This is a suspenseful, well-executed spin-off of [the author's] best-selling Myron Bolitar mystery series for adults.... Coben's semi-noir style translates well to YA, and the supporting cast is thoroughly entertaining. —*Publishers Weekly*

Cohen, Joshua
★ **Leverage**. By Joshua Cohen. Dutton Children's Books, 2011 304 p.
Grades: 10 11 12
1. Gymnasts; 2. Bullying and bullies; 3. Teenage abuse victims; 4. Violence; 5. Friendship; 6. Realistic fiction.
9780525423065

LC 2010013472

Booklist Editors' Choice: Books for Youth, 2011; YALSA Best Fiction for Young Adults, 2012.

High school sophomore Danny excels at gymnastics but is bullied, like the rest of the gymnasts, by members of the football team, until an emotionally and physically scarred new student joins the football team and forms an unlikely friendship with Danny.

Sports fans will love Cohen's style: direct, goal oriented, and filled with sensory detail. Characters and subplots are overly abundant yet add a deepness rarely found in comparable books. Drugs, rape, language, and violence make this book serious business, but those with experience will tell you that sports is serious business, too. —*Booklist*

Cohn, Rachel

Gingerbread. Rachel Cohn. Simon & Schuster Books for Young Readers, 2002 172 p. (Cyd Charisse trilogy, 1)
Grades: 9 10 11 12
1. Mothers and daughters; 2. Blended families; 3. Birthfathers; 4. Charisse, Cyd (Fictitious character); 5. Interpersonal relations; 6. New York City; 7. San Francisco, California; 8. Realistic fiction; 9. Teen chick lit; 10. Books for reluctant readers
9780689843372

LC 52225
YALSA Quick Picks for Reluctant Young Adult Readers, 2003; YALSA Best Books for Young Adults, 2003; School Library Journal Best Books, 2002.

After being expelled from a fancy boarding school, Cyd Charisse's problems with her mother escalate after Cyd falls in love with a sensitive surfer and is subsequently sent from San Francisco to New York City to spend time with her biological father.

Cohn works wonders with snappy dialogue, up-to-the-minute language, and funny repartee. Her contemporary voice is tempered with humor and deals with problems across two generations. Funny and irreverent reading with teen appeal that's right on target. —*School Library Journal*

Sequel: *Shrimp*.

★ **Nick** and Norah's infinite playlist. Rachel Cohn and David Levithan. Knopf, 2006 183 p.
Grades: 9 10 11 12
1. Teenage rock musicians; 2. Teenage romance; 3. Second chances; 4. Teenage boys; 5. Teenage girls; 6. New York City; 7. Coming-of-age stories; 8. Realistic fiction; 9. First person narratives; 10. Books for reluctant readers
9780375835315, hardback, US; 9780375935312, library, US; 9781405272438, print, UK; 9781741756968, Australia

LC 2005012413
Romantic Times Reviewers Choice Award, 2006; YALSA Best Books for Young Adults, 2007; YALSA Popular Paperbacks for Young Adults, 2008; YALSA Quick Picks for Reluctant Young Adult Readers, 2007.

High school student Nick O'Leary, member of a rock band, meets college-bound Norah Silverberg and asks her to be his girlfriend for five minutes in order to avoid his ex-sweetheart.

The would-be lovers are funny, do stupid things, doubt themselves, and teens will adore them. F-bombs are dropped throughout the book, but it works. These characters are not gosh or shucks people. —*Voice of Youth Advocates*

Cokal, Susann

★ The **kingdom** of little wounds. Susann Cokal. Candlewick Press, 2013 554 pages
Grades: 10 11 12 Adult
1. Household employees; 2. Rulers; 3. Seamstresses; 4. Intrigue; 5. Rape; 6. Scandinavia; 7. 16th century; 8. Historical fiction; 9. Multiple perspectives
9780763666941; 9781406360967, print, UK

LC Bl2013040324

YALSA Best Fiction for Young Adults, 2014; Michael L. Printz Honor Book, 2014.

The wedding festivities of Scandinavian Princess Sophia are thrown into turmoil by an illness plaguing the royal family and a courtier's plot that places a seamstress and a royal nursemaid at the center of an epic power struggle.

Despite the challenging content, the book's lyrical writing, enthralling characters, and compelling plot will give older readers lots to ponder. —*Booklist*

Coker, Rachel

Chasing Jupiter. Rachel Coker. Zondervan, 2012 221 p.
Grades: 9 10
1. Sixteen-year-old girls; 2. Dysfunctional families; 3. Teenage girls; 4. Boys with autism; 5. Faith (Christianity); 6. Georgia; 7. 1960s; 8. Historical romances.
9780310732938

Sixteen-year-old Scarlett Blaine discovers growing up on a farm and caring for her autistic brother amidst family tensions is far from peachy. When a tragic accident and financial difficulties place more pressures on Scarlett's shoulders, she has to find a hope to cling to before it's too late.

Minor confusions and repetitions mar Coker's sophomore effort, and not every storyline finds an organic conclusion. Yet the author's passion, along with her gift for description and pace, make up for these small imperfections, as does the pure charm of the narrative. —*Publishers Weekly*

Colasanti, Susane

Something like fate. Susane Colasanti. Viking, 2010 267 p. : Illustration
Grades: 7 8 9 10
1. Love triangles; 2. Interpersonal attraction; 3. Crushes in teenage girls; 4. Best friends; 5. Friendship; 6. Teen chick lit; 7. Realistic fiction; 8. First person narratives.
9780670011469

LC 2009024906
Lani and Jason, who is her best friend's boyfriend, fall in love, causing Lani tremendous anguish and guilt.

Colasanti provides credible and engaging character development for each cast member and interactions that spark just the right amount of tension to make this a romantic page-turner. —*Booklist*

Colbert, Brandy

Little & Lion. Brandy Colbert. Little, Brown and Company, 2017 336 p.
Grades: 9 10 11 12
1. African American teenage girls; 2. Bisexual teenage girls; 3. Mental illness; 4. Stepbrothers and stepsisters; 5. Brothers and sisters of people with mental illnesses; 6. Los Angeles, California; 7. California; 8. Realistic fiction; 9. LGBTQIA fiction.
9780316349000; 9780316318976, ebook, US; 9780316348980, ebook, US

LC 2016019838
Booklist Editors' Choice: Books for Youth, 2017; Stonewall Book Award for Children's and Young Adult Literature, 2018; YALSA Best Fiction for Young Adults, 2018; Rainbow List, 2018.

Returning home to Los Angeles from her New England boarding school, Suzette considers staying home for good so that she can be near her friends, her crush, and her recently diagnosed bipolar brother, a situation that is complicated by her growing feelings for the girl her brother loves.

One of many notable strengths here is Colbert's subtle, neatly interwoven exploration of intersectionality: Lion is desperate to be defined by something other than his bipolar disorder, and Suzette learns to navigate key elements of her identity—black, Jewish, bisexual—in a world that seems to want her to be only one thing. This superbly written novel teems with meaningful depth, which is perfectly balanced by romance and the languid freedom of summer. —*Booklist*

The **revolution** of Birdie Randolph. Brandy Colbert. Little, Brown and Company, 2019 325 p.
Grades: 8 9 10 11 12
1. African American teenage girls; 2. Expectation (Psychology); 3. Family secrets; 4. Family relationships; 5. African American families; 6. Chicago, Illinois; 7. Coming-of-age stories; 8. First person narratives; 9. African American fiction; 10. Books for reluctant readers
9780316448567, HRD, US; 9780316448574, ebook, US; 9780316448550, library ebook, US; 9780316448543, paperback, US
LC 2018022809
Booklist Editors' Choice: Books for Youth, 2019; YALSA Quick Picks for Reluctant Young Adult Readers, 2020.
Sixteen-year-old Dove "Birdie" Randolph's close bond with her parents is threatened by a family secret, and by hiding her relationship with Booker, who has been in juvenile detention.
Heavier topics like addiction, trauma, and the ills of juvenile justice system for teens of color are also explored in a refreshingly nuanced way that is handled with intelligence and care. —*Booklist*

★ The **voting** booth. Brandy Colbert. Disney-Hyperion 2020 304 p.
Grades: 9 10 11 12
1. African American teenagers; 2. Elections; 3. Teenage romance; 4. Teenage boy/girl relations; 5. Teenagers — Political activity; 6. Love stories; 7. Realistic fiction; 8. African American fiction.
9781368053297
LC 2019054677
The first year they are eligible to vote, Marva and Duke meet at their polling place and, over the course of one crazy day, fall in love.
Readers will find abundant food for thought in this vital fictional account of two teens intent on using their voices and engaging in a political system that makes it difficult for them to participate Publishers Weekly

Coles, Jay
★ **Tyler** Johnson was here. Jay Coles. Little, Brown and Company, 2018 304 p.
Grades: 9 10 11 12
1. Police shootings; 2. Brothers; 3. Racism; 4. African Americans; 5. Death; 6. Realistic fiction; 7. African American fiction; 8. Books for reluctant readers
9780316440776; 9780316472180; 9780316440783, ebook, US; 9780316472197, ebook, US
LC 2017027423
YALSA Quick Picks for Reluctant Young Adult Readers, 2019.
When Marvin Johnson's twin brother, Tyler, is shot and killed by a police officer, Marvin must fight injustice to learn the true meaning of freedom.

Collins, Suzanne
★ **Catching** fire. Suzanne Collins. Scholastic Press, 2009 400 p. (Hunger Games trilogy, 2)
Grades: 7 8 9 10
1. Dystopias; 2. Survival; 3. Contests; 4. Insurgency; 5. Revenge; 6. North America; 7. First person narratives; 8. Science fiction; 9. Books to movies

9780439023498; 9781407109367, UK; 9781407153346, print, UK; 9781743629864, print, Australia; 9781760159481, print, Australia; 9781407188911, Paperback, UK; 9781407132099, print, UK
LC 2008050493
Books I Love Best Yearly (BILBY), Older Reader, 2014; Golden Archer Awards (Wisconsin): Middle/Jr. High, 2012; Goodreads Choice Award, 2009; Indies' Choice Book Awards, Young Adult, 2010; Soaring Eagle Book Award (Wyoming), 2012; Golden Duck Awards: Hal Clement Award for Young Adult; YALSA Popular Paperbacks for Young Adults, 2015; Booklist Editors' Choice: Books for Youth, 2009; YALSA Best Books for Young Adults, 2010.
By winning the annual Hunger Games, District 12 tributes Katniss Everdeen and Peeta Mellark have secured a life of safety and plenty for themselves and their families, but because they won by defying the rules, they unwittingly become the faces of an impending rebellion.
Beyond the expert world building, the acute social commentary and the large cast of fully realized characters, there's action, intrigue, romance and some amount of hope in a story readers will find completely engrossing. —*Kirkus*
Film adaptation under the same name (2013).

★ The **Hunger** Games. By Suzanne Collins. Scholastic Press, 2008 374 p. (Hunger Games trilogy, 1)
Grades: 7 8 9 10
1. Survival; 2. Contests; 3. Dystopias; 4. Television programs; 5. Competition; 6. North America; 7. Science fiction; 8. Dystopian fiction; 9. First person narratives; 10. Books for reluctant readers
9780439023481; 9780329712716; 9780329789350; 9781743629857, print,Australia; 9781407109084, UK; 9781407153339, print, UK; 9781760159474,print, Australia; 9781760662103, Paperback,Australia; 9781407192086, Paperback
LC 2007039987
Abraham Lincoln Illinois High School Book Award, 2011; ALA Notable Children's Book, 2009; Amelia Bloomer List, 2009; Beehive Young Adult Book Award (Utah), 2010; Black-Eyed Susan Book Award (Maryland), High School, 2011; Blue Hen Book Award (Delaware) for Teen Books, 2010; Booklist Editors' Choice: Books for Youth, 2008; Books I Love Best Yearly (BILBY), Older Reader, 2012; California Young Reader Medal, Young Adult, 2011; Charlotte Award (New York), Young Adult, 2010; Colorado Blue Spruce YA Book Award, 2010; Eliot Rosewater Indiana High School Book Award (Rosie Award), 2011; Garden State Teen Book Award (New Jersey), Fiction (Grades 9-12), 2011; Gateway Readers Award (Missouri), 2011; Georgia Children's Book Award, 2012; Georgia Peach Book Award for Teen Readers, 2010; Golden Archer Awards (Wisconsin): Middle/Jr. High, 2011; Golden Duck Awards, Hal Clement Award for Young Adult; Golden Sower Award (Nebraska), Young Adult, 2011; Grand Canyon Reader Award (Arizona), Tween Book Category, 2011; Heartland Award, 2010; Inky Awards (Australia): Silver Inky, 2009; Iowa High School Book Award, 2011; Isinglass Teen Read Award (New Hampshire), 2009-2010. ; Kentucky Bluegrass Award for Grades 9-12, 2010; Land of Enchantment Book Award (New Mexico), Young Adult category, 2011; Maine Student Book Award, 2010; New York Times Notable Children's Book, 2008; Nutmeg Children's Book Award, Teen category, 2012; Pennsylvania Young Reader's Choice Awards, Young Adult, 2010; Rebecca Caudill Young Reader's Book Award (Illinois), 2011; Rhode Island Teen Book Award, 2010; Romantic Times Reviewers' Choice Award, 2008; School Library Journal Best Books, 2008; Sequoyah Book Awards (Oklahoma), High School Books, 2011; Sequoyah Book Awards (Oklahoma), Intermediate Books, 2011; Soaring Eagle Book Award (Wyoming), 2010; S
In a future North America, where the rulers of Panem maintain control through an annual televised survival competition pitting young people

from each of the twelve districts against one another, sixteen-year-old Katniss's skills are put to the test when she voluntarily takes her younger sister's place.

Collins's characters are completely realistic and sympathetic.... The plot is tense, dramatic, and engrossing. —*School Library Journal*

Mockingjay. Suzanne Collins. Scholastic Press, 2010 400 p. (Hunger Games trilogy, 3)
Grades: 7 8 9 10
1. Survival; 2. Contests; 3. Dystopias; 4. Television programs; 5. Competition; 6. North America; 7. First person narratives; 8. Science fiction; 9. Dystopian fiction
9780439023511; 9781407132105; 9781743628836, print, Australia; 9781407109374, UK; 9781407153353, print, UK; 9781743629871, print, Australia; 9781760159498, print, Australia; 9781407188928, Paperback, UK
Booklist Editors' Choice: Books for Youth, 2010; Books I Love Best Yearly (BILBY), Older Reader, 2016; Golden Archer Awards (Wisconsin): Middle/Jr. High, 2013; Goodreads Choice Award, 2010.

This concluding volume in Collins's Hunger Games trilogy accomplishes a rare feat, the last installment being the best yet, a beautifully orchestrated and intelligent novel that succeeds on every level. —*Publishers Weekly*

Combs, Sarah
Breakfast served anytime. Sarah Combs. Candlewick Press, 2014 272 p.
Grades: 7 8 9 10 11 12
1. Gifted teenagers; 2. Summer camps; 3. Teenage boy/girl relations; 4. Friendship; 5. High school seniors; 6. Kentucky; 7. Realistic fiction.
9780763667917
YALSA Best Fiction for Young Adults, 2015.

At a summer college program in Kentucky, a classroom of gifted students studying The Secrets of the Written Word grapples with life's big questions. Mercurial, dreamy, and verbose, protagonist Gloria narrates with intellectual enthusiasm and attention to emotional detail. Although the plot meanders, Gloria's open, genuine voice carries this debut novel to the end of a life-changing summer. —*Horn Book Guide*

Compestine, Ying Chang
★ A **banquet** for hungry ghosts. Ying Chang Compestine; illustrated by Coleman Polhemus. Henry Holt and Co, 2009 192 p.
Grades: 6 7 8 9 10
1. Ghosts; 2. Cooking, Chinese; 3. Families; 4. Recipes; 5. China; 6. Ghost stories; 7. Short stories
9780805082081

LC 2008050273
Presents an eight-course banquet of ghost stories centering around Chinese cooking and culture. Each story is followed by a recipe and historical notes.

The stories are laced with beautiful (as well as lurid) images and chilling illustrations of the ghosts and their victims. Like the ghosts themselves, Compestine's memorable stories should prove difficult to shake. —*Publishers Weekly*
Christy Ottaviano books.

Conaghan, Brian
When Mr. Dog bites. Brian Conaghan. 2014 320 p.
Grades: 10 11 12
1. Teenage boys; 2. Misunderstanding; 3. Tourette syndrome; 4. Sixteen-year-old boys; 5. Teenagers with Tourette syndrome; 6.

England; 7. Coming-of-age stories; 8. Realistic fiction; 9. First person narratives.
9781619633469; 9781681190181; 9781408838341, print, UK; 9781408838365, print, UK; 9781408843017, print, UK; 9781408838334, print, UK

LC 2013044567
YALSA Popular Paperbacks for Young Adults, 2017.
All seventeen-year-old Dylan Mint wants is to keep his Tourette's in check and live as a normal teen, but during a routine hospital visit he overhears that he is going to die, and in an attempt to claim the life he has always wanted he makes a list of "Cool Things To Do Before I Cack It" and sets out to have some fun.

Dylan's habitual use of Cockney slang may make for a tough reading experiencing for American teenagers, but Dylan is smart and caring, and beneath his realistically portrayed condition, he is a normal teenager with relatable concerns. As Dylan would say, this one is 'A-mayonnaise-ing.' —*Booklist*
First published in Great Britain in January 2014 by Bloomsbury Publishing Plc.

Condie, Allyson Braithwaite
The **last** voyage of Poe Blythe. Ally Condie. Dutton Books for Young Readers, 2019 336 p.
Grades: 7 8 9 10 11 12
1. Ship captains; 2. Revenge in teenage girls; 3. Gold mines and mining; 4. Grief; 5. Revenge; 6. Dystopian fiction; 7. Steampunk.
9780525426455; 9780698135611, ebook, US

LC 2018042052
Seeking to avenge the murder of her true love while on a dredge ship searching for gold, fifteen-year-old captain Poe Blythe becomes the architect of new defenses designed to destroy her enemies.

The plot moves across a well-thought-out dystopian backdrop, offering enough surprises to both intrigue and excite. Fans of Condie's *Matched* should find this a welcome and satisfying return to the author's YA roots. —*Publishers Weekly*

★ **Matched**. Ally Condie. Dutton Childrens Books, 2010 369 p; (Matched trilogy, 1)
Grades: 7 8 9 10
1. Matchmaking; 2. Dystopias; 3. Free will and determinism; 4. Mate selection; 5. Teenage boy/girl relations; 6. Dystopian fiction; 7. Science fiction; 8. First person narratives; 9. Books for reluctant readers
9780525423645; 9780141334783, print, UK
California Young Reader Medal, Young Adult, 2013; Maud Hart Lovelace Book Award (Minnesota), Division II (Grades 6-8), 2013; Pennsylvania Young Reader's Choice Awards, Young Adult, 2012; Rhode Island Teen Book Award, 2012; South Carolina Book Award, Young Adult Books, 2013; Teen Buckeye Book Award (Ohio), 2012; YALSA Popular Paperbacks for Young Adults, 2012; YALSA Quick Picks for Reluctant Young Adult Readers, 2011; YALSA Best Fiction for Young Adults, 2011.

Cassia has always trusted the Society to make the right choices for her, so when Xander appears on-screen at her Matching ceremony, Cassia knows he is her ideal mate—until Ky Markham's face appears for an instant before the screen fades to black.

Condie's enthralling and twisty dystopian plot is well served by her intriguing characters and fine writing. While the ending is unresolved.., Cassia's metamorphosis is gripping and satisfying. —*Publishers Weekly*

Reached. Ally Condie. Dutton Books, 2012 384 p. (Matched trilogy, 3)
Grades: 7 8 9 10

1. Dystopias; 2. Resistance to government; 3. Love triangles; 4. Teenage boy/girl relations; 5. Teenage girls; 6. Dystopian fiction; 7. Science fiction; 8. Multiple perspectives.
9780525423669; 9780141333083, print, UK

LC 2012031916

In search of a better life, Cassia joins a widespread rebellion against Society, where she is tasked with finding a cure to the threat of survival and must choose between Xander and Ky.

Connis, Dave
Suggested reading. Dave Connis. 2019 400 p.
Grades: 8 9 10 11 12
1. Teenage rebels; 2. Books and reading; 3. Censorship; 4. Banned books; 5. Protest movements; 6. Chattanooga, Tennessee; 7. Tennessee; 8. Realistic fiction.
9780062685254; 9780062685261

A bookworm finds a way to fight back when her school bans dozens of classic and meaningful books.

Connor, Leslie
The **things** you kiss goodbye. Leslie Connor. Katherine Tegen Books, an imprint of HarperCollinsPublishers, 2014 288 pages
Grades: 9 10 11 12
1. Greek Americans; 2. Dating violence; 3. Love triangles; 4. Automobile mechanics; 5. Basketball players; 6. Contemporary romances; 7. Teen chick lit; 8. First person narratives
9780060890919

LC 2013043191

High school junior Bettina Vasilisis is trapped in a relationship with her basketball star boyfriend when she meets Cowboy, a car mechanic whom her traditional father would not approve of.

Connor lets the story, and Bettina's realization of the situation, play out slowly, a choice that adds multiple subplots but also deepens characterization and elevates the book above simple problem-novel territory. Bettina begins finding herself through her art; her ensuing pride in her work is convincingly portrayed. A melodramatic ending and tendency to tie up all plot threads are somewhat distracting, but Bettina's situation creates much food for thought. —*Horn Book Guide*

Constable, Kate
The **singer** of all songs. Kate Constable. Arthur A. Levine Books, 2004 297 p; (Chanters of Tremaris trilogy, 1)
Grades: 7 8 9 10
1. Young women; 2. Women rulers; 3. Women priests; 4. Wizards; 5. Singers; 6. Fantasy fiction; 7. Australian fiction.
9780439554787; 9780439554794

LC 2003009034

Amelia Bloomer List, 2005; Booklist Editors' Choice: Books for Youth, 2004.

Calwyn, a young priestess of ice magic, or "chantment," joins with other chanters who have different magical skills to fight a sorcerer who wants to claim all powers for his own.

An impressive debut by an author who clearly has much to contribute to the fantasy genre. —*Booklist*

Cook, Eileen
The **education** of Hailey Kendrick. By Eileen Cook. Simon Pulse, 2011 256 p.
Grades: 7 8 9 10
1. Rich teenage girls; 2. Vandalism; 3. Resistance (Psychology) in teenage girls; 4. Janitors; 5. Dating (Social customs); 6. Vermont; 7. Realistic fiction; 8. Teen chick lit; 9. Canadian fiction.

9781442413252; 9781442413269

LC 2010025608

Dating a popular boy and adhering to every rule ever written, a high school senior at an elite Vermont boarding school begins to shed her good girl identity after an angry incident with her distant father.

Hailey is a likable character, and the events leading up to and away from her episode of vandalism are believable. Her emotions ring true as well.... The plot develops quickly, and readers will be madly flipping pages to find out what happens next. —*School Library Journal*

★ **With** malice. Eileen Cook. Houghton Mifflin Harcourt, 2016 320 p.
Grades: 9 10 11 12
1. Amnesia; 2. Accidents; 3. Rich teenage girls; 4. Death; 5. Best friends — Death; 6. Italy; 7. Mysteries; 8. Canadian fiction; 9. First person narratives
9780544805095; 9781328695314
YALSA Quick Picks for Reluctant Young Adult Readers, 2017.

Eighteen-year-old Jill Charron wakes up in a hospital, unable to remember the past six weeks, including the accident that killed her best friend, if it was, in fact, an accident.

Cook (Remember) believably portrays the struggles of girl who had it all and is left to pick up the pieces of a life she isnt sure is hers. —*Publishers Weekly*

Cook, Trish
Notes from the blender. Trish Cook and Brendan Halpin. Egmont USA, 2011 229 p.
Grades: 9 10 11 12
1. Loners; 2. Crushes in teenage boys; 3. Stepbrothers and stepsisters; 4. Children and remarriage; 5. Children of LGBTQIA parents; 6. Realistic fiction; 7. Humorous stories; 8. Multiple perspectives
9781606841402

LC 2010011315

Rainbow List, 2012.

Two teenagers—a heavy-metal-music-loving boy who is still mourning the death of his mother years earlier, and a beautiful, popular girl whose parents divorced because her father is gay—try to negotiate the complications of family and peer relationships as they get to know each other after learning that their father and mother are marrying each other.

This well developed story gives readers an opportunity to see teens taking the high road as they deal with both peers and parents in a novel teens will not want to put down. —*Library Media Connection*

Cooney, Caroline B.
The **face** on the milk carton. Caroline Cooney. Bantam Books, 1990 184 p. (Janie Johnson, 1)
Grades: 7 8 9 10
1. Missing children; 2. Child kidnapping victims; 3. Fifteen-year-old girls; 4. Teenage girls — Identity; 5. Books to movies; 6. Classics.
9780440220657; 9780553058536; 9780553289589

LC 89018311

Colorado Blue Spruce YA Book Award, 1996; Iowa Teen Award, 1993; Young Hoosier Book Award, Middle Books, 1993; Young Reader's Choice Award (Pacific Northwest), Senior, 1993.

A photograph of a missing girl on a milk carton leads Janie on a search for her real identity.

Cooney demonstrates an excellent ear for dialogue and a gift for portraying responsible middle-class teenagers trying to come to terms with very real concerns. —*School Library Journal*
Sequel: *Whatever Happened to Janie?*.

If the witness lied. Caroline B. Cooney. Delacorte Press, 2009 213 p;

Grades: 6 7 8 9 10
1. Protectiveness in teenagers; 2. Brothers and sisters; 3. Reality television programs; 4. Teenage orphans; 5. Grief in teenagers; 6. Connecticut; 7. Thrillers and suspense; 8. Psychological suspense
9780385904513

LC 2008023959

Torn apart by tragedies and the publicity they brought, siblings Smithy, Jack, and Madison, aged fourteen to sixteen, tap into their parent's courage to pull together and protect their brother Tris, nearly three, from further media exploitation and a much more sinister threat.

The pacing here is pure gold. Rotating through various perspectives to follow several plot strands...Cooney draws out the action, investing it with the slow-motion feel of an impending collision.... This family-drama-turned-thriller will have readers racing, heart in throat, to reach the conclusion. —*Horn Book Guide*

Janie face to face. Caroline B. Cooney. Delacorte Press, 2013 192 p. (Janie Johnson, 5)
Grades: 7 8 9 10
1. Women college students; 2. Child kidnapping victims; 3. Authors; 4. Kidnappers; 5. Dating (Social customs); 6. New York City; 7. Realistic fiction; 8. Multiple perspectives.
9780385742061

LC 2012006145

At college in New York City, Janie Johnson, aka Jennie Spring, seems to have successfully left behind her past as "The face on the milk carton," but soon she, her families, and friends are pursued by a true-crime writer who wants their help in telling her kidnapper's tale.

Cooper, Michelle
★ A **brief** history of Montmaray. Michelle Cooper. Alfred A. Knopf, 2009 286 p. (Montmaray journals, 1)
Grades: 7 8 9 10
1. Imaginary kingdoms; 2. Teenage girls; 3. Royal houses; 4. FitzOsborne, Sophia (Fictitious character); 5. Europe; 6. Diary novels; 7. Historical fiction; 8. Australian fiction
9780375858642; 9780375958649
NSW Premier's Literary Awards, Ethel Turner Prize for Young People's Literature, 2009; YALSA Best Books for Young Adults, 2010.

On her sixteenth birthday in 1936, Sophia begins a diary of life in a fictional island country off the coast of Spain, where she is among the last descendants of an impoverished royal family trying to hold their nation together on the eve of the second World War.

Cooper has crafted a sort of updated Gothic romance where sweeping adventure play equal with fluttering hearts. —*Booklist*

The **FitzOsbornes** at war. Michelle Cooper. Alfred A. Knopf, 2012 464 p. (Montmaray journals, 3)
Grades: 7 8 9 10
1. Teenagers and war; 2. Royal houses; 3. World War II; 4. Extended families; 5. Princesses; 6. London, England; 7. Second World War era (1939-1945); 8. Diary novels; 9. Historical fiction; 10. Australian fiction
9780375870507; 9780375970504; 9781742750323, Australia

In this third and final installment of the Montmaray Journals, Sophie and her family come together to support the war effort during World War I, meanwhile fighting to protect their beloved Montmaray.

The **FitzOsbornes** in exile. Michelle Cooper. Alfred A. Knopf, 2011 457 p. (Montmaray journals, 2)
Grades: 7 8 9 10

1. Princesses; 2. Royal houses; 3. Imaginary kingdoms; 4. Extended families; 5. Teenage girls; 6. England; 7. Great Britain; 8. 1930s; 9. Diary novels; 10. Historical fiction; 11. Australian fiction
9780375858659
Children's Book Council of Australia: Notable Australian Children's Book; Rainbow List, 2012; YALSA Best Fiction for Young Adults, 2012.

In January 1937, as Sophia FitzOsborne continues to record in her journal, the members of Montmaray's royal family are living in luxurious exile in England but, even as they participate in the social whirl of London parties and balls, they remain determined to free their island home from the occupying Germans despite growing rumors of a coming war that might doom their country forever.

Readers who enjoy their history enriched by immersion into the social milieu of the time period will find this a fascinating, utterly absorbing venture into English society of the late '30s. —*Bulletin of the Center for Children's Books*

Cooper, Susan
★ **Over** sea, under stone. Susan Cooper; illustrated by Margery Gill. Harcourt Brace Jovanovich, 1979 252 p. : Illustration (Dark is rising sequence, 1)
Grades: 5 6 7 8
1. Arthur; 2. Child adventurers; 3. Grail; 4. Treasure hunting; 5. Manuscripts; 6. Good and evil; 7. Cornwall, England; 8. England; 9. Fantasy fiction; 10. Classics.
9780152590345; 9780241377130, Paperback, UK

LC 79010489

Three children on a holiday in Cornwall find an ancient manuscript which sends them on a dangerous quest for a grail that would reveal the true story of King Arthur.

The air of mysticism and the allegorical quality of the continual contest between good and evil add much value to a fine plot, setting, and characterization. —*Horn Book Guide*

Cordova, Zoraida
Bruja born. Zoraida Cordova. 2018 352 p. (Brooklyn brujas, 2)
Grades: 9 10 11 12
1. Teenage witches; 2. Hispanic Americans; 3. Tragedy; 4. Accidents; 5. Black magic; 6. Paranormal fiction
9781492650652, Hardback, Australia

Still feeling broken after her family's battle in Los Lagos, Lula invokes a dark spell to bring her boyfriend and others back after a fatal bus crash, but unwittingly raises an army of hungry, half-dead casimuertos, instead.

Zombies and hunts for answers bring Lula and her circle across Brooklyn in this plot-driven novel. Lula's introspective narration shifts neatly to high action as the zombie outbreak heats up and Lula works to restore the balance between life and death. —*School Library Journal*

Labyrinth lost. Zoraida Cordova. 2016 336 pages (Brooklyn brujas, 1)
Grades: 9 10 11 12
1. Teenage witches; 2. Hispanic Americans; 3. Spells (Magic); 4. Witches; 5. Supernatural; 6. Paranormal fiction
9781492620945

LC 2016000723

YALSA Best Fiction for Young Adults, 2017; YALSA Quick Picks for Reluctant Young Adult Readers, 2017.

Alex is a bruja and the most powerful witch in her family. But she's hated magic ever since it made her father disappear into thin air. When a curse she performs to rid herself of magic backfires and her family vanishes, she must travel to Los Lagos, a land in-between as dark as Limbo and as strange as Wonderland, to get her family back.

A compelling must-have for teens. —*School Library Journal*

Cormier, Robert

★ **After** the first death. Robert Cormier. Pantheon Books, 1979 233 p.
Grades: 7 8 9 10
1. Child hostages; 2. Terrorism; 3. Hijacking of buses; 4. Teenagers; 5. Fathers and sons; 6. Multiple perspectives; 7. Realistic fiction.
9780394841229; 9780141368894, print, UK

LC 78011770

Events of the hijacking of a bus of children by terrorists seeking the return of their homeland are described from the perspectives of a hostage, a terrorist, an Army general involved in the rescue operation, and his son.

Beyond the chocolate war: a novel. Robert Cormier. Knopf, 1985 278 p.
Grades: 9 10 11 12
1. Student secret societies; 2. Bullying and bullies; 3. Manipulation by teenage boys; 4. Prep schools; 5. High schools; 6. Realistic fiction.
9780394873435; 9780394973432

LC 84022865

Obie tries to overcome the power of Archie Costello, the leader of a secret organization of students at Trinity High School.

Sequel to: *The chocolate war.*

★ The **chocolate** war: a novel. Robert Cormier. Dell Pub. Co, 1986 253 p.
Grades: 7 8 9 10
1. Teenage rebels; 2. Prep schools; 3. Bullying and bullies; 4. High schools; 5. School fund raising; 6. Realistic fiction; 7. Books to movies; 8. Classics.
9780440944591

LC 73015109

Jerry Renault is forced into a psychological showdown with Trinity School's gang leader, Archie Costello, for refusing to be bullied into selling chocolates for the annual fund raising.

★ **I** am the cheese. Robert Cormier. Knopf, 1977 233 p.
Grades: 7 8 9 10 11 12 Adult
1. Fourteen-year-olds; 2. Witnesses; 3. Memories; 4. Secrets; 5. Teenage boys; 6. Spy fiction; 7. Thrillers and suspense; 8. Books to movies
9780394834627; 9780141300511, print, UK

LC 76055948

Phoenix Award, 1997.

A young boy desperately tries to unlock his past yet knows he must hide those memories if he is to remain alive.

The suspense builds relentlessly to an ending that, although shocking, is entirely plausible. —*Booklist*

Cornwell, Betsy

The **Circus** Rose. Betsy Cornwell. Clarion Books, 2020 288 p.
Grades: 9 10 11 12
1. Twin sisters; 2. Circus; 3. Religious fanaticism; 4. Magic; 5. Families; 6. Fairy tale and folklore-inspired fiction; 7. Fantasy fiction; 8. Multiple perspectives.
9781328639509, HRD, US; 9780358164432, ebook, US

LC 2019029393

A retelling of Snow White and Rose Red in which teenage twins Ivory and Rosie battle evil religious extremists to save their loves and their circus family.

Tides. By Betsy Cornwell. Clarion Books, 2013 294 p;
Grades: 7 8 9 10 11 12
1. Selkies; 2. Islands; 3. Interpersonal attraction; 4. Internship programs; 5. Bulimia; 6. Isles of Shoals (Me. and N.H.); 7. Paranormal romances; 8. Mythological fiction; 9. Multiple perspectives
9780547927725

LC 2012022415

After moving to the Isles of Shoals for a marine biology internship, eighteen-year-old Noah learns of his grandmother's romance with a selkie woman, falls for the selkie's daughter, and must work with her to rescue her siblings from his mentor's cruel experiments.

Corrigan, Eireann

★ **Accomplice**. Eireann Corrigan. Scholastic Press, 2010 304 p.
Grades: 7 8 9 10
1. Hoaxes; 2. Consequences; 3. Guilt in teenage girls; 4. Guilt; 5. Deception; 6. New Jersey; 7. Realistic fiction; 8. Thrillers and suspense
9780545052368; 9781906427566, print, UK

LC 2009053869

High school juniors and best friends Finn and Chloe hatch a daring plot to fake Chloe's disappearance from their rural New Jersey town in order to have something compelling to put on their college applications, but unforeseen events complicate matters.

Corrigan has crafted a complex, heart-wrenchingly plausible YA thriller.... A fascinating character study of individuals and an entire town, this tension-filled story will entice readers with a single booktalk. —*Booklist*

Corthron, Kara Lee

★ **Daughters** of Jubilation. Kara Lee Corthron. Simon & Schuster, 2020 272 p.
Grades: 9 10 11 12
1. Superhuman abilities; 2. Familial love; 3. Teenage girls; 4. Earthquakes; 5. Rescues; 6. South Carolina; 7. 1960s; 8. Historical fantasy; 9. First person narratives; 10. Coming-of-age stories.
9781481459501

Emotional, magical worldbuilding, however, redeems the distressing narrative by weaving it with grounding bonds of familial love and protection. —*Publishers Weekly*

★ The **truth** of right now. Kara Lee Corthron. Simon Pulse, 2017 272 p.
Grades: 9 10 11 12
1. Teenage misfits; 2. Interracial romance; 3. African American teenage boys; 4. Teenage girl musicians; 5. Teenage romance; 6. New York City; 7. Manhattan, New York City; 8. Realistic fiction; 9. Multiple perspectives
9781481459471; 9781481459495, ebook, US

LC 2016018605

A heart-wrenching debut novel about relationships in its many forms—families, friendships, romance—and how Lily and Dari, coming from different backgrounds and different worlds, strive to find a connection through their differences as they fight against their own individual pasts.

A powerhouse of storytelling that feels timely and timeless. —*Kirkus*

Coulthurst, Audrey

★ **Of** fire and stars. Audrey Coulthurst. Balzer + Bray, an imprint of HarperCollins Publishers, 2016 389 p. (Of fire and stars, 1)
Grades: 8 9 10 11

1. Princesses; 2. Teenage girl/girl relations; 3. Assassination; 4. Superhuman abilities; 5. Magic; 6. High fantasy; 7. Fantasy fiction
9780062433251

A worthy debut that succeeds as both an adventure and a romance. —*Booklist*

Courtney, Nadine Jolie
★ **All-American** Muslim girl. Nadine Jolie Courtney. Farrar, Straus and Giroux, 2019 256 p.
Grades: 8 9 10 11 12
1. Muslim teenagers; 2. Teenage romance; 3. Islamophobia; 4. Self-acceptance; 5. Small towns; 6. Georgia; 7. Southern States; 8. Coming-of-age stories; 9. Realistic fiction
9780374309527, HRD, US

LC 2018056246

Sixteen-year-old Allie, aged seven when she knew her family was different and feared, struggles to claim her Muslim and Arabic heritage while finding her place as an American teenager.

Religion is rarely handled with such wisdom and depth in YA, or discussed so lovingly. A rich and memorable exploration of faith and family that is a first purchase for all collections. —*School Library Journal*

Cousins, Dave
Waiting for Gonzo. Dave Cousins. Flux, 2015 288 p.
Grades: 7 8 9 10
1. Moving, Household; 2. Brothers and sisters; 3. Teenage pregnancy; 4. Pregnancy; 5. Practical jokes; 6. England; 7. Realistic fiction; 8. Humorous stories.
9780738741994

LC 2014031277

Thirteen-year-old Oz struggles to fit in at his new school, stop causing trouble, and support his sister with her own unexpected problem.

In a darkly comic story written as Marcuss monologue to his unborn nephew (whom he nicknames Gonzo), Cousins (*15 Days Without a Head*) offers a vibrant, highly visual account of teen angst and backfiring schemes. Marcus makes more than a few mistakes at school and at home, but readers will never doubt that his heart is in the right place. —*Publishers Weekly*

Originally published by Oxford University Press, Oxford, UK, 2013.

Cowan, Jennifer
★ **Earthgirl**. By Jennifer Cowan. Groundwood Books, 2009 192 p.
Grades: 8 9 10 11 12
1. Teenage girls; 2. Teenage environmentalists; 3. Teenage boy/girl relations; 4. Sixteen-year-old girls; 5. Teenage social advocates; 6. Realistic fiction.
9780888998897

This novel with enormous teen appeal will inspire readers to question Sabine's tactics and their own impact on the earth. —*Kirkus*

Cranse, Pratima
All the major constellations. Pratima Cranse. Viking, 2015 304 p.
Grades: 9 10 11 12
1. Life change events; 2. Teenagers — Religious life; 3. Belonging; 4. Coma; 5. Friendship; 6. Vermont; 7. Realistic fiction; 8. Coming-of-age stories.
9780670016457

LC 2014044806

After Andrew's best friend is hit by a drunk driver and ends up in a coma, his enigmatic crush invites him to find comfort with her fundamentalist Christian group.

Andrew is prepared to graduate from high school, work his summer job, and finally escape his alcoholic father. His plans are thrown for a loop when one of his best friends, Sara, is in a coma after a car accident and his other best friend, Marcia, becomes distant as she helps to care for Sara. The fact that Andrew's older, baseball-star, bully brother is coming home from college only makes his home life more unbearable. A note slipped to him from his longtime crush, Laura, leads Andrew to a fundamentalist Christian youth group.... Older fans of realistic fiction will enjoy riding along with Andrew. —*School Library Journal*

Cronn-Mills, Kirstin
Beautiful music for ugly children. Kirstin Cronn-Mills. Flux, 2012 271 p.
Grades: 9 10 11 12
1. Transgender teenagers; 2. Friendship; 3. Coming out (Sexual or gender identity); 4. Teenagers — Sexuality; 5. Transgender persons; 6. LGBTQIA fiction
9780738732510

LC 2012019028

Rainbow List, 2013; Stonewall Book Award for Children's and Young Adult Literature, 2014; YALSA Best Fiction for Young Adults, 2013; YALSA Popular Paperbacks for Young Adults, 2014.

Gabe has always identified as a boy, but he was born with a girl's body. With his new public access radio show gaining in popularity, Gabe struggles with romance, friendships, and parents—all while trying to come out as transgendered. An audition for a station in Minneapolis looks like his ticket to a better life in the big city. But his entire future is threatened when several violent guys find out Gabe, the popular DJ, is also Elizabeth from school.

Cross, Gillian
Where I belong. Gillian Cross. Holiday House, 2011 245 p;
Grades: 7 8 9 10
1. Teenage fashion models; 2. Teenage immigrants; 3. Fashion design; 4. Kidnapping; 5. Ransom; 6. London, England; 7. England; 8. First person narratives; 9. Multiple perspectives; 10. Thrillers and suspense
9780823423323

LC 2010023671

YALSA Best Fiction for Young Adults, 2012.

Thirteen-year-old Khadija, a Somali refugee, becomes a model for a famous fashion designer to help her family back home, while the designer's daughter Freya and fourteen-year-old Abdi, whose family Khadija lives with in London, try to protect her.

This is a fast-paced adventure.... The fashion element will engage readers who would otherwise not read this genre.... This broadly appealing title has an engaging cover and is a worthy addition to any collection. —*School Library Journal*

Crossan, Sarah
Being Toffee. By Sarah Crossan. Bloomsbury Childrens Books 2020 416 p.
Grades: 8 9 10 11 12
1. Runaways; 2. Senior women; 3. Intergenerational friendship; 4. Child abuse; 5. Elder abuse; 6. Novels in verse; 7. Realistic fiction.
9781547603299

LC 2020014880

Allison runs away and, in what she thinks is an abandoned house, finds a home with Marla, an elderly woman with dementia who believes her to be an old friend named Toffee.

Breathe. Sarah Crossan. Greenwillow Books, 2012 400 p.
Grades: 7 8 9 10 11 12

1. Post-apocalypse; 2. Environmental degradation; 3. Insurgency; 4. Dystopias; 5. Survival; 6. Dystopian fiction; 7. Science fiction; 8. Multiple perspectives.
9780062118691

LC 2012017496

In a barren land, a shimmering glass dome houses the survivors of the Switch, the period when oxygen levels plunged and the green world withered. A state lottery meant a lucky few won safety, while the rest suffocated in the thin air. And now Alina, Quinn, and Bea—an unlikely trio, each with their own agendas, their own longings and fears—walk straight into the heart of danger. With two days' worth of oxygen in their tanks, they leave the dome. What will happen on the third day?

Sequel: *Resist*.

Moonrise. By Sarah Crossan. 2017 400 p.
Grades: 9 10 11 12
1. Brothers; 2. Capital punishment; 3. Family problems; 4. Death row prisoners; 5. Prisoners' families; 6. Texas; 7. Novels in verse; 8. Books for reluctant readers
9781408878439; 9781408867808, hardback; 9781681193663; 9781408867815, Paperback, UK

LC 2017025085

YALSA Quick Picks for Reluctant Young Adult Readers, 2019.

With little money or support, Joe Moon, seventeen, travels to Texas to help the older brother he barely knows through his last few weeks before being executed for murder.

Crossan's (*We Come Apart*, 2017, etc.) eloquent usage of language in this deeply affecting novel puts readers right at the heart of a very sensitive and timely story. —*Kirkus*

One. By Sarah Crossan. Greenwillow Books, an imprint of HarperCollinsPublishers, 2015 400 p.
Grades: 8 9 10 11 12
1. Conjoined twins; 2. Twin sisters; 3. Private schools; 4. High schools; 5. Schools; 6. Realistic fiction; 7. Novels in verse; 8. First person narratives
9780062118752; 9781408872345, print, UK; 9781408827215, print, UK

LC 2015004714

Carnegie Medal, 2016.

Despite problems at home, sixteen-year-old conjoined twins Tippi and Grace are loving going to school for the first time and making real friends when they learn that a cardiac problem will force them to have separation surgery, which they have never before considered.

Crossan trusts her characters and her readers to find their better selves through her gently paced story. —*Booklist*

Crowder, Melanie
Audacity. Melanie Crowder. Philomel Books, 2015 352 p.
Grades: 9 10 11 12
1. Lemlich, Clara, 1886-1982; 2. Labor movement; 3. Immigrants; 4. Women in the labor movement; 5. Immigrants, Russian; 6. Russian Americans; 7. New York City; 8. 1900s (Decade); 9. Historical fiction; 10. Novels in verse.
9780399168994; 9780147512499

LC 2014018466

Amelia Bloomer List, 2016; Jefferson Cup Award for Older Readers, 2016; Notable Books for a Global Society, 2016; YALSA Best Fiction for Young Adults: Top Ten, 2015; YALSA Best Fiction for Young Adults, 2016; YALSA Popular Paperbacks for Young Adults, 2017.

A historical fiction novel in verse detailing the life of Clara Lemlich and her struggle for women's labor rights in the early 20th century in New York.

Includes bibliographical references.

An **uninterrupted** view of the sky. Melanie Crowder. Philomel Books, 2017 304 p.
Grades: 7 8 9 10 11 12
1. Prisons; 2. Political corruption; 3. Indians of South America; 4. Aymara Indians; 5. Poverty; 6. Bolivia; 7. 1990s; 8. Historical fiction
9780399169007
YALSA Best Fiction for Young Adults, 2018.

When his father is sent to jail after being falsely convicted of a crime in 1999 Bolivia, teen Francisco is forced to choose between living with his father in prison and relocating to the mountains, where people have lived for centuries without education or modern conveniences.

Crowe, Chris
Mississippi trial, 1955. By Chris Crowe. P. Fogelman Books, 2002 231 p.
Grades: 7 8 9 10
1. Till, Emmett, 1941-1955; 2. Grandfather and child; 3. Fathers and sons; 4. Racism; 5. African Americans; 6. Mississippi; 7. 1950s
9780803727458

LC 2001040221

International Reading Association Children's Book Award for Young Adult Fiction, 2003; Golden Sower Award (Nebraska), Young Adult, 2005; Jefferson Cup Award, 2003; YALSA Best Books for Young Adults, 2003.

In Mississippi in 1955, a sixteen-year-old finds himself at odds with his grandfather over issues surrounding the kidnapping and murder of a fourteen-year-old African American from Chicago.

By combining real events with their impact upon a single fictional character, Crowe makes the issues in this novel hard-hitting and personal. The characters are complex. —*Voice of Youth Advocates*

Crowley, Cath
Words in deep blue. Cath Crowley. 2017 288 p.
Grades: 8 9 10 11
1. Love; 2. Best friends; 3. Bookstores; 4. Grief in teenagers; 5. Self-discovery in teenagers; 6. Melbourne, Victoria; 7. Australia; 8. Love stories; 9. Multiple perspectives; 10. Australian fiction.
9781101937648, hardcover, US; 9781101937655, library binding, US; 9781742612386, Australia
Children's Book Council of Australia: Notable Australian Children's Book, 2017; Inky Awards (Australia): Gold Inky, 2017; Prime Minister's Literary Awards: Young Adult Fiction, 2017; Queensland Literary Awards, Young Adult Book Award, 2017; USBBY Outstanding International Book, 2018; YALSA Best Fiction for Young Adults, 2018; CBCA Children's Book of the Year Awards Honour Book, 2017.

Teenagers Rachel and Henry find their way back to each other while working in an old bookstore full of secrets and crushes, love letters and memories, grief and hope.

This journey is original, wise, and essential...This love story is an ode to words and life. —*Kirkus*

Originally published in Sydney by Pan Macmillan Australia in 2016.

Crutcher, Chris
Angry management. Chris Crutcher. Greenwillow Books, 2009 246 p.
Grades: 9 10 11 12

1. Anger in teenagers; 2. Emotions in teenagers; 3. Misfits (Persons); 4. Emotions; 5. Hope; 6. Pacific Northwest; 7. LGBTQIA fiction; 8. Realistic fiction; 9. Short stories
9780060502478; 9780060502461

LC 2008052829

Rainbow List, 2010.

A collection of short stories featuring characters from earlier books by Chris Crutcher.

The stories are well-written, action packed, engrossing and at times humorous.... A good introduction to Crutcher, his latest book will certainly please current fans as well. —*Voice of Youth Advocates*

Period 8. Chris Crutcher. Greenwillow Books, 2013 320 p.
Grades: 7 8 9
1. Bullying and bullies; 2. Sex crimes; 3. Missing teenage girls; 4. Kidnapping; 5. High schools; 6. Mysteries; 7. Realistic fiction.
9780061914805; 9780061914812

LC 2012046726

Period 8 has always been a safe haven and high school senior Paulie "The Bomb" Baum a constant attendee, but as Paulie, Hannah, their friends, and a sympathetic teacher try to unravel the mystery of a missing classmate, the ultimate bully takes aim at the school.

Running loose. By Chris Crutcher. Greenwillow Books, 1983 190 p.
Grades: 7 8 9 10
1. High school football players; 2. Sportsmanship; 3. Teenagers and death; 4. Fatal traffic accidents; 5. Sports; 6. Idaho; 7. Realistic fiction; 8. Pacific Northwest fiction
9780688020026

LC 82020935

Louie, a high school senior in a small Idaho town, learns about sportsmanship, love, and death as he matures into manhood.

Louie Banks tells what happened to him in his senior year in a small town Idaho high school. Besides falling in love with Becky and losing her in a senseless accident, Louie takes a stand against the coach when he sets the team up to injure a black player on an opposing team, and learns that you can't be honorable with dishonorable men. —*Voice of Youth Advocates*

★ **Staying** fat for Sarah Byrnes. Chris Crutcher. Greenwillow Books, 1993 216 p.
Grades: 7 8 9 10
1. Overweight teenage boys; 2. Teenage girls with disfigurements; 3. Friendship; 4. Loyalty in teenage boys; 5. Emotional problems of teenagers; 6. Humorous stories; 7. Realistic fiction; 8. Pacific Northwest fiction
9780688115524

LC 91040097

California Young Reader Medal, Young Adult, 1997; YALSA Popular Paperbacks for Young Adults, 2010.

High school senior Eric Calhoune was a fat kid—a really fat kid—but has slimmed down since joining the swim team. Now the same people who used to call him "Moby" (as in Moby Dick, the whale) want to be his friends, but Eric remains loyal to Sarah Byrnes, who knows what it's like to be an outcast. When Sarah—who has horrible burn scars from a childhood accident—suddenly stops talking and is committed to a psych ward, Eric goes to visit her every day, but he can't figure out what has shaken the toughest girl he knows. Moments of humor give readers a breather from this novel's intense emotion and building suspense.

An obese boy and a disfigured girl suffer the emotional scars of years of mockery at the hands of their peers. They share a hard-boiled view of the world until events in their senior year hurl them in very different directions. A story about a friendship with staying power, written with pathos and pointed humor. —*School Library Journal*

Cummings, Priscilla
Blindsided. Priscilla Cummings. Dutton Children's Books, 2010 226 p;
Grades: 7 8 9 10
1. Teenagers who are blind; 2. Teenagers with disabilities; 3. Coping in teenage girls; 4. Coping; 5. Schools; 6. Maryland; 7. Realistic fiction.
9780525421610

LC 2009025092

After years of failing eyesight, fourteen-year-old Natalie reluctantly enters a school for the blind, where in spite of her initial resistance she learns the skills that will help her survive in the sighted world.

Natalie, 14, knows that her future is becoming dimmer as the loss of her eyesight is a nightmare she can't avoid.... Part of going from denial to acceptance is attending a boarding school for the blind.... Natalie is a credible character and her fear is palpable and painful.... Readers will enjoy the high drama and heroics. —*School Library Journal*

Title is also written in braille on t.p.

Cypess, Leah
Death sworn. By Leah Cypess. 2014 352 pages (Death sworn, 1)
Grades: 7 8 9 10 11 12
1. Assassins; 2. Secrets; 3. Murder; 4. Magic; 5. Teenage romance; 6. High fantasy; 7. Fantasy mysteries; 8. Fantasy fiction
9780062221216

LC 2013037379

When a young sorceress is exiled to teach magic to a clan of assassins, she will find that secrets can be even deadlier than swords.

As seventeen-year-old Ileni's magic begins to fade, she's sent to the Black Mountain to tutor assassins in sorcery. With the help of Sorin, her student and assigned protector, she must discover who killed her predecessors before someone kills her. Ileni proves a compelling protagonist, and the blend of romance, assassins, magic, and murder-mystery consistently raises the stakes. —*Horn Book Guide*

Mistwood. By Leah Cypess. Greenwillow Books, 2010 304 p.
Grades: 7 8 9 10
1. Rulers; 2. Shapeshifters; 3. Loyalty; 4. Memory; 5. Men/women relations; 6. Fantasy fiction.
9780061956997; 9780061957000

LC 2009023051

Brought back from the Mistwood to protect the royal family, a girl who has no memory of being a shape-shifter encounters political and magical intrigue as she struggles with her growing feelings for the prince.

A traditional premise is transformed into a graceful meditation on the ramifications of loyalty, duty and purpose.... Astonishing and inspiring. —*Kirkus*

Companion book: *Nightspell*.

Nightspell. By Leah Cypess. Greenwillow Books, 2011 336 p.
Grades: 7 8 9 10
1. Arranged marriage; 2. Ghosts; 3. Princes; 4. Dead; 5. Sisters; 6. Fantasy fiction.
9780061957024

Sent by her father, the king of Raellia, who is trying to forge an empire out of warring tribes, Darri arrives in Ghostland and discovers that her sister, whom she planned to rescue, may not want to leave this land where the dead mingle freely with the living.

Swordfights, blood, and double-dealing pack the pages as this action-filled story races to a surprising conclusion. —*Booklist*

Companion book to: *Mistwood*.

Damico, Gina

Hellhole. By Gina Damico. Houghton Mifflin Harcourt, 2014 352 p.
Grades: 9 10 11 12

1. Demons; 2. Children of sick persons; 3. Mothers and sons; 4. Personal conduct; 5. Interpersonal relations; 6. Paranormal fiction; 7. Humorous stories.
9780544307100

LC 2013042827

Max Kilgore has accidentally unleashed a devil—and now the big, evil oaf is living in his basement. If Max doesn't meet the devil's demands (which include providing unlimited junk food and a hot tub), everyone and everything he holds dear could go up in smoke.

The ending is somewhat rushed and leaves a few loose ends, but this remains a wild and unpredictable cautionary tale about ill-considered bargains and bad decisions. —*Publishers Weekly*

Rogue. Gina Damico. Graphia, Houghton Mifflin Harcourt, 2013 384 p. (Croak trilogy, 3)
Grades: 8 9 10

1. Death; 2. Life after death; 3. Ghosts; 4. Grim Reaper (Symbolic character); 5. Teenage girls; 6. Urban fantasy
9780544108844

LC 2013004154

Uncle Mort rounds up sixteen-year-old Lex, the other Junior Grims, and Grotton, the most powerful Grim of all time, for a journey to Necropolis, where only an impossible choice can save the Afterlife from destruction.

Scorch. By Gina Damico. Houghton Mifflin Harcourt, 2012 352 p. (Croak trilogy, 2)
Grades: 7 8 9 10

1. Death; 2. Life after death; 3. Soul; 4. Grim Reaper (Symbolic character); 5. Twin sisters; 6. Urban fantasy
9780547624570

LC 2012014799

Sixteen-year-old grim reaper Lex Bartleby tries to redeem herself among her fellow Grims by finding renegade Zara, who is indiscriminately damning souls, and stopping her once and for all.

Danforth, Emily M.

The **miseducation** of Cameron Post. Emily M. Danforth. Balzer + Bray, 2012 480 p.
Grades: 9 10 11 12

1. Lesbians; 2. Sexual orientation; 3. Secrets; 4. Lesbian teenagers; 5. Interpersonal relations; 6. Montana; 7. Books to movies; 8. LGBTQIA fiction
9780062020567; 9780141389165, print, UK

LC 2011001947

Booklist Editors' Choice: Books for Youth, 2012; Montana Book Award, 2012; Rainbow List, 2013; School Library Journal Best Books, 2012; YALSA Best Fiction for Young Adults, 2013; William C. Morris Debut Award finalist, 2013.

In the early 1990s, when gay teenager Cameron Post rebels against her conservative Montana ranch town and her family decides she needs to change her ways, she is sent to a gay conversion therapy center.

Daniels, April

★ **Dreadnought**. April Daniels. Diversion Books, 2017 300 p. (Nemesis (April Daniels), 1)
Grades: 8 9 10 11 12

1. Transgender teenagers; 2. Superheroes; 3. Identity (Psychology); 4. Gender identity; 5. Fifteen-year-old girls; 6. Superhero stories
9781682300688

Amelia Bloomer List, 2018; Rainbow List, 2018.

A thoroughly enjoyable, emotionally rich, action-packed story with the most exciting new superheroes in decades. —*Kirkus*

Danticat, Edwidge

Untwine: a novel. Edwidge Danticat. Scholastic Press, 2015 320 p.
Grades: 9 10 11 12

1. Grief in teenage girls; 2. Children of separated parents; 3. Twin sisters; 4. Haitian Americans; 5. Grief; 6. Miami, Florida; 7. Realistic fiction; 8. First person narratives
9780545423038, HRD, US

LC 2014046787

Identical twin teenagers Giselle and Isabelle Boyer have always been inseparable, and expected to stay that way even though their Haitian American parents are separating—but when when the entire family is caught in a car crash, everyone's world is shattered forever.

There's a lot quietly packed into this novel—Giselle's Haitian heritage, her parents' imminent separation, the complications and thrills of first love, music, and art—yet most interesting is Danticat's rendering of identical twins as unique individuals. This is a poignant story for thoughtful teens that explores what it means to be a twin and how to say good-bye without losing oneself. —*Booklist*

Dao, Julie C.

Kingdom of the blazing phoenix. Julie C. Dao. Philomel Books, 2018 384 p. (Rise of the Empress, 2)
Grades: 9 10 11 12

1. Prophecies; 2. Women rulers; 3. Insurgency; 4. Courts and courtiers; 5. Demons; 6. Fantasy fiction; 7. Fairy tale and folklore-inspired fiction; 8. Asian-influenced fantasy.
9781524738327

LC 2018009153

Westchester Fiction Award, 2019.

Following a changeable map and clues from folktales, Princess Jade embarks on a quest to summon the Dragon Lords, defeat her evil stepmother Empress Xifeng, and bring peace to the kingdoms of Feng Lu.

Darrows, Eva

The **awesome**. Eva Darrows. Simon & Schuster, 2015 352 p.
Grades: 9 10 11 12

1. Seventeen-year-old girls; 2. Virgins; 3. Vampires; 4. Teenage girls; 5. Monsters; 6. Massachusetts; 7. Paranormal fiction.
9781781083246

Maggie Cunningham, who wants to enter the family business of monster hunting, can't get her license until she loses her virginity, but finding a normal boy proves to be more difficult than she thought.

Blisteringly funny and unrepentantly crass, Maggie's hard-edged narration is the soul of Maggie's story, which thoughtfully explores her complicated relationships with her boyfriend and take-no-prisoners mother. —*Publishers Weekly*

Dead little mean girl. Eva Darrows. Harlequin Teen, 2017 250 p.
Grades: 7 8 9 10

1. Stepsisters; 2. Teenage girls and death; 3. Bullying and bullies; 4. Teenage girl misfits; 5. Death; 6. Realistic fiction
9780373212415

When proud geek-girl Emma's new stepsister, mean- girl Quinn, moves into the bedroom next door, Emma's world is turned upside down, but when Quinn dies suddenly, Emma realizes there was more to her stepsister than anyone ever realized.

Darrows (*The Awesome*, 2015) new YA novel is a seriously smart, funny, and empathetic look at how someones manufactured exterior might be hiding inner turmoil, and ultimately advocates for looking past labels and categories. —*Booklist*

Dashner, James

The **death** cure. James Dashner. Delacorte Press, 2011 256 p. (Maze runner trilogy, 3)

Grades: 7 8 9 10

1. Dystopias; 2. Post-apocalypse; 3. Survival; 4. Epidemics; 5. Virus diseases; 6. Dystopian fiction; 7. Science fiction; 8. Books to movies
9780385738774; 9781909489424, print, UK; 9781908435200, UK; 9781910655917, print, UK

Buckeye Children's Book Award (Ohio), Grades 6-8, 2013.

Dashner again displays his mastery of the action sequence, making readers turn pages even as they become further invested in the well-developed characters. Heart pounding to the very last moment. —*Kirkus*

Title adapted into a film in 2018.

The **kill** order. James Dashner. Delacorte Press, 2012 336 p. (Maze runner trilogy, Prequel)

Grades: 7 8 9 10 11 12

1. Post-apocalypse; 2. Dystopias; 3. Survival; 4. Epidemics; 5. Virus diseases; 6. Dystopian fiction; 7. Science fiction
9780385742887; 9780375990823; 9780307997917; 9781909489431, print, UK; 9781908435590, UK

LC 2012016790

Mark struggles to make sense of his new, post-disaster world in this prequel to *The Maze Runner*.

★ The **maze** runner. James Dashner. Delacorte Press, 2009 384 p. (Maze runner trilogy, 1)

Grades: 7 8 9 10 11 12

1. Labyrinths; 2. Amnesia; 3. Dystopias; 4. Cooperation; 5. Teenagers with amnesia; 6. Dystopian fiction; 7. Science fiction; 8. Books to movies; 9. Books for reluctant readers
9780385737944; 9780385907026; 9781909489400, print, UK; 9781910655108, print, UK

LC 2009001345

Abraham Lincoln Illinois High School Book Award, 2012; Books I Love Best Yearly (BILBY), Older Reader, 2015; Charlotte Award (New York), Young Adult, 2012; Delaware Diamonds (book award), Middle School, 2015; Garden State Teen Book Award (New Jersey), Fiction (Grades 6-8), 2012; Georgia Peach Book Award for Teen Readers, 2012; Grand Canyon Reader Award (Arizona), Tween Book Category, 2012; Isinglass Teen Read Award (New Hampshire), 2010-2011. ; Kentucky Bluegrass Award for Grades 9-12, 2011; Truman Readers Award (Missouri), 2012; West Australian Young Readers' Book Award (WAYRBA), Older Readers, 2015; YALSA Quick Picks for Reluctant Young Adult Readers, 2011; YALSA Popular Paperbacks for Young Adults, 2011; YALSA Best Fiction for Young Adults, 2011.

Sixteen-year-old Thomas wakes up with no memory in the middle of a maze and realizes he must work with the community in which he finds himself if he is to escape.

With a fast-paced narrative steadily answering the myriad questions that arise and an ever-increasing air of tension, Dashner's suspenseful adventure will keep readers guessing until the very end. —*Publishers Weekly*

Daud, Somaiya

Mirage. Somaiya Daud. Flatiron Books, 2018 320 p. (Mirage (Daud), 1)

Grades: 8 9 10 11 12

1. Royal pretenders; 2. Imaginary kingdoms; 3. Teenage kidnapping victims; 4. Impostors; 5. Mistaken identity; 6. First person narratives; 7. Science fiction; 8. Afrofuturism and Afrofantasy
9781250126429; 9781473672628, Hardback, UK; 9781473672635, Paperback, UK; 9781250126436; 9781473651746, Paperback, UK; 9781250126443, ebook, US

LC 2018013549

School Library Journal Best Books, 2018; YALSA Best Fiction for Young Adults, 2019; Children's Africana Book Awards Honor Book, Older Readers, 2019.

After being kidnapped by the Vathek, Amani is forced to work as a body double for the princess who is hated by her conquered people.

David, Keren

★ **When** I was Joe. Keren David. Frances Lincoln Children's, 2010 364 p. (When I was Joe, 1)

Grades: 7 8 9 10

1. Teenage murder witnesses; 2. Federal Witness Protection Program; 3. Teenage athletes; 4. Teenage runners; 5. New identities; 6. London, England; 7. England; 8. Realistic fiction.
9781847801005; 9781847801319

YALSA Best Fiction for Young Adults, 2011.

This book has an intriguing premise and a cast of likable and realistic characters. —*School Library Journal*

Sequel: *Almost true*.

Davies, Jacqueline

Lost. By Jacqueline Davies. Marshall Cavendish, 2009 256 p.

Grades: 7 8 9 10

1. Arnold, Dorothy Harriet Camille; 2. Heirs and heiresses; 3. Sisters; 4. Sixteen-year-old girls; 5. Blue collar workers; 6. Poor families; 7. New York City; 8. 1910s; 9. Historical fiction; 10. Parallel narratives
9780761455356

LC 2008040560

Westchester Fiction Award, 2009; YALSA Best Books for Young Adults, 2010.

In 1911 New York, sixteen-year-old Essie Rosenfeld must stop taking care of her irrepressible six-year-old sister when she goes to work at the Triangle Waist Company, where she befriends a missing heiress who is in hiding from her family and who seems to understand the feelings of heartache and grief that Essie is trying desperately to escape.

The unusual pacing adds depth and intrigue as the plot unfolds. There are many layers to this story, which will appeal to a variety of interests and age levels. —*School Library Journal*

Davies, Stephen

★ **Outlaw**. By Stephen Davies. Clarion Books, 2011 192 p.

Grades: 7 8 9 10

1. Hostages; 2. British in Africa; 3. Terrorism; 4. Hostage taking; 5. Survival; 6. Burkina Faso; 7. Sahara; 8. Adventure stories; 9. Survival stories
9780547390178

LC 2011009643

School Library Journal Best Books, 2011.

The children of Britain's ambassador to Burkina Faso, fifteen-year-old Jake, who loves technology and adventure, and thirteen-year-old Kas, a budding social activist, are abducted and spend time in the Sahara desert with Yakuuba Sor, who some call a terrorist but others consider a modern-day Robin Hood.

Stephen Davies has crafted a novel full of intrigue, fast-paced action, and sly humor. The fast moving story will draw in many readers, including those who usually shy away from books. —*Voice of Youth Advocates*

LIST OF FICTIONAL WORKS

Davis, Lane
I swear. Lane Davis. Simon & Schuster Books For Young Readers, 2012 288 p.
Grades: 9 10 11 12
1. Bullying and bullies; 2. Suicide; 3. Cruelty; 4. Options, alternatives, choices; 5. High school students; 6. Realistic fiction.
9781442435063

LC 2011046310

After Leslie Gatlin kills herself, her bullies reflect on how things got so far.

Davis, Tanita S.
A la carte. Tanita S. Davis. Alfred A. Knopf, 2008 281 p;
Grades: 7 8 9 10
1. Independence in teenage girls; 2. Teenage cooks; 3. African American teenage girls; 4. Cooks; 5. Friendship; 6. California; 7. Realistic fiction; 8. First person narratives
9780375948152

LC 2007049656

With such a shortage of cooking shows hosted by African-American female chefs, seventeen-year-old Lainey has high hopes that her dream will be fulfilled through her hard work and unique creations, but when her best friend and secret crush suddenly moves away, Lainey must find a way to deal with the painful loss in order to keep her focus.

The relationships and characters in this book are authentic. The actions and dialogue seem true to those represented. Even though it is a quick read, the story is a meaningful one. —*Voice of Youth Advocates*

Mare's war. Tanita S. Davis. Alfred A. Knopf, 2009 352 p.
Grades: 7 8 9 10
1. African-American women soldiers; 2. Grandmother and granddaughter; 3. Automobile travel; 4. African Americans; 5. Discrimination; 6. Europe; 7. 1940s; 8. First person narratives; 9. Historical fiction; 10. Epistolary novels
9780375957147

LC 2008033744

Amelia Bloomer List, 2010; YALSA Best Books for Young Adults, 2010; YALSA Popular Paperbacks for Young Adults, 2014; Coretta Scott King Honor Book for Authors, 2010.

Teens Octavia and Tali learn about strength, independence, and courage when they are forced to take a car trip with their grandmother, who tells about growing up Black in 1940s Alabama and serving in Europe during World War II as a member of the Women's Army Corps.

The parallel travel narratives are masterfully managed, with postcards from Octavia and Tali to the folks back home in San Francisco signaling the shift between then and now. Absolutely essential reading. —*Kirkus*

Dawn, Sasha
Splinter. By Sasha Dawn. Carolrhoda Lab, 2017 304 p.
Grades: 8 9 10 11
1. Mother-separated teenage girls; 2. Missing persons; 3. Family secrets; 4. Missing women; 5. Fathers; 6. Mysteries
9781512411515

LC 2016008994

Sami's mother disappeared ten years ago, and the police have always suspected that Sami's father killed her. But they've never had any convincing evidence...until now. Sami's sure her father's innocent. Or is she?

An absolute page-turner that uses well-paced suspense instead of graphic violence to craft an edgy tale. —*Booklist*

Dayton, Arwen
Stronger, faster, and more beautiful. Arwen Elys Dayton. Delacorte Press, 2018 384 p.
Grades: 9 10 11 12
1. Genetic engineering; 2. Posthumanism; 3. Ethics; 4. Perfection; 5. Humans; 6. Dystopian fiction; 7. Short stories; 8. Science fiction.
9780525580959

LC 2018022928

Westchester Fiction Award, 2020.

Six interconnected stories that ask how far we will go to remake ourselves into the perfect human specimens, and how hard that will push the definition of human—Provided by publisher.

De Goldi, Kate
The 10 p.m. question. Kate de Goldi. Candlewick Press, 2010 245 p.
Grades: 6 7 8 9 10
1. Worry in boys; 2. Agoraphobia; 3. New students; 4. Worry; 5. Families; 6. New Zealand; 7. Realistic fiction; 8. New Zealand fiction
9780763649395; 9781877460203; 9781848774667, print, UK
New Zealand Post Book Awards for Children and Young Adults, Young Adult Fiction Award, 2009; New Zealand Post Book Awards for Children and Young Adults, New Zealand Post Book of the Year, 2009; Storylines (New Zealand) Notable Book; YALSA Best Fiction for Young Adults, 2011; USBBY Outstanding International Book, 2011.

De Goldi's novel is an achingly poignant, wryly comic story of early adolescence.... Nearly every character...is a loving, talented, unforgettable eccentric whose dialogue, much like De Goldi's richly phrased narration, combines heart-stopping tenderness with perfectly timed, deliciously zany humor. —*Booklist*

De la Cruz, Melissa
The queen's assassin. Melissa De La Cruz. G.P. Putnam's Sons Books for Young Readers, 2020 384 p.
Grades: 9 10 11 12
1. Assassins; 2. Princesses; 3. Imaginary kingdoms; 4. Apprentices; 5. Alliances; 6. Fantasy fiction; 7. High fantasy; 8. Multiple perspectives
9780525515913, HRD, US

Caledon Holt is the kingdom's deadliest weapon. Shadow of the Honey Glade has been training all her life to join the Guild, hoping that one day she'll become an assassin as feared and revered as Cal. But Shadow's mother and aunts expect her to serve the crown as a lady of the Renovian Court. When a surprise attack brings Shadow and Cal together, they're forced to team up as assassin and apprentice.

De la Cruz's trademark tight construction, detailed world building, and action-packed romance are all at work in this sure-to-be-popular new series. —*Booklist*

De Leon, Jennifer
★ Don't ask me where I'm from. Jennifer De Leon. Atheneum Books for Young Readers, 2020 336 p.
Grades: 9 10 11 12
1. Hispanic American teenage girls; 2. Race relations; 3. Prejudice; 4. New students; 5. Family problems; 6. Boston, Massachusetts; 7. Realistic fiction.
9781534438248, HRD, US; 9781534438255, paperback, US; 9781534438262, ebook, US

LC 2019040448

Reinventing herself at a privileged white suburban high school to get by in the face of escalating racial tensions, a first-generation American-LatinX teen is forced to take a stand when she discovers that her absent father cannot legally return home.

De Lint, Charles

The **blue** girl. Charles de Lint. Viking, 2004 368 p; (Newford series (Young adult))

Grades: 7 8 9 10

1. Ghosts; 2. Misfits (Persons); 3. Teenage girls — Friendship; 4. Parallel universes; 5. New students; 6. Urban fantasy
9780670059249

LC 2004019051

Great Lakes Great Books Award (Michigan), Grades 9-12, 2007; White Pine Award (Ontario), 2006; YALSA Popular Paperbacks for Young Adults, 2008; YALSA Best Books for Young Adults, 2005.

New at her high school, Imogene enlists the help of her introverted friend Maxine and the ghost of a boy who haunts the school after receiving warnings through her dreams that soul-eaters are threatening her life.

The book combines the turmoil of high school intertwined with rich, detailed imagery drawn from traditional folklore and complex characters with realistic relationships.... This book is not just another ghost story, but a novel infused with the true sense of wonder and magic that is De Lint at his best. It is strongly recommended. —*Voice of Youth Advocates*

Deebs, Tracy

Phantom wheel. Tracy Deebs. Little Brown & Co, 2018 416 p. (Hackers, 1)

Grades: 9 10 11 12

1. Teenage hackers; 2. Computer viruses; 3. Cyberterrorism; 4. Hackers; 5. Friendship; 6. Cyber-thrillers; 7. Science fiction; 8. Science fiction thrillers.
9780316474412; 9780316474443

A group of teenage hackers has been conned into creating the most devastating virus the world has ever seen, and now it's up to them to take down the shadowy corporation behind it before it's too late.

Tempest rising. Tracy Deebs. Walker Books for Young Readers, 2011 352 p. (Tempest (Tracy Deebs), 1)

Grades: 8 9 10 11 12

1. Mermaids; 2. Surfing; 3. Options, alternatives, choices; 4. Decision-making; 5. War; 6. Paranormal romances.
9780802722317

LC 2010034339

On her seventeenth birthday, Tempest must decide whether to remain a human and live on land or submit to her mermaid half, like her mother before her, and enter into a long-running war under the sea.

Tempest is a gutsy, independent heroine with more than enough agency to save herself from danger.... For readers wanting a solid, familiar, but slightly different paranormal romance. —*Booklist*

Delaney, Joseph

A **new** darkness. Joseph Delaney. Greenwillow Books, 2014 416 pages (New Darkness, 1)

Grades: 7 8 9 10

1. Apprentices; 2. Monsters; 3. Witches; 4. Supernatural; 5. Teenage boys; 6. Fantasy fiction; 7. Horror
9780062334534; 9781782954088, print, UK; 9780370332215, print, UK; 9781849416382, print, UK

LC 2014011963

Although his apprenticeship was not done when John Gregory died, Tom Ward spent years learning to fight boggarts, witches, demons, and more and feels prepared to be the new county Spook, but while his youth causes many people to distrust him, Jenny is determined to be his apprentice.

A plethora of action involving ghastly creatures, sword fights, and magic coupled with just enough backstory and description make this novel engaging enough to keep even the most reluctant reader turning pages until the end. Tom's story has a doozy of a cliff-hanger that is sure to bring teens back for more. —*School Library Journal*

Delsol, Wendy

Stork. Wendy Delsol. Candlewick Press, 2010 368 p. (Stork trilogy, 1)

Grades: 7 8 9 10

1. Teenagers and moving; 2. Soul; 3. Rural teenagers; 4. Supernatural; 5. Teenage boy/girl relations; 6. Minnesota; 7. Paranormal romances; 8. Mythological fiction
9780763648442

LC 2009051357

Westchester Fiction Award, 2011.

After her parents' divorce, Katla and her mother move from Los Angeles to Norse Falls, Minnesota, where Kat immediately alienates two boys at her high school and, improbably, discovers a kinship with a mysterious group of elderly women—the Icelandic Stork Society—who "deliver souls."

This snappy, lighthearted supernatural romance blends Norse mythology and contemporary issues with an easy touch. —*Booklist*

Demetrios, Heather

Bad romance. Heather Demetrios. 2017 368 p.

Grades: 10 11 12

1. Emotional abuse; 2. Manipulation by teenagers; 3. Small towns; 4. Dating (Social customs); 5. Manipulation (Social sciences); 6. California; 7. Realistic fiction; 8. First person narratives
9781627797726; 9781250158772, Paperback, Australia

LC 2016035854

YALSA Best Fiction for Young Adults, 2018.

Desperate to escape her small California town and the home of her controlling parents, aspiring artist Grace falls in love with Gavin, a charming young man who gradually reveals a controlling and dangerous nature.

A realistic, worthwhile look at dating violence and unhealthy relationships. —*Kirkus*

Something real. Heather Demetrios. 2014 416 pages

Grades: 9 10 11 12

1. Reality television programs; 2. Families; 3. Teenage romance; 4. Brothers and sisters; 5. Seventeen-year-old girls; 6. Realistic fiction; 7. Books for reluctant readers
9780805097948; 9780805097962, ebook, US

LC 2013030798

YALSA Quick Picks for Reluctant Young Adult Readers, 2015.

Since the cancellation of her family's reality television show, seventeen-year-old Bonnie Baker, one of twelve siblings, has tried to live a normal life with real friends and a possible boyfriend, until her mother and the show's producers decide to bring *Baker's Dozen* back on the air.

It's been four years since the reality television show Baker's Dozen went off the air. Bonnie Baker, 17, feels lucky to have survived the tension and challenges from constantly being in the limelight with her 12 siblings... With likable protagonists and snappy dialogue, *Something Real* credibly zooms in on reality TV's impact on unwilling subjects-a shoo-in for teens drawn to contemporary romance and drama. —*School Library Journal*

Deming, Sarah

★ **Gravity**. Sarah Deming. Make Me a World, 2019 400 p.

Grades: 9 10 11 12

1. Teenage boxers; 2. Teenage girl athletes; 3. Olympic games; 4. Boxing; 5. Teenage children of alcoholics; 6. Brooklyn, New York City; 7. 2010s; 8. Realistic fiction; 9. Sports fiction

9780525581048, LIB, US; 9780525581031, HRD, US; 9780525581062

A young female boxer learns to fight for what she wants. A riveting pugilistic must-read. —*Kirkus*

Dennard, Susan

Something strange and deadly. Susan Dennard. HarperTeen, 2012 400 p. (Something strange and deadly trilogy, 1)
Grades: 7 8 9 10 11 12
1. Brothers and sisters; 2. Dead; 3. Magic (Occultism); 4. Teenage girls; 5. Magic; 6. United States; 7. Philadelphia, Pennsylvania; 8. Science fiction; 9. Horror; 10. Steampunk
9780062083265
LC 2011042114

In an alternate nineteenth-century Philadelphia, Eleanor Fitt sets out to rescue her brother, who seems to have been captured by an evil necromancer in control of an army of Undead.

Truthwitch. Susan Dennard. Tor Teen, 2016 415 p. (The Witchlands, 1)
Grades: 8 9 10 11 12
1. Witches; 2. Political intrigue; 3. Friendship; 4. Magic; 5. Imaginary empires; 6. High fantasy; 7. Fantasy fiction; 8. Multiple perspectives
9780765379283; 9781509825028, print, UK; 9781447282068, print, UK

On a continent ruled by three empires, some are born with a magical skill that sets them apart from others. Safiya is a Truthwitch, able to discern truth from lie; Iseult, a Threadwitch, can see the invisible ties that bind the lives around her. Safi and Iseult want to be free to live their own lives, but war is coming to the Witchlands. With the help of a Windwitch and the hindrance of a Bloodwitch bent on revenge, the friends must fight emperors, princes, and mercenaries alike, all of whom want to capture Safi.

A great choice for fans of fantasy adventure and strong female characters. —*School Library Journal*

Deonn, Tracy

Legendborn. By Tracy Deonn. Margaret K. McElderry Books 2020 432 p. (Legendborn, 1)
Grades: 9 10 11 12
1. Secret societies; 2. Demons; 3. African American teenage girls; 4. Monster hunters; 5. Magic; 6. North Carolina; 7. Fantasy fiction
9781534441606
LC 2020000642

John Steptoe Award for New Talent, Author Category, 2021; School Library Journal Best Books, 2020.

Wanting to escape her previous life after the accidental death of her mother, 16-year-old Bree enrolls in a program for high school students at the local university before her witness to a magical attack reveals her undiscovered powers as well as sinister truths about her mother's death.

Deonn adeptly employs the haunting history of the American South ('the low buzzing sound of exclusion') to explore themes of ancestral pain, grief, and love, balancing them with stimulating worldbuilding and multiple thrilling plot twists. —*Publishers Weekly*

Deracine, Anat

Driving by starlight. Anat Deracine. Henry Holt and Company, 2018 288 p.
Grades: 8 9 10 11 12
1. Teenage girls — Identity; 2. Resistance to government; 3. Women's role; 4. Sixteen-year-old girls; 5. Best friends; 6. Saudi Arabia; 7. Middle East; 8. Realistic fiction; 9. Coming-of-age stories

9781250133427; 9781250308955

Coming of age in a Saudi Arabia where they delight in small acts of rebellion against the Saudi cultural police, from secretly wearing Western clothing and listening to forbidden music to flirting and driving, best friends Leena and Mishie find themselves struggling against cultural restrictions that challenge their ambitions for college and independence.

The fast-paced narrative and unexpected twists make for an engaging yet educational novel with a powerful message about the complexities of being a woman in a man's world. —*Kirkus*

Derting, Kimberly

The **body** finder. By Kimberly Derting. Harper, 2010 336 p. (Body finder novels, 1)
Grades: 7 8 9 10 11 12
1. Extrasensory perception; 2. Serial murderers; 3. Violent deaths; 4. Murder; 5. Dead; 6. Washington (State); 7. Mysteries
9780061779817; 9780755378951, print, UK
LC 2009039675

YALSA Best Fiction for Young Adults, 2011.

High school junior Violet uses her uncanny ability to sense murderers and their victims to try to stop a serial killer who is terrorizing her town, and although her best friend and would-be boyfriend Jay promises to keep her safe, she becomes a target.

Violet Ambrose can find dead bodies. Their aura of sound, color, or even taste imprints itself on their murderers, and Violet's extrasensory perception picks up on those elements.... Derting has written a suspenseful mystery and sensual love story that will captivate readers who enjoy authentic high-school settings, snappy dialogue, sweet romance, and heart-stopping drama. —*Booklist*

Sequel: *Desires of the dead*.

Desires of the dead. Kimberly Derting. HarperCollins, 2011 368 p. (Body finder novels, 2)
Grades: 7 8 9 10
1. Teenage girl psychics; 2. Stalking victims; 3. Extrasensory perception; 4. Dead; 5. Murder; 6. Washington (State); 7. Mysteries
9780061779848; 9780755378968, print, UK
LC 2010017838

Sixteen-year-old Violet Ambrose's ability to find murder victims and their killers draws the attention of the FBI just as her relationship with Jay, her best-friend-turned-boyfriend, heats up.

The author paces the story beautifully, weaving together several story lines as she inches up to the final, desperate scene.... Imaginative, convincing and successful suspense. —*Kirkus*

Sequel to: *The body finder*.

The **last** echo. Kimberly Derting. HarperTeen, 2012 336 p. (Body finder novels, 3)
Grades: 7 8 9 10 11 12
1. Teenage girl psychics; 2. Serial murderers; 3. Extrasensory perception; 4. Psychic ability; 5. Serial murders; 6. Washington (State); 7. Mysteries
9780062082190; 9780755389155, print, UK
LC 2011044633

Violet, a high school junior, discovers the body of a teen killed by "the girlfriend collector" and is determined to solve the case, but the serial killer is on the lookout for a new "relationship" and Violet may have caught his eye.

As always, this author writes a gripping tale.... Personalities come across quite strongly, as several of the characters tend toward the eccentric. —*Kirkus*

The **pledge**. Kimberly Derting. Margaret K. McElderry Books, 2011 320 p. (Pledge trilogy, 1)

Grades: 7 8 9 10
1. Dystopias; 2. Language and languages; 3. Revolutions; 4. Ability; 5. Social classes; 6. Dystopian fiction; 7. Fantasy fiction.
9781442422018
YALSA Best Fiction for Young Adults, 2013.
Derting keeps her story consistently engaging through vivid description and brisk pacing.... Great suspense from a prolific new writer with a vibrant imagination. —*Kirkus*

Desai Hidier, Tanuja
Born confused. Tanuja Desai Hidier. Scholastic Press, 2002 413 p.
Grades: 8 9 10 11 12
1. East Indian American teenagers; 2. Teenage girl photographers; 3. Identity (Psychology); 4. Best friends; 5. Photography; 6. New Jersey; 7. Realistic fiction; 8. Coming-of-age stories.
9780439357623
LC 2002004515
YALSA Popular Paperbacks for Young Adults, 2013; YALSA Best Books for Young Adults, 2003.
Seventeen-year-old Dimple, whose family is from India, discovers that she is not Indian enough for the Indians and not American enough for the Americans, as she sees her hypnotically beautiful, manipulative best friend taking possession of both her heritage and the boy she likes.
This involving story...will reward its readers. The family background and richness in cultural information add a new level to the familiar girl-meets-boy story. —*School Library Journal*
Sequel: *Bombay blues*.

Despain, Bree
The **dark** Divine. Bree Despain. Egmont USA, 2010 372 p; (Dark Divine novels, 1)
Grades: 7 8 9 10 11
1. Children of clergy; 2. Christian teenage girls; 3. Teenage werewolves; 4. Supernatural; 5. Families; 6. Minnesota; 7. Paranormal romances.
9781606840658
LC 2009018680
YALSA Popular Paperbacks for Young Adults, 2011.
Grace Divine, almost seventeen, learns a dark secret when her childhood friend—practically a brother—returns, upsetting her pastor-father and the rest of her family, around the time strange things are happening in and near their small Minnesota town.
Despain raises complex issues of responsibility and forgiveness and offers no easy answers. Atmospheric and compelling. —*Booklist*

Dessen, Sarah
Along for the ride. Sarah Dessen. Viking, 2009 384 p.
Grades: 7 8 9 10
1. Children of divorced parents; 2. Self-discovery; 3. Guilt; 4. Teenage girls — Friendship; 5. Romantic love; 6. Realistic fiction.
9780670011940
Goodreads Choice Award, 2009; YALSA Popular Paperbacks for Young Adults, 2012; Young Reader's Choice Award (Pacific Northwest), Senior, 2012; YALSA Best Books for Young Adults, 2010.
When Auden impulsively goes to stay with her father, stepmother, and new baby sister the summer before she starts college, all the trauma of her parents' divorce is revived, even as she is making new friends and having new experiences such as learning to ride a bike and dating.
Dessen explores the dynamics of an extended family headed by two opposing, flawed personalities, revealing their parental failures with wicked precision yet still managing to create real, even sympathetic characters.... [This book] provides the interpersonal intricacies fans expect from a Dessen plot. —*Horn Book Guide*

Just listen: a novel. By Sarah Dessen. Viking Children's Books, 2006 384 p.
Grades: 9 10 11 12
1. Social isolation; 2. Ostracism; 3. High school students; 4. Misfits (Persons); 5. Interpersonal relations; 6. Realistic fiction; 7. Coming-of-age stories.
9780670061051
LC 2006000472
Gateway Readers Award (Missouri), 2009; Iowa High School Book Award, 2009; YALSA Best Books for Young Adults, 2007.
Isolated from friends who believe the worst because she has not been truthful with them, sixteen-year-old Annabel finds an ally in classmate Owen, whose honesty and passion for music help her to face and share what really happened at the end-of-the-year party that changed her life.
The author weaves a sometimes funny, mostly emotional, and very satisfying story. —*Voice of Youth Advocates*

Lock and key: a novel. By Sarah Dessen. Viking, 2008 422 p;
Grades: 7 8 9 10
1. Children of alcoholics; 2. Abandoned teenagers; 3. Sisters; 4. Emotional problems; 5. Seventeen-year-old girls; 6. Realistic fiction.
9780670010882
LC 2007025370
When she is abandoned by her alcoholic mother, high school senior Ruby winds up living with Cora, the sister she has not seen for ten years, and learns about Cora's new life, what makes a family, how to allow people to help her when she needs it, and that she too has something to offer others.
The dialogue, especially between Ruby and Cora, is crisp, layered, and natural. The slow unfolding adds to an anticipatory mood.... Recommend this one to patient, sophisticated readers. —*School Library Journal*

Once and for all: a novel. Sarah Dessen. Viking, an imprint of Penguin Group (USA), 2017 400 p.
Grades: 9 10 11 12
1. Summer romance; 2. Loss (Psychology); 3. Wedding planning; 4. Children of divorced parents; 5. Teenage romance; 6. Contemporary romances
9780425290330
LC Bl2017013587
Cynical about happy endings, Louna, the daughter of a wedding planner, initally holds Ambrose at arm's length, but Ambrose has finally found someone to save him from his serial dating ways, and he's not about be discouraged.
Romance, humor, kindhearted characters, and a touch of painful reality make this another sure bet for Dessen fans. —*Kirkus*

Saint Anything. Sarah Dessen. 2015 417 pages
Grades: 7 8 9 10 11 12
1. Self-discovery in teenage girls; 2. Family problems; 3. Brothers and sisters; 4. Friendship; 5. Self-discovery; 6. Realistic fiction
9780451474704; 9780141361734, print, Australia
LC 2014039813
Westchester Fiction Award, 2016; YALSA Best Fiction for Young Adults, 2016.
Sydney's charismatic older brother, Peyton, has always been the center of attention in the family but when he is sent to jail, Sydney struggles to find her place at home and the world until she meets the Chathams, including gentle, protective Mac, who makes her feel seen for the first time.

Once again, Dessen demonstrates her tremendous skill in evoking powerful emotions through careful, quiet prose, while delivering a satisfying romance. —*Publishers Weekly*

That summer. Sarah Dessen. Orchard Books, 1996 198 p.
Grades: 7 8 9 10
1. Children of divorced parents; 2. Weddings; 3. Family relationships; 4. Summer; 5. Fifteen-year-old girls; 6. Realistic fiction; 7. Books to movies
9780531095386
Booklist Editors' Choice: Books for Youth, 1996; YALSA Best Books for Young Adults, 1997.

During the summer of her divorced father's remarriage and her sister's wedding, fifteen-year-old Haven comes into her own by letting go of the myths of the past.

Dessen adds a fresh twist to a traditional sister-of-the-bride story with her keenly observant narrative full of witty ironies. Her combination of unforgettable characters and unexpected events generates hilarity as well as warmth. —*Publishers Weekly*

The 2003 film *How to deal* is based on Dessen's novels *That summer* and *Someone like you*.

What happened to goodbye. By Sarah Dessen. Viking Childrens Books, 2011 416 p.
Grades: 8 9 10 11 12
1. Children of divorced parents; 2. Identity (Psychology); 3. Self-discovery in teenage girls; 4. Self-discovery; 5. Moving, Household; 6. Realistic fiction.
9780670012947
LC 2010041041
YALSA Best Fiction for Young Adults, 2012.

Following her parents' bitter divorce as she and her father move from town to town, seventeen-year-old Mclean reinvents herself at each school she attends until she is no longer sure she knows who she is or where she belongs.

The novel nimbly weaves together familiar story lines of divorce, high-school happiness and angst, and teen-identity struggles with likable, authentic adult and teen characters and intriguing yet credible situations. —*Booklist*

DeStefano, Lauren
Fever. Lauren DeStefano. Simon & Schuster BFYR, 2012 368 p. (Chemical Garden trilogy, 2)
Grades: 9 10 11 12
1. Genetically engineered teenagers; 2. Separated friends, relatives, etc; 3. Dystopias; 4. Twin brothers and sisters; 5. Forced marriage; 6. Dystopian fiction; 7. Science fiction
9781442409071
LC 2011016961
In a future where genetic engineering has cured humanity of all diseases and defects but has also produced a virus that kills all females by age twenty and all males by the age twenty-five, teenaged Rhine escapes her forced marriage and journeys back to New York to find her twin brother.

Perfect ruin. Lauren DeStefano. SSBFYR, 2013 352 p. (Internment chronicles, 1)
Grades: 7 8 9 10
1. Dystopias; 2. Totalitarianism; 3. Murder; 4. Teenage girls; 5. Stockhour, Morgan (Fictitious character); 6. Dystopian fiction; 7. Science fiction.
9781442480612; 9781442480629, ebook, US
LC 2013014392
YALSA Best Fiction for Young Adults, 2014.

Sixteen-year-old Morgan Stockhour lives in Internment, a floating city utopia. But when a murder occurs, everything she knows starts to unravel.

Wither. Lauren DeStefano. Simon & Schuster Books for Young Readers, 2011 368 p. (Chemical Garden trilogy, 1)
Grades: 9 10 11 12
1. Genetically engineered teenagers; 2. Teenage girl kidnapping victims; 3. Polygamy; 4. Genetic engineering; 5. Forced marriage; 6. Florida; 7. Dystopian fiction; 8. Science fiction
9781442409057
YALSA Best Fiction for Young Adults, 2012; YALSA Popular Paperbacks for Young Adults, 2016.

After modern science turns every human into a genetic time bomb with men dying at age twenty-five and women dying at age twenty, girls are kidnapped and married off in order to repopulate the world.

This beautifully-written...fantasy, with its intriguing world-building, well-developed characters and intricate plot involving flashbacks as well as edge-of-the-seat suspense, will keep teens riveted to the plight of Rhine and her sister wives.... This thought-provoking novel will also stimulate discussion in science and ethics classes. —*Voice of Youth Advocates*

Deuker, Carl
Golden arm. Carl Deuker. Houghton Mifflin Harcourt, 2020 368 p.
Grades: 6 7 8 9 10
1. Baseball players; 2. Poverty; 3. Social classes; 4. Baseball; 5. Brothers; 6. Baseball stories; 7. Sports fiction; 8. Coming-of-age stories.
9780358012429, HRD, US
When his pitching talents land him a spot on a wealthier team where he has a chance to be drafted into the majors, a teen navigating poverty and a speech challenge struggles with leaving behind a brother who is increasingly influenced by drug gangs.

Deuker's realistic novel pits poverty, friendship, teamwork, self-reliance, and supportive adults against wealth, privilege, overambition, and overbearing helicopter parents. Even readers who don't like baseball will be riveted to this human-interest, underdog story. —*Booklist*

★ **Gym** candy. By Carl Deuker. Houghton Mifflin Company, 2007 313 p;
Grades: 7 8 9 10 11 12
1. High school football players; 2. Steroids; 3. Integrity; 4. Rehabilitation centers; 5. Teenage athletes; 6. Washington (State); 7. Sports fiction; 8. First person narratives; 9. Football stories
9780618777136
LC 2007012749
Iowa Teen Award, 2010; YALSA Popular Paperbacks for Young Adults, 2010.

Groomed by his father to be a star player, football is the only thing that has ever really mattered to Mick Johnson, who works hard for a spot on the varsity team his freshman year, then tries to hold onto his edge by using steroids, despite the consequences to his health and social life.

Deuker skillfully complements a sobering message with plenty of exciting on-field action and locker-room drama, while depicting Mick's emotional struggles with loneliness and insecurity as sensitively and realistically as his physical ones. —*Booklist*

Runner. Carl Deuker. Houghton Mifflin, 2005 216 p;
Grades: 7 8 9 10
1. Runners; 2. Teenage children of alcoholics; 3. Coping in teenagers; 4. Seventeen-year-old boys; 5. Teenage boys; 6. Puget Sound; 7. Sports fiction; 8. Realistic fiction; 9. First person narratives; 10. Books for reluctant readers
9780618542987

LC 2004015781
YALSA Quick Picks for Reluctant Young Adult Readers, 2006; YALSA Popular Paperbacks for Young Adults, 2010.

Living with his alcoholic father on a broken-down sailboat on Puget Sound has been hard on seventeen-year-old Chance Taylor, but when his love of running leads to a high-paying job, he quickly learns that the money is not worth the risk.

Writing in a fast-paced, action-packed, but at the same time reflective style, Deuker...uses running as a hook to entice readers into a perceptive coming-of-age novel. —*School Library Journal*

Swagger. Carl Deuker. Houghton Mifflin Harcourt, 2013 304 p.
Grades: 7 8 9 10 11 12
1. Teenage basketball players; 2. Sex crimes; 3. Basketball coaches; 4. Basketball; 5. Moving to a new state; 6. Sports fiction; 7. Basketball stories; 8. Books for reluctant readers
9780547974590

LC 2012045062
YALSA Quick Picks for Reluctant Young Adult Readers, 2015.

High school senior point guard Jonas Dolan is on the fast track to a basketball career until an unthinkable choice puts his future on the line.

When his family moves to Seattle, high school basketball star Jonas befriends new neighbor Levi, who plays power forward. Assistant coach Ryan Hartwell appreciates Jonas's fast-breaking style, but something about Hartwell feels wrong. Eventually his misdeeds lead to tragedy, and Jonas must find the courage to do what's right. Basketball fans will love the realistic hardwood action and the story's quick pacing. —*Horn Book Guide*

Devlin, Calla
Tell me some-thing real. Calla Devlin. Atheneum Books for Young Readers, 2016 304 p.
Grades: 9 10 11 12
1. Children of people with cancer; 2. Family secrets; 3. Mothers and daughters; 4. Sisters; 5. Betrayal; 6. San Diego, California; 7. Mexico; 8. 1970s; 9. Historical fiction
9781481461153
William C. Morris Debut Award finalist, 2017.

This is an intense read that explores the way illness can seep into the lives of everyone it touches, leaving behind confusion, fear, and anger, and a thoroughly engrossing story that will keep readers reevaluating everything they thought they knew about the Babcock family. —*School Library Journal*

DeWoskin, Rachel
Big girl small: a novel. Rachel DeWoskin. Farrar, Straus and Giroux, 2011 294 p.
Grades: 11 12 Adult
1. Teenage girls — Sexuality; 2. Date rape; 3. Humiliation; 4. Little people; 5. High school students; 6. Coming-of-age stories; 7. Adult books for young adults.
9780374112578; 9781443404754; 9781250002532; 9781611731132
LC 2010033106
Alex Award, 2012; Booklist Editors' Choice: Adult Books for Young Adults, 2011.

Sixteen-year-old Judy Lohden finds her three feet nine inches tall, incredibly talented self in the middle of a scandal, with the national media on her trail and the students at Darcy Academy, a local performing arts high school, involved in the mayhem.

Bright and sardonic Judy Lohden, a 16-year-old dwarf freshly enrolled in Ann Arbor's Darcy Arts Academy, falls victim to the worst Steven King Carrie prank in the history of dating at the hands of popular boy Jeff Legassic, who becomes an object of desire as soon as he and Judy meet cute the first week of school. The book opens with Judy hiding out in a seedy motel; throughout the novel, she slowly unveils her secret and reveals her two visions of herself—that of a pretty teenage girl with an hourglass figure who happens to be three feet nine inches tall, and that of a sideshow attraction. It's a rare author who is willing to subject her protagonist to the extreme ranges of degradation and redemption to which DeWoskin subjects Judy; thankfully, she manages it beautifully. —*Publishers Weekly*

Someday we will fly. By Rachel DeWoskin. Viking, published by Penguin Group, 2019 368 p.
Grades: 7 8 9 10
1. Jewish teenage girls; 2. Immigration and emigration; 3. Mother-separated children; 4. Sino-Japanese Conflict, 1937-1945; 5. Circus performers; 6. Shanghai (China); 7. China; 8. 1940s; 9. Historical fiction; 10. First person narratives
9780670014965; 9781984836243

LC 2018018516
National Jewish Book Award, 2019; Sydney Taylor Book Award for Teen Readers, 2020.

Lillia, fifteen, flees Warsaw with her father and baby sister in 1940 to try to make a new start in Shanghai, China, but the conflict grows more intense as America and Japan become involved.

DeWoskin captures the crushing destruction of war and occupation, the unfathomable resilience communities can muster through cross-cultural friendships and acts of kindness, andthe power of the performing arts to foster hope in times of struggle and desperation. —*Publishers Weekly*
Includes bibliographical references.

Dickerson, Melanie
The **merchant's** daughter. Melanie Dickerson. Zondervan, 2011 304 p. (Hagenheim, 2)
Grades: 7 8 9 10 11 12
1. Indentured servants; 2. Debt; 3. Bailiffs; 4. Christian life; 5. Romantic love; 6. Great Britain; 7. Medieval period (476-1492); 8. 14th century; 9. Christian historical fiction; 10. Fairy tale and folklore-inspired fiction
9780310727613

LC 2011034338
In 1352 England, seventeen-year-old Annabel, granddaughter of a knight and a would-be nun, eludes a lecherous bailiff but falls in love with Lord Le Wyse, the ferocious and disfigured man to whom her family owes three years of indentured servitude, in this tale loosely based on Beauty and the Beast.

Dickerson manages a heartfelt romance that will stick with readers, not only for its morality but also for the exploration of a woman's place within fourteenth-century English Christianity. —*Booklist*

Dickinson, Peter
★ **Eva**. Peter Dickinson. Delacorte Press, 1989 219 p.
Grades: 7 8 9 10
1. Thirteen-year-old girls; 2. Chimpanzees; 3. Transplantation of organs, tissues, etc; 4. Animal welfare; 5. Animal experimentation; 6. Science fiction.
9780385297028

LC 88029435
ALA Notable Children's Book, 1990; Phoenix Award, 2008; Young Reader's Choice Award (Pacific Northwest), Senior, 1992.

After a terrible accident, a young girl wakes up to discover that she has been given the body of a chimpanzee.

Diederich, Phillippe

Playing for the Devil's fire. By Phillippe Diederich. Cinco Puntos Press, 2016 232 p.

Grades: 7 8 9 10 11 12

1. Parent-separated teenagers; 2. Wrestlers; 3. Corruption; 4. Loss (Psychology); 5. Missing persons; 6. Mexico (City); 7. Mexico; 8. Coming-of-age stories; 9. Mysteries

9781941026298

LC 2015024951

Booklist Editors' Choice: Books for Youth, 2016; YALSA Best Fiction for Young Adults, 2017.

Thirteen-year-old Boli lives in a small pueblo near Mexico City, a landscape destroyed by drug crime, and when his parents leave town and are not heard from, Boli hopes to inspire a luchador to help him find them.

Striking imagery and symbolism, along with the timeliness of the subject, make this title a natural for classroom discussion, and a Spanish glossary will aid English-only speakers. Diederich, who grew up in Mexico City, brings firsthand experience as well as tremendous compassion to this poignant coming-of-age novel. —*Booklist*

Dimaline, Cherie

★ The **marrow** thieves. Cherie Dimaline. Dancing Cat Books, 2017 234 p.

Grades: 9 10 11 12

1. Dreams; 2. First Nations (Canada); 3. Post-apocalypse; 4. Bone marrow; 5. Procurement of organs, tissues, etc; 6. Canada; 7. Apocalyptic fiction; 8. Dystopian fiction; 9. Science fiction

9781770864863; 9781913090012, Paperback, UK

Amy Mathers Teen Book Award, 2018; Burt Award for First Nations, Metis, and Inuit Literature, 2018; Governor General's Literary Award for English-Language Children's Literature, 2017; Kirkus Prize for Young Readers' Literature, 2017; OLA Best Bets, 2017; School Library Journal Best Books, 2017; Sunburst Award for Excellence in Canadian Literature of the Fantastic, 2018; YALSA Best Fiction for Young Adults, 2018; American Indian Youth Literature Awards Honor Book, Young Adult Book, 2018.

In this futuristic dystopian novel for teens, the Indigenous people of North America are on the run in a fight for survival.

A dystopian world that is all too real and that has much to say about our own. —*Kirkus*

Dirkes, Craig

Sucktown, Alaska. By Craig Dirkes. 2017 352 pages

Grades: 9 10 11 12

1. Drug dealers; 2. Marijuana; 3. Newspapers; 4. Journalists; 5. Teenage boy/girl relations; 6. Alaska; 7. Realistic fiction; 8. Coming-of-age stories

9781630790554

LC 2016046406

When he is kicked out of his first year of college in Anchorage, eighteen-year-old Eddie Ashford promises the university officials to work for one year at the newspaper in Kusko, Alaska, which is a small, depressing town in back-of-beyond, where it requires either a plane or a dog-sled to get around for most of the time—but staying straight is a challenge, especially when he gets caught up in the local marijuana trade.

The author paints vivid, detailed pictures of life, both in rural Alaska and in the mind of a young man. —*Voice of Youth Advocates*

DiTerlizzi, Tony

★ The **search** for WondLa. Tony DiTerlizzi. Simon & Schuster Books for Young Readers, 2010 288 p. (WondLa trilogy, 1)

Grades: 5 6 7 8

1. Girl adventurers; 2. Robots; 3. Human/alien encounters; 4. Taxidermists; 5. Trees; 6. Science fiction.

9781416983101; 9780857073006, print, UK

LC 2010001326

Living in isolation with a robot on what appears to be an alien world populated with bizarre life forms, a twelve-year-old human girl called Eva Nine sets out on a journey to find others like her. Features "augmented reality" pages, in which readers with a webcam can access additional information about Eva Nine's world.

The abundant illustrations, drawn in a flat, two-tone style, are lush and enhance readers' understanding of this unique universe.... DiTerlizzi is pushing the envelope in his latest work, nearly creating a new format that combines a traditional novel with a graphic novel and with the interactivity of the computer. Yet, beneath this impressive package lies a theme readers will easily relate to: the need to belong, to connect, to figure out one's place in the world. The novel's ending is a stunning shocker that will leave kids frantically awaiting the next installment. —*School Library Journal*

Illustrated by the author.

Doctorow, Cory

★ **Little** brother. Cory Doctorow. Tor Teen, 2008 384 p.

Grades: 8 9 10 11 12

1. Hackers; 2. Terrorism; 3. Dystopias; 4. Near future; 5. Teenage boys; 6. California; 7. San Francisco, California; 8. Dystopian fiction; 9. Science fiction; 10. Cyber-thrillers

9780765319852

Booklist Editors' Choice: Books for Youth, 2008; Golden Duck Awards: Hal Clement Award for Young Adult; John W. Campbell Memorial Award for Best Science Fiction Novel, 2009; New York Times Notable Children's Book, 2008; OLA Best Bets, 2008; School Library Journal Best Books, 2008; Sunburst Award for Excellence in Canadian Literature of the Fantastic, 2009; White Pine Award (Ontario), 2009; YALSA Best Books for Young Adults, 2009; YALSA Popular Paperbacks for Young Adults, 2011.

Computer hacker Marcus spends most of his time outwitting school surveillance, until the day that San Francisco is bombed by terrorists—and he and his friends are arrested and brutally interrogated for days. When they release Marcus, the authorities threaten to come for him again if he breathes a word about his ordeal; meanwhile, America has become a police state where everyone is suspect. For Marcus, the only option left is to take down the power-crazed Department of Homeland Security with an underground online revolution.

The author manages to explain naturally the necessary technical tools and scientific concepts in this fast-paced and well-written story.... The reader is privy to Marcus's gut-wrenching angst, frustration, and terror, thankfully offset by his self-awareness and humorous observations. —*Voice of Youth Advocates*

Sequel: *Homeland.*

Pirate cinema. Cory Doctorow. Tor Teen, 2012 384 p.

Grades: 7 8 9 10

1. Runaway teenage boys; 2. Filmmakers; 3. Dystopias; 4. Copyright; 5. Creativity; 6. London, England; 7. England; 8. Science fiction; 9. Cyber-thrillers; 10. Science fiction thrillers.

9780765329080

In a dystopian, near-future Britain, sixteen-year-old Trent, obsessed with making movies on his computer, joins a group of artists and activists who are trying to fight a new bill that will criminalize even more harmless internet creativity.

Dogar, Sharon

Annexed: a novel. Sharon Dogar. Houghton Mifflin Harcourt, 2010 352 p.

Grades: 8 9 10 11 12

1. Pels, Peter van, 1926-1945; 2. Hiding; 3. Attics; 4. Jews — Amsterdam, Netherlands; 5. Teenage boys; 6. Anger in teenage boys; 7. Netherlands; 8. Second World War era (1939-1945); 9. 1940s; 10. Historical fiction.

9780547501956; 9781849391245, print, UK; 9781405664622, print, UK

School Library Journal Best Books, 2010.

Dogar reimagines what happened between the families who lived in the secret annex immortalized in Anne Frank's diary. In doing so, she creates a captivating historical novel and fully fleshes out the character of Peter, a boy whom teens will easily relate to. —*School Library Journal*

Doktorski, Jennifer Salvato

The **summer** after you and me. Jennifer Salvato Doktorski. 2015 293 pages

Grades: 9 10 11 12

1. Summer resorts; 2. First loves; 3. Love triangles; 4. Teenage boy/girl relations; 5. Friendship; 6. New Jersey; 7. Contemporary romances

9781492619031; 9781492619048; 9781492619055

LC 2014044296

A year after Superstorm Sandy, Lucy's life is returning to normal at the New Jersey shore, where she has grown up surfing with her twin brother, crabbing and long-boarding with friends, and working at Surf Taco, but the torch she holds for summer resident Connor, the center of The Big Mistake, still burns.

Doktorski has crafted a rich, multilayered novel with a strong sense of place and a good mix of characters and problems. —*Booklist*

Dole, Mayra L.

★ **Down** to the bone. Mayra Lazara Dole. HarperTeen, 2008 367 p; Grades: 8 9 10 11 12

1. Lesbian teenagers; 2. Lesbians; 3. Cuban Americans; 4. Homosexuality; 5. Coming out (Sexual or gender identity); 6. Miami, Florida; 7. LGBTQIA fiction; 8. Coming-of-age stories; 9. Realistic fiction

9780060843106

LC 2007033270

Rainbow List, 2009; YALSA Popular Paperbacks for Young Adults, 2014.

Laura, a seventeen-year-old Cuban American girl, is thrown out of her house when her mother discovers she is a lesbian, but after trying to change her heart and hide from the truth, Laura finally comes to terms with who she is and learns to love and respect herself.

Using Spanish colloquialisms and slang, this debut author pulls off the tricky task of dialect in a manner that feels authentic. As Dole tackles a tough and important topic, her protagonist will win over a range of teen audiences, gay and straight. —*Publishers Weekly*

Doller, Trish

The **devil** you know. By Trish Doller. Bloomsbury, 2015 304 p. Grades: 10 11 12

1. Psychopaths; 2. Murderers; 3. Automobile travel; 4. Murder; 5. Camping; 6. Florida; 7. Thrillers and suspense

9781619634169; 9781619634176, ebook, US

LC 2014023032

Exhausted and rebellious after three years of working for her father and mothering her brother, eighteen-year-old Arcadia "Cadie" Wells joins two cousins who are camping their way through Florida, soon learning that one is a murderer.

Cadie, 18, lives in a tiny Floridian town with her widowed dad and kid brother. She's spent the last couple years pining for an adventure to take her away from her boring home. When two cute cousins, Matt and Noah, show up at a campfire party, Cadie is so strongly attracted to Noah that it thrills and scares her. The next day, the guys invite her and her old friend to join them on their road trip. Even though they're not much more than strangers, Cadie just can't say no. What the teen thought was going to be a sexy and temporary getaway slowly turns out to be a dangerous, terrifying, and deadly experience.... This dark thriller features a strong female lead and a heap of sexy; a must-buy for readers looking for a healthy dose of drama. —*School Library Journal*

Donnelly, Jennifer

A **northern** light. Jennifer Donnelly. Harcourt, Inc, 2003 389 p; Grades: 9 10 11 12

1. Brown, Grace; 2. Teenage girls; 3. Teenage authors; 4. Hotel workers; 5. Women — History; 6. Farm life — History; 7. Adirondack Mountains, New York; 8. New York (State); 9. 1900s (Decade); 10. Historical fiction; 11. Coming-of-age stories.

9780152167059

LC 2002005098

Amelia Bloomer List, 2004; Booklist Editors' Choice: Books for Youth, 2003; Carnegie Medal, 2003; Charlotte Award (New York), Young Adult, 2006; Los Angeles Times Book Prize for Young Adult Fiction, 2003; YALSA Popular Paperbacks for Young Adults, 2011; YALSA Best Books for Young Adults, 2004; School Library Journal Best Books, 2003; Michael L. Printz Honor Book, 2004.

In 1906, sixteen-year-old Mattie, determined to attend college and be a writer against the wishes of her father and fiance, takes a job at a summer inn where she discovers the truth about the death of a guest. Based on a true story.

Donnelly's characters ring true to life, and the meticulously described setting forms a vivid backdrop to this finely crafted story. An outstanding choice for historical-fiction fans. —*School Library Journal*

★ **Revolution**. Jennifer Donnelly. Delacorte Press, 2010 471, 9 p; Grades: 9 10 11 12

1. Louis XVII, of France, 1785-1795; 2. Teenage girl musicians; 3. Grief in teenage girls; 4. Teenage actors and actresses; 5. Emotional problems; 6. Family problems; 7. Paris, France; 8. France; 9. Historical fiction

9780385737630; 9781408801512, print, UK

Amelia Bloomer List, 2012; Indies' Choice Book Awards, Young Adult, 2011; YALSA Popular Paperbacks for Young Adults, 2013; YALSA Best Fiction for Young Adults, 2011; School Library Journal Best Books, 2010.

Andi Alpers is so full of grief, rage, and antidepressants that nothing matters to her anymore—nothing except playing guitar and taking care of her severely depressed mother. She's on the verge of being expelled from her exclusive prep school when her distant father forces Andi to accompany him on a trip to Paris. In Paris, Andi finds the diary of Alexandrine, a young woman who lived during the French Revolution. She becomes obsessed with Alexandrine's life and the historical mystery it could solve.

The ambitious story, narrated in Andi's grief-soaked, sardonic voice, will wholly capture patient readers with its sharply articulated, raw emotions and insights into science and art; ambition and love; history's ever-present influence; and music's immediate, astonishing power. —*Booklist*

Stepsister. Jennifer Donnelly. Scholastic Press, 2019 342 p. Grades: 8 9 10 11 12

1. Stepsisters; 2. Options, alternatives, choices; 3. Beauty; 4. Ugliness; 5. Determination (Personal quality); 6. France; 7. 18th century; 8. Fairy tale and folklore-inspired fiction; 9. Historical fantasy; 10. Fantasy fiction.
9781338268461; 9781338268485; 9781471407970, Paperback, UK
LC 2019003322

Isabelle is one of Cinderella's ugly stepsisters, who cut off their toes in an attempt to fit into the glass slipper; but there is more to her story than a maimed foot, for the Marquis de la Chance is about to offer her a choice and the opportunity to change her fate—there will be blood and danger, but also the possibility of redemption and triumph, and most of all the chance to find her true self.

Printz Honor Book author Donnelly offers up a stunningly focused story that rips into the heart of a familiar fairy tale. The gorgeous prose and the fairy tale themes have obvious appeal; but the real strengths here are the depth of character across the board; the examination of the cost of beauty in a world that reveres it; and Isabelle herself, a shattered but not unredeemable girl with a warrior's heart. —*Booklist*

These shallow graves. Jennifer Donnelly. Delacorte Press, 2015 256 p.
Grades: 7 8 9 10
1. Social classes; 2. Gender role; 3. Fathers — Death; 4. Murder investigation; 5. Teenage romance; 6. New York City; 7. 1890s; 8. Gilded Age (1865-1898); 9. Historical mysteries
9780385737654; 9781471405143, print, UK; 9781471405174, print, UK; 9780307982919, ebook, US
LC 2014047825
Amelia Bloomer Lists, 2016; YALSA Best Fiction for Young Adults, 2016.

A young woman in nineteenth-century New York City must struggle against gender and class boundaries when her father is found dead of a supposed suicide, and she believes there is more than meets the eye, so in order to uncover the truth she will have to decide how much she is willing to risk and lose.

Melodrama and intrigue drive this fast-paced thriller with a Wharton-esque setting and a naive young protagonist willing to be exposed to the shadier side of life—prostitutes, uncouth men, and abject poverty—on her way to solving a mystery and asserting her right to claim her future for herself. The author keeps the clues coming at a rate that allows readers to be one small step ahead of Jo as the story races to its surprising conclusion. Readers who love costume dramas will relish this one. —*Kirkus*

Donoghue, Emma
★ **Room:** a novel. By Emma Donoghue. Little, Brown and Co, 2010 Ix, 321 p;
Grades: 10 11 12 Adult
1. Antisocial personality disorders; 2. Captives; 3. Boys; 4. Mother and child; 5. Captivity; 6. Psychological fiction; 7. Literary fiction; 8. Canadian fiction; 9. Adult books for young adults.
9780316098335; 9780316268356; 9780316391344; 9781554688326; 9781443449618; 9781443449625; 9781509803156, Oz; 9780330519021, UK; 9781786821768, print, UK
LC 2010006983
ALA Notable Book, 2011; Alex Award, 2011; CBA Libris Award for Fiction Book of the Year, 2011; Commonwealth Writers' Prize, Caribbean and Canada: Best Book, 2011; Evergreen Award (Ontario), 2011; Goodreads Choice Award, 2010; Indies' Choice Book Awards, Adult Fiction, 2011; Kentucky Bluegrass Award for Grades 9-12, 2012; Library Journal Best Books, 2010; New York Times Notable Book, 2010; Rogers Writers' Trust Fiction Prize, 2010; Shortlisted for the Man Booker Prize, 2010; Shortlisted for The Orange Prize for

Fiction, 2011; Governor General's Literary Awards, English-language Fiction finalist.

A 5-year-old narrates a riveting story about his life growing up in a single room where his mother aims to protect him from the man who has held her prisoner for seven years since she was a teenager.

Though the story's chilling circumstances reflect the horrors endured by tabloid-famous abductees, Donoghue avoids all sensationalism. Instead, she gracefully distills what it means to be a mother and what it's like for a child whose entire world measures just 11 x 11. —*Entertainment Weekly*

Dowd, Siobhan
★ **Bog** child. Siobhan Dowd. David Fickling Books, 2008 321 p.
Grades: 8 9 10 11 12
1. Bog bodies; 2. Smuggling; 3. Eighteen-year-old men; 4. Decision-making (Ethics); 5. Extortion; 6. Northern Ireland; 7. 1980s; 8. Historical fiction.
9780385751698; 9780385751704
LC 2008002998
Carnegie Medal, 2009; YALSA Best Books for Young Adults, 2009; USBBY Outstanding International Book, 2009.

In 1981, the height of Ireland's "Troubles," eighteen-year-old Fergus is distracted from his upcoming A-level exams by his imprisoned brother's hunger strike, the stress of being a courier for Sinn Fein, and dreams of a murdered girl whose body he discovered in a bog.

Dowd raises questions about moral choices within a compelling plot that is full of surprises, powerfully bringing home the impact of political conflict on innocent bystanders. —*Publishers Weekly*

A **swift** pure cry. Siobhan Dowd. David Fickling Books, 2007 309 p;
Grades: 9 10 11 12
1. Fifteen-year-old girls; 2. Resilience (Personal quality); 3. Pregnant teenagers; 4. Resilience in teenage girls; 5. Teenage girl caregivers; 6. Ireland; 7. 1980s; 8. Realistic fiction
9780385751087; 9780385751094; 9781909531185, print, UK; 9780241331200, Paperback, UK
LC 2006014562
YALSA Best Books for Young Adults, 2008.

Coolbar, Ireland, is a village of secrets and Shell, caretaker to her younger brother and sister after the death of their mother and with the absence of their father, is not about to reveal hers until suspicion falls on the wrong person.

This book, with its serious tone and inclusion of social issues, will have appeal for American readers desiring weightier material, and teachers might find it useful in the classroom. —*Voice of Youth Advocates*

Downham, Jenny
★ **Before** I die. Jenny Downham. David Fickling Books, 2007 326 p.
Grades: 8 9 10 11 12
1. Teenagers with terminal illnesses; 2. Teenage girls with leukemia; 3. Lists; 4. Leukemia; 5. Families; 6. England; 7. Realistic fiction; 8. First person narratives
9780385751551; 9780385751582; 9781909531161, print, UK
LC 2007020284
Booklist Editors' Choice: Books for Youth, 2007; YALSA Popular Paperbacks for Young Adults, 2015; YALSA Best Books for Young Adults, 2008; Inky Awards (Australia): Silver Inky, 2008.

A terminally ill teenaged girl makes and carries out a list of things to do before she dies.

Downham holds nothing back in her wrenchingly and exceptionally vibrant story. —*Publishers Weekly*

★ **You** against me. By Jenny Downham. David Fickling Books, 2011 416 p.
Grades: 9 10 11 12
1. Rape; 2. Families of rape victims; 3. Revenge in teenage boys; 4. Revenge; 5. Teenage rape victims; 6. England; 7. Realistic fiction.
9780385751605; 9780385751612; 9780385676311; 9781849920483, UK

LC 2010038226

YALSA Best Fiction for Young Adults, 2012.

When Mikey's sister claims a boy assaulted her, his world begins to fall apart. When Ellie's brother is charged with the offense, her world begins to unravel. When Mikey and Ellie meet, two worlds collide.

Crisp, revealing dialogue, measured pacing and candid, unaffected prose round out this illuminating novel in which any reader can find someone to root for or relate to. —*Kirkus*

Dowswell, Paul
Auslander. Paul Dowswell. Bloomsbury, 2009 295 p.
Grades: 7 8 9 10
1. Boy orphans; 2. Escapes; 3. Courage; 4. Identity (Psychology); 5. World War II — Children; 6. Germany; 7. Second World War era (1939-1945); 8. 1940s; 9. Historical fiction; 10. Thrillers and suspense
9780747589099

The characters are rich and nuanced;...the action is swift and suspenseful; and the juxtaposition of wartime nobility and wartime cruelty is timeless. —*Horn Book Guide*

Doyle, Eugenie
According to Kit. Eugenie Doyle. Front Street, 2009 215 p;
Grades: 7 8 9 10
1. Ballet; 2. Farm life; 3. Mothers and daughters; 4. Fifteen-year old girls; 5. Teenage girls; 6. Vermont; 7. Realistic fiction.
9781590784747

LC 2009007032

As fifteen-year-old Kit does chores on her family's Vermont farm, she puzzles over her mother's apparent unhappiness, complains about being homeschooled after a minor incident at school, and strives to communicate just how important dance is to her.

Doyle's characters are complicated and authentic.... Kit's obsession with ballet...will ring true for all teens equally focused on their own talents. —*Booklist*

Doyle, Marissa
★ **Bewitching** season. Marissa Doyle. Henry Holt, 2008 352 p. (Leland sisters, 1)
Grades: 7 8 9 10
1. Seventeen-year-old girls; 2. Missing persons; 3. Governesses; 4. Seventeen-year-olds; 5. Teenagers; 6. London, England; 7. Great Britain; 8. Georgian era (1714-1837); 9. 1830s; 10. Historical fantasy
9780805082517

LC 2007027317

In 1837, as seventeen-year-old twins, Persephone and Penelope, are starting their first London Season they find that their beloved governess, who has taught them everything they know about magic, has disappeared.

Doyle takes as much care with characters...as with story details. This [is a] delightful mlange of genres. —*Booklist*

Doyle, Roddy
★ A **greyhound** of a girl. Roddy Doyle. Amulet Books, 2012 192 p.
Grades: 7 8 9 10 11 12

1. Girls and ghosts; 2. Grandmothers; 3. Death; 4. Last days; 5. Mothers and daughters; 6. Dublin, Ireland; 7. Ireland; 8. Fantasy fiction.
9781419701689; 9781407129334, print, UK

LC 2011042200

USBBY Outstanding International Book, 2013.

Mary O'Hara is a sharp and cheeky twelve-year-old Dublin schoolgirl who is bravely facing the fact that her beloved Gran is dying. But Gran can't let go of life, and when a mysterious young woman turns up in Mary's street with a message for her Gran, Mary gets pulled into an unlikely adventure.

Drake, Julia
★ The **last** true poets of the sea. Julia Drake. Disney-Hyperion, 2019 400 p.
Grades: 9 10 11 12
1. Suicidal behavior; 2. Love triangles; 3. Self-discovery in teenagers; 4. Shipwrecks; 5. Searching; 6. Maine; 7. Realistic fiction.
9781368048088

From a stunning new voice in YA literature comes an epic, utterly unforgettable contemporary novel about a lost shipwreck, a missing piece of family history, and weathering the storms of life.

Wry, quick-witted, and filled with deep grief and fathomless joy in equal measure, this is a triumphant debut. —*Booklist*

Loosely based on *Twelfth Night*.

Draper, Sharon M.
★ The **battle** of Jericho. Sharon M. Draper. Atheneum Books for Young Readers, 2003 304 p. (Jericho trilogy, 1)
Grades: 7 8 9 10
1. Initiations (into trades, societies, etc.); 2. Friends' death; 3. High school juniors; 4. Sixteen-year-old boys; 5. Cousins; 6. Ohio; 7. African American fiction
9780689842320

LC 2002008612

Coretta Scott King Honor Book for Authors, 2004.

A high school junior and his cousin suffer the ramifications of joining what seems to be a "reputable" school club.

This title is a compelling read that drives home important lessons about making choices. —*School Library Journal*

Sequel: *November blues*.

Copper sun. Sharon Draper. Atheneum Books for Young Readers, 2006 302 p;
Grades: 8 9 10 11 12
1. Teenage slaves; 2. Interracial friendship; 3. Sexual slavery; 4. African American teenage girls; 5. Fifteen-year-old girls; 6. South Carolina; 7. Florida; 8. Historical fiction; 9. African American fiction
9780689821813

LC 2005005540

Coretta Scott King Award, Author Category, 2007; Heartland Award, 2007; School Library Journal Best Books, 2006.

Two fifteen-year-old girls—one a slave and the other an indentured servant—escape their Carolina plantation and try to make their way to Fort Moses, Florida, a Spanish colony that gives sanctuary to slaves.

This action-packed, multifaceted, character-rich story describes the shocking realities of the slave trade and plantation life while portraying the perseverance, resourcefulness, and triumph of the human spirit. —*Booklist*

Includes bibliographical references (p. [304]-[306]).

★ **Fire** from the rock. Sharon M. Draper. Dutton Children's Books, 2007 176 p.

Grades: 6 7 8 9

1. African American teenage girls; 2. School integration; 3. Race relations; 4. African Americans; 5. African American teenagers; 6. Little Rock, Arkansas; 7. Arkansas; 8. 1950s
9780525477204

LC 2006102952

In 1957, Sylvia Patterson's life—that of a normal African American teenager—is disrupted by the impending integration of Little Rock's Central High when she is selected to be one of the first black students to attend the previously all white school. Includes author's note and related websites.

This historical fiction novel is a must have. It keeps the reader engaged with vivid depictions of a time that most young people can only imagine. —*Voice of Youth Advocates*

Just another hero. Sharon M. Draper. Atheneum Books for Young Readers, 2009 288 p. (Jericho trilogy, 3)
Grades: 7 8 9 10

1. School shootings; 2. African American teenagers; 3. High school seniors; 4. Violence in schools; 5. Schools; 6. Ohio; 7. Coming-of-age stories; 8. Realistic fiction; 9. Books for reluctant readers
9781416907008

LC 2008030961

YALSA Quick Picks for Reluctant Young Adult Readers, 2010.

As Kofi, Arielle, Dana, November, and Jericho face personal challenges during their last year of high school, a misunderstood student brings a gun to class and demands to be taken seriously.

The author presents a timeless theme in a well-crafted, highly readable story. —*Voice of Youth Advocates*

Sequel to: *November blues*.

★ **November** blues. Sharon Draper. Atheneum Books for Young Readers, 2007 320 p. (Jericho trilogy, 2)
Grades: 8 9 10 11 12

1. African American teenagers; 2. Pregnant teenagers; 3. Mothers and daughters; 4. Pregnancy; 5. High schools; 6. Ohio; 7. Realistic fiction; 8. Multiple perspectives; 9. African American fiction
9781416906988

LC 2006101343

Delaware Diamonds (book award), High School, 2009; Coretta Scott King Honor Book for Authors, 2008.

A teenaged boy's death in a hazing accident has lasting effects on his pregnant girlfriend and his guilt-ridden cousin, who gives up a promising music career to play football during his senior year in high school.

Urban teens often ask, "Where are the books about us, Miss" and with this novel Draper has...given them something meaty and meaningful to read. —*School Library Journal*

Sequel to: *The battle of Jericho*; Sequel: *Just another hero*.

★ **Tears** of a tiger. Atheneum, 1994 162 p. (Hazelwood High trilogy, 1)
Grades: 7 8 9 10

1. Fatal traffic accidents; 2. African American teenagers; 3. Grief in teenage boys; 4. Traffic accidents; 5. Drunk driving; 6. Realistic fiction; 7. African American fiction
9780689318788

LC 94010278 /AC

Virginia Readers' Choice Award for High School, 1997; John Steptoe Award for New Talent, Author Category, 1995; YALSA Popular Paperbacks for Young Adults, 2009; YALSA Best Books for Young Adults, 1996.

The death of high school basketball star Rob Washington in an automobile accident affects the lives of his close friend Andy, who was driving the car, and many others in the school.

The story emerges through newspaper articles, journal entries, homework assignments, letters, and conversations that give the book immediacy; the teenage conversational idiom is contemporary and well written. Andy's perceptions of the racism directed toward young black males...will be recognized by African American YAs. —*Booklist*

Duane, Diane

So you want to be a wizard. Diane Duane. Harcourt Brace, 1996 369 p. (Young wizards, 1)
Grades: 6 7 8 9 10

1. Teenage wizards; 2. Good and evil; 3. Bullying and bullies; 4. Transformations (Magic); 5. Teenage girls; 6. Fantasy fiction.
9780152012397

LC 95-33451

Thirteen-year-old Nita, tormented by a gang of bullies because she won't fight back, finds the help she needs in a library book on wizardry which guides her into another dimension.

Dubosarsky, Ursula

The **golden** day. Ursula Dubosarsky. Candlewick Press, 2013 149 p.
Grades: 7 8 9 10

1. Scandals; 2. Missing persons; 3. Caves; 4. Poets; 5. Women teachers; 6. Sydney, New South Wales; 7. Australia; 8. 1960s; 9. Australian fiction
9780763663995; 9781742374710, Australia

Children's Book Council of Australia: Notable Australian Children's Book; Booklist Editors' Choice: Books for Youth, 2013; YALSA Best Fiction for Young Adults, 2014.

Spare and well written, this slim novel covers the days following a teacher's disappearance during a class outing. Eleven girls must make their way back to school where they are determined to keep their teacher's rendezvous with the local park's gardener a secret. The book's chilling atmosphere and mature tone are best suited for older readers. —*Horn Book Guide*

Duey, Kathleen

Sacred scars. Kathleen Duey; illustrated by Sheila Rayyan. Atheneum Books for Young Readers, 2009 560 p. (Resurrection of magic, 2)
Grades: 7 8 9 10

1. Wizards; 2. Loyalty; 3. Schools; 4. Magic; 5. Magicians; 6. Fantasy fiction; 7. Multiple perspectives; 8. First person narratives.
9780689840951

LC 2008056044

In alternate chapters, Sadima works to free captive boys forced to copy documents in the caverns of Limori, and Hahp makes a pact with the remaining students of a wizards' academy in hopes that all will survive their training, as both learn valuable lessons about loyalty.

The text so successfully portrays Hahp's experience in this grueling, cold-blooded wizard academyisolation, starvation, abuse and constant, unsolvable puzzlesthat readers may absorb his strain, confusion and desolation themselves.... Absorbing and unwaveringly suspenseful. —*Kirkus*

Sequel to: *Skin hunger.*

Skin hunger. By Kathleen Duey. Atheneum Books for Young Readers, 2007 368 p. (Resurrection of magic, 1)
Grades: 7 8 9 10

1. Hunger; 2. Punishment; 3. Magic — Study and teaching; 4. Fathers — Death; 5. Magicians; 6. Fantasy fiction; 7. Multiple perspectives; 8. First person narratives.
9780689840937

LC 2006034819

National Book Award for Young People's Literature finalist, 2007.

In alternate chapters, Sadima travels from her farm home to the city and becomes assistant to a heartless man who is trying to restore knowledge of magic to the world, and a group of boys fights to survive in the academy that has resulted from his efforts.

This is a compelling new fantasy.... Duey sweeps readers up in the page-turning excitement. —*Horn Book Guide*

Sequel: *Sacred scars.*

Duncan, Lois

I know what you did last summer. Lois Duncan. Little, 1973 199 p.
Grades: 7 8 9 10 11 12
1. Revenge; 2. Accidents; 3. Hit-and-run drivers; 4. Traffic accidents; 5. Teenagers; 6. Horror; 7. Books to movies; 8. Classics.
9780316195461

LC 73008829

Four teenagers who have desperately tried to conceal their responsibility for a hit-and-run accident are pursued by a mystery person seeking revenge.

This book has vivid characterization, good balance, and the boding sense of impending danger that adds excitement to the best mystery stories. —*Bulletin of the Center for Children's Books*

★ **Killing** Mr. Griffin. Lois Duncan. Little, Brown, 1978 243 p.
Grades: 7 8 9 10
1. High school students; 2. Teachers; 3. Death; 4. Teenagers; 5. High school teachers; 6. Thrillers and suspense; 7. Multiple perspectives
9780316195492

LC 77027658

Massachusetts Children's Book Award, 1982.

A teenager casually suggests playing a cruel trick on the English teacher, but did he intend it to end with murder?

The author's skillful plotting builds layers of tension that draws readers into the eye of the conflict. The ending is nicely handled in a manner which provides relief without removing any of the chilling implications. —*School Library Journal*

Locked in time. Lois Duncan. Dell, 1986 210 p.
Grades: 7 8 9 10
1. Plantations; 2. Blended families; 3. Haunted houses; 4. Seventeen-year-old girls; 5. Teenage girls; 6. Thrillers and suspense
9780440949428

LC 85000023

South Carolina Book Award, Young Adult Books, 1988.

Nore arrives at her stepmother's Louisiana plantation to find her new family odd and an aura of evil and mystery about the place.

The writing style is smooth, the characters strongly developed, and the plot, which has excellent pace and momentum, is an adroit blending of fantasy and realism. —*Bulletin of the Center for Children's Books*

Stranger with my face. Lois Duncan. Dell, 1982 235 p.
Grades: 7 8 9 10
1. Seventeen-year-old girls; 2. Paranormal phenomena; 3. Astral projection; 4. Teenage girls; 5. Twins; 6. Supernatural mysteries
9780440983569

California Young Reader Medal, Young Adult, 1984; Massachusetts Children's Book Award, 1983; South Carolina Book Award, Young Adult Books, 1984; Young Hoosier Book Award, Middle Books, 1986.

A seventeen-year-old senses she is being spied on and probably impersonated, but when she discovers what actually is occurring, it is more unbelievable than she ever imagined.

The ghostly Lia is deliciously evil; the idea of astral projection—Lia's method of travel—is novel; the island setting is vivid; and the relationships among the young people are realistic in the smoothly written supernatural tale. —*Horn Book Guide*

Dunker, Kristina

Summer storm. Kristina Dunker; translated by Margot Bettauer Dembo. AmazonCrossing, 2011 142 p;
Grades: 10 11 12
1. Missing persons; 2. Teenagers; 3. Blame; 4. Friendship; 5. Secrets; 6. Thrillers and suspense; 7. Translations
9781611090307

LC Bl2011021517

When ominous clouds begin to form on the horizon, Annie and her friends flee from the lake where they were spending the day, only to discover that Annie's cousin Gina has gone missing, and as the search for her wears on, accusations begin to fly.

Durham, David Anthony

★ **Gabriel's** story. David Anthony Durham. Doubleday, 2001 291 p;
Grades: 11 12 Adult
1. African American families; 2. African American cowboys; 3. Pioneer men; 4. Young men; 5. Homesteaders; 6. Kansas; 7. Westerns; 8. Coming-of-age stories; 9. African American fiction; 10. Adult books for young adults.
9780385498142, hardback, US; 9780385720335, paperback, US; 9780307425980, ebook, US

LC 25291

Alex Award, 2002; BCALA Literary Award for First Novelist, 2002; Booklist Editors' Choice, 2001; Hurston/Wright Legacy Award: Debut Fiction, 2002; New York Times Notable Book, 2001.

Reluctantly moving with his mother and younger brother from the urban East to join his stepfather, a Kansas homesteader, Gabriel hates their primitive, harsh new life and runs away to seek adventure as a cowboy, in a coming-of-age story of a young black man in the American West of the 1870s.

The moral gravity of Durham's narrative is offset by his attentiveness to the primacy of nature in the Western landscape. —*The New Yorker*

Durst, Sarah Beth

The **queen** of blood. Sarah Beth Durst. Harper Voyager, 2016 353 p. (Queens of Renthia, 1)
Grades: 11 12 Adult
1. Women students; 2. Warriors; 3. Quests; 4. Women rulers; 5. Spirits; 6. Epic fantasy; 7. Adult books for young adults.
9780062413345; 9780062474094; 9780062413369, ebook, US

LC 2015044319

Alex Award, 2017.

Daleina, a young student, joins forces with a disgraced warrior, Ven, to embark on an epic and treacherous quest to save their realm from the spirits that want to rid it of all human life.

In addition to a solid cast of characters and great political intrigue, Durst delivers some fascinating worldbuilding, and the spirits are malevolent, cunning, wild, and mysterious antagonists. —*Publishers Weekly*

Duyvis, Corinne

★ **Otherbound.** By Corinne Duyvis. Amulet Books, 2014 368 pages
Grades: 9 10 11 12
1. Fugitives; 2. People who are mute; 3. Healing; 4. Curses; 5. Princesses; 6. Arizona; 7. Fantasy fiction.
9781419709289

LC 2013029536

A seventeen-year-old boy finds that every time he closes his eyes, he is drawn into the body of a mute servant girl from another world—a world that is growing increasingly more dangerous, and where many things are not as they seem.

Whenever seventeen-year-old Nolan closes his eyes, he's transported into the body of Amara, a mute slave girl on an alien world who acts as decoy against would-be assassins of a princess. After years of being a helpless witness, Nolan suddenly becomes a player in the action. Duyvis keeps tensions high in both Nolan's Arizona and Amara's Dunelands. A humdinger of an adventure. —*Horn Book Guide*

Easton, T. S.

Boys don't knit. T.S. Easton. Feiwel & Friends, 2015 272 p.
Grades: 9 10 11 12
1. Knitting; 2. Contests; 3. Diaries; 4. Stealing; 5. Teenage romance; 6. England; 7. Humorous stories; 8. Diary novels; 9. Books for reluctant readers
9781250053312
YALSA Quick Picks for Reluctant Young Adult Readers, 2016.

Despite some unnecessary Americanization of the text, this wonderfully funny novel is infused with British slang, including dozens of terms easily understood in context. Wacky characters, a farcical plot and a fledgling romance are all part of the fun in this novel that will appeal to fans of *Angus, Thongs,* and *Full-Frontal Snogging.* —*Kirkus*

Edwardson, Debby Dahl

★ **My** name is not easy. Debby Dahl Edwardson. Marshall Cavendish, 2011 248 p.
Grades: 7 8 9 10
1. Inupiat; 2. Boarding schools; 3. Catholic schools; 4. Prejudice; 5. Homesickness; 6. Alaska; 7. 1960s; 8. Historical fiction; 9. Multiple perspectives
9780761459804
YALSA Best Fiction for Young Adults, 2012; Notable Books for a Global Society, 2012; School Library Journal Best Books, 2011; National Book Award for Young People's Literature finalist, 2011.

Alaskans Luke, Chickie, Sonny, Donna, and Amiq relate their experiences in the early 1960s when they are forced to attend a Catholic boarding school where, despite different tribal affiliations, they come to find a sort of family and home.

Edwardson's skillful use of dialogue and her descriptions of rural Alaska as well as boarding-school life invoke a strong sense of empathy and compassion in readers...Edwardson is to be applauded for her depth of research and her ability to portray all sides of the equation in a fair and balanced manner while still creating a very enjoyable read. —*School Library Journal*

Efaw, Amy

After. Amy Efaw. Viking, 2009 350 p.
Grades: 7 8 9 10
1. Pregnant teenagers; 2. Infanticide; 3. Denial (Psychology); 4. Attempted murder; 5. Trials (Attempted murder); 6. Realistic fiction; 7. Books for reluctant readers
9780670011834
LC Bl2009016839
YALSA Popular Paperbacks for Young Adults, 2016; YALSA Quick Picks for Reluctant Young Adult Readers, 2010; YALSA Best Books for Young Adults, 2010.

In complete denial that she is pregnant, straight-A student and star athlete Devon Davenport leaves her baby in the trash to die, and after the baby is discovered, Devon is accused of attempted murder.

Authentic dialogue and pithy writing allow teens to feel every prick of panic, embarrassment and fear. —*Kirkus*

Battle dress. Amy Efaw. HarperCollins, 2000 291 p.
Grades: 7 8 9 10
1. Military cadets; 2. Military education; 3. Self-confidence in teenage girls; 4. Self-confidence; 5. Self-esteem; 6. New York (State); 7. Realistic fiction; 8. Coming-of-age stories.
9780060279431; 9780060284114
LC 99034516
As a newly arrived freshman at West Point, seventeen-year-old Andi finds herself gaining both confidence and self esteem as she struggles to get through the grueling six weeks of new cadet training known as the Beast.

This book by a West Point graduate is a gripping, hard-to-put-down look at a young woman's struggle to succeed in a traditionally all-male environment. —*Voice of Youth Advocates*

Egan, Catherine

Julia defiant. Catherine Egan. Alfred A. Knopf, 2017 445 p. (Witch's child trilogy, 2)
Grades: 9 10 11 12
1. Assassins; 2. Witchcraft; 3. Superhuman abilities; 4. Magic; 5. Sixteen-year-old girls; 6. Fantasy fiction; 7. Canadian fiction
9780553533354; 9780385684682; 9780385684705, Paperback, Canada
A follow-up to *Julia Vanishes* finds Julia and her motley companions desperately fleeing a band of assassins while struggling to protect magic-bound Theo from power-hungry Casimir and navigating Julia's increasingly monstrous powers.

Complex and beautifully imagined, Julia's saga continues to thrill. —*Booklist*

★ **Julia** vanishes. Catherine Egan. Alfred A Knopf, 2016 384 p. (Witch's child trilogy, 1)
Grades: 9 10 11 12
1. Teenage spies; 2. Swindlers and swindling; 3. Witchcraft; 4. Occultism; 5. Secrets; 6. Fantasy fiction; 7. Canadian fiction
9780553524840; 9780385684651; 9780385684675
Julia, who has the unusual ability to be unseen, makes a living as a spy and a thief. For her latest job she is posing as a housemaid in the grand house of Mrs. Och where an odd assortment of characters live and work. And when a killer leaves a trail of bodies across the frozen city, she begins to suspect a frightening connection to the houseguests.

A beautifully rendered world and an exquisite sense of timing ensure a page-turning experience. —*Publishers Weekly*

Elkeles, Simone

Rules of attraction. By Simone Elkeles. Walker & Co, 2010 336 p. (Perfect chemistry series, 2)
Grades: 9 10 11 12
1. Hispanic American teenage boys; 2. Gangs; 3. Drug traffic; 4. Sexuality; 5. Teenage romance; 6. Colorado; 7. Contemporary romances; 8. Multicultural romances; 9. Books for reluctant readers
9780802720856
LC 2009049235
YALSA Quick Picks for Reluctant Young Adult Readers, 2011.

Living on the University of Colorado-Boulder campus with his older brother Alex, a college student and ex-gang member, high school senior Carlos is not ready to give up his wild ways until he meets a shy classmate named Kiara and becomes unwillingly involved in a drug ring.

The author delivers a steamy page-turner bound to make teens swoon. —*School Library Journal*

Elliott, David

★ **Bull**. By David Elliott. Houghton Mifflin Harcourt, 2017 200 p.
Grades: 9 10 11 12

1. Labyrinths; 2. Rulers; 3. Revenge; 4. Theseus (Greek mythology); 5. Minotaur (Greek mythology); 6. Novels in verse; 7. First person narratives; 8. Mythological fiction.
9780544610606

LC 2016014200

Booklist Editors' Choice: Books for Youth, 2017; YALSA Best Fiction for Young Adults, 2018.

A modern twist on the Theseus and Minotaur myth, told in verse.

Effective both for classrooms and pleasure reading, this modernization brings new relevancy to an old story. —*Booklist*

Voices: the final hours of Joan of Arc. By David Elliott. 2019 208 pages
Grades: 7 8 9 10

1. Joan of Arc, 1412-1431; 2. Women saints; 3. Christian teenage girl martyrs; 4. Faith in women; 5. Courage in women; 6. Leadership in women; 7. France; 8. 15th century; 9. Novels in verse; 10. Historical fiction; 11. Biographical fiction
9781328987594

LC 2018025855

Claudia Lewis Award, 2020.

A novel in verse explores how Joan of Arc changed the course of history and examines such timely issues as gender, misogyny, and the peril of speaking truth to power.

An elegant, spirited introduction to classical poetry and to a woman fighting not just for a cause but for a place in a world that undervalued her voice. —*Booklist*

Elliott, Laura

Hamilton and Peggy!: a revolutionary friendship. L. M. Elliott. Katherine Tegen Books, 2018 320 p.
Grades: 7 8 9 10 11 12

1. Hamilton, Alexander, 1757-1804; 2. American Revolu- tion, 1775-1783; 3. Van Rensselaer, Margarita, 1758-1801; 4. Rich families; 5. Friendship; 6. Men/women relations; 7. New York (State); 8. United States; 9. Revolutionary America (1775-1783); 10. Historical fiction
9780062671301; 9780062671318

Peggy Schuyler has always felt like she's existed in the shadows of her beloved sisters: the fiery, intelligent Angelica and beautiful, sweet Eliza. But it's in the throes of a chaotic war that Peggy finds herself a central figure amid Loyalists and Patriots, spies and traitors, friends and family.

But where the Broadway show shunted Peggy to the side, here she is showcased as a strong protagonist who is confident in the best possible ways. Her memorable story will keep readers interested from start to finish, even if they already know how it will end. —*Booklist*

Elliott, Patricia

The **traitor's** smile. Patricia Elliott. Holiday House, 2011 432 p. (Pimpernelles, 2)
Grades: 7 8 9 10

1. Aristocracy; 2. French Revolution, 1789-1799; 3. Spies; 4. Revolutions; 5. Politicians; 6. France; 7. Great Britain; 8. Georgian era (1714-1837); 9. 1790s; 10. Historical fiction.
9780823423613

LC 2011018988

In 1793, Eugenie de Boncoeur arrives at the home of her English uncle and cousin, but the French Revolution has pursued her in the form of Guy Deschamps, who is determined to bring her back to Paris to marry the Pale Assassin.

Ellis, Ann Dee

★ **This** is what I did. By Ann Dee Ellis. Little, Brown, 2007 176 p.
Grades: 6 7 8 9

1. Eighth-graders; 2. Teenage boys; 3. Teenagers; 4. New students; 5. Misfits (Persons); 6. Realistic fiction
9780316013635

LC 2006001388

YALSA Best Books for Young Adults, 2008.

Bullied because of an incident in his past, eighth-grader Logan is unhappy at his new school and has difficulty relating to others until he meets a quirky girl and a counselor who believe in him.

Part staccato prose, part transcript, this haunting first novel will grip readers right from the start.... A particularly attractive book design incorporates small drawings between each segment of text. —*Publishers Weekly*

Ellis, Deborah

My name is Parvana. Deborah Ellis. Groundwood Books, 2012 201 p. : Map (Breadwinner series, 4)
Grades: 5 6 7 8

1. Imprisonment; 2. Military bases; 3. Separated friends, relatives, etc; 4. Teenage girls; 5. Schools; 6. Afghanistan; 7. Canadian fiction
9781554982974; 9781743312988, Australia; 9781459664548; 9780192734044, print, UK

School Library Journal Best Books, 2012; USBBY Outstanding International Book, 2013.

Parvana is imprisoned and interrogated by American soldiers when she is found wandering around alone in a bombed-out school in Afghanistan.

Groundwood Books/House of Anansi Press.

★ **No** safe place. Deborah Ellis. Berkeley, Calif. : 2010 224 p.
Grades: 9 10 11 12

1. Teenage immigrants; 2. Stowaways; 3. Drug smuggling; 4. Heroin; 5. Boats; 6. France; 7. England; 8. Realistic fiction; 9. Canadian fiction.
9780888999733

OLA Best Bets, 2010.

This is the story of three teenagers—all orphans, all desperate to escape horrors in their home countries—whose paths converge on board a boat crossing the English Channel. Abdul is running from war-torn Baghdad, Iraq; Rosalia, a Romani girl, was sold into sexual slavery but escaped; and Cheslav is fleeing from the Russian military. All of them hope to start new lives in England...but they'll have to make it there alive first.

Ellis deftly uses flashbacks to fill in the backstories of each character, reminding readers of how they can never really know where people are coming from emotionally. Her writing is highly accessible, and yet understated. Orphans of the world and victims of human trafficking need all the press they can get, and this book does a great job of introducing the topic and allowing young people to see beyond the headlines of Another illegal accidentally dies in Chunnel. —*School Library Journal*

Ellis, Kat

Harrow Lake. Kat Ellis. Dial Books for Young Readers, 2020 304 p.
Grades: 9 10 11 12

1. Father-separated teenage girls; 2. Small towns; 3. Horror films; 4. Monsters; 5. Horror; 6. Mysteries.
9781984814531, HRD, US; 9781984814548, ebook, US; 9780241397046, Paperback, UK

LC 2019038738

Lola Nox is sent to live with her estranged maternal grandmother in the mining town where her horror movie director father's most iconic film was set, when paranormal incidents and whispers of a century-old monster make her question if she'll make it out alive.

A satisfying quasi-supernatural thriller. —*Kirkus*

Ellsworth, Loretta

★ **Unforgettable**. Loretta Ellsworth. Walker Books for Young Readers, 2011 256 p.
Grades: 6 7 8 9
1. Memory; 2. Synesthesia; 3. Crushes in teenage boys; 4. Teenage boy/girl relations; 5. High schools; 6. Minnesota; 7. Realistic fiction.
9780802723055

LC 2010049590

When Baxter Green was three years old he developed a condition that causes him to remember absolutely everything, and now that he is fifteen, he and his mother have moved to Minnesota to escape her criminal boyfriend and, Baxter hopes, to reconnect with a girl he has been thinking about since kindergarten.

A lot is going here—an exploration of of synesthesia and memory, a crime story, an environmental drama, family relationships and a sweet, earnest love story.... But everything works. —*Kirkus*

Elston, Ashley

The **lying** woods. Ashley Elston. 2018 336 p.
Grades: 9 10 11 12
1. Missing men; 2. Life change events; 3. Father-separated teenage boys; 4. Family secrets; 5. Family problems; 6. Louisiana; 7. Mysteries; 8. Parallel narratives; 9. Coming-of-age stories.
9781368014786

LC 2017058435

Owen Foster is pulled from his elite New Orleans boarding school when his father's assets are seized and, back in his small town, begins to piece together his father's past despite mounting danger.

The **rules** for disappearing. Ashley Elston. Hyperion, 2013 320 p.
Grades: 7 8 9 10 11 12
1. Witnesses — Protection; 2. Moving, Household; 3. Teenage romance; 4. New identities; 5. Federal Witness Protection Program; 6. Louisiana; 7. Natchitoches, Louisiana; 8. Realistic fiction; 9. Mysteries; 10. First person narratives
9781423168973

LC 2012035122

High school student "Meg" has changed identities so often that she hardly knows who she is anymore, and her family is falling apart, but she knows that two of the rules of witness protection are be forgettable and do not make friends—but in her new home in Louisiana a boy named Ethan is making that difficult.

The fresh first-person narration serves the story well, providing grounding in reality as events spin out of control. Though the plot may seem a bit far-fetched at times, the realistic setting, believable romance and spunky protagonist will make this one worth the trip for mystery and romance fans. —*Kirkus*

Sequel: *The Rules for Breaking*.

Emond, Stephen

Bright lights, dark nights. Stephen Emond. Roaring Brook Press, 2015 320 p.
Grades: 7 8 9 10
1. Children of police; 2. Race relations; 3. Interracial dating; 4. Scandals; 5. Racial profiling; 6. Realistic fiction; 7. Illustrated books
9781626722064; 9781626722071, ebook, US

LC 2014047413

Walter Wilcox's first love, Naomi, happens to be African American, so when Walter's policeman father is caught in a racial profiling scandal, the teens' bond and mutual love of the Foo Fighters may not be enough to keep them together through the pressures they face at school, at home, and online.

Readers coming to this story for romance may feel shortchanged, as the relationship here is more true-to-life and awkward than swooningly romantic, but thats what sets Emonds book apart. A real slice of contemporary teenage life thats painfully honest about the below-the-surface racism in todays America. —*Booklist*

Happyface. By Stephen Emond. Little, Brown and Co, 2010 307 p.
Grades: 7 8 9 10
1. Children of divorced parents; 2. Crushes in teenage boys; 3. Emotional problems of teenage boys; 4. Emotional problems; 5. Family problems; 6. Realistic fiction; 7. Diary novels; 8. First person narratives.
9780316041003

LC 2008047386

After going through traumatic times, a troubled, socially awkward teenager moves to a new school where he tries to reinvent himself.

The illustrations range from comics to more fleshed-out drawings. Just like Happyface's writing, they can be whimsical, thoughtful, boyishly sarcastic, off-the-cuff, or achingly beautiful. —*Publishers Weekly*

Winter town. By Stephen Emond. Little, Brown, 2011 336 p.
Grades: 7 8 9
1. Cartoonists; 2. Teenage boy/girl relations; 3. Self-fulfillment in teenagers; 4. Self-fulfillment; 5. Best friends; 6. Realistic fiction; 7. Multiple perspectives
9780316133326

LC 2011012966

Evan and Lucy, childhood best friends who grew apart after years of seeing one another only during Christmas break, begin a romance at age seventeen but his choice to mindlessly follow his father's plans for an Ivy League education rather than becoming the cartoonist he longs to be, and her more destructive choices in the wake of family problems, pull them apart.

This is a remarkable illustrated work of contemporary fiction.... Interspersed throughout are both realistic illustrations and drawings of a comic strip being created by Evan and Lucy; these black-and-white, almost chibi-style panels form an effective parallel with the plot and appeal mightily on their own. Compelling, honest and truethis musing about art and self-discovery, replete with pitch-perfect dialogue, will have wide appeal. —*Kirkus*

Engdahl, Sylvia

★ **Enchantress** from the stars. Sylvia Engdahl; drawings by Rodney Shackell. Collier Books, 1989 275 p.
Grades: 7 8 9 10 11 12
1. Space and time; 2. Responsibility; 3. Options, alternatives, choices; 4. Ethics; 5. Alien invasions; 6. Science fiction; 7. Classics.
9780020430315; 9780142500378

LC 8831743

Phoenix Award, 1990; Newbery Honor Book, 1971.

Three civilizations from different planets in widely varying stages of development clash in what could be either a mutually disastrous or beneficial encounter.

Emphasis is on the intricate pattern of events rather than on characterization, and readers will find fascinating symbolismand philosophical parallels to what they may have observed or thought. The book is completely absorbing and should have a wider appeal than much science fiction. —*Horn Book Guide*

Engle, Margarita
★ The **firefly** letters: a suffragette's journey to Cuba. Margarita Engle. Henry Holt and Co, 2010 160 p.
Grades: 7 8 9 10 11 12
1. Bremer, Fredrika; 2. Suffragists; 3. Teenage slaves; 4. Women — Suffrage; 5. Voyages and travels; 6. Slavery; 7. Cuba; 8. 1850s; 9. Novels in verse
9780805090826

LC 2009023445

ALA Notable Children's Book, 2011; Amelia Bloomer List, 2011; Notable Books for a Global Society, 2011; Pura Belpre Honor Book for Narrative, 2011.

This engaging title documents 50-year-old Swedish suffragette and novelist Fredrika Bremer's three-month travels around Cuba in 1851. Based in the home of a wealthy sugar planter, Bremer journeys around the country with her host's teenaged slave Cecilia, who longs for her mother and home in the Congo. Elena, the planter's privileged 12-year-old daughter, begins to accompany them on their trips into the countryside.... Using elegant free verse and alternating among each character's point of view, Engle offers powerful glimpses into Cuban life at that time. Along the way, she comments on slavery, the rights of women, and the stark contrast between Cuba's rich and poor. —*School Library Journal*

Hurricane dancers: the first Caribbean pirate shipwreck. Margarita Engle. Henry Holt & Co, 2011 154 p.
Grades: 6 7 8 9 10
1. Pirates; 2. Hurricanes; 3. Identity (Psychology); 4. Slaves; 5. Slavery; 6. Caribbean area; 7. 16th century; 8. First person narratives; 9. Novels in verse; 10. Historical fiction.
9780805092400
Americas Book Award for Children's and Young Adult Literature, 2012; Booklist Editors' Choice: Books for Youth, 2011; Pura Belpre Honor Book for Narrative, 2012.

This is an accomplished historical novel in verse set in the Caribbean.... The son of a Tano Indian mother and a Spanish father, [Quebrado] is taken in 1510 from his village on the island that is present-day Cuba and enslaved on a pirate's ship, where a brutal conquistador...is held captive for ransom. When a hurricane destroys the boat, Quebrado is pulled from the water by a fisherman, Narid, whose village welcomes him, but escape from the past proves nearly impossible.... Engle fictionalizes historical fact in a powerful, original story.... Engle distills the emotion in each episode with potent rhythms, sounds, and original, unforgettable imagery. —*Booklist*
Includes bibliographical references.

★ The **lightning** dreamer: Cuba's greatest abolitionist. Margarita Engle. Houghton Mifflin Harcourt, 2013 176 p.
Grades: 6 7 8 9 10
1. Gomez de Avellaneda y Arteaga, Gertrudis, 1814-1873; 2. Teenage girls; 3. Abolitionists; 4. Women; 5. Slavery; 6. Anti-slavery movements; 7. Cuba; 8. 19th century; 9. Historical fiction; 10. Biographical fiction; 11. Novels in verse
9780547807430
ALA Notable Children's Book, 2014; Amelia Bloomer List, 2014; Notable Books for a Global Society, 2014; YALSA Best Fiction for Young Adults, 2014; Pura Belpre Honor Book for Narrative, 2014.

A historical novel in verse by the Newbery Honor-winning author of The Surrender Tree presents the story of poet, abolitionist and women's rights pioneer Gertrudis Gomez de Avellaneda, who bravely resisted an arranged marriage at the age of 14 and was ultimately courageous enough to use her passionate, metaphorical verses to protest slavery in the dangerous political environment of 19th-century Cuba.

Engle's richly evocative verses conjure up a time when women, like slaves, were regarded as property to be sold into loveless marriages. This is the context for a splendid novel that celebrates one brave woman who rejected a constrained existence with enduring words that continue to sing of freedom. —*Booklist*

★ **Silver** people: voices from the Panama Canal. Margarita Engle. 2014 260 p.
Grades: 5 6 7 8
1. Teenage abuse victims; 2. Racism; 3. Discrimination; 4. Segregation; 5. Fourteen-year-old boys; 6. Panama Canal; 7. 1900s (Decade); 8. Novels in verse; 9. Multiple perspectives.
9780544109414

LC 2013037485

Americas Book Award for Children's and Young Adult Literature, 2015; Notable Books for a Global Society, 2015.

Fourteen-year-old Mateo and other Caribbean islanders face discrimination, segregation, and harsh working conditions when American recruiters lure them to the Panamanian rain forest in 1906 to build the great canal.

In melodic verses, Engle offers the voices of the dark-skinned workers (known as the 'silver people'), whose backbreaking labor helped build the Panama Canal, along with the perspective of a local girl. Interspersed are occasional echoes from flora and fauna as well as cameo appearances by historical figures. Together, they provide an illuminating picture of the project's ecological sacrifices and human costs. —*Horn Book Guide*
Includes bibliographical references.

Eshbaugh, Julie
Ivory and bone. Julie Eshbaugh... 2016 376 pages (Ivory and bone, 1)
Grades: 7 8 9 10
1. Ice age (Geology); 2. Prehistoric humans; 3. Clans; 4. Survival; 5. Love triangles; 6. Historical fantasy; 7. Classics-inspired fiction
9780062399250

LC 2015958594

Eshbaugh packs her debut with a classic love triangle, feuding clans, a well-drawn prehistoric setting, and a handful of fan fiction elements that will appeal to teens. —*School Library Journal*

Obsidian and stars. Julie Eshbaugh. 2017 359 pages (Ivory and bone, 2)
Grades: 7 8 9 10
1. Ice age (Geology); 2. Prehistoric humans; 3. Clans; 4. Runaways; 5. Survival; 6. Historical fantasy; 7. Classics-inspired fiction; 8. First person narratives
9780062399281

LC 2016961162

While working to secure her future with Kol, Mya finds herself facing an impossible choice when she learns her brother has arranged an unfavorable marriage

Eves, Rosalyn
Blood rose rebellion. Rosalyn Eves. Alfred A. Knopf, 2017 408 p. (Blood rose rebellion, 1)
Grades: 7 8 9 10
1. Nobility; 2. Social classes; 3. Revolutions; 4. Intrigue; 5. Magic; 6. Hungary; 7. Victorian era (1837-1901); 8. 1840s; 9. Historical fantasy
9781101935996
Accidentally breaking her sister's debutante spell, a 16-year-old non-magical girl from a powerful magic-wielding family is exiled to her father's native home in Hungary, where she confronts a difficult choice upon discovering her own latent power.

Intrigue, romance, and revolution, with enough unanswered questions that fans will cross fingers for a sequel. —*Kirkus*

Ewing, Eve L.
Electric arches. Eve L. Ewing. Haymarket Books, 2017 94 p.
Grades: 11 12 Adult
1. Identity (Psychology); 2. Gender identity; 3. Growing up; 4. Race (Social sciences); 5. Art and politics; 6. United States; 7. Literary fiction; 8. Experimental fiction; 9. Coming-of-age stories; 10. Adult books for young adults.
9781608468560
Alex Award, 2018.
Original meditations on race, gender, identity, and the joy and pain of growing up, from a distinctive new voice.

Extence, Gavin
The **universe** versus Alex Woods. Gavin Extence. Orbit, 2013 320 p.
Grades: 9 10 11 12 Adult
1. Misfits (Persons); 2. Teenage boys; 3. Intergenerational friendship; 4. Books and reading; 5. Widowers; 6. Coming-of-age stories; 7. Mainstream fiction; 8. Adult books for young adults.
9780316246576; 9780316246590; 9781444764611, UK; 9781444765885, print, UK; 9781444765892, print, UK
Alex Award, 2014; School Library Journal Best Books: Best Adult Books 4 Teens, 2013.
Alex Woods was struck by a meteorite when he was ten years old, leaving scars that marked him for an extraordinary life. The son of a fortune teller, bookish, and an easy target for bullies, he hasn't had the most conventional childhood. When he meets curmudgeonly widower Mr. Peterson, he finds an unlikely friend. Someone who teaches him that that you only get one shot at life. That you have to make it count. So when, aged seventeen, Alex is stopped at Dover customs with 113 grams of marijuana, an urn full of ashes on the passenger seat, and an entire nation in uproar, he's fairly sure he's done the right thing.
Most teens think the universe is against them at some point. Seventeen-year-old Alex Woods has plenty of evidence for his case: a tarot-reading witch for a mother, his father a one-night Solstice stand long since forgotten, a chunk of meteorite crashing through the roof and smashing into him, the onset of epileptic seizures, and school bullies eager to target him...A bittersweet, cross-audience charmer, this debut novel will appeal to guys, YA readers, and Vonnegut and coming-of-age fiction fans. —*Library Journal*
A tale of unlikely friendship

Falkner, Brian
The **project**. Brian Falkner. Random House Children's Books, 2011 288 p.
Grades: 6 7 8 9 10
1. Books; 2. Time machines; 3. Terrorists; 4. Time travel (Past); 5. Nazis; 6. Thrillers and suspense; 7. New Zealand fiction
9780375869457
Storylines (New Zealand) Notable Book.
After discovering a terrible secret hidden in the most boring book in the world, Iowa fifteen-year-olds Luke and Tommy find out that members of a secret Nazi organization intend to use this information to rewrite history.
The wacky unbelievability of this story in no way detracts from its enjoyment. It reads like an action movie, with plenty of chases, explosions, and by-a-hair escapes. —*School Library Journal*

Falls, Kat
Inhuman. Kat Falls. Scholastic Press, 2013 384 pages (Fetch, 1)
Grades: 7 8 9 10
1. Near future; 2. Dystopias; 3. Virus diseases; 4. Quarantine; 5. Survival; 6. Science fiction.
9780545370998
Years ago, the U.S. was bisected by a pandemic (spread by biting) that causes humans to mutate into feral human-animal hybrids. When pampered teenager Lane is blackmailed into the Feral Zone, she joins the search for a cure and discovers the gray area between human and feral. While Lane and her love triangle are bland, the zombie-apocalypse-meets-wereanimals-gone-wild setup captures the imagination. —*Horn Book Guide*

Fantaskey, Beth
Buzz kill. By Beth Fantaskey. Houghton Mifflin Harcourt, 2014 368 pages
Grades: 8 9 10 11 12
1. Teenage detectives; 2. Murder; 3. Teenage boy/girl relations; 4. Teenage journalists; 5. Quarterbacks (Football); 6. Mysteries; 7. Books for reluctant readers
9780547393100
LC 2013011423
YALSA Quick Picks for Reluctant Young Adult Readers, 2015.
Seventeen-year-old Millie joins forces with her classmate, gorgeous but mysterious Chase Colton, to try to uncover who murdered head football coach "Hollerin' Hank" Killdare—and why.
When the head football coach is killed, seventeen-year-old Millie, a school reporter obsessed with Nancy Drew, sets out to learn the truth and clear her assistant-coach father of any suspicion. She gets some unexpected help from dreamy quarterback Chase, who's hiding some secrets. This entertaining sleuth story is a good choice for teens now graduated from books featuring Millie's literary hero. —*Horn Book Guide*

Farish, Terry
★ The **good** braider: a novel. Terry Farish. Marshall Cavendish, 2012 221 p. : Map
Grades: 9 10 11 12
1. Refugees; 2. Teenage rape victims; 3. Civil war; 4. Immigrants; 5. Sudanese Americans; 6. Sudan; 7. Portland, Maine; 8. Realistic fiction.
9780761462675; 9781477816288
LC 2011033659
Lupine Award (Maine) for Juvenile/Young Adult, 2012; School Library Journal Best Books, 2012; YALSA Best Fiction for Young Adults, 2013; YALSA Popular Paperbacks for Young Adults, 2017.
Follows Viola as she survives brutality in war-torn Sudan, makes a perilous journey, lives as a refugee in Egypt, and finally reaches Portland, Maine, where her quest for freedom and security is hampered by memories of past horrors and the traditions hermother and other Sudanese adults hold dear. Includes historical facts and a map of Sudan.

Farizan, Sara
Here to stay. Sara Farizan. Algonquin Young Readers, 2018 272 p.
Grades: 9 10 11 12
1. Arab Americans; 2. High school students; 3. Cyberbullying; 4. Bullying and bullies; 5. Basketball; 6. Boston, Massachusetts; 7. Realistic fiction; 8. Basketball stories; 9. Books for reluctant readers
9781616207007; 9781616209858
LC 2018008382
YALSA Quick Picks for Reluctant Young Adult Readers, 2020.
When a cyberbully sends the entire high school a picture of basketball hero Bijan Majidi, photo-shopped to look like a terrorist, the school administration promises to find and punish the culprit, but Bijan just wants to pretend the incident never happened and move on.

★ **If** you could be mine: a novel. Sara Farizan. Algonquin, 2013 256 p.
Grades: 8 9 10 11 12
1. Lesbian teenagers; 2. Crushes in teenage girls; 3. Homosexuality; 4. Best friends; 5. Friendship; 6. Iran; 7. LGBTQIA romances; 8. Contemporary romances; 9. Realistic fiction
9781616202514; 9781443425728
LC 2013008931
Lambda Literary Award for Young Adult/Children, 2013; Rainbow List, 2014; YALSA Best Fiction for Young Adults, 2014.

In Iran, where homosexuality is punishable by death, seventeen-year-olds Sahar and Nasrin love each other in secret until Nasrin's parents announce their daughter's arranged marriage and Sahar proposes a drastic solution.

Rich with details of life in contemporary Iran, this is a GLBTQ story that we haven't seen before in YA fiction. —*School Library Journal*

Tell me again how a crush should feel: a novel. Sara Farizan. Algonquin Young Readers, 2014 256 p.
Grades: 9 10 11 12
1. Iranian Americans; 2. Lesbian teenagers; 3. Teenage girl/girl relations; 4. Coming out (Sexual or gender identity); 5. Friendship; 6. LGBTQIA romances; 7. Contemporary romances; 8. Coming-of-age stories; 9. Books for reluctant readers
9781616202842; 9781443439862; 9781443439879
LC 2014021580
Rainbow List, 2015; YALSA Quick Picks for Reluctant Young Adult Readers, 2015.

High school junior Leila's Persian heritage already makes her different from her classmates at Armstead Academy, and if word got out that she liked girls life would be twice as hard, but when a new girl, Saskia, shows up, Leila starts to take risks she never thought she would, especially when it looks as if the attraction between them is mutual, so she struggles to sort out her growing feelings by confiding in her old friends.

Farizan fashions an empowering romance featuring a lovable, awkward protagonist who just needs a little nudge of confidence to totally claim her multifaceted identity. —*Booklist*

Farmer, Nancy
★ The **Ear,** the Eye, and the Arm: a novel. Nancy Farmer. Orchard Book, 1994 311 p.
Grades: 6 7 8 9 10
1. Brothers and sisters; 2. Kidnapping; 3. Detectives; 4. Psychic ability; 5. Child adventurers; 6. Zimbabwe; 7. Africa; 8. Afrofuturism and Afrofantasy; 9. Science fiction; 10. Classics.
9780531068298, hardback, US; 9780531086797, lib. bdg, US; 9780141311098, paperback, US; 9780140376418, paperback, US
LC 93-11814
ALA Notable Children's Book, 1995; Golden Duck Awards, Hal Clement Award for Young Adult; Virginia Readers' Choice Award for Middle School, 1998; Newbery Honor Book, 1995.

In 2194 in Zimbabwe, General Matsika's three children are kidnapped and put to work in a plastic mine, while three mutant detectives use their special powers to search for them.

Throughout the story, it's the thrilling adventure that will grab readers, who will also like the comic, tender characterizations. —*Booklist*

★ A **girl** named Disaster. By Nancy Farmer. Orchard Books, 1996 309 p.
Grades: 6 7 8 9
1. Runaway girls; 2. Wilderness survival; 3. Eleven-year-old girls; 4. Girls; 5. Villages; 6. Zimbabwe; 7. Mozambique; 8. 1980s; 9. Adventure stories; 10. Survival stories
9780531095393

LC 9615141
ALA Notable Children's Book, 1997; School Library Journal Best Books, 1996; YALSA Best Books for Young Adults, 1997; National Book Award for Young People's Literature finalist, 1996; Newbery Honor Book, 1997.

While journeying to Zimbabwe from Mozambique, eleven-year-old Nhamo struggles to escape drowning and starvation and in so doing comes close to the luminous world of the African spirits.

This story is humorous and heartwrenching, complex and multilayered. —*School Library Journal*
History and peoples of Zimbabwe and Mozambique,

★ The **house** of the scorpion. Nancy Farmer. Atheneum Books for Young Readers, 2002 380 p;
Grades: 7 8 9 10
1. Clones and cloning; 2. Drug dealers; 3. Courage in boys; 4. Near future; 5. Courage; 6. Dystopian fiction; 7. Science fiction; 8. Coming-of-age stories
9780689852220
LC 2001056594
ALA Notable Children's Book, 2003; Booklist Editors' Choice: Books for Youth, 2002; Grand Canyon Reader Award (Arizona), Teen Book Category, 2005; National Book Award for Young People's Literature, 2002; Rhode Island Teen Book Award, 2004; Sequoyah Book Awards (Oklahoma), Young Adult Books, 2005; South Carolina Book Award, Junior Books, 2006; YALSA Best Books for Young Adults, 2003; Young Hoosier Book Award, Middle Books, 2006; Young Reader's Choice Award (Pacific Northwest), Senior, 2005; Michael L. Printz Honor Book, 2003; Newbery Honor Book, 2003.

In a future where humans despise clones, Matt enjoys special status as the young clone of El Patron, the 142-year-old leader of a corrupt drug empire nestled between Mexico and the United States.

This is a powerful, ultimately hopeful, story that builds on today's sociopolitical, ethical, and scientific issues and prognosticates a compelling picture of what the future could bring. —*Booklist*
Sequel: *The lord of Opium.*

★ The **lord** of Opium. Nancy Farmer. Atheneum Books for Young Readers, 2013 432 p.
Grades: 7 8 9 10
1. Clones and cloning; 2. Dystopias; 3. Drug traffic; 4. Near future; 5. Environmental degradation; 6. Science fiction.
9781442482548
LC 2012030418
In 2137, fourteen-year-old Matt is stunned to learn that, as the clone of El Patron, he is expected to take over as leader of the corrupt drug empire of Opium, where there is also a hidden cure for the ecological devastation faced by the rest of the world.
A Richard Jackson Book.

Farrey, Brian
With or without you. Brian Farrey. Simon Pulse, 2011 348 p;
Grades: 9 10 11 12
1. Gay teenagers; 2. Teenage artists; 3. AIDS (Disease); 4. Hate crimes; 5. Homosexuality; 6. Wisconsin; 7. Madison, Wisconsin; 8. Realistic fiction; 9. LGBTQIA fiction
9781442406995
LC 2010038722
Minnesota Book Award for Young People's Literature, 2012; Rainbow List, 2012; Stonewall Children's & Young Adult Literature Honor Book, 2012.

When eighteen-year-old best friends Evan and Davis of Madison, Wisconsin, join a community center group called "chasers" to gain acceptance and knowledge of gay history, there may be fatal consequences.

Farrey paces his story beautifully, covering many contemporary issues for teens about coming out, friendship, relationships, and following a dangerous crowd simply for a sense of belonging. —*School Library Journal*

Fawcett, Heather

Even the darkest stars. Heather Fawcett. Balzer & Bray, 2017 304 p. (Even the darkest stars, 1)
Grades: 8 9 10 11 12
1. Mountaineering; 2. Talismans; 3. Magic; 4. Voyages and travels; 5. Teenage girls; 6. Fantasy fiction; 7. Canadian fiction
9780062463388; 9780062463395

Kamzin has always dreamed of becoming one of the Emperor's royal explorers, the elite climbers tasked with mapping the wintry, mountainous Empire and spying on its enemies. She knows she could be the best in the world, if only someone would give her a chance.

Add in a detailed, well-realized setting, an unsettling villain that lingers just off the page, and buckets of danger to result in an utterly inventive and wholly original debut. —*Booklist*

Federle, Tim

The **great** American whatever. Tim Federle. 2016 288 pages
Grades: 9 10 11 12
1. Grief in teenage boys; 2. Gay teenagers; 3. Screenwriters; 4. Grief; 5. Teenage same-sex romance; 6. Realistic fiction; 7. LGBTQIA fiction
9781481404099; 9781481404105; 9781481404112
LC 2015015712
School Library Journal Best Books, 2016; YALSA Best Fiction for Young Adults, 2017; Rainbow List, 2017.

Teenaged Quinn, an aspiring screenwriter, copes with his sister's death while his best friend forces him back out into the world to face his reality.

It is cleverly plotted and smoothly written with many scenes presented in screenplay style. More important, while it has its serious aspects, it is whimsical, wry, and unfailingly funny a refreshing change from the often dour nature of much LGBTQ literature. Bright as a button, this is a treat from start to finish. —*Booklist*

Fehler, Gene

Beanball. By Gene Fehler. Clarion Books, 2008 119 p.
Grades: 7 8 9 10
1. High school students; 2. Sports injuries; 3. Baseball; 4. Teenagers; 5. Teenage boys; 6. Realistic fiction; 7. Sports fiction; 8. Baseball stories
9780618843480
LC 2007013058

Relates, from diverse points of view, events surrounding the critical injury of popular and talented high school athlete, Luke "Wizard" Wallace, when he is hit in the face by a fastball.

Feinstein, John

Last shot: a Final Four mystery. John Feinstein. Knopf, 2005 256 p. (Steve and Susan Carol sports mysteries, 1)
Grades: 6 7 8 9
1. Teenage detectives; 2. Basketball tournaments; 3. Sportswriters; 4. Basketball; 5. Thomas, Steve (Fictitious character); 6. New Orleans, Louisiana; 7. Sports fiction; 8. Mysteries; 9. Basketball stories
9780375831683; 9780375931680
LC 2004026535
Edgar Allan Poe Award for Best Young Adult Mystery Novel, 2006; YALSA Popular Paperbacks for Young Adults, 2008.

After winning a basketball reporting contest, eighth graders Stevie and Susan Carol are sent to cover the Final Four tournament, where they discover that a talented player is being blackmailed into throwing the final game.

The action on the court is vividly described.... Mystery fans will find enough suspense in this fast-paced narrative to keep them hooked. —*School Library Journal*
Sequel: *Vanishing Act*

Feldman, Ruth Tenzer

Blue thread. Ruth Tenzer Feldman. Ooligan Press, 2012 302 p. : Illustration
Grades: 7 8 9 10
1. Jewish teenage girls; 2. Suffragist movement; 3. Sixteen-year-old girls; 4. Magic shawls; 5. Teenage girls; 6. Portland, Oregon; 7. Oregon; 8. 1910s; 9. Historical fantasy
9781932010411
LC 2011024382
Amelia Bloomer List, 2013; Leslie Bradshaw Award for Young Adult Literature (Oregon), 2013.

When sixteen-year-old Miriam Josefsohn inherits her grandmother's prayer shawl, she is thrust into a time-traveling adventure where she is transported back in time to inspire the Daughters of Zelophehad, the first women in biblical history to own land.

Felin, M. Sindy

Touching snow. M. Sindy Felin. Atheneum Books for Young Readers, 2007 240 p.
Grades: 9 10 11 12
1. Haitian Americans; 2. African Americans; 3. African American teenage girls; 4. Seventh-grade girls; 5. Thirteen-year-old girls; 6. New York (State); 7. First person narratives; 8. Coming-of-age stories.
9781416917953
LC 2006014794
YALSA Best Books for Young Adults, 2008; National Book Award for Young People's Literature finalist, 2007.

After her stepfather is arrested for child abuse, thirteen-year-old Karina's home life improves but while the severity of her older sister's injuries and the urging of her younger sister, their uncle, and a friend tempt her to testify against him, her mother and other well-meaning adults pursuade her to claim responsibility.

Although the resolution is brutal, this story is a compelling read from an important and much-needed new voice. Readers will cheer for the young narrator. —*School Library Journal*

Fergus, Maureen

Recipe for disaster. Maureen Fergus. KCP Fiction, 2009 252 p.
Grades: 7 8 9
1. New students; 2. Growth (Psychology); 3. Friendship; 4. Baking; 5. High school students; 6. Canadian fiction; 7. Teen chick lit
9781554533206
YALSA Popular Paperbacks for Young Adults, 2011.

Francie's life is almost perfect before new girl Darlene shows up. She has her own business as a weekend baker, a best friend named Holly, and a crush on Tate Jarvis. But Darlene thinks Francie's obsession with baking is weird, she acts like Holly is her best friend, and she's somehow managed to steal Tate's attention away. Just as Francie's pastry-filled dreams are starting to slide, she gets a chance to meet celebrity baker Lorenzo LaRue....

Francie is a delight. Her own special brand of humor touches every aspect of the tale.... This breezy, appealing read covers personal growth, the sacrifices of friendship, and the mistakes made along the way. —*School Library Journal*

Fforde, Jasper
★ The **last** dragonslayer. Jasper Fforde. Harcourt, 2012 256 pages (Chronicles of Kazam, 1)
Grades: 7 8 9 10
1. Dragons; 2. Abandoned children; 3. Employment agencies; 4. Wizards; 5. Visions; 6. Fantasy fiction
9780547738475; 9781443407489; 9781443407496
YALSA Best Fiction for Young Adults, 2013.

Fifteen-year-old Jennifer Strange runs Kazam, an employment agency for soothsayers and sorcerers. Trouble starts when Jennifer has a vision that predicts the death of the last dragon at the hands of a dragonslayer.

Finn, Mary
Belladonna. Mary Finn. Candlewick Press, 2011 384 p.
Grades: 7 8 9 10
1. Stubbs, George; 2. Artists; 3. Lost horses; 4. Horses; 5. Animal anatomy; 6. Boy apprentices; 7. England; 8. Great Britain; 9. Georgian era (1714-1837); 10. 18th century; 11. Historical fiction.
9780763651060
LC 2010038707

In 1757 England, clever but unschooled Thomas Rose helps the spirited Ling seek Belladonna, the horse she rode in the circus, and in their quest they meet painter George Stubbs who euthanizes animals to study their anatomy, but he assures them her horse is safe at a nearby estate.

A touch of intrigue and interesting details about horses, early necropsy, and everyday life add a rich frame to this historical coming-of-age story, unique in both its setting and subject. —*Booklist*

Finneyfrock, Karen
The **sweet** revenge of Celia Door. By Karen Finneyfrock. Viking, 2013 272 p.
Grades: 7 8 9 10
1. Teenage girl misfits; 2. Teenage poets; 3. Revenge; 4. Gay teenagers; 5. Poetry; 6. Pennsylvania; 7. Hershey, Pennsylvania; 8. Realistic fiction.
9780670012756
LC 2011047221

Fourteen-year-old Celia, hurt by her parents' separation, the loss of her only friend, and a classmate's cruelty, has only her poetry for solace until newcomer Drake Berlin befriends her, comes out to her, and seeks her help in connecting with the boy he left behind.

Firkins, Jacqueline
Hearts, strings, and other breakable things. Jacqueline Firkins. Houghton Mifflin Harcourt, 2019 384 p.
Grades: 9 10 11 12
1. Dating (Social customs); 2. Vacations; 3. Love triangles; 4. Moving to a new state; 5. Teenage orphans; 6. Massachusetts; 7. Contemporary romances; 8. Classics-inspired fiction
9781328635198; 9780358156710
LC 2019001111

Living with her aunt's family in Mansfield, Massachusetts, for a few months before turning eighteen and starting college, Edie is torn between Sebastian, the boy next door, and playboy Henry.

Retellings of *Mansfield Park* are far less common than some other Austen-style reimaginings, and this one winningly upholds the spirit of its source material. —*Booklist*

Fisher, Catherine
Incarceron. By Catherine Fisher. Dial Books, 2010 442 p.
Grades: 7 8 9 10
1. Teenage prisoners; 2. Arranged marriage; 3. Dystopias; 4. Escapes; 5. Far future; 6. Dystopian fiction; 7. Steampunk; 8. Fantasy fiction.
9780803733961
LC 2008046254
YALSA Popular Paperbacks for Young Adults, 2012; YALSA Best Fiction for Young Adults, 2011; School Library Journal Best Books, 2010.

To free herself from an upcoming arranged marriage, Claudia, the daughter of the Warden of Incarceron, a futuristic prison with a mind of its own, decides to help a young prisoner escape.

Complex and inventive, with numerous and rewarding mysteries, this tale is certain to please. —*Publishers Weekly*
Sequel: *Sapphique*.

Fitzpatrick, Becca
Black ice. Becca Fitzpatrick. Simon & Schuster Books for Young Readers, 2014 400 p.
Grades: 9 10 11 12
1. Survival; 2. Hostages; 3. Storms; 4. Teenage girls; 5. Love; 6. Wyoming; 7. Grand Teton National Park; 8. Thrillers and suspense
9781442474260; 9781442474284, ebook, US
LC 2014004913

Britt goes hiking in the Grand Tetons of Wyoming with her ex-boyfriend Calvin, but trouble arises when she is caught in a blizzard, taken hostage by fugitives, finds evidence of murders, and learns whom to trust and whom to love.

While the romance between Britt and one of her captors is soapy, it dovetails nicely with the murder mystery. With an action-packed conclusion, capped off with a fairy-tale ending, this finds a good intersection between romance and suspense. —*Booklist*

Fitzpatrick, Huntley
My life next door. By Huntley Fitzpatrick. Dial Books, 2012 304 p.
Grades: 9 10 11 12
1. Children of politicians; 2. First loves; 3. Dilemmas; 4. Personal conduct; 5. Families; 6. Contemporary romances
9780803736993
LC 2011027166
YALSA Best Fiction for Young Adults, 2013.

When Samantha, the seventeen-year-old daugher of a wealthy, perfectionistic, Republican state senator, falls in love with the boy next door, whose family is large, boisterous, and just making ends meet, she discovers a different way to live, but when her mother is involved in a hit-and-run accident Sam must make some difficult choices.

Companion novel: *The boy most likely to.*

What I thought was true. By Huntley Fitzpatrick. Dial, 2014 409 pages
Grades: 9 10 11 12
1. First loves; 2. Social classes; 3. Islands; 4. Summer; 5. Families; 6. Connecticut; 7. Contemporary romances; 8. Teen chick lit
9780803739093
LC 2013027029

Seventeen-year-old Gwen Castle is a working-class girl determined to escape her small island town, but when rich-kid Cass Somers, with whom she has a complicated romantic history, shows up, she's forced to reassess her feelings about her loving, complex family, her lifelong best friends, her wealthy employer, the place she lives, and the boy she can't admit she loves.

Fixmer, Elizabeth
Down from the mountain. Elizabeth Fixmer. Albert Whitman & Company, 2015 276 p.
Grades: 9 10 11 12
  1. Cults; 2. Polygamy; 3. Fanaticism; 4. Pregnant women; 5. Mothers and daughters; 6. Realistic fiction; 7. First person narratives
9780807583708
LC 2014027714
Fourteen year-old Eva tries to be a good disciple of Righteous Path, a polygamy cult in Colorado, but her forays into the 'heathen world' cause her to question all she knows.
Teen readers fascinated by religious cults will be drawn in by Eva's story. —*Booklist*

Flack, Sophie
  ★ **Bunheads**. By Sophie Flack. Poppy, 2011 304 p.
Grades: 8 9 10 11 12
  1. Ballet; 2. Ballet dancers; 3. Ambition; 4. Discontent in teenage girls; 5. Discontent; 6. New York City; 7. Realistic fiction.
9780316126533
LC 2011009715
YALSA Popular Paperbacks for Young Adults, 2013.
Hannah Ward, nineteen, revels in the competition, intense rehearsals, and dazzling performances that come with being a member of Manhattan Ballet Company's corps de ballet, but after meeting handsome musician Jacob she begins to realize there could be more to her life.
Readers, both dancers and pedestrians (the corps' term for nondancers), will find Hannah's struggle a gripping read. —*Publishers Weekly*

Flake, Sharon
  Bang!. By Sharon G. Flake. Jump at the Sun/Hyperion Books for Children, 2005 298 p.
Grades: 8 9 10 11 12
  1. African American teenage boys; 2. Inner city teenage boys; 3. Identity (Psychology); 4. Survival; 5. Brothers — Death; 6. Coming-of-age stories; 7. African American fiction; 8. Realistic fiction; 9. Books for reluctant readers
9780786818440
LC 2005047434
YALSA Best Books for Young Adults, 2006; YALSA Quick Picks for Reluctant Young Adult Readers, 2006.
A teenage boy must face the harsh realities of inner city life, a disintegrating family, and destructive temptations as he struggles to find his identity as a young man.
This disturbing, thought-provoking novel will leave readers with plenty of food for thought and should fuel lively discussions. —*School Library Journal*

  Pinned. Sharon G. Flake. Scholastic Press, 2012 224 p.
Grades: 9 10 11 12
  1. Teenage boys with disabilities; 2. Teenage girl wrestlers; 3. African American teenagers; 4. Learning disabilities; 5. Teenage boy/girl relations; 6. Realistic fiction; 7. Multiple perspectives; 8. First person narratives
9780545057189
LC 2012009239
Adonis is smart, intellectually gifted, and born without legs; Autumn is strong, a great wrestler, and barely able to read in ninth grade—but Autumn is attracted to Adonis and determined to make him a part of her life whatever he or her best friend thinks.

Fleischman, Paul
  Seek. Paul Fleischman. Cricket Books, 2001 167 p.
Grades: 7 8 9 10
  1. Fathers and sons; 2. Radio; 3. Father-separated teenage boys; 4. High school seniors; 5. Fathers
9780812649000
LC 2001028869
ALA Notable Children's Book, 2002; YALSA Best Books for Young Adults, 2002; School Library Journal Best Books, 2001.
Rob becomes obsessed with searching the airwaves for his long-gone father, a radio announcer.
Fleischman has orchestrated a symphony that is both joyful and poignant with this book designed for reader's theatre. —*Voice of Youth Advocates*

Fletcher, Ralph
  The **one** o'clock chop. Ralph Fletcher. Holt, 2007 192 p.
Grades: 7 8 9 10
  1. Fourteen-year-old boys; 2. Fourteen-year-olds; 3. Teenage boys; 4. Teenagers; 5. Boats; 6. Long Island Sound; 7. Long Island, New York; 8. 1970s; 9. Coming-of-age stories
9780805081435
Plenty of universal teen fascinations and concerns exist for those readers willing to enter Matt's world and give themselves over to this smoothly paced and competently written novel. —*School Library Journal*

Fletcher, Susan
  Ancient, strange, and lovely. Susan Fletcher. Atheneum Books for Young Readers, 2010 315 p. (Dragon chronicles, 4)
Grades: 6 7 8 9
  1. Children of scientists; 2. Dragons; 3. Poaching; 4. Dragon babies; 5. Sisters; 6. Oregon; 7. Fantasy fiction.
9781416957867
LC 2009053797
Fourteen-year-old Bryn must try to find a way to save a baby dragon from a dangerous modern world that seems to have no place for something so ancient.
This book offers a wondrous mix of dystopic science fiction and magical fantasy.... Fletcher has done an outstanding job of creating a believable place and space for this story to unfold. The plot flows smoothly and quickly with a lot of action. —*School Library Journal*

  Dragon's milk. Susan Fletcher. Atheneum, 1989 242p. (Dragon chronicles, 1)
Grades: 7 8 9 10
  1. Girl adventurers; 2. Dragons; 3. Sisters; 4. Fantasy fiction.
9780689315794
LC 88035059
Leslie Bradshaw Award for Young Readers (Oregon), 1990.
Kaeldra, an outsider adopted by an Elythian family as a baby, possesses the power to understand dragons and uses this power to try to save her younger sister who needs dragon's milk to recover from an illness.
High-fantasy fans will delight in the clash of swords, the flash of magic, the many escape-and-rescue scenes. —*Booklist*
Sequel: *Sign of the dove.*

Flinn, Alex
  Beastly. Alex Flinn. HarperTeen, 2007 320 p. (Kendra chronicles, 1)
Grades: 6 7 8 9 10
  1. Self-fulfillment in teenage boys; 2. Pride and vanity; 3. Transformations, Personal; 4. Love; 5. Transformations (Magic); 6. Manhattan, New York City; 7. First person narratives; 8. Fantasy

fiction; 9. Fairy tale and folklore-inspired fiction; 10. Books for reluctant readers
9780060874162; 9780060874179

LC 2006036241

YALSA Popular Paperbacks for Young Adults, 2010; YALSA Popular Paperbacks for Young Adults, 2016; YALSA Quick Picks for Reluctant Young Adult Readers, 2008.

A modern retelling of "Beauty and the Beast" from the point of view of the Beast, a vain Manhattan private school student who is turned into a monster and must find true love before he can return to his human form.

This is creative enough to make it an engaging read.... [This is an] engrossing tale that will have appeal for fans of fantasy and realistic fiction. —*Voice of Youth Advocates*

★ **Breathing** underwater. Alexandra Flinn. Harper Collins Publishers, 2001 263 p.
Grades: 9 10 11 12
1. Sixteen-year-old boys; 2. Dating violence; 3. Anger in teenage boys; 4. Fathers and sons; 5. Teenage boys; 6. Realistic fiction; 7. Diaries; 8. Books for reluctant readers
9780060291983; 9780060291990

LC 44933

Black-Eyed Susan Book Award (Maryland), High School, 2004; YALSA Popular Paperbacks for Young Adults, 2016; YALSA Quick Picks for Reluctant Young Adult Readers, 2002; YALSA Best Books for Young Adults, 2002.

Sent to counseling for hitting his girlfriend, Caitlin, and ordered to keep a journal, sixteen-year-old Nick recounts his relationship with Caitlin, examines his controlling behavior and anger, and describes living with his abusive father.

Sequel: *Diva*.

Cloaked. Alex Flinn. HarperTeen, 2011 256 p.
Grades: 6 7 8 9
1. Witches; 2. Transformations (Magic); 3. Magic cloaks; 4. Missing persons; 5. Shoes — Repairing; 6. Miami, Florida; 7. Florida; 8. Fantasy fiction; 9. Fairy tale and folklore-inspired fiction
9780060874223

A diverting, whimsical romp through fairy-tale tropes. —*Bulletin of the Center for Children's Books*

A **kiss** in time. Alex Flinn. HarperTeen, 2009 371 p;
Grades: 7 8 9 10 11 12
1. Princesses; 2. Curses; 3. Self-awareness in teenagers; 4. Self-awareness; 5. Kissing; 6. Miami, Florida; 7. Europe; 8. Fantasy fiction; 9. Fairy tale and folklore-inspired fiction; 10. Multiple perspectives
9780060874193

LC 2008022582

Sixteen-year-old Princess Talia persuades seventeen-year-old Jack, the modern-day American who kissed her awake after a 300-year sleep, to take her to his Miami home, where she hopes to win his love before the witch who cursed her can spirit her away.

This is a clever and humorous retelling of "Sleeping Beauty".... Alternating between the teenagers' distinctive points of view, Flinn skillfully delineates how their upbringings set them apart while drawing parallels between their family conflicts. Fans of happily-ever-after endings will delight in the upbeat resolution. —*Publishers Weekly*

Flood, Bo
Soldier sister, fly home. Nancy Bo Flood. Charlesbridge, 2016 144 p.
Grades: 5 6 7 8

1. Multiracial teenage girls; 2. Identity (Psychology); 3. Navajo Indians; 4. Families; 5. Sisters; 6. Arizona; 7. Realistic fiction; 8. Coming-of-age stories
9781580897020; 9781607348214, ebook, US; 9781607348221, ebook, US

LC 2015018819

WILLA Literary Awards: Children's/Young Adult Fiction & Nonfiction, 2017.

Half-Navajo, half-white sisters Tess and Gaby are separated when Gaby drops out of college to join the army. Now as Gaby is deployed to Iraq, she asks Tess to care for Blue, the spirited horse that Tess dislikes. Tess struggles with her identity and with missing her sister, and she decides to spend the summer with her grandmother at sheep camp where tragedy strikes.

Flood lived and taught on the Navajo Nation for 15 years, and this quietly moving story of Tess's growing maturity as she searches for her cultural identity resounds with authenticity. —*Publishers Weekly*

Floreen, Tim
Willful machines. Tim Floreen. Simon Pulse, 2015 368 p.
Grades: 9 10 11 12
1. Gay teenagers; 2. Robots; 3. Near future; 4. Conservatives; 5. Terrorism; 6. Science fiction
9781481432771
Rainbow List, 2016.

An excellent debut thriller that will reach a wide range of readers. —*School Library Journal*

Flores-Scott, Patrick
★ **American** road trip. Patrick Flores-Scott. Christy Ottaviano Books, Henry Holt and Company, 2018 272 p.
Grades: 7 8 9 10 11 12
1. Families of military personnel; 2. Brothers; 3. Mental illness; 4. Automobile travel; 5. Post-traumatic stress disorder; 6. Realistic fiction; 7. Coming-of-age stories; 8. Pacific Northwest fiction
9781627797412; 9781250211651

LC 2018004255

YALSA Best Fiction for Young Adults, 2019.

Brothers Teodoro and Manny Avila take a road trip to address Manny's PTSD following his tour in Iraq, and to help T. change his life and win the heart of Wendy Martinez. Includes information and resources about PTSD.

Featuring a diverse cast of delightful characters, this novel bursts with much-needed optimism. —*Kirkus*

Jumped in. Patrick Flores-Scott. Christy Ottaviano Books, Henry Holt and Company, 2013 288 p.
Grades: 8 9 10
1. Slackers; 2. Poetry; 3. Mexican American teenage boys; 4. Mother-deserted children; 5. Poetry slams; 6. Washington (State); 7. Realistic fiction; 8. Pacific Northwest fiction
9780805095142
YALSA Best Fiction for Young Adults, 2014.

In the two years since his mother left him with his grandparents in Des Moines, Washington, Sam has avoided making friends and perfected the art of being a slacker, but being paired with a frightening new student for a slam poetry unit transforms his life.

While Flores-Scott targets reluctant readers at their point of entry with accessible language, style, and plot, it is the transcending heartbreak of Sam and Luis' deepening friendship that beckons every reader to heed his or her own inner voice. —*Booklist*

Foley, Jessie Ann

★ The **carnival** at Bray. Jessie Ann Foley. Elephant Rock Books, 2014 254 p.

Grades: 9 10 11 12

1. Americans in Ireland; 2. Teenage girls; 3. Life change events; 4. Uncle and niece; 5. Families; 6. Ireland; 7. 1990s; 8. Coming-of-age stories

9780989515597

YALSA Best Fiction for Young Adults, 2015; YALSA Best Fiction for Young Adults: Top Ten, 2015; YALSA Popular Paperbacks for Young Adults, 2017; William C. Morris Debut Award finalist, 2015; Michael L. Printz Honor Book, 2015.

The narrative subtly and carefully interweaves peer and family drama—much of it involving troubled Uncle Kevin—with the highs and lows of the grunge music scene, from the transformative glory of a Nirvana concert to the outpouring of grief around the death of Kurt Cobain. —*Kirkus*

Sorry for your loss. Jessie Ann Foley. HarperTeen, 2019 336 p.

Grades: 8 9 10 11 12

1. Teenage photographers; 2. Bereavement; 3. Large families; 4. Loss (Psychology); 5. Photography; 6. Chicago, Illinois; 7. Coming-of-age stories; 8. Realistic fiction.

9780062571915; 9780062571922

An awkward teen, the youngest of eight children, navigates the loss of a sibling throughout a photography assignment that leads him to secrets, opportunities and an unexpected connection.—

Written with Foley's keen ear for family dynamics, this is definitely a strong choice for fans of her work and those new to the author. —*School Library Journal*

Fombelle, Timothee de

★ **Between** sky and earth. Timothee de Fombelle. 2014 432 p. (Vango, 1)

Grades: 9 10 11 12

1. Treasure troves; 2. Monks; 3. Nazis; 4. Murder; 5. Murder suspects; 6. 1930s; 7. Between the Wars (1918-1939); 8. Historical mysteries

9780763671969; 9781406330922, print, UK

LC 2013955696

YALSA Best Fiction for Young Adults, 2015; YALSA Best Fiction for Young Adults: Top Ten, 2015.

A gripping mystery-adventure set in the 1930s interwar period about a character desperately searching for his identity.—Publisher's description.

de Fombelle has written a brilliant, wonderfully exciting story of flight and pursuit, filled with colorful characters and head-scratching mystery. As the novel proceeds, the suspense is ratcheted up to breathtaking levels as the boy remains only one step ahead of his relentless pursuers. —*Booklist*

A **prince** without a kingdom. Timothee de Fombelle. Candlewick Press, 2015 457 p. (Vango, 2)

Grades: 7 8 9 10 11 12

1. Identity (Psychology); 2. Voyages and travels; 3. Airships; 4. Parents; 5. Resistance to government; 6. 1930s; 7. Second World War era (1939-1945); 8. Historical mysteries; 9. Translations

9780763679507; 9781406331509

The story runs from 1936 through 1942, which means that it is touched by WWII and the German occupation of France, where meaningful portions of the story are set. But whatever the setting, the story is rich in mysteries, enlivened by surprises, and suffused with suspense. It is so beautifully wrought, it reminds us why we love to read, and there can be no higher praise. —*Booklist*

Translated from the French; Original French title: *Un prince sans royaume.*

Fontes, Justine

Benito runs. Justine Fontes. Darby Creek, 2011 104 p; (Surviving Southside)

Grades: 7 8 9 10

1. Hispanic American teenage boys; 2. Runaway teenage boys; 3. Post-traumatic stress disorder; 4. Children of military personnel; 5. Fathers; 6. Texas; 7. Urban fiction; 8. High interest-low vocabulary books

9780761361657

LC 2010023820

Benito's father, Xavier, returns from Iraq after more than a year suffering from PTSD—post-traumatic stress disorder—and yells constantly. He causes such a scene at a school function that Benny is embarrassed to go back to Southside High. Benny can't handle seeing his dad so crazy, so he decides to run away. Will Benito find a new life, or will he learn how to deal with his dad—through good times and bad?

This well-written [story reinforces] the importance of family, friends, values, and thoughtful decision-making.... [An] excellent [purchase, this book] will attract and engage reluctant readers. —*School Library Journal*

Summary adapted from p. [4] of cover; High interest story designed for reluctant readers or those reading below grade level.

Ford, John C.

★ The **morgue** and me. By John C. Ford. Viking Children's Books, 2009 288 p.

Grades: 8 9 10 11 12

1. Criminal investigation; 2. Murder; 3. Teenage detectives; 4. Murder investigation; 5. Police cover-ups; 6. Michigan; 7. Mysteries

9780670010967

LC 2009001956

Eighteen-year-old Christopher, who plans to be a spy, learns of a murder cover-up through his summer job as a morgue assistant and teams up with Tina, a gorgeous newspaper reporter, to investigate, despite great danger.

Ford spins a tale that's complex but not confusing, never whitewashing some of the harsher crimes people commit. The result is a story that holds its own as a mainstream mystery as well as a teen novel. —*Publishers Weekly*

Ford, Michael Thomas

Suicide notes: a novel. Michael Thomas Ford. HarperTeen, 2008 295 p.

Grades: 9 10 11 12 Adult

1. Gay teenagers; 2. Sexual orientation; 3. Self- acceptance; 4. Psychiatric hospital patients; 5. Teenagers — Sexuality; 6. LGBTQIA fiction; 7. Realistic fiction.

9780060737559; 9780060737566; 9780062043078

LC 2008019199

Rainbow List, 2009.

Brimming with sarcasm, fifteen-year-old Jeff describes his stay in a psychiatric ward after attempting to commit suicide.

Ford's characterizations run deep, and without too much contrivance the teens' interactions slowly dislodge clues about what triggered Jeff's suicide attempt. —*Publishers Weekly*

Z. Michael Thomas Ford. HarperTeen, 2010 208 p.

Grades: 7 8 9 10

1. Zombies; 2. Virtual reality games; 3. Drugs; 4. Near future; 5. Epidemics; 6. 21st century; 7. Science fiction.
9780060737580

This book is a thriller, and the clever plot and characters will have readers hoping for more. —*School Library Journal*

Forman, Gayle

I have lost my way. By Gayle Forman. 2018 304 p.
Grades: 9 10 11 12
1. Loss (Psychology); 2. Self-discovery in teenagers; 3. Teenagers; 4. Gay teenagers; 5. Friendship; 6. Central Park, New York City; 7. New York City; 8. Realistic fiction
9780425290774; 9780425290781

LC 2017058302

Three teengers, Freya, Harun, and Nathaniel feel lost in various ways and when they collide in Central Park, they begin to find purpose in their lives.

The intersections of love, family, and identity—and how loss impacts them all—lay the groundwork for the breathtaking empathy and friendship that takes root among these three seemingly dissimilar teens within hours of meeting each other. —*Kirkus*

I was here. Gayle Forman. Viking, published by the Penguin Group, 2015 288 p.
Grades: 9 10 11 12
1. Survivors of suicide victims; 2. Friends' death; 3. Guilt; 4. Suicide; 5. Grief; 6. Washington (State); 7. Mysteries
9780451471475

An engrossing and provocative look at the devastating finality of suicide, survivor's guilt, the complicated nature of responsibility and even the role of the Internet in life-and-death decisions. —*Kirkus*

★ **If** I stay: a novel. By Gayle Forman. Dutton Books, 2009 199 p. (If I stay, 1)
Grades: 7 8 9 10
1. Teenage girls in comas; 2. Fatal traffic accidents; 3. Teenage musicians; 4. Cellists; 5. Decision-making; 6. Oregon; 7. Realistic fiction; 8. First person narratives; 9. Books to movies; 10. Books for reluctant readers
9780525421030

LC 2008023938

Blue Hen Book Award (Delaware) for Teen Books, 2011; Great Lakes Great Books Award (Michigan), Grades 9-12, 2010; YALSA Popular Paperbacks for Young Adults, 2015; YALSA Quick Picks for Reluctant Young Adult Readers, 2010; YALSA Best Books for Young Adults, 2010.

While in a coma following an automobile accident that killed her parents and younger brother, seventeen-year-old Mia, a gifted cellist, weights whether to live with her grief or join her family in death.

Intensely moving, the novel will force readers to take stock of their lives and the people and things that make them worth living. —*Publishers Weekly*

Sequel: *Where she went* .

Where she went. By Gayle Forman. Dutton, 2011 208 p. (If I stay, 2)
Grades: 7 8 9 10
1. Teenage rock musicians; 2. Former girlfriends; 3. Reunions; 4. Cellists; 5. Interpersonal relations; 6. New York City; 7. Realistic fiction; 8. First person narratives
9780525422945; 9781849414289, print, UK
Goodreads Choice Award, 2011; YALSA Best Fiction for Young Adults, 2012; YALSA Popular Paperbacks for Young Adults, 2013.

Adam, now a rising rock star, and Mia, a successful cellist, reunite in New York and reconnect after the horrific events that tore them apart when Mia almost died in a car accident three years earlier.

Both characters spring to life, and their pain-filled back story and current realities provide depth and will hold readers fast. —*Kirkus*

Sequel to: *If I stay*.

Fowley-Doyle, Moira

★ The **accident** season. By Moïra Fowley-Doyle. Kathy Dawson Books, 2015 304 p.
Grades: 8 9 10 11 12
1. Teenagers; 2. Accidents; 3. Secrets; 4. Ghosts; 5. Seventeen-year-old girls; 6. Ireland; 7. Horror; 8. Ghost stories; 9. First person narratives.
9780525429487

LC 2014047858

School Library Journal Best Books, 2015.

Every October Cara and her family become mysteriously and dangerously accident-prone, but this year, the year Cara, her ex-stepbrother, and her best friend are 17, is when Cara will begin to unravel the accident season's dark origins.

Beautifully crafted and atmospheric, the magic realism of this book gradually peels away to expose secrets and reveal unexpected truths. Readers will be swept away by Fowley-Doyle's lyrical writing and entrancing premise in this tale of forbidden love and magic. —*Booklist*

Fox, Helena

★ **How** it feels to float. Helena Fox. Dial Books, 2019 384 p.
Grades: 9 10 11 12
1. Teenage girls with depression; 2. Hallucinations and illusions; 3. Fathers and daughters; 4. Loss (Psychology); 5. Post-traumatic stress disorder; 6. Realistic fiction; 7. First person narratives; 8. Australian fiction.
9780525554295; 9781760783303, Paperback, Australia; 9780525554356, ebook, US

LC 2018058425

Sixteen-year-old Biz sees her father every day, though he died when she was seven. When he suddenly disappears, she tumbles into a disaster-land of grief and depression from which she must find her way back.

Foxlee, Karen

★ The **anatomy** of wings. Karen Foxlee. Alfred A. Knopf, 2009 361 p.
Grades: 8 9 10 11 12
1. Death; 2. Suicide; 3. Grief; 4. Ten-year-old girls; 5. Sisters — Death; 6. Queensland; 7. Australia; 8. 1980s; 9. Realistic fiction; 10. Australian fiction
9780375856433
Commonwealth Writers' Prize, South East Asia and South Pacific: Best First Book, 2008; Dobbie Literary Award, 2008.

With her family falling apart from the sudden death of one of their own, ten-year-old Jennifer is left alone to look for answers to questions about what happened and why in the final month's of her beloved sister's short life in the hopes of finding the closure she so desperately seeks.

Jenny's observations are...poetic and washed with magic realism.... With heart-stopping accuracy and sly symbolism, Foxlee captures the small ways that humans reveal themselves, the mysterious intensity of female adolescence, and the surreal quiet of a grieving house, which slowly and with astonishing resilience fills again with sound and music. —*Booklist*

Frank, E. R.
Dime. E.R. Frank. Atheneum Books for Young Readers, 2015 336 p.
Grades: 9 10 11 12
1. Teenage prostitutes; 2. Prostitution; 3. Foster teenagers; 4. Hope; 5. Books and reading; 6. New Jersey; 7. Realistic fiction
9781481431606
Amelia Bloomer Lists, 2016; School Library Journal Best Books, 2015; YALSA Best Fiction for Young Adults, 2016.
Dime's desire to save her friend transcends artifice and approaches heroism, making for a tremendously affecting novel. —*Kirkus*

Frazier, Angie
Everlasting. By Angie Frazier. Scholastic Press, 2010 329 p.
Grades: 8 9 10 11 12
1. Mother-separated teenage girls; 2. Magic rocks; 3. Adventure; 4. Supernatural; 5. Shipwrecks; 6. Australia; 7. 1850s; 8. Historical fantasy
9780545114738
LC 2009020519
In 1855, seventeen-year-old Camille sets out from San Francisco, California, on her last sea voyage before entering a loveless marriage, but when her father's ship is destroyed, she and a friend embark on a cross-Australian quest to find her long-lost mother who holds a map to a magical stone.
Although this novel takes place in the nineteenth century, many of the themes are relevant for today's teens. The author does a nice job of developing strong and funny characters while keeping the plot moving at a readable pace. —*Voice of Youth Advocates*
Sequel: *The eternal sea.*

Fredericks, Mariah
Crunch time. Mariah Fredericks. Atheneum Books for Young Readers, 2006 317 p.
Grades: 9 10 11 12
1. Teenagers; 2. Teenage girls; 3. Teenage boys; 4. High school juniors; 5. Schools; 6. Realistic fiction.
9780689869389
Four students, who have formed a study group to prepare for the SAT exam, sustain each other through the emotional highs and lows of their junior year in high school.
Fredericks writes about high school academics and social rules with sharp insight and spot-on humor. —*Booklist*

The **girl** in the park. Mariah Fredericks. Schwartz & Wade Books, 2012 224 p.
Grades: 10 11 12
1. Teenage girl detectives; 2. Crimes against teenage girls; 3. Speech disorders; 4. Murder; 5. Murder investigation; 6. New York City; 7. Mysteries
9780375968433
LC 2011012309
When a teenaged girl with a bad reputation is murdered in New York City's Central Park after a party, her childhood friend is determined to solve the mystery of who caused her death.

Freitas, Donna
★ The **possibilities** of sainthood. Donna Freitas. Farrar, Straus and Giroux, 2008 272 p.
Grades: 7 8 9 10 11 12
1. Saints; 2. Teenagers — Personal conduct; 3. Teenage boy/girl relations; 4. Catholic teenagers; 5. Fifteen-year-old girls; 6. Rhode Island; 7. Realistic fiction; 8. Coming-of-age stories

9780374360870
LC 2007033298
While regularly petitioning the Vatican to make her the first living saint, fifteen-year-old Antonia Labella prays to assorted patron saints for everything from help with preparing the family's fig trees for a Rhode Island winter to getting her first kiss from the right boy.
With a satisfying ending, this novel about the realistic struggles of a chaste teen is a great addition to all collections. —*School Library Journal*
Frances Foster Books.

The **survival** kit. Donna Freitas. Farrar Straus Giroux, 2011 368 p.
Grades: 7 8 9 10
1. Sixteen-year-old girls; 2. Mothers — Death; 3. Grief in teenage girls; 4. Death; 5. Teenage girls; 6. Realistic fiction.
9780374399177
LC 2010041294
YALSA Best Fiction for Young Adults, 2012.
After her mother dies, sixteen-year-old Rose works through her grief by finding meaning in a survival kit that her mother left behind.
The premise of the survival kit, a real-life tradition from Freitas's own mother, begs to be discussed and glued-and-scissored with friends, students, teachers, and librarians. A copy of *The Survival Kit* would be a worthy addition for a teen coping with her own loss or struggling to help friends or family cope with theirs. —*Voice of Youth Advocates*
Frances Foster books.

Unplugged. Donna Freitas. Harperteen, 2016 448 p. (The wired (Donna Freitas), 1)
Grades: 8 9 10 11
1. Mother-separated teenage girls; 2. Paraphysics; 3. Virtual reality; 4. Teenage girls; 5. Dystopias; 6. Dystopian fiction; 7. Science fiction.
9780062118608
Years after being sent by her family to the extravagant virtual App World to live a life of wealth and privilege, Skylar relinquishes the glamour and prestige of her expensive downloads in favor of spending time with her family in the Real World, an effort that is dashed when the borders between worlds suddenly close.
Despite imperfections, one of the more ambitious and thought-provoking entries in a crowded genre. —*Kirkus*

French, Gillian
Grit. Gillian French. HarperTeen, 2017 294 p.
Grades: 9 10 11 12
1. Secrets; 2. Missing teenage girls; 3. Small towns; 4. Cousins; 5. Former friends; 6. Maine; 7. Realistic fiction
9780062642554
Lupine Award (Maine) for Juvenile/Young Adult, 2017.
Darcy, who has a reputation and is used to rumors swirling around her, wrestles with what happened the same night her friend disappeared the previous summer and struggles with the weight of the dark secret she and her cousin share.
Gorgeously written and helmed by a protagonist with an indelibly fierce heart. —*Kirkus*

Frick, Kit
I killed Zoe Spanos. Kit Frick. Margaret K. McElderry Books, 2020 384 p.
Grades: 9 10 11 12
1. Nannies; 2. Missing teenage girls; 3. Suspicion; 4. Memory; 5. Truthfulness and falsehood; 6. Hamptons, New York; 7. Psychological suspense; 8. Mysteries; 9. Multiple perspectives.
9781534449701; 9781534479241, Paperback, Australia

Hoping for a new start when she accepts a summer nanny job in the Hamptons, Anna is drawn into the disappearance case of a local teen who she eerily resembles while a local podcaster searches for answers, in a tale of suspense inspired by Daphne du Maurier's *Rebecca*.

There's a cunning balance of sunny and sinister, with beachside kid time counterbalanced with disturbing memories, threatening figures, and a touch of smoky arson. —*Bulletin of the Center for Children's Books*

Friedman, Aimee

The **year** my sister got lucky. Aimee Friedman. Scholastic, 2008 384 p.
Grades: 7 8 9 10
1. Fourteen-year-old girls; 2. Sisters; 3. Ballet dancers; 4. Moving, Household; 5. City life; 6. New York (State); 7. New York City; 8. First person narratives; 9. Realistic fiction; 10. Teen chick lit
9780439922272

LC 2007016416
When fourteen-year-old Katie and her older sister, Michaela, move from New York City to upstate New York, Katie is horrified by the country life-style but is even more shocked when her sister adapts effortlessly, enjoying their new life, unlike Katie.

Friedman gets the push and pull of the sister bond just right in this delightful, funny, insightful journey. —*Booklist*

Friend, Natasha

★ **Bounce**. Natasha Friend. Scholastic Press, 2007 188 p.
Grades: 6 7 8 9
1. Blended families; 2. Remarriage; 3. Popularity; 4. Moving to a new state; 5. Schools; 6. Boston, Massachusetts; 7. Massachusetts; 8. Realistic fiction.
9780439853507

LC 2006038126
Thirteen-year-old Evyn's world is turned upside-down when her father, widowed since she was a toddler, suddenly decides to remarry a woman with six children, move with Ev and her brother from Maine to Boston, and enroll her in private school.

The author presents, through hip conversations and humor, believable characters and a feel-good story with a satisfying amount of pathos. —*School Library Journal*

For keeps. By Natasha Friend. Viking, 2010 272 p.
Grades: 8 9 10 11 12
1. Father-separated teenage girls; 2. Mothers and daughters; 3. Trust in teenage girls; 4. Trust; 5. Dating (Social customs); 6. Massachusetts; 7. Realistic fiction.
9780670011902

LC 2009022472
Just as sixteen-year-old Josie and her mother finally begin trusting men enough to start dating seriously, the father Josie never knew comes back to town and shakes up what was already becoming a difficult mother-daughter relationship.

The book discusses sex and abortion, and includes adult language and underage drinking. Many readers will be able to relate to this protagonist, whose strength and maturity set a positive example. Friend skillfully portrays the challenges of adolescence while telling an engaging story with unique and genuine characters. —*School Library Journal*

How we roll. By Natasha Friend. Farrar Straus Giroux, 2018 272 p.
Grades: 7 8 9 10 11
1. Self-acceptance; 2. People with disabilities; 3. Love; 4. Alopecia areata; 5. People who have had amputations; 6. Massachusetts; 7. Contemporary romances; 8. Books for reluctant readers
9780374305666

LC 2017042313
YALSA Quick Picks for Reluctant Young Adult Readers, 2019.
After developing alopecia Quinn lost her friends along with her hair and former football player Jake lost his legs and confidence after an accident, but the two help each other believe in themselves and the possibility of love.

Lush. Natasha Friend. Scholastic Press, 2006 192 p.
Grades: 7 8 9 10
1. Children of alcoholic fathers; 2. Letter writing; 3. Family violence; 4. Alcoholism; 5. Fathers; 6. Realistic fiction; 7. Books for reluctant readers
9780439853460

LC 2005031333
Rhode Island Teen Book Award, 2008; YALSA Quick Picks for Reluctant Young Adult Readers, 2007.
Unable to cope with her father's alcoholism, thirteen-year-old Sam corresponds with an older student, sharing her family problems and asking for advice.

Friend adeptly takes a teen problem and turns it into a believable, sensitive, character-driven story, with realistic dialogue. —*Booklist*

My life in black and white. By Natasha Friend. Viking, 2012 304 p.
Grades: 8 9 10 11
1. Teenage girls with disfigurements; 2. Self-acceptance in teenage girls; 3. Teenage traffic accident victims; 4. Self-acceptance; 5. Beauty; 6. Realistic fiction.
9780670013036

LC 2011021436
When beautiful high school student Lexi is involved in an automobile accident that leaves her disfigured, she must learn who she really is beyond a pretty face, and she must also learn to forgive.

The **other** F-word. Natasha Friend. 2017 272 p.
Grades: 7 8 9 10 11 12
1. Children of sperm donors; 2. Half-brothers and sisters; 3. Identity (Psychology); 4. Children of LGBTQIA parents; 5. Families; 6. Realistic fiction; 7. Multiple perspectives
9780374302344; 9781250144157, Paperback, Australia

LC 2016009256
Rainbow List, 2018.
Two teens conceived via in vitro fertilization—one with extreme allergies and the other who recently lost her mother—team up to search for answers about their donor.

This is a joyful, emotional story full of love, humor, and the messiness of family, no matter the shape it takes. —*Publishers Weekly*

Perfect. Natasha Friend. Milkweed Editions, 2004 172 p;
Grades: 6 7 8 9
1. Bulimia; 2. Teenage girls with eating disorders; 3. Grief in teenage girls; 4. Grief; 5. Eating disorders; 6. Realistic fiction; 7. First person narratives
9781571316516; 9781571316523

LC 2004006371
Golden Sower Award (Nebraska), Young Adult, 2007; Isinglass Teen Read Award (New Hampshire), 2007-2008. ; YALSA Popular Paperbacks for Young Adults, 2010.
Following the death of her father, a thirteen-year-old uses bulimia as a way to avoid her mother's and ten-year-old sister's grief, as well as her own.

Isabelle's grief and anger are movingly and honestly portrayed, and her eventual empathy for her mother is believable and touching. —*Booklist*

Friesen, Gayle

The **Isabel** factor. By Gayle Friesen. Kids Can Press, 2005 256 p; Grades: 7 8 9 10

1. Summer camps; 2. Camp counselors; 3. Identity (Psychology); 4. Making friends; 5. Friendship; 6. Coming-of-age stories; 7. Canadian fiction.
9781553377375; 9781553377382

Anna and Zoe are inseparable—at least until Zoe breaks her arm and Anna finds herself on her way to summer camp without her best friend.... By the time Zoe arrives at camp (with her arm still in a sling), Anna is already embroiled in keeping peace between the individualistic Isabel and everyone else in Cabin 7.... Girls addicted to friendship stories will welcome this particularly well-crafted novel. —*Booklist*

Friesner, Esther M.

Nobody's princess. Esther Friesner. Random House, 2007 320 p. (Princesses of myth, 1)
Grades: 6 7 8 9 10

1. Helen of Troy (Greek mythology); 2. Princesses; 3. Young women; 4. Gods and goddesses; 5. Gender role; 6. Mediterranean Region; 7. Historical fiction; 8. Mythological fiction
9780375875281; 9780375975288; 9780375875298; 9780375875304
LC 2006006515

Determined to fend for herself in a world where only men have real freedom, headstrong Helen, who will be called queen of Sparta and Helen of Troy one day, learns to fight, hunt, and ride horses while disguised as a boy, and goes on an adventure throughout the Mediterranean world.

This is a fascinating portrait.... Along the way, Friesner skillfully exposes larger issues of women's rights, human bondage, and individual destiny. It's a rollicking good story. —*Booklist*

Nobody's princess. Esther Friesner. Random House, 2007 320 p. (Princesses of myth, 1)
Grades: 6 7 8 9 10

1. Helen of Troy (Greek mythology); 2. Princesses; 3. Young women; 4. Gods and goddesses; 5. Gender role; 6. Mediterranean Region; 7. Historical fiction; 8. Mythological fiction
9780375875281; 9780375975288; 9780375875298; 9780375875304
LC 2006006515

Determined to fend for herself in a world where only men have real freedom, headstrong Helen, who will be called queen of Sparta and Helen of Troy one day, learns to fight, hunt, and ride horses while disguised as a boy, and goes on an adventure throughout the Mediterranean world.

This is a fascinating portrait.... Along the way, Friesner skillfully exposes larger issues of women's rights, human bondage, and individual destiny. It's a rollicking good story. —*Booklist*

Sphinx's princess. Esther Friesner. Random House, 2009 370 p. (Princesses of myth, 3)
Grades: 8 9 10 11 12

1. Nefertiti, Queen of Egypt, active 14th century BCE; 2. Women rulers; 3. Power (Social sciences); 4. Duty; 5. Beauty; 6. Aunts; 7. Egypt; 8. Ancient Egypt (3100 BCE-640 CE); 9. Historical fiction; 10. First person narratives.
9780375956546
LC 2009013719

Although she is a dutiful daughter, Nefertiti's dancing abilities, remarkable beauty, and intelligence garner attention near and far, so much so that her family is summoned to the Egyptian royal court, where Nefertiti becomes a pawn in the power play of her scheming aunt, Queen Tiye.

Dramatic plot twists, a powerful female subject, and engrossing details of life in ancient Egypt make for lively historical fiction. —*Booklist*
Sequel: *Sphinx's queen.*

Sphinx's queen. Esther Friesner. Random House, 2010 288 p. (Princesses of myth, 4)
Grades: 8 9 10 11 12

1. Nefertiti, Queen of Egypt, active 14th century BCE; 2. Women rulers; 3. Malicious accusation; 4. Resource- fulness in teenage girls; 5. Resourcefulness; 6. Justice; 7. Egypt; 8. Ancient Egypt (3100 BCE-640 CE); 9. Historical fiction; 10. First person narratives.
9780375856570
LC 2010013769

Chased after by the prince and his soldiers for a crime she did not commit, Nefertiti finds temporary refuge in the wild hills along the Nile's west bank before returning to the royal court to plead her case to the Pharaoh.

This is written in fine prose that expresses the questioning of religion that most young people experience as they approach maturity.... This deeply moral book tells a good story; or, rather, this good story reveals deeply moral truths. —*School Library Journal*
Sequel to: *Sphinx's princess.*

Spirit's princess. Esther Friesner. Random House, 2012 464 p. (Princesses of myth, 5)
Grades: 7 8 9 10

1. Shamans; 2. Spirits; 3. Gender role; 4. Magic; 5. Teenage girls; 6. Japan; 7. 3rd century; 8. Historical fiction; 9. Mythological fiction; 10. Asian-influenced fantasy
9780375869075
LC 2011010468

In ancient Japan, Himiko, the privileged daughter of her clan's leader, fights the constraints and expectations imposed on young women and finds her own path, which includes secret shaman lessons.
Sequel: *Spirit's chosen.*

Frost, Helen

★ The **braid**. Helen Frost. Farrar, Straus and Giroux, 2006 112 p. Grades: 7 8 9 10

1. Teenage girls; 2. Teenagers; 3. Sisters; 4. Families; 5. Islands; 6. Mingulay, Scotland; 7. Cape Breton Island (N.S.); 8. 1850s; 9. Historical fiction; 10. First person narratives; 11. Multiple perspectives
9780374309626
LC 2005040148

School Library Journal Best Books, 2006; YALSA Best Books for Young Adults, 2007.

Two Scottish sisters, living on the western island of Barra in the 1850s, relate, in alternate voices and linked narrative poems, their experiences after their family is forcible evicted and separated with one sister accompanying their parents and younger siblings to Cape Breton, Canada, and the other staying behind with other family on the small island of Mingulay.

The book will inspire both students and teachers to go back and study how the taut poetic lines manage to contain the powerful feelings. —*Booklist*
Frances Foster books.

★ **Crossing** stones. Helen Frost. Farrar, Straus and Giroux, 2009 192 p.
Grades: 6 7 8 9 10

1. Neighbors; 2. World War I; 3. Interpersonal conflict; 4. Friendship; 5. Soldiers; 6. Michigan; 7. First World War era (1914-1918); 8. War stories; 9. Historical fiction; 10. Novels in verse.

9780374316532

LC 2008020755

Amelia Bloomer List, 2010; Booklist Editors' Choice: Books for Youth, 2009; YALSA Best Books for Young Adults, 2010.

In their own voices, four young people, Muriel, Frank, Emma, and Ollie, tell of their experiences during the first World War, as the boys enlist and are sent overseas, Emma finishes school, and Muriel fights for peace and women's suffrage.

Beautifully written in formally structured verse.... This [is a] beautifully written, gently told story. —*Voice of Youth Advocates*

Frances Foster Books.

★ **Keesha's** house. Helen Frost. Frances Foster Books/Farrar, Straus and Giroux, 2003 116 p.

Grades: 7 8 9 10

1. Teenagers; 2. Home (Concept); 3. Family problems; 4. Interpersonal relations; 5. Homosexuality; 6. Novels in verse; 7. Urban fiction; 8. Realistic fiction

9780374340643

LC 2002022698

YALSA Best Books for Young Adults, 2004; YALSA Popular Paperbacks for Young Adults, 2008; Michael L. Printz Honor Book, 2004.

Seven teens facing such problems as pregnancy, closeted homosexuality, and abuse each describe in poetic forms what caused them to leave home and where they found home again.

Spare, eloquent, and elegantly concise.... Public, private, or correctional educators and librarians should put this must-read on their shelves. —*Voice of Youth Advocates*

Fusco, Kimberly Newton

Chasing Augustus. Kimberly Newton Fusco. Random House Childrens Books, 2017 336 p.

Grades: 4 5 6 7 8

1. Determination in teenage girls; 2. Teenagers and dogs; 3. Searching; 4. Mother-deserted children; 5. Grandfather and granddaughter.

9780385754019; 9780571323029, Paperback, Australia

Rosie's led a charmed life with her loving dad, who runs the town donut shop. It's true her mother abandoned them when Rosie was just a baby, but her dad's all she's ever needed. But now that her father's had a stroke, Rosie lives with her tough-as-nails grandfather. And her beloved dog, Gloaty Gus, has just gone missing. Rosie's determined to find him. With the help of a new friend and her own determination, she'll follow the trail anywhere...no matter where it leads. If she doesn't drive the whole world crazy in the meantime.

Tending to Grace. Kimberly Newton Fusco. Knopf, 2004 167 p.

Grades: 7 8 9 10

1. Teenage neglect victims; 2. Stuttering; 3. Emotional problems of teenage girls; 4. Emotional problems; 5. Great-aunts; 6. Realistic fiction; 7. First person narratives.

9780375828621; 9780375928628

LC 2003060406

Schneider Family Book Award for Middle School, 2006; YALSA Best Books for Young Adults, 2005.

When Cornelia's mother runs off with a boyfriend, leaving her with an eccentric aunt, Cornelia must finally confront the truth about herself and her mother.

This quiet, beautiful first novel makes the search for home a searing drama. —*Booklist*

Gagnon, Michelle

Don't let go. Michelle Gagnon. Harper, an imprint of HarperCollins, 2014 352 pages (Persefone trilogy (Michelle Gagnon), 3)

Grades: 7 8 9 10 11 12

1. Hackers; 2. Human experimentation in medicine; 3. Foster children; 4. Experiments; 5. Corporations; 6. Thrillers and suspense; 7. Cyber-thrillers

9780062102966

LC 2014001880

In his final installment of the Don't Turn Around trilogy, Noa, Peter, and what is left of their army race across the country in their search to destroy Project Persephone before time runs out.

Don't look now. Michelle Gagnon. Harper, an imprint of HarperCollins, 2013 320 p. (Persefone trilogy (Michelle Gagnon), 2)

Grades: 7 8 9 10 11 12

1. Hackers; 2. Human experimentation in medicine; 3. Foster children; 4. Experiments; 5. Rich teenage boys; 6. Thrillers and suspense; 7. Cyber-thrillers

9780062102935

Still suffering strange side effects from her stint as a human lab rat at Pike & Dolan, Noa (*Don't Turn Around*) leads a group of homeless teens bent on sabotaging the corporation. In Boston, her hacktivist friend Peter and his ex-girlfriend, Amanda, uncover new evidence that places them all in danger. This tense, suspenseful tech-thriller will engage readers from beginning to end. —*Horn Book Guide*

Don't turn around. By Michelle Gagnon. Harper, 2012 400 p. (Persefone trilogy (Michelle Gagnon), 1)

Grades: 7 8 9 10 11 12

1. Hackers; 2. Conspiracies; 3. Human experimentation in medicine; 4. Rich teenage boys; 5. Teenage girl orphans; 6. Thrillers and suspense; 7. Cyber-thrillers

9780062102904

LC 2012009691

YALSA Best Fiction for Young Adults, 2013.

Noa Torson is a smart and tough computer hacker. As a runaway teenager, Noa thrives living "off the grid"—until the day she wakes up on an operating table with no memory of how she got there. Noa teams up with fellow hacker Peter to discover what happened to her, but the pair soon becomes the target of a dangerous corporation determined to keep them from exposing its deadly secrets.

Gaiman, Neil

The **sleeper** and the spindle. Neil Gaiman; illustrated by Chris Riddell. HarperCollins Children's Books, 2015 69 p.

Grades: 5 6 7 8 9 10

1. Princesses; 2. Enchantment; 3. Sleep; 4. Women rulers; 5. Quests; 6. Fairy tale and folklore-inspired fiction; 7. Fantasy fiction; 8. Illustrated books

9780062398246; 9781408878422, print, UK

Kate Greenaway Medal, 2016.

A brave young queen and her dwarf companions set out to rescue an enchanted princess who is not quite what she seems.

Each page is packed with marvelous details—vines claustrophobically twist everywhere and expressions convey far more emotion than the words let on. Gaiman's narrative about strength, sacrifice, choice, and identity is no simple retelling; he sends readers down one path then deliciously sends the story veering off in an unexpected direction. —*School Library Journal*

Galante, Cecilia

The **summer** of May. By Cecilia Galante. Aladdin, 2011 288 p.

Grades: 5 6 7 8
1. Mother-deserted children; 2. Teacher-student relationships; 3. Anger; 4. Anger in teenage girls; 5. Language arts; 6. Realistic fiction.
9781416980230

LC 2010015879

An angry thirteen-year-old girl and her hated English teacher spend a summer school class together, learning surprising things about each other.

May's voice is sometimes humorous, at times heartbreaking, and always authentic.... A taut and believable novel. —*School Library Journal*

Gansworth, Eric L.

Give me some truth: a novel with paintings. Eric Gansworth. 2018 400 p.
Grades: 8 9 10 11 12
1. Native American teenagers; 2. Indian reservations; 3. Teenage musicians; 4. Bands (Music); 5. Tuscarora Indians; 6. New York (State); 7. Tuscarora Nation Reservation (N.Y.); 8. 1980s; 9. Historical fiction; 10. Coming-of-age stories; 11. Multiple perspectives
9781338143546

LC 2017042555

School Library Journal Best Books, 2018.

In 1980 life is hard on the Tuscarora Reservation in upstate New York, and most of the teenagers feel like they are going nowhere: Carson Mastick dreams of forming a rock band, and Maggi Bokoni longs to create her own conceptual artwork instead of the traditional beadwork that her family sells to tourists—but tensions are rising between the reservation and the surrounding communities, and somehow in the confusion of politics and growing up Carson and Maggi have to make a place for themselves.

A rich, honest story of family and friends, of a Nation within a nation. —*Horn Book Guide*

Garber, Romina

★ **Lobizona**. Romina Garber. St Martins Pr 2020 400 p. (Wolves of no world, 1)
Grades: 9 10 11 12
1. Undocumented immigrants; 2. Werewolves; 3. Identity (Psychology); 4. Family secrets; 5. Magic; 6. Urban fantasy; 7. Fairy tale and folklore-inspired fiction.
9781250239129

LC 2019051880

When her mother is arrested by ICE, sixteen-year-old Argentinian Manu—who thinks she is hiding in a Miami apartment because she is an undocumented immigrant—discovers that her entire existence is illegal.

This layered novel blends languages and cultures to create a narrative that celebrates perseverance Publishers Weekly

Garber, Stephanie

★ **Caraval**. Stephanie Garber. Flatiron Books, 2017 400 p. (Caraval, 1)
Grades: 8 9 10 11
1. Circus; 2. Kidnapping; 3. Games; 4. Teenage romance; 5. Magic; 6. Fantasy fiction
9781250095251

Romantic Times Reviewer's Choice Award, 2017.

Believing that she will never be allowed to participate in the annual Caraval performance when her ruthless father arranges her marriage, Scarlett receives the invitation she has always dreamed of before her sister, Tella, is kidnapped by the show's mastermind organizer.

Garber's rich, vivid scene setting and descriptions make for entertaining reading, and the conclusion hints at a sequel focused on Tella. A colorful, imaginative fantasy with some steamy romance for good measure. —*Booklist*

Sequel: *Legendary*

Garcia, Kami

Beautiful darkness. By Kami Garcia & Margaret Stohl. Little, Brown, 2010 503 p; (Caster chronicles, 2)
Grades: 8 9 10 11 12
1. Teenage witches; 2. Psychic ability; 3. Decision-making; 4. Supernatural; 5. Teenage romance; 6. South Carolina; 7. Paranormal romances.
9780316077057; 9780141326092, print, UK

LC 2010007015

In a small southern town with a secret world hidden in plain sight, sixteen-year-old Lena, who possesses supernatural powers and faces a life-altering decision, draws away from her true love, Ethan, a mortal with frightening visions.

The southern gothic atmosphere, several new characters, and the surprising fate of one old favorite will keep readers going until the next book, which promises new surprises as 18 moons approaches. —*Booklist*

Gardner, Faith

★ The **second** life of Ava Rivers. Faith Gardner. Razorbill, 2018 416 p.
Grades: 9 10 11 12
1. Missing children; 2. Sisters; 3. Twins; 4. Family problems; 5. Former captives; 6. California; 7. Northern California; 8. Realistic fiction
9780451478306

LC 2018003873

Eighteen-year-old Vera, eager to start college and escape the celebrity her family has endured since her twin's disappearance twelve years earlier, finds her world turned upside-down again when Ava returns.

A teen girl's life is turned upside down when her missing twin reappears after 12 years... A deftly written examination of familial relationships, trauma, and post-adolescence. —*Kirkus*

Gardner, Kati

★ **Finding** balance. Kati Gardner. Flux, 2020 344 p.
Grades: 8 9 10 11 12
1. Cancer survivors; 2. Teenagers with disabilities; 3. Teenage boy/girl relations; 4. People who have had amputations; 5. Social acceptance; 6. Realistic fiction; 7. Multiple perspectives.
9781635830521, PAP, US; 9781635830538, ebook, US

LC 2019054447

Teenage cancer survivors Mari and Jase have flirted for years at Camp Chemo, but when she transfers to his high school their different approaches to their history cause trouble.

Gardner writes compellingly not only about the romance between these two teens, but also about the nuances in their navigation of survival. —*School Library Journal*

Gardner, Sally

The **red** necklace: a story of the French Revolution. Sally Gardner. Dial Books, 2008 378 p;
Grades: 8 9 10 11 12
1. Romanies; 2. Rescues; 3. Fourteen-year-old boys; 4. Teenage boys; 5. Twelve-year-old girls; 6. France; 7. Revolutionary France (1789-1799); 8. 1790s; 9. Historical fiction; 10. Adventure stories.
9780803731004

LC 2007039813

YALSA Best Books for Young Adults, 2009.

In the late eighteenth-century, Sido, the twelve-year-old daughter of a self-indulgent marquis, and Yann, a fourteen-year-old Gypsy orphan raised to perform in a magic show, face a common enemy at the start of the French Revolution.

Scores are waiting to be settled on every page; this is a heart-stopper. —*Booklist*

Sequel: *The silver blade.*

The **silver** blade. Sally Gardner. Dial Books, 2009 368 p.
Grades: 8 9 10 11 12
1. Romanies; 2. Rescues; 3. Magic; 4. Teenage boys; 5. Teenagers; 6. France; 7. Revolutionary France (1789-1799); 8. 1790s; 9. Historical fiction; 10. Adventure stories.
9780803733770

LC 2009009282

As the Revolution descends into the ferocious Reign of Terror, Yann, now an extraordinary practioner of magic, uses his skills to confound his enemies and help spirit refugees out of France, but the question of his true identity and the kidnapping of his true love, Sido, expose him to dangers that threaten to destroy him.

A luscious melodrama, rich in sensuous detail from horrific to sublime, with an iridescent overlay of magic. —*Kirkus*

Sequel to: *The red necklace*; First published in Great Britain in 2009 by Orion Children's Books.

Gardner, Scot
The **dead** I know. Scot Gardner. Houghton Mifflin Harcourt, 2015 208 p.
Grades: 9 10 11 12
1. Funeral homes; 2. Nightmares; 3. Sleep-walkers; 4. Sleep-walking; 5. Coping; 6. Realistic fiction; 7. Australian fiction
9780544232747; 9781742373843, paperback, Australia; 9780143182122, paperback, Australia
Children's Book of the Year Award for Older Readers (Children's Book Council of Australia), 2012; Children's Book Council of Australia: Notable Australian Children's Book.

Aaron Rowe, fresh out of high school and an apprentice to a funeral, searches for the truth about his sleepwalking and disturbing dreams before he falls asleep and never wakes up.

Originally published in Australia by Allen & Unwin in 2011.

Gardner, Whitney
★ **You're** welcome, universe. Whitney Gardner. Alfred A Knopf, 2017 297 p.
Grades: 8 9 10 11 12
1. Teenagers who are deaf; 2. Graffiti; 3. East Indian American teenagers; 4. Graffiti artists; 5. Street art; 6. Realistic fiction; 7. Canadian fiction
9780399551413
Schneider Family Book Award for Teens, 2018.

Gardner brings together Deaf culture, discrimination, sexuality, friendship, body image, trust, betrayal, and even a potential Banksy spotting for this fresh novel, brightened by black-and-white illustrations from Julias notebooks. —*Booklist*

Garrett, Camryn
Full disclosure. Camryn Garrett. Alfred A. Knopf, 2019 320 p.
Grades: 9 10 11 12
1. African American teenage girls; 2. HIV (Viruses); 3. Bullying and bullies; 4. Dating (Social customs); 5. Teenagers; 6. San Francisco Bay Area; 7. Realistic fiction; 8. African American fiction.
9781984829955; 9781984829962; 9781984829986

LC 2019031196

Simone, seventeen, HIV-positive and in love for the first time, decides that facing potential bullies head-on may be better than protecting her secret.

Garrett's debut novel not only successfully tackles discrimination through the lenses of race, sexuality, and having HIV, but also shows the possibility of living a full life despite it all. —*Kirkus*

Gaughen, A. C.
Imprison the sky. A. C. Gaughen. Bloomsbury, 2019 432 p. (Elementae, 2)
Grades: 9 10 11 12
1. Four elements; 2. Ship captains; 3. Women rulers; 4. Political intrigue; 5. Seafaring life; 6. High fantasy; 7. Fantasy fiction.
9781681191140

Aspasia, eighteen, an Elementae who controls air, gets caught in a battle between Cyrus, who forces her to capture slaves for market, and a queen whose husband experiments on Elementae.

In this breathtaking follow-up to Reign the Earth (2018), readers return to the same Elementae world with a protagonist who loves the sea as much as she loves her family Booklist..

Reign the Earth. By A.C. Gaughen. 2018 320 p. (Elementae, 1)
Grades: 9 10 11 12
1. Four elements; 2. Magic; 3. Princesses; 4. Political intrigue; 5. Teenage girls; 6. High fantasy; 7. Fantasy fiction
9781681191119

LC 2017024397

Having sacrificed her freedom to establish peace with a neighboring kingdom, Shalia discovers that she has the power to control earth the day she marries Calix, whose only motivation is to eliminate the Elementae.

Gaughen...delivers a tale of staggering magic, cutthroat royalty, and lethal intrigue. —*Booklist*

Geiger, J. C.
Wildman. J. C. Geiger. 2017 336 p.
Grades: 9 10 11 12
1. Overachievers; 2. Self-fulfillment; 3. Small towns; 4. Teenage boy/girl relations; 5. Self-fulfillment in teenage boys; 6. Washington (State); 7. Realistic fiction; 8. Coming-of-age stories
9781484749579

LC 2016029359

Lance Hendricks, eighteen, is an over-achiever headed to the last big party before graduation when his car breaks down in a remote Washington town, leading to life-changing experiences.

A thought-provoking, hilarious, eloquent story of a young man realizing that the world is much larger than the one set up for him. —*Kirkus*

George, Jessica Day
★ **Princess** of the Midnight Ball. Jessica Day George. Bloomsbury, 2009 280 p; (Princess books (Jessica Day George), 1)
Grades: 6 7 8 9 10
1. Princesses; 2. Curses; 3. Dancing; 4. Spells (Magic); 5. Magic; 6. 19th century; 7. Fantasy fiction; 8. Fairy tale and folklore-inspired fiction
9781599903224

LC 2008030310

Beehive Young Adult Book Award (Utah), 2011; YALSA Popular Paperbacks for Young Adults, 2016; YALSA Best Books for Young Adults, 2010.

A retelling of the tale of twelve princesses who wear out their shoes dancing every night, and of Galen, a former soldier now working in the king's gardens, who follows them in hopes of breaking the curse.

Fans of fairy-tale retellings...will enjoy this story for its magic, humor, and touch of romance. —*School Library Journal*

Gibney, Shannon

Dream country. By Shannon Gibney. Dutton, 2018 335 p.
Grades: 10 11 12
1. African American families; 2. Slavery; 3. Racism; 4. Families; 5. Liberia; 6. 19th century; 7. 20th century; 8. Family sagas.
9780735231672; 9780735231689; 9780735231696, ebook, US
LC 2017055923
Minnesota Book Award for Young People's Literature, 2019.

Spanning two centuries and two continents, *Dream Country* is the story of five generations of young people caught in a spiral of death and exile between Liberia and the United States.

See no color. By Shannon Gibney. 2015 196 p.
Grades: 7 8 9 10
1. Multiracial teenage girls; 2. Identity (Psychology); 3. Adopted girls; 4. Interracial families; 5. Sixteen-year-old girls; 6. Realistic fiction
9781467776820; 9781467788144, ebook, US
LC 2015001619
Minnesota Book Award for Young People's Literature, 2016.

Alex has always identified herself as a baseball player, the daughter of a winning coach, but when she realizes that is not enough she begins to come to terms with her adoption and her race.

Gier, Kerstin

Emerald green. Kerstin Gier; translated from the German by Anthea Bell. Henry Holt and Company, 2013 448 p. (Ruby red trilogy, 3)
Grades: 7 8 9 10
1. Time travel (Past); 2. Prophecies; 3. Secret societies; 4. Time machines; 5. Teenage romance; 6. London, England; 7. England; 8. Urban fantasy; 9. First person narratives; 10. Translations
9780805092677
LC 2013017885
Since learning she is the Ruby, the final member of the time-traveling Circle of Twelve, nothing has gone right for Gwen and she holds suspicions about both Count Saint-German and Gideon, but as she uncovers the Circle's secrets she finally learns her own destiny.

Sapphire blue. Kerstin Gier; translated from the German by Anthea Bell. Henry Holt, 2012 368 p. (Ruby red trilogy, 2)
Grades: 7 8 9 10
1. Time travel (Past); 2. Prophecies; 3. Secret societies; 4. Time machines; 5. Teenage romance; 6. London, England; 7. England; 8. Urban fantasy; 9. First person narratives; 10. Translations
9780805092660
LC 2011034011
Sixteen-year-old Gwen, the newest and final member of the secret time-traveling Circle of Twelve, searches through history for the other time-travelers, aided by friend Lesley, James the ghost, Xemerius the gargoyle demon, and Gideon, the Diamond, whose fate seems bound with hers.

Originally published in Germany in 2010 by Arena Verlag GmbH under the title *Saphirblau: Liebe geht durch alle Zeiten.*

Gilbert, Kelly Loy

Conviction. Kelly Loy Gilbert. 2015 342 pages
Grades: 9 10 11 12
1. Fathers and sons; 2. Faith (Christianity); 3. Trials (Murder); 4. Small towns; 5. Hit-and-run accidents; 6. Realistic fiction
9781423197386
LC 2014042087
School Library Journal Best Books, 2015; YALSA Best Fiction for Young Adults, 2016; William C. Morris Debut Award finalist, 2016.

A small-town boy questions everything he holds to be true when his father is accused of murder.

Picture us in the light. Kelly Loy Gilbert. 2018 368 p.
Grades: 9 10 11 12
1. Chinese-American teenage boys; 2. Children of immigrants; 3. Family secrets; 4. Best friends; 5. Teenage artists; 6. Silicon Valley, California; 7. California; 8. Realistic fiction
9781484726020; 9781484734117
LC 2017034519
School Library Journal Best Books, 2018; YALSA Best Fiction for Young Adults, 2019; Stonewall Children's & Young Adult Literature Honor Book, 2019.

Daniel, a Chinese-American teen, must grapple with his plans for the future, his feelings for his best friend Harry, and his discovery of a family secret that could shatter everything.

Family, art, love, duty, and longing collide in this painfully beautiful paean to the universal human need for connection. —*Kirkus*

Giles, Gail

Dark song. By Gail Giles. Little, Brown, 2010 304 p.
Grades: 8 9 10 11 12
1. Fifteen-year-old girls; 2. Family relationships; 3. Money — Psychological aspects; 4. Embezzlement; 5. Teenage girls; 6. Thrillers and suspense; 7. Psychological fiction; 8. Books for reluctant readers
9780316068864
YALSA Quick Picks for Reluctant Young Adult Readers, 2011.

Suspense lovers will savor this fast-paced psychological thriller. —*Voice of Youth Advocates*

★ **Girls** like us. Gail Giles. Candlewick Press, 2014 224 p.
Grades: 9 10 11 12
1. Children with developmental disabilities — Education; 2. Life change events; 3. Friendship; 4. Violence against children; 5. Violence against young women; 6. First person narratives; 7. Realistic fiction; 8. Multiple perspectives.
9780763662677
Amelia Bloomer List, 2015; Booklist Editors' Choice: Books for Youth, 2014; Schneider Family Book Award for Teens, 2015; YALSA Best Fiction for Young Adults, 2015.

In compelling, engaging, and raw voices, 18-year-olds Biddy and Quincy, newly independent, intellectually disabled high-school graduates, narrate their growing friendship and uneasy transition into a life of jobs, real world apartments, and facing cruel prejudice.... Giles offers a sensitive and affecting story of two young women learning to thrive in spite of their hard circumstances. —*Booklist*

Right behind you: a novel. By Gail Giles. Little, Brown, 2007 292 p.
Grades: 8 9 10 11 12
1. Guilt in teenage boys; 2. Secrets; 3. Redemption; 4. Fourteen-year-old boys; 5. Guilt; 6. Alaska; 7. Indiana; 8. Books for reluctant readers
9780316166362
LC 2007012336
YALSA Quick Picks for Reluctant Young Adult Readers, 2009.

After spending over four years in a mental institution for murdering a friend in Alaska, fourteen-year-old Kip begins a completely new life in Indiana with his father and stepmother under a different name, but not only has trouble fitting in, he finds there are still problems to deal with from his childhood.

The story-behind-the-headlines flavor gives this a voyeuristic appeal, while the capable writing and sympathetic yet troubled protagonist will suck readers right into the action. —*Bulletin of the Center for Children's Books*

Shattering glass. Gail Giles. Roaring Brook Press, 2002 215 p;.
Grades: 7 8 9 10
1. Teenage misfits; 2. Violence in teenagers; 3. Manipulation by teenagers; 4. Manipulation (Social sciences); 5. Teenage boys; 6. Thrillers and suspense; 7. Books for reluctant readers
9780761315810; 9780761326014

LC 2001041713
California Young Reader Medal, Young Adult, 2007; YALSA Popular Paperbacks for Young Adults, 2012; YALSA Quick Picks for Reluctant Young Adult Readers, 2003; YALSA Best Books for Young Adults, 2003.

When Rob, the charismatic leader of the senior class, turns the school nerd into Prince Charming, his actions lead to unexpected violence.

Tricky, surprising, and disquieting, this tension-filled story is a psychological thriller as well as a book about finding oneself and taking responsibility. —*Booklist*

★ **What** happened to Cass McBride? By Gail Giles. Little, Brown and Co, 2006 224 p.
Grades: 11 12
1. Revenge; 2. Teenage kidnapping victims; 3. College students; 4. Kidnapping; 5. Teenagers; 6. Thrillers and suspense; 7. Multiple perspectives; 8. Books for reluctant readers
9780316166386

LC 2005037298
YALSA Popular Paperbacks for Young Adults, 2015; YALSA Quick Picks for Reluctant Young Adult Readers, 2007; YALSA Best Books for Young Adults, 2007.

After his younger brother commits suicide, Kyle Kirby decides to exact revenge on the person he holds responsible.

Often brutal, this outstanding psychological thriller is recommended for older teens. —*Voice of Youth Advocates*

Giles, L. R.
Fake ID. L.R. Giles. 2014 320 pages
Grades: 8 9 10 11 12
1. African American teenage boys; 2. Federal Witness Protection Program; 3. Conspiracies; 4. Murder; 5. Teenage boys; 6. Virginia; 7. Mysteries; 8. African American fiction; 9. Books for reluctant readers
9780062121844

LC 2013032149
YALSA Quick Picks for Reluctant Young Adult Readers, 2015; Virginia Readers' Choice Award for High School, 2016.

An African-American teen in the Witness Protection Program moves to a new town and finds himself trying to solve a murder mystery when his first friend is found dead.

Teen readers will especially relate to the likable everyman and African American main character. His burgeoning relationship with Reya, despite being grounded in tragedy, is one of the more charming aspects of the plot. —*School Library Journal*

★ **Not** so pure and simple. Lamar Giles. HarperTeen, 2020 304 p.
Grades: 8 9 10 11 12
1. Virginity; 2. Masculinity; 3. Teenage boys; 4. High schools; 5. Dating (Social customs); 6. Virginia; 7. Coming-of-age stories; 8. Realistic fiction
9780062349194; 9780062349200

LC 2019025683
School Library Journal Best Books, 2020.

High school junior Del Rainey unwittingly joins a Purity Pledge class at church, hoping to get closer to his long-term crush, Kiera.

With true-to-life characters and a straightforward handling of sex, including often ignored aspects of male sexuality, Giles's thoughtful, hilarious read offers a timely viewpoint on religion, toxic masculinity, and teen sexuality. —*Kirkus*

Overturned. Lamar Giles. Scholastic Press, 2017 352 p.
Grades: 7 8 9 10 11 12
1. African American teenage girls; 2. Casinos; 3. Gambling; 4. Murder investigation; 5. Frameups; 6. Las Vegas, Nevada; 7. Mysteries; 8. African American fiction.
9780545812504

LC 2016035488
YALSA Best Fiction for Young Adults, 2018; YALSA Quick Picks for Reluctant Young Adult Readers, 2018.

When her father is cleared of murder charges and released from death row, Nikki, who has been saving money to get out of Vegas by playing illegal poker games, joins her father's obsessive search to find the person who framed him.

A fast-paced, compelling mystery and memorable characters and relationships make this selection a first choice for most YA collections. —*School Library Journal*

Spin. Lamar Giles. Scholastic Press, 2019 352 p.
Grades: 7 8 9 10
1. African American teenage girls; 2. Murder investigation; 3. Media fandom; 4. Interpersonal relations; 5. Secrets; 6. Thrillers and suspense; 7. Multiple perspectives; 8. First person narratives.
9781338219210

LC 2018044097
When DJ ParSec (Paris Secord), rising star of the local music scene, is found dead over her turntables, the two girls who found her, Kya (her pre-fame best friend) and Fuse (her current chief groupie) are torn between grief for Paris and hatred for each other—but when the lack of obvious suspects stalls the investigation, and the police seem to lose interest, despite pressure from social media and ParSec's loyal fans, the two girls unite, determined to find out who murdered their friend.

This is genre fiction at its best: a taut mystery with rich characterization and a strong sense of place. —*Kirkus*

Gill, David Macinnis
Black hole sun. By David Macinnis Gill. Greenwillow Books, 2010 368 p. (Black hole sun, 1)
Grades: 8 9 10 11 12
1. Mercenaries; 2. Mines and mineral resources; 3. Raids (Military science); 4. Cannibals; 5. Miners; 6. Mars (Planet); 7. Science fiction
9780061673047

LC 2009023050
School Library Journal Best Books, 2010.

On the planet Mars, sixteen-year-old Durango and his crew of mercenaries are hired by the settlers of a mining community to protect their most valuable resource from a feral band of marauders.

Durango is the 16-year-old chief of a team of mercenaries who eke out a living on Mars by earning meager commissions for their dangerous work. Their current job, and the main thrust of this high-energy, action-filled, science-fiction romp, is to protect South Pole miners from the Dru, a cannibalistic group who are after the miners' treasure.... Throughout the novel, the dialogue crackles with expertly delivered sarcastic wit and venom.... Readers will have a hard time turning the pages fast enough as the body count rises to the climactic, satisfying ending. —*Booklist*

Sequel: *Invisible Sun.*

Soul enchilada. By David Macinnis Gill. Greenwillow Books, 2009 368 p.
Grades: 7 8 9 10
1. Devil; 2. Repossessors; 3. Grandfathers; 4. Personal conduct; 5. Multiracial women; 6. Texas; 7. Fantasy fiction
9780061673023

LC 2008019486

YALSA Popular Paperbacks for Young Adults, 2011; YALSA Best Books for Young Adults, 2010.

When, after a demon appears to repossess her car, she discovers that both the car and her soul were given as collateral in a deal made with the Devil by her irrascible grandfather, eighteen-year-old Bug Smoot, given two-days' grace, tries to find ways to outsmart the Devil as she frantically searches for her conveniently absent relative.

Bug is a refreshingly gutsy female protagonist with an attitude that will win over readers searching for something different. —*Booklist*

Gilman, David
Blood sun. By David Gilman. Delacorte Press, 2011 336 p. (Danger zone, 3)
Grades: 7 8 9 10 11 12
1. Teenage boy adventurers; 2. Rain forests; 3. Assassins; 4. Drug smugglers; 5. Environmental protection; 6. England; 7. Central America; 8. Adventure stories.
9780385735629; 9780385665155

Desperate to uncover the secret of his mother's death, fifteen-year-old Max Gordon, pursued by enemies, travels from the bleakness of Dartmoor to the rainforest of Central America, where the environmental devastation hides a sinister secret.

Max Gordon is a likable character who faces tough challenges with determination, physical strength and a positive attitude.... This is...a solid read from start to breathless finish. —*Kirkus*

The **devil's** breath. David Gilman. Random House Childrens Books, 2008 336 p. (Danger zone, 1)
Grades: 7 8 9 10 11 12
1. Missing persons; 2. Father-separated teenage boys; 3. Environmentalism; 4. Missing persons investigation; 5. Kidnapping; 6. Namibia; 7. Adventure stories
9780385905466; 9780385669948

When fifteen-year-old Max Gordon's environmentalist-adventurer father goes missing while working in Namibia and Max becomes the target of a would-be assassin at his school in England, he decides he must follow his father to Africa and find him before they both are killed.

The action is relentless.... Gilman has a flair for making the preposterous seem possible. —*Booklist*

Ice claw. David Gilman. Random House Children's Books, 2010 336 p. (Danger zone, 2)
Grades: 7 8 9 10 11 12
1. Teenage boy adventurers; 2. Teenage murder witnesses; 3. Extreme sports; 4. Teenage boys; 5. Ecological disturbances — Prevention; 6. Pyrenees; 7. France; 8. Adventure stories.
9780385905473

The omniscient point of view...does a lot for clarity, which is his strong suitfew authors are able to depict action scenes so lucidly.... But it's Max's humanity...that makes Gilman's research and storytelling come alive. —*Booklist*

Gilmore, Kate
The **exchange** student. Houghton Mifflin 1999 217 p.
Grades: 7 8 9 10
1. Wildlife conservation; 2. Rare and endangered animals; 3. Aliens (Humanoid); 4. Exchange students; 5. Science fiction; 6. Books for reluctant readers
9780395575116

LC 97047162

YALSA Quick Picks for Reluctant Young Adult Readers, 2000; YALSA Best Books for Young Adults, 2000.

When her mother arranges to host one of the young people coming to Earth from Chela, Daria is both pleased and intrigued by the keen interest shown by the Chelan in her work breeding endangered species.

Gilmore makes a farfetched premise seem more reasonable with everyday details of life in the twenty-first century, sympathetic characters, and logical consequences.... A story that will appeal to readers on many levels. —*Booklist*

Girard, M-E
★ **Girl** mans up. M-E Girard. Katherine Tegen Books, 2016 384 p.
Grades: 9 10 11 12
1. Lesbian teenagers; 2. Gender identity; 3. Children of immigrants; 4. Loyalty; 5. Friendship; 6. Canada; 7. Ontario; 8. Realistic fiction; 9. LGBTQIA fiction; 10. Canadian fiction
9780062404176; 9781443447041; 9781443447058, Paperback, Canada

Amelia Bloomer List, 2017; Lambda Literary Award for Young Adult/Children, 2017; OLA Best Bets, 2016; Rainbow List, 2017; YALSA Best Fiction for Young Adults, 2017; William C. Morris Debut Award finalist, 2017.

Pen, who looks and acts like a boy, just wants is to be the kind of girl she is always been, but the people in her life have a problem with it? Old-world parents, faltering friendships, and strong feelings toward other girls lead Pen to see that in order to be who she truly wants to be, she'll have to man up.

A strong genderqueer lesbian character, imperfect, independent, and deserving of every cheer. —*Kirkus*

Glaser, Mechthild
The **book** jumper. Mechthild Gläser; [translated by Romy Fursland]. Henry Holt and Company, 2017 384 p.
Grades: 8 9 10
1. Books; 2. Characters and characteristics in literature; 3. Thieves; 4. Islands; 5. Fifteen-year-old girls; 6. Scotland; 7. Gateway fantasy; 8. Fantasy fiction; 9. Translations
9781250086662

LC 2016007363

A teen girl discovers she is a book jumper—she can leap directly into books, meet the characters, and experience the world of the book.

This offering is the first U.S. title from an award-winning German author and would be a good additional purchase for fans of Cornelia Funke's *Inkheart* or Kristin Kladstrup's *The Book of Story Beginnings.* —*School Library Journal*

Translated from the German.

Glasgow, Kathleen
★ **Girl** in pieces. Kathleen Glasgow. Delacorte Press, 2016 416 p.
Grades: 10 11 12
1. Homeless persons; 2. Self-harm; 3. Emotional problems; 4. Homeless teenage girls; 5. Cutting (Self-harm); 6. Arizona; 7. Realistic fiction
9781101934715; 9781101934722, ebook, US

LC 2015044136

Amelia Bloomer List, 2017; YALSA Best Fiction for Young Adults, 2017.

As she struggles to recover and survive, seventeen-year-old homeless Charlotte "Charlie" Davis cuts herself to dull the pain of abandonment and abuse.

This grittily provocative debut explores the horrors of self-harm and the healing power of artistic expression. —*Kirkus*

Gleason, Colleen

The **clockwork** scarab. Colleen Gleason. Chronicle Books, 2013 356 p. (Stoker & Holmes novels, 1)
Grades: 7 8 9 10

1. Secret societies; 2. Time travel; 3. Scarabs; 4. Vampire slayers; 5. Detectives; 6. London, England; 7. Great Britain; 8. Victorian era (1837-1901); 9. 19th century; 10. Historical mysteries; 11. Steampunk
9781452110707
YALSA Popular Paperbacks for Young Adults, 2015.

Roped into respective family businesses when two society girls go missing, Evaline, the sister of Bram Stoker, and Mina, the niece of Sherlock Holmes, overcome a fierce rivalry to investigate three mysterious gentlemen and a strange Egyptian relic.

Few answers are offered in this outing, but the author's writing exudes energy, romance, and humor, and she gives her heroines strong, vibrant personalities as they puzzle out the expansive mystery unfolding before them. —*Publishers Weekly*

Gleitzman, Morris

Now. Morris Gleitzman. Henry Holt, 2012 176 p. (Once series, 3)
Grades: 7 8 9 10

1. Parent-separated girls; 2. Wildfires; 3. Resilience in girls; 4. Resilience (Personal quality); 5. Grandfather and granddaughter; 6. Australia; 7. Victoria; 8. Realistic fiction; 9. Australian fiction
9780805093780, US; 9780670074372, Australia; 9780141329987, print, UK
Canberra's Own Outstanding List (COOL), Fiction for Years 7-9, 2011; Young Australians' Best Book Awards (YABBA), Fiction, Years 7-9, 2011; USBBY Outstanding International Book, 2013.

While her parents are working in Africa, Zelda is living with her grandfather, Holocaust survivor Felix Salinger, in Australia, when a disaster leads them both to deal with unresolved feelings about the first Zelda, Felix's childhood friend.

Once. Morris Gleitzman. Henry Holt, 2010 163 p. (Once series, 1)
Grades: 7 8 9 10

1. Runaway boys; 2. Book burning; 3. Holocaust (1933-1945); 4. World War II; 5. Hidden children (Holocaust); 6. Poland; 7. 1940s; 8. Historical fiction; 9. Australian fiction
9780805090260, US; 9780143301950, Australia; 9781405664462, print, UK; 9780141329888, print, UK
Kids Own Australian Literature Awards (KOALA), Fiction for Years 7-9, 2007; Young Australians' Best Book Awards (YABBA), Fiction, Years 7-9, 2007; YALSA Popular Paperbacks for Young Adults, 2014; YALSA Best Fiction for Young Adults, 2011; USBBY Outstanding International Book, 2011.

The horror of the Holocaust is told here through the eyes of a Polish Jewish child, Felix, who loses his innocence as he witnesses Nazi-led roundups, shootings, and deportations.... Most moving is the lack of any idealization.... Felix escapes, but one and a half million Jewish children did not, and this gripping novel will make readers want to find out more about them. —*Booklist*

Going, K. L.

★ **Fat** kid rules the world. K.L. Going. G.P. Putnam's Sons, 2003 187 p;
Grades: 7 8 9 10

1. Overweight teenage boys; 2. Teenage musicians; 3. Social acceptance in teenagers; 4. Homeless teenage boys; 5. Teenage boy misfits; 6. New York City; 7. Realistic fiction; 8. First person narratives; 9. Books to movies
9780399239908

LC 2002067956

Booklist Editors' Choice: Books for Youth, 2003; YALSA Best Books for Young Adults, 2004; YALSA Popular Paperbacks for Young Adults, 2012; Young Reader's Choice Award (Pacific Northwest), Senior, 2006; School Library Journal Best Books, 2003; Michael L. Printz Honor Book, 2004.

Seventeen-year-old Troy, depressed, suicidal, and weighing nearly 300 pounds, gets a new perspective on life when a homeless teenager who is a genius on guitar wants Troy to be the drummer in his rock band.

Going has put together an amazing assortment of characters.... This is an impressive debut that offers hope for all kids. —*Booklist*

Gong, Chloe

These violent delights. By Chloe Gong. Simon & Schuster 2020 400 p.
Grades: 9 10 11 12

1. Gang members; 2. Forbidden love; 3. Feuds; 4. Monsters; 5. Death; 6. Shanghai (China); 7. China; 8. 1920s; 9. Shakespeare-inspired fiction; 10. Historical fantasy
9781534457690; 9781529344554, Paperback, UK; 9781529344523, Hardback, UK

LC 2019055326

In 1926 Shanghai, eighteen-year-old Juliette Cai, heir of the Scarlet Gang, and her first love-turned-rival Roma Montagov, leader of the White Flowers, must work together when mysterious deaths threaten their city.

With a dazzling setting, a mysterious series of murders, and diverse, unapologetically criminal characters, this novel ranks with the greatest YA retellings. —*School Library Journal*

Goo, Maurene

I believe in a thing called love. Maurene Goo. 2017 336 p.
Grades: 7 8 9 10 11 12

1. Korean American teenage girls; 2. Overachievers; 3. Crushes in teenage girls; 4. Television programs; 5. Children of widowers; 6. Romantic comedies; 7. Contemporary romances
9780374304041

LC 2016035865

A disaster in romance, high school senior Desi Lee decides to tackle her flirting failures by watching Korean television dramas, where the hapless heroine always seems to end up in the arms of her true love by episode ten.

Plot-driven as the K dramas Goo's protagonist seeks to emulate, her funny, engaging narrative also delivers powerful messages of inclusion and acceptance. —*Kirkus*
Margaret Ferguson Books.

The **way** you make me feel. Maurene Goo. Farrar Straus & Giroux 2018 288 p.
Grades: 8 9 10 11 12

1. Summer employment; 2. Resistance (Psychology) in teenage girls; 3. Food trucks; 4. Making friends; 5. Growth (Psychology); 6. Realistic fiction; 7. Coming-of-age stories
9780374304089; 9780374311957; 9781250308801

Sentenced to a summer working on her father's food truck after taking a joke too far, prankster Korean-American Clara Shin unexpectedly bonds with a straitlaced co-worker and a cute boy on another food truck while reevaluating her relationship with her estranged mother.

With massive amounts of humor, heart, and soul, this love letter to L.A. and its diversity is a celebration of friends, family, and food trucks. —*Booklist*

Goodman, Alison
 The **Dark** Days Club. Alison Goodman. Viking, 2016 496 p. (Lady Helen novels, 1)
Grades: 8 9 10 11 12
 1. Charlotte, Queen, consort of George III, King of Great Britain, 1744-1818; 2. Demons; 3. Nobility; 4. Balls (Parties); 5. Courts and courtiers; 6. Missing persons; 7. London, England; 8. Great Britain; 9. Regency period (1811-1820); 10. Historical fantasy; 11. Australian fiction.
9780670785476; 9781406358964, print, UK; 9781460753866, Paperback, Australia
LC 2015006792
Children's Book Council of Australia: Notable Australian Children's Book, 2017.
 In April 1812, as she is preparing for her debut presentation to Queen Charlotte, Lady Helen Wrexhall finds herself in the middle of a conspiracy reaching to the very top of society, and learns the truth about her mother, who died ten years ago.
 Readers willing to embrace the deep, deliberately paced journey will find the pace and tension increasing until the end leaves them eager for the next volume. —*Kirkus*
 Published in Australia as *Lady Helen and the Dark Days Club*. Reissued in 2019 (HarperCollins).

 ★ **Eon:** Dragoneye reborn. Alison Goodman. Viking Children's Books, 2008 544 p.
Grades: 7 8 9 10
 1. Teenage girls with disabilities; 2. Disguises; 3. Dragons; 4. Gender role; 5. Magic; 6. High fantasy; 7. Fantasy fiction; 8. Australian fiction
9780670062270; 9780732288006, Australia
LC Bl2008017708
Aurealis Awards, Best Fantasy Novel, 2008; Children's Book Council of Australia: Notable Australian Children's Book; Amelia Bloomer List, 2010; YALSA Best Books for Young Adults, 2010; USBBY Outstanding International Book, 2009.
 Supernatural "energy dragons" control all of Earth's energies. Young men compete for the honor of being apprenticed to one of the Dragoneyes, powerful men who communicate and bargain with the dragons on behalf of the people. Sixteen-year-old Eon has been training hard, but, due to an old injury and the fact that "he" is really a girl in disguise, is the least likely to be chosen.
 Entangled politics and fierce battle scenes provide a pulse-quickening pace, while the intriguing characters add interest and depth. —*Booklist*

 Eona: return of the dragoneye. Alison Goodman. Viking, 2011 531 p;
Grades: 7 8 9 10
 1. Teenage girls with disabilities; 2. Dragons; 3. Gender role; 4. Betrayal; 5. Sexuality; 6. High fantasy; 7. Fantasy fiction; 8. Australian fiction
9780670063116; 9780670064144; 9780552572163, print, UK; 9780732284947, Paperback, Australia
 Facing the ultimate battle for control of the land she calls home, Eona finds herself waging an internal battle every bit as devastating as the war threatening to break out across the kingdom.

One of those rare and welcome fantasies that complicate black-and-white morality. —*Kirkus*
 Sequel to: *Eon.*

Goodman, Shawn
 Kindness for weakness. Shawn Goodman. Delacorte Press, 2013 272 p.
Grades: 9 10 11 12
 1. Juvenile delinquents (Boys); 2. Juvenile detention; 3. Teenage abuse victims; 4. Self-esteem; 5. Drug dealers; 6. New York (State); 7. Realistic fiction; 8. Books for reluctant readers
9780385743242
LC 2012015772
YALSA Quick Picks for Reluctant Young Adult Readers, 2014; YALSA Best Fiction for Young Adults, 2014.
 A fifteen-year-old boy from an abusive home desperately seeking his older brother's love and approval starts pushing drugs for him and suffers the consequences.

Goslee, S. J.
 How not to ask a boy to prom. S. J. Goslee. Henry Holt & Co, 2019 288 p.
Grades: 9 10 11 12
 1. Gay teenagers; 2. Proms; 3. Dating (Social customs); 4. Teenage romance; 5. Sixteen-year-old boys; 6. Romantic comedies; 7. First person narratives
9781626724013
 A teenager bravely contends with hormones, homosexuality, and high school in this uproarious romantic comedy of errors that breathes new life into the prom story. —*Kirkus*

 ★ **Whatever:** a novel. By S.J. Goslee. Roaring Brook Press, 2016 304 p.
Grades: 9 10 11 12
 1. Questioning (Sexual or gender identity); 2. Bisexual teenagers; 3. Slackers; 4. Friendship; 5. Dating (Social customs); 6. Realistic fiction; 7. LGBTQIA fiction
9781626723993; 9781250115140; 9781626724006, ebook, US
LC 2015023376
Booklist Editors' Choice: Books for Youth, 2016.
 Junior year is going to be the best ever for slacker Mike until he loses his girlfriend, gets roped into school activities, and becomes totally confused about his sexual orientation after sharing a drunken kiss with a guy.
 A humorous account of a teen's reluctant and awkward journey to acceptance of his emerging bisexuality. —*Kirkus*

Gottfred, B. T.
 ★ The **nerdy** and the dirty. B.t. gottfred. 2016 304 pages
Grades: 10 11 12
 1. Self-acceptance; 2. Teenage boy/girl relations; 3. Dating (Social customs); 4. Identity (Psychology); 5. Self-acceptance in teenagers; 6. Contemporary romances; 7. Multiple perspectives; 8. First person narratives
9781627798501
LC 2016001531
 A cool girl—with an X-rated internal life—and a socially-inept guy prove that opposites attract in this honest look at love, sexuality, and becoming your true self.
 This is a love story that is genuine, explicit, passionate, and often adorable. Pens and Benedicts ability to accept their true selves transcends their hormones, their parents burdens, and their peers expectations, and makes for a reading experience not soon forgotten. —*Booklist*

Grant, Helen

The **glass** demon. Helen Grant. Bantam Dell, 2011 320 p.

Grades: 11 12 Adult

1. Fathers and daughters; 2. Relics; 3. Demons; 4. Supernatural; 5. Teenage girls; 6. Germany; 7. Horror; 8. Adult books for young adults.

9780385344203; 9780345527585; 9780141325767, print, UK

Booklist Editors' Choice, 2011; School Library Journal Best Books: Best Adult Books 4 Teens, 2011.

When seventeen-year-old Lin and her family move to an ancient German castle for a year while her medievalist father searches for the famed Allerheiligen glass—lost stained glass windows that are said to be haunted by a terrifying demon—she becomes involved in a horrific murder mystery.

With its fascinating information on medieval folklore, unique setting, and increasingly claustrophobic sense of terror, this is an exhilarating page-turner that offers a cerebral blend of horror and mystery. —*Booklist*

The **vanishing** of Katharina Linden. Helen Grant. Delacorte, 2010 304 p.

Grades: 11 12 Adult

1. Villages; 2. Missing persons; 3. Secrets; 4. Ten-year-old girls; 5. Bullying and bullies; 6. Germany; 7. Mysteries; 8. Coming-of-age stories; 9. Adult books for young adults.

9780385344173; 9780385344180; 9780440339618

Alex Award, 2011; Booklist Editors' Choice: Adult Books for Young Adults, 2010.

Reviled in her German village home where her only friends are a fellow outcast and an elderly storyteller, eleven-year-old Pia investigates the disappearances of three local girls whom she believes are tied to unsolved missing persons cases from decades earlier.

Set in the small German town of Bad Mnstereifel during a cold, dreary winter when little girls seem to be disappearing left and right, this dark story gains immeasurably from Grant's choice of narrator: Pia Kolvenbach, who is socially ostracized (shunned as the Potentially Explosive Schoolgirl) after her grandmother dies in a bizarre accident. Feeling even more isolated when her English mother and German father begin quarreling, Pia finds companionship with StinkStefan, the most unpopular boy in the class, and Herr Schiller, a kindly old gent who spins terrifying but oddly comforting horror stories. Although thin on plot, the novel has nice atmosphere and takes a tender view of lonely children trying to make sense of a grown-up world. —*New York Times Book Review*

Grant, Michael

Eve & Adam. Michael Grant and Katherine Applegate. Feiwel and Friends, 2012 291 p.

Grades: 7 8 9 10

1. Biomedical engineering; 2. Traffic accident victims; 3. Healing; 4. Corporations; 5. Mothers and daughters; 6. San Francisco, California; 7. Science fiction.

9780312583514

A story told from alternating viewpoints by the husband-and-wife team creators of the Animorphs series follows the efforts of a car accident patient who, while recovering in her mother's research facility, is given the task of creating a perfect boy using detailed simulation technologies.

Observant, smart, and unencumbered by emotion, this is a tasty read that readers will devour in a flash. Lucky for them, there's a sequel planned. —*Publishers Weekly*

Front lines. Michael Grant. Harpercollins Childrens Books, 2016 400 p. (Front lines (Michael Grant), 1)

Grades: 9 10 11 12

1. Women soldiers; 2. Battles; 3. World War II; 4. War; 5. Women in combat; 6. Alternative histories; 7. Multiple perspectives

9780062342157

An epic, genre-bending, and transformative new series that reimagines World War II with girl soldiers fighting on the front lines.

Bestselling science-fiction author Grant did his research (an extensive bibliography is provided), but the odd and likely unintended consequence of his premise is the erasure of thousands of military women who historically served and fought and died. Still, an engrossing portrayal of ordinary women in extraordinary circumstances. —*Kirkus*

Messenger of Fear. Michael Grant. Katherine Tegen Books, 2014 272 pages (Messenger of Fear, 1)

Grades: 9 10 11 12

1. Justice; 2. Teenage apprentices; 3. Fear; 4. Good and evil; 5. Games; 6. Urban fantasy

9780062207401; 9781405265157, print, UK; 9781405276221, print, UK; 9781405265171, print, UK

LC 2014013832

The Messenger of Fear brings justice to those who do wrong, creating frightening games where the players earn their redemption—or lose their sanity—and somehow Mara, fifteen, has become his apprentice.

Grant explores bullying, family problems, suicide, and more, and several painful passages will have readers cringing, even as they make them think about what they would do in the same situation. This is a solid beginning to a series that is likely to be quite popular with horror and paranormal fans. —*Booklist*

★ **Silver** stars: a Front lines novel. Michael Grant. Katherine Tegen Books, an imprint of HarperCollinsPublishers, 2017 548 p. (Front lines (Michael Grant), 2)

Grades: 10 11 12

1. Women soldiers; 2. Prejudice; 3. Sexism; 4. Espionage; 5. Racism; 6. Alternative histories; 7. Multiple perspectives

9780062342188

This series continues to be a fascinating, stunningly written examination of both war and womens role in it, and this installment only adds to its already considerable depth. —*Booklist*

Graudin, Ryan

★ **Blood** for blood. By Ryan Graudin. 2016 496 p. (Wolf by wolf, 2)

Grades: 9 10 11 12

1. Hitler, Adolf, 1889-1945; 2. Jewish teenage girls; 3. Shapeshifters; 4. Resistance to government; 5. Assassins; 6. Nazis; 7. 1950s; 8. Alternative histories

9780316405157; 9780316405133, ebook, US; 9780316405140, ebook, US

LC 2015043452

In this alternate version of the 1950s, after the Axis powers win World War II, Yael, a Jewish skinshifter, fails in her mission to kill Hitler and finds herself being hunted while trying to finish what she started.

Highly recommended for fans of historical fiction, alternate history, or works of espionage and intrigue. —*School Library Journal*

Invictus. By Ryan Graudin. Little, Brown and Company, 2017 416 p.

Grades: 9 10 11 12

1. Time travel; 2. Thieves; 3. Sabotage; 4. Teenage romance; 5. Teenagers; 6. Science fiction; 7. Multiple perspectives

9780316503075; 9780316503082; 9780316503136, ebook, US; 9780316503235, ebook, US

LC 2017000174

YALSA Best Fiction for Young Adults, 2018.

A group of time-traveling teens races through history to try to stop time and the multiverse from unraveling.

A madcap, vivid time-travel tale with a strong ensemble, both indebted and cheekily alluding to *Doctor Who* and *Firefly*. —*Kirkus*

The **walled** city. By Ryan Graudin. Little, Brown and Company, 2014 432 p.
Grades: 9 10 11 12
1. Brothels; 2. Gangs; 3. Homeless children; 4. Violence; 5. Sisters; 6. Hong Kong; 7. Thrillers and suspense; 8. Multiple perspectives
9780316405058; 9781780622002, print, UK
Vivid descriptions add color and infuse the story with realism. While there are mature situations dealing with drugs, violence, and rape, they are skillfully relayed without being graphic. This complex, well-written novel is full of tension, twists, and turns, and teens will not be able to put it down. —*School Library Journal*

Gray, Claudia

Defy the worlds. Claudia Gray. 2018 400 p. (Constellation trilogy, 2)
Grades: 7 8 9 10 11 12
1. Teenage soldiers; 2. Robots; 3. Purpose in life; 4. Love; 5. Loyalty; 6. Space opera; 7. Science fiction; 8. Multiple perspectives.
9780316394109; 9780316394079; 9780316394086, ebook library edition), US
LC 2017034001
Sophisticated robot Abel must save teenaged soldier Noemi from capture on a hidden planet, while outwitting armies of deranged service robots and securing medical aid for a plague on Noemi's home world.
Romantic and adventurous, this novel contains a plethora of STEM-related content and is a worthy discussion starter for conversations about the ethics of technology. —*Booklist*

Evernight. Claudia Gray. HarperTeen, 2008 327 p; (Evernight, 1)
Grades: 8 9 10 11 12
1. Teenage vampires; 2. Teenage misfits; 3. Crushes in teenage girls; 4. Vampire slayers; 5. Teenage boy/girl relations; 6. Paranormal romances; 7. First person narratives
9780061284397; 9780732293222, Australia
LC 2007036733
YALSA Popular Paperbacks for Young Adults, 2013.
Sixteen-year-old Bianca, a new girl at the sinister Evernight boarding school, finds herself drawn to another outsider, Lucas, but dark forces threaten to tear them apart and destroy Bianca's entire world.
Gray's writing hooks readers from the first page and reels them in with surprising plot twists and turns.... A must-have for fans of vampire stories. —*School Library Journal*
Sequel: *Stargazer*

Steadfast: a Spellcaster novel. Claudia Gray. 2014 384 p. (Spellcaster series (Claudia Gray), 2)
Grades: 8 9 10 11 12
1. Witches; 2. Magic; 3. Curses; 4. Demons; 5. Good and evil; 6. Rhode Island; 7. Urban fantasy
9780061961229
LC 2013015445
Nadia must stop the evil sorceress Elizabeth before she lures the One Beneath to Captive's Sound, destroying the town and everyone Nadia holds dear at the same time.
Gray uses unique and lyrical free-verse spells, spoken by both Nadia and the dark sorceress Elizabeth, as inroads to sets of memoriesa clever tactic that helps readers understand motivation while providing backstories that make it easy to bond with Nadia and her friends. The ending will provide terrific fodder for book discussions, so make sure you have enough copies to go around. —*Booklist*
Sequel to: *Spellcaster.*

A **thousand** pieces of you. Claudia Gray. HarperTeen, an imprint of HarperCollinsPublishers, 2014 368 p. (Firebird trilogy (Claudia Gray), 1)
Grades: 8 9 10 11
1. Interdimensional travel; 2. Revenge; 3. Children of scientists; 4. Space and time; 5. Families; 6. Science fiction; 7. First person narratives
9780062278968
LC 2014001894
When eighteen-year-old Marguerite Caine's father is killed, she must leap into different dimensions and versions of herself to catch her father's killer and avenge his murder.
Readers will appreciate Marguerite's determination to help her parents, even though she is a misfit, the lone artist in a family of scientific geniuses. The secondary players are equally well rounded, and their various incarnations in each dimension make for intriguing character explorations. In resourceful Marguerite's first-person narration, the story moves quickly, and the science is explained enough to make the plot clear, but not so much as to bog things down. —*Booklist*

Green, John

★ An **abundance** of Katherines. John Green. Dutton Books, 2006 256 p.
Grades: 9 10 11 12
1. Teenage boy prodigies; 2. Rejection (Psychology) in teenagers; 3. Automobile travel; 4. Teenage boys; 5. Teenagers; 6. Chicago, Illinois; 7. Tennessee; 8. Coming-of-age stories; 9. Realistic fiction.
9780525476887
LC 2006004191
Booklist Editors' Choice: Books for Youth, 2006; YALSA Popular Paperbacks for Young Adults, 2009; YALSA Best Books for Young Adults, 2007; Michael L. Printz Honor Book, 2007.
Having been recently dumped for the nineteenth time by a girl named Katherine, recent high school graduate and former child prodigy Colin sets off on a road trip with his best friend to try to find some new direction in life while also trying to create a mathematical formula to explain his relationships.
This is an enjoyable, thoughtful novel that will attract readers interested in romance, math, or just good storytelling. —*Voice of Youth Advocates*

★ The **fault** in our stars. John Green. Dutton Childrens Books 2012 272 p.
Grades: 9 10 11 12
1. Teenagers with cancer; 2. Group psychotherapy; 3. Teenage romance; 4. Authors; 5. Teenage boy/girl relations; 6. Indiana; 7. Netherlands; 8. Realistic fiction; 9. Love stories; 10. Books to movies
9780525478812; 9780329946203; 9780143567592, Oz; 9780141355078, print, UK; 9780141345659, print, UK
Abraham Lincoln Illinois High School Book Award, 2014; Blue Hen Book Award (Delaware) for Teen Books, 2014; Booklist Editors' Choice: Books for Youth, 2012; Black-Eyed Susan Book Award (Maryland), High School, 2014; Buckeye Teen Book Award (Ohio), Grades 9-12, 2014; California Young Reader Medal, Young Adult, 2015; Colorado Blue Spruce YA Book Award, 2016; Garden State Teen Book Award (New Jersey), Fiction (Grades 9-12), 2015; Gateway Readers Award (Missouri), 2015; Georgia Peach Book Award for Teen Readers, 2014; Goodreads Choice Award, 2012; Golden Archer Awards (Wisconsin): Middle/Jr. High, 2015; Green Mountain Book Award (Vermont), 2014; Indies' Choice Book Awards, Young Adult, 2013; Inky Awards (Australia): Silver Inky, 2012; Keystone to Reading Book Award (Pennsylvania), High School level, 2014; Pennsylvania Young Reader's Choice Awards, Young Adult, 2013; Rhode Island Teen Book Award, 2014; Romantic Times

Reviewer's Choice Award, 2012; Sequoyah Book Awards (Oklahoma), High School Books, 2015; School Library Journal Best Books, 2012; Soaring Eagle Book Award (Wyoming), 2015; Thumbs Up! Award (Michigan), 2012; Virginia Readers' Choice Award for High School, 2014; West Australian Young Readers' Book Award (WAYRBA), Older Readers, 2013; Westchester Fiction Award, 2013; YALSA Best Fiction for Young Adults, 2013; YALSA Popular Paperbacks for Young Adults, 2015; Young Reader's Choice Award (Pacific Northwest), Senior, 2015.

Sixteen-year-old Hazel, a stage IV thyroid cancer patient, has accepted her terminal diagnosis until a chance meeting with a boy at cancer support group forces her to reexamine her perspective on love, loss, and life.

If there's a knock on John Green (and it's more of a light tap considering he's been recognized twice by the Printz committee) it's that he keeps writing the same book: nerdy guy in unrequited love with impossibly gorgeous girl, add road trip. His fourth novel departs from that successful formula to even greater success: this is his best work yet. —*Publishers Weekly*

★ **Looking** for Alaska. John Green. Dutton Children's Books, 2005 237 p.
Grades: 9 10 11 12
1. Loss (Psychology); 2. Boarding schools; 3. Self-destructive behavior in teenagers; 4. Sixteen-year-old boys; 5. Teenage boys; 6. Alabama; 7. Realistic fiction; 8. Books to TV; 9. Books for reluctant readers
9780525475064; 9780007523160, UK; 9780007424832, print, UK; 9780008384128, Paperback, UK
LC 2004010827
Booklist Editors' Choice: Books for Youth, 2005; Green Mountain Book Award (Vermont), 2008; Kentucky Bluegrass Award for Grades 9-12, 2006; Michael L. Printz Award, 2006; YALSA Best Books for Young Adults, 2006; YALSA Popular Paperbacks for Young Adults, 2009; YALSA Quick Picks for Reluctant Young Adult Readers, 2006; Inky Awards (Australia): Silver Inky, 2007; School Library Journal Best Books, 2005.

Sixteen-year-old Miles' first year at Culver Creek Preparatory School in Alabama includes good friends and great pranks, but is defined by the search for answers about life and death after a fatal car crash.

The language and sexual situations are aptly and realistically drawn, but sophisticated in nature. Miles's narration is alive with sweet, self-deprecating humor, and his obvious struggle to tell the story truthfully adds to his believability. —*School Library Journal*

Paper towns. John Green. Dutton Books, 2008 352 p.
Grades: 9 10 11 12
1. Missing persons; 2. Teenage boy/girl relations; 3. High school seniors; 4. Revenge; 5. Neighbors; 6. Orlando, Florida; 7. Coming-of-age stories; 8. Mysteries; 9. Realistic fiction
9780525478188; 9780732289003, Australia; 9781408865682, print, UK; 9781408806593, print, UK
LC 2007052659
Booklist Editors' Choice: Books for Youth, 2008; Edgar Allan Poe Award for Best Young Adult, 2009; Nutmeg Children's Book Award, High School category, 2014; School Library Journal Best Books, 2008; YALSA Popular Paperbacks for Young Adults, 2012; YALSA Best Books for Young Adults, 2009.

One month before graduating from his Central Florida high school, Quentin "Q" Jacobsen basks in the predictable boringness of his life until the beautiful and exciting Margo Roth Spiegelman, Q's neighbor and classmate, takes him on a midnight adventure and then mysteriously disappears.

The writing is...stellar, with deliciously intelligent dialogue and plenty of mind-twisting insights.... Language and sex issues might make this book more appropriate for older teens, but it is still a powerfully great read. —*Voice of Youth Advocates*

★ **Turtles** all the way down. John Green. Dutton Books, 2017 286 p.
Grades: 9 10 11 12
1. Obsessive-compulsive disorder in teenage girls; 2. Teenagers with mental illnesses; 3. Fugitives; 4. Friendship; 5. High school girls; 6. Indianapolis, Indiana; 7. Realistic fiction
9780525555360; 9780241335437, print, UK; 9780141346045, Paperback, UK
Booklist Editors' Choice: Books for Youth, 2017; Westchester Fiction Award, 2018; School Library Journal Best Books, 2017; YALSA Best Fiction for Young Adults, 2018.

Aza Holmes, a high school student with obsessive-compulsive disorder, becomes focused on searching for a fugitive billionaire.

With its attention to ideas and trademark introspection, its a challenging but richly rewarding read. It is also the most mature of Greens work to date and deserving of all the accolades that are sure to come its way. —*Booklist*

Green, Sally

Half bad. Sally Green. Viking, published by the Penguin Group, 2014 352 pages (Half bad trilogy, 1)
Grades: 9 10 11 12
1. Witches; 2. Captives; 3. Fathers and sons; 4. Captivity; 5. Escapes; 6. England; 7. Urban fantasy
9780670016785; 9780141350868, print, UK
LC 2013041190
Booklist Editors' Choice: Books for Youth, 2014; YALSA Best Fiction for Young Adults, 2015.

In modern-day England, where witches live alongside humans, Nathan, son of a White witch and the most powerful Black witch, must escape captivity before his seventeenth birthday and receive the gifts that will determine his future.

Told at times in first- and second-person, the story allows unique insights into Nathan's perspectives, including the fast-paced escapes and heart-wrenching torment. An interesting spin on the paranormal that runs adjacent to some important social issues, Half Bad leaves readers questioning if the division between good and evil is ever as simple as black and white. —*Voice of Youth Advocates*

Gregorio, I. W.

This is my brain in love. I. W. Gregorio. Little, Brown and Company, 2020 384 p.
Grades: 8 9 10 11 12
1. Restaurants; 2. Family businesses; 3. Cooking, Chinese; 4. Anxiety in teenagers; 5. Teenagers with depression; 6. New York State; 7. Romantic comedies; 8. Contemporary romances; 9. Multiple perspectives
9780316423823, HRD, US; 9780316423847, ebook, US
LC 2019033954
Schneider Family Book Award for Teens, 2021.

Rising high school juniors Jocelyn Wu and Will Domenici fall in love while trying to save the Wu family restaurant, A-Plus Chinese Garden.

Deftly navigating issues of race and mental health, as well as giving voice to the reality of American teens born to immigrant families, many of whom grapple with different cultural and familial expectations, Gregorio, a founding member of We Need Diverse Books, has written a heartwarming foodie rom-com. —*School Library Journal*

LIST OF FICTIONAL WORKS

Grey, Melissa

The **girl** at midnight. Melissa Grey. Delacorte Press, 2015 368 p. (Girl at midnight, 1)
Grades: 9 10 11 12
1. Imaginary wars and battles; 2. Runaway teenage girls; 3. Pickpockets; 4. Magic; 5. Teenage girls; 6. New York City; 7. Urban fantasy; 8. Multiple perspectives
9780385744652

The well-built world, vivid characters, and perfect blend of action and amour should have readers eagerly seeking the sequel. —*Kirkus*

Griffin, Adele

The **unfinished** life of Addison Stone. Adele Griffin. Soho Teen, 2014 256 pages
Grades: 9 10 11 12
1. Teenage girl artists; 2. Fame; 3. Artists; 4. Celebrities; 5. Teenage girls — Death; 6. New York City; 7. Mysteries
9781616953607

LC 2014009576
School Library Journal Best Books: Fiction, 2014; YALSA Best Fiction for Young Adults, 2015.

When a celebrated New York City teenager, known for her subversive street art, mysteriously dies, her life is examined in a series of interviews with her parents, friends, boyfriends, mentors, and critics.

This novel is...a terrific experiment, something fresh and hard to put down. It gives a sense of both the artistic temperament and the nature of madnessand the sometimes thin line in between. —*Booklist*

Griffin, N.

Just wreck it all. N. Griffin. A Caitlyn Dlouhy Book/Atheneum, 2018 336 p.
Grades: 7 8 9 10 11
1. Self-destructive behavior in teenage girls; 2. Guilt; 3. Compulsive eating; 4. Teenage girls; 5. Teenage runners; 6. Realistic fiction
9781481465182; 9781481465205; 9781481465199

LC 2018008167
Crippled with guilt after causing a horrific accident two years earlier, sixteen-year-old Bett's life is a series of pluses and minuses. But when the pluses become too much to outweigh the minuses, Bett is forced to confront her self-harming behavior—Provided by publisher.

Griffin, Paul

Adrift. Paul Griffin. Scholastic, 2015 240 p.
Grades: 9 10 11 12
1. Survival; 2. Sailing; 3. Class conflict; 4. Oceans; 5. Summer; 6. Survival stories; 7. Adventure stories.
9780545709392; 9781925240160, print, Australia

Working in Montauk for the summer, Matt and Mike meet three teens who invite them to their Hamptons mansion, where the group decides to sail out into the ocean in a small boat, become lost at sea, and must learn to work together to survive.

Burning blue. By Paul Griffin. Dial Books, 2012 288 p.
Grades: 9 10 11 12
1. Teenage hackers; 2. Teenage girls with disfigurements; 3. Crushes in teenage boys; 4. Teenage boy/girl relations; 5. Rich teenage girls; 6. New Jersey; 7. Mysteries; 8. First person narratives; 9. Books for reluctant readers
9780803738157; 9781922079145

LC 2012003578
YALSA Quick Picks for Reluctant Young Adult Readers, 2014.

When beautiful, smart Nicole, disfigured by acid thrown in her face, and computer hacker Jay meet in the school psychologist's office, they become friends and Jay resolves to find her attacker.

Stay with me. By Paul Griffin. Dial Books for Young Readers, 2011 304 p.
Grades: 10 11 12
1. First loves; 2. High school dropouts; 3. Dogs; 4. Breaking up (Interpersonal relations); 5. Anger in teenage boys; 6. Contemporary romances; 7. Multiple perspectives
9780803734487

LC 2011001287
YALSA Popular Paperbacks for Young Adults, 2015; School Library Journal Best Books, 2011.

Fifteen-year-olds Mack, a high school drop-out but a genius with dogs, and Cece, who hopes to use her intelligence to avoid a life like her mother's, meet and fall in love at the restaurant where they both work, but when Mack lands in prison he pushes Cece away and only a one-eared pit-bull can keep them together.

A stellar story, with genuine dialogue and drama, this is a book that will appeal greatly to teens, especially dog lovers. —*School Library Journal*

Grimes, Nikki

★ **Bronx** masquerade. Nikki Grimes. Dial Books, 2002 167 p.
Grades: 7 8 9 10
1. African American students; 2. Identity (Psychology); 3. Bonding (Interpersonal relations); 4. Ethnicity; 5. African Americans; 6. Bronx, New York City; 7. Novels in verse; 8. Multiple perspectives; 9. First person narratives; 10. Books for reluctant readers
9780803725690

LC 31701
Coretta Scott King Award, Author Category, 2003; YALSA Best Books for Young Adults, 2003; YALSA Popular Paperbacks for Young Adults, 2007; YALSA Quick Picks for Reluctant Young Adult Readers, 2003.

While studying the Harlem Renaissance, students at a Bronx high school read aloud poems they've written, revealing their innermost thoughts and fears to their formerly clueless classmates.

Funny and painful, awkward and abstract, the poems talk about race, abuse, parental love, neglect, death, and body image.... Readers will enjoy the lively, smart voices that talk bravely about real issues and secret fears. A fantastic choice for readers' theater. —*Booklist*
Companion novel: *Between the lines.*

★ **Jazmin's** notebook. Nikki Grimes. Dial Books, 1998 102 p.
Grades: 6 7 8 9
1. African American girls; 2. Fourteen-year-old girls; 3. Sisters; 4. African American families; 5. Harlem, New York City; 6. 1960s; 7. Realistic fiction; 8. African American fiction
9780803722248

LC 97005850
Booklist Editors' Choice: Books for Youth, 1998; Coretta Scott King Honor Book for Authors, 1999.

Jazmin, a fourteen-year-old Afro-American girl who lives with her sister in a Harlem apartment, finds strength in writing poetry and keeping a diary.

An articulate, admirable heroine, Jazmin leaps over life's hurdles with agility and integrity. —*Publishers Weekly*

Groth, Darren

Munro vs. the Coyote. Darren Groth. 2017 276 p.
Grades: 7 8 9 10 11 12

1. Grief in teenage boys; 2. Student exchange programs; 3. Guilt in teenage boys; 4. Anger in teenage boys; 5. Death; 6. Australia; 7. Realistic fiction; 8. First person narratives; 9. Australian fiction
9781459814097

Since the sudden death of his younger sister, Munro Maddux has been having flashbacks and anger-management issues. And there's a harsh and cruel voice he calls "the Coyote." To move beyond his troubled past, Munro goes to Australia on a student exchange. In Brisbane, Munro discovers the Coyote can be silenced at an assisted living residence called Fair Go Community Village, where he is a volunteer.

Characters that will steal readers' hearts with their humor and resilience, smooth writing, and a satisfying and hopeful ending make this a book to enjoy both emotionally and critically. —*Kirkus*

Grove, S. E.
The **crimson** skew. S.E. Grove. Viking, an imprint of Penguin Random House LLC, 2016 432 p. (Mapmakers trilogy, 3)
Grades: 6 7 8 9 10
1. Parent-separated teenage girls; 2. Maps; 3. Pirates; 4. Imaginary wars and battles; 5. Teenage girls; 6. 1890s; 7. Fantasy fiction.
9780670785049
LC 2015036703
In a world transformed by 1799's Great Disruption—when all of the continents were flung into different time periods, Sophia Tims journeys home to Boston, anticipating her runion with Theo, but he has been conscripted to fight in the Western War, Prime Minister Broadgirldle's twisted vision of Manifest Destiny.

Pirates, sea captains, fortunetellers, a dragon, poisonous red fog, former slave traders, and healers populate a story that may introduce young readers to the old-fashioned pleasure of settling into a long, rich, and complicated tale. A triumphant conclusion to a prodigious feat of storytelling. —*Kirkus*

The **glass** sentence. S.E. Grove. Viking, an imprint of Penguin Group (USA), 2014 512 p. (Mapmakers trilogy, 1)
Grades: 6 7 8 9 10
1. Maps; 2. Kidnapping; 3. Adventure; 4. Teenage girls; 5. Tims, Sophia (Fictitious character); 6. 1890s; 7. Fantasy fiction.
9780670785025
In a world fractured into disparate eras during the Great Disruption, Sophia Tims is entrusted with the Tracing Glass (containing a memory thought to be the cause of the Disruption) when her uncle, the cartographer Shadrack Elli, is kidnapped. An intricate fantasy with a Gilded-Age feel, this solidly constructed quest features maps of all kinds and unusual steampunk-flavored elements. —*Horn Book Guide*

The **golden** specific. S.E. Grove; maps by Dave A. Stevenson. Viking, an imprint of Penguin Group (USA), 2015 528 p. (Mapmakers trilogy, 2)
Grades: 6 7 8 9 10
1. Parent-separated teenage girls; 2. Maps; 3. Missing persons; 4. Plague; 5. Adventure; 6. 1890s; 7. Fantasy fiction.
9780670785032
Thirteen-year-old Sophia Tims and her friend Theo continue to search for her parents, explorers who have vanished, as the borders shift within a world transformed by the Great Disruption of 1799.

Brilliantly imagined and full of wonder. —*Kirkus*

Guene, Faiza
Kiffe kiffe tomorrow. Faiza Guene; translated from the French by Sarah Adams. Harcourt, 2006 156 p.
Grades: 11 12 Adult

1. Fifteen-year-old girls; 2. Mothers and daughters; 3. Muslims; 4. Public housing; 5. Low-rent housing; 6. Translations
9780156030489
LC 2005030456
Booklist Editors' Choice: Adult Books for Young Adults, 2006.
Struggling with an overworked mother, an absent father, and the challenges of life within the infamous Paradise projects of suburban Paris, fifteen-year-old French Muslim Doria endures a parade of social workers, experiences a first kiss, and assumes a philosophical outlook regarding her circumstances.

Doria, 15, a child of Muslim immigrants, describes her daily struggle in Paris' rough housing projects in a contemporary narrative that's touching, furious, and very funny. —*Booklist*

Haddix, Margaret Peterson
Just Ella. Margaret Peterson Haddix. Simon & Schuster Books for Young Readers, 1999 185 p. (Palace chronicles, 1)
Grades: 7 8 9 10
1. Princesses; 2. Independence in teenage girls; 3. Engagement; 4. Princes; 5. Gender role; 6. Fantasy fiction; 7. Fairy tale and folklore-inspired fiction; 8. Books for reluctant readers
9780689821868
LC 98008384
YALSA Popular Paperbacks for Young Adults, 2016; YALSA Quick Picks for Reluctant Young Adult Readers, 2000; YALSA Best Books for Young Adults, 2000.
In this continuation of the "Cinderella" story, fifteen-year-old Ella finds that accepting Prince Charming's proposal ensnares her in a suffocating tangle of palace rules and royal etiquette, so she plots to escape.

In lively prose, with well-developed characters, creative plot twists, wit, and drama, Haddix transforms the "Cinderella" tale into an insightful coming-of-age story. —*Booklist*
Companion novel: *Palace of Mirrors.*

★ **Uprising**. Margaret Peterson Haddix. Simon & Schuster Books for Young Readers, 2007 346 p;
Grades: 6 7 8 9 10
1. Women employees; 2. Sweatshops; 3. Factories; 4. Immigrants; 5. Labor disputes; 6. New York City; 7. 1910s; 8. Historical fiction; 9. Multiple perspectives
9781416911715
Amelia Bloomer List, 2008.
In 1927, at the urging of twenty-one-year-old Harriet, Mrs. Livingston reluctantly recalls her experiences at the Triangle Shirtwaist factory, including miserable working conditions that led to a strike, then the fire that took the lives of her two best friends, when Harriet, the boss's daughter, was only five years old. Includes historical notes.

This deftly crafted historical novel unfolds dramatically with an absorbing story and well-drawn characters who readily evoke empathy and compassion. —*School Library Journal*
Includes bibliographical references.

Hahn, Mary Downing
Mister Death's blue-eyed girls. By Mary Downing Hahn. Clarion Books, 2012 384 p.
Grades: 8 9 10 11 12
1. Crimes against teenage girls; 2. Grief in teenage girls; 3. Murder; 4. Former boyfriends; 5. Teenage murder victims; 6. Baltimore, Maryland; 7. 1950s; 8. Historical fiction; 9. Coming-of-age stories; 10. Multiple perspectives.
9780547760629
LC 2011025950

Narrated from several different perspectives, tells the story of the 1956 murder of two teenaged girls in suburban Baltimore, Maryland.

Hahn, Rebecca

A **creature** of moonlight. Rebecca Hahn. 2014 320 p.
Grades: 7 8 9 10 11 12
1. Identity (Psychology); 2. Dragons; 3. Princesses; 4. Forests; 5. Revenge; 6. Fantasy fiction.
9780544109353
LC 2013020188
Marni, a young flower seller who has been living in exile, must choose between claiming her birthright as princess of a realm whose king wants her dead, and a life with the father she has never known—a wild dragon.

Marni lives in a shack at the edge of the woods with her Gramps, where she tends flowers, as she's done for most of her life. Yet change is afoot... This book's greatest strength lies in the vivid woodland scenes and the rich detail that describes the mystical pieces of Marni's tale. —*School Library Journal*

Haines, Kathryn Miller

The **girl** is murder. Kathryn Miller Haines. Roaring Brook Press, 2011 352 p. (Iris Anderson mysteries, 1)
Grades: 7 8 9 10
1. Teenage detectives; 2. Missing persons; 3. Fifteen-year-old girls; 4. Grief in teenage girls; 5. Fathers and daughters; 6. New York City; 7. 1940s; 8. Historical mysteries; 9. Mysteries
9781596436091
LC 2010032935
In 1942 New York City, fifteen-year-old Iris grieves for her mother who committed suicide and for the loss of her life of privilege, and secretly helps her father with his detective business since he, having lost a leg at Pearl Harbor, struggles to make ends meet.

This is a smart offering that gives both mysteries and historical fiction a good name.... The mystery is solid, but what makes this such a standout is the cast.... The characters, young and old, leap off the pages. —*Booklist*

Hale, Shannon

★ **Book** of a thousand days. By Shannon Hale; [illustrations by James Noel Smith].. Bloomsbury Children's Books, 2007 305 p.
Grades: 7 8 9 10
1. Teenage girl orphans; 2. Imprisonment; 3. Household employees; 4. Nobility; 5. Punishment; 6. Central Asia; 7. Fairy tale and folklore-inspired fiction; 8. Fantasy fiction; 9. Diary novels.
9781599900513
LC 2006036999
School Library Journal Best Books, 2007; YALSA Popular Paperbacks for Young Adults, 2016; YALSA Best Books for Young Adults, 2008.

Fifteen-year-old Dashti, sworn to obey her sixteen-year-old mistress, the Lady Saren, shares Saren's years of punishment locked in a tower, then brings her safely to the lands of her true love, where both must hide who they are as they work as kitchen maids.

This is a captivating fantasy filled with romance, magic, and strong female characters. —*Booklist*

The **goose** girl. By Shannon Hale. Bloomsbury Children's Books, 2003 383 p. (Books of Bayern, 1)
Grades: 6 7 8 9
1. Princesses; 2. Inheritance and succession; 3. Courage in teenage girls; 4. Courage; 5. Human/animal communica- tion; 6. Fairy tale and folklore-inspired fiction; 7. Fantasy fiction.

9781582348438; 9780747598008, UK; 9780747571230, print, UK
LC 2002028336
Josette Frank Award, 2004; YALSA Popular Paperbacks for Young Adults, 2010.

On her way to marry a prince she's never met, Princess Anidori is betrayed by her guards and her lady-in-waiting and must become a goose girl to survive until she can reveal her true identity and reclaim the crown that is rightfully hers.

A fine adventure tale full of danger, suspense, surprising twists, and a satisfying conclusion. —*Booklist*
Sequel: *Enna burning*.

Kind of a big deal. Shannon Hale. Roaring Brook Press, 2020 391 p.
Grades: 9 10 11 12
1. High school dropouts; 2. Nannies; 3. Books and reading; 4. Characters and characteristics in literature; 5. Interpersonal relations; 6. Missoula, Montana; 7. Fantasy fiction; 8. Coming-of-age stories
9781250206237
Dropping out of high school to pursue her Broadway ambitions, a talented performer lands in a directionless job before a visit to the library catapults her into the plotlines of the books she reads. —*OCLC*

The post-high-school setting pushes this into the still woefully scant new adult category, and it's a solid pick for readers who are finding that the course they're on isn't the one they'd planned for. —*Booklist*

Hall, Kate Hazel

From darkness. Kate Hazel Hall. Duet Books, an imprint of Interlude Press, 2020 324 p.
Grades: 9 10 11 12
1. Teenage girls; 2. Death; 3. Life after death; 4. Coastal towns; 5. Teenage girl/girl relations; 6. Fantasy fiction; 7. Australian fiction
9781945053986
Sixteen-year-old Ari Wyndham lost her best friend in the sea. Everybody told her it was an accident, but Ari can't forgive herself. Her own life is cut short when a tiger-snake delivers a deathly bite, and a beautiful, ghostly and strangely familiar young woman appears, summoning Ari's soul to the underworld. Ari, however, refuses to go. Though she knows there will be a terrible price to pay for her transgression, the mysterious guide chooses to save Ari. Their rebellion upsets the balance of life and death in Ari's remote coastal village.

A rift opens from the underworld, unleashing dark magic: savage dog packs emerge at night, fishermen catch ghostly bodies in their nets, and children go missing. Together, Ari and her guide battle the dark powers of the underworld and heal the rift. Though their bond seems unbreakable, it may not be enough. It is up to Ari to find the courage to do the one thing that will save the world from darkness.

Ari's journey is clear, heartrending, and shot through with sweetness and eerie beauty. —*Publishers Weekly*

Halpern, Julie

Get well soon. Julie Halpern. Feiwel and Friends, 2007 193 p.
Grades: 7 8 9 10
1. Sixteen-year-old girls; 2. Overweight teenage girls; 3. Teenage girls; 4. Teenagers; 5. Mental illness; 6. Illinois; 7. Epistolary novels; 8. First person narratives; 9. Realistic fiction; 10. Books for reluctant readers
9780312367954
YALSA Quick Picks for Reluctant Young Adult Readers, 2008.

When her parents confine her to a mental hospital, an overweight teenage girl, who suffers from panic attacks, describes her experiences in a series of letters to a friend.

Halpern creates a narrative that reflects the changes in Anna with each passing day that includes self-reflection and a good dose of humor. —*Voice of Youth Advocates*
Sequel: *Have a nice day.*

Into the wild nerd yonder. By Julie Halpern. Feiwel and Friends, 2009 247 p.
Grades: 9 10 11 12
1. Best friends; 2. Friendship; 3. Popularity; 4. High schools; 5. Schools; 6. Realistic fiction.
9780312382520

LC 2008034751
South Carolina Book Award, Young Adult Books, 2012; YALSA Popular Paperbacks for Young Adults, 2012; YALSA Best Books for Young Adults, 2010.

As her sophomore year begins, Jess knows she's growing apart from her best friends, Char and Bizza, a situation made much worse when Bizza goes poseur-punk in order to pursue Jess' long-time crush. When Jess, who loves math, sewing, and audiobooks, is invited to play Dungeons and Dragons by class nerd Dottie, she discovers that embracing life as a nerd isn't so bad—especially when there's a cute boy involved who loves role-playing games, too.

Descriptions of high school cliques...are hilarious and believable.... This novel is particularly strong in showing how teen friendships evolve and sometimes die away, and how adolescents redefine themselves. —*School Library Journal*

Hamilton, Alwyn
Hero at the fall. Alwyn Hamilton. Viking, 2018 464 p. (Rebel of the sands, 3)
Grades: 9 10 11 12
1. Teenage girl orphans; 2. Captives; 3. Rulers; 4. Teenage romance; 5. Teenage girls; 6. High fantasy; 7. Fantasy fiction; 8. First person narratives
9780451477866; 9780147519108

Armed with only her revolver, her wits, and the Demdji powers she's struggling to control, Amani must rally a crew of rebels to take on the bloodthirsty sultan of Miraji and free the imprisoned prince Ahmed. But as the rescue mission travels through the unforgiving desert to a place that, according to maps, doesn't exist, Amani questions whether she is leading them all to their deaths. —*OCLC*

Hamilton is a master of twists and unexpected surprises, and she again delivers shocking alliances, reappearances of characters long thought gone, and deadly choices. —*Booklist*

Rebel of the sands. By Alwyn Hamilton. 2016 320 pages (Rebel of the sands, 1)
Grades: 9 10 11 12
1. Teenage girl orphans; 2. Sharpshooters; 3. Disguises; 4. Princes; 5. Sixteen-year-old girls; 6. High fantasy; 7. Fantasy fiction; 8. Middle Eastern-influenced fantasy
9780451477538; 9780571325252, print, UK

LC 2015026037
Goodreads Choice Award, 2016.

Amani is desperate to leave the dead-end town of Dustwalk, and she's counting on her sharpshooting skills to help her escape. But after she meets Jin, the mysterious rebel running from the Sultan's army, she unlocks the powerful truth about the desert nation of Miraji...and herself.

Traitor to the throne. Alwyn Hamilton. Viking, 2017 518 p. (Rebel of the sands, 2)
Grades: 9 10 11 12

1. Teenage girl orphans; 2. Captives; 3. Rulers; 4. Teenage romance; 5. Teenage girls; 6. High fantasy; 7. Fantasy fiction; 8. First person narratives
9780451477859; 9780571325412, print, UK

Desperate to uncover the Sultan's secrets by spying on his court, gunslinger Amani is taken captive by the forces of the Sultan, whose agenda seems less tyrannical than originally believed

Hamilton's strong and exciting sophomore novel is full of compelling twists and turns, and the ending will leave readers highly anticipating the final volume in the Rebel of the Sands trilogy. —*Booklist*

Hamilton, Steve
★ The **lock** artist. Steve Hamilton. Minotaur Books, 2010 304 p.
Grades: 11 12 Adult
1. Safecrackers; 2. Men who are mute; 3. Psychic trauma in men; 4. Former convicts; 5. Criminals; 6. Crime fiction; 7. Adult books for young adults.
9780312380427; 9780752883311, UK

LC 2009034523
Alex Award, 2011; Edgar Allan Poe Award for Best Novel, 2011; Ian Fleming Steel Dagger Award, 2011.

Traumatized at the age of eight and pushed into a life of crime by reason of his unforgiveable talent—lock picking—Michael sees his chance to escape, and with one desperate gamble risks everything to come back home to the only person he ever loved, and to unlock the secret that has kept him silent for so long.

Hammonds Reed, Christina
★ The **black** kids. Christina Hammonds Reed. Simon & Schuster 2020 368 p.
Grades: 9 10 11 12
1. Race relations; 2. African American teenagers; 3. RIch people; 4. Race riots; 5. Families; 6. Los Angeles, California; 7. 1990s; 8. Realistic fiction; 9. Coming-of-age stories; 10. African American fiction
9781534462724

LC 2019035025
School Library Journal Best Books, 2020; William C. Morris Debut Award finalist, 2021.

With the Rodney King riots closing in on high school senior Ashley and her family, the privileged bubble she has enjoyed, protecting her from the difficult realities most black people face, begins to crumble.

The explorations of race and socio-economic privilege are valuable and will speak to readers who have not previously confronted or thought about these issues. A timely exploration of '90s Los Angeles during racial upheaval and one girl's awakening. —*Kirkus*

Han, Jenny
Always and forever, Lara Jean. Jenny Han. Simon & Schuster BFYR, 2017 325 p. (To all the boys I've loved before, 3)
Grades: 9 10 11 12
1. Multiracial teenage girls; 2. Korean American teenage girls; 3. Children and remarriage; 4. Dating (Social customs); 5. High school seniors; 6. Contemporary romances; 7. Teen chick lit
9781481430487; 9781534497252, Paperback, US; 9781407177663, print, UK; 9781760666095, Paperback, UK; 9781501942204, EBOOK

While helping plan her father's wedding, senior Lara Jean struggles with choosing a college and questions how graduation is going to change her relationship with her boyfriend Peter.

It's not summer without you: a summer novel. Jenny Han. Simon & Schuster Books for Young Readers, 2010 288 p. (Summer novels (Jenny Han), 2)

Grades: 7 8 9 10

1. Grief in teenagers; 2. Crushes in teenage girls; 3. Summer romance; 4. Vacation homes; 5. Grief; 6. Realistic fiction; 7. Coming-of-age stories.

9781416995555

LC 2009042180

Teenaged Isobel "Belly" Conklin, whose life revolves around spending the summer at her mother's best friend's beach house, reflects on the tragic events of the past year that changed her life forever.

Han artfully weaves together Belly's and Jeremiah's back stories, recent and long past, to create a solid fabric of relationship and longing. Flashes of humor, realistic (and often salty) dialogue and growing-up moments both painful and authentic create a convincing and poignant read. —*Publishers Weekly*

Sequel to: *The summer I turned pretty.*

The **summer** I turned pretty. Jenny Han. Simon & Schuster Books for Young Readers, 2009 288 p. (Summer novels (Jenny Han), 1)

Grades: 7 8 9 10

1. Crushes in teenage girls; 2. Summer romance; 3. Growing up; 4. Beaches; 5. Vacation homes; 6. Realistic fiction; 7. Coming-of-age stories

9781416968238; 9780141353821, print, UK; 9780141330532, print, Australia

LC 2008027070

YALSA Best Books for Young Adults, 2010.

Belly spends the summer she turns sixteen at the beach just like every other summer of her life, but this time things are very different.

Romantic and heartbreakingly real.... The novel perfectly blends romance, family drama, and a coming-of-age tale, one that is substantially deeper than most. —*School Library Journal*

Sequel: *It's not summer without you.*

★ **To** all the boys I've loved before. Jenny Han. 2014 288 pages (To all the boys I've loved before, 1)

Grades: 9 10 11 12

1. Love triangles; 2. Multiracial teenage girls; 3. Letters; 4. Dating (Social customs); 5. Children of widowers; 6. Contemporary romances; 7. Teen chick lit; 8. Books to movies

9781442426702; 9781407149073, print, UK; 9781407177687, Paperback, UK; 9781760665951, Paperback, Australia; 9781442426726, ebook, US

LC 2013022311

School Library Journal Best Books: Fiction, 2014.

Lara Jean writes love letters to all the boys she has loved and then hides them in a hatbox until one day those letters are accidentally sent—Provided by publisher.

Lara Jean writes letters to boys she's liked without thinking they'll ever be sent. When she discovers that the letters have been mailed, she pretends to date one of those boys to save face in front of another (who also dated her studying-abroad sister). What follows is a sweet, honest, and beautifully written story about sisterly bonds and true first love. —*Horn Book Guide*

Title adapted into a film by the same name in 2018.

We'll always have summer: a summer novel. Jenny Han. Simon & Schuster BFYR, 2011 291 p. (Summer novels (Jenny Han), 3)

Grades: 7 8 9 10

1. Women college students; 2. Love triangles; 3. Engagement; 4. Brothers; 5. Beaches; 6. Realistic fiction; 7. First person narratives.

9781416995586

LC 2010046670

The summer after her first year of college, Isobel "Belly" Conklin is faced with a choice between Jeremiah and Conrad Fisher, brothers she has always loved, when Jeremiah proposes marriage and Conrad confesses that he still loves her.

In Han's conclusion to the trilogy that began with *The Summer I Turned Pretty*, she both underscores the folly of getting engaged too young and vividly depicts the emotions of a girl on the brink of womanhood. —*Publishers Weekly*

Hand, Cynthia

The **how** & the why. Cynthia Hand. Harperteen, 2019 464 p.

Grades: 7 8 9 10 11 12

1. Teenage girls; 2. Searching; 3. Adoption; 4. Identity (Psychology); 5. Teenage pregnancy; 6. Idaho; 7. Coming-of-age stories; 8. Realistic fiction; 9. Multiple perspectives

9780062693167

A novel told from the viewpoints of an adoptee and the teen mother who gave her up 18 years earlier follows Cassandra's search for clues about her true identity in the letters left behind by her birth mother.

Hand explores adoption's multiple dimensions with great insight and sensitivity. Inclusive and illustrative an engaging lesson in timeless family values. —*Kirkus*

My Calamity Jane. . HarperTeen, 2020 544 p. (Lady Janies)

Grades: 7 8 9 10 11

1. Calamity Jane, 1856-1903; 2. Gunfighters; 3. Were- wolves; 4. Frontier and pioneer life; 5. Wild West shows; 6. Monster hunters; 7. The West (United States); 8. American Westward Expansion (1803-1899); 9. 1870s; 10. Westerns; 11. Historical fantasy.

9780062652812

A side-splitting follow-up to My Plain Jane finds Wild Bill's Traveling Show performer Calamity Jane incurring a suspicious bite in the wake of a garou hunt gone wrong before seeking a cure in Deadwood, where she encounters a life-threatening surprise.

★ **My** Lady Jane. . HarperTeen, an imprint HarperCollins Publishers, 2016 491 p. (Lady Janies, 1)

Grades: 7 8 9 10 11

1. Grey, Jane, Lady, 1537-1554; 2. Conspiracies; 3. Shapeshifters; 4. Rulers; 5. Intrigue; 6. Courts and courtiers; 7. Great Britain; 8. Tudor period (1485-1603); 9. 16th century; 10. Historical fantasy; 11. Multiple perspectives

9780062391742

Amelia Bloomer List, 2017; Booklist Editors' Choice: Books for Youth, 2016; YALSA Best Fiction for Young Adults, 2017.

On the eve of her marriage to a stranger, sixteen-year-old Lady Jane Grey is swept in a conspiracy to usurp the throne from her cousin.

Wonky, offbeat, and happily anachronisticthe references run the gamut from Shakespeare to Monty Python, with plenty of nods to The Princess Bridethis fantasy adventure politely tips its hat to history before joyfully punting it out of the way. An utter delight. —*Booklist*

My plain Jane. . Harpercollins Childrens Books 2018 512 p. (Lady Janies, 2)

Grades: 7 8 9 10 11

1. Governesses; 2. Men/women relations; 3. Ghosts; 4. Orphans; 5. Mischief; 6. 19th century; 7. Paranormal romances; 8. Historical fantasy; 9. Gothic fiction.

9780062652775

YALSA Best Fiction for Young Adults, 2019.

A fun, supernatural mashup of different literary novels that shines on its own merit. —*Kirkus*

Handler, Daniel

★ **Why** we broke up. . Little, Brown, 2011 368 p.
Grades: 8 9 10 11 12
1. Breaking up (Interpersonal relations); 2. Souvenirs (Keepsakes); 3. Former boyfriends; 4. Letters; 5. Teenage boy/girl relations; 6. Realistic fiction; 7. Illustrated books.
9780316127257; 9781443401890; 9781405261357, print, UK
Booklist Editors' Choice: Books for Youth, 2011; YALSA Best Fiction for Young Adults, 2012; School Library Journal Best Books, 2011; Michael L. Printz Honor Book, 2012.

Sixteen-year-old Min Green writes a letter to Ed Slaterton in which she breaks up with him, documenting their relationship and how items in the accompanying box, from bottle caps to a cookbook, foretell the end.

Hardinge, Frances

★ **Cuckoo** song. Frances Hardinge. Amulet Books, 2015 416 p.
Grades: 7 8 9 10 11 12
1. Supernatural; 2. Sisters; 3. Grief; 4. Postwar life; 5. Identity (Psychology); 6. England; 7. Great Britain; 8. Between the Wars (1918-1939); 9. 1920s; 10. Historical fantasy
9781419714801; 9780330519731, print, UK
LC 2014045264
ALA Notable Children's Book, 2016; School Library Journal Best Books, 2015.

In post-World War I England, eleven-year-old Triss nearly drowns in a millpond known as "The Grimmer" and emerges with memory gaps, aware that something is terribly wrong, and to try to set things right, she must meet a twisted architect who has designs on her family.

Nuanced and intense, this painstakingly created tale mimics the Escher-like constructions of its villainous Architect, fooling the eyes and entangling the emotions of readers willing and able to enter into a world like no other. —*Kirkus*

First published in Great Britain in 2014 by Macmillan UK.

Deeplight. Frances Hardinge. Amulet, 2020 416 p.
Grades: 7 8 9 10 11 12
1. Gods and goddesses; 2. Best friends; 3. Sea monsters; 4. Islands; 5. Scavenging; 6. Fantasy fiction
9781419743207; 9781509836956, Hardback, UK; 9781529014570, Paperback, UK; 9781509897568, Paperback, UK

The gods are dead. Decades ago, they turned on one another and tore each other apart. Nobody knows why. But are they really gone forever? When 15-year-old Hark finds the still-beating heart of a terrifying deity, he risks everything to keep it out of the hands of smugglers, military scientists, and a secret fanatical cult so that he can use it to save the life of his best friend, Jelt. But with the heart, Jelt gradually and eerily transforms. How long should Hark stay loyal to his friend when he's becoming a monster? And what is Hark willing to sacrifice to save him?

Equal parts dazzling fantasy, swashbuckling adventure, and tender coming-of-age tale, this ambitious standalone from Hardinge (*A Skinful of Shadows*) cautions against xenophobia, zealotry, and greed while using boldly drawn characters to illustrate storytelling's power and fear's role in faith. —*Publishers Weekly*

★ A **face** like glass. Frances Hardinge. Amulet Books, 2017 496 p.
Grades: 6 7 8 9 10
1. Strangers; 2. Tunnels; 3. Artisans; 4. Civilization, Subterranean; 5. Royal houses; 6. Fantasy fiction.
9781419724848; 9781509818723, print, UK
ALA Notable Children's Books, 2018; USBBY Outstanding International Book, 2018; YALSA Best Fiction for Young Adults, 2018.

Hardinge's characteristically lush and sophisticated language will entrance readers, and she makes wonderful use of her singular setting and wildly eccentric cast to pose haunting questions about reality, artifice, and the things we attempt to conceal. —*Publishers Weekly*

★ The **lie** tree. Frances Hardinge. 2016 384 p.
Grades: 7 8 9 10 11 12
1. Magic trees; 2. Dishonesty; 3. Fathers — Death; 4. Truth; 5. Islands; 6. Victorian era (1837-1901); 7. Historical fantasy; 8. Fantasy mysteries
9781419718953
LC 2015028326
ALA Notable Children's Book, 2017; Amelia Bloomer List, 2017; Booklist Editors' Choice: Books for Youth, 2016; Boston Globe-Horn Book Award for Fiction and Poetry, 2016; Costa Book of the Year Award, 2015; Costa Children's Book Award, 2015; Los Angeles Times Book Prize for Young Adult Literature, 2016; School Library Journal Best Books, 2016; USBBY Outstanding International Book, 2017; YALSA Best Fiction for Young Adults, 2017.

On an island off the south coast of Victorian England, fourteen-year-old Faith investigates the mysterious death of her father, who was involved in a scandal, and discovers a tree that feeds upon lies and gives those who eat its fruit visions of truth.

Smart, feminist, and shadowy, Hardinge's talents are on full display here. —*School Library Journal*

★ The **lost** conspiracy. Frances Hardinge. Bowen Press, 2009 576 p.
Grades: 6 7 8 9 10
1. Intrigue; 2. Revenge; 3. Sisters; 4. Escapes; 5. Secrets; 6. High fantasy; 7. Fantasy fiction
9780060880415; 9780060880422; 9781509818730, print, UK
LC 2008045380
ALA Notable Children's Book, 2010; YALSA Best Books for Young Adults, 2010; School Library Journal Best Books, 2009.

When a lie is exposed and their tribe turns against them, Hathin must find a way to save her sister Arilou—once considered the tribe's oracle—and herself.

A deeply imaginative story, with nuanced characters, intricate plotting, and an amazingly original setting.... A perfectly pitched, hopeful ending caps off this standout adventure. —*Booklist*

Published in the United Kingdom as *Gullstruck Island*.

★ A **skinful** of shadows. Frances Hardinge. Amulet Books, an imprint of ABRAMS, 2017 432 p.
Grades: 7 8 9 10
1. Spirit possession; 2. Family secrets; 3. Illegitimacy; 4. Aristocracy; 5. Spirits; 6. England; 7. Historical fantasy
9781419725722; 9781509835508, Paperback, UK
USBBY Outstanding International Book, 2018; School Library Journal Best Books, 2017; YALSA Best Fiction for Young Adults, 2019.

Makepeace, the illegitimate daughter of a rich father, must fight the spirit that possesses her, her family's terrible secret, and the dangers of of a war-torn country.

Hardinge's writing is stunning, and readers will be taken hostage by its intensity, fascinating developments, and the fierce, compassionate girl leading the charge. —*Booklist*

Harland, Richard

Liberator. Richard Harland. Simon & Schuster Book for Young Reades, 2012 496 p.
Grades: 6 7 8 9 10
1. Social classes; 2. Cities and towns; 3. Ghettoes; 4. Sabotage; 5. Murder; 6. 19th century; 7. Steampunk; 8. Science fiction; 9. Alternative histories.
9781442423336; 9781442423350; 9781848772519, print, UK

LC 2010050911

After the Filthies seize control of the massive juggernaut Worldshaker, now called Liberator, members of the former elite, Swanks, remain to teach them, but class differences continue to cause strife and even Col and Riff may be unable to bring unity.

Harrison, Margot

The **killer** in me. Margot Harrison. 2016 368 p.
Grades: 9 10 11 12
1. Serial murderers; 2. Adopted teenage girls; 3. Dreams; 4. Survival; 5. Seventeen-year-old girls; 6. Vermont; 7. New Mexico; 8. Thrillers and suspense; 9. Paranormal fiction; 10. Multiple perspectives
9781484727997; 9781484728369, ebook, US

LC 2015030822

A girl's unsettling connection with a serial killer leads her on a potentially deadly manhunt.

Taut storytelling and believable characters make this a standout mystery, with paranormal notes adding another layer of complexity. —*Publishers Weekly*

Harrison, Rory

Looking for group. Rory Harrison. HarperTeen, an imprint of HarperCollinsPublishers, 2017 356 p.
Grades: 9 10 11 12
1. Gay teenagers; 2. Transgender teenagers; 3. Teenage romance; 4. Transgender teenage girls; 5. Video gamers; 6. Contemporary romances; 7. LGBTQIA romances; 8. First person narratives
9780062453075

A teen in remission from cancer embarks on a mysterious ocean adventure in the hope of making a connection with his online best friend, who is secretly discovering the gender identity her father refuses to acknowledge.

This book is a triumph, allowing honesty, excitement, humor, and heart to step over gender and sexuality constraints and tell a beautiful story. —*Kirkus*

Harstad, Johan

172 hours on the moon. Johan Harstad; translation by Tara F. Chace. Little, Brown and Company, 2012 368 p.
Grades: 9 10 11 12
1. Teenage astronauts; 2. Survival; 3. Space flight to the moon; 4. Astronauts; 5. Secrets; 6. Moon; 7. Science fiction; 8. Horror; 9. Translations
9780316182881; 9781907411519, print, UK

LC 2011025414

In 2019, teens Mia, Antoine, and Midori are selected by lottery to join experienced astronauts on a NASA mission to the once top-secret moon base, DARLAH 2, while in a Florida nursing home, a former astronaut struggles to warn someone of the terrible danger there.

Translated from the Norwegian.

Hartinger, Brent

Three truths and a lie. Brent Hartinger. 2016 288 p.
Grades: 9 10 11 12
1. Cabins; 2. Gay teenagers; 3. Secrets; 4. Dating (Social customs); 5. Friendship; 6. Washington (State); 7. Olympic Peninsula, Washington; 8. Thrillers and suspense.
9781481449601; 9781481449625, ebook, US

LC 2015042737

YALSA Quick Picks for Reluctant Young Adult Readers, 2017.

When friends Rob, Liam, Mia, and Galen gather for a weekend of fun deep in the forest, one is hiding a lie and not everyone will live to find out which one it is.

The story is suspenseful, with excellent pacing, self-aware humor, and a twist that Hartinger pulls off as well as the best slasher films. —*Kirkus*

Hartley, A. J.

Firebrand. A. J. Hartley. Tor Teen, 2017 336 p. (Alternative detective, 2)
Grades: 8 9 10 11 12
1. Undercover operations; 2. Conspiracies; 3. Refugees; 4. Teenage girls; 5. Sutonga, Anglet (Fictitious character); 6. South Africa; 7. Fantasy mysteries; 8. Steampunk; 9. First person narratives
9780765388131

When government plans for a secret weapon are stolen and sold to a rogue enemy, Anglet goes undercover as a foreign princess to infiltrate an exclusive social club while navigating formidable political and cultural challenges.

Hartley has composed another electrifying fantasy that buzzes with intrigue and timely political and social issues, making this a must-have addition to any collection. —*Booklist*

Steeplejack. A.J. Hartley. Tor Teen, 2016 334 p. (Alternative detective, 1)
Grades: 8 9 10 11 12
1. Teenage girl detectives; 2. Race relations; 3. Conspiracies; 4. Intrigue; 5. Murder; 6. Fantasy mysteries; 7. Steampunk; 8. Afrofuturism and Afrofantasy
9780765383426, hardback, US; 9780765383433, paperback, US
Booklist Editors' Choice: Books for Youth, 2016; Thriller Award for Best YA Novel, 2017; YALSA Best Fiction for Young Adults, 2017.

Repairing roof fixtures in her ethnically diverse industrial city in an alternate world resembling Victorian South Africa, 17-year-old Anglet Sutonga investigates the death of a young apprentice while caring for her sister's baby against a backdrop of racial tensions, political secrets and a stolen historical icon.

Hartley's (the Darwen Arkwright series) story is a thought-provoking blend of action and intrigue, with a competent and ethical heroine in Ang and a fully imagined setting whose atmosphere and cultural cues also play important roles. The result is an unforgettable page-turner built on surprises and full of potential. —*Publishers Weekly*

Hartman, Rachel

★ **Seraphina**: a novel. By Rachel Hartman. Random House, 2012 480 p. (Seraphina, 1)
Grades: 7 8 9 10 11 12
1. Dragons; 2. Musicians; 3. Conspiracies; 4. Identity (Psychology); 5. Secrets; 6. High fantasy; 7. Fantasy fiction; 8. First person narratives.
9780375866562, hardback, US; 9780375866227, paperback, US; 9780375896583,ebook, US; 9780375966569, library, US; 9780385668392, hardback, Canada; 9780385668415, paperback, Canada; 9780552566001, paperback, UK; 978085573156

LC 2011003015

ALA Notable Children's Book, 2013; Booklist Editors' Choice: Books for Youth, 2012; Monica Hughes Award for Science Fiction and Fantasy, 2013; OLA Best Bets, 2012; School Library Journal Best Books, 2012; Sunburst Award for Excellence in Canadian Literature of the Fantastic, 2013; William C. Morris YA Debut Award, 2013; YALSA Best Fiction for Young Adults, 2013.

In a world where dragons and humans coexist in an uneasy truce and dragons can assume human form, Seraphina, whose mother died giving birth to her, grapples with her own identity amid magical secrets and royal scandals, while she struggles to accept and develop her extraordinary musical talents.

Shadow scale: a companion to Seraphina. Rachel Hartman. Random House, 2015 480 p. (Seraphina, 2)
Grades: 7 8 9 10 11 12
1. Half-human hybrids; 2. War; 3. Dragons; 4. Courts and courtiers; 5. Civilization, Medieval; 6. High fantasy; 7. Fantasy fiction; 8. First person narratives.
9780375866579; 9780385668606; 9780552557351 1, print, UK; 9780857531599, print, UK; 9780552566018, print, UK; 9780375896590, ebook, US

LC 2014017953

Seraphina, half-dragon and half-human, searches for others like her who can make the difference in the war between dragons and humans in the kingdom of Goredd.

From graceful language to high stakes to daring intrigue, this sequel shines with the same originality, invention, and engagement of feeling that captivated readers in Hartman's debut. —*Horn Book Guide*

★ **Tess** of the road. Rachel Hartman. 2018 536 p.
Grades: 7 8 9 10 11 12
1. Courts and courtiers; 2. Runaways; 3. Disguises; 4. Dragons; 5. Voyages and travels; 6. High fantasy; 7. Fantasy fiction
9781101931288; 9781101931301; 9781101931295; 9780385685887, print, Canada

LC 2016041764

Booklist Editors' Choice: Books for Youth, 2018; Sunburst Award for Excellence in Canadian Literature of the Fantastic, 2019.

Tiring of the oppressive limits imposed on women in the medieval kingdom of Goredd, strong-minded Tess flees when her family decides to send her to a nunnery and embarks on a journey in the Southlands, pretending to be a boy, before running into a dragon friend who helps her find purpose and a way to make peace with a troubling secret past.

Like Tess' journey, surprising, rewarding, and enlightening, both a fantasy adventure and a meta discourse on consent, shame, and female empowerment. —*Kirkus*

Hartnett, Sonya
Golden boys. Sonya Hartnett. Candlewick Press, 2016 256 p.
Grades: 10 11 12 Adult
1. Families; 2. New neighbors; 3. Suburban life; 4. Family violence; 5. Family secrets; 6. Australia; 7. Australian fiction; 8. Domestic fiction; 9. Literary fiction
9780763679491; 9781926428611, paperback (Australia); 9780143572831, paperback (Australia)
Booklist Editors' Choice: Books for Youth, 2016; Shortlisted for the Miles Franklin Literary Award, 2015.

The menacing dynamics present in so many of the relationships are persistently disquieting but also authentic, and a tone of dread pervades, though in the end, events are understated. Sophisticated teen readers will be wowed by this gorgeous, tension-filled novel, but its more natural audience may be adults. —*Kirkus*

Surrender. Sonya Hartnett. Candlewick Press, 2006 248 p.
Grades: 9 10 11 12
1. Men with terminal illnesses; 2. Arson; 3. Dogs as pets; 4. Dogs; 5. Boys — Friendship; 6. Australia; 7. Psychological fiction; 8. First person narratives; 9. Coming-of-age stories.
9780763627683

LC 2005054259

USBBY Outstanding International Book, 2007; Victorian Premier's Literary Awards, Vance Palmer Prize for Fiction, 2005; YALSA

Popular Paperbacks for Young Adults, 2016; YALSA Best Books for Young Adults, 2007; Michael L. Printz Honor Book, 2007.

As he is dying, a twenty-year-old man known as Gabriel recounts his troubled childhood and his strange relationship with a dangerous counterpart named Finnigan.

From the gripping cover showing a raging inferno to the blood-chilling revelation of the final chapter, this page-turner is a blistering yet dense psychological thriller. —*Voice of Youth Advocates*

Hartzler, Aaron
What we saw. Aaron Hartzler. 2015 336 pages
Grades: 9 10 11 12
1. Rape; 2. Witnesses; 3. Small towns; 4. Teenage basketball players; 5. Teenage romance; 6. Realistic fiction
9780062338747

LC 2015005619

Amelia Bloomer Lists, 2016; YALSA Quick Picks for Reluctant Young Adult Readers, 2017.

The story of a town torn apart by the events surrounding the rape of drunk girl at a house party, from the perspective of the partygoers who witnessed it.

Even minor characters here are carefully conceived, and every bit of dialogue and social media activity is chillingly note-perfect. Classroom scenes and conversations offer frameworks for understanding what has happened and why, but the touch is so light and the narrative voice so strong that even a two-page passage breaking down the sexism in Grease! avoids seeming didactic. A powerful tale of betrayal and a vital primer on rape culture. —*Kirkus*

Haston, Meg
The **end** of our story. Meg Haston. Harpercollins Childrens Books, 2017 288 p.
Grades: 9 10 11 12
1. Teenage boy/girl relations; 2. Loss (Psychology); 3. Betrayal; 4. Fathers — Death; 5. High school students; 6. Florida; 7. Love stories; 8. Multiple perspectives; 9. First person narratives.
9780062335777

Instead, the source of the novel's tension comes from Wil and Bridge's attempts to figure out how to address their fractured relationship and whether their futures will involve each other. —*Publishers Weekly*

Hattemer, Kate
The **feminist** agenda of Jemima Kincaid. Kate Hattemer. Alfred A. Knopf, 2020 304 p.
Grades: 9 10 11 12
1. High school seniors; 2. Private schools; 3. Social action; 4. Feminism; 5. Feminists; 6. Virginia; 7. Coming-of-age stories; 8. Teen chick lit.
9781984849137; 9781984849120

In her last few weeks at Northern Virginia's elite Chawton School, eighteen-year-old Jemima Kincaid works to up-end its patriarchal traditions and, in the process, finds the freedom she has always sought. —*OCLC*

Through her fast-paced narrative and lively dialogue, Hattemer (*The Vigilante Poets of Selwyn Academy*, 2014) conveys Jemima's growing understanding of (and sometimes resistance to) the nuances, exploring white feminism and internalized misogyny. A clever, insightful, and sharply funny story. —*Booklist*

The **vigilante** poets of Selwyn Academy. Kate Hattemer. Alfred A. Knopf, 2014 336 p.
Grades: 8 9 10 11 12

1. Reality television programs; 2. Creativity in teenagers; 3. Art schools; 4. Schools; 5. Friendship; 6. Minnesota; 7. Realistic fiction
9780385753784
YALSA Best Fiction for Young Adults, 2015.

Relying on the passion and ideals that drive adolescence, this has a vibrancy and authenticity that will resonate with anyone who has fought for their beliefs—or who has loved a hamster. —*Booklist*

Hautman, Pete
Blank confession. Pete Hautman. Simon & Schuster Books for Young Readers, 2010 176 p.
Grades: 7 8 9 10
1. Teenage drug dealers; 2. Bullying and bullies; 3. Teenage murderers; 4. Confession (Law); 5. High schools; 6. Realistic fiction; 7. Multiple perspectives; 8. Books for reluctant readers
9781416913276

LC 2009050169
Minnesota Book Award for Young People's Literature, 2011; YALSA Quick Picks for Reluctant Young Adult Readers, 2011.

A new and enigmatic student named Shayne appears at high school one day, befriends the smallest boy in the school, and takes on a notorious drug dealer before turning himself in to the police for killing someone.

Masterfully written with simple prose, solid dialogue and memorable characters, the tale will grip readers from the start and keep the reading in one big gulp, in the hope of seeing behind Shayne's mask. A sure hit with teen readers. —*Kirkus*

★ The **Cydonian** Pyramid. Pete Hautman. Candlewick Press, 2013 361 pages; (Klaatu diskos, 2)
Grades: 7 8 9 10 11 12
1. Time travel; 2. Human sacrifice; 3. Pyramids; 4. Escapes; 5. Space and time; 6. Minnesota; 7. Science fiction; 8. Multiple perspectives
9780763654047

A sequel to *The Obsidian Blade* finds an escaped Tucker Feye and Lah Lia hurtling through time while relating their stories from alternating viewpoints that converge at crucial moments.

★ **Godless**. Pete Hautman. Simon & Schuster Books for Young Readers, 2004 198 p.
Grades: 7 8 9 10
1. Belief and doubt; 2. Idols and images; 3. Religion; 4. Water towers; 5. Spirituality; 6. Realistic fiction.
9780689862786

LC 2003010468
Minnesota Book Award for Young Adult Books, 2005; National Book Award for Young People's Literature, 2004; Booklist Editors' Choice: Books for Youth, 2004; YALSA Popular Paperbacks for Young Adults, 2007; YALSA Best Books for Young Adults, 2005.

When sixteen-year-old Jason Bock and his friends create their own religion to worship the town's water tower, what started out as a joke begins to take on a power of its own.

The witty text and provocative subject will make this a supremely enjoyable discussion-starter as well as pleasurable read. —*Bulletin of the Center for Children's Books*

Invisible. Pete Hautman. Simon & Schuster Books for Young Readers, 2005 149 p.
Grades: 7 8 9 10
1. Loners; 2. Teenagers with mental illnesses; 3. Social isolation; 4. Best friends; 5. Mental illness; 6. Realistic fiction
9780689868009

LC 2004002484

Elizabeth Burr/Worzalla Award (Wisconsin), 2006; YALSA Popular Paperbacks for Young Adults, 2016; YALSA Best Books for Young Adults, 2006.

Doug and Andy are unlikely best friends—one a loner obsessed by his model trains, the other a popular student involved in football and theater—who grew up together and share a bond that nothing can sever.

With its excellent plot development and unforgettable, heartbreaking protagonist, this is a compelling novel of mental illness. —*School Library Journal*

The **Klaatu** terminus: a Klaatu Diskos novel. Pete Hautman. Candlewick Press, 2014 358 p. (Klaatu diskos, 3)
Grades: 7 8 9 10 11 12
1. Time travel; 2. Pyramids; 3. Space and time; 4. Love triangles; 5. Teenage boys; 6. Minnesota; 7. Science fiction; 8. Multiple perspectives
9780763654054

Pulling together elaborate strands of the first two books, this conclusion rewards readers with a surprising yet cogent and satisfying chronicle across time. —*Horn Book Guide*

Hawkins, Rachel
Hex Hall. Rachel Hawkins. Disney/Hyperion Books, 2010 323 p. (Hex Hall novels, 1)
Grades: 7 8 9 10
1. Father-separated teenage girls; 2. Teenage witches; 3. Crimes against teenagers; 4. Teenage vampires; 5. Supernatural; 6. Georgia; 7. Urban fantasy
9781423121305
YALSA Popular Paperbacks for Young Adults, 2012.

After a prom-night spell goes badly wrong, witch Sophie Mercer is exiled to an isolated reform school for wayward Prodigium, supernaturally gifted teenagers, where she learns that an unknown predator has been attacking students.

Sixteen-year-old Sophie Mercer, whose absentee father is a warlock, discovered both her heritage and her powers at age 13. While at her school prom, Sophie happens upon a miserable girl sobbing in the bathroom and tries to perform a love spell to help her out. It misfires, and Sophie finds herself at Hecate (aka Hex) Hall, a boarding school for delinquent Prodigium (witches, warlocks, faeries, shape-shifters, and the occasional vampire). What makes this fast-paced romp work is Hawkins' wry humor and sharp eye for teen dynamics. —*Booklist*

School spirits. Rachel Hawkins. Hyperion, 2013 304 p. (School spirits, 1)
Grades: 7 8 9 10
1. Haunted schools; 2. Ghosts; 3. Monsters; 4. Supernatural; 5. Magic; 6. Mississippi; 7. Urban fantasy
9781423148494

LC 2012046402
Fifteen-year-old Izzy, who comes from a long line of monster hunters, investigates a series of hauntings at her new high school.

Headley, Justina Chen
Return to me. By Justina Chen. Little, Brown, 2013 352 p.
Grades: 7 8 9 10
1. Teenage girl psychics; 2. Children of divorced parents; 3. Self-fulfillment in teenage girls; 4. Self-fulfillment; 5. Architecture; 6. Realistic fiction.
9780316102551

LC 2012001549
Always following her parents' wishes and ignoring her psychic inner voice takes eighteen-year-old Rebecca Muir from her beloved cottage and

boyfriend on Puget Sound to New York City, where revelations about herself and her family help her find a path to becoming the architect she wants to be.

Healey, Karen

Guardian of the dead. By Karen Healey. Little, Brown, 2010 345 p.
Grades: 9 10 11 12
1. Teenage martial artists; 2. Immortality; 3. Crushes in teenage girls; 4. Murder; 5. Maori (New Zealand people); 6. New Zealand; 7. Urban fantasy; 8. New Zealand fiction
9780316044301

LC 2009017949
Aurealis Awards, Best Young Adult Novel, 2010; YALSA Popular Paperbacks for Young Adults, 2013; YALSA Best Fiction for Young Adults, 2011; William C. Morris Debut Award finalist, 2011.

A production of *A Midsummer Night's Dream* turns into a nightmare for 17-year-old Ellie when she discovers that some of the actors playing fairies in the play actually are fairies—specifically, menacing creatures known as patupaiarehe—and that they're determined to become immortal, even at the cost of countless human lives. Set in New Zealand against a backdrop of Maori mythology, this intriguing debut features thrilling twists, star-crossed romance, and a smart, tenacious heroine.

Fast-paced adventure and an unfamiliar, frightening enemy set a new scene for teen urban fantasy. —*Kirkus*

When we wake. Karen Healey. Little, Brown Books for Young Readers, 2013 304 p.
Grades: 7 8 9 10 11 12
1. Sixteen-year-old girls; 2. Undead; 3. Low temperature engineering; 4. Gunshot victims; 5. Greed; 6. Australia; 7. Science fiction; 8. New Zealand fiction.
9780316200769; 9781742378084

LC 2012028739
New Zealand Post Children's Book Awards, Children's Choice, Young Adult Fiction Category, 2014; YALSA Best Fiction for Young Adults, 2014; Storylines (New Zealand) Notable Book.

In 2027, sixteen-year-old Tegan is just like every other girl—playing the guitar, falling in love, and protesting the wrongs of the world with her friends. But then Tegan dies, waking up 100 years in the future as the unknowing first government guinea pig to be cryogenically frozen and successfully revived. Appalling secrets about her new world come to light, and Tegan must choose to either keep her head down or fight for a better future.

Sequel: *While we run.*

Heath, Jack

The **lab**. Jack Heath. Scholastic, 2008 311 p. (Six of Hearts, 1)
Grades: 7 8 9 10
1. Teenage spies; 2. Dystopias; 3. Genetic engineering; 4. Clones and cloning; 5. Vigilantes; 6. Dystopian fiction; 7. Science fiction; 8. Australian fiction
9780545068604

Far into the future, the world is devastated by pollution, and the single walled city that remains is controlled entirely by the corrupt ChaoSonic corporation. The only hope for the downtrodden populace is the Deck, a secret organization that's sworn to take down ChaoSonic—and whose best operative is a product of ChaoSonic's lab, genetically enhanced Agent Six of Hearts. But Agent Six has just been captured.

A gritty dystopic world exists under the iron rule of the mega-corporation Chao-Sonic, with only a few vigilante groups around to act as resistance. Six of Hearts is easily the best agent on one such group, the Deck, and he is fiercely dedicated to justice, using his extensive genetic modifications to his advantage.... The compelling and memorable protagonist stands out even against the intricately described and disturbing city whose vividness makes the place's questionable fate a suspenseful issue in its own right. —*Bulletin of the Center for Children's Books*

Remote control. Jack Heath. Scholastic Press, 2010 326 p; (Six of Hearts, 2)
Grades: 7 8 9 10
1. Teenage spies; 2. Trust in teenage boys; 3. Twin brothers; 4. Kidnapping; 5. Rescues; 6. Dystopian fiction; 7. Science fiction; 8. Australian fiction
9780545075916

LC Bl2009035265
Teenage agent Six of Hearts is suspected of being a double agent, which has him on the run from his fellow agents at the Deck while also trying to track down his brother's kidnappers.

The technothriller begun in *The Lab* (2008) takes several intriguing twists...on its way to a satisfying, if temporary, resolution. —*Booklist*

Heilig, Heidi

The **girl** from everywhere. Heidi Heilig. Greenwillow Books, 2016 464 p. (Girl from everywhere, 1)
Grades: 9 10 11 12
1. Time travel (Past); 2. Fathers and daughters; 3. Pirates; 4. Seafaring life; 5. Time travel; 6. Honolulu, Hawaii; 7. 1860s; 8. Fantasy fiction
9780062380753
YALSA Best Fiction for Young Adults, 2017.

Growing up beside her father on a time-traveling ship that ventures to real and imaginary places, 16-year-old Nix struggles to preserve her life when her father obsessively pursues a map in a past time period in ways that threaten her existence.

With time travel, fantasy, Hawaiian history, mythology, cute animals, and a feisty protagonist, romance and fantasy readers will find much to enjoy in this quick read. —*Booklist*

A **kingdom** for a stage. Heidi Heilig. Greenwillow Books, 2019 464 p. (For a muse of fire, 2)
Grades: 9 10 11 12
1. Teenage girls; 2. Magic; 3. Resistance to government; 4. Treason; 5. Teenage fugitives; 6. Asian-influenced fantasy; 7. Fantasy fiction
9780062651976

Finds Jetta caught in a war between the rebels and invading colonizers who force her to choose between saving her people and protecting her sanity.

Sequel to: *For a Muse of Fire*

Hemphill, Stephanie

Sisters of glass. Stephanie Hemphill. Alfred A. Knopf, 2012 150 p;
Grades: 7 8 9 10
1. Glass blowing; 2. Teenage romance; 3. Families; 4. Fifteen-year-old girls; 5. Teenage girls; 6. Venice, Italy; 7. Murano, Italy; 8. 15th century; 9. Historical fiction; 10. Novels in verse.
9780375861093

LC Bl2012004819
When a new glassblower arrives to help in the family business, the attraction Maria feels for him causes a web of conflicting emotions to grow even more tangled.

★ **Your** own, Sylvia: a verse portrait of Sylvia Plath. By Stephanie Hemphill. Alfred A. Knopf, 2007 272 p.
Grades: 8 9 10 11 12
1. Plath, Sylvia; 2. Authors, American; 3. Poets, American; 4. Rejection (Psychology); 5. Family relationships; 6. Poets
9780375837999

LC 2006007253

Booklist Editors' Choice: Books for Youth, 2007; YALSA Best Books for Young Adults, 2008; Michael L. Printz Honor Book, 2008.

Hemphill's verse, like Plath's, is completely compelling: every word, every line, worth reading. —*Horn Book Guide*

Henderson, Eleanor

Ten thousand saints. Eleanor Henderson. Ecco, 2011 336 p.
Grades: 11 12 Adult
   1. Family relationships; 2. Teenagers; 3. Former drug addicts; 4. Parent and child; 5. AIDS (Disease); 6. New York City; 7. Vermont; 8. 1980s; 9. Mainstream fiction; 10. Coming-of-age stories; 11. Books to movies; 12. Adult books for young adults.
9780062021021; 9781780872179, print, UK; 9781780872193, print, UK

New York Times Notable Book, 2011; School Library Journal Best Books: Best Adult Books 4 Teens, 2011.

Sometimes too much of a good thing is just not enough. When his friend Teddy dies of an overdose, disaffected adolescent Jude puts suburban Vermont in his rearview mirror and makes for New York City—where a decade's hopes and foibles spin madly about him.

Henderson is a versatile ventriloquist, taking us briskly and believably into the minds and hearts of most of her major characters (though Eliza, while briefly vivid, turns into exactly what the boys treat her as, which is a passive plot device). Though it loses some steam as it hurtles toward a happy ending, *Ten Thousand Saints* is at its best when depicting the punk scene in New York in the 1980s and its amalgam of homeless junkies, vegan Hinduists, early AIDS victims, and antigentrification activists. It's an auspicious debut, and gives us reason to hope that Eleanor Henderson will mature as satisfyingly as her subjects do. —*Boston Globe*

Hendriks, Jenni

Unpregnant. Jenni Hendriks and Ted Caplan. HarperTeen, 2019 320 p.
Grades: 9 10 11 12
   1. Former friends; 2. Cross-country automobile trips; 3. Abortion; 4. Unplanned pregnancy; 5. Pregnant teenagers; 6. Realistic fiction; 7. Books to movies; 8. Books for reluctant readers
9780062876249; 9781912626168, Paperback, UK

YALSA Quick Picks for Reluctant Young Adult Readers, 2020.

Finding herself unexpectedly pregnant, a 17-year-old girl from a conservative community teams up with her wild former friend to get an out-of-state abortion that is complicated by unexpected challenges, kind strangers and reckonings with the past.

The authors' background in television and film shows, with scene after hilarious scene normalizing the most serious of subjects: how far women must often go to exercise control over their own bodies. Not surprisingly, this is being made into a movie. —*Publishers Weekly*

Made into an HBO Max movie in 2020.

Henry, April

The lonely dead. April Henry. Henry Holt & Co, 2019 240 p.
Grades: 7 8 9 10 11 12
   1. Former friends; 2. Mediums; 3. Murder investigation; 4. Murder victims; 5. Ghosts; 6. Supernatural mysteries; 7. Thrillers and suspense.
9781250157577, HRD, US

LC 2018021064

When schizophrenic Adele, who possesses a paranormal gift, is implicated in an investigation that involves the murder of her ex-best friend Tori, Adele must work with Tori's ghost to find the killer.

A thriller that manages to be both creepy and fun. —*Kirkus*

Henry, Katie

★ **Heretics** anonymous. Katie Henry. Harpercollins Childrens Books 2018 336 p.
Grades: 8 9 10 11 12
   1. Atheists; 2. Misfits (Persons); 3. Catholic schools; 4. Belief and doubt; 5. Secret societies; 6. Realistic fiction
9780062698872; 9780062698889

The story adeptly asks readers to question what they believe and why, without being preachy, judgmental, or dismissive. Humor interlaced with more serious ideas make for an interesting and enjoyable read. —*School Library Journal*

★ **Let's** call it a doomsday. Katie Henry. Katherine Tegen Books, an imprint of HarperCollinsPublishers, 2019 400 p.
Grades: 9 10 11 12
   1. Mormons; 2. End of the world; 3. Anxiety disorders; 4. Anxiety in teenagers; 5. Faith in teenage girls; 6. Realistic fiction; 7. First person narratives.
9780062698902

Ellis Kimball, sixteen, whose anxiety disorder causes her to prepare for the imminent end of the world, meets Hannah, who claims to know when it will happen.

A too-rare, well-rounded portrayal of a contemporary religious adolescent. —*Horn Book Guide*

Hensley, Joy N.

Rites of passage. Joy N. Hensley. HarperTeen, 2014 416 pages
Grades: 7 8 9 10
   1. Military education; 2. Hazing; 3. Gender role; 4. Bullying and bullies; 5. Schools; 6. Blue Ridge Mountains; 7. Realistic fiction
9780062295194

LC 2014010022

Sixteen-year-old Sam McKenna discovers that becoming one of the first girls to attend the revered Denmark Military Academy means living with a target on her back.

The narrative flows along terrifically as Sam courageously battles to make it even while the forces against her increase. The characters stand out as individual and real; readers will cheer Sam on throughout. Absolutely compelling. —*Kirkus*

Henstra, Sarah

We contain multitudes. Sarah Henstra. 2019 400 p.
Grades: 9 10 11 12
   1. Dating (Social customs); 2. Love; 3. Gay teenagers; 4. Teenage boy/boy relations; 5. Homophobia; 6. LGBTQIA fiction; 7. Realistic fiction; 8. Canadian fiction.
9780316524650; 9780735264212, print, Canada; 9780316524643, ebook, US

LC 2018022802

As penpals for a high school English assignment, poetry-loving sophomore Jonathan and popular-athlete senior Adam explore their growing relationship through a series of letters.

Graphic toxic masculinity, familial abuse, drug use, and sexual betrayal are balanced (not obliterated) by the beauty of love between two boys who never expected the best from each other. Your reason to root for love—and the power of the pen. —*Kirkus*

Heppermann, Christine

★ **Ask** me how I got here. Christine Heppermann. Greenwillow Books, an imprint of HarperCollins Publishers, 2016 225 p.
Grades: 9 10 11 12

1. Abortion; 2. Teenage pregnancy; 3. Cross-country runners; 4. Dating (Social customs); 5. Catholics; 6. Realistic fiction; 7. Coming-of-age stories; 8. Novels in verse
9780062387950
Amelia Bloomer List, 2017; YALSA Best Fiction for Young Adults, 2017; YALSA Quick Picks for Reluctant Young Adult Readers, 2017.

Addie's future is laid out in front of her—become the best runner in the state and go to college on a scholarship—but after getting pregnant with her boyfriend her decision to have an abortion affects her life greatly.

Heppermann's free-verse poems glide over many of the stickier parts, pausing meaningfully to focus on Addie's emotions, which are brought into sharpest relief in the presence of a bullish antiabortion classmate. While her abortion is a catalyzing event, ultimately this thought-provoking novel in verse is more about well-rounded Addie's gratifying process of self-determination than her choice to end her pregnancy. —*Booklist*

Herbach, Geoff
Nothing special. Geoff Herbach. Sourcebooks Fire, 2012 290 p. (Felton Reinstein trilogy, 2)
Grades: 6 7 8 9 10
1. Teenage boys; 2. Families; 3. Brothers; 4. Fame; 5. Runaways.
9781402265075
Minnesota Book Award for Young People's Literature, 2013.

When Felton Reinstein's little brother Andrew goes missing, Felton puts his football aspirations on hold to travel cross-country to Florida to find him.

The combination of outrageous circumstances and humor expertly balances out the very serious issues of guilt, anger, and mental and emotional collapse. Felton's voice is fresh and believable as a teen on the edge of manhood. Boys especially will discover kindred spirits in Felton and Andrew. Kudos to Herbach for this deep, moving, LOL funny, and completely original story. —*School Library Journal*

Stupid fast: the summer I went from a joke to a jock. Geoff Herbach. Sourcebooks Fire, 2011 311 p; (Felton Reinstein trilogy, 1)
Grades: 6 7 8 9 10
1. Survivors of suicide victims; 2. High school football; 3. First loves; 4. Teenage boy/girl relations; 5. Family problems; 6. Wisconsin; 7. Realistic fiction; 8. First person narratives.
9781402256301
LC 2011020274
YALSA Best Fiction for Young Adults, 2012.

Just before his sixteenth birthday, Felton Reinstein has a sudden growth spurt that turns him from a small, jumpy, picked-on boy with the nickname of "Squirrel Nut" to a powerful athlete, leading to new friends, his first love, and the courage to confront his family's past and current problems.

Herbach is at his peak limning the confusion and frustration of a young man who no longer recognizes his own body, and Felton's self-deprecating take on his newly awarded A-list status is funny and compelling. —*Bulletin of the Center for Children's Books*

Herlong, Madaline
The **great** wide sea. By Madaline Herlong. Viking Childrens Books, 2008 240 p.
Grades: 7 8 9 10
1. Sailing; 2. Grief; 3. Seafaring life; 4. Family relationships; 5. Brothers; 6. Caribbean Sea; 7. Survival stories; 8. Adventure stories; 9. First person narratives
9780670063307
LC 2008008384
YALSA Best Books for Young Adults, 2010.

Still mourning the death of their mother, three brothers go with their father on an extended sailing trip off the Florida Keys and have a harrowing adventure at sea.

Herlong makes the most of the three boys' characters, each exceptionally well developed here, to make this as much a novel of brotherhood as a sea story. —*Bulletin of the Center for Children's Books*

Hernandez, David
Suckerpunch. David Hernandez. HarperTeen, 2008 217 p;
Grades: 9 10 11 12
1. Child abuse; 2. Brothers; 3. Fathers and sons; 4. Drug abuse; 5. Family relationships; 6. California; 7. Coming-of-age stories; 8. Books for reluctant readers
9780061173318
LC 2007024182
YALSA Quick Picks for Reluctant Young Adult Readers, 2009; YALSA Best Books for Young Adults, 2009.

Shy, seventeen-year-old Marcus and his sixteen-year-old brother, Enrique, accompanied by two friends, drive from their home in southern California to Monterey to confront the abusive father who walked out a year earlier, and who now wants to return home.

The author's imagery, sometimes subtle, sometimes searing, invariably hits its mark. —*Publishers Weekly*

Herrick, Steven
By the river. Steven Herrick. Front Street, 2006 238 p.
Grades: 8 9 10 11 12
1. Teenage boys; 2. Teenagers; 3. Children of single parents; 4. Single-parent families; 5. Death; 6. Australia; 7. 1960s; 8. Novels in verse; 9. Historical fiction; 10. Coming-of-age stories
9781932425727; 9781741143577, Australia
NSW Premier's Literary Awards, Ethel Turner Prize for Young People's Literature, 2005; USBBY Outstanding International Book, 2007.

The poems are simple but potent in their simplicity, blending together in a compelling, evocative story of a gentle, intelligent boy growing up and learning to deal with a sometimes-ugly little world that he...will eventually escape. —*Voice of Youth Advocates*

Hesse, Karen
Safekeeping. Karen Hesse. Feiwel and Friends, 2012 304 p.
Grades: 7 8 9 10 11 12
1. Survival; 2. Parent-separated teenage girls; 3. Dystopias; 4. Friendship; 5. Seventeen-year-old girls; 6. New England; 7. First person narratives.
9781250011343
LC Bl2012021621
When Radley returns to the United States after volunteering abroad, she comes back to a country under military rule with strict travel restrictions, and she must find her way back to her Vermont home through the New England woods.

Hesse, Monica
Girl in the blue coat. Monica Hesse. 2016 320 p.
Grades: 9 10 11 12
1. Black market; 2. Missing teenage girls; 3. World War II; 4. Resistance to military occupation; 5. Holocaust (1933-1945); 6. Netherlands; 7. Second World War era (1939-1945); 8. Historical fiction
9780316260602; 9780316260640, ebook, US
LC 2015020565

Edgar Allan Poe Award for Best Young Adult, 2017; Notable Books for a Global Society, 2017; YALSA Best Fiction for Young Adults, 2017.

In 1943 Nazi-occupied Amsterdam, teenage Hanneke—a 'finder' of black market goods—is tasked with finding a Jewish girl a customer had been hiding, who has seemingly vanished into thin air, and is pulled into a web of resistance activities and secrets as she attempts to solve the mystery and save the missing girl.

In 1943 Amsterdam, Hanneke nurses a broken heart—her boyfriend has died in the war—while delivering black market goods (foodstuffs, cigarettes, etc.) to her neighbors. One customer, Mrs. Janssen, implores Hanneke to find a missing girl whom the woman had been sheltering, leading to an engaging mystery that shakes Hanneke from her emotional stupor. An author's note includes useful information about the Dutch Resistance. —*Horn Book Guide*

They went left. Monica Hesse. Little, Brown and Company, 2020 384 p.
Grades: 9 10 11 12
1. Holocaust survivors; 2. Postwar life; 3. Separated friends, relatives, etc; 4. Searching; 5. Brothers and sisters; 6. Germany; 7. 1940s; 8. Historical fiction.
9780316490573
Sydney Taylor Honor Book for Teen Readers, 2021.

Zofia, a teenage Holocaust survivor, travels across post-war Europe as she searches for her younger brother and seeks to rebuild her shattered life.

Hesse (*The War Outside*) has written several YA novels that touch on WWII traumas, and this one shows her gift at coming at an oft-told story from a new angle, as well as her compelling language, characterization, and ability to fill a story with realistic details and tension. —*Publishers Weekly*

★ The **war** outside. Monica Hesse. 2018 336 p.
Grades: 8 9 10 11 12
1. Teenage girls; 2. Concentration camps; 3. Japanese Americans — Forced removal and incarceration, 1942-1945; 4. German Americans; 5. Friendship; 6. Texas; 7. Second World War era (1939-1945); 8. Historical fiction; 9. Multiple perspectives
9780316316699; 9780316316712; 9780316316705, ebook, US; 9780316445238, ebook, US
LC 2018005733
Notable Books for a Global Society, 2019; YALSA Best Fiction for Young Adults, 2019.

Teens Haruko, a Japanese American, and Margot, a German American, form a life-changing friendship as everything around them starts falling apart in the Crystal City family internment camp during World War II.

Interned in a Texas camp during World War II, Japanese-American Haruko and German-American Margot watch their families fall apart and are driven to depend on each other, even if they should not. —*Kirkus*

Hiaasen, Carl

Skink—no surrender. Carl Hiaasen. Alfred A. Knopf, 2014 288 pages
Grades: 8 9 10 11 12
1. Missing teenage girls; 2. Internet predators; 3. Wilderness areas; 4. Cousins; 5. Former governors; 6. Florida; 7. Mysteries; 8. Books for reluctant readers
9780375870514; 9780307974068, ebook, US; 9781780622194, print, UK
LC 2014006036
YALSA Quick Picks for Reluctant Young Adult Readers, 2016.

With the help of an eccentric ex-governor, a teenaged boy searches for his missing cousin in the Florida wilds.

Higgins, Jack

★ **Sure** fire. By Jack Higgins with Justin Richards. HarperCollins, 2006 256 p. (Rich and Jade, 1)
Grades: 6 7 8 9
1. Twin brothers and sisters; 2. Spies; 3. Kidnapping; 4. Fifteen-year-olds; 5. Mothers — Death; 6. London, England; 7. Spy fiction; 8. Thrillers and suspense
9780007244096
LC 2007008144
YALSA Popular Paperbacks for Young Adults, 2009.

Resentful of having to go and live with their estranged father after the death of their mother, fifteen-year-old twins, Rich and Jade, soon find they have more complicated problems when their father is kidnapped and their attempts to rescue him involve them in a dangerous international plot to control the world's oil.

This is a standout YA spy novel.... Each chapter ends with a cliff-hanger, maintaining the high level of suspense. —*Publishers Weekly*

Higson, Charles

The **dead**. Charlie Higson. Hyperion, 2011 485 p. (Enemy series (Charlie Higson), 2)
Grades: 8 9 10
1. Post-apocalypse; 2. Zombies; 3. Survival (after epidemics); 4. Dystopias; 5. Fires; 6. London, England; 7. Horror; 8. Multiple perspectives
9781423134121; 9780141384658, print, UK

With the book's immense cast and substantial body count, it doesn't pay to get too attached to any one character, while the intense descriptions of violence and sickness will get under readers' skin. —*Publishers Weekly*

★ The **enemy**. Charlie Higson. Hyperion, 2010 440 p. (Enemy series (Charlie Higson), 1)
Grades: 9 10 11 12
1. Post-Apocalypse; 2. Zombies; 3. Survival (after epidemics); 4. Dystopias; 5. Death; 6. London, England; 7. Horror
9781423131755; 9781484721469; 9780141931845, print, UK
YALSA Popular Paperbacks for Young Adults, 2017.

After a disease turns everyone over sixteen into brainless, decomposing, flesh-eating creatures, a group of teenagers leave their shelter and set out on a harrowing journey across London to the safe haven of Buckingham Palace.

Nearly two years ago, the world changed; everyone over 16 became horrifically ill and began to crave fresh meat. As supplies are exhausted and the vicious grown-ups grow braver, Arrum and Maxie, along with their band of refugees, must embark on a perilous journey across London to reach the safest spot in the city: Buckingham Palace.... Intrigue, betrayal and the basic heroic-teens-against-marauding-adults conflict give this work a high place on any beach-reading list. —*Kirkus*

Hill, C. J.

Slayers. C.J. Hill. Feiwel and Friends, 2011 384 p. (Slayers (C.J. Hill), 1)
Grades: 7 8 9 10 11 12
1. Sixteen-year-old girls; 2. Teenage girls; 3. Dragons; 4. Interpersonal relations; 5. Ability; 6. Fantasy fiction.
9780312614140; 9780312675141
LC 2011023559

At a rustic summer camp, sixteen-year-old Tori, a senator's daughter, learns that she is descended from medieval dragon slayers, that dragons still exist, and that she is expected to hone her special abilities to join her fellow campers in battling the beasts and the man who controls them.

The dragon mythos has a good dollop of modern science, and Hill offers cunning peeks into the minds of characters on all sides of the power struggle.... The character development, plotting, and ethical quandries make this more than a worthy equal to the works of Rick Riordan or Christopher Paolini. —*Booklist*

Hinton, S. E.

★ The **outsiders**. By S. E. Hinton. Puffin Books, 1997 180 p.
Grades: 7 8 9 10
1. Gangs; 2. Brothers; 3. Teenagers; 4. Teenage boys; 5. Bullying and bullies; 6. Realistic fiction; 7. Books to movies; 8. Classics.
9780140385724; 9780141189116, UK; 9780141314570, print, UK; 9780141368887, print, UK

LC 67013606

Virginia Readers' Choice Award for High School, 1985.

Three brothers struggle to stay together after their parents' death, as they search for an identity among the conflicting values of their adolescent society in which they find themselves "outsiders."

This remarkable novel by a seventeen-year-old girl gives a moving, credible view of the outsiders from the inside—their loyalty to each other, their sensitivity under tough crusts, their understanding of self and society. —*Horn Book Guide*

Hirsch, Jeff

The **eleventh** plague. Jeff Hirsch. Scholastic Press, 2011 304 p.
Grades: 7 8 9 10
1. Post-apocalypse; 2. Survival; 3. Dystopias; 4. Practical jokes; 5. Communities; 6. Dystopian fiction; 7. Science fiction; 8. First person narratives.
9780545290142

LC 2010048966

YALSA Popular Paperbacks for Young Adults, 2016.

Twenty years after the start of the war that caused the Collapse, fifteen-year-old Stephen, his father, and grandfather travel post-Collapse America scavenging, but when his grandfather dies and his father decides to risk everything to save the lives of two strangers, Stephen's life is turned upside down.

This novel is an impressive story with strong characters.... Hirsch delivers a tight, well-crafted story. —*Publishers Weekly*

Hobbs, Will

Beardance. Will Hobbs. Atheneum, 1993 197 p.
Grades: 7 8 9 10
1. Native American teenage boys; 2. Wilderness survival; 3. Wildlife rescue; 4. Grizzly bear; 5. Self-discovery in teenage boys; 6. Colorado; 7. San Juan Mountains (Colo. and N.M.); 8. Adventure stories; 9. Realistic fiction.
9780689318672

LC 92-44874

While accompanying an elderly rancher on a trip into the San Juan Mountains, Cloyd, a Ute Indian boy, tries to help two orphaned grizzly cubs survive the winter and, at the same time, completes his spirit mission.

The story offers plenty of action and memorable characters, and the descriptions of Ute rituals and legends, the setting, and Cloyd's first experiences with spirit dreams are particularly well done. —*Horn Book Guide*
Sequel to: *Bearstone*.

★ **Bearstone**. Will Hobbs. Atheneum, 1989 154 p.
Grades: 7 8 9 10
1. Native American teenage boys; 2. Boys and senior men; 3. Ranch life; 4. Ranchers; 5. Ute teenage boys; 6. Colorado; 7. Coming-of-age stories; 8. Realistic fiction; 9. Classics.
9780689314964

LC 89006641

A troubled teenage Indian boy goes to live with an elderly rancher whose caring ways help the boy become a man.

Rebellious at being forced to abandon his family and his Ute Indian heritage to attend high school, Cloyd is sent to spend a summer with a lonely old rancher in Colorado. Upon arriving, Cloyd accidentally finds a turquoise bear totem in an Anasazi grave site, which serves as a touchstone between his cultural roots and his feelings. As time goes by, he also develops a mutual respect and friendship for the old man. The growth and maturity that Cloyd acquires as the summer progresses is juxtaposed poetically against the majestic Colorado landscape. Hobbs has creatively blended myth and reality as Cloyd forges a new identity for himself. —*Voice of Youth Advocates*
Sequel: *Beardance*.

Crossing the wire. By Will Hobbs. HarperCollins, 2006 216 p.
Grades: 5 6 7 8
1. Mexicans; 2. Undocumented workers; 3. Drug smugglers; 4. Fifteen-year-old boys; 5. Teenage boys; 6. Mexico; 7. Arizona; 8. Survival stories; 9. Adventure stories; 10. Realistic fiction.
9780060741389; 9780060741396

LC 2005019697

Heartland Award, 2008.

Fifteen-year-old Victor Flores journeys north in a desperate attempt to cross the Arizona border and find work in the United States to support his family in central Mexico.

This is an exciting story in a vital contemporary setting. —*Voice of Youth Advocates*

Downriver. Will Hobbs. Atheneum, 1991 204 p;
Grades: 7 8 9 10
1. Teenage rebels; 2. White-water rafting; 3. Wilderness survival; 4. Change (Psychology); 5. Teenagers; 6. Colorado River; 7. Grand Canyon; 8. Adventure stories; 9. Realistic fiction; 10. Classics.
9780689316906

LC 90001044

California Young Reader Medal, Young Adult, 1995; Colorado Blue Spruce YA Book Award, 1997-1998.

Fifteen-year-old Jessie and the other rebellious teenage members of a wilderness survival school team abandon their adult leader, hijack his boats, and try to run the dangerous white water at the bottom of the Grand Canyon.

The book is exquisitely plotted, with nail-biting suspense and excitement. —*School Library Journal*
Sequel: *River thunder*.

The **maze**. Will Hobbs. Morrow Junior Books, 1998 198 p;
Grades: 7 8 9 10
1. Foster teenagers; 2. Wildlife reintroduction; 3. Boys and men; 4. Fourteen-year-old boys; 5. Teenage boys; 6. Utah; 7. Canyonlands National Park; 8. Adventure stories; 9. Realistic fiction; 10. Books for reluctant readers
9780688150921

LC 98010791

YALSA Quick Picks for Reluctant Young Adult Readers, 1999; YALSA Best Books for Young Adults, 1999.

Rick, a fourteen-year-old foster child, escapes from a juvenile detention facility near Las Vegas and travels to Canyonlands National Park in Utah where he meets a bird biologist working on a project to reintroduce condors to the wild.

Hobbs spins an engrossing yarn, blending adventure with a strong theme, advocating the need for developing personal values. —*Horn Book Guide*

Take me to the river. By Will Hobbs. HarperCollins, 2011 192 p.
Grades: 5 6 7 8

1. White-water rafting; 2. Fugitives; 3. Boy cousins; 4. Hurricanes; 5. Kidnappers; 6. Rio Grande; 7. Texas; 8. Adventure stories.
9780060741440

The story unfolds in a disarming manner. The pace is quick, and the challenges are relentless, but the writing is so grounded in physical details and emotional realism that every turn of events seems convincing within the context of the story. —*Booklist*

Wild man island. Will Hobbs. HarperCollins Publishers, 2002 184 p. Illustration; Map
Grades: 6 7 8 9
1. Wilderness survival; 2. Resourcefulness in teenage boys; 3. Men recluses; 4. Resourcefulness; 5. Fourteen-year-old boys; 6. Alaska; 7. Admiralty Island, Alaska; 8. Survival stories; 9. Adventure stories.
9780688174736; 9780060298104
LC 2001039818

After fourteen-year-old Andy slips away from his kayaking group to visit the wilderness site of his archaeologist father's death, a storm strands him on Admiralty Island, Alaska, where he manages to survive, encounters unexpected animal and human inhabitants, and looks for traces of the earliest prehistoric immigrants to America.

A well-paced adventure, this novel combines survival saga, mystery, and archaeological expedition. —*Voice of Youth Advocates*

Hodge, Rosamund

Cruel beauty. Rosamund Hodge. Balzer + Bray, an imprint of HarperCollinsPublishers, 2014 336 p.
Grades: 8 9 10 11 12
1. Arranged marriage; 2. Interpersonal attraction; 3. Duty; 4. Household employees; 5. Teenage girls; 6. Fantasy fiction; 7. Mythological fiction; 8. Fairy tale and folklore-inspired fiction
9780062224736
YALSA Popular Paperbacks for Young Adults, 2016.

Hodge's story infuses elements of Greek mythology and classic fairy tales. The plot moves quickly, and the characters are well formed; their transgressions make them interesting and authentic. The complex relationship between Nyx and Ignifex is especially engaging. An entertaining read for teens who enjoy romantic fantasy. —*School Library Journal*

Hodkin, Michelle

The **unbecoming** of Mara Dyer. Michelle Hodkin. Simon & Schuster, 2011 272 p. (Mara Dyer trilogy, 1)
Grades: 7 8 9 10 11 12
1. Post-traumatic stress disorder; 2. Supernatural; 3. Murder; 4. Teenage boy/girl relations; 5. High schools; 6. Florida; 7. Paranormal fiction.
9781442421769
LC 2010050862
YALSA Popular Paperbacks for Young Adults, 2016.

Seventeen-year-old Mara cannot remember the accident that took the lives of three of her friends but, after moving from Rhode Island to Florida, finding love with Noah, and more deaths, she realizes that uncovering something buried in her memory might save her family and her future.

The characters are real and wonderful, and the supernatural story is riveting. —*School Library Journal*

Hoffman, Nina Kiriki

A **stir** of bones. By Nina Kiriki Hoffman. Viking, 2003 244 p.
Grades: 7 8 9 10
1. Haunted houses; 2. Teenage girls and ghosts; 3. Family problems; 4. Teenage boy ghosts; 5. Abusive men; 6. Oregon; 7. Pacific Northwest; 8. Ghost stories; 9. Pacific Northwest fiction
9780670035519
LC 2003005029
YALSA Best Books for Young Adults, 2004.

After discovering the secrets that lie in an abandoned house, fourteen-year-old Susan Backstrom, with the help of some new friends, has the ability to make a safe, new life for herself.

Fourteen-year-old Susan Blackstrom begins the painful process of breaking away from her abusive father, with help from allies both human and supernatural. A chance encounter with three classmates leads Susan to an abandoned house that...harbors an uncommonly substantial ghost named Nathan.... Richly endowed with complex relationships, a strange and subtle brand of magic, evocative language, and suspenseful storytelling, this will draw readers into a world less safe and simple than it seems at first glance. —*Booklist*
Prequel to: author's adult title: *A red heart of memories*.

Hoffmeister, Peter Brown

This is the part where you laugh. Peter Brown Hoffmeister. Alfred A. Knopf, 2016 370 p.
Grades: 9 10 11 12
1. Children of drug abusers; 2. Poverty; 3. Family problems; 4. Friendship; 5. Basketball; 6. Oregon; 7. Realistic fiction
9780553538106; 9780553538120, ebook, US
LC 2015022147
YALSA Best Fiction for Young Adults, 2017.

Rising sophomore Travis and his best friend, Creature, spend a summer in a Eugene, Oregon, trailer park dealing with cancer, basketball, first love, addiction, gang violence, and a reptilian infestation.

In this tragicomic YA debut from adult author Hoffmeister (Let Them Be Eaten by Bears), a young man contends with anger, family troubles, and romance over a few increasingly chaotic months. Travis's summer goals are simple: improve his basketball skills, stay out of trouble, and try to cheer up his grandmother, who's dying from cancer. He also hangs out with his best friend Creature, spends time with a mercurial girl named Natalie, and searches for his drug-addicted mother in the homeless camps around the area.... The result is a raw, offbeat novel with an abundance of honesty and heart. —*Publishers Weekly*

Holder, Nancy

Crusade. By Nancy Holder and Debbie Viguie. Simon Pulse, 2010 384 p. (Crusade trilogy, 1)
Grades: 7 8 9 10 11
1. Vampire slayers; 2. Vampires; 3. Courage in teenage girls; 4. Courage; 5. Betrayal; 6. New Orleans, Louisiana; 7. San Francisco, California; 8. Urban fantasy
9781416998020
LC 2010009094

An international team of six teenaged vampire hunters, trained in Salamanca, Spain, goes to New Orleans seeking to rescue team-member Jenn's younger sister as the vampires escalate their efforts to take over the Earth.

The cinematic writing and apocalyptic scenario should find a ready audience. —*Publishers Weekly*

Holland, Sara

Everless. Sara Holland. HarperTeen, 2018 336 p.
Grades: 8 9 10 11 12
1. Imaginary kingdoms; 2. Time; 3. Debt; 4. Rulers; 5. Teenage girls; 6. High fantasy; 7. Fantasy fiction

9780062653659; 9781408353622, paperback, UK; 9781408353394, hardback, UK; 9781408349151, Paperback, Australia

In the kingdom of Sempera, time is currency—extracted from blood, bound to iron, and consumed to add time to one's own lifespan. The rich aristocracy, like the Gerlings, tax the poor to the hilt, extending their own lives by centuries.

Holland's debut is set in an intricate and immersive fantasy world, a world she skillfully builds through layers of flashbacks and memories. —*Booklist*

Holt, Kimberly Willis

Part of me: stories of a Louisiana family. Kimberly Willis Holt. H. Holt, 2006 224 p.
Grades: 7 8 9 10
1. Holt, Kimberly Willis; 2. Rural life; 3. Women authors; 4. Books and reading; 5. Families; 6. Bookmobiles; 7. Louisiana; 8. Short stories; 9. Autobiographical fiction
9780805063608

LC 2005029676

Ten stories trace the connections between four generations of one Louisiana family from 1939 when a young girl leaves school to help support her family to 2006 when an eighty-year-old woman embarks on a book tour.

Holt once again excels at creating character and an evocative sense of place. —*School Library Journal*

Hoover, P. J.

Tut: my epic battle to save the world. P.J. Hoover. Starscape, 2017 329 p. (Tut (P.J. Hoover), 2)
Grades: 5 6 7 8
1. Tutankhamen, King of Egypt; 2. Gods and goddesses, Egyptian; 3. Immortality; 4. Prisoners; 5. Brothers; 6. Missing persons; 7. Fantasy fiction; 8. Mythological fiction
9780765390820

Embarking on a mission to find his missing brother, eighth-grade immortal Tut discovers that his brother is being held prisoner by the vengeful Egyptian god Apep, who is plotting to swallow the sun to plunge the world into eternal darkness

A sequel that doesn't disappoint; purchase where there are fans of the first book, or buy the series for readers looking for history and adventure. —*School Library Journal*

Hopkins, Ellen

★ **Burned**. Ellen Hopkins. Margaret K. McElderry Books, 2006 532 p.
Grades: 9 10 11 12
1. Mormons; 2. Anger in teenage girls; 3. Family violence; 4. Fear in teenage girls; 5. Mormon teenage girls; 6. Nevada; 7. Realistic fiction; 8. First person narratives; 9. Novels in verse.
9781416903543

LC 2005032461

YALSA Popular Paperbacks for Young Adults, 2012.

Seventeen-year-old Pattyn, the eldest daughter in a large Mormon family, is sent to her aunt's Nevada ranch for the summer, where she temporarily escapes her alcoholic, abusive father and finds love and acceptance, only to lose everything when she returns home.

The free verses, many in the form of concrete poems, create a compressed and intense reading experience with no extraneous dialogue or description.... This book will appeal to teens favoring realistic fiction and dramatic interpersonal stories. —*Voice of Youth Advocates*

Sequel: *Smoke*.

Identical. Ellen Hopkins. Margaret K. McElderry Books, 2008 565 p;
Grades: 10 11 12
1. Identical twin sisters; 2. Child sexual abuse; 3. Self-destructive behavior in teenage girls; 4. Self-destructive behavior; 5. Family problems; 6. California; 7. Realistic fiction; 8. Novels in verse; 9. First person narratives; 10. Books for reluctant readers
9781416950059

LC 2007032463

YALSA Popular Paperbacks for Young Adults, 2016; YALSA Quick Picks for Reluctant Young Adult Readers, 2009.

Sixteen-year-old identical twin daughters of a district court judge and a candidate for the United States House of Representatives, Kaeleigh and Raeanne Gardella desperately struggle with secrets that have already torn them and their family apart.

This book tells the twins' story in intimate and often-graphic detail. Hopkins packs in multiple issues including eating disorders, drug abuse, date rape, alcoholism, sexual abuse, and self-mutilation as she examines a family that puts the dys in dysfunction.... Gritty and compelling, this is not a comfortable read, but its keen insights make it hard to put down. —*School Library Journal*

Smoke. Ellen Hopkins. Margaret K. McElderry Books, 2013 560 p.
Grades: 9 10 11 12
1. Mormons; 2. Runaway teenage girls; 3. Guilt; 4. Teenage rape victims; 5. Sisters; 6. Realistic fiction; 7. Novels in verse; 8. Multiple perspectives
9781416983286

After the death of her abusive father and loss of her beloved Ethan and their unborn child, Pattyn runs away, desperately seeking peace, as her younger sister, a sophomore in high school, also tries to put the pieces of her life back together.

The poems are sparse, each word and phrase carefully chosen, each line and stanza designed to convey both girls' desperation and resilience...Hopkins also tackles issues of immigration, homosexuality, bullying, Mormon extremism, and America's shadowy antigovernment militia, making for a compelling and thought-provoking read. —*Booklist*

Sequel to: *Burned*.

Tricks. Ellen Hopkins. Margaret K. McElderry Books, 2009 640 p.
Grades: 10 11 12
1. Teenage prostitutes; 2. Emotional problems of teenagers; 3. Despair; 4. Prostitution; 5. Family problems; 6. LGBTQIA fiction; 7. Realistic fiction; 8. Novels in verse.
9781416950073

LC 2009020297

Rainbow List, 2010.

Five troubled teenagers fall into prostitution as they search for freedom, safety, community, family, and love.

Hopkins's pithy free verse reveals shards of emotion and quick glimpses of physical detail. It doesn't matter that the first-person voices blur, because the stories are distinct and unmistakable. Graphic sex, rape, drugs, bitter loneliness, despairand eventually, blessedly, glimmers of hope. —*Kirkus*

Sequel: *Traffick*.

★ **The you** I've never known. Ellen Hopkins. Margaret K. McElderry Books, 2017 608 p.
Grades: 9 10 11 12
1. Fathers and daughters; 2. Questioning (Sexual or gender identity); 3. Identity (Psychology); 4. Sexual orientation; 5. Teenage girl/girl relations; 6. California; 7. Realistic fiction; 8. Novels in verse; 9. Multiple perspectives
9781481442909

Hopkins creates a satisfying and moving story, and her carefully structured poems ensure that each word and phrase is savored. —*Publishers Weekly*

Hopkinson, Nalo
The **Chaos**. Nalo Hopkinson. Margaret K. McElderry Books, 2012 320 p.
Grades: 7 8 9 10 11 12
   1. Multiracial teenage girls; 2. Identity (Psychology); 3. Missing persons; 4. Supernatural; 5. Brothers and sisters; 6. Toronto, Ontario; 7. Canada; 8. Urban fantasy; 9. Canadian fiction; 10. Afrofuturism and Afrofantasy
9781416954880

LC 2011018154
   Struggling to fit in because of her mixed-race heritage, 16-year-old Scotch is baffled when her skin becomes covered by a sticky black substance that cannot be removed at the same time her brother is swallowed up by a mysterious bubble of light and their town is overcome by a malevolent supernatural force.

Hornby, Nick
   ★ **Slam**. Nick Hornby. G.P. Putnam's Sons, 2007 370 p.
Grades: 8 9 10 11 12
   1. Hawk, Tony; 2. Skateboarders; 3. Teenage fathers; 4. Posters; 5. Growing up; 6. Teenage boy/girl relations; 7. London, England; 8. Coming-of-age stories; 9. Realistic fiction.
9780399250484

LC 2007014146
Booklist Editors' Choice: Books for Youth, 2007; YALSA Best Books for Young Adults, 2008; School Library Journal Best Books, 2007.
   At the age of fifteen, Sam Jones's girlfriend gets pregnant and Sam's life of skateboarding and daydreaming about Tony Hawk changes drastically.
   The author pens a first novel for teens that is a sweet and funny story about mistakes and choices.... Recommend this delightful and poignant novel to older teens who will laugh and weep with Sam. —*Voice of Youth Advocates*

Houston, Julian
   New boy. Julian Houston. Houghton Mifflin, 2005 282 p;
Grades: 8 9 10 11 12
   1. Fifteen-year-old boys; 2. African American teenage boys; 3. High school sophomores; 4. Boarding school students; 5. Boarding schools; 6. Connecticut; 7. Harlem, New York City; 8. 1950s; 9. Historical fiction; 10. Coming-of-age stories; 11. First person narratives.
9780618432530

LC 2004027207
   As a new sophomore at an exclusive boarding school, a young black man is witness to the persecution of another student with bad acne.
   As the first black student in an elite Connecticut boarding school in the late 1950s, Rob Garrett, 16, knows he is making history.... When his friends in the South plan a sit-in against segregation, he knows he must be part of it.... The honest first-person narrative makes stirring drama.... This brings up much for discussion about then and now. —*Booklist*

Howard, J. J.
   That time I joined the circus. J.J. Howard. Point, 2013 272 p.
Grades: 7 8 9 10
   1. Mother-deserted children; 2. Fathers — Death; 3. Circus; 4. Best friends; 5. Friendship; 6. Florida; 7. New York City; 8. Coming-of-age stories.
9780545433815

LC 2012016715
   After her father's sudden death and a break-up with her best friends, seventeen-year-old Lexi has no choice but to leave New York City seeking her long-absent mother, rumored to be in Florida with a traveling circus, where she just may discover her destiny.

   Tracers. J.J. Howard. G.P. Putnam's Sons, an imprint of Penguin Group (USA), 2015 279 p.
Grades: 9 10 11 12
   1. Parkour; 2. Teenage boy orphans; 3. Criminals; 4. Gangs; 5. Gangsters; 6. New York City; 7. Thrillers and suspense; 8. Books for reluctant readers
9780399173738; 9781407159317, print, UK

LC 2014031563
YALSA Quick Picks for Reluctant Young Adult Readers, 2016.
   Cam is a New York City bike messenger with no family or strings attached to anyone, but when he meets a mysterious stranger and is pulled into her dangerous world of parkour, he is torn between following his heart and sacrificing everything to pay off his debts.

Howe, Katherine
   Conversion. Katherine Howe. G. P. Putnam's Sons, 2014 448 pages
Grades: 7 8 9 10 11 12
   1. Epidemics; 2. Private schools; 3. Trials (Witchcraft); 4. Schools; 5. Friendship; 6. Massachusetts; 7. Mysteries; 8. Multiple perspectives; 9. Parallel narratives
9780399167775

LC 2014000397
Massachusetts Book Awards, Children's/YA Literature Literature Award, 2015; YALSA Best Fiction for Young Adults, 2015.
   When girls start experiencing strange tics and other mysterious symptoms at Colleen's high school, her small town of Danvers, Massachusetts, falls victim to rumors that lead to full-blown panic, and only Colleen connects their fate to the ill-fated Salem Village, where another group of girls suffered from a similarly bizarre epidemic three centuries ago.
   St. Joan's Academy in Danvers, Massachusetts, a well-to-do private girls school for the best and brightest, is usually only home to hysteria of the college-admissions kind. But when Clara starts convulsing in class, a media frenzy fixates on the St. Joan's mystery disease...A simmering blend of relatable high-school drama with a persistent pinprick of unearthliness in the background. —*Booklist*

Howell, Simmone
   Girl defective. Simmone Howell. Atheneum Books for Young Readers, 2014 320 p.
Grades: 9 10 11 12
   1. Eccentric families; 2. Music stores; 3. Suburbs; 4. Families; 5. Friendship; 6. Melbourne, Victoria; 7. St. Kilda, Victoria; 8. Realistic fiction; 9. Australian fiction.
9781442497603; 9780330426176
   Funny, observant, a relentless critic of the world's (and her own) flaws, Sky is original, thoroughly authentic and great company, decorating her astute, irreverent commentary with vivid Aussie references; chasing these down should provide foreign readers with hours of online fun. —*Kirkus*
Originally published in 2013 in Australia by Pan Macmillan Australia Pty Limited

Howland, Leila
   Nantucket blue. Leila Howland. Hyperion, 2013 304 p. (Nantucket (Leila Howland), 1)
Grades: 8 9 10 11 12

1. Interpersonal attraction; 2. First loves; 3. Children of divorced parents; 4. Best friends; 5. Grief; 6. Nantucket, Massachusetts; 7. Contemporary romances; 8. Teen chick lit.
9781423160519

LC 2012035121

Seventeen-year-old Cricket Thompson is planning on spending a romantic summer on Nantucket Island near her long time crush, Jay—but the death of her best friend's mother, and her own sudden intense attraction to her friend's brother Zach are making this summer complicated.

Lacrosse-champ Cricket Thompson has always been welcomed by her best friend Jules's affluent family. But when Nina, Jules's mother, dies suddenly, big changes ensue. Expecting her usual warm reception, Cricket shows up at Jules's family home on Nantucket to find herself shunned. There's some emotional heaviness to the story, but it's also a breezy, beach-ready tale of self-awakening and first love. —*Horn Book Guide*
Sequel: *Nantucket red.*

Hrdlitschka, Shelley
Allegra. Shelley Hrdlitschka. Orca Book Publishers, 2013 268 p.
Grades: 7 8 9 10
1. Teenage girl dancers; 2. High school teachers; 3. Teenage girls — Relations with older men; 4. High school students; 5. Children of divorced parents; 6. Realistic fiction; 7. Canadian fiction.
9781459801974

LC 2012952952

Allegra wants to dance, but when her music-theory teacher insists she undertake a composition project, their collaboration brings unforeseen changes in both their lives.

Hubbard, Jennifer R.
Try not to breathe. By Jennifer Hubbard. Viking, 2012 272 p.
Grades: 10 11 12
1. Teenage boys; 2. Secrets; 3. Suicide; 4. Interpersonal relations
9780670013906

LC 2011012203

The summer Ryan is released from a mental hospital following his suicide attempt, he meets Nicki, who gets him to share his darkest secrets while hiding secrets of her own.

Hubbard, Jenny
★ **And** we stay. Jenny Hubbard. Delacorte Press, 2014 240 p.
Grades: 9 10 11 12
1. Boarding schools; 2. Survivors of suicide victims; 3. Guilt in teenage girls; 4. Poetry; 5. Guilt; 6. Massachusetts; 7. Amherst, Massachusetts; 8. Realistic fiction.
9780385740579
YALSA Best Fiction for Young Adults, 2015; Michael L. Printz Honor Book, 2015.

Budding poets may particularly appreciate Emily's story, but there is certainly something for anyone looking for a good read with a strong, believable female lead who is working her hardest to overcome tragedy. —*School Library Journal*

★ **Paper** covers rock. Jenny Hubbard. Delacorte Press, 2011 192 p.
Grades: 9 10 11 12
1. Boarding school students; 2. Guilt in teenage boys; 3. Guilt; 4. Death; 5. Teachers; 6. North Carolina; 7. 1980s; 8. Realistic fiction.
9780385740555
Booklist Editors' Choice: Books for Youth, 2011; School Library Journal Best Books, 2011; William C. Morris Debut Award finalist, 2012.

In 1982 Buncombe County, North Carolina, sixteen-year-old Alex Stromm writes of the aftermath of the accidental drowning of a friend, as his English teacher reaches out to him while he and a fellow boarding school student try to cover things up.

This is a powerful story of how the truth can easily be manipulated, how actions can be misinterpreted, and how fragile adolescent friendships and alliances can be. —*Voice of Youth Advocates*

Hughes, Dean
★ **Four-Four-Two.** Dean Hughes. Atheneum Books for Young Readers, 2016 256 p.
Grades: 7 8 9 10
1. World War II; 2. Japanese Americans — Forced removal and incarceration, 1942-1945; 3. Prejudice; 4. Soldiers; 5. Loyalty; 6. United States; 7. War stories; 8. Historical fiction.
9781481462525

LC 2015043700
YALSA Quick Picks for Reluctant Young Adult Readers, 2018.

Forced into an internment camp at the start of World War II, eighteen-year-old Yuki enlists in the Army to fight for the Allies as a member of the "Four-Four-Two," a segregated Japanese American regiment.

Nuanced and riveting in equal parts. —*Kirkus*
Includes bibliographical references.

Hughes, Pat
★ **Five** 4ths of July. By Pat Raccio Hughes. Viking Childrens Books, 2011 278 p.
Grades: 7 8 9 10
1. Teenage prisoners; 2. Freedom; 3. Imprisonment; 4. Soldiers; 5. Fourteen-year-old boys; 6. Connecticut; 7. United States; 8. Revolutionary America (1775-1783); 9. 18th century; 10. Historical fiction.
9780670012077

LC 2010049521

On July 4th, 1777, fourteen-year-old Jake Mallory and his friends are celebrating their new nation's independence, but over the next four years Jake finds himself in increasingly adventurous circumstances as he battles British forces, barely survives captivity on a prison ship, and finally returns home to Connecticut, war-torn and weary, but hopeful for America's future.

This is a straightforward and well-conceived novel.... A fine addition to collections on the war and an eye-opening look at the horrors of British prison ships. —*Kirkus*

Hunter, John P.
Red thunder. By John P. Hunter. Colonial Williamsburg Foundation, 2007 234 p;
Grades: 7 8 9 10
1. Teenage boys; 2. Spies; 3. Adventure; 4. Teenagers; 5. African American men; 6. United States; 7. Yorktown, Virginia; 8. Revolutionary America (1775-1783); 9. Historical fiction; 10. Adventure stories.
9780879352318

LC 2006030730

In Virginia in 1781, fourteen-year-old Nate Chandler and his dog Rex join James Armistead Lafayette, a slave, as spies for the Continental Army as the battle of Yorktown and the end of the Revolutionary War approach.

Huntley, Amy
The **everafter.** Amy Huntley. HarperCollins, 2009 256 p.
Grades: 7 8 9 10

1. Teenage girls; 2. Death; 3. Life after death; 4. Seventeen-year-old girls; 5. Purpose in life.
9780061776793

LC 2008046149

After her death, seventeen-year-old Maddy finds a way to revisit moments in her life by using objects that she lost while she was alive, and by so doing she tries to figure out the complicated emotions, events, and meaning of her existence.

This fresh take on a teen's journey of self-exploration is a compelling and highly enjoyable tale. Huntley expertly combines a coming-of-age story with a supernatural mystery that keeps readers engrossed until the climactic ending. This touching story will appeal to those looking for a ghost story, romance, or family drama. —*School Library Journal*

Hurley, Tonya

★ **Ghostgirl**. By Tonya Hurley. Little Brown, 2008 328 p. : Illustration (Ghostgirl, 1)
Grades: 7 8 9 10
1. Teenage girl ghosts; 2. Life after death; 3. Crushes in teenage girls; 4. Popularity; 5. Death; 6. Paranormal fiction.
9780316113571

LC 2007031541

After dying, high school senior Charlotte Usher is as invisible to nearly everyone as she always felt, but despite what she learns in a sort of alternative high school for dead teens, she clings to life while seeking a way to go to the Fall Ball with the boy of her dreams.

Hurley combines afterlife antics, gothic gore, and high school hell to produce an original, hilarious satire.... Tim Burton and Edgar Allan Poe devotees will die for this fantastic, phantasmal read. —*School Library Journal*

Hurwitz, Gregg Andrew

The **Rains**. Gregg Hurwitz. Tor Teen, 2016 352 p.
Grades: 8 9 10 11
1. Brothers; 2. Survival; 3. Small towns; 4. Teenage boys; 5. Science fiction; 6. Horror
9780765382672; 9780143788621, print, Australia
Thriller Award for Best YA Novel, 2018.

When the adults in Creek's Cause turn into ferocious, inhuman beings, Chance Rain and his older brother, Patrick, take refuge with other kids at the school, where they work to find the source of the plague.

This zombie-esque sci-fi novel will feed the needs of readers looking for a fast-paced, adrenaline-pumping story with elements of horror. —*Kirkus*

Sequel: *Last chance*

Hutchinson, Shaun David

The **apocalypse** of Elena Mendoza. Shaun David Hutchinson. Simon Pulse, 2018 448 p.
Grades: 9 10 11 12
1. Teenagers; 2. Free will and determinism; 3. Interpersonal relations; 4. Options, alternatives, choices; 5. Virgins; 6. Science fiction; 7. Mysteries.
9781481498548; 9781481498555
Booklist Editors' Choice: Books for Youth, 2018; YALSA Best Fiction for Young Adults, 2019.

A creative and original tale shot through with quirky humor that entertains while encouraging readers to ponder questions of free will and social responsibility. —*Kirkus*

★ **At** the edge of the universe. Shaun David Hutchinson. Simon & Schuster, 2017 304 p.

Grades: 9 10 11 12
1. Teenage boy/boy relations; 2. Missing persons; 3. Grief in teenage boys; 4. Small towns; 5. Gay teenagers.
9781481449663
Rainbow List, 2018.

An earthy, existential coming-of-age gem. —*Kirkus*

The **five** stages of Andrew Brawley. Shaun David Hutchinson; illustrations by Christine Larsen. Simon Pulse, 2015 336 p.
Grades: 9 10 11 12
1. Guilt; 2. Grief in teenage boys; 3. Gay teenagers; 4. Hospitals; 5. Guilt in teenage boys; 6. Realistic fiction; 7. Graphic novel hybrids; 8. LGBTQIA fiction
9781481403108

LC 2014022200

Rainbow List, 2016.

Convinced he should have died in the accident that killed his parents and sister, sixteen-year-old Drew lives in a hospital, hiding from employees and his past, until Rusty, set on fire for being gay, turns his life around. Includes excerpts from the superhero comic Drew creates.

Hutchinson's latest is an unflinching look at loss, grief, and recovery. Seventeen-year-old Drew Brawley has been hiding from death for months in the Florida hospital where the rest of his family died. He passes the time working at the cafeteria and making friends with teen patients in the oncology ward.... Dark and frequently grim situations are lightened by realistic dialogue and genuineness of feeling. The rapid-fire back-and-forth snark between Drew and his hospital family rings true, and the mystery of Drew's past will keep readers turning the pages. This is a heartbreaking yet ultimately hopeful work from a writer to watch. —*Booklist*

★ **We** are the ants. Shaun David Hutchinson. Simon Pulse, 2016 304 p.
Grades: 9 10 11 12
1. Gay teenagers; 2. Teenage boys with depression; 3. Dilemmas; 4. End of the world; 5. Teenage same-sex romance; 6. LGBTQIA fiction; 7. Science fiction
9781481449632
Westchester Fiction Award, 2018; School Library Journal Best Books, 2016; YALSA Best Fiction for Young Adults, 2017; Rainbow List, 2017.

After the suicide of his boyfriend, Henry deals with depression and family issues, all while wondering if he was really abducted and told he has 144 days to decide whether or not the world is worth saving.

Hutchinson's excellent novel of ideas invites readers to wonder about their place in a world that often seems uncaring and meaningless. The novel is never didactic; on the contrary, it is unfailingly dramatic and crackling with characters who become real upon the page. —*Booklist*

Hutton, Keely

★ **Soldier** boy. Keely Hutton. Farrar Straus Giroux, 2017 224 p.
Grades: 8 9 10 11 12
1. Anywar, Ricky Richard; 2. Teenage soldiers; 3. Teenage kidnapping victims; 4. Teenage boy orphans; 5. Teenagers and war; 6. Teenage boys; 7. Uganda; 8. War stories; 9. Historical fiction; 10. Biographical fiction
9780374305635; 9781250158444

LC 2016035897

Booklist Editors' Choice: Books for Youth, 2017; YALSA Best Fiction for Young Adults, 2018; Children's Africana Book Awards Notable Book, Older Readers, 2018.

Follows Ricky from 1987-1991, and Samuel in 2006, as they are abducted to serve as child-soldiers in Joseph Kony's Lord's Resistance Army in Uganda. Includes historical notes and information about Friends of Orphans, an organization founded by Ricky Richard Anywar, on whose life the story is partly based.

The novel is a visceral indictment of man's inhumanity to man, while also celebrating human beings' ability to empathize and to rescue those who desperately need saving. —*Booklist*

Hyde, Catherine Ryan

The **year** of my miraculous reappearance. Catherine Ryan Hyde. Alfred A. Knopf, 2007 240 p.
Grades: 7 8 9 10
1. Alcoholism; 2. Alcoholic women; 3. Children of alcoholics; 4. Alcoholic teenagers; 5. Thirteen-year-old girls; 6. Coming-of-age stories.
9780375832574

LC 2006029194

Thirteen-year-old Cynnie has had to deal with her mother's alcoholism and stream of boyfriends all her life, but when her grandparents take custody of her brother, who has Down Syndrome, Cynnie becomes self-destructive and winds up in court-mandated Alcoholics Anonymous meetings.

Cynnie's love for and devotion to Bill are wholly believable, as are her attempts to snare a stable adult presence in her life. Secondary characters are multidimensional and well drawn. —*Booklist*

Ibbitson, John

★ The **landing**. John Ibbitson. Kids Can Press, 2008 160 p;
Grades: 7 8 9 10
1. Rich people; 2. Violinists; 3. Wealth; 4. Teenage boys; 5. Teenage musicians; 6. Canada; 7. 1930s; 8. Historical fiction; 9. Canadian fiction.
9781554532346; 9781554532384; 9781525300257, Paperback, Canada
Geoffrey Bilson Award for Historical Fiction, 2009; Governor General's Literary Award for English-Language Children's Literature, 2008; OLA Best Bets, 2008; USBBY Outstanding International Book, 2009.

After the Great Depression, Ben, who sneaks in violin practice between chores, gets a new job fixing up a grand old cottage on nearby Pine Island where he is introduced to a world of wealth and privilege, making him even more desperate to escape Cook's Landing.

With lovely prose, Ibbitson brings to life the rugged beauty and the devastating poverty of the Lake Muskoka region. His characters are as strong and remote as their surroundings. —*Voice of Youth Advocates*

Ifueko, Jordan

Raybearer. Jordan Ifueko. Amulet Books, 2020 368 p.
Grades: 8 9 10 11 12
1. Mothers and daughters; 2. Courts and courtiers; 3. Competition; 4. Fate and fatalism; 5. Social isolation; 6. Afrofuturism and Afrofantasy; 7. High fantasy; 8. Fantasy fiction
9781419739828, HRD, US; 9781683357193, ebook, US; 9781471409271, Paperback, UK

LC 2019053872

School Library Journal Best Books, 2020.

Raised in isolation, Tarisai yearns for the closeness she could have as one of the Crown Prince's Council of 11, but her mother, The Lady, has magically compelled Tarisai to kill the Crown Prince.

The nuanced experiences of the fantasy communities will resonate with global, contemporary marginalized peoples and their struggles against discrimination. A fresh, phenomenal fantasy that begs readers to revel in its brilliant world. —*Kirkus*

Iloh, Candice

★ **Every** body looking. Candice Iloh. Penguin Group USA, 2020 416 p.
Grades: 9 10 11 12
1. Self-discovery in women; 2. Dancing; 3. Child sexual abuse; 4. Young women; 5. African American teenage girls; 6. Novels in verse; 7. Coming-of-age stories.
9780525556206
Michael L. Printz Honor Book, 2020.

With complex relationship dynamics and heavy-hitting issues like rape, overbearing and neglectful parents, and addiction, this book will leave readers deeply affected. A young woman's captivating, sometimes heartbreaking, yet ultimately hopeful story about coming into her own. —*Kirkus*

Ingold, Jeanette

Hitch. Jeanette Ingold. Harcourt, 2005 272 p;
Grades: 7 8 9 10
1. Teenage boys; 2. Younger brothers and sisters; 3. Children of alcoholic fathers; 4. Teenage employees; 5. Families; 6. Montana; 7. United States; 8. Depression era (1929-1941); 9. 1930s; 10. Coming-of-age stories; 11. Historical fiction.
9780152047474

LC 2004019447

To help his family during the Depression and avoid becoming a drunk like his father, Moss Trawley joins the Civilian Conservation Corps, helps build a new camp near Monroe, Montana, and leads the other men in making the camp a success.

This is a credible, involving story.... Both [the author's] writing style and her 1930s setting feels totally true to the time. —*Booklist*

Ireland, Justina

Deathless divide. Justina Ireland. Balzer + Bray, 2020 551 pages; (Dread nation, 2)
Grades: 9 10 11 12
1. Zombies; 2. African Americans; 3. Voyages and travels; 4. Alliances; 5. Young women; 6. The West (United States); 7. American Westward expansion (1803-1899); 8. 1880s; 9. Historical fantasy; 10. Horror; 11. African American fiction.
9780062570635, HRD, US; 9781789090895, Paperback, UK

LC 2019944665

After the fall of Summerland, Jane McKeene hoped her life would get simpler: Get out of town, stay alive, and head west to California to find her mother. But nothing is easy when you're a girl trained in putting down the restless dead, and a devastating loss on the road to a protected village called Nicodemus has Jane questioning everything she thought she knew about surviving in 1880s America.

Shambler attacks, narrow escapes, and heartbreaking decisions keep the pace riding high in the first part, but the transition to the girls' separate journeys west pulls in the reins, giving thoughtful consideration to the layers of racism and oppression that continue to plague a society already literally plagued by the past. —*Bulletin of the Center for Children's Books*

★ **Dread** nation. Justina Ireland. Balzer + Bray, an imprint of HarperCollinsPublishing, 2018 464 p. (Dread nation, 1)
Grades: 9 10 11 12
1. Zombies; 2. African Americans; 3. Oppression (Psychology); 4. Schools; 5. Missing persons; 6. United States; 7. American Civil War era (1861-1865); 8. 1880s; 9. African American fiction; 10. Historical fantasy; 11. Horror
9780062570604; 9781789090871, Paperback, UK
Locus Young Adult Book Award, 2019; School Library Journal Best Books, 2018; YALSA Best Fiction for Young Adults, 2019.

When families go missing in Baltimore County, Jane McKeene, who is studying to become an Attendant, finds herself in the middle of a conspiracy that has her fighting for her life against powerful enemies.

This absorbing page-turner works on multiple levels: as unflinching alternate history set in post-Reconstruction-era Maryland and Kansas; as a refreshingly subversive action story starring a badass (and biracial and bisexual) heroine; as zombie fiction suspenseful and gory enough to please any fan of the genre; and as a compelling exhortation to scrutinize the racist underpinnings of contemporary American sociopolitical systems. —*Kirkus*

Isbell, Tom
The **prey**. Tom Isbell. HarperTeen, an imprint of HarperCollinsPublishers, 2015 352 p. (Prey trilogy, 1)
Grades: 7 8 9 10
1. Teenage boy orphans; 2. Twin sisters; 3. Dystopias; 4. Human experimentation in medicine; 5. Post-apocalypse; 6. Science fiction; 7. Dystopian fiction; 8. Multiple perspectives
9780062216014

An electromagnetic pulse followed by radiationthey called it Omega, the enddestroyed civilization as it once existed. The survivors established the Republic of the True America. But the future still looks like a dead end for Book and Hope, two teens who find themselves in the camps that purport to be orphanages...Careful readers will appreciate the irony and subtle, deeper meanings in character and location names as Isbell shapes his own vision of a dark world... —*Booklist*

Iturbe, Antonio
★ The **librarian** of Auschwitz. Antonio Iturbe; translated by Lilit Thwaites. Henry Holt and Company, 2017 432 p.
Grades: 7 8 9 10 11 12
1. Kraus, Dita, 1929-; 2. Teenage girls; 3. Concentration camps; 4. Books and reading; 5. Jews, Czech; 6. Jews; 7. Prague, Czech Republic; 8. Poland; 9. Second World War era (1939-1945); 10. Historical fiction; 11. Translations
9781627796187; 9781250217677, Paperback, UK
Sydney Taylor Book Award for Teen Readers, 2018; YALSA Best Fiction for Young Adults, 2018.

Follows the true story of Dita Kraus, a fourteen-year-old girl from Prague who after being sent to Auschwitz is chosen to protect the eight volumes prisoners have smuggled past the guards.

Despite being a fictional retelling of a true story, this novel is one that could easily be recommended or taught alongside Elie Wiesel's *Night* and *The Diary of Anne Frank* and a text that, once read, will never be forgotten. —*School Library Journal*
First published in Spain by Editorial Planeta in 2012

Jackson, Tiffany D.
Allegedly. Tiffany D. Jackson. Katherine Tegen Books, 2017 400 p.
Grades: 9 10 11 12
1. African American teenage girls; 2. Group homes; 3. Guilt (Law); 4. Juvenile delinquents; 5. Mothers and daughters; 6. African American fiction; 7. Realistic fiction.
9780062422644
School Library Journal Best Books, 2017; YALSA Best Fiction for Young Adults, 2018; YALSA Quick Picks for Reluctant Young Adult Readers, 2018.

Complicated family loyalties, the lasting effects of media sensationalism, and the privileges inherent with whiteness all come into play here, and Mary herself is a carefully crafted character, unreliable at times and sympathetic at others, who will not be forgotten. —*Booklist*

★ **Grown**. Tiffany D. Jackson. Katherine Tegen Books, 2020 384 p.
Grades: 9 10 11 12
1. Rhythm and blues musicians; 2. Teenage girls; 3. Control (Psychology); 4. Dominance (Psychology); 5. Fame; 6. Thrillers and suspense; 7. African American fiction; 8. First person narratives
9780062840356

When legendary R&B artist Korey Fields spots Enchanted Jones at an audition, her dreams of being a famous singer take flight. Until Enchanted wakes up with blood on her hands and zero memory of the previous night. Who killed Korey Fields?

Expertly juxtaposing the glamour of Enchanted's potential fame against the harshness of her private moments with Korey, Jackson builds the story gradually and painfully to an astonishing, chilling climax. —*Publishers Weekly*

★ **Let** me hear a rhyme. Malik-16. Katherine Tegen Books, 2019 380 p.
Grades: 8 9 10 11 12
1. Rap musicians; 2. Murder victims; 3. Hip-hop culture; 4. African American teenagers; 5. Music industry and trade; 6. Brooklyn, New York City; 7. New York City; 8. 1990s; 9. Historical fiction; 10. Urban fiction; 11. Mysteries.
9780062840325, HRD, US
LC 2018968472
Booklist Editors' Choice: Books for Youth, 2019.

After their friend Steph is murdered, Quadir, Jarrell, and Steph's sister Jasmine promote his music under a new rap name, the Architect, but when his demo catches a music label rep's attention, the trio must prove his talent from beyond the grave.

From obscure rap and hip-hop references to invocations of scalding hot combs, Jackson scores a bull's-eye with her passionate homage to black city life in the late '90s, yet it's her earnest takes on creativity, love, and loss that are timeless. —*Publishers Weekly*

★ **Monday's** not coming. Tiffany D. Jackson. Katherine Tegen Books, 2018 320 p.
Grades: 8 9 10 11 12
1. Missing persons; 2. Child abuse; 3. Loss (Psychology); 4. Bullying and bullies; 5. Dyslexia; 6. African American fiction; 7. Mysteries; 8. Realistic fiction.
9780062422675; 9780062422682
John Steptoe Award for New Talent, Author Category, 2019; School Library Journal Best Books, 2018; YALSA Best Fiction for Young Adults, 2019; Walter Honor Book, Teen, 2019.

Monday Charles is missing, and only Claudia seems to notice. Claudia and Monday have always been inseparable?more sisters than friends. So when Monday doesn't turn up for the first day of school, Claudia's worried.

This is a powerful and emotional novel that is gripping and heartbreaking and hits upon serious topics. —*Booklist*

Jaffe, Michele
Rosebush. Michele Jaffe. Razorbill, 2010 304 p.
Grades: 8 9 10 11 12
1. Hospital patients; 2. Hit-and-run victims; 3. Rich teenage girls; 4. Hit-and-run accidents; 5. Attempted murder; 6. Mysteries
9781595143532

Compulsively readable, the novel bristles with red herrings, leading readers down one tempting plot branch after another, each one blooming with plausibility. The characters are skillfully cultivated through flashbacks, and the insecure, people-pleasing Jane grows believably as she takes on the mystery. —*Booklist*

Jaigirdar, Adiba

The **henna** wars. Adiba Jaigirdar. Page Street Kids, 2020 400 p.
Grades: 8 9 10 11 12

1. Lesbian teenagers; 2. Bengalis; 3. Mehndi (Body painting); 4. Crushes (Interpersonal relations); 5. Competition; 6. Ireland; 7. Realistic fiction; 8. LGBTQIA fiction
9781624149689, HRD, US; 9781444962208, Paperback, UK

Nishat doesn't want to lose her family, but she also doesn't want to hide who she is, and it only gets harder once a childhood friend walks back into her life. Flavia is beautiful and charismatic, and Nishat falls for her instantly. —*OCLC*

Readers of YA #WeNeedDiverseBooks need this on their shelves—a wholly uncontrived story with lesbians who aren't just brown but diverse in a multitude of ways. —*Booklist*

Jansen, Hanna

★ **Over** a thousand hills I walk with you. By Hanna Jansen; translated from the German by Elizabeth D. Crawford. Carolrhoda Books, 2006 342 p.
Grades: 7 8 9 10

1. Umubyeyi, Jeanne d'Arc; 2. Adopted children; 3. Genocide — History; 4. Civil war; 5. Adopted girls; 6. Adoptive families; 7. Rwanda; 8. 1990s; 9. Translations; 10. Historical fiction; 11. War stories
9781575059273; 9781842706732, print, UK

LC 2005021123
Booklist Editors' Choice: Books for Youth, 2006; USBBY Outstanding International Book, 2007; YALSA Best Books for Young Adults, 2007.

Jeanne and her family, who are Tutsis living in Rwanda during a time of civil war, flee their home in hopes of evading Hutu soldiers as political events threaten to overtake them.

Eight-year-old Jeanne was the only one of her family to survive the 1994 Rwanda genocide. Then a German family adopted her, and her adoptive mother now tells Jeanne's story in a compelling fictionalized biography that stays true to the traumatized child's bewildered viewpoint. —*Booklist*

Jarzab, Anna

All unquiet things. Anna Jarzab. Delacorte Press, 2010 352 p.
Grades: 8 9 10 11 12

1. Murder; 2. Boarding schools; 3. Secrets; 4. Social classes; 5. Teenage boy/girl relations; 6. Northern California; 7. Mysteries; 8. Multiple perspectives
9780385738354

LC 2009011557
After the death of his ex-girlfriend Carly, northern California high school student Neily joins forces with Carly's cousin Audrey to try to solve her murder.

A year after Carly's murder, friends Neily and Audrey team up to find her killer. Their investigation exposes unsettling secrets about her final months. Jarzab's deft construction of alternating narratives by Neily and Audrey reveals not only Carly's mysterious last days but also the girls' relationship with one another. The murder mystery, while suspenseful, is not as well developed as the fully realized characters. —*Horn Book Guide*

Jayne, Hannah

Truly, madly, deadly. Hannah Jayne. Sourcebooks Fire, 2013 272 p.
Grades: 8 9 10 11 12

1. Teenage girls; 2. Dating violence; 3. Stalkers; 4. Obsession; 5. High school students; 6. Thrillers and suspense
9781402281211

LC 2012046383
When her abusive boyfriend dies in what seems to be a drunk-driving accident, Sawyer is secretly relieved until she opens her locker and finds a note from a secret admirer that says "You're welcome."

Jenkins, A. M.

Beating heart: a ghost story. A.M. Jenkins. Harper Collins, 2006 244 p;
Grades: 9 10 11 12

1. Haunted houses; 2. Ghosts; 3. Sexuality; 4. Divorce; 5. Seventeen-year-old boys; 6. Coming-of-age stories; 7. Ghost stories; 8. Books for reluctant readers
9780060546076; 9780060546083

LC 2005005071
YALSA Quick Picks for Reluctant Young Adult Readers, 2007.

After 17-year-old Evan's parents divorce, he moves with his mother and sister into a broken-down Victorian house that his mom is renovating. Evan doesn't expect much to change in his life; the move hasn't required him to attend a new school or be separated from his girlfriend, Carrie. But then Evan starts having disturbing and erotic dreams about a girl he doesn't know. Turns out, the house he and his family moved into wasn't empty—it still imprisons the ghost of Cora, a teenager who died there over 100 years before. Cora has mistaken Evan for her long-departed lover...and she wants him back.

Both accessible and substantive, this book will be an easy sell to teens. —*Booklist*

Jensen, Danielle L.

Dark skies. Danielle L. Jensen. Tor Teen, 2020 480 p. (Dark shores, 2)
Grades: 9 10 11 12

1. Gods and goddesses; 2. Imaginary empires; 3. Political intrigue; 4. Warriors; 5. Princesses; 6. High fantasy; 7. Fantasy fiction; 8. Multiple perspectives.
9781250317766

While the scholar Lydia flees death threats only to become entangled in a foreign war where her burgeoning powers are sought by both sides, a disgraced Killian swears fealty to the crown princess before political intrigues test his loyalty.

Responsibility is the grounding theme that unites the protagonists in their heroic strivings; trauma and the fully rounded characters' emotional vulnerabilities take their tolls. —*Kirkus*

Jimenez, Francisco

★ **Breaking** through. Francisco Jimenez. Houghton Mifflin, 2001 195 p.
Grades: 7 8 9 10 11 12

1. Mexican American teenage boys; 2. Immigrants, Mexican; 3. Deportation; 4. Migrant agricultural laborers; 5. Mexican American families; 6. California; 7. Autobiographical fiction; 8. Short stories.
9780618011735

LC 2001016941
ALA Notable Children's Book, 2002; Americas Book Award for Children's and Young Adult Literature, 2001; Booklist Editors' Choice: Books for Youth, 2001; Tomas Rivera Mexican American Children's Book Award, 2002; YALSA Best Books for Young Adults, 2002; Pura Belpre Honor Book for Narrative, 2002.

Having come from Mexico to California ten years ago, fourteen-year-old Francisco is still working in the fields but fighting to improve his life and complete his education.

For all its recounting of deprivation, this is a hopeful book, told with rectitude and dignity. —*Horn Book Guide*
Sequel to: *The circuit*; Sequel: *Reaching out*.

★ The **circuit:** stories from the life of a migrant child. Francisco Jimenez. Houghlin Mifflin Co, 1999 116 p;
Grades: 7 8 9 10 11 12
1. Jimenez, Francisco; 2. Mexican American boys; 3. Immigrants, Mexican; 4. Migrant agricultural laborers; 5. Undocumented workers; 6. Mexican American families; 7. California; 8. Autobiographical fiction; 9. Short stories; 10. Realistic fiction
9780395979020
Americas Book Award for Children's and Young Adult Literature, 1997; Boston Globe-Horn Book Award for Fiction, 1998; Booklist Editors' Choice: Books for Youth, 1997; YALSA Best Books for Young Adults, 1999.
A realistic portrayal of the lives of migrant workers, based on the author's own experiences, movingly chronicles a family's perseverance in the face of extreme hardship.
The story begins in Mexico when the author is very young and his parents inform him that they are going on a very long trip to El Norte. What follows is a series of stories of the family's unending migration from one farm to another as they search for the next harvesting job. Each story is told from the point of view of the author as a young child. The simple and direct narrative stays true to this perspective.... Lifting the story up from the mundane, Jimnez deftly portrays the strong bonds of love that hold this family together. —*Publishers Weekly*
Sequel: *Taking hold*.

Jinks, Catherine
Babylonne. Catherine Jinks. Candlewick Press, 2008 400 p. (Pagan chronicles, 5)
Grades: 7 8 9 10 11 12
1. Teenage girl orphans; 2. Sieges; 3. Disguises; 4. Trust; 5. Trust in teenage girls; 6. France; 7. 13th century; 8. Historical fiction; 9. Australian fiction
9780763636500
LC 2007021958
Children's Book Council of Australia: Notable Australian Children's Book.
In the violent and predatory world of thirteenth-century Languedoc, Pagan's sixteen-year-old daughter disguises herself as a boy and runs away with a priest who claims to be a friend of her dead father and mother, not knowing whether or not she can trust him, or anyone.
Complete with snappy dialogue, humorous asides, and colorful descriptions...this novel stands on its own as a very fine historical fiction book about a period in history that is not commonly written about for teens. —*Voice of Youth Advocates*

★ **Evil** genius. Catherine Jinks. Harcourt, 2007 486 pages (Evil genius books, 1)
Grades: 7 8 9 10
1. Genius; 2. Hackers; 3. Gifted teenagers; 4. Teenage boy prodigies; 5. Identity (Psychology); 6. Australia; 7. Science fiction; 8. Australian fiction
9780152059880; 9781741144598, Paperback, Australia
LC 2006014476
Davitt Awards, Best YA Novel, 2006; YALSA Popular Paperbacks for Young Adults, 2009; School Library Journal Best Books, 2007.
Child prodigy Cadel Piggott, an antisocial computer hacker, discovers his true identity when he enrolls as a first-year student at an advanced crime academy.
Cadel's turnabout is convincingly hampered by his difficulty recognizing appropriate outlets for rage, and Jinks' whiplash-inducing sus-

pense writing will gratify fans of Anthony Horowitz's high-tech spy scenarios. —*Booklist*

Living hell. Catherine Jinks. Harcourt, 2010 256 p.
Grades: 7 8 9 10
1. Space vehicles; 2. Machinery; 3. Survival; 4. Escapes; 5. Seventeen-year-old boys; 6. Science fiction; 7. Australian fiction
9780152061937
LC 2009018938
Chronicles the transformation of a spaceship into a living organism, as seventeen-year-old Cheney leads the hundreds of inhabitants in a fight for survival while machines turn on them, treating all humans as parasites.
Jinks' well-thought-out environs and rational characters help ground this otherwise out-of-control interstellar thriller. —*Booklist*

John, Antony
Five flavors of Dumb. By Antony John. Dial Books, 2010 337 p.
Grades: 7 8 9 10
1. Rock groups; 2. Teenagers who are deaf; 3. Resentfulness; 4. Teenage girls with disabilities; 5. Supervisors; 6. Seattle, Washington; 7. Washington (State); 8. Realistic fiction.
9780803734333
LC 2009044449
Schneider Family Book Award for Teens, 2011; YALSA Popular Paperbacks for Young Adults, 2013; Notable Books for a Global Society, 2011.
Eighteen-year-old Piper becomes the manager for her classmates' popular rock band, called Dumb, giving her the chance to prove her capabilities to her parents and others, if only she can get the band members to get along.
Readers interested in any of the narrative strands...will find a solid, satisfyingly complex story here. —*Bulletin of the Center for Children's Books*

Johnson, Angela
★ A **certain** October. Angela Johnson. Simon & Schuster Books For Young Readers, 2012 144 p.
Grades: 7 8 9 10 11 12
1. Guilt in teenage girls; 2. Accidents; 3. Children with autism; 4. Guilt; 5. Death; 6. Ohio; 7. Realistic fiction; 8. First person narratives; 9. African American fiction
9780689865053
LC 2012001595
YALSA Best Fiction for Young Adults, 2013.
Scotty compares herself to tofu: no flavor unless you add something. And it's true that Scotty's friends, Misha and Faclone, and her brother, Keone, make life delicious. But when a terrible accident occurs, Scotty feels responsible for the loss of someone she hardly knew, and the world goes wrong. She cannot tell what is a dream and what is real. Her friends are having a hard time getting through to her and her family is preoccupied with their own trauma. But the prospect of a boy, a dance, and the possibility that everything can fall back into place soon help Scotty realize that she is capable of adding her own flavor to life—Provided by publisher.

★ The **first** part last. Angela Johnson. Simon & Schuster Books for Young Readers, 2003 144 p. (Heaven trilogy, 2)
Grades: 7 8 9 10
1. Teenage fathers; 2. African American teenage boys; 3. Father and child; 4. Sixteen-year-old boys; 5. Teenage parents; 6. New York City; 7. Coming-of-age stories; 8. Realistic fiction; 9. African American fiction; 10. Books for reluctant readers
9780689849220; 9780689849237, paperback, US
LC 2002036512

Coretta Scott King Award, Author Category, 2004; Georgia Peach Book Award for Teen Readers, 2005; Green Mountain Book Award (Vermont), 2006; Michael L. Printz Award, 2004; YALSA Quick Picks for Reluctant Young Adult Readers, 2004; Booklist Editors' Choice: Books for Youth, 2003; YALSA Popular Paperbacks for Young Adults, 2008; YALSA Best Books for Young Adults, 2004.

When his girlfriend Nia announces that she is pregnant, sixteen-year-old Bobby, a typical urban New York City teenager, must cast aside his life of partying to visit obstetricians and social workers, who try to convince them to give their baby up for adoption, until tragedy strikes.

Brief, poetic, and absolutely riveting. —*School Library Journal*

★ **Sweet,** hereafter. Angela Johnson. Simon and Schuster Books for Young Readers, 2010 128 p. (Heaven trilogy, 3)
Grades: 7 8 9 10
1. African American teenage girls; 2. Identity (Psychology); 3. Unhappiness; 4. Soldiers; 5. Interpersonal relations; 6. Realistic fiction.
9780689873850

LC 2009027618

Sweet leaves her family and goes to live in a cabin in the woods with the quiet but understanding Curtis, to whom she feels intensely connected, just as he is called back to serve again in Iraq.

With heartfelt empathy, we share in Shoogy's personal loss and her need for a new direction. Characters from the two other titles reappear, and we get a glimpse of how their lives are moving forward. This book belongs in all junior and senior high school collections, especially those who already own the first two titles.... Johnson now has one more well-woven character development novel to her name. —*Library Media Connection*

Johnson, Harriet McBryde
★ **Accidents** of nature. Harriet McBryde Johnson. Holt, 2005 240 p.
Grades: 9 10 11 12
1. Seventeen-year-old girls; 2. Teenage girls with disabilities; 3. People with disabilities; 4. Camps; 5. Cerebral palsy; 6. North Carolina; 7. 1970s
9780805076349

LC 2005024598

School Library Journal Best Books, 2006; YALSA Best Books for Young Adults, 2007.

Having always prided herself on blending in with "normal" people despite her cerebral palsy, seventeen-year-old Jean begins to question her role in the world while attending a summer camp for children with disabilities.

This book is smart and honest, funny and eye-opening. A must-read. —*School Library Journal*

Johnson, Kim
This is my America. Kim Johnson. Random House Children's Books, 2020 416 p.
Grades: 9 10 11 12
1. African American teenage girls; 2. Malicious accusation; 3. Innocence (Law); 4. Injustice; 5. Racism; 6. Mysteries; 7. Realistic fiction; 8. African American fiction.
9780593118764, hardback, US; 9780593118771, library, US; 9780593118788, ebook, US

LC 2019024787

Sending weekly letters to an organization she hopes will save her innocent father from death row, 17-year-old Tracy uncovers racist community secrets when her track star brother is wrongly accused of murder.

Johnson, Maureen
13 little blue envelopes. Maureen Johnson. Harper Collins, 2005 317 p. (Little blue envelopes, 1)
Grades: 8 9 10 11 12
1. Teenage travelers; 2. Growth (Psychology); 3. Letters; 4. Seventeen-year-old girls; 5. Teenage girls; 6. Europe; 7. Realistic fiction; 8. Teen chick lit
9780060541415; 9780060541422

LC 2005002658

YALSA Popular Paperbacks for Young Adults, 2009; YALSA Best Books for Young Adults, 2006.

When seventeen-year-old Ginny receives a packet of mysterious envelopes from her favorite aunt, she leaves New Jersey to criss-cross Europe on a sort of scavenger hunt that transforms her life.

Equal parts poignant, funny and inspiring, this tale is sure to spark wanderlust. —*Publishers Weekly*

Sequel: *The last little blue envelope.*

The **hand** on the wall. Maureen Johnson. Katherine Tegen Books, 2020 384 p. (Truly Devious, 3)
Grades: 8 9 10 11 12
1. Teenage girl detectives; 2. Boarding schools; 3. Murder investigation; 4. Murder; 5. Riddles; 6. Vermont; 7. Mysteries.
9780062338112, HRD, US; 9780062338129

A conclusion to the series that includes *The Vanishing Stair* finds another death compelling Stevie to navigate mysterious riddles and track down a missing David at the same time a massive storm forces her to confront a killer.

In this hotly anticipated trilogy finale (beginning with Truly Devious, 2018), Johnson pulls out all the stops, filling the thrillingly nimble narrative with classic mystery conventions. —*Booklist*

The **name** of the star. Maureen Johnson. G. P. Putnam's Sons, 2011 384 p. (Shades of London, 1)
Grades: 6 7 8 9 10
1. Teenage murder witnesses; 2. Copycat murders; 3. Ghosts; 4. Serial murders; 5. Supernatural; 6. London, England; 7. England; 8. Paranormal fiction
9780399256608

LC 2011009003

YALSA Popular Paperbacks for Young Adults, 2013.

Rory, of Boueuxlieu, Louisiana, is spending a year at a London boarding school when she witnesses a murder by a Jack the Ripper copycat and becomes involved with the very unusual investigation.

Johnson's trademark sense of humor serves to counterbalance some grisly murders in this page-turner, which opens her Shades of London series.... As one mutilated body after another turns up, Johnson...amplifies the story's mysteries with smart use of and subtle commentary on modern media shenanigans and London's infamously extensive surveillance network.... Readers looking for nonstop fun, action, and a little gore have come to the right place. —*Publishers Weekly*

Truly, Devious. Maureen Johnson. HarperCollins Children's Books, 2018 320 p. (Truly Devious, 1)
Grades: 8 9 10 11 12
1. Boarding schools; 2. Murder; 3. Teenage girl detectives; 4. Crime; 5. Teenage girls; 6. Vermont; 7. Mysteries
9780062338051; 9780062338068

Pennsylvania Young Reader's Choice Awards, Young Adult, 2020; YALSA Best Fiction for Young Adults, 2019.

Ellingham Academy is a famous private school in Vermont for the brightest thinkers, inventors, and artists. It was founded by Albert Ellingham, an early twentieth century tycoon, who wanted to make a wonderful place full of riddles, twisting pathways, and gardens. "A place," he said, "where learning is a game."

Johnson deftly twists two mysteries together—Stevies investigation is interspersed with case files and recollections from the Ellington kidnapping—and the result is a suspenseful, attention-grabbing mystery with no clear solution. Invested readers, never fearthis is just the first in a series. —*Booklist*

The **vanishing** stair. Maureen Johnson. HarperCollins Children's Books, 2019 384 p. (Truly Devious, 2)
Grades: 8 9 10 11 12
1. Boarding schools; 2. Murder; 3. Teenage girl detectives; 4. Investigations; 5. Teenage girls; 6. Vermont; 7. Mysteries
9780062338082
Pulled out of Ellingham Academy by her overprotective parents, aspiring detective Stevie Bell makes a deal with the despicable Edward King in hopes of reuniting with her friends and solving the Truly Devious case.

In this second trilogy installment, Johnson gives and she takes away: a few major mysteries are satisfying solved, but other long-standing riddles remain tantalizingly indecipherable, and several new ones come into play by the enigmatic end. —*Booklist*

Johnston, E. K.
Exit, pursued by a bear. By E.K. Johnston. 2016 256 pages
Grades: 9 10 11 12
1. Teenage rape victims; 2. Abortion; 3. Pregnant teenagers; 4. Psychic trauma; 5. Cheerleaders; 6. Ontario; 7. Canada; 8. Realistic fiction; 9. Shakespeare-inspired fiction
9781101994580
LC 2015020645
Amelia Bloomer List, 2017; Amy Mathers Teen Book Award, 2017; Booklist Editors' Choice: Books for Youth, 2016; OLA Best Bets, 2016; YALSA Quick Picks for Reluctant Young Adult Readers, 2017.

At cheerleading camp, Hermione is drugged and raped, but she is not sure whether it was one of her teammates or a boy on another team—and in the aftermath she has to deal with the rumors in her small Ontario town, the often awkward reaction of her classmates, the rejection of her boyfriend, the discovery that her best friend, Polly, is gay, and above all the need to remember what happened so that the guilty boy can be brought to justice.

A beautifully written portrait of a young woman facing the unthinkable. —*School Library Journal*

That inevitable Victorian thing. E.K. Johnston. Dutton Books for Young Readers, 2017 326 p.
Grades: 9 10 11 12
1. Near future; 2. Princesses; 3. Heirs and heiresses; 4. Nobility; 5. Disguises; 6. Canada; 7. Toronto, Ontario; 8. Science fiction; 9. Alternative histories; 10. Canadian fiction
9781101994979, Hardback, US; 9781101994566, Paperback, US
Preparing for her arranged marriage and coronation in an alternate-universe near-future where the British Empire never fell, crown princess Victoria-Margaret, a descendent of Victoria I, embarks on a final summer filled with balls and freedom before forging an unusual bond with a geneticist's daughter and a shipping heir.

A thoughtful exploration of class consciousness, genetics, and politics that doesn't lose track of the human story. —*Kirkus*

Jones, Adam Garnet
Fire song. Adam Garnet Jones. Annick Press, 2018 232 p.
Grades: 9 10 11 12
1. Gay teenagers; 2. First Nations (Canada); 3. Grief in families; 4. Sisters — Death; 5. Self-discovery in teenagers; 6. Realistic fiction; 7. LGBTQIA fiction; 8. Canadian fiction
9781554519781, hardback, Canada; 9781554519774, paperback, Canada
OLA Best Bets, 2018.
Fire Song tells about the struggles of two Indigenous gay teenagers trying to find their place in the world.

A touching story that has been a long time coming for the Indigenous community. —*Kirkus*

Jones, Patrick
★ **Bridge**. Patrick Jones. Lerner Pub Group, 2014 92 p. (The alternative)
Grades: 6 7 8 9 10 11 12
1. Hispanic American teenage boys; 2. Immigrant families; 3. Responsibility in teenage boys; 4. High school students; 5. Truancy; 6. Realistic fiction; 7. High interest-low vocabulary books
9781467744829, PAP, US
The authors effective use of flashbacks and crisp portraits of positive adult characters add further emotional depth to this emotional glimpse at the high-pressure difficulties facing children in immigrant families. References to O'Brien's book will likely spark the interest of readers in that title as well. —*Publishers Weekly*

Jordan, Dream
Hot girl. Dream Jordan. St. Martin's Griffin, 2008 214 p;
Grades: 7 8 9 10
1. Foster teenagers; 2. African American teenage girls; 3. Friendship; 4. Foster care; 5. Personal conduct; 6. Brooklyn, New York City; 7. Urban fiction; 8. African American fiction; 9. Realistic fiction; 10. Books for reluctant readers
9780312382841
LC 2008024995
YALSA Quick Picks for Reluctant Young Adult Readers, 2009; YALSA Popular Paperbacks for Young Adults, 2010.
Kate, a fourteen-year-old Brooklyn girl and former gang member, risks losing her first good foster family when she adopts the risqué ways of her flirtatious new friend, Naleejah.
Sequel: *Bad boy.*

Juby, Susan
★ The **fashion** committee. By Susan Juby. Viking Books for Young Readers, 2017 304 p.
Grades: 7 8 9 10
1. Competition; 2. Fashion; 3. Small towns; 4. Children of drug abusers; 5. Scholarships and fellowships; 6. Canada; 7. Realistic fiction; 8. Canadian fiction; 9. Multiple perspectives
9780451468789
OLA Best Bets, 2017; YALSA Best Fiction for Young Adults, 2018.
Charlie and John are both gunning for the same scholarship to a private arts high school. For this coveted spot, they must compete in a fashion competition—and only one can win.

Juby's thoughtful bildungsroman excels in showcasing and normalizing those on society's fringewhether it be in her bold portrayal of differing socio-economic class issues or subtle examination of gender identity. —*Kirkus*

★ The **truth** commission. Susan Juby; illustrations by Trever Cooper. Viking, an imprint of Penguin Group (USA), 2015 304 p.
Grades: 9 10 11 12

1. Art schools; 2. Truthfulness and falsehood; 3. Dysfunctional families; 4. Friendship; 5. Gossiping and gossips; 6. Realistic fiction; 7. Canadian fiction; 8. Illustrated books
9780451468772; 9780670067596
Amy Mathers Teen Book Award, 2016; BC Book Prizes, Sheila A. Egoff Children's Literature Prize, 2016; YALSA Best Fiction for Young Adults, 2016.

Normandy Pale writes about the Truth Commission, whose purpose is to ask a question and get an honest answer, as a project for her junior year of high school at Green Pastures Academy of Art and Applied Design.

Best friends and art-school students Normandy (a girl), Dusk (a girl), and Neil (a boy, duh!) form a de facto truth commission: each week, each of them will ask someone to give them the straight truth. The experiments results will constitute Normandy's creative nonfiction project. The novel, then, is presented as that project, complete with footnotes and the occasional piece of spot art...The problem, as Juby expertly shows, is that truth is messy and sometimes—like a hot potato—hard to handle. Though it comes dangerously close to melodrama by the end, the story is clever, the characters appealing, and the theme is thought-provoking. —*Horn Book Guide*

Jung, Jessica

Shine. Jessica Jung. 2020 352 p.
Grades: 9 10 11 12
1. Popular music; 2. Korean-American teenage girls; 3. Fame; 4. Girl groups (Musical groups); 5. Scandals; 6. South Korea; 7. Contemporary romances
9781534462519

LC 2020027204
Seventeen-year-old Rachel Kim confronts the dark underbelly of the K-pop world as she strives to become a K-pop star.

Debut author Jung's background as a former Korean American K-pop star informs this world of catty, sabotaging antagonists; elite private school classmates; and parental pressure. —*Kirkus*

Kagawa, Julie

The **eternity** cure. Julie Kagawa. Harlequin Teen, 2013 304 p. (Blood of Eden, 2)
Grades: 7 8 9 10 11 12
1. Vampires; 2. Immortality; 3. Viruses; 4. Zombies; 5. Urban fantasy; 6. Apocalyptic fiction
9780373210695; 9781743566299, print, Australia
Elevated to Queen of the Underworld after attaining immortality, Kate Winters resolves to win the love of Henry despite his increasing secretiveness, a situation that escalates when Henry is abducted by the King of the Titans, triggering a dangerous war and a pact with Henry's first wife, Persephone.

The **forever** song. Julie Kagawa. Harlequin Teen, 2014 304 p. (Blood of Eden, 3)
Grades: 7 8 9 10 11 12
1. Vampires; 2. Immortality; 3. Viruses; 4. Zombies; 5. Urban fantasy; 6. Apocalyptic fiction
9780373211128; 9781743568071, print, Australia
Embracing her vampire side after the death of her beloved Zeke, Allie teams up with her companions to hunt the psychopathic vampire responsible for his murder only to be confronted with brutal surprises.

★ The **immortal** rules. Julie Kagawa. Harlequin Teen, 2012 512 p. (Blood of Eden, 1)
Grades: 7 8 9 10 11 12
1. Vampires; 2. Immortality; 3. Zombies; 4. Near future; 5. Viruses; 6. Urban fantasy; 7. Apocalyptic fiction
9780373210510; 9780373210800; 9781743566282, print, Australia
YALSA Best Fiction for Young Adults, 2013; YALSA Popular Paperbacks for Young Adults, 2017.

After Allison is forced to flee the city, she joins a band of humans who are seeking a legend—a possible cure to the disease that killed off most of humankind and created the creatures threatening humans and vampires alike.

Kagawa wraps excellent writing and skillful plotting around a well-developed concept and engaging characters, resulting in a fresh and imaginative thrill-ride that deserves a wide audience. —*Publishers Weekly*

Shadow of the fox. Julie Kagawa. Harlequin Teen, 2018 416 p. (Shadow of the fox, 1)
Grades: 9 10 11 12
1. Mythical creatures; 2. Fate and fatalism; 3. Half-human hybrids; 4. Yokai (Japanese folklore); 5. Samurai; 6. Japan; 7. Asian-influenced fantasy; 8. Fantasy fiction; 9. Multiple perspectives.
9781335145161; 9781335142382; 9781489267368, Paperback, Australia
A debut entry in a lush fantasy series inspired by Japanese mythology follows the adventures of a secret shapeshifter who escapes an attack on her temple with a piece of an ancient scroll before meeting a samurai who would kill her for it.

Talon. Julie Kagawa. Harlequin Books Teen, 2014 400 p. (Talon saga, 1)
Grades: 8 9 10 11
1. Dragons; 2. Shapeshifters; 3. Twin brothers and sisters; 4. Love triangles; 5. Teenagers; 6. California; 7. Urban fantasy; 8. Multiple perspectives
9780373211395; 9781848453371, print, UK; 9781760371791, print, Australia
Young love, sibling rivalry, rogue dragons, and plots for world domination create an intriguing mix in this new series. —*Horn Book Guide*

Kamata, Suzanne

Gadget Girl: the art of being invisible. Suzanne Kamata. GemmaMedia, 2013 256 p. (Aiko Cassidy novels, 1)
Grades: 9 10 11 12
1. Artists; 2. People with disabilities; 3. Voyages and travels; 4. Life change events; 5. Self-discovery; 6. Paris, France; 7. France; 8. Coming-of-age stories
9781936846382

LC 2012051566
Aiko Cassidy, a fourteen-year-old with cerebral palsy, tired of posing for the sculptures that have made her mother famous, dreams of going to Japan to meet her father and become a great manga artist, but takes a life-changing trip to Paris, instead.

For Aiko Cassidy, it's hard enough sitting at the invisible table and dealing with trespassing geeks. It's harder when her cerebral palsy makes guys notice her in all the wrong ways...Awkwardly and believably, this sensitive novel reveals an artistic teen adapting to family, disability and friendships in all their flawed beauty. —*Kirkus*

Gadget Girl began as a novella published in *Cicada*. The story won the SCBWI Magazine Merit Award in Fiction and was included in an anthology of the best stories published in *Cicada* over the past ten years

Indigo girl. Suzanne Kamata. 2019 240 pages (Aiko Cassidy novels, 2)
Grades: 9 10 11 12

1. People with disabilities; 2. Self-discovery; 3. Birthfathers; 4. Life change events; 5. Multiracial children; 6. Michigan; 7. Japan; 8. Coming-of-age stories
9781936846733, PAP, US

LC 2019005490

Fifteen-year-old Aiko Cassidy, a manga enthusiast with cerebral palsy, spends a summer in Japan, learning about her father's family and making new friends, while avoiding her stepfather and baby half-sister.
Sequel to: *Gadget Girl (2013).*

Kantor, Melissa
The **breakup** bible: a novel. By Melissa Kantor. Hyperion, 2007 265 p.
Grades: 8 9 10 11 12
1. High school girls; 2. Teenage boy/girl relations; 3. Student newspapers and periodicals; 4. High schools; 5. Advice; 6. Teen chick lit; 7. Realistic fiction.
9780786809622

Written with wit and featuring a few fine plot twists, this will have teen girls nodding sympathetically. —*Booklist*

Kaplan, A. E.
Grendel's guide to love and war. A.E. Kaplan. Alfred A. Knopf, 2017 312 p.
Grades: 9 10 11 12
1. Bullying and bullies; 2. Loss (Psychology); 3. Crushes in teenage boys; 4. Friendship; 5. Jewish teenage boys; 6. Virginia; 7. Realistic fiction; 8. Classics-inspired fiction
9780399555541

A teen misfit resolves to defeat a local bully who upsets the senior community by constantly throwing wild parties, an effort that is complicated by the teen's father's PTSD, his unrequited feelings for the bully's sister and an existential crisis related to his mother's death.

Deep and uproarious all at once, this doesn't require familiarity with the source material for readers to have a fine time with it. A clever spin on a weighty classic. —*Kirkus*

We regret to inform you. A.E. Kaplan. Alfred A. Knopf, 2018 352 p.
Grades: 9 10 11 12
1. Hackers; 2. College applicants; 3. College choice; 4. Identity (Psychology); 5. Private schools; 6. Realistic fiction
9781524773700; 9781524773717

LC 2018013862
YALSA Best Fiction for Young Adults, 2019.

When high-achiever Mischa is rejected from every college she applies to, she teams up with a group of hacker girls to find who altered her transcript and set things right.

Kaplan, Ariel
★ **We** are the perfect girl. Ariel Kaplan. Alfred A. Knopf Books for Young Readers, 2019 374 p;
Grades: 9 10 11 12
1. Self-acceptance in teenagers; 2. Deception; 3. Teenage boy/girl relations; 4. Dating (Social customs); 5. Female friendship; 6. Classics-inspired fiction; 7. Romantic comedies; 8. First person narratives.
9780525647102, HRD, US; 9780525647119, LIB, US

LC 2019942294
Booklist Editors' Choice: Books for Youth, 2019.

A warmhearted retelling of Cyrano de Bergerac finds two teens, the outgoing Aphra and the beautiful Bethany, working together in an unintentionally escalating deception to win the heart of a mutual crush.

The story progresses rapidly and instantly hooks readers while holding interest from beginning to end, and the novel hits on relevant themes including self-esteem, body image, and leaving your comfort zone...A must-have for library shelves. —*School Library Journal*

Karim, Sheba
That thing we call a heart. Sheba Karim. 2017 275 p.
Grades: 9 10 11 12
1. Pakistani Americans; 2. Muslim teenagers; 3. Teenage romance; 4. Friendship; 5. Summer; 6. New Jersey; 7. Realistic fiction; 8. Coming-of-age stories
9780062445704

LC 2016949962
Amelia Bloomer List, 2018.

When Shabnab's best friend starts wearing a Muslim headscarf, she feels alienated until taking a summer job that leads to falling in love with a friend in ways that remind her of the rose and nightingale of classic Urdu poetry.

Funny, fresh, and poignant, Karim's (*Skunk Girl*, 2009) novel is noteworthy for its authentic depiction of a Pakistani American teen coming of age and falling in love. —*Booklist*

Katcher, Brian
Deacon Locke went to prom. Brian Katcher. Harpercollins Childrens Books, 2017 304 p.
Grades: 7 8 9 10
1. Grandmother and grandson; 2. Proms; 3. Popularity; 4. Fame; 5. First loves; 6. Coming-of-age stories.
9780062422521

The love life of an awkward teen takes an unforgettable turn after he brings his grandmother to prom in this funny, offbeat, and smile-inducing contemporary romance that is pitch perfect for fans of Jesse Andrews and Robyn Schneider.

The **improbable** theory of Ana and Zak. Brian Katcher. Katherine Tegen Books, an imprint of HarperCollinsPublishers, 2015 336 p.
Grades: 7 8 9 10 11 12
1. Fan conventions; 2. Contests; 3. Missing teenage boys; 4. Science fiction fandom; 5. Genius; 6. Seattle, Washington; 7. Washington (State); 8. Contemporary romances; 9. Romantic comedies; 10. Multiple perspectives
9780062272775

LC 2014030718
Ana is an honor student obsessed with being successful at everything academic, Clayton is her thirteen-year-old genius brother, the youngest student in their high school and Zak is gamer who is forced to join the quiz team by his teacher—but when Clayton sneaks off to a science fiction convention in Seattle while they are all there for a quiz bowl tournament, Ana is forced to rely on the unreliable Zak to find him.

Type-A Ana and relaxed geek Zak take turns narrating as they spend a night searching for Ana's younger brother at a comic-book convention. The he said/she said romance has been done before, of course, but the unconventional setting, quirky convention-goers, and many over-the-top hijinks (e.g, multiple fights, a sci-fi-themed gay wedding, inadvertent drug-running) give this one a unique twist. —*Horn Book Guide*

Playing with matches. Brian Katcher. Delacorte Press, 2008 294 p.
Grades: 8 9 10 11 12
1. Teenage boy misfits; 2. Teenage girls with disfigurements; 3. Burn victims; 4. Dating (Social customs); 5. Teenage romance; 6. Missouri; 7. Realistic fiction
9780385905251

YALSA Popular Paperbacks for Young Adults, 2010; YALSA Best Books for Young Adults, 2009.

While trying to find a girl who will date him, Missouri high school junior Leon Sanders befriends a lonely, disfigured female classmate.

This is a strong debut novel with a cast of quirky, multidimensional characters struggling with issues of acceptance, sexuality, identity, and self-worth. —*School Library Journal*

Kate, Lauren

The **betrayal** of Natalie Hargrove. Lauren Kate. Penguin Young Readers Group, 2009 235 p.
Grades: 9 10 11 12
1. Ambition in teenage girls; 2. Practical jokes; 3. Accidental death; 4. Ambition; 5. Proms; 6. South Carolina; 7. Thrillers and suspense; 8. Realistic fiction.
9781595142658

LC 2009018481

South Carolina high school senior Nat has worked hard to put her trailer-park past behind her, and when she and her boyfriend are crowned Palmetto Prince and Princess everything would be perfect, except that a prank they played a few nights before went horribly awry.

Lots of adjectives can be applied to this debut effortmean, smutty, decadentand all of them should be taken as compliments. —*Booklist*

Katsoulis, Gregory Scott

Access restricted. Gregory Scott Katsoulis. Harlequin Books 2018 304 p. (Word$, 2)
Grades: 7 8 9 10 11 12
1. Silence and silent things; 2. Resistance to government; 3. Escapes; 4. Sisters; 5. Parent-separated teenage girls; 6. Dystopian fiction; 7. Science fiction
9781335016256

After taking down Silas Rog and freeing the city from his grasp, Speth journeys outside the dome in search of her parents, who were sold into indentured servitude years earlier.

All rights reserved. Gregory Scott Katsoulis. Harlequin Books Teen, 2017 392 p. (Word$, 1)
Grades: 7 8 9 10 11 12
1. Silence and silent things; 2. Resistance to government; 3. Speech; 4. Fifteen-year-old girls; 5. Teenage girls; 6. Dystopian fiction; 7. Science fiction
9780373212446; 9781489242167, print, Australia; 9781335017222
YALSA Best Fiction for Young Adults, 2018.

Preparing to deliver her Last Day speech to celebrate her new adulthood in a world where every word and gesture is copyrighted, patented or trademarked, a 15-year-old girl elects to remain silent rather than pay to speak, a decision that threatens to unravel the fabric of society.

A fresh and detailed dystopian tale that will capture and make demands upon the attention of its readers, as the genre should, with a conclusion that sets readers up for the sequel. —*Kirkus*

Kaufman, Amie

Aurora burning. Amie Kaufman and Jay Kristoff. Alfred A. Knopf, 2020 512 p. (Aurora cycle, 2)
Grades: 9 10 11 12
1. Fugitives; 2. Teenage soldiers; 3. Space warfare; 4. Space vehicles; 5. Misfits (Persons); 6. Space; 7. Space opera; 8. Science fiction thrillers; 9. Science fiction.
9781524720926; 9781524720933; 9781786077745, Hardback, UK; 9781760295745, Australia

Aurora, the human trigger for an ancient weapon built to destroy a world-conquering power, and the members of the Aurora Legion must evade a variety of forces, all out to control her if she does not succeed in managing her new powers.

★ **Aurora** rising. Amie Kaufman and Jay Kristoff. Alfred A. Knopf, 2019 480 p. (Aurora cycle, 1)
Grades: 8 9 10 11 12
1. Military cadets; 2. Stowaways; 3. Space vehicles; 4. Fugitives; 5. Misfits (Persons); 6. Space; 7. Space opera; 8. Science fiction thrillers; 9. Science fiction.
9781524720971; 9781524720964; 9781760295738, Paperback, Australia; 9781786075338, Hardback, UK

LC 2018026944

Relegated by a misguided act of heroism to a squad comprised of his school's hopeless misfits, a graduating cadet in a 24th-century space academy rescues a centuries-hibernating girl from interdimensional space only to be swept up in an interstellar war millions of years in the making.

Rotating perspectives and never-flagging energy propel this narrative forward, which, if it werent compelling enough on its own, is given illustrious life by its ragtag, always-at-odds cast. —*Booklist*

Gemina. Amie Kaufman & Jay Kristoff; journal illustrations by Marie Lu. Alfred A. Knopf, 2016 672 p. (Illuminae files, 2)
Grades: 8 9 10 11 12
1. Space vehicles; 2. Artificial intelligence; 3. Space flight; 4. Space stations; 5. Corporations; 6. Space opera; 7. Science fiction; 8. Australian fiction.
9780553499155; 9781925266573, Oz; 9781780749815, print, UK; 9781780749822, ebook; 9780553499186, Canada; 9781760875954, Paperback, Australia
Aurealis Awards, Best Science Fiction Novel, 2016.

An action-packed thrill ride and stellar head trip. —*Kirkus*

★ **Illuminae**. Amie Kaufman; Jay Kristoff. 2015 608 p. (Illuminae files, 1)
Grades: 8 9 10 11 12
1. Space flight; 2. Artificial intelligence; 3. Plague; 4. Electronic records; 5. Refugees; 6. Space opera; 7. Science fiction; 8. Science fiction thrillers.
9780553499117; 9780553499124; 9780553499148; 9781760113803; 9781780748375, print, UK; 9781780748382, ebook; 9781760875404, Paperback, Australia

LC 2014017908

Aurealis Awards, Best Science Fiction Novel, 2015; Australian Book Industry Awards, Book of the Year for Older Children, 2016; YALSA Best Fiction for Young Adults, 2016; Inky Awards (Australia): Gold Inky, 2016.

The planet Kerenza is attacked, and Kady and Ezra find themselves on a space fleet fleeing the enemy, while their ship's artificial intelligence system and a deadly plague may be the end of them all.

This sci-fi romance novel's minimalist, dynamic format—the story is told entirely through instant messages, transcripts, letters, reports, etc.—increases the sense of tension and adds the reading experience. —*Horn Book Guide*

Obsidio. Amie Kaufman & Jay Kristoff; with journal illustrations by Marie Lu. 2018 608 p. (Illuminae files, 3)
Grades: 8 9 10 11 12
1. Space vehicles; 2. Artificial intelligence; 3. Space flight; 4. Space stations; 5. Corporations; 6. Space opera; 7. Science fiction; 8. Australian fiction.
9780553499209; 9780553499193; 9780553499223; 9781925266726, Paperback, Australian; 9781760875961, Paperback, Australia

LC Bl2018020416

Kady, Ezra, Hanna, Nik reluctantly return to Kerenza with other refugees, while Asha has joined Kerenza's ragtag underground resistance, and when she reconnects with her old flame Rhys, the two find themselves on opposite sides of the conflict.

★ The **other** side of the sky. Amie Kaufman & Meagan Spooner. 2020 471 p. (Other side of the sky, 1)
Grades: 9 10 11 12
1. Princes; 2. Gods and goddesses; 3. Prophecies; 4. Magic; 5. Fate and fatalism; 6. Science fiction; 7. Fantasy fiction; 8. Australian fiction
9780062893338; 9781760637675, Paperback, Australia
A first entry in a planned duology by two best-selling authors finds the prince of a sky city and an earth goddess linked by a terrifying prophecy that forces them to choose between saving their people or succumbing to their forbidden love.
Turbid worldbuilding abounds, but evocative prose, escalating intrigue, and charismatic, predominantly olive- and brown-skinned characters with diverse sexual orientations and gender identities keep the pages turning. —*Publishers Weekly*

Kelly, Tara
Harmonic feedback. Tara Kelly. Henry Holt, 2010 280 p.
Grades: 9 10 11 12
1. Asperger's syndrome; 2. Self-perception in teenage girls; 3. Bands (Music); 4. Self-perception; 5. Interpersonal relations; 6. Washington (State); 7. Bellingham, Washington; 8. Realistic fiction.
9780805090109
LC 2009024150
YALSA Best Fiction for Young Adults, 2011.
When Drea and her mother move in with her grandmother in Bellingham, Washington, the sixteen-year-old finds that she can have real friends, in spite of her Asperger's, and that even when you love someone it does not make life perfect.
The novel's strength lies in Drea's dynamic personality: a combination of surprising immaturity, childish wonder, and profound insight. Her search for stability and need to escape being labeled is poignant and convincing. —*Publishers Weekly*

Kemmerer, Brigid
A **heart** so fierce and broken. By Brigid Kemmerer. Bloomsbury, 2020 450 pages : Map (Cursebreaker series, 2)
Grades: 8 9 10 11 12
1. Heirs and heiresses; 2. Inheritance and succession; 3. Princes; 4. People with post-traumatic stress disorder; 5. Post-traumatic stress disorder; 6. Fairy tale and folklore-inspired fiction; 7. Fantasy fiction; 8. Multiple perspectives
9781681195117, Hardback, US; 9781681195124, ebook, US; 9781408885086, Paperback, UK
The curse is finally broken, but Prince Rhen of Emberfall faces darker troubles still. Rumors circulate that he is not the true heir and that forbidden magic has been unleashed in Emberfall. Loyalties are tested and new love blooms in a kingdom on the brink of war.
This sweeping, romantic epic repeatedly turns the tables on the fantasy tropes that readers might be expecting. —*Kirkus*
Sequel to: *A curse so dark and lonely.*

More than we can tell. By Brigid Kemmerer. Bloomsbury, 2018 304 p.
Grades: 9 10 11 12
1. Adopted teenage boys; 2. Child abuse; 3. Computer games; 4. Teenage boy/girl relations; 5. Harassment; 6. Realistic fiction
9781681190143; 9781681199917

LC 2017025086
When Rev Fletcher and Emma Blue meet, they both long to share secrets, his of being abused by his birth father, hers of her parents' failing marriage and an online troll who truly frightens her.
Mature topics, including foster parenting and divorce, creativity and autonomy, religion gone awry, the politics of trust, and facing one's most intimate fears, make this an absorbing, emotional roller coaster of a read. —*Booklist*

Kenneally, Miranda
Coming up for air. Miranda Kenneally. Sourcebooks Fire, an imprint of Sourcebooks, Inc, 2017 288 p. (Hundred Oaks, 8)
Grades: 10 11 12
1. Swimmers; 2. Best friends; 3. Swimming; 4. Friendship; 5. High schools; 6. Contemporary romances
9781492630111
When high school senior Maggie realizes there is more to life than swimming, she may be placing her long-term friendship with teammate Levi and her hope of an Olympic tryout at risk.
Fans of the author's Hundred Oaks series won't be disappointed as they watch Maggie's and Levi's friendship move in a new direction, and the competitive and uncertain element of Maggie's future in swimming makes the page turning all the more enjoyable. —*Publishers Weekly*

Racing Savannah. Miranda Kenneally. Sourcebooks Fire, 2013 304 p. (Hundred Oaks, 4)
Grades: 8 9 10 11 12
1. Teenage equestrians; 2. Teenage girls and horses; 3. Horse farms; 4. Moving to a new state; 5. Teenage romance; 6. Tennessee; 7. Franklin, Tennessee; 8. Contemporary romances; 9. Teen chick lit.
9781402284762
Kenneally (*Stealing Parker*, 2012) again looks at sports through a female lens, this time tackling male-dominated horse racing, in this fourth Hundred Oaks novel. Savannah, her widowed horse-trainer father, and her father's pregnant girlfriend move to Tennessee's Cedar Hill, a farm that trains horses for races including the Kentucky Derby...The author's knack for weaving forbidden romance, breezy dialogue, and details of this lesser-known sports venue places it in the winner's circle for reluctant readers and chick-lit fans. —*Booklist*

Kephart, Beth
Dangerous neighbors. Beth Kephart. Egmont USA, 2010 192 p.
Grades: 7 8 9 10
1. Twin sisters; 2. Death; 3. Grief; 4. Sisters; 5. Suicide; 6. Philadelphia, Pennsylvania; 7. Historical fiction
9781606840801
LC 2010011249
Set against the backdrop of the 1876 Centennial Exhibition in Philadelphia, Katherine cannot forgive herself when her beloved twin sister dies, and she feels that her only course of action is to follow suit.
Exceptionally graceful prose...and flashbacks are so realistically drawn and deftly integrated that readers will be as startled as Katherine to find themselves yanked out of morose memories and surrounded by noisy fairgoers. —*Bulletin of the Center for Children's Books*

★ **Going** over. Beth Kephart. Chronicle Books, 2014 262 p. : Map
Grades: 8 9 10 11 12
1. Berlin Wall; 2. Separated friends, relatives, etc; 3. Graffiti; 4. Immigrants; 5. Families; 6. Berlin, Germany; 7. Germany; 8. 1980s; 9. Historical fiction; 10. Multiple perspectives
9781452124575
LC 2012046894
Booklist Editors' Choice: Books for Youth, 2014.

In the early 1980s Ada and Stefan are young, would-be lovers living on opposite sides of the Berlin Wall—Ada lives with her mother and grandmother and paints graffiti on the Wall, and Stefan lives with his grandmother in the East and dreams of escaping to the West.

In a present-tense narration alternating between Ada's first-person and Stefan's second-person, the young lovers on opposite sides of the Berlin Wall in 1983 plan for Stefan's escape to the West. Kephart works romantic chemistry into a danger-packed plot with moving results in this captivating glimpse into an underrepresented era that will appeal to older readers with a taste for literary historical fiction. —*Horn Book Guide*
Includes bibliographical references (p. [259]-262).

★ The **heart** is not a size. Beth Kephart. HarperTeen/Balzer & Bray, 2010 256 p.
Grades: 7 8 9 10
1. Self-perception in teenage girls; 2. Teenage volunteers; 3. Poverty; 4. Volunteers; 5. Fifteen-year-old girls; 6. Mexico; 7. Pennsylvania; 8. Realistic fiction.
9780061470486; 9780061470493
LC 2008055721
YALSA Best Fiction for Young Adults, 2011.
Fifteen-year-old Georgia learns a great deal about herself and her troubled best friend Riley when they become part of a group of suburban Pennsylvania teenagers that go to Anapra, a squatters village in the border town of Juarez, Mexico, to undertake a community construction project.

Kephart's prose is typically poetic. She pens a faster-paced novel that explores teens' inner selves.... The writing is vivid, enabling readers to visualize Anapra's desolation and hope. —*Voice of Youth Advocates*

House of Dance. Beth Kephart. HarperTeen, 2008 272 p.
Grades: 7 8 9 10
1. Grandfathers — Death; 2. Senior men; 3. Sick persons; 4. Fifteen-year-old girls; 5. Teenage girls; 6. Coming-of-age stories.
9780061429293
Having spent a lot of time with her grandfather before his passing and listening to his wonderful tales, a young girl finally understands his love of music and motion when she enters the House of Dance and gets to experience it for herself.

This is distinguished more by its sharp, eloquent prose than by its plot.... Poetically expressed memories and moving dialogue both anchor and amplify the characters' emotions. —*Publishers Weekly*

One thing stolen. Beth Kephart. Chronicle Books, 2015 272 p.
Grades: 9 10 11 12
1. Americans in Italy; 2. Kleptomania; 3. Teenage girls with mental illnesses; 4. Compulsive behavior; 5. Families; 6. Florence, Italy; 7. Italy; 8. Realistic fiction; 9. Multiple perspectives
9781452128313
LC 2014005286
Nadia Cara is in Florence, Italy with her family because her professor father is researching the 1966 flood, but Nadia herself is in trouble—she has turned into a kleptomaniac and she feels detached from everything, except for an elusive Italian boy whom no one but herself has seen.

Fans of Jandy Nelson's dense, unique narratives will lose themselves in Kephart's enigmatic, atmospheric, and beautifully written tale. —*Booklist*

★ **Small** damages. Beth Kephart. Philomel Books, 2012 304 p.
Grades: 10 11 12
1. Pregnant teenagers; 2. Americans in Spain; 3. Ranch life; 4. Adoption; 5. Interpersonal relations; 6. Spain; 7. Realistic fiction; 8. First person narratives
9780399257483
LC 2011020947

Eighteen-year-old Kenzie of Philadelphia, pregnant by Yale-bound Kevin, is bitter when her mother sends her to Spain to deliver and give her baby away, but discovers a makeshift family with the rancher who takes her in, his cook, and the young man they have raised together.

This is the story of you. Beth Kephart. 2016 264 p.
Grades: 7 8 9 10 11 12
1. Hurricanes; 2. Survival (after hurricanes); 3. Mother-separated teenage girls; 4. Island life; 5. Seventeen-year-old girls; 6. New Jersey; 7. Realistic fiction; 8. Survival stories.
9781452142845
LC 2015003765
Seventeen-year-old Mira lives in a small island beach town off the coast of New Jersey year-round, and when a devastating superstorm strikes she will face the storm's wrath and the destruction it leaves behind alone.

At once an exploration of the unrelenting power of nature and a reminder of the one thing in the world that is irreplaceable: family. —*Booklist*

★ **Undercover**. Beth Kephart. HarperTeen, 2007 278 p;
Grades: 8 9 10 11 12
1. High school students; 2. Teenagers; 3. Teenage girls; 4. Teenage girl authors; 5. Ghostwriters; 6. Contemporary romances; 7. Classics-inspired fiction
9780061238932; 9780061238949
LC 2007002981
School Library Journal Best Books, 2007.
High school sophomore Elisa is used to observing while going unnoticed except when classmates ask her to write love notes for them, but a teacher's recognition of her talent, a "client's" desire for her friendship, a love of ice skating, and her parent's marital problems draw her out of herself.

Kephart tells a moving story.... Readers will fall easily into the compelling premise and Elisa's memorable, graceful voice. —*Booklist*
Laura Geringer Books.

Keplinger, Kody
Lying out loud. Kody Keplinger. Scholastic Press, 2015 304 p.
Grades: 9 10 11 12
1. Truthfulness and falsehood; 2. Dishonesty in teenage girls; 3. Crushes in teenage girls; 4. Teenage boy/girl relations; 5. Dishonesty; 6. Contemporary romances; 7. Teen chick lit
9780545831093
Sonny is a realistic and very human character, and even though she is a liar, her motivations are all too believable. One of the strong points of the book is the emphasis on female friendship. —*School Library Journal*
Companion book to: The DUFF.

Run. Kody Keplinger. Scholastic Press, 2016 304 p.
Grades: 7 8 9 10 11 12
1. Runaway teenage girls; 2. Teenagers who are blind; 3. Female friendship; 4. Bisexual teenagers; 5. Children of drug abusers; 6. Kentucky; 7. Realistic fiction; 8. Multiple perspectives
9780545831130
A good unlikely friendship story with compelling characters and a nuanced portrait of disability and small-town life. —*School Library Journal*

That's not what happened. Kody Keplinger. Scholastic Press, 2018 336 p.
Grades: 7 8 9 10 11 12
1. School shootings; 2. Truthfulness and falsehood; 3. Teenage girl murder victims; 4. Memories; 5. Loss (Psychology); 6. Realistic

fiction; 7. First person narratives; 8. Multiple perspectives; 9. Books for reluctant readers
9781338186529; 9781444933628, Paperback, UK

LC 2017060501

YALSA Quick Picks for Reluctant Young Adult Readers, 2019.

In the three years since the Virgil County High School Massacre, a story has grown up around one of the victims, Sarah McHale, that says she died proclaiming her Christian faith—but Leanne Bauer was there, and knows what happened, and she has a choice: stay silent and let people believe in Sarah's martyrdom, or tell the truth.

Kerr, M. E.
Gentlehands. M.E. Kerr. Harper & Row, 1978 183 p.
Grades: 7 8 9 10
1. Teenage boys; 2. Nazi fugitives; 3. Teenage boy/girl relations; 4. Children of police; 5. Teenage romance; 6. Love stories
9780060231767

LC 77011860

To impress his rich girlfriend, Buddy Boyle takes her to visit his estranged grandfather. But he discovers that his grandfather's culture and sophistication hide a long-buried secret reaching back to Auschwitz.
An Ursula Nordstrom book.

Night kites. M.E. Kerr. Harper & Row, 1986 216 p.
Grades: 7 8 9 10
1. Seventeen-year-old boys; 2. People with AIDS — Family relationships; 3. Teenage boy/girl relations; 4. Brothers; 5. Best friends; 6. Realistic fiction.
9780060232535

LC 85045386

California Young Reader Medal, Young Adult, 1991.

Seventeen-year-old Erick's comfortable and well-ordered life begins to fall apart when he is forced to keep two secrets: the identity of his new girlfriend and the nature of his brother's debilitating disease.

Pete and his methods of coping with his disease and its effects on himself, his friends, his family, and ultimately, his community, are sensitively and non-sentimentally drawn, and seem to be portrayed accurately. This is sure to be a popular title, and will be a natural for booktalks. —*Voice of Youth Advocates*

Keyser, Amber
★ **Pointe,** claw. Amber J. Keyser. Carolrhoda Lab, 2017 278 pages;
Grades: 8 9 10 11 12
1. Teenage girl ballet dancers; 2. Former friends; 3. Diseases; 4. Friendship; 5. Zoonoses; 6. Realistic fiction; 7. Multiple perspectives
9781467775915

LC 2016006114

After eight years of separation childhood best friends are reunited. One is studying to be a professional ballerina, the other has a rare disease that is rapidly taking its toll.

Keyser's writing shimmers with raw emotion and empathy, and her finale, much like in dance, is poetic, bittersweet, and life affirming. —*Publishers Weekly*

The **way** back from broken. By Amber J. Keyser. 2015 196 p.
Grades: 9 10 11 12
1. Grief in teenage boys; 2. Grief; 3. Camping; 4. Fifteen-year-old boys; 5. Ten-year-old girls; 6. Canada; 7. Portland, Oregon; 8. Realistic fiction
9781467775908; 9781467788175, ebook, US

LC 2015001617

After losing his infant sister, Rakmen's family is devastated. While his parents figure things out, they send Rakmen on a camping trip in the Canadian wilderness with another grieving family. Rakmen is far from thrilled about the trip, and he has to decide whether it's too late to find his way back from broken.

With a cast of diverse and well-rounded characters, poignant relationships that never become schmaltzy, and a compelling high-stakes adventure, this vivid, moving exploration of grief and recovery hits all the right notes. —*Booklist*

Khan, Sabina
The **love** and lies of Rukhsana Ali. Sabina Khan. 2019 336 p.
Grades: 9 10 11 12
1. Lesbian teenagers; 2. Muslim families; 3. Identity (Psychology); 4. Muslims; 5. Coming out (Sexual or gender identity); 6. Bangladesh; 7. LGBTQIA fiction; 8. Realistic fiction; 9. Coming-of-age stories; 10. Books for reluctant readers
9781338227017

LC 2018033253

YALSA Quick Picks for Reluctant Young Adult Readers, 2020.

After her conservative Muslim parents catch her kissing her girlfriend Ariana, Rukhsana Ali finds herself whisked off to Bangladesh and must find the courage to fight for the right to choose her own path.

With an up-close depiction of the intersection of the LGBTQIA+ community with Bengali culture, this hard-hitting and hopeful story is a must-purchase for any YA collection. —*School Library Journal*

Khanani, Intisar
Thorn. Intisar Khanani. HarperTeen, 2020 512 p.
Grades: 9 10 11 12
1. Princesses; 2. Body swapping; 3. Arranged marriage; 4. Imaginary kingdoms; 5. Princes; 6. Fairy tale and folklore-inspired fiction; 7. Middle Eastern-influenced fantasy; 8. Fantasy fiction.
9780062835703; 9781471408724

A fantasy retelling of the "Goose Girl" fairy tale follows the experiences of a betrothed princess who is robbed of her identity by a mysterious sorceress before a threat against her betrothed prince compels her to make a dangerous choice.

A measured romance and an awareness of contemporary social issues elevate the text, but most alluring of all is Alyrra's strong, sensible heart. —*Booklist*

Khorram, Adib
Darius the Great deserves better. Adib Khorram. 2020 352 p.
Grades: 9 10 11 12
1. Iranian American teenagers; 2. Teenage boy/boy relations; 3. Gay teenagers; 4. Depression; 5. Iranian Americans; 6. Portland, Oregon; 7. Realistic fiction; 8. LGBTQIA fiction
9780593108239

LC 2020008231

Darius Kellner has everything he thought he wanted—a new boyfriend, a new internship, and a spot on the soccer team—but growing up makes him question everything.

Blending broad themes like consent and toxic masculinity with the specificity of Darius' intersectional identity (gay, white and Iranian), this coming-of-age masterpiece packs a multitude of truth and heart. —*Kirkus*
Sequel of: *Darius the Great is not okay*

★ **Darius** the Great is not okay. Adib Khorram. 2018 320 p.
Grades: 7 8 9 10 11 12
1. Iranian American teenagers; 2. Depression; 3. Identity (Psychology); 4. Family visits; 5. Iranian Americans; 6. Iran; 7. Realistic fiction; 8. Coming-of-age stories; 9. Books for reluctant readers

9780525552963; 9780525553809, Paperback, UK

LC 2018009825

Asian Pacific American Asian Pacific American Award for Literature: Young Adult Literature, 2019; Westchester Fiction Award, 2019; William C. Morris YA Debut Award, 2019; YALSA Best Fiction for Young Adults, 2019; YALSA Quick Picks for Reluctant Young Adult Readers, 2020; Middle East Book Award, Youth Literature Winner, 2019.

Clinically-depressed Darius Kellner, a high school sophomore, travels to Iran to meet his grandparents, but it is their next-door neighbor, Sohrab, who changes his life.

Darius is a well-crafted, awkward but endearing character, and his cross-cultural story will inspire reflection about identity and belonging. —*School Library Journal*

Sequel: *Darius the Great deserves better*

Kiely, Brendan

★ The **gospel** of winter: a novel. Brendan Kiely. Margaret K. McElderry Books, 2014 296 p.

Grades: 9 10 11 12

1. Priests; 2. Sex crimes; 3. Teenage abuse victims; 4. Family problems; 5. Drug abuse; 6. Connecticut; 7. Realistic fiction
9781442484894

YALSA Best Fiction for Young Adults, 2015; YALSA Best Fiction for Young Adults: Top Ten, 2015.

Managing the challenges of his dysfunctional family by taking Adderall, sneaking drinks from his father's bar and confiding in a local priest who shatteringly abuses him, 16-year-old Aidan finds support from a crew of new friends including a crush, a wild girl and a charismatic swim-team captain with secrets of his own.

Kiely's gutsy debut addresses abuse in the Catholic Church. The year is 2001, the events of 9/11 are only two months old, and 16-year-old Aidan's family is falling apart. Aidan finds comfort in snorting lines of Adderall, swiping drinks from his father's wet bar, and forming a friendship with Father Greg of Most Precious Blood, the town's Catholic church. The scandal among the Boston archdiocese in early 2002 gets Aidan's town's attention, and when it does, Aidan's feelings of rage and denial and fear come to a head. This is challenging, thought-provoking material, presented in beautiful prose that explores the ways in which acts rendered in the name of love can both destroy and heal. —*Booklist*

Last true love story. Brendan Kiely. 2016 288 pages

Grades: 9 10 11 12

1. Grandfather and grandson; 2. People with Alzheimer's disease; 3. Adopted teenage girls; 4. Self-fulfillment; 5. Teenage musicians; 6. Realistic fiction
9781481429887; 9781481429894

LC 2015036953

YALSA Best Fiction for Young Adults, 2017.

Hendrix and Corrina bust Hendrix's grandfather out of assisted living, and leave LA for New York in pursuit of freedom, truth, and love.

Readers will be swept up in Kiely's musical prose as Teddy learns about love, romance, forgiveness, and reconciliation. —*Kirkus*

Tradition. Brendan Kiely. Simon & Schuster 2018 352 p.

Grades: 7 8 9 10 11 12

1. Boarding schools; 2. Sexism; 3. High school students; 4. Rites and ceremonies; 5. Teenage boy/girl relations; 6. Realistic fiction
9781481480345; 9781481480352; 9781481480369, ebook, US

A thoughtfully crafted argument for feminism and allyship. —*Kirkus*

Kiem, Elizabeth

Dancer, daughter, traitor, spy. By Elizabeth Kiem. Soho Teen, 2013 288 p. (Bolshoi saga, 1)

Grades: 9 10 11 12

1. Spies; 2. Teenage psychics; 3. Teenage girls; 4. Clairvoyance; 5. Russian Americans; 6. Soviet Union; 7. United States; 8. 1980s; 9. Spy fiction; 10. Thrillers and suspense
9781616952631

LC 2013006502

After a harrowing defection to the United States in 1982, Russian teenager Marya and her father settle in Brooklyn, where Marya is drawn into a web of intrigue involving her gift of foresight, her mother's disappearance, and a boy she cannot bring herself to trust.

The pacing is somewhat uneven, but there are enough twists to surprise and engage readers to the end. A compelling portrait of a young woman on the verge of adulthood, caught up in the domestic secrets of her parents and the enmity of two countries. —*Kirkus*

Kincaid, S. J.

The **Diabolic**. S. J. Kincaid. Simon & Schuster Books for Young Readers, 2016 320 p. (Diabolic trilogy, 1)

Grades: 8 9 10 11 12

1. Genetically engineered teenagers; 2. Courts and courtiers; 3. Hostages; 4. Genetic engineering; 5. Teenage romance; 6. Science fiction; 7. First person narratives
9781481472678; 9781471147142, print, UK; 9781471147159, print, UK; 9781471147166, ebook

LC 2016003698

Westchester Fiction Award, 2018; YALSA Best Fiction for Young Adults, 2018.

Nemesis is a Diabolic, a humanoid teenager and the galaxy's most deadly weapon, who masquerades as Sidonia, a senator's daughter, and becomes a hostage of the galactic court.

Kincaid has crafted incredible characters who readers can relate to and care for even if they range from privileged, bratty children to creations designed to kill. The imagery used in establishing these protagonists and the complex setting will thrill the YA audience. —*School Library Journal*

Sequel: *The empress.*

The **empress**. S.J. Kincaid. 2017 378 p; (Diabolic trilogy, 2)

Grades: 8 9 10 11 12

1. Genetically engineered teenagers; 2. Courts and courtiers; 3. Hostages; 4. Genetic engineering; 5. Teenage romance; 6. Science fiction; 7. First person narratives
9781534409927; 9781534409934; 9781534409941, ebook, US

LC 2017023825

Nemesis, the Diabolic, and Tyrus face new challenges and old enemies as Tyrus ascends to the throne, and the two struggle to prove Nemesis' humanity to those who oppose her position as Empress and keep them from full power over the galaxy.

Kincaid deftly juggles high-octane action with emotionally devastating punches, and readers will riot for the next installment. —*Kirkus*

Sequel to: *The diabolic.*

Kindl, Patrice

Keeping the castle. By Patrice Kindl. Viking Childrens Books, 2012 224 p.

Grades: 7 8 9 10 11

1. Seventeen-year-old girls; 2. Castles; 3. Teenage girls; 4. Rich men; 5. Nobility; 6. England; 7. Great Britain; 8. Georgian era (1714-1837); 9. Historical romances.
9780670014385

LC 2011033185

Booklist Editors' Choice: Books for Youth, 2012; School Library Journal Best Books, 2012; YALSA Best Fiction for Young Adults, 2013.

In order to support her family and maintain their ancient castle in Lesser Hoo, seventeen-year-old Althea bears the burden of finding a wealthy suitor who can remedy their financial problems.

Companion book: A school for brides

A **school** for brides: a story of maidens, mystery, and matrimony. Patrice Kindl. Viking, an imprint of Penguin Group (USA) LLC, 2015 272 p.
Grades: 7 8 9 10
1. Boarding schools; 2. Schools; 3. Marriage; 4. Courtship; 5. Teenage girls; 6. England; 7. Yorkshire, England; 8. Georgian era (1714-1837); 9. 1800s (Decade); 10. Historical fiction
9780670786084

This affectionate homage to the genre delivers what's missing: a witty, intelligent plot whose characterscomplex, conniving, hypocritical, and hilariousseek happiness within an ordered world. This airy souffl of a tale, garnished with quirky charm, is an unmitigated delight from start to finish. —*Kirkus*

Companion book to: *Keeping the castle*

King, A. S.

★ **Ask** the passengers: a novel. By A.S. King. Little, Brown, 2012 304 p.
Grades: 9 10 11 12
1. Questioning (Sexual or gender identity); 2. Gossiping and gossips; 3. Prejudice; 4. Family problems; 5. Small towns; 6. Pennsylvania; 7. Realistic fiction; 8. Magical realism; 9. LGBTQIA fiction
9780316194686
LC 2011053207
Carolyn W. Field Award (Pennsylvania), 2013; James Cook Book Award (Ohio), 2013; Los Angeles Times Book Prize for Young Adult Literature, 2012; Rainbow List, 2013; School Library Journal Best Books, 2012; YALSA Best Fiction for Young Adults, 2013.

Imagining that she is sending love to passengers in airplanes flying overhead, Astrid Jones, a teen from a small town torn by gossip and narrow-mindedness, struggles with her family's dysfunction and hides her love for another girl.

Dig. A. S. King. Dutton Books for Young Readers, 2019 400 p.
Grades: 9 10 11 12
1. Cousins; 2. Family reunions; 3. Dysfunctional families; 4. Racism; 5. Rich families; 6. Pennsylvania; 7. Family sagas; 8. Magical realism; 9. Multiple perspectives.
9781101994917; 9781925773521, Australia
Michael L. Printz Award, 2020; School Library Journal Best Books, 2019.

Five white teenage cousins who are struggling with the failures and racial ignorance of their dysfunctional parents and their wealthy grandparents, reunite for Easter.

This visceral examination of humanity's flaws and complexity, especially where the adult characters are concerned, nevertheless cultivates hope in a younger generation that's wiser and stronger than its predecessors. —*Booklist*

★ **Everybody** sees the ants. By A.S. King. Little, Brown, 2012 288 p.
Grades: 9 10 11 12
1. Dreams; 2. Bullying and bullies; 3. Self-confidence in teenage boys; 4. Self-confidence; 5. Family problems; 6. Arizona; 7. Realistic fiction; 8. Magical realism
9780316129282
LC 2010049434

YALSA Best Fiction for Young Adults, 2012.

Overburdened by his parents' bickering and a bully's attacks, fifteen-year-old Lucky Linderman begins dreaming of being with his grandfather, who went missing during the Vietnam War, but during a visit to Arizona, his aunt and uncle and their beautiful neighbor, Ginny, help him find a new perspective.

★ **Glory** O'Brien's history of the future: a novel. By A.S. King. 2014 320 pages
Grades: 9 10 11 12
1. Visions; 2. Survivors of suicide victims; 3. Feminism; 4. Women's rights; 5. Best friends; 6. Magical realism
9780316222723
LC 2013041670
Amelia Bloomer List, 2015; Booklist Editors' Choice: Books for Youth, 2014; School Library Journal Best Books: Fiction, 2014; YALSA Best Fiction for Young Adults, 2015.

As her high school graduation draws near, Glory O'Brien begins having powerful and terrifying visions of the future as she struggles with her long-buried grief over her mother's suicide.

Imbuing Glory's narrative with a graceful, sometimes dissonant combination of anger, ambivalence, and hopefulness that resists tidy resolution, award-winning King presents another powerful, moving, and compellingly complex coming-of-age story. —*Booklist*

I crawl through it. By A.S. King. Little, Brown and Company, 2015 336 p.
Grades: 9 10 11 12
1. Coping; 2. Loss (Psychology); 3. Reality; 4. Teenage rape victims; 5. Examinations; 6. Multiple perspectives
9780316334099
Booklist Editors' Choice: Books for Youth, 2015.

Characters unfold like riddles before the reader, while King uses magical realism and a motif of standardized testing to emphasize the flaw in obtaining answers without confronting reality's hard questions. Beautiful prose, poetry, and surreal imagery combine for an utterly original story that urges readers to question, love, and believe—or risk explosion. —*Booklist*

Please ignore Vera Dietz. By A.S. King. Alfred A. Knopf, 2010 304 p.
Grades: 9 10 11 12
1. Children of alcoholic fathers; 2. Grief in teenage girls; 3. Anger; 4. Betrayal; 5. Fathers and daughters; 6. Pennsylvania; 7. Realistic fiction; 8. Magical realism
9780375865862
LC 2010012730
YALSA Best Fiction for Young Adults, 2011; Michael L. Printz Honor Book, 2011.

When her best friend, whom she secretly loves, betrays her and then dies under mysterious circumstances, high school senior Vera Dietz struggles with secrets that could help clear his name.

This is a gut-wrenching tale about family, friendship, destiny, the meaning of words, and self-discovery. —*Voice of Youth Advocates*

Kinsella, Sophie

Finding Audrey. Sophie Kinsella. 2015 272 p.
Grades: 9 10 11 12
1. Anxiety disorders; 2. Teenage boy/girl relations; 3. Teenage romance; 4. Teenage girls; 5. Fourteen-year-old girls; 6. Realistic fiction
9780553536515; 9780385684996; 9780385685016; 9780553536539; 9780553536522, ebook, US
LC 2014048476

YALSA Popular Paperbacks for Young Adults, 2017.

Audrey has developed an anxiety disorder but she sees a therapist and is making slow but steady progress. She meets Linus, her brother's teammate and finds she can talk through her fears with him in a way she's never been able to do with anyone before.

A deep and sensitive portrayal of a British teen's recovery from a traumatic experience. Expect requests! School Library Journal.

Kirby, Matthew J.
★ A **taste** for monsters. Matthew J. Kirby. Scholastic Press, 2016 352 p.
Grades: 7 8 9 10
1. Merrick, Joseph Carey, 1862-1890; 2. People with disfigurements; 3. Household employees; 4. Serial murders; 5. Ghosts; 6. Phosphorus — Physiological effect; 7. London, England; 8. Great Britain; 9. Victorian era (1837-1901); 10. 1880s; 11. Historical fiction; 12. Paranormal fiction
9780545817844

LC 2015048826

In 1888 seventeen-year-old Evelyn Fallow, herself disfigured by the phosphorus in the match factory where she worked, has been hired as a maid to Joseph Merrick, the Elephant Man—but when the Jack the Ripper murders begin she and Merrick find themselves haunted by the ghosts of the slain women, and Evelyn is caught up in the mystery of Jack's identity.

A lovely, suspenseful, lyrical, imperfect paranormal mystery. —*Kirkus*

Kisner, Adrienne
Dear Rachel Maddow. Adrienne Kisner. Feiwel & Friends, 2018 272 p.
Grades: 7 8 9 10 11
1. Maddow, Rachel; 2. Lesbian teenagers; 3. Equality; 4. Grief in teenage girls; 5. High schools; 6. School politics; 7. Realistic fiction; 8. LGBTQIA fiction; 9. Epistolary novels
9781250146021; 9781250308832
International Literacy Association Children's Book Award for Young Adult Fiction, 2019; YALSA Best Fiction for Young Adults, 2019.

A teen slogging through remedial courses at school in the wake of her sibling's death, a breakup with her first girlfriend and her parents' dysfunctions writes unsent e-mails to her favorite news anchor before becoming involved in a moral and political dilemma involving an honor student's controversial opinions.

Kittle, Katrina
Reasons to be happy. Katrina Kittle. Sourcebooks, Inc, 2011 281 p.
Grades: 7 8 9 10
1. Teenage girls; 2. Eating disorders; 3. Belonging; 4. Beauty; 5. Self-esteem in teenage girls; 6. Los Angeles, California; 7. Africa
9781402260209
Hannah's believability as a character as well as the realistic, painful depiction of bulimia make this a standout. —*Booklist*

Kizer, Amber
A **matter** of days. Amber Kizer. Delacorte Press, 2013 288 p.
Grades: 7 8 9 10
1. Epidemics; 2. Near future; 3. Transcontinental journeys; 4. Survival; 5. Virus diseases; 6. Science fiction.
9780385739733

LC 2012012200

In the not-too-distant future when a global pandemic kills most of humanity, a teenaged girl and her younger brother struggle to survive.

This post-apocalyptic tale is particularly frightening as it doesn't take place in some distant, imagined future. A solid, realistically imagined survival tale with a strong female protagonist. —*Kirkus*

Meridian. Amber Kizer. Delacorte Press, 2009 320 p. (Meridian saga (Amber Kizer), 1)
Grades: 7 8 9 10
1. Angels; 2. Soul; 3. Death; 4. Supernatural; 5. Good and evil; 6. Colorado; 7. Paranormal romances; 8. Urban fantasy
9780385906210

On her sixteenth birthday, Meridian Sozu is whisked off to her great-aunt's home in Revelation, Colorado, where she learns that she is a Fenestra, the half-human, half-angel link between the living and the dead, and must learn to help human souls to the afterlife before the dark forces reach them.

The author brings a fresh voice to the realm of teen paranormal romantic fiction.... The characters are compelling and the themes of good and evil, life and death will keep readers engaged. —*School Library Journal*
Sequel: *Wildcat fireflies*.

Wildcat fireflies: a Meridian novel. Amber Kizer. Delacorte Press, 2011 528 p. (Meridian saga (Amber Kizer), 2)
Grades: 7 8 9 10
1. Angels; 2. Soul; 3. Protectiveness in teenagers; 4. Death; 5. Supernatural; 6. Indiana; 7. Paranormal romances; 8. Urban fantasy
9780385739719

Teenaged Meridian Sozu, a half-human, half-angel link between the living and the dead known as a Fenestra, hits the road with Tens, her love and sworn protector, in hopes of finding another person with Meridian's ability to help souls transition safely into the afterlife.

Some of the day-to-day events may be hard to believe, but this is a book about angels and demons after all; fans will forgive. —*Kirkus*
Sequel to: *Meridian*.

Klass, David
Firestorm. David Klass. Frances Foster Books, 2006 304 p. (Caretaker trilogy, 1)
Grades: 8 9 10 11 12
1. Young men; 2. Eighteen-year-old men; 3. Heroes and heroines; 4. Ninja; 5. Shapeshifters; 6. Science fiction.
9780374323073

LC 2005052112

YALSA Best Books for Young Adults, 2008; School Library Journal Best Books, 2006.

After learning that he has been sent from the future for a special purpose, eighteen-year-old Jack receives help from an unusual dog and a shape-shifting female fighter.

The sobering events and tone are leavened with engaging humor, and the characters are multidimensional. The relentless pace, coupled with issues of ecology, time travel, self-identity, and sexual awakening, makes for a thrilling and memorable read. —*School Library Journal*

Timelock. David Klass. Farrar, Straus and Giroux, 2009 256 p. (Caretaker trilogy, 3)
Grades: 8 9 10 11 12
1. Environmentalism; 2. Time travel; 3. Young men; 4. Eighteen-year-old men; 5. Heroes and heroines; 6. Science fiction; 7. First person narratives.
9780374323097

LC 2008023280

Jack discovers that the only way to protect the Earth from ecological disaster at the hands of the Dark Army is to lock time, and he must choose between staying in the present or returning to the future world from which he came.

Every bit as fast paced, thrilling, and similar to a gripping computer game as its predecessors, this final volume in the trilogy will keep readers absorbed while presenting them with a valuable warning about the need for environmental awareness. —*School Library Journal*

Frances Foster books.

Whirlwind. David Klass. Farrar Straus Giroux, 2008 293 p; (Caretaker trilogy, 2)
Grades: 8 9 10 11 12
1. Time travel; 2. Adventure; 3. Environmentalism; 4. Young men; 5. Eighteen-year-old men; 6. Science fiction.
9780374323080

LC 2007014160

Jack finds himself embroiled in another dangerous adventure when, after a six-month absence, he returns to the Hudson River town where he grew up to find his girlfriend PJ only to discover that she is missing and everyone believes him to be responsible for her disappearance and the death of his family.

The fast-paced, gripping plot is an excellent vehicle for presenting a significant environmental message to an audience that might not hear it otherwise. —*School Library Journal*

Frances Foster Books.

Klass, Sheila Solomon

★ **Soldier's** secret: the story of Deborah Sampson. Sheila Solomon Klass. Henry Holt, 2009 215 p.
Grades: 6 7 8 9 10
1. Gannett, Deborah Sampson, 1760-1827; 2. Deception; 3. Gender role; 4. Women soldiers; 5. Soldiers; 6. Women and war; 7. United States; 8. Revolutionary America (1775-1783); 9. 18th century; 10. Biographical fiction; 11. Historical fiction
9780805082005

LC 2008036783

Flicker Tale Children's Book Award (North Dakota) for Juvenile Fiction, 2010.

During the Revolutionary War, a young woman named Deborah Sampson disguises herself as a man in order to serve in the Continental Army.

In this novel, Sampson is strong, brave, and witty.... Klass doesn't shy away from the horrors of battle; she also is blunt regarding details young readers will wonder about, like how Sampson dealt with bathing, urination, and menstruation.... Sampson's romantic yearnings for a fellow soldier...is given just the right notes or restraint and realism. —*Booklist*

Christy Ottaviano books.

Klause, Annette Curtis

★ **Blood** and chocolate. Annette Curtis Klause. Delacorte Press, 1997 264 p.
Grades: 7 8 9 10
1. Teenage werewolves; 2. Identity (Psychology); 3. Crushes in teenage girls; 4. Supernatural; 5. Secret identity; 6. Maryland; 7. Fantasy fiction; 8. Paranormal romances; 9. Books to movies; 10. Books for reluctant readers
9780385323055

LC 96-35247

Garden State Teen Book Award (New Jersey), Fiction (Grades 9-12), 2000; South Carolina Book Award, Young Adult Books, 2000; YALSA Quick Picks for Reluctant Young Adult Readers, 1998; Booklist Editors' Choice: Books for Youth, 1997; YALSA Popular Paperbacks for Young Adults, 2008; YALSA Best Books for Young Adults, 1998; School Library Journal Best Books, 1997.

Having fallen for a human boy, a beautiful teenage werewolf must battle both her packmates and the fear of the townspeople to decide where she belongs and with whom.

Klause's imagery is magnetic, and her language fierce, rich, and beautiful.... Passion and philosophy dovetail superbly in this powerful, unforgettable novel for mature teens. —*Booklist*

Klein, Lisa

Cate of the lost colony. By Lisa Klein. Bloomsbury Children's Books : 2010 336 p.
Grades: 8 9 10 11 12
1. Raleigh, Walter, Sir, 1552?-1618; 2. Nobility; 3. Exile (Punishment); 4. Wilderness survival; 5. Lumbee Indians; 6. Indians of North America; 7. Roanoke Island, North Carolina; 8. Roanoke Colony; 9. Colonial America (1600-1775); 10. Tudor period (1485-1603); 11. Historical romances.
9781599905075

LC 2010008299

When her dalliance with Sir Walter Ralegh is discovered by Queen Elizabeth in 1587, lady-in-waiting Catherine Archer is banished to the struggling colony of Roanoke, where she and the other English settlers must rely on a Croatoan Indian for their survival. Includes author's note on the mystery surrounding the Lost Colony.

This robust, convincing portrait of the Elizabethan world with complex, rounded characters wraps an intriguingly plausible solution to the lost colony mystery inside a compelling love story of subtle thematic depth. —*Kirkus*

Includes bibliographical references.

Klune, TJ

The **Extraordinaries**. TJ Klune. Tor Teen, 2020 400 p. (Extraordinaries, 1)
Grades: 9 10 11 12
1. Fans (Persons); 2. Superheroes; 3. Teenage boy/boy relations; 4. Crushes (Interpersonal relations); 5. LGBTQIA teenagers; 6. Superhero stories; 7. Coming-of-age stories.
9781250203656; 9781473693043, Hardback, UK; 9781473693050, Paperback, UK

A successful fan-fiction writer has a chance encounter with a superhero crush who challenges him to remake himself in ways that compromise his bond with a best friend, who is becoming something more.

There's plenty in this lighthearted, superhero-interested teen dramedy for kids who feel like they're sometimes on the outside, including the positive representation of a teen with ADHD. —*Publishers Weekly*

Knowles, Johanna

Jumping off swings. Jo Knowles. Candlewick Press, 2009 230 p;
Grades: 10 11 12
1. Teenage pregnancy; 2. Family problems; 3. Emotional problems of teenagers; 4. Sexuality; 5. Pregnancy; 6. Realistic fiction; 7. Multiple perspectives; 8. First person narratives; 9. Books for reluctant readers
9780763639495

LC 2009004587

YALSA Quick Picks for Reluctant Young Adult Readers, 2010; YALSA Quick Picks for Reluctant Young Adult Readers, 2010; YALSA Best Books for Young Adults, 2010.

Tells, from four points of view, the ramifications of a pregnancy resulting from a "one-time thing" between Ellie, who feels loved when boys touch her, and Josh, an eager virgin with a troubled home life.

With so many protagonists in the mix, it is no small feat that each character is fully developed and multidimen- sional—there are no villains or heroes here, only kids groping their way through a desperate situation.... [This is] a moving tale with a realistically unresolved ending. —*Kirkus*

Sequel: *Living with Jackie Chan*.

Read between the lines. Jo Knowles. Candlewick Press, 2015 336 p.
Grades: 9 10 11 12

1. Teenagers; 2. Social perception; 3. Small town life; 4. Teachers; 5. Social status; 6. Realistic fiction; 7. Books for reluctant readers
9780763663872

YALSA Quick Picks for Reluctant Young Adult Readers, 2016.

Issues of absent parents, conflicted sexuality, eating disorders, and various forms of abuse are dealt with succinctly but tenderly, and some nuances are subtle enough that multiple levels of reading are possible, with a twist at the end so understated you may miss it. This is likely to speak to any teenager in a stage of transition. —*Booklist*

★ **See** you at Harry's. Jo Knowles. Candlewick Press, 2012 310 p.
Grades: 6 7 8 9 10 11

1. Grief; 2. Family problems; 3. Brothers and sisters; 4. Homosexuality; 5. Grief in children.
9780763654078

LC 2011018619

ALA Notable Children's Book, 2013; Rainbow List, 2013; YALSA Best Fiction for Young Adults, 2013.

Twelve-year-old Fern feels invisible in her family, where grumpy eighteen-year-old Sarah is working at the family restaurant, fourteen-year-old Holden is struggling with school bullies and his emerging homosexuality, and adorable, three-year-old Charlie is always the center of attention, and when tragedy strikes, the fragile bond holding the family together is stretched almost to the breaking point.

Knox, Elizabeth

Dreamhunter: book one of the Dreamhunter duet. Elizabeth Knox. Farrar, Straus and Giroux, 2006 384 p. (Dreamhunter duet, 1)
Grades: 7 8 9 10

1. Fifteen-year-old girls; 2. Dreams; 3. Parallel universes; 4. Missing persons; 5. Fourteen-year-old girls; 6. 20th century; 7. Fantasy fiction; 8. New Zealand fiction
9780374318536; 9780732281939, print, UK

LC 2005046366

LIANZA Children's Book Awards, Esther Glen Award, 2006; Booklist Editors' Choice: Books for Youth, 2006; YALSA Best Books for Young Adults, 2007.

In a world where select people can enter "The Place" and find dreams of every kind to share with others for a fee, a fifteen-year-old girl is training to be a dreamhunter when her father disappears, leaving her to carry on his mysterious mission.

This first of a two-book series is a highly original exploration of the idea of a collective unconscious, mixed with imagery from the raising of Lazarus and with the brave, dark qualities of the psyche of an adolescent female. —*Horn Book Guide*

Frances Foster books

Dreamquake: book two of the Dreamhunter duet. Elizabeth Knox. Farrar, Straus and Giroux, 2007 464 p. (Dreamhunter duet, 2)
Grades: 7 8 9 10

1. Fifteen-year-old girls; 2. Dreams; 3. Parallel universes; 4. Families; 5. Missing persons; 6. Coming-of-age stories; 7. Fantasy fiction; 8. New Zealand fiction
9780374318543

LC 2006048109

Booklist Editors' Choice: Books for Youth, 2007; YALSA Best Books for Young Adults, 2008; Michael L. Printz Honor Book, 2008.

Aided by her family and her creation, Nown, Laura investigates the powerful Regulatory Body's involvement in mysterious disappearances and activities and learns, in the process, the true nature of the Place in which dreams are found.

The author's haunting, invigorating storytelling will leave readers eager to return to its puzzles—and to reap its rewards. —*Booklist*

Frances Foster books.

Mortal fire. Elizabeth Knox. Frances Foster Books, 2013 336 p.
Grades: 7 8 9 10 11

1. Gifted teenagers; 2. Magic; 3. Imprisonment; 4. Genius; 5. Stepbrothers and stepsisters; 6. New Zealand; 7. Islands of the Pacific; 8. 1950s; 9. Fantasy fiction; 10. New Zealand fiction
9780374388294; 9781877579530

LC 2012040872

New Zealand Post Book Awards for Children and Young Adults, Young Adult Fiction Award, 2014; Storylines (New Zealand) Notable Book.

When sixteen-year-old Canny of the Pacific island, Southland, sets out on a trip with her stepbrother and his girlfriend, she finds herself drawn into enchanting Zarene Valley where the mysterious but dark seventeen-year-old Ghislain helps her to figure out her origins.

Knutsson, Catherine

Shadows cast by stars. Catherine Knutsson. Atheneum Books for Young Readers, 2012 320 p.
Grades: 7 8 9 10

1. Native American teenage girls; 2. Spirits; 3. Plague; 4. Dystopias; 5. Indians of North America; 6. Science fiction; 7. Mythological fiction; 8. Canadian fiction.
9781442401914

LC 2011038419

OLA Best Bets, 2012.

To escape a government that needs antigens in aboriginal blood to stop a plague, sixteen-year-old Cassandra and her family flee to the Island, where she not only gets help in communicating with the spirit world, she learns she has been chosen to be their voice and instrument.

Koertge, Ronald

Now playing: Stoner & Spaz II. Ron Koertge. Candlewick Press, 2011 208 p.
Grades: 8 9 10 11 12

1. Teenage boys with disabilities; 2. Teenage girl drug abusers; 3. Documentary filmmakers; 4. Teenage filmmakers; 5. Cerebral palsy; 6. Realistic fiction.
9780763650810

LC 2010040151

Booklist Editors' Choice: Books for Youth, 2011.

High schooler Ben Bancroft, a budding filmmaker with cerebral palsy, struggles to understand his relationship with drug-addict Colleen while he explores a new friendship with A.J, who shares his obsession with movies and makes a good impression on Ben's grandmother.

Koertge writes sharp dialogue and vivid scenes. —*Publishers Weekly*
Sequel to: *Stoner & Spaz.*

Koja, Kathe

★ **Headlong**. Kathe Koja. Farrar, Straus and Giroux, 2008 195 p;
Grades: 8 9 10 11 12

1. Social classes; 2. Boarding schools; 3. Self-perception in teenage girls; 4. High school students; 5. High school sophomores; 6. Realistic fiction; 7. First person narratives
9780374329129

LC 2007023612

High school sophomore Lily opens herself to new possibilities when, despite warnings, she becomes friends with "ghetto girl" Hazel, a new student at the private Vaughn School which Lily, following in her elitist mother's footsteps, has attended since preschool.

Class, identity and friendship are the intersecting subjects of this intelligent novel.... [The author] relays this story with her usual insight and, through her lightning-fast characterizations, an ability to project multiple perspectives simultaneously. —*Publishers Weekly*

Frances Foster books.

Kokie, E. M.

Radical. E. M. Kokie. 2016 437 pages
Grades: 9 10 11 12
1. Lesbian teenagers; 2. Survivalists; 3. Teenage girl/girl relations; 4. Imprisonment; 5. Survival; 6. Michigan; 7. Realistic fiction; 8. LGBTQIA fiction; 9. First person narratives
9780763669621

LC 2016944081

A hard, clear-eyed look at coming of age in a prejudiced world. —*Kirkus*

Konen, Leah

Love and other train wrecks. Leah Konen. Katherine Tegen Books, 2018 320 p.
Grades: 7 8 9 10 11
1. First loves; 2. Teenage romance; 3. Trains; 4. Love; 5. Voyages and travels; 6. Contemporary romances
9780062402509

Noah is a hopeless romantic. He's traveling home for one last chance with his first love, and he needs a miracle to win her back. Ammy doesn't believe in true love—just look at her parents. If there's one thing she's learned about love in the last year, it's that it ends.

An absurdly charming, funny, and romantic odyssey. —*Kirkus*

The **Romantics**. By Leah Konen. Amulet Books, 2016 336 p.
Grades: 8 9 10
1. Children of divorced parents; 2. Breaking up (Interpersonal relations); 3. Love; 4. Teenage romance; 5. Divorce; 6. Contemporary romances; 7. Romantic comedies
9781419721939

LC 2016012076

When his first big relationship crumbles on the heels of his parents' painful separation, seventeen-year-old Gael is heartbroken until Love intervenes.

A smart, snappy look at romance tropes and a feel-good love story all in one. —*Booklist*

Konigsberg, Bill

★ **Honestly** Ben. Bill Konigsberg. Arthur A. Levine Books, 2017 336 p. (Openly straight, 2)
Grades: 7 8 9 10 11 12
1. Boarding school students; 2. Questioning (Sexual or gender identity); 3. Identity (Psychology); 4. Teenage baseball players; 5. Boarding schools; 6. Massachusetts; 7. Realistic fiction; 8. LGBTQIA fiction.
9780545858267; 9780545858335

LC 2016008865

Rainbow List, 2018.

Ben Carver returns for the spring semester at the exclusive Natick School in Massachusetts determined to put his relationship with Rafe Goldberg behind him and concentrate on his grades and the award that

will mean a full scholarship—but Rafe is still there, there is a girl named Hannah whom he meets in the library, and behind it all is his relationship with his distant, but demanding father.

Packed with literary references, pranks, heady conversations, humor, honesty, and tribulation, this is one that will be remembered. A fresh, insightful, inspiring take on what it means to come out. —*Kirkus*

Companion to: *Openly straight*.

★ The **music** of what happens. Bill Konigsberg. Arthur A. Levine Books, 2019 320 p.
Grades: 9 10 11 12
1. Gay teenagers; 2. Hispanic American teenagers; 3. Homophobia; 4. Teenage boy/boy relations; 5. Racism; 6. Phoenix, Arizona; 7. Realistic fiction; 8. LGBTQIA fiction; 9. Multiple perspectives.
9781338215502

LC 2018016859

Booklist Editors' Choice: Books for Youth, 2019.

A cool and popular gay teen who harbors a secret, intense crush and a poetic youth who is looking for Mr. Right in spite of his troubled family weigh what they are willing to risk while working together at an organic food truck during a blistering Arizona summer.

Konigsberg's character-driven novel is expert in revealing the boys growth and changes, as well as examining their innermost thoughts, the evolving nature of their relationship, and the music of what happens in their lives. —*Booklist*

★ **Openly** straight. Bill Konigsberg. Arthur A. Levine Books, 2013 336 p. (Openly straight, 1)
Grades: 8 9 10 11
1. Gay teenagers; 2. Identity (Psychology); 3. Boarding school students; 4. Soccer; 5. Homosexuality; 6. Massachusetts; 7. Realistic fiction; 8. LGBTQIA romances
9780545509893

LC 2012030552

Notable Books for a Global Society, 2014; Rainbow List, 2014; YALSA Best Fiction for Young Adults, 2014.

Tired of being known as "the gay kid, Rafe Goldberg decides to assume a new persona when he comes east and enters an elite Massachusetts prep school—but trying to deny his identity has both complications and unexpected consequences.

Rafe is sick of being the poster child for all things gay at his uber-liberal Colorado high school, so when he gets into a Massachusetts boarding school for his junior year, he decides to reboot himself as openly straight. Konigsberg slyly demonstrates how thoroughly assumptions of straightness are embedded in everyday interactions. For a thought-provoking take on the coming-out story, look no further. —*Horn Book Guide*

Companion book: *Honestly Ben*.

★ The **porcupine** of truth. Bill Konigsberg. Arthur A. Levine Books, 2015 325 pages
Grades: 9 10 11 12
1. Dysfunctional families; 2. Children of alcoholic fathers; 3. African American teenage girls; 4. Lesbian teenagers; 5. Friendship; 6. Montana; 7. Billings, Montana; 8. Realistic fiction
9780545648936; 9780545648943; 9780545754927

LC 2014027136

Booklist Editors' Choice: Books for Youth, 2015; Rainbow List, 2016; Stonewall Book Award for Children's and Young Adult Literature, 2016; YALSA Best Fiction for Young Adults, 2016.

Seventeen-year-old Carson Speier is bored of Billings, Montana, and resentful that he has to help his mother take care of his father, a dying alcoholic whom he has not seen in fourteen years—but then he meets Aisha, a beautiful African American girl who has run away from her own difficult family, and together they embark on a journey of discovery that may help them both come to terms with their lives.

Visiting small-town Montana to care for his long-absent alcoholic father, also the child of estranged parents, Carson becomes obsessed with discovering the reason for his grandfather's abandonment. New friend Aisha, homeless since coming out to her family, joins his cross-country scavenger hunt. Smart-alecky dialogue and quirky roadside characters lighten the commentary on religion, secrets, family, and forgiveness. —*Horn Book Guide*

Konigsburg, E. L.
Silent to the bone. E. L. Konigsburg. Atheneum Books for Young Readers, 2000 261 p.
Grades: 7 8 9 10
1. Elective mutism; 2. Thirteen-year-old boys; 3. Emotional problems; 4. Traffic accident victims — Family relationships; 5. Remarriage; 6. Realistic fiction
9780689836015

LC 20043
New York Times Notable Children's Book, 2000; Booklist Editors' Choice: Books for Youth, 2000; YALSA Best Books for Young Adults, 2001; School Library Journal Best Books, 2000.

When he is wrongly accused of gravely injuring his baby half-sister, thirteen-year-old Branwell loses his power of speech and only his friend Connor is able to reach him and uncover the truth about what really happened.

A compelling mystery that is also a moving story of family, friendship, and seduction. —*Booklist*

A Jean Karl book.

Korman, Gordon
★ The **juvie** three. By Gordon Korman. Hyperion, 2008 256 p.
Grades: 7 8 9 10
1. Group homes; 2. Juvenile delinquents; 3. Cooperation; 4. Second chances; 5. Juvenile detention; 6. New York City; 7. Realistic fiction; 8. Canadian fiction.
9781423101581; 9781423101628; 9781443157469
LC 2008019087
YALSA Popular Paperbacks for Young Adults, 2015.

Gecko, Arjay, and Terence, all in trouble with the law, must find a way to keep their halfway house open in order to stay out of juvenile detention.

Korman keeps lots of balls in the air as he handles each boy's distinct voice and characteras well as the increasingly absurd situationwith humor and flashes of sadness. —*Booklist*

★ **Son** of the mob. Gordon Korman. Hyperion, 2002 262 p;
Grades: 7 8 9 10
1. Organized crime; 2. Seventeen-year-old girls; 3. Teenage boys; 4. Teenage boy/girl relations; 5. Crime bosses; 6. New York City; 7. Realistic fiction; 8. Canadian fiction; 9. Books for reluctant readers
9780786807697; 9780786826162; 9780439967556
LC 2002068672
Grand Canyon Reader Award (Arizona), Teen Book Category, 2007; Heartland Award, 2004; Kentucky Bluegrass Award for Grades 9-12, 2005; YALSA Popular Paperbacks for Young Adults, 2012; Young Reader's Choice Award (Pacific Northwest), Intermediate, 2005; YALSA Quick Picks for Reluctant Young Adult Readers, 2003; YALSA Best Books for Young Adults, 2003.

Seventeen-year-old Vince's life is constantly complicated by the fact that he is the son of a powerful Mafia boss, a relationship that threatens to destroy his romance with the daughter of an FBI agent.

The fast-paced, tightly focused story addresses the problems of being an honest kid in a family of outlawsand loving them anyway. Korman doesn't ignore the seamier side of mob life, but even when the subject matter gets violent...he keeps things light by relating his tale in the first-person voice of a humorously sarcastic yet law-abiding wise guy. —*Horn Book Guide*

Sequel: *Son of the mob: Hollywood hustle.*

Kostick, Conor
Edda. Conor Kostick. Viking, 2011 440 p. (Avatar chronicles, 3)
Grades: 7 8 9 10
1. Weapons; 2. Computer games; 3. Independence (Personal quality); 4. Fantasy games — Computer methods; 5. Role playing; 6. Science fiction.
9780670012183
LC 2011003000
In the virtual world of Edda, ruler Scanthax decides he wants to invade another virtual world, embroiling the universes of Edda, Saga, and Epic in war, with only three teenagers to try to restore peace.

Humans, electronic beings and servers are separated by light years and metaphysics, but Kostick's action-filled series conclusion is immediate and relevant. —*Kirkus*

★ **Epic**. Conor Kostick. Viking, 2007 320 p. (Avatar chronicles, 1)
Grades: 7 8 9 10
1. Computer games; 2. Fantasy games — Computer methods; 3. Exile (Punishment); 4. Role playing; 5. Role playing games; 6. Dystopian fiction; 7. Science fiction
9780670061792
LC 2006019958
School Library Journal Best Books, 2007; YALSA Popular Paperbacks for Young Adults, 2011.

On New Earth, a world based on a video role-playing game, fourteen-year-old Erik pursuades his friends to aid him in some unusual gambits in order to save Erik's father from exile and safeguard the futures of each of their families.

There is intrigue and mystery throughout this captivating page-turner. Veins of moral and ethical social situations and decisions provide some great opportunities for discussion. Well written and engaging. —*School Library Journal*

Sequel: *Saga*

Saga. Conor Kostick. Penguin, 2008 368 p. (Avatar chronicles, 2)
Grades: 7 8 9 10
1. Computer games; 2. Fantasy games — Computer methods; 3. Immortality; 4. Women rulers; 5. Role playing; 6. Dystopian fiction; 7. Science fiction
9780670062805
As the Dark Queen and controller of Saga sets out to enslave the people of New Earth, Ghost and his street hacker airboard gang of friends must find a way to stop her before the world they have always known is gone forever.

The plot and pacing are near perfect in this tale of a world cramped by fear and tradition.... Compulsively readable and palpable (the descriptions of airboarding are a near-physical experience), it will appeal to SF fans across the board. —*Voice of Youth Advocates*

Sequel to: *Epic*

Kraus, Daniel
At the edge of empire. Daniel Kraus. Simon & Schuster, 2015 688 p. (Death and life of Zebulon Finch, 1)
Grades: 9 10 11 12

1. Undead; 2. Redemption; 3. Seventeen-year-old boys; 4. Soldiers; 5. Gangsters; 6. Horror; 7. Historical fiction.
9781481411394

A hefty volume for fans of historical fiction with an undead twist. —*School Library Journal*

Krisher, Trudy

Fallout. Holiday House, 2006 364 p.
Grades: 7 8 9 10

1. Nonconformists; 2. Teenage nonconformists; 3. Teenage poets; 4. Teenage girls; 5. Teenagers; 6. North Carolina; 7. 1950s; 8. Coming-of-age stories; 9. Historical fiction.
9780823420353

This is an excellent novel for teens searching for a good story with a well-paced and action-filled plot that challenges them to think about the importance of voicing their opinions. —*School Library Journal*

Kristoff, Jay

Dev1at3. Jay Kristoff. Knopf Books for Young Readers, 2019 448 p.
(Lifel1k3, 2)
Grades: 8 9 10 11

1. Former friends; 2. Robots; 3. Identity (Psychology); 4. Memory; 5. Secrets; 6. Science fiction; 7. Science fiction thrillers; 8. Apocalyptic fiction.
9781524713966; 9781524713973; 9781760295714, Paperback, Australia

While Eve searches for the real Ana Monrova in the hope of creating an army of lifelikes, her former best friend, Lemon, joins a group of people with genetic powers like her own only to discover that not all of her new associates are trustworthy.

The author delights in futuristic slang that may be a way into the book for teens who don't think they like sci-fi or fantasy. —*Booklist*

Lifel1k3. Jay Kristoff. Knopf Books for Young Readers, 2018 416 p.
(Lifel1k3, 1)
Grades: 7 8 9 10 11 12

1. Memory; 2. Robots; 3. Secrets; 4. Paranormal phenomena; 5. Islands; 6. Science Fiction; 7. Science fiction thrillers; 8. Apocalyptic fiction.
9781524713928, hardback, US; 9781524713935, hardback, US; 9781760295691, Paperback, Australia

Aurealis Awards, Best Science Fiction Novel, 2018; Librarians' Choice (Australia), 2018; YALSA Best Fiction for Young Adults, 2019.

Kuehn, Stephanie

★ **Charm** & strange. Stephanie Kuehn. St. Martin's Griffin, 2013 216 p.
Grades: 9 10 11 12

1. Emotional abuse; 2. Boarding school students; 3. Mental illness; 4. Sex crimes; 5. Secrets; 6. Vermont; 7. Virginia
9781250021946; 9781250021939, ebook, US

LC 2013003247

William C. Morris YA Debut Award, 2014; YALSA Popular Paperbacks for Young Adults, 2016.

A lonely teenager exiled to a remote Vermont boarding school in the wake of a family tragedy must either surrender his sanity to the wild wolves inside his mind or learn that surviving means more than not dying.

Kuehn...keeps us on constant edge regarding exactly what genre of book it is that we're reading. —*Booklist*

Complicit. Stephanie Kuehn. St. Martin's Griffin, 2014 224 pages
Grades: 8 9 10 11 12

1. Amnesia; 2. Adopted teenagers; 3. Mental illness; 4. Brothers and sisters; 5. Private schools; 6. California; 7. Psychological suspense; 8. First person narratives
9781250044594; 9781250044600; 9781466843059, ebook, US

LC 2014008117

YALSA Best Fiction for Young Adults, 2015; YALSA Popular Paperbacks for Young Adults, 2017.

Jamie's mother was murdered when he was six, about seven years later his sister Cate was incarcerated for burning down a neighbor's barn, and now Jamie, fifteen, learns that Cate has been released and is coming back for him, blaming him for all the bad things that led to her arrest.

...every page shows a firm, surprising choice, whether you like it or not. Cate, naturally, is the main event, the alternatingly irrational, gentle, explosive, and enigmatic center of this fast, black whirlpool of a novel. —*Booklist*

Delicate monsters. Stephanie Kuehn. St. Martin's Griffin, 2015 240 p.
Grades: 10 11 12

1. Guilt; 2. Visions; 3. Missing persons; 4. Teenage boy/girl relations; 5. Brothers; 6. California; 7. Psychological fiction; 8. Multiple perspectives
9781250063847

Like her previous YA novels, Kuehn's latest benefits from tight construction, expert pacing, and voices that ring especially true for contemporary teenagers, particularly Sadie's entrancing, gleefully acerbic tone. Intelligent, compulsively readable literary fiction with a dark twist. —*Booklist*

When I am through with you. Stephanie Kuehn. Dutton Books, 2017 304 p.
Grades: 9 10 11 12

1. Hiking; 2. Teenage prisoners; 3. Survival; 4. Teenage boy/girl relations; 5. Teenagers; 6. California; 7. Northern California; 8. Thrillers and suspense
9781101994733; 9781101994740, ebook, US

LC 2016040902

A simple mountain hike in northern California turns deadly for a group of high school students, one of whom has killed before.

Full of secrets and plot twists, Kuehn's latest is a satisfying, sophisticated study in complicated relationships. —*Kirkus*

Kuhn, Sarah

I love you so mochi. Sarah Kuhn. Scholastic Press, 2019 320 pages
Grades: 8 9 10 11 12

1. Asian American teenage girls; 2. Self-discovery in teenage girls; 3. Grandparents; 4. Family problems; 5. Dating (Social customs); 6. Japan; 7. Teen chick lit; 8. Romantic comedies; 9. First person narratives
9781338302882

Eagerly visiting her estranged grandparents in Japan to distance herself from the mother who disapproves of her fashion ambitions, a talented young designer immerses herself in Kyoto's markets and cherry blossom festival and bonds with a cute med student while uncovering illuminating family secrets.

Kuhn...has brought together travel, fashion, food, romance, and family to create an incredibly sweet and heartwarming coming of age romantic comedy. weaving in Japanese vocabulary and slang, she also subtly addresses racism and differences between Japanese and Japanese-American cultures. —*Kirkus*

Kwaymullina, Ambelin

The **things** she's seen. By Ambelin Kwaymullina and Ezekiel Kwaymullina. 2019 208 p.

Grades: 7 8 9 10 11 12

1. Dead; 2. Murder; 3. Racism; 4. Aboriginal Australians; 5. Grief in men; 6. Australia; 7. Psychological suspense; 8. Paranormal fiction; 9. Multiple perspectives.

9781984849373; 9781984848789; 9781760631628, Paperback, Australia; 9780241380079, Paperback, UK

Aurealis Awards, Best Young Adult Novel, 2018; Children's Book Council of Australia: Notable Australian Children's Book, 2019; Librarians' Choice (Australia), 2018; Victorian Premier's Literary Awards, Prize for Young Adult Fiction, 2019; USBBY Outstanding International Books, 2020.

Nothing's been the same for Beth Teller since she died. Her dad, a detective, is the only one who can see and hear her—and he's drowning in grief. But now they have a mystery to solve together regarding a fire at a children's home. As Beth unravels the mystery, she finds a shocking story lurking beneath the surface of a small town, and a friendship that lasts beyond one life and into another. Told in two unforgettable voices, this gripping novel interweaves themes of grief, colonial history, violence, love and family.

L'Engle, Madeleine

★ A **wrinkle** in time. Madeleine L'Engle. Farrar, Straus, and Giroux, 1962 211 p. (Time quintet, 1)

Grades: 5 6 7 8 9 10

1. Time travel; 2. Father-separated children; 3. Brothers and sisters; 4. Space and time; 5. Rescues; 6. Science fiction; 7. Classics; 8. Books to movies

9780374386139; 9780141354934, print, UK

LC 62007203

Newbery Medal, 1963.

Meg and Charles Wallace set out with their friend Calvin in a search for their father. His top secret job as a physicist for the government has taken him away and the children search through time and space to find him.

This book makes unusual demands on the imagination and consequently gives great rewards. —*Horn Book Guide*

Sequel: *A Wind in the Door.*

LaBan, Elizabeth

The **Tragedy** Paper. Elizabeth LaBan. Alfred A. Knopf, 2013 272 p.

Grades: 7 8 9 10 11 12

1. Boarding school students; 2. Albinos and albinism; 3. Research papers; 4. Teenage boy/girl relations; 5. Boarding schools; 6. Realistic fiction; 7. Coming-of-age stories.

9780375970405

LC 2012011294

YALSA Best Fiction for Young Adults, 2014.

While preparing for the most dreaded assignment at the prestigious Irving School, the Tragedy Paper, Duncan gets wrapped up in the tragic tale of Tim Macbeth, a former student who had a clandestine relationship with the wrong girl, and his own ill-fated romance with Daisy.

LaCour, Nina

Everything leads to you. Nina Lacour. Penguin Group USA, 2014 304 p.

Grades: 9 10 11 12

1. Interns; 2. Lesbians — Interpersonal relations; 3. Film industry and trade; 4. Motion picture art directors; 5. Lesbian teenagers; 6. Hollywood, California; 7. Los Angeles, California; 8. LGBTQIA romances; 9. Coming-of-age stories; 10. Realistic fiction.

9780525425885

Rainbow List, 2015; YALSA Best Fiction for Young Adults, 2015.

Eighteen-year-old production design intern Emi is getting over her first love and trying to establish her place in the Los Angeles film industry...When she and her best friend Charlotte find a letter hidden in the possessions of a recently deceased Hollywood film legend at an estate sale, they begin searching for its intended recipient. Eventually that leads to Ava, a beautiful teen to whom Emi is immediately attracted. ... This one is highly enjoyable and highly recommended. —*School Library Journal*

Hold still. Nina LaCour; with illustrations by Mia Nolting. Dutton Books, 2009 229 p.

Grades: 9 10 11 12

1. Survivors of suicide victims; 2. Loss (Psychology); 3. Grief in teenage girls; 4. Grief; 5. Bereavement; 6. San Francisco, California; 7. Realistic fiction; 8. First person narratives.

9780525421559

YALSA Best Books for Young Adults, 2010.

Interspersed with drawings and journal entries, the story of Caitlin's journey through her grief is both heart-wrenching and realistic.... LaCour strikes a new path through a familiar story, leading readers with her confident writing and savvy sense of prose. —*Kirkus*

★ **Watch** over me. Nina LaCour. Dutton Books, 2020 272 p.

Grades: 9 10 11 12

1. Former foster children; 2. Internship programs; 3. Psychic trauma; 4. Farms; 5. Tutors; 6. California; 7. Psychological fiction; 8. First person narratives

9780593108970

A newly graduated Mila emerges from foster care to accept a job on an isolated Northern California Coast farm where she confronts haunting memories and the traumas of her fellow residents.

Printz Medalist LaCour's (We Are Okay) portrait of a young woman yearning to belong and facing her past while navigating the liminal space between childhood and adulthood brims with tender moments and sensory details. —*Publishers Weekly*

★ **We** are okay: a novel. By Nina LaCour. Dutton Books, 2017 234 p.

Grades: 8 9 10 11 12

1. Women college students; 2. Best friends; 3. Grief; 4. College freshmen; 5. Mexican American teenage girls; 6. New York (State); 7. Realistic fiction; 8. LGBTQIA fiction; 9. First person narratives

9780525425892; 9780702262562, Paperback, Australia

Booklist Editors' Choice: Books for Youth, 2017; Michael L. Printz Award, 2018; YALSA Best Fiction for Young Adults, 2018; Rainbow List, 2018.

After leaving her life behind to go to college in New York, Marin must face the truth about the tragedy that happened in the final weeks of summer when her friend Mabel comes to visit.

Though there's little action, with most of the writing devoted to Marin's memories, thoughts, and musings, the author's nuanced and sensitive depiction of the protagonist's complex and turbulent inner life makes for a rich narrative. Marin is a beautifully crafted character, and her voice is spot-on, conveying isolation, grief, and, eventually, hope. —*School Library Journal*

You know me well. Nina LaCour and David Levithan. St. Martin's Griffin, 2016 256 p.

Grades: 9 10 11 12

1. Gay teenagers; 2. Lesbian teenagers; 3. Unrequited love; 4. Friendship; 5. Crushes (Interpersonal relations); 6. San Francisco, California; 7. Realistic fiction; 8. LGBTQIA fiction; 9. Multiple perspectives

9781250098641; 9781925355529, print, Australia
YALSA Best Fiction for Young Adults, 2017; Rainbow List, 2017.

A once-upon-a-time reminder that life sucks and love stinks but ain't they grand? Kirkus.

LaFaye, A.
Stella stands alone. A. LaFaye. Simon & Schuster Books for Young Readers, 2008 245 p. : Map
Grades: 7 8 9 10
1. Teenage girl orphans; 2. Plantations; 3. Reconstruction (United States history); 4. Swindlers and swindling; 5. Freed slaves; 6. Mississippi; 7. 1860s; 8. Alternative histories.
9781416911647
LC 2007038725

Fourteen-year-old Stella, orphaned just after the Civil War, fights to keep her family's plantation and fulfill her father's desire to turn the land over to the people who have worked on it for generations, but first she must find her father's hidden deed and will.

Readers will be drawn along by Stella's refusal to act helpless and sweet and her discovery of strength and kindness in unexpected places. The sadness and anger, and the wrenching legacy of slavery are present throughout. —*Booklist*

LaFevers, R. L.
Dark triumph. By Robin LaFevers. Houghton Mifflin, Houghton Mifflin Harcourt, 2013 400 p. (His fair assassin, 2)
Grades: 9 10 11 12
1. Assassins; 2. Political corruption; 3. Courts and courtiers; 4. Convents; 5. Death (Personification); 6. Brittany, France; 7. France; 8. 15th century; 9. Historical fantasy
9780547628387
LC 2012033555

School Library Journal Best Books, 2013; YALSA Best Fiction for Young Adults, 2014.

The extremely damaged Lady Sybella serves Mortain, the god of Death, by killing those who have been "marqued" by His hand. When Sybella is ordered back to her childhood home (and personal hell) to spy on her wicked father, she waits hopefully for the order to kill him—but Mortain has other plans and instead orders her to rescue her father's enemy, the Beast of Waroch. Set in 15th-century France, this story is packed with action, adventure, and unexpected romance.

LaFevers weaves the 'crazed, tangled web' of Sybella's life...with force, suspense and subtle tenderness. The prose's beauty inspires immediate re-reads of many a sentence, but its forward momentum is irresistible. An intricate, masterful page-turner about politics, treachery, religion, love and healing. —*Kirkus*

Grave mercy. Robin Lafevers. Houghton Mifflin, 2012 416 p. (His fair assassin, 1)
Grades: 9 10 11 12
1. Assassins; 2. Political corruption; 3. Courts and courtiers; 4. Convents; 5. Poisoning; 6. Brittany, France; 7. France; 8. 15th century; 9. Historical fantasy
9780547628349; 9780544022492
Booklist Editors' Choice: Books for Youth, 2012; School Library Journal Best Books, 2012; YALSA Best Fiction for Young Adults, 2013.

In the fifteenth-century kingdom of Brittany, seventeen-year-old Ismae escapes from the brutality of an arranged marriage into the sanctuary of the convent of St. Mortain, where she learns that the god of Death has blessed her with dangerous gifts—and a violent destiny.

★ **Mortal** heart. By Robin LaFevers. 2014 464 p. (His fair assassin, 3)
Grades: 9 10 11 12
1. Assassins; 2. Convents; 3. Courts and courtiers; 4. Nuns; 5. Death (Personification); 6. Brittany, France; 7. France; 8. 15th century; 9. Historical fantasy
9780547628400
LC 2014001877

LibraryReads Favorites, 2014; School Library Journal Best Books: Fiction, 2014; YALSA Best Fiction for Young Adults, 2015.

This thrilling series conclusion narrates the fate of 17-year-old convent-raised Annith who impatiently awaits her assignment to serve as the god Mortain's Handmaiden of Death...The protagonists' sometimes-contradictory natures enrich their characters, and the intertwined relationships of realistic and Netherworld personages add depth to their personal stories. A plethora of strong females and their romantic relationships will have wide appeal for teens, making this a definite purchase where *Grave Mercy* (2012) and *Dark Triumph* (2013, both Houghton Harcourt) are popular and a strong story that can stand on its own. —*School Library Journal*

Lai, Thanhha
★ **Butterfly** yellow. Thanhha Lai. Harper, 2019 284 pages;
Grades: 8 9 10 11 12
1. Separated friends, relatives, etc; 2. Refugees; 3. Reunions; 4. Vietnamese in the United States; 5. Brothers and sisters; 6. Texas; 7. 1980s; 8. Historical fiction.
9780062229212, HRD, US; 9780062229229, paperback, US; 9780062229236, ebook, US; 9780702262890, Paperback, Australia
Booklist Editors' Choice: Books for Youth, 2019; Scott O'Dell Historical Fiction Award, 2020.

A Vietnam War refugee in Texas partners with a rodeo aspirant to track down the younger brother she was forced to leave behind before discovering that he no longer remembers her.

Remarkable. Told with ample grace, Lai's finely drawn narrative and resilient characters offer a memorable, deeply felt view of the Vietnam War's impact. —*Publishers Weekly*

Lake, Nick
★ **Hostage** Three. By Nick Lake. Bloomsbury, 2013 320 p.
Grades: 9 10 11 12
1. Hostages; 2. Pirates; 3. Yachts; 4. Survival; 5. Crushes in teenage girls; 6. Survival stories; 7. Adventure stories; 8. First person narratives
9781619631236; 9781408828212
LC 2013002686

School Library Journal Best Books, 2013; YALSA Best Fiction for Young Adults, 2014.

Seventeen-year-old Amy, her father, and her stepmother become hostages when Somalian pirates seize their yacht, but although she builds a bond with one of her captors it becomes brutally clear that the price of life and its value are two very different things.

The last way seventeen-year-old Amy wants to spend the summer after high school is sailing around the world with her father and new stepmother. When Somali pirates hijack the family's yacht, the sullen, entitled teen forms a surprising bond with one of their captors. Lake's sensitive character development and sophisticated storytelling (including alternate endings) helps elicit readers' sympathies for his complex characters. —*Horn Book Guide*

In darkness. By Nick Lake. Bloomsbury, 2012 341 p.
Grades: 8 9 10 11 12

1. Toussaint Louverture, 1743-1803; 2. Gang members; 3. Separated friends, relatives, etc; 4. Earthquakes; 5. Survival (after earthquakes); 6. Haiti Earthquake, Haiti, 2010; 7. Haiti; 8. First person narratives. 9781599907437; 9781408824184, UK; 9781408819944, UK; 9781471204173, UK; 9781408819975, UK

LC 2011022350

Michael L. Printz Award, 2013; YALSA Best Fiction for Young Adults, 2013.

In the aftermath of the Haitian earthquake, fifteen-year-old Shorty, a poor gang member from the slums of Site Soleil, is trapped in the rubble of a ruined hospital, and as he grows weaker he has visions and memories of his life of violence, his lost twin sister, and of Toussaint L'Ouverture, who liberated Haiti from French rule in the 1804.

Lanagan, Margo
Black juice. Margo Lanagan. Eos, 2005 208 p.
Grades: 7 8 9 10

1. Life change events; 2. Personal conduct; 3. Human nature; 4. Good and evil; 5. Brothers and sisters; 6. Short stories; 7. Australian fiction. 9780060743901; 9780060743918; 9780575079243, print, UK

LC 2004008715

USBBY Outstanding International Book, 2006; Victorian Premier's Literary Awards, Prize for Young Adult Fiction, 2004; YALSA Best Books for Young Adults, 2006; Michael L. Printz Honor Book, 2006.

Provides glimpses of the dark side of civilization and the beauty of the human spirit through ten short stories that explore significant moments in people's lives, events leading to them, and their consequences.

This book will satisfy readers hungry for intelligent, literary fantasies that effectively twist facets of our everyday world into something alien. —*School Library Journal*

★ **Tender** morsels. Margo Lanagan. Alfred A. Knopf, 2008 224 p.
Grades: 10 11 12

1. Supernatural; 2. Parallel universes; 3. Mothers and daughters; 4. Good and evil; 5. Rape; 6. Fantasy fiction; 7. Fairy tale and folklore-inspired fiction; 8. Australian fiction
9780375848117

Booklist Editors' Choice: Books for Youth, 2008; Ditmar Award, 2009; World Fantasy Award, 2009; YALSA Best Books for Young Adults, 2009; YALSA Popular Paperbacks for Young Adults, 2016; School Library Journal Best Books, 2008; Michael L. Printz Honor Book, 2009.

A young woman who has endured unspeakable cruelties is magically granted a safe haven apart from the real world and allowed to raise her two daughters in this alternate reality, until the barrier between her world and the real one begins to break down.

The author touches on nightmarish adult themes, including multiple rape scenarios and borderline human-animal sexual interactions, which reserve this for the most mature readers.... Drawing alternate worlds that blur the line between wonder and horror, and characters who traverse the nature of human and beast, this challenging, unforgettable work explores the ramifications of denying the most essential and often savage aspects of life. —*Booklist*

Lancaster, Mike A.
The **future** we left behind. Mike A. Lancaster. Egmont USA, 2012 384 p.
Grades: 7 8 9 10

1. Technological innovations; 2. Human/computer interaction; 3. Scientists; 4. Superhuman abilities; 5. Computer programs; 6. England; 7. Science fiction.
9781606844106; 9781606844113

LC 2012003794

A thousand years after the release of the Straker Tapes, when Peter and Alpha discover that stories of human upgrades are true, they strive to stop a group of scientists from making a decision that could destroy humanity.

Sequel to: *Human.4*.

Landers, Melissa
Starflight. Melissa Landers. Hyperion, 2016 368 p. (Starflight, 1)
Grades: 10 11 12

1. Space vehicles; 2. Space flight; 3. Teenage girl orphans; 4. Rich teenage boys; 5. Criminals; 6. Science fiction; 7. Multiple perspectives
9781484723241

Desperate to relocate to an off-world place where nobody cares about her humble working status or her criminal past, Solara Brooks indentures herself to a rich bully who pretends to be her servant on a starship full of eccentric crewmates after he is framed for conspiracy on Earth

Landers has a firm hand on the plot, which includes a rousing fight scene or two, as well as a nifty twist at the end. —*Booklist*

Landman, Tanya
★ **Hell** and high water. Tanya Landman. 2017 320 p;
Grades: 7 8 9 10

1. Multiracial persons; 2. Fathers — Death; 3. Family secrets; 4. Poor people; 5. Prejudice; 6. Devon, England; 7. 18th century; 8. Georgian era (1714-1837); 9. Historical mysteries; 10. Coming-of-age stories.
9780763688752; 9781406356618, (hbk.) (London); 9781406366914, print, UK

Set in eighteenth-century Devon, this is the story of Caleb, the son of a poor puppeteer. When his father is wrongfully accused of theft and sentenced to transportation, Caleb is left all alone in the world. As a mixed race boy living in an age of slavery, he has always been treated with fear and mistrust. Without his father he is more vulnerable than ever, and is forced to seek out his estranged aunt. After a body washes up on a nearby beach, a shattered Caleb finds himself involved in a dastardly plot: a plot that places him and his newfound family in mortal danger.

Murder and mystery abound in this engrossing and atmospheric tale set in 18th-century England. —*Kirkus*

Lane, Dakota
Gothic Lolita. Dakota Lane. Atheneum Books for Young Readers, 2008 208 p.
Grades: 8 9 10 11 12

1. Sixteen-year-old girls; 2. Grief in teenage girls; 3. Girls — Identity; 4. Blogs; 5. Grief; 6. Hollywood, California; 7. Japan; 8. Realistic fiction
9781416913962

LC 2008015390

Sixteen-year-olds Chelsea and Miya have a lot in common, from their love of blogging, loss of loved ones, and the Shonin rainbow warrior books, to nationalities, even though they are half-way across the world from each other.

Lane focuses on two half-Japanese, half-American girls who forge an unusual bond over their blogs, loneliness and fascination with the gothic Lolita subculture. Chelsea is in L.A. and Miya is in Japan.... Readers will find themselves quickly engrossed. —*Publishers Weekly*

Ginee Seo books.

Lange, Erin Jade
Butter. Erin Jade Lange. Bloomsbury, 2012 296 p;
Grades: 8 9 10 11 12

1. Overweight teenage boys; 2. Obesity; 3. Loneliness in teenage boys; 4. Loneliness; 5. Internet; 6. Arizona; 7. Scottsdale, Arizona; 8. Realistic fiction.
9781599907802

LC 2011045509

Unable to control his binge eating, a morbidly obese teenager nick-named Butter decides to make a live webcast of his last meal as he attempts to eat himself to death.

Dead ends. By Erin Jade Lange. Bloomsbury, 2013 336 p.
Grades: 8 9 10
1. Father-separated teenage boys; 2. Teenagers with Down syndrome; 3. Bullying and bullies; 4. Friendship; 5. Single-parent families; 6. Missouri; 7. Realistic fiction.
9781619630802; 9780571308828, print, UK; 9780571308293, print, UK; 9781619630819, ebook, US

LC 2013009593

When Dane, a bully, refuses to hit Billy D because he has Down syndrome, Billy takes that as a sign of friendship and enlists Dane's help in solving riddles left in an atlas by his missing father, sending the pair on a risky adventure.

Lange writes realistically about teens with rough lives, and readers will believe in the friendships, feel Billy's pain of abandonment, and appreciate the honesty of the not-tied-up-with-a-bow ending. —*School Library Journal*

Larbalestier, Justine
★ **Liar**. By Justine Larbalestier. Bloomsbury, 2009 376 p.
Grades: 9 10 11 12
1. African American teenage girls; 2. Truthfulness and falsehood; 3. Murder; 4. Dishonesty in teenage girls; 5. Dishonesty; 6. First person narratives; 7. Thrillers and suspense; 8. Paranormal fiction
9781599903057; 9781742375380, Australia

LC 2009012581

Davitt Awards, Best YA Novel, 2010; Western Australian Premier's Book Awards, Young Adult category, 2009; YALSA Popular Paperbacks for Young Adults, 2016; YALSA Best Books for Young Adults, 2010; School Library Journal Best Books, 2009.

Micah is an admitted compulsive liar—and a suspect in the case of her boyfriend's Zach's murder. Now she says she wants to come clean and tell the whole, true story of her family, her special talents, and what happened to Zach. But when someone lies all the time, about everything, it can take a while to get to the real story...and you may not recognize it when you hear it.

Micah's narrative is convincing, and in the end readers will delve into the psyche of a troubled teen and decide for themselves the truths and lies. This one is sure to generate discussion. —*School Library Journal*

★ **My** sister Rosa. Justine Larbalestier. Soho Teen, 2016 320 p.
Grades: 9 10 11 12
1. Psychopaths; 2. Brothers and sisters; 3. Deception; 4. Australians in the United States; 5. Moving to a new country; 6. New York City; 7. Psychological suspense; 8. Australian fiction.
9781616956745; 9781760112226, paperback, Australia
Adelaide Festival Awards (South Australia), YA Fiction Award, 2018; YALSA Best Fiction for Young Adults, 2017.

When his father's business takes the family to New York City, a seventeen-year-old Australian boy must balance his desire to protect his ten-year-old sister, a diagnosable psychopath, from the world with the desperate need to protect the world from her.

Larbalestier's novel is a slow boil, moody and tense, with just the right amount of creep factor and a casually diverse cast of characters (Leilani is half-Korean, half-white; her girlfriend's best friend is black and gender-fluid; and Sojourner is a black, sexually experienced Chris-

tian)... Che's journey toward self-awareness is at times enlightening, at times devastating, and the threat of violence from Rosa is suspenseful and truly terrifying. —*Horn Book Guide*

Razorhurst. Justine Larbalestier. Soho Teen, 2015 320 p.
Grades: 9 10 11 12
1. Organized crime; 2. Ghosts; 3. Criminals; 4. Spirits; 5. Paranormal phenomena; 6. Sydney, New South Wales; 7. Australia; 8. 1930s; 9. Urban fantasy; 10. Historical fantasy; 11. Australian fiction.
9781616955441; 9781743319437, paperback, Australia; 9781616955458, ebook, US
Aurealis Awards, Best Horror Novel, 2014; Children's Book Council of Australia: Notable Australian Children's Book; YALSA Best Fiction for Young Adults, 2016.

In 1932, in Sydney's deadly Razorhurst neighborhood, where crime and razor-wielding men rule, two girls with contrasting lives who share the ability to see ghosts meet over a dead body and find themselves on the run from mob bosses.

Larbalestier pulls no punches with the gruesome, gory details about the violence of poverty, and the result is a dark, unforgettable and blood-soaked tale of outlaws and masterminds. —*Kirkus*
Originally published in Australia by Allen and Unwin in 2014.

Team Human. Justine Larbalestier and Sarah Rees Brennan. HarperTeen, 2012 368 p.
Grades: 8 9 10 11 12
1. Vampires; 2. Crushes in teenage girls; 3. Best friends; 4. Teenage romance; 5. High schools; 6. Maine; 7. Urban fantasy; 8. Humorous stories
9780062089649

LC 2011026149

YALSA Best Fiction for Young Adults, 2013.

Residing in New Whitby, Maine, a town founded by vampires trying to escape persecution, Mel finds her negative attitudes challenged when her best friend falls in love with one, another friend's father runs off with one, and she herself is attracted to someone who tries to pass himself off as one.

Laskas, Gretchen Moran
The **miner's** daughter. Gretchen Moran Laskas. Simon & Schuster Books for Young Readers, 2007 256 p.
Grades: 8 9 10 11 12
1. Coal mines and mining; 2. Coal miners; 3. Sixteen-year-old girls; 4. Teenage girls; 5. Teenagers; 6. West Virginia; 7. Arthurdale, West Virginia; 8. Depression era (1929-1941); 9. 1930s; 10. Coming-of-age stories; 11. Historical fiction.
9781416912620

LC 2006000684

Sixteen-year-old Willa, living in a Depression-era West Virginia mining town, works hard to help her family, experiences love and friendship, and finds an outlet for her writing when her family becomes part of the Arthurdale, West Virginia, community supported by Eleanor Roosevelt.

Richly drawn characters and plot make this an excellent novel that explores the struggles endured by many in America in the 1930s. —*School Library Journal*

Laskin, Pamela L.
Ronit & Jamil. Pamela L. Laskin. Katherine Tegen Books, 2017 240 p.
Grades: 7 8 9 10 11 12
1. Israeli-Palestinian relations; 2. Teenage romance; 3. Muslim boys; 4. Jewish girls; 5. Israel; 6. Shakespeare- inspired fiction; 7. Novels in verse; 8. Contemporary romances

9780062458544

Ronit, an Israeli girl, lives on one side of the fence. Jamil, a Palestinian boy, lives on the other side. Only miles apart but separated by generations of conflict—much more than just the concrete blockade between them. Their fathers, however, work in a distrusting but mutually beneficial business arrangement, a relationship that brings Ronit and Jamil together. And lightning strikes. The kind of lightning that transcends barrier fences, war, and hatred.

At once romantic and revealing, an important window into contemporary conditions in the Middle East. —*Kirkus*

Latham, Jennifer
   Dreamland burning. By Jennifer Latham. 2017 384 p.
Grades: 8 9 10 11 12
   1. Teenage detectives; 2. Murder; 3. Racism; 4. Skeleton; 5. Amateur detectives; 6. Tulsa, Oklahoma; 7. Mysteries; 8. Parallel narratives; 9. Multiple perspectives.
9780316384933; 9780316384926, ebook, US; 9780316384940, ebook, US
                              LC 2015049682
YALSA Quick Picks for Reluctant Young Adult Readers, 2018.

When Rowan finds a skeleton on her family's property, investigating the brutal, century-old murder leads to painful discoveries about the past. Alternating chapters tell the story of William, another teen grappling with the racial firestorm leading up to the 1921 Tulsa race riot, providing some clues to the mystery.

An unflinching, superbly written story about family, friendship, and integrity, set during one of America's deadliest race riots. —*Kirkus*

   Scarlett undercover. Jennifer Latham. 2015 320 p.
Grades: 9 10 11 12
   1. Teenage girl detectives; 2. Genies; 3. Curses; 4. Muslim teenagers; 5. Supernatural; 6. Supernatural mysteries; 7. Books for reluctant readers
9780316283939; 9780316283892, ebook, US; 9780316283953, ebook, US
                              LC 2014013252
YALSA Quick Picks for Reluctant Young Adult Readers, 2016.

Scarlett, a sixteen-year-old private detective in the fictional city of Las Almas, finds herself at the center of a mysterious case—involving ancient curses, priceless artifacts, and jinn—as she discovers that her own family secrets may have more to do with the situation than she thinks.

This whip-smart, determined, black Muslim heroine brings a fresh hard-boiled tone to the field of teen mysteries. —*Kirkus*

Laure, Estelle
   Mayhem. Estelle Laure. St Martins Pr 2020 304 p.
Grades: 9 10 11 12
   1. Vigilantes; 2. Family curses; 3. Magic; 4. Ability; 5. Women; 6. California; 7. 1980s; 8. Urban fantasy.
9781250297938
                              LC 2020005578
In 1987, when sixteen-year-old Mayhem and her mother leave her abusive stepfather and return to Santa Maria, California, May learns she is heir to magical power, destined to stop evildoers.

Patient readers will be rewarded with a vivid tale that deftly explores pain and empowerment. A compelling, unrelenting work of magical realism that will enthrall fans of nuanced feminist revenge fantasies. —*School Library Journal*

Lauren, Christina
   Autoboyography. Christina Lauren. Simon & Schuster Books for Young Readers, 2017 288 p.
Grades: 9 10 11 12
   1. Bisexual teenagers; 2. Mormons; 3. Teenage boy/boy relations; 4. Writing; 5. Bisexual teenage boys; 6. Utah; 7. Contemporary romances; 8. LGBTQIA romances
9781481481687
Rainbow List, 2018.

While avoiding any demonizing of any religious groups, this manages to take on the intricacies of sexuality versus organized religion in an intense but ultimately inspirational narrative. Lauren successfully tackles a weighty subject with both ferocity and compassion. —*Booklist*

Laurie, Victoria
   Forever, again. Victoria Laurie. Hyperion, 2016 368 p.
Grades: 7 8 9 10
   1. Reincarnation; 2. Teenage boy/girl relations; 3. Murder; 4. Suicide; 5. Teenagers; 6. Supernatural mysteries; 7. Multiple perspectives.
9781484700099
                              LC 2015045683
Sixteen-year-old Lily Bennett becomes wrapped up in a murder mystery that she learns might be linked to her past...and future.

With plot twist after plot twist, the book never dulls, and readers will be totally entertained page after page. —*Voice of Youth Advocates*

Lavender, William
   Aftershocks. William Lavender. Harcourt, 2006 343 p;
Grades: 8 9 10 11 12
   1. Gender role; 2. Fathers and daughters; 3. Fourteen-year-old girls; 4. Teenage girls; 5. Teenagers; 6. San Francisco, California; 7. California; 8. 1900s (Decade); 9. Diary novels; 10. Historical fiction.
9780152058821
                              LC 2005019695
In San Francisco from 1903 to 1908, teenager Jessie Wainwright determines to reach her goal of becoming a doctor while also trying to care for the illegitimate child of a liaison between her father and their Chinese maid.

This is readable historical fiction about an engrossing event in U.S. history. —*Voice of Youth Advocates*

Lawlor, Laurie
   Dead reckoning: a pirate voyage with Captain Drake. Laurie Lawlor. Simon & Schuster Books for Young Readers, 2005 254 p. : Map
Grades: 7 8 9 10
   1. Drake, Francis; 2. Fifteen-year-old boys; 3. Orphans; 4. Boy orphans; 5. Cousins; 6. Voyages and travels; 7. Age of exploration (1419-1610); 8. 16th century; 9. Sea stories; 10. Historical fiction.
9780689865770
                              LC 2004021682
Emmet, a fifteen-year-old orphan, learns hard lessons about survival when he sails from England in 1577 as a servant aboard the Golden Hind—the ship of his cousin, the explorer and pirate Francis Drake—on its three-year circumnavigation of the world.

The tone is dark and grim, and there are scenes that might horrify younger readers.... But the story is authentic and harrowing, and the historical details are well done. This book would be perfect for older teens who love historical fiction, or want more on pirates. —*School Library Journal*

Lawson, Liz
   The **lucky** ones. Liz Lawson. Delacorte Press, 2020 352 p.

Grades: 9 10 11 12
1. Twins — Death; 2. Survivor guilt; 3. Healing — Psychological aspects; 4. School shootings; 5. Mass shootings; 6. Realistic fiction; 7. Multiple perspectives.
9780593118504; 9780593118498

In the aftermath of a school tragedy, May and Zach struggle with grief, survivor's guilt, and the complex emotional impact of the event, learning how to heal and hope in the face of it all.

Wildly ambitious and wholly empathetic, devastatingly raw, and impossibly gentle; a must-read in this moment. —*Kirkus*

Le Guin, Ursula K.

Gifts. Ursula K. Le Guin. Harcourt, 2004 288 p. (Annals of the Western Shore, 1)
Grades: 7 8 9 10
1. Magic; 2. Power (Social sciences); 3. People who are blind; 4. Young men; 5. Fathers; 6. Fantasy fiction.
9780152051235; 9781842551073, print, UK
LC 2003021449
Booklist Editors' Choice: Books for Youth, 2004.

When a young man in the Uplands blinds himself rather than use his gift of "unmaking"—a violent talent shared by members of his family—he upsets the precarious balance of power among rival, feuding families, each of which has a strange and deadly talent of its own.

Although intriguing as a coming-of-age allegory, Orrec's story is also rich in...earthy magic and intelligent plot twists. —*Booklist*

★ The **left** hand of darkness. Ursula Le Guin. Ace Books, 1969 286 p. (Hainish series, 6)
Grades: 9 10 11 12 Adult
1. Far future; 2. Androgyny (Psychology); 3. Life on other planets; 4. Culture conflict; 5. Ethnologists; 6. Science fiction classics; 7. Social science fiction; 8. Science fiction
9780441007318; 9780802713025; 9781473225947, Paperback, UK
Hugo Award for Best Novel, 1970; James Tiptree, Jr. Award, 1995; Nebula Award for Best Novel, 1969.

While on a mission to the planet Gethen, earthling Genly Ai is sent by leaders of the nation of Orgoreyn to a concentration camp from which the exiled prime minister of the nation of Karhide tries to rescue him.

Powers. Ursula K. Le Guin. Harcourt, 2007 502 p. : Map (Annals of the Western Shore, 3)
Grades: 7 8 9 10
1. Grief; 2. Psychic ability; 3. Slavery; 4. Teenage boy psychics; 5. Fourteen-year-old boys; 6. Fantasy fiction.
9780152057701; 9781842555316, print, UK
LC 2006013549
Nebula Award for Best Novel, 2008; Booklist Editors' Choice: Books for Youth, 2007.

When young Gavir's sister is brutally killed, he escapes from slavery and sets out to explore the world and his own psychic abilities.

Le Guin uses her own prodigious power as a writer to craft lyrical, precise sentences, evoking a palpable sense of place and believable characters. —*School Library Journal*

Voices. Ursula K. Le Guin. Harcourt, 2006 352 p. (Annals of the Western Shore, 2)
Grades: 7 8 9 10
1. Magic; 2. Power (Social sciences); 3. Revenge; 4. Censorship; 5. Resistance to government; 6. Fantasy fiction.
9780152056780; 9781842555071, print, UK
LC 2005020753

Young Memer takes on a pivotal role in freeing her war-torn homeland from its oppressive captors.

While her prose is simple and unadorned, Le Guin's superior narrative voice and storytelling power make even small moments ring with truth, and often with beauty. —*School Library Journal*

Leavitt, Martine

★ **Calvin**. Martine Leavitt. Margaret Ferguson Books, Farrar Straus Giroux, 2015 224 p.
Grades: 7 8 9 10 11 12
1. Watterson, Bill; 2. Teenagers with schizophrenia; 3. Mental illness; 4. Schizophrenia; 5. Teenage boys with mental illnesses; 6. High schools; 7. Lake Erie; 8. Realistic fiction; 9. Canadian fiction
9780374380731; 9781554987207
LC 2015002574
Governor General's Literary Award for English-Language Children's Literature, 2016; YALSA Best Fiction for Young Adults, 2016; OLA Best Bets, 2015.

Seventeen-year-old Calvin, who was born on the day that the last Calvin and Hobbes comic strip was published, is stricken by a schizophrenic episode and begins having conversations with the tiger, Hobbes. Struggling to regain control of his mind and destiny, Calvin becomes convinced that he'll get better if the strip's creator, Bill Watterson, will draw just one more comic.

Funny, intellectual, and entertaining, its a sensitive yet irreverent adventure about a serious subject. —*Publishers Weekly*

My book of life by Angel. Martine Leavitt. Margaret Ferguson Books/Farrar Straus Giroux, 2012 352 p.
Grades: 8 9 10 11
1. Teenage prostitutes; 2. Drug abuse; 3. Prostitution; 4. Missing persons; 5. Sixteen-year-old girls; 6. Vancouver, British Columbia; 7. Canada; 8. Novels in verse; 9. Realistic fiction; 10. Canadian fiction.
9780374351236; 9781554981175
LC 2011044563
Booklist Editors' Choice: Books for Youth, 2012; Canadian Library Association Young Adult Book Award, 2013; YALSA Best Fiction for Young Adults, 2013; Notable Books for a Global Society, 2013.

Angel, a sixteen-year-old girl working the streets of Vancouver's Downtown Eastside, befriends Melli, an 11-year-old girl in the same situation and realizes she must do all that she can to save Melli and perhaps save herself at the same time.

Lecesne, James

★ **Absolute** brightness. James Lecesne. HarperTeen, 2008 472 p;
Grades: 7 8 9 10
1. Gay teenagers; 2. Difference (Psychology); 3. Homophobia; 4. Adolescence; 5. Teenagers; 6. New Jersey; 7. Coming-of-age stories; 8. Realistic fiction.
9780061256288
LC 2007002988
In the beach town of Neptune, New Jersey, Phoebe's life is changed irrevocably when her gay cousin moves into her house and soon goes missing.
Laura Geringer books.

Lee, C. B.

Not your sidekick. C.B. Lee; book design and illustrations by CB Messer. Interlude Press, 2016 283 p. (Sidekick squad, 1)
Grades: 7 8 9 10
1. Interns; 2. Asian American girls; 3. Superheroes; 4. Supervillains; 5. Bisexuals; 6. Superhero stories
9781945053030

Resigned to a life without superpowers in a world full of them, Jess takes a paid internship where she helps a heinous supervillain and works with her longtime crush, but she soon stumbles on a massive plot.

Lee (*Seven Tears at High Tide*) offers up a fast-paced, engaging tale set in a quasi-dystopian 22nd-century America where the line between hero and villain is often blurred. With a diverse cast of characters, both in terms of sexuality and ethnic background, and a wholly adorable romance for Jess, it's a lively exploration of morality in a superpowered age. —*Publishers Weekly*

Lee, Lyla

I'll be the one. Lyla Lee. Katherine Tegen Books, 2020 336 p.
Grades: 8 9 10 11 12

1. Overweight teenage girls; 2. Schools; 3. Popular music; 4. Singers; 5. Dancers; 6. Romantic comedies; 7. Realistic fiction
9780062936929

A nuanced celebration of body positivity by the author of the Mindy Kim series follows the experiences of a plus-sized teen girl who shatters expectations on a televised competition to become the next big K-pop star.

Lee's debut whips up intense Dumplin' vibes with a main character you want to reach into the pages for and honestly just hug for hours. —*Booklist*

Lee, Mackenzi

★ The **gentleman's** guide to vice and virtue. Mackenzi Lee. 2017 528 p. (Montague siblings, 1)
Grades: 7 8 9 10 11 12

1. Rich teenage boys; 2. Teenage boy/boy relations; 3. Pirates; 4. Multiracial teenage boys; 5. Brothers and sisters; 6. Europe; 7. 18th century; 8. Historical fantasy; 9. LGBTQIA fiction; 10. First person narratives
9780062382801, hardback, US

LC 2016949692
Booklist Editors' Choice: Books for Youth, 2017; Rainbow List, 2018; YALSA Best Fiction for Young Adults, 2018; Romantic Times Reviewer's Choice Award, 2017; Stonewall Children's & Young Adult Literature Honor Book, 2018.

Two friends on a Grand Tour of 18th-century Europe stumble across a magical artifact that leads them from Paris to Venice in a dangerous manhunt shaped by pirates, highwaymen and their growing attraction to one another.

Austen, Wilde, and Indiana Jones converge in this deliciously anachronistic bonbon. —*Kirkus*

★ The **lady's** guide to petticoats and piracy. Mackenzi Lee. Katherine Tegen Books, 2018 464 p. (Montague siblings, 2)
Grades: 9 10 11 12

1. Women physicians; 2. Former friends; 3. Piracy; 4. Gender role; 5. Women pirates; 6. Europe; 7. 18th century; 8. Historical fiction; 9. Adventure stories; 10. First person narratives.
9780062795328; 9780062890122, Paperback, UK

Amelia Bloomer List, 2019; YALSA Best Fiction for Young Adults, 2019.

Hoping to travel to Germany to ask for help enrolling in medical school, Felicity has no money for the trip until a mysterious woman offers to travel with her and pay her way, which ends up entangling Felicity in a perilous quest across Europe.

Loki: where mischief lies. By Mackenzi Lee; illustrated by Stephanie Hans. Disney Press, 2019 336 p.
Grades: 6 7 8 9 10

1. Sibling rivalry; 2. Murder; 3. Assassins; 4. Loki (Norse deity); 5. Secret societies; 6. London, England; 7. 19th century; 8. Historical fantasy; 9. Superhero stories; 10. Franchise books.
9781368022262

After the banishment of his only friend, the sorceress Amora, to Earth, a young Loki travels to nineteenth-century London to investigate a string of murders but finds much more than he expects.

This deft, nuanced examination of identity, destiny, and agency is a surprisingly tender addition to the Marvel canon. —*Kirkus*

Lee, Stacey

★ The **downstairs** girl. Stacey Lee. G.P. Putnam's Sons, 2019 384 p.
Grades: 7 8 9 10 11 12

1. Chinese American teenage girls; 2. Household employees; 3. Advice columns; 4. Teenage girl journalists; 5. Social reformers; 6. Atlanta, Georgia; 7. Southern States; 8. 1890s; 9. 19th century; 10. Historical fiction; 11. First person narratives.
9781524740955, HRD, US; 9781524740962, ebook, US; 9780349423609, Paperback, UK

LC 2018018881
Booklist Editors' Choice: Books for Youth, 2019; Notable Books for a Global Society, 2020; School Library Journal Best Books, 2019; Westchester Fiction Award, 2020.

1890, Atlanta. By day, seventeen-year-old Jo Kuan works as a lady's maid for the cruel Caroline Payne, the daughter of one of the wealthiest men in Atlanta. But by night, Jo moonlights as the pseudonymous author of a newspaper advice column for 'the genteel Southern lady'.

Unflinching in its portrayals of racism yet ultimately hopeful and heartfelt, this narrative places voices frequently left out of historical fiction center stage. —*School Library Journal*

Outrun the moon. Stacey Lee. 2016 400 pages
Grades: 7 8 9 10

1. Chinese American teenage girls; 2. Earthquakes; 3. Boarding schools; 4. Survival; 5. San Francisco Earthquake and Fire, Calif, 1906; 6. San Francisco, California; 7. Chinatown, San Francisco, California; 8. 1900s (Decade); 9. Historical fiction
9780399175411

LC 2015032478
Amelia Bloomer List, 2017; Asian Pacific American Asian Pacific American Award for Literature: Young Adult Literature, 2017; YALSA Best Fiction for Young Adults, 2017.

On the eve of the San Francisco Earthquake of 1906, Mercy Wong—daughter of Chinese immigrants—is struggling to hold her own among the spoiled heiresses at prestigious St. Clare's School. When tragedy strikes, everyone must band together to survive.

Under a painted sky. By Stacey Lee. G. P. Putnam's Sons, an imprint of Penguin Group (USA), 2015 384 p.
Grades: 9 10 11 12

1. Runaway teenage girls; 2. Chinese American teenage girls; 3. African American girls; 4. Disguises; 5. Slavery; 6. The West (United States); 7. Oregon Trail; 8. American Westward Expansion (1803-1899); 9. 1840s; 10. Westerns
9780399168031

Amelia Bloomer List, 2016; Westchester Fiction Award, 2016; YALSA Best Fiction for Young Adults, 2016.

Lee packs the plot with plenty of peril and Wild West excitement, and Sammy's fixation on fate, luck, and the Chinese zodiac adds a unique flavor. A great fit for fans of historical adventure with a touch of romance. —*Booklist*

Lee, Stephan
K-pop confidential. Stephan Lee. Point, 2020 336 p.
Grades: 9 10 11 12
1. Korean American girls; 2. Popular music; 3. Love triangles; 4. Dating (Social customs); 5. Teenage girl singers; 6. Seoul, Korea; 7. Romantic comedies
9781338640021, LIB, US; 9781338639933, PAP, US; 9781913322298, Paperback, UK
Hiding a secret passion for singing beneath a veneer of an obedient straight-A student, Candace enters a K-pop audition on a dare before plunging headfirst into the grueling world of training and rehearsals, before a fellow trainee and a hot boy-band star challenge a strict no-dating rule.
This wish-fulfillment story twines 'Cinderella' moments with intersectional issues—class, racism, sexism—but it's Candace's sense of self-worth that will get readers to cheer. —*Publishers Weekly*

Lee, Y. S.
The body at the tower. Y.S. Lee. Candlewick Press, 2010 352 p. (The Agency, 2)
Grades: 8 9 10 11 12
1. Teenage girl detectives; 2. Role reversal; 3. Poor boys; 4. Teenage girl orphans; 5. Teenage girls; 6. Great Britain; 7. London, England; 8. Victorian era (1837-1901); 9. 1850s; 10. Historical mysteries; 11. Canadian fiction; 12. Mysteries
9780763649685; 9780763656430
As a nearly full-fledged member of the Agency, the all-female detective unit based in Miss Scrimshaw's Academy for Girls, Mary Quinn, disguised as a poor apprentice builder, must brave the sinister underworld of Victorian London in order to unmask a murderer.
Mary Quinn returns in another case for the Agency, a covert all-female detective agency in Victorian London. A man has recently fallen out of the soon-to-be-completed clock tower of the Houses of Parliament. Mary disguises herself as an errand boy and attempts to infiltrate the work site to discover potential suspects.... This second book is much stronger than the first, both in terms of character development and the central mystery. —*School Library Journal*

A spy in the house. Y.S. Lee. Candlewick Press, 2010 352 p. (The Agency, 1)
Grades: 8 9 10 11 12
1. Teenage girl orphans; 2. Swindlers and swindling; 3. Girl thieves; 4. Smuggling; 5. Seventeen-year-old girls; 6. Great Britain; 7. London, England; 8. Victorian era (1837-1901); 9. 1850s; 10. Historical mysteries; 11. Canadian fiction; 12. Mysteries
9780763640675; 9780763687489
LC 2009032736
John Spray Mystery Award (Canada), 2011; YALSA Popular Paperbacks for Young Adults, 2015.
Mary graduates from Miss Scrimshaw's Academy for Girls with admirable skills, including being an undercover investigator. Working in the guise of a lady's companion, she infiltrates a merchant's home to try to trace his missing cargo ships. She then finds that that household is full of dangerous secrets.
Lee fills the story with classic elements of Victorian mystery and melodrama. Class differences, love gone awry, racial discrimination, London's growing pains in the 1850s, and the status of women in society are all addressed. Historical details are woven seamlessly into the plot, and descriptive writing allows readers to be part of each scene. —*School Library Journal*

Legrand, Claire
Furyborn. Claire Legrand. Sourcebooks Fire, 2018 512 p. (Empirium trilogy, 1)
Grades: 9 10 11 12
1. Prophecies; 2. Women rulers; 3. Bounty hunters; 4. End of the world; 5. Imaginary empires; 6. High fantasy; 7. Fantasy fiction; 8. Parallel narratives
9781492656623
LC 2017034431
LibraryReads Favorites, 2018.
Legrand excels at world building, deftly integrating the religion and history of this imaginary world into a dark yet rousing adventure story that combines passion and danger at every turn. —*Booklist*

Lightbringer. Claire Legrand. Sourcebooks Inc 2020 480 p. (Empirium trilogy, 3)
Grades: 9 10 11 12
1. Prophecies; 2. Women rulers; 3. End of the world; 4. Fate and fatalism; 5. Good and evil; 6. High fantasy; 7. Fantasy fiction; 8. Parallel narratives
9781492656685
LC 2020025070
Two queens, separated by a thousand years, must face their ultimate destinies—a second chance for salvation, or the destruction their world has been dreading. Provided by publisher.
A rousing conclusion to a series studded with unforgettable heroes and villains. —*Booklist*

★ Sawkill girls. Claire Legrand. Katherine Tegen Books, 2018 464 p.
Grades: 9 10 11 12
1. Missing teenage girls; 2. Islands; 3. Monsters; 4. Good and evil; 5. Disappearances (Parapsychology); 6. Horror; 7. Multiple perspectives.
9780062696601; 9780062696618
YALSA Best Fiction for Young Adults, 2019.
A lovelorn newcomer, a grief-stricken pariah and a privileged liar intersect on the island of Sawkill Rock, where they become unlikely defenders against an insidious monster that has been preying upon the girls in their community for decades.
Through this dank, atmospheric, and genuinely frightening narrative, Legrand weaves powerful threads about the dangerous journey of growing up female. In a world where monsters linger at the edges, this is an intensely character-driven story about girls who support each other, girls who betray each other, and girls who love each other in many complicated ways. Strange, eerie, and unforgettable. —*Booklist*

Lennon, Tom
When love comes to town. Tom Lennon. Albert Whitman, 2013 288 p.
Grades: 8 9 10 11 12
1. Gay teenagers; 2. Coming out (Sexual or gender identity); 3. Rejection (Psychology); 4. Closeted gay teenagers; 5. Teenage boys; 6. Ireland; 7. 1990s; 8. Realistic fiction; 9. LGBTQIA fiction
9780807589168
LC 2012020160
Neil Byrne, a teenager in Dublin, Ireland, in the 1990s, comes to terms with the fact that he is gay and seeks acceptance from his friends and family.

Leno, Katrina
Everything all at once. Katrina Leno. Harpercollins Childrens Books, 2017 304 p.

Grades: 8 9 10 11 12
1. Risk-taking (Psychology); 2. Grief in teenagers; 3. Anxiety in teenagers; 4. Aunts — Death; 5. Scavenger hunts; 6. Low fantasy; 7. Fantasy fiction.
9780062493095
When her struggles with anxiety worsen in the aftermath of a family death, Lottie is bequeathed a series of letters from her late aunt, a best-selling author, who leaves instructions to help Lottie overcome her fears and explore her own literary voice.

Horrid. Katrina Leno. New York : 2020 304 p.
Grades: 9 10 11 12
1. Ghosts; 2. Manors; 3. Grief; 4. Teenage girls; 5. Mothers and daughters; 6. Maine; 7. Horror
9780316537247

LC 2019055174
Following her father's sudden death, Jane North-Robinson and her mother are forced to move to the old North house in Maine, where Jane uncovers her family's disturbing secrets.
With less focus on character development and more on creating a rich atmosphere and sense of foreboding, this is a great choice for those interested in a gripping but speedy read. —*School Library Journal*

The **lost** & found. Katrina Leno. HarperTeen, an imprint of HarperCollinsPublishers, 2016 352 p.
Grades: 7 8 9 10 11
1. Loss (Psychology); 2. Automobile travel; 3. Lost articles; 4. Teenagers; 5. Realistic fiction
9780062231208
Forging a friendship through an online support group, Frannie and Louis, teens whose losses are tied to mysterious disappearances, search for answers during a road trip to Austin, where they find magical things that the other has lost.
This is a beautiful exploration of loss in many forms and the emotional toll it can take on those who are affected.... An emotional journey that's well worth the ride. —*School Library Journal*

You must not miss. Katrina Leno. Little, Brown, and Company, 2019 304 p.
Grades: 9 10 11 12
1. Sexual violence victims; 2. Ostracism; 3. Emotional problems of teenage girls; 4. Revenge; 5. Family problems; 6. New England; 7. Magical realism; 8. Horror.
9780316449779
When seventeen-year-old Magpie Lewis discovers a magical world in her backyard, she uses it and its powers to enact her revenge on all those who have wronged her. —Provided by publisher.
Leno doesn't shy away from challenging themes—including substance abuse, toxic friendships, rape, and suicide—and she brings lyrically haunting language to a story filled with inherent darkness. —*Publishers Weekly*

Lester, Julius
★ **Day** of tears: a novel in dialogue. Hyperion Books for Children, 2005 176 p.
Grades: 7 8 9 10
1. Slave trade; 2. Cruelty; 3. Slaves; 4. African Americans; 5. Slaveholders; 6. Savannah, Georgia; 7. Southern States; 8. Antebellum America (1820-1861); 9. 19th century; 10. Historical fiction; 11. First person narratives.
9780786804900
Coretta Scott King Award, Author Category, 2006; ALA Notable Children's Book, 2006; Booklist Editors' Choice: Books for Youth, 2005; YALSA Best Books for Young Adults, 2006.

The horror of the auction and its aftermath is unforgettable.... The racism is virulent (there's widespread use of the n-word). The personal voices make this a stirring text for group discussion. —*Booklist*

★ **Guardian**. By Julius Lester. Amistad/HarperTeen, 2008 160 p.
Grades: 7 8 9 10
1. Lynching; 2. Racism; 3. Race relations; 4. Judicial error; 5. African Americans; 6. Southern States; 7. 1940s; 8. Historical fiction
9780061558900
YALSA Best Books for Young Adults, 2009.
In a rural southern town in 1946, a white man and his son witness the lynching of an innocent black man. Includes historical note on lynching.
The author's understated, haunting prose is as compelling as it is dark;...[the story] leaves a deep impression. —*Publishers Weekly*
Includes bibliographical references.

Time's memory. Julius Lester. Farrar Straus Giroux, 2006 240 p.
Grades: 8 9 10 11 12
1. Slavery; 2. African Americans — History; 3. Loss (Psychology); 4. African American families; 5. Dogon (African people) — Religion; 6. Virginia; 7. 1860s; 8. Historical fiction; 9. African American fiction; 10. Mythological fiction
9780374371784

LC 2005047716
Ekundayo, a Dogon spirit brought to America from Africa, inhabits the body of a young African American slave on a Virginia plantation, where he experiences loss, sorrow, and reconciliation in the months preceding the Civil War.
More than a picture of slavery through the eyes of those enslaved or their captors, Lester's narrative evokes spiritual images of Mali's Dogon people. —*School Library Journal*

Levenseller, Tricia
Daughter of the pirate king. Tricia Levenseller. Feiwel & Friends, 2017 272 p. (Daughter of the pirate king, 1)
Grades: 8 9 10 11
1. Girl pirates; 2. Maps; 3. Undercover operations; 4. Captivity; 5. Pirates; 6. Fantasy fiction.
9781250095961
Resourceful and confident, Alosa swaggers through the pages with style and panache, and her supporting cast is just as delightful. —*Publishers Weekly*

Levine, Gail Carson
Fairest. Gail Carson Levine. Harper Collins, 2006 336 p.
Grades: 6 7 8 9
1. Self-acceptance in teenage girls; 2. Teenage girl singers; 3. Ugliness; 4. Fifteen-year-old girls; 5. Teenage girls; 6. Fantasy fiction; 7. Fairy tale and folklore-inspired fiction
9780060734084; 9780060734091

LC 2006000337
Booklist Editors' Choice: Books for Youth, 2006; School Library Journal Best Books, 2006.
In a land where beauty and singing are valued above all else, Aza eventually comes to reconcile her unconventional appearance and her magical voice, and learns to accept herself for who she truly is.
The plot is fast-paced, and Aza's growth and maturity are well crafted and believable. —*School Library Journal*

Levithan, David
★ **19** love songs. David Levithan. Alfred A. Knopf, 2019 320 p.
Grades: 9 10 11 12

1. Valentine's Day; 2. Love; 3. Gay couples; 4. Compassion; 5. Individuality; 6. Short stories; 7. Autobiographical fiction; 8. LGBTQIA fiction
9781984848642, LIB, US; 9781984848635, HRD, US; 9781922268921, Paperback, Australia; 9781405298056, Paperback, UK

LC 2019019912

A collection of fiction, nonfiction, and a story in verse celebrating love.

The well-read reader will catch allusions to classic literature and children's books as well as Levithan's novels, reinforcing an intertextuality that allows the book to express a love of stories alongside its stories of love. —*Bulletin of the Center for Children's Books*

★ **Boy** meets boy. David Levithan. Alfred A. Knopf, 2003 185 p;
Grades: 9 10 11 12
1. Gay teenagers; 2. Crushes in teenage boys; 3. Teenage same-sex romance; 4. High school sophomores; 5. Teenage boys; 6. Contemporary romances; 7. LGBTQIA romances; 8. Realistic fiction; 9. Books for reluctant readers
9780375824005; 9780375924002

LC 2002073154

Lambda Literary Award for Young Adult/Children, 2003; YALSA Quick Picks for Reluctant Young Adult Readers, 2004; Booklist Editors' Choice: Books for Youth, 2003; YALSA Best Books for Young Adults, 2004.

When Paul falls hard for Noah, he thinks he has found his one true love, but when Noah walks out of his life, Paul has to find a way to get him back and make everything right once more.

Though at times arch and even precious, this wacky, charming, original story is never outrageous, and its characters are fresh, real, and deeply engaging. In its blithe acceptance and celebration of human differences, this is arguably the most important gay novel since Nancy Garden's *Annie on My Mind;* it certainly seems to represent a revolution in the publishing of gay-themed books for adolescents. —*Booklist*

★ **Every** day. By David Levithan. Alfred A. Knopf, 2012 304 p. (Every day, 1)
Grades: 9 10 11 12
1. Body swapping; 2. Love; 3. Interpersonal attraction; 4. Dating (Social customs); 5. Interpersonal relations; 6. Magical realism; 7. Books to movies
9780307931887, hardback, US; 9781921922954, Australia; 9781925773033, paperback, Australia

LC 2012004173

Booklist Editors' Choice: Books for Youth, 2012; Nutmeg Children's Book Award, High School category, 2015; School Library Journal Best Books, 2012; Virginia Readers' Choice Award for High School, 2015; YALSA Best Fiction for Young Adults, 2013; YALSA Popular Paperbacks for Young Adults, 2014.

Known to him/herself only as "A," the narrator of this philosophically electrifying novel wakes up every morning in the body of a different person. This constant, inexplicable change—A is usually around the same age but has experienced different genders, ethnicities, personality types, etc.—has made A unusually circumspect, mature, and careful not to alter anything that would impact the lives of those whose bodies s/he's inhabited. It makes for a lonely existence...until A falls in love with a girl named Rhiannon and breaks those rules, just to see her again.

Levithan's self-conscious, analytical style marries perfectly with the plot...Readers will devour his trademark poetic wordplay and cadences that feel as fresh as they were when he wrote Boy Meets Boy (2003). —*Kirkus*

Title adapted into a film in 2018.

Someday. David Levithan. Alfred A. Knopf, 2018 400 p. (Every day, 3)
Grades: 9 10 11 12
1. Body swapping; 2. Belonging; 3. Loneliness; 4. Love; 5. Identity (Psychology); 6. Magical realism; 7. Multiple perspectives.
9780399553066; 9780399553059; 9780399553080; 9780399553073, ebook, US

LC 2018017815

When A discovers there are others who wake up in a different person's body every day, A gains new understanding of the extremes where love and loneliness can lead. Told from multiple perspectives.

Companion book to: *Every day* and *Another day.*

★ **Two** boys kissing. David Levithan. Alfred A. Knopf, 2013 208 p.
Grades: 8 9 10 11 12
1. Gay teenagers; 2. Kissing; 3. AIDS (Disease); 4. Dating (Social customs); 5. Former boyfriends; 6. LGBTQIA romances; 7. Realistic fiction; 8. Contemporary romances
9780307931900; 9781922147486; 9781405264433, print, UK; 9780307975645, ebook, US

LC 2012047089

Lambda Literary Award for Young Adult/Children, 2013; Rainbow List, 2014; YALSA Best Fiction for Young Adults, 2014; Stonewall Children's & Young Adult Literature Honor Book, 2014.

A chorus of men who died of AIDS observes and yearns to help a cross-section of today's gay teens who navigate new love, long-term relationships, coming out, self-acceptance, and more in a society that has changed in many ways.

Craig and Harry attempt to break the world record for longest kiss, which, in turn, affects the lives of the people around them. Narrated by a ghostly chorus of past generations of gay men who died of AIDS, Levithan's latest novel weaves together an informed (sometimes melodramatic) perspective on the past with the present-day stories of seven boys constructing their own sexual identities. —*Horn Book Guide*

Lim, Elizabeth

Spin the dawn. Elizabeth Lim. Random House Children's Books, 2019 416 p. (Blood of stars, 1)
Grades: 9 10 11 12
1. Seamstresses; 2. Contests; 3. Enchantment; 4. Imaginary empires; 5. Disguises; 6. Asian-influenced fantasy; 7. High fantasy; 8. Fantasy fiction.
9780525646990, HRD, US; 9780525647003, LIB, US; 9780593118443, Paperback, UK; 9781529362909, Paperback, UK

Risking her life by disguising herself as a boy to secure the position of imperial tailor, Maia is given the impossible task of sewing three magic gowns representing the sun, moon and stars for the emperor's reluctant bride-to-be.

Beautifully written with a can't-wait-for-the-sequel ending, this breathtaking and fast-paced Silk-road inspired fantasy from the author of Mulan-retelling Reflection is sure to enchant readers beginning to end. —*Booklist*

Lindelauf, Benny

Fing's war. Benny Lindelauf; translated from the Dutch by John Nieuwenhuizen. Consortium Book Sales & Dist, 2019 411 p.
Grades: 4 5 6
1. Families; 2. War; 3. Anger in teenagers; 4. Eccentrics and eccentricities; 5. Teenage girls — Career aspirations; 6. Netherlands; 7. Second World War era (1939-1945); 8. Historical fiction; 9. Translations
9781592702695

LC 2019011185

Follows teenaged Fing Boon and her large, impoverished, eccentric family as they navigate the changes World War II visits upon their little town on the border of the Netherlands and Germany.

First published in 2010 in Dutch in the Netherlands by Em. Querido's Kinderboeken Uitgeverij as *De hemel van Heivisj*

Lindstrom, Eric

Not if I see you first. Eric Lindstrom. Little, Brown and Company, 2016 320 p.

Grades: 9 10 11 12

1. Teenagers who are blind; 2. Teenage girl orphans; 3. Loss (Psychology); 4. Teenage boy/girl relations; 5. Teenage girls with disabilities; 6. Realistic fiction

9780316259859; 9780008146306, print, UK; 9780008146344, print, UK; 9780008146313, print, UK

YALSA Best Fiction for Young Adults, 2017; YALSA Quick Picks for Reluctant Young Adult Readers, 2017.

Demanding to be treated the same as everyone else in spite of her blindness, Parker doles out tough-love advice to her peers, refuses to cry after losing her father, and stubbornly shuns a boy who broke her heart years earlier.

While Lindstrom's debut understandably contains plenty of melancholy, angst, and self-doubt, it also possesses crackling wit, intense teen drama, and a lively pace that pulls readers in, as do the everyday details of Parker's world: spoken-word texts, clever methods of finding her way, and a guide runner who helps Parker when she considers joining the school track team. This unique coming-of-age tale is off and running from the start. —*Booklist*

Link, Kelly

★ **Pretty** monsters: stories. By Kelly Link; decorations by Shaun Tan. Viking, 2008 416 p.

Grades: 9 10 11 12

1. Magic; 2. Monsters; 3. Fantasy fiction; 4. Horror; 5. Short stories.

9780670010905; 9781406330298, print, UK

LC 2008033251

Booklist Editors' Choice: Books for Youth, 2008; YALSA Best Books for Young Adults, 2009.

Nine short stories take readers into worlds with elements that mix fantasy with reality.

Readers as yet unfamiliar with Link...will be excited to discover her singular voice in this collection of nine short stories, her first book for young adults.... [Subjects] range from absurd to mundane, all observed with equidistant irony.... The author mingles the grotesque and the ethereal to make magic on the page. —*Publishers Weekly*

Lipsyte, Robert

★ The **contender**. Robert Lipsyte. Harper & Row, 1967 182 p.

Grades: 7 8 9 10

1. African American teenage boys; 2. Persistence in teenage boys; 3. Boxing; 4. Courage in teenage boys; 5. Gangs; 6. Sports fiction.

9780060239206

LC 67019623

Against great odds, a black high school drop-out trains to become a championship boxer.

Littke, Lael

Lake of secrets. Lael Littke. H. Holt, 2002 202 p;

Grades: 7 8 9 10

1. Brothers and sisters; 2. Reincarnation; 3. Missing persons; 4. Fifteen-year-old girls; 5. Teenage girls; 6. Mysteries

9780805067309

LC 2001039933

Having arrived in her mother's home town to try to find her long-missing brother, who disappeared three years before she was born, fifteen-year-old Carlene finds herself haunted by memories from a past life.

The realistic characters and plot make the idea compelling, and the story will intrigue teens. —*Booklist*

Littlefield, Sophie

Infected. Sophie Littlefield. Delacorte Press, 2015 256 p.

Grades: 7 8 9 10

1. Teenage girl orphans; 2. Viruses; 3. Survival; 4. Antidotes; 5. Uncles — Death; 6. Thrillers and suspense

9780385741064

Nail-biting action with a scientifically and technologically involved plotline gives this novel an edge, and, moreover, the character development is surprisingly rich given the fast pace of the narrative. The weight of the themes also keeps the story from reading like a movie script. Red herrings keep the reader guessing until the end. —*Booklist*

Littman, Sarah

Backlash. Sarah Darer Littman. Scholastic Press, 2015 336 p.

Grades: 7 8 9

1. Cyberbullying; 2. Suicide; 3. Teenage girls; 4. Teenage boy/girl relations; 5. Social status; 6. Realistic fiction.

9780545651264

LC 2014020226

Grand Canyon Reader Award (Arizona), Tween Book Category, 2019; Iowa Teen Award, 2017.

When Christian, a boy she knows only through Facebook, posts a lot of nasty comments on her page, fifteen-year-old Lara tries to kill herself—but that is only the beginning of the backlash for her sister, Sydney; her former friend Bree; and her classmates.

The depression and bullying are handled realistically without sugar-coating, and fortunately, consequences are applied. An excellent choice for any antibullying campaign. —*Booklist*

Lloyd, Saci

★ The **carbon** diaries 2015. By Saci Lloyd. Holiday House, 2009 330 p.

Grades: 8 9 10 11 12

1. Rationing; 2. Energy conservation; 3. Climate change; 4. Global warming; 5. Families; 6. London, England; 7. Diary novels; 8. Science fiction

9780823421909

LC 2008019712

YALSA Popular Paperbacks for Young Adults, 2016; School Library Journal Best Books, 2009.

In 2015, when England becomes the first nation to introduce carbon dioxide rationing in a drastic bid to combat climate change, sixteen-year-old Laura documents the first year of rationing as her family spirals out of control.

Deeply compulsive and urgently compulsory reading. —*Booklist*

The **carbon** diaries 2017. Saci Lloyd. Holiday House, 2010 326 p. : Illustration; Map

Grades: 8 9 10 11 12

1. Women college students; 2. Rationing; 3. Energy conservation; 4. Protest movements; 5. Climate change; 6. London, England; 7. Diary novels; 8. Science fiction

9780823422609

LC 2009020412

In 2017, two years after England introduces carbon dioxide rationing to combat climatic change, eighteen-year-old Laura chronicles her first year at a London university as natural disasters and political upheaval disrupt her studies.

The friction of living life in times of radical upheaval remains potent, sobering, and awfully exciting. —*Booklist*

Lloyd-Jones, Emily

The **bone** houses. Emily Lloyd-Jones. Little, Brown and Company, 2019 352 p.
Grades: 7 8 9 10 11
1. Teenage girl orphans; 2. Apprentices; 3. Undead; 4. Curses; 5. Villages; 6. Fantasy fiction; 7. Horror.
9780316418416, HRD, US

When risen corpses called 'bone houses' threaten Ryn's village because of a decades-old curse, she teams up with a mapmaker named Ellis to solve the mystery of the curse and destroy the bone houses forever.

The story serves as a meditation on the complicated relationship between the living and the dead, combining fear, humor and enchantment in equal measure, and alloying them with humor. —*Publishers Weekly*

Lo, Malinda

Ash. By Malinda Lo. Little, Brown and Co, 2009 264 p.
Grades: 8 9 10 11
1. Teenage girl orphans; 2. Lesbian teenagers; 3. Balls (Parties); 4. Fairies; 5. Enchantment; 6. Fantasy fiction; 7. LGBTQIA fiction; 8. Fairy tale and folklore-inspired fiction
9780316040099; 9780340988374, UK
LC 2009017471
YALSA Popular Paperbacks for Young Adults, 2014; Rainbow List, 2010.

In this variation on the Cinderella story, Ash grows up believing in the fairy realm that the king and his philosophers have sought to suppress, until one day she must choose between a handsome fairy cursed to love her and the King's Huntress whom she loves.

Part heart-pounding lesbian romance and part universal coming-of-age story, Lo's powerful tale is richly embroidered with folklore and glittering fairy magic that will draw fans of Sharon Shinn's earthy, herb-laced fantasies. —*Booklist*
Prequel: *Huntress*.

Huntress. Malinda Lo. Little, Brown, 2011 384 p.
Grades: 9 10 11 12
1. Lesbian teenagers; 2. Sages; 3. Visions; 4. Interpersonal attraction; 5. Voyages and travels; 6. Fantasy fiction; 7. LGBTQIA fiction; 8. Asian-influenced fantasy
9780316040075
LC 2010038827
Rainbow List, 2012; YALSA Best Fiction for Young Adults, 2012.

Seventeen-year-olds Kaede and Taisin are called to go on a dangerous and unprecedented journey to Tanlili, the city of the Fairy Queen, in an effort to restore the balance of nature in the human world.

A Tam Lin-inspired rendition of fairy society blends nicely with the author's Chinese and I Ching-inspired human society, creating a delicate, unusual setting; and although the expeditionary plot has an overly deliberate pace, the episodes are varied and emotional enough to retain interest. Most notably, the inclusion of gay characters in a young adult fantasy, and the natural unfolding of their relationship, comes as a refreshing change. —*Horn Book Guide*
Prequel to: *Ash*.

A **line** in the dark. Malinda Lo. Dutton Books, 2017 288 p.
Grades: 8 9 10 11

1. Chinese American teenage girls; 2. Lesbian teenagers; 3. Social classes; 4. Jealousy; 5. Best friends; 6. Massachusetts; 7. Mysteries; 8. First person narratives
9780735227422

In this unusually structured murder mystery, Lo (Inheritance) explores the knotty jealousies, romantic longings, and class disparities among students at a pair of Massachusetts high schools. —*Publishers Weekly*

Lockhart, E.

★ **Again** again. E. Lockhart. Delacorte Press, 2020 304 p.
Grades: 8 9 10 11 12
1. Teenage girls; 2. Dating (Social customs); 3. Possibilities; 4. Family problems; 5. Boarding schools; 6. Contemporary romances
9780385744799, hardcover, US; 9780375991851, library binding, US; 9780385391399, ebook, US; 9781760295943, Paperback, Australia
LC 2019041060

Rising high school senior Adelaide Buchwald grapples with a family catastrophe and romantic upheaval while confronting secrets she keeps, her ideas about love, and the weird grandiosity of the human mind.

Lockhart takes her penchant for plot twists to a new level, with a narrative that explores the idea of the multiverse, those infinite worlds loosed by paths taken and not taken. —*Publishers Weekly*

The **boy** book: a study of habits and behaviors, plus techniques for taming them. E. Lockhart. Delacorte Press, 2006 208 p. (Ruby Oliver novels, 2)
Grades: 8 9 10 11 12
1. Self-discovery in teenage girls; 2. Making friends; 3. Psychotherapy; 4. Sixteen-year-old girls; 5. Teenage girls; 6. Seattle, Washington; 7. Realistic fiction; 8. First person narratives; 9. Teen chick lit
9780385732086; 9780385902397; 9781471405983, print, UK
LC 2006004601

A high school junior continues her quest for relevant data on the male species, while enjoying her freedom as a newly licensed driver and examining her friendship with a clean-living vegetarian classmate.

Lockhart achieves the perfect balance of self-deprecating humor and self-pity in Ruby, and thus imbues her with such realism that she seems almost to fly off the page. —*Voice of Youth Advocates*
Sequel to: *The boyfriend list*.

The **boyfriend** list: (15 guys, 11 shrink appointments, 4 ceramic frogs, and me, Ruby Oliver). E. Lockhart. Delacorte Press, 2005 229 p. (Ruby Oliver novels, 1)
Grades: 9 10 11 12
1. Self-discovery in teenage girls; 2. Breaking up (Interpersonal relations); 3. Psychotherapy; 4. Self-esteem in teenage girls; 5. Self-discovery; 6. Seattle, Washington; 7. Realistic fiction; 8. First person narratives; 9. Teen chick lit; 10. Books for reluctant readers
9780385732062; 9780385902380; 9781471405969, print, UK
LC 2004006691
YALSA Quick Picks for Reluctant Young Adult Readers, 2006.

A Seattle fifteen-year-old explains some of the reasons for her recent panic attacks, including breaking up with her boyfriend, losing all her girlfriends, tensions between her performance-artist mother and her father, and more.

Readers will find many of Ruby's experiences familiar, and they'll appreciate the story as a lively, often entertaining read. —*Booklist*
Sequel: *The boy book*.

★ The **disreputable** history of Frankie Landau-Banks. E. Lockhart. Hyperion, 2008 345 p.

Grades: 7 8 9 10 11 12
1. Self-perception in teenage girls; 2. Secret societies; 3. Social acceptance; 4. Dating (Social customs); 5. Teenage girls; 6. Coming-of-age stories; 7. Realistic fiction; 8. Teen chick lit
9780786838189; 9781471404405, print, UK
Amelia Bloomer List, 2009; Booklist Editors' Choice: Books for Youth, 2008; New York Times Notable Children's Book, 2008; School Library Journal Best Books, 2008; YALSA Best Books for Young Adults, 2009; YALSA Popular Paperbacks for Young Adults, 2013; Michael L. Printz Honor Book, 2009; National Book Award for Young People's Literature finalist, 2008.

Tells of the life and transformation of Frankie Landau-Banks who began her teenage years as a quiet member of the Debate Club and grew to become a sixteen-year-old criminal mastermind with an attitude to match.

On her return to Alabaster Prep...[Frankie] attracts the attention of gorgeous Matthew...[who] is a member of the Loyal Order of the Basset Hounds, an all-male Alabaster secret society.... Frankie engineers her own guerilla membership by assuming a false online identity.... Lockhart creates a unique, indelible character.... Teens will be galvanized. —*Booklist*

★ **Genuine** fraud. E. Lockhart. Delacorte, 2017 288 p.
Grades: 7 8 9 10 11 12
1. Impostors; 2. Social classes; 3. Disguises; 4. Impersonation; 5. Murderers; 6. Thrillers and suspense
9780385744775; 9780375991844; 9781760295936, paperback, Australia; 9781471406638, ePub ebook, UK; 9781760526283, Paperback, Australia

Imogen is a runaway heiress, an orphan, a cook, and a cheat. Jule is a fighter, a social chameleon, and an athlete. An intense friendship. A disappearance. A murder, or maybe two. A bad romance, or maybe three. Blunt objects, disguises, blood, and chocolate. The American dream, superheroes, spies, and villains. A girl who refuses to give people what they want from her. A girl who refuses to be the person she once was.

This quietly unsettling, cinematic novel is deliciously suspenseful, and while its slim, it packs a real punch. —*Booklist*

How to be bad. . HarperTeen, 2008 325 p;
Grades: 9 10 11 12
1. Automobile travel; 2. Christian teenage girls; 3. Quarreling; 4. Social acceptance; 5. Friendship; 6. Florida; 7. Realistic fiction; 8. First person narratives; 9. Multiple perspectives
9780061284236
LC 2007052946
Told in alternating voices, Jesse, Vicks, and Mel, hoping to leave all their worries and woes behind, escape their small town by taking a road trip to Miami.

Whip-smart dialogue and a fast-moving, picaresque plot that zooms from lump-in-the-throat moments to all-out giddiness will keep readers going, and it's a testimony to how real these girls seem that the final chapters are profoundly satisfying rather than tidy. —*Publishers Weekly*

★ **We** were liars. E. Lockhart. Delacorte Press, 2014 240 pages
Grades: 7 8 9 10 11 12
1. Rich families; 2. Amnesia; 3. Islands; 4. Friendship; 5. Teenage romance; 6. Massachusetts; 7. Thrillers and suspense
9780385741262, hardback, US; 9780375989940, hardback, US; 9780385741279,paperback, US; 9781524764586, hardback, US; 9780375984402, ebook, US; 9781471403989,paperback, UK; 9781471406911, hardback, UK; 9781471403996, ebook
LC 2013042127
Abraham Lincoln Illinois High School Book Award, 2016; Blue Hen Book Award (Delaware) for Teen Books, 2017; Goodreads Choice Award, 2014; Great Lakes Great Books Award (Michigan), Grades 9-12, 2015; LibraryReads Favorites, 2014; School Library Journal

Best Books: Fiction, 2014; YALSA Best Fiction for Young Adults, 2015; YALSA Best Fiction for Young Adults: Top Ten, 2015.

Spending the summers on her family's private island off the coast of Massachusetts with her cousins and a special boy named Gat, teenaged Cadence struggles to remember what happened during her fifteenth summer.

Cadence Sinclair Easton comes from an old-money family, headed by a patriarch who owns a private island off of Cape Cod. Each summer, the extended family gathers at the various houses on the island, and Cadence, her cousins Johnny and Mirren, and friend Gat (the four Liars), have been inseparable since age eight....The story, while lightly touching on issues of class and race, more fully focuses on dysfunctional family drama, a heart-wrenching romance between Cadence and Gat, and, ultimately, the suspense of what happened during that fateful summer. The ending is a stunner that will haunt readers for a long time to come. —*School Library Journal*

London, Alex
Black wings beating. Alex London. Farrar Straus Giroux, 2018 432 p. (Skybound saga, 1)
Grades: 8 9 10 11 12
1. Twin brothers and sisters; 2. Quests; 3. Falconry; 4. Twins; 5. Birds; 6. Fantasy fiction; 7. Asian-influenced fantasy; 8. Multiple perspectives.
9780374306823; 9781250211484
LC 2018001439
Twins Kylee and Brysen must fight for survival in a remote valley called Six Villages as war approaches, she by rejecting her ancient gifts for falconry and Brysen by striving to find greatness.

Red skies falling. Alex London. Farrar Straus Giroux, 2019 480 p. (Skybound saga, 2)
Grades: 8 9 10 11 12
1. Twin brothers and sisters; 2. Birds; 3. Political intrigue; 4. Imaginary wars and battles; 5. Falconry; 6. Fantasy fiction; 7. Asian-influenced fantasy; 8. Multiple perspectives.
9780374306847, HRD, US
LC 2018046457
Orphaned twins Kylee and Brysen continue to fight for survival and power in the remote valley of the Six Villages.

Readers clamoring for a YA Game of Thrones will easily fall prey to this trilogy and await the final installment. Arresting. —*Kirkus*

Longo, Jennifer
What I carry. Jennifer Longo. Random House, 2020 336 p.
Grades: 8 9 10 11 12
1. Foster teenagers; 2. Control (Psychology); 3. Belonging; 4. Familial love; 5. Foster family; 6. Washington (State); 7. Bainbridge Island, Washington; 8. Coming-of-age stories; 9. Realistic fiction.
9780553537727; 9780553537710; 9780553537734
LC 2019001923
In her final year in foster care, seventeen-year-old Muir tries to survive her senior year before aging out of the system.

The power of relationship both those experienced and those denied is expertly explored throughout this novel with nuance and humanity. —*Kirkus*

Lord, Emery
The **map** from here to there. By Emery Lord. Bloomsbury, 2020 368 p.
Grades: 9 10 11 12

1. High school seniors; 2. Options, alternatives, choices; 3. Change; 4. High schools; 5. Small towns; 6. Indiana; 7. Coming-of-age stories; 8. Realistic fiction.
9781681199382; 9781526606648, Paperback, UK

LC 2019019170

High school senior Paige knows there is so much more to life after high school, but is it so terrible to want everything to stay the same forever?

The well-developed ensemble cast includes diverse family structures and shifting friendship dynamics that mirror Paige's own evolution in this satisfying story that ties up all the loose ends. —*Kirkus*

Sequel to: *The start of me and you.*

The **names** they gave us. By Emery Lord. 2017 400 p.
Grades: 9 10 11 12
1. Family secrets; 2. Belief and doubt; 3. Camps; 4. Faith; 5. Dating (Social customs); 6. Realistic fiction; 7. Coming-of-age stories
9781619639584; 9781408877814, Paperback, UK

LC 2016024917

YALSA Best Fiction for Young Adults, 2018.

When her perfectly planned summer of quality time with her parents, her serious boyfriend, and her Bible camp unravels and long-hidden family secrets emerge, Lucy must figure out what she is made of and what grace really means.

Comfortingly familiar, vibrant, and, at times, wrenching, this belongs on all shelves. —*Booklist*

The **start** of me and you. By Emery Lord. Bloomsbury, 2015 336 p.
Grades: 9 10 11 12
1. Self-fulfillment; 2. Children of divorced parents; 3. Loss (Psychology); 4. Self-fulfillment in teenage girls; 5. Teenage romance; 6. Indiana; 7. Realistic fiction
9781619633599; 9781619633605, ebook, US

LC 2014014376

Paige Hancock starts junior year with a list of ways to take back her life, rather than spending another year as "The Girl Whose Boyfriend Drowned," and finding out that Ryan Chase, her long-term crush, is available again might be the key.

Sequel: *The map from here to there*

When we collided. By Emery Lord. Bloomsbury, 2016 380 p.
Grades: 8 9 10 11 12
1. Teenage girls with mental illnesses; 2. Grief; 3. Children of people with depression; 4. Family problems; 5. Teenagers with bipolar disorder; 6. California; 7. Realistic fiction; 8. Love stories; 9. Multiple perspectives
9781619638457; 9781619638464, ebook, US

LC 2015011933

Schneider Family Book Award for Teens, 2017; YALSA Best Fiction for Young Adults, 2017; YALSA Quick Picks for Reluctant Young Adult Readers, 2017; Georgia Peach Honor Book for Teen Readers, 2017.

Can seventeen-year-old Jonah save his family restaurant from ruin, his mother from her sadness, and his danger-seeking girlfriend Vivi from herself?

As much about the fragility of the human experience as it is about mental illness, this offers a refreshing perspective on a spectrum of mental health disorders. This love story veers away from tragedy, instead firmly entrenching itself in hope and possibility. —*Booklist*

Lord, Emma
Tweet cute. Emma Lord. Wednesday Books, 2020 362 p.
Grades: 7 8 9 10 11 12

1. Business competition; 2. Social media; 3. Teenagers — Interpersonal relations; 4. Teenage boy/girl relations; 5. Fast food restaurants, chains, etc; 6. New York City; 7. Romantic comedies; 8. Teen chick lit; 9. Multiple perspectives
9781250237323, (hardcover), US

LC 2019036362

A reimagining of *You've Got Mail* follows the unlikely romance between an overachiever from a successful family and the class clown, who exchange snarky tweets that escalate into a viral Twitter war.

This plugged-in romance will likely be seen as a precursor to the way teen love stories will be told for years to come. —*Booklist*

Lowry, Lois
Gathering blue. Lois Lowry. Houghton Mifflin, 2000 215 p. (Giver quartet, 2)
Grades: 5 6 7 8
1. Dystopias; 2. Girl orphans; 3. Embroidery; 4. Girls with disabilities; 5. Far future; 6. Dystopian fiction; 7. Science fiction.
9780618055814

LC 24359

Booklist Editors' Choice: Books for Youth, 2000.

Lame and suddenly orphaned, Kira is mysteriously removed from her squalid village to live in the palatial Council Edifice, where she is expected to use her gifts as a weaver to do the bidding of the all-powerful Guardians.

Lowry has once again created a fully realized world full of drama, suspense, and even humor. —*School Library Journal*

★ The **giver**. Lois Lowry. Houghton Mifflin, 1993 180 p. (Giver quartet, 1)
Grades: 5 6 7 8 9 10
1. Dystopias; 2. Twelve-year-old boys; 3. Memories; 4. Far future; 5. Dystopian fiction; 6. Coming-of-age stories; 7. Books to movies.
9780395645666; 9780440237686

LC 92015034

ALA Notable Children's Book, 1994; Black-Eyed Susan Book Award (Maryland), Grades 6-9, 1995; Buckeye Children's Book Award (Ohio), Grades 6-8, 1997; Eliot Rosewater Indiana High School Book Award (Rosie Award), 1997; Garden State Teen Book Award (New Jersey), Fiction (Grades 6-8), 1996; Golden Archer Awards (Wisconsin): Middle/Jr. High, 1996; Golden Duck Awards: Hal Clement Award for Young Adult; Golden Sower Award (Nebraska), Young Adult, 1995; Grand Canyon Reader Award (Arizona), Teen Book Category, 1996; Great Stone Face Children's Book Award (New Hampshire), 1996; Land of Enchantment Book Award (New Mexico), General category, 1997; Maine Student Book Award, 1995; Newbery Medal, 1994; Pennsylvania Young Reader's Choice Awards, Grades 3-8, 1995; Rebecca Caudill Young Reader's Book Award (Illinois), 1996; Sequoyah Book Awards (Oklahoma), Young Adult Books, 1996; Surrey Book of the Year Award (British Columbia), 1996; Virginia Readers' Choice Award for Middle School, 1996; William Allen White Children's Book Award (Kansas), 1996; Young Reader's Choice Award (Pacific Northwest), Senior, 1996.

Given his lifetime assignment at the Ceremony of Twelve, Jonas becomes the receiver of memories shared by only one other in his community and discovers the terrible truth about the society in which he lives.

A riveting, chilling story that inspires a new appreciation for diversity, love, and even pain. Truly memorable. —*School Library Journal*

★ **Son**. By Lois Lowry. Houghton Mifflin, 2012 288 p. (Giver quartet, 4)
Grades: 6 7 8 9 10 11 12

1. Utopias; 2. Birthmothers; 3. Mother and child; 4. Separation (Psychology); 5. Coastal towns; 6. Dystopian fiction; 7. Science fiction; 8. Books to movies
9780547887203; 9780007597307, print, UK

LC 2012014034

ALA Notable Children's Book, 2013; School Library Journal Best Books, 2012.

Unlike the other Birthmothers in her utopian community, teenaged Claire forms an attachment to her baby, feeling a great loss when he is taken to the Nurturing Center to be adopted by a family unit.

Lu, Marie

Batman: Nightwalker. Marie Lu. 2018 304 p. (DC icons, 2)
Grades: 7 8 9 10

1. Superheroes; 2. Batman (Fictitious character); 3. Teenage boys; 4. Villains; 5. Superhero stories; 6. Multiple perspectives; 7. Franchise books
9780399549786; 9780399549779; 9780141386836, print, UK; 9780399549793, ebook, US

LC 2017021544

The Nightwalkers are terrorizing Gotham City, and Bruce Wayne is next on their list.... Bruce will walk the dark line between trust and betrayal as the Nightwalkers circle closer.

A fast-paced story line, action-packed fight sequences, and hi-tech gadgetry expected from any Batman story make this a fun read with wide appeal. —*School Library Journal*

Batman created by Bob Kane with Bill Finger

The **Kingdom** of Back. Marie Lu. G.P. Putnam's Sons, 2020 336 p.
Grades: 7 8 9 10 11 12

1. Berchtold zu Sonnenburg, Maria Anna Mozart, Reichsfreiin von, 1751-1829; 2. Musicians; 3. Faustian bargains; 4. Women's role; 5. Brothers and sisters; 6. Fairies; 7. Austria; 8. Europe; 9. 18th century; 10. Historical fantasy.
9781524739010

Nannerl Mozart has just one wish—to be remembered forever. But she has little hope she'll ever become the acclaimed composer she longs to be. As Nannerl's hope grows dimmer with each passing year, the talents of her beloved younger brother, Wolfgang, only seem to shine brighter. His brilliance begins to eclipse her own, until one day a mysterious stranger from a magical land appears with an irresistible offer—but his help may cost her everything.

★ **Legend**. Marie Lu. G. P. Putnam's Sons, 2011 336 p. (Legend (Marie Lu), 1)
Grades: 8 9 10 11 12

1. Post-apocalypse; 2. Plague; 3. Dystopias; 4. Revenge; 5. Resistance to government; 6. Los Angeles, California; 7. 22nd century; 8. Dystopian fiction; 9. Science fiction; 10. Multiple perspectives
9780399256752; 9780141339603, print, UK

LC 2011002003

Garden State Teen Book Award (New Jersey), Fiction (Grades 6-8), 2014; Golden Sower Award (Nebraska), Young Adult, 2014; Iowa Teen Award, 2014; Kentucky Bluegrass Award for Grades 6-8, 2013; Rebecca Caudill Young Reader's Book Award (Illinois), 2015; Sunshine State Young Reader's Award (Florida), 2014; Truman Readers Award (Missouri), 2014; YALSA Best Fiction for Young Adults, 2012; YALSA Popular Paperbacks for Young Adults, 2016.

In a dark future, when North America has split into two warring nations, fifteen-year-olds Day, a famous criminal, and prodigy June, the brilliant soldier hired to capture him, discover that they have a common enemy.

The characters are likable, the plot moves at a good pace, and the adventure is solid. —*School Library Journal*

★ **Prodigy:** a Legend novel. Marie Lu. G. P. Putnam's Sons, 2012 288 p. (Legend (Marie Lu), 2)
Grades: 8 9 10 11 12

1. Post-apocalypse; 2. Dystopias; 3. Fugitives; 4. Resistance to government; 5. Assassination; 6. Los Angeles, California; 7. 22nd century; 8. Dystopian fiction; 9. Science fiction
9780399256769; 9780141339573, print, UK

LC 2012003773

YALSA Best Fiction for Young Adults, 2014.

June and Day make their way to Las Vegas where they join the rebel Patriot group and become involved in an assassination plot against the Elector in hopes of saving the Republic.

This is a well-molded mixture of intrigue, romance, and action, where things can change with almost any turn of the page, and frequently do. —*Booklist*

Rebel. Marie Lu. Roaring Brook Press, 2019 378 pages; (Legend (Marie Lu), 4)
Grades: 8 9 10 11 12

1. Post-apocalypse; 2. Dystopias; 3. Brothers; 4. Far future; 5. Hiding; 6. Antarctica; 7. Dystopian fiction; 8. Science fiction
9781250221704; 9781250620880; 9780241436479, Paperback, UK

LC Bl2019024462

As Day and Eden struggle with who they've become since their time in the Republic, a new danger creeps into the distance between them, and Eden finds himself drawn into Ross City's dark side, where his legendary brother may not be able to save him.

This tale of intrigue, alliances, and love will draw Legend fans and new readers into a fascinating world whose combined layers of privilege and surveillance draw comparisons to many present-day social ills. —*Kirkus*

The **Rose** Society. Marie Lu. 2015 416 p. (Young elites, 2)
Grades: 9 10 11 12

1. Teenage girl heroes; 2. Imaginary kingdoms; 3. Survival (after epidemics); 4. Plague; 5. Pariahs; 6. High fantasy; 7. Fantasy fiction.
9780399167843

LC Bl2015034693

Vengeful in the aftermath of cruel betrayals by both family and friends, Adelina flees with her sister to build an army of fellow Young Elites in an effort to strike down the white-cloaked Inquisition Axis soldiers who nearly killed her.

The Young Elites was both an instant best-seller and critically acclaimed, and the success is sure to hop to this even-stronger sequel. —*Booklist*

★ **Skyhunter**. Marie Lu. Roaring Brook Press, 2020 384 p. (Skyhunter duology, 1)
Grades: 9 10 11 12

1. Warriors; 2. Prisoners; 3. Mutants; 4. Genetic engineering; 5. Post-apocalypse; 6. Dystopian fiction; 7. First person narratives
9781250221681

Talin is a Striker, a member of an elite fighting force that stands as the last defense for Mara, the only free nation in the world, but when a mysterious prisoner is brought from the front to Mara's capital, Talin senses there is more to him than meets the eye.

Readers will eagerly await a follow-up to this engrossing dystopian novel, which searingly interrogates traumas of war, immigration, and imperialism. —*Publishers Weekly*

★ **Warcross**. Marie Lu. G.P. Putnam's Sons Books for Young Readers, 2017 416 p. (Warcross, 1)

Grades: 8 9 10 11 12

1. Computer games; 2. Teenage hackers; 3. Undercover operations; 4. Computer crimes; 5. Virtual reality games; 6. Tokyo, Japan; 7. Japan; 8. Science fiction; 9. STEM fiction
9780399547966; 9780241321430, paperback, UK; 9780241321423, hardcover, UK; 9780241321454, ebook, UK; 9780241321447, Paperback, UK
Westchester Fiction Award, 2018; YALSA Best Fiction for Young Adults, 2018; YALSA Quick Picks for Reluctant Young Adult Readers, 2018; Best STEM Books, 2018.

After hacking into the Warcross Championships' opening game to track illegal betting, bounty hunter Emika Chen is asked by the game's creator to go undercover to investigate a security problem, and she uncovers a sinister plot.

Readers will move effortlessly through Lu's fantastic writing, and they will enjoy getting to know this international cast of characters. The author adeptly weaves together exciting video games scenes, virtual reality, and romance. —*School Library Journal*

Wildcard. Marie Lu. G.P. Putnam's Sons Books for Young Readers, 2018 352 p. (Warcross, 2)
Grades: 8 9 10 11 12

1. Computer games; 2. Teenage hackers; 3. Undercover operations; 4. Computer crimes; 5. Virtual reality games; 6. Tokyo, Japan; 7. Japan; 8. Science fiction; 9. STEM fiction
9780399547997; 9780399548000; 9781432857653; 9780241342428; 9780241342442, Paperback, UK; 9780399548017, ebook, US
LC 2018011748

For the millions who log in every day, Warcross isn't just a game it's a way of life. And teenage hacker Emika Chen has found herself caught up in a conflict that could change the world. Warcross creator, Hideo Tanaka, wants to use to the game to control peoples' thoughts and feelings, effectively ending free will Zero, a mysterious (and dangerous) hacker, wants to stop him. Now Emika must decide who she will fight for. The game is on!

The plotting is exquisite, with tiny details connecting back to the first book, big twists that never feel forced, and emotional power drawn from character growth. —*Kirkus*
Sequel to: *Warcross.*

The **young** elites. Marie Lu. G. P. Putnam's Sons, 2014 336 p. (Young elites, 1)
Grades: 8 9 10 11 12

1. Teenage girl heroes; 2. Imaginary kingdoms; 3. Survival (after epidemics); 4. Plague; 5. Pariahs; 6. High fantasy; 7. Fantasy fiction.
9780399167836
YALSA Best Fiction for Young Adults, 2015; YALSA Best Fiction for Young Adults: Top Ten, 2015.

Scarred and cast out after surviving the blood plague, Adelina finds a place for herself among the Young Elites who use their magic to advocate on behalf of young innocents and who are targeted by the soldiers of the Inquisition Axis.

In a gorgeously constructed world that somewhat resembles Renaissance Italy but with its own pantheon, geography and fauna, the multiethnic and multisexual Young Elites offer a cinematically perfect ensemble of gorgeous-but-unusual illusionists, animal speakers, fire summoners and wind callers. A must for fans of Kristin Cashore's *Fire* (2009) and other totally immersive fantasies. —*Kirkus*

Lubar, David

★ **Character,** driven. David Lubar. Tor Teen, a Tom Doherty Associates book, 2016 300 p.
Grades: 8 9 10 11 12

1. Children of unemployed parents; 2. Fathers and sons; 3. Teenage boy/girl relations; 4. High school seniors; 5. Virginity; 6. New Jersey; 7. Realistic fiction; 8. Coming-of-age stories
9780765316332
School Library Journal Best Books, 2016; YALSA Best Fiction for Young Adults, 2017.

In his last year of high school, seventeen-year-old virgin Cliff Sparks has to figure out what to do with his life, including how to meet new girl Jillian and how to deal with old issues with his unemployed father.

This exquisitely crafted coming-of-age novel gets down and dirty—and even rebellious—without sacrificing honesty, thoughtfulness, or respect. —*Booklist*

Sleeping freshmen never lie. By David Lubar. Dutton Children's Books, 2005 279 p. (Scott Hudson books, 1)
Grades: 7 8 9 10

1. High school freshmen; 2. Teenage authors; 3. Self-confidence in teenage boys; 4. High school students; 5. New students; 6. Pennsylvania; 7. Realistic fiction.
9780525473114
LC 2004023067
Thumbs Up! Award (Michigan), 2006; YALSA Popular Paperbacks for Young Adults, 2014; YALSA Best Books for Young Adults, 2006.

While navigating his first year of high school and awaiting the birth of his new baby brother, Scott loses old friends and gains some unlikely new ones as he hones his skills as a writer.

The plot is framed by Scott's journal of advice for the unborn baby. The novel's absurd, comical mood is evident in its entries.... The author brings the protagonist to three-dimensional life by combining these introspective musings with active, hilarious narration. —*School Library Journal*

Lucier, Makiia

A **death-struck** year. Makiia Lucier. Houghton Mifflin Harcourt, 2014 282 pages;
Grades: 9 10 11 12

1. Epidemics; 2. Diseases; 3. Self-reliance in teenage girls; 4. Death; 5. Red Cross workers; 6. Portland, Oregon; 7. Historical fiction; 8. First person narratives.
9780544164505
LC 2013037482
When the Spanish influenza epidemic reaches Portland, Oregon, in 1918, seventeen-year-old Cleo leaves behind the comfort of her boarding school to work for the Red Cross.

A teen girl struggles to survive the Spanish influenza pandemic of 1918...Readers will be swept up in the story as Cleo builds friendships and manages to find hope amid disease and death. A notable debut. —*Kirkus*
Includes bibliographical references (page 280).

★ **Isle** of blood and stone. Makiia Lucier. 2018 400 p. (Tower of winds, 1)
Grades: 7 8 9 10 11 12

1. Cartographers; 2. Riddles; 3. Missing persons; 4. Political intrigue; 5. Maps; 6. High fantasy; 7. Sea stories; 8. Fantasy fiction
9780544968578
LC 2017015656
YALSA Best Fiction for Young Adults, 2019.

When two maps surface, each bearing the same hidden riddle, nineteen-year-old Elias, a royal mapmaker, sets sail with King Ulises to uncover long-held secrets behind the mysterious disappearance of the king's two young brothers eighteen years earlier.

A romantic maritime epic and a charming tribute to mapmakers, calligraphers, and explorers. —*Kirkus*

Song of the abyss. Makiia Lucier. Houghton Mifflin Harcourt 2019 368 p. (Tower of winds, 2)

Grades: 7 8 9

1. Explorers; 2. Missing persons; 3. Seafaring life; 4. Cartographers; 5. Inheritance and succession; 6. High fantasy; 7. Sea stories; 8. Fantasy fiction.

9780544968585; 9780544968615, ebook, US

LC 2018052136

When men start vanishing at sea without a trace, seventeen-year-old Reyna, a Master Explorer, must travel to a country shrouded in secrets to solve the mystery before it is too late.

Lundin, Britta

Ship it. By Britta Lundin. 2018 384 p.

Grades: 7 8 9 10 11 12

1. Actors and actresses; 2. Media fandom; 3. Prejudice; 4. Blogs; 5. Popularity; 6. Coming-of-age stories; 7. LGBTQIA fiction; 8. Realistic fiction.

9781368003131; 9781368021159

LC 2017034202

Told from two viewpoints, Forest, a television actor who needs more fans, and Claire, a teen fan fiction blogger, are teamed to raise his profile despite their disagreement over whether his character is gay.

Luper, Eric

Seth Baumgartner's love manifesto. By Eric Luper. Balzer & Bray, 2010 304 p.

Grades: 8 9 10 11 12

1. Love; 2. Dating (Social customs); 3. Interpersonal relations; 4. Teenage boys; 5. Teenage boy/girl relations.

9780061827532; 9780061827549

LC 2009029706

After his girlfriend breaks up with him and he sees his father out with another woman, high school senior Seth Baumgartner, who has a summer job at the country club and is preparing for a father-son golf tournament, launches a podcast in which he explores the mysteries of love.

Luper weaves together many themes—trust and secrets, lies and truth, love, lust and, of course, golf—in a way that even the most introspection-hating male reader will eat with a spoon. —*Kirkus*

Lurie, April

The **latent** powers of Dylan Fontaine. April Lurie. Delacorte Press, 2008 211 p;

Grades: 8 9 10 11 12

1. Family problems; 2. Brothers; 3. Bands (Music); 4. Marijuana; 5. Fifteen-year-old boys; 6. New York City; 7. Coming-of-age stories; 8. First person narratives; 9. Realistic fiction

9780385731256

LC 2007032313

Fifteen-year-old Dylan's friend Angie is making a film about him while he is busy trying to keep his older brother from getting caught with drugs, to deal with his mother having left the family, and to figure out how to get Angie to think of him as more than just a friend.

Ly, Many

Roots and wings. Many Ly. Delacorte Press, 2008 262 p;

Grades: 6 7 8 9 10

1. Cambodian Americans; 2. Mothers and daughters; 3. Identity (Psychology); 4. Grandmothers; 5. Fourteen-year-old girls; 6. St. Petersburg, Florida; 7. Coming-of-age stories; 8. Realistic fiction

9780385735001

Asian Pacific American Award for Literature: Young Adult Literature, 2009.

While in St. Petersburg, Florida, to give her grandmother a Cambodian funeral, fourteen-year-old Grace, who was raised in Pennsylvania, finally gets some answers about the father she never met, her mother's and grandmother's youth, and her Asian-American heritage.

The book is beautifully written...[and] the author allows family secrets to unfold carefully and explores them with sincerity. —*School Library Journal*

Lyga, Barry

★ The **astonishing** adventures of Fanboy & Goth Girl. By Barry Lyga. Houghton Mifflin, 2006 311 p.

Grades: 8 9 10 11 12

1. Teenage misfits; 2. Comic book writers; 3. Self-perception in teenagers; 4. Fifteen-year-old boys; 5. Teenagers; 6. Realistic fiction.

9780618723928

LC 2005033259

School Library Journal Best Books, 2006; YALSA Best Books for Young Adults, 2008; YALSA Popular Paperbacks for Young Adults, 2012.

A fifteen-year-old "geek" who keeps a list of the high school jocks and others who torment him, and pours his energy into creating a great graphic novel, encounters Kyra, Goth Girl, who helps change his outlook on almost everything, including himself.

This engaging first novel has good characterization with genuine voices.... The book is compulsively readable. —*Voice of Youth Advocates*

Sequel: *Goth Girl rising*.

★ **Bang:** a novel. By Barry Lyga. 2017 304 p.

Grades: 9 10 11 12

1. Guilt in teenage boys; 2. Interfaith friendship; 3. Prejudice; 4. Friendship; 5. Hope; 6. Realistic fiction.

9780316315500; 9780316315524, ebook, US; 9780316315531, ebook, US

LC 2016019843

YALSA Best Fiction for Young Adults, 2018; YALSA Quick Picks for Reluctant Young Adult Readers, 2018.

A new friend and their YouTube cooking channel help fourteen-year-old Sebastian move on from accidentally shooting his infant sister ten years earlier.

Its a raw exploration of persistent social stigmas, a beautiful study of forgiveness, and an unflinching portrait of a parents worst nightmare. —*Publishers Weekly*

Blood of my blood. Barry Lyga. 2014 480 pages (Jasper Dent trilogy, 3)

Grades: 9 10 11 12

1. Children of murderers; 2. Serial murderers; 3. Fathers and sons; 4. Dating (Social customs); 5. Best friends; 6. New York City; 7. Thrillers and suspense; 8. Multiple perspectives

9780316198707

LC 2014003643

Jazz Dent, who has been shot and left to die in New York City, his girlfriend, Connie, who is in the clutches of Jazz's serial killer father, Billy, and his best friend, Howie, who is bleeding to death on the floor of Jazz's own home in tiny Lobo's Nod, must all rise above the horrors their lives have become and find a way to come together in pursuit of Billy.

You can't stop reading...Lyga's strength is a plot that rockets with blood-slicked assurance and with the intercut speed (and splatter) of Thomas Harris' *The Silence of the Lambs* (1988). Will Jazz end up a Crow or just another 'prospect? Here's hoping the Edgar Awards retroactively present Lyga a trio of statuettes for his chilling three-book answer. —*Booklist*

Boy toy. By Barry Lyga. Houghton Mifflin, 2007 410 p;
Grades: 10 11 12
1. Sexually abused teenagers; 2. Emotional problems of teenagers; 3. Coping in teenage boys; 4. Eighteen-year-old men; 5. Young men — Sexuality; 6. Realistic fiction; 7. First person narratives
9780618723935
LC 2006039840
YALSA Best Books for Young Adults, 2008.

After five years of fighting his way past flickers of memory about the teacher who molested him and the incident that brought the crime to light, eighteen-year-old Josh gets help in coping with his molestor's release from prison when he finally tells his best friends the whole truth.

The author tackles this incredibly sensitive story with boldness and confidence. He does not shy away from graphic descriptions of Josh's past and even makes the audacious choice of showing young Josh enjoying the attention...[Josh] works hard at healing himself and moving into healthy adulthood, and by the end of this well-written, challenging novel, the reader has high hopes that he will make it. —*Voice of Youth Advocates*

★ **I** hunt killers. By Barry Lyga. Little, Brown, 2012 368 p. (Jasper Dent trilogy, 1)
Grades: 10 11 12
1. Children of murderers; 2. Serial murder investigation; 3. Psychopaths; 4. Serial murderers; 5. Murder; 6. Thrillers and suspense; 7. Books for reluctant readers
9780316125840
LC 2011025418
Kentucky Bluegrass Award for Grades 9-12, 2014; YALSA Best Fiction for Young Adults, 2013; YALSA Popular Paperbacks for Young Adults, 2015; YALSA Quick Picks for Reluctant Young Adult Readers, 2013.

Jasper "Jazz" Dent is the son of Billy Dent, the country's most notorious serial killer, and "Dear Old Dad" taught him everything he knew. But Billy's in prison now and Jazz wants to convince the world—and himself—that he's not like his father. When several murders occur in his town, Jazz and his friend Howie try to track down the killer before he strikes again.

Lynch, Chris
The **Big** Game of Everything. Chris Lynch. HarperTeen, 2008 275 p;
Grades: 7 8 9 10
1. Self-discovery; 2. Summer employment; 3. Grandfather and grandson; 4. Golf courses; 5. Eccentric families; 6. Realistic fiction
9780060740344
LC 2007049578
Jock and his eccentric family spend the summer working at Grampus's golf complex, where they end up learning the rules of "The Big Game of Everything."

This Printz Honor-winning author offers up another touching and off-beat novel full of delightfully skewed humor. —*Voice of Youth Advocates*

Hit count: a novel. By Chris Lynch. Algonquin Young Readers, 2015 368 p.
Grades: 8 9 10 11 12
1. Football players; 2. High school football; 3. Sports injuries; 4. Dating (Social customs); 5. Football; 6. Football stories; 7. Sports fiction
9781616202507
LC 2014043009
Arlo Brodie loves being at the heart of the action on the football field, and while his dad cheers him on, his mother quotes head injury statistics

and refuses to watch, but Arlo's winning plays, the cheering crowds, and the adrenaline rush are enough to convince him that everything is OK, in spite of the pain, the pounding, the dizziness, and the confusion.

This intense, timely story provides incredible insight into the reasons why knowledge of football's potential danger is not enough to keep young players from taking the field. —*Kirkus*

★ **Inexcusable**. Chris Lynch. Atheneum Books for Young Readers, 2005 165 p. (Inexcusable, 1)
Grades: 8 9 10 11 12
1. High school football players; 2. Date rape; 3. Self-deception; 4. Teenage boy/girl relations; 5. Violence in teenage boys; 6. Realistic fiction; 7. First person narratives.
9780689847899
LC 2004030874
Booklist Editors' Choice: Books for Youth, 2005; School Library Journal Best Books, 2005; YALSA Popular Paperbacks for Young Adults, 2016; YALSA Best Books for Young Adults, 2006; National Book Award for Young People's Literature finalist, 2005.

High school senior and football player Keir sets out to enjoy himself on graduation night, but when he attempts to comfort a friend whose date has left her stranded, things go terribly wrong.

This finely crafted and thought-provoking page-turner carefully conveys that it is simply inexcusable to whitewash wrongs, and that those responsible should (and hopefully will) pay the price. —*School Library Journal*

Maaren, Kari
★ **Weave** a circle round. Kari Maaren. Tor, 2017 336 p.
Grades: 11 12 Adult
1. Misfits (Persons); 2. Time travel (Past); 3. High school students; 4. Chaos; 5. Neighbors; 6. Gateway fantasy; 7. Fantasy fiction; 8. Canadian fiction; 9. Adult books for young adults
9780765386281, paperback, US
Loan Stars Favourites, 2017.

When she runs afoul of her eccentric new neighbors, teen Freddy is sent traveling through time where she encounters numerous versions of her neighbors, Josiah and Cuerva, and she realizes that she might be the third in their group of immortals.

This is an ambitious, intricate, joyful coming-of-age tale, with memorable characters and a powerful sense of wonder. —*Publishers Weekly*

Maas, Sarah J.
Catwoman: Soulstealer. Sarah J. Maas. 2018 320 p; (DC icons, 3)
Grades: 7 8 9 10
1. Superheroes; 2. Women criminals; 3. Catwoman (Fictitious character); 4. Women villains; 5. Supervillains; 6. Superhero stories; 7. Multiple perspectives; 8. Franchise books
9780399549694; 9780399549700; 9780141386898, Paperback, UK; 9780141386881, Hardback, UK; 9780399549717, ebook, US

Two years after escaping Gotham City's slums, Selina Kyle returns as the mysterious and wealthy Holly Vanderhees. She quickly discovers that with Batman off on a vital mission, Gotham City looks ripe for the taking.

A **court** of thorns and roses. By Sarah J. Maas. Bloomsbury, 2015 432 p. (A court of thorns and roses, 1)
Grades: 9 10 11 12
1. Fairies; 2. Curses; 3. Shapeshifting; 4. Imaginary places; 5. Love; 6. High fantasy; 7. Fantasy fiction.
9781619634442; 9781619634459; 9781408857861, UK; 9781408891995, print, UK; 9781547604173; 9781526605399, Paperback, UK; 9781526630780, Paperback, UK
LC 2014020071

LibraryReads Favorites, 2015; YALSA Best Fiction for Young Adults, 2016.

Dragged off to a treacherous magical land as retribution for killing a wolf, huntress Feyre learns that her captor is one of the lethal, immortal faeries who once ruled her world.

Also published as a collector's edition in 2019.

Throne of glass. By Sarah J. Maas. Bloomsbury, 2012 416 p. (Throne of glass novels, 1)
Grades: 10 11 12

1. Assassins; 2. Princes; 3. Teenage prisoners; 4. Competition; 5. Courts and courtiers; 6. High fantasy; 7. Fantasy fiction.
9781599906959; 9781408832332

LC 2012011229

YALSA Best Fiction for Young Adults, 2013.

After she has served a year of hard labor in the salt mines of Endovier for her crimes, Crown Prince Dorian offers eighteen-year-old assassin Celaena Sardothien her freedom on the condition that she act as his champion in a competition to find a new royal assassin.

Maberry, Jonathan
★ **Rot** & Ruin. Jonathan Maberry. Simon & Schuster Books for Young Readers, 2010 458 p; (Benny Imura books, 1)
Grades: 9 10 11 12

1. Zombies; 2. Bounty hunters; 3. Stepbrothers; 4. Rationing; 5. Survival; 6. California; 7. Apocalyptic fiction; 8. Science fiction; 9. Horror
9781442402324

LC 2009046041

Gateway Readers Award (Missouri), 2013; Nutmeg Children's Book Award, Teen category, 2013; YALSA Popular Paperbacks for Young Adults, 2016; YALSA Best Fiction for Young Adults, 2011.

After the zombie apocalypse, teens must find work by the age of 15 if they want to keep their food ration. And that's why lazy, resentful, 15-year-old Benny reluctantly leaves the safety of home and joins his bounty-hunting half-brother Tom in the zombie-riddled wilds of the Rot and Ruin. As the brothers encounter villains far more inhuman than the undead, Benny begins to question his understanding not only of Tom, but also of life, death, and what bravery really means.

In turns mythic and down-to-earth, this intense novel combines adventure and philosophy to tell a truly memorable zombie story. —*Publishers Weekly*

Sequel: *Dust & decay.*

Mabry, Samantha
All the wind in the world. Samantha Mabry. Algonquin Young Readers, 2017 288 p.
Grades: 9 10 11 12

1. Ranches; 2. Ranch life; 3. Curses; 4. Secrets; 5. Teenage romance; 6. Texas; 7. Southwest (United States); 8. Magical realism
9781616206666; 9781616208554

LC 2017020570

Booklist Editors' Choice: Books for Youth, 2017; Longlisted for the National Book Award for Young People's Literature, 2017.

Working in the maguey fields of the Southwest, Sarah Jac and James are in love but forced to start over on a ranch that is possibly cursed where the delicate balance in their relationship begins to give way.

A gripping, fablelike story of a love ferocious enough to destroy and a world prepared to burn with it. —*Booklist*

★ **Tigers**, not daughters. Samantha Mabry. Algonquin Books of Chapel Hill, 2020 289 p.
Grades: 9 10 11 12

1. Sisters — Death; 2. Fathers and daughters; 3. Grief; 4. Ghosts; 5. Children of widowers; 6. San Antonio, Texas; 7. Paranormal fiction; 8. Multiple perspectives
9781616208967, HRD, US; 9781643750545, ebook, US

LC 2019037812

School Library Journal Best Books, 2020.

Three sisters in San Antonio are shadowed by guilt and grief over the loss of their oldest sister, who still haunts their house.

The book's structure moves like contained chaos, jumping among timelines, focalizing through different sisters, and offering the first-person perspective of an unnamed neighborhood boy, all so that the reader never quite knows Ana but only witnesses the wreckage her death left behind. —*Bulletin of the Center for Children's Books*

Mac, Carrie
★ **10** things I can see from here. Carrie Mac. Alfred A. Knopf, 2017 320 p.
Grades: 7 8 9 10 11 12

1. Lesbian teenagers; 2. Anxiety disorders; 3. Anxiety in teenagers; 4. Fathers and daughters; 5. Love; 6. Vancouver, British Columbia; 7. Realistic fiction; 8. LGBTQIA fiction; 9. First person narratives.
9780399556258; 9780399556289, Paperback, US

LC 2015046690

OLA Best Bets, 2017; Rainbow List, 2018.

Maeve, a sufferer of severe anxiety, moves in with her recovering alcoholic father and her very pregnant stepmother and falls for a girl who is not afraid of anything.

With Maeve, Mac delivers a character who's heart- warmingly real and sympathetic, and her story provides a much needed mirror for anxious queer girls everywhere. —*Kirkus*

MacColl, Michaela
Nobody's secret. By Michaela MacColl. Chronicle Books, 2013 288 p.
Grades: 7 8 9 10

1. Dickinson, Emily; 2. Poets; 3. Murder investigation; 4. Teenage poets; 5. Fifteen-year-old girls; 6. Teenage girls; 7. Amherst, Massachusetts; 8. 1840s; 9. 19th century; 10. Historical mysteries
9781452108605

LC 2012030364

When fifteen-year-old Emily Dickinson meets a charming, enigmatic young man who playfully refuses to tell her his name, she is intrigued—so when he is found dead in her family's pond in Amherst she is determined to discover his secret, no matter how dangerous it may prove to be.

MacCullough, Carolyn
Always a witch. By Carolyn MacCullough. Clarion Books, 2011 276 p;
Grades: 8 9 10 11 12

1. Teenage witches; 2. Time travel (Past); 3. Prophecies; 4. Ability; 5. Household employees; 6. New York City; 7. 1880s; 8. Urban fantasy
9780547224855

LC 2011008148

Haunted by her grandmother's prophecy that she will soon be forced to make a terrible decision, witch Tamsin Greene risks everything to travel back in time to 1887 New York to confront the enemy that wants to destroy her family.

This is an enjoyable magical adventure. —*Kirkus*

Sequel to: *Once a witch .*

Macdonald, Maryann
Odette's secrets. By Maryann Macdonald. Bloomsbury, 2013 240 p.

Grades: 6 7 8 9

1. Meyers, Odette; 2. Jewish girls; 3. World War II; 4. Identity (Psychology); 5. Parent-separated girls; 6. Holocaust (1933-1945); 7. France; 8. Second World War era (1939-1945); 9. 1940s; 10. Historical fiction; 11. Novels in verse; 12. First person narratives
9781599907505

LC 2012015549

When Odette Meyer's father is sent to a Nazi work camp, her mother sends Odette from Paris to the French countryside where she must pretend to be a Catholic peasant to remain safe, while secrets burn within her.

MacHale, D. J.

Black water. D.J. MacHale. Aladdin Paperbacks, 2004 427 p; (Pendragon series, 5)
Grades: 7 8 9 10

1. Teenage heroes and heroines; 2. Shapeshifters; 3. Plague; 4. Antidotes; 5. Demons; 6. Fantasy fiction; 7. Gateway fantasy.
9780689869112

LC Bl2004107497

Bobby Pendragon must choose whether to endanger himself and the other residents of Halla in order to save the residents of Eelong who are infected with a mysterious plague.

The **lost** city of Faar. D.J. MacHale. Aladdin Paperbacks, 2003 385 p; (Pendragon series, 2)
Grades: 7 8 9 10

1. Teenage heroes and heroines; 2. Shapeshifters; 3. Demons; 4. Imaginary wars and battles; 5. Underwater cities; 6. Fantasy fiction; 7. Gateway fantasy.
9780743437325

LC 2002108580

The ideas are clever and the descriptions inviting and easy to picture.... The teenaged protagonists enlist readers' sympathy and involvement and the nonstop plot developments keep the many pages turning and readers wanting more. —*School Library Journal*

Aladdin fantasy

The **merchant** of death. By D.J. MacHale. Aladdin, 2002 375 p; (Pendragon series, 1)
Grades: 7 8 9 10

1. Teenage heroes and heroines; 2. Parallel universes; 3. Shapeshifters; 4. Demons; 5. Imaginary wars and battles; 6. Fantasy fiction; 7. Gateway fantasy.
9780743437318

LC 2002210164

YALSA Popular Paperbacks for Young Adults, 2012.

Bobby Pendragon is a seemingly normal fourteen-year-old boy. He has a family, a home, and even Marley, his beloved dog. But there is something very special about Bobby. He is going to save the world. ...Before he can object, he is swept off to an alternate dimension known as Denduron, a territory inhabited by strange beings, ruled by a magical tyrant, and plagued by dangerous revolution.

The **never** war. D.J. MacHale. Aladdin Paperbacks, 2003 336 p; (Pendragon series, 3)
Grades: 7 8 9 10

1. Teenage heroes and heroines; 2. Shapeshifters; 3. Time travel; 4. Demons; 5. Space and time; 6. New York City; 7. 1930s; 8. Fantasy fiction; 9. Gateway fantasy.
9780743437332

LC 2002116463

Bobby and the Traveler from Cloral—Spader—have flumed to New York City, 1937. Against a backdrop of gangsters, swing music, and the distant sound of a brewing war, the two must uncover the evil Saint Dane's newest plot.

This book has a fast pace, suspenseful plotting, and cliffhanger chapter endings that will make it popular. —*School Library Journal*

★ The **pilgrims** of Rayne. D.J. MacHale. Simon & Schuster Books for Young Readers, 2007 547 p. (Pendragon series, 8)
Grades: 7 8 9 10

1. Teenage heroes and heroines; 2. Shapeshifters; 3. Demons; 4. Rescues; 5. Imaginary places; 6. Fantasy fiction; 7. Gateway fantasy.
9781416914167

LC 2006038131

With Saint Dane seemingly on the verge of toppling all of the territories, Pendragon and Courtney set out to rescue Mark and find themselves traveling—and battling—their way through different worlds as they try to save all of Halla.

This is packed...with nonstop action, mind-boggling plot twists, and well-imagined locales. —*Voice of Youth Advocates*

Journal of an adventure through time and space.

The **Quillan** games. By D.J. MacHale. Simon & Schuster Books for Young Readers, 2006 486 p. (Pendragon series, 7)
Grades: 7 8 9 10

1. Teenage heroes and heroines; 2. Shapeshifters; 3. Games; 4. Demons; 5. Imaginary places; 6. Fantasy fiction; 7. Gateway fantasy.
9781416914235

LC 2005029902

With more questions than answers about Saint Dane, Bobby travels to the territory of Quillan and is forced to play games where only the winner survives.

Raven rise. D.J. MacHale. Simon & Schuster Books for Young Readers, 2008 544 p. (Pendragon series, 9)
Grades: 7 8 9 10

1. Teenage heroes and heroines; 2. Shapeshifters; 3. Demons; 4. Imaginary wars and battles; 5. Imaginary places; 6. Fantasy fiction; 7. Gateway fantasy.
9781416914181

LC 2007046886

While Pendragon is trapped on Ibara, Alder returns to Denduron and reluctantly goes into battle again, and other Travelers face obstacles of various sorts, Saint Dane gains the power he seeks on Second Earth and makes his push to destroy and rebuild Halla.

Journal of an adventure through time and space.

The **reality** bug. D.J. MacHale. Aladdin Paperbacks, 2003 375 p. (Pendragon series, 4)
Grades: 7 8 9 10

1. Teenage heroes and heroines; 2. Shapeshifters; 3. Virtual reality; 4. Demons; 5. Space and time; 6. Fantasy fiction; 7. Gateway fantasy.
9780743437349

LC 2003105075

The **rivers** of Zadaa. D.J. MacHale. Simon & Schuster, 2005 405 p. (Pendragon series, 6)
Grades: 7 8 9 10

1. Teenage heroes and heroines; 2. Shapeshifters; 3. Droughts; 4. Demons; 5. Imaginary wars and battles; 6. Fantasy fiction; 7. Gateway fantasy.
9781416907107

LC 2004031120

Taking advantage of a severe drought and the long-standing distrust between two tribes, the demonic Saint Dane attempts to take over Loor's home planet of Zadaa, opposed once again by the teenaged Pendragon and other Travelers.

This is a fast-moving, rip-roaring...story.... The action never stops for long, and [this book] is sure to hold the interest of fans of the series. —*School Library Journal*

An adventure through time and space.

The **soldiers** of Halla. D.J. MacHale. Aladdin, 2009 560 p. (Pendragon series, 10)
Grades: 7 8 9 10
1. Teenage heroes and heroines; 2. Shapeshifters; 3. Demons; 4. Imaginary wars and battles; 5. Imaginary places; 6. Fantasy fiction; 7. Gateway fantasy.
9781416914204

LC 2008053573

Each of the Travelers returns home to learn the truth about their origins before being reunited for a final, inevitable confrontation with Saint Dane, whose efforts to control Halla are destroying its very foundations.

Journal of an adventure through time and space.

Maciel, Amanda

Tease. Amanda Maciel. Balzer + Bray, an imprint of HarperCollinsPublishers, 2014 352 pages
Grades: 9 10 11 12
1. Bullying and bullies; 2. Suicide; 3. High school students; 4. High schools; 5. Schools; 6. Realistic fiction
9780062305305; 9781444918717, print, UK

LC 2013043067

YALSA Best Fiction for Young Adults, 2015.

A teenage girl faces criminal charges for bullying after a classmate commits suicide.

A complex and thought-provoking examination of modern teen bullying. —*Horn Book Guide*

Mackler, Carolyn

★ The **Earth,** my butt, and other big, round things. Carolyn Mackler. Candlewick Press, 2003 246 p; (Earth, my butt, and other big, round things, 1)
Grades: 7 8 9 10
1. Fifteen-year-old girls; 2. Self-perception in teenage girls; 3. Assertiveness in teenage girls; 4. Family problems; 5. Weight control; 6. New York City; 7. Realistic fiction; 8. Teen chick lit
9780763619589; 9781408897058, Paperback, UK

LC 2002073921

Amelia Bloomer List, 2005; YALSA Popular Paperbacks for Young Adults, 2010; YALSA Best Books for Young Adults, 2004; Michael L. Printz Honor Book, 2004.

Virginia Shreves is insecure—and comparing herself to the tall, dark, and slender over-achievers who make up the rest of her family doesn't help. Add in even more criticism than usual from her exercise-obsessed mom and the fact that Virginia's best friend has moved away, and it's sure be a bad year of epic proportions. Or is it? This funny, sexy, no-holds-barred story of a girl who's about to learn that her "perfect" family isn't so perfect.

The e-mails [Virginia] exchanges... and the lists she makes (e.g, The Fat Girl Code of Conduct) add both realism and insight to her character. The heroine's transformation into someone who finds her own style and speaks her own mind is believable—and worthy of applause. —*Publishers Weekly*

★ **Infinite** in between. Carolyn Mackler. HarperTeen, an imprint of HarperCollins Publishers, 2015 462 p.
Grades: 9 10 11 12

1. High school students; 2. Teenage boy/girl relations; 3. Children of divorced parents; 4. Gay teenagers; 5. Teenage musicians; 6. Realistic fiction; 7. Coming-of-age stories; 8. Multiple perspectives
9780061731075
YALSA Best Fiction for Young Adults, 2016.

Things happen, for the most part, no more dramatically than they do in high schools every day. A clear, true portrait of life as it is for many teenagers. —*Booklist*

Tangled. Carolyn Mackler. HarperTeen, 2010 308 p.
Grades: 8 9 10 11 12
1. Self-confidence in teenagers; 2. Growth (Psychology); 3. Emotional problems of teenagers; 4. Emotional problems; 5. Americans in the Caribbean Area; 6. Caribbean Area; 7. Realistic fiction; 8. First person narratives; 9. Multiple perspectives
9780061731044

The various viewpoints weave together to create a compelling and cohesive whole. Themes of understanding, respecting others, and the power of good communication are carefully and effectively woven throughout a story that begs for discussion. —*School Library Journal*

MacLean, Sarah

The **season**. By Sarah MacLean. Orchard Books, 2009 352 p.
Grades: 7 8 9 10
1. Aristocracy; 2. Murder; 3. Courtship; 4. Seventeen-year-old girls; 5. Teenage girls; 6. London, England; 7. Great Britain; 8. Regency period (1811-1820); 9. 19th century; 10. Historical mysteries; 11. Historical romances; 12. Mysteries
9780545048866

Showing no interest in the sumptuous balls, lavish dinner parties, and country weekends enjoyed by the rest of early nineteenth-century London society, seventeen-year-old Lady Alexandra Stafford seeks adventure as she investigates the puzzling murder of the Earl of Blackmoor, father of devilishly handsome Gavin.

Macvie, Meagan

The **ocean** in my ears. Meagan Macvie. 2017 300 p.
Grades: 10 11 12
1. Small town life; 2. High school seniors; 3. Teenage boy/girl relations; 4. Small towns; 5. Seventeen-year-old girls; 6. Alaska; 7. 1990s; 8. Coming-of-age stories; 9. Pacific Northwest fiction; 10. First person narratives
9781932010947

LC 2017005062

In small-town Alaska in the 1990s, high school senior Meri's determination to escape for a more exciting place wanes as she struggles with family, grief, friends, and hormones.

An unforgettable journey to adulthood. —*Kirkus*

Madigan, L. K.

★ **Flash** burnout: a novel. By L. K. Madigan. Houghton Mifflin, 2009 332 p;
Grades: 9 10 11 12
1. Teenage photographers; 2. Children of drug abusers; 3. Friendship; 4. Homeless persons; 5. Teenage boy/girl relations; 6. Realistic fiction.
9780547194899

LC Bl2009026698

William C. Morris YA Debut Award, 2010; YALSA Best Books for Young Adults, 2010.

After he takes a photograph of a woman who is living on the streets and discovers it to be the meth-addicted mother of his closest friend

Marissa, Blake finds himself spending more time with Marissa than with his girlfriend.

This rich romance explores the complexities of friendship and love, and the all-too-human limitations of both. It's a sobering, compelling, and satisfying read for teens. —*Booklist*

Includes bibliographical references (p. 331-332).

Mae, Natalie

The **kinder** poison. Natalie Mae. Razorbill, 2020 416 p.
Grades: 8 9 10 11 12
1. Magic; 2. Rulers; 3. Teenage girls; 4. Imaginary kingdoms; 5. Running races; 6. Fantasy fiction; 7. Middle Eastern-influenced fantasy; 8. First person narratives
9781984835215, HRD, US; 9781984835239, ebook, US
LC 2019051803

When her magical kingdom's ailing ruler invokes an ancient tradition to identify his successor, a lowly stable girl who possesses the ability to commune with animals is chosen as a human sacrifice during a high-risk desert crossing involving three ruthless heirs.

Maetani, Valynne E.

Ink & ashes. Valynne E. Maetani. 2015 386 pages
Grades: 7 8 9 10
1. Japanese American teenage girls; 2. Organized crime; 3. Grief in teenage girls; 4. Fathers — Death; 5. Blended families; 6. Utah; 7. Thrillers and suspense
9781620142110
LC 2015006632

When Japanese American Claire Takata finds out that her deceased father was once a member of the yakuza, a Japanese crime syndicate, danger enters her life that could end up killing someone.

Maetani's fast-paced debut will appeal to readers who like their intrigue with a generous helping of romance. —*Booklist*

Mafi, Tahereh

★ A **very** large expanse of sea. Tahereh Mafi. 2018 304 p.
Grades: 8 9 10 11 12
1. First loves; 2. Prejudice; 3. Muslim girls; 4. Sixteen-year-old girls; 5. Stereotypes (Social psychology); 6. Realistic fiction; 7. Love stories.
9780062866561, hardback, US; 9780062866578
LC 2018945999

Booklist Editors' Choice: Books for Youth, 2018.

Shirin and Ocean's interactions are palpable, and the discussions and exploration of what it means to be a Muslim in politically charged America will resonate with many teens and will be enlightening for some. —*School Library Journal*

Magoon, Kekla

37 things I love (in no particular order). Kekla Magoon. Henry Holt, 2012 208 p.
Grades: 9 10 11 12
1. People in comas; 2. Emotions in teenage girls; 3. Grief in teenage girls; 4. Grief; 5. Interpersonal relations; 6. Realistic fiction; 7. First person narratives; 8. African American fiction
9780805094657
LC 2011031998

Rainbow List, 2013.

Fifteen-year-old Ellis recalls her favorite things as her mother's desire to turn off the machines that have kept Ellis's father alive for two years fill the last four days of her sophomore year with major changes in herself and her relationships.

★ **How** it went down. Kekla Magoon. Henry Holt and Company, 2014 224 p.
Grades: 9 10 11 12
1. Violence and guns; 2. Race relations; 3. Communities; 4. Murder; 5. African American teenage boys; 6. Realistic fiction; 7. Multiple perspectives; 8. Books for reluctant readers
9780805098693

YALSA Best Fiction for Young Adults, 2015; YALSA Quick Picks for Reluctant Young Adult Readers, 2015; Notable Books for a Global Society, 2015; Coretta Scott King Honor Book for Authors, 2015.

When 16-year-old Tariq, a black teen, is shot and killed by a white man, every witness has a slightly different perception of the chain of events leading up to the murder. Family, friends, gang members, neighbors, and a well-meaning but self-serving minster make up the broad cast of characters...With a great hook and relatable characters, this will be popular for fans of realistic fiction. The unique storytelling style and thematic relevance will make it a potentially intriguing pick for classroom discussion. —*School Library Journal*

★ **Light** it up. Kekla Magoon. Henry Holt and Company, 2019 336 p.
Grades: 9 10 11 12
1. Violence and guns; 2. Police shootings; 3. Race relations; 4. Communities; 5. Death; 6. Realistic fiction; 7. Multiple perspectives; 8. African American fiction.
9781250128898
LC 2019002033

School Library Journal Best Books, 2019.

Told from multiple viewpoints, Shae Tatum, an unarmed, thirteen-year-old black girl, is shot by a white police officer, throwing their community into upheaval and making it a target of demonstrators.

Magoon's latest novel houses an unapologetic, poignant narrative that forces readers to come face-to-face with the harsh realities of racial violence and racial profiling in America A clarion call for action. —*Booklist*

★ The **rock** and the river. Kekla Magoon. Aladdin, 2009 290 p;
Grades: 7 8 9 10
1. Civil Rights Movement; 2. Racism; 3. Brothers; 4. African Americans; 5. Fourteen-year-old boys; 6. Chicago, Illinois; 7. United States; 8. 1960s; 9. Historical fiction; 10. African American fiction
9781416975823
LC 2008029170

John Steptoe Award for New Talent, Author Category, 2010; ALA Notable Children's Book, 2010; YALSA Best Books for Young Adults, 2010.

It's 1968, and Chicago teen Sam is torn. He's always looked up to his father, a civil rights leader dedicated to nonviolence. His older brother Stick, however, has left home to join the revolutionary Black Panther Party. At first Sam is skeptical of the Panthers' militant approach to ending racial injustice, but after one of his friends is brutally beaten by the police, Sam starts to question his father's nonviolent beliefs.

This novel will make readers feel what it was like to be young, black, and militant 40 years ago, including the seething fury and desperation over the daily discrimination that drove the oppressed to fight back. —*Booklist*

Sequel: *Fire in the streets*.

Maguire, Gregory

★ **Egg** & spoon. Gregory Maguire. Candlewick Press, 2014 496 p.
Grades: 7 8 9 10 11 12

1. Mistaken identity; 2. Witches; 3. Baba Yaga (Legendary character); 4. Princes; 5. Social classes; 6. Russia; 7. 1900s (Decade); 8. Historical fantasy; 9. Metafiction.
9780763672201
School Library Journal Best Books: Fiction, 2014; YALSA Best Fiction for Young Adults, 2015.

With one brother conscripted into the Tsar's army and another bound to serve a local landowner, Elena is left alone to care for her widowed and ailing mother in early 20th-century Russia. When an elegant train bearing a noble her age rolls through their barren village, Elena and her counterpart, Cat, accidentally swap places.... The author weaves a lyrical tale full of magic and promise, yet checkered with the desperation of poverty and the treacherous prospect of a world gone completely awry. *Egg and Spoon* is a beautiful reminder that fairy tales are at their best when they illuminate the precarious balance between lighthearted childhood and the darkness and danger of adulthood. —*School Library Journal*

Maizel, Rebecca

Infinite days. Rebecca Maizel. St. Martins Press, 2010 320 p. (Vampire queen novels (Rebecca Maizel), 1)
Grades: 7 8 9 10
1. Vampires; 2. Betrayal; 3. Transformations (Magic); 4. Covens; 5. Humans; 6. Urban fantasy
9780312649913; 9780330520423, print, UK

The story is filled with action, romance, longing, deception, and sacrifice. It will leave vampire fans thirsting for more. —*School Library Journal*

Stolen nights: a Vampire queen novel. Rebecca Maizel. St. Martins Press, 2013 320 p. (Vampire queen novels (Rebecca Maizel), 2)
Grades: 7 8 9 10
1. Vampires; 2. Boarding schools; 3. Love triangles; 4. Humans; 5. Schools; 6. Urban fantasy
9780312649920

At first, this novel seems to lack luster in its genre, but timeless themes of love and the search for identity, in addition to the cliff-hanger ending, leave readers pondering Lenah's choices and keenly anticipating the next installment. —*School Library Journal*

Malley, Gemma

The **resistance**. Gemma Malley. Bloomsbury, 2008 323 p. (Declaration trilogy, 2)
Grades: 7 8 9 10
1. Immortality; 2. Population control; 3. Reproductive rights; 4. Human reproduction; 5. Spies; 6. England; 7. Dystopian fiction; 8. Science fiction
9781599903026

In a future England where young people, or "Surpluses," are heavily regulated and everyone takes a drug called Longevity, a member of the Underground infiltrates the Pincent Pharma manufacturing plant, and uncovers horrific acts being committed in an attempt to create eternal youth.

The novel is well written and will be enjoyed by readers who liked the first book. —*Voice of Youth Advocates*
Sequel to: *The Declaration*

Mandanna, Sangu

Color outside the lines: stories about love. Edited by Sangu Mandanna. 2019 312 p.
Grades: 8 9 10 11 12
1. Hope; 2. Teenage romance; 3. Love; 4. Interpersonal relations; 5. Interracial romance; 6. Anthologies; 7. Love stories; 8. LGBTQIA romances

9781641290463
LC 2019017621
This modern, groundbreaking YA anthology explores the complexity and beauty of interracial and LGBTQ+ relationships where differences are front and center.

From dealing with a racist bully to facing the impact of colonialism and handling Asian fever, the authors delve into a number of cultures, races, religions, and ethnicities Moroccan, Indian, black, Hmong, Chinese, Jewish, Latinx, Palestinian, and Irish, among others. —*Kirkus*

Maniscalco, Kerri

Stalking Jack the Ripper. Kerri Maniscalco. JIMMY Patterson Books/Little, Brown and Company, 2016 336 p. (Stalking Jack the Ripper, 1)
Grades: 10 11 12
1. Jack the Ripper; 2. Serial murder investigation; 3. Forensic sciences; 4. Gender role; 5. Serial murderers; 6. Teenage romance; 7. London, England; 8. Great Britain; 9. Victorian era (1837-1901); 10. Historical mysteries; 11. Gothic fiction
9780316273497; 9781538761182, Paperback, Australia

An entertaining debut full of twists and turns, perfect for fans of historical fiction and mystery. —*School Library Journal*

Mann, Jennifer Ann

What every girl should know: Margaret Sanger's journey : a novel. By J. Albert Mann. Atheneum, 2019 240 p.
Grades: 7 8 9 10 11 12
1. Sanger, Margaret, 1879-1966; 2. Children of sick persons; 3. Poor families; 4. Gender role; 5. Feminists; 6. Women social reformers; 7. New York (State); 8. 19th century; 9. Biographical fiction; 10. Historical fiction
9781534419322; 9781534419339

In this fictionalized biography, a teenage Maggie Higgins struggles to balance her responsibilities to her family, society's expectations for women, and her desire to pursue her education and plan for the future.

An important, readable novel about Sanger, who changed the fate of millions of women through access to contraception. —*Kirkus*

Mantchev, Lisa

Eyes like stars. By Lisa Mantchev. Feiwel and Friends, 2009 368 p. (Theatre Illuminata trilogy, 1)
Grades: 8 9 10 11 12
1. Parent-separated teenagers; 2. Magical books; 3. Theater; 4. Magic; 5. Actors and actresses; 6. Fantasy fiction; 7. Shakespeare-inspired fiction.
9780312380960
LC 2008015317
Seventeen-year-old Bertie strives to save Theater Illuminata, the only home she has ever known, but is hindered by the Players who magically live on there, especially Ariel, who is willing to destroy the Book at the center of the magic in order to escape into the outside world.

The story contains enough mystery and mayhem to keep readers engaged, even as they analyze. —*Voice of Youth Advocates*

Perchance to dream. Lisa Mantchev. Feiwel & Friends, 2010 337 p. (Theatre Illuminata trilogy, 2)
Grades: 8 9 10 11 12
1. Parent-separated teenagers; 2. Fairies; 3. Theater; 4. Spirits; 5. Kidnapping; 6. Fantasy fiction; 7. Shakespeare-inspired fiction.
9780312380977
LC Bl2010011542

Bertie, who is blessed with word magic, and her fairy sidekicks seek to save Nate, who has been kidnapped by the Sea Witch, but Bertie is torn between Nate and Ariel, an air spirit who loves Bertie enough to die for her.

The pace is fast and furious...but it's Mantchev's fresh, intelligent style that delights most.... This fantastical rompan absolute must for theater buffsmight stand alone, but it'd be a pity not to start with the first. —*Kirkus*

So silver bright. Lisa Mantchev. Feiwel and Friends, 2011 368 p. (Theatre Illuminata trilogy, 3)
Grades: 8 9 10 11 12
1. Parent-separated teenagers; 2. Fairies; 3. Theater; 4. Magical books; 5. Magic; 6. Fantasy fiction; 7. Shakespeare-inspired fiction.
9780312380984
LC 2011023907
Bertie thinks that to complete her quest to have a true family she need only reunite her father, the Scrimshander, with her mother, Ophelia, but complications arise and she is torn between her responsibilities and the dream of flying free, just as she is torn between Nate and Ariel.

Manzano, Sonia
★ The **revolution** of Evelyn Serrano. Sonia Manzano. Scholastic, 2012 224 p.
Grades: 6 7 8 9 10
1. Puerto Ricans; 2. Protest movements; 3. Grandmothers; 4. Identity (Psychology); 5. Families; 6. New York City; 7. East Harlem, New York City; 8. 1960s; 9. Historical fiction.
9780545325059
LC 2012009240
ALA Notable Children's Book, 2013; Amelia Bloomer List, 2013; Americas Book Award for Children's and Young Adult Literature, 2013; Notable Books for a Global Society, 2013; Pura Belpre Honor Book for Narrative, 2013.
It is 1969 in Spanish Harlem, and fourteen-year-old Evelyn Serrano is trying hard to break free from her conservative Puerto Rican surroundings, but when her activist grandmother comes to stay and the neighborhood protests start, things get a lot more complicated—and dangerous.

Marchetta, Melina
★ **Finnikin** of the rock. Melina Marchetta. Candlewick Press, 2010 399 p. (Lumatere chronicles, 1)
Grades: 8 9 10 11 12
1. Royal houses; 2. Curses; 3. Heirs and heiresses; 4. Imaginary kingdoms; 5. Impostors; 6. High fantasy; 7. Fantasy fiction; 8. Australian fiction
9780763643614; 9781406355895, print, UK
Aurealis Awards, Best Young Adult Novel, 2008; Australian Book Industry Awards, Book of the Year for Older Children, 2009; Blue Hen Book Award (Delaware) for Teen Books, 2012; YALSA Popular Paperbacks for Young Adults, 2012; YALSA Best Fiction for Young Adults, 2011; School Library Journal Best Books, 2010.
Now on the cusp of manhood, Finnikin, who was a child when the royal family of Lumatere was brutally murdered and replaced by an imposter, reluctantly joins forces with an enigmatic young novice and fellow-exile, who claims that her dark dreams will lead them to a surviving royal child and a way to regain the throne of Lumatere.
The skillful world building includes just enough detail to create a vivid sense of place, and Marchetta maintains suspense with unexpected story arcs. It is the achingly real characters, though, and the relationships that emerge through the captivating dialogue that drive the story. Filled with questions about the impact of exile and the human need to belong,

this standout fantasy quickly reveals that its real magic lies in its accomplished writing. —*Booklist*

★ **Froi** of the exiles. Melina Marchetta. Candlewick Press, 2012 400 p. (Lumatere chronicles, 2)
Grades: 8 9 10 11 12
1. Princesses; 2. Inheritance and succession; 3. Curses; 4. Prophecies; 5. Loyalty; 6. High fantasy; 7. Fantasy fiction; 8. Australian fiction
9780763647599; 9781406356137, print, UK; 9780143567738, print, Australia; 9780670076086, Australia
YALSA Best Fiction for Young Adults, 2013.
Fiercely loyal to the Queen and Finnikin, Froi has been taken roughly and lovingly in hand by the Guard sworn to protect the royal family but is soon sent on a secretive mission to the kingdom of Charyn where he must unravel both the dark bonds of kinship and the mysteries of a half-mad princess.

★ **Jellicoe** Road. Melina Marchetta. HarperTeen, 2008 419 p.
Grades: 9 10 11 12
1. Mother-separated teenage girls; 2. Identity (Psychology); 3. Emotional problems of teenage girls; 4. Abandoned children; 5. Boarding schools; 6. Australia; 7. Realistic fiction; 8. Australian fiction
9780061431838; 9780061431845; 9780143011194, Australia
LC 2008000760
Michael L. Printz Award, 2009; West Australian Young Readers's Book Awards (WAYRBA), Avis Page Award, 2008; YALSA Best Books for Young Adults, 2009.
Abandoned by her drug-addicted mother at the age of eleven, high school student Taylor Markham struggles with her identity and family history at a boarding school in Australia.
Readers may feel dizzied and disoriented, but as they puzzle out exactly how Hannah's narrative connects with Taylor's current reality, they will find themselves ensnared in the story's fascinating, intricate structure. A beautifully rendered mystery. —*Kirkus*
Previously published in 2006 in Australia under the title: *On the Jellicoe Road.*

Marks, Graham
Zoo: a novel. By Graham Marks. Bloomsbury : 2005 266 p;
Grades: 9 10 11 12
1. Seventeen-year-old boys; 2. Teenage boys; 3. Kidnapping victims; 4. Kidnapping; 5. Suspicion; 6. California; 7. San Diego, California; 8. Adventure stories; 9. Thrillers and suspense
9781582349916
LC 2004062366
After seventeen-year-old Cam Stewart escapes from the kidnappers who took him from right in front of his San Diego home, he continues a dangerous adventure that includes finding a mysterious chip in his arm which leads him to question his identity.

Marquardt, Marie F.
Dream things true. Marie Marquardt. St Martins Press, 2015 320 p.
Grades: 9 10 11 12
1. Undocumented immigrants; 2. Teenagers; 3. Small towns; 4. Mexicans in the United States; 5. Immigration and emigration; 6. Southern States; 7. Love stories.
9781250070456
A debut romance for libraries looking to diversify their offerings. —*School Library Journal*

★ The **radius** of us. Marie Marquardt. St. Martin's Griffin, 2017 295 p.
Grades: 9 10 11 12

1. Immigration and emigration; 2. Interethnic romance; 3. Victims of crimes; 4. Teenage romance; 5. Teenage crime victims; 6. Georgia; 7. Atlanta, Georgia; 8. Realistic fiction; 9. Multiple perspectives; 10. First person narratives
9781250096890

Tackling the issues of gang violence, immigration, mental health, and cultural bias, this is a compelling story that delivers profound messages through engaging, accessible prose. —*School Library Journal*

Marr, Melissa

Darkest mercy. Melissa Marr. Harper, 2011 336 p. (Wicked lovely, 5)
Grades: 8 9 10 11 12
1. Fairies; 2. Women rulers; 3. Loyalty; 4. Love triangles; 5. Good and evil; 6. Urban fantasy
9780061659256; 9780061659263
LC 2010033584

The political and romantic tensions that began when Aislin became Summer Queen threaten to boil over as the Faerie Courts brace against the threat of all-out war.

Fragile eternity. Melissa Marr. Bowen Press, 2009 400 p. (Wicked lovely, 3)
Grades: 8 9 10 11 12
1. Fairies; 2. Women rulers; 3. Crushes in teenagers; 4. Immortality; 5. Teenage boy/girl relations; 6. Urban fantasy
9780061214721
LC 2008034420

Aislinn and Seth struggle with the unforeseen consequences of Aislinn's transformation from mortal girl to faery queen as the world teeters on the brink of cataclysmic violence.

Ink exchange. Melissa Marr. HarperTeen, 2008 325 p. (Wicked lovely, 2)
Grades: 8 9 10 11 12
1. Fairies; 2. Tattooing; 3. Teenage rape victims; 4. Options, alternatives, choices; 5. Slavery; 6. Urban fantasy
9780061214684; 9780061214691
LC 2007040106

Seventeen-year-old Leslie wants a tattoo as a way of reclaiming control of herself and her body, but the eerie image she selects pulls her into the dangerous Dark Court of the faeries, where she draws on inner strength to make a horrible choice.

Readers will be drawn in by Marr's darkly poetic imagery and language, her vivid portrayal of the art of tattooing, and her shadowy love triangle. This is indeed a delicious, smoky delight. —*Bulletin of the Center for Children's Books*

Sequel to: *Wicked lovely.*

Radiant shadows. Melissa Marr. HarperCollins, 2010 340 p. (Wicked lovely, 4)
Grades: 8 9 10 11 12
1. Fairies; 2. Assassins; 3. Women rulers; 4. Courage; 5. Magic; 6. Urban fantasy
9780061659225; 9780061659232; 9780007346141, print, UK
LC 2009053458
Romantic Times Reviewers' Choice Award, 2010.

The author's Wicked Lovely series continues with the fourth—and penultimate—installment in the story about the collision of the mortal and faery worlds.

This is a worthy addition to a fine series. Readers who have enjoyed the early books will find this a satisfying read. —*School Library Journal*

Wicked lovely. Melissa Marr. HarperTeen, 2007 328 p. (Wicked lovely, 1)

Grades: 8 9 10 11 12
1. Fairies; 2. Rulers; 3. Options, alternatives, choices; 4. Secrets; 5. Magic; 6. Urban fantasy
9780061214653; 9780061214660
LC 2007009143
RITA Award for Best Young Adult Romance, 2008; YALSA Popular Paperbacks for Young Adults, 2011.

Seventeen-year-old Aislinn, who has the rare ability to see faeries, is drawn against her will into a centuries-old battle between the Summer King and Winter Queen, and the survival of her life, her love, and summer all hang in the balance.

This story explores the themes of love, commitment, and what it really means to give of oneself for the greater good to save everyone else. It is the unusual combination of past legends and modern-day life that gives a unique twist to this fairy tale. —*School Library Journal*

Sequel: *Fragile eternity.*

Marsden, Carolyn

My own revolution. Carolyn Marsden. Candlewick Press, 2012 192 p.
Grades: 7 8 9 10 11 12
1. Thirteen-year-old boys; 2. Communism; 3. Resistance to government; 4. Resistance (Psychology) in teenage boys; 5. Teenage boy/girl relations; 6. Czechoslovakia; 7. 1960s; 8. Historical fiction.
9780763653958

Quietly rebelling against the communist regime in 1960s Czechoslovakia, fourteen-year-old Patrick listens to contraband Beatles records and spray-paints slogans until party interference forces his family to make a dangerous decision.

Marsden's carefully researched and engrossing story will be of obvious classroom use but will also appeal to thoughtful independent readers. —*Booklist*

Marsden, John

While I live. John Marsden. Scholastic Press, 2007 304 p. (Ellie chronicles, 1)
Grades: 7 8 9 10
1. Teenage girl orphans; 2. Family farms; 3. Grief in teenage girls; 4. Grief; 5. Resourcefulness in teenage girls; 6. Australia; 7. Adventure stories; 8. Australian fiction
9780439783187
USBBY Outstanding International Book, 2008.

Fans of 16-year-old Ellie Linton...will be overjoyed that she's back in an exciting series of her own. The realistic and shocking war-related violence that characterized the earlier titles is just as prevalent here. —*School Library Journal*

Marsh, Katherine

★ **Jepp,** who defied the stars. Katherine Marsh. Hyperion, 2012 384 p.
Grades: 6 7 8 9 10
1. Little people; 2. Courts and courtiers; 3. Quests; 4. Teenage boys; 5. Fate and fatalism; 6. Europe; 7. Renaissance (1300-1600); 8. 16th century; 9. Historical fiction; 10. Coming-of-age stories.
9781423135005
LC 2011053065

Jepp, a teenage dwarf living in sixteenth-century Europe, leaves home to seek his destiny.

Marsh, Sarah Glenn

Reign of the fallen. Sarah Glenn Marsh. Razorbill, 2018 303 p. (Reign of the Fallen, 1)

Grades: 7 8 9 10 11 12
1. Magic (Occultism); 2. Spirits; 3. Grief in teenage girls; 4. Death; 5. Teenage girls; 6. High fantasy; 7. Fantasy fiction; 8. First person narratives
9780448494395

Odessa is one of Karthia's master necromancers, catering to the kingdom's ruling Dead. Whenever a noble dies, it's Odessa's job to raise them by retrieving their soul from a dreamy and dangerous shadow world called the Deadlands. But there is a cost to being raised: the Dead must remain shrouded. If even a hint of flesh is exposed, a grotesque transformation begins, turning the Dead into terrifying, bloodthirsty Shades.

Marshall, Kate Alice
I am still alive. Kate Alice Marshall. Viking Books for Young Readers, 2018 352 p.
Grades: 8 9 10 11
1. Wilderness survival; 2. Revenge; 3. Fathers — Death; 4. Endurance in women; 5. Grief in women; 6. Canada; 7. Survival stories; 8. Adventure stories.
9780425290989, hardback, US; 9780425291009

Stranded in the woods with few supplies and survival skills, a disabled girl and her dog fervently prepare for the coming winter while evaluating how her mother's death, a dysfunctional foster-care system and her survivalist father led to her predicament.

Martin, Darragh
The **keeper**. Darragh Martin. Little Island, 2013 267 pages;
Grades: 7 8 9 10
1. Magical books; 2. Mythology, Celtic; 3. Kidnapping; 4. Magic; 5. Brothers and sisters; 6. Dublin, Ireland; 7. Fantasy fiction; 8. Mythological fiction
9781908195845
LC 2014407173

Fans of Percy Jackson and Harry Potter will enjoy this fast-paced high fantasy adventure that adds a refreshing twist to Celtic myths and legends. —*School Library Journal*

Martin, Maggie Ann
To be honest. Maggie Ann Martin. 2018 304 p.
Grades: 8 9 10 11 12
1. Body image; 2. High school seniors; 3. Mothers and daughters; 4. Overweight teenage girls; 5. Sisters; 6. Realistic fiction
9781250183156
LC Bl2018180829

After her older sister goes to college, Savannah is left home alone with her weight-obsessed mother, and must find consolation in a new relationship with George, who has insecurities of his own.

Martin, T. Michael
The **end** games. T. Michael Martin. Balzer + Bray, 2013 400 p.
Grades: 9 10 11 12
1. Survival; 2. Brothers; 3. Zombies; 4. Boys with autism; 5. Teenage romance; 6. West Virginia; 7. Horror
9780062201805
LC 2012038108

YALSA Best Fiction for Young Adults, 2014.
In the rural mountains of West Virginia, seventeen-year-old Michael Faris tries to protect his fragile younger brother from the horrors of the zombie apocalypse.

Martinez, Claudia Guadalupe
Pig park. Claudia Guadalupe Martinez. 2014 248 p.
Grades: 8 9 10 11
1. Neighborhoods; 2. Bakeries; 3. Hispanic Americans; 4. Families; 5. Building; 6. Chicago, Illinois; 7. Coming-of-age stories; 8. Realistic fiction
9781935955764
LC 2013040645

Seventeen-year-old Masi Burciaga's barrio becomes more like a ghost town every day, but when she and other youths are recruited to erect a giant pyramid in hopes of attracting tourists, she wonders about the entrepreneur behind the scheme—and his attractive son.

Martinez uses nicely specific physical details to relate Masi's experiences, and the moments in the bakery seem particularly authentic and are suffused with love. The warm, diverse community setting and the realistic family interactions help overcome the somewhat jumbled plotlines. —*Kirkus*

Martinez, Jessica
★ **Virtuosity**. Jessica Martinez. Simon Pulse, 2011 294 p;
Grades: 8 9 10 11 12
1. Teenage musicians; 2. Competition; 3. Mothers and daughters; 4. Teenage boy/girl relations; 5. Home schooled teenage girls; 6. Chicago, Illinois; 7. Realistic fiction; 8. Canadian fiction.
9781442420526; 9781442420533; 9780857072849, print, UK
LC 2010042513
YALSA Best Fiction for Young Adults, 2012; YALSA Popular Paperbacks for Young Adults, 2013.

Just before the most important violin competition of her career, seventeen-year-old prodigy Carmen faces critical decisions about her anti-anxiety drug addiction, her controlling mother, and a potential romance with her most talented rival.

This is a riveting novel.... The portrayal of Carmen's world...is unique and convincing.... Even readers without much interest in music will enjoy this exceptional novel. —*School Library Journal*

Martinez, Victor
★ **Parrot** in the oven: mi vida : a novel. Victor Martinez. HarperCollins, 1996 216 p.
Grades: 7 8 9 10
1. Teenage boys; 2. Gangs; 3. Alcoholic fathers; 4. Mexican American teenagers; 5. High school students; 6. California; 7. Coming-of-age stories; 8. Realistic fiction.
9780060267049; 9780060267063; 9780064471862
LC 962119
Americas Book Award for Children's and Young Adult Literature, 1996; National Book Award for Young People's Literature, 1996; Pura Belpre Award for Narrative, 1998.

Manny relates his coming of age experiences as a member of a poor Chicano family in which the alcoholic father only adds to everyone's struggle.

The author maintains the authenticity of his setting and characterizations through a razor-sharp combination of tense dialogue, coursing narrative and startlingly elegant imagery. —*Publishers Weekly*

Mason, Simon
Running girl. Simon Mason. David Fickling Books/Scholastic Inc, 2016 432 p. (Garvie Smith, 1)
Grades: 9 10 11 12
1. Multiracial teenage boys; 2. Genius; 3. Slackers; 4. Murder investigation; 5. Gifted teenagers; 6. England; 7. Mysteries
9781338036428; 9781338036442, ebook, US

LC 2016005739

Garvie Smith is a sixteen-year-old with a genius level IQ, who can not be bothered with school, smokes cannabis, and hangs out with the bad boys—but when fifteen-year-old Chloe Dow is murdered he comes up against the ambitious Detective Inspector Singh,and both of them are determined to solve the case.

Mason (*Moon Pie*) grounds the story in reality as Garvie grows to better understand that actions have real and sometimes permanent consequences, seamlessly melding British teen drama with a believable and suspenseful plot full of well-executed twists. —*Publishers Weekly*

First published in the United Kingdom in 2014 by David Fickling Books

Masood, Syed M.
★ **More** than just a pretty face. Syed Masood. Little Brown & Co 2020 352 p.
Grades: 9 10 11 12
1. Muslim teenagers; 2. Arranged marriage; 3. Tutors; 4. Crushes (Interpersonal relations); 5. Teenage romance; 6. California; 7. Romantic comedies; 8. Multicultural romances; 9. Contemporary romances.
9780316492355; 9781529311334, Paperback, UK
LC 2019023874
When self-proclaimed 'not very bright' nineteen-year-old Danyal Jilani is chosen for a prestigious academic contest, he hopes to impress a potential arranged marriage match, only to begin falling for the girl helping him study instead.

This delightful debut will make a fine addition to any YA collection, and includes a much-needed historical and contemporary perspective of Western culture through a South Asian lens School Library Journal

Mass, Wendy
Heaven looks a lot like the mall: a novel. By Wendy Mass. Little, Brown, 2007 251 p;
Grades: 8 9 10 11 12
1. People in comas; 2. Near-death experience; 3. Self-discovery in teenage girls; 4. Self-discovery; 5. Shopping malls; 6. Novels in verse; 7. First person narratives.
9780316058513
LC 2007012333
When high school junior Tessa Reynolds falls into a coma after getting hit in the head during gym class, she experiences heaven as the mall where her parents work, and she revisits key events from her life, causing her to reevaluate herself and how she wants to live.

Tessa's journey and authentic voice is one that readers will appreciate.... Funny, thought-provoking, and at times heartbreaking, this story will entertain and inspire readers. —*School Library Journal*

Mather, Janice Lynn
Learning to breathe. Janice Lynn Mather. 2018 336 p.
Grades: 9 10 11 12
1. Teenage rape victims; 2. Teenage pregnancy; 3. Individuality; 4. Pregnant teenagers; 5. Rape; 6. Nassau, Bahamas; 7. Bahamas; 8. Realistic fiction
9781534406018, hardback, US; 9781534406032; 9781534406025
LC 2017047526
Amelia Bloomer List, 2019; YALSA Best Fiction for Young Adults, 2019.

Sixteen-year-old Indy struggles to conceal that she is pregnant by rape and then, turned out by relatives, must find a way to survive on her own in Nassau.

Mathieu, Jennifer
The **liars** of Mariposa Island. Jennifer Mathieu. Henry Holt & Co, 2019 256 p.
Grades: 9 10 11 12
1. Dishonesty; 2. Control (Psychology); 3. Self-fulfillment in teenagers; 4. Secrets; 5. Teenage boy/girl relations; 6. Cuba; 7. 1980s; 8. Multiple perspectives; 9. Parallel narratives; 10. Historical fiction.
9781626726338; 9781444946062, Paperback, UK
With a touch of romance, this gentle, multilayered novel comes with a dash of the unexpected thanks to the deeply unreliable nature of its narrators. A beautiful portrayal of a Cuban American family during a crossroads summer. —*Kirkus*

★ **Moxie**. Jennifer Mathieu. Roaring Brook Press, 2017 336 p.
Grades: 8 9 10 11 12
1. Feminism; 2. Sexism; 3. Zines; 4. Small towns; 5. Misogyny; 6. Texas; 7. Realistic fiction
9781626726352; 9781444940633, paperback, UK
LC 2016057288
YALSA Best Fiction for Young Adults, 2018; Amelia Bloomer List, 2018; YALSA Quick Picks for Reluctant Young Adult Readers, 2018.

In a small Texas town where high school football reigns supreme, Viv, sixteen, starts a feminist revolution using anonymously-written zines.

Matson, Morgan
Amy & Roger's epic detour. Morgan Matson. Simon & Schuster BFYR, 2010 343 p. : Illustration; Map
Grades: 9 10 11 12
1. Grief in teenage girls; 2. Guilt in teenage girls; 3. Transcontinental journeys; 4. Automobile travel; 5. Grief; 6. Realistic fiction.
9781416990659; 9780857072689, print, UK
LC 2009049988
YALSA Popular Paperbacks for Young Adults, 2012; YALSA Best Fiction for Young Adults, 2011.

After the death of her father, Amy, a high school student, and Roger, a college freshman, set out on a carefully planned road trip from California to Connecticut, but wind up taking many detours, forcing Amy to face her worst fears and come to terms with her grief and guilt.

This entertaining and thoughtful summertime road trip serves up slices of America with a big scoop of romance on the side. —*Kirkus*

Since you've been gone. Morgan Matson. 2014 400 pages
Grades: 7 8 9 10
1. Self-discovery in teenage girls; 2. Separated friends, relatives, etc; 3. Teenage boy/girl relations; 4. Self-discovery; 5. Self-reliance; 6. Connecticut; 7. Realistic fiction.
9781442435001; 9781442435025, ebook, US
LC 2013041617
Quiet Emily's sociable and daring best friend, Sloane, has disappeared leaving nothing but a random list of bizarre tasks for her to complete, but with unexpected help from popular classmate Frank Porter, Emily gives them a try.

Emily feels lost when her best friend, Sloane, disappears without explanation. But Sloane left Emily a daunting to-do list (with items like 'kiss a stranger'), and Emily bravely takes on each task, finding new friends, confidence, and a crush along the way. A perfectly awkward protagonist; well-rounded, quirky supporting characters; and spot-on dialogue make this novel of self-discovery stand out. —*Horn Book Guide*

Maxwell, Lisa
The **last** magician. Lisa Maxwell. Simon & Schuster, 2017 352 p. (Last magician, 1)
Grades: 10 11 12

1. Thieves; 2. Time travel; 3. Magicians; 4. Immigrants; 5. Magic; 6. New York City; 7. 1900s (Decade); 8. Historical fantasy; 9. High fantasy; 10. Multiple perspectives.
9781481432078; 9781481432085

In modern day New York, magic is all but extinct. The remaining few who have an affinity for magic—the Mageus—live in the shadows, hiding who they are from the Brink, a dark energy barrier that confines them to the island. Crossing it means losing their power—and often their lives. Esta is a talented thief. And all of Esta's training has been for one final job: traveling back to 1902 to steal an ancient book containing the secrets of the Order—and the Brink—before the Magician can destroy it and doom the Mageus to a hopeless future.

May, Kyla

Kiki: my stylish life. By Kyla May. Scholastic, 2013 96 p. (Lotus Lane, 1)
Grades: 7 8 9 10 11 12
1. Fashion design; 2. Competition; 3. New neighbors; 4. Clubs; 5. Best friends; 6. Realistic fiction; 7. Diary novels; 8. Australian fiction.
9780545496131

LC 2012034246

Kiki and her best friends, Coco and Lulu, all live on Lotus Lane, attend Amber Acres Elementary School, and have their own club, so when a when a Japanese girl named Mika moves in next door and also chooses fashion design for her art project, Kiki is seriously annoyed.

Mayhew, Julie

The **big** lie. Julie Mayhew. Candelwick Press, 2015 352 p.
Grades: 9 10 11 12
1. Nazis; 2. Sexuality; 3. Best friends; 4. Lesbians; 5. Women/women relations; 6. Great Britain; 7. Alternative histories; 8. Coming-of-age stories
9780763691257; 9781471404702, London
Sidewise Awards for Alternate History, 2015; USBBY Outstanding International Book, 2018.

A tale set in an alternate-world modern England under a Nazi regime finds the sheltered teen daughter of the Greater German Reich questioning what it means to be good and how far she is willing to go to break the rules.

Red ink. Julie Mayhew. Candlewick Pressr 2016 297 p.
Grades: 9 10 11 12
1. Loss (Psychology); 2. Grief in teenage girls; 3. Coping in teenage girls; 4. Grief; 5. Death; 6. London, England; 7. Realistic fiction
9780763677312

Melon tells her own story interspersed with her mother's in fractured, chaotic vignettes that circle the day of the accident: 17 days since, 3 days since, 6 years before. As a narrator, she is harsh and abrasive but always sympathetic. Gritty and sad as this may be, it certainly rings true. —*Booklist*

Mazer, Harry

A **boy** at war: a novel of Pearl Harbor. Harry Mazer. Simon & Schuster Books for Young Readers, 2001 104 p.
Grades: 7 8 9 10
1. Pearl Harbor, Attack on, 1941; 2. Fathers and sons; 3. Missing in action; 4. Teenage children of military personnel; 5. World War II — Teenagers; 6. Hawaii
9780689841613

LC 49687

Nene Award (Hawaii), 2007.

While fishing with his friends off Honolulu on December 7, 1941, teenaged Adam is caught in the midst of the Japanese attack and through the chaos of the subsequent days tries to find his father, a naval officer who was serving on the U.S.S. *Arizona* when the bombs fell.

Mazer's graphic, sensory descriptions give the narrative immediacy, putting readers alongside Adam, watching with him as pieces of the ship and pieces of men rained down around him.... This is a thought-provoking, sobering account of the human costs of war. —*Horn Book Guide*
Sequel: *A boy no more.*

A **boy** no more. Harry Mazer. Simon & Schuster Books for Young Readers, 2004 144 p.
Grades: 7 8 9 10
1. Teenage children of military personnel; 2. Fifteen-year-old boys; 3. Japanese American boys; 4. Fathers and sons; 5. Fathers — Death; 6. California; 7. Hawaii
9781416914044; 9780689855337

LC 2003021130

After his father is killed in the attack on Pearl Harbor, Adam, his mother, and sister are evacuated from Hawaii to California, where he must deal with his feelings about the war, Japanese internment camps, his father, and his own identity.

A satisfying coming-of-age story in a well-documented historical setting. —*Booklist*
Sequel to: *A Boy at War*; Sequel: *Heroes Don't Run.*

Heroes don't run: a novel of the Pacific War. Harry Mazer. Simon & Schuster Books for Young Readers, 2005 128 p.
Grades: 7 8 9 10
1. Seventeen-year-old boys; 2. Teenage boys; 3. Teenage soldiers; 4. Children of military personnel; 5. Loss (Psychology); 6. Hawaii; 7. Okinawa Island, Japan; 8. Second World War era (1939-1945); 9. War stories; 10. First person narratives; 11. Historical fiction.
9780689855344; 9781416933946

LC 2004010935

To honor his father who died during the Japanese invasion of Pearl Harbor, seventeen-year-old Adam eagerly enlists in the Marines in 1944, survives boot camp, and faces combat on the tiny island of Okinawa.

The clear first-person narrative is terse and gripping, graphic about the slaughter and heartfelt about the loss. —*Booklist*
Sequel to: *A Boy No More.*

★ The **last** mission. Harry Mazer. Delacorte Press, 1979 182 p.
Grades: 7 8 9 10
1. Jewish American teenage boys; 2. Teenage soldiers; 3. Fifteen-year-olds; 4. World War II — Aerial operations; 5. World War II — Prisoners and prisons, German; 6. 1940s; 7. Historical fiction; 8. War stories
9780385286626

LC 79050674

Jack is a freshman in high school when he decides that he wants to be a hero. One small lie gets him a job as a gunner in a B-17 flying combat mission across Europe in 1944. But he wasn't prepared for the terror of night missions or getting shot down.

Told in a rapid journalistic style, occasionally peppered with barrack-room vulgarities, the story is a vivid and moving account of a boy's experience during World War II as well as a skillful, convincing portrayal of his misgivings as a Jew on enemy soil and of his ability to size upin mature human fashionthe misery around him. —*Horn Book Guide*

Somebody please tell me who I am. Harry Mazer and Peter Lerangis. Simon & Schuster Books for Young Readers, 2012 160 p.
Grades: 6 7 8 9 10 11 12
1. Men with brain injuries; 2. Memory; 3. Rehabilitation; 4. Soldiers; 5. Coma; 6. Realistic fiction

9781416938958

LC 2011006010

Schneider Family Book Award for Teens, 2013; YALSA Best Fiction for Young Adults, 2013; YALSA Popular Paperbacks for Young Adults, 2014.

Wounded in Iraq while his Army unit is on convoy and treated for many months for traumatic brain injury, the first person Ben remembers from his earlier life is his autistic brother.

Mazer, Norma Fox

★ The **missing** girl. Norma Fox Mazer. HarperTeen, 2008 284 p.
Grades: 7 8 9 10
1. Stalkers; 2. Sisters; 3. Kidnapping victims; 4. Teenagers; 5. Teenage girls; 6. New York (State); 7. Psychological suspense; 8. Multiple perspectives
9780066237763
YALSA Popular Paperbacks for Young Adults, 2011; YALSA Best Books for Young Adults, 2009.

Fans of...classic tales of high-tension peril will appreciate the way this successfully plays on their deepest fears. —*Bulletin of the Center for Children's Books*

McBride, Lish

Hold me closer, necromancer. Lish McBride. Henry Holt, 2010 342 p. (Necromancer (Lish McBride), 1)
Grades: 9 10 11 12
1. Werewolves; 2. College dropouts; 3. Dead; 4. Supernatural; 5. Magic; 6. Seattle, Washington; 7. Urban fantasy; 8. Pacific Northwest fiction
9780805090987
Great Lakes Great Books Award (Michigan), Grades 9-12, 2012; YALSA Popular Paperbacks for Young Adults, 2014; YALSA Best Fiction for Young Adults, 2011; William C. Morris Debut Award finalist, 2011.

Sam LaCroix, a Seattle fast-food worker and college dropout, discovers that he is a necromancer, part of a world of harbingers, werewolves, satyrs, and one particular necromancer who sees Sam as a threat to his lucrative business of raising the dead.

With fine writing, tight plotting, a unique and uniquely odd cast of teens, adults, and children, and a pace that smashes through any curtain of disbelief, this sardonic and outrageous story's only problem is that it must, like all good things, come to an end. —*Booklist*

Sequel: *Necromancing the stone.*

McCaffrey, Anne

Dragonflight. Anne McCaffrey. Ballantine Books, 1968 303 p. (Dragonriders of Pern, 1)
Grades: 8 9 10 11 12 Adult
1. Women rulers; 2. Household employees; 3. Dragons; 4. Biological invasions; 5. Survival; 6. Science fiction; 7. Science fantasy; 8. Adult books for young adults.
9780345276940; 9780552084536; 9780345484260; 9780345277497

At a time when the number of Dragonriders has fallen too low for safety and only one Weyr trains the creatures and their riders, the Red Star approaches Pern, threatening it with disaster.

The short stories *Weyr Search* and *Dragonrider* are incorporated in this book.

McCahan, Erin

The **lake** effect. Erin McCahan. Penguin Group USA, 2017 391 p.
Grades: 7 8 9 10 11 12

1. Self-fulfillment; 2. Growing up; 3. Risk-taking (Psychology); 4. Eighteen-year-old men; 5. Personal assistants; 6. Michigan; 7. Coming-of-age stories; 8. Realistic fiction.
9780803740525

It's the summer after senior year, and Briggs Henry is out the door. He's leaving behind his ex-girlfriend and his parents' money troubles for Lake Michigan and its miles of sandy beaches, working a summer job as a personal assistant, and living in a gorgeous Victorian on the shore. But then he gets there. And his eighty-four-year-old boss tells him to put on a suit for her funeral. So begins a summer of social gaffes, stomach cramps, fraught beach volleyball games, moonlit epiphanies, and a drawer full of funeral programs. Add to this Abigail, the mystifying girl next door on whom Briggs's charms just won't work, and "the lake effect" is taking on a whole new meaning.

Observant, sarcastic, compelling, and very funny, narrator Briggs is entirely convincing and, ably abetted by an abundance of diverse characters, never less than good company. —*Kirkus*

McCall, Guadalupe Garcia

All the stars denied. By Guadalupe Garcia McCall. Tu Books, an imprint of Lee & Low Books Inc, 2018 336 p.
Grades: 6 7 8 9 10
1. Mexican American families; 2. Deportation; 3. Racism; 4. Mexican American girls; 5. Race relations; 6. Texas; 7. Mexico (City); 8. 1930s; 9. Historical fiction; 10. Diary novels.
9781620142813

LC 2017058034

When resentment surges during the Great Depression in a Texas border town, Estrella, fifteen, organizes a protest against the treatment of tejanos and soon finds herself witih her mother and baby brother in Mexico.

A companion novel to *Shame the stars.*

Shame the stars. Guadalupe Garcia McCall. Tu Books, 2016 320 p.
Grades: 6 7 8 9
1. Mexican Americans; 2. Racism; 3. Corruption; 4. Family feuds; 5. Race relations; 6. Texas; 7. Mexican-American Border Region; 8. Mexican Revolution (1910-1920); 9. Historical fiction; 10. Love stories
9781620142783

Pura Belpr winner McCall delivers an ambitious, sardonically relevant historical novela must-read, complex twist on a political Shakespearean tragedy. —*Kirkus*

★ **Under** the mesquite. By Guadalupe Garcia McCall. Lee & Low Books, 2011 224 p.
Grades: 7 8 9 10 11 12
1. Mexican American teenage girls; 2. Children of people with cancer; 3. Responsibility in teenage girls; 4. Responsibility; 5. Acting; 6. Texas; 7. Realistic fiction; 8. Novels in verse; 9. First person narratives.
9781600604294

LC 2010052567

Booklist Editors' Choice: Books for Youth, 2011; Pura Belpre Award for Narrative, 2012; Tomas Rivera Mexican American Children's Book Award, 2013; YALSA Best Fiction for Young Adults, 2012; Notable Books for a Global Society, 2012; William C. Morris Debut Award finalist, 2012.

Throughout her high school years, as her mother battles cancer, Lupita takes on more responsibility for her house and seven younger siblings, while finding refuge in acting and writing poetry. Includes glossary of Spanish terms.

With poignant imagery and well-placed Spanish, the author effectively captures the complex lives of teenagers in many Latino and/or immigrant families. —*Kirkus*

McCarry, Sarah

About a girl. Sarah Mccarry. St. Martin's Griffin, 2015 256 p. (Metamorphoses trilogy, 3)
Grades: 9 10 11 12
1. Adopted teenage girls; 2. Small towns; 3. Family secrets; 4. Identity (Psychology); 5. Friendship; 6. Washington (State); 7. Urban fantasy; 8. Mythological fiction
9781250068620
Rainbow List, 2016.
As in other books in the trilogy, McCarry inflects the Pacific Northwest setting with Greek mythology, weaving ancient magic throughout Tally's story and adding an enchanting dose of magic realism. Tally's imagistic, melodic narrative roils with urgent emotion, and readers who loved the first two installments in the series will be richly rewarded by this series ender. —*Booklist*

All our pretty songs. Sarah McCarry. St. Martin's Griffin, 2013 224 p. (Metamorphoses trilogy, 1)
Grades: 9 10 11 12
1. Best friends; 2. Good and evil; 3. Love triangles; 4. Friendship; 5. Musicians; 6. Urban fantasy; 7. Mythological fiction
9781250027085; 9781250040886; 9781250027092, ebook, US
LC 2013003451
In the Pacific Northwest, the bond between two best friends is challenged when a mysterious and gifted musician comes between them and awakens an ancient evil.
Art and music run rampant through an unnamed narrator's journey with her best friend, strikingly beautiful Aurora, as frightening and elusive strangers promise drugs, fame, and love. The writing is rich and lush, yet conveys immediacy and is comprehensible even when the events are not...The descent into the underworld is riveting as the heroine tries to fight for her loved ones' fates. Raw sex and foul language accompany the shadow world that promises fame and one's heart's desire, and only faith in the narrator makes the journey endurable. Brilliant in concept and execution. —*School Library Journal*

Dirty wings. Sarah McCarry. St. Martin's Griffin, 2014 288 p. (Metamorphoses trilogy, 2)
Grades: 9 10 11 12
1. Runaway teenagers; 2. Teenage prodigies; 3. Automobile travel; 4. Teenage pianists; 5. Friendship; 6. New York City; 7. Mexico; 8. Urban fantasy; 9. Mythological fiction; 10. Multiple perspectives.
9781250049384; 9781250027108, ebook, US
LC 2014000136
In this retelling of the Persephone myth, an unlikely friendship develops between Cass, a teenaged runaway, and Maia, a piano prodigy imprisoned in the oppressive silence of her adoptive parents' house. When Cass frees Maia from her sheltered life and the hypnotic blue-eyed rocker Jason appears on the scene, an ancient evil is awakened.
The mothers of the girls featured in *All Our Pretty Songs* (2013) receive their own girlhood story in this beautifully constructed and grim tale...Identity, musical talent, and poisonous relationships between parents and children are depicted in a bravura retelling of a classic myth. —*Booklist*
Prequel to: *All our pretty songs.*

McCarthy, Andrew

Just fly away. By Andrew McCarthy. Algonquin Young Readers, 2017 272 p.

Grades: 7 8 9 10 11 12
1. Family secrets; 2. Betrayal; 3. Fathers and daughters; 4. Grandfather and granddaughter; 5. Half-brothers and sisters; 6. New Jersey; 7. Maine; 8. Realistic fiction; 9. First person narratives
9781616206291
LC 2016038077
Fifteen-year-old Lucy Willows discovers that her father had an illegitimate child, now an eight-year-old boy who lives in the same town, and she begins to question everything she thought she knew about her family and life.
This is a moving coming-of-age story for young adults who enjoy calm, character-driven reading. —*Voice of Youth Advocates*

McCaughrean, Geraldine

The **white** darkness. By Geraldine McCaughrean. Oxford University Press, 2005 264 p.
Grades: 8 9 10 11 12
1. Oates, Lawrence Edward Grace, 1880-1912; 2. Expeditions; 3. Uncle and niece; 4. Shyness in teenage girls; 5. Shyness; 6. Imaginary playmates; 7. Antarctica; 8. Survival stories; 9. Adventure stories; 10. Coming-of-age stories.
9780192719836
Michael L. Printz Award, 2008; Booklist Editors' Choice: Books for Youth, 2007; YALSA Best Books for Young Adults, 2008.
When her uncle takes her on a dream trip to the Antarctic wilderness, Sym's obsession with Captain Oates and the doomed expedition becomes a reality as she herself is soon in a fight for her life in some the harshest terrain on the planet.
McCaughrean's lyrical language actively engages the senses, plunging readers into a captivating landscape that challenges the boundaries of reality. —*Booklist*

McCauley, Kyrie

If these wings could fly. Kyrie McCauley. Katherine Tegen Books, 2020 400 p.
Grades: 9 10 11 12
1. High school seniors; 2. Family violence; 3. Family relationships; 4. Sisters; 5. Crows; 6. Pennsylvania; 7. Magical realism; 8. First person narratives.
9780062885029
William C. Morris YA Debut Award, 2021.
In Auburn, Pennsylvania, a farming community overrun with crows, high school senior Leighton struggles to keep herself and her sisters safe from her abusive father even as she starts a relationship. —*OCLC*
There are titles for teens that address the realities of dating violence, but it's more difficult to find stories of family violence; in her debut, McCauley traverses the tender ground with grace. —*Booklist*

McClintock, Norah

Masked. Written by Norah McClintock. Orca Book Publishers, 2010 108 p.
Grades: 7 8 9 10
1. Life change events; 2. Fathers and daughters; 3. Convenience stores; 4. Thieves; 5. Robbery; 6. High interest-low vocabulary books; 7. Canadian fiction.
9781554693658; 9781554693641
Tight plotting, swift pacing, and tension that intensifies with each page mark this entry in the always-reliable Orca Soundings series for reluctant readers. —*Booklist*
High interest story designed for reluctant readers or those reading below grade level.

Out of tune. Norah McClintock. 2017 222 p. (Riley Donovan mysteries, 3)
Grades: 7 8 9 10
1. Teenage detectives; 2. Murder; 3. Murder suspects; 4. Violinists; 5. Donovan, Riley (Fictitious character); 6. Mysteries; 7. Canadian fiction.
9781459814653

When Alicia, a talented violinist at Riley Donovan's high school, is found dead, Riley goes searching for the truth.

The plot is complex and tightly woven, the reveal is both surprising and satisfying, the violence is prominent but tastefully presented, and Riley continues to be a strong and relatable protagonist with good moral fiber. —*Booklist*

Trial by fire: a Riley Donovan mystery. Norah McClintock. Orca Book Publishers, 2016 240 p. (Riley Donovan mysteries, 1)
Grades: 7 8 9 10
1. Immigrants; 2. Arson; 3. Farms; 4. Small towns; 5. Prejudice; 6. Mysteries; 7. Canadian fiction.
9781459809369

After Riley saves her neighbor from a barn fire he is accused of setting the fire himself. Riley believes he is innocent and becomes determined to prove his innocence.

The mystery is compelling, the ending surprising, the protagonist plucky, and the language appealing for reluctant and avid readers alike, while the small-town race issues ground it as a discussion piece. —*Booklist*

McCormick, Patricia
Purple heart. By Patricia McCormick. Balzer & Bray, 2009 176 p.
Grades: 7 8 9 10
1. Soldiers; 2. People with brain injuries; 3. Iraq War, 2003-2011; 4. Memory; 5. Suspicion; 6. Iraq; 7. War stories
9780061730900; 9780061730917
LC 2009001757
YALSA Best Books for Young Adults, 2010.

While recuperating in a Baghdad hospital from a traumatic brain injury sustained during the Iraq War, eighteen-year-old soldier Matt Duffy struggles to recall what happened to him and how it relates to his ten-year-old friend, Ali.

Strong characters heighten the drama.... McCormick raises moral questions without judgment and will have readers examining not only this conflict but the nature of heroism and war. —*Publishers Weekly*

★ **Sold**. Patricia McCormick. Hyperion, 2006 272 p.
Grades: 9 10 11 12
1. Sexually abused girls; 2. Prostitution; 3. Sexual slavery; 4. Teenage prostitutes; 5. Stepfathers; 6. Nepal; 7. India; 8. First person narratives; 9. Realistic fiction; 10. Books to movies; 11. Books for reluctant readers
9780786851713
LC 2006049594
Amelia Bloomer List, 2007; Booklist Editors' Choice: Books for Youth, 2006; California Young Reader Medal, Young Adult, 2009; Delaware Diamonds (book award), High School, 2009; YALSA Best Books for Young Adults, 2007; YALSA Popular Paperbacks for Young Adults, 2010; YALSA Quick Picks for Reluctant Young Adult Readers, 2007; National Book Award for Young People's Literature finalist, 2006.

When she is tricked by her stepfather and sold into prostitution, thirteen-year-old Lakshmi becomes submerged in a nightmare where her only comfort is the friendship she forms with the other girls, which helps her survive and eventually escape.

In beautiful clear prose and free verse that remains true to the child's viewpoint, first-person, present-tense vignettes fill in Lakshmi's story. The brutality and cruelty are ever present (I have been beaten here, / locked away, / violated a hundred times / and a hundred times more), but not sensationalized.... An unforgettable account of sexual slavery as it exists now. —*Booklist*

McCoy, Chris
The **prom** goer's interstellar excursion. Chris Mccoy. Alfred A. Knopf, 2015 272 p.
Grades: 8 9 10 11 12
1. UFO abductions; 2. Aliens (Non-humanoid); 3. Bands (Music); 4. Space flight; 5. Teenage boys; 6. Science fiction
9780375855993

Readers will root for Bennett to get the girl and even for crusty band member Skark to accomplish his dream of becoming better than the one billionth and sixteenth band in the universe. The book's ending is a nicely placed, realistic surprise. Witty and action-packed, the plot boldly glazes over science-fiction details in favor of well-wrought characters. —*School Library Journal*

McCoy, Mary
Camp So-and-So. Mary McCoy. Carolrhoda Lab, 2017 424 p.
Grades: 9 10 11 12
1. Friendship; 2. Camps; 3. Survival; 4. Courage in girls; 5. Supernatural; 6. Paranormal fiction; 7. Thrillers and suspense.
9781512415971
LC 2016006371
Booklist Editors' Choice: Books for Youth, 2017.

Twenty five girls are invited to attend the mysterious Camp So-and-So over the summer where they work with their cabin mates to compete in the All-Camp Sports 7 Follies.

All the world's a stage in this clever compendium of horror and fantasy tropes, set at an Appalachian summer camp for girls. —*Booklist*

★ **I**, Claudia. Mary McCoy. Carolrhoda Lab, 2018 424 p.
Grades: 8 9 10 11 12
1. High school students; 2. Betrayal; 3. Student government; 4. Historians; 5. Power (Social sciences); 6. Los Angeles, California; 7. First person narratives; 8. Psychological fiction
9781512448467; 9781541530690; 9781541523753
LC 2017038714
Booklist Editors' Choice: Books for Youth, 2018; Michael L. Printz Honor Book, 2019.

Over the course of her high school years, awkward Claudia McCarthy finds herself unwittingly drawn into the dark side of her school's student government, with dire consequences—Provided by publisher.

Smart, witty, and featuring an unforgettable (and possibly unreliable) narrator, as well as a seamless stream of political history, the audience that finds this novel will be unable to put it down. —*Booklist*

McCreight, Kimberly
The **outliers**. Kimberly McCreight. HarperTeen, an imprint of HarperCollinsPublishers, 2016 368 p. (Outliers trilogy, 1)
Grades: 9 10 11 12
1. Missing teenage girls; 2. Anxiety in teenagers; 3. Best friends; 4. Mothers — Death; 5. Teenage girls; 6. Maine; 7. Thrillers and suspense
9780062359094

Best-selling author McCreight makes her YA debut with a heart-pounding thriller that ends on a cliff-hanger. —*Booklist*

McCullough, Joy

Blood water paint. Joy McCullough. Dutton Books, 2018 304 p. Grades: 10 11 12

1. Gentileschi, Artemisia, 1593-1652 or 1653; 2. Artists; 3. Gender role; 4. Child abuse victims; 5. Women artists; 6. Rape; 7. Italy; 8. 17th century; 9. Novels in verse; 10. Historical fiction.
9780735232112; 9780735232129; 9780735232136

LC 2017020678

Amelia Bloomer List, 2019; Booklist Editors' Choice: Books for Youth, 2018; Great Lakes Great Books Award (Michigan), Grades 9-12, 2019; School Library Journal Best Books, 2018; YALSA Best Fiction for Young Adults, 2019; William C. Morris Debut Award finalist, 2019.

By the time she was seventeen, Artemisia did more than grind pigment. She was one of Rome's most talented painters, even if no one knew her name. But Rome in 1610 was a city where men took what they wanted from women, and in the aftermath of rape Artemisia faced another terrible choice: a life of silence or a life of truth, no matter the cost.

McDaniel, Lurlene

Hit and run. Lurlene McDaniel. Delacorte Press, 2007 180 p. Grades: 8 9 10 11 12

1. Teenage athletes; 2. Hit-and-run accidents; 3. Guilt in teenage boys; 4. Guilt; 5. Popularity; 6. North Carolina; 7. Asheville, North Carolina; 8. Realistic fiction; 9. Multiple perspectives; 10. First person narratives.
9780385731614

Events surrounding the hit and run accident of a popular high school student are told from the viewpoints of those involved, including the victim.

This demonstrates the power of love and making choices. McDaniel, known for her inspiring novels, has a simplistic style, but a weighty message—it's the way you respond to a given situation that defines who you are and who you will be. —*School Library Journal*

McDonald, Abby

The **anti-prom**. Abby McDonald. Candlewick Press, 2011 288 p. Grades: 8 9 10 11

1. Proms; 2. Father-deserted children; 3. Revenge in teenage girls; 4. Revenge; 5. Resentfulness; 6. Realistic fiction; 7. Multiple perspectives
9780763649562

LC 2010039170

On prom night, Bliss, Jolene, and Meg, students from the same high school who barely know one another, band together to get revenge against Bliss's boyfriend and her best friend, whom she caught together in the limousine they rented.

McDonald instills more intelligence than you'd expect from such a plot while not skimping on the simple pleasures, either. —*Booklist*

McDonald, Janet

Harlem Hustle. Janet McDonald. Frances Foster Books, 2006 192 p. Grades: 8 9 10 11

1. African American teenage boys; 2. Rap musicians; 3. Hip-hop culture; 4. Seventeen-year-old boys; 5. Teenage boys; 6. New York City; 7. Harlem, New York City.
9780374371845

LC 2005052108

Eric "Hustle" Samson, a smart and street-wise seventeen-year-old dropout from Harlem, aspires to rap stardom, a dream he naively believes is about to come true.

The author nails the hip-hop lingo and the street slang, and her characters strike just the right attitude.... Young adults will love this book. —*School Library Journal*

Off-color. Janet McDonald. Farrar, Straus and Giroux, 2007 163 p. Grades: 7 8 9 10 11 12

1. Multiracial persons; 2. Teenage girls; 3. Identity (Psychology); 4. Fifteen-year-old girls; 5. Teenagers; 6. Brooklyn, New York City
9780374371968

LC 2006047334

Fifteen-year-old Cameron living with her single mother in Brooklyn finds her search for identity further challenged when she discovers that she is the product of a biracial relationship.

McDonald dramatizes the big issues from the inside, showing the hard times and the joy in fast-talking dialogue that is honest, insulting, angry, tender, and very funny. —*Booklist*

Frances Foster book.

McEntire, Myra

Hourglass. Myra McEntire. Egmont USA, 2011 400 p. (Hourglass novels, 1)
Grades: 7 8 9 10

1. Seventeen-year-old girls; 2. Superhuman abilities; 3. Space and time; 4. Ghosts; 5. Men/women relations; 6. Science fiction
9781606841440; 9781606842546

LC 2010043618

Just before her parents died in a car accident, 17-year-old Emerson Cole began seeing ghosts, and now, four years later, she's desperate for relief. (Her tendency to have conversations with thin air has resulted in her dismissal from two schools and her hospitalization for a nervous breakdown.) When Emerson's older brother Thomas hires handsome Michael Weaver, a consultant from a shadowy organization called Hourglass, to help her, Emerson doesn't think it'll do any good. But she doesn't realize that Michael wants to help her use her gift, not get rid of it.

Em is an entertainingly cheeky narrator and appealingly resilient heroine.... McEntire deftly juggles plot, characters and dialogue; her portrait of grief is particularly poignant. —*Kirkus*

McGarry, Katie

★ **Dare** you to. Katie McGarry. Harlequin Teen, 2013 468 p. (Pushing the limits, 2)
Grades: 9 10 11 12

1. Teenage baseball players; 2. Children of drug abusers; 3. Dysfunctional families; 4. Teenage romance; 5. Teenage boy/girl relations; 6. Kentucky; 7. Louisville, Kentucky; 8. Contemporary romances; 9. Multiple perspectives
9780373210633

Romantic Times Reviewer's Choice Award, 2013.

When an intervention forces her to move in with an aunt, Beth becomes a misfit in a new school and unexpectedly falls for star athlete Ryan, whose secrets and compulsion to engage in daring behaviors prompts an intense relationship.

Sex, drugs, profanity, and violence, as well as subplots about loved ones who escaped town for emotional survival, heighten the dramatic tension but don't disguise the wholesome, girl-next-door quality of this well-paced, satisfying romance. —*Publishers Weekly*

Only a breath apart. Katie McGarry. Tor Teen, 2019 368 p. Grades: 8 9 10 11 12

1. Former friends; 2. Inheritance and succession; 3. Farms; 4. Secrets; 5. Love; 6. Kentucky; 7. Contemporary romances; 8. Realistic fiction; 9. Multiple perspectives.
9781250193858; 9781250193872, ebook, US

LC 2018044554
Told in two voices, childhood best friends Jessie and Scarlett reconnect at his grandmother's funeral and start to share their secrets and feelings for each other.

The novel manages to tackle domestic violence in a way that never feels clichd, and the romance is sure to win over even the most cynical reader. —*Booklist*

A Tom Doherty Associates Book.

Pushing the limits. Harlequin Teen, 2012 384 p. (Pushing the limits, 1)
Grades: 9 10 11 12
1. Teenagers; 2. Secrets; 3. Life change events; 4. Memory; 5. Tutoring; 6. Contemporary romances; 7. Books for reluctant readers
9780373210497
YALSA Quick Picks for Reluctant Young Adult Readers, 2013.

Former popular girl, Echo, finds herself mysteriously cast as an outsider at school and has scars on her arms with no memory of how they got there. When she meets bad boy, Noah Hutchinson, she is surprised that he is able to understand. Sparks fly and the two have a hard time fighting their attraction despite secrets they are both keeping.

McGhee, Alison
★ **What** I leave behind. Alison McGhee. Simon & Schuster 2018 128 p.
Grades: 9 10 11 12
1. Fathers — Suicide; 2. Helpfulness in teenage boys; 3. Teenagers and death; 4. Grief in teenage boys; 5. Sixteen-year-old boys; 6. Los Angeles, California; 7. Realistic fiction; 8. Books for reluctant readers
9781481476560
Booklist Editors' Choice: Books for Youth, 2018; YALSA Quick Picks for Reluctant Young Adult Readers, 2019.

McGhee skillfully evokes sense memory, as Will attempts to find solace in his nighttime wanderings. Ultimately, the piercing narrative offers an affirmation of remaining connected to others through loss as Will embraces his relationships and begins to heal. —*Publishers Weekly*

McGinnis, Mindy
Be not far from me. Mindy McGinnis. Katherine Tegen Books, 2020 240 p.
Grades: 8 9 10 11
1. Wilderness survival; 2. Wilderness areas; 3. Infection; 4. Wounds and injuries; 5. Survival; 6. Great Smoky Mountains (N.C. and Tenn.); 7. Tennessee; 8. Survival stories.
9780062561626
Lost in the Great Smoky Mountains, rising high school senior Ashley Hawkins must fight for survival without any tools, growing in awareness that the world is not tame, and neither are people. —*OCLC*

★ The **female** of the species. Mindy McGinnis. 2016 341 pages
Grades: 10 11 12
1. Revenge; 2. Rural teenagers; 3. Small towns; 4. High school seniors; 5. Murder; 6. Ohio; 7. Thrillers and suspense; 8. Multiple perspectives
9780062320896
LC 2016932089
Romantic Times Reviewer's Choice Award, 2016; School Library Journal Best Books, 2016; Sequoyah Book Awards (Oklahoma), High School Books, 2018; YALSA Best Fiction for Young Adults, 2017.

McGinnis explores how one teen uses violence for justice in this gripping story that should be read and discussed by teens, as well as those who work with them. —*Booklist*

A **madness** so discreet. Mindy McGinnis. 2015 376 pages

Grades: 9 10 11 12
1. Psychiatric hospitals; 2. Criminal investigation; 3. Physicians; 4. Teenage rape victims; 5. Teenage girls; 6. 19th century; 7. Historical fiction; 8. Thrillers and suspense
9780062320865
LC 2014041255
Edgar Allan Poe Award for Best Young Adult, 2016.

Near the turn of the nineteenth century, Dr. Thornhollow helps teenaged Grace Mae escape from the Boston asylum where she was sent after becoming pregnant by rape, and takes her to Ohio where they put her intelligence and remarkable memory to use in trying to catch murderers.

Readers will wish they could watch [Grace] and Thornhollow solve murders for pages and pages more. A dark study of the effects of power in the wrong hands, buoyed by a tenacious heroine and her colorful companions. —*Kirkus*

McGovern, Cammie
Just breathe. Cammie McGovern. HarperTeen, 2020 352 p.
Grades: 9 10 11 12
1. Teenagers with depression; 2. Sick persons; 3. Teenage romance; 4. People with cystic fibrosis; 5. Cystic fibrosis; 6. Contemporary romances; 7. Realistic fiction; 8. Multiple perspectives.
9780062463357
David Scheinman is the popular president of his senior class, battling cystic fibrosis. Jamie Turner is a quiet sophomore, struggling with depression. The pair soon realizes that they're able to be more themselves with each other than they can be with anyone else, and their unlikely friendship starts to turn into something so much more. But neither Jamie nor David can bring themselves to reveal the secrets that weigh most heavily on their hearts, and their time for honesty may be running out.—Publisher description.

McGovern skillfully imbues her characters with realistic voices; her teenagers sound like real teenagers and less like how some authors want teenagers to sound. —*Booklist*

★ A **step** toward falling. Cammie McGovern. HarperTeen, an imprint of HarperCollinsPublishers, 2015 364 p.
Grades: 9 10 11 12
1. People with disabilities; 2. Community service (Punishment); 3. Teenage girls with developmental disabilities; 4. High school football players; 5. Teenage boy/girl relations; 6. Realistic fiction; 7. Multiple perspectives
9780062271136
No mere empathy builder for Emily and Lucas, Belinda is a fully developed character—good at some things (better than Emily and Lucas, in fact), bad at others. Without evading or sugarcoating difficult topics, McGovern...shows that disabled and able aren't binary states but part of a continuum—a human one. —*Publishers Weekly*

McGovern, Kate
★ **Fear** of missing out. Kate McGovern. Farrar Straus Giroux, 2019 320 p.
Grades: 9 10 11 12
1. Teenagers with cancer; 2. Terminal illness; 3. Options, alternatives, choices; 4. Cancer; 5. Cryonics; 6. Realistic fiction; 7. First person narratives.
9780374305475
LC 2018020372
Despite the loving intentions of her mother and boyfriend, sixteen-year-old Astrid wants to make the decisions about her life and death when her cancer returns, including exploring the possibility of cryopreservation.

A heartbreaking story of loss and grief peopled with nuanced, endearing characters that ultimately leaves the reader with a feeling of triumph. —*Kirkus*

McGuigan, Mary Ann
Morning in a different place. Mary Ann McGuigan. Front Street, 2009 195 p;
Grades: 7 8 9 10
1. Interracial friendship; 2. Race relations; 3. Racism; 4. Eighth-grade girls; 5. Teenage girls; 6. Bronx, New York City; 7. New York City; 8. 1960s; 9. Historical fiction
9781590785515
LC 2007017547
In 1963 in the Bronx, New York, eighth-graders Fiona and Yolanda help one another face hard decisions at home despite family and social opposition to their interracial friendship, but Fiona is on her own when popular classmates start paying attention to her and give her a glimpse of both a different way of life and a new kind of hatefulness.
This book is never didactic. McGuigan's writing is spare and low-key, and her metaphors are acute. —*Booklist*

McKay, Sharon E.
Thunder over Kandahar. Sharon E. McKay; photographs by Rafal Gerszak. Annick Press, 2010 260 p. : Illustration
Grades: 7 8 9 10 11 12
1. Runaway teenage girls; 2. Arranged marriage; 3. Religious persecution; 4. Best friends; 5. Friendship; 6. Afghanistan; 7. Realistic fiction; 8. Canadian fiction.
9781554512676
LC Bl2010021366
Notable Books for a Global Society, 2011; Amelia Bloomer List, 2011; USBBY Outstanding International Book, 2011.
Teenage best friends Tamanna and Yasmine face arranged marriages and persecution by the Taliban in their Afghan village, so they flee through dangerous mountain passes with only one another to rely upon.
When her British and American-educated parents' return to Afghanistan is cut short by a terrible attack, 14-year-old Yasmine is sent to Kandahar for safety. Instead, the driver abandons her and her friend Tamanna along the way, and they must travel on their own through Taliban-controlled mountains.... In spite of unrelenting violence, along with grinding poverty, restrictive customs, and the horrors of war, what shines through this sad narrative is the love Afghans have for their country.... [The author] traveled to Afghanistan and provides numerous credits for this gripping tale. —*School Library Journal*

McKenzie, Paige
The **awakening** of Sunshine girl. . Perseus Books Group, 2016 320 p. (Haunting of Sunshine girl, 2)
Grades: 7 8 9
1. Dead; 2. Fathers and daughters; 3. Birthfathers; 4. Adoptive mothers; 5. Love triangles; 6. Horror
9781602862746; 9781509801855, print, UK
Sixteen-year-old Sunshine is reluctantly gaining control over her powers as a Luiseach. But while she explores her mystical lineage, Sunshine discovers a dangerous discordance—one only she can heal.

McKernan, Victoria
Shackleton's stowaway. Victoria McKernan. Knopf, 2005 317 p;
Grades: 7 8 9 10
1. Blackborow, W. Perce, 1894-1949; 2. Shackleton, Ernest Henry, Sir, 1874-1922; 3. Survival (after airplane accidents, shipwrecks,

etc.); 4. Expeditions; 5. Voyages and travels; 6. Cold; 7. Antarctica; 8. Survival stories; 9. Adventure stories; 10. Historical fiction.
9780375826917; 9780375926914
LC 2004010313
A fictionalized account of the adventures of eighteen-year-old Perce Blackborow, who stowed away for the 1914 Shackleton Antarctic expedition and, after their ship Endurance was crushed by ice, endured many hardships, including the loss of the toes of his left foot to frostbite, during the nearly two-year return journey across sea and ice.
This book provides historical information for history and geography classes who are interested in exploration, the Antarctic, and early history of great sea voyages. —*Library Media Connection*
Includes bibliographical references.

McKinley, Robin
★ **Beauty:** a retelling of the story of Beauty & the beast. Robin McKinley. Harper & Row, 1978 247 p;
Grades: 7 8 9 10
1. Enchantment; 2. Self-sacrifice; 3. Spells (Magic); 4. Love; 5. Kindness; 6. Fantasy romances; 7. Fairy tale and folklore-inspired fiction
9780060241490; 9780060241506
LC 77025636
YALSA Popular Paperbacks for Young Adults, 2016; YALSA Popular Paperbacks for Young Adults, 2010.
Kind Beauty grows to love the Beast at whose castle she is compelled to stay and through her love releases him from the spell which had turned him from a handsome prince into an ugly beast.

Chalice. Robin McKinley. G.P. Putnam's Sons, 2008 272 p.
Grades: 7 8 9 10 11 12
1. Beekeepers; 2. Nature; 3. Duty; 4. Women political consultants; 5. Priests; 6. Fantasy fiction.
9780399246760
LC 2008000704
A beekeeper by trade, Mirasol's life changes completely when she is named the new Chalice, the most important advisor to the new Master, a former priest of fire.
The fantasy realm is evoked in thorough and telling detail.... A lavish and lasting treat. —*Publishers Weekly*

The **door** in the hedge. By Robin McKinley. Greenwillow Books, 1981 216 p;
Grades: 7 8 9 10
1. Princesses; 2. Enchantment; 3. Good and evil; 4. Animals; 5. Magic; 6. Fantasy fiction; 7. Short stories; 8. Fairy tale and folklore-inspired fiction
9780688003128
LC 80021903
The author presents four romantic tales that elaborate—to a greater or lesser degreeupon the supernatural lore of fairy tale, myth, and legend. Two of the stories are original in plot and in characters.... The other two stories are literary recastings of Grimm tales, "The Princess and the Frog"...and The "Twelve Dancing Princesses." —*Horn Book Guide*

★ **Fire:** tales of elemental spirits. Robin McKinley and Peter Dickinson. G. P. Putnam's Sons, 2009 304 p. (Tales of elemental spirits, 2)
Grades: 7 8 9 10
1. Imaginary creatures; 2. Fire; 3. Four elements; 4. Supernatural; 5. Self-discovery; 6. Fantasy fiction; 7. Short stories
9780399252891
LC 2009004730
YALSA Best Books for Young Adults, 2010.

The settings of these five tales range from ancient to modern, but they are all united by encounters with magical creatures with an affinity for fire.... This collection of beautifully crafted tales will find a warm welcome from fans of either author, as well as from fantasy readers in general. —*School Library Journal*

★ The **outlaws** of Sherwood. Robin McKinley. Greenwillow Books, 1988 282 p;
Grades: 8 9 10 11 12
1. Richard I, King of England, 1157-1199; 2. Robin Hood (Legendary character); 3. Outlaws; 4. Nobility — History; 5. Heroes and heroines; 6. Adventurers; 7. England; 8. Sherwood Forest, England; 9. 12th century; 10. Historical fiction; 11. Fairy tale and folklore-inspired fiction
9780688071783
LC 88045227
ALA Notable Children's Book, 1989.
The author retells the adventures of Robin Hood and his band of outlaws who live in Sherwood Forest in twelfth-century England.
McKinley takes a fresh look at a classic, changing some of the events or deviating from standard characterization to gain new dimensions. Her afterword explains her artistic compromise with myth and history, her wish to write a version that is historically unembarrassing. With a few exceptions, she has done that admirably, creating a story that has pace and substance and style, and that is given nuance and depth by the characterization. —*Bulletin of the Center for Children's Books*

Pegasus. Robin McKinley. G.P. Putnam's Sons, 2010 400 p.
Grades: 8 9 10 11 12
1. Princesses; 2. Winged horses; 3. Telepathy; 4. Wizards; 5. Alliances; 6. High fantasy; 7. Fantasy fiction.
9780399246777
LC 2010002279
Because of a thousand-year-old alliance between humans and pegasi, Princess Sylvi is ceremonially bound to Ebon, her own pegasus, on her twelfth birthday, but the closeness of their bond becomes a threat to the status quo and possibly to the safety of their two nations.
McKinley's storytelling is to be savored. She lavishes page after page upon rituals and ceremonies, basks in the awe of her intricately constructed world, and displays a masterful sense of pegasi physicality and mannerisms. —*Booklist*

Rose daughter. Robin McKinley. Greenwillow Books, 1997 306 p;
Grades: 7 8 9 10
1. Enchantment; 2. Roses; 3. Love; 4. Beauty; 5. Rose growing; 6. Fantasy romances; 7. Fairy tale and folklore-inspired fiction
9780688154394
LC 96048783
Booklist Editors' Choice: Books for Youth, 1997; YALSA Best Books for Young Adults, 1998.
Beauty grows to love the Beast at whose castle she is compelled to stay, and through her love he is released from the curse that had turned him from man to beast.
Compared to *Beauty*, this is fuller bodied, with richer characterizations and a more mystical, darker edge.... There is more background on the Beast in this version...and Beauty's choice at the end, a departure from that in *Beauty*, is just so right. Readers will be enchanted, in the best sense of the word. —*Booklist*

McKinney, L. L.
A **dream** so dark. L. L. McKinney. Imprint, 2019 416 p. (Nightmare-verse, 2)
Grades: 9 10 11 12

1. Demon slayers; 2. Parallel universes; 3. African American teenage girls; 4. Monsters; 5. Good and evil; 6. Atlanta, Georgia; 7. Gateway fantasy; 8. Urban fantasy; 9. Classics-inspired fiction.
9781250153920; 9781789093049, Paperback, UK
A high-suspense follow-up to A Blade So Black continues the dark adventures of Alice, whose efforts to save her Wonderland friends are complicated by a Nightmare-summoning poet's schemes to raise the dead.
The twists and turns of this novel are explosive from start to finish and guaranteed to send readers gleefully down a rabbit hole from which they'll emerge begging for a third installment. —*Booklist*

McKissack, Fredrick
Shooting star. Fredrick L. McKissack. Atheneum Books for Young Readers, 2009 288 p.
Grades: 8 9 10 11 12
1. High school football players; 2. Anabolic steroids in sports; 3. African Americans; 4. High schools; 5. High school football; 6. Sports fiction; 7. Coming-of-age stories; 8. Realistic fiction
9781416947455
LC 2008055525
Sophomore defensive back Jomo Rogers trains hard to be the best—but is it enough? Discouraged by his football coach and friends' constant comments about his size, Jomo loses patience and considers using steroids to bulk up, despite the risks. More than a play-by-play of gridiron action, this is a story about difficult choices and their effects on other people, especially loved ones. But don't worry, Shooting Star isn't sentimental or overly dramatic—it's an honest, layered novel about complex, believable characters grappling with real-life issues.
Profane and scatological language abounds, but it is not outside the realm of what one could hear any day in a school locker room. Top-notch sports fiction. —*School Library Journal*

McLaughlin, Lauren
The **free**. Lauren McLaughlin. Soho Teen, 2017 288 p.
Grades: 8 9 10 11 12
1. Juvenile detention; 2. Psychic trauma in teenagers; 3. Self-fulfillment; 4. Juvenile delinquency; 5. Secrets; 6. Realistic fiction
9781616957315; 9781616957322, ebook, US
LC 2016020652
Teenaged Isaac, who steals to give his younger sister the basic necessities that his alcoholic mother cannot provide, is sentenced to a juvenile detention center and during therapy sessions with fellow criminals, a repressed memory surfaces that changes everything.
Compassionate, compelling, gritty, and redeeming, this storys broad appeal will hit the mark with mystery or realistic fiction fans and those who care about social justice. —*Booklist*

McLemore, Anna-Marie
Blanca & Roja. Anna-Marie McLemore. Feiwel & Friends, 2018 320 p.
Grades: 8 9 10 11
1. Curses; 2. Sisters; 3. Love; 4. Swans; 5. Duty; 6. Magical realism.
9781250162717
School Library Journal Best Books, 2018; YALSA Best Fiction for Young Adults, 2019.

Dark and deepest red. Anna-Marie McLemore. Feiwel & Friends, 2020 320 p.
Grades: 9 10 11 12

1. Shoes; 2. Magic shoes; 3. Dancing; 4. Magic (Occultism); 5. Difference (Psychology); 6. Magical realism; 7. Fairy tale and folklore-inspired fiction; 8. Parallel narratives
9781250162748; 9781250162731

LC 2019940845

Trapped in a pair of red shoes that compel her to dance uncontrollably, Rosella is drawn to a youth of questionable intent whose family was blamed for witchcraft centuries earlier.

The author spins a tale of first love, misfits forging their own places in the world, and the inherent prejudices of people who fear what they don't understand. —*Kirkus*

The **weight** of feathers. Anna-Marie McLemore. St. Martin's Press, 2015 320 p.
Grades: 9 10 11 12
1. Family feuds; 2. Circus performers; 3. Teenage romance; 4. Magic; 5. Rescues; 6. Magical realism
9781250058652
YALSA Best Fiction for Young Adults, 2016; William C. Morris Debut Award finalist, 2016.

Lace Paloma and Cluck Corbeau, from feuding families of traveling performers, fall in love.

The enchanting setup and the forbidden romance that blooms between these two outcasts will quickly draw readers in, along with the steady unspooling of the families' history and mutual suspicions in this promising first novel. —*Publishers Weekly*

When the moon was ours. Anna-Marie McLemore. St. Martin's Griffin, 2016 273 p.
Grades: 9 10 11 12
1. Latin Americans; 2. Transgender teenagers; 3. Gender identity; 4. Friendship; 5. Teenage boy/girl relations; 6. Magical realism
9781250058669
Booklist Editors' Choice: Books for Youth, 2016; James Tiptree, Jr. Award, 2016; YALSA Best Fiction for Young Adults, 2017; Rainbow List, 2017; Stonewall Children's & Young Adult Literature Honor Book, 2017.

Readers who stick with this novel will be rewarded with a love story that is as endearingly old-fashioned as it is modern and as fantastical as it is real. —*School Library Journal*

Wild beauty. Anna-Marie McLemore. Feiwel and Friends, 2017 320 p.
Grades: 9 10 11 12
1. Curses; 2. Gardens; 3. Love; 4. Families; 5. Cousins; 6. Magical realism
9781250124555; 9781250180735
Booklist Editors' Choice: Books for Youth, 2017; School Library Journal Best Books, 2017.

For nearly a century, the Nomeolvides women have tended the grounds of La Pradera, hiding a terrible legacy, until mysterious Fel arrives and Estrella helps him explore his dangerous past.

This is not only a powerful exploration of truth and family...but also gender identity, sexuality...and love itself. Sheer magic: fierce, bright, and blazing with possibility. —*Booklist*

McMann, Lisa
Gone. By Lisa McMann. Simon Pulse, 2010 224 p. (Wake trilogy (Lisa McMann), 3)
Grades: 8 9 10 11
1. Children of alcoholic mothers; 2. Dreams; 3. People in comas; 4. Lucid dreams; 5. Fathers and daughters; 6. Supernatural mysteries
9781416979180

LC 2009018682

While eighteen-year-old Janie ponders her future with Cabe, knowing that her being a dream-catcher means eventual blindness and crippling, she encounters her past as the father she never knew is hospitalized with brain trauma and seems to need her help.

McMann wraps up the trilogy that began with *Wake* (2008) and *Fade* (2009).... Janie...learns that the father she never knew has been living in an isolated house not far from her and now lies in a hospital bed. By entering his unconscious, she also learns that he is a dream catcher too, while a search through his home reveals that he has avoided the debilitating blindness and gnarled hands of Janie's dream-catching mentor, Miss Stubin, but has sacrificed love in the process.... A fitting completion to this popular series. —*Kirkus*

Wake. Lisa McMann. Simon Pulse, 2008 210 p; (Wake trilogy (Lisa McMann), 1)
Grades: 7 8 9 10
1. Children of alcoholic mothers; 2. Dreams; 3. Teenagers and seniors; 4. Lucid dreams; 5. High schools; 6. Supernatural mysteries; 7. Books for reluctant readers
9781416953579
YALSA Quick Picks for Reluctant Young Adult Readers, 2009.

Ever since she was eight years old, high school student Janie Hannagan has been uncontrollably drawn into other people's dreams, but it is not until she befriends an elderly nursing home patient and becomes involved with an enigmatic fellow-student that she discovers her true power.

A fast pace, a great mix of teen angst and supernatural experiences, and an eerie, attention-grabbing cover will make this a hit. —*Booklist*
Sequel: *Fade*.

McManus, Karen M.
★ The **cousins**. Karen M. McManus. Delacorte Press, 2020 336 p.
Grades: 9 10 11 12
1. Cousins; 2. Family secrets; 3. Grandmothers; 4. Islands; 5. Resorts; 6. Massachusetts; 7. Thrillers and suspense
9780525708001; 9780525708018

After receiving an invitation to spend the summer with their estranged grandmother, the Story cousins arrive at her house only to discover that she is not there, and the longer they stay on the island, the more they realize their mysterious family history has some deadly secrets. —*OCLC*

In classic McManus fashion, perspectives shift, providing insights into the three cousins' distinct stories and personal motives while maintaining a steady pace that leaves readers flipping pages. —*Kirkus*

★ **One** of us is lying. Karen M. McManus. 2017 368 pages (Bayview High series, 1)
Grades: 9 10 11 12
1. Teenage murder suspects; 2. High school students; 3. Murder; 4. Application software; 5. School detention; 6. California; 7. San Diego, California; 8. Mysteries; 9. Multiple perspectives
9781524714680, hardcover; 9781524714697, library binding; 9781524764722, paperback; 9780141375632, paperback, UK; 9780141375649, ebook, UK

LC 2016032495

Black-Eyed Susan Book Award (Maryland), High School, 2019; Garden State Teen Book Award (New Jersey), Fiction (Grades 9-12), 2020; Rhode Island Teen Book Award, 2020; South Carolina Book Award, Young Adult Books, 2020; Westchester Fiction Award, 2018; YALSA Quick Picks for Reluctant Young Adult Readers, 2018.

When one of five students in detention is found dead, his high-profile classmates—including a brainy intellectual, a popular beauty, a drug dealer on probation and an all-star athlete—are investigated and revealed to be the subjects of the victim's latest gossip postings.

McManus captures the power of social media among high school students and the tangled web of ever-changing relationships that is the fabric of adolescent life. Give to readers looking for mysteries set securely in the teen world. —*Voice of Youth Advocates*

★ **One** of us is next. Karen M. McManus. Delacorte Press, 2020 384 p. (Bayview High series, 2)
Grades: 9 10 11 12
1. High school students; 2. Murder; 3. Revenge; 4. Friendship; 5. Online social networks; 6. California; 7. San Diego, California; 8. Mysteries; 9. Multiple perspectives
9780525707974; 9780525707967; 9780241376928, Paperback, UK
Finds the Bayview friends targeted by an anonymous adversary who uses an increasingly dangerous truth-or-dare app to keep the late Simon's gossip legacy alive.
A can't put down read. —*Kirkus*
Sequel to: *One of Us is Lying*.

Two can keep a secret. Karen M. McManus. Delacorte Press, 2019 336 p.
Grades: 9 10 11 12
1. Murder; 2. Missing persons; 3. Small towns; 4. Community life; 5. Multiracial teenagers; 6. Thrillers and suspense; 7. Multiple perspectives; 8. Books for reluctant readers
9781524714734; 9781524714727; 9780141375656, Paperback, UK
LC 2018022931
YALSA Quick Picks for Reluctant Young Adult Readers, 2020.
While true-crime aficionado Ellery and her twin brother are staying with their grandmother in a Vermont community known for murder, a new friend goes missing and Ellery may be next.

McNab, Andy
Meltdown: the final chapter of the Watts family adventures!. Andy McNab and Robert Rigby. G.P. Putnam's Sons, 2007 248 p; (Watts family adventures, 4)
Grades: 7 8 9 10
1. Spies; 2. Drugs; 3. Terrorism; 4. Grandfather and grandson; 5. Orphans; 6. England; 7. Thrillers and suspense; 8. Adventure stories
9780399246869
LC 2007022674
Eighteen-year-old Danny Watts and his grandfather Fergus, an ex-SAS explosives expert, travel to England, Spain, and Germany, in a life-or-death race to save the population from the spread of a lethal new drug that has been unleashed by terrorists.
This compelling, fast-paced, plot-driven dose of espionage and intrigue features a bit of appropriately gruesome violence thrown in for good measure. —*Voice of Youth Advocates*

Payback. By Andy McNab and Robert Rigby. G. P. Putnam's Sons, 2006 250 p. (Watts family adventures, 2)
Grades: 7 8 9 10
1. Seventeen-year-old boys; 2. Teenage boys; 3. Teenage girls; 4. Teenagers; 5. Teenage spies; 6. England; 7. London, England; 8. Spy fiction; 9. Thrillers and suspense; 10. Adventure stories
9780399244650
LC 2005032657
As teenage suicide bombers terrorize England, seventeen-year-old Danny tries to help his grandfather, an ex-SAS explosives expert falsely accused of being a traitorous spy by the government's intelligence agencies.
Teens will...enjoy the fast-paced, action-laden plot and the wealth of details about tricks of the spy trade. —*Booklist*
Sequel to: *Traitor*; Sequel: *Avenger*.

Traitor. By Andy McNab and Robert Rigby. G.P. Putnam's Sons, 2005 288 p. (Watts family adventures, 1)
Grades: 7 8 9 10
1. Seventeen-year-old boys; 2. Seventeen-year-olds; 3. Teenage girls; 4. Teenagers; 5. Spies; 6. England; 7. London, England; 8. 2000s (Decade); 9. Spy fiction; 10. Thrillers and suspense; 11. Adventure stories
9780399244643
LC 2005006701
YALSA Popular Paperbacks for Young Adults, 2009.
A boy who believes his grandfather to be a traitor, a spy who turned against England and then disappeared, tracks down his grandfather and finds out the truth.
Orphaned Londoner Danny Watts wants nothing to do with his estranged grandfather, a traitor who went MIA years ago, until the British military offers Danny a proposition: find his grandfather and he'll receive a scholarship.... With help from his best friend, Elena, he sets off to find his relative and the truth.... The well-crafted language includes a few coarse phrases.... With its brisk plot and unpredictable characters, this story of intrigue rises above many standard adventure stories. —*Booklist*

McNally, Janet
Girls in the moon. Janet McNally. HarperTeen, an imprint of HarperCollinsPublishers, 2016 338 p.
Grades: 8 9 10 11
1. Sisters; 2. Children of rock musicians; 3. Fathers and daughters; 4. Bands (Music); 5. Musicians; 6. New York City; 7. Realistic fiction; 8. Coming-of-age stories; 9. Multiple perspectives
9780062436245
McNally is a polished storyteller, her prose alive with vivid descriptions, the excitement of romance, and an artists yearning to create. —*Publishers Weekly*

The **looking** glass. Janet McNally. HarperTeen, 2018 288 p.
Grades: 7 8 9 10
1. Sisters; 2. Runaways; 3. Missing girls; 4. Teenage girls; 5. Prescription drug abuse; 6. Realistic fiction
9780062436276
LC 2017034545
A copy of *Grimms' Fairy Tales* sends Sylvie, a sixteen-year-old ballerina-in-training, in search of her runaway older sister amid strange happenings, such as a woman leaving a shoe behind while running.

McNeal, Tom
★ **Far** far away. By Tom McNeal. Alfred A. Knopf Books for Young Readers, 2013 371 p.
Grades: 7 8 9 10
1. Grimm, Jacob; 2. Revenge; 3. Ghosts; 4. Bakers; 5. Supernatural; 6. Friendship; 7. Fantasy fiction; 8. Fairy tale and folklore-inspired fiction
9780375849725; 9780375896989, ebook, US
LC 2012020603
ALA Notable Children's Book, 2014; Booklist Editors' Choice: Books for Youth, 2013; School Library Journal Best Books, 2013; YALSA Best Fiction for Young Adults, 2014; YALSA Best Fiction for Young Adults: Top Ten, 2014; National Book Award for Young People's Literature finalist, 2013.
After his mother left and his father became a recluse, Jeremy Johnson Johnson (whose mother and father both had the same last name) was left to support the family, but he's been aided by the ghost of Jacob Grimm, one half of the infamous Brothers Grimm writing duo, and when provocative local girl Ginger Boultinghouse takes an interest in Jeremy (and his unique abilities), a grim chain of events is put into motion.

LIST OF FICTIONAL WORKS

McNeil, Gretchen
  #murdertrending. Freeform Books, 2018 352 p. (#MurderTrending, 1)
Grades: 9 10 11 12
  1. Teenage prisoners; 2. Reality television programs; 3. Executions and executioners; 4. Social media; 5. Murder; 6. Horror; 7. Dystopian fiction; 8. Thrillers and suspense; 9. Books for reluctant readers
9781368013703; 9781368010023, Hardback, UK
YALSA Quick Picks for Reluctant Young Adult Readers, 2019.

  Falsely accused of murdering her stepsister, seventeen-year-old Dee fights to survive paid assassins on Alcatraz 2.0, the most popular prison on social media.

  McNeil offers a tense, fast-paced tale that balances gore (numerous people die in creative, occasionally graphic ways), pop culture, and dark comedy. —*Publishers Weekly*

  I'm not your manic pixie dream girl. Gretchen McNeil. Balzer + Bray, an imprint of HarperCollinsPublishers, 2016 352 p.
Grades: 8 9 10 11
  1. Multiracial teenage girls; 2. Breaking up (Interpersonal relations); 3. Former boyfriends; 4. Mathematics; 5. Gay teenagers; 6. Contemporary romances
9780062409119
  The love rhombus crafted here is a tad predictable, but the excitement's in the execution: the author's strong characterizations and smart humor put this above most similar titles. —*Kirkus*

McQuein, Josin L.
  Arclight. Josin L. McQuein. Greenwillow Books, an imprint of HarperCollins Publishers, 2013 400 p. (Arclight, 1)
Grades: 8 9 10 11 12
  1. Dystopias; 2. Colonies; 3. Amnesia; 4. Identity (Psychology); 5. Teenage girls; 6. Apocalyptic fiction; 7. Science fiction.
9780062130143
LC 2013002929
  The first person to cross the barrier that protects Arclight from the Fade, teenaged Marina has no memory when she is rescued but when one of the Fade infiltrates Arclight, she recognizes it and begins to unlock secrets she never knew she had.

McQuerry, Maureen
  The **Peculiars**: a novel. Maureen Doyle McQuerry. Amulet Books, 2012 288 p.
Grades: 7 8 9 10 11 12
  1. Father-separated teenage girls; 2. Librarians; 3. Identity (Psychology); 4. Eighteen-year-old women; 5. Teenage girls; 6. Steampunk
9781419701788
LC 2012000844
Westchester Fiction Award, 2013; YALSA Best Fiction for Young Adults, 2013.
  Eighteen-year-old Lena Mattacascar sets out for Scree, a weird place inhabited by Peculiars, seeking the father who left when she was young, but on the way she meets young librarian Jimson Quiggley and handsome marshall Thomas Saltre, who complicate her plans.

McStay, Moriah
  Everything that makes you. Moriah McStay. Katherine Tegen Books, an imprint of HarperCollins Children's Books, 2015 352 p.
Grades: 8 9 10 11
  1. Teenage girls with disfigurements; 2. Lacrosse players; 3. Self-confidence; 4. Self-discovery; 5. Teenage boy/girl relations; 6.

Tennessee; 7. Memphis, Tennessee; 8. Realistic fiction; 9. Parallel narratives
9780062295484
  Entertaining and intellectually stimulating, the novel invites discussion about how much of a persons life is determined by events and whether some tendencies are inborn. —*Publishers Weekly*

McVoy, Terra Elan
  Pure. Terra Elan McVoy. Simon Pulse, 2009 330 p;
Grades: 8 9 10 11 12
  1. Christian teenage girls; 2. Virginity; 3. Loyalty in teenage girls; 4. Loyalty; 5. Chastity; 6. Christian fiction; 7. Realistic fiction; 8. First person narratives
9781416978725
LC 2008033404
  Fifteen-year-old Tabitha and her four best friends all wear purity rings to symbolize their pledge to remain virgins until they marry, but when one admits that she has broken the pledge each girl must reexamine her faith, friendships, and what it means to be pure.
  Tabitha's blooming romance with Jake and her positive relationship with her supportive, if somewhat quirky, parents add pleasant undercurrents to a book that girls of a spiritual bent will enjoy. —*School Library Journal*

McWilliams, Kelly
  Agnes at the end of the world. Kelly McWilliams. Little, Brown, and Company, 2020 432 p.
Grades: 8 9 10 11 12
  1. Prophets; 2. Cults; 3. End of the world; 4. Belief and doubt; 5. Faith; 6. Apocalyptic fiction; 7. Coming-of-age stories; 8. Multiple perspectives.
9780316487337
  Dutifully embracing her faith while tirelessly caring for her younger siblings, including one who needs forbidden insulin to survive, a teen who is unaware that she lives within a strict cult meets an Outsider boy and begins to question what is and is not a sin.
  This ambitious novel covers much ground, masterfully addressing the sexism and patriarchy so deeply imbedded in Agnes' mind and her journey to break free from it. —*Bulletin of the Center for Children's Books*

Medina, Meg
  ★ **Burn** baby burn. Meg Medina. Candlewick Press, 2016 308 p.
Grades: 9 10 11 12
  1. Cuban Americans; 2. Power failures; 3. Serial murders; 4. Teenage romance; 5. Single-parent families; 6. New York City; 7. 1970s; 8. Historical fiction; 9. Coming-of-age stories; 10. First person narratives
9780763674670
Amelia Bloomer List, 2017; School Library Journal Best Books, 2016; Booklist Editors' Choice: Books for Youth, 2016; Westchester Fiction Award, 2017; YALSA Best Fiction for Young Adults, 2017; Kirkus Prize for Young Readers' Literature finalist, 2016.
  During the summer of 1977 when New York City is besieged by arson, a massive blackout, and a serial killer named Son of Sam, seventeen-year-old Nora must also face her family's financial woes, her father's absence, and her brother's growing violence.
  Powerfully moving, this stellar piece of historical fiction emphasizes the timeless concerns of family loyalty and personal strength while highlighting important issues that still resonate today. —*Booklist*

★ **Yaqui** Delgado wants to kick your ass. Meg Medina. Candlewick Press, 2013 272 p.
Grades: 9 10 11 12
1. Bullying and bullies; 2. Hispanic American teenage girls; 3. New students; 4. Moving, Household; 5. Fifteen-year-old girls; 6. Realistic fiction; 7. First person narratives; 8. Books for reluctant readers
9780763658595
ALA Notable Children's Book, 2014; Pura Belpre Award for Narrative, 2014; School Library Journal Best Books, 2013; Westchester Fiction Award, 2014; YALSA Best Fiction for Young Adults, 2014; YALSA Quick Picks for Reluctant Young Adult Readers, 2014.

Informed that a bully she does not know is determined to beat her up, Latin American teen Piddy Sanchez struggles to learn more about the father she has never met, until the bully's gang forces her to confront more difficult challenges.

With issues of ethnic identity, class conflict, body image, and domestic violence, this could have been an overstuffed problem novel; instead, it transcends with heartfelt, truthful writing that treats the complicated roots of bullying with respect. —*Booklist*

Meehl, Brian
★ **Suck** it up. Brian Meehl. Delacorte Press, 2008 323 p.
Grades: 8 9 10 11
1. Teenage vampires; 2. Teenage boy misfits; 3. Publicity agents; 4. Teenage boy/girl relations; 5. Public relations; 6. Urban fantasy
9780385733007

A teenage vampire sets out to prove that not all vampires are the same by demonstrating his non-violent attitude, his sensitive nature, and his desperate need for understanding as the soy-blood substitute drinking guy and Vampire Pride Parade participant that he is.

This an original and light variation on the current trend in brooding teen vampire protagonists.... Puns abound in this lengthy, complicated romp.... Teens will find it delightful. —*Booklist*
Sequel: *Suck it up and die.*

Mejia, Tehlor Kay
Miss Meteor. Tehlor Kay Mejia and Anna-Marie McLemore. HarperTeen, 2020 400 p.
Grades: 9 10 11 12
1. Hispanic American teenage girls; 2. Beauty contests; 3. Former friends; 4. Competition; 5. Self-acceptance; 6. New Mexico; 7. Magical realism; 8. Multiple perspectives
9780062869913

A teen who secretly arrived with the meteor that gave her small hometown its name discovers that she is turning back into stardust and teams up with her best friend in an effort to secure her human existence by entering a local beauty pageant that has always been won by thin, blonde, white girls.

Extended metaphors of stardust and space magic could grow tired in less capable hands, but they work powerfully in Mejia and McLemore's descriptions of teenage emotional urgency when courage can be as a fleeting as a shooting star.... A love letter to misfits who have been scared to let their stardust shine. —*Kirkus*

★ **We** set the dark on fire. Tehlor Kay Mejia. Katherine Tegen Books, 2019 384 p. (We set the dark on fire, 1)
Grades: 9 10 11 12
1. Husband and wife; 2. Polygamy; 3. Political intrigue; 4. Bisexual women; 5. Latin Americans; 6. Dystopian fiction; 7. Fantasy fiction
9780062691316, HRD, US; 9780062691323, PAP, US
Booklist Editors' Choice: Books for Youth, 2019; School Library Journal Best Books, 2019.

A society wife-in-training has an uncomfortable awakening about her strictly polarized society after being recruited into a band of rebel spies and falling for her biggest rival.

The first in a duology, this fierce, feminist novel throws memorable characters into a provocative set of circumstances, and the constant twists will leave readers yearning for the conclusion. —*Publishers Weekly*

★ **We** unleash the merciless storm. Tehlor Kay Mejia. Katherine Tegen Books, 2020 388 pages; (We set the dark on fire, 2)
Grades: 9 10 11 12
1. Women spies; 2. Political intrigue; 3. Insurgency; 4. Latin Americans; 5. Bisexual women; 6. Dystopian fiction; 7. Fantasy fiction.
9780062691347, HRD, US
LC 2020288562
A sequel to *We Set the Dark on Fire* finds La Voz operative, Carmen, forced to choose between the girl she loves and the success of a rebellion that has escalated to the point of civil war.

Tragedy and heroism interweave in a story about revolution, resistance, and beautiful queer love.... Thrilling, timely, and terrific. —*Kirkus*

Meldrum, Christina
Madapple. Christina Meldrum. Alfred A. Knopf, 2008 416 p.
Grades: 9 10 11 12
1. Miracles; 2. Mothers and daughters; 3. Trials (Murder); 4. Teenage girls; 5. Teenagers; 6. Maine; 7. Mysteries; 8. Psychological suspense
9780375951763
LC 2007049653
Booklist Editors' Choice: Books for Youth, 2008; YALSA Best Books for Young Adults, 2009.

A girl who has been brought up in near isolation is thrown into a twisted web of family secrets and religious fundamentalism when her mother dies and she goes to live with relatives she never knew she had.

A markedly intelligent offering mixing lush descriptions of plants, history, science and religion, this should surely spark interest among a wide array of readers. —*Kirkus*

Melling, O. R.
The **Light-Bearer's** daughter. By O.R. Melling. Amulet Books, 2007 304 p. (Chronicles of Faerie, 3)
Grades: 7 8 9 10 11
1. Rulers; 2. Teenage girls; 3. Quests; 4. Good and evil; 5. Magic; 6. Ireland; 7. Gateway fantasy; 8. Fantasy fiction; 9. Canadian fiction.
9780810907812
LC 2006033517
In exchange for the granting of her heart's desire, twelve-year-old Dana agrees to make an arduous journey to Lugnaquillia through the land of Faerie in order to warn King Lugh, second in command to the High King, that an evil destroyer has entered the Mountain Kingdom.

The richly integrated, vivid fantasy scenes balance the strident calls for environmental protection and world peace, and the characters' private passages through layers of storied memory will bring the issues home for readers. —*Booklist*

Meminger, Neesha
Shine, coconut moon. Neesha Meminger. Margaret K. McElderry Books, 2009 253 p;
Grades: 7 8 9 10
1. East Indian American teenagers; 2. Ethnic identity; 3. Self-discovery in teenage girls; 4. Identity (Psychology); 5. East Indian Americans; 6. Realistic fiction
9781416954958

LC 2008009836
YALSA Popular Paperbacks for Young Adults, 2013.

In the days and weeks following the terrorist attacks on September 11, 2001, Samar, who is of Punjabi heritage but has been raised with no knowledge of her past by her single mother, wants to learn about her family's history and to get in touch with the grandparents her mother shuns.

Meminger's debut book is a beautiful and sensitive portrait of a young woman's journey from self-absorbed navet to selfless, unified awareness. —*School Library Journal*

Mendez, Yamile Saied

Furia. Yamile Saied Mendez. 2020 368 p.
Grades: 9 10 11 12

1. Teenage girl soccer players; 2. Soccer; 3. Athletic ability; 4. Conflict in families; 5. Fathers and daughters; 6. Argentina; 7. Sports fiction; 8. Realistic fiction; 9. Coming-of-age stories
9781616209919

LC 2020020758
Pura Belpre Young Adult Author Award for Narrative, 2021.

Seventeen-year-old Camila Hassan, a rising soccer star in Rosario, Argentina, dreams of playing professionally, in defiance of her fathers' wishes and at the risk of her budding romance with Diego.

In this stirring novel by Argentine American author Mendez, passion for sports and personal growth intersect in Camila's powerful, feminist first-person narrative. —*Kirkus*

Menon, Sandhya

10 things I hate about Pinky. Sandhya Menon. Simon Pulse, 2020 368 p.
Grades: 7 8 9 10 11

1. East Indian Americans; 2. Summer; 3. Coastal towns; 4. Dating (Social customs); 5. Teenage boy/girl relations; 6. Cape Cod, Massachusetts; 7. Romantic comedies; 8. Multicultural romances; 9. Multiple perspectives.
9781534416819; 9781529325379, Paperback, UK

A latest entry in the series that includes There's Something About Sweetie finds Ashish's friends, Pinky and Samir, pretending to date each other to achieve respective goals during a Cape Cod summer, with disastrously uproarious results.

Companion to: There's something about Sweetie

★ **From** Twinkle, with love. Sandhya Menon. 2018 336 p.
Grades: 7 8 9 10 11 12

1. Teenage filmmakers; 2. Twin brothers; 3. Filmmaking; 4. East Indian Americans; 5. Teenage girls; 6. Romantic comedies; 7. Epistolary novels
9781481495400; 9781473667440, Paperback, UK; 9781481495417; 9781481495424, ebook, US

LC 2017048138
Told through letters, aspiring filmmaker and wallflower Twinkle Mehra learns a lesson about love while directing a movie for the Midsummer Night arts festival, in which her longtime crush and his twin brother are also participating.

This is an often laugh-out-loud funny journey through the tribulations of high school thats tempered by Twinkles very real feelings of isolation...A charming addition to the rom-com canon. —*Booklist*

There's something about Sweetie. By Sandhya Menon. Simon Pulse, 2019 384 p.
Grades: 7 8 9 10

1. Dating (Social customs); 2. East Indian Americans; 3. Teenage boy/girl relations; 4. Self-discovery in teenagers; 5. Families; 6.

Romantic comedies; 7. Contemporary romances; 8. Multicultural romances
9781534416789; 9781529325294, Paperback, UK

LC 2019004082
Told in two voices, disappointed-in-love Ashish Patel and self-proclaimed fat athlete Sweetie Nair begin to find their true selves while dating under contract.

This companion book to her successful debut, *When Dimple Met Rishi* (2017), hits all the right notes and delivers a joyful relationship that discards societys dictates about appearance in favor of loving the whole person. Give this to readers who love a good rom-com with a message. —*Booklist*

Companion to: *When Dimple met Rishi*; Companion to: *10 things I hate about Pinky*

When Dimple met Rishi. Sandhya Menon. 2017 384 p.
Grades: 7 8 9 10

1. Arranged marriage; 2. East Indian Americans; 3. First loves; 4. East Indian American teenagers; 5. Teenage romance; 6. California; 7. Contemporary romances; 8. Romantic comedies; 9. Multicultural romances
9781481478687

LC 2016023129
School Library Journal Best Books, 2017; YALSA Best Fiction for Young Adults, 2018; Amelia Bloomer List, 2018.

When Dimple Shah and Rishi Patel meet at a Stanford University summer program, Dimple is avoiding her parents' obsession with "marriage prospects" but Rishi hopes to woo her into accepting arranged marriage with him.

The strength of the story comes from its blending of Indian culture and values into a modern-day romance that scores of readers can enjoy. This novel touches on issues of identity while remaining light and fun. —*School Library Journal*

Meriano, Anna

This is how we fly. Anna Meriano. Philomel Books, 2020 304 p.
Grades: 9 10 11 12

1. Multiracial teenagers; 2. Blended families; 3. Sports; 4. Summer; 5. Fans (Persons); 6. Texas; 7. Coming-of-age stories; 8. Realistic fiction; 9. First person narratives
9780593116876, hardback, US; 9780593116883, ebook, US

LC 2020034433
Grounded for the summer by her sometimes-evil stepmother, seventeen-year-old vegan feminist Ellen Lopez-Rourke gets permission to join a Quidditch team, where she makes new, if nerdy, friends.

This clever, subtle reimagining of a beloved fairy tale is both subversive and empowering. —*Kirkus*

Merullo, Roland

The **talk-funny** girl: a novel. Roland Merullo. Crown, 2011 320 p.
Grades: 11 12 Adult

1. Teenage girl abuse victims; 2. Isolationism; 3. Self-fulfillment in young women; 4. Courage in young women; 5. Cult leaders; 6. New Hampshire; 7. Psychological suspense; 8. Adult books for young adults.
9780307452924, HRD, US

LC 2011003328
Alex Award, 2012.

Raised by parents so intentionally isolated that they speak their own hybrid dialect, abused youth Marjorie witnesses a nearby town's economic ruin and her parents' submission to a sadistic cult leader before she is rescued by another abuse survivor who teaches her stoneworking skills.

Mesrobian, Carrie

Cut both ways. Carrie Mesrobian. HarperTeen, 2015 304 p.
Grades: 10 11 12
1. Interpersonal relations; 2. Bisexuality; 3. Self-discovery; 4. Friendship; 5. Teenage boy/boy relations; 6. LGBTQIA fiction; 7. Coming-of-age stories; 8. First person narratives.
9780062349880

LC 2014047809
Rainbow List, 2016.

Senior Will Caynes must face unsettling feelings for his best friend Angus after they share a drunken kiss, while also embarking on his first real relationship with sophomore Brandy—all as the burden of home-life troubles weigh heavily.

Intense, honestly described, and sometimes awkward sexual encounters will ring true for teen readers, and many will identify with the family strife, too. Pitch perfect, raw, and moving. —*Kirkus*

★ **Just** a girl. Carrie Mesrobian. Harper, an imprint of HarperCollinsPublishers, 2017 304 p.
Grades: 9 10 11 12
1. Children of divorced parents; 2. Small towns; 3. Sexuality; 4. Families; 5. Russians in the United States; 6. Minnesota; 7. Realistic fiction
9780062349910

Struggling with societal conventions that frown on her sexual activities at the same time her estranged parents begin living together again, high school senior Rianne becomes increasingly determined to escape her small town and pursue a relationship with a compassionate Russian student.

Rianne's rich inner life, especially when it's at odds with what's expected of her, is captivatingly full of meaningful, compelling drama, and Mesrobian's frank, realistic depiction of teenage sexuality is a particular bright spot. —*Booklist*

Sex and violence: a novel. Carrie Mesrobian. Carolrhoda Lab, 2013 298 p;
Grades: 10 11 12
1. Sexuality; 2. Assault and battery; 3. Emotional problems of teenage boys; 4. Emotional problems; 5. Interpersonal relations; 6. Minnesota; 7. Realistic fiction; 8. First person narratives.
9781467705974

LC 2012047181
Minnesota Book Award for Young People's Literature, 2014; William C. Morris Debut Award finalist, 2014.

Sex has always come without consequences for Evan, until the night when all the consequences land at once, leaving him scarred inside and out.

The absence of sentimentality and melodrama in favor of frank dialogue and bruising honesty is a gasp of fresh air. —*Booklist*

Metzger, Lois

A **trick** of the light. Lois Metzger. Balzer + Bray, 2013 272 p.
Grades: 9 10 11 12
1. Eating disorders; 2. Family problems; 3. Crushes in teenage boys; 4. Anorexia nervosa; 5. Teenagers with eating disorders; 6. Realistic fiction.
9780062133083

LC 2012019039
YALSA Best Fiction for Young Adults, 2014.

Fifteen-year-old Mike desperately attempts to take control as his parents separate and his life falls apart.

This is a somewhat familiar story told in a new way.... A chilling, straightforward novel written with depth and understanding. —*School Library Journal*

Meyer, Carolyn

Beware, Princess Elizabeth. Carolyn Meyer. Harcourt, 2001 214 p. (Young royals, 2)
Grades: 7 8 9 10
1. Elizabeth I, Queen of England, 1533-1603; 2. Princesses; 3. Rulers; 4. Sisters; 5. Thirteen-year-old girls; 6. Great Britain; 7. Tudor period (1485-1603); 8. 16th century; 9. Historical fiction; 10. Biographical fiction
9780152026592

LC 11700
After the death of her father, King Henry VIII, in 1547, thirteen-year-old Elizabeth must endure the political intrigues and dangers of the reigns of her half-brother Edward and her half-sister Mary before finally becoming Queen of England eleven years later.

Duchessina, a novel of Catherine de Medici. Carolyn Meyer. Harcourt, 2007 272 p. (Young royals, 5)
Grades: 7 8 9 10
1. Catherine de Médicis, Queen, consort of Henry II, King of France, 1519-1589; 2. Nobility; 3. Women's role; 4. Arranged marriage; 5. Teenage girls; 6. Young women; 7. Italy; 8. Renaissance (1300-1600); 9. 16th century; 10. Historical fiction.
9780152055882

LC 2006028876
While her tyrannical family is out of favor in Italy, young Catherine de Medici is raised in convents, then in 1533, when she is fourteen, her uncle, Pope Clement VII, arranges for her marriage to prince Henri of France, who is destined to become king.

With meticulous historical detail, sensitive characterizations, and Catherine's strong narration, Meyer's memorable story of a fascinating young woman who relies on her intelligence, rather than her beauty, will hit home with many teens. —*Booklist*

Meyer, Joanna Ruth

Echo north. Joanna Ruth Meyer. Page Street Kids, 2019 400 p.
Grades: 9 10 11 12
1. Enchantment; 2. Wolves; 3. Books and reading; 4. Talking animals; 5. Father-separated teenage girls; 6. Fairy tale and folklore-inspired fiction; 7. Fantasy fiction.
9781624147159

After her father disappears, Echo meets a wolf who promises to make sure her father is returned home safely if Echo agrees to live with the wolf in his enchanted house for one year.

Meyer, L. A.

★ **Bloody** Jack: being an account of the curious adventures of Mary. L.A. Meyer. Harcourt, 2002 278 p. : Illustration (Bloody Jack adventures, 1)
Grades: 7 8 9 10
1. Teenage girl orphans; 2. Impostors; 3. Teenage girl impostors; 4. Thirteen-year-old girls; 5. Teenage girls; 6. 1790s; 7. 18th century; 8. Historical fiction; 9. Adventure stories; 10. Sea stories.
9780152167318

LC 2002000759
Amelia Bloomer List, 2003; Booklist Editors' Choice: Books for Youth, 2002; Georgia Peach Book Award for Teen Readers, 2006; YALSA Best Books for Young Adults, 2004; YALSA Popular Paperbacks for Young Adults, 2012.

Reduced to begging and thievery in the streets of London, a thirteen-year-old orphan disguises herself as a boy and connives her way onto a British warship set for high sea adventure in search of pirates.

From shooting a pirate in battle to foiling a shipmate's sexual attack to surviving when stranded alone on a Caribbean island, the action in Jacky's tale will entertain readers with a taste for adventure. —*Booklist*
Sequel: *Curse of the blue tattoo*.

Curse of the blue tattoo: being an account of the misadventures of Jacky Faber, midshipman and fine lady. L.A. Meyer. Harcourt, 2004 488 p; (Bloody Jack adventures, 2)
Grades: 7 8 9 10
1. Teenage girl orphans; 2. Girls' schools; 3. Women's role; 4. Gender role; 5. Friendship; 6. Boston, Massachusetts; 7. 1800s (Decade); 8. Historical fiction; 9. Adventure stories; 10. First person narratives
9780152051150
LC 2003019032
YALSA Popular Paperbacks for Young Adults, 2013; YALSA Best Books for Young Adults, 2005.
In 1803, after being exposed as a girl and forced to leave her ship, Jacky Faber finds herself attending school in Boston, where, instead of learning to be a lady, she battles her snobbish classmates, roams the city in search of adventure, and learns to ride a horse.
Meyer does an excellent job of conveying life in Boston in 1803, particularly the rights, or lack thereof, of women.... The narrative is full of lecherous men, and Jacky herself is free in her ways. This fact and the sometimes-strong language make this book more appropriate for older readers. —*School Library Journal*
Sequel to: *Bloody Jack*.

In the belly of the bloodhound: being an account of a particularly peculiar adventure in the life of Jacky Faber. L. A. Meyer. Harcourt, 2006 528 p. (Bloody Jack adventures, 4)
Grades: 7 8 9 10
1. Teenage girl orphans; 2. Kidnapping; 3. Resourcefulness in teenage girls; 4. Resourcefulness; 5. Teenage girls; 6. Boston, Massachusetts; 7. 19th century; 8. 1800s (Decade); 9. Historical fiction; 10. Adventure stories; 11. Sea stories.
9780152055578
LC 2005033562
Jacky Faber and her classmates at the Lawson Peabody School for Young Girls in Boston are kidnapped while on a school outing and transported in the hold of a slave ship bound for the slave markets of North Africa.
This plot-driven novel... is one more fabulous adventure for Jacky and friends and a thoroughly delightful story. —*Voice of Youth Advocates*

My bonny light horseman: being an account of the further adventures of Jacky Faber, in love and war. L.A. Meyer. Harcourt, 2008 448 p. (Bloody Jack adventures, 6)
Grades: 7 8 9 10
1. Napoleonic Wars, 1800-1815; 2. Teenage girl orphans; 3. Girl spies; 4. Teenage girls; 5. Sixteen-year-old girls; 6. France; 7. 19th century; 8. 1800s (Decade); 9. Historical fiction; 10. Adventure stories; 11. Sea stories.
9780152061876
LC 2007049582
While trying to run a respectable shipping business in 1806, teenaged Jacky Faber finds herself in France, spying for the British Crown in order to save her friends.
Jacky's wit and lots of action make it an engaging read. —*Voice of Youth Advocates*

Under the Jolly Roger: being an account of the further nautical adventures of Jacky Faber. L.A. Meyer. Harcourt, 2005 518 p; (Bloody Jack adventures, 3)
Grades: 7 8 9 10

1. Girl pirates; 2. Resourcefulness in teenage girls; 3. Resourcefulness; 4. Teenage boy/girl relations; 5. Fifteen-year-old girls; 6. London, England; 7. 19th century; 8. 1800s (Decade); 9. Historical fiction; 10. Adventure stories; 11. Sea stories.
9780152053451
LC 2004022463
In 1804, fifteen-year-old Jacky Faber heads back to sea where she gains control of a British warship and eventually becomes a privateer.
Readers will root for resilient Jacky and her memorable friends as she cannily makes the best of even the least-promising situations. A swashbuckling saga with a decidedly unconventional heroine. —*Booklist*
A Bloody Jack adventure.

Meyer, Marissa
★ **Cinder**. Marissa Meyer. Feiwel & Friends, 2012 400 p. (Lunar chronicles, 1)
Grades: 7 8 9 10 11 12
1. Cyborgs; 2. Plague; 3. Mind control; 4. Aliens; 5. Princes; 6. Science fiction; 7. Fairy tale and folklore-inspired fiction
9780312641894
California Young Reader Medal, Young Adult, 2016; Charlotte Award (New York), Young Adult, 2014; Colorado Blue Spruce YA Book Award, 2015; Golden Duck Awards, Hal Clement Award for Young Adult; YALSA Best Fiction for Young Adults, 2013; YALSA Popular Paperbacks for Young Adults, 2016.
As plague ravages the overcrowded Earth, observed by a ruthless lunar people, Cinder, a gifted mechanic and cyborg, becomes involved with handsome Prince Kai and must uncover secrets about her past in order to protect the world in this futuristic take on the Cinderella story.

★ **Cress**. Marissa Meyer. Feiwel & Friends, 2014 552 p. (Lunar chronicles, 3)
Grades: 7 8 9 10 11 12
1. Cyborgs; 2. Hackers; 3. Imprisonment; 4. Aliens; 5. Mechanics; 6. Science fiction; 7. Fairy tale and folklore-inspired fiction
9780312642976
Cress is locked away in a floating satellite. She dreams of visiting Earth, the planet she has been forced to spy on, and meeting Carswell Thorne, the handsome ship captain who teamed up with Cinder in *Scarlet* (Feiwel & Friends, 2013)....Cress fills in more historical details about Earth and Luna's relationship—most of which will be of no surprise to the reader—and Cinder's rebirth as a cyborg. Fans of Scarlet and Wolf may be disappointed that their relationship takes a backseat to the newly introduced pairing. As always, Meyer excels at interweaving new characters that extend beyond the archetypes of their fairy tale into the main story. Readers will eagerly await the final installment of this highly appealing and well-constructed series. —*School Library Journal*

Heartless. Marissa Meyer. 2016 464 pages
Grades: 7 8 9 10
1. Rulers; 2. Fools and jesters; 3. Characters and characteristics in literature; 4. Teenage romance; 5. Women rulers; 6. Fantasy fiction; 7. Classics-inspired fiction
9781250044655
LC 2015021393
Blue Hen Book Award (Delaware) for Teen Books, 2018; YALSA Best Fiction for Young Adults, 2017.
In this prequel to *Alice in Wonderland*, Cath would rather open a bakery and marry for love than accept a proposal from the King of Hearts, especially after meeting the handsome and mysterious court jester.
If you only read one fractured fairy tale this year, make it *Heartless*. A must-have title. —*School Library Journal*

★ **Instant** karma. Marissa Meyer. Feiwel & Friends, 2020 512 p.

Grades: 9 10 11 12

1. Karma; 2. Teenage girls; 3. Overachievers; 4. High school students; 5. Magic; 6. Romantic comedies

9781250618818

A girl is suddenly gifted with the ability to cast instant karma on those around her—both good and bad.

A satisfying romance and an unsanctimonious lesson about the importance of changing one's ideas about oneself and others when needed. —*Publishers Weekly*

Renegades. Marissa Meyer. Feiwel & Friends 2017 416 p. (Renegades, 1)

Grades: 8 9 10 11 12

1. Supervillains; 2. Superheroes; 3. Revenge; 4. Teenage boy/girl relations; 5. Good and evil; 6. Superhero stories.

9781250044662; 9781250180636

West Australian Young Readers' Book Award (WAYRBA), Older Readers, 2019.

In a ruined world where humans with extraordinary abilities have become the world's champions of justice, a vengeance-seeking girl and a justice-seeking boy team up against a villain who has the power to destroy everything they have worked to protect.

Fans of Marissa Meyer and teens who enjoy a deep storyline will be more than satisfied with all the clever details, plot twists, and thought-provoking dilemmas that fill the pages of this first book in a new series. —*Voice of Youth Advocates*

★ **Scarlet**. Marissa Meyer. Feiwel and Friends, 2013 464 p. (Lunar chronicles, 2)

Grades: 7 8 9 10 11 12

1. Cyborgs; 2. Missing persons; 3. Imprisonment; 4. Aliens; 5. Mechanics; 6. Science fiction; 7. Fairy tale and folklore-inspired fiction

9780312642969

LC 2012034060

Grand Canyon Reader Award (Arizona), Teen Book Category, 2015; YALSA Best Fiction for Young Adults, 2014.

Scarlet Benoit and Wolf, a street fighter who may have information about her missing grandmother, join forces with Cinder as they try to stay one step ahead of the vicious Lunar Queen Levana in this story inspired by "Little Red Riding Hood."

★ **Winter**. Marissa Meyer. Feiwel and Friends, 2015 824 p. (Lunar chronicles, 4)

Grades: 7 8 9 10 11 12

1. Princesses; 2. Cyborgs; 3. Women rulers; 4. Stepmothers; 5. Teenage romance; 6. Science fiction; 7. Fairy tale and folklore-inspired fiction

9780312642983; 9780141340241, print, Australia

Like the previous entries in this widely appealing series, this title features strong heroines taking control of their destinies set against a fully developed and imaginative world. —*School Library Journal*

Meyer, Stephenie

Breaking dawn. Stephenie Meyer. Little, Brown and Co, 2008 768 p. (Twilight saga, 4)

Grades: 8 9 10 11 12

1. Eighteen-year-old women; 2. Teenage vampires; 3. Pregnant teenagers; 4. Marriage; 5. Teenage girls; 6. Washington (State); 7. Seattle, Washington; 8. Paranormal romances; 9. First person narratives; 10. Multiple perspectives

9780316067928; 9781907411892, UK; 9781405664370, print, UK

LC 2008928027

British Book Award for Children's Book of the Year, 2009.

For those who find it hard to say farewell to Bella and company, take heart: it may not be goodbye. —*Booklist*

★ **Midnight** sun. Stephenie Meyer. Little Brown & Co 2020 662 p. (Twilight saga, 5)

Grades: 9 10 11 12

1. Teenage vampires; 2. Teenage girls; 3. Teenage boy/girl relations; 4. Interpersonal attraction; 5. High school students; 6. Washington (State); 7. Paranormal romances; 8. First person narratives; 9. Books to movies; 10. Books for reluctant readers

9780316707046; 9780316592635; 9780349003627, Hardback, UK

LC Bl2020016379

The story of Bella and Edward from *Twilight* told from Edward's point of view takes on a new and decidedly dark twist. Meeting Bella is both the most unnerving and intriguing event he has experienced in all his years as a vampire. As we learn more fascinating details about Edward's past and the complexity of his inner thoughts, we understand why this is the defining struggle of his life. How can he justify following his heart if it means leading Bella into danger?—Provided by publisher.

Megan Tingley books.

New moon. By Stephenie Meyer. Little, Brown and Co, 2006 576 p. (Twilight saga, 2)

Grades: 8 9 10 11 12

1. Teenage werewolves; 2. Breaking up (Interpersonal relations); 3. Teenage girls with depression; 4. Eighteen-year-old women; 5. Friendship; 6. Washington (State); 7. Paranormal romances; 8. First person narratives; 9. Books to movies; 10. Books for reluctant readers

9780316160193; 9781405663571, print, UK; 9781904233886, Paperback, UK

LC 2006012309

Books I Love Best Yearly (BILBY), Older Reader, 2010; Soaring Eagle Book Award (Wyoming), 2008; South Carolina Book Award, Young Adult Books, 2009; YALSA Quick Picks for Reluctant Young Adult Readers, 2007; Young Reader's Choice Award (Pacific Northwest), Senior, 2009.

When the Cullens, including her beloved Edward, leave Forks rather than risk revealing that they are vampires, it is almost too much for eighteen-year-old Bella to bear, but she finds solace in her friend Jacob until he is drawn into a "cult" and changes in terrible ways.

Vampire aficionados will voraciously consume this mighty tome in one sitting, then flip back and read it once more. It maintains a brisk pace and near-genius balance of breathtaking romance and action. —*Voice of Youth Advocates*

★ **Twilight**. Stephenie Meyer. Little, Brown and Co, 2005 498 p. (Twilight saga, 1)

Grades: 8 9 10 11 12

1. Teenage vampires; 2. First loves; 3. Crushes in teenagers; 4. Vampires; 5. Teenage boy/girl relations; 6. Washington (State); 7. Paranormal romances; 8. First person narratives; 9. Books to movies; 10. Books for reluctant readers

9780316160179; 9781904233657, UK; 9781408428351, print, UK

LC 2004024730

Abraham Lincoln Illinois High School Book Award, 2008; Black-Eyed Susan Book Award (Maryland), High School, 2008; Books I Love Best Yearly (BILBY), Older Reader, 2009; Delaware Diamonds (book award), Middle School, 2009; Eliot Rosewater Indiana High School Book Award (Rosie Award), 2008; Garden State Teen Book Award (New Jersey), Fiction (Grades 9-12), 2008; Gateway Readers Award (Missouri), 2008; Georgia Peach Book Award for Teen Readers, 2008; Golden Archer Awards (Wisconsin): Middle/Jr. High, 2010; Golden Sower Award (Nebraska), Young Adult, 2009; Grand Canyon Reader Award (Arizona), Teen Book

Category, 2008; Iowa High School Book Award, 2008; Isinglass Teen Read Award (New Hampshire), 2006-2007. ; Kentucky Bluegrass Award for Grades 9-12, 2007; Pennsylvania Young Reader's Choice Awards, Young Adult, 2009; Rhode Island Teen Book Award, 2007; South Carolina Book Award, Young Adult Books, 2008; West Australian Young Readers's Book Award (WAYRBA), Older Readers, 2008; YALSA Popular Paperbacks for Young Adults, 2012; YALSA Quick Picks for Reluctant Young Adult Readers, 2006; YALSA Best Books for Young Adults, 2006; School Library Journal Best Books, 2005.

When seventeen-year-old Bella leaves Phoenix to live with her father in Forks, Washington, she meets an exquisitely handsome boy at school for whom she feels an overwhelming attraction and who she comes to re-alize is not wholly human.

Realistic, subtle, succinct, and easy to follow,...[this book] will have readers dying to sink their teeth into it. —*School Library Journal*

Michaels, Rune

★ **Genesis** Alpha: a thriller. Rune Michaels. Atheneum Books for Young Readers, 2007 193 p.
Grades: 7 8 9 10
1. Cancer survivors; 2. Role playing; 3. Guilt in teenage boys; 4. Guilt; 5. Donation of organs, tissues, etc; 6. Thrillers and suspense
9781416918868

LC 2007001446

When thirteen-year-old Josh's beloved older brother, Max, is arrested for murder, the victim's sister leads Josh to evidence of Max's guilt—and her own—hidden in their favorite online role-playing game and Josh, who was conceived to save Max's life years earlier, must consider whether he shares that guilt.

Skillfully interweaving science fiction and cyberspace into a murder mystery, Michaels gives readers a story that is not only difficult to put down but also poses questions that will linger long after the last page is turned. —*Voice of Youth Advocates*

Ginee Seo Books.

Mieville, China

★ **Railsea**. China Mieville. Del Rey/Ballantine Books, 2012 424 p.
Grades: 7 8 9 10
1. Trains; 2. Monsters; 3. Orphans; 4. Prairies; 5. Treasure hunting; 6. Fantasy fiction.
9780345524522; 9780345524546; 9780230765122, UK

LC 2012009516

Booklist Editors' Choice: Books for Youth, 2012; YALSA Best Fiction for Young Adults, 2013; Locus Young Adult Book Award, 2013.

On board the moletrain Medes, Sham Yes ap Soorap watches in awe as he witnesses his first moldywarpe hunt: the giant mole bursting from the earth, the harpoonists targeting their prey, the battle resulting in one's death & the other's glory. But no matter how spectacular it is, Sham can't shake the sense that there is more to life than traveling the endless rails of the railsea—even if his captain can think only of the hunt for the ivory-colored mole she's been chasing since it took her arm all those years ago. When they come across a wrecked train, at first it's a welcome dis-traction. But what Sham finds in the derelict—a kind of treasure map indi-cating a mythical place untouched by iron rails—leads to considerably more than he'd bargained for. Soon he's hunted on all sides, by pirates, trainsfolk, monsters, & salvage-scrabblers. & it might not be just Sham's life that's about to change. It could be the whole of the railsea. Here is a novel for readers of all ages, a gripping & brilliantly imagined take on Herman Melville's *Moby-Dick* that confirms China Mieville's status as

"the most original & talented voice to appear in several years." —*Science Fiction Chronicle*

★ **Un** lun dun. China Mieville. Del Rey, 2007 448 p.
Grades: 5 6 7 8 9
1. Parallel universes; 2. Prophecies; 3. Twelve-year-old girls; 4. Good and evil; 5. Heroes and heroines; 6. London, England; 7. Gateway fantasy; 8. Fantasy fiction
9780345495167

LC 2006048500

Locus Young Adult Book Award, 2008; YALSA Popular Paperbacks for Young Adults, 2011; YALSA Best Books for Young Adults, 2008.

Stumbling into an alternate funhouse version of her home city, twelve-year-old Londoner Deeba finds herself trapped in a world of killer giraffes, animated umbrellas, and ghost children, and must take on the role of savior to prevent utter destruction.

Mieville's fantastical city is vivid and splendidly crafted.... The story is exceptional and the action moves along at a quick pace. —*School Li-brary Journal*

Mikaelsen, Ben

Ghost of Spirit Bear. Ben Mikaelsen. HarperCollins, 2008 154 p;
Grades: 6 7 8 9
1. Self-fulfillment in teenage boys; 2. Bullying and bullies; 3. Change (Psychology); 4. Self-fulfillment; 5. High schools; 6. Minneapolis, Minnesota; 7. Realistic fiction.
9780060090074

LC 2007036732

After a year in exile on an Alaskan island as punishment for severely beating a fellow student, Cole Matthews returns to school in Minneapolis having made peace with himself and his victim—but he finds that surviv-ing the violence and hatred of high school is even harder than surviving in the wilderness.

Sequel to: *Touching Spirit Bear.*

Touching Spirit Bear. By Ben Mikaelsen. HarperCollins, 2001 241 p.
Grades: 6 7 8 9
1. Juvenile delinquents (Boys); 2. Anger in teenage boys; 3. Wilderness survival; 4. Self-fulfillment in teenage boys; 5. Self-fulfillment; 6. Alaska; 7. Survival stories; 8. Adventure stories; 9. Coming-of-age stories.
9780380977444; 9780060291495

LC 40702

Beehive Young Adult Book Award (Utah), 2003; California Young Reader Medal, Middle School, 2003; Flicker Tale Children's Book Award (North Dakota) for Juvenile Fiction, 2002. ; Golden Archer Awards (Wisconsin): Middle/Jr. High, 2004; Golden Sower Award (Nebraska), Young Adult, 2004; Maud Hart Lovelace Book Award (Minnesota), Division II (Grades 6-8), 2004; Soaring Eagle Book Award (Wyoming), 2006; Sunshine State Young Reader's Award (Florida), 2004; YALSA Best Books for Young Adults, 2002.

After his anger erupts into violence, Cole, in order to avoid going to prison, agrees to participate in a sentencing alternative based on the native American Circle Justice, and he is sent to a remote Alaskan Island where an encounter with a huge Spirit Bear changes his life.

Mikaelsen's portrayal of this angry, manipulative, damaged teen is dead on.... Gross details about Cole eating raw worms, a mouse, and worse will appeal to fans of the outdoor adventure/survival genre. —*School Li-brary Journal*

Sequel: *Ghost of Spirit Bear.*

Milan, Maura

Eclipse the skies. By Maura Milan. Albert Whitman and Company, 2019 400 p. (Ignite the Stars, 2)

Grades: 7 8 9 10

1. Space warfare; 2. Military academies; 3. Teenage pilots; 4. Far future; 5. Imaginary wars and battles; 6. Space opera; 7. Science fiction; 8. Multiple perspectives.

9780807536384

LC 2019021474

Criminal mastermind and unrivaled pilot Ia Cocha and her allies make unpredictable choices as they fight to keep darkness from eclipsing the skies.

The bittersweet ending is satisfyingly complete yet ambiguous, leaving open a possibility but not the certainty of more. —*Kirkus*

Ignite the stars. Maura Milan. Albert Whitman & Company, 2018 400 p. (Ignite the Stars, 1)

Grades: 7 8 9 10

1. Space warfare; 2. Military academies; 3. Girl pilots; 4. Far future; 5. Imaginary wars and battles; 6. Space opera; 7. Science fiction; 8. Multiple perspectives

9780807536254; 9780807536261

When the notorious Ia Cocha is captured by the Olympus Commonwealth and revealed to be a sixteen-year-old girl, she is sentenced to correctional rehabilitation at a training ground for the elite Star Force where she forms unlikely alliances—Provided by publisher.

Milford, Kate

★ The **Boneshaker**. Kate Milford; with illustrations by Andrea Offermann. Clarion Books, 2010 372 p. : Illustration

Grades: 5 6 7 8 9

1. Courage in teenage girls; 2. Machinery; 3. Courage; 4. Medicine shows; 5. Supernatural; 6. Missouri; 7. 1910s; 8. Historical fantasy; 9. Steampunk

9780547241876

LC 2009045350

YALSA Best Fiction for Young Adults, 2011.

When Jake Limberleg brings his traveling medicine show to a small Missouri town in 1913, thirteen-year-old Natalie senses that something is wrong and, after investigating, learns that her love of automata and other machines makes her the only one who can set things right.

Natalie is a well-drawn protagonist with sturdy supporting characters around her. The tension built into the solidly constructed plot is complemented by themes that explore the literal and metaphorical role of crossroads and that thin line between good and evil. —*Kirkus*

Prequel: *The Broken Lands*.

The **Broken** Lands. By Kate Milford; with illustrations by Andrea Offermann. Clarion Books, 2012 384 p.

Grades: 5 6 7 8 9 10

1. Orphans; 2. Bridges; 3. Supernatural; 4. Good and evil; 5. Demons; 6. Coney Island, New York City; 7. New York City; 8. 19th century; 9. 1870s; 10. Historical fantasy

9780547739663

LC 2011049466

Set in the seedy underworld of nineteenth-century Coney Island during the construction of the Brooklyn Bridge, two orphans are determined to stop evil forces from claiming the city of New York.

Prequel to: *The Boneshaker*.

Miller, Ashley Edward

Colin Fischer. Ashley Edward Miller & Zack Stentz. Razorbill, 2012 256 p.

Grades: 9 10 11

1. Teenagers with autism; 2. Asperger's syndrome; 3. Bullying and bullies; 4. Guns; 5. Schools and guns; 6. Mysteries

9781595145789

LC 2012014274

A boy with autism teams up with the high school bully to get to the bottom of a cafeteria crime—Provided by publisher.

Miller, Kirsten

All you desire: can you trust your heart? Kirsten Miller. Razorbill, 2011 423 p. (Eternal ones novels (Kirsten Miller), 2)

Grades: 6 7 8 9 10

1. Reincarnation; 2. Missing teenage boys; 3. Fate and fatalism; 4. Love triangles; 5. Teenage romance; 6. New York City; 7. Paranormal romances

9781595143235

A multi-layered mystery with (mostly) rounded characters. —*Kirkus*

Sequel to: *The eternal ones*.

★ The **eternal** ones. Kirsten Miller. Razorbill, 2010 411 p. (Eternal ones novels (Kirsten Miller), 1)

Grades: 6 7 8 9 10

1. Reincarnation; 2. Murder suspects; 3. Teenage romance; 4. Dressmakers; 5. Identity (Psychology); 6. New York City; 7. Tennessee; 8. Paranormal romances

9781595143082

LC 2010022775

Miller's writing elevates the supernatural romance well beyond typical fare, and Haven's mix of navet and determination makes her a solid, credible heroine. —*Publishers Weekly*

Sequel: *All you desire*.

Miller, Samuel

A **lite** too bright. Samuel Miller. Katherine Tegen Books, 2018 368 p.

Grades: 9 10 11 12

1. Grandfathers; 2. Authors; 3. Voyages and travels; 4. Secrets; 5. People with Alzheimer's disease; 6. Realistic fiction

9780062662002

YALSA Best Fiction for Young Adults, 2019.

Arthur Louis Pullman the Third is on the verge of a breakdown. He's been stripped of his college scholarship, is losing his grip on reality, and has been sent away to live with his aunt and uncle.

Beautifully conceived and executed, it has an irresistible premise; an ingenious plot tinged with mystery; compelling, multidimensional characters; and a haunting ethos that will linger in readers' minds long after they have finished. —*Booklist*

Miller, Sarah Elizabeth

The **lost** crown. Sarah Miller. Atheneum Books for Young Readers, 2011 448 p.

Grades: 8 9 10 11 12

1. Nicholas II, Emperor of Russia, 1868-1918 — Family; 2. Sisters; 3. Revolutions; 4. World War I; 5. Rulers; 6. Teenage girls; 7. Russia; 8. Romanov Dynasty (1613-1917); 9. 1910s; 10. Historical fiction; 11. Multiple perspectives

9781416983408

LC 2010037001

In alternating chapters, Grand Duchesses Olga, Tatiana, Maria, and Anastasia tell how their privileged lives as the daughters of the tsar in early twentieth-century Russia are transformed by world war and revolution.

Each Grand Duchess comes across as a unique personality.... Like the best historical novels, this allows modern-day teens to see themselves in very different people. —*Booklist*

★ **Miss** Spitfire: reaching Helen Keller. Sarah Miller. Atheneum, 2007 240 p.
Grades: 7 8 9 10 11
1. Sullivan, Annie, 1866-1936; 2. Teacher-student relationships; 3. People who are blind and deaf; 4. People who are blind; 5. People who are deaf; 6. People with disabilities; 7. Alabama; 8. Historical fiction; 9. First person narratives.
9781416925422
Booklist Editors' Choice: Books for Youth, 2007; YALSA Best Books for Young Adults, 2008.
This excellent novel is compelling reading even for those familiar with the Keller/Sullivan experience. —*School Library Journal*

Miller-Lachmann, Lyn
Gringolandia. By Lyn Miller-Lachmann. Curbstone Press, 2009 279 p.
Grades: 9 10 11 12
1. Chilean Americans; 2. Fathers and sons; 3. Seventeen-year-old boys; 4. Hispanic American families; 5. Political activists; 6. Chile; 7. Wisconsin; 8. 1980s; 9. Historical fiction; 10. Coming-of-age stories
9781931896498
LC 2008036990
YALSA Best Books for Young Adults, 2010.
In 1986, when seventeen-year-old Daniel's father arrives in Madison, Wisconsin, after five years of torture as a political prisoner in Chile, Daniel and his eighteen-year-old "gringa" girlfriend, Courtney, use different methods to help this bitter, self-destructive stranger who yearns to return home and continue his work.
This poignant, often surprising and essential novel illuminates too-often ignored political aspects of many South Americans' migration to the United States. —*Kirkus*

Mills, Emma
Famous in a small town. Emma Mills. Henry Holt & Co, 2018 320 p.
Grades: 7 8 9 10 11
1. New neighbors; 2. Small town life; 3. Celebrities; 4. Marching bands; 5. Crushes in teenage girls; 6. Illinois; 7. Realistic fiction; 8. Teen chick lit.
9781250179630
Loving her small community, school and best friends, Sophie develops an unexpected crush on a quiet, alluring new next-door neighbor, August, who seems to prefer keeping others at arm's length.—
A comfortable, readable tale of deep friendship, small towns, and big love in all its guises. —*Booklist*

Lucky caller. Emma Mills. Henry Holt Books for Young Readers, 2020 336 p.
Grades: 9 10 11 12
1. Childhood friends; 2. High school seniors; 3. Radio; 4. Interpersonal relations; 5. Friendship; 6. Indiana; 7. Teen chick lit; 8. Realistic fiction.
9781250179654
A high school senior's decision to take a radio broadcasting class is complicated by the very different approaches of her broadcast team and the presence of a childhood former friend she had hoped to avoid.
Proving once again that a teen's life is anything but simple, veteran romance writer Mills (*Famous in a Small Town*) delivers a well-crafted, bittersweet comedy of errors filled with realistically flawed characters and taut, witty dialogue. —*Publishers Weekly*

This adventure ends. Emma Mills. 2016 320 pages
Grades: 8 9 10 11
1. Friendship; 2. Hispanic American teenagers; 3. Children of authors; 4. Twin brothers and sisters; 5. Moving to a new state; 6. Florida; 7. Realistic fiction
9781627799355
LC 2016001536
Sloane isn't expecting to fall in with a group of friends when she moves from New York to Florida especially not a group of friends so intense, so in love, so all-consuming.
Mild in every way but language, this tale of privileged teens offers a fairly satisfying glimpse of an almost alternate universe in which mundane life can be ignored. —*Kirkus*

Mills, Wendy
All we have left. Wendy Mills. Bloomsbury USA, 2016 272 p.
Grades: 8 9 10 11 12
1. September 11 Terrorist Attacks, 2001; 2. Muslim teenagers; 3. Prejudice; 4. Terrorism; 5. Sixteen-year-old girls; 6. New York City; 7. Realistic fiction; 8. Parallel narratives; 9. Multiple perspectives
9781619633438
This outstanding, touching look at a national tragedy promotes healing and understanding and belongs in every Library. —*School Library Journal*

Minchin, Adele
★ The **beat** goes on. Adele Minchin. Simon & Schuster Books for Young Readers, 2004 212 p;
Grades: 9 10 11 12
1. Girl musicians; 2. Cousins; 3. Musicians; 4. Teenage girls — Sexuality; 5. Teenage girls — Friendship.
9780689866111
LC BL2004002359
Fifteen-year-old Leyla, a shy musician, has always looked up to her gorgeous and confident cousin, sixteen-year-old Emma, but when Emma learns she's HIV positive after having unprotected sex just once, everything changes.
In spite of its heavy Briticisms and a didactic tone, this is one of the better YA books about HIV. The facts of transmission and symptoms are clearly presented, as are Emma's struggles to lead a normal, healthy life.... Minchin educates young readers while telling a gripping story that will keep personal tragedy aficionados turning the pages to the hopeful yet realistic conclusion. —*Booklist*
Originally published in Great Britain in 2001 by Livewire Books, The Women's Press Limited

Miranda, Megan
Come find me. Megan Miranda. Crown, 2019 336 p.
Grades: 9 10 11 12
1. Grief in teenagers; 2. Searching; 3. Life change events; 4. Family problems; 5. Brothers; 6. Psychological suspense; 7. Multiple perspectives.
9780525578291; 9780525578307; 9780525578314, ebook, US
Told in two voices, sixteen-year-old Kennedy Jones and seventeen-year-old Nolan Chandler are drawn together by strange signals related to family tragedies, and find they are more connected than they could have imagined.

Mitchell, Saundra
All out: the no-longer-secret stories of queer teens throughout the ages. Saundra Mitchell. Harlequin Books, 2018 384 p.
Grades: 9 10 11 12

1. Forbidden love; 2. Gay teenagers; 3. Lesbian teenagers; 4. Transgender teenagers; 5. Asexuality; 6. LGBTQIA fiction; 7. Historical fiction; 8. Short stories.
9781335470454

YALSA Best Fiction for Young Adults, 2019.

LGBTQIA story collections are scarce, but even if they werent, this one would be essential. —*Booklist*

Sequel: *Out now*

Miyabe, Miyuki

Brave story. Miyuki Miyabe; translated by Alexander O. Smith. VIZ Media, 2007 824 p.
Grades: 6 7 8 9

1. Teenage boys; 2. Father-deserted children; 3. Imaginary creatures; 4. Enemies; 5. Gods and goddesses; 6. Japan; 7. Gateway fantasy; 8. Fantasy fiction; 9. Translations
9781421511962

LC 2007008829

Mildred L. Batchelder Award, 2008; ALA Notable Children's Book, 2008.

After his father abandons them and his mother tries to commit suicide, young Wataru decides to try to navigate the magical world of Vision, collecting five elusive gemstones along the way, in order to claim the Demon's Bane that will change his fate.

Translated from the Japanese.

Mlynowski, Sarah

Don't even think about it. Sarah Mlynowski. 2014 336 p.
Grades: 7 8 9 10

1. Extrasensory perception; 2. Teenage psychics; 3. Teenage boy/girl relations; 4. High school sophomores; 5. High schools; 6. New York City; 7. Tribeca (New York City); 8. Paranormal fiction; 9. First person narratives
9780385737388; 9780385906623; 9780385737395; 9781408331569, print, UK

LC 2012050777

Stellar Awards (British Columbia), 2016.

A group of Tribeca high school kids go in for flu shots...and they discover that they now have telepathic abilities.

When a group of Manhattan 10th graders inadvertently receives telepathic abilities from tainted flu shots, things rapidly get chaotic (and noisy). Finding out too much information dramatically upends family relationships, friendships, and romances.... Filled with heartbreak, hilarity, and some brutal truths, Mlynowski's novel will leave readers thinking about the gaps between our private and public selves and the lies we tell others and ourselves. —*Publishers Weekly*

Ten things we did (and probably shouldn't have). Sarah Mlynowski. HarperTeen, 2011 368 p.
Grades: 7 8 9 10

1. Parent-separated teenage girls; 2. Independence (Personal quality); 3. Self-reliance in teenage girls; 4. Self-reliance; 5. Sexuality; 6. Connecticut; 7. Teen chick lit; 8. Realistic fiction; 9. Books for reluctant readers
9780061701245; 9780061701269

LC 2010045556

YALSA Quick Picks for Reluctant Young Adult Readers, 2012.

Sixteen-year-old April, a high school junior, and her friend Vi, a senior, get a crash course in reality as the list of things they should not do becomes a list of things they did while living parent-free in Westport, Connecticut, for the semester.

With wit, energy, and an uncanny understanding of teenage logic, Mlynowski...weighs the pros and cons of independence in this modern cautionary tale.... Mlynowski avoids sermonizing, offering 10 madcap and remarkably tense escapades that will have readers laughing, cringing, and guessing how April will get out of the next pickle. —*Publishers Weekly*

Molope, Kagiso Lesego

This book betrays my brother. Kagiso Lesego Molope. Mawenzi House Pub 2018 187 p.
Grades: 8 9 10 11 12

1. Brothers and sisters; 2. Teenage girls; 3. Rape; 4. Family relationships; 5. Personal conduct; 6. South Africa; 7. Coming-of-age stories; 8. Realistic fiction; 9. Canadian fiction
9781988449296

All her life, Naledi has been in awe of Basi, her charming and outgoing older brother. They've shared their childhood, with its jokes and secrets, the alliances and stories about the community. Having reached thirteen, she is preparing to go to the school dance. Then she sees Basi commit an act that violates everything she believes about him. How will she live her life now? —Excerpted from publisher description

Monaghan, Annabel

A girl named Digit. Annabel Monaghan. Houghton Mifflin Harcourt, 2012 187 p.
Grades: 7 8 9

1. Teenage girl detectives; 2. Mathematics; 3. Chases; 4. FBI agents; 5. Eco-terrorists; 6. New York City; 7. Thrillers and suspense
9780547668529

Farrah "Digit" Higgins is trying to shed her middle-school nickname now that she's in high school, so she hides the fact that she's a math genius who's already been accepted into MIT. But then Farrah notices some odd strings of numbers in the credits of a TV show and inadvertently cracks a terrorist group's code, and before she knows what's happening, she's working for the FBI...with hot rookie agent John Bennett.

Sequel: *Double Digit.*

Monir, Alexandra

The girl in the picture. Alexandra Monir. Delacorte Press, 2016 272 p.
Grades: 7 8 9 10

1. Prep schools; 2. Teenage girl musicians; 3. Rich teenagers; 4. Murder; 5. Secrets; 6. Supernatural mysteries; 7. Multiple perspectives
9780385743907; 9780385372527, ebook, US

LC 2015042550

When a popular high school boy is found murdered, everyone is surprised he carried pictures of himself with Nicole Morgan, a shy "music geek" no one knew was close to him.

Teens will enjoy the cleverly crafted ride of this whodunit. —*School Library Journal*

Moon, Sarah

Sparrow. Sarah Moon. Arthur A. Levine Books, an imprint of Scholastic Inc, 2017 272 p.
Grades: 7 8 9 10 11

1. Grief; 2. Psychotherapy; 3. African American teenage girls; 4. Coping; 5. Loss (Psychology); 6. Brooklyn, New York City; 7. Realistic fiction
9781338032581

LC 2017017322

YALSA Best Fiction for Young Adults, 2018.

Fourteen-year-old Sparrow Cooke struggles with emotional issues and suicidal feelings following the death of her school librarian, who was the only person who seemed to understand her.

An elegantly told and important novel about learning to cope, live, and be happy with depression and anxiety. —*Booklist*

Moore, Lisa

★ **Flannery**. Lisa Moore. Groundwood Books, 2016 256 p.
Grades: 9 10 11 12
1. Mothers and daughters; 2. Teenage boy/girl relations; 3. Poverty; 4. Friendship; 5. Teenage girls; 6. Newfoundland and Labrador; 7. Realistic fiction; 8. Canadian fiction
9781554980765
OLA Best Bets, 2016.

Story of a sixteen-year-old girl, Flannery, struggling with love, friendship, and growing up.

An engaging story and strong purchase with some valuable lessons about love, friendship, and growing up. —*School Library Journal*

Moore, Peter

Red moon rising. Peter Moore. Hyperion, 2011 328 p.
Grades: 7 8 9 10
1. Teenage boy misfits; 2. Teenage vampires; 3. Teenage werewolves; 4. Prejudice; 5. Genetics; 6. Urban fantasy
9781423116653

LC 2009040375

In a world where vampires dominate and werewolves are despised, a teenaged half-vampire discovers his recessive werewolf genes are developing with the approaching full moon.

The details are imaginative and believable, as are the social interactions at school and in Danny's home. —*Booklist*

Moore, Stephanie Perry

Always upbeat. Stephanie Perry Moore; All that / Stephanie Perry Moore & Derrick Moore. Saddleback, 2012 Ix, 155, ix, 149 p; (Lockwood Lions)
Grades: 7 8 9 10 11 12
1. Cheerleaders; 2. High school football players; 3. African American teenagers; 4. Dating (Social customs); 5. Sexuality; 6. Atlanta, Georgia; 7. Realistic fiction; 8. Reversible books; 9. African American fiction
9781616518844

LC Bl2012022088

Two novels recount from different perspectives the challenges Charli Black and Blake Strong face in their relationship, personal lives, and at school.

High interest story designed for reluctant readers or those reading below grade level.

Moracho, Cristina

A **good** idea. Cristina Moracho. Penguin Group, 2017 384 p.
Grades: 9 10 11 12
1. Revenge; 2. Small towns; 3. Murder investigation; 4. Bisexual teenagers; 5. Best friends — Death; 6. Maine; 7. 1990s; 8. Mysteries
9780451476241

LC 2016020075

A girl returns to her small hometown in Maine seeking revenge for the death of her childhood best friend.

Edgy, atmospheric, and sometimes steamy, this is a thoughtful portrait of grief and an engaging examination of the risks we take for the ones we love. Ideal for mystery enthusiasts and noir newcomers. —*Booklist*

Moreno, Nina

Don't date Rosa Santos. Nina Moreno. Hyperion, 2019 336 p.
Grades: 8 9 10 11
1. Cuban Americans; 2. Studying abroad; 3. Family curses; 4. Dating (Social customs); 5. Family relationships; 6. Florida; 7. Romantic comedies; 8. Multicultural romances; 9. Teen chick lit.
9781368039703

Rosa Santos, a Cuban American, works to save her Florida town, seeks admittance to study abroad in her homeland, and wonders if love can break her family's curse.

Full of complex family relationships, a diverse community, and plenty of swoonworthy moments, fans of rom-coms won't be able to put this one down. —*Kirkus*

Morgan, Page

The **beautiful** and the cursed. Page Morgan. Delacorte Press, 2013 400 p. (The dispossessed, 1)
Grades: 7 8 9 10 11 12
1. Gargoyles; 2. Missing persons; 3. British in France; 4. Protectiveness; 5. Demons; 6. Paris, France; 7. France; 8. 1890s; 9. Historical fantasy
9780385743112; 9780385679084; 9780307980816, ebook, US

LC 2012022378

Ingrid Waverly was forced to leave her life in London with her mother and her younger sister, Gabby. In Paris the house rented by Ingrid's twin brother, Grayson, isn't a house at all. It's an abbey. And to top it all off, Grayson is missing. Yet no one seems to be concerned about Grayson's whereabouts save for Luc, a servant who has some deep and dark secrets of his own. Ingrid is sure her twin isn't dead, and that it's up to her and Gabby to find him before all hope is lost.

Morgenroth, Kate

★ **Echo**. Kate Morgenroth. Simon & Schuster Books for Young Readers, 2007 144 p.
Grades: 7 8 9 10
1. Death; 2. Brothers — Death; 3. Fifteen-year-old boys; 4. Teenage boys; 5. Teenagers; 6. Psychological suspense
9781416914389

LC 2005032984

After Justin witnesses his brother's accidental shooting death, he must live with the repercussions, as the same horrific day seems to happen over and over.

Moriarty, Jaclyn

★ A **corner** of white. Jaclyn Moriarty. Arthur A. Levine Books, 2013 384 p. (Colors of Madeleine trilogy, 1)
Grades: 7 8 9 10 11 12
1. Parallel universes; 2. Princesses; 3. Pen pals; 4. Color; 5. Magic; 6. Cambridge, England; 7. England; 8. Fantasy fiction; 9. Australian fiction; 10. Gateway fantasy.
9780545397360; 9781742611396; 9780545397377

LC 2012016582

Children's Book Council of Australia: Notable Australian Children's Book; NSW Premier's Literary Awards, Ethel Turner Prize for Young People's Literature, 2013; Queensland Literary Awards, Young Adult Book Award, 2013; School Library Journal Best Books, 2013.

Fourteen-year-old Madeleine of Cambridge, England, struggling to cope with poverty and her mother's illness, and fifteen-year-old Elliot of the Kingdom of Cello in a parallel world where colors are villainous and his father is missing, begin exchanging notes through a crack between their worlds and find they can be of great help to each other.

Australian writer Moriarty's marvelously original fantasy is quirky and clever... [she] captures the proud iconoclasm of many homeschoolers and does not shy away from tenderness and poignancy. —*Booklist*

★ The **cracks** in the Kingdom. Jaclyn Moriarty. Arthur A. Levine Books, an imprint of Scholastic Inc, 2014 480 p. (Colors of Madeleine trilogy, 2)
Grades: 7 8 9 10 11 12
1. Parallel universes; 2. Teenagers; 3. Searching; 4. Teenage boys; 5. Rural boys; 6. Fantasy fiction; 7. Australian fiction; 8. Gateway fantasy.
9780545397384; 9781742612874
Aurealis Awards, Best Young Adult Novel, 2014; Children's Book Council of Australia: Notable Australian Children's Book; NSW Premier's Literary Awards, Ethel Turner Prize for Young People's Literature, 2015; Queensland Literary Awards, Young Adult Book Award, 2014.

In this lively follow-up to *A Corner of White* (Scholastic, 2013), Moriarty chronicles the ever-intertwining lives of Cambridge resident Madeline Tully and her secret correspondent Elliot Baranski, a quick-witted farm boy from the Kingdom of Cello...The RYA's work around Cello expands an already complex and intricately drawn world. Readers will be clamoring for the next title after the thrilling yet satisfying conclusion. —*School Library Journal*

Feeling sorry for Celia: a novel. Jaclyn Moriarty. St. Martin's Press, 2001 276 p; (Ashbury/Brookfield books, 1)
Grades: 7 8 9 10 11 12
1. Teenage girls; 2. Letter writing; 3. Friendship; 4. Fathers and daughters; 5. High school students; 6. Australia; 7. Coming-of-age stories; 8. Teen chick lit; 9. Epistolary novels
9780312269234
LC 45969
NSW Premier's Literary Awards, Ethel Turner Prize for Young People's Literature, 2001; YALSA Best Books for Young Adults, 2002.

Life is pretty complicated for Elizabeth Clarry. Her best friend Celia keeps disappearing, her absent father suddenly reappears, and her communication with her mother consists entirely of wacky notes left on the fridge. On top of everything else, because her English teacher wants to re-kindle the "Joy of the Envelope," a Complete and Utter Stranger knows more about Elizabeth than anyone else.

Moriarty poignantly captures the trials of adolescent friendships and the bittersweet evolution of the teenage subconscious. —*Booklist*

A **tangle** of gold. Jaclyn Moriarty. Arthur A. Levine Books, an imprint of Scholastic Inc, 2016 480 p. (Colors of Madeleine trilogy, 3)
Grades: 9 10 11 12
1. Parallel universes; 2. Royal houses; 3. Captives; 4. Magic; 5. Missing persons; 6. England; 7. Cambridge, England; 8. Fantasy fiction; 9. Australian fiction; 10. Gateway fantasy.
9780545397407; 9781743533239, print, Australia; 9780545777353, ebook, US; 9780545777377, ebook, US
LC 2015027754
In Cambridge, England, Madeleine Tully is still working to gather the Royal Family, and get them back to their parallel world—but in Cello, Elliot Baranski is being held captive, the Hostiles are working against the Royal Family, and the World Severance Unit is trying to stop all contact between Cello and the World for good.

Readers may find themselves slowing down to savor Moriarty's distinctive language and humor in this final outing. This remains a series unlike any other, with frequent pockets of beautiful imagery and a unique rhythm all its own. —*Booklist*

Morpurgo, Michael

An **elephant** in the garden. Michael Morpurgo; illustrated by Michael Foreman. HarperCollins Children's, 2010 232 p.
Grades: 6 7 8 9
1. Girls and war; 2. Elephants; 3. World War II; 4. Zoos; 5. Wildlife rescue; 6. Dresden, Germany; 7. Germany; 8. Second World War era (1939-1945); 9. 1940s; 10. Historical fiction.
9780007339570; 9781405664776, print, UK; 9780007876013, print, UK
USBBY Outstanding International Book, 2012.

This well-paced, heartwarming narrative by a master storyteller will appeal to readers on several levelsas a tale of adventure and suspense, as a commentary on human trauma and animal welfare during war, as a perspective on the hardships facing the German people in the final months of World War II, and as a tribute to the rich memories and experiences of an older generation. —*School Library Journal*

★ **Listen** to the moon. Michael Morpurgo. Feiwel & Friends, 2014 352 p.
Grades: 5 6 7 8 9
1. Convalescence; 2. Families; 3. War; 4. Forgiveness; 5. Hope; 6. First World War era (1914-1918); 7. 1910s
9781250042040; 9780007339631; 9780007339655, print, UK
A framing device, built around the research of Lucy's future grandson, allows Morpurgo to shift among multiple narrators as he unspools the mystery of where she came from. Along the way, Morpurgo offers powerful descriptions of shipwreck, mass drowning, and devastation, as well as healing and growth. —*Publishers Weekly*

★ **Private** Peaceful. By Michael Morpurgo. Scholastic Press, 2004 202 p.
Grades: 7 8 9 10
1. Teenage soldiers; 2. Duty; 3. World War I; 4. Trench warfare; 5. Brothers; 6. England; 7. France; 8. First World War era (1914-1918); 9. War stories; 10. Historical fiction; 11. First person narratives.
9780439636483; 9780439636537; 9780007150076, print, UK; 9780008191740, print, UK
LC 2003065347
California Young Reader Medal, Young Adult, 2008; Booklist Editors' Choice: Books for Youth, 2004; YALSA Best Books for Young Adults, 2005; School Library Journal Best Books, 2004.

When Thomas Peaceful's older brother is forced to join the British Army, Thomas decides to sign up as well, although he is only fourteen years old, to prove himself to his country, his family, his childhood love, Molly, and himself.

In this World War I story, the terse and beautiful narrative of a young English soldier is as compelling about the world left behind as about the horrific daily details of trench warfare.... Suspense builds right to the end, which is shocking, honest, and unforgettable. —*Booklist*

Morris, Brittney

Slay. Brittney Morris. Simon Pulse, 2019 336 p.
Grades: 9 10 11 12
1. African American teenage girls; 2. Video gamers; 3. Ethnic identity; 4. Internet games; 5. Role playing games; 6. Realistic fiction; 7. African American fiction.
9781534445420; 9781534445437; 9781444951721, Paperback, UK
Westchester Fiction Award, 2020.

An honors student at Jefferson Academy, seventeen-year-old Keira enjoys developing and playing Slay, a secret, multiplayer online role-playing game celebrating black culture, until the two worlds collide.

So often, Black gamer girls and Black girls in STEAM are overlooked. However, Morris unapologetically brings both identities front and center with her explosive debut. —*Booklist*

Morris, Gerald

The **ballad** of Sir Dinadan. Gerald Morris. Houghton Mifflin Co, 2003 245 p; (Squire's Tale series, 5)
Grades: 6 7 8 9

1. Knights and knighthood; 2. Minstrels; 3. Honor; 4. Tristan (Legendary character); 5. Iseult (Legendary character); 6. Great Britain; 7. Historical fantasy; 8. Arthurian fantasy
9780618190997

LC 2002010818

Though he would rather pursue his talent as a minstrel, eighteen-year-old Dinadan is forced to follow his older brother Tristram's path and become a knight, and while on a quest with Sir Kai and Sir Bedivere, he learns that honor is often found not in spectacular, heroic deeds of song, but in quite simpler ways. Set at the time of King Arthur.

Written in accessible prose and laced with occasional magic, the novel moves at a quick pace and showcases a continually maturing hero. —*Horn Book Guide*

The **legend** of the king. Gerald Morris. Houghton Mifflin Books for Children, 2010 304 p. (Squire's Tale series, 10)
Grades: 6 7 8 9

1. Arthur, King; 2. Knights and knighthood; 3. Rulers; 4. Conspiracies; 5. Camelot (Legendary place); 6. Gareth (Legendary character); 7. Great Britain; 8. Arthurian fantasy; 9. Historical fantasy
9780547144207

LC 2009039316

Sir Dinadan and his friend Sir Palomides, Sir Gaheris, Sir Terence, and other knights of the Round Table and their associates try to stop Mordred and his White Horsemen from ending King Arthur's rule of Great Britain.

Morris pulls off a spectacular conclusion to his humane and witty Squire's Tales series. —*Kirkus*

The **lioness** and her knight. Written by Gerald Morris. Houghton Mifflin, 2005 352 p. (Squire's Tale series, 7)
Grades: 6 7 8 9

1. Teenage girls; 2. Teenagers; 3. Knights and knighthood; 4. Adventurers; 5. Cousins; 6. Great Britain; 7. Historical fantasy; 8. Arthurian fantasy
9780618507726

LC 2004015782

Headstrong sixteen-year-old Lady Luneta and her distant cousin, Sir Ywain, travel to Camelot and beyond finding more adventure than they hoped for until, with the help of a fool, Luneta discovers what she really wants from life.

Adventure, magic, love, and knights of the realm collide in this delightfully witty tale. —*School Library Journal*

Parsifal's page. Gerald Morris. Houghton Mifflin, 2001 232 p; (Squire's Tale series, 4)
Grades: 6 7 8 9

1. Arthur, King; 2. Knights and knighthood; 3. Royal pages; 4. Eleven-year-old boys; 5. Perceval (Legendary character); 6. Great Britain; 7. Historical fantasy; 8. Arthurian fantasy
9780618055098

LC 31894

In medieval England, eleven-year-old Piers' dream comes true when he becomes page to Parsifal, a peasant whose quest for knighthood reveals important secrets about both of their families.

Filled with action and laced with humor, the entertaining story proceeds at a rollicking pace. —*Horn Book Guide*

Sequel to: *The Savage Damsel and the Dwarf;* Sequel: *The Ballad of Sir Dinadan.*

The **princess,** the crone, and the dung-cart knight. Gerald Morris. Houghton Mifflin, 2004 310 p; (Squire's Tale series, 6)
Grades: 6 7 8 9

1. Thirteen-year-old girls; 2. Teenage orphans; 3. Knights and knighthood; 4. Fairies; 5. Revenge; 6. Great Britain; 7. Historical fantasy; 8. Arthurian fantasy
9780618378234

LC 2003012296

Determined to find the knight responsible for the terrible deaths of her mother and the Jewish peddler who had given them a home, thirteen-year-old Sarah is helped in her quest by a strange old woman, a magical sword, a young faery, and an unkempt knight with little armor and no horse.

The novel is driven by a keen sense of justice and lightened by droll wit. A terrific cast of characters energizes the story, which plays out against a colorful, well-developed historical background. —*Booklist*

Sequel to: *The Ballad of Sir Dinadan.*

The **quest** of the fair unknown. By Gerald Morris. Houghton Mifflin, 2006 278 p. (Squire's Tale series, 8)
Grades: 6 7 8 9

1. Innocence (Personal quality); 2. Knights and knighthood; 3. Heroes and heroines; 4. Adventurers; 5. Father-separated teenage boys; 6. Great Britain; 7. Historical fantasy; 8. Arthurian fantasy
9780618631520

LC 2005034850

Having grown up in an isolated forest, Beaufils sets off for Camelot to find his father and winds up undertaking quests with Sirs Gawain and Galahad, visiting various hermits, and traveling to the fairy world.

Morris' language is sly and charming and funny; his characters embody both the tale and the gentle lessons he imparts. —*Booklist*

The **savage** damsel and the dwarf. Houghton Mifflin Co, 2000 213 p. (Squire's Tale series, 3)
Grades: 6 7 8 9

1. Arthur; 2. Teenage girls; 3. Courage in girls; 4. Knights and knighthood; 5. Magic; 6. Gareth (Legendary character); 7. Great Britain; 8. Historical fantasy; 9. Arthurian fantasy
9780395971260

LC 99016457

YALSA Best Books for Young Adults, 2001.

Lynet, a feisty young woman, journeys to King Arthur's court in order to find a champion to rescue her beautiful older sister, and she is joined in her quest by a clever dwarf and a bold kitchen knave, neither of whom are what they seem.

The whimsical narrative features wry dialogue and memorable characterizations. —*Horn Book Guide*

The **squire's** quest. Gerald Morris. Houghton Mifflin, 2009 275 p; (Squire's Tale series, 9)
Grades: 6 7 8 9

1. Arthur, King; 2. Squires; 3. Knights and knighthood; 4. Fairies; 5. Teenage boys; 6. Rulers; 7. Great Britain; 8. Greece; 9. Arthurian fantasy; 10. Historical fantasy
9780547144245

LC 2008045903

Terence worries about the lengthy absence of his faery friends as he travels to Greece to aid the Emperor Alexander and attempts to thwart a nefarious plot by Mordred to assume the throne held by King Arthur.

Morris misses no opportunity to poke fun at knightly traditions and the more ridiculous conventions of courtly love, but there is also a serious undertone here, foreshadowing events to come later in the Arthurian cycle.... Morris's treatment of the Byzantine Empire is also fresh and interesting. —*School Library Journal*

★ The **squire's** tale. Houghton Mifflin, 1998 212 p. (Squire's Tale series, 1)
Grades: 6 7 8 9
1. Arthur, King; 2. Boys — Identity; 3. Friendship; 4. Wizards; 5. Orphans; 6. Identity (Psychology); 7. Great Britain; 8. Historical fantasy; 9. Arthurian fantasy
9780395869598

LC 97012447

In medieval England, fourteen-year-old Terence finds his tranquil existence suddenly changed when he becomes the squire of the young Gawain of Orkney and accompanies him on a long quest, proving Gawain's worth as a knight and revealing an important secret about his own true identity.

Well-drawn characters, excellent, snappy dialogue, detailed descriptions of medieval life, and a dry wit put a new spin on this engaging tale of the characters and events of King Arthur's time. —*Booklist*

The **squire**, his knight, and his lady. Houghton Mifflin, 1999 232 p. (Squire's Tale series, 2)
Grades: 6 7 8 9
1. Arthur, King; 2. Knights and knighthood; 3. Magic; 4. Squires; 5. Quests; 6. Gawain (Legendary character); 7. Great Britain; 8. Historical fantasy; 9. Arthurian fantasy
9780395912119
YALSA Best Books for Young Adults, 2000.

After several years at King Arthur's court, Terence, as Sir Gawain's squire and friend, accompanies him on a perilous quest that tests all their skills and whose successful completion could mean certain death for Gawain.

Laced with magic, humor, and chivalry, this reworking of Sir Gawain and the Green Knight, in which Gawain learns humility and Terence discovers his true place in the world, provides an engaging introduction to the original tale. —*Horn Book Guide*
Sequel to: *The Squire's Tale;* Sequel: *The Savage Damsel and the Dwarf.*

Morrow, Bethany C.

A **song** below water. Bethany C. Morrow. Tor Teen, 2020 288 p.
Grades: 8 9 10 11 12
1. African American teenage girls; 2. Sirens (Mythology); 3. Trials (Murder); 4. Murder investigation; 5. Discrimination; 6. Portland, Oregon; 7. Fantasy fiction; 8. Multiple perspectives; 9. African American fiction.
9781250315328

A metaphorical tale follows the experiences of a black teen siren and her haunted best friend, who find themselves targeted by violence when they are unable to hide their supernatural identities in an alternate world that discriminates against magic.

Empowering and innovative, Morrow elevates mermaids and sirens to legitimate and compelling vanguards for social change. —*School Library Journal*

Morton-Shaw, Christine

The **riddles** of Epsilon. Christine Morton-Shaw. Katherine Tegen Books, 2005 375 p. : Illustration; Map
Grades: 7 8 9 10
1. Fourteen-year-old girls; 2. Fourteen-year-olds; 3. Parent and child; 4. Parent and teenager; 5. Mothers; 6. England; 7. Horror; 8. Ghost stories
9780060728199; 9780060728205; 9780007199815, print, UK

LC 2004014641

After moving with her parents to a remote English island, fourteen-year-old Jess attempts to dispel an ancient curse by solving a series of riddles, aided by Epsilon, a supernatural being.

Moses, Shelia P.

Joseph. Shelia P. Moses. Margaret K. McElderry Books, 2008 176 p.
Grades: 7 8 9 10
1. Family problems; 2. Mothers and sons; 3. Homeless persons; 4. Alcoholism; 5. Drug abuse; 6. Realistic fiction; 7. African American fiction
9781416917526

LC 2007046464

Fourteen-year-old Joseph tries to avoid trouble and keep in touch with his father, who is serving in Iraq, as he and his alcoholic, drug-addicted mother move from one homeless shelter to another.

Moses creates a compelling character in Joseph. His struggle to survive his current situation intact is fascinating to read.... Negative influences such as drug dealers and users are described in a clear, cold light. Education and hard work are praised for their positive influences. Middle school and junior high teens will enjoy this story. —*Voice of Youth Advocates*
Sequel to: *Joseph's grace.*

The **legend** of Buddy Bush. Shelia P. Moses. Margaret K. McElderry Books, 2004 216 p.
Grades: 6 7 8 9
1. Twelve-year-old girls; 2. African American girls; 3. African American men; 4. Sick persons; 5. Race relations; 6. Rich Square, North Carolina; 7. North Carolina; 8. Coming-of-age stories.
9780689858390

LC 2003008024

Coretta Scott King Honor Book for Authors, 2005; National Book Award for Young People's Literature finalist, 2004.

In 1947, twelve-year-old Pattie Mae is sustained by her dreams of escaping Rich Square, North Carolina, and moving to Harlem when her Uncle Buddy is arrest for attempted rape of a white woman and her grandfather is diagnosed with a terminal brain tumor.

Patti Mae's first-person voice, steeped in the inflections of the South, rings true, and her observations richly evoke a time, place, and a resilient African American community. —*Booklist*
Sequel: *The return of Buddy Bush.*

The **return** of Buddy Bush. Shelia P. Moses. Margaret K. McElderry Books, 2006 143 p. : Illustration
Grades: 6 7 8 9
1. Twelve-year-old girls; 2. African American girls; 3. Grandfather and granddaughter; 4. Grandfathers — Death; 5. Uncle and niece; 6. North Carolina; 7. Harlem, New York City; 8. 1940s; 9. African American fiction
9780689874314

LC 2004020503

Following her grandfather's death in rural North Carolina in 1947, twelve-year-old Pattie Mae learns more about her family after reading her grandmother's collection of obituaries and traveling to Harlem, New York, to find her uncle who has escaped from the Ku Klux Klan.

Pattie Mae's voice is fresh and colloquial, and her spunky narration will speak to readers. —*School Library Journal*
Sequel to: *The Legend of Buddy Bush.*

Mosier, Paul

Train I ride. Paul Mosier. Harper, an imprint of HarperCollinsPublishers,s, 2017 192 p.
Grades: 6 7 8 9 10

1. Self-acceptance; 2. Railroad travel; 3. Loss (Psychology); 4. Self-acceptance in teenage girls; 5. Thirteen-year-old girls; 6. Realistic fiction
9780062455734
Booklist Editors' Choice: Books for Youth, 2017; International Reading Association Children's Book Award for Intermediate Fiction, 2018.

Taking a train journey from her elderly grandmother's home in California to live in Chicago with an unknown relative, young Rydr holds a suitcase filled with memories and bonds with fellow passengers while seeking the hope and forgiveness she needs to start over.

A harrowing, moving, immersive, and ultimately uplifting debut novel. —*Kirkus*

Moskowitz, Hannah
Sick kids in love. Hannah Moskowitz. Entangled Teen, 2019 317 pages;
Grades: 8 9 10 11 12
1. People with chronic illnesses; 2. Teenage romance; 3. Dating (Social customs); 4. Teenage boy/girl relations; 5. Chronic pain; 6. New York City; 7. Contemporary romances
9781640637320, HRD, US; 9781640637368, ebook, US
Sydney Taylor Honor Book for Teen Readers, 2020.

Isabel has one rule: no dating. She's got issues. She's got secrets. She's got rheumatoid arthritis. But then she meets another sick kid. He's got a chronic illness Isabel's never heard of, something she can't even pronounce. He understands what it means to be sick. He understands her more than her healthy friends. He understands her more than her own father who's a doctor. He's gorgeous, fun, and foul-mouthed. And totally into her."—adapted from publisher's description.

Thoughtful without being heavy-handed or improbable in its teen characterization, *Sick Kids In Love* has a cinematic feel reminiscent of mid-00s romantic comedies, without feeling dated. —*Booklist*

Mosley, Walter
47. By Walter Mosley. Little, Brown, 2005 232 p;
Grades: 7 8 9 10
1. Slaves; 2. Aliens (Humanoid); 3. Boy slaves; 4. African American teenage boys; 5. Fourteen-year-old boys; 6. Georgia; 7. 19th century; 8. Afrofuturism and Afrofantasy; 9. Science fiction; 10. First person narratives.
9780316110358
LC 2004012500
Number 47, a fourteen-year-old slave boy growing up under the watchful eye of a brutal master in 1832, meets the mysterious Tall John, who introduces him to a magical science and also teaches him the meaning of freedom.

Time travel, shape-shifting, and intergalactic conflict add unusual, provocative elements to this story. And yet, well-drawn characters; lively dialogue filled with gritty, regional dialect; vivid descriptions; and poignant reflections ground it in harsh reality. —*School Library Journal*

Moulite, Maika
Dear Haiti, Love Alaine. . Harlequin Books, 2019 384 p.
Grades: 9 10 11 12
1. Family secrets; 2. Voyages and travels; 3. Family relationships; 4. Student suspension; 5. Loss (Psychology); 6. Haiti; 7. Epistolary novels; 8. Coming-of-age stories.
9781335777096
The setting takes on a life of its own, plunging readers into Haiti's rich cultural traditions, breathtaking landscape, and vibrant people along-side Alaine, who will quickly become a beloved character among teens. —*Booklist*

Moulton, Courtney Allison
Angelfire. Courtney Allison Moulton. Katherine Tegen Books, 2011 384 p. (Angelfire trilogy, 1)
Grades: 7 8 9 10
1. Angels; 2. Reincarnation; 3. Soul; 4. Demons; 5. Good and evil; 6. Urban fantasy
9780062002327
The author has introduced a dark and compelling world of action and intrigue, albeit with enough normal drama and humor sprinkled throughout to lighten it.... Older junior and senior high school readers will find themselves engrossed in the story until its powerful conclusion—then anxiously awaiting the second installment. —*Voice of Youth Advocates*

Mowll, Joshua
Operation typhoon shore. Joshua Mowll. Candlewick Press, 2006 288 p. (Guild of Specialists trilogy, 2)
Grades: 7 8 9 10
1. Parent-separated teenagers; 2. Teenagers; 3. Brothers and sisters; 4. Uncles; 5. Adventurers; 6. South China Sea; 7. China; 8. 1920s; 9. Historical mysteries; 10. Adventure stories
9780763631222
LC 2006047481
In the spring of 1920, teenaged siblings Rebecca and Doug MacKenzie continue their adventures on their uncle's ship, sailing through a typhoon into the Celebes Sea in pursuit of a missing "gyrolabe" which may be connected to the disappearance of their parents.

This book rolls along with plenty of action and fun. Readers will be captivated by the story line, but also will be intrigued by all of the sketches, photographs, newspaper clippings, and foldout information on technology. —*School Library Journal*

Mukherjee, Sonya
Gemini. Sonya Mukherjee. Simon & Schuster Books for Young Readers, 2016 384 p.
Grades: 8 9 10 11 12
1. Conjoined twins; 2. Identity (Psychology); 3. High school seniors; 4. Small towns; 5. High schools; 6. California; 7. Realistic fiction; 8. Multiple perspectives
9781481456777; 9781481456791, ebook, US
LC 2015019774
YALSA Quick Picks for Reluctant Young Adult Readers, 2017.
In a small town, as high school graduation approaches, two conjoined sisters must weigh the importance of their dreams as individuals against the risk inherent in the surgery that has the potential to separate them forever.

Even for sisters, Clara and Hailey are close. They have to be—theyre conjoined twins attached at the spine.... [T]his debut is a well-researched and particularly heartfelt account of a rare medical condition and the people it affects. Though they share a body, Clara and Hailey are two very different people with different dreams, and their fight for a normal life will resonate with many. —*Booklist*

Munda, Rosaria
★ **Fireborne.** Rosaria Munda. G. P. Putnam's Sons, 2019 448 p. (Aurelian cycle, 1)
Grades: 7 8 9 10 11 12
1. Teenage orphans; 2. Dragons; 3. Power (Social sciences); 4. Competition; 5. Social classes; 6. High fantasy; 7. Fantasy fiction.
9780525518211, HRD, US

When a brutal revolution opens dragonrider classes to everyone, two orphans from very different backgrounds become rising stars in a new regime that is challenged by violent survivors of the former government.

Munda seamlessly moves between breathless action and an unflinching examination of horrors inflicted in pursuit of noble ideals, and the difficulty of escaping cycles of power and violence. —*Publishers Weekly*

Murdock, Catherine Gilbert
★ **Dairy** queen: a novel. By Catherine Gilbert Murdock. Houghton Mifflin, 2006 275 p. (Dairy queen trilogy, 1)
Grades: 7 8 9 10
1. Rural teenagers; 2. Girl football players; 3. Self-discovery in teenage girls; 4. Self-discovery; 5. Teenage girl athletes; 6. Wisconsin; 7. Sports fiction; 8. Realistic fiction; 9. First person narratives.
9780618683079
LC 2005019077
Great Lakes Book Awards, Children's category, 2007; Pennsylvania Young Reader's Choice Awards, Young Adult, 2008; School Library Journal Best Books, 2006; YALSA Best Books for Young Adults, 2007; YALSA Popular Paperbacks for Young Adults, 2008; YALSA Popular Paperbacks for Young Adults, 2014.

After spending her summer running the family farm and training the quarterback for her school's rival football team, sixteen-year-old D.J. decides to go out for the sport herself, not anticipating the reactions of those around her.

D. J.'s voice is funny, frank, and intelligent, and her story is not easily pigeonholed. —*Voice of Youth Advocates*

Sequel: *The off season.*

★ **Princess** Ben: being a wholly truthful account of her various discoveries and misadventures, recounted to the best of her recollection, in four parts. Written by Catherine Gilbert Murdock. Houghton Mifflin, 2008 344 p;
Grades: 7 8 9 10
1. Princesses; 2. Arranged marriage; 3. Self-fulfillment in teenage girls; 4. Self-fulfillment; 5. Magic; 6. Fantasy fiction; 7. Coming-of-age stories; 8. First person narratives.
9780618959716
LC 2007034300
School Library Journal Best Books, 2008.

A girl is transformed, through instruction in life at court, determination, and magic, from sullen, pudgy, graceless Ben into Crown Princess Benevolence, a fit ruler of the kindgom of Montagne as it faces war with neighboring Drachensbett.

Murdock's prose sweeps the reader up and never falters, blending a formal syntax and vocabulary with an intimate tone that bonds the reader with Ben. —*Horn Book Guide*

Murphy, Julie
Dumplin'. Julie Murphy. Balzer + Bray, an imprint of HarperCollins Publishers, 2015 375 pages;
Grades: 8 9 10 11 12
1. Overweight teenage girls; 2. Beauty contests; 3. Self-esteem; 4. Self-esteem in teenage girls; 5. Friendship; 6. Texas; 7. Realistic fiction; 8. Books to movies; 9. Books for reluctant readers
9780062327185; 9781760890414, Paperback, Australia
Amelia Bloomer Lists, 2016; Booklist Editors' Choice: Books for Youth, 2015; Romantic Times Reviewer's Choice Award, 2015; YALSA Best Fiction for Young Adults, 2016; YALSA Quick Picks for Reluctant Young Adult Readers, 2016; YALSA Quick Picks for Reluctant Young Adult Readers: Top Ten, 2016.

Sixteen-year-old Willowdean wants to prove to everyone in her small Texas town that she is more than just a fat girl, so, while grappling with her feelings for a co-worker who is clearly attracted to her, Will and some other misfits prepare to compete in the beauty pageant her mother runs.

The story's set piece is the beauty contest, which Will and several other misfits decide to enter, ready to take the ridicule in trade for their right to the spotlight, but there are also splendid subplots involving friendships, the push-pull of the mother-daughter relationship, and the kindness of strangers, including an encouraging drag queen. —*Booklist*

★ **Ramona** Blue. Julie Murphy. 2017 432 p.
Grades: 8 9 10 11
1. Lesbian teenagers; 2. Questioning (Sexual or gender identity); 3. Swimming; 4. African American teenage boys; 5. Teenage boy/girl relations; 6. Mississippi; 7. Realistic fiction; 8. Coming-of-age stories; 9. LGBTQIA fiction
9780062418357
LC 2016950250
YALSA Best Fiction for Young Adults, 2018; Rainbow List, 2018.

Struggling with the loss of her home and her dysfunctional family after Hurricane Katrina, gay teen Ramona finds solace in a new swimming hobby while developing confusing feelings for a boy who challenges her perceptions.

An exquisite, thoughtful exploration of the ties that bind and the fluidity of relationships, sexuality, and life. —*Kirkus*

Mussi, Sarah
★ The **door** of no return. Sarah Mussi. Margaret K. McElderry Books, 2008 394 p.
Grades: 8 9 10 11 12
1. Treasure hunting; 2. Political corruption; 3. Murder; 4. Sixteen-year-old boys; 5. Teenage boys; 6. Ghana; 7. Adventure stories; 8. First person narratives.
9781416915508
School Library Journal Best Books, 2008.

Sixteen-year-old Zac Baxter never believed his grandfather's tales about their enslaved ancestors being descended from an African king, but when his grandfather is murdered and the villains come after Zac, he sets out for Ghana to find King Baktu's long-lost treasure before the murderers do.

This exciting narrative takes place in England and Africa; in jungles, dark caves, and on the sea.... Overall, this is a complex, masterful story for confident readers. —*School Library Journal*

Myers, E. C.
The **silence** of six. E. C. Myers. Adaptive Books, 2014 368 p. (SOS thrillers, 1)
Grades: 9 10 11 12
1. Conspiracies; 2. Hackers; 3. Surveillance; 4. Teenagers; 5. National security; 6. Cyber-thrillers; 7. Books for reluctant readers
9780996066624
YALSA Quick Picks for Reluctant Young Adult Readers, 2016; YALSA Quick Picks for Reluctant Young Adult Readers: Top Ten, 2016.

After his best friend Evan kills himself, Max Stein finds himself the target of a corporate-government witch-hunt and is forced to go on the run.

Along with pleasing fans of Cory Doctorow's *Homeland* (2013) and like "hacktion" thrillers, this offers sobering insight into how fragile our privacy really is.

Myers, Walter Dean

All the right stuff. By Walter Dean Myers. HarperTeen, 2012 224 p.
Grades: 8 9 10 11 12

1. Soup kitchens; 2. Mentors; 3. Social contract; 4. African Americans; 5. Teenage mothers; 6. Harlem, New York City; 7. Realistic fiction.
9780061960888

After his father is killed in a shooting, Paul volunteers at a soup kitchen where he hears about the social contract from an elderly African American man, and mentors an unwed mother who wants to make it to college on a scholarship.

Myers's bold novel gives readers the same gift Elijah gives Paul: the chance to think. Specifically, it asks them to contemplate social contract theory as formulated by Locke, Hobbs, Rousseau, and now Jones. —*Horn Book Guide*

★ **Darius** & Twig. Walter Dean Myers. Harper, an imprint of HarperCollinsPublishers, 2013 208 p.
Grades: 8 9 10 11 12

1. Best friends; 2. Teenage authors; 3. Bullying and bullies; 4. Friendship; 5. Teenage runners; 6. Harlem, New York City; 7. New York City; 8. First person narratives; 9. Books for reluctant readers
9780061728235; 9780061728242

LC 2012050678

Booklist Editors' Choice: Books for Youth, 2013; YALSA Quick Picks for Reluctant Young Adult Readers, 2014; ALA Notable Children's Book, 2014; Coretta Scott King Honor Book for Authors, 2014.

Two best friends, a writer and a runner, deal with bullies, family issues, social pressures, and their quest for success coming out of Harlem.

This encouraging text may inspire teens who feel trapped by their surroundings...Told in Darius's voice, the prose is poetic but concise. This would be a worthwhile addition to any middle or high school media center or public Library shelf and would make a valuable book for discussion in a middle school classroom. —*Voice of Youth Advocates*

Dope sick. Walter Dean Myers. HarperTeen/Amistad, 2009 192 p.
Grades: 8 9 10 11 12

1. Teenage boys; 2. Options, alternatives, choices; 3. Second chances; 4. Seventeen-year-old boys; 5. Personal conduct; 6. Harlem, New York City; 7. Magical realism; 8. Literary fiction; 9. African American fiction; 10. Books for reluctant readers
9780061214783; 9780061214776

LC 2008010568

YALSA Quick Picks for Reluctant Young Adult Readers, 2010.

Seeing no way out of his difficult life in Harlem, seventeen-year-old Jeremy "Lil J" Dance flees into a house after a drug deal goes awry and meets a weird man who shows different turning points in Lil J's life when he could have made better choices.

Myers uses street-style lingo to cover Lil J's sorry history of drug use, jail time, irresponsible fatherhood and his own childhood grief. A didn't-see-that-coming ending wraps up the story on a note of well-earned hope and will leave readers with plenty to think about. —*Publishers Weekly*

★ **Fallen** angels. Walter Dean Myers. Scholastic, 1988 309 p.
Grades: 8 9 10 11 12

1. Vietnam War, 1961-1975 — African-American troops; 2. Vietnam War, 1961-1975; 3. Seventeen-year-old boys; 4. African-American teenage soldiers; 5. Battles; 6. War stories; 7. Coming-of-age stories; 8. African American fiction
9780590409421

LC 87023236

Charlotte Award (New York), Young Adult, 1992; Coretta Scott King Award, Author Category, 1989; Keystone to Reading Book Award (Pennsylvania), General category, 1994; South Carolina Book Award, Young Adult Books, 1991.

Seventeen-year-old Richie Perry, just out of his Harlem high school, enlists in the Army in the summer of 1967 and spends a devastating year on active duty in Vietnam.

Except for occasional outbursts, the narration is remarkably direct and understated; and the dialogue, with morbid humor sometimes adding comic relief, is steeped in natural vulgarity, without which verisimilitude would be unthinkable. In fact, the foul talk, which serves as the story's linguistic setting, is not nearly as obscene as the events. —*Horn Book Guide*

Game. Walter Dean Myers. HarperTeen, 2008 218 p.
Grades: 8 9 10 11 12

1. Inner city; 2. Basketball players; 3. Competition; 4. Seventeen-year-old boys; 5. Teenage boys; 6. Harlem, New York City; 7. Realistic fiction; 8. African American fiction
9780060582951; 9780060582944

Basketball fans will love the long passages of detailed court action.... The authentic thoughts of a strong, likable, African American teen whose anxieties, sharp insights, and belief in his own abilities will captivate readers of all backgrounds. —*Booklist*

★ **Hoops**: a novel. Walter Dean Myers. Delacorte Press, 1981 183 p.
Grades: 7 8 9 10

1. African American basketball players; 2. Sports betting; 3. Teenage athletes; 4. Sports — Corrupt practices; 5. Seventeen-year-old boys; 6. Realistic fiction; 7. African American fiction
9780440938842

LC 81065497

A teenage basketball player from Harlem is befriended by a former professional player who, after being forced to quit because of a point shaving scandal, hopes to prevent other young athletes from repeating his mistake.

Growing up in the streets of Harlem, seventeen-year-old Lonnie Jackson dreams of making a better life. He has a game, and sees basketball as his way out of the ghetto. ALAN,This story offers the reader some fast, descriptive basketball action, a love story between Lonnie and girlfriend Mary-Ann, peer friendship problems, and gangster intrigues. Most importantly, however, it portrays the growth of a trusting and deeply caring father-son relationship between [the coach] Cal and [fatherless] Lonnie. —*Voice of Youth Advocates*

Sequel: *The outside shot.*

Juba!. Walter Dean Myers. HarperTeen, 2015 208 p.
Grades: 7 8 9 10

1. Lane, William Henry; 2. Dancers; 3. African American teenage boys; 4. Prejudice; 5. New York City; 6. Five Points (New York City); 7. 1840s; 8. 19th century; 9. Historical fiction; 10. Biographical fiction; 11. African American fiction
9780062112712, HRD, US

LC 2014042527

In Five Points, New York, in the 1840s, African American teenager William Henry "Juba" Lane works hard to achieve his dream of becoming a professional dancer but his real break comes when he is invited to perform in England. Based on the life of Master Juba; includes historical note.

Juba is presented as a thoughtful, proud young man who means well and works hard; Myers gives him a direct and sympathetic voice, depicting the struggles and successes of his short life in the Five Points neighborhood of New York City, and later in London, with warmth and convincing detail. —*Publishers Weekly*

Kick. Walter Dean Myers and Ross Workman. HarperTeen, 2011 208 p.
Grades: 7 8 9 10
1. Thirteen-year-old boys; 2. Personal conduct; 3. Criminal investigation; 4. Police; 5. Soccer; 6. New Jersey; 7. Multiple perspectives; 8. Realistic fiction; 9. African American fiction
9780062004895

Told in their separate voices, thirteen-year-old soccer star Kevin and police sergeant Brown, who knew his father, try to keep Kevin out of juvenile hall after he is arrested on very serious charges.

Workman is a genuine talent, writing short, declarative sentences that move that narrative forward with assurance and a page-turning tempo. Myers, of course, is a master.... The respective voices and characters play off each other as successfully as a high-stakes soccer match. —*Booklist*

Lockdown. Walter Dean Myers. HarperTeen/Amistad, 2010 256 p.
Grades: 8 9 10 11 12
1. Juvenile delinquents (Boys); 2. African American teenage boys; 3. Juvenile jails; 4. Self-perception in teenage boys; 5. Personal conduct; 6. Realistic fiction; 7. African American fiction; 8. Books for reluctant readers
9780061214813
LC 2009007287
YALSA Popular Paperbacks for Young Adults, 2015; YALSA Quick Picks for Reluctant Young Adult Readers, 2011; YALSA Best Fiction for Young Adults, 2011; National Book Award for Young People's Literature finalist, 2010; Coretta Scott King Honor Book for Authors, 2011.

Teenage Reese, serving time at a juvenile detention facility, gets a lesson in making it through hard times from an unlikely friend with a harrowing past.

Reese's first-person narration rings with authenticity.... Myers' storytelling skills ensure that the messages he offers are never heavy-handed. —*Booklist*

★ **Monster**. By Walter Dean Myers; illustrations by Christopher Myers. Harper Collins, 1999 281 p.
Grades: 7 8 9 10
1. Teenage prisoners; 2. Trials (Murder); 3. Prisons; 4. Teenage murder suspects; 5. African-American teenage prisoners; 6. Realistic fiction; 7. African American fiction; 8. Books to movies; 9. Books for reluctant readers
9780060280772; 9780060280789; 9780064407311
LC 98040958 /AC
Booklist Editors' Choice: Books for Youth, 1999; Isinglass Teen Read Award (New Hampshire), 2002-2003; Kentucky Bluegrass Award for Grades 9-12, 2002; Michael L. Printz Award, 2000; New York Times Notable Children's Book, 1999; YALSA Best Books for Young Adults, 2000; YALSA Popular Paperbacks for Young Adults, 2015; YALSA Quick Picks for Reluctant Young Adult Readers, 2000; Coretta Scott King Honor Book for Authors, 2000; National Book Award for Young People's Literature finalist, 1999.

While on trial as an accomplice to a murder, sixteen-year-old Steve Harmon records his experiences in prison and in the courtroom in the form of a film script as he tries to come to terms with the course his life has taken.

Balancing courtroom drama and a sordid jailhouse setting with flashbacks to the crime, Myers adeptly allows each character to speak for him or herself, leaving readers to judge for themselves the truthfulness of the defendants, witnesses, lawyers, and, most compellingly, Steve himself. —*Horn Book Guide*

Written in screenplay format; Movie version entitled: *All Rise*.

Scorpions. By Walter Dean Myers. Harper & Row, 1988 216 p.

Grades: 6 7 8 9
1. African American gangs; 2. Ghettoes, African American; 3. African American teenage boys; 4. Gangs; 5. Harlem, New York City; 6. Realistic fiction; 7. African American fiction; 8. Classics.
9780060243647
LC 85045815
ALA Notable Children's Book, 1989; Newbery Honor Book, 1989.

After reluctantly taking on the leadership of the Harlem gang, the Scorpions, Jamal finds that his enemies treat him with respect when he acquires a gun until a tragedy occurs.

Myracle, Lauren
The **infinite** moment of us. By Lauren Myracle. Amulet Books, 2013 376 p.
Grades: 9 10 11 12
1. Foster teenagers; 2. High school students; 3. Crushes in teenage boys; 4. Dating (Social customs); 5. Teenage romance; 6. Atlanta, Georgia; 7. Contemporary romances; 8. Teen chick lit; 9. Multiple perspectives; 10. Books for reluctant readers
9781419707933
LC 2013017135
YALSA Quick Picks for Reluctant Young Adult Readers, 2014.

As high school graduation nears, Wren Gray is surprised to connect with gentle Charlie Parker, a boy with a troubled past who has loved her for years, while she considers displeasing her parents for the first time and changing the plans for her future.

Peace, love & baby ducks. By Lauren Myracle. Dutton Children's Books, 2009 192 p.
Grades: 8 9 10 11 12
1. Rich teenage girls; 2. Jealousy in teenage girls; 3. Sibling rivalry; 4. Identity (Psychology); 5. Family relationships; 6. Atlanta, Georgia; 7. Realistic fiction; 8. First person narratives; 9. Teen chick lit
9780525477433
LC 2008034221
Fifteen-year-old Carly's summer volunteer experience makes her feel more real than her life of privilege in Atlanta ever did, but her younger sister starts high school pretending to be what she is not, and both find their relationships suffering.

Myracle empathetically explores issues of socioeconomic class, sibling rivalry, and parental influence in a story that is deeper and more nuanced than the title and cutesy cover. —*Booklist*

Shine. By Lauren Myracle. Amulet Books, 2011 208 p.
Grades: 10 11 12
1. Hate crimes; 2. Gay teenagers; 3. Best friends; 4. Small towns; 5. Justice; 6. North Carolina; 7. Coming-of-age stories; 8. Mysteries
9780810984172
LC 2010045017
Rainbow List, 2012; Westchester Fiction Award, 2011; YALSA Best Fiction for Young Adults, 2012; YALSA Popular Paperbacks for Young Adults, 2014.

When her best friend falls victim to a vicious hate crime, sixteen-year-old Cat sets out to discover the culprits in her small North Carolina town.

Readers will find themselves thinking about Cat's complicated rural community long after the mystery has been solved. —*Publishers Weekly*

This boy. Lauren Myracle. Walker Books US, a division of Candlewick Press, 2020 288 p.
Grades: 9 10 11 12
1. Misfits (Persons); 2. Best friends; 3. Addiction; 4. High school students; 5. Teenage drug abusers; 6. Coming-of-age stories; 7. Psychological fiction; 8. First person narratives.

9781536206050

Informed in no uncertain terms that he is a far cry from the alpha male types that dominate his high school, Paul makes an unexpected new friend and captures the attention of his crush while gradually succumbing to addiction.

Myracle's depiction of Paul, his deep friendship with Roby, his relationship with his mom, and his first love with Natalia (a strong and multidimensional young woman) will snag readers, both reluctant and voracious, as they root for each of them to make it through the difficult realities of life, high school, and love. —*School Library Journal*

Ttyl. Lauren Myracle. Amulet Books, 2004 224 p. (Internet girls books, 1)
Grades: 9 10 11 12
1. Instant messaging; 2. High school sophomores; 3. Teacher-student relationships; 4. Christian teenage girls; 5. Teenage girls — Friendship; 6. Realistic fiction; 7. Teen chick lit; 8. Books for reluctant readers
9780810948211
LC 2003016280
YALSA Quick Picks for Reluctant Young Adult Readers, 2005.

Chronicles, in "instant message" format, the day-to-day experiences, feelings, and plans of three friends, Zoe, Maddie, and Angela, as they begin tenth grade.

Yolo. Lauren Myracle. Amulet Books, 2014 240 p. (Internet girls books, 4)
Grades: 9 10 11 12
1. Women college students; 2. Separated friends, relatives, etc; 3. Best friends; 4. Instant messaging; 5. Friendship; 6. Realistic fiction; 7. Teen chick lit
9781419708718; 9781613125045, ebook, US
LC 2014014986
Through "instant messages," chronicles the struggles best friends Maddie, Angela, and Zoe face during their freshman year in college, each of them in a different state, two wondering if their romantic relationships will last, and one determining that roller derby is the key to keeping the trio close.

The story, which can stand independently from the rest of the Internet Girls series, offers readers realistic, engaging, and provocative perspectives on scary first semesters away from home and sage advice about drinking, partying, and shutting down socially, all without ever leaving the perfectly crafted text-message flow. —*Booklist*

Na, An
Wait for me. An Na. G. P. Putnam's Sons, 2006 240 p.
Grades: 8 9 10 11 12
1. High school seniors; 2. Korean American teenage girls; 3. Expectation (Psychology); 4. Seventeen-year-old girls; 5. Korean Americans; 6. California; 7. Realistic fiction; 8. Coming-of-age stories; 9. Multiple perspectives
9780399242755
LC 2005030931
YALSA Best Books for Young Adults, 2007.

As her senior year in high school approaches, Mina yearns to find her own path in life but working at the family business, taking care of her little sister, and dealing with her mother's impossible expectations are as stifling as the southern California heat, until she falls in love with a man who offers a way out.

This is a well-crafted tale, sensitively told.... The mother-daughter conflict will resonate with teens of any culture who have wrestled parents for the right to choose their own paths. —*Bulletin of the Center for Children's Books*

Namey, Laura Taylor
A **Cuban** girl's guide to tea and tomorrow. Laura Taylor Namey. Simon & Schuster 2020 320 p.
Grades: 9 10 11 12
1. Hispanic American teenage girls; 2. Loss (Psychology); 3. Grief; 4. Women bakers; 5. Voyages and travels; 6. England; 7. Contemporary romances; 8. Coming-of-age stories
9781534471245
LC 2019055585
Seventeen-year-old Lila Reyes, furious when her parents send her to the English countryside to recover from grief and heartbreak, unexpectedly falls in love with a teashop clerk—and England, itself.

This book has it all: the recipe for new, lasting, happy friendships, a dash of romance, and some gentle (albeit hard) lessons about honoring yourself and letting go of people as perspectives shift. —*Booklist*

Napoli, Donna Jo
Storm. Donna Jo Napoli. Simon & Schuster Books for Young Readers, 2014 350 pages;
Grades: 8 9 10 11 12
1. The Flood; 2. Noah's ark; 3. Survival; 4. Millennium (2000 A.D.); 5. Stowaways; 6. Bible novels; 7. Historical fiction; 8. First person narratives
9781481403023; 9781481403047, ebook, US
LC 2013026808
Sydney Taylor Book Award for Teen Readers, 2015.

Having lost her family in a massive flood, sixteen-year-old Sebah finds her way onto a gigantic ark, where she must conceal herself from Noah and his family until it is safe for her and another stowaway to slip away.

Sixteen-year-old Sebah, a Canaanite girl, survives a massive flood that kills her family. As the rains continue, she encounters a giant boat—Noah's ark. Exhausted and grief-stricken, Sebah finds herself in a cage with a pair of bonobos, with whom she soon bonds. The characters that Napoli creates to flesh out her retelling of the classic story add depth. —*Horn Book Guide*

A Paula Wiseman book.

Zel. Dutton Children's Books, 1996 227 p.
Grades: 7 8 9 10
1. Teenage romance; 2. Mothers and daughters; 3. Nobility; 4. Switzerland; 5. 15th century; 6. Fantasy romances; 7. Fairy tale and folklore-inspired fiction
9780525456124
LC 96-15135
School Library Journal Best Books, 1996.

Based on the fairy tale *Rapunzel*, the story is told in alternating chapters from the point of view of Zel, her mother, and the prince, and delves into the psychological motivations of the characters.

This version, with its Faustian overtones, will challenge readers to think about this old story on a deeper level. It begs for discussion in literature classes. —*School Library Journal*

Nayeri, Daniel
★ **Everything** sad is untrue: a true story. Daniel Nayeri. Levine Querido, 2020 368 p.
Grades: 7 8 9 10 11 12
1. Refugees; 2. Everyday life; 3. Storytelling; 4. Storytellers; 5. Memory; 6. Oklahoma; 7. Biographical fiction; 8. Realistic fiction.
9781646140008
Michael L. Printz Award, 2021; Walter Honor Book, Younger Readers, 2020.

At the front of a middle school classroom in Oklahoma, a boy named Khosrou (whom everyone calls "Daniel) stands, trying to tell a story. His story. But no one believes a word he says. To them he is a dark-skinned, hairy-armed boy with a big butt whose lunch smells funny; who makes things up and talks about poop too much. Like Scheherazade in a hostile classroom, Daniel weaves a tale to save his own life: to stake his claim to the truth.

It's the book's focus on the themes of storytelling and memory and the stubborn authenticity of young Khousrou/Daniel's child view that result in a story that soars sometimes despite, sometimes because of, its sorrows. —*Bulletin of the Center for Children's Books*

★ **Straw** house, Wood house, Brick house, Blow. Daniel Nayeri. Candlewick Press, 2011 432 p.
Grades: 8 9 10 11 12
1. Farmers; 2. Detectives; 3. Death; 4. Love; 5. Short stories.
9780763655266
LC 2011013675
A collection of four novellas in different genres, including a western about a farmer who grows living toys and a rancher who grows half-living people; a science fiction story of the near-future in which the world is as easy to manipulate as the Internet; a crime story in which every wish comes true and only the Imaginary Crimes Unit can stop them; and a comedic love story in which Death describes himself as a charismatic hero.

Four stylistically brilliant novellas offer readers a range of exquisite reading experiences in this collection. —*Bulletin of the Center for Children's Books*

Nazemian, Abdi
Like a love story. Abdi Nazemian. Balzer + Bray, 2019 432 pages
Grades: 8 9 10 11 12
1. Gay teenagers; 2. Iranians in the United States; 3. Teenage boy/boy relations; 4. Teenage same-sex romance; 5. First loves; 6. New York City; 7. 1980s; 8. LGBTQIA fiction; 9. Historical fiction; 10. Multiple perspectives
9780062839367
Stonewall Children's & Young Adult Literature Honor Book, 2020.
An Iranian youth who hides his sexual orientation from his family, an openly gay photographer and an aspiring fashion designer with an HIV-positive uncle fall in love and find their voices as activists during the height of the AIDS crisis in New York City.

This is a beautifully written exploration of first loves fragility in the face of a world full of hate and fear. But just as compelling is its look into a friendship that isnt shattered by a betrayal; instead, its cracks are revealed as two friends grow into the people theyre meant to be. —*Booklist*

Nelson, Jandy
★ **I'll** give you the sun. By Jandy Nelson. Dial Books for Young Readers, an imprint of Penguin Group (USA) Inc, 2014 416 pages
Grades: 8 9 10 11 12
1. Artists; 2. Twin brothers and sisters; 3. Gay teenagers; 4. Teenage artists; 5. Grief; 6. California; 7. Realistic fiction; 8. LGBTQIA fiction; 9. Multiple perspectives
9780803734968; 9781406326499, print, UK
LC 2014001596
Booklist Editors' Choice: Books for Youth, 2014; Great Lakes Great Books Award (Michigan), Grades 9-12, 2016; Inky Awards (Australia): Silver Inky, 2016; James Cook Book Award (Ohio), 2015; Josette Frank Award, 2015; Michael L. Printz Award, 2015; Nutmeg Children's Book Award, High School category, 2017; Rainbow List, 2015; School Library Journal Best Books: Fiction, 2014; Virginia Readers' Choice Award for High School, 2017; YALSA Best Fiction for Young Adults, 2015; YALSA Best Fiction for Young Adults: Top

Ten, 2015; Stonewall Children's & Young Adult Literature Honor Book, 2015.

A story of first love, family, loss, and betrayal told from different points in time, and in separate voices, by artists Jude and her twin brother Noah.

Nelson, Vaunda Micheaux
No crystal stair. By Vaunda Micheaux Nelson; illustrated by R. Gregory Christie. Carolrhoda Lab, 2012 208 p.
Grades: 6 7 8 9 10 11 12
1. Michaux, Lewis H,; 2. African Americans; 3. Bookstores; 4. Books and reading; 5. Booksellers; 6. African American men; 7. Harlem, New York City; 8. New York City; 9. Biographical fiction; 10. Historical fiction.
9780761361695
LC 2011021251
Boston Globe-Horn Book Award for Fiction and Poetry, 2012; Notable Books for a Global Society, 2013; School Library Journal Best Books, 2012; YALSA Best Fiction for Young Adults, 2013; Coretta Scott King Honor Book for Authors, 2013.

Neri, Greg
Knockout games. G. Neri. 2014 304 p.
Grades: 7 8 9 10
1. Violence; 2. Gangs; 3. Urban teenagers; 4. Mothers and daughters; 5. Children of separated parents; 6. St. Louis, Missouri; 7. Realistic fiction
9781467732697
LC 2013036855
As a gang of urban teenagers known as the TKO Club makes random attacks on bystanders, Erica, who is dating the gang leader, wrestles with her dark side and "good kid" identity.

Kalvin may seem like every parent's worst nightmare for their daughter, but the author draws him with a complexity that helps illustrate the larger themes being explored. Neri's main concern is the 'post-racial' urban landscape, raising many talking points while letting readers come to their own conclusions. Harsh and relentless, a tough but worthy read. —*Kirkus*

Ness, Patrick
★ **And** the ocean was our sky. Patrick Ness; illustrated by Rovina Cai. HarperTeen, 2018 176 p.
Grades: 7 8 9 10 11 12
1. Whales; 2. Ships; 3. Hostages; 4. Prisoners; 5. Oceans; 6. Fantasy fiction; 7. Classics-inspired fiction
9780062860729; 9781406383560, Hardback, UK; 9781406385861, Paperback, UK
With harpoons strapped to their backs, the proud whales of Bathsheba's pod live for the hunt, fighting in the ongoing war against the world of men. When they attack a ship bobbing on the surface of the Abyss, they expect to find easy prey. Instead, they find the trail of a myth, a monster, perhaps the devil himself...

Ness mines *Moby-Dick* for incidents and motifs, pitting men against whales in a futuristic alternate world.... The story, though far shorter than its progenitor, conjures similar allegorical weight by pairing the narrative's rolling cadences with powerful, shadowy illustrations featuring looming whales, an upside-down ship in full sail, and swarms of red-eyed sharks, all amid dense swirls of water and blood. —*Kirkus*

The **Ask** and the Answer: a novel. By Patrick Ness. Candlewick Press, 2009 528 p. (Chaos walking, 2)
Grades: 8 9 10 11 12

1. Space colonies; 2. Telepathy; 3. Dystopias; 4. Teenagers; 5. Teenage boy/girl relations; 6. Dystopian fiction; 7. Science fiction; 8. Multiple perspectives
9780763644901; 9781406357998, print, UK; 9781406339864, print, UK

LC 2009007329

Costa Children's Book Award, 2009; Booklist Editors' Choice: Books for Youth, 2009; USBBY Outstanding International Book, 2010.

Alternate chapters follow teenagers Todd and Viola, who become separated as the Mayor's oppressive new regime takes power in New Prentisstown, a space colony where residents can hear each other's thoughts.

Provocative questions about gender bias, racism, the meaning of war and the price of peace are thoughtfully threaded throughout a breathless, often violent plot peopled with heartbreakingly real characters. —*Kirkus*

★ The **knife** of never letting go. Patrick Ness. Candlewick Press, 2008 492 p. (Chaos walking, 1)
Grades: 8 9 10 11 12
1. Dystopias; 2. Telepathy; 3. Space colonies; 4. Social problems; 5. Human/animal communication; 6. Dystopian fiction; 7. Science fiction; 8. Books to movies
9780763639310; 9781406357981, print, UK; 9781406339857, print, UK

LC 2007052334

Booklist Editors' Choice: Books for Youth, 2008; Green Mountain Book Award (Vermont), 2012; James Tiptree, Jr. Award, 2008; USBBY Outstanding International Book, 2009; Virginia Readers' Choice Award for High School, 2012; YALSA Popular Paperbacks for Young Adults, 2011; YALSA Best Books for Young Adults, 2009.

Pursued by power-hungry Prentiss and mad minister Aaron, young Todd and Viola set out across New World searching for answers about his colony's true past and seeking a way to warn the ship bringing hopeful settlers from Old World.

This troubling, unforgettable opener to the Chaos Walking trilogy is a penetrating look at the ways in which we reveal ourselves to one another, and what it takes to be a man in a society gone horribly wrong. —*Booklist*

★ A **monster** calls: a novel. By Patrick Ness; inspired by an idea from Siobhan Dowd; illustrations by Jim Kay. Candlewick Press, 2011 224 p.
Grades: 6 7 8 9 10
1. Monsters; 2. Children of people with cancer; 3. Self-fulfillment in teenage boys; 4. Self-fulfillment; 5. Schools; 6. England; 7. Magical realism; 8. Illustrated books; 9. Books to movies.
9780763655594; 9780763692155; 9781406365856, UK; 9781406336511, print, UK

LC 2010040741

ALA Notable Children's Book, 2012; Booklist Editors' Choice: Books for Youth, 2011; British Book Award for Children's Book of the Year, 2011; Carnegie Medal, 2012; Kate Greenaway Medal, 2012; School Library Journal Best Books, 2011; Westchester Fiction Award, 2011; YALSA Best Fiction for Young Adults, 2012.

Thirteen-year-old Conor awakens one night to find a monster outside his bedroom window, but not the one from the recurring nightmare that began when his mother became ill—an ancient, wild creature that wants him to face truth and loss.

This is a profoundly moving, expertly crafted tale of unaccountable loss.... A singular masterpiece, exceptionally well-served by Kay's atmospheric and ominous illustrations. —*Publishers Weekly*

More than this. Patrick Ness. Candlewick Press, 2013 472 p.
Grades: 9 10 11 12

1. Guilt; 2. Drowning victims; 3. Death; 4. Guilt in teenage boys; 5. Sexuality; 6. England; 7. Science fiction.
9780763662585; 9781406331158; 9781406350487, print, UK
Rainbow List, 2014; School Library Journal Best Books, 2013; YALSA Best Fiction for Young Adults, 2014.

Awakening inexplicably in the suburban English town of his early childhood after drowning, Seth is baffled by changes in the community and suffers from agonizing memories that reveal sinister qualities about the world around him.

Ness' knack for cliff-hangers, honed in the Chaos Walking series, remains strong, while the spare, gradual, anytime, anyplace quality of the story recalls A Monster Calls (2011). Repeated, similar battles with an antagonist feel like a distraction; nevertheless, Ness has crafted something stark and uncompromising. —*Booklist*

★ **Release**. Patrick Ness. HarperTeen, an imprint of HarperCollinsPublishers, 2017 352 p.
Grades: 9 10 11 12
1. Gay teenagers; 2. Ghosts; 3. Revenge; 4. Murder victims; 5. Grief; 6. Magical realism; 7. LGBTQIA fiction; 8. Multiple perspectives
9780062403193; 9781406331172, hardback, UK; 9781406377279, paperback, UK
YALSA Best Fiction for Young Adults, 2018.

Struggling with his family's religious beliefs, an employer's ultimatum and his unrequited love for his ex, Adam struggles to move on with a best friend and a new relationship while trying to find the courage to stay true to himself.

Part character study, part reckoning, this is a painful, magical gem of a novel that, even when it perplexes, will rip the hearts right out of its readers. —*Booklist*

Neumeier, Rachel
The **keeper** of the mist. Rachel Neumeier. Alfred A. Knopf, 2016 400 p.
Grades: 7 8 9 10 11 12
1. Rulers; 2. Inheritance and succession; 3. Illegitimate children of royalty; 4. Magic; 5. Imaginary places; 6. High fantasy; 7. Fantasy fiction
9780553509281

Required by ancient magic to assume the dangerous position previously held by the father she barely knew, Keri relies on her three clever guides and struggles to outmaneuver her treacherous half-brothers while working to repair a failing boundary between her people and land-hungry neighbors.

This is a beautifully written story that emphasizes intelligence and diplomacy. Recommend to fans of Patricia Wrede and Tamora Pierce, as well as lovers of traditional fantasy. —*School Library Journal*

The **white** road of the moon. Rachel Neumeier. Alfred A. Knopf, 2017 376 p.
Grades: 7 8 9 10 11 12
1. Ghosts; 2. Teenage girl orphans; 3. Psychic ability; 4. Fifteen-year-old girls; 5. Teenage girls; 6. High fantasy; 7. Fantasy fiction
9780553509328

A girl who is hated by her family and community because of her ability to see and communicate with ghosts runs away to escape being sold into an abusive apprenticeship before encountering a mysterious stranger and a ghost boy who are desperate for her help.

A richly rewarding stand-alone story evoking far more color than its titular tint might suggest. —*Kirkus*

Newman, Leslea

October mourning: a song for Matthew Shepard. Leslea Newman. Candlewick, 2012 128 p.
Grades: 10 11 12
1. Shepard, Matthew; 2. Hate crimes; 3. Gay men; 4. Crimes against gay men and lesbians; 5. Murder; 6. Young men; 7. Laramie, Wyoming; 8. 1990s; 9. LGBTQIA fiction; 10. Novels in verse; 11. Multiple perspectives.
9780763658076

LC 2011048358
Rainbow List, 2013; YALSA Best Fiction for Young Adults, 2013; Stonewall Children's & Young Adult Literature Honor Book, 2013.

Relates, from various points of view, events from the night of October 6, 1998, when twenty-one-year-old Matthew Shepard, a gay college student, was lured out of a Wyoming bar, savagely beaten, tied to a fence, and left to die.

Includes bibliographical references.

Nicholson, William

Seeker. William Nicholson. Harcourt, 2006 432 p. (Noble warriors, 1)
Grades: 7 8 9 10
1. Self-fulfillment; 2. Personal conduct; 3. Faith; 4. Sixteen-year-old boys; 5. Teenage boys; 6. Fantasy fiction; 7. Multiple perspectives
9780152057688; 9781405218955, print, UK

LC 2005017171
Having been rejected by the Nomana—the revered warrior-monk order they long to join—sixteen-year-olds Seeker and Morning Star, along with a curious pirate named Wildman, attempt to prove that they are worthy of joining the community, after all.

The classic coming-of-age tale is combined with a rich setting of cold villains, strange powers, and disturbing warriors. —*Voice of Youth Advocates*

Nielsen, Jennifer A.

Resistance. Jennifer A. Nielsen. Scholastic Press, 2018 400 p.
Grades: 6 7 8 9 10
1. Jewish teenage girls; 2. Resistance to military occupation; 3. Ghettoes, Jewish; 4. Jewish resistance and revolts; 5. Jews — Persecutions; 6. Poland; 7. Warsaw, Poland; 8. Second World War era (1939-1945); 9. Historical fiction; 10. War stories.
9781338148473, HRD, US
Georgia Children's Book Award, 2020.

After a smuggling mission to an isolated Jewish ghetto goes wrong and her colleagues are arrested, Chaya Lindner, a Jewish girl living in Nazi-occupied Poland, decides to go to Warsaw, where an uprising is in the works.

Historical fiction at its finest, this informs, enlightens, and engages young readers. A first purchase. —*School Library Journal*

Nielsen, Susin

No fixed address. Susin Nielsen. Wendy Lamb Books, 2018 288 p.
Grades: 6 7 8 9
1. Homelessness; 2. Mothers and sons; 3. Self-reliance in boys; 4. Television game shows; 5. Community life; 6. Vancouver, British Columbia; 7. Realistic fiction; 8. First person narratives; 9. Canadian fiction.
9781524768348, hardback, US; 9781783447213, hardback, UK; 9780735226751, print, Canada; 9781783448326, Paperback, UK
BC Book Prizes, Sheila A. Egoff Children's Literature Prize, 2019; Chocolate Lily Book Awards (British Columbia), Chapter Book/Novel category, 2020; National Chapter of Canada IODE Violet

Downey Book Award, 2019; OLA Best Bets, 2018; Red Maple Fiction Award (Ontario), 2020; Rocky Mountain Book Award (Alberta), 2020; USBBY Outstanding International Books, 2019.

Twelve-year-old Felix's appearance on a television game show reveals that he and his mother have been homeless for a while, but also restores some of his faith in other people.

Optimists die first. Susin Nielsen. Wendy Lamb Books, 2017 224 p.
Grades: 7 8 9 10 11 12
1. Art therapy; 2. Emotional problems; 3. Loss (Psychology); 4. Fear in teenage girls; 5. Teenage romance; 6. Vancouver, British Columbia; 7. Realistic fiction
9780553496918

LC 2016014407
OLA Best Bets, 2017.

When Petula de Wilde, who is anything but wild, meets Jacob in their school's dorky art therapy program, his friendship (and something more) helps her overcome intense fears since her sister died. And he has a secret of his own.

Heartbreaking and hopeful, this is a solid choice for readers looking for a book to make them cry and laugh at the same time. —*Booklist*

We are all made of molecules. Susin Nielsen. Wendy Lamb Books, 2015 256 p.
Grades: 9 10 11 12
1. Children and single parent dating; 2. Children of divorced parents; 3. Loss (Psychology); 4. Bullying and bullies; 5. Thirteen-year-old boys; 6. Realistic fiction; 7. Canadian fiction; 8. First person narratives
9780553496864; 9780553496895; 9781770497801; 9781783442324, print, UK
Rainbow List, 2016; Ruth and Sylvia Schwartz Children's Book Award for YA-Middle Reader, 2016; USBBY Outstanding International Book, 2016; OLA Best Bets, 2015.

Thirteen-year-old brilliant but socially-challenged Stewart and mean-girl Ashley must find common ground when, two years after Stewart's mother died, his father moves in with his new girlfriend—Ashley's mother, whose gay ex-husband lives in their guest house.

Nijkamp, Marieke

Before I let go. Marieke Nijkamp. Sourcebooks Fire, 2018 304 p.
Grades: 9 10 11 12
1. Death; 2. Grief in teenage girls; 3. Best friends; 4. Teenage girls with mental illnesses; 5. Artists; 6. Alaska; 7. Coming-of-age stories; 8. Realistic fiction
9781492642282; 9781492668077

Best friends Corey and Kyra were inseparable in their snow-covered town of Lost Creek, Alaska. When Corey moves away, she makes Kyra promise to stay strong during the long, dark winter, and wait for her return. Just days before Corey is to return home to visit, Kyra dies. Corey is devastated—and confused.

The time line of the book alternates among the aftermath of Kyra's death, letters Kyra sent to Corey, and moments between the friends before Corey left. Nijkamp writes about the highs and lows of the mental illness and how even the best-intentioned people can do harm. —*School Library Journal*

★ **Even** if we break. Marieke Nijkamp. Sourcebooks Fire, 2020 352 p.
Grades: 9 10 11 12
1. Best friends; 2. Fantasy games; 3. Transgender teenagers; 4. Teenagers with autism; 5. Cabins; 6. Thrillers and suspense; 7. Multiple perspectives
9781492636113

LC 2020005284
Friends Finn, Liva, Maddy, Carter, and Ever begin a farewell round of the game they have played for three years, but each is hiding secrets and the game itself seems to turn against them.

[This] darkly twisted ode to self-discovery briskly whisks an intersectionally inclusive group through a reasonably stormy, emotionally charged scenario that considers the sometimes-steep price of growing up and growing apart. —*Publishers Weekly*

This is where it ends. Marieke Nijkamp. Sourcebooks Fire 2016 304 p.
Grades: 9 10 11 12
1. School shootings; 2. Revenge; 3. Violence; 4. Interpersonal relations; 5. Brothers and sisters; 6. Alabama; 7. Realistic fiction; 8. First person narratives; 9. Multiple perspectives
9781492622468
Flicker Tale Children's Book Award (North Dakota) for YA Fiction, 2018; YALSA Quick Picks for Reluctant Young Adult Readers, 2017.

Strong characterizations capture diversity in gender, race, ability, and sexuality. Even reluctant readers will anxiously pursue the ending, unable to turn away from the tragedy and in desperate hope for a resolution, knowing there cannot be a happy ending. —*Booklist*

Niven, Jennifer
★ **All** the bright places. Jennifer Niven. Alfred A. Knopf, 2015 384 p.
Grades: 9 10 11 12
1. Suicide; 2. Bipolar disorder; 3. Grief in teenage girls; 4. Friendship; 5. Emotional problems; 6. Indiana; 7. Realistic fiction; 8. Multiple perspectives; 9. Books to movies.
9780385755887; 9780385755917; 9780241395967, Paperback, UK
Eliot Rosewater Indiana High School Book Award (Rosie Award), 2017; YALSA Best Fiction for Young Adults, 2016; YALSA Popular Paperbacks for Young Adults, 2017.

Meeting on the ledge of their school's bell tower, misfit Theodore Finch and suicidal Violet Markey find acceptance and healing that are overshadowed by Finch's fears about Violet's growing social world.

The journey to, through, and past tragedy is romantic and heartbreaking, as characters and readers confront darkness, joy, and the possibilities—and limits—of love in the face of mental illness. —*Publishers Weekly*

★ **Holding** up the universe. Jennifer Niven. Alfred A. Knopf, 2016 384 p.
Grades: 9 10 11 12
1. Multiracial teenage boys; 2. Prosopagnosia; 3. Overweight teenage girls; 4. Obesity; 5. Obesity in teenagers; 6. Contemporary romances; 7. Multiple perspectives
9780385755924; 9780141357058, print, UK
LC 2016003865
A boy with face blindness and a girl who struggles with weight fall in love.

More a story about falling in love with yourself than with a romantic interest, this novel will resonate with all readers whove struggled to love themselves. —*Kirkus*

Nix, Garth
★ **Abhorsen**. Garth Nix. HarperCollins Publishers, 2003 358 p. (Old Kingdom, 3)
Grades: 7 8 9 10
1. Teenage girl orphans; 2. Wizards; 3. Courage in teenagers; 4. Courage; 5. Good and evil; 6. High fantasy; 7. Fantasy fiction; 8. Australian fiction

9780060278250; 9780060278267; 9781743316603, print, Australia; 9780007137343, print, UK
LC 2002003151
Aurealis Awards, Best Fantasy Novel, 2003; Aurealis Awards, Best Young Adult Novel, 2003.

Abhorsen-In-Waiting Lirael and Prince Sameth, a Wallmaker, must confront and bind the evil spirit Oranis before it can destroy all life.

The tension throughout the story is palatable, and despite a solid, satisfying conclusion, Nix leaves himself a bit of room to revisit his intricately designed universe. —*Booklist*

★ **Across** the wall: tales of the Old Kingdom and beyond. Garth Nix. EOS, 2005 Xii, 305 p.
Grades: 7 8 9 10
1. Magic; 2. Espionage; 3. Monsters; 4. Fantasy fiction; 5. Short stories; 6. Australian fiction.
9780060747138; 9780060747145; 9781760290603, print, Australia; 9781741147018, Australia
LC 2004028086
A collection of fantasy short stories plus a novella that is set in the world of the Abhorsen trilogy (Old Kingdom).

In Nicholas Sayre and the creature of case, the opening novella, Nick encounters a bloodsucking Free Magic monster during a visit to Ancelstierre's top-secret intelligence agency. The story teasingly refers to British mysteries and spy fiction, parodic elements that will appeal most to Nix's adult fans. Even less-experienced readers, though, will enjoy getting to know Nick on his own terms.... The remaining 11 stories...include selections clearly intended for middle-graders as well as more sophisticated offerings containing frank references to sex and violence spattered with blood and brains and urine. Buy this with the understanding that the packaging will attract the full spectrum of Nix's fans but that the younger ones may get more than they bargained for. —*Booklist*

★ **Clariel**: the lost Abhorsen. Garth Nix. Harper, an imprint of HarperCollinsPublishers, 2014 400 p. (Old Kingdom, 4)
Grades: 7 8 9 10
1. Revenge; 2. Good and evil; 3. Murder; 4. Parents — Death; 5. Spirits; 6. High fantasy; 7. Fantasy fiction; 8. Australian fiction.
9780061561559; 9781471403842, print, UK; 9781741758627, print, Australia
Ignoring rumors about her family's claim to the throne after moving to the city of Belisaere, Clariel dreams of escaping to a hunter's life while trying to outmaneuver a Free Magic creature, an unwanted betrothal and a plot against King Orrikan.

Nix's intricate world building reveals more Old Kingdom history and its ever-shifting alliance between the political and magical. Themes of freedom and destiny underpin Clariel's harrowing, bittersweet story, and readers will delight in the telling. —*Booklist*

A **confusion** of princes. By Garth Nix. HarperTeen, 2012 352 p.
Grades: 8 9 10 11
1. Princes; 2. Inheritance and succession; 3. Interplanetary relations; 4. Teenage romance; 5. Nineteen-year-old men; 6. Science fiction; 7. Australian fiction; 8. First person narratives
9780060096946; 9781743314791, print, Australia; 9781473231306, Paperback, UK
YALSA Best Fiction for Young Adults, 2013.

Battling aliens, space pirates, and competitors, Prince Khemri meets a young woman, named Raine, and learns more than he expected about the hidden workings of a vast, intergalactic Empire, and about himself.

In this single volume he manages to tell a tale that is grand in scope with vivid characters and imaginative technology. —*Library Journal*

Frogkisser!. Garth Nix. Scholastic Press, 2017 384 p.
Grades: 8 9 10

1. Princesses; 2. Transformations (Magic); 3. Wizards; 4. Sisters; 5. Magic; 6. Fantasy fiction; 7. Australian fiction.
9781338052084; 9781760293512, print, Australia; 9781848126374, print, UK

LC 2016026559

YALSA Best Fiction for Young Adults, 2018; Children's Book Council of Australia: Notable Australian Children's Book, 2018; Mythopoeic Award for Children's Literature, 2017.

Princess Anya has a big problem: Duke Rikard, her step-stepfather is an evil wizard who wants to rule the kingdom and has a habit of changing people into frogs, and her older sister Morven, the heir, is a wimp—so with the help of the librarian Gotfried (who turns into an owl when he is upset), and the Royal Dogs, she must find away to defeat Rikard, save her sister, and maybe even turn Prince Denholm back into a human being.

Well-developed characters, an unfailing sense of humor, and polished prose make Nix's uproarious adventure a pleasure to read. —*Publishers Weekly*

★ **Goldenhand:** an Old Kingdom novel. Garth Nix; maps by Mike Schley. Harper,, 2016 344 p. (Old Kingdom, 5)
Grades: 7 8 9 10
1. Imaginary kingdoms; 2. Magic; 3. Rescues; 4. Good and evil; 5. Teenage girls; 6. High fantasy; 7. Fantasy fiction; 8. Multiple perspectives
9780061561580; 9781741758634; 9781471404443, print, UK; 9781760528300, Paperback, Australia

A masterfully spun tale well worth the yearslong wait. —*Kirkus*

The **left-handed** booksellers of London. Garth Nix. Katherine Tegen Books, 2020 416 p.
Grades: 9 10 11 12
1. Father-separated children; 2. Missing persons; 3. Booksellers; 4. Parallel universes; 5. Quests; 6. London, England; 7. 1980s; 8. Fantasy fiction; 9. Australian fiction
9780062683250; 9781760631246, Australia

Searching for the father she has never met in an alternate-world 1983 London, Susan is drawn into an extended family of magical, left-handed, fighting booksellers who police intruders from the mythical Old World of England.

The broad, immersive world and the specific rules for types of booksellers maintain a sense of discovery, and Susan and Merlin, the heroic protagonists, have vibrant, entertaining personalities (and a realistic romantic storyline). —*Kirkus*

★ **Lirael,** daughter of the Clayr. Garth Nix. HarperCollins, 2001 487 p; (Old Kingdom, 2)
Grades: 7 8 9 10
1. Teenage girl orphans; 2. Courage in teenagers; 3. Imaginary wars and battles; 4. Courage; 5. Princes; 6. High fantasy; 7. Fantasy fiction; 8. Australian fiction
9780060278236; 9780060278243

LC 59707

Adelaide Festival Award for Children's Literature (South Australia), 2002; Ditmar Award, 2002; West Australian Young Readers's Book Award (WAYRBA), Older Readers, 2003; YALSA Best Books for Young Adults, 2002.

When a dangerous necromancer threatens to unleash a long-buried evil, Lirael and Prince Sameth are drawn into a battle to save the Old Kingdom and reveal their true destinies.

The Clayr Lirael is 14, but is unable to be initiated as a Clayr because she has not had a vision. To ease her disappointment, Lirael is made Third Assistant Librarian. This allows Lirael an opportunity to study volumes of forgotten magic, and she uses one spell to turn a stone carving of a dog into a living creature. Lirael gradually increases her knowledge, and, with

Disreputable Dog, explores forgotten passages in the Library.... With her special powers, Lirael leaves the enclave to help save the Old Kingdom. Book Rep,Sound world-building, swift plotting, and superb characterization, including some of the strongest animal characters in recent fantasy, make this sequel must reading for those who have read the first volume and a brisk, involving experience for those who have not. —*Voice of Youth Advocates*

Mister Monday. Garth Nix. Scholastic, 2003 361 p; (Keys to the kingdom, 1)
Grades: 6 7 8 9
1. Magic keys; 2. Plague; 3. Boy heroes; 4. Seventh-grade boys; 5. Boys with asthma; 6. Fantasy fiction; 7. Australian fiction
9780439551236; 9780007179015, print, UK

LC BL2003009595

Aurealis Awards, Best Children's Long Fiction, 2003.

Although Arthur Penhaligon is supposed to die, he is saved by a key shaped like the minute hand of a clock, and now some bizarre creatures—including Mister Monday, his avenging messengers, and an army of dog-faced Fetchers—will stop at nothing to get the key.

The first in a seven part series for middle graders is every bit as exciting and suspenseful as the author's previous young adult novels. —*School Library Journal*

★ **Sabriel**. Garth Nix. HarperCollins, 1995 Xi, 292 p; (Old Kingdom, 1)
Grades: 7 8 9 10
1. Wizards; 2. Courage in teenage girls; 3. Spirits; 4. Good and evil; 5. Teenage girls; 6. High fantasy; 7. Fantasy fiction; 8. Australian fiction
9780060273224; 9780060273231; 9781743316580, print, Australia; 9780007137305, print, UK

LC 96001295

Aurealis Awards, Best Fantasy Novel, 1995; Aurealis Awards, Best Young Adult Novel, 1995; ALA Notable Children's Book, 1997; YALSA Popular Paperbacks for Young Adults, 2009; YALSA Best Books for Young Adults, 1997.

Sabriel, daughter of the necromancer Abhorsen, must journey into the mysterious and magical Old Kingdom to rescue her father from the Land of the Dead.

The final battle is gripping, and the bloody cost of combat is forcefully presented. The story is remarkable for the level of originality of the fantastic elements...and for the subtle presentation, which leaves readers to explore for themselves the complex structure and significance of the magic elements. —*Horn Book Guide*

First published in 1995 by HarperCollins

★ **To** hold the bridge. Garth Nix. HarperCollins Children's Books, 2015 416 p.
Grades: 6 7 8 9 10 11 12
1. Fantasy fiction; 2. Science fiction; 3. Horror
9780062292520; 9781743316559

This anthology's titular novella is a suspenseful prequel to The Old Kingdom Chronicles. Eighteen other tales are organized by theme, with a satisfying variety of genres and tones. Some pay homage to famous speculative fiction (Hellboy; John Carter of Mars), others are companion pieces to Nix's own work; the majority stand alone. Nix's superb world-building and tight plotting are evident here. —*Horn Book Guide*

Noel, Alyson
Unrivaled. Alyson Noel. Katherine Tegen Books, an imprint of HarperCollinsPublishers, 2016 420 p. (Beautiful idols, 1)
Grades: 9 10 11 12

1. Contests; 2. Actors and actresses; 3. Missing teenage girls; 4. Celebrities; 5. Nightclubs; 6. Los Angeles, California; 7. Mysteries; 8. Teen chick lit
9780062324528

This is a suspenseful, scandalous, and consumable novel that is sure to gain instant fandom and leave readers eagerly awaiting the next installment. —*School Library Journal*

Nolan, Han

A **summer** of Kings. Han Nolan. Harcourt, 2006 334 p;
Grades: 6 7 8 9

1. Fourteen-year-old girls; 2. Fourteen-year-olds; 3. Eighteen-year-old men; 4. Eighteen-year-olds; 5. African Americans; 6. Westchester County, New York; 7. Washington, D.C; 8. 1960s; 9. Historical fiction.
9780152051082

LC 2005019487

After being accused of killing a white man in Alabama and sent north by his mother to escape a lynch mob, King-Roy finds his way to a home where he meets Esther, a young white girl looking for excitement and attention, where an unexpected friendship develops that transforms both of their lives while coming to terms with what they deem just and right.

Infused with rhetoric that is as meaningful today as it was two generations ago, this young teen's account of a life-changing summer not only opens a window to history, but also displays Nolan's brilliant gift for crafting profoundly appealing protagonists. —*School Library Journal*

North, Pearl

Libyrinth. Pearl North. Tor, 2009 332 p; (Libyrinth trilogy, 1)
Grades: 7 8 9 10

1. Teenage apprentices; 2. Books; 3. Libraries; 4. Book burning; 5. Dystopias; 6. Science fiction.
9780765320964

LC 2009001514

Amelia Bloomer List, 2011.

In a distant future where Libyrarians preserve and protect the ancient books that are housed in the fortress-like Libyrinth, Haly is imprisoned by Eradicants, who believe that the written word is evil, and she must try to mend the rift between the two groups before their war for knowledge destroys them all.

Among this novel's pleasures are the many anonymous quotations scattered throughout, snatches of prose that Haly hears as she goes about her chores...all of which are carefully identified at the end. The complex moral issues posed by this thoughtful and exciting tale are just as fascinating. —*Publishers Weekly*

A Tom Doherty Associates book.

North, Phoebe

Starglass. Phoebe North. Simon & Schuster Books for Young Readers, 2013 448 p. (Starglass, 1)
Grades: 7 8 9 10

1. Jews; 2. Dystopias; 3. Space flight; 4. Space vehicles; 5. Insurgency; 6. Dystopian fiction; 7. Science fiction.
9781442459533

LC 2012021171

For all of her sixteen years, Terra has lived on a city within a spaceship that left Earth five hundred years ago seeking refuge, but as they finally approach the chosen planet, she is drawn into a secret rebellion that could change the fate of her people.

North, Ryan

Romeo and/or Juliet: a chooseable-path adventure. Ryan North. Riverhead Books, 2016 476 pages : Illustration; Color
Grades: 9 10 11 12 Adult

1. Shakespeare, William; 2. Swordplay; 3. Family feuds; 4. Political intrigue; 5. Men/women relations; 6. Options, alternatives, choices; 7. Plot-your-own stories; 8. Canadian fiction; 9. Adult books for young adults.
9781101983300

Alex Award, 2017.

A choose-your-own-path adaptation of Shakespeare's classic imagines riotous "what if" scenarios, inviting readers to explore the alternate stories of the star-crossed lovers as they fall for other partners, pursue unconventional interests and team up to take over Verona in robot suits.

North has turned Shakespeare's play about star-crossed lovers into a seemingly endless game of choices, with the ability to play as either Romeo or Juliet and a guarantee that any path taken will turn into an outrageously silly adventure. For some threads, North cleverly inserts original passages from Shakespeare's work to heighten the comic effect. —*School Library Journal*

Norton, Preston

Neanderthal opens the door to the universe. Preston Norton. 2018 416 p.
Grades: 9 10 11 12

1. Survivors of suicide victims; 2. Alliances; 3. Bullying and bullies; 4. Visions; 5. Suicide; 6. Realistic fiction; 7. Coming-of-age stories
9781484790625; 9781484798683

LC 2017032265

YALSA Best Fiction for Young Adults, 2019.

Nearly a year after his brother's suicide, sixteen-year-old Cliff "Neanderthal" Hubbard gets recruited to make life better at Happy Valley High by the school's quarterback, who claims he had a vision from God.

At the story's core is an unsentimental treatment of a bullied kid and his one-time bully discovering their commonalities. That Norton accomplishes this without moralizing and in inventively rhythmic and pop-culture-saturated language only adds to the fun. —*Publishers Weekly*

Novic, Sara

Girl at war. Sara Novic. Random House, 2015 320 p.
Grades: 11 12 Adult

1. War — Psychological aspects; 2. Loss (Psychology); 3. Memory; 4. Yugoslav War, 1991-1995; 5. Secrets; 6. Croatia; 7. New York City; 8. 1990s; 9. Coming-of-age stories; 10. Adult books for young adults
9780812996340; 9781408706541, print, UK; 9780349140988, print, UK

Alex Award, 2016; Longlisted for the Baileys Women's Prize for Fiction, 2016.

When her happy life in 1991 Croatia is shattered by civil war, 10-year-old Ana Juric is embroiled in a world of guerilla warfare and child soldiers before making a daring escape to America, where years later she struggles to hide her past.

Elegiac, and understandably if unrelievedly so, with a matter-of-factness about death and uprootedness. A promising start. —*Kirkus*

Noyes, Deborah

★ The **ghosts** of Kerfol. Deborah Noyes. Candlewick Press, 2008 163 p;
Grades: 8 9 10 11 12

1. Haunted houses; 2. Ghosts; 3. Supernatural; 4. Manors; 5. France; 6. Ghost stories; 7. Short stories
9780763630003

LC 2007051884

Over the centuries, the inhabitants of author Edith Wharton's fictional mansion, Kerfol, are haunted by the ghosts of dead dogs, fractured relationships, and the bitter taste of revenge.

This collection includes five wonderfully chilling short stories. —*Publishers Weekly*

Nunn, Malla

When the ground is hard. Malla Nunn. G.P. Putnam's Sons Books for Young Readers, 2019 272 p.
Grades: 8 9 10 11
1. Boarding school students; 2. Social classes; 3. Multi- racial persons; 4. Human skin color — Social aspects; 5. Christian schools; 6. Swaziland; 7. 1960s; 8. Coming-of- age stories; 9. Historical fiction.
9780525515579; 9781760524814, Paperback, Australia; 9780525515586, ebook, US

LC 2018040602

Los Angeles Times Book Prize for Young Adult Literature, 2019; Josette Frank Award, 2020; Westchester Fiction Award, 2020.

At Swaziland's Keziah Christian Academy, where the wealth and color of one's father determines one's station, once-popular Adele bonds with poor Lottie over a book and a series of disasters.

In Swaziland, wealth and privilege are tightly bound to race. as a mixed-race girl, Adele considers herself above the native Zulus, but her relatively privileged status is compromised by the fact that her white father lives with his 'real' family in Johannesburg. —*Booklist*

Nussbaum, Susan

★ **Good** kings, bad kings: a novel. Susan Nussbaum. Algonquin Books of Chapel Hill, 2013 336 p.
Grades: 10 11 12 Adult
1. Institutional care — Employees; 2. Teenagers with disabilities; 3. Children with developmental disabilities; 4. Children with disabilities; 5. Wheelchair users; 6. Chicago, Illinois; 7. Multiple perspectives; 8. Mainstream fiction; 9. First person narratives; 10. Adult books for young adults.
9781616202637

LC 2013001350

Bellwether Prize for Fiction, 2012.

The residents at a facility for disabled young people in Chicago build trust and make friends in an effort to fight against their living conditions and mistreatment in this debut novel from the playwright behind "Mishuganismo."

Nussbaum charms, outrages, and enlightens readers as she cycles among these and other characters, boldly contrasting the transcendence of love with the harsh realities of a negligent for-profit nursing home. —*Booklist*

Nwaubani, Adaobi Tricia

Buried beneath the baobab tree. Adaobi Tricia Nwaubani and Viviana Mazza. Katherine Tegen Books, 2018 402 p.
Grades: 9 10 11 12
1. Rape victims; 2. Forced marriage; 3. Kidnapping victims; 4. Teenage girls; 5. Violence; 6. Nigeria; 7. Realistic fiction
9780062696724; 9780062696748, ebook, US
Notable Books for a Global Society, 2019; YALSA Best Fiction for Young Adults, 2019; Booklist Editors' Choice: Books for Youth, 2018.

Based on interviews with young women who were kidnapped by Boko Haram, this poignant novel tells the timely story of one girl who was taken from her home in Nigeria and her harrowing fight for survival. Includes an afterword by award-winning journalist Viviana Mazza.

Nye, Naomi Shihab

★ **Habibi**. Naomi Shihab Nye. Simon & Schuster Books for Young Readers, 1997 259 p.
Grades: 7 8 9 10
1. Fourteen-year-old girls; 2. Arab American families; 3. Palestinian Americans; 4. Arab American teenage girls; 5. Teenagers; 6. Jerusalem, Israel; 7. Realistic fiction
9780689801495

LC 97010943

Jane Addams Book Award for Books for Older Children, 1998; ALA Notable Children's Book, 1998; YALSA Best Books for Young Adults, 1998; Middle East Book Award, Youth Literature Winner, 2000.

When fourteen-year-old Liyanna, her younger brother, and her parents move from St. Louis to a new home between Jerusalem and the Palestinian village where her father was born, they face many changes and must deal with the tensions between Jews and Palestinians.

Poetically imaged and leavened with humor, the story renders layered and complex history understandable through character and incident. —*School Library Journal*

O'Brien, Caragh M.

★ **Birthmarked**. Caragh M. O'Brien. Roaring Brook Press, 2010 368 p. (Birthmarked trilogy, 1)
Grades: 6 7 8 9 10
1. Teenage apprentices; 2. Midwives; 3. Dystopias; 4. Infants; 5. Genetic engineering; 6. Dystopian fiction; 7. Science fiction.
9781596435698
Amelia Bloomer List, 2011; YALSA Best Fiction for Young Adults, 2011.

In future world decimated by climate change, apprentice midwife Gaia lives along the shore of what used to be Lake Michigan, helping her mother deliver babies and making sure to "advance" the required three newborns per month to the exclusive, walled-in Enclave. Gaia is forced to infiltrate the Enclave herself after her parents are arrested as traitors, and though she finds help (maybe even love?) from someone unexpected, she also uncovers devastating secrets that shatter her understanding of her society.

Readers who enjoy adventures with a strong heroine standing up to authority against the odds will enjoy this compelling tale. —*School Library Journal*

O'Brien, Robert C.

★ **Z** for Zachariah. Robert C. O'Brien. Atheneum, 1975 249 p.
Grades: 7 8 9 10
1. Survival (after nuclear warfare); 2. Nuclear holocaust survivors; 3. Escapes; 4. Radiation victims; 5. Dystopias; 6. Apocalyptic fiction; 7. Science fiction; 8. Books to movies
9780689304422; 9780141368986, print, UK

LC 74076736

Edgar Allan Poe Award for Best Juvenile Mystery Novel, 1976.

Seemingly the only person left alive after a nuclear war, a sixteen-year-old girl is relieved to see a man arrive into her valley until she realizes that he is a tyrant and she must somehow escape.

The journal form is used by O'Brien very effectively, with no lack of drama and contrast, and the pace and suspense of the story are adroitly maintained until the dramatic and surprising ending. —*Bulletin of the Center for Children's Books*

LIST OF FICTIONAL WORKS

O'Neill, Louise
★ **Asking** for It. Louise O'Neill. Quercus, 2016 324 p.
Grades: 9 10 11 12
1. Teenage rape victims; 2. Rape culture; 3. Small towns; 4. Rape; 5. Shame; 6. Ireland; 7. Realistic fiction
9781681445373; 9781784293208, print, UK; 9781848668201, ebook
Amelia Bloomer List, 2017; School Library Journal Best Books, 2016; YALSA Best Fiction for Young Adults, 2017; Michael L. Printz Honor Book, 2017.

O'Neill's treatment of how communities mishandle sexual assault and victimize its victims is unforgiving, and readers will despair to see Emma helpless in the face of injustice. It's a brutal, hard-to-forget portrait of human cruelty that makes disturbingly clear the way women and girls internalize sexist societal attitudes and unwarranted guilt. —*Publishers Weekly*

O'Sullivan, Joanne
★ **Between** two skies. Joanne O'Sullivan. Candlewick Press, 2017 272 p.
Grades: 7 8 9 10 11 12
1. Hurricane Katrina, 2005; 2. Teenage boy/girl relations; 3. Teenagers; 4. Sixteen-year-old girls; 5. Social classes; 6. Louisiana; 7. Love stories; 8. Historical fiction.
9780763690342

Enjoying a quiet life in a tiny Louisiana fishing town, six-teen-year-old Evangeline is set adrift by Hurricane Katrina and must work through difficult political and cultural challenges to regain her sense of belonging.

Told in a strong, purposeful voice filled with controlled emotion and hope, the impact of Katrina on families is as compelling as Evangeline's drive to regain her sense of self and belonging. —*Booklist*

Oakes, Stephanie
The **arsonist**. Stephanie Oakes. Dial Books, 2017 400 p.
Grades: 7 8 9
1. Diaries; 2. Mother-separated teenage girls; 3. Murder investigation; 4. Kuwaiti Americans; 5. Teenagers with epilepsy; 6. East Germany; 7. Mysteries
9780803740716
LC 2016032499
YALSA Best Fiction for Young Adults, 2018.

Molly Mavity and Pepper Yusef are dealing with their own personal tragedies when they are tasked by an anonymous person with solving the decades-old murder of Ava Dryman, an East German teenager whose diary was published after her death.

Packed with dynamic characters, thoughtful writing, and a de-cades-spanning mystery, this will appeal to readers looking for something off the beaten path. —*Booklist*

★ The **sacred** lies of Minnow Bly. By Stephanie Oakes. 2015 384 p.
Grades: 9 10 11 12
1. Cults; 2. Juvenile detention; 3. Teenage girls; 4. Polygamy; 5. Fanaticism; 6. Montana; 7. Realistic fiction; 8. Fairy tale and folklore-inspired fiction
9780803740709
LC 2014033187
Booklist Editors' Choice: Books for Youth, 2015; YALSA Best Fiction for Young Adults, 2016; Golden Kite Award Honor Book for Fiction, 2016; William C. Morris Debut Award finalist, 2016.

A handless teen escapes from a cult, only to find herself in juvenile detention and suspected of knowing who murdered her cult leader.

Based on Grimm's fairy tale, "The Handless Maiden," the powerful, fluent writing; engrossing and well-layered mystery; compelling charac-ters; and provocative ideas about family, faith, honesty, loyalty, and friendship are engaging. —*School Library Journal*

Dark and not just a little sensational but hugely involving neverthe-less. —*Kirkus*

Oates, Joyce Carol
Two or three things I forgot to tell you. Joyce Carol Oates. HarperTeen, 2012 320 p.
Grades: 9 10 11 12
1. Self-harm in teenage girls; 2. Survivors of suicide victims; 3. Teenagers and death; 4. Self-harm; 5. Secrets; 6. Realistic fiction; 7. Multiple perspectives.
9780062110473
LC 2012009699
When their best friend, Tink, dies from an apparent suicide, high school seniors Merissa and Nadia are alienated by their secrets, adrift from each other and from themselves—Provided by publisher.

Ockler, Sarah
The **book** of broken hearts. By Sarah Ockler. Simon Pulse, 2013 352 p.
Grades: 9 10 11 12
1. Summer romance; 2. People with Alzheimer's disease; 3. Fathers and daughters; 4. Teenage boy/girl relations; 5. Automobile mechanics; 6. Realistic fiction; 7. Coming-of-age stories.
9781442430389
Jude has learned a lot from her older sisters, the most important thing being that the Vargas brothers are notorious heartbreakers, but as Jude be-gins to fall for Emilio Vargas, she wonders if her sisters were wrong.

Oelke, Lianne
Nice try, Jane Sinner. Lianne Oelke. 2018 432 p.
Grades: 9 10 11 12
1. High school dropouts; 2. Reality television programs; 3. Faith in teenage girls; 4. Universities and colleges; 5. Community colleges; 6. Canada; 7. Realistic fiction; 8. Diary novels; 9. Canadian fiction
9780544867857; 9780358097563, Paperback, US
LC 2016035569
OLA Best Bets, 2018.

Jane Sinner sets out to redefine herself through a series of schemes and stunts, including participating in a low-budget reality TV show at her local community college.

Character-driven, humorous, and deceptively profound. —*Kirkus*

Oh, Ellen
A **thousand** beginnings and endings: 15 retellings of Asian myths and legends. . Greenwillow Books, 2018 328 pages;
Grades: 6 7 8 9 10 11 12
1. Mythology, Asian; 2. Asia; 3. Short stories; 4. Anthologies; 5. Mythology — Collection (mixed); 6. Folklore — Collection (mixed).
9780062671158, HRD, US
YALSA Best Fiction for Young Adults, 2019.

Fifteen authors of Asian descent reimagine the folklore and mythol-ogy of East and South Asia, in short stories ranging from fantasy to sci-ence fiction to contemporary, from romance to tales of revenge.

A marvelous anthology of retold Asian myths and legends tying the traditional and modern together and accessible to all teens of all back-grounds. —*Kirkus*

Okorafor, Nnedi
Akata warrior. Nnedi Okorafor. Viking, 2017 496 p. (Akata series, 2)

Grades: 6 7 8 9 10
1. Secret societies; 2. Nigerian Americans; 3. Imaginary wars and battles; 4. Magic; 5. Nwazue, Sunny (Fictitious character); 6. Nigeria; 7. Africa; 8. Fantasy fiction; 9. African American fiction; 10. Gateway fantasy
9780670785612
Booklist Editors' Choice: Books for Youth, 2017; Locus Young Adult Book Award, 2018; Children's Africana Book Awards Honor Book, Older Readers, 2018.

Now stronger, feistier, and a bit older, Sunny Nwazue, along with her friends from the the Leopard Society, travel through worlds, both visible and invisible, to the mysterious town of Osisi, where they fight in a climactic battle to save humanity.

Okorafor's novel will ensnare readers and keep them turning pages until the very end to see if and how Sunny fulfills the tremendous destiny that awaits her. —*Booklist*

★ **Akata** witch. Nnedi Okorafor. Viking, 2011 352 p. (Akata series, 1)
Grades: 6 7 8 9 10
1. Girl misfits; 2. Albinos and albinism; 3. Witches; 4. Witchcraft; 5. Nigerian Americans; 6. Nigeria; 7. Africa; 8. Fantasy fiction; 9. African American fiction; 10. Afrofuturism and Afrofantasy
9780670011964
Amelia Bloomer List, 2012; YALSA Best Fiction for Young Adults, 2012.

Twelve-year-old Sunny Nwazue, an American-born albino child of Nigerian parents, moves with her family back to Nigeria, where she learns that she has latent magical powers which she and three similarly gifted friends use to catch a serial killer.

This vividly imagined, original fantasy shows what life is like in today's Nigeria, while it beautifully explores an alternate magical reality. Sunny must deal with cultural stereotypes, a strict father who resents her being female, and older brothers who pick on her because she's better at soccer than they are. This is a consistently surprising, inventive read that will appeal to more thoughtful, patient fantasy readers because it relies less on action and more on exploring the characters' gradual mastery of their talents. —*School Library Journal*

The **shadow** speaker. Nnedi Okorafor-Mbachu. Jump at the Sun/Hyperion Books for Children, 2007 336 p;
Grades: 7 8 9 10
1. Teenage girl heroes; 2. Muslim teenagers; 3. Technology; 4. Biological terrorism; 5. Magic; 6. Sahara; 7. Sahara; 8. 21st century; 9. Fantasy fiction; 10. African American fiction; 11. Afrofuturism and Afrofantasy
9781423100331
Amelia Bloomer List, 2009.

Okorafor-Mbachu does an excellent job of combining both science fiction and fantasy elements into this novel.... The action moves along at a quick pace and will keep most readers on their toes and wanting more at the end of the novel. —*Voice of Youth Advocates*

Older, Daniel Jose
★ **Shadowhouse** fall. Daniel Jose Older. Arthur A. Levine Books, an imprint of Scholastic Inc, 2017 304 p. (Shadowshaper cypher, 2)
Grades: 9 10 11 12
1. Puerto Ricans; 2. Spirits; 3. Teenage artists; 4. Good and evil; 5. Magic; 6. Brooklyn, New York City; 7. New York City; 8. Urban fantasy
9780545952828; 9780545952835, ebook, US

LC 2017016620

After channeling hundreds of spirits through herself to defeat Wick, Sierra Santiago discovers she woke up something powerful and unfriendly that put her loved ones at risk.

The expanding cast of well-rounded characters, clearly choreographed action, and foreshadowing of installments to come will have fantasy fans eagerly awaiting more of this dynamic, smart series. —*Booklist*

★ **Shadowshaper**. Daniel Jose Older. Arthur A. Levine Books, 2015 304 p. (Shadowshaper cypher, 1)
Grades: 9 10 11 12
1. Teenage artists; 2. Ancestors; 3. Zombies; 4. Grandfather and granddaughter; 5. Puerto Ricans; 6. Brooklyn, New York City; 7. New York City; 8. Urban fantasy; 9. Books for reluctant readers
9780545591614
Booklist Editors' Choice: Books for Youth, 2015; School Library Journal Best Books, 2015; YALSA Best Fiction for Young Adults, 2016; YALSA Best Fiction for Young Adults: Top Ten, 2015; YALSA Quick Picks for Reluctant Young Adult Readers, 2016; YALSA Quick Picks for Reluctant Young Adult Readers: Top Ten, 2016; Kirkus Prize for Young Readers' Literature finalist, 2015.

Excellent diverse genre fiction in an appealing package. —*School Library Journal*

Shadowshaper legacy. Daniel José Older. Scholastic Press, 2020 432 p. : Illustration (Shadowshaper cypher, 3)
Grades: 9 10 11 12
1. Teenage artists; 2. Ancestors; 3. Spirits; 4. Imaginary wars and battles; 5. Consequences; 6. Brooklyn, New York City; 7. New York City; 8. Urban fantasy; 9. Multiple perspectives; 10. Books for reluctant readers.
9780545953009, HRD, US; 9780545953016, ebook, US

LC 2019030317

A war is brewing among the different Houses, some of Sierra's shadowshapers are still in jail, and the House of Shadow and Light has been getting threatening messages from whisper wraiths, and even though one spy was exposed Sierra is not quite sure who she can trust—but the deal with Death made by one of her ancestors has given her power, and she will need to control it and confront her family's past if she has any hope of saving the future.

Older knocks it out of the park with his thrilling conclusion to the Shadowshaper Cypher series. —*Booklist*

Oliver, Ben
The **loop**. Benjamin Oliver. Chicken House, an imprint of Scholastic Inc, 2020 368 p. (Loop (Ben Oliver), 1)
Grades: 9 10 11 12
1. Human experimentation in medicine; 2. Death row prisoners; 3. Artificial intelligence; 4. Teenage boys; 5. Survival; 6. Dystopian fiction; 7. Science fiction; 8. Books for reluctant readers
9781338589306, HRD, US; 9781912626557
Enduring a tortuous existence on a futuristic death row for teens where inmates can delay their execution date in exchange for becoming laboratory subjects, Luka uncovers rumors about chaos spreading throughout the outside world before he becomes targeted by his crazed fellow prisoners.

Oliver's debut presents a terrifying futurescape at the heart-stopping intersection of *The Matrix* and *The Maze Runner*, kicking off a trilogy sure to prove dystopian sci-fi still has more to offer. —*Booklist*

Oliver, Jana G.
The **demon** trapper's daughter: a Demon trapper novel. Jana Oliver. St. Martin's Griffin, 2011 X, 355 p; (Demon trapper novels, 1)
Grades: 7 8 9 10

1. Demon slayers; 2. Teenage apprentices; 3. Demons; 4. Supernatural; 5. Fathers — Death; 6. Atlanta, Georgia; 7. Georgia; 8. Urban fantasy
9780312614782

LC 2010038860

When 17-year-old Riley Blackthorne, an apprentice demon-trapper in 2018 Atlanta, Georgia, attempts a routine Grade-One demon extraction in a university library, things go awry despite her careful attention to procedure. Soon after, a much more dangerous demon kills Riley's father (a renowned demon-trapper himself), and it becomes clear that something very big—and very bad—is afoot, and Riley is in grave danger.

With a strong female heroine, a fascinating setting, and a complex, thrill-soaked story, this series is off to a strong start. —*Publishers Weekly*

Oliver, Lauren

★ **Before** I fall. Lauren Oliver. 2010 470 p.
Grades: 9 10 11 12
1. Traffic accident victims; 2. Redemption; 3. Self-perception in teenage girls; 4. Self-perception; 5. Fatal traffic accidents; 6. Books to movies
9780061726804; 9781473654785, Oz; 9780340980903, UK

LC 2009007288

Garden State Teen Book Award (New Jersey), Fiction (Grades 9-12), 2013; Goodreads Choice Award, 2010; YALSA Popular Paperbacks for Young Adults, 2012; YALSA Best Fiction for Young Adults, 2011.

After she dies in a car crash, teenage Samantha relives the day of her death over and over again until, on the seventh day, she finally discovers a way to save herself.

This is a compelling book with a powerful message that will strike a chord with many teens. —*Booklist*
Title adapted into a film by the same name in 2017.

★ **Delirium**. Lauren Oliver. HarperCollins, 2011 320 p. (Delirium trilogy, 1)
Grades: 8 9 10 11
1. Crushes in teenage girls; 2. Love; 3. Dystopias; 4. Surgery; 5. Resistance to government; 6. Maine; 7. Dystopian fiction; 8. Science fiction.
9780061726828; 9780340980910, print, UK; 9780340980934, print, UK

LC 2010017839

YALSA Best Fiction for Young Adults, 2012; YALSA Popular Paperbacks for Young Adults, 2016.

High school senior Lena Haloway is counting the 95 days until her appointment to undergo the operation that every citizen has at age 18 to prevent them from contracting amor deliria nervosa—love, which is seen as a deadly disease. At first, Lena is eager for the surgery, believing it will make her life happy and safe. But then she meets handsome and enigmatic Alex, and she's not so sure anymore.

This book is a deft blend of realism and fantasy.... The story bogs down as it revels in romanceAlex is standard-issue perfectionbut the book never loses its *A Clockwork Orange*-style bite regarding safety versus choice. —*Booklist*

Panic. Lauren Oliver. Harper, 2014 416 p.
Grades: 9 10 11 12
1. Games; 2. Risk-taking (Psychology); 3. Small towns; 4. Competition; 5. High school graduates; 6. New York (State); 7. Thrillers and suspense; 8. Multiple perspectives
9780062014559; 9781444723052, print, UK
LibraryReads Favorites, 2014.

The bleak setting, tenacious characters, and anxiety-filled atmosphere will draw readers right into this unique story. Oliver's powerful re-

turn to a contemporary realistic setting will find wide a readership with this fast-paced and captivating book. —*School Library Journal*

Replica.. Lauren Oliver. Harper, an imprint of HarperCollins Publishers, 2016 236, 284 pages. (Replica (Lauren Oliver), 1)
Grades: 8 9 10 11 12
1. Clones and cloning; 2. Government conspiracies; 3. Near future; 4. Research institutes; 5. Teenage girls; 6. Florida; 7. Science fiction; 8. Reversible books
9780062394163; 9781473614956, London

With Oliver's clever crafting, readers will be clamoring for the next book in the projected series. —*Horn Book Guide*
Titles from separate title pages; works issued back-to-back and inverted.

Vanishing girls. Lauren Oliver. Harper, 2015 480 p.
Grades: 9 10 11 12
1. Sisters; 2. Missing girls; 3. Dissociative disorders; 4. Teenage boy/girl relations; 5. Traffic accident victims; 6. Mysteries
9780062224101; 9780062224118

LC 2014028437

LibraryReads Favorites, 2015; YALSA Popular Paperbacks for Young Adults, 2017.

Perfect for readers who devoured *We Were Liars*, it's the sort of novel that readers will race to finish, then return to the beginning to marvel at how it was constructed—and at everything they missed. —*Publishers Weekly*

Onyebuchi, Tochi

War girls. Tochi Onyebuchi. 2019 464 p. (War girls, 1)
Grades: 9 10 11 12
1. Sisters; 2. Cyborgs; 3. Civil war; 4. Dystopias; 5. Post-apocalypse; 6. Nigeria; 7. Africa; 8. Afrofuturism and Afrofantasy; 9. Science fiction; 10. African American fiction
9780451481672; 9780451481696

LC 2019016805

Children's Africana Book Awards Honor Book, Older Readers, 2020.

In 2172, when much of the world is unlivable, sisters Onyii and Ify dream of escaping war-torn Nigeria and finding a better future together but are, instead, torn apart.

The intense plot is narrated in alternating third-person perspectives, and the author explores themes surrounding colonization, family, and the injustices of war. The story culminates in an unexpected, heart-wrenching end. —*Kirkus*

Oppel, Kenneth

Airborn. Kenneth Oppel. Eos, 2004 368 p. (Airborn adventures, 1)
Grades: 7 8 9 10
1. Airships; 2. Cabin boys; 3. Rich girls; 4. Teenage boy/girl relations; 5. Teenagers; 6. Fantasy fiction; 7. Steampunk; 8. Canadian fiction; 9. Books for reluctant readers
9780060531805; 9780060531812; 9781554682812; 9780006392590; 9780002005371; 9780340878552, print, UK

LC 2003015642

ALA Notable Children's Book, 2005; Beehive Young Adult Book Award (Utah), 2006; Governor General's Literary Award for English-Language Children's Literature, 2004; OLA Best Bets, 2004; Red Cedar Book Awards (British Columbia), Fiction category, 2007; Red Maple Fiction Award (Ontario), 2005; Rocky Mountain Book Award (Alberta), 2006; Ruth and Sylvia Schwartz Children's Book Award for YA-Middle Reader, 2005; Thumbs Up! Award (Michigan), 2005; Virginia Readers' Choice Award for Middle School, 2009; YALSA Quick Picks for Reluctant Young Adult Readers, 2005;

YALSA Popular Paperbacks for Young Adults, 2011; YALSA Best Books for Young Adults, 2005; School Library Journal Best Books, 2004; Michael L. Printz Honor Book, 2005.

Matt, a young cabin boy aboard an airship, and Kate, a wealthy young girl traveling with her chaperone, team up to search for the existence of mysterious winged creatures reportedly living hundreds of feet above the Earth's surface.

This rousing adventure has something for everyone: appealing and enterprising characters, nasty villains, and a little romance. —*School Library Journal*

Bloom. Kenneth Oppel. Knopf Books for Young Readers, 2020 320 p. (Overthrow, 1)
Grades: 5 6 7 8 9
1. Plant invasions; 2. Carnivorous plants; 3. Teenagers; 4. Plants; 5. Alien plants; 6. Vancouver, British Columbia; 7. British Columbia; 8. Science fiction; 9. Apocalyptic fiction; 10. Canadian fiction
9781524773014; 9781524773007; 9781524773038; 9781443450317, print, Canada

The invasion begins—but not as you'd expect. It begins with rain. Rain that carries seeds. Seeds that sprout—overnight, everywhere. These new plants take over crop fields, twine up houses, and burrow below streets. They bloom—and release toxic pollens. They bloom—and form Venus flytrap-like pods that swallow animals and people. They bloom—everywhere, unstoppable. Or are they? Three kids on a remote island seem immune to the toxic plants. Anaya, Petra, Seth. They each have strange allergies—and yet not to these plants. What's their secret? Can they somehow be the key to beating back this invasion? They'd better figure it out fast, because it's starting to rain again....

In this fast-paced thriller, Oppel spins a richly drawn, incredibly fascinating world. Beginning with the brilliantly unique premise of a botanical alien invasion, the plot unravels satisfyingly, building readers' curiosity by creating 10 new questions for every answer given. —*Kirkus*

Every hidden thing. Kenneth Oppel. Simon & Schuster Books for Young Readers, 2016 256 p.
Grades: 9 10 11 12
1. Fossils; 2. Paleontology; 3. Dinosaurs; 4. Dakota Indians; 5. Families; 6. Badlands Region; 7. 19th century; 8. Historical fiction; 9. Multiple perspectives; 10. First person narratives
9781481464161; 9781443410298; 9781443410304; 9781910989579, print, UK; 9781481464185, ebook, US

LC 2015045436
OLA Best Bets, 2016.

In the late nineteenth century, a budding romance develops between Rachel and Samuel, two teenagers from rival families of fossil hunters heading out to the badlands in seach of a rare dinosaur skeleton.

Suspense, romance, and the excitement of discovery make this Western thoroughly enjoyable. —*Kirkus*

★ **This** dark endeavor. Kenneth Oppel. Simon & Schuster Books for Young Readers, 2011 304 p. (Apprenticeship of Victor Frankenstein, 1)
Grades: 7 8 9 10
1. Twin brothers; 2. Alchemy; 3. Alchemists; 4. Love triangles; 5. Sick teenage boys; 6. Geneva (Republic); 7. 18th century; 8. Horror; 9. Gothic fiction; 10. Canadian fiction.
9781442403154; 9781554683390

LC 2011016974
YALSA Best Fiction for Young Adults, 2012.

When his twin brother falls ill in the family's chateau in the independent republic of Geneva in the eighteenth century, sixteen-year-old Victor Frankenstein embarks on a dangerous and uncertain quest to create the forbidden Elixir of Life described in an ancient text in the family's secret Biblioteka Obscura.

Written in a readable approximation of early 19th-century style, Oppel's...tale is melodramatic, exciting, disquieting, and intentionally over the top. —*Publishers Weekly*

Ormsbee, Kathryn
Tash hearts Tolstoy. Katie Ormsbee. 2017 384 p.
Grades: 9 10 11 12
1. Fame; 2. Internet television — Production and direction; 3. Asexuals; 4. Internet personalities; 5. Teenage boy/girl relations; 6. Realistic fiction; 7. LGBTQIA fiction; 8. Coming-of-age stories
9781481489331; 9781481489348

LC 2016032661
Rainbow List, 2018.

When a shout-out by a famed vlogger causes her own web series to go viral, Tash embarks on an ambitious project marked by her love of Tolstoy, adoring fans, high pressure, a cyber-flirtation with a fellow award nominee and her secret asexual orientation.

Whip-smart, funny, flawed, and compassionate, these are characters readers will want to know and cheer for. A clever, thoroughly enjoyable addition to the growing body of diverse teen literature. —*Kirkus*

Oseman, Alice
Solitaire. Alice Oseman. HarperTeen, 2015 368 p.
Grades: 9 10 11 12
1. Sixteen-year-old girls; 2. Teenage girls with depression; 3. Practical jokes; 4. Alienation (Social psychology); 5. Brothers and sisters; 6. Great Britain; 7. Realistic fiction.
9780062335685; 9780007559220, print, UK

LC 2014026695
Tori Spring feels completely disconnected from her life—until she meets the relentlessly cheerful Michael Holden, and a series of schoolwide pranks starts to draw her out of her shell.

The obvious nod to *The Catcher in the Rye* provides another pull to readers who will enjoy parsing the parallels. —*Booklist*

Oshiro, Mark
Anger is a gift: a novel. Mark Oshiro. Tor Teen, 2018 464 p.
Grades: 8 9 10 11 12
1. African American teenage boys; 2. Gay teenagers; 3. Protests, demonstrations, vigils, etc; 4. High schools; 5. Racism; 6. Oakland, California; 7. California; 8. Realistic fiction
9781250167026; 9781250167033
Schneider Family Book Award for Teens, 2019.

A young adult debut by the popular social media personality and critic reflects the racial and economic struggles of today's teens in the story of high school junior Moss, who in the face of a racist school administration decides to organize a protest that escalates into violence.

Oshiro deftly captures the simmering rage that ultimately transforms Moss from a quiet teenager to a committed activist against a brutal, menacing system. —*Publishers Weekly*

Each of us a desert. Mark Oshiro. St Martins Pr 2020 431 pages : Illustration
Grades: 9 10 11 12
1. Storytellers; 2. Lesbian teenagers; 3. Deserts; 4. Quests; 5. Post-apocalypse; 6. Fantasy fiction; 7. First person narratives
9781250169211

Destined to a solitary life in the desert, a storyteller longing for a kindred spirit encounters the cold and beautiful daughter of her village's murderous conqueror before nightmarish threats challenge their unlikely relationship.

This ambitious, organically Spanish-studded examination of trauma stays adventurous and accessible, resulting in a grace-filled, loving declaration of human value and worth. —*Publishers Weekly*

Ostrovski, Emil

Away we go. Emil Ostrovski. Harpercollins Childrens Books, 2016 432 p.
Grades: 9 10 11 12
1. Purpose in life; 2. Teenage boy/boy relations; 3. Teenagers with terminal illnesses; 4. End of the world; 5. Near future; 6. Apocalyptic fiction.
9780062238559

Noah's snarky repartee and constant jokes belie the depth of his struggle, and the oscillation between his heartfelt interior thoughts and sometimes careless actions and words is both moving and infuriatingin other words, vividly human. An intelligent, thought-provoking exploration of living in spite of futility. —*Booklist*

Owen, Margaret

The **merciful** Crow. Margaret Owen. 2019 384 p. (Merciful Crow, 1)
Grades: 7 8 9 10
1. Witches; 2. Fugitives; 3. Staged deaths; 4. Teenage girls; 5. Euthanasia; 6. Fantasy fiction
9781250191922
LC 2018038716

Fie, a sixteen-year-old chieftain from a lowly caste of mercy-killers, must rely on her wits and bone magic to smuggle the crown prince of Sabor to safety.

Memorable and filled with diverse characters with fluid sexualities and identities, this tale is both a satisfying standalone and the first half of a planned duology. —*Publishers Weekly*

Padian, Maria

How to build a heart. Maria Padian. Algonquin, 2020 352 p.
Grades: 8 9 10 11 12
1. Home (Concept); 2. Multiracial teenage girls; 3. Social classes; 4. Hispanic American families; 5. Neighbors; 6. Realistic fiction; 7. First person narratives.
9781616208493
LC 2019007625

Izzy Crawford's family has been selected for a new home by Habitat for Humanity, near where the very attractive Sam lives, but just when her neighbor and best friend needs her most.

While navigating the remnants of her Methodist father's legacy and her mother's deeply rooted Catholicism, Izzy must also explore her relationship with both sides of her family. —*Kirkus*

Wrecked. By Maria Padian. Algonquin Young Readers, 2016 320 p.
Grades: 9 10 11 12
1. Rape investigation; 2. Rape; 3. Violence in universities and colleges; 4. Rape victims; 5. College students; 6. Realistic fiction; 7. Multiple perspectives
9781616206246
LC 2016020315

Offers a kaleidoscopic view of a sexual assault on a college campus that will leave readers thinking about how memory and identity, what's at stake, and who sits in judgment shape what we all decide to believe about the truth.

All characters are realistically flawed and human as they struggle to do what's right. In the face of recent college rape trials, readers will be rapt and emotionally spent by the end. —*Kirkus*
Published simultaneously in Canada by Thomas Allen & Son Limited.

Pan, Emily X. R.

★ The **astonishing** color of after. By Emily X.R. Pan. Little, Brown and Company, 2018 400 p.
Grades: 9 10 11 12
1. Children of suicide victims; 2. Grief in teenagers; 3. Self-discovery in teenagers; 4. Suicide; 5. Children of people with mental illnesses; 6. Taiwan; 7. Magical realism.
9780316463997; 9780316464017; 9780316464000; 9780316464925
LC 2017022920

Booklist Editors' Choice: Books for Youth, 2018; School Library Journal Best Books, 2018; Walter Honor Book, Teen, 2019.

After her mother's suicide, grief-stricken Leigh Sanders travels to Taiwan to stay with grandparents she never met, determined to find her mother who she believes turned into a bird.

An evocative novel that captures the uncertain, unmoored feeling of existing between worlds—culturally, linguistically, ethnically, romantically, and existentially—it is also about seeking hope and finding beauty even in one's darkest hours. —*Kirkus*

Paolini, Christopher

★ **Eragon**. Christopher Paolini. Alfred A. Knopf, 2003 528 p. (Inheritance cycle (Christopher Paolini), 1)
Grades: 7 8 9 10
1. Dragons; 2. Fifteen-year-old boys; 3. Revenge; 4. Boys and dragons; 5. Magic; 6. High fantasy; 7. Fantasy fiction; 8. Books to movies
9780375826689; 9780375926686; 9780552552097, UK; 9780385607926, UK
LC 2003047481

Beehive Young Adult Book Award (Utah), 2005; Books I Love Best Yearly (BILBY), Older Reader, 2007; Book Sense Book of the Year for Children's Literature, 2004; Buckeye Children's Book Award (Ohio), Grades 6-8, 2007; Colorado Blue Spruce YA Book Award, 2005; Colorado Children's Book Award, Junior Book, 2005; Eliot Rosewater Indiana High School Book Award (Rosie Award), 2006; Gateway Readers Award (Missouri), 2006; Golden Archer Awards (Wisconsin): Middle/Jr. High, 2006; Grand Canyon Reader Award (Arizona), Teen Book Category, 2006; Iowa Teen Award, 2008; Isinglass Teen Read Award (New Hampshire), 2004-2005. ; Nene Award (Hawaii), 2006; Rebecca Caudill Young Reader's Book Award (Illinois), 2006; Rhode Island Teen Book Award, 2005; Pennsylvania Young Reader's Choice Awards, Grades 6-8, 2005; Sequoyah Book Awards (Oklahoma), Young Adult Books, 2006; Soaring Eagle Book Award (Wyoming), 2005; South Carolina Book Award, Young Adult Books, 2006; Surrey Book of the Year Award (British Columbia), 2007; Virginia Readers' Choice Award for Middle School, 2006; YALSA Popular Paperbacks for Young Adults, 2012; Young Reader's Choice Award (Pacific Northwest), Intermediate, 2006.

When fifteen-year-old Eragon comes to learn that he is a gifted Dragon Rider, he realizes that his destiny is to fight the evil powers that will bring complete destruction to the Empire and so leaves his quiet life as a farm boy to succeed in his one true mission in life.

This unusual, powerful tale...is the first book in the planned Inheritance trilogy.... The telling remains constantly fresh and fluid, and [the author] has done a fine job of creating an appealing and convincing relationship between the youth and the dragon. —*Booklist*

Paquette, Ammi-Joan

Nowhere girl. A.J. Paquette. Walker Books for Young Readers, 2011 256 p.

Grades: 6 7 8 9

1. Children of prisoners; 2. Identity (Psychology); 3. Belonging; 4. Voyages and travels; 5. Americans in Thailand; 6. Realistic fiction.

9780802722973

LC 2010049591

Fair-skinned and blond-haired, thirteen-year-old Luchi was born in a Thai prison where her American mother was being held and she has never had any other home, but when her mother dies Luchi sets out into the world to search for the family and home she has always dreamed of.

The classic quest story gets expanded here with contemporary details in spare lyrical prose that intensify the perilous, archetypal journey.... The realistic specifics...make the story of betrayal and kindness immediate and universal. —*Booklist*

Park, Linda Sue

★ **A long** walk to water: based on a true story. By Linda Sue Park. Clarion Books, 2009 128 p.

Grades: 6 7 8 9 10

1. Dut, Salva, 1974-; 2. Refugees; 3. Civil war; 4. Survival; 5. Eleven-year-old boys; 6. Water; 7. Sudan; 8. Realistic fiction; 9. Multiple perspectives.

9780547251271; 9781786074621, Paperback, UK

LC 2009048857

Jane Addams Book Award for Books for Older Children, 2011; Notable Books for a Global Society, 2011.

When the Sudanese civil war reaches his village in 1985, eleven-year-old Salva becomes separated from his family and must walk with other Dinka tribe members through southern Sudan, Ethiopia, and Kenya in search of safe haven. Based on the life of Salva Dut, who, after emigrating to America in 1996, began a project to dig water wells in Sudan.

This is a spare, immediate account.... Young readers will be stunned by the triumphant climax of the former refugee who makes a difference. —*Booklist*

Parker, Morgan

★ **Who** put this song on? Morgan Parker. Delacorte Press, 2019 325 pages;

Grades: 7 8 9 10 11

1. African American teenage girls; 2. Teenage girls with depression; 3. Misfits (Persons); 4. Depression; 5. Christian schools; 6. California; 7. Coming-of-age stories; 8. Realistic fiction; 9. African American fiction.

9780525707516, HRD, US; 9780525707530, LIB, US; 9780525707523, ebook, US; 9781472154217, Paperback, UK

LC 2018051979

Seventeen-year-old Morgan is a black teen triumphantly figuring out her identity when her conservative town deems depression as a lack of faith, and blackness as something to be politely ignored.

This fresh read provides a positive and inclusive take on mental health and wellness and offers readers some tools to survive on their own. —*Booklist*

Parker, Natalie C.

Seafire. Natalie C. Parker. Razorbill, 2018 384 p. (Seafire trilogy, 1)

Grades: 7 8 9 10 11 12

1. Women ship captains; 2. Revenge; 3. Seafaring life; 4. Ship captains; 5. Insurgency; 6. Sea stories; 7. Dystopian fiction.

9780451478801, HRD, US; 9780451478825, PAP, US; 9781474966580, Paperback, UK

LC 2018012935

Follows Caledonia Styx, captain of her own ship, the Mors Navis, and its all-female crew as they strive to defeat the powerful fleet of Aric Athair, the vicious warlord who has taken their homes and families.

Along with openly feminist themes, the crew is racially diverse and in this future world, skin color appears to carry no connotations. —*Kirkus*

Parker, Robert B.

Chasing the bear: a young Spenser novel. Robert B. Parker. Philomel Books, 2009 169 p;

Grades: 7 8 9 10

1. Kidnapping; 2. Child abuse; 3. Bullying and bullies; 4. Friendship; 5. Dysfunctional families; 6. Mysteries

9780399247767

LC 2008052725

Spenser reflects back to when he was fourteen years old and how he helped his best friend Jeannie when she was abducted by her abusive father.

A clean, sharp jab of a read. —*Booklist*

Parker, S. M.

The rattled bones. S.M. Parker. Simon Pulse, 2017 368 p.

Grades: 10 11 12

1. Racism; 2. Ghosts; 3. Archaeology; 4. Islands; 5. Lobster fishers; 6. Maine; 7. Paranormal fiction

9781481482042, HRD, US; 9781481482059, PAP, US

After her father's death, Rilla Brae puts off thoughts of college to take over his lobstering business, while helping an archaeology student excavate nearby Malaga, an uninhabited island with a ghost that beckons her.

Parker's vivid descriptions of life on Maine's coast and the lobstering business ground a haunting and atmospheric tale about the sea and reckoning with a community's past. —*Publishers Weekly*

Parks, Kathy

Notes from my captivity. Kathy Parks. Harpercollins Childrens Books, 2018 352 p.

Grades: 9 10 11 12

1. Missing persons; 2. Teenage journalists; 3. Survival; 4. Captivity; 5. Seventeen-year-old girls; 6. Siberia; 7. Magical realism.

9780062394002; 9780062394019

Adrienne Cahill cares about three things: getting into a great college; becoming a revered journalist like her idol, Sydney Declay; and making her late father proud of her. So when Adrienne is offered the chance to write an article that will get her into her dream school and debunk her foolish stepfather's belief that a legendary family of hermits is living in the Siberian wilderness, there's no question that she's going to fly across the world. But the Russian terrain is even less forgiving than Adrienne. And when disaster strikes, none of their extensive preparations seem to matter. Now Adrienne's being held captive by the family she was convinced didn't exist, and her best hope for escape is to act like she cares about them, even if it means wooing the youngest son.

Patel, Sonia

Rani Patel in full effect. Sonia Patel. Cinco Puntos Press,, 2016 224 p.

Grades: 9 10 11 12

1. East Indian American teenagers; 2. Hip-hop culture; 3. Children of immigrants; 4. Sex crimes; 5. Teenage incest victims; 6. Hawaii; 7. Molokai, Hawaii; 8. 1990s; 9. Historical fiction

9781941026496; 9781941026502

Amelia Bloomer List, 2017; YALSA Best Fiction for Young Adults, 2017; YALSA Quick Picks for Reluctant Young Adult Readers, 2017; William C. Morris Debut Award finalist, 2017.

Vivid, bold, and passionate. —*Booklist*

Paterson, Katherine

The **day** of the pelican. By Katherine Paterson. Clarion Books, 2009 160 p.

Grades: 6 7 8 9

1. Refugees; 2. Albanians in Kosovo, Serbia; 3. Kosovo War, 1998-1999; 4. Refugee camps; 5. Muslims; 6. Kosovo, Serbia; 7. Realistic fiction.

9780547181882

LC 2009014998

In 1998 when the Kosovo hostilities escalate, thirteen-year-old Meli's life as an ethnic Albanian, changes forever after her brother escapes his Serbian captors and the entire family flees from one refugee camp to another until they are able to immigrate to America.

Paterson offers a realistic and provocative account of these refugees' plight, balanced by the hope of new beginnings and the resilience of the human spirit. —*Publishers Weekly*

Houghton Mifflin Harcourt.

Patneaude, David

Thin wood walls. By David Patneaude. Houghton Mifflin, 2004 231 p;

Grades: 7 8 9 10

1. Eleven-year-old boys; 2. Japanese American boys; 3. Brothers; 4. Friendship; 5. Prejudice; 6. Seattle, Washington; 7. Second World War era (1939-1945); 8. 1940s; 9. Diary novels; 10. First person narratives; 11. Historical fiction.

9780618342907

LC 2004001014

When the Japanese bomb Pearl Harbor, Joe Hamada and his family face growing prejudice, eventually being torn away from their home and sent to a relocation camp in California, even as his older brother joins the United States Army to fight in the war.

Basing his story on extensive research and interviews, the author does a fine job of bringing the daily experience up close through the story of an American kid torn from home. —*Booklist*

Patrick, Cat

Forgotten: a novel. By Cat Patrick. Little, Brown, 2011 304 p.

Grades: 7 8 9 10 11

1. Memory; 2. Visions; 3. Amnesia; 4. High schools; 5. Schools; 6. Mysteries

9780316094610

LC 2010043032

Sixteen-year-old London Lane forgets everything each night and must use notes to struggle through the day, even to recall her wonderful boyfriend, but she "remembers" future events and as her "flashforwards" become more disturbing she realizes she must learn more about the past lest it destroy her future.

Patrick raises philosophical issues of real interest.... Thoughtful readers will enjoy the mind games, romance readers will enjoy the relationship dynamics, and all readers will find themselves inexorably pulled into a logical yet surprising and compelling finish. —*Booklist*

The **originals**. Cat Patrick. Little, Brown, 2013 304 p.

Grades: 8 9 10 11 12

1. Clones and cloning; 2. Individuality; 3. Sisters; 4. Single-parent families; 5. Dating (Social customs); 6. Science fiction.

9780316219433

LC 2012029853

Seventeen-year-olds Lizzie, Ella, and Betsy Best are clones, raised as identical triplets by their surrogate mother but living as her one daughter, Elizabeth, until their separate abilities and a romantic relationship force a change.

Revived. By Cat Patrick. Little, Brown, 2012 352 p.

Grades: 7 8 9 10 11 12

1. Death; 2. Emotions in teenage girls; 3. Teenagers and death; 4. Fifteen-year-old girls; 5. Drugs; 6. Science fiction; 7. Books for reluctant readers

9780316094627; 9781405253628, print, UK

LC 2011026950

YALSA Quick Picks for Reluctant Young Adult Readers, 2013.

Having been brought back from the dead repeatedly by a top-secret government super drug called Revive, and forced to move so the public does not learn the truth, fifteen-year-old Daisy meets people worth living for and begins to question the heavy-handed government controls she has dealt with for eleven years.

Patterson, James

Homeroom diaries. By James Patterson and Lisa Papademetriou; illustrated by Keino. 2014 272 pages

Grades: 7 8 9 10

1. Foster teenagers; 2. Teenage girl misfits; 3. Cliques; 4. High schools; 5. Schools; 6. Realistic fiction; 7. Diary novels; 8. Illustrated books.

9780316207621; 9780099596257, print, UK; 9780316207638, ebook, US

LC 2013016061

Seventeen-year-old Margaret "Cuckoo" Clark keeps a journal detailing the trials and tribulations of high school life as she and her close-knit group of outcast friends try to break down the barriers between their school's "warring nations."

Despite the fact that serious issues (a negligent mother, an attempted sexual assault, and an incident of cyberbullying) are at play, the light-hearted tone adds levity to the work. The novel is fully illustrated with humorous artwork that contributes to the story in a meaningful way. Fans of the popular diary fiction genre (as well as those simply looking for an approachable and quick read) will find much to enjoy here. —*School Library Journal*

★ **Middle** school: the worst years of my life. James Patterson and Chris Tebbetts; illustrated by Laura Park. Little, Brown, 2011 288 p. (Middle school (James Patterson), 1)

Grades: 4 5 6 7

1. Rules; 2. Misbehavior in boys; 3. Children and single parent dating; 4. Misbehavior; 5. Personal conduct; 6. Realistic fiction; 7. Books to movies; 8. Books for reluctant readers

9780316101875

LC 2010022852

Delaware Diamonds (book award), Middle School, 2013; Nene Award (Hawaii), 2013; YALSA Quick Picks for Reluctant Young Adult Readers, 2012.

When Rafe Kane enters middle school, he teams up with his best friend, "Leo the Silent," to create a game to make school more fun by trying to break every rule in the school's code of conduct.

The book's ultrashort chapters, dynamic artwork, and message that normal is boring should go a long way toward assuring kids who don't fit the mold that there's a place for them, too. —*Publishers Weekly*

Paulsen, Gary

Brian's hunt. Gary Paulsen. Wendy Lamb Books, 2003 112 p. (Brian's saga, 5)
Grades: 6 7 8 9
1. Wilderness survival; 2. Humans and wild animals; 3. Hunting; 4. Wilderness areas; 5. Dogs; 6. Canada; 7. Adventure stories.
9780385746472; 9780385908825; 9780307929594

LC 2003019477

Two years after having survived a plane crash into the Canadian wilderness, a sixteen-year-old returns to the wild to befriend a wounded dog and hunt a rogue bear.

Paulsen's latest will satisfy his many fans. —*Booklist*

Brian's return. Delacorte Press, 1999 117 p. (Brian's saga, 4)
Grades: 6 7 8 9
1. Self-reliance in teenagers; 2. Wilderness survival; 3. Self-reliance; 4. Teenage boys; 5. Children of divorced parents; 6. Adventure stories; 7. Books for reluctant readers
9780385325004; 9780307929600

LC 9824278

YALSA Quick Picks for Reluctant Young Adult Readers, 2000.

After having survived alone in the wilderness, Brian finds that he can no longer live in the city but must return to the place where he really belongs.

This work is bold, confident and persuasive, its transcendental themes powerfully seductive. —*Publishers Weekly*

Brian's winter. Delacorte Press, 1996 133 p. (Brian's saga, 3)
Grades: 6 7 8 9
1. Wilderness survival; 2. Survival (after airplane accidents, shipwrecks, etc.); 3. Winter; 4. Children of divorced parents; 5. Thirteen-year-old boys; 6. Canada; 7. Adventure stories; 8. Survival stories; 9. Books for reluctant readers
9780385321983; 9780307929587

LC 95041337 /AC

Garden State Teen Book Award (New Jersey), Fiction (Grades 6-8), 1999; Golden Archer Awards (Wisconsin): Middle/Jr. High, 1999; Iowa Teen Award, 1998; YALSA Quick Picks for Reluctant Young Adult Readers, 1997.

Instead of being rescued from a plane crash, as in the author's book Hatchet, this story portrays what would have happened to Brian had he been forced to survive a winter in the wilderness with only his survival pack and hatchet.

The same formula that worked before is successful here: the driving pace of the narration, the breathtaking descriptions of nature, and the boy who triumphs on the merits of efficient problem solving. The author's ability to cast a spell, mesmerize his audience, and provide a clinic in winter survival is reason enough to buy this novel. —*School Library Journal*

Companion book to: *Hatchet* and *The River*.

★ **Dogsong**. Gary Paulsen. Bradbury Press, 1985 177 p.
Grades: 6 7 8 9
1. Wilderness survival; 2. Dogsledding; 3. Inuit teenage boys; 4. Inuit; 5. Inuit girls; 6. Coming-of-age stories
9780027701807

LC 84020443

ALA Notable Children's Book, 1986; Newbery Honor Book, 1986.

A fourteen-year-old Inuit boy who feels assailed by the modernity of his life takes a 1400-mile journey by dog sled across ice, tundra, and mountains seeking his own "song" of himself.

The author's mystical tone and blunt prose style are well suited to the spare landscape of his story, and his depictions of Russell's icebound existence add both authenticity and color to a slick rendition of the vi-

sion-quest plot, which incorporates human tragedy as well as promise. —*Booklist*

★ **Harris** and me: a summer remembered. Harcourt Brace, 1993 157 p.
Grades: 5 6 7 8
1. Farm life; 2. Cousins; 3. Children of alcoholics; 4. Eleven-year-old boys; 5. Boys — Friendship; 6. Humorous stories
9780152928773

LC 93019788 /AC

Golden Archer Awards (Wisconsin): Middle/Jr. High, 1997; Iowa Teen Award, 1997; South Carolina Book Award, Young Adult Books, 1997; Young Hoosier Book Award, Middle Books, 1996.

Sent to live with relatives on their farm because of his unhappy home life, an eleven-year-old city boy meets his distant cousin Harris and is given an introduction to a whole new world.

Readers will experience hearts as large as farmers' appetites, humor as broad as the country landscape and adventures as wild as boyhood imaginations. All this adds up to a hearty helping of old-fashioned, rip-roaring entertainment. —*Publishers Weekly*

★ **Hatchet**. Gary Paulsen. Bradbury Press, 1987 195 p. (Brian's saga, 1)
Grades: 6 7 8 9
1. Airplane accidents; 2. Wilderness survival; 3. Survival (after airplane accidents, shipwrecks, etc.); 4. Children of divorced parents; 5. Thirteen-year-old boys; 6. Canada; 7. Survival stories; 8. Adventure stories; 9. Books to movies
9780027701302; 9780330439725, UK; 9781509838790, print, UK; 9781442403321, ebook

LC 87006416

ALA Notable Children's Book, 1988; Buckeye Children's Book Award (Ohio), Grades 6-8, 1991; Flicker Tale Children's Book Award (North Dakota) for Juvenile Fiction, 1990; Georgia Children's Book Award, 1991; Indian Paintbrush Book Award (Wyoming), 1990; Iowa Teen Award, 1990; Massachusetts Children's Book Award, 1995; Maud Hart Lovelace Book Award (Minnesota), 1991; Minnesota Book Award for Young Adult Books, 1988; Sequoyah Book Awards (Oklahoma), Young Adult Books, 1990; Soaring Eagle Book Award (Wyoming), 1997; Surrey Book of the Year Award (British Columbia), 1990; Virginia Readers' Choice Award for Middle School, 1990; William Allen White Children's Book Award (Kansas), 1990; Young Hoosier Book Award, Middle Books, 1991; Newbery Honor Book, 1988.

After a plane crash, thirteen-year-old Brian spends fifty-four days in the wilderness, learning to survive initially with only the aid of a hatchet given him by his mother, and learning also to survive his parents' divorce.

Paulsen's knowledge of our national wilderness is obvious and beautifully shared. —*Voice of Youth Advocates*

A Cry in the Wild

Nightjohn. Gary Paulsen. Delacorte Press, 1993 92 p.
Grades: 7 8 9 10
1. African American girls; 2. Girl slaves; 3. Slavery; 4. Reading; 5. Cruelty; 6. Southern States; 7. Historical fiction
9780385308380

LC 92001222

Young Hoosier Book Award, Middle Books, 1997; ALA Notable Children's Book, 1994.

Twelve-year-old Sarny's brutal life as a slave becomes even more dangerous when a newly arrived slave offers to teach her how to read.

Paulsen is at his best here: the writing is stark and bareboned, without stylistic pretensions of any kind. The narrator's voice is strong and true, the violence real but stylized with an almost mythic tone.... The simplicity of the text will make the book ideal for older reluctant readers who can handle violence but can't or won't handle fancy writing in long books. Best of all, the metaphor of reading as an act of freedom speaks for itself through striking action unembroidered by didactic messages. —*Bulletin of the Center for Children's Books*

Notes from the dog. Gary Paulsen. Wendy Lamb Books, 2009 133 p; Grades: 5 6 7 8
1. People with breast cancer; 2. House sitters; 3. Neighbors; 4. Teenage boys; 5. Self-confidence; 6. Realistic fiction.
9780385738453
LC 2009013300
When Johanna shows up at the beginning of summer to house-sit next door to Finn, he has no idea of the profound effect she will have on his life by the time summer vacation is over.

The plot is straightforward, but Paulsen's thoughtful characters are compelling and their interactions realistic. This emotional, coming-of-age journey about taking responsibilty for one's own happiness and making personal connections will not disappoint. —*Publishers Weekly*

Paintings from the cave: three novellas. Gary Paulsen. Wendy Lamb Books, 2011 160 p.
Grades: 4 5 6 7
1. Violence; 2. Art; 3. Dogs; 4. Foster children; 5. Sculptors; 6. Realistic fiction
9780385746847
LC 2011016287
In these three novellas, Gary Paulsen explores how children can survive the most difficult circumstances through art and the love of dogs. —Provided by publisher.

These novellas portray an unflinching look at children who have endured neglectful and abusive homes and are surviving on their own. The atmospheric first tale, *Man of the Iron Heads*, is narrated by Jake, a boy of about 11, who hides from the local gang until he finds the courage to outsmart its violent leader. *Jo-Jo the Dog-Faced Girl* presents a lonely girl with three adopted dogs who finds acceptance in befriending a girl with leukemia. Finally, *Erik's Rules* celebrates the power of art and is told by Jamie, the younger of two homeless brothers, whose unstable existence changes after a chance encounter with a friendly volunteer at the animal shelter. By incorporating the solace found in dogs, art, libraries, and new friends into these tales of heartache and redemption, Paulsen provides his readers with hope of a better life. —*School Library Journal*

Soldier's heart:being the story of the enlistment and due serviceof the boy Charley Goddard in the First MinnesotaVolunteers: a novel of the Civil War. Delacorte Press, 1998 106 p.
Grades: 7 8 9 10
1. Children and war; 2. Post-traumatic stress disorder; 3. Fifteen-year-old boys; 4. Teenage boys; 5. Teenage soldiers; 6. United States; 7. American Civil War era (1861-1865); 8. Historical fiction; 9. War stories; 10. Classics; 11. Books for reluctant readers
9780385324984
LC 98010038
Jefferson Cup Award, 1999; Minnesota Book Award for Young Adult Books, 1999; YALSA Quick Picks for Reluctant Young Adult Readers, 1999; Booklist Editors' Choice: Books for Youth, 1998; YALSA Best Books for Young Adults, 1999.

Eager to enlist, fifteen-year-old Charley has a change of heart after experiencing both the physical horrors and mental anguish of Civil War combat.

The **Transall** saga. Delacorte Press, 1998 248 p.
Grades: 5 6 7 8

1. Time travel; 2. Thirteen-year-old boys; 3. Wilderness survival; 4. Teenagers; 5. Survival; 6. Science fiction; 7. Books for reluctant readers
9780385321969
LC 97040773
Golden Sower Award (Nebraska), Young Adult, 2002; Iowa Teen Award, 2002; YALSA Quick Picks for Reluctant Young Adult Readers, 1999.

While backpacking in the desert, thirteen-year-old Mark falls into a tube of blue light and is transported into a more primitive world, where he must use his knowledge and skills to survive.

A riveting tale of adventure and action. —*Voice of Youth Advocates*

★ The **winter** room. Gary Paulsen. Orchard Books, 1989 103 p; Grades: 5 6 7 8
1. Norwegian Americans; 2. Uncles; 3. Logging; 4. Farm life; 5. Lumber workers; 6. Minnesota
9780531084397; 9780531058398
LC 89042541
ALA Notable Children's Book, 1990; Northeastern Minnesota Book Awards, 1989; Newbery Honor Book, 1990.

A young boy growing up on a northern Minnesota farm describes the scenes around him and recounts his old Norwegian uncle's tales of an almost mythological logging past.

While this seems at first to be a collection of anecdotes organized around the progression of the farm calendar, Paulsen subtly builds a conflict that becomes apparent in the last brief chapters, forceful and well-prepared.... Lyrical and only occasionally sentimental, the prose is clean, clear, and deceptively simple. —*Bulletin of the Center for Children's Books*
A Richard Jackson Book

Peacock, Shane
Death in the air. Shane Peacock. Tundra Books of Northern New York, 2008 254 p. (Boy Sherlock Holmes, 2)
Grades: 6 7 8 9 10
1. Teenage boy detectives; 2. Murder investigation; 3. Acrobats; 4. Murder; 5. Thirteen-year-old boys; 6. London, England; 7. England; 8. Victorian era (1837-1901); 9. 19th century; 10. Historical mysteries; 11. Canadian fiction; 12. Mysteries
9780887768514
LC 2007927388
OLA Best Bets, 2008.
Young Sherlock Holmes finds himself immersed in a new mystery when he attends a trapeze performance at the magnificent Crystal Palace where the troupe's star falls to his death.

The mystery is solid, the characters compelling, and the historical background is convincing but not overwhelming. Peacock paints a vivid picture of Victorian England, including interesting details about the criminal underground and the lives of the high-trapeze performers in this strong addition to a very promising series. —*Voice of Youth Advocates*

The **dragon** turn. By Shane Peacock. Tundra Books, 2011 264 p. (Boy Sherlock Holmes, 5)
Grades: 6 7 8 9 10
1. Teenage boy detectives; 2. Magicians; 3. Murder suspects; 4. Investigations; 5. Teenage boys; 6. London, England; 7. England; 8. Victorian era (1837-1901); 9. 19th century; 10. Historical mysteries; 11. Canadian fiction; 12. Mysteries
9781770492318; 9781770494114
When Inspector Lestrade and his son arrest magician Alistair Hemsworth for the murder of his rival the Wizard of Nottingham, Sherlock Holmes isn't so sure that they have the right man. The Wizard is missing and his spectacles have been discovered along with pools of

blood in Hemsworth's secret workshop, but no body has been found, and when Holmes digs deeper, he finds that the clues don't add up to a closed case.

★ **Eye** of the crow. Shane Peacock. Tundra Books of Northern New York, 2007 251 p. (Boy Sherlock Holmes, 1)
Grades: 6 7 8 9 10
1. Teenage boy detectives; 2. Murder investigation; 3. Murder suspects; 4. Murder; 5. Thirteen-year-old boys; 6. London, England; 7. England; 8. Victorian era (1837-1901); 9. 19th century; 10. Historical mysteries; 11. Canadian fiction; 12. Mysteries
9780887768507
LC 2006940128
Arthur Ellis Award for Best Juvenile Mystery, 2008; National Chapter of Canada IODE Violet Downey Book Award, 2008; OLA Best Bets, 2007.

Young Sherlock finds comfort studying the world around him and re-constructing events, but when he decides to snoop around for clues to solve a sensational murder, Sherlock is accused of the crime and now must use all his mystery-solving clues to save himself.

A young woman is brutally murdered in a dark back street of White-chapel; a young Arab is discovered with the bloody murder weapon; and a thirteen-year-old Sherlock Holmes, who was seen speaking with the al-leged killer as he was hauled into jail, is suspected to be his accomplice.... Although imaginative reconstruction of Holmes childhood has been the subject of literary and cinematic endeavors, Peacock's take ranks among the most successful. —*Bulletin of the Center for Children's Books*

The **secret** fiend. Shane Peacock. Tundra Books, 2010 Ix, 244 p. : Map (Boy Sherlock Holmes, 4)
Grades: 6 7 8 9 10
1. Teenage boy detectives; 2. Assault and battery; 3. Investigations; 4. Suspicion; 5. Friendship; 6. London, England; 7. England; 8. Victorian era (1837-1901); 9. 19th century; 10. Historical mysteries; 11. Canadian fiction; 12. Mysteries
9780887768538; 9781770493858
LC Bl2010011545
It is 1868, the week that Benjamin Disraeli becomes Prime Minister of the Empire. Sherlock's beautiful but poor admirer, Beatrice appears at the door late at night. She is terrified, claiming that she and her friend have just been attacked by the Spring Heeled Jack on Westminster Bridge and the fiend has made off with her friend.

The **vanishing** girl. Shane Peacock. Tundra Books, 2009 307 p. (Boy Sherlock Holmes, 3)
Grades: 6 7 8 9 10
1. Teenage boy detectives; 2. Kidnapping investigation; 3. Missing girls; 4. Kidnapping; 5. Thirteen-year-old boys; 6. London, England; 7. England; 8. Victorian era (1837-1901); 9. 19th century; 10. Historical mysteries; 11. Canadian fiction; 12. Mysteries
9780887768521
Geoffrey Bilson Award for Historical Fiction, 2010; National Chapter of Canada IODE Violet Downey Book Award, 2010; Ruth and Sylvia Schwartz Children's Book Award for YA-Middle Reader, 2010; OLA Best Bets, 2009.

When a wealthy young girl vanishes in Hyde Park, Sherlock is once again driven to prove himself; in a heart-stopping race against time, an in-nocent boy's survival depends on Sherlock's ability to solve the mysteri-ous puzzle, leading him on a search as complex as the maze that protects the missing girl's hiding place.

The richly descriptive prose offers a vivid sense of both Victorian life and the diverse characters, especially complex, intriguing, and sympa-thetic Sherlock, an outsider conflicted between arrogance and self-doubt,

reason and emotion, and driven by his desire for justice and sorrow over past tragedies. —*Booklist*

Pearsall, Shelley
All shook up. Shelley Pearsall. Alfred A. Knopf, 2008 261 p. : Illustration
Grades: 6 7 8 9
1. Fathers and sons; 2. Embarrassment in teenagers; 3. Children of divorced parents; 4. Children and single parent dating; 5. Single-parent families; 6. Chicago, Illinois; 7. Realistic fiction; 8. Humorous stories
9780375836985
LC 2007022931
When thirteen-year-old Josh goes to stay with his father in Chicago for a few months, he discovers—to his horror—that his dad has become an Elvis impersonator.

This affecting story of a typical, clever middle-school boy dealing with divorce and the new families that sometimes replace the old is also a very funny tale told by a terrifically engaging young narrator. —*Voice of Youth Advocates*

Pearson, Mary
★ The **adoration** of Jenna Fox. Mary E. Pearson. Henry Holt, 2008 272 p. (Jenna Fox chronicles, 1)
Grades: 7 8 9 10 11 12
1. Biotechnology; 2. People in comas; 3. Self-perception in teenage girls; 4. Self-perception; 5. Traffic accident victims; 6. Science fiction; 7. First person narratives.
9780805076684; 9781741756401, Australia
LC 2007027314
School Library Journal Best Books, 2008; Westchester Fiction Award, 2009; YALSA Best Books for Young Adults, 2009; YALSA Popular Paperbacks for Young Adults, 2010.

In the not-too-distant future, when biotechnological advances have made synthetic bodies and brains possible but illegal, a seven-teen-year-old girl, recovering from a serious accident and suffering from memory lapses, learns a startling secret about her existence.

The science...and the science fiction are fascinating, but what will hold readers most are the moral issues of betrayal, loyalty, sacrifice, and survival. —*Booklist*

Dance of thieves. Mary E. Pearson. Henry Holt and Company, 2018 512 p. (Dance of thieves, 1)
Grades: 8 9 10 11 12
1. Outlaws; 2. Guards; 3. Loyalty; 4. Imaginary kingdoms; 5. Thieves; 6. High fantasy; 7. Fantasy fiction; 8. Multiple perspectives
9781250159014; 9781250308979
When outlaw leader meets reformed thief, a cat-and-mouse game of false moves ensues, bringing them intimately together in a battle that may cost them their lives—and their hearts.

Fox forever. Mary E. Pearson. Henry Holt and Company, 2013 304 p. (Jenna Fox chronicles, 3)
Grades: 7 8 9 10 11 12
1. Resistance to government; 2. Biotechnology; 3. Medical ethics; 4. Bioethics; 5. Dystopias; 6. Science fiction; 7. First person narratives.
9780805094343
LC 2012027677
Before he can start a life with Jenna, seventeen-year-old Locke, who was brought back to life in a newly bioengineered body after an accident destroyed his body 260 years ago, must do a favor for the resistance move-ment opposing the nightmarish medical technology.

Vow of thieves. Mary E. Pearson. Henry Holt and Company, 2019 496 p. (Dance of thieves, 2)
Grades: 9 10 11 12
1. Thieves; 2. Warriors; 3. Loyalty; 4. Imaginary wars and battles; 5. Enemies; 6. High fantasy; 7. Fantasy fiction; 8. Multiple perspectives.
9781250162656
A sequel to *Dance of Thieves* finds an ominous warning overshadowing Kazi and Jase's return to Tor's Watch before a violent attack separates the pair, forcing them to pursue unexpected alliances.
The two volumes work most effectively as a pair?the seeds for this book were planted skillfully throughout the first, but it is here that they take glorious root. —*Booklist*

Peck, Richard
Are you in the house alone? Richard Peck. Viking, 1976 156 p.
Grades: 8 9 10 11 12
1. Stalking; 2. Teenage rape victims; 3. Threat (Psychology); 4. Rape case prosecution; 5. High school girls; 6. New York (State); 7. Realistic fiction; 8. Thrillers and suspense
9780440902270
LC 76028810
Edgar Allan Poe Award for Best Juvenile Mystery Novel, 1977.
Gail, a rape victim, learns she must prove her assailant's guilt in order to see him convicted.

★ The **river** between us. Richard Peck. Dial Books, 2003 164 p;
Grades: 7 8 9 10
1. Twin brothers and sisters; 2. Multiracial persons; 3. Civil war; 4. Families; 5. Race relations; 6. United States; 7. New Orleans, Louisiana; 8. American Civil War era (1861-1865); 9. Historical fiction
9780803727359
LC 2002034815
Scott O'Dell Historical Fiction Award, 2004; ALA Notable Children's Book, 2004; Booklist Editors' Choice: Books for Youth, 2003; YALSA Best Books for Young Adults, 2004; National Book Award for Young People's Literature finalist, 2003.
During the early days of the Civil War, the Pruitt family takes in two mysterious young ladies who have fled New Orleans to come north to Illinois.
The harsh realities of war are brutally related in a complex, always surprising plot that resonates on mutiple levels. —*Horn Book Guide*

Peck, Robert Newton
★ A **day** no pigs would die. Knopf 1972 150 p.
Grades: 6 7 8 9
1. Thirteen-year-old boys; 2. Boys and pigs; 3. Children and death; 4. Children and pets; 5. Farm life; 6. Vermont; 7. Classics.
9780394482354
LC 72000259
Colorado Children's Book Award, 1977.
To a thirteen-year-old Vermont farm boy whose father slaughters pigs for a living, maturity comes early as he learns "doing what's got to be done," especially regarding his pet pig who cannot produce a litter.

Peet, Mal
Beck. Mal Peet with Meg Rosoff. 2017 266 p;
Grades: 10 11 12
1. Beck; 2. Multiracial men; 3. Belonging; 4. Depressions; 5. Multiracial boys; 6. Young men; 7. Canada; 8. Historical fiction; 9. Coming-of-age stories; 10. Multiple perspectives
9780763678425; 9781406331127, London

Both harrowing and life-affirming, the final novel from Carnegie Medal-winning author Mal Peet is the sweeping coming-of-age adventure of a mixed race boy transported to North America. Born from a street liaison between a poor young woman and an African soldier in the 1900s, Beck is soon orphaned and sent to the Catholic Brothers in Canada. Shipped to work on a farm, his escape takes him across the continent in a search for belonging. Enduring abuse and many hardships, Beck has times of comfort and encouragement, eventually finding Grace, the woman with whom he can finally forge his life and shape his destiny as a young man. A picaresque novel set during the Depression as experienced by a young black man, it depicts great pain but has an uplifting and inspiring conclusion. Ages 14+
Harrowing but hopeful, its a memorable portrait of a boy struggling to love, be loved, and find his way against overwhelming odds. —*Publishers Weekly*

★ **Tamar:** a novel of espionage, passion and betrayal. Mal Peet. Candlewick Press, 2007 424 p.
Grades: 8 9 10 11 12
1. Soldiers; 2. Granddaughters; 3. Undercover operations; 4. World War II; 5. Resistance to military occupation; 6. Netherlands; 7. Second World War era (1939-1945); 8. 1990s; 9. Love stories; 10. Historical fiction; 11. Parallel narratives
9780763634889
Carnegie Medal, 2005; Booklist Editors' Choice: Books for Youth, 2007; School Library Journal Best Books, 2007; USBBY Outstanding International Book, 2008; YALSA Best Books for Young Adults, 2008.
Peet's plot is tightly constructed, and striking, descriptive language, full of metaphor, grounds the story. —*Booklist*

Peevyhouse, Parker
Where futures end. Parker Peevyhouse. Kathy Dawson Books, 2016 304 p.
Grades: 9 10 11 12
1. Parallel universes; 2. Social media; 3. Teenagers; 4. Science fiction.
9780803741607
LC 2015022984
Five interconnected stories that weave a subtle science-fictional web stretching out from the present into the future, presenting eerily plausible possibilities for social media, corporate sponsorship, and humanity, as our world collides with a mysterious alternate universe.

Pellegrino, Marge
Journey of dreams. Marge Pellegrino. Frances Lincoln Children's Books, 2009 256 p.
Grades: 6 7 8 9
1. Mayan girls; 2. Civil war; 3. Storytelling; 4. State-sponsored terrorism; 5. Hiding; 6. Guatemala; 7. 1980s; 8. Historical fiction.
9781847800619
USBBY Outstanding International Book, 2010.
This novel will captivate both Latin American survivors of civil war and their peers. Outstanding. —*Kirkus*

Pena, Matt de la
Mexican whiteboy. Matt de la Pena. Delacorte Press, 2008 249 p;
Grades: 8 9 10 11 12
1. Father-separated teenage boys; 2. Multiracial teenage boys; 3. Baseball; 4. Identity (Psychology); 5. Self-acceptance; 6. California; 7. Realistic fiction
9780385733106
LC 2007032302

YALSA Popular Paperbacks for Young Adults, 2013; YALSA Best Books for Young Adults, 2009.

Sixteen-year-old Danny searches for his identity amidst the confusion of being half-Mexican and half-white while spending a summer with his cousin and new friends on the baseball fields and back alleys of San Diego County, California.

The author juggles his many plotlines well, and the portrayal of Danny's friends and neighborhood is rich and lively. —*Booklist*

Pennington, Kate
Brief candle. Hodder Children's Books, 2005 262 p.
Grades: 6 7 8 9
1. Bronte, Emily, 1818-1848; 2. Teenage girls; 3. Brothers and sisters; 4. Fourteen-year-old girls; 5. Teenagers; 6. Misfits (Persons); 7. Yorkshire, England; 8. England; 9. Historical fiction.
9780340873700

Along with losing herself in romantic poetry, 14-year-old Emily Bronte loves to wander the wild landscape around her father's parsonage.... Her two passions thrillingly collide when she encounters a distraught young man, whose courtship of a girl outside his station has left him jobless and desperate.... Pennington's homage offers the most to teens familiar with Bronte's *Wuthering Heights*.... But even readers without much previous knowledge about the book's underpinnings...will enjoy the universally accessible view of an ill-fated love and the dreamy restless teen who acts on its behalf. —*School Library Journal*

Perez, Ashley Hope
Out of darkness. By Ashley Hope Perez. Carolrhoda Lab, 2015 396 p.
Grades: 9 10 11 12
1. Interracial romance; 2. Racism; 3. Explosions; 4. Race relations; 5. African American teenage boys; 6. Texas; 7. New London, Texas; 8. 1930s; 9. Historical fiction; 10. Multiple perspectives
9781467742023
Americas Book Award for Children's and Young Adult Literature, 2016; School Library Journal Best Books, 2015; Tomas Rivera Mexican American Children's Book Award, 2016; YALSA Best Fiction for Young Adults, 2016; Michael L. Printz Honor Book, 2016.

Elegant prose and gently escalating action will leave readers gasping for breath at the tragic climax and moving conclusion. —*Booklist*

What can(t) wait. By Ashley Hope Perez. Carolrhoda, 2011 234 p.
Grades: 7 8 9 10
1. Mexican American teenage girls; 2. Options, alternatives, choices; 3. Self-fulfillment in teenage girls; 4. Self-fulfillment; 5. Expectation (Psychology); 6. Texas; 7. Houston, Texas; 8. Realistic fiction.
9780761361558
LC 2010028175
YALSA Best Fiction for Young Adults, 2012.

Marooned in a broken-down Houston neighborhood—and in a Mexican immigrant family where making ends meet matters much more than making it to college—smart, talented Marissa seeks comfort elsewhere when her home life becomes unbearable.

Prez fills a hole in YA lit by giving Marisa an authentic voice that smoothly blends Spanish phrases into dialogue and captures the pressures of both Latina life and being caught between two cultures. —*Kirkus*

Perez, Marlene
Dead is a battlefield. Marlene Perez. Graphia, 2012 208 p. (Dead is— (Spin-off), 1)
Grades: 7 8 9 10

1. Zombies; 2. Crushes in teenage girls; 3. Teenage singers; 4. Perfumes; 5. Teenage boy/girl relations; 6. California; 7. Supernatural mysteries; 8. First person narratives
9780547607344
LC 2011031489
Nightshade High freshman Jessica Walsh's hope of finding normalcy in high school is crushed when fellow students develop zombie-like crushes on a new boy, and she learns that she is a Virago, a woman warrior who fights when her city is in trouble.

Dead is just a dream. Marlene Perez. Harcourt Children's Books, 2013 208 p. (Dead is— (Spin-off), 3)
Grades: 8 9 10
1. Psychics; 2. Nightmares; 3. Murder; 4. Supernatural; 5. High schools; 6. California; 7. Fantasy mysteries; 8. Urban fantasy; 9. First person narratives
9780544102620
LC 2013003883
Paranormal warrior Jessica Walsh enlists the help of her psychic neighbor, Daisy Giordano, to help discover who or what is causing Nightshade, California, residents to die in their sleep with horrified looks on their faces.

Jessica and her virago friends are back in this latest Dead Is series entry. This time they're in the midst of four murders, all seemingly connected to creepy paintings being installed in the homes of Nightshade's most influential citizens. Just when the girls think they've solved the mystery, a bloody clown begins to stalk Jessica, confounding their original suspicions...Girl drama, sweet romance, and murder—what more could young teens want in a breezy read? Booklist.

Perkins, Lynne Rae
★ **As** easy as falling off the face of the earth. Lynne Rae Perkins. Greenwillow Books, 2010 368 p.
Grades: 8 9 10 11 12
1. Teenage boys; 2. Disasters, Minor; 3. Voyages and travels; 4. Accidents; 5. Bad luck; 6. Montana; 7. Realistic fiction.
9780061870903
LC 2009042524
Booklist Editors' Choice: Books for Youth, 2010; YALSA Best Fiction for Young Adults, 2011.

A teenaged boy encounters one comedic calamity after another when his train strands him in the middle of nowhere, and everything comes down to luck.

The real pleasure is Perkins' relentlessly entertaining writing.... Wallowing in the wry humor, small but potent truths, and cheerful implausibility is an absolute delight. —*Booklist*

Perkins, Mitali
Secret keeper. Mitali Perkins. Delacorte Press, 2009 272 p.
Grades: 7 8 9 10
1. Sisters; 2. Arranged marriage; 3. Gender role; 4. Individuality in teenage girls; 5. Family relationships; 6. India; 7. 1970s; 8. First person narratives
9780385733403
LC 2008021475
Notable Books for a Global Society, 2010; Amelia Bloomer List, 2010.

In 1974 when her father leaves New Delhi, India, to seek a job in New York, Ashi, a tomboy at the advanced age of sixteen, feels thwarted in the home of her extended family in Calcutta where she, her mother, and sister must stay, and when her father dies before he can send for them, they must remain with their relatives and observe the old-fashioned traditions that Ashi hates.

The plot is full of surprising secrets rooted in the characters' conflicts and deep connections with each other. The two sisters and their mutual sacrifices are both heartbreaking and hopeful. —*Booklist*

You bring the distant near. Mitali Perkins. Farrar Straus Giroux, 2017 256 p.
Grades: 9 10 11 12
1. East Indian Americans; 2. Immigrants; 3. Families; 4. East Indian American families; 5. Social action; 6. New York City; 7. 1960s; 8. 1990s; 9. Family sagas; 10. Historical fiction; 11. Multiple perspectives
9780374304904
LC 2016057822
Amelia Bloomer List, 2018; School Library Journal Best Books, 2017; YALSA Best Fiction for Young Adults, 2018; Longlisted for the National Book Award for Young People's Literature, 2017; Walter Honor Book, Teen, 2018.
From 1965 through the present, an Indian American family adjusts to life in New York City, alternately fending off and welcoming challenges to their own traditions.
Full of sisterhood, diversity, and complex, strong women, this book will speak to readers as they will undoubtedly find a kindred spirit in at least one of the Das women. —*Booklist*

Perkins, Stephanie

★ **Anna** and the French kiss. Stephanie Perkins. Dutton, 2010 384 p.
Grades: 7 8 9 10
1. Children of authors; 2. Studying abroad; 3. Crushes in teenage girls; 4. Teenage boy/girl relations; 5. Boarding schools; 6. Paris, France; 7. France; 8. Contemporary romances; 9. Teen chick lit.
9780525423270
LC 2009053290
YALSA Best Fiction for Young Adults, 2012; YALSA Popular Paperbacks for Young Adults, 2012.
Who wouldn't jump at the chance to spend her senior year at a boarding school in Paris? Anna Oliphant, that's who. Besides barely speaking French, Anna is perfectly happy at home in Atlanta, Georgia. But Anna's father insists, so Paris it is. And Anna does warm up to the city...especially after she meets gorgeous Etienne St. Clair, who seems to return her interest but already has a girlfriend.
Perkin's debut surpasses the usual chick-lit fare with smart dialogue, fresh characters and plenty of tingly interactions, all set amid pastries, parks and walks along the Seine in arguably the most romantic city in the world. —*Kirkus*

Isla and the happily ever after. Stephanie Perkins. Dutton Books, 2014 352 p.
Grades: 9 10 11 12
1. Studying abroad; 2. Boarding school students; 3. Children of politicians; 4. Teenage romance; 5. Americans in Paris, France; 6. Paris, France; 7. Contemporary romances; 8. Teen chick lit.
9780525425632
Romantic Times Reviewer's Choice Award, 2014.
These choppy waters of neurosis will snag the soaring hearts of readers who have been there (and who hasn't?), and they'll ache upon Isla and Josh's rite-of-passage first doubts about their relationship. Fans of literary heart flutters will love it. —*Booklist*

Lola and the boy next door. Stephanie Perkins. Dutton Books, 2011 384 p.
Grades: 9 10 11 12
1. Former boyfriends; 2. First loves; 3. Costume design; 4. Neighbors; 5. Inventors; 6. Contemporary romances; 7. Teen chick lit.
9780525423287
LC 2011015533
Rainbow List, 2013.
Budding costume designer Lola lives an extraordinary life in San Francisco with her two dads and beloved dog, dating a punk rocker, but when the Bell twins return to the house next door Lola recalls both the friendship-ending fight with Calliope, a figure skater, and the childhood crush she had on Cricket.
Perkins's novel goes a bit deeper than standard chick-lit fare, and Lola is a sympathetic protagonist even when readers disagree with her decisions.... Step back—it's going to fly off the shelves. —*School Library Journal*

Peterfreund, Diana

Across a star-swept sea. Diana Peterfreund. 2013 464 pages
Grades: 9 10 11 12
1. Social classes; 2. Spies; 3. Resistance to government; 4. Rescues; 5. Dystopias; 6. Science fiction; 7. Classics-inspired fiction.
9780062006165
LC 2013003082
Sixteen-year-old Persis Blake struggles to balance her life as a socialite and a secret spy in a future where Regs, or regular people, have power over the Reduced—those genetically engineered or drugged into physical and mental impairments.

For darkness shows the stars. Diana Peterfreund. Balzer + Bray, 2012 384 p.
Grades: 9 10 11 12
1. Dystopias; 2. Social classes; 3. Genetic engineering; 4. Family problems; 5. Teenage romance; 6. Science fiction; 7. Classics-inspired fiction.
9780062006141
LC 2011042126
Elliot North fights to save her family's land and her own heart in this post-apocalyptic reimaging of Jane Austen's Persuasion.
The story stands on its own, a richly envisioned portrait of a society in flux, a steely yet vulnerable heroine, and a young man who does some growing up. —*Publishers Weekly*

Petrus, Junauda

The **stars** and the blackness between them. By Junauda Petrus. Dutton Books for Young Readers, 2019 320 p.
Grades: 9 10 11 12
1. African American teenage girls; 2. Sick persons; 3. Teenage girl/girl relations; 4. Lesbian teenagers; 5. Identity (Psychology); 6. Minneapolis, Minnesota; 7. Minnesota; 8. LGBTQIA romances; 9. Love stories; 10. Magical realism.
9780525555483
LC 2019003294
Coretta Scott King Honor Book for Authors, 2020.
Told in two voices, sixteen-year-old Audre and Mabel, both young women of color from different backgrounds, fall in love and figure out how to care for each other as one of them faces a fatal illness.
Told through unflinching prose and poetry laced with astrological themes, Petrus' work breaks the mold of traditional writing and uses unconventional dialogue and voice to bring life to the story of two authentic, unapologetic Black girls as they face the hardest truths head on and discover everlasting love that reaches even the most distant corners of the cosmos. —*Booklist*

Philbin, Joanna

The **daughters**. Joanna Philbin. Poppy, 2010 275 p; (Daughters (Joanna Philbin), 1)

Grades: 6 7 8 9
1. Children of celebrities; 2. Rich teenage girls; 3. Teenage fashion models; 4. Fame; 5. Best friends; 6. New York City; 7. Realistic fiction; 8. Teen chick lit
9780316049009

LC 2009045621

In New York City, three fourteen-year-old best friends who are all daughters of celebrities watch out for each other as they try to strike a balance between ordinary high school events, such as finding a date for the homecoming dance, and family functions like walking the red carpet with their famous parents.

This is a fun, quick read.... Readers will be intrigued by the well-drawn characters and their growth over the course of several months. —*School Library Journal*

Philippe, Ben

Charming as a verb. Ben Philippe. Balzer and Bray 2020 392 p.
Grades: 9 10 11 12
1. High school students; 2. Teenage boys; 3. Neighbors; 4. Swindlers and swindling; 5. Haitian Americans; 6. Romantic comedies; 7. First person narratives
9780062824141
School Library Journal Best Books, 2020.

Henri "Halti" Haltiwanger can charm just about anyone. But his easy smiles mask a burning ambition to attend his dream college, Columbia University. There is only one person who seems immune to Henri's charms: his "intense" classmate and neighbor Corinne Troy. When she uncovers Henri's less-than-honest dog-walking scheme, she blackmails him into helping her change her image at school. Henri agrees, seeing a potential upside for himself. Soon what started as a mutual hustle turns into something more surprising than either of them ever bargained for....

This humorous, first-person narrative with a conversational, almost conspiratorial, tone will captivate readers even with the almost-too-neat ending. —*Kirkus*

The **field** guide to the North American teenager. Ben Philippe. Balzer + Bray, 2018 384 p.
Grades: 8 9 10
1. Stereotypes (Social psychology); 2. New students; 3. Moving, Household; 4. Cynicism; 5. Making friends; 6. Austin, Texas; 7. Texas; 8. Coming-of-age stories; 9. Realistic fiction; 10. Black Canadian fiction.
9780062824110

LC 2018014221
OLA Best Bets, 2019; William C. Morris YA Debut Award, 2020.

When Norris, a Black French Canadian, starts his junior year at an Austin, Texas, high school, he views his fellow students as cliches from "a bad 90s teen movie."

Philpot, Chelsey

Even in paradise. Chelsey Philpot. 2014 368 pages
Grades: 9 10 11 12
1. Female friendship; 2. Artists; 3. Social acceptance; 4. Boarding schools; 5. Schools; 6. Realistic fiction
9780062293695

LC 2013047956
Seventeen-year-old Charlotte "Charlie" Ryder, a girl from a working class family whose talent for the arts has gained her entry into the exclusive St. Anne's school, is drawn into the circle of the larger-than-life Julia Buchanan, a former senator's daughter.

There is nothing in this Gatsbyesque world we havent seen before, but Philpot knows that and happily hands over the tragic goods: disaffected, charming, well-drawn characters; gauzy tuxedo-and-gown parties;

and a wistful, melancholy tone that makes it all seem achingly fleeting. —*Booklist*

Pierce, Tamora

Alanna: the first adventure. By Tamora Pierce. Atheneum, 1983 241 p. (Song of the lioness, 1)
Grades: 7 8 9 10
1. Girl adventurers; 2. Knights and knighthood; 3. Disguises; 4. Girl healers; 5. Tortall (Imaginary place); 6. High fantasy; 7. Fantasy fiction; 8. Classics.
9780689309946; 9781442426412; 9781481416498; 9781481439589; 9780606361033; 9780689853234; 9780689878558; 9780807287729; 9780844670027; 9781417720613; 9781439120293; 9781439529638; 9781448748402

LC 83002595
Eleven-year-old Alanna, who aspires to be a knight even though she is a girl, disguises herself as a boy to become a royal page, and learns many hard lessons along her path to high adventure.

Bloodhound. Tamora Pierce. Random House, 2009 240 p. (Beka Cooper, 2)
Grades: 7 8 9 10
1. Counterfeits and counterfeiting; 2. Rookie police; 3. Girl psychics; 4. Criminal investigation; 5. Police; 6. High fantasy; 7. Fantasy fiction; 8. Diary novels
9780375814693
Amelia Bloomer List, 2010.

Having been promoted from "Puppy" to "Dog," Beka, now a full-fledged member of the Provost's Guard, and her former partner head to a neighboring port city to investigate a case of counterfeit coins.

Quirky, endearing characters save the story. —*Booklist*

Briar's book. Scholastic Press, 1999 258 p. (Circle of magic (Tamora Pierce), 4)
Grades: 6 7 8 9
1. Teenage wizards; 2. Teenage misfits; 3. Plague; 4. Wizards; 5. Diseases; 6. Fantasy fiction.
9780590553599

LC 98026148
Briar, a young mage-in-training, and his teacher Rosethorn must use their magic to fight a deadly plague that is ravaging Summersea.

This fast-paced, imaginative fantasy could be read and enjoyed on its own, but it works better as part of the quartet, which covers the span of a year and begins with Sandry's Book. —*School Library Journal*

Daja's book. Scholastic Press, 1998 234 p. (Circle of magic (Tamora Pierce), 3)
Grades: 6 7 8 9
1. Teenage wizards; 2. Teenage misfits; 3. Forest fires; 4. Wizards; 5. Teenagers — Friendship; 6. Fantasy fiction.
9780590553582

While at Gold Ridge Castle, Daja and 3 other mages-in-training develop their unique magical talents as they try to stop a devastating forest fire.

The fantasy elements of the series as a whole are satisfyingly well imagined, as are the main characters, and readers who have not read the first two novels will understand what is going on. —*School Library Journal*

★ **First** test. Random House, 1999 216 p. (Protector of the small, 1)
Grades: 6 7 8 9
1. Knights and knighthood; 2. Gender role; 3. Royal pages; 4. Determination in girls; 5. Ten-year-old girls; 6. High fantasy; 7. Fantasy fiction.

9780679889144

LC 98030903

Ten-year-old Keladry of Mindelan, daughter of nobles, serves as a page but must prove herself to the males around her if she is ever to fulfill her dream of becoming a knight.

Pierce spins a whopping good yarn, her plot balanced on a solid base of action and characterization. —*Bulletin of the Center for Children's Books*

Lady knight. Tamora Pierce. Random House, 2002 429 p. Illustration; Map (Protector of the small, 4)
Grades: 6 7 8 9
1. Knights and knighthood; 2. Gender role; 3. Refugee camps; 4. Women knights; 5. Tortall (Imaginary place); 6. High fantasy; 7. Fantasy fiction.
9780375814655; 9780375914652

LC 2002069862

When she became a knight, eighteen-year-old Kel hoped to be given a combat post, but instead she finds herself named commander of an outpost of refugees, where she must face the unnatural forces of the evil Balyce.

Kel's world is completely realized in quick, precise detail. —*Booklist*

Page. Random House, 2000 257 p. (Protector of the small, 2)
Grades: 6 7 8 9
1. Knights and knighthood; 2. Gender role; 3. Royal pages; 4. Eleven-year-old girls; 5. Tortall (Imaginary place); 6. High fantasy; 7. Fantasy fiction.
9780679889151; 9780679989158

LC 99089894

Keladry of Mindelan continues her training to become a squire with the aid of a new maid, the support of her friends, interference from some other pages, and some serious, even dangerous opposition. Includes "Cast of characters" and glossary.

The plot is engaging and Kel's character growth continues. —*School Library Journal*

Illustrated with map.

★ **Sandry's** book. Tamora Pierce. Scholastic, 1997 252 p. (Circle of magic (Tamora Pierce), 1)
Grades: 6 7 8 9
1. Teenage wizards; 2. Teenage misfits; 3. Orphans; 4. Misfits (Persons); 5. Wizards; 6. Fantasy fiction.
9780590553568

LC 95039540

Pierce has created an excellent new world where magic is a science and utterly believable and populated it with a cast of well-developed characters. —*Booklist*

Squire. By Tamora Pierce. Random House, 2001 399 p. Map (Protector of the small, 3)
Grades: 6 7 8 9
1. Knights and knighthood; 2. Gender role; 3. Squires; 4. Tortall (Imaginary place); 5. Keladry of Mindelan (Fictitious character); 6. High fantasy; 7. Fantasy fiction.
9780679889168; 9780679989165

LC 2001019280

YALSA Best Books for Young Adults, 2002.

After becoming a squire to Lord Raoul, commander of the King's Own, Kel of Mindelan, must face a terrifying test in the Chamber of the Ordeal before she can be a knight.

The novel expertly juxtaposes outward action and introspection, as Kel matures in both her knightly skills and personal outlook. —*Horn Book Guide*

★ **Terrier**. Tamora Pierce. Random House, 2006 592 p. (Beka Cooper, 1)
Grades: 7 8 9 10
1. Girl psychics; 2. Extrasensory perception; 3. Rookie police; 4. Cooper, Rebakah (Fictitious character); 5. Teenage girls; 6. High fantasy; 7. Fantasy fiction; 8. First person narratives.
9780375814686

LC 2006014834

West Australian Young Readers's Book Award (WAYRBA), Older Readers, 2009; YALSA Best Books for Young Adults, 2007.

When sixteen-year-old Beka becomes "Puppy" to a pair of "Dogs," as the Provost's Guards are called, she uses her police training, natural abilities, and a touch of magic to help them solve the case of a murdered baby in Tortall's Lower City.

Pierce deftly handles the novel's journal structure, and her clear homage to the police-procedural genre applies a welcome twist to the girl-legend-in-the-making story line. —*Booklist*

★ **Trickster's** choice. Tamora Pierce. Random House, 2003 422 p. : Map (Trickster series (Tamora Pierce), 1)
Grades: 7 8 9 10
1. Sixteen-year-old girls; 2. Girl spies; 3. Girl slaves; 4. Tortall (Imaginary place); 5. Alianne; 6. Fantasy fiction; 7. Asian-influenced fantasy
9780375814662; 9780375828799; 9780375914669; 9780375814723; 9780439968089, print, UK

LC 2003005202

YALSA Popular Paperbacks for Young Adults, 2012; YALSA Best Books for Young Adults, 2004.

Alianne must call forth her mother's courage and her father's wit in order to survive on the Copper Isles in a royal court rife with political intrigue and murderous conspiracy.

This series opener is packed with Pierce's alluring mix of fantasy, adventure, romance, and humor, making the book an essential purchase for school and public libraries. —*Voice of Youth Advocates*

★ **Wild** magic. Tamora Pierce. Atheneum, 1992 259 p. (Immortals (Tamora Pierce), 1)
Grades: 6 7 8 9 10
1. Thirteen-year-old girls; 2. Human/animal communication; 3. Women knights; 4. Magic; 5. Wizards; 6. High fantasy; 7. Fantasy fiction.
9780689317613; 9780008304072, Paperback, UK

LC 91043909

The mage Numair, the knight Alanna, and Queen Thayet enlist thirteen-year-old Daine's help to battle the dreadful immortal creatures that have recently begun to attack the kingdom of Tortall.

Pignat, Caroline

Wild geese. Caroline Pignat. Red Deer Press, 2010 288 p.
Grades: 7 8 9 10
1. Immigrants, Irish; 2. Separated friends, relatives, etc; 3. Disguises; 4. Best friends; 5. Immigration and emigration; 6. Canada; 7. 19th century; 8. Historical fiction; 9. First person narratives; 10. Canadian fiction.
9780889954328

Kit, pursued as a criminal, has safely made it on board an immigrant coffin ship bound for Canada, disguised as a boy and accompanied by Mick, her best friend. Along the way, with historically gritty authenticity, she encounters a lethal fever, near-starvation conditions and terrifying storms.... When she finally reaches Canada, there is more disease and separation. —*Kirkus*

Sequel to: *Greener grass*; Sequel: *Timber wolf*.

Pink, Randi

Girls like us. Randi Pink. Feiwel and Friends, 2019 320 p.
Grades: 9 10 11 12
1. Teenage pregnancy; 2. Reproductive rights; 3. Female friendship;
4. Unplanned pregnancy; 5. Teenage girls; 6. 1970s; 7. Historical
fiction; 8. Multiple perspectives
9781250155856; 9781250155863

LC 2019002029

School Library Journal Best Books, 2019.

In the summer of 1972, three girls from very different backgrounds
struggle to come to terms with being pregnant.

As women s right to choose is placed under scrutiny once again, these
stories are a reminder of what horrors lie ahead if history repeats itself.
—*Booklist*

Into white. Randi Pink. 2016 288 pages
Grades: 8 9 10 11
1. Racism; 2. Identity (Psychology); 3. Bullying and bullies; 4.
Self-discovery; 5. Body image; 6. Alabama; 7. Montgomery, Alabama
9781250070210; 9781250086907

LC 2016937797

This debut ought to inspire readers to have conversations among
themselves about family, empathy, community, and respect for others.
—*Booklist*

Pitcher, Annabel

My sister lives on the mantelpiece. By Annabel Pitcher. Little, Brown
& Co, 2012 214 p.
Grades: 6 7 8 9 10
1. Grief in families; 2. Terrorism; 3. Children of alcoholic fathers; 4.
Grief; 5. Prejudice; 6. England; 7. Realistic fiction.
9780316176903; 9781444001839; 9781780620299, print, UK
ALA Notable Children's Book, 2013.

With his family still grieving over his sister's death in a terrorist
bombing seven years earlier, twelve-year-old Jamie is far more interested
in his cat, Roger, his birthday Spiderman T-shirt, and keeping his new
Muslim friend Sunya a secret from his father.

Silence is goldfish: a novel. By Annabel Pitcher. 2016 352 p.
Grades: 7 8 9 10
1. Teenage girls who are mute; 2. Family secrets; 3. Identity
(Psychology); 4. Fathers; 5. Bullying and bullies; 6. England; 7.
Manchester, England; 8. Realistic fiction; 9. Coming-of-age stories.
9780316370752; 9780316370745, ebook, US; 9780316406369,
ebook, US

LC 2015024312

Fifteen-year-old Tess Turner of Manchester, England, decides to stop
speaking in the wake of discovering a heartbreaking family secret.

Tess, fifteen, is an offbeat English introvert with a highly involved
dad. After she discovers his startling blog post recounting her own birth
('It wasn't my daughter. It was...some sperm donor's'), her anger embold-
ens her to stand up against Dad's expectations. Her rebellion of choice is
silence, but her narrative voice speaks loudly—Tess is a witty and appealing protagonist. —*Horn Book Guide*

Originally published in Great Britain in 2015 by Orion Publishing
Group

Pixley, Marcella Fleischman

Ready to fall. Marcella Pixley. Farrar Straus Giroux, 2017 320 p.
Grades: 9 10 11 12
1. Grief; 2. Theater; 3. Loss (Psychology); 4. Friendship; 5. Grief in
teenage boys; 6. Realistic fiction
9780374303587; 9781250180711

LC 2016058779

Seventeen-year-old Max, struggling to come to terms with his
mother's death, is cast as the ghost in Hamlet and finds strength in his new
theater friends.

...this work is ultimately an affecting novel about parental relationships, grieving, and recovery. —*School Library Journal*

Margaret Ferguson Books.

Plozza, Shivaun

Tin heart. Shivaun Plozza. 2018 320 p.
Grades: 8 9 10 11 12
1. Transplant recipients; 2. Identity (Psychology); 3. Chronic diseases;
4. Second chances; 5. Family feuds; 6. Coming-of-age stories; 7.
Romantic comedies; 8. Australian fiction.
9780143786276; 9781760146719; 9781250312761; 9781250312778,
ebook, US

Funny and direct, this book by Plozza...is capable of balancing heartbreak, first love, mortality, and the absurd. —*Publishers Weekly*

Poblocki, Dan

The **haunting** of Gabriel Ashe. Dan Poblocki. Scholastic Press, 2013
288 p.
Grades: 6 7 8
1. Monsters; 2. Neighbors; 3. Imagination; 4. Friendship; 5. Games; 6.
Massachusetts; 7. Horror
9780545402705

LC 2013004009

YALSA Best Fiction for Young Adults, 2014.

Since eighth-grader Gabriel Ashe moved into his grandmother's
house he has been spending a lot of time playing in the woods with his
new friend Seth, but the games Seth invents involve a child-eating monster called the Hunter, and Gabriel is not sure how much is imagination
and how much real.

Podos, Rebecca

The **wise** and the wicked. Rebecca Podos. 2019 368 pages
Grades: 9 10 11 12
1. Precognition; 2. Mother-separated teenage girls; 3. Fate and
fatalism; 4. Extrasensory perception; 5. Family feuds; 6. Paranormal
fiction
9780062699022

LC 2018055696

Growing up hearing stories about her magically powerful women ancestors, a Russian-American girl who has inherited a family ability to see
her own death contemplates a life of free will when an aunt's passing is
contrary to her visions.

A beautifully rendered story about sacrifice, vengeance, survival, secrets, and lies. Recommended for all collections. —*Library Journal*

Polisner, Gae

In sight of stars. Gae Polisner. Wednesday Books, 2018 288 p.
Grades: 10 11 12
1. Grief in teenage boys; 2. Psychiatric hospital patients; 3. Teenage
boys with mental illnesses; 4. Mental illness; 5. Death; 6. Realistic
fiction
9781250143839

Seventeen-year-old Klee's father was the center of his life. He introduced Klee to the great museums of New York City and the important artists on their walls, he told him stories made of myths and magic. Until his
death.

An intense, sometimes graphic, totally heartbreaking portrait of a character who will keep pages turning. —*Booklist*

The **pull** of gravity. Gae Polisner. Frances Foster Books, 2011 208 p.
Grades: 6 7 8 9
1. Steinbeck, John; 2. Family problems; 3. Death; 4. Grief; 5. Grief in teenagers; 6. Teenagers; 7. Rochester, New York; 8. Realistic fiction; 9. Coming-of-age stories.
9780374371937
LC 2010021749
When their friend Scooter dies of a rare disease, teenagers Nick Gardner and Jaycee Amato set out on a secret journey to find the father who abandoned "The Scoot" when he was an infant, and give him a signed first edition of *Of Mice and Men.*

Polisner's first novel begins with a bang and ends with another .... There is a great deal to enjoy throughout, and literary kids will surely enjoy a subplot involving John Steinbeck. —*Booklist*

Pollen, Samuel
★ The **year** I didn't eat. Samuel Pollen. Yellow Jacket, 2019 400 p.
Grades: 6 7 8 9
1. People with anorexia; 2. Teenage boys; 3. Eating disorders; 4. Anorexia nervosa; 5. Fourteen-year-old boys; 6. England; 7. Realistic fiction; 8. First person narratives
9781499808087; 9781999863357
A 14-year-old boy with anorexia records his efforts to control his eating disorder in a therapist-prescribed journal that documents the progression of his illness and its impact on his perspectives and family.

Max is a thoughtful, appealing narrator to whom readers will relate, and his story brings attention to an illness most commonly associated with girls and older teens or adults. —*Booklist*

Polonsky, Ami
★ **Gracefully** Grayson. Ami Polonsky. Disney/Hyperion, 2014 256 p.
Grades: 6 7 8 9
1. Transgender children; 2. Girl orphans; 3. School plays; 4. Theater; 5. Self-acceptance; 6. Chicago, Illinois; 7. Realistic fiction; 8. LGBTQIA fiction
9781423185277
LC 2014010155
Rainbow List, 2016.
Grayson, a transgender twelve-year-old, learns to accept her true identity and share it with the world.

Sixth grader Grayson daydreams about being a girl, despite being seen by everyone as male. Grayson keeps people at a distance until Amelia moves to town. After landing the (female) lead in a play, Grayson fights for the right to present her truest self to others—both on and off stage. Polonsky captures her protagonist's loneliness, then courage, in an immediate and intimate narrative. —*Horn Book Guide*

Pon, Cindy
Fury of the phoenix. By Cindy Pon. Greenwillow Books, 2011 416 p.
Grades: 9 10 11 12
1. Teenage girl adventurers; 2. Father-separated teenage boys; 3. Spirits; 4. Monsters; 5. Courage; 6. China; 7. Fantasy fiction; 8. Asian-influenced fantasy
9780061730252
LC 2010011700
When Ai Ling leaves her home and family to accompany Chen Yong on his quest to find his father, haunted by the ancient evil she thought she had banished to the underworld, she must use her growing supernatural powers to save Chen Yong from the curses that follow her.

Sequel to: *Silver phoenix.*

★ **Silver** phoenix: beyond the Kingdom of Xia. Cindy Pon. Greenwillow Books, 2009 338 p.
Grades: 9 10 11 12
1. Father-separated teenage girls; 2. Demons; 3. Fate and fatalism; 4. Extortion; 5. Martial arts; 6. China; 7. Fantasy fiction; 8. Asian-influenced fantasy
9780061730214
Booklist Editors' Choice: Books for Youth, 2009.
With her father long overdue from his journey and a lecherous merchant blackmailing her into marriage, seventeen-year-old Ai Ling becomes aware of a strange power within her as she goes in search of her parent.

Pon's writing, both fluid and exhilarating, shines whether she's describing a dinner delicacy or what it feels like to stab an evil spirit in the gut. There's a bit of sex here, including a near rape, but it's all integral to a saga that spins and slashes as its heroine tries to find her way home. —*Booklist*

Sequel: *Fury of the phoenix.*

Pool, Katy Rose
★ **There** will come a darkness. Katy Rose Pool. Henry Holt and Company, 2019 496 p. (Age of Darkness (Katy Rose Pool), 1)
Grades: 8 9 10 11 12
1. Prophets; 2. Prophecies; 3. End of the world; 4. Fate and fatalism; 5. Free will and determinism; 6. High fantasy; 7. Fantasy fiction.
9781250211750; 9781250619853; 9780356513713, Paperback, UK; 9780356513539, Paperback, UK
LC 2019017243
William C. Morris Debut Award finalist, 2020.
For generations the Seven Prophets guided humanity with their visions, ending wars and uniting nations—until the day they vanished, leaving behind the promise of a looming Age of Darkness and the birth of a Prophet who could be the world's salvation...or the cause of its destruction.

A well-crafted, surprising, and gripping start to a new trilogy. —*Kirkus*

Porter, Sarah
★ **Vassa** in the night. Sarah Porter. Tor Teen, a Tom Doherty and Associates book, 2016 303 p.
Grades: 9 10 11 12
1. Witches; 2. Baba Yaga (Legendary character); 3. Retail stores; 4. Magic; 5. Dolls; 6. Brooklyn, New York City; 7. Urban fantasy; 8. Fairy tale and folklore-inspired fiction
9780765380548
YALSA Best Fiction for Young Adults, 2017.
Inspired by the Russian folktale classic "Vassilissa the Beautiful," a modern fairy tale finds a girl from a working-class section of a magical Brooklyn tapping the powers of her dead mother's protective doll to defend against the evil of a murderous owner of a local convenience store.

Sixteen-year-old Vassa Lisa Lowenstein's mother is dead, and her father is gone. She has a stepmother and two stepsisters. It's an odd living arrangement but no more peculiar than a lot of things in her working-class Brooklyn neighborhood. The nights have been especially strange, growing longer and longer. When her stepsister sends Vassa out in the middle of the night for lightbulbs, the only store that's still open is the local BY's. Everyone knows about BY's, and its owner Babs Yagg, but people do tend to remember a store that dances around on chicken legs and has a habit of decapitating shoplifters.... A deliberate lack of romantic tension makes this a refreshing read, and elements of traditional horror blend well with high-concept fantasy in this surprising and engaging tale. A must-have for YA urban fantasy collections. —*School Library Journal*

Portes, Andrea

Anatomy of a misfit. Andrea Portes. HarperTeen, an imprint of HarperCollinsPublishers, 2014 336 p.

Grades: 9 10 11 12

1. Teenage girls; 2. Popularity; 3. Teenage boy/girl relations; 4. Misfits (Persons); 5. Teenagers; 6. Nebraska; 7. Love stories; 8. First person narratives

9780062313645

LC 2014008722

The third most popular girl in school's choice between the hottest boy in town and a lonely but romantic mistfit ends in tragedy and self-realization.

Anika Dragomir looks like the All-American girl-next-door, but 'nobody knows that on the inside I am spider soup.' 'Nerd-ball turned goth romance hero' Logan McDonough and God's-gift-to-Nebraska, Jared Kline, vie for her affections. A dramatic climax is foreshadowed by sections in italics that hint at tragedy. Anika's observations are razor-sharp, especially when she's describing other people (and especially when she's ragging on her family). —*Horn Book Guide*

Portman, Frank

King Dork. Frank Portman. Delacorte Press, 2006 352 p.

Grades: 10 11 12

1. Salinger, J. D; 2. High school students; 3. Losers (Persons); 4. Fathers — Death; 5. Teenagers; 6. Teenage boys; 7. Mysteries; 8. Realistic fiction

9780385732918; 9780385903127; 9780141322803, print, UK

LC 2005012556

YALSA Popular Paperbacks for Young Adults, 2012; YALSA Best Books for Young Adults, 2007.

High school loser Tom Henderson discovers that *The Catcher in the Rye* may hold the clues to the many mysteries in his life.

Mature situations, casual sexual experiences, and allusions to Salinger suggest an older teen audience, who will also best appreciate the appended bandography and the very funny glossary. —*Booklist*

Sequel: *King Dork approximately.*

Powell, Laura

Burn mark. By Laura Powell. Bloomsbury Children's Books : 2012 304 p. (Burn mark, 1)

Grades: 7 8 9 10 11 12

1. Witches; 2. Conspiracies; 3. Undercover operations; 4. Crime; 5. Fifteen-year-olds; 6. London, England; 7. England; 8. Urban fantasy

9781599908434; 9781408815229, print, UK

LC 2011034464

In an alternate London, England, the lives of a fifteen-year-old girl eagerly awaiting the development of her "fae," or witch abilities, and the son of a man who sentences witches to death by burning, intersect when the son makes a startling discovery.

Sequel: *Witch fire.*

The **game** of triumphs. Laura Powell. Alfred A. Knopf, 2011 288 p.

Grades: 7 8 9 10

1. Tarot; 2. Teenage girl orphans; 3. Interdimensional travel; 4. Supernatural; 5. Murder; 6. London, England; 7. Urban fantasy

9780375865879

Fifteen-year-old Cat and three other London teens are drawn into a dangerous game in which Tarot cards open doorways into a different dimension and while there is everything to win, losing can be fatal.

Original and engrossing. —*Kirkus*

Sequel: *The Master of Misrule.*

Powell, Patricia Hruby

★ **Loving** vs. Virginia: a documentary novel of the landmark civil rights case. By Patricia Hruby Powell; artwork by Shadra Strickland. Chronicle Books, 2017 260 p.

Grades: 7 8 9 10

1. Loving, Richard Perry; 2. Interracial marriage; 3. Race relations; 4. Civil Rights Movement; 5. African American women; 6. Imprisonment; 7. Virginia; 8. 1950s; 9. 1960s; 10. Historical fiction; 11. Novels in verse; 12. First person narratives

9781452125909

A powerful and riveting account of an American couple in love when that love was ruled illegal in many American states. —*Kirkus*

Powell, Randy

Swiss mist. Randy Powell. Farrar, Straus and Giroux, 2008 224 p.

Grades: 6 7 8 9 10

1. Loners; 2. Family relationships; 3. Divorce; 4. Teenage boys; 5. High school sophomores; 6. Washington (State); 7. Coming-of-age stories; 8. Pacific Northwest fiction

9780374373566

LC 2007027680

Follows Milo from fifth grade, when his mother and philosopher father get divorced, through tenth grade, when his mother has married a wealthy businessman and Milo is still a bit of a loner, looking for the meaning of life.

This book is rewardingly remarkable for the characters and bits of truth that Milo never stops pursuing, even as he learns that truth is not what matters most. —*School Library Journal*

Three clams and an oyster. Randy Powell. Farrar Straus Giroux, 2002 216 p.

Grades: 7 8 9 10

1. Teenage boys; 2. Friendship; 3. Flag football; 4. High school juniors; 5. Sixteen-year-old boys; 6. Seattle, Washington; 7. Washington (State); 8. Humorous stories; 9. Realistic fiction; 10. Pacific Northwest fiction

9780374375263

LC 2001054833

YALSA Best Books for Young Adults, 2003.

During their humorous search to find a fourth player for their flag football team, three high school juniors are forced to examine their long friendship, their individual flaws, and their inability to try new experiences.

Powell, William Campbell

Expiration day. William Campbell Powell. 2014 320 p.

Grades: 8 9 10 11 12

1. Robots; 2. Diaries; 3. Teenage girls; 4. Near future; 5. Infertility; 6. England; 7. Science fiction; 8. Coming-of-age stories; 9. Diary novels.

9780765338280

LC 2013025453

Golden Duck Awards, Hal Clement Award for Young Adult, 2015.

It is the year 2049, and humanity is on the brink of extinction. Tania Deeley has always been told that she's a rarity: a human child in a world where most children are sophisticated androids manufactured by Oxted Corporation.

The author pays homage to the genre's giants while combining realistic characters (both human and android) and detailed worldbuilding with an unpredictably optimistic conclusion. In the end, the thoughtful balance of narrative and description and the well-paced plot are marred only by a mildly distracting subplot that unreels in interstitial Intervals. An auspicious debut. —*Kirkus*

A Tom Doherty Associates book.

Power, Rory

Burn our bodies down. Rory Power. Delacorte Press, 2020 352 p.
Grades: 9 10 11 12

1. Mothers and daughters; 2. Family secrets; 3. Emotional abuse; 4. Manipulation (Social sciences); 5. Intergenerational relations; 6. Nebraska; 7. Psychological suspense; 8. Horror; 9. First person narratives.
9780525645627; 9780525645634; 9781529022834, Paperback, UK

Growing up alongside a mother who refuses to speak about the past, a teen who longs for a family discovers a photograph that leads to her mother's hometown, where she encounters disturbing revelations.

Power creates a vivid world with a gothic horror?like setting, where mutant corn stalks produce double helix cobs with pink flesh and where grandmothers are not exactly what they seem.... A riveting, often frightening read. —*Publishers Weekly*

★ **Wilder** girls. Rory Power. Random House Childrens Books, 2019 368 p.
Grades: 8 9 10 11 12

1. Quarantine; 2. Survival; 3. Climate change; 4. Diseases; 5. Missing persons; 6. Maine; 7. Thrillers and suspense; 8. Horror
9780525645580, HRD, US; 9781529021264, Paperback, UK

Friends Hetty, Byatt, and Reece go to extremes trying to uncover the dark truth about the mysterious disease that has had them quarantined at their boarding school on a Maine island.

Power's evocative, haunting, and occasionally gruesome debut will challenge readers to ignore its bewitching presence. —*Booklist*

Powers, J. L.

This thing called the future: a novel. By J.L. Powers. Cinco Puntos Press, 2011 213 p;
Grades: 8 9 10 11 12

1. Children of sick persons; 2. Zulu (African people); 3. Medical care; 4. Sick mothers; 5. Healers; 6. South Africa; 7. Realistic fiction.
9781933693958

LC 2010037399

YALSA Best Fiction for Young Adults, 2012.

Fourteen-year-old Khosi's mother wants her to get an education to break out of their South African shantytown, although she herself is wasting away from an untreated illness, while Khosi's grandmother, Gogo, seeks help from a traditional Zulu healer.

Powers composes a compelling, often harrowing portrait of a struggling country, where old beliefs and rituals still have power, but can't erase the problems of the present. Readers will be fully invested in Khosi's efforts to secure a better future. —*Publishers Weekly*

Pratchett, Terry

★ **Dodger**. By Terry Pratchett. HarperCollins, 2012 336 p.
Grades: 7 8 9 10

1. Dickens, Charles, 1812-1870; 2. Homeless teenagers; 3. Criminals; 4. Todd, Sweeney (Legendary character); 5. Fourteen-year-old boys; 6. Teenage boys; 7. London, England; 8. Great Britain; 9. Victorian

era (1837-1901); 10. 19th century; 11. Humorous stories; 12. Historical fiction.
9780062009494, hardback, US; 9780385619271, UK; 9780552577205, Paperback, UK

LC 2012022155

Booklist Editors' Choice: Books for Youth, 2012; YALSA Best Fiction for Young Adults, 2013; Michael L. Printz Honor Book, 2013.

Surviving by his wits in an alternative-universe London ruled by a young Queen Victoria, the intrepid young Dodger inadvertently foils a murderous Sweeney Todd's operation and encounters numerous fictional and historical characters, including Darwin, Disraeli and Dickens.

★ **I** shall wear midnight. Terry Pratchett. Harper, 2010 272 p. (Discworld (Young adult), 5)
Grades: 7 8 9 10

1. Teenage witches; 2. Hate; 3. Memory; 4. Villains; 5. Witches; 6. Fantasy fiction; 7. Humorous stories.
9780061433047

LC Bl2010019256

Amelia Bloomer List, 2012; Nebula Awards: Andre Norton Award, 2010.

Combines comedy and action in the final adventure of Tiffany Aching and the Wee Free Men as the young witch faces an insidious new foe, one who whispers threats of violence and quietly unleashes mayhem.

The final adventure in Pratchett's Tiffany Aching series brings this subset of Discworld novels to a moving and highly satisfactory conclusion. —*Publishers Weekly*

★ **Nation**. Terry Pratchett. HarperCollins, 2008 272 p.
Grades: 7 8 9 10 11 12

1. Tsunamis; 2. Survival; 3. Interpersonal relations; 4. Island life; 5. Survival (after environmental catastrophe); 6. Survival stories; 7. Adventure stories
9780061433016; 9780552577199, Paperback, UK

ALA Notable Children's Book, 2009; Booklist Editors' Choice: Books for Youth, 2008; Boston Globe-Horn Book Award for Fiction and Poetry, 2009; Los Angeles Times Book Prize for Young Adult Fiction, 2008; USBBY Outstanding International Book, 2009; YALSA Best Books for Young Adults, 2009; School Library Journal Best Books, 2008; Michael L. Printz Honor Book, 2009.

After a devastating tsunami destroys all that they have ever known, Mau, an island boy, and Daphne, an aristocratic English girl, together with a small band of refugees, set about rebuilding their community and all the things that are important in their lives.

Quirky wit and broad vision make this a fascinating survival story on many levels. —*Booklist*

★ The **Wee** Free Men. Terry Pratchett. Harper Collins Publishers, 2003 263 p; (Discworld (Young adult), 2)
Grades: 7 8 9 10

1. Preteen girls; 2. Miniature persons (Imaginary characters); 3. Fairies; 4. Witches; 5. Warriors; 6. Fantasy fiction; 7. Humorous stories
9780060012366; 9780060012373; 9780552576307, print, UK; 9780857535450, hbk.

LC 2002015396

ALA Notable Children's Book, 2004; Amelia Bloomer List, 2004; YALSA Best Books for Young Adults, 2004; School Library Journal Best Books, 2003.

A young witch-to-be named Tiffany teams up with the Wee Free Men, a clan of six-inch-high blue men, to rescue her baby brother and ward off a sinister invasion from Fairyland.

Pratchett invites readers into his well-established realm of Discworld where action, magic, and characters are firmly rooted in literary reality.

Humor ripples throughout, making tense, dangerous moments stand out in stark contrast. —*Bulletin of the Center for Children's Books*
Sequel: *A Hat full of sky.*

Preston, Caroline

The **scrapbook** of Frankie Pratt. Caroline Preston. Ecco Press, 2011 240 p.
Grades: 11 12 Adult
1. Scrapbooks; 2. Women authors; 3. Men/women relations; 4. Growing up; 5. Moving to a new city; 6. 1920s; 7. Historical fiction; 8. Diary novels; 9. Illustrated books; 10. Adult books for young adults.
9780061966903
Alex Award, 2012.

Using an array of vintage memorabilia, a novel told in the form of a scrapbook follows Frankie Pratt, who goes to Vassar in 1920 with dreams of becoming a writer, which becomes a stepping stone to an international adventure.

Preus, Margi

Enchantment Lake: a Northwoods mystery. Margi Preus. University of Minnesota Press, 2015 200 p. (Enchantment Lake mysteries, 1)
Grades: 6 7 8 9 10
1. Murder investigation; 2. Parent-separated teenage girls; 3. Small towns; 4. Lakes; 5. Treasure troves; 6. Minnesota; 7. Mysteries
9780816683024
Preus offers intriguing characters, suspenseful moments, and a love interest—plenty to keep readers involved. —*Booklist*

★ **Shadow** on the mountain: a novel inspired by the true adventures of a wartime spy. By Margi Preus. Amulet Books, 2012 286 p.
Grades: 6 7 8 9
1. Spies; 2. World War II; 3. Resistance to military occupation; 4. Underground newspapers; 5. Fourteen-year-old boys; 6. Norway; 7. Second World War era (1939-1945); 8. 1940s; 9. Historical fiction.
9781419704246
LC 2012015623
Notable Books for a Global Society, 2013.

In Nazi-occupied Norway, fourteen-year-old Espen joins the resistance movement, graduating from deliverer of illegal newspapers to courier and spy.

Price, Charlie

The **interrogation** of Gabriel James. Charlie Price. Farrar Straus Giroux, 2010 176 p.
Grades: 9 10 11 12
1. Teenage witnesses; 2. Murder; 3. Responsibility; 4. Witnesses; 5. Questioning; 6. Montana; 7. Mysteries; 8. Books for reluctant readers
9780374335458
LC 2009037309
Edgar Allan Poe Award for Best Young Adult, 2011; YALSA Quick Picks for Reluctant Young Adult Readers, 2011.

As an eyewitness to two murders, a Montana teenager relates the shocking story behind the crimes in a police interrogation interspersed with flashbacks.

The author writes intriguing and believable characters and keeps a stream of realism moving through the story even when neither readers nor Gabriel are really sure what's going on. Patience from readers won't be required, though, as plenty of action keeps the narrative moving while the plot details unfold. The result is not only suspense but a memorable and believable characterization. Top notch. —*Kirkus*

Priest, Cherie

★ **I** am Princess X. By Cherie Priest; illustrated by Kali Ciesemier. Arthur A. Levine, 2015 256 p.
Grades: 7 8 9 10 11 12
1. Best friends — Death; 2. Subcultures; 3. Suspicion; 4. Teenage girls; 5. Traffic accidents; 6. Seattle, Washington; 7. Mysteries; 8. Graphic novel hybrids; 9. Pacific Northwest fiction; 10. Books for reluctant readers
9780545620857
Westchester Fiction Award, 2016; YALSA Quick Picks for Reluctant Young Adult Readers, 2016.

Best friends Libby Deaton and May Harper invented Princess X when they were in fifth grade, but when the car Libby is in goes off a bridge, she is presumed dead, and the story came to an end—except now, three years later, Princess X is suddenly everywhere, with a whole underground culture focused on a webcomic, and May believes her friend must be alive

May and Libby created Princess X on the day they met in fifth grade. That was before Libby and her mother died in a car crash. Now May is 16 and looking at another long, lonely summer in Seattle when she spots a Princess X sticker on the corner of a store window. Suddenly she starts seeing Princess X everywhere, including in a webcomic at IAmPrincessX.com, where the princess story is eerily similar to Libby's.... An excellent book with loads of cross-genre and cross-format appeal. —*School Library Journal*

Prinz, Yvonne

The **vinyl** princess. By Yvonne Prinz. HarperTeen, 2010 320 p.
Grades: 8 9 10 11 12
1. Records, Phonograph; 2. Music lovers; 3. Blogs; 4. Zines; 5. Music; 6. Berkeley, California; 7. First person narratives; 8. Coming-of-age stories; 9. Realistic fiction.
9780061715839
LC 2009014270
OLA Best Bets, 2010.

Allie, a sixteen-year-old who is obsessed with LPs, works at the used record store on Telegraph Ave. and deals with crushes—her own and her mother's—her increasingly popular blog and zine, and generally grows up over the course of one summer in her hometown of Berkeley, California.

Prinz writes with a genuine passion for music that readers who live to listen will recognize, and in this heartfelt, often-hilarious story, she shows the profound ways that music can shape lives. —*Booklist*

Pullman, Philip

The **amber** spyglass. Philip Pullman. A. A. Knopf, 2000 518 p. (His dark materials, 3)
Grades: 7 8 9 10 11 12
1. Girl heroes; 2. Familiars (Spirits); 3. Quests; 4. Fathers and daughters; 5. Dark matter (Astronomy); 6. Fantasy fiction; 7. Steampunk; 8. Classics.
9780679879268; 9781407153308, print, UK; 9781407154176, print, UK; 9780590542449, print, UK; 9781407104065, print, UK; 9781743837139, Paperback, UK
LC 44776
ALA Notable Children's Book, 2001; British Book Award for Children's Book of the Year, 2000; West Australian Young Readers's Book Award (WAYRBA), Older Readers, 2002; Whitbread Book Award for Children's Book of the Year, 2001; Whitbread Book of the Year Award, 2001; YALSA Best Books for Young Adults, 2002.

Lyra and Will find themselves at the center of a battle between the forces of the Authority and those gathered by Lyra's father, Lord Asriel.
Sequel to: *The Subtle Knife*; Sequel: *Lyra's Oxford*.

★ The **book** of dust; Volume 1,. Philip Pullman. Alfred A. Knopf Books for Young Readers, 2017 464 p. (Book of dust, 1)
Grades: 8 9 10 11 12
1. Familiars (Spirits); 2. Eleven year old boys; 3. Totalitarianism; 4. Dust; 5. Freedom of speech; 6. Oxford, England; 7. England; 8. Fantasy fiction.
9780375815300; 9780857561084, paperback, UK; 9780385604413, hardback, UK; 9781984830579
Booklist Editors' Choice: Books for Youth, 2017; School Library Journal Best Books, 2017; YALSA Best Fiction for Young Adults, 2018.
Magisterial storytelling will sweep readers along; the cast is as vividly drawn as ever; and big themes running beneath the surface invite profound responses and reflection. —*Kirkus*

★ The **book** of dust; Volume 2,. Philip Pullman. Alfred A. Knopf, 2019 656 p. (Book of dust, 2)
Grades: 8 9 10 11 12
1. Familiars (Spirits); 2. Young women; 3. College teachers; 4. College students; 5. Dark matter (Astronomy); 6. Oxford, England; 7. England; 8. Fantasy fiction
9780553510669; 9780553510676; 9780241373347, Paperback, UK; 9780241373330, Hardback, UK; 9780241373354, Paperback, UK
Unaware of her professor's role in bringing her and the alethiometer to Jordan College, 20-year-old undergraduate Lyra and her daemon, Pantalaimon, receive secrets from a dying man about a daemon-haunted city and the origins of Dust.
Magisterial storytelling will sweep readers along; the cast is as vividly drawn as ever; and big themes running beneath the surface invite profound responses and reflection. —*Kirkus*

★ The **golden** compass. Philip Pullman. A.A. Knopf, 1995 399 p. (His dark materials, 1)
Grades: 7 8 9 10 11 12
1. Familiars (Spirits); 2. Girl heroes; 3. Quests; 4. Child kidnapping victims; 5. Transformations (Magic); 6. Arctic regions; 7. Fantasy fiction; 8. Steampunk; 9. Books to movies
9780679879244; 9780593178553, PAP,US; 9781407154169, UK; 9781407153322,print, UK; 9781407186108, Paperback, UK; 9781405663489, print, UK; 9780439951784,print, UK; 9781407104058, print, UK; 9780439944663, print, UK
ALA Notable Children's Book, 1997; Booklist Editors' Choice: Books for Youth, 1996; British Book Award for Children's Book of the Year, 1996; Carnegie Medal, 1995; YALSA Best Books for Young Adults, 1997.
Accompanied by her shape-shifting daemon, Lyra Belacqua sets out to prevent her best friend and other kidnapped children from becoming the subject of gruesome experiments in the Far North.
This first title in a fantasy trilogy introduces the characters and sets up the basic conflict, namely, a race to unlock the mystery of a newly discovered type of charged particles simply called dust that may be a bridge to an alternate universe. The action follows 11-year-old protagonist Lyra Belacqua from her home at Oxford University to the frozen wastes of the North on a quest to save dozens of kidnapped children from the evil Gobblers, who are using them as part of a sinister experiment involving dust. —*Library Journal*
First published 1995 by Scholastic Children's Books under title: *His dark materials: northern lights*.

The **subtle** knife. Philip Pullman. A.A. Knopf, 1997 326 p. (His dark materials, 2)

Grades: 7 8 9 10 11 12
1. Girl heroes; 2. Familiars (Spirits); 3. Quests; 4. Magic; 5. Transformations (Magic); 6. Fantasy fiction; 7. Steampunk; 8. Classics.
9780679879251; 9781407153315, print, UK; 9781407154183, print, UK; 9781405663496, print, UK; 9780439994132, print, UK; 9781407104072, print, UK; 9781743837122, Paperback, UK
LC 97673
Booklist Editors' Choice: Books for Youth, 1997; YALSA Best Books for Young Adults, 1998.
As the boundaries betweens worlds begin to dissolve, Lyra and her daemon help Will Parry in his search for his father and for a powerful, magical knife.
More than fulfilling the promise of *The Golden Compass*, this second volume in the His Dark Materials trilogy starts off at a heart-thumping pace and never slows down. —*Publishers Weekly*
Sequel to: *The Golden Compass*.

Pung, Alice
Lucy and Linh. Alice Pung. 2016 352 p.
Grades: 9 10 11 12
1. Girls' schools; 2. Asian Australians; 3. Children of immigrants; 4. Peer pressure in teenagers; 5. Bullying and bullies; 6. Australia; 7. Realistic fiction; 8. Coming-of-age stories; 9. Australian fiction
9780399550485; 9780399550492; 9781863956925, paperback, Australia; 9781922231581, ebook, Australia; 9780399550508, ebook, US
Children's Book Council of Australia: Notable Australian Children's Book; NSW Premier's Literary Awards, Ethel Turner Prize for Young People's Literature, 2016; YALSA Best Fiction for Young Adults, 2017.
In Australia, Lucy tries to balance her life at home surrounded by her Chinese immigrant family, with her life at a pretentious private school.
A bracing, enthralling gut-punch and an essential read for teens, teachers, and parents alike. —*Kirkus*
Originally published in Australia by Black Inc. in 2014 under title: *Laurinda*.

Pyle, Howard
The **story** of King Arthur and his knights. Written and illustrated by Howard Pyle. C. Scribner's Sons, 1954 312 p. (King Arthur series (Howard Pyle), 1)
Grades: 8 9 10 11 12
1. Arthur, King; 2. Merlin (Legendary character); 3. Queen Guinevere (Legendary character); 4. Great Britain; 5. Arthurian legends; 6. Illustrated books.
9780684148144
LC 76019113
Retells the adventures of Sir Gawaine, Sir Pellias, Merlin, and King Arthur, and describes how the Round Table came into being.

Qamar, Amjed
Beneath my mother's feet. Amjed Qamar. Atheneum Books for Young Readers, 2008 198 p;
Grades: 7 8 9 10
1. Women; 2. Women's role; 3. Determination in teenage girls; 4. Fourteen-year-old girls; 5. Teenage girls; 6. Pakistan
9781416947288
LC 2007019001
Amelia Bloomer List, 2009.
When her father is injured, fourteen-year-old Nazia is pulled away from school, her friends, and her preparations for an arranged marriage, to

help her mother clean houses in a wealthy part of Karachi, Pakistan, where she finally rebels against the destiny that is planned for her.

This novel provides a fascinating glimpse into a world remarkably distant from that of most American teens, and would be an excellent suggestion for readers who want to know about how other young people live. —*School Library Journal*

Quick, Matthew

Every exquisite thing. By Matthew Quick. Little, Brown and Company, 2016 272 p.
Grades: 9 10 11 12
1. Teenage girls; 2. Resistance (Psychology) in teenage girls; 3. Self-fulfillment; 4. Nonconformity; 5. Risk-taking in teenagers; 6. First person narratives; 7. Realistic fiction.
9780316379595; 9780316379588, ebook, US; 9780316379625, ebook, US
LC 2015011641
YALSA Best Fiction for Young Adults, 2017.

Nanette O'Hare, a star student and athlete, is given a mysterious out-of-print cult classic novel by her beloved teacher that sparks the rebel within her, but as she befriends the reclusive author and attempts to insert her true self into the world with wild abandon, Nanette learns the hard way that sometimes rebellion comes at a high price.

Conventional high-schooler Nanette's life changes after she befriends Nigel Booker, elderly author of a classic cult novel about nonconformity. Booker sets her up with fellow teen fan Alex, a poet with a troubled, violent past. This is an ode to revolutionary literature—its power to inspire change and incite action (positive and otherwise); it's also an engaging bildungsroman as Nanette comes into her own. —*Horn Book Guide*

Forgive me, Leonard Peacock. By Matthew Quick. Little, Brown and Company, 2013 288 p.
Grades: 9 10 11 12
1. Suicide; 2. Former friends; 3. Neighbors; 4. Teachers; 5. Violinists; 6. Realistic fiction; 7. First person narratives.
9780316221337
YALSA Best Fiction for Young Adults, 2014.

Eighteen-year-old Leonard Peacock is packing a handgun and planning to kill his former best friend, then himself. Over the course of one intense day (with flashbacks), Leonard's existential crisis is delineated through an engaging first-person narrative supplemented with letters from the future that urge Leonard to believe in a life beyond the ubermorons at school. Complicated characters and ideas mark this memorable story. —*Horn Book Guide*

Quigley, Dawn

Apple in the middle. Dawn Quigley. North Dakota State University Press, 2018 264 p.
Grades: 6 7 8 9 10
1. Multiracial teenage girls — Identity; 2. Indian reservations; 3. Adjustment (Psychology); 4. Native American teenage girls; 5. Native American families; 6. North Dakota; 7. Coming-of-age stories; 8. Realistic fiction.
9781946163073
American Indian Youth Literature Awards Honor Book, Young Adult Book, 2020.

Apple in the Middle is a coming-of-age novel with an unexpected look at what happens when two cultures collide and our only tour guide is a quirky, offbeat outcast.—

Quintero, Isabel

★ **Gabi,** a girl in pieces. By Isabel Quintero. Cinco Puntos Press, 2014 208 p.
Grades: 9 10 11 12
1. Mexican American teenage girls; 2. Children of drug abusers; 3. Teenage pregnancy; 4. Gay teenagers; 5. High schools; 6. Realistic fiction; 7. Diary novels; 8. Coming-of-age stories; 9. Books for reluctant readers
9781935955948; 9781935955955
LC 2014007658
Amelia Bloomer List, 2015; Booklist Editors' Choice: Books for Youth, 2014; Land of Enchantment Book Award (New Mexico): Black bears (Grades 9-12), 2018; School Library Journal Best Books: Fiction, 2014; Tomas Rivera Mexican American Children's Book Award, 2015; William C. Morris YA Debut Award, 2015; YALSA Best Fiction for Young Adults, 2015; YALSA Quick Picks for Reluctant Young Adult Readers, 2015; YALSA Quick Picks for Reluctant Young Adult Readers: Top Ten, 2015.

Sixteen-year-old Gabi Hernandez chronicles her senior year in high school as she copes with her friend Cindy's pregnancy, friend Sebastian's coming out, her father's meth habit, her own cravings for food and cute boys, and especially, the poetry that helps forge her identity.

A fresh, authentic and honest exploration of contemporary Latina identity. —*Kirkus*

Quintero, Sofia

Efrain's secret. Sofia Quintero. Alfred A. Knopf, 2010 240 p.
Grades: 8 9 10 11 12
1. Ambition in teenage boys; 2. Urban teenagers; 3. Teenage drug dealers; 4. Drug traffic; 5. College choice; 6. Bronx, New York City; 7. Realistic fiction.
9780375947063

Ambitious high school senior and honor student Efrain Rodriguez makes some questionable choices in pursuit of his dream to escape the South Bronx and attend an Ivy League college.

Quintero imbues her characters with unexpected grace and charm.... Mostly, though, it is Quintero's effortless grasp of teen slang that gives her first-person story its heart. —*Booklist*

Rabb, Margo

Kissing in America. Margo Rabb. HarperCollinsPublishers, 2015 256 p.
Grades: 9 10 11 12
1. Grief in teenage girls; 2. Cross-country automobile trips; 3. Best friends; 4. Grief; 5. Teenage boy/girl relations; 6. Realistic fiction; 7. First person narratives
9780062322371
Amelia Bloomer Lists, 2016; YALSA Best Fiction for Young Adults, 2016.

A lineup of friends and meddling relatives adds humor and depth beyond the romance plot, giving Eva a chance to repair her relationships. —*Horn Book Guide*

Raina, Arushi

★ **When** morning comes. Arushi Raina. Tradewind Books, 2016 232 p.
Grades: 8 9 10 11 12
1. Resistance to government; 2. High school students; 3. Race relations; 4. Apartheid; 5. Soweto Uprising, June 16, 1976; 6. South Africa; 7. 1970s; 8. Historical fiction; 9. Multiple perspectives
9781896580692
Children's Africana Book Awards, Older Readers, 2018.

It's 1976 in South Africa, and four young people are living in Johannesburg and its black township, Soweto: Zanele, a black female student organizer; Meena, a South Asian girl working at her father's shop; Jack, an Oxford-bound white student; and Thabo, a teen-gang member, or tsotsi. From each of their points of view, this book explores the roots of the Soweto Uprising and the edifice of apartheid in a South Africa about to explode.

A sophisticated political thriller that challenges readers and offers no pat endings. The appended historical note and glossary are essential. —*Booklist*

Randall, Thomas
   Dreams of the dead. By Thomas Randall. Bloomsbury Children's Books, 2009 304 p. (Waking, 1)
Grades: 8 9 10 11 12
   1. Death; 2. Nightmares; 3. Murder; 4. Supernatural; 5. Fathers and daughters; 6. Japan; 7. Horror
9781599902500
                                        LC 2008030844
   After her mother dies, sixteen-year-old Kara and her father move to Japan, where he teaches and she attends school, but she is haunted by a series of frightening nightmares and deaths that might be revenge—or something worse.
   The story has suspense, mystery, and horror. It will be a great hit with fans of manga, anime, or Japanese culture. —*School Library Journal*
   Christopher Golden writing as Thomas Randall.

   Spirits of the Noh. By Thomas Randall. Bloomsbury Children's Books, 2010 272 p. (Waking, 2)
Grades: 8 9 10 11 12
   1. Missing teenagers; 2. Demons; 3. Curses; 4. School plays; 5. Demonic possession; 6. Japan; 7. Horror
9781599902517
                                        LC 2009018251
   Just as Kara and her friends at the Monju-no-Chie school in Japan are beginning to get over the horrifying deaths of two students, another monster emerges to terrorize the school.
   Using all the usual horror elements, Randall constructs a fine teen chiller complete with mean-girl drama, a dash of romance and the angst of teens who believe that adults do not understand them. —*Kirkus*

Redgate, Riley
   Final draft. Riley Redgate. Amulet Books, 2018 336 p.
Grades: 9 10 11 12
   1. Teenage girl authors; 2. Creativity; 3. Risk-taking (Psychology); 4. Approval-craving in women; 5. Eighteen-year-old women; 6. Realistic fiction.
9781419728723; 9781419734878
                                        LC 2017057158
   Eighteen-year-old Laila Piedra is a biracial aspiring author whose creative writing teacher always told her she has a special talent, so when he suddenly dies and is replaced by Nadiya Nazarenko, a Pulitzer Prize-winning novelist who is sadistically critical and perpetually unimpressed, Laila grows obsessed with gaining the woman's approval and is led to believe she must choose between perfection and sanity, but rejecting her all-powerful mentor may be the only way for Laila to thrive.

   ★ **Note** worthy. Riley Redgate. Amulet Books, 2017 384 p.
Grades: 9 10 11 12
   1. Choirs; 2. Disguises; 3. Teenage girl singers; 4. Chinese American teenage girls; 5. Bisexual teenage girls; 6. New York (State); 7. Realistic fiction; 8. First person narratives
9781419723735

Amelia Bloomer List, 2018.
   Feeling undervalued because of musical talents that place her outside the spotlight, Jordan disguises herself as a boy to gain entry into a competitive, all-male a cappella group that is looking for a singer with her vocal range.
   A heart song for all readers who have ever felt like strangers in their own skins. —*Kirkus*

Reed, Amy Lynn
   Clean. Amy Reed. Simon Pulse, 2011 272 p;
Grades: 9 10 11 12
   1. Teenage girls with anorexia; 2. Alcoholic teenagers; 3. Rehabilitation; 4. Rehabilitation centers; 5. Interpersonal relations; 6. Seattle, Washington; 7. Washington (State); 8. Realistic fiction; 9. Multiple perspectives; 10. First person narratives; 11. Books for reluctant readers
9781442413443
                                        LC 2010026771
YALSA Quick Picks for Reluctant Young Adult Readers, 2012.
   A group of teens in a Seattle-area rehabilitation center form an unlikely friendship as they begin to focus less on their own problems with drugs and alcohol by reaching out to help a new member, who seems to have even deeper issues to resolve.

   ★ The **Nowhere** Girls. By Amy Reed. Simon Pulse, 2017 416 p.
Grades: 9 10 11 12
   1. Rape culture; 2. Sexism; 3. Rape; 4. New students; 5. Teenagers with Asperger's syndrome; 6. Oregon; 7. Realistic fiction; 8. Multiple perspectives
9781481481731; 9781481481755, ebook, US
                                        LC 2016044338
Amelia Bloomer List, 2018; Westchester Fiction Award, 2019.
   Three misfit girls come together to avenge the rape of a girl none of them knew and in the process start a movement that transforms the lives of everyone around them.
   ...a highly nuanced and self-reflective narrative that captures rape culture's ubiquitous harm without swerving into didactic, one-size-fits-all solutions or relying on false notions of homogenous young womanhood. Scandal, justice, romance, sex positivity, subversive anti-sexism just try to put it down. —*Kirkus*

Reed, Jaime
   Living violet: the Cambion chronicles. Jaime Reed. Dafina KTeen Books/Kensington Pub. Corp, 2012 Viii, 311 p; (Cambion chronicles, 1)
Grades: 9 10 11 12
   1. Summer romance; 2. Paranormal phenomena; 3. Multiracial teenage girls; 4. Secrecy; 5. Heart attack; 6. Virginia; 7. Paranormal romances; 8. First person narratives; 9. African American fiction
9780758269249
   Samara is intrigued by her flirtatious co-worker, Caleb, but his secrets draw Samara into a world that places her loved ones in danger, forcing her to take a risk that will change her life forever.
   The novel explores issues of self-control, peer pressure, and relationship boundaries amid drama in the human and paranormal worlds, and when Sam's eyes turn green at the end of book, teens will want the next installment in the series immediately. —*School Library Journal*

Reeve, Philip
   ★ **Fever** Crumb. By Philip Reeve. Scholastic Press, 2010 336 p. (Hungry city chronicles, 1)
Grades: 6 7 8 9 10

1. Abandoned children; 2. Prejudice; 3. Identity (Psychology); 4. Girl apprentices; 5. Orphans; 6. London, England; 7. England; 8. Science fiction; 9. Steampunk
9780545207195; 9781407193212, Paperback, UK

LC 2009015457

YALSA Popular Paperbacks for Young Adults, 2012; ALA Notable Children's Book, 2011; Booklist Editors' Choice: Books for Youth, 2010; YALSA Best Fiction for Young Adults, 2011; USBBY Outstanding International Book, 2011; School Library Journal Best Books, 2010.

Foundling Fever Crumb has been raised as an engineer although females in the future London, England, are not believed capable of rational thought, but at age fourteen she leaves her sheltered world and begins to learn startling truths about her past while facing danger in the present.

Reeve's captivating flights of imagination play as vital a role in the story as his endearing heroine, hiss-worthy villains, and nifty array of supporting characters. —*Booklist*

★ **Here** lies Arthur. Philip Reeve. Scholastic, 2007 289 p.
Grades: 7 8 9 10
1. Arthur, King; 2. Bards and bardism; 3. Storytelling; 4. Queen Guinevere (Legendary character); 5. Girls; 6. Merlin (Legendary character); 7. Great Britian; 8. 6th century; 9. Arthurian fantasy; 10. Historical fantasy
9780439955331; 9781407103587, print, UK; 9781407195995, Paperback, UK
ALA Notable Children's Book, 2009; Booklist Editors' Choice: Books for Youth, 2008; Carnegie Medal, 2008; Nestle Children's Book Prize for Nine to Eleven Year Olds, 2007; School Library Journal Best Books, 2008; USBBY Outstanding International Book, 2009; YALSA Best Books for Young Adults, 2009.

When her village is attacked and burned, Gwyna seeks protection from the bard Myrddin, who uses Gwyna in his plan to transform young Arthur into the heroic King Arthur.

Powerfully inventive.... Events rush headlong toward the inevitable ending, but Gwyna's observations illuminate them in a new way. —*Booklist*

Reger, Rob
Dark times. Rob Reger and Jessica Gruner; illustrated by Rob Reger and Buzz Parker. Harper, 2010 256 p. (Emily the Strange novels, 3)
Grades: 7 8 9 10
1. Teenage nonconformists; 2. Antiheroes and antiheroines; 3. Time travel (Past); 4. Magic; 5. Families; 6. 1790s; 7. Diary novels; 8. First person narratives
9780061452352; 9780007365913, print, UK

LC 2009032256

Traveling in her homemade Time-Out Machine, Emily journeys to the eighteenth century to uncover the truth behind a Strange family rumor.

Entertaining and thought-provoking, Emily's adventures maintain the series' popularity and present an interesting choice for a mother/daughter reading group. —*Voice of Youth Advocates*

Stranger and stranger. Rob Reger and Jessica Gruner; illustrated by Rob Reger and Buzz Parker. Bowen Press, 2010 272 p. (Emily the Strange novels, 2)
Grades: 7 8 9 10
1. Clones and cloning; 2. Teenage nonconformists; 3. Goth culture (Subculture); 4. Antiheroes and antiheroines; 5. Teenage girls; 6. Diary novels; 7. First person narratives
9780061452338; 9780061452321
Emily's second journal, a sequel to *The Lost Days* (HarperCollins, 2009), is a dark delight, filled with all kinds of Strangeness.... Fans of the

first book and newcomers alike will thoroughly enjoy the zaniness and clamor for more. —*School Library Journal*

Reichs, Brendan
Chrysalis. Brendan Reichs. G.P. Putnam's Sons Books for Young Readers, 2019 416 p. (Project Nemesis, 3)
Grades: 8 9 10 11 12
1. Survival; 2. Cooperation; 3. Teenagers; 4. Alliances; 5. Conspiracies; 6. Idaho; 7. Apocalyptic fiction; 8. Science fiction; 9. Multiple perspectives
9780525517054; 9781529022995, Paperback, UK

LC 2018051632

After the test subjects of Project Nemesis find themselves in the dangerous Fire Lake valley and discover that they may not be alone, they realize that they have to overcome their old conflicts and work together if they hope to survive.

Genesis. Brendan Reichs. G. P. Putnam's Sons, 2018 320 p. (Project Nemesis, 2)
Grades: 8 9 10 11 12
1. Survival; 2. Conspiracies; 3. Couples; 4. Betrayal; 5. Computer programs; 6. Idaho; 7. Science fiction; 8. Science fiction thrillers; 9. Multiple perspectives.
9780399544965

LC 2017028972

Min, Noah, and the sophomores of Fire Lake must fight to survive in the second phase of Project Nemesis.

Nemesis was a page-turner, and Genesis has plenty of fevered action and startling surprises, especially as the book nears its conclusion. ...Fans of the first book will certainly want to read this and look forward to the trilogys conclusion. Booklist..

★ **Nemesis**. Brendan Reichs. G.P. Putnam's Sons, 2017 320 p. (Project Nemesis, 1)
Grades: 8 9 10 11 12
1. Asteroids — Collisions with Earth; 2. Conspiracies; 3. Experimental medicine; 4. Survival; 5. Murder; 6. Idaho; 7. Apocalyptic fiction; 8. Science fiction; 9. Multiple perspectives
9780399544934; 9781509860302, print, UK

LC 2016021737

As the Anvil, an enormous asteroid, threatens to end all life on Earth, sixteen-year-old Min begins to uncover a lifetime of lies, a sinister conspiracy involving all students in her sophomore class in Fire Lake, Idaho.

Reichs's new novel offers readers a glimpse into the final moments of a preapocalyptic world, as seen through the eyes of two radically different teens. —*School Library Journal*

Reinhardt, Dana
★ The **things** a brother knows. Dana Reinhardt. Wendy Lamb Books, 2010 288 p.
Grades: 7 8 9 10 11 12
1. Soldiers; 2. Post-traumatic stress disorder; 3. Walking; 4. Brothers; 5. Former Marines; 6. Boston, Massachusetts; 7. Washington, D.C; 8. Realistic fiction
9780375844553

LC 2009035867

Sydney Taylor Book Award for Teen Readers, 2011; YALSA Popular Paperbacks for Young Adults, 2014; Booklist Editors' Choice: Books for Youth, 2010; YALSA Best Fiction for Young Adults, 2011; School Library Journal Best Books, 2010.

Although they have never gotten along well, seventeen-year-old Levi follows his older brother Boaz, an ex-Marine, on a walking trip from

Boston to Washington, D.C. in hopes of learning why Boaz is completely withdrawn.

Reinhardt's poignant story of a soldier coping with survivor's guilt and trauma, and his Israeli American family's struggle to understand and help, is timely and honest. —*Booklist*

Renn, Diana

Tokyo heist. By Diana Renn. Viking, 2012 384 p.
Grades: 7 8 9 10 11 12

1. Gogh, Vincent van; 2. Art thefts; 3. Children of artists; 4. Fathers and daughters; 5. Summer; 6. Sixteen-year-old girls; 7. Seattle, Washington; 8. Tokyo, Japan; 9. Mysteries
9780670013326
LC 2011043364

After a high-profile art heist of three van Gogh drawings in her home town of Seattle, sixteen-year-old Violet Rossi finds herself in Japan with her artist father, searching for the related van Gogh painting.

The plot has lots of twists and turns, leaving readers on edge, and a hint of romance... Teens will learn about Japanese culture, and fans of manga and art students will rejoice that they can relate to the protagonist and story. —*Library Journal*

Rennison, Louise

Angus, thongs and full-frontal snogging: confessions of Georgia Nicolson. Louise Rennison... HarperCollins Publishers, 2000 247 pages (Confessions of Georgia Nicolson, 1)
Grades: 7 8 9 10

1. Teenage girls; 2. Teenage boy/girl relations; 3. Teenage romance; 4. Fourteen-year-old girls; 5. Nicolson, Georgia (Fictitious character); 6. England; 7. Diary novels; 8. Realistic fiction; 9. Teen chick lit; 10. Books for reluctant readers
9780060288143; 9780060288716
LC 99040591

Booklist Editors' Choice: Books for Youth, 2000; Garden State Teen Book Award (New Jersey), Fiction (Grades 9-12), 2003; Nestle Children's Book Prize for Nine to Eleven Year Olds, 1999; Virginia Readers' Choice Award for High School, 2003; YALSA Best Books for Young Adults, 2001; YALSA Popular Paperbacks for Young Adults, 2015; YALSA Quick Picks for Reluctant Young Adult Readers, 2001; Michael L. Printz Honor Book, 2001.

Presents the humorous journal of a year in the life of a four-teen-year-old British girl who tries to reduce the size of her nose, stop her mad cat from terrorizing the neighborhood animals, and win the love of handsome hunk Robbie.

Georgia is a wonderful character whose misadventures are not only hysterically funny but universally recognizable. —*Booklist*

Stop in the name of pants!: the confessions of Georgia Nicolson. Louise Rennison. HarperTeen, 2008 256 pages (Confessions of Georgia Nicolson, 9)
Grades: 7 8 9 10

1. Teenage girls; 2. Teenage boy/girl relations; 3. Teenage romance; 4. Fourteen-year-old girls; 5. Dating (Social customs); 6. England; 7. Diary novels; 8. Realistic fiction; 9. Teen chick lit
9780061459320; 9780007275847, UK

This ninth installment in the hilarious series finds Georgia Nicolson wondering if Dave the Laugh is merely a good mate, especially since gorgeous Masimo has told Georgia that he wants her to be his one and only.

Teens will enjoy the detailed dance instructions that are included at the end from the main character's new career path. Although she is on her ninth series book, the author keeps things fresh with new drama and her usual hilarious wit. —*Voices of Youth Advocates*

The **taming** of the tights. Louise Rennison. HarperTeen, 2013 256 p. (Misadventures of Tallulah Casey, 3)
Grades: 7 8 9 10 11 12

1. Teenage actors and actresses; 2. Performing arts; 3. Teenage boy/girl relations; 4. Schools; 5. Teenage girls; 6. England; 7. Yorkshire, England; 8. Realistic fiction; 9. Teen chick lit
9780062226204; 9780007323937, print, UK
LC 2013021359

Tullulah Casey has returned for another term at her performing arts school, but after sharing a secret kiss with the local bad boy, Tallulah is now determined to find her perfect leading man.

Tallulah (A Midsummer Tights Dream) and the Tree Sisters are back for another term at performing arts college where they comically reinter-pret another Shakespeare play. But drama follows Tallulah offstage as she debates who is better boyfriend material: Cain or Charlie. Though the book is light on plot, readers will welcome the return of Tallulah's humorous musings and this distinctly British, quirky cast of characters. —*Horn Book Guide*

Resau, Laura

★ The **Queen** of Water. By Laura Resau and Maria Virginia Farinango. Delacorte Press, 2011 304 p.
Grades: 8 9 10 11 12

1. Indentured servants; 2. Social classes; 3. Quechua Indians; 4. Schools; 5. Reading; 6. Ecuador; 7. Coming-of-age stories; 8. First person narratives.
9780385907613

Amelia Bloomer List, 2012; YALSA Best Fiction for Young Adults, 2012; School Library Journal Best Books, 2011.

The complexities of class and ethnicity within Ecuadorian society are explained seamlessly within the context of the first-person narrative, and a glossary and pronunciation guide further help to plunge readers into the novel's world. By turns heartbreaking, infuriating and ultimately inspiring. —*Kirkus*

Revis, Beth

★ **Across** the universe. Beth Revis. Razorbill, 2011 398 p. (Across the universe trilogy, 1)
Grades: 7 8 9 10

1. Space vehicles; 2. Cryonics; 3. Dystopias; 4. Space flight; 5. Teenage romance; 6. Dystopian fiction; 7. Science fiction; 8. Multiple perspectives
9781595143976

Romantic Times Reviewers' Choice Award, 2011.

Revis's tale hits all of the standard dystopian notes, while presenting a believable romance and a series of tantalizing mysteries that will hold readers' attention. —*Publishers Weekly*

Bid my soul farewell. Beth Revis. Razorbill, 2019 336 p. (Give the dark my love, 2)
Grades: 9 10 11 12

1. Twins; 2. Magic (Occultism); 3. Undead; 4. Soul; 5. Good and evil; 6. Fantasy fiction; 7. Multiple perspectives.
9781595147196
LC 2019023069

Told in two voices, Grey hopes to revitalize plague-ravaged Lunar Island, but knows that his alliance with the emperor threatens his love for necromancer Nedra, who wants to keep her revenant sister with her even as she tries to free the souls of the dead.

A slow burn that does not disappoint. —*Kirkus*

Give the dark my love. Beth Revis. Razorbill, an imprint of Penguin Random House LLC, 2018 320 p. (Give the dark my love, 1)

Grades: 9 10 11 12

1. Magic (Occultism); 2. Plague; 3. Risk-taking (Psychology); 4. Teenagers; 5. Anger in teenage girls; 6. Fantasy fiction; 7. Multiple perspectives.

9781595147172; 9781595147189

LC 2018013398

Told in two voices, seventeen-year-old alchemy student Nedra turns to dark magic when a deadly plague sweeps through her homeland leaving her new friend, Grey, to pull her from the darkness.

Rex, Adam

★ **Cold** cereal. Adam Rex. Balzer + Bray, 2012 288 p. (Cold cereal saga, 1)

Grades: 4 5 6 7

1. Boy misfits; 2. Experiments; 3. Corporations; 4. Breakfast cereals; 5. Twin brothers and sisters; 6. New Jersey; 7. Fantasy fiction.

9780062060020

LC 2011019538

A boy who may be part changeling, twins involved in a bizarre secret experiment, and a clurichaun in a red tracksuit try to save the world from an evil cereal company whose ultimate goal is world domination.

The author tucks in portrait illustrations and hilariously odd TV-commercial storyboards, along with a hooded Secret Society, figures from Arthurian legend, magical spells and potions, a certain amount of violence, many wonderful throwaway lines.... All in all, it's a mad scramble that culminates in the revelation of a dastardly plot that will require sequels to foil. —*Kirkus*

Fat vampire: a never-coming-of-age story. Adam Rex. Balzer + Bray, 2010 324 p.

Grades: 9 10 11 12

1. Teenage vampires; 2. Overweight teenage boys; 3. Crushes in teenage boys; 4. Teenage boy misfits; 5. Television programs; 6. Philadelphia, Pennsylvania; 7. Humorous stories; 8. Coming-of-age stories.

9780061920905

LC 2010009616

After being bitten by a vampire, not only is fifteen-year-old Doug doomed eternally to be fat, but now he must also save himself from the desperate host of a public-access-cable vampire-hunting television show that is on the verge of cancellation.

Rex successfully sustains the wonderfully dry humor and calculated silliness and then surprises the reader with a thoughtful, poignant, ambiguous ending that is bound to inspire discussion. —*Booklist*

Reynolds, Alastair

Revenger. Alastair Reynolds. Orbit, 2017 560 p. (Revenger novels, 1)

Grades: 11 12 Adult

1. Far future; 2. Treasure hunters; 3. Spaceship captains; 4. Life on other planets; 5. Revenge in women; 6. Solar system; 7. Space; 8. Science fiction; 9. Space opera; 10. Adult books for young adults.

9780316555562; 9780316555623; 9780316555630; 9780575090538, print, UK; 9780575090552, print, UK

LC 2016037813

Locus Young Adult Book Award, 2017.

Adrana and Fura Ness are new on Captain Rackamore's ship, and they are using their Bone Reader abilities to their advantage while trying to avoid the feared Bosa Sennen.

The award-winning Reynolds' newest action-packed science fiction novel is a tale of sisterly devotion, heartbreaking loss, and brutal vengeance. —*Booklist*

Reynolds, Jason

★ **All** American boys: a novel. . Atheneum Books for Young Readers, 2015 240 p.

Grades: 8 9 10 11 12

1. African American teenage boys; 2. Race relations; 3. Prejudice; 4. Police; 5. Violence; 6. Realistic fiction; 7. African American fiction; 8. Multiple perspectives

9781481463331

School Library Journal Best Books, 2015; Thumbs Up! Award (Michigan), 2016; Westchester Fiction Award, 2016; Walter Award, 2016; YALSA Quick Picks for Reluctant Young Adult Readers, 2017; Coretta Scott King Honor Book for Authors, 2016; Georgia Peach Honor Book for Teen Readers, 2017.

When sixteen-year-old Rashad is mistakenly accused of stealing, classmate Quinn witnesses his brutal beating at the hands of a police officer who happens to be the older brother of his best friend. Told through Rashad and Quinn's alternating viewpoints.

Police brutality and race relations in America are issues that demand debate and discussion, which this superb book powerfully enables. —*Booklist*

★ The **boy** in the black suit. Jason Reynolds. Atheneum Books for Young Readers, 2015 272 p.

Grades: 7 8 9 10

1. African American teenage boys; 2. Grief in teenage boys; 3. Funeral homes; 4. Grief; 5. Funerals; 6. Brooklyn, New York City; 7. Realistic fiction; 8. African American fiction

9781442459502; 9780571356126, Paperback, UK

YALSA Best Fiction for Young Adults: Top Ten, 2015; YALSA Best Fiction for Young Adults, 2016; Coretta Scott King Honor Book for Authors, 2016.

High-school senior Matt has a job at Mr. Ray's funeral home, but he's also in mourning, for his mother who died and his long-on-the-wagon father who's returned to drink. While all this sounds like heavy problem-novel territory, it isn't. Reynolds writes about urban African American kids in a warm and empathetic way that the late Walter Dean Myers would have applauded. —*Horn Book Guide*

★ **Long** way down. Jason Reynolds. Atheneum, 2017 240 p.

Grades: 6 7 8 9 10 11 12

1. Revenge; 2. Grief; 3. Violence and guns; 4. Loss (Psychology); 5. Ghosts; 6. Novels in verse; 7. African American fiction

9781481438254, HRD, US; 9780571335121, Paperback, UK

ALA Notable Children's Books, 2018; Edgar Allan Poe Award for Best Young Adult, 2018; Flicker Tale Children's Book Award (North Dakota) for YA Fiction, 2019; Great Lakes Great Books Award (Michigan), Grades 9-12, 2018; Los Angeles Times Book Prize for Young Adult Literature, 2018; Nutmeg Children's Book Award, High School category, 2020; School Library Journal Best Books, 2017; Soaring Eagle Book Award (Wyoming), 2019; Walter Award, Teen, 2018; YALSA Best Fiction for Young Adults, 2018; YALSA Quick Picks for Reluctant Young Adult Readers, 2018; Coretta Scott King Honor Book for Authors, 2018; Longlisted for the National Book Award for Young People's Literature, 2017; Michael L. Printz Honor Book, 2018; Newbery Honor Book, 2018.

Driven by the secrets and vengeance that mark his street culture, 15-year-old Will contemplates over the course of 60 psychologically suspenseful seconds whether or not he is going to murder the person who killed his brother.

Teens are left with an unresolved ending that goes beyond the simple question of whether Will will seek revenge. Told in verse, this title is fabulistic in its simplicity and begs to be discussed. —*School Library Journal*

Miles Morales. Jason Reynolds. Marvel Press, 2017 416 p.
Grades: 7 8 9 10 11 12
1. Multiracial teenage boys; 2. Teenage superheroes; 3. Identity (Psychology); 4. Prep schools; 5. Schools; 6. Brooklyn, New York City; 7. Superhero stories; 8. African American fiction; 9. Books to movies
9781484787489
YALSA Quick Picks for Reluctant Young Adult Readers, 2018.

After a misunderstanding leads him to be suspended from school, Miles Morales feels conflicted about his identity as the new Spider-Man, but when his scholarship is threatened, he uncovers a plot that puts his friends and neighborhood at risk.

Reynolds builds on a comic book plot and neatly ties in Miles' Marvel Universe background, but he focuses more on his 16-year-old protagonist's struggle with self-doubt in a vividly rendered urban setting stocked with engaging supporting characters. —*Booklist*

When I was the greatest. Jason Reynolds. Atheneum Books for Young Readers, 2014 240 p.
Grades: 9 10 11 12
1. African Americans; 2. Brothers and sisters; 3. Neighborhoods; 4. Parties; 5. Tourette syndrome; 6. Brooklyn, New York City; 7. African American fiction
9781442459472
John Steptoe Award for New Talent, Author Category, 2015.

Avoiding the violence that has given his neighborhood a bad name, urban youth Ali spends busy days attending school, boxing and helping his family while looking out for a troublesome friend and a Tourette's-afflicted brother only to be brutally targeted in the aftermath of a misunderstanding. A first novel.—Publisher's description.

Sixteen-year-old Ali is a walking contradiction. He's a lauded boxer-in-training who's afraid of stepping into the ring; a straight-laced, head-down kind of kid on a bad block in Bed-Stuy, a neighborhood rife with drugs and violence...With fresh, fast-paced dialogue, Reynolds' debut novel chronicles Ali's friendship with next-door brothers Needles and Noodles, flawed but unforgettable characters all their own, as the three prepare for the party of a lifetime and pay the consequences for thrusting themselves into a more sordid encounter than any of them could have envisioned. *When I Was the Greatest* is urban fiction with heart, a meditation on the meaning of family, the power of friendship, and the value of loyalty. —*Booklist*

Reynolds, Justin A.
Early departures. Justin A. Reynolds. Harpercollins Childrens Books 2020 320 p.
Grades: 9 10 11 12
1. Loss (Psychology; 2. Friendship; 3. Resurrection; 4. Second chances; 5. Life after death; 6. Ohio; 7. Science fiction; 8. Multiple perspectives.
9780062748409

This is a page-turning narrative with a cast of fully realized characters and realistic dialogue. The skillful use of flashbacks and social media content fully engages readers. Despite the seriousness of the story, humor and moments of pathos will elicit empathy and connection. —*Kirkus*

Ribay, Randy
★ **Patron** saints of nothing. Randy Ribay. 2019 352 pages
Grades: 8 9 10 11 12
1. Murder; 2. Cousins; 3. Filipino American boys; 4. Drug traffic; 5. Identity (Psychology); 6. Philippines; 7. Realistic fiction; 8. Coming-of-age stories; 9. First person narratives; 10. Books for reluctant readers
9780525554912; 9780525554936; 9781788951548, Paperback, UK

LC 2018044009
YALSA Quick Picks for Reluctant Young Adult Readers, 2020; Westchester Fiction Award, 2020; National Book Award for Young People's Literature finalist, 2019.

When seventeen-year-old Jay Reguero learns his Filipino cousin and former best friend, Jun, was murdered as part of President Duterte's war on drugs, he flies to the Philippines to learn more.

By deftly weaving key details into Jay's quest for the truth, Ribay provides a much-needed window for young people of the West to better understand the Filipino history of colonization, occupation, and revolution. —*Booklist*
Includes bibliographical references.

Richards, Jame
★ **Three** rivers rising: a novel of the Johnstown flood. Jame Richards. Alfred A. Knopf, 2010 293 p. : Map
Grades: 6 7 8 9 10
1. Rich teenage girls; 2. Floods; 3. Classism; 4. Social classes; 5. Teenage boy/girl relations; 6. Pennsylvania; 7. 1880s; 8. Novels in verse; 9. Historical fiction; 10. Multiple perspectives
9780375958854
LC 2009004251
YALSA Best Fiction for Young Adults, 2011; School Library Journal Best Books, 2010.

Sixteen-year-old Celestia is a wealthy member of the South Fork Fishing and Hunting Club, where she meets and falls in love with Peter, a hired hand who lives in the valley below, and by the time of the torrential rains that lead to the disastrous Johnstown flood of 1889, she has been disowned by her family and is staying with him in Johnstown. Includes an author's note and historical timeline.

This is a striking novel in verse.... Richards builds strong characters with few words and artfully interweaves the lives of these independent thinkers. —*Publishers Weekly*

Richards, Natalie D.
Six months later. Natalie D. Richards. 2013 336 p.
Grades: 9 10 11 12
1. High school students; 2. Amnesia; 3. Memory; 4. High schools; 5. Teenage girls; 6. Psychological suspense
9781402285516
LC 2013012470
Chloe didn't think about it much when she nodded off in study hall on that sleepy summer day. But when she wakes up, snow is on the ground and she can't remember the last six months of her life. Before, she'd been a mediocre student. Now, she's on track for valedictorian and being recruited by Ivy League schools. Before, she never had a chance with super jock Blake. Now he's her boyfriend. Before, she and Maggie were inseparable. Now her best friend won't speak to her. What happened to her? And why can't she remember?

Richards constructs Chloe's fear, paranoia, and scheming with great care. Her novel has the feel of a high-stakes poker game in which every player has something to hide, and the cards are held until the very end. —*Publishers Weekly*

Riggs, Ransom
Hollow City: the second novel of Miss Peregrine's Home for Peculiar Children. Ransom Riggs. Quirk Books, 2014 400 p. (Miss Peregrine, 2)
Grades: 6 7 8 9 10
1. Orphans; 2. Animals; 3. Escapes; 4. Supernatural; 5. Teenage boys; 6. London, England; 7. Wales; 8. 1940s; 9. Fantasy fiction; 10. Illustrated books.
9781594746123; 9781594747359

In 1940, Jacob and his new friends escape from Miss Peregrine's island and travel to London where they encounter new allies, a menagerie of peculiar animals, and other unexpected surprises.

Like the first volume, this one is generously illustrated with peculiar period photographs that capture and enhance the eerie mood and mode. —*Booklist*

Library of souls: the third novel of Miss Peregrine's peculiar children. Ransom Riggs. Quirk Books, 2015 400 p. (Miss Peregrine, 3)
Grades: 6 7 8 9 10
  1. Orphans; 2. Rescues; 3. Supernatural; 4. Teenage boys; 5. London, England; 6. Wales; 7. 1940s; 8. Fantasy fiction; 9. Illustrated books.
9781594747588

The adventure that began with Miss Peregrine's *Home for Peculiar Children* and continued in *Hollow City* comes to a thrilling conclusion with Library of Souls. As the story opens, sixteen-year-old Jacob discovers a powerful new ability, and soon he's diving through history to rescue his peculiar companions from a heavily guarded fortress. Accompanying Jacob on his journey are Emma Bloom, a girl with fire at her fingertips, and Addison MacHenry, a dog with a nose for sniffing out lost children.—From publisher description.

As in the previous books, Riggs builds atmosphere with eerie vintage photos that amplify the curious nature of his imagined world. This novel proves perhaps too neat a conclusion to Jacob's story arc, but satisfying answers are given to long-standing questions about peculiardom, and all major story lines see resolution. Fans will easily lose themselves in this most peculiar tale of all. —*Booklist*

A **map** of days. Ransom Riggs. Dutton Children's Books, 2018 496 p. (Miss Peregrine, 4)
Grades: 6 7 8 9 10
  1. Orphanages; 2. Time travel (Past); 3. Abandoned property; 4. Grandfathers — Death; 5. Supernatural; 6. Florida; 7. Fantasy fiction; 8. Illustrated books; 9. Books to movies.
9780735232143; 9780141385907, Hardback, Australia; 9780141385921, Paperback, UK

LC Bl2018179834

Jacob Portman is back in Florida and this time Miss Peregrine, Emma, and their peculiar friends are with him, but when he finds a secret underground bunker owned by his grandfather Abe, Jacob is thrust into a new adventure.

★ **Miss** Peregrine's home for peculiar children: a novel. By Ransom Riggs. Quirk Books, 2011 352 p. (Miss Peregrine, 1)
Grades: 6 7 8 9 10
  1. Orphanages; 2. Time travel (Past); 3. Abandoned property; 4. Grandfathers — Death; 5. Islands; 6. Wales; 7. Fantasy fiction; 8. Illustrated books; 9. Books to movies.
9781594744761; 9781594745744; 9781594748387; 9781594748905; 9781594746062
Books I Love Best Yearly (BILBY), Older Reader, 2017; Pennsylvania Young Reader's Choice Awards, Young Adult, 2014; YALSA Best Fiction for Young Adults, 2012.

After a family tragedy, Jacob feels compelled to explore an abandoned orphanage on an island off the coast of Wales, discovering disturbing facts about the children who were kept there.

Nearly 50 unsettling vintage photographs appear throughout, forming the framework of this dark but empowering tale, as Riggs creates supernatural backstories and identities for those pictured in them.... It's an enjoyable, eccentric read, distinguished by well-developed characters, a believable Welsh setting, and some very creepy monsters. —*Publishers Weekly*

Tales of the Peculiar. Ransom Riggs; illustrated by Andrew Davidson. Dutton Books for Young Readers, 2016 208 p. (Miss Peregrine, Related works)
Grades: 7 8 9 10
  1. Time travel; 2. Secrets; 3. Shapeshifters; 4. Cannibals; 5. Princesses; 6. Fantasy fiction; 7. Short stories; 8. Illustrated books.
9780399538537; 9780141373409, print, UK; 9780141371658, print, UK
YALSA Quick Picks for Reluctant Young Adult Readers, 2017.

Elegantly detailed engravings from Davidson open each story, setting the tone for the tale that follows. —*Publishers Weekly*

Rinaldi, Ann

The **redheaded** princess. Ann Rinaldi. Harper Collins Publishers, 2008 224 p.
Grades: 6 7 8 9
  1. Elizabeth I, Queen of England, 1533-1603; 2. Princesses; 3. Rulers; 4. Teenage girls; 5. Great Britain; 6. Tudor period (1485-1603); 7. 16th century; 8. Historical fiction
9780060733742; 9780060733759

LC 2007018577

In 1542, nine-year-old Lady Elizabeth lives on an estate near London, striving to get back into the good graces of her father, King Henry VIII, and as the years pass she faces his death and those of other close relatives until she finds herself next in line to ascend the throne of England in 1558.

The rich scene-setting and believable, appealing heroine will satisfy Rinaldi's many fans. —*Booklist*

Ritter, William

Beastly bones: a Jackaby novel. By William Ritter. Algonquin Young Readers, 2015 304 p. (Jackaby, 2)
Grades: 7 8 9 10
  1. Detectives; 2. Serial murder investigation; 3. Shapeshifters; 4. Supernatural; 5. Serial murderers; 6. New England; 7. 1890s; 8. 19th century; 9. Supernatural mysteries; 10. First person narratives
9781616203542; 9781616206369

LC 2015010990

YALSA Best Fiction for Young Adults, 2016.

When dinosaur bones from a recent dig mysteriously go missing, and an unidentified beast starts attacking animals and people, leaving their mangled bodies behind, Abigail and her eccentric employer R. F. Jackaby, investigators of the supernatural in 1892 New England, find themselves hunting for a thief, a monster, and a murderer.

With one case closed but two unsolved, the well-matched, well-written duo will undoubtedly return to fight a more fearsome foe. A witty and weird adventure equal parts Sherlock and Three Stooges. —*Kirkus*

The **dire** king. William Ritter. Algonquin Young Readers, 2017 352 p. (Jackaby, 4)
Grades: 7 8 9 10
  1. Detectives; 2. Shapeshifters; 3. Eccentrics and eccentricities; 4. Rulers; 5. Zombies; 6. New England; 7. 1890s; 8. Supernatural mysteries; 9. Historical mysteries.
9781616206703; 9781616208547

LC 2017002941

In this conclusion to the Jackaby series, the eccentric detective and his assistant Abigail Rook find themselves in the middle of a war between magical worlds.

A humorous, energetic, action-packed, and magical conclusion. —*Kirkus*

Series complete in 4 volumes.

Jackaby. R. William Ritter. Algonquin Young Readers, 2014 304 pages (Jackaby, 1)
Grades: 7 8 9 10 11 12
1. Serial murder investigation; 2. Serial murderers; 3. Murder; 4. Supernatural; 5. Imaginary creatures; 6. New England; 7. 1890s; 8. 19th century; 9. Supernatural mysteries; 10. First person narratives
9781616203535
LC 2014014706
YALSA Best Fiction for Young Adults, 2015; YALSA Best Fiction for Young Adults: Top Ten, 2015.
Newly arrived in 1892 New England, Abigail Rook becomes assistant to R. F. Jackaby, an investigator of the unexplained with the ability to see supernatural beings, and she helps him delve into a case of serial murder which, Jackaby is convinced, is due to a nonhuman creature.

Rivers, Karen
Love, Ish. Karen Rivers. Algonquin Young Readers, 2017 304 p.
Grades: 6 7 8 9
1. Children with cancer; 2. Adopted girls; 3. Friendship; 4. Brain — Tumors; 5. New students; 6. Mars (Planet); 7. Realistic fiction; 8. First person narratives
9781616205706
LC 2016038086
Twelve-year-old Mischa "Ish" Love's longtime dream has been to someday live on Mars, but when she collapses on the first day of seventh grade, Ish receives a diagnosis which threatens her future plans.

Roat, Sharon Huss
How to disappear. Sharon Huss Roat. HarperTeen, an imprint of HarperCollins Publishers, 2017 377 p.
Grades: 7 8 9 10 11 12
1. Introverts; 2. Social media; 3. Kindness; 4. Anxiety; 5. Loneliness; 6. Realistic fiction
9780062291752; 9780062291769
YALSA Best Fiction for Young Adults, 2018.
Living life strictly below the radar after her only friend moves away, Vicky, determined to put off her mother's intervention, Photoshops herself into pictures that she posts online before meeting numerous people who feel just as alone and ignored as she does.
This is a witty, hard-to-put-down novel that's appropriate for younger teens. However, the lack of grittiness won't deter older teens, who will be carried along by familiar lingo and references to social networks and celebrities. —*School Library Journal*

Robinson, Gary
Little Brother of War. Gary Robinson. 7th Generation, 2013 120 p.
Grades: 6 7 8
1. Native American teenage boys; 2. Teenage athletes; 3. Fathers and sons; 4. Individuality; 5. Ball games; 6. Mississippi; 7. Realistic fiction.
9781939053022; 9781939053886, ebook, US
LC 2013013182
Sixteen-year-old Mississippi Choctaw Randy Cheska lives under the shadow of his brother who was a football hero, later killed in Iraq, until proves himself to his parents and others through the ancient game of stickball.

Standing strong. Gary Robinson. Orca Book Pub 2019 120 p.
Grades: 7 8 9
1. Native American teenage girls; 2. Protests, demonstrations, vigils, etc; 3. Suicidal behavior; 4. Environmental protection; 5. Oil industry

and trade; 6. Standing Rock Reservation, North Dakota; 7. Montana; 8. Realistic fiction; 9. Books for reluctant readers.
9781939053220
LC 2019002633
After a failed suicide attempt, seventeen-year-old Rhonda Runningcrane is inspired to help a crew protesting against an oil company running a pipeline through sacred Native land in North Dakota.
A book for reluctant readers that highlights the heroism of young activists. —*Kirkus*
Inspired by Actual Events.

Rocco, John
Swim that rock. John Rocco & Jay Primiano. Candlewick Press, 2014 293 p.
Grades: 7 8 9 10
1. Money-making projects; 2. Father-separated teenage boys; 3. Money lenders; 4. Diners (Restaurants); 5. Clamming; 6. Rhode Island; 7. Narragansett Bay region, Rhode Island; 8. Realistic fiction; 9. Coming-of-age stories.
9780763669058
When his fisherman father went missing, Jake and his mother lost their house, and now the family diner is in danger of being repossessed. A mysterious character named Captain and seasoned fisherman Gene Hassard help Jake earn money by learning the ways of the bay. With a lushly detailed sense of place and character, the story examines a boy coming to terms with his situation. —*Horn Book Guide*

Roe, Robin
★ A **list** of cages. Robin Roe. 2017 320 p.
Grades: 8 9 10 11
1. Teenage abuse victims; 2. Child abuse; 3. Teenage boy orphans; 4. Teenage boys with ADHD; 5. Teenagers with dyslexia; 6. Realistic fiction; 7. Multiple perspectives; 8. First person narratives
9781484763803
LC 2015045422
Landing a coveted elective to serve as an aide to the school psychologist, Adam, a student struggling with ADHD, is assigned to track down a troubled freshman he discovers is the foster brother he has not seen in five years.
A triumphant story about the power of friendship and of truly being seen. —*Kirkus*

Roecker, Lisa
The **Liar** Society. Lisa & Laura Roecker. Sourcebooks Fire, 2011 361 p; (Liar Society, 1)
Grades: 7 8 9 10
1. Secret societies; 2. Murder investigation; 3. Grief in teenage girls; 4. Email; 5. Best friends — Death; 6. Mysteries
9781402256332
LC Bl2011006431
When Kate receives a mysterious e-mail from her dead friend Grace, she must prove that Grace's death was not an accident, but finds that her elite private school holds secrets so big people are willing to kill to protect them.
This is a smartly paced and plotted first novel, full of twists, clues, and sleuthing. Add this to your go-to list of mysteries. —*Booklist*

Roehrig, Caleb
The **fell** of dark. Caleb Roehrig. Feiwel & Friends, 2020 416 p.
Grades: 9 10 11 12
1. Gay teenagers; 2. Vampires; 3. Teenage same-sex romance; 4. Good and evil; 5. Supernatural; 6. Paranormal romances.

9781250155849, HRD, US

Trying to keep his head down in a supernaturally charged community that is populated mostly by vampires, August is unexpectedly attracted to a mysterious vampire boy who draws him into a conflict with an ancient and terrible power.

Roesch, Mattox

Sometimes we're always real same-same. Mattox Roesch. Unbridled Books, 2009 317 p.

Grades: 11 12 Adult

1. Former gang members; 2. Inuit; 3. Moving to a new state; 4. Boy cousins; 5. Boys — Friendship; 6. Alaska; 7. Coming-of-age stories; 8. First person narratives; 9. Adult books for young adults.
9781932961874

Booklist Editors' Choice: Adult Books for Young Adults, 2009.

Roesch's compelling story, exotic setting and eccentric characters make this coming-of-age tale a fresh, welcome read. —*Publishers Weekly*

Rogerson, Margaret

An **enchantment** of ravens. Margaret Rogerson. Margaret K. McElderry Books, 2017 300 pages

Grades: 7 8 9 10

1. Teenage girl artists; 2. Portraits; 3. Fairies; 4. Princes; 5. Imaginary kingdoms; 6. High fantasy; 7. Fantasy fiction
9781481497589; 9781481497596

A superbly skilled portrait artist who includes among her patrons the sinister, immortal fair folk who covet her talents, Isobel makes the terrible mistake of revealing an autumn faerie prince's sorrow in his portrait, a choice that strands them both in a hostile land where they risk their lives to pursue forbidden feelings for each other.

Rogerson ably builds this fantasy world through canny details and contemporary dialogue, allowing for an enjoyable read by fantasy and non-fantasy readers alike. She also craftily depicts the power imbalance between Isobel and Rook, offering a refreshing dynamic in which Isobel often comes out on top. —*School Library Journal*

Sorcery of thorns. Margaret Rogerson. Margaret K. McElderry Books, 2019 464 p.

Grades: 9 10 11 12

1. Librarians; 2. Wizards; 3. Magical books; 4. Conspiracies; 5. Demons; 6. High fantasy; 7. Fantasy fiction.
9781481497619; 9781481497626, Paperback, UK

When apprentice librarian Elisabeth is implicated in sabotage that released the library's most dangerous grimoire, she becomes entangled in a centuries-old conspiracy that could mean the end of everything.

In her second novel, Rogerson proves herself a worthy successor to Diana Wynne Jones in this moody, atmospheric, and lively classic fantasy. Elisabeth was raised in a magical library, providing her with limitless book smarts but very little life experience. This enchanting story is sure to appeal to teen readers eager for more of the world-building, fierce friendships, and feminist heroines of Robin LaFevers and Naomi Novik. —*School Library Journal*

Rorby, Ginny

The **outside** of a horse: a novel. By Ginny Rorby. Dial Books for Young Readers, 2010 343 p;

Grades: 7 8 9 10

1. Girls and horses; 2. Veterans with disabilities; 3. Equestrian therapy; 4. Girl volunteers; 5. Human/animal relationships; 6. Realistic fiction.
9780803734784

LC 2009025101

When her father returns from the Iraq War as an amputee with post-traumatic stress disorder, Hannah escapes by volunteering to work with rescued horses, never thinking that the abused horses could also help her father recover.

Hannah comes across as a believable teen. As a backdrop to the story, Rorby has interwoven a good deal of disturbing information about animal cruelty. Horse lovers and most others will saddle up right away with this poignant tale. —*Booklist*

Rosen, Renee

★ **Every** crooked pot. Renee Rosen. St. Martin's Griffin, 2007 227 p.

Grades: 7 8 9 10

1. Teenage girls; 2. Fathers and daughters; 3. Self-acceptance in girls; 4. Beauty; 5. Popularity; 6. Akron, Ohio; 7. Ohio; 8. Coming-of-age stories
9780312365431

LC 2007010457

Booklist Editors' Choice: Books for Youth, 2007; YALSA Popular Paperbacks for Young Adults, 2010.

Rosen looks back at the life of Nina Goldman, whose growing up is tied to two pillars: a port-wine stain around her eye and her inimitable father, Artie. The birthmark, she hates; her father, she loves. Both shape her in ways that merit Rosen's minute investigation.... There's real power in the writing. —*Booklist*

Rosenfield, Kat

Amelia Anne is dead and gone. Kat Rosenfield. Dutton Books, 2012 304 p.

Grades: 9 10 11 12

1. Teenage girl murder victims; 2. Dating violence; 3. Small towns; 4. Murder; 5. Dating (Social customs); 6. Mysteries
9780525423898

LC 2011029958

Unveils the details of a horrific murder, its effects on permanent and summer residents of the small Appalachian town where the body is discovered, and especially how the related violence shakes eighteen-year-old Becca's determination to leave home as soon as possible.

Rosoff, Meg

★ **How** I live now. Meg Rosoff. Wendy Lamb Books, 2004 208 p.

Grades: 7 8 9 10

1. Separated friends, relatives, etc; 2. Teenagers and war; 3. Survival; 4. Cousins; 5. Farms; 6. England; 7. Science fiction; 8. First person narratives; 9. Books to movies
9780385746779; 9780385909082; 9780141380759, print, UK; 9780141925080, print, UK

LC 2004006443

Booklist Editors' Choice: Books for Youth, 2004; Michael L. Printz Award, 2005; YALSA Best Books for Young Adults, 2005.

To get away from her pregnant stepmother in New York City, fifteen-year-old Daisy goes to England to stay with her aunt and cousins, with whom she instantly bonds, but soon war breaks out and rips apart the family while devastating the land.

Teens may feel that they have experienced a war themselves as they vicariously witness Daisy's worst nightmares. Like the heroine, readers will emerge from the rubble much shaken, a little wiser and with perhaps a greater sense of humanity. —*Publishers Weekly*

Title adapted into a film by the same name (2013).

★ **Picture** me gone. Meg Rosoff. G.P. Putnam's Sons, an imprint of Penguin Group (USA) Inc, 2013 256 p.

Grades: 7 8 9

1. Missing persons; 2. Fathers and daughters; 3. Observation (Psychology); 4. Twelve-year-old girls; 5. Preteen girls; 6. New York (State); 7. Mysteries; 8. Coming-of-age stories.
9780399257650; 9780141344041; 9780385681896
Booklist Editors' Choice: Books for Youth, 2013; YALSA Best Fiction for Young Adults, 2014; National Book Award for Young People's Literature finalist, 2013.

Mila has an exceptional talent for reading a room, sensing hidden facts and unspoken emotions from clues that others overlook. So when her fathers best friend, Matthew, goes missing from his upstate New York home, Mila and her beloved father travel from London to find him.

Sensitive Londoner Mila, twelve, travels with her father, Gil, to upstate New York to search for Gil's boyhood friend, who has inexplicably disappeared. The subject of this road-trip novel—how much guilt and tragedy can a person bear before he gives up on life?—is adult, but the writing is up to Rosoff's usual standards of originality, depth, wit, and insight. —*Horn Book Guide*

★ **There** is no dog. Meg Rosoff. Doubleday Canada, 2011 242 p.
Grades: 7 8 9
1. God; 2. Mothers and sons; 3. Creation; 4. Teenage boy/girl relations; 5. Personal conduct; 6. Earth; 7. Humorous stories
9780385668293; 9780385668316; 9780141327167, print, UK

In this story, God is a teenage boy named Bob and he created the Earth in six days. Unfortunately, Bob is a typical teenage boy, meaning that he is lazy, careless, self-obsessed, sex-mad, and about to meet a girl and fall in love.

Rossi, Veronica

Riders. Veronica Rossi. Tom Doherty Associates, 2016 368 p. (Riders (Veronica Rossi), 1)
Grades: 8 9 10 11 12
1. Four Horsemen of the Apocalypse; 2. Demons; 3. Angels; 4. Supernatural; 5. Teenage romance; 6. Urban fantasy
9780765382542, HRD, US; 9781466887794, ebook, US; 9780765382559, paperback, US

Recovering from an accident that actually killed him, Gideon Blake, who aspired to be a U.S. Army Ranger, discovers that he is manifesting strange new powers and has become one of the four legendary horsemen of the apocalypse who, along with his fellow riders, must save humanity from an ancient evil force.

Under the never sky. Veronica Rossi. Harpercollins Childrens Books, 2012 400 p. (Under the never sky trilogy, 1)
Grades: 6 7 8 9 10 11 12
1. Post-apocalypse; 2. Dystopias; 3. Quests; 4. Teenage boy/girl relations; 5. Seventeen-year-old girls; 6. Multiple perspectives; 7. Science fiction; 8. Apocalyptic fiction.
9780062072030
School Library Journal Best Books, 2012; YALSA Best Fiction for Young Adults, 2013.

Aria and Perry, two teens from radically different societies—one highly advanced, the other primitive—hate being dependent on one another until they overcome their prejudices and fall in love, knowing they can't stay together.

Roth, Veronica

Allegiant. Veronica Roth. Katherine Tegen Books, 2013 544 pages (Divergent trilogy, 3)
Grades: 9 10 11 12
1. Social classes; 2. Dystopias; 3. Civil war; 4. Loyalty; 5. Teenage girls; 6. Chicago, Illinois; 7. Dystopian fiction; 8. Science fiction; 9. Books to movies.

9780062024060; 9780007534944, print, UK
Goodreads Choice Award, 2013.

Roth shakes up her storytelling (and will do the same to some readers) in this highly anticipated, largely satisfying wrap-up to the Divergent trilogy...for those who have faithfully followed these five factions, and especially the Dauntless duo who stole hearts two books ago, this final installment will capture and hold attention until the divisive final battle has been waged. —*Publishers Weekly*

Carve the mark. Veronica Roth. Katherine Tegen Books, an imprint of HarperCollinsPublishers, 2017 528 p. (Carve the mark, 1)
Grades: 8 9 10 11 12
1. Superhuman abilities; 2. Kidnapping victims; 3. Political intrigue; 4. Survival; 5. Pain; 6. Science fiction; 7. Fantasy fiction; 8. Multiple perspectives
9780062348630; 9780008157821

LC Bl2016051945
Living on a violent planet where everyone develops a unique power meant to shape the future, Akos and Cyra, youths from enemy nations, resent gifts that render them vulnerable to others' control before they become unlikely survival partners.

Roth offers a richly imagined, often-brutal world of political intrigue and adventure, with a slow-burning romance at its core. —*Booklist*

★ **Divergent**. Veronica Roth. Katherine Tegen Books, 2011 384 pages (Divergent trilogy, 1)
Grades: 9 10 11 12
1. Social classes; 2. Dystopias; 3. Options, alternatives, choices; 4. Identity (Psychology); 5. Courage; 6. Chicago, Illinois; 7. Dystopian fiction; 8. Science fiction; 9. Books to movies; 10. Books for reluctant readers
9780062024022; 9780007420421; 9780007538065, print, UK
LC 2010040579
Amelia Bloomer List, 2012; Black-Eyed Susan Book Award (Maryland), High School, 2013; California Young Reader Medal, Young Adult, 2014; Colorado Blue Spruce YA Book Award, 2014; Eliot Rosewater Indiana High School Book Award (Rosie Award), 2014; Garden State Teen Book Award (New Jersey), Fiction (Grades 9-12), 2014; Gateway Readers Award (Missouri), 2014; Georgia Peach Book Award for Teen Readers, 2013; Goodreads Choice Award, 2011; Grand Canyon Reader Award (Arizona), Teen Book Category, 2014; Great Lakes Great Books Award (Michigan), Grades 9-12, 2013; Green Mountain Book Award (Vermont), 2013; Iowa High School Book Award, 2014; Isinglass Teen Read Award (New Hampshire), 2012-2013. ; Kentucky Bluegrass Award for Grades 9-12, 2013; Land of Enchantment Book Award (New Mexico), Young Adult category, 2014; Nutmeg Children's Book Award, Teen category, 2014; Rhode Island Teen Book Award, 2013; Romantic Times Reviewers' Choice Award, 2011; School Library Journal Best Books, 2011; Sequoyah Book Awards (Oklahoma), High School Books, 2014; Soaring Eagle Book Award (Wyoming), 2013; South Carolina Book Award, Young Adult Books, 2014; YALSA Best Fiction for Young Adults, 2012; YALSA Popular Paperbacks for Young Adults, 2015; YALSA Quick Picks for Reluctant Young Adult Readers, 2012; Young Reader's Choice Award (Pacific Northwest), Senior, 2014.

In a future Chicago, sixteen-year-old Beatrice Prior must choose among five predetermined factions to define her identity for the rest of her life, a decision made more difficult when she discovers that she is an anomaly who does not fit into any one group, and that the society she lives in is not perfect after all.

Roth's nonstop action, excellent voice, and simple yet accessible writing style will draw in many new readers to the genre. The themes are particularly poignant for young adults trying to identify their place in the

worldhaving the choice to follow in your parents' footsteps or do something new.... This is a fast-paced and fun read. —*Voice of Youth Advocates*
Title adapted into a film by the same name (2014).

The **fates** divide. Veronica Roth. 2018 464 p. (Carve the mark, 2)
Grades: 8 9 10 11 12
1. Superhuman abilities; 2. Political intrigue; 3. Survival; 4. Teenagers; 5. Fate and fatalism; 6. Science fiction; 7. Fantasy fiction; 8. Multiple perspectives
9780062426956, US; 9780062426963; 9780008192204, UK; 9780008192211, Paperback, UK
When Cyra's father Lazmet Noavek, a soulless tyrant thought to be dead, reclaims the throne, Cyra Noavek and Akos Kereseth are desperate to stop him from igniting a barbaric war.

Four: a Divergent collection. Veronica Roth. 2014 304 pages (Divergent trilogy)
Grades: 9 10 11 12
1. Social classes; 2. Dystopias; 3. Options, alternatives, choices; 4. Identity (Psychology); 5. Courage; 6. Chicago, Illinois; 7. Dystopian fiction; 8. Science fiction; 9. First person narratives.
9780062345219; 9780007584642, print, UK; 9780007560691, print, UK; 9780007582891, print, UK
LC 2014934784
Young Reader's Choice Award (Pacific Northwest), Senior, 2017.
Told from Tobias's point of view, *Four* shares details of his transfer from Abnegation to Dauntless, his initiation, and claiming his place in the Dauntless hierarchy.

Insurgent. Veronica Roth. Katherine Tegen Books, 2012 544 pages (Divergent trilogy, 2)
Grades: 9 10 11 12
1. Social classes; 2. Dystopias; 3. Civil war; 4. Guilt; 5. Identity (Psychology); 6. Chicago, Illinois; 7. Dystopian fiction; 8. Science fiction; 9. First person narratives.
9780062024046; 9780007442928
LC 2011053287
Goodreads Choice Award, 2012; Romantic Times Reviewer's Choice Award, 2012.
As war surges in the dystopian society around her, sixteen-year-old Divergent Tris Prior must continue trying to save those she loves—and herself—while grappling with haunting questions of grief and forgiveness, identity and loyalty, politics and love.

Rothenberg, Jess
The **Kingdom**. Jess Rothenberg. Henry Holt & Co 2019 343 p.
Grades: 7 8 9 10
1. Cyborgs; 2. Trials (Murder); 3. Amusement parks; 4. Posthumanism; 5. Artificial intelligence; 6. Science fiction.
9781250293855; 9781509899388, Paperback, UK
LC 2018038696
Ana, a half-android, half-human employee of a futuristic fantasy theme park, the Kingdom, faces a charge of murder in a tale told through flashbacks and court transcripts.
A layered and fast-paced mystery with an ethical backbone. —*Booklist*

Roux, Madeleine
House of furies. Madeleine Roux. HarperTeen, an imprint of HarperCollinsPublishers, 2017 407 p. (House of furies, 1)
Grades: 9 10 11 12
1. Boarding houses; 2. Household employees; 3. Runaways; 4. Supernatural; 5. England; 6. Great Britain; 7. Georgian era

(1714-1837); 8. 1800s (Decade); 9. Horror; 10. Gothic fiction; 11. Historical fiction
9780062498618
Escaping from her harsh school before finding work as a maid in an English boarding house, Louisa realizes that her mysterious employer and his staff execute cruel judgments on the guests.
Atmospheric and troubling, this series starter will sink its hooks into readers as surely as it frightens them. —*Booklist*

Rowell, Rainbow
★ **Carry** on: a novel. Rainbow Rowell. Griffin, 2015 528 p. (Simon Snow, 1)
Grades: 8 9 10 11 12
1. Wizards; 2. Boarding schools; 3. Monsters; 4. Teenage boy/boy relations; 5. Magic; 6. Fantasy fiction
9781250049551; 9781447298908, print, UK; 9781447266945, print, UK; 9781529013009, Paperback, UK
Booklist Editors' Choice: Books for Youth, 2015; School Library Journal Best Books, 2015; Rainbow List, 2016; YALSA Best Fiction for Young Adults, 2016.
During his last year at Watford School of Magicks, Simon Snow, the Chosen One, faces a magic-eating monster wearing his face, a break-up, and a missing nemesis.
The novel playfully twists genre conventions—there are plenty of wink-wink, nudge-nudge moments to satisfy faithful fantasy readers—but it also stands alone as a modern bildungsroman. —*Kirkus*

★ **Eleanor** & Park. Rainbow Rowell. St. Martin's Griffin, 2013 328 p.
Grades: 9 10 11 12
1. First loves; 2. Multiracial teenage boys; 3. Romantic love; 4. High school students; 5. Misfits (Persons); 6. Omaha, Nebraska; 7. 1980s; 8. Historical fiction; 9. Love stories; 10. Teen chick lit; 11. Books for reluctant readers
9781250012579; 9781409116325; 9781409120544; 9781409116332
Abraham Lincoln Illinois High School Book Award, 2015; Black-Eyed Susan Book Award (Maryland), High School, 2015; Blue Hen Book Award (Delaware) for Teen Books, 2015; Booklist Editors' Choice: Books for Youth, 2013; Boston Globe-Horn Book Award for Fiction and Poetry, 2013; Garden State Teen Book Award (New Jersey), Fiction (Grades 9-12), 2016; Georgia Peach Book Award for Teen Readers, 2015; Goodreads Choice Award, 2013; Indies' Choice Book Awards, Young Adult, 2014; International Reading Association Children's Book Award for Young Adult Fiction, 2014; Iowa High School Book Award, 2015; Land of Enchantment Book Award (New Mexico): Black bears (Grades 9-12), 2017; Pennsylvania Young Reader's Choice Awards, Young Adult, 2015; Rhode Island Teen Book Award, 2015; School Library Journal Best Books, 2013; Thumbs Up! Award (Michigan), 2014; YALSA Quick Picks for Reluctant Young Adult Readers, 2014; YALSA Best Fiction for Young Adults, 2014; YALSA Best Fiction for Young Adults: Top Ten, 2014; Michael L. Printz Honor Book, 2014.
Set over the course of one school year in 1986, this is the story of two star-crossed misfits—smart enough to know that first love almost never lasts, but brave and desperate enough to try.
Through Eleanor and Park's alternating voices, readers glimpse the swoon-inducing, often hilarious aspects of first love.... Funny, hopeful, foulmouthed, sexy and tear-jerking, this winning romance will captivate teen and adult readers alike. —*Kirkus*

★ **Fangirl**. Rainbow Rowell. St. Martin's Griffin, 2013 448 p.
Grades: 9 10 11 12

1. Teenage girl authors; 2. Fans (Persons); 3. Twin sisters; 4. Identical twin sisters; 5. Women college students; 6. Realistic fiction; 7. Coming-of-age stories.
9781250030955; 9781447263227, Oz; 9781529012996, Paperback, UK
Buckeye Teen Book Award (Ohio), Grades 9-12, 2015; Inky Awards (Australia): Silver Inky, 2015; LibraryReads Favorites, 2013; School Library Journal Best Books, 2013; YALSA Best Fiction for Young Adults, 2014.

Change-resistant college freshman Cather holes up in her dorm room, writing fantasy fanfiction. But as the year progresses, she is pushed outside her comfort zone by her snarky roommate, Reagan; by Levi, Reagan's ex-boyfriend (and eventually Cath's first love interest); and by her manic but well-meaning father. Rowell transitions seamlessly between Cath's strong interior voice and clever dialogue in this sophisticated coming-of-age novel. —*Horn Book Guide*

Wayward son. Rainbow Rowell. Wednesday Books, 2019 368 p. (Simon Snow, 2)
Grades: 8 9 10 11 12
1. Cross-country automobile trips; 2. Misadventures; 3. Wizards; 4. Vampires; 5. Teenage boy/boy relations; 6. United States; 7. Fantasy fiction.
9781250146076, HRD, US; 9781250146090, ebook, US; 9781509896882, Hardback, UK; 9781509896899, Paperback, UK; 9781509896905, Paperback, UK
LC 2019028910
Finds an overwhelmed Simon joining Penny and Baz on a trip to the American West in a vintage convertible, only to be confronted by dragons, vampires and gun-toting skunks.

Carefully plotted, the book is a classic page-turner right to the open ending which, o frabjous day, promises a sequel to the sequel! One can hardly wait. —*Booklist*

Rowling, J. K.
Harry Potter and the Chamber of Secrets. J. K. Rowling; illustrations by Mary GrandPre. Arthur A. Levine Books, 1999 341 p. (Harry Potter (Original series), 2)
Grades: 4 5 6 7 8 9 10
1. Child wizards; 2. Boarding schools; 3. Magic — Study and teaching; 4. Schools; 5. Potter, Harry (Fictitious character); 6. England; 7. Fantasy fiction; 8. Books to movies; 9. Classics.
9780439064866, HRD, US; 9781551923703; 9781408855669; 9781408855904; 9781408810552; 9780606191814; 9780756903169; 9781594130014; 9787020033447; 9780786222735; 9780747545774; 9781408894637, paperback, UK
LC 98-46370
Booklist Editors' Choice: Books for Youth, 1999; Books I Love Best Yearly (BILBY), Older Reader, 2001; Books I Love Best Yearly (BILBY), Younger Reader, 2001; British Book Award for Children's Book of the Year, 1998; Mythopoeic Award for Children's Literature, 2008; Nestle Children's Book Prize for Nine to Eleven Year Olds, 1998; New York Times Notable Children's Book, 1999; School Library Journal Best Books, 1999; YALSA Best Books for Young Adults, 2000.

When the Chamber of Secrets is opened again at the Hogwarts School for Witchcraft and Wizardry, second-year student Harry Potter finds himself in danger from a dark power that has once more been released on the school.

Harry Potter and the deathly hallows. J. K. Rowling; illustrated by Mary GrandPré. Arthur A. Levine Books, 2007 784 p. (Harry Potter (Original series), 7)
Grades: 4 5 6 7 8 9 10

1. Teenage wizards; 2. Boarding schools; 3. Self- fulfillment; 4. Magic — Study and teaching; 5. Schools; 6. England; 7. Fantasy fiction; 8. Books to movies; 9. Classics.
9780545010221; 9780545029377; 9780545029360; 9781408855959; 9781408855713; 9781408810606; 9780747591054; 9780747595830; 9781408810293; 9781408835029; 9780747591061, print, UK; 9780747591092, print, UK
LC 2007925449
ALA Notable Children's Book, 2008; Books I Love Best Yearly (BILBY), Older Reader, 2008; Mythopoeic Award for Children's Literature, 2008; Nebula Awards: Andre Norton Award, 2007; New York Times Notable Book, 2007; New York Times Notable Children's Book, 2007; Booklist Editors' Choice: Books for Youth, 2007; YALSA Best Books for Young Adults, 2008; USBBY Outstanding International Book, 2008.

The seventh and final book of the blockbuster Harry Potter series follows the wizard's last year at Hogwarts School of Witchcraft and Wizardry.

Throughout, Rowling returns to and embellishes the hallmark themes of the series: the importance of parental influences, the redemptive power of sacrifice, and the strength found in love. These truths are the underpinnings of a finale that is worthy of fans' hopes and expectations. —*Booklist*

Harry Potter and the goblet of fire. J. K. Rowling; illustrations by Mary GrandPre. A. A. Levine Books, 2000 734 p. (Harry Potter (Original series), 4)
Grades: 4 5 6 7 8 9 10
1. Teenage wizards; 2. Boarding schools; 3. Magic — Study and teaching; 4. Schools; 5. Potter, Harry (Fictitious character); 6. England; 7. Fantasy fiction; 8. Books to movies; 9. Classics.
9780439139595, HRD, US; 9781408810576; 9781408834992; 9781408855683; 9781408855928; 9780747582380; 9781408894651, Paperback, UK; 9780747550990, print, UK; 9781408845677, Hardback, UK
ALA Notable Children's Book, 2001; Books I Love Best Yearly (BILBY), Older Reader, 2001; Books I Love Best Yearly (BILBY), Older Reader, 2018; Books I Love Best Yearly (BILBY), Younger Reader, 2001; Golden Archer Awards (Wisconsin): Middle/Jr. High, 2002; Hugo Award for Best Novel, 2001; Indian Paintbrush Book Award (Wyoming), 2002; Mythopoeic Award for Children's Literature, 2008; New York Times Notable Children's Book, 2000; West Australian Young Readers' Book Award (WAYRBA), Younger Readers, 2001; Booklist Editors' Choice: Books for Youth, 2000; YALSA Popular Paperbacks for Young Adults, 2009.

Fourteen-year-old Harry Potter joins the Weasleys at the Quidditch World Cup, then enters his fourth year at Hogwarts Academy where he is mysteriously entered in an unusual contest that challenges his wizarding skills, friendships and character, amid signs that an old enemy is growing stronger.
Sequel to: *Harry Potter and the prisoner of Azkaban; Sequel: Harry Potter and the Order of the Phoenix.*

Harry Potter and the half-blood prince. J. K. Rowling; illustrated by Mary GrandPre. Arthur A. Levine Books, 2005 672 p. (Harry Potter (Original series), 6)
Grades: 4 5 6 7 8 9 10
1. Teenage wizards; 2. Boarding schools; 3. Teenage boy orphans; 4. Magic — Study and teaching; 5. Schools; 6. England; 7. Fantasy fiction; 8. Books to movies; 9. Classics.
9780439784542; 9781551929859; 9780439786775; 9780439791328; 9780439785969; 9781408855942; 9780747598466; 9781408810583; 9781408855706, print, UK; 9781408835012,print, UK; 9781408894767, Paperback, UK; 978
LC 2005921149

Booklist Editors' Choice: Books for Youth, 2005; Books I Love Best Yearly (BILBY), Older Reader, 2006; British Book Award for Book of the Year, 2006; Colorado Blue Spruce YA Book Award, 2008; Golden Archer Awards (Wisconsin): Middle/Jr. High, 2008; Mythopoeic Award for Children's Literature, 2008; New York Times Notable Book, 2005; New York Times Notable Children's Book, 2005; YALSA Best Books for Young Adults, 2006.

Harry Potter begins his sixth year at Hogwarts School of Witchcraft and Wizardry in an atmosphere of uncertainty, as the magical world begins to face the fact that the evil wizard Voldemort is alive and active once again.

Once again, Rowling capably blends literature, mythology, folklore, and religion into a delectable stew. This sixth book may be darker and more difficult, but Potter fans will devour it and begin the long and bittersweet wait for the final installment. —*School Library Journal*

Harry Potter and the Order of the Phoenix. J. K. Rowling; illustrated by Mary GrandPre. Arthur A. Levine Books, 2003 896 p. (Harry Potter (Original series), 5)
Grades: 4 5 6 7 8 9 10
1. Boarding schools; 2. Teenage boy orphans; 3. Magic — Study and teaching; 4. Schools; 5. Potter, Harry (Fictitious character); 6. England; 7. Fantasy fiction; 8. Classics; 9. Books to movies
9780439358064; 9781408855935; 9780747591269; 9781408855690, print, UK; 9781408894750, Paperback, UK; 9780747551003, print, UK; 9780747569404,print, UK; 9780747561071, print, UK; 9780747570738, print, UK; 97814088

LC 2003102525
Anthony Award for Best Young Adult Mystery, 2004; Books I Love Best Yearly (BILBY), Older Reader, 2004; Colorado Blue Spruce YA Book Award, 2006; Golden Archer Awards (Wisconsin): Middle/Jr. High, 2005; Mythopoeic Award for Children's Literature, 2008; ALA Notable Children's Book, 2004; Booklist Editors' Choice: Books for Youth, 2003; YALSA Best Books for Young Adults, 2004.

When the government of the magic world and authorities at Hogwarts School of Witchcraft and Wizardry refuse to believe in the growing threat of a freshly revived Lord Voldemort, fifteen-year-old Harry Potter finds support from his loyal friends in facingthe evil wizard and other new terrors.

Sequel to: *Harry Potter and the Goblet of Fire*; Originally published: 2003.

Harry Potter and the prisoner of Azkaban. J. K. Rowling; illustrations by Mary GrandPre. A. A. Levine Books, 1999 435 p. (Harry Potter (Original series), 3)
Grades: 4 5 6 7 8 9 10
1. Boarding schools; 2. Teenage boy orphans; 3. Magic — Study and teaching; 4. Schools; 5. Potter, Harry (Fictitious character); 6. England; 7. Fantasy fiction; 8. Classics; 9. Books to movies
9780439136358, HRD, US; 9781408810569; 9781408855676; 9781408855911; 9781480614994; 9780747573760; 9780747574491; 9781408894644, paperback, UK; 9780747546290, print, UK
Booklist Editors' Choice: Books for Youth, 1999; Books I Love Best Yearly (BILBY), Older Reader, 2001; Books I Love Best Yearly (BILBY), Older Reader, 2005; Books I Love Best Yearly (BILBY), Younger Reader, 2001; Colorado Blue Spruce YA Book Award, 2004; Golden Archer Awards (Wisconsin): Intermediate, 2001; Indian Paintbrush Book Award (Wyoming), 2004; Locus Award for Fantasy Novel, 1999. ; Maine Student Book Award, 2001; Mythopoeic Award for Children's Literature, 2008; Nestle Children's Book Prize for Nine to Eleven Year Olds, 1999; Soaring Eagle Book Award (Wyoming), 2002; Whitbread Book Award for Children's Book of the Year, 1999; YALSA Best Books for Young Adults, 2000.

During his third year at Hogwarts School for Witchcraft and Wizardry, Harry Potter must confront the devious and dangerous wizard responsible for his parents' death.

Sequel to: *Harry Potter and the Chamber of Secrets; Sequel: Harry Potter and the goblet of fire.*

★ **Harry** Potter and the sorcerer's stone. J. K. Rowling; illustrations by Mary GrandPre. A. A. Levine Books, 1997 Vi, 309 p. : Illustration (Harry Potter (Original series), 1)
Grades: 4 5 6 7 8 9 10
1. Child wizards; 2. Boarding schools; 3. Magic — Study and teaching; 4. Schools; 5. Eleven-year-old boys; 6. England; 7. Fantasy fiction; 8. Classics; 9. Books to movies
9780590353403, hardback, US; 9780747532699, Hardback, UK; 9780747545729,Hardback, UK; 9780747554561, Hardback, UK; 9780747532743; 9781551923963; 9781551927282; 9781408866184; 9781408855652, paperback, UK; 978140

LC 9739059
ABBY Award for Children's Books, 1999; ALA Notable Children's Book, 1999; Booklist Editors' Choice: Books for Youth, 1998; Books I Love Best Yearly (BILBY), Older Reader, 2001; Books I Love Best Yearly (BILBY), Younger Reader, 2001; Blue Hen Book Award (Delaware) for Chapter Books, 2001; Book Sense Book of the Year for Children's Literature, 1999; British Book Award for Children's Book of the Year, 1997; Charlotte Award (New York), Young Adult, 2000; Colorado Blue Spruce YA Book Award, 2001; Eliot Rosewater Indiana High School Book Award (Rosie Award), 2001; Golden Archer Awards (Wisconsin): Middle/Jr. High, 2000; Grand Canyon Reader Award (Arizona), Teen Book Category, 2000; Great Stone Face Children's Book Award (New Hampshire), 2000; Indian Paintbrush Book Award (Wyoming), 2000; Massachusetts Children's Book Award, 2000; Mythopoeic Award for Children's Literature, 2008; Nene Award (Hawaii), 2000; Nestle Children's Book Prize for Nine to Eleven Year Olds, 1997; Rebecca Caudill Young Reader's Book Award (Illinois), 2001; School Library Journal Best Books, 1998; South Carolina Book Award, Junior Books, 2001; Surrey Book of the Year Award (British Columbia), 2000; West Australian Young Readers' Book Award (WAYRBA), Younger Readers, 2000; West Virginia Children's Choice Book Award, 2001; YALSA Best Books for Young Adults, 1999.

Rescued from the outrageous neglect of his aunt and uncle, a young boy with a great destiny proves his worth while attending Hogwarts School of Witchcraft and Wizardry.

This is a brilliantly imagined and beautifully written fantasy. —*Booklist*

Roy, Jennifer Rozines
★ **Mindblind**. Jennifer Roy. Marshall Cavendish, 2010 248 p;
Grades: 7 8 9 10 11
1. Gifted teenagers; 2. Rock groups; 3. Asperger's syndrome; 4. Songwriting; 5. Genius; 6. Realistic fiction.
9780761457169

LC 2010006966
Westchester Fiction Award, 2011; YALSA Best Fiction for Young Adults, 2011.

Fourteen-year-old Nathaniel Clark, who has Asperger's Syndrome, tries to prove that he is a genius by writing songs for his rock band, so that he can become a member of the prestigious Aldus Institute, the premier organization for the profoundly gifted.

Mature readers will empathize with Nathaniel as his friends, Jessa and Cooper, do. This book is for teens who appreciate a story about self-discovery, dreams, and friendship. —*Voice of Youth Advocates*

Rubens, Michael

The **bad** decisions playlist. Michael Rubens. 2016 368 p.
Grades: 9 10 11 12

   1. Slackers; 2. Fathers and sons; 3. Musicians; 4. Rock music; 5. Teenage romance; 6. Realistic fiction
9780544096677

LC 2015028509

Sixteen-year-old Austin, a self-described screw-up, finds out that his allegedly dead father happens to be the very-much-alive rock star Shane Tyler. Austin—a talented musician himself—is sucked into his newfound father's alluring music-biz orbit, pulling his true love, Josephine, along with him.

Funny and painful, its a sharply etched portrait of fallible human beings living, loving, screwing up, and making doand a fine look at the Twin Cities music scene. —*Publishers Weekly*

Rubin, Lance

   Crying laughing. Lance Rubin. Alfred A. Knopf, 2019 336 p.
Grades: 7 8 9 10 11

   1. Improvisation (Acting); 2. Teenage girls; 3. Family problems; 4. Stand-up comedy; 5. High school students; 6. Realistic fiction; 7. Coming-of-age stories
9780525644682; 9780525644675

The author of Denton Little's Deathdate gives us a tragicomic story of bad dates, bad news, bad performances, and one girl's determination to find the funny in high school.

This book is for anyone who's ever attended high school, had a crush, gotten news they weren't prepared to deal with, or learned that someone close to them isn't quite who they thought they were—in short, for everyone. —*Booklist*

   Denton Little's deathdate: a novel. By Lance Rubin. Alfred A. Knopf, 2015 352 p. (Denton Little, 1)
Grades: 9 10 11 12

   1. Genetic screening; 2. Genetic engineering; 3. Identity (Psychology); 4. Seventeen-year-old boys; 5. Near future; 6. Science fiction; 7. First person narratives
9780553496963

International Reading Association Children's Book Award for Young Adult Fiction, 2016; YALSA Best Fiction for Young Adults, 2016.

In a world where everyone knows the day they will die, a teenage boy is determined to outlive his upcoming expiration date.

While this seems to be a stand-alone novel, and a satisfying one at that, there is plenty of fodder for a sequel. Rubin's is a new voice on the YA literature scene and is well-worth reading. —*School Library Journal*

   Denton Little's still not dead. Lance Rubin. Random House Childrens Books, 2017 352 p. (Denton Little, 2)
Grades: 9 10 11 12

   1. High school seniors; 2. Death; 3. Secrets; 4. Genetic screening; 5. Mothers; 6. New York City; 7. Humorous stories; 8. Science fiction; 9. First person narratives
9780553497007

Denton and his quirky friends are laugh-out-loud funny, even as their riotous adventures raise deeper questions about science, government control, life, and death. —*School Library Journal*

Ruby, Laura

   ★ **Bone** Gap. Laura Ruby. 2015 368 pages
Grades: 9 10 11 12

   1. Kidnapping; 2. Small towns; 3. Bullying and bullies; 4. Love; 5. Face perception; 6. Magical realism; 7. Multiple perspectives
9780062317605; 9780571332755, print, UK

LC 2014013676

YALSA Best Fiction for Young Adults: Top Ten, 2015; Booklist Editors' Choice: Books for Youth, 2015; Michael L. Printz Award, 2016; School Library Journal Best Books, 2015; YALSA Best Fiction for Young Adults, 2016; National Book Award for Young People's Literature finalist, 2015.

Eighteen-year-old Finn, an outsider in his quiet Midwestern town, is the only witness to the abduction of town favorite Roza, but his inability to distinguish between faces makes it difficult for him to help with the investigation, and subjects him to even more ridicule and bullying.

In Ruby's refined and delicately crafty hand, reality and fantasy dont fall neatly into place. She compellingly muddles the two together right through to the end. Even then, after she reveals many secrets, magic still seems to linger in the real parts of Bone Gap, and the magical elements retain their frightening reality. Wonder, beauty, imperfection, cruelty, love, and pain are all inextricably linked but bewitchingly so. —*Booklist*

   The **clockwork** ghost. Laura Ruby. Walden Pond Press, an imprint of HarperCollinsPublishers, 2019 464 pages (York (Laura Ruby), 2)
Grades: 5 6 7 8

   1. Codes (Communication); 2. Puzzles; 3. Twin brothers and sisters; 4. Neighbors; 5. Jewish children; 6. New York City; 7. Fantasy mysteries; 8. Steampunk
9780062306968; 9780062306975

Continuing their efforts to solve the Morningstarr cipher in the aftermath of their home's destruction, the Biedermann twins and their friend Jaime encounter dangerous enemies who are attempting to claim the cipher's treasure.

Ruby takes a classic puzzle mystery and compellingly draws it out, both in the time the puzzles take and by giving the characters room to contemplate their feelings. —*Booklist*

   The **shadow** cipher. Laura Ruby. Walden Pond Press, an imprint of HarperCollinsPublishers, 2017 476 p. (York (Laura Ruby), 1)
Grades: 5 6 7 8 9

   1. Codes (Communication); 2. Puzzles; 3. Twin brothers and sisters; 4. Neighbors; 5. Real estate developers; 6. New York City; 7. Fantasy mysteries; 8. Steampunk
9780062306937

YALSA Best Fiction for Young Adults, 2018.

A debut entry in an alternate-history series depicts three kids who try to solve a modern-world puzzle and complete a treasure hunt laid into the streets and buildings of New York City.

   Thirteen doorways, wolves behind them all. Laura Ruby. Balzer + Bray, 2019 384 p.
Grades: 9 10 11 12

   1. Depressions; 2. Orphanages; 3. Ghosts; 4. Teenage girls; 5. Abandonment (Psychology); 6. Chicago, Illinois; 7. 1940s; 8. Historical fantasy
9780062317643, hardback, US

School Library Journal Best Books, 2019; National Book Award for Young People's Literature finalist, 2019.

Abandoned in a Depression-era Chicago orphanage with her sister, a young woman endures injustice, poverty and violence while struggling to survive in the years leading up to World War II.

Though a slow unspooling may frustrate some, the women s resonant journeys, marked by desire and betrayal, thoughtfully illuminate the deep harm that women and girls suffer at the hands of a patriarchal society as well as the importance of living fully. —*Publishers Weekly*

Ruiz Zafon, Carlos

   ★ **Marina**. Carlos Ruiz Zafon. Little, Brown and Company, 2014 336 pages;

Grades: 8 9 10 11 12

1. Boarding school students; 2. Secrets; 3. Tombs; 4. Loyalty; 5. Mansions; 6. Barcelona, Spain; 7. Spain; 8. Gothic fiction; 9. Translations

9780316044714; 9780297856474; 9781922079152; 9781780224268, print, UK

Set in Barcelona, Spain from late 1979 to May 1980, this gothic novel centers around 15-year-old boarding school student Oscar Drai. Instead of studying during his free time, the teen explores the city, and one day ends up in an area that seems deserted. Drawn in by music coming from an old dilapidated house, Oscar is given a scare by the owner, an eccentric and haunted German artist...With elements of romance, mystery, and horror, none of them overwhelming the other, this complex volume that hints at Mary Shelley's *Frankenstein* manages to weave together three separate stories for a cohesive and eerie result. —*School Library Journal*

★ The **prince** of mist. Carlos Ruiz Zafon. Little, Brown, 2010 208 p.
Grades: 6 7 8 9 10

1. Coastal towns; 2. Shipwrecks; 3. Magicians; 4. Good and evil; 5. Gardens; 6. Horror

9780316044776

YALSA Best Fiction for Young Adults, 2011.

In 1943, in a seaside town where their family has gone to be safe from war, thirteen-year-old Max Carver and sister, fifteen-year-old Alicia, with new friend Roland, face off against an evil magician who is striving to complete a bargain made before he died.

Zafon is a master storyteller. From the first page, the reader is drawn into the mystery and suspense that the young people encounter when they move into the Fleischmann house.... This book can be read and enjoyed by every level of reader. —*Voice of Youth Advocates*

Runyon, Brent
Surface tension: a novel in four summers. Brent Runyon. Alfred A. Knopf, 2009 197 p;
Grades: 8 9 10 11

1. Vacations; 2. Teenage boys; 3. Growing up; 4. Summer; 5. Families; 6. New York (State); 7. Realistic fiction; 8. Coming-of-age stories; 9. First person narratives

9780375844461

LC 2008009193

YALSA Best Books for Young Adults, 2010.

During the summer vacations of his thirteenth through his sixteenth year at the family's lake cottage, Luke realizes that although some things stay the same over the years that many more change.

With sensitivity and candor, Runyon reveals how life changes us all and how these unavoidable changes can be full of both turmoil and wonder. —*Kirkus*

Rush, Jennifer
Altered. By Jennifer Rush. Little, Brown, 2013 336 p. (Altered series, 1)
Grades: 7 8 9 10 11 12

1. Genetic engineering; 2. Human experimentation in medicine; 3. Conspiracies; 4. Runaways; 5. Memory; 6. Science fiction

9780316197083

LC 2012007545

Seventeen-year-old Anna finds herself on the run from her father's enigmatic Agency, along with the four teen boys the Agency had been experimenting on, as they try to make sense of erased memories, secret identities, and genetic alteration.

[T]his debut's strengths—pacing and plot twists, especially—outweigh the deficits. Riveting. —*Kirkus*

Russell, Chris
Songs about a girl. Chris Russell. Flatiron Books, 2017 362 p.
Grades: 7 8 9 10

1. Boy bands; 2. Photographers; 3. Best friends; 4. Bullying and bullies; 5. Teenage girl photographers; 6. England; 7. Realistic fiction

9781250095169; 9781444929157, print, UK

Accepting a job taking band photos for a former classmate, aspiring photographer Charlie Bloom is surprised when the unexpectedly popular band catapults her into the world of fandom and paparazzi before a love triangle, a creative rivalry and a personal secret threaten her prospects.

Russo, Meredith
Birthday: a novel. Meredith Russo. Flatiron Books, 2019 275 p.
Grades: 9 10 11 12

1. Transgender teenagers; 2. Birthdays; 3. Best friends; 4. Childhood friends; 5. Transitioning (Gender identity); 6. Tennessee; 7. Love stories; 8. LGBTQIA fiction; 9. Coming-of-age stories.

9781250129833; 9781474967419, Paperback, UK; 9781250129840, ebook, US

LC 2019007978

Born in the same hospital on the same day, Eric and Morgan grow up together as best friends, through six years of birthdays they discover who they are meant to be, and if they are meant to be together.

Stonewall Award winner Russo (If I Was Your Girl) tackles teen love, heartbreak, sexuality, and gender identity in this novel told over the course of six years through the alternating voices of transgender girl Morgan and cisgender boy Eric, two childhood best friends who share the same birthday.... Russo weaves together a series of short stories, encapsulating each year of development in a snapshot without losing character depth. —*Publishers Weekly*

★ **If** I was your girl. Meredith Russo. Flatiron Books, 2016 280 p.
Grades: 9 10 11 12

1. Transgender teenagers; 2. New students; 3. Teenage romance; 4. Transgender persons; 5. Secrets; 6. Tennessee; 7. Realistic fiction; 8. LGBTQIA fiction

9781250078407; 9781474923835, print, UK

Rainbow List, 2017; Stonewall Book Award for Children's and Young Adult Literature, 2017; YALSA Best Fiction for Young Adults, 2017; YALSA Quick Picks for Reluctant Young Adult Readers, 2017; Walter Honor Book, 2017.

A newcomer to a Tennessee community hides the secret about her gender reassignment that forces her to keep potential new friends at arm's length before meeting easygoing Grant, who captures her heart and who she fears will not accept the complicated realities of her life.

After being beaten up in a mall bathroom, eighteen-year-old transgender woman Amanda goes to live with her previously unsupportive father in Lambertville, Tennessee, where no one knows her from her pre-transition life. Though she's determined to lie low while finishing high school, she finds unexpected friendships with a trio of church-going Baptist girls and with art classmate Bee, a bisexual girl secretly in a relationship with one of them. Even more unexpected is her blossoming relationship with tender and respectful Grant, who has a complicated past of his own.... Flashbacks to Amanda's life pre-, during, and post-suicide attempt and subsequent transition are interspersed throughout the narrative. There is no gratuitous trauma, and Amanda's story is neither overly sentimental nor didactic. Russo, herself a trans woman living in Tennessee, crafts a thoughtful, truthful, and much needed coming-of-age tale. —*Horn Book Guide*

Rutkoski, Marie
The **Celestial** Globe. Marie Rutkoski. Farrar, Straus and Giroux, 2009 304 p. (Kronos chronicles, 2)

Grades: 5 6 7 8

1. Spies; 2. Murder investigation; 3. Globes; 4. Pirates; 5. Romanies; 6. Historical fantasy
9780374310271

LC 2008035599

Thirteen-year-old Petra, her tin spider Astrophil, and their Roma friends Neel and Tomik are surprised by revelations about Dee, Kit, and Petra's father as they face Prince Rodolfo of Bohemia, who will do anything to possess a powerful object, the Celestial Globe.

This stellar sequel to *The Cabinet of Wonders* surpasses its predecessor by navigating the intelligent fantasy adventure outside 16th-century Bohemia and deepening the scope of its magic.... Strong characters and fast-paced plotting let this compelling installment stand independently, but the ending will leave readers eager for the next. —*Publishers Weekly*

The **Jewel** of the Kalderash. Marie Rutkoski. Farrar, Straus and Giroux, 2011 352 p. (Kronos chronicles, 3)
Grades: 5 6 7 8

1. Inheritance and succession; 2. Transformations (Magic); 3. Romanies; 4. Spiders; 5. Magic; 6. Historical fantasy
9780374336783

LC 2010037716

Fourteen-year-old Petra, her tin spider Astrophil, and their friends become entangled in the competition for the Roma crown, then set out for Prague in hopes of finally finding a cure for Petra's father.

Short, action-packed chapters lead to a climax of heroic courage, violent horror and tragic sacrifice, and an epilogue perfectly admixes restrained melancholy and tender hope. Thrilling, heartrending and unexpectedly sweet; Petra's adventures could not have had a more satisfying conclusion. —*Kirkus*

The **midnight** lie. Marie Rutkoski. Farrar Straus & Giroux 2020 368 p.
Grades: 9 10 11 12

1. Teenage girl/girl relations; 2. Truthfulness and falsehood; 3. Social classes; 4. Caste; 5. Secrets; 6. Fantasy fiction.
9780374306380; 9781529357509, Paperback, UK; 9781529357479, Hardback, UK

LC 2019024764

Nirrim endures a grim and punishing life as a Half Caste until she encounters Sid, a rakish traveler from far away who whispers rumors that the High Caste possess magic and tempts Nirrim to seek that magic for herself.

It is difficult to find teen fantasy novels where LGBTQ+ romance isn't tangential, but in this adventure set in the same world as Rutkoski's Winner's series, girl-girl love and attraction drive the plot as much as Sid's secret mission and Nirrim's need to understand her uncommon talents, and each narrative thread complements the others. —*Booklist*

The **winner's** crime. Marie Rutkoski. Farrar Straus Giroux Books for Young Readers, 2015 352 p. (Winner's trilogy, 2)
Grades: 7 8 9 10 11 12

1. Aristocracy; 2. Spies; 3. Loyalty; 4. Secrets; 5. Engagement; 6. High fantasy; 7. Fantasy fiction
9780374384708; 9780374384715, ebook, US

LC 2014025185

The engagement of Lady Kestrel to Valoria's crown prince is the event of a lifetime, but to Kestrel it means living in a cage of her own making, so as she aches to tell the truth about her engagement, she becomes a skilled practitioner of deceit and as a spy passes information and gets close to uncovering a shocking secret.

A rich and complex story of political intrigue, missed opportunities, and thwarted trust fill the pages of this sequel to *The Winner's Curse*

(2014). Rutkoski's world is splendid in its cruelty and beauty, with characters that continue to claim our hearts. —*Booklist*

★ The **winner's** curse. Marie Rutkoski. Farrar, Straus and Giroux, 2014 368 p. (Winner's trilogy, 1)
Grades: 7 8 9 10 11 12

1. Slavery; 2. Aristocracy; 3. Loyalty; 4. Slaves; 5. Interpersonal attraction; 6. High fantasy; 7. Fantasy fiction
9780374384678
YALSA Best Fiction for Young Adults, 2015.

Full-bodied characters explore issues of loyalty, class, and values (for example, arts versus military strengths), without sacrificing any of the relationship-related tension that is a hallmark of this kind of story. —*Booklist*

The **winner's** kiss. Marie Rutkoski. Farrar Straus Giroux Books for Young Readers, 2016 352 p. (Winner's trilogy, 3)
Grades: 7 8 9 10 11 12

1. Aristocracy; 2. Slavery; 3. Imaginary wars and battles; 4. Secrets; 5. Teenage girls; 6. High fantasy; 7. Fantasy fiction
9780374384739

Arin fights in the war between the East and the Empire as he tries to forget Kestrel, the woman he believes betrayed her people, while Kestrel struggles to escape from a labor camp before discovering terrible secrets.

Ryan, Amy Kathleen

Flame: a Sky chasers novel. Amy Kathleen Ryan. 2014 326 pages (Sky chasers, 3)
Grades: 8 9 10 11 12

1. Space flight; 2. Enemies; 3. Parent-separated teenagers; 4. Space vehicles; 5. Religion; 6. Science fiction; 7. Multiple perspectives
9780312621360

LC 2013039416

Waverly, Kieran, and Seth struggle to survive on board the New Horizon—and take down their enemies before it's too late.

When this meaty, harrowing conclusion to the Sky Chasers series opens, the inhabitants of the vessel Empyrean are fleeing their destroyed spacecraft to join their former enemies on board the New Horizon. Action begins immediately, and the story shifts mainly among the points of view of Waverly, Kieran and Seth...The pace is at times methodical, and much of the suspense comes from characters' and readers' uncertainty as to whom to trust. Stakes are high, however, and readers witness graphic (though generally not gory) violence and bodily harm as the three teens work to both overthrow and defend Pastor Anne Mather, the New Horizon's leader. It all comes to a head in a climax that is tense and viscerally frightening. Detailed and gripping, with a thorough and satisfying resolution. —*Kirkus*

Glow. Amy Kathleen Ryan. St. Martin's Griffin, 2011 307 p. (Sky chasers, 1)
Grades: 8 9 10 11 12

1. Human fertility; 2. Religion; 3. Teenage girl kidnapping victims; 4. Kidnapping; 5. Space vehicles; 6. Science fiction; 7. Books for reluctant readers
9780312590567

LC 2011020385

School Library Journal Best Books, 2011; YALSA Quick Picks for Reluctant Young Adult Readers, 2013.

Part of the first generation to be conceived in deep space, fifteen-year-old Waverly is expected to marry young and have children to populate a new planet, but a violent betrayal by the dogmatic leader of their sister ship could have devastating consequences.

The themes of survival, morality, religion, and power are well developed, and the characters are equally complex. The author has also created a unique and vivid outer-space setting that is exciting and easy to imagine. —*School Library Journal*

Spark: a Sky chasers novel. Amy Kathleen Ryan. St. Martin's Griffin, 2012 320 p. (Sky chasers, 2)
Grades: 8 9 10 11 12
1. Parent-separated teenagers; 2. Explosions; 3. Space flight; 4. Space vehicles; 5. Teenage boy/girl relations; 6. Science fiction.
9780312621353; 9781447208051, print, UK

Waverly and Kieran are finally reunited on the Empyrean, but when Seth is mysteriously released from the brig the night of a strange explosion that sends the ship off-course, tensions between Kieran and Seth reach a boiling point, as Waverly ponders following her heart, even if it puts lives at risk.

Ryan, Carrie
The **dark** and hollow places. Carrie Ryan. Delacorte Press, 2011 384 p. (Forest of Hands and Teeth trilogy, 3)
Grades: 9 10 11 12
1. Twin sisters; 2. Zombies; 3. Separated friends, relatives, etc; 4. Survival; 5. Undead; 6. Horror; 7. Fantasy fiction.
9780385738590; 9780385907385; 9780575094833, print, UK; 9780575094857, print, UK

LC 2010045776

Alone and listening to the moaning of the Dark City dying around her, Annah wants to find her way back home, to her sister and family and their village in the Forest of Hands and Teeth.

The **dead-tossed** waves. Carrie Ryan. Delacorte Press, 2010 407 p. (Forest of Hands and Teeth trilogy, 2)
Grades: 9 10 11 12
1. Teenagers and death; 2. Cults; 3. Undead; 4. Zombies; 5. Imprisonment; 6. Horror; 7. Fantasy fiction.
9780385906326; 9780575090927, print, UK

LC 2009030113

Gabry lives a quiet life in a town trapped between a forest and the ocean, hemmed in by the dead who hunger for the living, but her mother Mary's secrets, a cult of religious zealots who worship the dead, and a stranger from the forest who seems to know Gabry threaten to destroy her world.

Like its predecessor, this book features a breach of the town, an escape into the Forest, a love triangle, the ever-present and inexhaustible Mudo, and an extraordinarily bleak mood. But it also offers an expansion of postapocalyptic detail...and a few inspired surprises.... Readers are sure to be hooked. —*Publishers Weekly*

Sequel to: *The Forest of Hands and Teeth.*

★ The **Forest** of Hands and Teeth. Carrie Ryan. Delacorte Press, 2009 310 p. (Forest of Hands and Teeth trilogy, 1)
Grades: 9 10 11 12
1. Teenage girl orphans; 2. Undead; 3. Survival; 4. Zombies; 5. Escapes; 6. Horror; 7. Fantasy fiction
9780385736817; 9780385736824

LC 2008006494

YALSA Best Books for Young Adults, 2010; YALSA Popular Paperbacks for Young Adults, 2017; YALSA Popular Paperbacks for Young Adults, 2011.

Through twists and turns of fate, orphaned Mary seeks knowledge of life, love, and especially what lies beyond her walled village and the surrounding forest, where dwell the Unconsecrated, aggressive flesh-eating people who were once dead.

Mary's observant, careful narration pulls readers into a bleak but gripping story of survival and the endless capacity of humanity to persevere.... Fresh and riveting. —*Publishers Weekly*

Sequel: *The dead-tossed waves.*

Ryan, Pam Munoz
★ **Echo.** Pam Munoz Ryan. Scholastic Press, 2015 592 p.
Grades: 4 5 6 7 8
1. Harmonica; 2. Music; 3. Fate and fatalism; 4. Curses; 5. Orphans; 6. Germany; 7. Pennsylvania; 8. Historical fiction.
9780439874021

ALA Notable Children's Book, 2016; Americas Book Award for Children's and Young Adult Literature, 2016; California Young Reader Medal, Middle School, 2019; Garden State Teen Book Award (New Jersey), Fiction (Grades 6-8), 2018; Grand Canyon Reader Award (Arizona), Tween Book Category, 2017; Kirkus Prize for Young Readers' Literature, 2015; Notable Books for a Global Society, 2016; Virginia Readers' Choice Award for Middle School, 2017; Newbery Honor Book, 2016.

Decades after a man is entwined in a prophecy-based quest involving three mysterious sisters and a harmonica, three individuals from different areas of the world confront daunting challenges involving the same harmonica.

The harmonica and the love of music serve as the unifying threads for these tales of young people who save the lives and spirits of their families and neighbors, each in a time marked by bigotry and violence. It's an ambitious device, but Ryan's storytelling prowess and vivid voice lead readers expertly through a hefty tome illuminated by layers of history, adventure, and the seemingly magical but ultimately very human spirit of music. —*Horn Book Guide*

Saedi, Sara
Americanized: rebel without a green card. Sara Saedi. Alfred A. Knopf, 2018 280 pages;
Grades: 9 10 11 12
1. Teenage immigrants; 2. Undocumented immigrants; 3. Anxiety in teenagers; 4. Iranian Americans; 5. Families; 6. California; 7. 1990s; 8. Autobiographical fiction
9781524717797; 9781524717803, library, US; 9781524717827, PAP, US; 9781524717810, ebook, US

LC 2016057751

School Library Journal Best Books, 2018.

In San Jose, California, in the 1990s, teenaged Sara keeps a diary of life as an Iranian American and her discovery that she and her family entered as undocumented immigrants.

Filled with pop culture references, journal excerpts, photographs, and relatable coming-of-age content, this book will keep readers fully entertained while pushing them to deeper cultural understandings. —*School Library Journal*

Saeed, Aisha
Written in the stars. Aisha Saeed. 2015 304 pages
Grades: 9 10 11 12
1. Forced marriage; 2. Pakistani Americans; 3. Children of immigrants; 4. Dating (Social customs); 5. Love; 6. Pakistan; 7. Realistic fiction; 8. First person narratives; 9. Books for reluctant readers
9780399171703; 9780147513939

LC 2014019860

California Young Reader Medal, Young Adult, 2019; Westchester Fiction Award, 2016; YALSA Quick Picks for Reluctant Young Adult Readers, 2016; YALSA Popular Paperbacks for Young Adults, 2017.

Naila's vacation to visit relatives in Pakistan turns into a nightmare when she discovers her parents want to force her to marry a man she's never met.

Naila's harrowing story is compellingly told, and Saeed includes an afterword about the problem of forced marriages not only in Pakistan but among immigrant communities in the U.S. Stirring, haunting, and ultimately hopeful. —*Booklist*

Includes bibliographical references.

Saeed, Jamal

Yara's spring. Jamal Saeed & Sharon E. McKay. Annick Press, 2020 264 p.
Grades: 6 7 8 9
1. Girl refugees; 2. Survival; 3. Arab Spring, 2010-; 4. Parent-separated children; 5. Children and war; 6. Jordan; 7. Syria; 8. Realistic fiction; 9. Coming-of-age stories; 10. Canadian fiction
9781773214405; 9781773214399

Coming of age against all odds in the midst of the Arab Spring.

The narrative is fast-paced and descriptive, and the dialogue so charged with the characters' emotions that readers will be immediately drawn into Yara's plight. They will not only learn about how the Syrian war is affecting ordinary lives but also how people rely on social media to connect and keep abreast—and how they have to negotiate myriad complications in order to gain refuge. —*Booklist*

Saenz, Benjamin Alire

★ **Aristotle** and Dante discover the secrets of the universe. Benjamin Alire Sáenz. Simon & Schuster Books for Young Readers, 2012 368 p.
Grades: 9 10 11 12
1. Loners; 2. Mexican American teenage boys; 3. Gay teenagers; 4. Families; 5. Friendship; 6. Texas; 7. El Paso, Texas; 8. 1980s; 9. Coming-of-age stories; 10. LGBTQIA fiction; 11. First person narratives.
9781442408920

LC 2010033649
ALA Notable Children's Book, 2013; Lambda Literary Award for Young Adult/Children, 2012; Pura Belpre Award for Narrative, 2013; Rainbow List, 2013; School Library Journal Best Books, 2012; Stonewall Book Award for Children's and Young Adult Literature, 2013; Westchester Fiction Award, 2013; YALSA Best Fiction for Young Adults, 2013; Michael L. Printz Honor Book, 2013.

Fifteen-year-old Ari Mendoza is an angry loner with a brother in prison, but when he meets Dante and they become friends, Ari starts to ask questions about himself, his parents, and his family that he has never asked before.

★ **He** forgot to say good-bye. Benjamin Alire Saenz. Simon & Schuster Books for Young Readers, 2008 321 p.
Grades: 8 9 10 11
1. Father-separated teenage boys; 2. Emotional problems of teenage boys; 3. Family problems; 4. Interpersonal relations; 5. Teenage boys; 6. El Paso, Texas; 7. Texas; 8. First person narratives; 9. Realistic fiction; 10. Multiple perspectives
9781416949633

LC 2007021959
Tomas Rivera Mexican American Children's Book Award, 2009.

Two teenaged boys with very different lives find that they share a common bond—fathers they have never met who left when they were small boys—and in spite of their differences, they become close when they each need someone who understands.

The affirming and hopeful ending is well-earned for the characters and a great payoff for the reader.... Characters are well-developed and

complex.... Overall it is a strong novel with broad teenage appeal. —*Voice of Youth Advocates*

★ The **inexplicable** logic of my life: a novel. By Benjamin Alire Saenz. 2017 464 p.
Grades: 8 9 10 11 12
1. Adopted teenage boys; 2. Identity (Psychology); 3. Mexican American families; 4. Families; 5. Friendship; 6. Realistic fiction
9780544586505

LC 2016001079
YALSA Best Fiction for Young Adults, 2018.

A story set on the American border with Mexico, about family and friendship, life and death, and one teen struggling to understand what his adoption does and doesn't mean about who he is.

The themes of love, social responsibility, death, and redemption are expertly intertwined with well-developed characters and a compelling story line. This complex, sensitive, and profoundly moving book is beautifully written and will stay with readers. —*School Library Journal*

Safi, Aminah Mae

Not the girls you're looking for. Aminah Mae Safi. Feiwel & Friends, 2018 304 p.
Grades: 9 10 11 12
1. Friendship; 2. Muslim teenagers; 3. Identity (Psychology); 4. Sexual consent; 5. Teenagers — Sexuality; 6. Coming-of-age stories; 7. Realistic fiction.
9781250151810

A Muslim-American teen goes into denial mode about her role in an out-of-control party that occurred during Ramadan, a situation that escalates until she incurs damage that is harder to repair, forcing her to come to terms with her true self.—From publisher description

Safi's debut novel offers Arab and Muslim readers a teenager they can relate to as they too learn to navigate racial and religious tensions in a predominantly white society. Delightful and funny but still giving voice to serious issues of sexual consent and xenophobia. —*Kirkus*

Tell me how you really feel. Aminah Mae Safi. Feiwel & Friends, 2019 320 pages
Grades: 9 10 11 12
1. Mexican American teenage girls; 2. Asian American teenage girls; 3. Teenage girl/girl relations; 4. Lesbian teenagers; 5. Teenage romance; 6. Romantic comedies; 7. LGBTQIA romances; 8. Multiple perspectives
9781250299482

A tale told in alternative viewpoints and inspired by classic romantic comedies follows the unlikely on-camera romance between an overachieving cheerleader and the senior film project director who secretly hates her.

While Sana and Rachel's sexual orientation is an important part of the story, it is just one part, allowing Safi to create layered, nuanced characters who keep readers enthralled. A queer romance that will sweep readers away. —*Kirkus*

This is all your fault. Aminah Mae Safi. Feiwel & Friends 2020 320 p.
Grades: 9 10 11 12
1. Teenage girls; 2. Interpersonal relations; 3. Small business; 4. Quarreling; 5. Young women; 6. Multiple perspectives.
9781250242341

An energizing, character-driven celebration of belonging, acceptance, and sisterhood with a clear nod to the importance of community spaces. —*Publishers Weekly*

Safier, David

28 days: a novel of resistance in the Warsaw Ghetto. David Safier; translated by Helen MacCormac. Feiwel & Friends 2020 416 p.
Grades: 9 10 11 12

1. Jewish teenage girls; 2. Jewish resistance and revolts; 3. World War II — Underground movements; 4. Warsaw ghetto uprising, 1943; 5. Jews — Persecutions; 6. Warsaw, Poland; 7. Poland; 8. Second World War era (1939-1945); 9. Historical fiction; 10. First person narratives; 11. Translations
9781250237149

LC 2019018302

In Warsaw, Poland, in 1942, Mira faces impossible decisions after learning that the Warsaw ghetto is to be "liquidated," but a group of young people are planning an uprising against their Nazi captors.

Throughout this complex novel, rich in evocative detail, Mira's view evolves from a narrow focus on herself and her family to consideration of the larger community around her, reflected in her first-person narrative. —*Booklist*

Salisbury, Graham

★ **Eyes** of the emperor. Graham Salisbury. Wendy Lamb Books, 2005 229 p. (Prisoners of the empire, 2)
Grades: 7 8 9 10

1. Japanese American teenage boys; 2. Teenage soldiers; 3. Japanese Americans; 4. Dogs — War use; 5. Racism; 6. Hawaii; 7. United States; 8. Second World War era (1939-1945); 9. Historical fiction; 10. War stories; 11. First person narratives.
9780385729710; 9780385908740

LC 2004015142

Leslie Bradshaw Award for Young Adult Literature (Oregon), 2006; ALA Notable Children's Book, 2006; YALSA Best Books for Young Adults, 2006.

Following orders from the United States Army, several young Japanese-American men train K-9 units to hunt Asians during World War II.

Based on the experiences of 26 Hawaiian-Americans of Japanese ancestry, this novel tells an uncomfortable story. Yet it tells of belief in honor, respect, and love of country. —*Library Media Connection*

Companion book: *Under the blood-red sun.*

Lord of the deep. Graham Salisbury. Delacorte Press, 2001 182 p;
Grades: 5 6 7 8

1. Stepfather and stepson; 2. Deep-sea fishing; 3. Bribery; 4. Forgiveness; 5. Stepfathers; 6. Hawaii; 7. Realistic fiction; 8. Coming-of-age stories.
9780385729185

LC 60280

Boston Globe-Horn Book Award for Fiction and Poetry, 2002; Booklist Editors' Choice: Books for Youth, 2001; YALSA Best Books for Young Adults, 2002; School Library Journal Best Books, 2001.

Working for his stepfather on a charter fishing boat in Hawaii teaches thirteen-year-old Mikey about fishing, and about taking risks, making sacrifices, and facing some of life's difficult choices.

With its vivid Hawaiian setting, this fine novel is a natural for book-discussion groups that enjoy pondering moral ambiguity. Its action-packed scenes will also lure in reluctant readers. —*School Library Journal*

Salisbury, Melinda

The **Sin** Eater's daughter. Melinda Salisbury. Scholastic Press, an imprint of Scholastic Inc, 2015 336 p. (Sin Eater's daughter, 1)
Grades: 9 10 11 12

1. Gods and goddesses; 2. Executions and executioners; 3. Intrigue; 4. Poisons; 5. Princes; 6. High fantasy; 7. Fantasy fiction

9780545810623; 9781407147635, print, UK

LC 2014038970

For four years sixteen-year-old Twylla has lived in the castle of Lormere, the goddess-embodied, whose touch can poison and kill, and hence the Queen's executioner—but when Prince Merek, her betrothed, who is immune to her touch returns to the kingdom she finds herself caught up in palace intrigues, unsure if she can trust him or the bodyguard who claims to love her.

Salisbury weaves a complex tale of romance, religion, fairy tales and politics. A slow but satisfying read with impressive depth and emotion. —*Kirkus*

Sanchez, Alex

Rainbow boys. Alex Sanchez. Simon & Schuster Books for Young Readers, 2001 224 p. (Rainbow trilogy, 1)
Grades: 10 11 12

1. Gay teenagers; 2. Self-acceptance in teenage boys; 3. First loves; 4. Friendship; 5. Homosexuality; 6. Coming-of-age stories; 7. Realistic fiction; 8. LGBTQIA fiction
9780689841002

LC 2001020952

YALSA Best Books for Young Adults, 2002.

Three high school seniors, a jock with a girlfriend and an alcoholic father, a closeted gay, and a flamboyant gay rights advocate, struggle with family issues, gay bashers, first sex, and conflicting feelings about each other.

Some of the language and sexual situations may be too mature for some readers, but overall there's enough conflict, humor and tenderness to make this story believableand touching. —*Publishers Weekly*

Sanchez, Erika L.

★ **I** am not your perfect Mexican daughter. Erika L. Sanchez. Knopf Books for Young Readers, 2017 352 p.
Grades: 9 10 11 12

1. Mexican American teenagers; 2. Expectation (Psychology); 3. Grief; 4. Sisters. — Death; 5. Secrets; 6. Realistic fiction; 7. Coming-of-age stories.
9781524700485; 9781524700492

School Library Journal Best Books, 2017; YALSA Best Fiction for Young Adults, 2018; Tomas Rivera Mexican American Children's Book Award, 2018; National Book Award for Young People's Literature finalist, 2017.

When the sister who delighted their parents by her faithful embrace of Mexican culture dies in a tragic accident, Julia, who longs to go to college and move into a home of her own, discovers from mutual friends that her sister may not have been as perfect as believed.

The depiction of Julia as she processes her losses is hauntingly memorable and noteworthy in its authentic representation of culture and experience too rarely written. —*Horn Book Guide*

Sanderson, Brandon

The **Rithmatist**. Brandon Sanderson. Tor Teen, 2013 384 p. (Rithmatist, 1)
Grades: 7 8 9 10

1. Drawing; 2. Kidnapping; 3. Magic; 4. Schools; 5. Teenage boys; 6. Fantasy fiction.
9780765320322; 9780765338440; 9781429953160, ebook, US

LC 2012043417

YALSA Best Fiction for Young Adults, 2014; YALSA Popular Paperbacks for Young Adults, 2015.

As Wild Chalklings threaten the American Isles and Rithmatists are humanity's only defense, Joel can only watch as Rithmatist students learn the magical art that he would do anything to practice.
A Tom Doherty Associates Book.

Skyward. Brandon Sanderson. 2018 513 pages : Illustration (Skyward (Brandon Sanderson), 1)
Grades: 7 8 9 10
1. Survival; 2. War; 3. Pilots; 4. Girls; 5. Courage in girls; 6. Science fiction.
9780399555770; 9780399555787; 9781473217867, Paperback, UK; 9781473217850, Hardback, UK; 9781473217874, Paperback, UK
LC 2018026175
When a long-term attack against her world by the alien Krell escalates, Spensa's dream of becoming a pilot may come true, despite her deceased father being labeled a deserter.

Steelheart. Brandon Sanderson. Random House Childrens Books, 2013 400 p. (Reckoners trilogy, 1)
Grades: 8 9 10 11 12
1. Teenage boy orphans; 2. Supervillains; 3. Dystopias; 4. Revenge; 5. Teenage boys; 6. Superhero stories
9780385743563; 9780575103993, print, UK
Garden State Teen Book Award (New Jersey), Fiction (Grades 6-8), 2016; Kentucky Bluegrass Award for Grades 6-8, 2015; Rhode Island Teen Book Award, 2015; YALSA Best Fiction for Young Adults, 2014.
At age eight, David watched as his father was killed by an Epic, a human with superhuman powers, and now, ten years later, he joins the Reckoners—the only people who are trying to kill the Epics and end their tyranny.

Sandler, Karen
Rebellion. Karen Sandler. Tu Books, an imprint of Lee & Low Books, 2014 400 p. (Tankborn novels, 3)
Grades: 7 8 9 10
1. Genetic engineering; 2. Captivity; 3. Terrorists; 4. Teenagers; 5. Social classes; 6. Science fiction
9781600609848
Sandler tackles caste systems, slavery and terrorism (including its muddled logic) head-on.... With rebellions, ideological questions and a nonwhite, not-entirely-heterosexual cast, this series is a strong addition to the genre. —*Kirkus*

Tankborn. Karen Sandler. Tu Books, 2011 373 p. (Tankborn novels, 1)
Grades: 7 8 9 10
1. Genetic engineering; 2. Social classes; 3. Conspiracies; 4. Missing children; 5. Slaves; 6. Science fiction.
9781600606625
LC 2011014589
Kayla and Mishalla, two genetically engineered non-human slaves (GENs), fall in love with higher-status boys, discover deep secrets about the creation of GENs, and in the process find out what it means to be human.
Sandler has created a fascinating dystopian world.... The author's speculative vision of the darker side of future possibilities in genetic engineering and mind control is both chilling and thought-provoking. —*School Library Journal*

Savage, Kim
★ **Beautiful** broken girls. Kim Savage. Farrar, Straus, Giroux, 2017 320 p.
Grades: 9 10 11 12

1. Grief in teenage boys; 2. Survivors of suicide victims; 3. Suicide; 4. Death; 5. Grief; 6. Massachusetts; 7. Mysteries; 8. Multiple perspectives
9780374300593
LC 2016001909
Ben learns why the love of his life Mira and her sister drowned themselves when he receives a post-mortem letter from Mira challenging him to find and decode notes hidden in the seven places where they secretly touched.
Even though the truth can be seen before it's revealed, the girls' secrets pack a gut punch that lingers. Haunting and mesmerizing. —*Kirkus*

Savit, Gavriel
Anna and the Swallow Man. Gavriel Savit. 2016 240 p.
Grades: 8 9 10 11 12
1. Girl orphans; 2. Seven-year-old girls; 3. World War II; 4. Bonding (Interpersonal relations); 5. Innocence (Psychology); 6. Poland; 7. Germany; 8. Second World War era (1939-1945); 9. Historical fiction.
9780553513349; 9780552575270, print, UK; 9781782300526, print, UK; 9780141376646, print, UK
Indies' Choice Book Awards, Young Adult, 2016; Sydney Taylor Book Award for Teen Readers, 2017.
Left alone when her intellectual father is arrested by the Germans during World War II, Anna, a child growing up in occupied Krakow, Poland, finds shelter with a talented illusionist who hides a sinister nature.
Full of sophisticated questions and advanced vocabulary, Savits debut occasionally feels like an adult novel, but young readers with the patience for his gauzy pacing and oblique plot turns will be rewarded by a moving, thought-provoking story about coming-of-age in the midst of trauma. —*Booklist*

Scelsa, Kate
Fans of the impossible life. Kate Scelsa. Balzer + Bray, an imprint of HarperCollins Publishers, 2015 336 p.
Grades: 9 10 11 12
1. Gay teenagers; 2. Teenage girls with depression; 3. Foster teenagers; 4. Best friends; 5. Friendship; 6. New Jersey; 7. Realistic fiction; 8. Multiple perspectives
9780062331755; 9781509805143, print, UK
LC 2015005754
Rainbow List, 2016.
At Saint Francis Prep school in Mountain View, New Jersey, Mira, Jeremy, and Sebby come together as they struggle with romance, bullying, foster home and family problems, and mental health issues.
So much more than a love triangle novel, Scelsa's debut is filled with teens discovering how to handle life's situations. —*School Library Journal*

Schlitz, Laura Amy
★ The **hired** girl. Laura Amy Schlitz. Candlewick Press, 2015 400 p.
Grades: 7 8 9 10
1. Household employees; 2. Catholics; 3. Jewish families; 4. Crushes in teenage girls; 5. Fourteen-year-old girls; 6. Baltimore, Maryland; 7. Pennsylvania; 8. 1910s; 9. Historical fiction; 10. Coming-of-age stories; 11. Diary novels
9780763678180
ALA Notable Children's Book, 2016; Booklist Editors' Choice: Books for Youth, 2015; Scott O'Dell Historical Fiction Award, 2016; Sydney Taylor Book Award for Teen Readers, 2016; YALSA Best Fiction for Young Adults, 2016; National Jewish Book Award, 2015.
A wonderful look into the life of strong girl who learns that she needs the love of others to truly grow up. —*School Library Journal*

Schmatz, Pat

★ **Bluefish**. Pat Schmatz. Candlewick Press, 2011 240 p.
Grades: 7 8 9 10
1. Loners; 2. Illiteracy; 3. Resentfulness in teenagers; 4.
Resentfulness; 5. Family problems; 6. Realistic fiction; 7. Multiple
perspectives
9780763653347

LC 2010044815

Booklist Editors' Choice: Books for Youth, 2011; Josette Frank
Award, 2012; Elizabeth Burr/Worzalla Award (Wisconsin), 2012.

Everything changes for thirteen-year-old Travis, a new student who is
trying to hide his illiteracy, when he meets a sassy classmate with her own
secrets and a remarkable teacher.

A cast of richly developed characters peoples this work of contemporary fiction, told in the third person from Travis' point of view, with
first-person vignettes from Velveeta's perspective peppered throughout....
A story rife with unusual honesty and hope. —*Kirkus*

Lizard Radio. Pat Schmatz. Candlewick Press, 2015 288 p.
Grades: 9 10 11 12
1. Gender identity; 2. Camps; 3. Crushes (Interpersonal relations); 4.
Fifteen-year-old girls; 5. Teenage girls; 6. Dystopian fiction; 7.
Science fiction; 8. Coming-of-age stories.
9780763676353

James Tiptree, Jr. Award, 2015; Rainbow List, 2016.

An entertaining and thought-provoking read, this title will be a big hit
for those who want something deeper from their dystopian fiction.
—*School Library Journal*

Schmidt, Gary D.

★ **Orbiting** Jupiter. Gary D. Schmidt. 2015 192 pages cm
Grades: 6 7 8 9
1. Teenage fathers; 2. Father-separated children; 3. Foster children; 4.
Friendship; 5. Emotional problems; 6. Realistic fiction
9780544462229

LC 2015001338

ALA Notable Children's Book, 2016; Great Lakes Great Books
Award (Michigan), Grades 6-8, 2016; Land of Enchantment Book
Award (New Mexico): Lizards (Grades 6-8), 2018; Nutmeg
Children's Book Award, Teen category, 2018; Notable Books for a
Global Society, 2016; Westchester Fiction Award, 2017; YALSA Best
Fiction for Young Adults, 2017; Grand Canyon Reader Award
(Arizona), Tween Book Category, 2018; Young Hoosier Book Award,
Middle Books, 2018.

Jack, 12, tells the gripping story of Joseph, 14, who joins his family as
a foster child. Damaged in prison, Joseph wants nothing more than to find
his baby daughter, Jupiter, whom he has never seen. When Joseph has begun to believe he'll have a future, he is confronted by demons from his
past that force a tragic sacrifice.

The matter-of-fact narrative voice ensures that the tragic plot never
overwhelms this wrenching tale of growth and loss. —*School Library
Journal*

★ The **Wednesday** wars. By Gary D. Schmidt. Clarion Books, 2007
256 p.
Grades: 5 6 7 8
1. Shakespeare, William, 1564-1616; 2. Teacher-student relationships;
3. Growth (Psychology); 4. Junior high schools; 5. Schools; 6.
Families; 7. Long Island, New York; 8. 1960s; 9. Coming-of-age
stories; 10. Historical fiction.
9780618724833

LC 2006023660

ALA Notable Children's Book, 2008; Booklist Editors' Choice:
Books for Youth, 2007; YALSA Best Books for Young Adults, 2008;

YALSA Popular Paperbacks for Young Adults, 2013; Newbery Honor
Book, 2008.

During the 1967 school year, on Wednesday afternoons when all his
classmates go to either Catechism or Hebrew school, seventh-grader
Holling Hoodhood stays in Mrs. Baker's classroom where they read the
plays of William Shakespeare and Holling learns much of value about the
world he lives in.

The serious issues are leavened with ample humor, and the supporting cast...is fully dimensional. Best of all is the hero. —*Publishers Weekly*
Companion novel: *Okay for now.*

Schneider, Robyn

★ The **beginning** of everything. Robyn Schneider. Katherine Tegen
Books, 2013 336 p.
Grades: 9 10 11 12
1. Teenage athletes; 2. Cheating (Interpersonal relations); 3. Traffic
accident victims; 4. Interpersonal relations; 5. Friendship; 6.
California; 7. Realistic fiction.
9780062217134

LC 2012030976

Star athlete and prom king Ezra Faulkner's life is irreparably transformed by a tragic accident and the arrival of eccentric new girl Cassidy
Thorpe.

Schrefer, Eliot

The **deadly** sister. Eliot Schrefer. Scholastic Press, 2010 310 p;
Grades: 8 9 10 11 12
1. Protectiveness; 2. Determination in teenage girls; 3. Teenage drug
dealers; 4. Missing teenage girls; 5. Sisters; 6. Florida; 7. Mysteries
9780545165747

LC Bl2010011576

Abby Goodwin is used to covering up for her rebellious sister Maya's
frequent misdemeanors, but she is baffled when Maya is accused of murder and resolves to clear her sister's name, with unexpectedly dangerous
results.

Well-drawn characters, realistic dialogue, and suspenseful twists and
turns add to the appeal. Teens crave mystery, and this book will suit them
just fine. —*School Library Journal*

★ **Endangered**. Eliot Schrefer. Scholastic Press, 2012 264 p. (Ape
quartet, 1)
Grades: 7 8 9 10 11 12
1. Bonobos; 2. Wilderness survival; 3. Coups d'etat; 4. Rescues; 5.
Animal rescue; 6. Congo (Democratic Republic); 7. Adventure
stories.
9780545165761

LC 2012030877

Amelia Bloomer List, 2013; Notable Books for a Global Society,
2013; YALSA Best Fiction for Young Adults, 2013; National Book
Award for Young People's Literature finalist, 2012.

Sophie is not happy to be back in the Congo for the summer, but when
she rescues an abused baby bonobo she becomes more involved in her
mother's sanctuary—and when fighting breaks out and the sanctuary is attacked, it is up to Sophie to rescue the apes and somehow survive in the
jungle.

★ **Threatened**. Eliot Schrefer. Scholastic Press, 2014 288 p. (Ape
quartet, 2)
Grades: 7 8 9 10 11 12
1. Chimpanzees; 2. Teenage boy orphans; 3. Jungles; 4. Survival; 5.
Teenage boys; 6. Africa; 7. Gabon; 8. Adventure stories.
9780545551434

YALSA Best Fiction for Young Adults, 2015; National Book Award for Young People's Literature finalist, 2014.

Escaping his jailer by fleeing into the forest with a scientist who is not entirely what he seems, an African street youth helps the scientist with his studies of chimpanzees and must join the chimps to save their habitat from unwelcome intruders.

The book is filled with sensory detail—the city and jungle settings pulse with vitality—and the characters, human and nonhuman alike, are well drawn. —*Horn Book Guide*

Schreiber, Joe

Au revoir, crazy European chick. By Joe Schreiber. Houghton Mifflin, 2011 240 p.
Grades: 9 10 11 12
1. Assassins; 2. Exchange students; 3. High school seniors; 4. Lithuanians in the United States; 5. Families; 6. New York City; 7. Spy fiction; 8. Teen chick lit; 9. Books for reluctant readers
9780547577388

LC 2011009845

YALSA Best Fiction for Young Adults, 2013; YALSA Quick Picks for Reluctant Young Adult Readers, 2012.

Perry's parents insist that he take Gobi, their quiet, Lithuanian exchange student, to senior prom but after an incident at the dance he learns that Gobi is actually a trained assassin who needs him as a henchman, behind the wheel of his father's precious Jaguar, on a mission in Manhattan.

Perfect for action adventure junkies who will enjoy the car chases, thugs, graphic killing scenes, explosions, and a random bear fight, Schreiber's debut novel also contains enough humor, sexual tension, distinctive language, and character development to make this more than just a quick thrill read. —*Horn Book Guide*
Sequel: *Perry's killer playlist.*

★ **Perry's** killer playlist. Written by Joe Schreiber. Houghton Mifflin, 2012 192 p.
Grades: 9 10 11 12
1. Rock musicians; 2. Assassins; 3. Espionage; 4. Eighteen-year-old men; 5. Teenage boy/girl relations; 6. Europe; 7. Adventure stories.
9780547601175

LC 2011041392

As his rock band tours Italy, eighteen-year-old Perry says a reluctant "bonjour" to Gobi, his former exchange student/Lithuanian assassin, who enlists his help on a justice-dispensing rampage all over Europe.

Schrieve, Hal

Out of Salem. Hal Schrieve. Random House Inc 2019 448 p.
Grades: 9 10 11 12
1. Zombies; 2. Genderqueer; 3. Totalitarianism; 4. Werewolves; 5. Lesbians; 6. Salem, Oregon; 7. Oregon; 8. 1990s; 9. Urban fantasy; 10. Allegories; 11. Multiple perspectives.
9781609809010; 9781609809027

LC 2018029438

Longlisted for the National Book Award for Young People's Literature, 2019.

When a local psychiatrist is murdered by what seems to be werewolves, a small town becomes even more hostile to "monsters," and Z, a genderqueer orphaned zombie, and Aysel, an unregistered werewolf, are driven together in an attempt to survive a place where most people wish that neither of them existed.

Shrieve conjures intricate magic vital to the plot, pushes the book's leads to grow amid the book's ratcheting tension, and provides incisive social commentary via monster-tale tropes. Any reader who has felt it necessary to hide their true identity will find strong characters to connect with in this fun, powerful story. —*Publishers Weekly*

Schroder, Monika

The **dog** in the wood. Monika Schroder. Front Street, 2009 163 p.
Grades: 6 7 8 9
1. Parent-separated boys; 2. Children and war; 3. Farm life; 4. Courage in boys; 5. Ten-year-old boys; 6. Germany; 7. Second World War era (1939-1945); 8. Historical fiction
9781590787014

LC 2009004970

As World War II draws to an end, Russian soldiers occupy Schwartz, Germany, bringing both friendship and hardship to the family of ten-year-old Fritz, whose grandfather was a Nazi sympathizer, eventually forcing them to leave their farm, then arresting Fritz's mother and her hired hand.

The action in this important addition of WWII literature will grab readers, and Schroder's story is an excellent, authentic portrait of children in war. —*Booklist*

My brother's shadow. Monika Schroder. Farrar Straus Giroux, 2011 240 p.
Grades: 6 7 8 9 10
1. Teenage boys; 2. Personal conduct; 3. World War I; 4. War; 5. Sixteen-year-old boys; 6. Germany; 7. War stories; 8. Historical fiction; 9. First person narratives.
9780374351229

LC 2010033107

In 1918 Berlin, Germany, sixteen-year-old Moritz struggles to do what is right on his newspaper job, in his relationship with his mother and sister who are outspoken socialists, and with his brother, who returns from the war physically and emotionally scarred.

In this nuanced and realistic work of historical fiction, Schrder...immerses readers in her setting with meticulous details and dynamic characters that contribute to a palpable sense of tension. —*Publishers Weekly*
Frances Foster Books.

Schroeder, Lisa

All we have is now. Lisa Schroeder. Scholastic, 2015 272 p.
Grades: 9 10 11 12
1. Homeless teenagers; 2. End of the world; 3. Wishing and wishes; 4. Asteroids; 5. Portland, Oregon; 6. Science fiction.
9780545802536

Since she ran away from home Emerson has been living on the streets of Portland, relying on her wits and her friend Vince to get by, but as a meteor approaches North America they meet Carl, who tells them he has been granting people's wishes—so what will they do if this is their last day on Earth, and, more important, what will they do if it is not?

Cleverly plotted with strong characters and interspersed with Emerson's free-verse poetry, this at times far-fetched novel will capture many teen readers' hearts. Schroeder deftly explores a variety of themes—family, romance, forgiveness, friendship—and uses wit and the promise of hope to keep the story from becoming overwhelming. —*Booklist*

Chasing Brooklyn. Lisa Schroeder. Simon Pulse, 2010 432 p.
Grades: 7 8 9 10
1. Grief in teenagers; 2. Teenagers and death; 3. Nightmares; 4. Grief; 5. Death; 6. Novels in verse.
9781416991687

LC 2009019442

As teenagers Brooklyn and Nico work to help each other recover from the deaths of Brooklyn's boyfriend—Nico's brother Lucca—and their friend Gabe, the two begin to rediscover their passion for life, and a newly blossoming passion for one another.

Chasing Brooklyn is told in a verse format that enables the author to cut right to the emotional quick. The short sentences and minimal dialogue keep the focus on the pain and fear of the two main characters....

While the wrenching impact will leave readers raw, the ultimately hopeful ending is comforting. A quick read, but one with substance. —*School Library Journal*

Schwab, Victoria

The **Near** Witch. Victoria Schwab. Hyperion Books, 2011 288 p.
Grades: 7 8 9 10
1. Witches; 2. Missing children; 3. Moors and heaths; 4. Villages; 5. Supernatural; 6. Paranormal fiction; 7. First person narratives
9781423137870; 9781789091922, Paperback, UK; 9781789091120, Hardback, UK

LC 2010036289

Sixteen-year-old Lexi, who lives on an enchanted moor at the edge of the village of Near, must solve the mystery when, the day after a mysterious boy appears in town, children start disappearing.

Part fairy tale, part legend with a little romance, this well-written mystery will capture the attention of teens. —*School Library Journal*

Our dark duet. Victoria Schwab. Greenwillow Books, an imprint of HarperCollinsPublishers, 2017 510 p. (Monsters of Verity, 2)
Grades: 9 10 11 12
1. Monsters; 2. Violence; 3. Soul; 4. Teenagers; 5. Harker, Kate (Fictitious character); 6. Urban fantasy
9780062380883

When a new monster, who feeds on chaos and brings out its victim's inner demon, emerges from the shadows, Kate finds herself lured home to face a monster she thought she killed, a boy she thought she knew, and a demon all her own.

Masterly writing, a fast-moving plot, and just the right amount of bittersweet romance make this book hard to put down. —*School Library Journal*

★ **This** savage song. Victoria Schwab. Greenwillow Books, an imprint of HarperCollins Publishers, 2016 427 p. (Monsters of Verity, 1)
Grades: 9 10 11 12
1. Monsters; 2. Conspiracies; 3. Post-apocalypse; 4. Magic; 5. Music; 6. Urban fantasy
9780062380852; 9781785652745, print, UK; 9781785652752, ebook
Booklist Editors' Choice: Books for Youth, 2016.
Crackling with energy, just the ticket for an all-night read. —*Kirkus*

Scott, Elizabeth

★ **Living** dead girl. Elizabeth Scott. Simon Pulse, 2008 170 p;
Grades: 9 10 11 12
1. Kidnapping; 2. Sexually abused teenagers; 3. Sex crimes; 4. Captivity; 5. Captives; 6. Psychological fiction; 7. Multiple perspectives; 8. First person narratives; 9. Books for reluctant readers
9781416960591

LC Bl2008023118

YALSA Quick Picks for Reluctant Young Adult Readers, 2009; Amelia Bloomer List, 2009; YALSA Popular Paperbacks for Young Adults, 2010; YALSA Best Books for Young Adults, 2009.

After being abducted when she was ten and abused for five years by her kidnapper, Ray, Alice's only hope of freedom is in death, but her only way to achieve such an escape is to help Ray find the next girl for his collection.

Scott's prose is spare and damning, relying on suggestive details and their impact on Alice to convey the unimaginable violence she repeatedly experiences. Disturbing but fascinating, the book exerts an inescapable grip on readerslike Alice, they have virtually no choice but to continue until the conclusion sets them free. —*Publishers Weekly*

Scott, Michael

★ The **alchemyst**. Michael Scott. Delacorte Press, 2007 400 p. (Secrets of the immortal Nicholas Flamel, 1)
Grades: 7 8 9 10
1. Flamel, Nicolas, 1330-1418; 2. Twin brothers and sisters; 3. Alchemists; 4. Rare books; 5. Magic; 6. Supernatural; 7. San Francisco, California; 8. California; 9. Fantasy fiction.
9780385733571; 9780385903721; 9780552562522, print, UK

LC 2006024417

Rhode Island Teen Book Award, 2009; YALSA Popular Paperbacks for Young Adults, 2012.

Having discovered the secret to eternal youth, 14th-century alchemist Nicholas Flamel and his wife are alive and well in present-day San Francisco, California. But they won't stay well if 15-year-old twins Sophie and Josh Newman don't fulfill their prophesied role of either saving or destroying the world, starting by getting back an ancient text stolen from Flamel's bookstore. (The stolen volume contains the key to the Flamels' immortality, which they must renew every month.)

Scott uses a gigantic canvas for this riveting fantasy.... A fabulous read. —*School Library Journal*
Sequel: *The magician*.

The **enchantress**. Michael Scott. Delacorte Press, 2012 416 p. (Secrets of the immortal Nicholas Flamel, 6)
Grades: 7 8 9 10
1. Flamel, Nicolas, 1330-1418; 2. Alchemists; 3. Twin brothers and sisters; 4. Prophecies; 5. Immortality; 6. Supernatural; 7. Fantasy fiction.
9780385905183; 9780385619004, print, UK

With the twins of prophecy split, Nicholas Flamel near death, and John Dee in possession of the swords of power, Danu Talis has yet to fall and the future of the human race lies in the balance.

[Scott] fully fleshes out his main characters in their final roles, realistically and sometimes surprisingly melding their lives, their deaths, and their futures. This is a powerful and tidy conclusion to [the] series. —*Booklist*

The **magician**. Michael Scott. Delacorte Press, 2008 455 p; (Secrets of the immortal Nicholas Flamel, 2)
Grades: 7 8 9 10
1. Flamel, Nicolas, 1330-1418; 2. Twin brothers and sisters; 3. Alchemists; 4. Jealousy in teenage boys; 5. Monsters; 6. Immortality; 7. Paris, France; 8. Fantasy fiction.
9780385733588; 9780552562539, print, UK; 9780385613101, print, UK

LC 2007051598

Fifteen-year-old twins Sophie and Josh Newman continue their magical training in Paris with Nicholas Flamel, Scatty, and the Comte de Sant Germaine, pursued by Doctor Dee and the immortal Niccolo Machiavelli.

Although the novel is essentially plot driven, the book's characters are well developed and engaging. The addition of historical figures in the story...add an appealing intrigue to the book. Teens who like fast-paced fantasies with lots of action...are sure to enjoy this new addition to the genre. —*Voice of Youth Advocates*
Sequel to: *The Alchemyst*.

The **necromancer**. Michael Scott. Delacorte Press, 2010 416 p. (Secrets of the immortal Nicholas Flamel, 4)
Grades: 7 8 9 10
1. Flamel, Nicolas, 1330-1418; 2. Twin brothers and sisters; 3. Alchemists; 4. Monsters; 5. Trust; 6. Magic; 7. London, England; 8. San Francisco, California; 9. Fantasy fiction.
9780385735315; 9780385905169; 9780375896606; 9780385619035, print, UK

LC 2010003372
Back in London, fifteen-year-old twins Sophie and Josh Newman must determine whom they can and cannot trust as they search for both Scatty and an immortal who can teach Josh the magic of fire, while Doctor Dee and Machiavelli continue to seek power.

The **sorceress**. Michael Scott. Delacorte Press, 2009 488 p. (Secrets of the immortal Nicholas Flamel, 3)
Grades: 7 8 9 10
1. Flamel, Nicolas, 1330-1418; 2. Twin brothers and sisters; 3. Alchemists; 4. Women wizards; 5. Magic; 6. Supernatural; 7. England; 8. Fantasy fiction.
9780385735292; 9780552557245, print, UK
While armies of the Shadowrealms gather and Machiavelli goes to Alcatraz to kill Perenelle Flamel, fifteen-year-old twins Sophie and Josh Newman accompany the Alchemist to England to seek Gilgamesh.

Master yarnspinner that he is, Scott expertly cranks up the suspense while keeping his now-large cast in quick motion.... Ending in a welter of revelations, reunions and unresolved plotlines, this page-turner promises plenty of action to come. —*Kirkus*

The **warlock**. Michael Scott. Delacorte Press, 2011 400 p. (Secrets of the immortal Nicholas Flamel, 5)
Grades: 7 8 9 10
1. Flamel, Nicolas, 1330-1418; 2. Alchemists; 3. Twin brothers and sisters; 4. Monsters; 5. Immortality; 6. Supernatural; 7. San Francisco, California; 8. Alcatraz Island, California; 9. Fantasy fiction.
9780385735339; 9780385905176; 9780375899546; 9780552562560, print, UK; 9780857530264, print, UK
LC 2011005716
Fifteen-year-old Josh has chosen to side neither with his twin sister Sophie nor with the Alchemyst, Nicholas Flamel, but rather to fight alongside Dr. John Dee and the mysterious Virginia Dare, while the immortal Machiavelli and Billy the Kid follow the Elders' plans to set loose the monsters of Alcatraz on San Francisco and trigger the end of the human race.

Sedgwick, Marcus
★ The **ghosts** of heaven. Marcus Sedgwick. Roaring Brook Press, 2015 256 p.
Grades: 9 10 11 12
1. Cave-drawings; 2. Psychiatric hospitals; 3. Stone age; 4. Spirals; 5. Signs and symbols; 6. England; 7. Science fiction; 8. Parallel narratives
9781626721258; 9781780622217, print, UK; 9781626721265, ebook, US
LC 2014040471
Booklist Editors' Choice: Books for Youth, 2015; Michael L. Printz Honor Book, 2016.
Four linked stories of discovery and survival begin with a Paleolithic-era girl who makes the first written signs, continue with Anna, who people call a witch, then a mad twentieth-century poet who watches the ocean knowing the horrors it hides, and concluding with an astronaut on the first spaceship from Earth sent to colonize another world.

What openly draws these stories together is a spiral and spinning symbolism that presents itself through vivid details, from the seemingly mundane to literary references. Individually they conform to conventions; together they defy expectations as they raise questions about humanity and its connections to the universe and one another. —*Kirkus*
First published in the United Kingdom in 2014 by Orion Children's Books, London.

★ **Midwinterblood**. Marcus Sedgwick. Roaring Brook Press, 2013 272 p.

Grades: 7 8 9 10 11 12
1. Reincarnation; 2. Islands; 3. Love; 4. Painters; 5. Journalists; 6. Scandinavia; 7. Magical realism
9781596438002; 9781780620091, print, UK
LC 2012013302
Booklist Editors' Choice: Books for Youth, 2013; Michael L. Printz Award, 2014; YALSA Best Fiction for Young Adults, 2014; YALSA Best Fiction for Young Adults: Top Ten, 2014; YALSA Popular Paperbacks for Young Adults, 2015.
Seven linked vignettes unfold on a Scandinavian island inhabited—throughout various time periods—by Vikings, vampires, ghosts, and a curiously powerful plant—Provided by publisher.

★ **Revolver**. Marcus Sedgwick. Roaring Brook Press, 2010 204 p.
Grades: 7 8 9 10
1. Decision-making; 2. Guns; 3. Cabins; 4. Gold rush; 5. Fathers — Death; 6. Alaska; 7. Arctic regions; 8. 1910s; 9. Historical mysteries; 10. Adventure stories; 11. Mysteries
9781596435926; 9781405664356, print, UK
YALSA Best Fiction for Young Adults, 2011; Michael L. Printz Honor Book, 2011.
Tight plotting and a wealth of moral concerns—good versus evil; faith, love, and hope; the presence of God; survival in a bleak landscape; trusting the lessons parents teach—make this a memorable tale. —*Horn Book Guide*

★ **Saint** death. Marcus Sedgwick. Roaring Brook Press, 2017 240 p.
Grades: 9 10 11 12
1. Santa Muerte; 2. Gangs; 3. Drug traffic; 4. Human trafficking; 5. Card games; 6. Gambling; 7. Mexico; 8. Mexican-American Border Region.
9781626725492
LC 2016035286
YALSA Best Fiction for Young Adults, 2018.
An unsparing tale set in the grimly violent world of the human and drug trade on the U.S.-Mexican border finds Arturo enduring a hardscrabble existence before helping his friend, who has stolen money from the narcos to smuggle his girlfriend and baby into the U.S.

This well-researched novel is an absorbing, heart-rending read and a scathing indictment of the conditions that have allowed the drug trade and human trafficking to flourish in Mexico. —*School Library Journal*
First published in the United Kingdom in 2016 by Orion Children's Books, London

★ **She** is not invisible. Marcus Sedgwick. 2014 224 p.
Grades: 7 8 9 10 11 12
1. Teenagers who are blind; 2. Father-separated children; 3. Missing persons; 4. Brothers and sisters; 5. Blindness; 6. New York City; 7. London, England; 8. Mysteries; 9. First person narratives
9781596438019; 9781780621098; 9781780621340, print, UK
LC 2013029561
YALSA Best Fiction for Young Adults, 2015.
A London teenager who is blind and her younger brother travel to New York to find their missing father, using clues from his notebook.

Laureth is sixteen, smart, self-doubting, and blind. She is also desperate to find her missing famous writer father—desperate enough to boost her mother's credit card to buy two plane tickets from London to New York City, forge travel documents, and abduct her beloved seven-year-old brother in order to disguise her blindness... Laureth herself is worth the journey. The tricks she uses to negotiate in a sighted world. her determination to fight the tendency of sighted people to treat blind people as stupid or deaf or, most insidiously, invisible—all are presented matter-of-factly and sympathetically. Readers will applaud Laureth's believable evolution into a more confident—and definitely more visible—young woman. —*Horn Book Guide*

★ **White** crow. Marcus Sedgwick. Roaring Brook Press, 2011 240 p.
Grades: 8 9 10 11 12
1. Life after death; 2. Priests; 3. Coastal towns; 4. Good and evil; 5. Friendship; 6. England; 7. East Anglia, England; 8. Horror
9781596435940

LC 2010034053

YALSA Best Fiction for Young Adults, 2012; School Library Journal Best Books, 2011.

Sixteen-year-old Rebecca moves with her father from London to a small, seaside village, where she befriends another motherless girl and they spend the summer together exploring the village's sinister history.

Showing his customary skill with a gothic setting and morally troubled characters, Sedgwick keeps readers guessing to the very end. —*Publishers Weekly*

Selfors, Suzanne

Mad love. Suzanne Selfors. Walker Books for Young Readers, 2010 336 p.
Grades: 7 8 9 10
1. Children of people with mental illnesses; 2. Cupid (Roman deity); 3. Writing; 4. Love; 5. Creativity — Mental health aspects; 6. Seattle, Washington; 7. Washington (State); 8. Teen chick lit; 9. Mythological fiction; 10. Pacific Northwest fiction
9780802784506

LC 2010023261

When her famous romance-novelist mother is secretly hospitalized in an expensive mental facility, sixteen-year-old Alice tries to fulfill her mother's contract with her publisher by writing a love story—with the help of Cupid.

There's a bit of mythology, a bit of romance, a bit of the paranormal, and some real-life problems, but Selfors juggles them all assuredly. Serious ideas are handled carefully, while real humor is spread throughout the whole book. This book has real charm with great depth. —*Voice of Youth Advocates*

The **sweetest** spell. By Suzanne Selfors. Walker Books for Young Readers, 2012 416 p.
Grades: 7 8 9 10 11 12
1. Teenage girls with disabilities; 2. Prejudice; 3. Chocolate; 4. Magic; 5. Floods; 6. Fantasy fiction; 7. Multiple perspectives
9780802723765

LC 2011034591

YALSA Best Fiction for Young Adults, 2013.

Scorned in her Flatlands village because of a deformed foot, Emmeline Thistle's life changes when she is taken in by Wanderlands dairy farmers and discovers her magical ability to make chocolate, which is more precious and rare than gold or jewels in the kingdom of Anglund.

Selfors's story line initially comes across as chaotic, but the pacing is strong, and the elements of her tale fall into place in a logical and entirely satisfying manner. An exhilarating, romantic, and frequently funny story of self-discovery. —*Publishers Weekly*

Selzer, Adam

How to get suspended and influence people. By Adam Selzer. Delacorte Press, 2007 192 p.
Grades: 6 7 8 9
1. Films — Production and direction; 2. Filmmaking; 3. Gifted children; 4. Middle school students; 5. Eighth-grade boys; 6. Humorous stories; 7. First person narratives.
9780385733694

LC 2006020438

Gifted eighth-grader Leon Harris becomes an instant celebrity when the film he makes for a class project sends him to in-school suspension.

This funny, fast-paced novel is filled with characters who epitomize the middle school experience, and it presents a lesson or two about free speech as well. —*School Library Journal*

Sequel: *Pirates of the Retail Wasteland.*

Sendak, Maurice

★ **My** brother's book. Maurice Sendak. Michael di Capua Books, 2013 32 p.
Grades: 4 5 6 7 8
1. Brothers; 2. Separated brothers; 3. Familial love; 4. Separated friends, relatives, etc; 5. Desire; 6. Picture books.
9780062234896

New York Times Best Illustrated Children's Book, 2013.

Presents a poem Sendak wrote to pay homage to his late brother, Jack, whom he credited for his passion for writing and drawing.

As the ultimate not-for-little-children Sendak, this profoundly personal book about loss and healing should find its audience among thoughtful adults (and perhaps some teenagers). —*Horn Book Guide*

Illustrated by the author.

Sepetys, Ruta

★ **Between** shades of gray. Ruta Sepetys. Philomel Books, 2011 352 p.
Grades: 8 9 10 11 12
1. Teenage girl artists; 2. Forced labor; 3. Survival; 4. Fifteen-year-old girls; 5. Teenage girls; 6. Lithuania; 7. Siberia; 8. 1940s; 9. Historical fiction; 10. Books to movies
9780399254123; 9780141335889, print, UK

LC 2009050092

ALA Notable Children's Book, 2012; Booklist Editors' Choice: Books for Youth, 2011; Golden Kite Award for Fiction, 2011; Indies' Choice Book Awards, Young Adult, 2012; International Reading Association Children's Book Award for Young Adult Fiction, 2012; Notable Books for a Global Society, 2012; YALSA Best Fiction for Young Adults, 2012; YALSA Popular Paperbacks for Young Adults, 2014; School Library Journal Best Books, 2011; William C. Morris Debut Award finalist, 2012.

In 1941, fifteen-year-old Lina, her mother, and brother are pulled from their Lithuanian home by Soviet guards and sent to Siberia, where her father is sentenced to death in a prison camp while she fights for her life, vowing to honor her family and the thousands like hers by burying her story in a jar on Lithuanian soil. Based on the author's family, includes a historical note.

A harrowing page-turner, made all the more so for its basis in historical fact, the novel illuminates the persecution suffered by Stalin's victims (20 million were killed), while presenting memorable characters who retain their will to survive even after more than a decade in exile. —*Publishers Weekly*

Produced as a movie titled: *Ashes in the Snow.*

★ The **fountains** of silence. Ruta Sepetys. Philomel Books. 2019 512 p.
Grades: 9 10 11 12
1. Photographers; 2. Tourists; 3. Postwar life; 4. Fascism; 5. Teenagers; 6. Madrid, Spain; 7. Spain; 8. 1950s; 9. Historical fiction
9780399160318; 9780241422236, Paperback, UK; 9780241421871, Hardback, UK; 9780241421857, Paperback, UK

Drawn back to his mother's homeland by the utopian promises of the Franco regime in 1957 Madrid, the photographer son of an oil tycoon bonds with a girl who raises his awareness about the lingering shadows of the Spanish Civil War.

As Sepetys slowly unspools hard truths about the era, such as the prevalence of babies stolen from poor, Republican families, the facts become increasingly impossible to ignore, both for the reader and for Daniel. The romance ultimately takes center stage, but the troubling events in the margins add terrifyingly high stakes to Daniel and Ana's relationship. —*Booklist*

★ **Out** of the Easy. Ruta Sepetys. Philomel Books, 2013 288 p.
Grades: 9 10 11 12 Adult
1. Children of prostitutes; 2. Murder investigation; 3. Teenage romance; 4. Seventeen-year-old girls; 5. Teenage girls; 6. New Orleans, Louisiana; 7. French Quarter (New Orleans, La.); 8. 1950s; 9. Historical mysteries; 10. Mysteries
9780399256929
LC 2012016062
YALSA Best Fiction for Young Adults, 2014; YALSA Best Fiction for Young Adults: Top Ten, 2014.

Josie, the seventeen-year-old daughter of a French Quarter prostitute, is striving to escape 1950 New Orleans and enroll at prestigious Smith College when she becomes entangled in a murder investigation.

★ **Salt** to the sea: a novel. Ruta Sepetys. Philomel Books, 2016 391 pages : Map
Grades: 8 9 10 11 12
1. Refugees; 2. World War II; 3. Nurses; 4. Pregnant teenagers; 5. Soldiers; 6. Europe; 7. Second World War era (1939-1945); 8. 1940s; 9. Historical fiction; 10. Multiple perspectives
9780399160301; 9780141347400, print, UK
California Young Reader Medal, Young Adult, 2018; Carnegie Medal, 2017; Golden Kite Award for Fiction, 2017; Goodreads Choice Award, 2016; Grand Canyon Reader Award (Arizona), Teen Book Category, 2018; Indies' Choice Book Awards, Young Adult, 2017; LibraryReads Favorites, 2016; Notable Books for a Global Society, 2017; School Library Journal Best Books, 2016; Virginia Readers' Choice Award for High School, 2018; YALSA Best Fiction for Young Adults, 2017.

As World War II draws to a close, refugees try to escape the war's final dangers, only to find themselves aboard a ship with a target on its hull.

Sepetys describes an almost unknown maritime disaster whose nearly 9,000 casualties dwarfed those of both the Titanic and the Lusitania. Told alternately from the perspective of each of the main characters, the novel also highlights the struggle and sacrifices that ordinary people—children— were forced to make. At once beautiful and heart-wrenching, this title will remind readers that there are far more casualties of war than are recorded in history books. —*Library Journal*

Shabazz, Ilyasah

★ **X:** a novel. . Candlewick Press, 2015 384 p.
Grades: 8 9 10 11 12
1. Malcolm X; 2. African American boys; 3. Separated friends, relatives, etc; 4. Segregation; 5. Black Muslims; 7. Lansing, Michigan; 8. Historical fiction; 9. First person narratives; 10. Coming-of-age stories.
9780763669676
Booklist Editors' Choice: Books for Youth, 2015; School Library Journal Best Books, 2015; YALSA Best Fiction for Young Adults, 2016; YALSA Best Fiction for Young Adults: Top Ten, 2016; Coretta Scott King Honor Book for Authors, 2016; Walter Honor Book, 2016.

Malcolm X was born Malcolm Little. The story opens with his departure from Michigan as a teen, though there are flashbacks to his younger years. It follows Malcolm through his time in Boston and Harlem, culminating with his conversion to Islam and his decision to change his name

while in prison in 1948.... The author's honesty about his early troubles serves to convey that it is possible to rise through adversity to make a positive difference in this world. —*School Library Journal*

Shan, Darren

The **thin** executioner. By Darren Shan. Little, Brown, 2010 483 p.
Grades: 10 11 12
1. Executions and executioners; 2. Slaves; 3. Kindness; 4. Quests; 5. Warriors; 6. Fantasy fiction; 7. Classics-inspired fiction; 8. Middle Eastern-influenced fantasy
9780316078658
LC 2009045606
In a nation of warriors where weakness is shunned and all crimes, no matter how minor, are punishable by beheading, young Jebel Rum, along with a slave who is fated to be sacrificed, sets forth on a quest to petition the Fire God for invincibility, but when the long and arduous journey is over, Jebel has learned much about fairness and the value of life.

Readers will hate the villains, feel sorry for the innocent, and root for Tel Hesani and Jebel to complete their mission. This is a must-read for thrill seekers with a strong stomach looking for an action-packed adventure with a host of fantastical creatures. —*Voice of Youth Advocates*

Sharpe, Tess

Far from you. Tess Sharpe. 2014 384 p.
Grades: 9 10 11 12
1. Murder; 2. Best friends; 3. Drug addiction; 4. Friendship; 5. Drug addicts; 6. Mysteries; 7. LGBTQIA fiction
9781423184621; 9781780621654, print, UK; 9781780621630, print, UK
LC 2013037960
Rainbow List, 2015.

After Sophie Winters survives a brutal attack in which her best friend, Mina, is murdered, she sets out to find the killer. At the same time she must prove she is free of her past Oxy addiction and in no way to blame for Mina's death.

Sophie was there when her best friend, Mina, was murdered, but she doesn't know by whom, or why. So Sophie launches her own investigation, knowing that Mina's death isn't related to Sophie's painkiller addiction, as everyone else seems to think. This tense, tragic page-turner has plenty of chills, but just as compelling is the depth of Sophie's physical and emotional pain. —*Horn Book Guide*

Shaw, Susan

★ **Safe**. By Susan Shaw. Dutton Children's Books, 2007 208 p.
Grades: 7 8 9 10
1. Thirteen-year-old girls; 2. Mother-separated teenage girls; 3. Teenage rape victims; 4. Rape; 5. Mothers; 6. Realistic fiction; 7. Books for reluctant readers
9780525478294
LC 2006036428
YALSA Quick Picks for Reluctant Young Adult Readers, 2008.

When thirteen-year-old Tracy, whose mother died when she was three years old, is raped and beaten on the last day of school, all her feelings of security disappear and she does not know how to cope with the fear and dread that engulf her.

This is an extraordinarily tender novel.... Intimate, first-person narrative honestly expresses Tracy's full range of emotions. —*Publishers Weekly*

Tunnel vision. Susan Shaw. Margaret K. McElderry Books, 2011 272 p.
Grades: 5 6 7 8

1. Teenage murder witnesses; 2. Federal Witness Protection Program; 3. Organized crime; 4. Crime; 5. Murder; 6. Thrillers and suspense
9781442408395

After witnessing her mother's murder, sixteen-year-old high school student Liza Wellington and her father go into the witness protection program.

The author creates a completely believable character in Liza, who often reverts to childlike emotions only to learn the hard way that cold reality takes precedence over even dearly held wishes. Kudos for the unexpected double ending, both illusory and realistic, giving readers a choice. —*Kirkus*

Shecter, Vicky

Cleopatra's moon. By Vicky Alvear Shecter. Arthur A. Levine Books, 2011 355 p;
Grades: 8 9 10 11 12

1. Cleopatra; 2. Princesses; 3. Parents — Death; 4. Imprisonment; 5. Love triangles; 6. Ancient Egypt; 7. Rome; 8. Roman Empire (27 BCE-476 CE); 9. Ancient Egypt (3100 BCE-640 CE); 10. Historical fiction
9780545221306; 9780545221313

Cleopatra Selene, the only surviving daughter of Cleopatra and Marc Antony, recalls her life of pomp and splendor in Egypt and, after her parents' deaths, capitivity and treachery in Rome.

This novel has romance, drama, heartbreak, and adventure, all rooted in an accurate and descriptive historical setting. Shecter writes about the world of ancient Egypt and Rome with wonderful detail.... Her characters are skillfully fictionalized. —*School Library Journal*

Sheehan, Anna

A **long,** long sleep. Anna Sheehan. Candlewick Press, 2011 352 p.
Grades: 8 9 10 11 12

1. Parent-separated teenage girls; 2. Robots; 3. Assassins; 4. Inheritance and succession; 5. Corporations; 6. Science fiction; 7. Fairy tale and folklore-inspired fiction; 8. First person narratives
9780763652609

LC 2010040146

Golden Duck Awards: Hal Clement Award for Young Adult; YALSA Popular Paperbacks for Young Adults, 2016.

Sixteen-year-old Rosalinda Fitzroy, heir to the multiplanetary corporation UniCorp, is awakened after sixty years in stasis to find that everyone she knew has died and as she tries to make a new life for herself, learns she is the target of a robot assassin.

With well-developed characters, a touch of romance, and a believable future that, for once, is not entirely dystopian, Sheehan's tale should please many readers. —*Publishers Weekly*

Sheinmel, Courtney

The **survival** list. Courtney Sheinmel. Katherine Tegen Books, 2019 320 p.
Grades: 9 10 11 12

1. Family secrets; 2. Suicide; 3. Grief in teenage girls; 4. Sisters; 5. Jewish teenage girls; 6. Realistic fiction
9780062655004

Devastated by her older sister's inexplicable suicide, a teen searches for answers on a mysterious list of names and places in California, where she teams up with a boy who helps her uncover astonishing family secrets.

Shepard, Sara

The **amateurs.** Sara Shepard. 2016 320 p. (The amateurs (Sara Shepard), 1)
Grades: 9 10 11 12

1. Teenage detectives; 2. Cold cases (Criminal investigation); 3. Murder investigation; 4. Stalking; 5. Friendship; 6. Mysteries
9781484742273

LC 2015044197

Four teens who met on an online cold-case solving forum attempt to solve another teen's murder.

A twisty and ultimately satisfying romantic whodunit. —*Kirkus*

The **lying** game. Sara Shepard. HarperTeen, 2010 352 p. (Lying game novels, 1)
Grades: 9 10 11 12

1. Foster teenagers; 2. Murder victims; 3. Identical twins; 4. Teenage girl ghosts; 5. Mistaken identity; 6. Supernatural mysteries; 7. Teen chick lit; 8. Books for reluctant readers
9780061869709

YALSA Quick Picks for Reluctant Young Adult Readers, 2012.

Shepard keeps the action rolling and the clues confusing as she spends this installment uncovering the twins' characters but not solving the murder yet. Naturally, boys and fashion also figure into the story, fleshing out a distinctive scenario that should appeal to many teen girls. —*Kirkus*

Sequel: *Never have I ever.*

Shepherd, Megan

Her dark curiosity. Megan Shepherd. Balzer + Bray, 2014 368 pages (Madman's daughter trilogy, 2)
Grades: 9 10 11 12

1. Serial murders; 2. Conspiracies; 3. Experiments; 4. Characters and characteristics in literature; 5. Teenage romance; 6. London, England; 7. Horror; 8. Gothic fiction; 9. Classics-inspired fiction.
9780062128058

While the novel can be read independently of the first title, as enough of the backstory is given to make what is happening clear, readers will have a more satisfying experience if familiar with the previous installment. The psychological questions that Prince/Jekyll raises as to evil, desire, and nature vs. nurture add a depth of richness not often seen in young adult literature. —*School Library Journal*

The **madman's** daughter. Megan Shepherd. Balzer + Bray, 2013 368 pages (Madman's daughter trilogy, 1)
Grades: 9 10 11 12 Adult

1. Fathers and daughters; 2. Human experimentation in medicine; 3. Mad scientist (Concept); 4. Characters and characteristics in literature; 5. Love triangles; 6. Horror; 7. Gothic fiction; 8. Classics-inspired fiction.
9780062128027; 9780062128034

LC 2012004281

YALSA Best Fiction for Young Adults, 2014; YALSA Popular Paperbacks for Young Adults, 2017.

Dr. Moreau's daughter, Juliet, travels to her estranged father's island, only to encounter murder, medical horrors, and a love triangle.

Midnight beauties. By Megan Shepherd. Houghton Mifflin Harcourt 2019 448 p. (Grim lovelies, 2)
Grades: 9 10 11 12

1. Magic (Occultism); 2. Witches; 3. Princes; 4. Transformations (Magic); 5. Enemies; 6. Paris, France; 7. London, England; 8. Urban fantasy; 9. Fairy tale and folklore-inspired fiction.
9781328811905; 9780358173045; 9781328811912, ebook, US

LC 2018060799

Seventeen-year-old Anouk is forced into a sinister deal with Crown Prince Rennar in order to help her friends, who are trapped in their animal forms, and save Paris from the Coven at Oxford.

Sheth, Kashmira
   ★ **Keeping** corner. Kashmira Sheth. Hyperion, 2007 288 p.
Grades: 7 8 9 10 11 12
   1. Gandhi, Mahatma, 1869-1948; 2. Families; 3. Widows; 4. National self-determination; 5. Child marriage; 6. Mourning customs; 7. India; 8. British Raj (1858-1947); 9. 1940s
9780786838592
                                  LC 2007015314
Amelia Bloomer List, 2009; YALSA Best Books for Young Adults, 2009.
   In India during World War I, thirteen-year-old Leela's happy, spoiled childhood ends when her husband since age nine, whom she barely knows, dies, leaving her a widow whose only hope of happiness could come from Mahatma Ghandi's social and political reforms.
   Sheth sets up a thrilling premise in which politics become achingly personal. —*Booklist*

Shinn, Sharon
   ★ **Gateway**. Sharon Shinn. Viking, 2009 288 p.
Grades: 6 7 8 9 10
   1. Chinese American teenage girls; 2. Parallel universes; 3. Social classes; 4. Adopted teenage girls; 5. Space and time; 6. St. Louis, Missouri; 7. Gateway fantasy; 8. Fantasy fiction; 9. Asian-influenced fantasy
9780670011780
                                    LC 2009014002
YALSA Best Fiction for Young Adults, 2011.
   While passing through the Arch in St. Louis, Missouri, a Chinese American teenager is transported to a parallel world where she is given a dangerous assignment.
   The author's fantasy finds the right balance between adventure and romance, while illuminating how seductive evil can be and that sometimes the best weapon one can possess is a skeptical mind. —*Publishers Weekly*

Shirvington, Jessica
   Embrace. Jessica Shirvington. Sourcebooks, 2012 397 p. (Violet Eden chapters, 1)
Grades: 10 11 12
   1. Angels; 2. Crushes in teenage girls; 3. Love triangles; 4. Teenage boy/girl relations; 5. Teenage romance; 6. Paranormal romances; 7. First person narratives; 8. Australian fiction
9781402268403
   On her 17th birthday, everything will change for Violet Eden. The boy she loves will betray her. Her enemy will save her. And she will have to make a choice that could cost not only her life, but her eternity...
   ...this absorbing debut, the first in a series, features an appealing, well-written protagonist; diversely drawn characters; intricate (if somewhat convoluted) mythology; and an exploration of free will versus destiny. While coarse language, some sexual content, and violence gear this more towards mature readers, fans of otherworldly stories will likely enjoy this edgy, suspenseful romance and anticipate its follow-up. —*Booklist*

   Entice. Jessica Shirvington. Sourcebooks, 2012 464 p. (Violet Eden chapters, 2)
Grades: 10 11 12
   1. Angels; 2. Crushes in teenage girls; 3. Love triangles; 4. Teenage boy/girl relations; 5. Teenage romance; 6. Paranormal romances; 7. Australian fiction
9781402268434; 9780734411853, Australia
   Protecting humans from the vengeance of exiled angels, half-angel Violet Eden discovers that her reinforcements, including Lincoln, are hid-

ing secrets that may tilt the balance of power during a battle against the forces of Phoenix.

Shreve, Susan Richards
   The **lovely** shoes. Susan Shreve. Arthur A. Levine Books, 2011 256 p.
Grades: 6 7 8 9
   1. Teenage girls with disabilities; 2. Shoes; 3. Self-acceptance; 4. Mothers and daughters; 5. School dances; 6. Ohio; 7. Florence, Italy; 8. 1950s; 9. Historical fiction.
9780439680493
                                    LC 2010027937
   In 1950s Ohio, ninth-grader Franny feels isolated and self-conscious at high school because of her deformed leg and feet, but her irrepressibly high-spirited mother is determined to find shoes for Franny to wear at the school dances.
   Celebrating the rewards of determination and a positive attitude, this atmospheric novel credibly depicts Franny's internal growth and changing attitude. The contrast between smalltown Ohio and splendorous Florence provides an intriguing framework for the book's classic themes. —*Publishers Weekly*

Shrum, Brianna R.
   Never never. Brianna R. Shrum. Spencer Hill Press, 2015 356 pages;
Grades: 9 10 11 12
   1. Pirates; 2. Parallel universes; 3. Imaginary places; 4. Aging; 5. Hook, Captain (Fictitious character); 6. Fantasy fiction; 7. Classics-inspired fiction; 8. Gateway fantasy
9781633920392
                                    LC Bl2015039427
   James Hook, a child who only wants to become an adult, finds himself trapped in Neverland, a world where children are never to grow up, held against his will by Peter Pan.

Shulman, Mark
   ★ **Scrawl**. Mark Shulman. Roaring Brook Press, 2010 240 p.
Grades: 6 7 8 9 10
   1. Bullying and bullies; 2. Punishment; 3. Writing; 4. Diaries; 5. Student counselors; 6. Realistic fiction; 7. Books for reluctant readers
9781596434172
                                    LC 2010010521
YALSA Quick Picks for Reluctant Young Adult Readers, 2011; YALSA Best Fiction for Young Adults, 2011.
   When eighth-grade school bully Tod and his friends get caught committing a crime on school property, his penalty—staying after school and writing in a journal under the eye of the school guidance counsellor—reveals aspects of himself that he prefers to keep hidden.
   Blackmail, cliques, and a sense of hopelessness from both students and teachers sets up an unexpected ending that will leave readers with a new appreciation for how difficult high school can be. With the potential to occupy the rarified air of titles like S.E. Hinton's *The Outsiders* and Chris Crutcher's *Staying Fat for Sarah Byrnes*..., Scrawl paints the stereotypical school bully in a different, poignant light. —*Voice of Youth Advocates*
   A Neal Porter Book.

Shusterman, Neal
   ★ **Antsy** does time. By Neal Shusterman. Dutton Children's Books, 2008 256 p. (Antsy Bonano, 2)
Grades: 7 8 9 10

1. Teenagers with terminal illnesses; 2. Death; 3. Interpersonal attraction; 4. Family problems; 5. Fourteen- year-old boys; 6. Brooklyn, New York City; 7. Realistic fiction.
9780525478256

LC 2008000459

YALSA Best Books for Young Adults, 2009.

Fourteen-year-old Anthony "Antsy" Bonano learns about life, death, and a lot more when he tries to help a friend with a terminal illness feel hopeful about the future.

Featuring a terrific supporting cast led by Antsy's wise, acerbic mother, an expert blend of comedy and near tragedy, and the wry observations of a narrator...this will keep tween readers hooked from start to finish. —*Booklist*

Sequel to: *The Schwa Was Here*

Bruiser. Neal Shusterman. HarperTeen, 2010 336 p.
Grades: 8 9 10 11 12

1. Twin brothers and sisters; 2. Teenage boy misfits; 3. Supernatural; 4. Child abuse; 5. Bullying and bullies; 6. Paranormal fiction; 7. Multiple perspectives
9780061134081; 9780061134098

LC 2009030930

Eliot Rosewater Indiana High School Book Award (Rosie Award), 2013; YALSA Popular Paperbacks for Young Adults, 2012.

Inexplicable events start to occur when sixteen-year-old twins Tennyson and Bronte befriend a troubled and misunderstood outcast, aptly nicknamed Bruiser, and his little brother, Cody.

Narrated in turns by Tennyson, Bronte, Bruiser, and Bruiser's little brother, Cody, the story is a fascinating study in the art of self-deception and the way our best intentions for others are often based in the selfish desires of our deepest selves.... This eloquent and thoughtful story will most certainly leave its mark. —*Bulletin of the Center for Children's Books*

Challenger deep. Neal Shusterman. Harpercollins Childrens Books 2015 320 p.
Grades: 9 10 11 12

1. Teenagers with mental illnesses; 2. Schizophrenia; 3. Psychiatric hospitals; 4. Teenage boys; 5. Paranoia; 6. Realistic fiction; 7. Psychological fiction.
9780061134111; 9780061134142; 9781406396119, Paperback, UK
Booklist Editors' Choice: Books for Youth, 2015; Golden Kite Award for Fiction, 2016; James Cook Book Award (Ohio), 2017; National Book Award for Young People's Literature, 2015; School Library Journal Best Books, 2015; YALSA Best Fiction for Young Adults, 2016; YALSA Best Fiction for Young Adults: Top Ten, 2015; YALSA Popular Paperbacks for Young Adults, 2017.

This novel is a challenge to the reader from its first lines: author Shusterman takes us into the seemingly random, rambling, and surreal fantasies of fifteen-year-old Caden Bosch (yes, it makes sense to associate him with artist Hieronymus) as mental illness increasingly governs his consciousness.... Clearly written with love, the novel is moving; but it's also funny, with dry, insightful humor. Illustrations by the author's son Brendan, drawn during his own time in the depths of mental illness, haunt the story with scrambling, rambling lines, tremulousness, and intensity. —*Horn Book Guide*

Dry. Neal Shusterman and Jarrod Shusterman. 2018 352 p.
Grades: 7 8 9 10 11 12

1. Droughts; 2. Survival; 3. Nature — Effect of humans on; 4. Ecology; 5. Brothers and sisters; 6. California; 7. Survival stories; 8. Realistic fiction; 9. Multiple perspectives; 10. Books for reluctant readers
9781481481960; 9781406386851, Paperback, Australia; 9781481481977

Keystone to Reading Book Award (Pennsylvania), High School level, 2020; Sequoyah Book Awards (Oklahoma), High School Books, 2020; Westchester Fiction Award, 2019; YALSA Best Fiction for Young Adults, 2019; YALSA Quick Picks for Reluctant Young Adult Readers, 2020.

The drought-or the Tap-Out, as everyone calls it-has been going on for a while now. Everyone's lives have become an endless list of don'ts : don't water the lawn, don't fill up your pool, don't take long showers. Until the taps run dry. Suddenly, Alyssa's quiet suburban street spirals into a warzone of desperation; neighbours and families turned against each other on the hunt for water. And when her parents don't return and her life-and the life of her brother-is threatened, Alyssa has to make impossible choices if she's going to survive.

Everlost. Neal Shusterman. Simon & Schuster Books for Young Readers, 2006 320 p. (Skinjacker trilogy, 1)
Grades: 8 9 10 11 12

1. Life after death; 2. Soul; 3. Spirit possession; 4. Teenagers; 5. Fatal traffic accidents; 6. New York City; 7. Fantasy fiction.
9780689872372

LC 2005032244

YALSA Popular Paperbacks for Young Adults, 2009; School Library Journal Best Books, 2006.

When Nick and Allie are killed in a car crash, they end up in Everlost, or limbo for lost souls, where although Nick is satisfied, Allie will stop at nothing—even skinjacking—to break free.

Shusterman has reimagined what happens after death and questions power and the meaning of charity. While all this is going on, he has also managed to write a rip-roaring adventure complete with monsters, blimps, and high-diving horses. —*School Library Journal*

Everwild. Neal Shusterman. Simon & Schuster Books for Young Readers, 2009 432 p. (Skinjacker trilogy, 2)
Grades: 8 9 10 11 12

1. Rescues; 2. Life after death; 3. Spirit possession; 4. Dead; 5. Soul; 6. Fantasy fiction.
9781416958635

LC 2008051348

Nick, known as the dreaded "chocolate ogre," is trying to find all the children in Everlost and release them from the limbo they are in, while Mikey and Allie have joined a band of skinjackers and are putting themselves in danger by visiting the world of the living.

A fascinating read penned by an expert hand. —*Kirkus*

The **Schwa** was here. Neal Shusterman. Dutton Children's Books, 2004 228 p. (Antsy Bonano, 1)
Grades: 7 8 9 10

1. Mischief in boys; 2. Social acceptance; 3. Self-perception; 4. Eighth-grade boys; 5. Friendship; 6. Brooklyn, New York City; 7. Coming-of-age stories; 8. Realistic fiction.
9780525471820

LC 2004045072

ALA Notable Children's Book, 2005; Boston Globe-Horn Book Award for Fiction and Poetry, 2005; California Young Reader Medal, Middle School, 2008; YALSA Popular Paperbacks for Young Adults, 2007; YALSA Best Books for Young Adults, 2005.

A Brooklyn eighth-grader nicknamed Antsy befriends the Schwa, an "invisible-ish" boy who is tired of blending into his surroundings and going unnoticed by nearly everyone.

Antsy is one funny narrator.... Shusterman has created yet another very readable and refreshingly different story. —*Voice of Youth Advocates*

Sequel: *Antsy does time.*

★ **Scythe**. Neal Shusterman. Simon & Schuster Books for Young Readers, 2016 352 p. (Arc of a scythe, 1)

Grades: 8 9 10 11 12

> 1. Death; 2. Murder; 3. Teenage apprentices; 4. Competition; 5. Corruption; 6. Dystopian fiction; 7. Science fiction; 8. Multiple perspectives
> 9781442472426; 9781442472440, ebook, US

LC 2016006502

Blue Hen Book Award (Delaware) for Teen Books, 2020; California Young Reader Medal, Young Adult, 2020; Colorado Blue Spruce YA Book Award, 2019; Gateway Readers Award (Missouri), 2019; Golden Sower Award (Nebraska), Young Adult, 2019; Green Mountain Book Award (Vermont), 2018; Land of Enchantment Book Award (New Mexico): Black bears (Grades 9-12), 2019; Nutmeg Children's Book Award, High School category, 2019; Rhode Island Teen Book Award, 2018; School Library Journal Best Books, 2016; Soaring Eagle Book Award (Wyoming), 2018; Westchester Fiction Award, 2018; YALSA Best Fiction for Young Adults, 2017; YALSA Quick Picks for Reluctant Young Adult Readers, 2018; Young Hoosier Book Award, Middle Books, 2019; Michael L. Printz Honor Book, 2017.

In a world where disease has been eliminated, the only way to die is to be randomly killed ('gleaned') by professional reapers ('scythes'). Two teens must compete with each other to become a scythe—a position neither of them wants. The one who becomes a scythe must kill the one who doesn't.

Elegant and elegiac, brooding but imbued with gallows humor, Shusterman's dark tale thrusts realistic, likable teens into a surreal situation and raises deep philosophic questions. —*Kirkus*

Ship out of luck. Neal Shusterman. Dutton Books, an imprint of Penguin Group (USA) Inc, 2013 256 p. (Antsy Bonano, 3)
Grades: 6 7 8

> 1. Pleasure cruises; 2. Stowaways; 3. Undocumented immigrants; 4. Cruise ships; 5. Teenage boys; 6. Caribbean Area; 7. Realistic fiction.
> 9780525422266

LC 2013000031

Brooklyn-native Antsy Bonano embarks on the largest cruise ship in the world, where mischief, adventure, and deportation await.

★ **Thunderhead**. Neal Shusterman. Simon & Schuster, 2018 352 p. (Arc of a scythe, 2)
Grades: 8 9 10 11 12

> 1. Death; 2. Murder; 3. Competition; 4. Corruption; 5. Teenagers; 6. Dystopian fiction; 7. Science fiction; 8. Multiple perspectives
> 9781442472457; 9781406379532, Paperback, UK; 9781442472464; 9781442472471, ebook, US

Rowan and Citra take opposite stances on the morality of the Scythedom, putting them at odds, in the chilling sequel to the Printz Honor Book Scythe from New York Times bestseller Neal Shusterman, author of the Unwind dystology.

★ **The toll**. Neal Shusterman. Simon & Schuster Books for Young Readers, 2019 640 p. (Arc of a scythe, 3)
Grades: 7 8 9 10 11 12

> 1. Fugitives; 2. Artificial intelligence; 3. Death; 4. Executions and executioners; 5. Corruption; 6. Dystopian fiction; 7. Science fiction; 8. Multiple perspectives.
> 9781481497060; 9781481497084, (ebook); 9781406385670, Paperback, UK

LC 2019035943

Citra and Rowan have disappeared. Endura is gone. It seems like nothing stands between Scythe Goddard and absolute dominion over the world scythedom. With the silence of the Thunderhead and the reverberations of the Great Resonance still shaking the earth to its core, the question

remains: Is there anyone left who can stop him? The answer lies in the Tone, the Toll, and the Thunder.

Long but strong, a furiously paced finale that reaches for the stars. —*Kirkus*

UnDivided. Neal Shusterman. Simon & Schuster Books for Young Readers, 2014 432 p. (Unwind dystology, 4)
Grades: 6 7 8 9 10 11 12

> 1. Fugitives; 2. Human body parts industry and trade; 3. Revolutionaries; 4. Dystopias; 5. Teenagers; 6. Dystopian fiction; 7. Science fiction.
> 9781481409759; 9781471122538, print, UK; 9781471122545, ebook; 9781481409773, ebook, US

LC 2014003060

Three teens band together in order to sway the government to repeal all rulings in support of a procedure in which unwanted teenagers are captured and are unwound into parts that can be reused for transplantation.

UnSouled. Neal Shusterman. Simon & Schuster Books for Young Readers, 2013 416 p. (Unwind dystology, 3)
Grades: 6 7 8 9 10 11 12

> 1. Fugitives; 2. Human body parts industry and trade; 3. Dystopias; 4. Survival; 5. Revolutionaries; 6. Dystopian fiction; 7. Science fiction.
> 9781442423695

LC 2013022703

After the destruction of the Graveyard, Connor and Lev are on the run, seeking a woman who may be the key to bringing down unwinding forever while Cam, the rewound boy, tries to prove his love for Risa by bringing Proactive Citizenry to its knees.

In the third of his projected four-volume Unwind dystology Shusterman brings most of his central cast of teenage fugitives together and introduces an important new character, who is exempt from being unwound (legally disassembled for body parts) because she has a mild spectrum disorder. Frequent references to events in previous episodes slow the pace somewhat but the present-tense tale remains suspenseful, the overall premise is as hauntingly plausible as ever, and an electrifying revelation at the end points the way to a possible resolution. —*Booklist*

UnWholly. Neal Shusterman. Simon & Schuster Books For Young Readers, 2012 352 p. (Unwind dystology, 2)
Grades: 6 7 8 9 10 11 12

> 1. Fugitives; 2. Human body parts industry and trade; 3. Dystopias; 4. Survival; 5. Revolutionaries; 6. Dystopian fiction; 7. Science fiction.
> 9781442423664

LC 2012002729

After Connor, Lev, and Risa's high-profile revolt against unwinding, using teens to provide tissues for transplant, a sadistic bounty hunter who takes "trophies" from the unwinds he captures starts to pursue them.

Unwind. Neal Shusterman. Simon & Schuster Books for Young Readers, 2007 352 p. (Unwind dystology, 1)
Grades: 6 7 8 9 10 11 12

> 1. Human body parts industry and trade; 2. Runaway teenagers; 3. Dystopias; 4. Escapes; 5. Revolutionaries; 6. Dystopian fiction; 7. Science fiction; 8. Books for reluctant readers
> 9781416912040

LC 2006032689

Black-Eyed Susan Book Award (Maryland), High School, 2010; Eliot Rosewater Indiana High School Book Award (Rosie Award), 2010; Green Mountain Book Award (Vermont), 2010; Nutmeg Children's Book Award, Teen category, 2011; Sequoyah Book Awards (Oklahoma), Intermediate Books, 2010; Virginia Readers' Choice Award for High School, 2010; YALSA Best Books for Young Adults, 2008; YALSA Popular Paperbacks for Young Adults, 2011; YALSA

Quick Picks for Reluctant Young Adult Readers, 2008; YALSA Quick Picks for Reluctant Young Adult Readers: Top Ten: 2008.

In a future world where those between the ages of thirteen and eighteen can have their lives "unwound" and their body parts harvested for use by others, three teens go to extreme lengths to uphold their beliefs—and, perhaps, save their own lives.

Poignant, compelling, and ultimately terrifying. —*Voice of Youth Advocates*

Silver, Eve

Rush. Eve Silver. Katherine Tegen Books, 2013 352 p. (The game, 1)
Grades: 9 10 11 12
1. Virtual reality games; 2. Parallel universes; 3. Teenagers; 4. Combat; 5. Aliens; 6. Cyber-thrillers; 7. Science fiction; 8. Canadian fiction.
9780062192134

LC 2012025496

White Pine Award (Ontario), 2015; OLA Best Bets, 2013.

Rochester, New York, high schooler Miki Jones is pulled into a sort of a game in which she and other teens battle real-life aliens and the consequences of each battle could be deadly.

Silvera, Adam

★ **History** is all you left me. Adam Silvera. Soho Teen, 2017 320 p.
Grades: 9 10 11 12
1. Grief in teenage boys; 2. Loss (Psychology); 3. Gay teenagers; 4. First loves; 5. Grief; 6. Realistic fiction; 7. LGBTQIA fiction
9781616956929; 9781616956936, ebook, US

LC 2016020598

Rainbow List, 2018.

Secrets are revealed as OCD-afflicted Griffin grieves for his first love, Theo, who died in a drowning accident.

The talented author of *More Happy than Not* (2015) returns with a moving novel that explores friendship, grief, and trust among four young men. —*Kirkus*

Infinity son. Adam Silvera. HarperTeen, 2020 368 p. (Infinity cycle, 1)
Grades: 8 9 10 11 12
1. Twin brothers; 2. Gangs; 3. Magic; 4. Teenage boys; 5. Ability; 6. New York City; 7. Urban fantasy; 8. Fantasy fiction; 9. Multiple perspectives
9780062457820; 9781471191565, Paperback, UK; 9781471187803, Paperback, UK

LC 2019033533

Manifesting supernatural phoenix fire abilities when he turns 18, Emil becomes a reluctant defender against the specters that overshadow his world and reluctantly joins a vigilante team that his powerless brother idolizes.

Fans of Cassandra Clare, Mackenzie Lee's Loki, Brandon Sanderson's Steelheart, Kiersten White's Slayer and Marissa Meyer's Renegades series will love this magical book that embodies it all: romance, heartbreak, deceit, shifting loyalties, revenge, power struggles, violence, and complicated origin stories. —*School Library Journal*

★ **More** happy than not. Adam Silvera. 2015 304 pages
Grades: 9 10 11 12
1. Near future; 2. Memory; 3. Gay teenagers; 4. Survivors of suicide victims; 5. Dating (Social customs); 6. Bronx, New York City; 7. New York City; 8. Science fiction; 9. LGBTQIA fiction
9781616955601; 9781616956776; 9781471175848, Paperback, Australia

LC 2014044586

Booklist Editors' Choice: Books for Youth, 2015; YALSA Best Fiction for Young Adults: Top Ten, 2015; School Library Journal Best Books, 2015; Rainbow List, 2016; YALSA Best Fiction for Young Adults, 2016; YALSA Popular Paperbacks for Young Adults, 2017.

After enduring his father's suicide, his own suicide attempt, broken friendships, and more in the Bronx projects, Aaron Soto, sixteen, is already considering the Leteo Institute's memory-alteration procedure when his new friendship with Thomas turns to unrequited love.

Silvera pulls no punches in this portrait of a boy struggling with who he is in the face of immense cultural and societal pressure to be somebody else. —*Publishers Weekly*

★ **They** both die at the end. Adam Silvera. Harper, an imprint of HarperCollinsPublishers, 2017 336 p.
Grades: 9 10 11 12
1. Near future; 2. Death; 3. Teenage boy/boy relations; 4. Hispanic American teenage boys; 5. Friendship; 6. New York City; 7. Science fiction; 8. Multiple perspectives; 9. First person narratives
9780062457790; 9781471166204, London

LC 2016053514

Abraham Lincoln Illinois High School Book Award, 2020; Booklist Editors' Choice: Books for Youth, 2017; School Library Journal Best Books, 2017; YALSA Best Fiction for Young Adults, 2018; Rainbow List, 2018.

In a near-future New York City where a service alerts people on the day they will die, teenagers Mateo Torrez and Rufus Emeterio meet using the Last Friend app and are faced with the challenge of living a lifetime on their End Day.

Engrossing, contemplative, and as heart-wrenching as the title promises. —*Kirkus*

Silvey, Craig

★ **Jasper** Jones: a novel. Craig Silvey. Alfred A. Knopf, 2011 312 p.
Grades: 6 7 8 9 10
1. Teenage boys; 2. Misfits (Persons); 3. Life change events; 4. Small towns; 5. Secrets; 6. Western Australia; 7. Australia; 8. 1960s; 9. Literary fiction; 10. Coming-of-age stories; 11. Australian fiction; 12. Adult books for young adults.
9780375866661; 9781760295929, Australia; 9781742372624, Australia

Australian Book Industry Awards, Book of the Year, 2010; Australian Book Industry Awards, Literary Fiction Book of the Year, 2010; Nielsen BookData Australian Booksellers' Choice Award, 2010; Western Australian Premier's Book Awards, Fiction category, 2009; YALSA Best Fiction for Young Adults, 2012; School Library Journal Best Books, 2011; Shortlisted for the Miles Franklin Literary Award, 2010; Shortlisted for the International IMPAC Dublin Literary Award, 2011; Michael L. Printz Honor Book, 2012.

In small-town Australia, teens Jasper and Charlie form an unlikely friendship when one asks the other to help him cover up a murder until they can prove who is responsible.

Silvey infuses his prose with a musician's sensibility Charlie's pounding heart is echoed in the terse staccato sentences of the opening scenes, alternating with legato phrases laden with meaning. The author's keen ear for dialogue is evident in the humorous verbal sparring between Charlie and Jeffrey, typical of smart 13-year-old boys.... A richly rewarding exploration of truth and lies by a masterful storyteller. —*Kirkus*

Sim, Tara

Scavenge the stars. Tara Sim. Disney-Hyperion, 2020 336 p. (Scavenge the stars, 1)
Grades: 9 10 11 12

1. Escapes; 2. Prisoners; 3. Revenge; 4. Pirates; 5. Sailors; 6. Classics-inspired fiction; 7. Adventure stories; 8. Multiple perspectives
9781368051415

Rescuing a mysterious stranger from drowning, a vengeful captive on a debtor ship is offered a means to escape by the man she saved, only to find herself in a perilous region of old-world opulence and desperate gamblers.

Captivating worldbuilding and empathetically etched characters make *Scavenge the Stars* a light and enjoyable read. —*Kirkus*

Simmons, Kristen

Article 5. Kristen Simmons. Tor, 2012 364 p; (Article 5 trilogy, 1)
Grades: 9 10 11
1. Resistance to government; 2. Dystopias; 3. Teenage boy/girl relations; 4. Single mothers; 5. Ethics; 6. Dystopian fiction; 7. Science fiction.
9780765329585; 9780765329615

LC 2011035411

Seventeen-year-old Ember Miller has perfected the art of keeping a low profile in a future society in which Moral Statutes have replaced the Bill of Rights and offenses carry stiff penalties, but when Chase, the only boy she has ever loved, arrests her rebellious mother, Ember must take action.
A Tom Doherty Associates Book.

Metaltown. Kristen Simmons. Tor Teen, 2016 384 p.
Grades: 10 11 12
1. Factories; 2. Corruption; 3. Post-apocalypse; 4. Intrigue; 5. Industrial accidents; 6. Science fiction; 7. Multiple perspectives
9780765336620

In this gritty tale of intrigue, corruption, greed, and human rights, Simmons offers readers a savvy take on a post-apocalyptic society. —*Kirkus*

Three. Kristen Simmons. Tor Teen, 2014 400 p. (Article 5 trilogy, 3)
Grades: 9 10 11 12
1. Resistance to government; 2. Dystopias; 3. Teenage fugitives; 4. Fugitives; 5. Teenage boy/girl relations; 6. Dystopian fiction; 7. Science fiction.
9780765329608

LC 2013026344

When Ember and Chase finally arrive at the safe house and find it in ruins, they follow tracks leading away until they find a group of refugees and join forces with them to seek the rumored settlement known as Three.

Teen activists Ember and Chase (Article 5; Breaking Point) are on the run from a dangerous government bureau and find their safe house in ruins. With only a few clues to go on, they search for Three, a mysterious organization they hope will take them in. Despite clumsy exposition, romance, dystopia, and suspense mingle to create a gripping conclusion to the trilogy. —*Horn Book Guide*
A Tom Doherty Associates Book.

Simner, Janni Lee

Faerie after. Janni Lee Simner. Random House, 2013 288 p. (Bones of Faerie trilogy, 3)
Grades: 7 8 9 10
1. Fairies; 2. Parallel universes; 3. Environmental degradation; 4. Shapeshifters; 5. Magic; 6. Fantasy fiction.
9780375870699

LC 2012006430

Liza must journey to the Faerie realm in order to save both the fairy and human worlds from impending doom.

Faerie winter. Janni Lee Simner. Random House Children's Books, 2011 272 p. (Bones of Faerie trilogy, 2)
Grades: 7 8 9 10
1. Fairies; 2. Post-apocalypse; 3. Winter; 4. Quests; 5. Shapeshifters; 6. Fantasy fiction.
9780375866715

Simner tells a more streamlined story this time around and keeps up the dark atmospherics of her high-appeal blend of unsettling speculative-fiction scenarios. —*Booklist*
Sequel to: *Bones of Faerie*.

Thief eyes. Janni Lee Simner. Random House Children's Books, 2010 259 p.
Grades: 7 8 9 10
1. Women wizards; 2. Spells (Magic); 3. Missing women; 4. Magic; 5. Protectiveness in teenagers; 6. Iceland; 7. Fantasy fiction; 8. Mythological fiction
9780375966705

LC 2009018166

Haley's mother disappeared while on a trip to Iceland, and a year later, when her father takes her there to find out what happened, Haley finds herself deeply involved in an ancient saga that began with her Nordic ancestors.

Simner skillfully weaves Haley and Ari's modern emotional struggles into the ancient saga and enlivens the story with an intriguing cast of characters from the original tale. —*Booklist*

Simon, Charnan

Plan B. Charnan Simon. Darby Creek, 2011 104 p; (Surviving Southside)
Grades: 7 8 9 10
1. Pregnant teenagers; 2. Teenage pregnancy; 3. Decision-making; 4. Dating (Social customs); 5. High schools; 6. Urban fiction; 7. High interest-low vocabulary books
9780761361633

LC 2010023819

Lucy has her life planned out: she'll graduate and then join her boyfriend, Luke, at college in Austin. She'll become a Spanish teacher, and they'll get married. Deciding there's no reason to wait, and despite trying to be careful, Lucy gets pregnant. Now, none of Lucy's options are part of her picture-perfect plan. Together, she and Luke will have to make the most difficult decision of their lives.

This well-written [story reinforces] the importance of family, friends, values, and thoughtful decision-making.... [An] excellent [purchase, this book] will attract and engage reluctant readers. —*School Library Journal*
Summary adapted from p. [4] of cover; High interest story designed for reluctant readers or those reading below grade level.

Simukka, Salla

As red as blood. . Amazon Pub, 2014 265 p. (Snow White trilogy, 1)
Grades: 9 10 11 12
1. Seventeen-year-old girls; 2. Murder investigation; 3. Drug traffic; 4. Money; 5. Drug cartels; 6. Finland; 7. Mysteries; 8. Fairy tale and folklore-inspired fiction; 9. Translations
9781477847718; 9781524713416; 9781471402463, print, UK

The starkly powerful opening paragraph of the *Grimms Snow White* provides the narrative frame, and it's no flimsy high concept—rather, Simukka's onto something: Fairy tales, like mysteries, present uncompromising moral imperatives—no soft, comforting shades of gray for even the youngest readers. Limned in stark red, white and black, this cold, delicate snowflake of a tale sparkles with icy magic. —*Kirkus*

Sitomer, Alan Lawrence

The **downside** of being up. Alan Lawrence Sitomer. G.P. Putnam's Sons, 2011 224 p.
Grades: 6 7 8 9

1. Puberty; 2. Crushes in boys; 3. Middle school students; 4. Erections; 5. Families; 6. Realistic fiction; 7. Humorous stories.
9780399254987

LC 2010044203

ALA Notable Children's Book, 2012.

All Bobby Connor wants is to survive middle school, but puberty is making that difficult for him as his body conspires against him.

It is impossible to dislike this pun-filled tale.... This fiction provides some long-needed realism, served up by a narrator who knows what he is talking about. —*Booklist*

Homeboyz. By Alan Lawrence Sitomer. Jump at the Sun/Hyperion Books For Children, 2007 283 p; (Hoopster trilogy, 3)
Grades: 7 8 9 10

1. Revenge; 2. Violence; 3. Loss (Psychology); 4. Grief in teenage boys; 5. African Americans; 6. Urban fiction; 7. Books for reluctant readers
9781423100300

YALSA Quick Picks for Reluctant Young Adult Readers, 2008.

When his attempt to exact revenge on his little sister's killer places him under house arrest, Teddy Anderson is forced by his probation officer to tutor a twelve-year-old orphan—a community service assignment that eventually helps him to save his family and himself.

Still, the tale's violent, rough-hewn plot and street-inflected language supply sufficient intensity to carry the heavy agenda. —*Booklist*

The **secret** story of Sonia Rodriguez. By Alan Lawrence Sitomer. Jump at the Sun/Hyperion Books For Children, 2008 320 p.
Grades: 7 8 9 10

1. Mexican American teenage girls; 2. Determination in teenage girls; 3. Family problems; 4. Undocumented immigrants; 5. Mexican American families; 6. First person narratives; 7. Realistic fiction; 8. Books for reluctant readers
9781423110729

LC 2007045265

YALSA Popular Paperbacks for Young Adults, 2013; YALSA Quick Picks for Reluctant Young Adult Readers, 2009.

Tenth-grader Sonia reveals secrets about her life and her Hispanic family as she studies hard to become the first Rodriguez to finish high school.

Sonia's immediate voice will hold teens with its mix of anger, sorrow, tenderness, and humor. —*Booklist*

Skelton, Matthew

★ **Endymion** Spring. Matthew Skelton. Delacorte Press, 2006 400 p.
Grades: 5 6 7 8

1. Gutenberg, Johann, 1397?-1468; 2. Twelve-year-old boys; 3. Brothers and sisters; 4. Books and reading; 5. Magical books; 6. Apprentices; 7. Oxford, England; 8. England; 9. Fantasy fiction; 10. Canadian fiction.
9780385733809

LC 2006046259

Having reluctantly accompanied his academic mother and pesky younger sister to Oxford, twelve-year-old Blake Winters is at loose ends until he stumbles across an ancient and magical book, secretely brought to England in 1453 by Gutenberg's mute apprentice to save it from evil forces, and which now draws Blake into a dangerous and life-threatening quest.

This book is certain to reach an audience looking for a page-turner, and it just might motivate readers to explore the... facts behind the fiction. —*School Library Journal*

Skovron, Jon

Man made Boy. By Jon Skovron. Viking, 2013 384 p. (Man made Boy, 1)
Grades: 7 8 9 10

1. Runaway teenage boys; 2. Monsters; 3. Computer viruses; 4. Transcontinental journeys; 5. Teenage boys; 6. Science fiction; 7. Classics-inspired fiction.
9780670786206; 9781743315132

LC 2012043217

Tired of being sheltered from humans, seventeen-year-old Boy, son of Frankenstein's monster and the Bride of Frankenstein, runs away from home and embarks on a wild road trip that takes him across the country and deep into the heart of America.

Boy, the son of Frankenstein's monster, lives at a Broadway theater with the cast and crew of *The Show*. Restless, Boy runs away, then tries to evade an out-of-control computer virus he created. Eventually he must face his creation to destroy it. Readers will willingly suspend disbelief for this creative sci-fi/action/road-trip/coming-of-age story that includes a colorful cast of mythical characters. —*Horn Book Guide*

Sequel: *This broken wondrous world.*

Skrutskie, Emily

The **abyss** surrounds us. Emily Skrutskie. Flux, 2016 288 p. (Abyss surrounds us, 1)
Grades: 8 9 10 11

1. Sea monsters; 2. Pirates; 3. Ships; 4. Secrets; 5. Piracy; 6. Science fiction; 7. Teenagers' writings.
9780738746913

LC 2015032027

YALSA Quick Picks for Reluctant Young Adult Readers, 2017.

Cassandra Leung—a seventeen-year-old trainer of Reckoners, sea beasts bred to defend ships—is kidnapped by the pirate queen Santa Elena and ordered to train a Reckoner pup to defend Santa Elena's ship.

Bonds of brass. Emily Skrutskie. Del Rey Publishing, 2020 304 p. (Bloodright trilogy, 1)
Grades: 10 11 12 Adult

1. Space warfare; 2. Fighter pilots; 3. Friendship; 4. Rebels; 5. Teenage romance; 6. Science fiction; 7. Space opera; 8. Adult books for young adults.
9780593128893, HRD, US

A young pilot risks everything to save his best friend?the man he trusts most and might even love?only to learn that he's secretly the heir to a brutal galactic empire.

Despite an out-of-the-blue twist at the end, Skrutskie's sympathetic characters, perfectly-tuned pop-culture references, and harsh glimpses into the realities of empire and war keep the pages turning. This inspired tale will please fantasy fans and has cross-over YA appeal. —*Publishers Weekly*

Skrypuch, Marsha Forchuk

Making bombs for Hitler. Marsha Forchuk Skrypuch. Scholastic Press, 2017 230 p.
Grades: 5 6 7 8

1. Separated sisters; 2. Concentration camps; 3. World War II — Children; 4. Concentration camp inmates; 5. Child prisoners; 6. Second World War era (1939-1945); 7. Historical fiction; 8. Canadian fiction.

9780545931915; 9781443107303
Iowa Teen Award, 2019; Manitoba Young Readers' Choice Award, 2014; Silver Birch Award (Ontario), Fiction, 2013; OLA Best Bets, 2012.

When Lida and her sister are caught by the Nazis they are separated. Lida is sent to a slave labour camp and must work from dawn to dusk on bread and soup, without shoes and wearing only a thin dress. Even if she survives the war, will Lida ever see her sister again?

A well-told story of persistence, lost innocence, survival, and hope. —*Kirkus*

Sleator, William

The **duplicate**. William Sleator. Dutton, 1988 154 p.
Grades: 7 8 9 10
1. Clones and cloning; 2. Competition; 3. Deception; 4. Consequences; 5. Sibling rivalry; 6. Science fiction.
9780525443902

LC 87030562

Sixteen-year-old David, finding a strange machine that creates replicas of living organisms, duplicates himself and suffers the horrible consequences when the duplicate turns against him.

There are some points in the story when the roles of the clones (referred to as Duplicates A and B) become congested to the detriment of the book's pace, but fantasy fans will doubtless find the concept fresh enough and eerie enough to compensate for this, and Sleator is, as always, economical in casting and structuring his story. —*Bulletin of the Center for Children's Books*

★ **Interstellar** pig. William Sleator. Dutton, 1984 197 p.
Grades: 5 6 7 8
1. Aliens (Non-humanoid); 2. Board games; 3. Treasure troves; 4. Science fiction games; 5. Ship captains; 6. New England; 7. Science fiction.
9780525440987; 9780140375954

LC 84004132

ALA Notable Children's Book, 1985; California Young Reader Medal, Young Adult, 1988.

Barney's boring seaside vacation suddenly becomes more interesting when the cottage next door is occupied by three exotic neighbors who are addicted to a game they call "Interstellar Pig."

The author draws the reader in with intimations of danger and horror, but the climactic battle is more slapstick than horrific, and the victor's prize could scarcely be more ironic. Problematic as straight science fiction but great fun as a spoof on human-alien contact. —*Booklist*

Sequel: *Parasite Pig*.

Singularity. William Sleator. Puffin Books, 1995 170 p.
Grades: 7 8 9 10
1. Twin brothers; 2. Space and time; 3. Competition in teenage boys; 4. Identical twins; 5. Competition; 6. Illinois; 7. Science fiction.
9780140375985

Sixteen-year-old twins Harry and Barry stumble across a gateway to another universe, where a distortion in time and space causes a dramatic change in their competitive relationship.

The book has a title with a fine double entendre and is an unusual, suspenseful yarn told by a master storyteller. —*Horn Book Guide*

Sloan, Holly Goldberg

★ **I'll** be there. By Holly Goldberg Sloan. Little, Brown, 2011 400 p.
Grades: 7 8 9 10
1. Teenage musicians; 2. Survival; 3. Violence in men; 4. Elective mutism; 5. Boys who are mute; 6. Realistic fiction.
9780316122795; 9781760152888, print, Australia

LC 2010042994

YALSA Best Fiction for Young Adults, 2012.

Raised by an unstable father who keeps constantly on the move, Sam Border has long been the voice of his silent younger brother, Riddle, but everything changes when Sam meets Emily Bell and, welcomed by her family, the brothers are faced with normalcy for the first time.

This riveting story will keep readers interested and guessing until the end. —*School Library Journal*

Smelcer, John E.

Edge of nowhere. . Leapfrog Press, 2014 154 p.
Grades: 8 9 10 11 12
1. Castaways; 2. Shipwrecks; 3. Survival; 4. Resourcefulness; 5. Teenagers and dogs; 6. Alaska; 7. Survival stories; 8. Adventure stories; 9. Coming-of-age stories
9781935248576

This is an example of authentic Native Alaskan storytelling at its best. Readers are drawn immediately into this realistic modern-day vision-quest scenario and easily identify and empathize with the characters. The excitement and fast pace of the action are reminiscent of Jack London stories. This novel would make a versatile addition to any secondary English or multicultural curriculum. Not to be missed. —*School Library Journal*

Smith, Alexander Gordon

Death sentence. Alexander Gordon Smith. Farrar Straus Giroux, 2011 272 p. (Escape from Furnace, 3)
Grades: 7 8 9 10
1. Monsters; 2. Cruelty; 3. Teenage prisoners; 4. Prisoners; 5. Fourteen-year-old boys; 6. Science fiction; 7. Horror; 8. Books for reluctant readers
9780374324940; 9780571245611, print, UK

LC 2010010938

YALSA Quick Picks for Reluctant Young Adult Readers, 2012.

After his failed attempt to escape from Furnace Penitentiary, Alex struggles to survive the bloodstained laboratories beneath where monsters are manufactured, with a death sentence—or worse—hanging over his head.

Smith strikes the ideal balance between action and introspection. Readers will feel genuine sympathy for antihero Alex. —*Kirkus*

Hellraisers. Alexander Gordon Smith. Farrar Straus Giroux, 2015 320 p. (Devil's engine, 1)
Grades: 9 10 11 12
1. Faustian bargains; 2. Imaginary wars and battles; 3. Monsters; 4. Teenagers with asthma; 5. Soldiers; 6. New York City; 7. Horror; 8. Fantasy fiction
9780374301699; 9780374301712, ebook, US

LC 2015007190

Marlow Green is a high school boy in New York who is always in trouble for vandalism and acting out, until one day he stumbles into the middle of a battle with a demon, and learns about The Devil's engine—an ancient machine which can grant anything you wish for, in exchange for your soul.

Marlow is a likable, flawed underdog of a hero, and his many comrades in arms gradually gain dimension as the plot progresses. First in a planned trilogy, Smith's latest is largely going to appeal to readers in it for the gritty action and horror. —*Booklist*

Lockdown. Alexander Gordon Smith. Farrar, Straus and Giroux, 2009 273 p. (Escape from Furnace, 1)
Grades: 7 8 9 10

1. Prisons; 2. Teenage prisoners; 3. False imprisonment; 4. Escapes; 5. Monsters; 6. Horror; 7. Science fiction; 8. Books for reluctant readers
9780374324919; 9780571240807, print, UK

LC 2008043439

YALSA Popular Paperbacks for Young Adults, 2015; YALSA Quick Picks for Reluctant Young Adult Readers, 2010.

When fourteen-year-old Alex is framed for murder, he becomes an inmate in the Furnace Penitentiary, where brutal inmates and sadistic guards reign, boys who disappear in the middle of the night sometimes return weirdly altered, and escape might just be possible.

Once a plot is hatched, readers will be turning pages without pause, and the cliffhanger ending will have them anticipating the next installment. Most appealing is Smith's flowing writing style, filled with kid-speak, colorful adjectives, and amusing analogies. —*School Library Journal*

Solitary. Alexander Gordon Smith. Farrar Straus Giroux, 2010 240 p. (Escape from Furnace, 2)
Grades: 7 8 9 10
1. Teenage prisoners; 2. Solitary confinement; 3. False imprisonment; 4. Judicial error; 5. Prisons; 6. Horror; 7. Science fiction; 8. Books for reluctant readers
9780374324926

LC 2009030843

YALSA Quick Picks for Reluctant Young Adult Readers, 2011.

Imprisoned for a murder he did not commit, fourteen-year-old Alex Sawyer thinks that he has escaped the hellish Furnace Penitentiary, but instead he winds up in solitary confinement, where new horrors await him.

The author knows what keeps his readers locked to the page and delivers it soundly. —*Kirkus*

Smith, Andrew
★ The **Alex** crow: a novel. By Andrew Smith. 2015 304 pages
Grades: 9 10 11 12
1. Teenage refugees; 2. Camps; 3. Ships; 4. Expeditions; 5. Bombers (Persons); 6. West Virginia; 7. 19th century; 8. Science fiction; 9. Parallel narratives
9780525426530

LC 2014039366

YALSA Best Fiction for Young Adults, 2016.

The story of Ariel, a Middle Eastern refugee who lives with an adoptive family in Sunday, West Virginia, is juxtaposed against those of a schizophrenic bomber, the diaries of a failed arctic expedition from the late nineteenth century, and a depressed, bionic reincarnated crow.

Anchored by Smith's reliably strong prose with a distinct teenage-boy sensibility, the whole is a smartly cohesive exploration of survival and extinction, and the control humans have (or shouldn't have) over such matters. —*Horn Book Guide*

Exile from Eden: Or, After the hole. Andrew Smith. Simon & Schuster, 2019 368 p.
Grades: 9 10 11 12
1. Post-apocalypse; 2. Survival; 3. Teenage romance; 4. Genetically engineered insects; 5. Sixteen-year-old boys; 6. Humorous stories; 7. Survival stories; 8. Apocalyptic fiction.
9781534422230; 9781405293969, Paperback, UK

Arek, having lived his sixteen years in a hole with his small family, sets out into a monster-filled world with his friend Mel to find his fathers and, perhaps, another human.

Smith's latest is a marvel endlessly inventive, witty stand-alone postapocalyptic fiction that delivers a happy ending and will inspire deep discussions. —*Booklist*

Illustrated by the author; Sequel to: *Grasshopper Jungle.*

Grasshopper jungle: a history. By Andrew Smith. Dutton Books, an imprint of Penguin Group (USA), 2014 432 pages
Grades: 9 10 11 12
1. Bisexuality; 2. Teenage boys; 3. Genetically engineered insects; 4. Survival; 5. Sexuality; 6. Iowa; 7. Science fiction; 8. Apocalyptic fiction
9780525426035; 9781742978802, print, Australia; 9781405295932, Paperback, UK

LC 2013030265

Boston Globe-Horn Book Award for Fiction and Poetry, 2014; Rainbow List, 2015; School Library Journal Best Books: Fiction, 2014; YALSA Best Fiction for Young Adults, 2015; YALSA Popular Paperbacks for Young Adults, 2016; Michael L. Printz Honor Book, 2015.

Austin Szerba narrates the end of humanity as he and his best friend Robby accidentally unleash an army of giant, unstoppable bugs and uncover the secrets of a decades-old experiment gone terribly wrong.

Award-winning author Smith has cleverly used a B movie science fiction plot to explore the intricacies of teenage sexuality, love, and friendship. Austin's desires might garner buzz and controversy among adults but not among the teenage boys who can identify with his internal struggles. This novel is proof that when an author creates solely for himself—as Smith notes in the acknowledgments section— the result is an original, honest, and extraordinary work that speaks directly to teens as it pushes the boundaries of young adult literature. —*School Library Journal*

The **Marbury** lens. Andrew Smith. Feiwel and Friends, 2010 368 p.
Grades: 10 11 12
1. Cannibals; 2. Parallel universes; 3. Magic eyeglasses; 4. Emotional problems; 5. Kidnapping; 6. London, England; 7. England; 8. Horror
9780312613426

LC 2010013007

Booklist Editors' Choice: Books for Youth, 2010; YALSA Best Fiction for Young Adults, 2011.

After being kidnapped and barely escaping, sixteen-year-old Jack goes to London with his best friend Connor, where someone gives him a pair of glasses that send him to an alternate universe where war is raging, he is responsible for the survival of two younger boys, and Connor is trying to kill them all.

This bloody and genuinely upsetting book packs an enormous emotional punch. Smith's characters are very well developed and the ruined alternate universe they travel through is both surreal and believable. —*Publishers Weekly*

Sequel: *Passenger.*

★ **Passenger**. Andrew Smith. Feiwel and Friends, 2012 465 p.
Grades: 9 10 11 12
1. Parallel universes; 2. Magic eyeglasses; 3. Survival; 4. Best friends; 5. Teenage boys; 6. London, England; 7. England; 8. Horror
9781250004871

Jack and Conner are drawn back to Marbury to rescue other friends and attempt to destroy the lens that transports them to the alternate world.

The menacing, post-apocalyptic world of Marbury is again richly imagined in this stunning sequel to *The Marbury Lens* (2010). —*Kirkus*

Sequel to: *The Marbury Lens.*

★ **Stand-off**. Andrew Smith. Simon & Schuster Books for Young Readers, 2015 448 p. (Winger, 2)
Grades: 9 10 11 12
1. Rugby football; 2. Boarding school students; 3. Grief; 4. Panic attacks; 5. Coping; 6. Oregon; 7. Realistic fiction.
9781481418294; 9780141354774, print, UK; 9781481418317, ebook, US

LC 2015002163

Now a senior at Pine Mountain Academy, fifteen-year-old Ryan Dean West becomes captain of the rugby team, shares his dormitory room with a twelve-year-old prodigy, Sam Abernathy, and through the course of the year learns to appreciate things he has tried to resist, including change.

A brave, wickedly funny novel about grief and finding a way to live with it, with sweetly realistic first sexual experiences. —*Kirkus*

Winger. Andrew Smith. Simon & Schuster Books for Young Readers, 2013 448 p. (Winger, 1)
Grades: 9 10 11 12
1. Boarding school students; 2. Rugby football; 3. Crushes in teenage boys; 4. Boarding schools; 5. Schools; 6. Oregon; 7. Realistic fiction; 8. Coming-of-age stories; 9. First person narratives.
9781442444928
                                LC 2011052750
Booklist Editors' Choice: Books for Youth, 2013; Rainbow List, 2014; YALSA Best Fiction for Young Adults, 2014; YALSA Best Fiction for Young Adults: Top Ten, 2014.

Two years younger than his classmates at a prestigious boarding school, fourteen-year-old Ryan Dean West grapples with living in the dorm for troublemakers, falling for his female best friend who thinks of him as just a kid, and playing wing on the Varsity rugby team with some of his frightening new dorm-mates.

Smith deftly builds characters—readers will suddenly realize they've effortlessly fallen in love with them—and he laces meaning and poignantly real dialogue into uproariously funny scatological and hormonally charged humor, somehow creating a balance between the two that seems to intensify both extremes. Bawdily comic but ultimately devastating, this is unforgettable. —*Kirkus*

Smith, Cynthia Leitich
    Blessed. Cynthia Leitich Smith. Candlewick Press, 2011 480 p. (Tantalize series, 3)
Grades: 9 10 11 12
1. Teenage vampires; 2. Guardian angels; 3. Restaurants; 4. Supernatural; 5. Cooks; 6. Austin, Texas; 7. Texas; 8. Urban fantasy
9780763643263
                                LC 2010038697
Even as teenaged Quincie Morris adjusts to her appetites as a neophyte vampire, she must clear her true love, the hybrid-werewolf Kieren, of murder charges; thwart the apocalyptic ambitions of Bradley Sanguini, the vampire-chef who "blessed" her; and keep her dead parents' restaurant up and running before she loses her own soul.

A satisfying blend of excitement and intrigue, Blessed provides a fun and entertaining read. Appealing to high schoolers with a flair for fantasy, this book provides a twist on life as an eternal. —*Voice of Youth Advocates*

    Eternal. Cynthia Leitich Smith. Candlewick Press, 2009 307 p. (Tantalize series, 2)
Grades: 8 9 10 11
1. Teenage vampires; 2. Guardian angels; 3. Redemption; 4. Angels; 5. Death; 6. Chicago, Illinois; 7. Dallas, Texas; 8. Urban fantasy
9780763635732
                                LC 2008027658
When Miranda's guardian angel Zachary recklessly saves her from falling into an open grave and dying, the result is that she turns into a vampire and he is left to try to reinstate his reputation by finally doing the right thing.

Readers should be hooked by this fully formed world, up through the action-packed finale. —*Publishers Weekly*

    Feral curse. Cynthia Leitich Smith. Candlewick Press, 2014 272 p. (Feral series, 2)
Grades: 9 10 11 12

1. Shapeshifters; 2. Teenagers; 3. Identity (Psychology); 4. Magic; 5. Prejudice; 6. Austin, Texas; 7. Urban fantasy; 8. Multiple perspectives
9780763659103
After touching the carousel-animal cougar in his Grams's antique store, Yoshi (*Feral Nights*) is transported to Pine Ridge, home of secret werecat Kayla. Within a few days, more Shifters show up, all inexplicably drawn to her. Debut character Kayla—level-headed, religious, but also quietly proud of her shifter nature—holds her own. Witty banter keeps the tone light even as the stakes ramp up. —*Horn Book Guide*

    Feral nights. Cynthia Leitich Smith. Candlewick Press, 2013 304 p. (Feral series, 1)
Grades: 9 10 11 12
1. Shapeshifters; 2. Missing persons; 3. Kidnapping; 4. Islands; 5. Teenagers; 6. Austin, Texas; 7. Urban fantasy; 8. Multiple perspectives
9780763659097
Tracking his sister to Austin only to discover that she is a key suspect in a murder case, werecat Yoshi embarks on a search for answers, while werepossum Clyde and Aimee pursue their own investigation in an effort to avenge the killing.

Smith's fantasy smoothly switches between the three protagonists' perspectives, while expertly blending the mythical and the modern. The story's sharp banter and edgy plot make for an entertaining and clever story about loyalty and reconciling differences. —*Publishers Weekly*

    Hearts unbroken. Cynthia Leitich Smith. Candlewick Press, 2018 286 p.
Grades: 9 10 11 12
1. Teenage boy/girl relations; 2. Multiculturalism; 3. Racism; 4. First loves; 5. Native American teenagers; 6. Realistic fiction.
9780763681142, hardback, US; 9781536202007, ebook, US
Amelia Bloomer List, 2019; American Indian Youth Literature Awards, Best Young Adult Book, 2020.

Breaking up with her first real boyfriend when he makes racist remarks about her Native American heritage, high school senior Louise Wolfe teams up with a fellow school newspaper editor to cover a multicultural casting of the school play and the racial hostilities it has exposed.

Blending teen romance with complex questions of identity, equality, and censorship, this is an excellent choice for most collections. —*School Library Journal*

    ★ **Tantalize**. Cynthia Leitich Smith. Candlewick Press, 2007 310 p. (Tantalize series, 1)
Grades: 9 10 11 12
1. Teenage werewolves; 2. Murder suspects; 3. Restaurants; 4. Seventeen-year-old girls; 5. Teenage girls; 6. Austin, Texas; 7. Texas; 8. Urban fantasy
9780763627911
                                LC 2005058124
YALSA Popular Paperbacks for Young Adults, 2011.

When multiple murders in Austin, Texas, threaten the grand re-opening of her family's vampire-themed restaurant, seventeen-year-old, orphaned Quincie worries that her best friend-turned-love interest, Keiren, a werewolf-in-training, may be the prime suspect.

Horror fans will be hooked by Kieren's quiet, hirsute hunkiness, and Texans by the premise that nearly everybody in their capitol is a shapeshifter. —*Publishers Weekly*

Smith, Jennifer E.
    Field notes on love. Jennifer E. Smith. Delacorte Press, 2019 288 p.
Grades: 7 8 9 10 11 12

1. British in the United States; 2. Teenage filmmakers; 3. Railroad travel; 4. Strangers; 5. New experiences; 6. Coming-of-age stories; 7. Contemporary romances; 8. Romantic comedies.
9780399559419; 9780399559433; 9781529014563, Paperback, UK; 9781509831715, Paperback, UK

LC 2018023440

Two teens, Hugo and Mae, are strangers until they share a cross-country train trip that teaches them about love, each other, and the futures they can build for themselves.

A coming-of-age story as well as a romance, it offers authentic, complementary protagonists while capturing the thrill of exploring new territory. —*Booklist*

The **geography** of you and me. Jennifer E. Smith. Little, Brown and Company, 2014 352 p.
Grades: 7 8 9 10 11 12
1. Long-distance romance; 2. Loss (Psychology); 3. Power failures; 4. Voyages and travels; 5. Teenagers; 6. New York City; 7. Contemporary romances; 8. Books for reluctant readers
9780316254779; 9781472206299, print, UK
YALSA Quick Picks for Reluctant Young Adult Readers, 2015.

Owen and Lucy meet during a citywide blackout in New York and spend a memorable (chaste) night together. Soon afterward, Lucy's parents take her to Europe, and Owen and his dad move to San Francisco, but even on opposite sides of the world, they think about each other. Smith's fans will recognize the alternating narration; reflective, deliberate writing style; and serendipitous coincidences. —*Horn Book Guide*

Hello, goodbye, and everything in between. Jennifer E. Smith. 2015 288 p.
Grades: 9 10 11 12
1. Teenagers; 2. Couples; 3. Change; 4. Breaking up (Interpersonal relations); 5. Long-distance romance; 6. Love stories; 7. Realistic fiction.
9780316334426; 9780316334440, ebook, US; 9780316334457, ebook, US

LC 2014043210

High school sweethearts Clare and Aidan spend the night before they leave for college reminiscing about their relationship and deciding whether they should stay together or break up.

Students approaching the college transition, those who have already experienced it, and fans of romantic, realistic fiction will most enjoy this relatable, emotive story. —*School Library Journal*

The **statistical** probability of love at first sight. By Jennifer E. Smith. Little, Brown, 2012 256 p.
Grades: 9 10 11 12
1. Seventeen-year-old girls; 2. Children and remarriage; 3. Teenage boy/girl relations; 4. Love; 5. Children of divorced parents; 6. London, England; 7. England; 8. Contemporary romances.
9780316122382; 9780755384020; 9780755384037, print, UK; 9780755392179, print, UK

LC 2010048704

Seventeen-year-old Hadley's father is getting remarried, and while Hadley is (much) less than thrilled about it, she's traveling to England to be a part of his wedding. After missing her flight to London by just four minutes, Hadley gets rebooked on another flight...where she meets Oliver.

This is what happy looks like. Jennifer E. Smith. Poppy, 2013 416 p.
Grades: 9 10 11
1. Teenage celebrities; 2. Family secrets; 3. Email; 4. Fame; 5. Teenage boy/girl relations; 6. Maine; 7. Contemporary romances; 8. Teen chick lit; 9. Multiple perspectives.
9780316212823

LC 2012028755

Young Reader's Choice Award (Pacific Northwest), Senior, 2016.

Perfect strangers Graham Larkin and Ellie O'Neill meet online when Graham accidentally sends Ellie an e-mail about his pet pig, Wilbur. The two 17-year-olds strike up an e-mail relationship from opposite sides of the country and don't even know each other's first names. What's more, Ellie doesn't know Graham is a famous actor, and Graham doesn't know about the big secret in Ellie's family tree. When the relationship goes from online to in-person, they find out whether their relationship can be the real thing.

Windfall. Jennifer E. Smith. Delacorte Press, 2017 320 p.
Grades: 9 10 11 12
1. Lottery winners; 2. Loss (Psychology); 3. Teenage girl orphans; 4. Wealth; 5. Best friends; 6. Chicago, Illinois; 7. Realistic fiction
9780399559372

A story that could have easily skimmed the surface of emotions plunges head-on into the complexities of grief, loss, and love. —*School Library Journal*

Smith, Lindsay

Dreamstrider. Lindsay Smith. Roaring Brook Press, 2015 320 p.
Grades: 9 10 11 12
1. Dreams; 2. Spirit possession; 3. Espionage; 4. Spies; 5. Nightmares; 6. Paranormal fiction; 7. Spy fiction; 8. Thrillers and suspense
9781626720428; 9781626720435, ebook, US

LC 2015011848

Livia can enter other people's bodies through their dreams, an ability that makes her an invaluable and dangerous spy for her kingdom.

An engaging stand-alone fantasy spy thriller. —*School Library Journal*

Sekret. Lindsay Smith. 2014 352 p. (Sekret, 1)
Grades: 8 9 10 11 12
1. Teenage psychics; 2. Espionage; 3. Supernatural; 4. Cold War; 5. Psychic ability; 6. Soviet Union; 7. 1960s; 8. Spy fiction; 9. Historical fiction.
9781596438927

LC 2013027913

Follows a group of psychic teenagers in 1960s Soviet Russia who are forced to use their powers to spy for the KGB.

We the Living meets Genius Squad, this novel follows the misfortunes of Yulia, one of a group of psychic teens pressed into the service of the 1960s KGB. The concept is ambitious and the heroine fiery, but there is a surfeit of plot elements (including a hokey love triangle) and the writing is frequently turgid. —*Horn Book Guide*

Smith, Roland

The **edge**. By Roland Smith. 2015 266 p. (Peak, 2)
Grades: 6 7 8 9 10
1. Teenage mountaineers; 2. Survival; 3. Kidnapping; 4. Mountaineering; 5. Hindu Kush Mountains; 6. Afghanistan; 7. Adventure stories; 8. Survival stories
9780544341227

LC 2014044086

Fifteen-year-old Peak Marcello is invited to participate in an "International Peace Ascent" in the Hindu Kush, with a team made up of under-eighteen-year-old climbers from around the world—but from the first something seems wrong, so when the group is attacked, and most of the climbers are either killed or kidnapped, Peak finds himself caught up in a struggle to survive, shadowed by the Shen, a mysterious snow leopard.
Sequel to: *Peak.*

Smith, Sherri L.

Orleans. Sherri L. Smith. G.P. Putnam's Sons, 2013 336 p.
Grades: 9 10 11 12
1. Post-apocalypse; 2. Dystopias; 3. Virus diseases; 4. Teenage girl orphans; 5. Scientists; 6. New Orleans, Louisiana; 7. Afrofuturism and Afrofantasy; 8. Science fiction; 9. Multiple perspectives
9780399252945
LC 2012009634
YALSA Popular Paperbacks for Young Adults, 2016.
Set in a futuristic, hostile Orleans landscape, Fen de la Guerre must deliver her tribe leader's baby over the Wall into the Outer States before her blood becomes tainted with Delta Fever—Provided by publisher.

Smith-Ready, Jeri

Shade. Jeri Smith-Ready. Simon Pulse, 2010 320 p. (Shade trilogy, 1)
Grades: 9 10 11 12
1. Teenage girls and ghosts; 2. Teenage boy ghosts; 3. Teenage musicians; 4. Trials (Wrongful death); 5. Ghosts; 6. Baltimore, Maryland; 7. Maryland; 8. Paranormal romances
9781416994060
LC 2009039487
Sixteen-year-old Aura of Baltimore, Maryland, reluctantly works at her aunt's law firm helping ghosts with wrongful death cases file suits in hopes of moving on, but it becomes personal when her boyfriend, a promising musician, dies and persistently haunts her.
Although Smith-Ready's occasionally racy...[book] resolves almost none of the issues surrounding the Shift, leaving the door open for future books, it is a fully satisfying read on its own, with well-developed, believable characters.... Perhaps even more impressive is the understatement of the paranormal premise Smith-Ready changes the world completely by simply changing our ability to see. —*Publishers Weekly*
Sequel: *Shift*.

Shift. Jeri Smith-Ready. Simon Pulse, 2011 367 p; (Shade trilogy, 2)
Grades: 9 10 11 12
1. Teenage girls and ghosts; 2. Teenage boy ghosts; 3. Former boyfriends; 4. Supernatural; 5. Teenage boy/girl relations; 6. Baltimore, Maryland; 7. Maryland; 8. Paranormal romances
9781416994084; 9780857071866, print, UK
LC 2010036784
Logan returns as a ghost, complicating sixteen-year-old Aura's budding relationship with Zachary, especially when they discover that Logan might be able to become solid again.
Smith-Ready's strengths are well-developed core characters, dialogue, and the clever narrative tone. Mature language and content make this better suited for older teens. —*School Library Journal*
Sequel to: *Shade*.

This side of salvation. Jeri Smith-Ready. Simon Pulse, 2014 384 pages
Grades: 9 10 11 12
1. Grief; 2. End of the world; 3. Faith; 4. Families; 5. Missing persons; 6. Pennsylvania; 7. Realistic fiction.
9781442439481; 9781442439504, ebook, US
LC 2013019948
After his older brother is killed, David turns to anger and his parents to religion, but just as David's life is beginning to make sense again his parents press him and his sister to join them in cutting worldly ties to prepare for the Rush, when the faithful will be whisked off to heaven.
Following the death of his soldier brother, David's grief-stricken parents have turned to religion—specifically a fundamentalist cult—for solace. His recovering-alcoholic father speaks only in Bible verses; his mother is fixated on the upcoming Rapture, or Rush. When his parents disappear, David must untangle the mystery. Chapter flashbacks to Before the Rush alternate with Now in this nuanced study of relationships, religion, and faith. —*Horn Book Guide*

Somper, Justin

Black heart. By Justin Somper. Little, Brown, 2009 504 p; (Vampirates, 4)
Grades: 6 7 8 9
1. Twin brothers and sisters; 2. Pirates; 3. Vampires; 4. Seafaring life; 5. Pirate ships; 6. Fantasy fiction
9780316020879
LC B12009008073
When the destructive behavior of a new ship of vampirates results in the death of a prominent pirate, the Pirate Federation trains a new crew of vampire hunters that includes newly-appointed captain Cheng Li and pirate prodigy Connor Tempest.
This is a fast-paced adventure story with a few surprises along the way. —*School Library Journal*

Blood captain. By Justin Somper. Little, Brown and Co, 2008 569 p; (Vampirates, 3)
Grades: 6 7 8 9
1. Twin brothers and sisters; 2. Pirates; 3. Vampires; 4. Teenage girl healers; 5. Blindness; 6. Fantasy fiction
9780316020855; 9781407451275, large print, UK; 9781912979134, Paperback, UK
LC 2007031538
While Connor faces trouble in the form of an obnoxious new crewmate, Grace, his twin sister, seeks out a vampirate guru who might be able to heal their dear friend Lorcan's blindness.
The haunting characters, both new and from earlier books, are again well rounded and believable, each described with care and an attention to detail that should allow new readers to follow the story. —*Voice of Youth Advocates*

Demons of the ocean. By Justin Somper. Little, Brown, 2006 330 p. (Vampirates, 1)
Grades: 6 7 8 9
1. Twin brothers and sisters; 2. Pirates; 3. Vampires; 4. Pirate ships; 5. Seafaring life; 6. Australia; 7. Fantasy fiction
9780316013734
This winning fantasy features both pirates and vampires with adventure, bloodcurling action, and sinister characters. —*Voice of Youth Advocates*

Empire of night. By Justin Somper; [interior illustrations by Jon Foster].. Little, Brown, 2010 490 p. (Vampirates, 5)
Grades: 6 7 8 9
1. Twin brothers and sisters; 2. Pirates; 3. Vampires; 4. Seafaring life; 5. Pirate ships; 6. Fantasy fiction
9780316033220
LC 2010019251
Evil Sidorio continues to expand his empire across the oceans, but as he faces growing opposition from both the Pirate Federation and the vampirate realm, twins Grace and Connor Tempest are caught in the conflict.
Readers looking for suspense and gore won't be disappointed; those wanting character development will find some satisfaction too. —*Horn Book Guide*

Tide of terror. Justin Somper. Little, Brown, 2007 459 p. (Vampirates, 2)
Grades: 6 7 8 9
1. Twin brothers and sisters; 2. Pirates; 3. Vampires; 4. Pirate ships; 5. Seafaring life; 6. Fantasy fiction

9780316013741; 9781912979127, Paperback, UK

Sones, Sonya

Stop pretending: what happened when my big sister went crazy. Sonya Sones. HarperCollins, 1999 149 p.
Grades: 6 7 8 9

1. Teenage girls with mental illnesses; 2. Sisters; 3. Healing; 4. Families; 5. Friendship; 6. Novels in verse; 7. Realistic fiction; 8. First person narratives; 9. Books for reluctant readers
9780060283872; 9780060283865

LC 99011473

Claudia Lewis Award, 2000; YALSA Best Books for Young Adults, 2000; YALSA Quick Picks for Reluctant Young Adult Readers, 2000.

A younger sister has a difficult time adjusting to life after her older sister has a mental breakdown.

Based on the journals Sones wrote at the age of 13 when her 19-year-old sister was hospitalized due to manic depression, the simply crafted but deeply felt poems reflect her thoughts, fears, hopes, and dreams during that troubling time. —*School Library Journal*

★ **What** my girlfriend doesn't know. Sonya Sones. Simon & Schuster Books for Young Readers, 2007 304 p.
Grades: 7 8 9 10

1. Teenage artists; 2. Social acceptance in teenagers; 3. Self-esteem in teenage boys; 4. Dating (Social customs); 5. Teenagers; 6. Boston, Massachusetts; 7. Novels in verse; 8. Realistic fiction; 9. First person narratives; 10. Books for reluctant readers
9780689876028

LC 2006014682

YALSA Quick Picks for Reluctant Young Adult Readers, 2008.

Fourteen-year-old Robin Murphy is so unpopular at high school that his name is slang for "loser," and so when he begins dating the beautiful and popular Sophie her reputation plummets, but he finds acceptance as a student in a drawing class at Harvard.

Robin's believable voice is distinctive, and Sones uses her spare words (and a few drawings) to expert effect. —*Booklist*
Sequel to: *What my mother doesn't know.*

What my mother doesn't know. By Sonya Sones. Simon & Schuster Books for Young Readers, 2001 259 p.
Grades: 7 8 9 10

1. Crushes in teenage girls; 2. Love; 3. Teenage boy/girl relations; 4. Crushes (Interpersonal relations); 5. Dating (Social customs); 6. Novels in verse; 7. Realistic fiction; 8. First person narratives; 9. Books for reluctant readers
9780689841149

LC 52634

Iowa Teen Award, 2006; YALSA Quick Picks for Reluctant Young Adult Readers, 2002; Booklist Editors' Choice: Books for Youth, 2001; YALSA Best Books for Young Adults, 2002.

A series of poems reflect the thoughts and feelings of Sophie, a fifteen-year-old-girl, as she describes her relationships with a series of boys and as she searches for Mr. Right.

Fourteen-year-old Sophia is searching for Mr. Right. In a story written in poetry form, Sophia describes her relationships with sexy Dylan, suspicious cyberboy, and, finally, with the mysterious masked stranger who dances with her on Halloween and then disappears. Book Rep,This is a fast, funny, touching book.... The very short, sometimes rhythmic lines make each page fly. Sophie's voice is colloquial and intimate. —*Booklist*
Sequel: *What my girlfriend doesn't know.*

Sonnenblick, Jordan

★ **Falling** over sideways. Jordan Sonnenblick. Scholastic Press, 2016 272 p.
Grades: 7 8 9 10

1. Girl dancers; 2. Children of parents with disabilities; 3. Fathers and daughters; 4. Families; 5. People who have had strokes; 6. Realistic fiction; 7. First person narratives.
9780545863247

LC 2016022926

Booklist Editors' Choice: Books for Youth, 2016.

Harassed at her middle school, not taken seriously at home, and with a "perfect" older brother, Matthew, to live up to, thirteen-year-old Claire has always felt like her life was cursed—then one morning, when she are her beloved father are talking at breakfast, her father suddenly falls over with a stroke, and suddenly everything changes.

In Claire, Sonnenblick crafts a convincing, lightly sardonic narrator, and her bittersweet and hopeful story will likely stay with readers for some time. —*Horn Book Guide*

★ **Notes** from the midnight driver. By Jordan Sonnenblick. Scholastic Press, 2006 272 p.
Grades: 8 9 10 11 12

1. Sixteen-year-old boys; 2. Intergenerational friendship; 3. Community service (Punishment); 4. Teenage boys; 5. Senior men; 6. Realistic fiction.
9780439757799

LC 2005027972

YALSA Best Books for Young Adults, 2008.

After being assigned to perform community service at a nursing home, sixteen-year-old Alex befriends a cantankerous old man who has some lessons to impart about jazz guitar playing, love, and forgiveness.

The author deftly infiltrates the teenage mind to produce a first-person narrative riddled with enough hapless confusion, mulish equivocation, and beleaguered deadpan humor to have readers nodding with recognition, sighing with sympathy, and gasping with laughter—often on the same page. —*Horn Book Guide*

★ **Zen** and the art of faking it. By Jordan Sonnenblick. Scholastic Press, 2007 264 p.
Grades: 5 6 7 8

1. Fourteen-year-old boys; 2. Identity (Psychology); 3. Zen Buddhism; 4. Teenage boys; 5. Chinese American boys; 6. Pennsylvania; 7. Realistic fiction; 8. First person narratives.
9780439837071

LC 2006028841

YALSA Popular Paperbacks for Young Adults, 2014.

When thirteen-year-old San Lee moves to a new town and school for the umpteenth time, he is looking for a way to stand out when his knowledge of Zen Buddhism, gained in his previous school, provides the answer—and the need to quickly become a convincing Zen master.

The author gives readers plenty to laugh at.... Mixed with more serious scenes,...lighter moments take a basic message about the importance of honesty and forgiveness and treat it with panache. —*Publishers Weekly*

Soria, Destiny

★ **Iron** cast. Destiny Soria. 2016 384 pages
Grades: 9 10 11 12

1. Nightclubs; 2. Hallucinations and illusions; 3. Criminals; 4. Swindlers and swindling; 5. Superhuman abilities; 6. Boston, Massachusetts; 7. 1910s; 8. Historical fantasy
9781419721922

LC 2016013279

In 1919 Boston, best friends Corinne and Ada perform illegally as illusionists in an infamous gangster's nightclub, using their "afflicted" blood to con Boston's elite, until the law closes in.

Energetic and original, this alternative history, fantasy, and mystery mashup with its pair of smart, resourceful, flawed but engaging heroines never disappoints. —*Kirkus*

Sorosiak, Carlie
Wild blue wonder. Carlie Sorosiak. Harpercollins Childrens Books 2018 320 p.
Grades: 7 8 9 10 11
1. Best friends; 2. Survivor guilt; 3. Boating accidents; 4. Grief; 5. Teenage boys — Death; 6. Maine; 7. Realistic fiction
9780062563996

Following a tragic boating accident during the summer before her senior year of high school, Quinn goes through life in a daze of grief until the new boy in town, Alexander, helps her begin to understand the truth about love and loss.

Sparks, Lily
Teen killers club: novel. Lily Sparks. 2020 263 p.
Grades: 9 10 11 12
1. Teenage assassins; 2. Murder; 3. Judicial error; 4. Frameups; 5. Misfits (Persons); 6. Thrillers and suspense
9781643852294

Framed for the murder of her best friend, a young girl joins a super-secret society of teenage assassins to avoid a lifetime behind bars—and discovers her own true self.

Sparks crafts a page-turner with a disturbingly unusual premise, snappy dialogue, and characters that go deeper than their heinous crimes. —*Kirkus*

Speare, Elizabeth George
★ The **witch** of Blackbird Pond. Elizabeth George Speare. Houghton, 1958 249 p.
Grades: 6 7 8 9
1. Puritans — History; 2. Independence (Personal quality); 3. Witchcraft; 4. Prejudice; 5. Connecticut; 6. United States; 7. Colonial America (1600-1775); 8. 18th century; 9. Historical fiction; 10. Classics.
9780395071144

LC 58011063
Newbery Medal, 1959.

A young woman brought up in Barbados comes to live with her uncle in Connecticut, and find their Puritan way of life difficult after her unconventional upbringing.

Spears, Katarina M.
Breakaway: a novel. Kat Spears. St. Martin's Griffin, 2015 320 p.
Grades: 10 11 12
1. Best friends; 2. Loss (Psychology); 3. Teenage romance; 4. Soccer players; 5. Dating (Social customs); 6. Realistic fiction
9781250065513; 9781466872479, ebook, US

LC 2015019024
Readers will be hard-pressed to find a more realistic portrait of friends finding themselves while losing one another. A rare study of growing pains that gives equal weight to humor and hardship. —*Kirkus*

Spiegler, Louise
The **Jewel** and the key. By Louise Spiegler. Clarion Books, 2011 464 p.

Grades: 8 9 10 11 12
1. Time travel (Past); 2. Theater; 3. World War I; 4. Earthquakes; 5. Sixteen-year-old girls; 6. Seattle, Washington; 7. Washington (State); 8. First World War era (1914-1918); 9. 1910s; 10. Fantasy fiction.
9780547148793

LC 2011008149
After an earthquake, Seattle sixteen-year-old Addie McNeal finds herself jolted back to 1917 just as the United States is entering World War I, where she is drawn to the grand old Jewel Theater which is threatened both then and in the present time, as the United States again is about to enter a war.

Spinelli, Jerry
★ **Crash**. Jerry Spinelli. Knopf, 1996 162 p.
Grades: 5 6 7 8
1. Empathy; 2. Aggressiveness (Psychology); 3. Racing; 4. Bullying and bullies; 5. Empathy in boys; 6. Realistic fiction; 7. First person narratives.
9780679979579

LC 95-30942
Golden Archer Awards (Wisconsin): Intermediate, 2000; Indian Paintbrush Book Award (Wyoming), 1998; Iowa Teen Award, 1999; Massachusetts Children's Book Award, 1998; Maud Hart Lovelace Book Award (Minnesota), Division II (Grades 6-8), 1999; North Carolina Children's Book Award, Junior Books category, 2000; Pennsylvania Young Reader's Choice Awards, Grades 6-8, 1999; School Library Journal Best Books, 1996; South Carolina Book Award, Junior Books, 1999; Virginia Readers' Choice Award for Middle School, 1999; YALSA Best Books for Young Adults, 1997.

Seventh-grader John "Crash" Coogan has always been comfortable with his tough, aggressive behavior, until his relationship with an unusual Quaker boy and his grandfather's stroke make him consider the meaning of friendship and the importance of family.

Crash is a star football player. He torments Penn, a classmate who is everything Crash is not friendly, small, and a pacifist. When his beloved grandfather comes to live with his family and suffers a debilitating stroke, Crash begins to see value in many of the things he has scorned. —*Horn Book Guide*

Love, Stargirl. Jerry Spinelli. Alfred A. Knopf, 2007 274 p.
Grades: 7 8 9 10
1. Eccentric teenage girls; 2. Unhappiness in teenagers; 3. Breaking up (Interpersonal relations); 4. Unhappiness; 5. Fifteen-year-old girls; 6. Pennsylvania; 7. Realistic fiction; 8. Epistolary novels.
9780375813757; 9780375913754

LC 2007002308
Still moping months after being dumped by her Arizona boyfriend Leo, fifteen-year-old Stargirl, a home-schooled free spirit, writes "the world's longest letter" to Leo, describing her new life in Pennsylvania.

Smiles to go. Jerry Spinelli. Joanna Cotler Books, 2008 248 p;
Grades: 6 7 8 9 10
1. Self-fulfillment in teenage boys; 2. Insecurity (Psychology); 3. Brothers and sisters; 4. Love triangles; 5. Insecurity in teenagers; 6. Coming-of-age stories; 7. Realistic fiction.
9780060281335

LC 2007029563
Will Tuppence's life has always been ruled by science and common sense but in ninth grade, shaken up by the discovery that protons decay, he begins to see the entire world differently and gains new perspective on his relationships with his little sister and two closest friends.

What makes a Spinelli novel isn't plotting so much as character, dialogue, voice and humor. The Spinelli touch remains true in this funny and thoroughly enjoyable read. —*Publishers Weekly*

★ **Stargirl**. Jerry Spinelli. Alfred A. Knopf, 2000 176 p.
Grades: 7 8 9 10
1. Nonconformity; 2. Popularity; 3. First loves; 4. Eccentric teenage girls; 5. Teenagers; 6. Arizona; 7. Realistic fiction; 8. Classics; 9. Books to movies.
9780679886372; 9780679986379; 9781408341025, print, UK

LC 99087944

Charlotte Award (New York), Young Adult, 2004; Garden State Teen Book Award (New Jersey), Fiction (Grades 6-8), 2003; Grand Canyon Reader Award (Arizona), Teen Book Category, 2003; Iowa Teen Award, 2003; Young Hoosier Book Award, Middle Books, 2003; YALSA Best Books for Young Adults, 2001.

In this story about the perils of popularity, the courage of nonconformity, and the thrill of first love, an eccentric student named Stargirl changes Mica High School forever.

As always respectful of his audience, Spinelli poses searching questions about loyalty to one's friends and oneself and leaves readers to form their own answers. —*Publishers Weekly*

This book was made into the 2020 Disney Plus movie of the same name.

St. Crow, Lili
Betrayals: a strange angels novel. Lili St. Crow. Razorbill, 2009 304 p. (Strange angels, 2)
Grades: 8 9 10 11 12
1. Supernatural; 2. Betrayal; 3. Psychic ability; 4. Teenagers; 5. Teenage girls; 6. Urban fantasy
9781595142528

LC 2009021856

For her own protection, sixteen-year-old Dru is taken to a secret training facility that feels more like a prison, but she faces great danger there and learns that a traitor who was involved in her mother's death now wants Dru dead.

Defiance: a Strange angels novel. Lili St. Crow. Razorbill, 2011 259 p; (Strange angels, 4)
Grades: 8 9 10 11 12
1. Teenage girl orphans; 2. Psychic ability; 3. Kidnapping; 4. Rescues; 5. Werewolves; 6. Urban fantasy
9781595143921

LC 2010054253

When sixteen-year-old Dru's worst fears come true and Sergej kidnaps her best friend Graves, she embarks on a suicidal rescue mission in which she will test Christophe's training and try to defeat her mother's betrayer, Anna, for good.

Strange angels. By Lili St. Crow. Razorbill, 2009 293 p. (Strange angels, 1)
Grades: 8 9 10 11 12
1. Supernatural; 2. Psychic ability; 3. Girl heroes; 4. Werewolves; 5. Vampires; 6. Urban fantasy; 7. Coming-of-age stories.
9781595142511

LC 2008039720

YALSA Popular Paperbacks for Young Adults, 2011.

Sixteen-year-old Dru's psychic abilities helped her father battle zombies and other creatures of the "Real World," but now she must rely on herself, a "werwulf-bitten friend, and a half-human vampire hunter to learn who murdered her parents, and why.

The book grabs readers by the throat, sets hearts beating loudly and never lets go. —*Kirkus*

St. James, James
Freak show. James St. James. Dutton Children's Books, 2007 224 p.
Grades: 8 9 10 11 12
1. Drag queens; 2. Gay teenagers; 3. Seventeen-year-old boys; 4. Homosexuality; 5. Prejudice; 6. Fort Lauderdale, Florida; 7. LGBTQIA fiction; 8. Realistic fiction; 9. Books to movies; 10. Books for reluctant readers
9780525477990

LC 2006029716

Rainbow List, 2008; School Library Journal Best Books, 2007; YALSA Best Books for Young Adults, 2008; YALSA Popular Paperbacks for Young Adults, 2009; YALSA Quick Picks for Reluctant Young Adult Readers, 2008.

Having faced teasing that turned into a brutal attack, Christianity expressed as persecution, and the loss of his only real friend when he could no longer keep his crush under wraps, seventeen-year-old Billy Bloom, a drag queen, decides the only way to become fabulous again is to run for Homecoming Queen at his elite, private school near Fort Lauderdale, Florida.

Though the subject matter and language will likely prove controversial, it's nearly impossible to remain untouched after walking a mile in the stilettos of someone so unfailingly true to himself and so blisteringly funny. —*Publishers Weekly*

Title adapted into a film by the same name in 2017.

Stamper, Phil
The **gravity** of us. Phil Stamper. Bloomsbury, 2020 352 p.
Grades: 8 9 10 11 12
1. Journalism; 2. Family problems; 3. Teenage boy/boy relations; 4. Astronauts; 5. Teenage romance; 6. LGBTQIA romances; 7. Realistic fiction
9781547600144, HRD, US; 9781526619945, Paperback, UK

LC 2019019167

When his volatile father is picked to become an astronaut for NASA's mission to Mars, seventeen-year-old Cal, an aspiring journalist, reluctantly moves from Brooklyn to Houston, Texas, and looks for a story to report, finding an ally (and crush) in Jeremy, the son of another astronaut.

In his debut novel, Stamper crafts a sweet fish-out-of-water tale that also shrewdly explores the intersection between social class and modern media culture. —*Kirkus*

Stamper, Vesper
What the night sings. Vesper Stamper. 2018 272 p.
Grades: 9 10 11 12
1. Refugees; 2. Holocaust survivors; 3. Singing; 4. Jewish teenagers; 5. Teenage boy/girl relations; 6. Germany; 7. Historical fiction
9781524700386; 9781524700393

LC 2017020646

Sydney Taylor Book Award for Teen Readers, 2019; YALSA Best Fiction for Young Adults, 2019; Golden Kite Honor Book for Fiction, 2019; William C. Morris Debut Award finalist, 2019.

Liberated from Bergen-Belsen Concentration Camp in 1945, sixteen-year-old Gerta tries to make a new life for herself, aided by Lev, a fellow survivor, and Michah, who helps Jews reach Palestine.

A well-researched, elegant, and fittingly melodic exploration of reclaiming ones voiceand the many kinds of faith it can spark. —*Booklist*

Illustrated by the author.

Staples, Suzanne Fisher
The **house** of djinn. Suzanne Fisher Staples. Farrar, Straus and Giroux, 2008 Ix, 207 p;
Grades: 8 9 10 11 12

1. Fifteen-year-olds; 2. Families; 3. Culture conflict; 4. Mothers and daughters; 5. Aunt and nephew; 6. Pakistan; 7. Realistic fiction.
9780374399368

LC 2007005093

An unexpected death brings Shabanu's daughter, Mumtaz, and nephew, Jameel, both aged fifteen, to the forefront of an attempt to modernize Pakistan, but the teens must both sacrifice their own dreams if they are to meet family and tribal expectations.

As atmospheric and suspenseful as its predecessors, Shabanu and Haveli, this evocative novel transports readers to an intriguing corner of the universe to provide an insightful look at modern Middle Eastern culture. —*Publishers Weekly*

Frances Foster books.

★ **Under** the persimmon tree. Suzanne Fisher Staples. Farrar, Straus and Giroux, 2005 288 p.
Grades: 7 8 9 10
1. Girls; 2. Afghans; 3. Refugees; 4. Child refugees; 5. Women; 6. Afghanistan; 7. Peshawar, Pakistan; 8. 21st century; 9. War stories; 10. Multiple perspectives; 11. First person narratives.
9780374380250

LC 2004053256

ALA Notable Children's Book, 2006; YALSA Best Books for Young Adults, 2006.

Alternating between the stories of Najmah, a 12-year-old Afghan girl, and Nusrat, a young American woman, this powerful, poignant novel depicts the emotional cost of the war in Afghanistan. Nusrat longs for the return of her husband, Faiz, who left to open a medical clinic in Afghanistan. Meanwhile, Najmah, whose mother and baby brother were killed by American bombs, desperately searches for her father and older brother, who were forced to fight for the Taliban. When Najmah and Nusrat meet at a refugee camp in Pakistan, they forge a friendship that reveals the heartbreak and hope of surviving the devastation of war.

Staples weaves a lot of history and politics into her story.... But...it's the personal story...that compels as it takes readers beyond the modern stereotypes of Muslims as fundamentalist fanatics. There are no sweet reunions, but there's hope in heartbreaking scenes of kindness and courage. —*Booklist*

Frances Foster books.

Starmer, Aaron
Spontaneous. By Aaron Starmer. Dutton, 2016 368 p.
Grades: 9 10 11 12
1. Spontaneous human combustion; 2. Teenagers and death; 3. FBI agents; 4. High school seniors; 5. Dating (Social customs); 6. New Jersey; 7. Humorous stories; 8. Books to movies
9780525429746; 9781460753149, print, Australia; 9781460707791, ebook; 9781786890610, Paperback, UK
YALSA Best Fiction for Young Adults, 2017.

A blood-soaked, laugh-filled, tear-drenched, endlessly compelling read. —*Kirkus*

Stead, Rebecca
First light. Rebecca Stead. Wendy Lamb Books, 2007 328 p.
Grades: 5 6 7 8
1. Children of scientists; 2. Global warming; 3. Underground areas; 4. Secrets; 5. Adventure; 6. Greenland; 7. Adventure stories; 8. Multiple perspectives; 9. First person narratives.
9780375840173; 9780375940170; 9781783441129, print, UK
LC 2006039733

When twelve-year-old Peter and his family arrive in Greenland for his father's research, he stumbles upon a secret his mother has been hiding from him all his life, and begins an adventure he never imagines possible.

This novel is an exciting, engaging mix of science fiction, mystery, and adventure.... Peter and Thea are fully developed main characters. —*School Library Journal*

Steiger, A. J.
When my heart joins the thousand. A. J. Steiger. Harpercollins Childrens Books, 2018 336 p.
Grades: 9 10 11 12
1. Teenagers with autism; 2. Teenage orphans; 3. Teenage romance; 4. Autism; 5. Teenagers with disabilities; 6. Contemporary romances
9780062656476
YALSA Best Fiction for Young Adults, 2019.

Alvie Fitz doesn't fit in, and she doesn't care. She's spent years swallowing meds and bad advice from doctors and social workers. Adjust, adapt. Pretend to be normal. It sounds so easy.

A gorgeous love story of depth and raw emotion that beautifully dismantles the ugly perceptions of autism. —*Kirkus*

Sternberg, Libby
The **case** against my brother. Libby Sternberg. Bancroft Press, 2007 224 p.
Grades: 6 7 8 9
1. Racism; 2. Race relations; 3. Prejudice; 4. Religious persecution; 5. Teenagers; 6. Portland, Oregon; 7. Oregon; 8. 1920s; 9. Historical mysteries.
9781890862510

LC 2007936856

In 1922, when their widowed mother dies, Carl Matiuski and his older brother, Adam, move to Portland, OR, to live with an uncle.... When [Adam] is accused of a crime he didn't commit, Carl steps in...to try to clear his brother's name.... Readers are easily swept up in the adventure as the eye-opening mystery unfolds. —*School Library Journal*

Steven, Laura
The **exact** opposite of okay. Laura Steven. HarperTeen, 2019 352 p.
Grades: 9 10 11 12
1. Bloggers; 2. Scandals; 3. Sexuality; 4. Gossiping and gossips; 5. Shame; 6. First person narratives; 7. Realistic fiction.
9780062877529; 9781405288446, Paperback, UK

Izzy O'Neill is an aspiring comic, an impoverished orphan, and a Slut Extraordinaire. Or at least, that's what the malicious website flying round the school says. Izzy can try all she wants to laugh it off—after all, her sex life, her terms—but when pictures emerge of her doing the dirty with a politician's son, her life suddenly becomes the centre of a national scandal. Izzy's never been ashamed of herself before, and she's not going to start now. But keeping her head up will take everything she has.—

With dark humor, Steven dispels the myth of the Nice Guy and examines the stigma still attached to female sexuality. Izzy's wry voice and fierce spirit make her impossible not to root for. —*Booklist*

Stewart, Martin J.
Riverkeep: a novel. Martin Stewart. Viking, an imprint of Penguin Random House LLC, 2016 416 p.
Grades: 6 7 8 9 10
1. Rivers; 2. Demonic possession; 3. Sea monsters; 4. Fathers; 5. Rescues; 6. Fantasy fiction
9781101998298; 9780141362038, print, UK

Filled with wild adventure and hilarious dialogue (Tillinghast has a particularly saucy mouth), this vivid, engrossing fantasy will delight readers, even those who occasionally find the dialect tricky to navigate. —*Publishers Weekly*

The **sacrifice** box. Martin Stewart. Penguin Group USA 2018 304 p.

Grades: 8 9 10 11 12

1. Friendship; 2. Magic boxes; 3. Consequences; 4. Magic; 5. Betrayal; 6. 1980s; 7. Coming-of-age stories; 8. Horror

9780425289532

In the summer of 1982, five friends discover an ancient stone box hidden deep in the woods. They seal inside of it treasured objects from their childhoods, and they make a vow. Four years later, a series of strange and terrifying events begin to unfold. Someone broke the rules of the box, and now everyone has to pay.

Stiefvater, Maggie

All the crooked saints. By Maggie Stiefvater. Scholastic Press, 2017 288 p.

Grades: 9 10 11 12

1. Self-awareness; 2. Mexican Americans; 3. Miracles; 4. Saints; 5. Self-fulfillment; 6. Magical realism

9780545930802; 9781407164793, print, UK; 9781407188836, Paperback, UK

True history blends with traditional and fanciful folklore as fallen saints find salvation in the lyrical power of family, community, and rock-'n'-roll. —*Kirkus*

Ballad: a gathering of faerie. Maggie Stiefvater. Flux, 2009 353 p; (Books of Faerie, 2)

Grades: 8 9 10 11 12

1. Fairies; 2. Teenage musicians; 3. Inspiration; 4. Bagpipers; 5. Supernatural; 6. Fantasy fiction; 7. Multiple perspectives

9780738714844; 9781443113632

LC 2009019393

When music prodigy James Morgan and his best friend, Deirdre, join a private conservatory for musicians, his talent attracts Nuala, a faerie muse who fosters and feeds on creative energies, but soon he finds himself battling the Queen of the Fey for the very lives of Deirdre and Nuala.

The themes of music, faerie, and romance combined with a smart male voice wil satisfy realistic fantasy readers as well as existing and new readers of the series. —*Library Media Connection*

★ **Blue** Lily, Lily Blue. Maggie Stiefvater. Scholastic Press, 2014 416 p. (Raven cycle, 3)

Grades: 9 10 11 12

1. Clairvoyance; 2. Dreams; 3. Trust; 4. Psychics; 5. Supernatural; 6. Urban fantasy

9780545424967; 9781407136639, print, UK

School Library Journal Best Books: Fiction, 2014.

This atmospheric fantasy is far more character driven than the former book, with increased and especially satisfying interactions among players.... The books luminous and lively prose takes unanticipated paths, some new and surprising, with others connecting to previous events, demonstrating meticulous plot design. —*Voice of Youth Advocates*

★ **Call** down the hawk. Maggie Stiefvater. Scholastic Press, 2019 480 p. (Dreamer trilogy, 1)

Grades: 7 8 9 10 11 12

1. Dreams; 2. End of the world; 3. Prophecies; 4. Brothers; 5. Magic; 6. Washington, D.C; 7. Urban fantasy; 8. Multiple perspectives

9781338188325, HRD, US; 9781407194462, Paperback, UK

While dreamers Ronan Lynch and Jordan Hennessy work to control their powers and stop destructive dreaming, government agent Carmen Farooq-Lane is hunting dreamers to prevent the prophesied apocalypse.

Stiefvater delivers a stunningly imaginative tale that is by turns dark, funny, tragic, romantic, and surreal. Exquisitely drawn characters and witty, graceful prose complement the artfully crafted plot, which thrills

while examining issues of individuality and mortality. —*Publishers Weekly*

★ The **dream** thieves. Maggie Stiefvater. Scholastic Press, 2013 416 p. (Raven cycle, 2)

Grades: 8 9 10 11 12

1. Dreams; 2. Family secrets; 3. Gay teenagers; 4. Clairvoyance; 5. Rich teenage boys; 6. Urban fantasy

9780545424943

School Library Journal Best Books, 2013; YALSA Best Fiction for Young Adults, 2014.

In this darker second book (*The Raven Boys*), Gansey, Blue, and the search for Glendower take a backseat to the exploration of Ronan's and Adam's tortured personalities. Stiefvater's descriptive prose reveals a complicated plot, multiple viewpoints, and detailed backstories. Many mysteries remain, but the cliffhanger ending makes it clear that Glendower will resurface as the main focus of book three. —*Horn Book Guide*

Forever. Maggie Stiefvater. Scholastic Press, 2011 390 p. (Wolves of Mercy Falls trilogy, 3)

Grades: 9 10 11 12

1. Shapeshifters; 2. Wolves; 3. Hunting; 4. Supernatural; 5. Teenage romance; 6. Paranormal romances.

9780545259088; 9781407121116, print, UK

Stiefvater's emotional prose is rich without being melodramatic, and she clearly shares her fans' love of these characters. —*Booklist*

Linger. Maggie Stiefvater. Scholastic Press, 2010 362 p. (Wolves of Mercy Falls trilogy, 2)

Grades: 8 9 10 11 12

1. Shapeshifters; 2. Wolves; 3. Crushes in teenagers; 4. Secrets; 5. Supernatural; 6. Paranormal romances.

9780545123280; 9781407121086, print, UK

LC 2009039500

As Grace hides the vast depth of her love for Sam from her parents and Sam struggles to release his werewolf past and claim a human future, a new wolf named Cole wins Isabel's heart but his own past threatens to destroy the whole pack.

This riveting narrative, impossible to put down, is not only an excellent addition to the current fangs and fur craze but is also a beautifully written romance that, along with Shiver, will have teens clamoring for the third and final entry. —*Voice of Youth Advocates*

★ The **raven** boys. Maggie Stiefvater. Scholastic Press, 2012 390 p. (Raven cycle, 1)

Grades: 8 9 10 11 12

1. Clairvoyance; 2. Rich teenage boys; 3. Psychics; 4. Spirits; 5. Love; 6. Urban fantasy

9780545424929; 9781407134611, print, UK

Inky Awards (Australia): Silver Inky, 2013; School Library Journal Best Books, 2012; YALSA Best Fiction for Young Adults, 2013.

Blue Sargent's gift seems to be that she makes other people's talents stronger, and when she meets Gansey, one of the Raven Boys from the Aglionby Academy, she discovers that together their talents are a dangerous mix.

★ The **raven** king. Maggie Stiefvater. Scholastic Press, 2016 400 p. (Raven cycle, 4)

Grades: 8 9 10 11 12

1. Clairvoyance; 2. Psychics; 3. Rich teenage boys; 4. Dreams; 5. Supernatural; 6. Urban fantasy

9780545424981

School Library Journal Best Books, 2016.

Stiefvater excels at building an intricately layered narrative with twisting, unpredictable turns, and her ability to introduce new, complex characters and storylines while also tying up previous loose ends is remarkable. —*Voice of Youth Advocates*

★ The **Scorpio** races. Maggie Stiefvater. Scholastic Press, 2011 400 p.
Grades: 8 9 10 11 12
1. Horse racing; 2. Competition; 3. Teenage girl orphans; 4. Horses; 5. Islands; 6. Fantasy fiction; 7. Multiple perspectives.
9780545224901; 9781407178967, print, UK
LC 2011015775
Booklist Editors' Choice: Books for Youth, 2011; YALSA Best Fiction for Young Adults, 2012; Westchester Fiction Award, 2011; School Library Journal Best Books, 2011; Michael L. Printz Honor Book, 2012.
Nineteen-year-old returning champion Sean Kendrick competes against Puck Connolly, the first girl ever to ride in the annual Scorpio Races, both trying to keep hold of their dangerous water horses long enough to make it to the finish line.
Stiefvater's narration is as much about atmospherics as it is about event, and the water horses are the environment in which Sean and Puck move, allies and rivals to the end. It's not a feel-good story—dread, loss, and hard choices are the islanders' lot. As a study of courage and loyalty tested, however, it is an utterly compelling read. —*Publishers Weekly*

★ **Shiver**. Maggie Stiefvater. Scholastic, 2009 400 p. (Wolves of Mercy Falls trilogy, 1)
Grades: 9 10 11 12
1. Shapeshifters; 2. Wolves; 3. Crushes in teenagers; 4. Supernatural; 5. Seasons; 6. Paranormal romances; 7. Books for reluctant readers
9780545123266
LC 2009005257
Georgia Peach Book Award for Teen Readers, 2011; Inky Awards (Australia): Silver Inky, 2010; YALSA Quick Picks for Reluctant Young Adult Readers, 2010; YALSA Popular Paperbacks for Young Adults, 2011; YALSA Best Books for Young Adults, 2010.
In all the years she has watched the wolves in the woods behind her house, Grace has been particularly drawn to an unusual yellow-eyed wolf who, in his turn, has been watching her with increasing intensity.
Stiefvater skillfully increases the tension throughout; her take on werewolves is interesting and original while her characters are refreshingly willing to use their brains to deal with the challenges they face. —*Publishers Weekly*

Sinner. Maggie Stiefvater. Scholastic Press, 2014 368 p.
Grades: 9 10 11 12
1. Teenage musicians; 2. Shapeshifters; 3. Fame; 4. Wolves; 5. Teenage romance; 6. Los Angeles, California; 7. Paranormal romances.
9780545654579; 9781407145754, print, UK; 9781407145730, print, UK
The relationship between the richly drawn characters is the heart of the book—it is light on paranormal and wolf action. Cole and Isabel are both jerks, but they are jerks with hearts, and they keep up with each other's witty banter. The ending wraps up a bit too neatly, but getting there is an absolute delight. A spectacularly messy, emotionally oh-so-human romance. —*Kirkus*
Companion book to the Shiver trilogy.

Stirling, Tricia
When my heart was wicked. Tricia Stirling. Scholastic Press, 2015 192 p.
Grades: 9 10 11 12

1. Mothers and daughters; 2. Options, alternatives, choices; 3. Stepmothers; 4. Magic; 5. Sixteen-year-old girls; 6. California; 7. Paranormal fiction
9780545695732
LC 2014021741
After her father dies, leaving sixteen-year-old Lacy with her much-loved stepmother, Lacy's birth mother suddenly shows up wanting Lacy back—and she will stop at nothing, not even dark magic, to control her daughter and draw her into her own twisted life.
Stirling does a wonderful job of making the reader care for Lacy, who is not beyond casting spells herself. Her Northern California world of idiosyncratic personalities and oddball beauty is memorable and will be sure to appeal to teens who like their realism tempered with the otherworldly. —*Booklist*

Stohl, Margaret
Forever red. Margaret Stohl. Marvel, 2015 304 p. (Black Widow (Margaret Stohl), 1)
Grades: 7 8 9 10 11 12
1. Superheroines; 2. Assassins; 3. Secret societies; 4. Teenage girls; 5. Black Widow (Fictitious character); 6. Superhero stories; 7. Franchise books; 8. Books for reluctant readers
9781484726433; 9781484776452
YALSA Quick Picks for Reluctant Young Adult Readers, 2016.
Trained from a young age in the arts of death and deception, elite assassin Natasha reluctantly reunites with a Russian quantum physicist's daughter she once rescued in order to stop her former master's abductions of children throughout Eastern Europe.
Great fight sequences, plenty of action, twists in the plot, and characters motivated by strong emotions will keep readers engaged and entertained. —*School Library Journal*
Based on the characters from the Avengers series.

Stokes, Paula
Girl against the universe. Paula Stokes. Harperteen, an imprint of HarperCollinsPublishers,, 2016 379 p.
Grades: 8 9 10 11
1. Tennis players; 2. Psychotherapy; 3. Survivor guilt; 4. Bad luck; 5. Teenage romance; 6. Contemporary romances; 7. First person narratives
9780062379962
Stokes' engaging prose and sympathetic characters serve up great lessons in acceptance for teens dealing with trauma. —*Kirkus*

Stolarz, Laurie Faria
Jane Anonymous. Laurie Faria Stolarz. Wednesday Books, 2020 320 p.
Grades: 9 10 11 12
1. Kidnapping victims; 2. Memory; 3. Healing — Psychological aspects; 4. Psychic trauma; 5. Self-deception; 6. Thrillers and suspense; 7. Parallel narratives; 8. Diary novels.
9781250303707, HRD, US; 9781250303721, ebook), US
LC 2019037603
In chapters alternating between "then" and "now," seventeen-year-old Jane Anonymous chronicles the events leading up to her abduction and seven-month captivity and her painful return to family and friends.
A story about lingering trauma, loss, and the journey toward healing, this gripping crime novel could be a documentary from the Investigation Discovery channel. A must-read. —*School Library Journal*

Stone, Nic

Dear Justyce. Nic Stone. 2020 288 p.
Grades: 9 10 11 12

1. Juvenile correctional institutions; 2. Teenage prisoners; 3. African American college students; 4. Juvenile justice system; 5. Family problems; 6. Realistic fiction; 7. African American fiction
9781984829672; 9781984829665

LC 2020020509

Incarcerated teen Quan Banks writes letters to Justyce McCallister, with whom he bonded years before over family issues, about his experiences in the American juvenile justice system.

A powerful, raw must-read told through the lens of a Black boy ensnared by our broken criminal justice system. —*Kirkus*

Companion novel to: *Dear Martin*.

★ **Dear** Martin. Nic Stone. 2017 224 pages
Grades: 9 10 11 12

1. King, Martin Luther; 2. African American teenage boys; 3. Racism; 4. Race relations; 5. Racial profiling; 6. Police brutality; 7. Realistic fiction; 8. African American fiction
9781101939499, hardcover; 9781101939505, hardcover library edition; 9781101939529, paperback; 9781101939512, ebook; 9781471175565, Paperback, UK

LC 2016058582

Georgia Peach Book Award for Teen Readers, 2019; YALSA Best Fiction for Young Adults, 2018; YALSA Quick Picks for Reluctant Young Adult Readers, 2018; William C. Morris Debut Award finalist, 2018.

Writing letters to the late Dr. Martin Luther King Jr, seventeen-year-old college-bound Justyce McAllister struggles to face the reality of race relations today and how they are shaping him.

Odd one out. Nic Stone. 2018 320 p.
Grades: 9 10 11 12

1. Love triangles; 2. Sexual orientation; 3. Self-discovery in teenagers; 4. Dating (Social Customs); 5. Best friends; 6. Georgia; 7. First person narratives; 8. Multiple perspectives; 9. LGBTQIA romances
9781101939536; 9781101939543; 9781471175589, Paperback, UK
YALSA Best Fiction for Young Adults, 2019.

High school juniors and best friends Courtney and Jupe, and new sophomore Rae, explore their sexuality and their budding attractions for one another. —*OCLC*

Stone, Peter

The **perfect** candidate. Peter Stone. Simon & Schuster Books for Young Readers, 2018 384 p.
Grades: 7 8 9 10

1. Conspiracies; 2. Interns; 3. FBI agents; 4. Political intrigue; 5. Secrets; 6. Washington, D.C; 7. Thrillers and suspense.
9781534422179

When Cameron Carter goes straight from high school in small-town California to a summer internship with a powerful U.S. Congressman he admires, he soon learns that not everything in Washington, D.C. is as it appears.

Stone, Tamara Ireland

Little do we know. Tamara Ireland Stone. 2018 416 p.
Grades: 9 10 11 12

1. Former friends; 2. Boyfriends; 3. Quarreling; 4. Neighbors; 5. Christian teenage girls; 6. Realistic fiction
9781484768211

LC 2018004933

Told from two viewpoints, neighbors and former best friends Hannah and Emory, seventeen, must face what caused their rift after Hannah saves the life of Emory's boyfriend, Luke.

Time between us. Tamara Ireland Stone. Hyperion, 2012 384 p.
Grades: 7 8 9 10

1. Sixteen-year-old girls; 2. Teenage romance; 3. Time travel; 4. Teenage girls; 5. Space and time; 6. Illinois; 7. Evanston, Illinois; 8. 1990s; 9. Fantasy romances
9781423159568

LC 2011053368

In 1995 Evanston, Illinois, sixteen-year-old Anna's perfectly normal life is turned upside-down when she meets Bennett, whose ability to travel through space and time creates complications for them both.

Sequel: *Time after time.*

Stork, Francisco X.

Disappeared. Francisco X. Stork. Arthur A. Levine Books, 2017 336 p. (Disappeared (Stork), 1)
Grades: 7 8 9 10

1. Journalists; 2. Missing persons; 3. Criminals; 4. Crime; 5. Poverty; 6. Mexico; 7. Ciudad Juarez, Mexico; 8. Thrillers and suspense
9780545944472

LC 2017017320

YALSA Best Fiction for Young Adults, 2018; Walter Honor Book, Teen, 2018.

Four months ago Sara Zapata's best friend, Linda, disappeared from the streets of Juarez, and ever since Sara has been using her job as a reporter to draw attention to the girls who have been kidnapped by the criminals who control the city, but now she and her family are being threatened—meanwhile her younger brother, Emiliano, is being lured into the narcotics business by the promise of big money, and soon the only way for both of them to escape is to risk the dangerous trek across the desert to the United States border.

Stork (*The Memory of Light*) crafts a narrative that is both riveting and eye-opening. Part thriller, part sociological study, the novel sheds light on poverty, corruption, and greed while bringing readers intimately close to the plight of those who illegally cross borders with the hope of a brighter future. —*Publishers Weekly*

★ The **last** summer of the Death Warriors. Francisco X. Stork. Arthur A. Levine Books, 2010 352 p.
Grades: 8 9 10 11 12

1. People with cancer; 2. Caregivers; 3. Revenge; 4. Seventeen-year-old boys; 5. Teenage boys; 6. New Mexico; 7. Classics-inspired fiction.
9780545151337; 9780545151344; 9781407120980, print, UK; 9781407121024, print, UK

LC 2009019853

Westchester Fiction Award, 2010; YALSA Best Fiction for Young Adults, 2011.

Seventeen-year-old Pancho is bent on avenging the senseless death of his sister, but after he meets D.Q, who is dying of cancer, and Marisol, one of D.Q.'s caregivers, both boys find their lives changed by their interactions.

This novel, in the way of the best literary fiction, is an invitation to careful reading that rewards serious analysis and discussion. Thoughtful readers will be delighted by both the challenge and Stork's respect for their abilities. —*Booklist*

★ **Marcelo** in the real world. Francisco X. Stork. Arthur A. Levine Books, 2009 320 p.
Grades: 8 9 10 11 12

1. God (Christianity) — Will; 2. Teenagers with autism; 3. Injustice; 4. Romantic love; 5. Teenage boys; 6. Realistic fiction.
9780545054744

LC 2008014729

James Cook Book Award (Ohio), 2011; Schneider Family Book Award for Teens, 2010; Notable Books for a Global Society, 2010; Booklist Editors' Choice: Books for Youth, 2009; YALSA Best Books for Young Adults, 2010; School Library Journal Best Books, 2009.

Marcelo Sandoval, a seventeen-year-old boy on the high-functioning end of the autistic spectrum, faces new challenges, including romance and injustice, when he goes to work for his father in the mailroom of a corporate law firm.

Stork introduces ethical dilemmas, the possibility of love, and other real world conflicts, all the while preserving the integrity of his characterizations and intensifying the novel's psychological and emotional stakes. —*Publishers Weekly*

★ The **memory** of light. Francisco X. Stork. Arthur A. Levine Books, an imprint of Scholastic Inc, 2016 336 p.
Grades: 9 10 11 12

1. Mexican American teenage girls; 2. Depression; 3. Suicidal behavior; 4. Psychotherapy patients; 5. Families; 6. Texas; 7. Realistic fiction; 8. First person narratives
9780545474320

Tomas Rivera Mexican American Children's Book Award, 2017; YALSA Best Fiction for Young Adults, 2017.

Stork remains loyal to his characters, their moments of weakness, and their pragmatic views, and he does not shy away from such topics as domestic violence, social-class struggles, theology, and philosophy. —*Kirkus*

Strasser, Todd

Boot camp. Todd Strasser. Simon & Schuster Books for Young Readers, 2007 256 p.
Grades: 8 9 10 11 12

1. Fifteen-year-old boys; 2. Juvenile delinquency; 3. Prison boot camps; 4. Teenage boys; 5. Teenagers; 6. Realistic fiction; 7. Books for reluctant readers
9781416908487

LC 2006013634

YALSA Popular Paperbacks for Young Adults, 2015; YALSA Quick Picks for Reluctant Young Adult Readers, 2008.

After ignoring several warnings to stop dating his teacher, Garrett is sent to Lake Harmony, a boot camp that uses unorthodox and brutal methods to train students to obey their parents.

The ending is both realistic and disturbing.... Writing in the teen's mature and perceptive voice, Strasser creates characters who will provoke strong reactions from readers.... [This is a] fast-paced and revealing story. —*School Library Journal*

Famous. Todd Strasser. Simon & Schuster BFYR, 2011 259 p;
Grades: 7 8 9 10

1. Teenage girl photographers; 2. Fame; 3. Celebrities; 4. Paparazzi; 5. Actors and actresses; 6. Hollywood, California; 7. Realistic fiction.
9781416975113

LC 2009048163

Sixteen-year-old Jamie Gordon had a taste of praise and recognition at age fourteen when her unflattering photograph of an actress was published, but as she pursues her dream of being a celebrity photographer, she becomes immersed in the dark side of fame.

The book makes some astute observations about America's reality-television culture and its obsession with fame.... This well-crafted novel clearly belongs in all public, junior high, and high school libraries. —*Voice of Youth Advocates*

No place. Todd Strasser. Simon & Schuster, 2014 272 p.
Grades: 7 8 9 10

1. High school seniors; 2. Poverty; 3. Homelessness; 4. Young men; 5. Teenage boys; 6. Realistic fiction.
9781442457218

Rendered homeless by circumstances beyond his middle-class family's control, Dan, a popular school baseball star, is forced to move to Tent City, where he becomes involved in the efforts of people fighting for better conditions only to be targeted by an adversary who wants to destroy the impoverished region.

With the consummate skill of the best young adult writers, Strasser avoids sermonizing as he seamlessly combines real-time information about the social and economic conditions in contemporary society with a realistic and readable story of high school life. This exceptionally thought-provoking novel should be part of all collections serving teens. —*Voice of Youth Advocates*

Price of duty. Todd Strasser. Simon & Schuster, 2018 224 p.
Grades: 8 9 10 11

1. Veterans; 2. Post-traumatic stress disorder; 3. War; 4. Heroes and heroines; 5. Addiction; 6. Realistic fiction; 7. Books for reluctant readers
9781481497091; 9781481497107; 9781481497114, ebook, US

Hailed as a hero, twenty-year-old Jake returns to his pro-military hometown and family injured physically and emotionally, unsure if he can return to active duty but uncomfortable with the alternative.

Wish you were dead. Todd Strasser. Egmont USA, 2009 236 p; (Thrillogy, 1)
Grades: 8 9 10 11 12

1. Missing persons; 2. Stalking; 3. Revenge; 4. Guilt in teenage girls; 5. High school students; 6. New York (State); 7. Thrillers and suspense; 8. Books for reluctant readers
9781606840078

LC 2009014641

YALSA Quick Picks for Reluctant Young Adult Readers, 2011.

Madison, a senior at a suburban New York high school, tries to uncover who is responsible for the disappearance of her friends, popular students mentioned in the posts of an anonymous blogger, while she, herself, is being stalked online and in-person.

The themes of bullying, tolerance, and friendship are issues to which readers can relate, as well as the inclusion of the IMing, blogging, texting, and social networking. This thriller will be popular and passed from one reader to another. —*Voice of Youth Advocates*

Stratton, Allan

★ **Borderline**. Allan Stratton. HarperTeen, 2010 320 p.
Grades: 6 7 8 9 10

1. Prejudice; 2. Terrorism; 3. Fathers and sons; 4. Identity (Psychology); 5. Muslims; 6. Mysteries; 7. Coming-of-age stories; 8. Canadian fiction.
9780061451119; 9780061451126; 9781443410502

LC 2009005241

YALSA Popular Paperbacks for Young Adults, 2013; YALSA Best Fiction for Young Adults, 2011.

Sami Sabiri risks his life to uncover the truth when his father is implicated in a terrorist plot.

This is a powerful story and excellent resource for teaching tolerance, with a message that extends well beyond the timely subject matter. —*Publishers Weekly*

★ **Chanda's** secrets. Allan Stratton. Annick, 2004 193 p.
Grades: 7 8 9 10
1. Sixteen-year-old girls; 2. Children of people with AIDS; 3. Family secrets; 4. Parent-separated teenagers; 5. Caregivers; 6. Sub-Saharan Africa; 7. Canadian fiction.
9781550378351; 9781550378344
Booklist Editors' Choice: Books for Youth, 2004; Children's Africana Book Awards, Older Readers, 2005; Willow Awards, Snow Willow category, 2005; YALSA Best Books for Young Adults, 2005; Michael L. Printz Honor Book, 2005.

The details of sub-Saharan African life are convincing and smoothly woven into this moving story of poverty and courage, but the real insight for readers will be the appalling treatment of the AIDS victims. Strong language and frank description are appropriate to the subject matter. —*School Library Journal*

Chanda's wars. By Allan Stratton. Harper Collins Publishers, 2008 400 p.
Grades: 8 9 10 11 12
1. Teenage girls; 2. Child kidnapping victims; 3. Courage in teenage girls; 4. Brothers and sisters; 5. Orphans; 6. Africa; 7. Canadian fiction.
9780060872625
LC 2007010829
Canadian Library Association Young Adult Book Award, 2009.

Chandra Kabelo, a teenaged African girl, must save her younger siblings after they are kidnapped and forced to serve as child soldiers in General Mandiki's rebel army.

The characters are drawn without sentimentality, and the story is a moving portrayal of betrayal and love. The army's brutality and the traumas of the child soldiers are graphic and disturbing. —*Booklist*

Strickland, AdriAnne
Shadow run. AdriAnne Strickland & Michael Miller. Delacorte Press, 2017 336 p. (Kaitan chronicles, 1)
Grades: 7 8 9 10 11 12
1. Princes; 2. Far future; 3. Disguises; 4. Energy; 5. Space vehicles; 6. Space; 7. Science fiction.
9780399552533
LC 2015044876
The captain of a starship and a prince are forced to revise their ideas of family and loyalty, with the fate of their worlds hanging in the balance.

The world-building is excellent, with a convincingly unique source of cosmic energy that has the potential for extraordinary power. The writing is accomplished; the plot, though familiar, has good twists; and the pace is appropriately fast. —*School Library Journal*

Strohmeyer, Sarah
How Zoe made her dreams (mostly) come true. Sarah Strohmeyer. Balzer + Bray, 2013 336 p.
Grades: 7 8 9 10
1. Amusement parks; 2. Summer employment; 3. Competition; 4. Teenage romance; 5. Cousins; 6. New Jersey; 7. Contemporary romances; 8. Romantic comedies; 9. Teen chick lit.
9780062187451
LC 2012038163
Seventeen-year-old Zoe and her cousin Jess eagerly start summer jobs at New Jersey's Fairyland theme park, but Jess does not get her dream role and Zoe is assigned to be personal assistant to the park's "Queen," winning her no friends.

Smart girls get what they want. By Sarah Strohmeyer. Balzer + Bray, 2012 256 p.

Grades: 7 8 9 10 11 12
1. High school sophomores; 2. Theater; 3. Best friends; 4. High schools; 5. Schools; 6. Realistic fiction.
9780061953408
LC 2011026094
Three sophomore best friends use their brains—and their wits—to find happiness in high school.

Stroud, Jonathan
★ The **amulet** of Samarkand. Jonathan Stroud. Hyperion Books For Children, 2003 464 p. (Bartimaeus trilogy, 1)
Grades: 7 8 9 10
1. Boy apprentices; 2. Genies; 3. Revenge; 4. Magic; 5. Twelve-year-old boys; 6. London, England; 7. Fantasy fiction; 8. Multiple perspectives; 9. First person narratives.
9780786818594
LC 2003049904
ALA Notable Children's Book, 2004; Booklist Editors' Choice: Books for Youth, 2003; Mythopoeic Award for Children's Literature, 2006; YALSA Best Books for Young Adults, 2004.

Nathaniel, a magician's apprentice, summons up the djinni Bartimaeus and instructs him to steal the Amulet of Samarkand from the powerful magician Simon Lovelace.

There is plenty of action, mystery, and humor to keep readers turning the pages. This title, the first in a trilogy, is a must for fantasy fans. —*School Library Journal*
Sequel: *The Golem's eye.*

The **golem's** eye. By Jonathan Stroud. Hyperion Books for Children, 2004 574 p. (Bartimaeus trilogy, 2)
Grades: 7 8 9 10
1. Teenage apprentices; 2. Power (Social sciences); 3. Genies; 4. Golem; 5. Fourteen-year-old boys; 6. London, England; 7. Prague, Czech Republic; 8. Fantasy fiction; 9. Multiple perspectives; 10. First person narratives.
9780786818600
LC 2004054232
Mythopoeic Award for Children's Literature, 2006; New York Times Notable Children's Book, 2004; YALSA Best Books for Young Adults, 2005.

In their continuing adventures, magician's apprentice Nathaniel, now fourteen years old, and the djinni Bartimaeus travel to Prague to locate the source of a golem's power before it destroys London.

The characters are well developed and the action never lets up. A must-purchase for all fantasy collections. —*School Library Journal*
Miramax books.

★ **Heroes** of the valley. Jonathan Stroud. Hyperion, 2009 480 p.
Grades: 7 8 9 10
1. Teenage adventurers; 2. Practical jokes; 3. Hero worship; 4. Quests; 5. Fifteen-year-old boys; 6. Fantasy fiction; 7. Coming-of-age stories.
9781423109662
Booklist Editors' Choice: Books for Youth, 2009; YALSA Best Books for Young Adults, 2010.

When young Halli Sveinsson takes one of his practical jokes too far, he is forced to leave the House of Svein and go on a hero's quest where he encounters highway robbers, terrifying monsters, and a girl who may be as fearless as he is.

Smart, funny dialogue and prose, revealing passages about the exploits of the hero Svein, bouts of action and a touch of romance briskly move the story along. —*Publishers Weekly*

Ptolemy's gate. Jonathan Stroud. Hyperion Books For Children, 2006 512 p. (Bartimaeus trilogy, 3)

Grades: 7 8 9 10

1. Teenage magicians; 2. Genies; 3. Conspiracies; 4. Seventeen-year-old boys; 5. Magic; 6. London, England; 7. Egypt; 8. Fantasy fiction; 9. Multiple perspectives; 10. First person narratives.
9780786818617

LC 2005052655

Mythopoeic Award for Children's Literature, 2006; Booklist Editors' Choice: Books for Youth, 2006.

Dangerous adventures continue for the djinni Bartimaeus and his master, seventeen-year-old Nathaniel, a powerful magician who is serving as England's minister of information.

This is an exciting and eminently satisfying conclusion to the trilogy.... literate, entertaining, and exciting. —*School Library Journal*
Miramax books.

★ The **ring** of Solomon: a Bartimaeus novel. By Jonathan Stroud. Disney/Hyperion Books, 2010 512 p. (Bartimaeus trilogy, Prequel)
Grades: 7 8 9 10

1. Solomon; 2. Genies; 3. Magic rings; 4. Women assassins; 5. Magic; 6. Wizards; 7. Jerusalem, Israel; 8. Fantasy fiction; 9. Multiple perspectives; 10. First person narratives.
9781423123729; 9780385619158, print, UK

LC 2010015468

Booklist Editors' Choice: Books for Youth, 2010; School Library Journal Best Books, 2010.

Wise-cracking djinni Bartimaeus finds himself at the court of King Solomon with an unpleasant master, a sinister servant, and King Solomon's magic ring.

In this exciting prequel set in ancient Israel, Stroud presents an early adventure of his sharp-tongued djinn, Bartimaeus.... This is a superior fantasy that should have fans racing back to those books. —*Publishers Weekly*

Stuber, Barbara

★ **Crossing** the tracks. Barbara Stuber. Margaret K. McElderry Books, 2010 258 p;
Grades: 6 7 8 9

1. Families; 2. Live-in companions; 3. Trust; 4. Grief in teenage girls; 5. Teenage girls; 6. Missouri; 7. 1920s; 8. Historical fiction.
9781416997030

LC 2009042672

YALSA Best Fiction for Young Adults, 2011; William C. Morris Debut Award finalist, 2011.

In Missouri in 1926, fifteen-year-old Iris Baldwin discovers what family truly means when her father hires her out for the summer as a companion to a country doctor's invalid mother.

Thought-provoking and tenderhearted, Iris's story is one of a mature young woman who faces life with courage and common sense.... This thoughtful novel offers strong character development and an engaging protagonist. —*School Library Journal*

Sugiura, Misa

It's not like it's a secret. Misa Sugiura. 2017 400 p.
Grades: 7 8 9 10 11

1. Japanese American teenage girls; 2. Secrets; 3. First loves; 4. Teenage romance; 5. Extramarital affairs; 6. California; 7. Realistic fiction; 8. Coming-of-age stories; 9. First person narratives
9780062473417

LC 2016961849

Asian Pacific American Asian Pacific American Award for Literature: Young Adult Literature, 2018; YALSA Best Fiction for Young Adults, 2018; Rainbow List, 2018.

A girl whose life revolves around big and small secrets struggles with differences between two diverse groups of friends, a boy's sweet but unrequited affection, her crush on her best friend and her father's increasingly obvious affair.

Well-paced, brimming with drama, and utterly vital. —*Kirkus*

This time will be different. Misa Sugiura. 2019 400 p.
Grades: 8 9 10 11 12

1. Florists; 2. Self-discovery in teenage girls; 3. Japanese Americans; 4. Teenage girls; 5. Flower arrangement; 6. Silicon Valley, California; 7. California; 8. Realistic fiction; 9. Coming-of-age stories
9780062473448

LC 2018964875

Preferring a simple future to her mother's ambitions for her, a 17-year-old Japanese-American teen discovers her talent for flower arranging before her mother tries to sell the flower shop to the swindlers responsible for their hardships.

In Silicon Valley, Japanese American CJ Katsuyama, 17, has yet to show an interest in or an aptitude for anything, except perhaps working at the family's failing flower shop Heart's Desire, with her aunt Hannah, much to her overachieving venture capitalist mother Mimi's chagrin. —*Publishers Weekly*

Sullivan, Tara

★ The **bitter** side of sweet. Tara Sullivan. Penguin Group USA, 2016 320 p.
Grades: 9 10 11 12

1. Brothers; 2. Slavery; 3. Survival; 4. Fifteen-year-old boys; 5. Life change events; 6. Cote d'Ivoire; 7. Africa.
9780399173073

ALA Notable Children's Book, 2017; YALSA Best Fiction for Young Adults, 2017; Children's Africana Book Awards Honor Book, Older Readers, 2017.

Frantically working to escape punishment by their overseers, Ivory Coast child slaves Amadou and Seydou befriend a slave newcomer whose constant attempts to escape compel the brothers to plan their own flight.

There are so few stories for teenagers that provide a glimpse into the complex global systems, such as cocoa production, that they unwittingly participate in every day and likely take for granted. An author's note, glossary, and source material provide further context to engage readers and teachers. Absorbing and important. —*Booklist*

Golden boy. Tara Sullivan. G. P. Putnam's Sons, an imprint of Penguin Group (USA) Inc, 2013 384 p.
Grades: 7 8 9 10 11 12

1. Albinos and albinism; 2. Apprentices; 3. Poverty; 4. Human skin color; 5. Human rights; 6. Tanzania; 7. Realistic fiction.
9780399161124

LC 2012043310

YALSA Best Fiction for Young Adults, 2014; YALSA Best Fiction for Young Adults: Top Ten, 2014.

A Tanzanian albino boy finds himself the ultimate outsider, hunted because of the color of his skin.

Sullivan, Tricia

Shadowboxer. Tricia Sullivan. Ravenstone, 2014 286 p.
Grades: 9 10 11 12

1. Mixed martial arts; 2. Teenage martial artists; 3. Americans in Thailand; 4. Human trafficking; 5. Supernatural; 6. Thailand; 7. Urban fantasy; 8. First person narratives
9781781082829

SF author Sullivan (Lightborn) spins a kinetic, violent, and magical tale that makes excellent use of Jades hard-edged voice. Sullivan brings to life the beauty of Thailand and the sweat and blood of the gym, infusing them with magic and danger. —*Publishers Weekly*

Suma, Nova Ren
17 & gone. Nova Ren Suma. Dutton, 2013 320 p.
Grades: 9 10 11 12
1. Missing teenage girls; 2. Mental illness; 3. Visions; 4. Supernatural; 5. Schizophrenia; 6. Psychological suspense; 7. Paranormal fiction.
9780525423409

LC 2012029324

The missing girls are all different, except for two things: they all disappeared when they were 17, and they're all haunting Lauren Woodman. Lauren isn't sure why she's seeing visions of the girls, but she feels compelled to find out what happened to them. As she spirals deeper into obsession, and her own 17th birthday approaches, Lauren can't help but wonder: what if she's next?

Mature without being graphic, with a complex and intriguing plot, this novel should have no trouble finding readers. —*School Library Journal*

Imaginary girls. Nova Ren Suma. Dutton, 2011 304 p.
Grades: 9 10 11 12
1. Sisters; 2. Dead; 3. Supernatural; 4. Reservoirs; 5. Family relationships; 6. New York (State); 7. Hudson Valley; 8. Paranormal fiction
9780525423386

LC 2010042758

YALSA Popular Paperbacks for Young Adults, 2016.

Two years after sixteen-year-old Chloe discovered classmate London's dead body floating in a Hudson Valley reservoir, she returns home to be with her devoted older sister Ruby, a town favorite, and finds that London is alive and well, and that Ruby may somehow have brought her back to life and persuaded everyone that nothing is amiss.

The author uses the story's supernatural, horror movie-ready elements in the best of ways; beneath all the strangeness lies beauty, along with a powerful statement about the devotion between sisters. Not your average paranormal novel. —*Publishers Weekly*

★ The **walls** around us: a novel. By Nova Ren Suma. 2015 336 pages
Grades: 9 10 11 12
1. Juvenile jails; 2. Ballet dancers; 3. Teenage prisoners; 4. Supernatural; 5. Teenage girl ballet dancers; 6. Thrillers and suspense; 7. Paranormal fiction; 8. Multiple perspectives
9781616203726

LC 2014031972

School Library Journal Best Books, 2015; YALSA Best Fiction for Young Adults, 2016.

Orianna and Violet are ballet dancers and best friends, but when the ballerinas who have been harassing Violet are murdered, Orianna is accused of the crime and sent to a juvenile detention center where she meets Amber and they experience supernatural events linking the girls together.

This haunting and evocative tale of magical realism immerses readers in two settings that seem worlds apart. The book is told in alternating first-person voices from the perspective of two teenagers: lonely Amber, who at age 13 was convicted of murdering her abusive stepfather and sent to Aurora Hills, a juvenile detention facility, and Vee, an insecure yet ruthlessly ambitious Julliard-bound ballerina.... A powerful story that will linger with readers. —*School Library Journal*

Summers, Courtney
All the rage. By Courtney Summers. St. Martin's Griffin, 2015 336 p.
Grades: 9 10 11 12

1. Teenage rape victims; 2. Small towns; 3. Missing teenage girls; 4. Diners (Restaurants); 5. Teenage waitresses; 6. Realistic fiction; 7. Canadian fiction
9781250021915
Amelia Bloomer List, 2016; YALSA Best Fiction for Young Adults, 2016; OLA Best Bets, 2015.

Summers takes victim-shaming to task in this timely story, and the cruelties not only of Romy's classmates but also the adults she should be able to trust come heartbreakingly to the fore. Romy's breathy internal monologue is filled with bitter indignation, and while the narrative style may require some patience, older teens who like gritty realism will find plenty to ponder. —*Booklist*

Fall for anything. Courtney Summers. St. Martin's Griffin, 2011 224 p.
Grades: 9 10 11 12
1. Suicide; 2. Fathers and daughters; 3. Grief; 4. Interpersonal relations; 5. Photographers; 6. Mysteries; 7. Canadian fiction; 8. Books for reluctant readers
9780312656737

LC 2010037873

YALSA Quick Picks for Reluctant Young Adult Readers, 2012.

As she searches for clues that would explain the suicide of her successful photographer father, Eddie Reeves meets the strangely compelling Culler Evans who seems to know a great deal about her father and could hold the key to the mystery surrounding his death.

Readers may find the book fascinating or mesmerizingly melancholy depending on their moods, but there is no denying that Summers has brought Eddie's intense experience into the world of her readers. An unusual, bold effort that deserves attention. —*Kirkus*

★ **Sadie**. Courtney Summers. Wednesday Books, 2018 311 p.
Grades: 9 10 11 12
1. Podcasts; 2. Small towns; 3. Murder investigation; 4. Stuttering; 5. Missing girls; 6. Thrillers and suspense; 7. Multiple perspectives; 8. Canadian fiction; 9. Books for reluctant readers
9781250105714, hardback, US
Amelia Bloomer List, 2019; Edgar Allan Poe Award for Best Young Adult, 2019; John Spray Mystery Award (Canada), 2019; School Library Journal Best Books, 2018; White Pine Award (Ontario), 2020; YALSA Best Fiction for Young Adults, 2019; YALSA Quick Picks for Reluctant Young Adult Readers, 2019.

Told from the alternating perspectives of nineteen-year-old Sadie who runs away from her isolated small Colorado town to find her younger sister's killer, and a true crime podcast exploring Sadie's disappearance.

This is not a test. Courtney Summers. St. Martin's Griffin, 2012 326 p.
Grades: 7 8 9 10 11 12
1. Zombies; 2. Survival (after disaster); 3. End of the world; 4. High schools; 5. Family problems; 6. Apocalyptic fiction; 7. Horror; 8. Canadian fiction; 9. Books for reluctant readers
9780312656744
YALSA Best Fiction for Young Adults, 2013; YALSA Quick Picks for Reluctant Young Adult Readers, 2013; YALSA Popular Paperbacks for Young Adults, 2017.

Sloane Price is barricaded in Cortege High with five other teens while zombies try to get in. She observes her fellow captives become more unpredictable and violent as time passes although they each have much more reason to live than she has.

Sun, Amanda
Ink. Amanda Sun. Harlequin Books, 2013 304 p. (Paper gods, 1)
Grades: 7 8 9 10 11 12

1. Americans in Japan; 2. Sixteen-year-old girls; 3. Strangers; 4. Paranormal phenomena; 5. Teenage girls; 6. Japan; 7. Urban fantasy; 8. Canadian fiction; 9. Asian-influenced fantasy
9780373210718

After a family tragedy in Deep River, Canada Katie Greene is sent to live with her aunt in Shizuoka, Japan. There she feels lost and alone until she meets the mysterious Tomohiro and strange things begin to happen whenever they are together : ink drips from nowhere, drawings come to life, etc. As their relationship deepens, Katie becomes drawn into Tomo's world, that is somehow connected to the kami— powerful ancient Japanese beings.

Katie's tendency to jump to conclusions, cry, and act before she thinks is frustrating, but it leaves plenty of room for growth. The descriptions of life in Japan—particularly teen life—create a strong sense of place, and set a vivid backdrop for this intriguing series opener by a debut author. —*Booklist*

Supplee, Suzanne
Somebody everybody listens to. Suzanne Supplee. Dutton Books, 2010 245 p;
Grades: 7 8 9 10 11 12
1. Teenage girl singers; 2. Country music; 3. Ambition in teenage girls; 4. Ambition; 5. Country musicians; 6. Tennessee; 7. Nashville, Tennessee; 8. Realistic fiction; 9. First person narratives; 10. Teen chick lit
9780525422426
LC 2009025089
YALSA Popular Paperbacks for Young Adults, 2013; YALSA Best Fiction for Young Adults, 2011.

Upon graduating from high school in the tiny town of Starling, Tennessee, aspiring country singer Retta Lee Jones manages to get herself to Nashville, where, in spite of some bad luck and hard times, she tries to persevere in pursuing her dreams.

While a must read for country music lovers,...[this book] will appeal to a wide audience, especially those who long to pursue a dream against the odds. —*Publishers Weekly*

Sutherland, Tui
So this is how it ends. Tui T. Sutherland. Eos, 2006 368 p. (Avatars, 1)
Grades: 7 8 9 10
1. Teenage girls; 2. Teenage boys; 3. Teenagers; 4. Teenage superheroes; 5. Earthquakes; 6. Central Park, New York City; 7. 21st century; 8. Apocalyptic fiction; 9. Fantasy fiction.
9780060750244; 9780060750282
LC 2006020122
During an earthquake in the year 2012 five teens are transported seventy-five years into the future, where the end of the world is imminent, and are drawn together by a mysterious force.

The complexities of time travel and possibilities of biotechnology run amok are realized with verve, making this a good choice for discussion. —*Booklist*

Sutton, Kelsey
Some quiet place. Kelsey Sutton. Flux, 2013 331 p;
Grades: 7 8 9 10
1. Emotions; 2. Fear; 3. Children of alcoholic fathers; 4. Supernatural; 5. Family problems; 6. Wisconsin; 7. Paranormal romances
9780738736433
LC 2013005021
Seventeen-year-old Elizabeth Caldwell sees, rather than feels, emotions; they're beings who walk among us. The only emotion who engages with her now is Fear, and he's as desperate as Elizabeth is to figure out how she became this way.

Haunting, chilling and achingly romantic, Sutton's debut novel for teens will keep readers up until the wee hours, unable to tear themselves away from this strange and beautifully crafted story. Elizabeth Caldwell can't feel emotions, yet she sees them everywhere, human in appearance, standing alongside their summons....Chills and goose bumps of the very best kind accompany this haunting, memorable achievement. —*Kirkus*
Sequel: *Where silence gathers* (2014).

Sweeney, Diana
The **minnow**. By Diana Sweeney. 2014 263 pages
Grades: 8 9 10 11 12
1. Pregnant teenagers; 2. Grief; 3. Teenage girl orphans; 4. Floods; 5. Grief in teenage girls; 6. Realistic fiction; 7. Australian fiction.
9781922182012
Children's Book Council of Australia: Notable Australian Children's Book; CBCA Children's Book of the Year Awards Honour Book, 2015.

Readers who can accept the ambiguous chronology and Tom's glib ability to communicate beyond worlds will be rewarded: the universe into which Minnow is born and will undoubtedly thrive is engaging and extraordinary. A promising and welcome debut. —*Booklist*

Tahir, Sabaa
★ An **ember** in the ashes: a novel. By Sabaa Tahir. 2015 464 pages (Ember in the ashes, 1)
Grades: 9 10 11 12
1. Spies; 2. Resistance to government; 3. Political intrigue; 4. Slaves; 5. Supernatural; 6. Fantasy fiction.
9781595148032; 9780008108427, UK; 9780007593279, print, UK
LC 2014029687
YALSA Best Fiction for Young Adults, 2016.

Laia is a Scholar living under the iron-fisted rule of the Martial Empire. When her brother is arrested for treason, Laia goes undercover as a slave at the empire's greatest military academy in exchange for assistance from rebel Scholars who claim that they will help to save her brother from execution—Provided by publisher.

Nuanced, multileveled world-building provides a dynamic backdrop for an often brutal exploration of moral ambiguity and the power of empathy. —*Horn Book Guide*
Sequel: *A torch against the night*

A **reaper** at the gates. Sabaa Tahir. 2018 480 p. (Ember in the ashes, 3)
Grades: 9 10 11 12
1. Spies; 2. Resistance to government; 3. Protectiveness; 4. Prisons; 5. Political intrigue; 6. Fantasy fiction.
9780448494500; 9780008288754, Hardback, UK; 9780008288792, Paperback, UK
LC 2018006968
Beyond the Empire and within it, the threat of war looms ever larger as the Blood Shrike, Helene Aquilla, Laia of Serra, and Elias Veturius all face increasing dangers.

A **torch** against the night. Sabaa Tahir. Razorbill, 2016 464 p. (Ember in the ashes, 2)
Grades: 9 10 11 12
1. Spies; 2. Resistance to government; 3. Rescues; 4. Prisons; 5. Political intrigue; 6. Fantasy fiction.
9781101998878; 9781101998885
Laia and Elias fight their way north to liberate Laia's brother from the horrors of Kauf Prison, a mission that is complicated by hunting Empire

soldiers, the manipulations of the Commandant and lingering ghosts from their pasts.

Infusing her story with magic, Tahir proves to be a master of suspense and a canny practitioner of the cliff-hanger, riveting readers' attention throughout. —*Booklist*

Sequel to: *An ember in the ashes*

Talley, Robin

Our own private universe. Robin Talley. Harlequin Teen, 2017 376 p.
Grades: 7 8 9 10 11 12

1. African American teenage girls; 2. Bisexual teenagers; 3. Christian teenagers; 4. Christian missions; 5. Children of clergy; 6. Mexico; 7. Contemporary romances; 8. LGBTQIA romances; 9. First person narratives
9780373211982; 9781335013361, Paperback, Canada
Rainbow List, 2018.

Fifteen-year-old Aki Simon has a theory. And it's mostly about sex. No, it isn't that kind of theory. Aki already knows she's bisexual, even if, until now, it's mostly been in the hypothetical sense. Aki has dated only guys so far, and her best friend, Lori, is the only person who knows she likes girls, too. Actually, Aki's theory is that she's got only one shot at living an interesting life—and that means she's got to stop sitting around and thinking so much. It's time for her to actually do something. Or at least try. So when Aki and Lori set off on a church youth-group trip to a small Mexican town for the summer and Aki meets Christa—slightly older, far more experienced—it seems her theory is prime for the testing. But it's not going to be easy. For one thing, how exactly do two girls have sex, anyway? And more important, how can you tell if you're in love? It's going to be a summer of testing theories, and the result may just be love—Provided by publisher.

An important and heartfelt contribution to contemporary teen lit about queer women: hopeful, realistic, and romantic, Talley's newest is sure to satisfy. —*Kirkus*

Pulp. Robin Talley. Harlequin Teens, 2018 406 p.
Grades: 8 9 10 11 12

1. Lesbian teenagers; 2. Women authors; 3. Books and reading; 4. Young women; 5. Teenage same sex romance; 6. Washington, D.C; 7. 1950s; 8. Love stories; 9. Parallel narratives; 10. Novels-within-novels.
9781335012906; 9781848457126, Paperback, UK

Duel narratives follow an eighteen-year-old closeted lesbian in 1955 keeping a secret romance and wanting to write her own stories and another young woman sixty-two years later studying 1950s lesbian pulp fiction for her senior project.

Tamaki, Mariko

Saving Montgomery Sole. Mariko Tamaki. Roaring Brook Press, 2016 288 p.
Grades: 7 8 9 10

1. Children of LGBTQIA parents; 2. Clubs; 3. Homophobia; 4. Self-perception; 5. Friendship; 6. California; 7. Realistic fiction; 8. First person narratives
9781626722712, HRD, US; 9781626722729, (ebook), US
LC 2015004007
Rainbow List, 2017.

An outcast teen girl explores the mysteries of friendship, family, faith, and phenomena, including the greatest mystery of all—herself.

Montgomery's slow confrontation with reality creates a realistic, satisfying arc, and Tamaki's economical storytelling results in dimensional characters whose struggles feel viscerally real. —*Publishers Weekly*

Tamani, Liara

All the things we never knew. Liara Tamani. Greenwillow Books, 2020 384 p.
Grades: 8 9 10 11 12

1. African American teenagers; 2. First loves; 3. Basketball; 4. Teenage basketball players; 5. Teenage romance; 6. Texas; 7. Multicultural romances; 8. Contemporary romances; 9. Multiple perspectives.
9780062656919, HRD, US; 9780062656933, ebook, US
LC 2019060207

Carli and Rex have an immediate connection, an understanding that must mean first love, but family secrets, disappointments—and basketball, which holds center stage in both their lives—all create complications.

The immediacy of Tamani's writing, imbued with wonderful sensory moments as the two protagonists let their guards down, will ensure that this engaging story has wide appeal. —*School Library Journal*

Calling my name. Liara Tamani. Harpercollins Childrens Books, 2017 384 p.
Grades: 9 10 11 12

1. African American teenage girls; 2. Self-discovery in teenage girls; 3. Christian life; 4. Spirituality; 5. Virginity; 6. Houston, Texas; 7. 1990s; 8. Coming-of-age stories; 9. Realistic fiction; 10. African American fiction
9780062656865
YALSA Best Fiction for Young Adults, 2018; Golden Kite Honor Book for Fiction, 2018.

This unforgettable novel tells a universal coming-of-age story about Taja Brown, a young African American girl growing up in Houston, Texas, and it deftly and beautifully explores the universal struggles of growing up, battling family expectations, discovering a sense of self, and finding a unique voice and purpose.

An excellent portrayal of African American culture, gorgeous lyrical prose, strong characters, and societal critique make Tamanis debut a must-read. —*Booklist*

Tan, Shaun

Cicada. Shaun Tan. 2019 32 p. : Illustration
Grades: 6 7 8 9

1. Cicadas; 2. Office workers; 3. Ingratitude; 4. Offices; 5. Insects; 6. Picture books for children; 7. Australian fiction.
9781338298390; 9780734418630, Hardback, Australia; 9781444946208, Hardback, UK
Books I Love Best Yearly (BILBY), Younger Reader, 2019; Children's Book Council of Australia: Notable Australian Children's Book, 2019; Children's Book of the Year Award (Children's Book Council of Australia), Picture Book of the Year, 2019.

Cicada works in an office, dutifully toiling day after day for unappreciative bosses and being bullied by his coworkers. But one day, Cicada goes to the roof of the building, and something truly extraordinary happens.

Tarttelin, Abigail

★ **Golden** boy: a novel. By Abigail Tarttelin. Atria Books, 2013 352 p.
Grades: 11 12 Adult

1. People who are intersex; 2. Gender identity; 3. Rape; 4. Identity (Psychology); 5. Brothers; 6. LGBTQIA fiction; 7. Coming-of-age stories; 8. Adult books for young adults.
9781476705804; 9780297870944, print, UK
LC 2012049192

Booklist Editors' Choice, 2013; Booklist Editors' Choice: Adult Books for Young Adults, 2013; School Library Journal Best Books: Best Adult Books 4 Teens, 2013; Alex Award, 2014.

Presenting themselves to the world as an effortlessly excellent family, successful criminal lawyer Karen, her Parliament candidate husband and her intelligent athlete son, Max, find their world crumbling in the wake of a friend's betrayal and the secret about Max's intersexual identity.

Tash, Sarvenaz

The **geek's** guide to unrequited love. Sarvenaz Tash. Simon & Schuster Books for Young Readers, 2016 256 p.
Grades: 9 10 11 12
1. Fan conventions; 2. Unrequited love; 3. Comic book fans; 4. Fans (Persons); 5. Teenage boy/girl relations; 6. New York City; 7. Contemporary romances
9781481456531; 9781481456548; 9781481456555, ebook, US
YALSA Quick Picks for Reluctant Young Adult Readers, 2017.

As Tash introduces a cast of charming, goofy, and diverse characters, she uses the hopeful voice of a young man in the throes of first love to gently poke fun at fandom while celebrating the passion and camaraderie of the community. —*Publishers Weekly*

Tashjian, Janet

The **gospel** according to Larry. Janet Tashjian. Henry Holt and Co, 2001 227 p. : Illustration (Gospel according to Larry, 1)
Grades: 7 8 9 10
1. Secret identity; 2. Websites; 3. Crushes in teenage boys; 4. Consumerism; 5. Fame; 6. Coming-of-age stories; 7. Realistic fiction.
9780805063783
LC 2001024568
Booklist Editors' Choice: Books for Youth, 2001; YALSA Best Books for Young Adults, 2002.

Seventeen-year-old Josh, a loner-philosopher who wants to make a difference in the world, tries to maintain his secret identity as the author of a web site that is receiving national attention.

Tashjian fabricates a cleverly constructed scenario and expertly carries it out to the bittersweet end. —*Horn Book Guide*
Sequel: *Vote for Larry.*

Larry and the meaning of life. Janet Tashjian. Henry Holt and Co, 2008 211 p. (Gospel according to Larry, 3)
Grades: 7 8 9 10
1. Thoreau, Henry David; 2. Political activists; 3. Gurus; 4. Spiritual journeys; 5. Identity (Psychology); 6. Interpersonal relations; 7. Walden Woods, Massachusetts; 8. Realistic fiction; 9. First person narratives.
9780805077353
LC 2007046936
Larry (otherwise known as Josh) is in the doldrums, but after meeting a spiritual guru at Walden Pond who convinces him to join his study group, he starts to question his grasp of reality.
Christy Ottaviano Books.

Vote for Larry. Janet Tashjian. Henry Holt and Co, 2004 Xi, 224 p; (Gospel according to Larry, 2)
Grades: 7 8 9 10
1. Presidential candidates; 2. Elections; 3. Political activists; 4. Crushes in teenage boys; 5. Practical politics; 6. Realistic fiction.
9780805072013
LC 2003056578
Not yet eighteen years old, Josh, a.k.a. Larry, comes out of hiding and returns to public life, this time to run for President as an advocate for issues of concern to youth and to encourage voter turnout.

A solid and timely work that will make readers laugh, but more important, will make them think. —*Voice of Youth Advocates*
Sequel to: *The Gospel According to Larry.*

Taub, Melinda

Still star-crossed. Melinda Taub. Delacorte Press, 2013 352 p.
Grades: 7 8 9 10 11 12
1. Characters and characteristics in literature; 2. Family feuds; 3. Arranged marriage; 4. Grief; 5. Teenagers; 6. Verona, Italy; 7. Historical fiction; 8. Shakespeare-inspired fiction.
9780385743501
Struggling to maintain the peace between the rivaling Montagues and Capulets after the suicides of Romeo and Juliet, Prince Escalus of Verona arranges a marriage between Romeo's best friend, Benvolio, and Juliet's cousin, Rosaline, whose unwilling match forges unexpected bonds.

Rosaline and Benvolio's tale is equal parts historical fiction, detective story and high adventure, relayed in accurate but not overwhelming period language, informed by Romeo and Juliet and Shakespeare's other works but offering an expanded and original perspective. A perfect blend of the intimate and the epic, the story both honors its origin and works in its own right. —*Kirkus*

Taylor, Greg

Killer Pizza: a novel. Greg Taylor. Feiwel and Friends, 2009 346 p. (Killer Pizza, 1)
Grades: 6 7 8 9
1. Pizzeria workers; 2. Secret societies; 3. Monsters; 4. Shapeshifters; 5. Pizzerias; 6. Horror
9780312373795
LC 2008028543
While working as summer employees in a local pizza parlor, three teenagers are recruited by an underground organization of monster hunters.

Toby is an easygoing and relatable young adult, and young teens will enjoy the fun, slightly scary read. —*Voice of Youth Advocates*

The **slice**. Greg Taylor. Feiwel and Friends, 2011 352 p. (Killer Pizza, 2)
Grades: 6 7 8 9
1. Monsters; 2. Shapeshifters; 3. Snakes; 4. Pizzeria workers; 5. Secret societies; 6. Ohio; 7. Horror
9780312580889
LC 2010048928
Having passed the tests to become Monster Combat Officers, teens Toby, Annabel, and Strobe are sent on a secret mission to deliver to the Monster Protection Program a beautiful fourteen-year-old monster who wants to defect, regardless of the considerable dangers this poses.

Taylor, Laini

★ **Daughter** of smoke and bone. By Laini Taylor. Little, Brown, 2011 432 p. (Daughter of smoke and bone trilogy, 1)
Grades: 8 9 10 11 12
1. Teenage girl artists; 2. Angels; 3. Chimera (Greek mythology); 4. Mythical creatures; 5. Supernatural; 6. Prague, Czech Republic; 7. Czech Republic; 8. Urban fantasy
9780316134026; 9781444722659, print, UK; 9781529353969, Paperback, UK
LC 2010045802
YALSA Best Fiction for Young Adults, 2012; School Library Journal Best Books, 2011.

Seventeen-year-old Karou, a lovely, enigmatic art student in a Prague boarding school, carries a sketchbook of hideous, frightening monsters—the chimaerae who form the only family she has ever known.

Taylor again weaves a masterful mix of reality and fantasy with cross-genre appeal. Exquisitely written and beautifully paced. —*Publishers Weekly*

★ **Days** of blood & starlight. Laini Taylor. Little, Brown Books for Young Readers, 2012 528 p. (Daughter of smoke and bone trilogy, 2)
Grades: 9 10 11 12
1. Angels; 2. Chimera (Greek mythology); 3. Imaginary wars and battles; 4. Demons; 5. Revenge; 6. Morocco; 7. Urban fantasy
9780316133975; 9781444722703, UK
YALSA Best Fiction for Young Adults, 2014.
A sequel to *Daughter of Smoke* and *Bone* finds Karou struggling to come to terms with her nature while pursuing revenge for her people.

Dreams of gods & monsters. Laini Taylor. Little, Brown, 2014 304 p. (Daughter of smoke and bone trilogy, 3)
Grades: 8 9 10 11 12
1. Angels; 2. Chimera (Greek mythology); 3. Imaginary wars and battles; 4. Supernatural; 5. Parallel universes; 6. Urban fantasy
9780316134071; 9781444722727, print, UK
Romantic Times Reviewer's Choice Award, 2014.
Karou and Akiva join their rival human armies against brutal angel invaders, an alliance that is tested by Karou's inability to forgive Akiva for killing the only family she has ever known.

New revelations, characters, multiple love stories, and constant plot twists and suspense will not disappoint Taylor's many fans, who will also appreciate the novel's subtle philosophical undercurrents about racial harmony and the profound difficulty of making choices that reconcile duty, the greater good, and personal happiness. —*Booklist*

★ **Lips** touch: three times. By Laini Taylor; illustrations by Jim Di Bartolo. Arthur A. Levine Books, 2009 265 p.
Grades: 8 9 10 11 12
1. Kissing; 2. Curses; 3. Goblins; 4. Shapeshifters; 5. Supernatural; 6. Urban fantasy; 7. Short stories; 8. Illustrated books.
9780545055857; 9780545055864
LC 2009005458
YALSA Best Books for Young Adults, 2010; National Book Award for Young People's Literature finalist, 2009.
Presents a collection of three short stories in which three girls face very different circumstances while pursuing romance as powerful supernatural forces impact their lives and first loves.

Taylor offers a powerful trio of tales, each founded upon the consequences of a kiss.... Contemporary Kizzy, who so yearns to be a normal, popular teenager that she forgets the rules of her Old Country upbringing and is seduced by a goblin in disguise; Anamique, living in British colonial India, silenced forever due to a spell cast upon her at birth; and Esme, who at 14 discovers she is host to another—nonhuman—being.... Each is, in vividly distinctive fashion, a mesmerizing love story that comes to a satisfying but never predictable conclusion. Di Bartolo's illustrations provide tantalizing visual preludes to each tale. —*Publishers Weekly*

Muse of nightmares. Laini Taylor. 2018 528 p. (Strange the dreamer, 2)
Grades: 9 10 11 12
1. Dreams; 2. Demigods; 3. Ghosts; 4. Hostages; 5. Revenge; 6. Middle Eastern-influenced fantasy; 7. Fantasy fiction.
9780316341714; 9780316341691; 9781444789041, Paperback, UK; 9781444789034, Hardback, UK; 9781444789065, Paperback, UK; 9781444789072, Paperback, UK
Booklist Editors' Choice: Books for Youth, 2018.

In the aftermath of the citadel's near fall, a new enemy reveals itself and the mysteries of the Mesarthim are resurrected.

★ **Strange** the dreamer. Laini Taylor. Little, Brown and Company, 2016 536 p. (Strange the dreamer, 1)
Grades: 9 10 11 12
1. Dreams; 2. Demigods; 3. Orphans; 4. Librarians; 5. Loss (Psychology); 6. Middle Eastern-influenced fantasy; 7. Fantasy fiction.
9780316341684; 9781444788983, hardback, UK; 9781444788976, UK; 9781444788969, ebook, UK
Librarians' Choice (Australia), 2017; Booklist Editors' Choice: Books for Youth, 2017; Leslie Bradshaw Award for Young Adult Literature (Oregon), 2018; YALSA Best Fiction for Young Adults, 2018; Michael L. Printz Honor Book, 2018.
In the aftermath of a war between gods and men, a hero, a librarian, and a girl must battle the fantastical elements of a mysterious city stripped of its name.

Lovers of intricate worldbuilding and feverish romance will find this enthralling. —*Kirkus*

Taylor, Mildred D.

★ **All** the days past, all the days to come. Mildred D. Taylor. Viking Childrens Books, 2020 496 p. (Logan family (Mildred D. Taylor), 9)
Grades: 8 9 10 11 12
1. Racism; 2. African American families; 3. Civil Rights Movement; 4. Interracial marriage; 5. Grief in women; 6. Southern States; 7. 20th century; 8. Historical fiction; 9. Family sagas; 10. African American fiction
9780399257308
Coretta Scott King Honor Book for Authors, 2021.
A long-awaited conclusion to the story that began in the Newbery Medal-winning *Roll of Thunder, Hear My Cry* finds young adult Cassie Logan searching for a sense of belonging before joining the civil rights movement in 1960s Mississippi.

Taylor is unsparing in her depiction of the years of segregation and of the Black experience of white racism, bigotry, and injustice. —*Booklist*

★ The **land**. Mildred D. Taylor. Phyllis Fogelman Books, 2001 375 p. (Logan family (Mildred D. Taylor), 8)
Grades: 7 8 9 10
1. Racism; 2. African American families; 3. Multiracial persons; 4. Prejudice; 5. Fathers and sons; 6. Mississippi; 7. Southern States; 8. 19th century; 9. Historical fiction; 10. Family sagas; 11. Coming-of-age stories.
9780803719507
LC 39329
Los Angeles Times Book Prize for Young Adult Fiction, 2001; Scott O'Dell Historical Fiction Award, 2002; Coretta Scott King Award, Author Category, 2002; ALA Notable Children's Book, 2002; Booklist Editors' Choice: Books for Youth, 2001; YALSA Best Books for Young Adults, 2002.
After the Civil War, Paul, the son of a white father and a black mother, finds himself caught between the two worlds of colored folks and white folks as he pursues his dream of owning land of his own.

Taylor masterfully uses harsh historical realities to frame a powerful coming-of-age story that stands on its own merits. —*Horn Book Guide*

★ **Roll** of thunder, hear my cry. Mildred D. Taylor. Dial Press, 1976 276 p. (Logan family (Mildred D. Taylor), 2)
Grades: 4 5 6 7 8 9
1. African American families; 2. Racism; 3. Rural families; 4. African American girls; 5. African American children; 6. Southern States; 7.

1930s; 8. Historical fiction; 9. Family sagas; 10. African American fiction

9780140348934; 9780141354873, print, UK

LC 76002287

Newbery Medal, 1977; Young Reader's Choice Award (Pacific Northwest), Junior, 1979.

A Black family living in the South during the 1930s is faced with prejudice and discrimination which their children don't understand.

Taylor, Nandi

Given. Nandi Taylor. Wattpad Books, 2020 352 p.

Grades: 7 8 9 10 11 12

1. Women warriors; 2. Dragons; 3. Fate and fatalism; 4. Imaginary empires; 5. Warriors; 6. Afrofuturism and Afrofantasy; 7. Mythological fiction; 8. Fantasy fiction.

9781989365045, HRD, US; 9780241455753, Paperback, UK

Yenni has never been this far from home. With only her wits, her strength, and her sacred runelore, the fierce Yirba warrior princess is alone in the Empire of Cresh. It's a land filled with strange magics and even stranger people?all of whom mistrust anyone who's different. But Yenni will prove herself, and find the cure for her father's wasting illness. She will not fail. But no one warned her about the dragons. Especially not about him.

The captivating worldbuilding of magical lands and well-paced plot and character development combined with intriguing twists will have readers looking forward to more. —*Kirkus*

Taylor, S. S.

The **expeditioners** and the treasure of Drowned Man's Canyon. By S.S. Taylor; illustrated by Katherine Roy. McSweeneys McMullens, 2012 375 p. (Expeditioners, 1)

Grades: 5 6 7 8

1. Orphans; 2. Maps; 3. Codes (Communication); 4. Treasure troves; 5. Adventure; 6. Fantasy fiction; 7. Steampunk

9781938073069

After an explorer with a clockwork hand gives Kit West an old book from his father, he and his siblings must evade government agents while solving the puzzle their father sent.

Teller, Janne

★ **Nothing**. Janne Teller; translated by Martin Aitken. Atheneum Books for Young Readers, 2010 240 p.

Grades: 7 8 9 10 11 12

1. Semantics (Philosophy); 2. Purpose in life; 3. Self-sacrifice; 4. Interpersonal relations; 5. Schools; 6. Realistic fiction; 7. Books for reluctant readers

9781416985792

LC 2009019784

ALA Notable Children's Book, 2011; Booklist Editors' Choice: Books for Youth, 2010; YALSA Best Fiction for Young Adults, 2011; YALSA Quick Picks for Reluctant Young Adult Readers, 2011; Batchelder Honor Book, 2011.

When thirteen-year-old Pierre Anthon leaves school to sit in a plum tree and train for becoming part of nothing, his seventh grade classmates set out on a desperate quest for the meaning of life.

Indelible, elusive, and timeless, this uncompromising novel has all the marks of a classic. —*Booklist*

Translated from the Danish.

Temblador, Alex

Secrets of the Casa Rosada. By Alex Temblador. Pinata Books, an imprint of Arte Publico Press, 2018 160 p.

Grades: 8 9 10 11 12

1. Grandmother and granddaughter; 2. Healers; 3. Mexican American teenage girls; 4. Family secrets; 5. Healing; 6. Texas; 7. 1990s; 8. Coming-of-age stories; 9. Realistic fiction.

9781558858701

LC 2018029355

Sixteen-year-old Martha's life is transformed when her mother leaves her in Laredo, Texas, in 1990 with a grandmother she never knew, who is a revered curandera.

Templeman, McCormick

The **glass** casket. McCormick Templeman. Delacorte Press, 2014 352 p.

Grades: 9 10 11 12

1. Witches; 2. Murder; 3. Supernatural; 4. Cousins; 5. Communities; 6. Fantasy fiction

9780385743457

YALSA Best Fiction for Young Adults, 2015.

After the brutal murder of her cousin, everything changes for sixteen-year-old Rowan, who must not only seek the evil forces responsible before they destroy her family and village, but also set aside her studies when she becomes betrothed to her best friend, Tom.

With stylish prose, richly developed characters and well-realized worldbuilding, Templeman plumbs archetypes of folklore to create a compelling blend of mythic elements and realistic teen experience. —*Kirkus*

Terrill, Cristin

All our yesterdays. Cristin Terrill. Hyperion, 2013 368 p.

Grades: 7 8 9 10 11 12

1. Time travel (Past); 2. Assassination; 3. Imprisonment; 4. Time machines; 5. Murder; 6. Science fiction.

9781423176374

LC 2013008007

Thriller Award for Best YA Novel, 2014; YALSA Best Fiction for Young Adults, 2014.

Em must travel back in time to prevent a catastrophic time machine from ever being invented, while Marina battles to prevent the murder of the boy she loves—Provided by publisher.

Terry, Teri

Fractured. Teri Terry. Nancy Paulsen Books, 2013 336 p. (Slated trilogy, 2)

Grades: 7 8 9 10

1. Memory; 2. Dystopias; 3. Terrorism; 4. Identity (Psychology); 5. Near future; 6. England; 7. Dystopian fiction; 8. Science fiction; 9. Canadian fiction.

9780399161735; 9780142425046

Although Kyla has recovered some of her memories, she is not sure how they all fit together, whether she was really a terrorist, or why she is able to remember anything at all from before she was "slated—but she is determined to find the answers.

Kyla's memories, wiped by the government in Slated, are slowly returning; she's been found by an anti-government group that claims she's a member and wants her to complete one last mission. Kyla's struggles to uncover her identity and think through the consequences of her actions are realistic and add an emotional backbone to this fast-paced middle volume of the trilogy. —*Horn Book Guide*

Slated. Teri Terry. Nancy Paulsen Books, 2013 368 p. (Slated trilogy, 1)

Grades: 7 8 9 10

1. Memory; 2. Dystopias; 3. Near future; 4. Identity (Psychology); 5. Dating (Social customs); 6. England; 7. Dystopian fiction; 8. Science fiction; 9. Canadian fiction.
9780399161728; 9780142425039; 9781408319468, print, UK

LC 2012020873

In a future England, sixteen-year-old Kyla is one of the "Slated," those whose memories have been erased usually because they have committed serious crimes, but as she observes more and more strange events, she also gains more memories which put her and her boyfriend, Ben in danger.

Testa, Maria

Something about America. Maria Testa. Candlewick Press, 2005 96 p.
Grades: 6 7 8 9

1. Thirteen-year-old girls; 2. Teenage girls; 3. Burn victims; 4. Refugees; 5. Serbian Americans; 6. Novels in verse.
9780763625283

LC 2005047064

Testa's distilled poetry never seems forced, and her stirring words enhance a sense of the characters' experiences and emotions.... Based on an actual incident, this is an excellent choice for readers' theater and classroom discussion. —*Booklist*

Tharp, Tim

Badd. By Tim Tharp. Alfred A. Knopf, 2011 308 p.
Grades: 9 10 11 12

1. Post-traumatic stress disorder; 2. Iraq War, 2003-2011; 3. Coping; 4. Soldiers; 5. Brothers and sisters; 6. Realistic fiction.
9780375864445; 9780375964442

LC 2010012732

A teenaged girl's beloved brother returns home from the Iraq War completely unlike the person she remembers.

With convincing three-dimensional characters, Tharp paints a sympathetic portrait of the constraints of small town life, the struggles of PTSD, and the challenges of faith. —*Publishers Weekly*

Knights of the hill country. Tim Tharp. Alfred A. Knopf, 2006 233 p.
Grades: 8 9 10 11 12

1. Children of single parents; 2. High school football players; 3. Self-discovery in teenage boys; 4. High school football; 5. High school seniors; 6. Oklahoma; 7. Coming-of-age stories; 8. Football stories; 9. Sports fiction
9780375836534; 9780375936531

LC 2005033279

Oklahoma Book Award, Young Adult, 2007; YALSA Popular Paperbacks for Young Adults, 2009; YALSA Best Books for Young Adults, 2007.

In his senior year, high school star linebacker Hampton Greene finally begins to think for himself and discovers that he might be interested in more than just football.

Taut scenes on the football field and the dilemmas about choosing what feels right over what's expected are all made memorable by Hamp's unforgettable, colloquial voice. —*Booklist*

Thomas, Aiden

★ **Cemetery** boys. Aiden Thomas. Swoon Reads, 2020 352 p.
Grades: 9 10 11 12

1. Transgender teenage boys; 2. Witches; 3. Ghosts; 4. Magic; 5. Murder victims; 6. Paranormal fiction; 7. LGBTQIA fiction.
9781250250469, HRD, US

LC 2019036381

Yadriel, a trans boy, summons the angry spirit of his high school's bad boy, and agrees to help him learn how he died, thereby proving himself a brujo, not a bruja, to his conservative family.

Thomas marries concept and execution in a romantic mystery as poignant as it is spellbinding, weaved in a mosaic of culture, acceptance, and identity, where intricately crafted characters are the pieces and love—platonic, romantic, familial, and communal—is the glue. —*Publishers Weekly*

Thomas, Angie

★ The **hate** u give. Angie Thomas. Balzer + Bray, 2017 444 p.
Grades: 8 9 10 11 12

1. African American teenage girls; 2. Racism; 3. Police shootings; 4. Interracial dating; 5. Prep schools; 6. Realistic fiction; 7. African American fiction; 8. Books to movies.
9780062498533, HRD, US; 9780062871350; 9781406389463, Hardback,UK; 9781406377286, paperback, UK; 9781406372151, paperback, UK; 9781406387162,Paperback, UK; 9781406375114, ebook, UK; 9781406387933, Paperback, Australia
Abraham Lincoln Illinois High School Book Award, 2019; Blue Hen Book Award (Delaware) for Teen Books, 2019; Booklist Editors' Choice: Books for Youth, 2017; Boston Globe-Horn Book Award for Fiction and Poetry, 2017; Buckeye Teen Book Award (Ohio), Grades 9-12, 2018; Colorado Blue Spruce YA Book Award, 2018; Eliot Rosewater Indiana High School Book Award (Rosie Award), 2020; Garden State Teen Book Award (New Jersey), Fiction (Grades 9-12), 2019; Gateway Readers Award (Missouri), 2020; Georgia Peach Book Award for Teen Readers, 2018; Golden Archer Awards (Wisconsin): Senior, 2020; Goodreads Choice Award, 2017; Grand Canyon Reader Award (Arizona), Teen Book Category, 2019; Indies' Choice Book Awards, Young Adult, 2018; Kentucky Bluegrass Award for Grades 9-12, 2019; Pennsylvania Young Reader's Choice Awards, Young Adult, 2019; Rhode Island Teen Book Award, 2019; School Library Journal Best Books, 2017; Sequoyah Book Awards (Oklahoma), High School Books, 2019; Soaring Eagle Book Award (Wyoming), 2020; Thumbs Up! Award (Michigan), 2018; William C. Morris YA Debut Award, 2018; YALSA Best Fiction for Young Adults, 2018; YALSA Quick Picks for Reluctant Young Adult Readers, 2018; Romantic Times Reviewer's Choice Award, 2017; Inky Awards (Australia): Silver Inky, 2018; Goodreads Choice Award, 2018; Young Reader's Choice Award (Pacific Northwest), Senior, 2020; Coretta Scott King Honor Book for Authors, 2018; Kirkus Prize for Young Readers' Literature finalist, 2017; Longlisted for the National Book Award for Young People's Literature, 2017; Michael L. Printz Honor Book, 2018.

After witnessing her friend's death at the hands of a police officer, Starr Carter's life is complicated when the police and a local drug lord try to intimidate her in an effort to learn what happened the night Kahlil died.

With smooth but powerful prose delivered in Starr's natural, emphatic voice, finely nuanced characters, and intricate and realistic relationship dynamics, this novel will have readers rooting for Starr and opening their hearts to her friends and family. —*Kirkus*
Prequel: *Concrete rose*

★ **On** the come up. Angie Thomas. Balzer + Bray, 2019 447 pages;
Grades: 9 10 11 12

1. Rap musicians; 2. African American teenage girls; 3. Freedom of speech; 4. Community life; 5. Poverty; 6. Realistic fiction; 7. African American fiction.
9780062498564, HRD, US; 9781406372168, UK

LC Bl2018194793

Booklist Editors' Choice: Books for Youth, 2019; Buckeye Teen Book Award (Ohio), Grades 9-12, 2020; Westchester Fiction Award, 2020; Kirkus Prize for Young Readers' Literature finalist, 2019.

Sixteen-year-old Bri hopes to become a great rapper, and after her first song goes viral for all the wrong reasons, must decide whether to sell out or face eviction with her widowed mother.

Set in the same neighborhood as Thomas's electrifying *The Hate U Give*, this visceral novel makes cogent observations about the cycle of poverty and the inescapable effects of systemic racism. Though the book never sands over the rough realities of Garden Heights, such as gang warfare, it imbues its many characters with warmth and depth. While acknowledging that society is quick to slap labels onto black teens, the author allows her heroine to stumble and fall before finding her footing and her voice. Thomas once again fearlessly speaks truth to power; a compelling coming-of-age story for all teens. —*School Library Journal*

Thomas, Kara

The **darkest** corners. Kara Thomas. Delacorte Press, 2016 336 p.
Grades: 9 10 11 12
1. Serial murderers; 2. Small towns; 3. Friendship; 4. Murder; 5. Teenage girls; 6. Pennsylvania; 7. Mysteries
9780553521450

Equally concerned with a quest for the truth and the powerful motivation of guilt, this compelling novel wont linger on the shelf. —*Booklist*

Little monsters. Kara Thomas. Delacorte Press, 2017 336 p.
Grades: 10 11 12
1. Missing teenage girls; 2. Revenge; 3. Manipulation (Social sciences); 4. Friendship; 5. Moving, Household; 6. Wisconsin; 7. Mysteries
9780553521498; 9780553521511, ebook, US
LC 2016032457

When Kacey moves in with her estranged father and his new family, her new friend goes missing and Kacey finds herself at the center of the investigation.

Thomas, Leah

Nowhere near you. By Leah Thomas. Bloomsbury, 2017 352 p. (Because you'll never meet me, 2)
Grades: 9 10 11 12
1. Epilepsy; 2. Teenagers who are blind; 3. Teenage boys with disabilities; 4. Automobile travel; 5. Pen pals; 6. Science fiction; 7. Epistolary novels
9781681191782; 9781408885376, London
LC 2016022577

Ollie and Moritz might never meet, but their friendship knows no bounds. Their letters carry on as Ollie embarks on his first road trip away from the woods—no easy feat for a boy allergic to electricity—and Moritz decides which new school would best suit an eyeless boy who prefers to be alone. Along the way they meet other teens like them, other products of strange science who lead seemingly normal lives in ways Ollie and Moritz never imagined possible.

A fantastic novel that will be especially resonant for readers who struggle with being or feeling outside of 'normal.' —*Booklist*

Thomas, Rhiannon

Long may she reign. Rhiannon Thomas. HarperTeen, an imprint of HarperCollinsPublishers, 2017 422 p.
Grades: 7 8 9 10 11 12
1. Courts and courtiers; 2. Assassination; 3. Rulers; 4. Scientists; 5. Intrigue; 6. Fantasy fiction.
9780062418685

Unexpectedly elevated to the throne when a devastating massacre ends the lives of those in succession before her, Freya is targeted by manipulative nobles and corrupt councilors while she struggles to identify the assassins.

A clever, absorbing mystery of court intrigue, intense friendships, and newfound courage. —*Booklist*

Thomas, Sherry

The **burning** sky. Sherry Thomas. Balzer + Bray, an imprint of HarperCollinsPublishers, 2013 432 p. (Elemental trilogy (Sherry Thomas), 1)
Grades: 7 8 9 10 11 12
1. Teenage wizards; 2. Rulers; 3. Resistance to government; 4. Rebels; 5. Magic; 6. High fantasy; 7. Fantasy fiction; 8. Multiple perspectives
9780062207296
LC 2013014504

A young elemental mage named Iaolanthe Seabourne discovers her shocking power and destiny when she is thrown together with a deposed prince to lead a rebellion against a tyrant.

When sixteen-year-old elemental mage Iolanthe summons a lightning bolt, she draws the unwelcome attention of the Inquisitor of Atlantis. She also draws the eye of resistance fighter Prince Titus, who rescues her and disguises her as a boy. Heightened action combined with Scarlet Pimpernel-esque cleverness will keep readers eagerly turning pages, while the romantic tension adds juiciness to the fantasy plot. —*Horn Book Guide*

The **magnolia** sword: a ballad of Mulan. Sherry Thomas. Tu Books, 2019 352 p.
Grades: 7 8 9 10
1. Women warriors; 2. Impostors; 3. Martial arts; 4. Battles; 5. Power (Social sciences); 6. China; 7. 5th century; 8. Fairy tale and folklore-inspired fiction; 9. Historical fiction.
9781620148044, HRD, US; 9781760876685, Paperback, Australia
LC 2019003668

When her ailing father is conscripted to fight invaders from the north, Mulan dresses as a man to take his place in the army, but an old enemy and an attraction for her troop's commander complicate her mission.

Skillful martial arts scenes combine with crucial discourse on power, gender, and the impact of language on history in this gripping, thoughtfully layered reinterpretation. —*Publishers Weekly*

Thompson, Holly

The **language** inside. Holly Thompson. Delacorte Press, 2013 528 p.
Grades: 7 8 9 10 11 12
1. Teenage volunteers; 2. Moving to a new country; 3. Children of people with cancer; 4. Tsunamis; 5. Refugees; 6. Massachusetts; 7. Japan; 8. Realistic fiction; 9. Novels in verse.
9780385739795
LC 2012030596

Notable Books for a Global Society, 2014; YALSA Best Fiction for Young Adults, 2014.

Raised in Japan, American-born tenth-grader Emma is disconcerted by a move to Massachusetts for her mother's breast cancer treatment, because half of Emma's heart remains with her friends recovering from the tsunami.

Orchards. Holly Thompson. Delacorte Press, 2011 320 p.
Grades: 7 8 9 10
1. Multiracial teenage girls; 2. Suicide; 3. Guilt in teenage girls; 4. Guilt; 5. Orchards; 6. Japan; 7. Manhattan, New York City; 8. Realistic fiction; 9. Novels in verse.
9780385908061

LC 2010023724

Asian Pacific American Asian Pacific American Award for Literature: Young Adult Literature, 2012; YALSA Best Fiction for Young Adults, 2012; YALSA Popular Paperbacks for Young Adults, 2013.

Sent to Japan for the summer after an eighth-grade classmate's suicide, half-Japanese, half-Jewish Kana Goldberg tries to fit in with relatives she barely knows and reflects on the guilt she feels over the tragedy back home.

Kanako's urgent teen voice, written in rapid free verse and illustrated with occasional black-and-white sketches, will hold readers with its nonreverential family story. —*Booklist*

Thompson, Kate
The **new** policeman. Kate Thompson. Greenwillow Books, 2007 442 p. (New policeman trilogy, 1)
Grades: 7 8 9 10
1. Teenage musicians; 2. Fairies; 3. Time; 4. Fifteen-year-old boys; 5. Music; 6. Ireland; 7. Fantasy fiction.
9780061174278, hardback, US; 9780370328232, hardback, UK
ALA Notable Children's Book, 2008; School Library Journal Best Books, 2007; USBBY Outstanding International Book, 2008; Whitbread Book Award for Children's Book of the Year, 2005; YALSA Best Books for Young Adults, 2008.

Irish teenager JJ Liddy discovers that time is leaking from his world into Tir na Nog, the land of the fairies, and when he attempts to stop the leak he finds out a lot about his family history, the music that he loves, and a crime his great-grandfather may or may not have committed.

Mesmerizing and captivating, this book is guaranteed to charm fantasy fans. —*Voice of Youth Advocates*

Thompson, Mary G.
Amy Chelsea Stacie Dee. Mary G. Thompson. 2016 304 pages
Grades: 9 10 11 12
1. Teenage girl kidnapping victims; 2. Former captives; 3. Secrets; 4. Cousins; 5. Sixteen-year-old girls; 6. Psychological suspense
9781101996805

LC 2016008732

Westchester Fiction Award, 2017.

Amy and her cousin Dee were kidnapped six years ago, and when Amy finds her way home, she's desperate to protect the ones she loves at any cost.

Thompson expertly builds the novels tension to an unbearable pitch as she guides readers to a bittersweet, satisfying conclusion. —*Publishers Weekly*

Thomson, Jamie
Dark Lord, the early years. By Jamie Thomson. Walker & Co, 2012 304 p. (Dark Lord, 1)
Grades: 6 7 8 9
1. Villains; 2. Identity (Psychology); 3. Spells (Magic); 4. Magic; 5. Twelve-year-old boys; 6. Fantasy fiction; 7. Humorous stories
9780802728494

LC 2012007152

Evil Dark Lord tries to recover his dignity, his power, and his lands when an arch-foe transports him to a small town, into the body of a thirteen-year-old boy.

Thor, Annika
Deep sea. Annika Thor; translated from the Swedish by Linda Schenck. Delacorte Press, 2015 224 p. (Steiner sisters quartet, 3)
Grades: 7 8 9 10 11 12

1. World War II — Refugees; 2. Refugees; 3. Jews; 4. Sisters; 5. Schools; 6. Sweden; 7. Goteborg, Sweden; 8. Second World War era (1939-1945); 9. Historical fiction; 10. Translations
9780385743853; 9780385371346, ebook, US

LC 2014005586

USBBY Outstanding International Book, 2016.

Nearly four years after leaving Vienna to escape the Nazis, Stephie Steiner, now sixteen, and her sister Nellie, eleven, are still living in Sweden, worrying about their parents and striving to succeed in school, and at odds with each other despite their mutual love.

This novel about coming of age during a complicated, tragic time in history is both delicate and poignant, as when Stephie and Nellie sit on the dock, remembering a lullaby their mother sang. Thor's novel capably demonstrates the loneliness, powerlessness, and prejudice Stephie faces, as well as her growing inner strength. —*Publishers Weekly*

Originally published in Sweden as *Havets djup* by Annika Thor, copyright 1998 by Annika Thor, by Bonnier Carlsen, Stockholm, in 1998.

A **faraway** island. Annika Thor; translated by Linda Schenck. Delacorte Press, 2009 256 p. (Steiner sisters quartet, 1)
Grades: 4 5 6 7
1. Jewish children; 2. Sisters; 3. World War II; 4. Children and war; 5. Parent-separated children; 6. Sweden; 7. Second World War era (1939-1945); 8. Historical fiction.
9780385905909

Mildred L. Batchelder Award, 2010; ALA Notable Children's Book, 2010; USBBY Outstanding International Book, 2010.

In 1939 Sweden, two Jewish sisters wait in seperate foster homes for their parents to join them in fleeing the Nazis in Austria, but while eight-year-old Nellie settles in quickly, twelve-year-old Stephie feels stranded at the end of the world, with a foster mother who is as cold and unforgiving as the island on which they live.

Children will readily empathize with Stephie's courage. Both sisters are well-drawn, likable characters. This is the first of four books Thor has written about the two girls. —*School Library Journal*

The **lily** pond. Annika Thor; translated from the Swedish by Linda Schenck. Delacorte Press, 2011 256 p. (Steiner sisters quartet, 2)
Grades: 4 5 6 7
1. Jewish girls; 2. World War II; 3. Children and war; 4. Foster family; 5. City life; 6. Sweden; 7. Second World War era (1939-1945); 8. Historical fiction; 9. Translations
9780385908382

ALA Notable Children's Book, 2012; Batchelder Honor Book, 2012.

Having left Nazi-occupied Vienna a year ago, thirteen-year-old Jewish refugee Stephie Steiner adapts to life in the cultured Swedish city of Gothenburg, where she attends school, falls in love, and worries about her parents who were not allowed to emigrate.

Thornburgh, Blair
★ **Ordinary** girls. Blair Thornburgh. HarperTeen, 2019 368 pages
Grades: 7 8 9 10 11 12
1. Sisters; 2. Family problems; 3. Mothers and daughters; 4. Father-separated teenage girls; 5. Single mothers; 6. Philadelphia, Pennsylvania; 7. Realistic fiction; 8. Coming-of-age stories; 9. Classics-inspired fiction
9780062447814, HRD, US

Booklist Editors' Choice: Books for Youth, 2019.

A lighthearted contemporary retelling of *Sense and Sensibility* finds two sisters, complete opposites in temperament, who discover that the secrets they have been keeping make them more alike than they realized.

A smart, character-driven contemporary novel with a timeless feel. —*School Library Journal*

Tingle, Tim
House of purple cedar. By Tim Tingle. Cinco Puntos Press, 2014 192 p.
Grades: 10 11 12
1. Choctaw Indians; 2. Indians of North America; 3. Race relations; 4. Culture conflict; 5. Christianity; 6. Oklahoma; 7. 1890s; 8. Historical fiction; 9. Adult books for young adults
9781935955696; 9781935955245
LC 2013010570
American Indian Youth Literature Awards, Best Young Adult Book, 2016; Notable Books for a Global Society, 2015.

In 1896, as white settlers hungry for land flooded into Indian territory in what is now Oklahoma, a boarding school for Indian girls called the New Hope Academy was burned to the ground with a severe loss of life. It presaged the destruction of the Choctaw community, related here by fire survivor Rose Goode in measured but heartfelt language. —*Library Journal*

When a ghost talks, listen: a Choctaw Trail of Tears story. Tim Tingle. RoadRunner Press, 2018 188 p. (How I became a ghost, 2)
Grades: 7 8 9 10
1. Native American boys; 2. Visions; 3. Choctaw Indians — Relocation; 4. Ghosts; 5. Boy ghosts; 6. Oklahoma; 7. Washington, D.C; 8. 1830s; 9. 19th century; 10. Historical fiction; 11. Ghost stories.
9781937054519
Ten-year-old Isaac, now a ghost, continues with his people as they walk the Choctaw Trail of Tears headed to Indian Territory in what will one day become Oklahoma. There have been surprises aplenty on their trek, but now Isaac and his three Choctaw comrades learn they can time travel—making for an unexpected adventure. The foursome heads back in time to Washington, D.C, to bear witness for Choctaw Chief Pushmataha who has come to the nation's capital at the invitation of Andrew Jackson..

Tintera, Amy
Reboot. Amy Tintera. HarperTeen, an imprint of HarperCollinsPublishers, 2013 365 p; (Reboot duology, 1)
Grades: 9 10 11 12
1. Survival (after epidemics); 2. Resurrection; 3. Teenage romance; 4. Adventurers; 5. Dead; 6. Dystopian fiction; 7. Science fiction; 8. Books for reluctant readers
9780062217073
LC 2012051741
YALSA Quick Picks for Reluctant Young Adult Readers, 2014.
Seventeen-year-old Wren rises from the dead as a Reboot and is trained as an elite crime-fighting soldier until she is given an order she refuses to follow.

Tokuda-Hall, Maggie
★ The **mermaid,** the witch, and the sea. Maggie Tokuda-hall. Candlewick Press, 2020 368 p.
Grades: 9 10 11 12
1. Pirates; 2. Seafaring life; 3. Imperialism; 4. Colonialism; 5. Magic; 6. High fantasy; 7. Fantasy fiction.
9781536204315; 9781406395501, Paperback, UK
School Library Journal Best Books, 2020.
In a world divided by colonialism and threaded with magic, a desperate orphan turned pirate and a rebellious imperial lady find a connection on the high seas.

Tomlinson, Heather
★ **Toads** and diamonds. Heather Tomlinson. Henry Holt, 2010 288 p.

Grades: 8 9 10 11 12
1. Stepsisters; 2. Curses; 3. Ability; 4. Gifts; 5. Gods and goddesses; 6. India; 7. Historical fantasy; 8. Fairy tale and folklore-inspired fiction; 9. Asian-influenced fantasy
9780805089684
LC 2009023448
YALSA Best Fiction for Young Adults, 2011; School Library Journal Best Books, 2010.
A retelling of the Perrault fairy tale set in pre-colonial India, in which two stepsisters receive gifts from a goddess and each walks her own path to find her gift's purpose, discovering romance along the way.
The author creates a vivid setting. Lavish details starkly contrast the two girls' lives and personalities.... The complexities of the cultural backstory pose a challenge to readers, but this beautifully embroidered adventure is well worth the effort. —*Booklist*

Toro, Guillermo del
Pan's labyrinth: the labyrinth of the faun. Guillermo del Toro and Cornelia Funke. Katherine Tegen Books, an imprint of HarperCollinsPublishers, 2019 272 pages
Grades: 6 7 8 9
1. Imaginary places; 2. Fauns (Roman mythology); 3. Thirteen-year-old girls; 4. Labyrinths; 5. Fairies; 6. Spain; 7. Second World War era (1939-1945); 8. 1940s; 9. Historical fantasy; 10. Media tie-ins
9780062414465; 9781526609557, Hardback, UK; 9781526609571, Paperback, UK
Del Toro's Oscar-winning film *Pan's Labyrinth* is a natural pick for novelization, steeped as it is in books and storytelling. But perhaps novelization is too limiting a word, for Funke beautifully expands the story's mythologies and deftly transposes Del Toro's highly visual world to the page. —*Booklist*

Torres Sanchez, Jenny
Death, Dickinson, and the demented life of Frenchie Garcia. By Jenny Torres Sanchez. RP Teens, 2013 271 p;
Grades: 9 10 11 12
1. Suicide; 2. Teenage girl artists; 3. Teenagers and death; 4. Crushes in teenage girls; 5. Hispanic American teenage girls; 6. Realistic fiction
9780762446803
LC Bl2013020764
Struggling to come to terms with the suicide of her crush, Andy Cooper, Frenchie obsessively retraces each step of their tumultuous final encounter and looks to the poetry of Emily Dickinson for guidance.
An exceptionally well-written journey to make sense of the senseless. —*Kirkus*

★ **We** are not from here. Jenny Torres Sanchez. Philomel Books, 2020 368 p.
Grades: 9 10 11 12
1. Teenage refugees; 2. Voyages and travels; 3. Immigration and emigration; 4. Survival; 5. American dream; 6. Mexican-American Border Region; 7. Survival stories; 8. Magical realism; 9. Multiple perspectives.
9781984812261, HRD, US; 9781984812278, ebook, US
LC 2020934990
School Library Journal Best Books, 2020; Pura Belpre Honor Book for Narrative, 2021.
Teens from Guatelama escape through Mexico and attempt to reach the U.S. border.
Melding the adventure with bouts of magical realism recalling the works of Gabriel Garcia Marquez—and writing with respect and sympa-

thy for the plight of these people—Sanchez takes readers on a frightening pursuit of the American dream, and whether or not the trio is successful, we must keep them company every difficult step of the way. —*Booklist*

Toten, Teresa

Beware that girl. Teresa Toten. Delacorte Press, 2016 272 p.
Grades: 9 10 11 12
1. Psychopaths; 2. Rich teenage girls; 3. Private schools; 4. Schools; 5. Friendship; 6. New York City; 7. Thrillers and suspense; 8. Multiple perspectives
9780553507904; 9780385684743, Paperback, Canada; 9780553507928, ebook, US

LC 2015028074

OLA Best Bets, 2016.

When a scholarship girl and a wealthy classmate become friends, their bond is tested when a handsome young teacher separately influences the girls in order to further his less-than-admirable interests.

Complete with a disturbing yet satisfying conclusion, this is a must-have for teen fans of psychological thrillers such as Gillian Flynn's *Gone Girl*. —*School Library Journal*

The **unlikely** hero of room 13B. Teresa Toten. Delacorte Press, 2015 289 p.
Grades: 9 10 11 12
1. Obsessive-compulsive disorder; 2. Dysfunctional families; 3. Support groups; 4. Fourteen-year-old boys; 5. Teenagers; 6. Realistic fiction; 7. Canadian fiction; 8. Books for reluctant readers
9780553507867; 9780385678346
Governor General's Literary Award for English-Language Children's Literature, 2013; Ruth and Sylvia Schwartz Children's Book Award for YA-Middle Reader, 2014; Schneider Family Book Award for Teens, 2016; YALSA Best Fiction for Young Adults, 2016; YALSA Quick Picks for Reluctant Young Adult Readers, 2016; OLA Best Bets, 2013.

Adam not only is trying to understand his OCD, while trying to balance his relationship with his divorced parents, but he's also trying to navigate through the issues that teenagers normally face, namely the perils of young love.

Fifteen-year-old Adam falls for Robyn in his teen OCD therapy group. Adam's insightful, steadfast support helps Robyn (and several other groupmates) improve—but Adam actually seems to get worse. While the tone is light overall (superhero group names!), there are plenty of touching, even wrenching, moments as Adam struggles to accept his own limitations and those of his loved ones. —*Horn Book Guide*

Originally published in paperback by Doubleday Canada, Toronto, Ontario, in 2013.

Trigiani, Adriana

Viola in reel life. Written by Adriana Trigiani. HarperTeen, 2009 282 p. (Viola Chesterton books, 1)
Grades: 7 8 9 10
1. Self-reliance in teenage girls; 2. Filmmakers; 3. Videos — Production and direction; 4. Teenage filmmakers; 5. Teenage boy/girl relations; 6. Indiana; 7. Realistic fiction; 8. Teen chick lit; 9. First person narratives.
9780061451027; 9781847389268, print, UK

LC 2009014269

When fourteen-year-old Viola is sent from her beloved Brooklyn to boarding school in Indiana for ninth grade, she overcomes her initial reservations as she makes friends with her roommates, goes on a real date, and uses the unsettling ghost she keeps seeing as the subject of a short film—her first.

This is a sweet, character-driven story. Viola is very real, as are her feelings, hopes, desires, and dreams. —*School Library Journal*

Viola in the spotlight. Adriana Trigiani. HarperTeen, 2011 288 p. (Viola Chesterton books, 2)
Grades: 7 8 9 10
1. Theater; 2. Internship programs; 3. Crushes in teenage girls; 4. Summer; 5. Interpersonal relations; 6. Brooklyn, New York City; 7. New York City; 8. Realistic fiction; 9. Teen chick lit; 10. First person narratives.
9780061451058; 9780857070203, print, UK

LC 2010045553

Back home in Brooklyn, fifteen-year-old Viola has big summer plans but with one best friend going to camp and the other not only working but experiencing her first crush, Viola is glad to be overworked as an unpaid lighting intern when her grandmother's play goes to Broadway.

An equally enjoyable follow-up to Viola in Reel Life. —*Booklist*
Sequel to: *Viola in reel life*.

Tripp, Ben

The **accidental** highwayman: being the tale of Kit Bristol, his horse Midnight, a mysterious princess, and sundry magical persons besides. Ben Tripp. Tor Teen, 2014 304 p. (Accidental highwayman trilogy, 1)
Grades: 7 8 9 10
1. Teenage boy orphans; 2. Princesses; 3. Voyages and travels; 4. Fairies; 5. Teenage boys; 6. England; 7. Ireland; 8. 18th century; 9. Historical fantasy; 10. First person narratives; 11. Illustrated books
9780765335494
YALSA Best Fiction for Young Adults, 2015.

Donning his wounded master's riding cloak to seek help in 18th-century England, young Kit Bristol is mistaken as an outlaw and catapulted into a world of magic, imperiled princesses and dark omens.

Readers will root for star-crossed lovers, Kit and Morgana, and delight in their 'opposites attract' romance, drawn onward by a rollicking plot...Fantasy readers, especially fans of Cathrynne Valente's work, will enjoy the author's elegant turns of phrase. A first purchase for all fantasy collections. —*School Library Journal*

Tromly, Stephanie

Trouble is a friend of mine. By Stephanie Tromly. Kathy Dawson Books, an imprint of Penguin Group (USA) LLC, 2015 320 p. (Trouble (Stephanie Tromly), 1)
Grades: 9 10 11 12
1. Kidnapping investigation; 2. Teenage misfits; 3. Children of divorced parents; 4. Missing children; 5. Moving, Household; 6. New York (State); 7. Mysteries; 8. First person narratives
9780525428404

LC 2014040605

Arthur Ellis Award for Best Juvenile Mystery, 2016; OLA Best Bets, 2015.

After her parents' divorce, Zoe Webster moves from Brooklyn to upstate New York where she meets the weirdly compelling misfit, Philip Digby, and soon finds herself in a series of hilarious and dangerous situations as he pulls her into his investigation into the kidnapping of a local teenage girl which may be related to the disappearance of his kid sister eight years ago.

Sequel: *Trouble makes a comeback*.

Trueman, Terry

★ **Cruise** control. Terry Trueman. Harper Tempest, 2004 149 p;
Grades: 7 8 9 10

1. Father-separated teenage boys; 2. Teenage athletes; 3. Anger in teenage boys; 4. Brothers; 5. Family relationships; 6. Realistic fiction; 7. First person narratives.
9780066239606; 9780066239613

LC 2003019822

A talented basketball player struggles to deal with the helplessness and anger that come with having a brother rendered completely dysfunctional by severe cerebral palsy and a father who deserted the family.

This powerful tale is extremely well written and will give readers an understanding of what it's like to have a challenged sibling. —*School Library Journal*

Companion to: *Stuck in neutral.*

★ **Inside** out. Terry Trueman. Harper Tempest, 2003 117 p;
Grades: 7 8 9 10
1. People with schizophrenia; 2. Hostages; 3. Robbery; 4. Children of unemployed parents; 5. Children of people with cancer; 6. Thrillers and suspense; 7. Realistic fiction; 8. First person narratives; 9. Books for reluctant readers
9780066239620; 9780066239637

LC 2002151604

YALSA Quick Picks for Reluctant Young Adult Readers, 2004; YALSA Best Books for Young Adults, 2004.

A sixteen-year-old with schizophrenia is caught up in the events surrounding an attempted robbery by two other teens who eventually hold him hostage.

Trueman sometimes captures moments of heartbreaking truth, and his swift, suspenseful plot will have particular appeal to reluctant readers. —*Booklist*

Life happens next: a novel. By Terry Trueman. HarperTeen, 2012 128 p.
Grades: 7 8 9 10
1. Teenagers with cerebral palsy; 2. People with disabilities; 3. Crushes in teenage boys; 4. Cerebral palsy; 5. Down syndrome; 6. Seattle, Washington; 7. Realistic fiction; 8. First person narratives.
9780062028037

LC 2011044627

Shawn McDaniel, almost fifteen, cannot speak and has no control over his body due to severe cerebral palsy, but he forms a strong connection with his mother's cousin Debi, who has Down Syndrome, and her dog Rusty.

Sequel to: *Stuck in neutral.*

Stuck in neutral. Terry Trueman. Harper Collins Publishers, 2000 Ix, 114 p.
Grades: 7 8 9 10
1. Father-separated teenage boys; 2. Teenage boys with disabilities; 3. Euthanasia; 4. Gifted teenagers; 5. Dilemmas; 6. Seattle, Washington; 7. Realistic fiction; 8. First person narratives; 9. Books for reluctant readers
9780060285197

LC 99037098

Booklist Editors' Choice: Books for Youth, 2000; Kentucky Bluegrass Award for Grades 6-8, 2002; YALSA Best Books for Young Adults, 2001; YALSA Popular Paperbacks for Young Adults, 2010; YALSA Quick Picks for Reluctant Young Adult Readers, 2001; Michael L. Printz Honor Book, 2001.

Fourteen-year-old Shawn McDaniel, who suffers from severe cerebral palsy and cannot function, relates his perceptions of his life, his family, and his condition, especially as he believes his father is planning to kill him.

Trueman has created a compelling novel that poses questions about ability and existence while fostering sympathy for people with severe physical limitations. —*Bulletin of the Center for Children's Books*

Sequel: *Life happens next*; Companion novel: *Cruise Control.*

Tubb, Kristin O'Donnell
★ **Selling** hope. Kristin O'Donnell Tubb. Feiwel and Friends, 2010 224 p.
Grades: 6 7 8
1. Keaton, Buster; 2. Vaudeville; 3. Hoaxes; 4. Magicians; 5. Single-parent families; 6. Halley's Comet; 7. Chicago, Illinois; 8. 1910s; 9. Historical fiction.
9780312611224

LC 2010012571

In 1910, just before the Earth passes through the tail of Halley's Comet, thirteen-year-old Hope McDaniels, whose father is a magician in a traveling vaudeville show, tries to earn enough money to quit the circuit by selling "anti-comet pills," with the help of fellow-performer Buster Keaton.

Tubb deftly ingrains a thoughtful ethical question into the story...but never overdoes it in this bouncy tale populated by a terrific cast of characters. —*Booklist*

Tucholke, April Genevieve
Between the devil and the deep blue sea. By April Genevieve Tucholke. Dial Books, 2013 368 p.
Grades: 7 8 9 10
1. Devil; 2. Family secrets; 3. Small towns; 4. Twin brothers and sisters; 5. Good and evil; 6. Maine; 7. Gothic fiction; 8. Paranormal fiction
9780803738898

LC 2012035586

Violet is in love with River, a mysterious seventeen-year-old stranger renting the guest house behind the rotting seaside mansion where Violet lives, but when eerie, grim events begin to happen, Violet recalls her grandmother's frequent warnings about the devil and wonders if River is evil.

It's no coincidence that when the alluring River West shows up to rent the guesthouse of Violet's dilapidated seaside mansion, eerie and brutal things begin to happen in town. Yet love-struck Violet finds herself powerless to act, or really care. A highly atmospheric and unreliable narrative wends its way between scenes alternately homey and macabre to a twisty ending. —*Horn Book Guide*

Sequel: *Between the spark and the burn*

Between the spark and the burn. April Genevieve Tucholke. Dial Books, 2014 368 p.
Grades: 7 8 9 10
1. Devil; 2. Twin brothers and sisters; 3. Good and evil; 4. Quests; 5. Seventeen-year-old girls; 6. Gothic fiction; 7. Paranormal fiction
9780803740471

The faded opulence of the setting is an ideal backdrop for this lushly atmospheric gothic thriller, which, happily, comes with a satisfying conclusion. Darkly romantic and evocative. —*Kirkus*

Sequel to: *Between the devil and the deep blue sea*

The **Boneless** Mercies. April Genevieve Tucholke. Farrar Straus Giroux, 2018 352 p.
Grades: 7 8 9 10 11 12
1. Women warriors; 2. Monsters; 3. Mercenaries; 4. Voyages and travels; 5. Ambition in women; 6. High fantasy; 7. Mythological fiction.
9780374307066; 9781471170003, Paperback, UK

LC 2018003350
Four female mercenaries known as Boneless Mercies, weary of roaming Vorseland, ignored and forgotten until they are needed for mercy killings, decide to seek glory by going after a legendary monster in this reimagining of Beowulf.

Frey's earnest narrative voice creates a strong sense of the center of this fantasy: female solidarity. Bodily closeness, a shared quest for justice, and sheer joy in physical capacity are only part of it: collaboration and attentive respect are the true underpinning of Tucholke's creation. —*Horn Book Guide*

Seven endless forests. April Genevieve Tucholke. Farrar, Straus & Giroux, 2020 330 p.
Grades: 8 9 10 11 12
1. Sisters; 2. Kidnapping; 3. Rescues; 4. Imaginary creatures; 5. Quests; 6. Arthurian fantasy; 7. High fantasy; 8. Fantasy fiction.
9780374307097, hardback, US; 9780374307103, ebook, US; 9781250762917, paperback, US; 9781471170027, Paperback, UK

A fierce and lyrical retelling of the King Arthur legend. On the heels of a devastating plague, Torvi's sister Morgunn is stolen from the family farm by Uther, a flame-loving wolf-priest who leads a pack of ragged, starving girls. Torvi leaves the only home she's ever known and joins a shaven-headed druid and a band of roaming Elsh artists known as the Butcher Bards. They set out on a quest to rescue Torvi's sister, and find a mythical sword. On their travels, Torvi and her companions will face wild, dangerous magic that leads to love, joy, tragedy, and death....

References to the Arthur legend loosely make their way into the narrative—a sword lodged in a stone tree, Mort Darthur River, a wizard who unlocks the path to Avalon—but even readers without an intimate knowledge of the legend will fall beneath Tucholke's spell. A lovely tale of quests and camaraderie. —*Booklist*

Companion to *The Boneless Mercies*.

Turner, Megan Whalen

A **conspiracy** of kings. By Megan Whalen. Greenwillow Books, 2010 316 p. (Queen's thief, 4)
Grades: 7 8 9 10
1. Princes; 2. Kidnapping victims; 3. Slavery; 4. Power (Social sciences); 5. Rulers; 6. High fantasy; 7. Fantasy fiction.
9780061870934; 9780061870941

LC 2009023052
Los Angeles Times Book Prize for Young Adult Literature, 2010; YALSA Best Fiction for Young Adults, 2011; School Library Journal Best Books, 2010.

Kidnapped and sold into slavery, Sophos, an unwilling prince, tries to save his country from being destroyed by rebellion and exploited by the conniving Mede empire.

Given the complexity of Turner's plot, readers should reread the first three books before beginning this one, which derives its power from the intricate construction of Turner's imagined world, a realm in which her founding mythology is as impressive as her descriptions of the land itself.... Strong evidence emerges that the story doesn't end here, and fans will savor this while they wait for more. —*Publishers Weekly*

The **king** of Attolia. Megan Whalen Turner. Greenwillow Books, 2006 387 p. (Queen's thief, 3)
Grades: 7 8 9 10
1. Guards; 2. Rulers; 3. Attempted assassination; 4. Soldiers; 5. Eugenides; 6. High fantasy; 7. Fantasy fiction.
9780060835774; 9780060835781

LC 2005040303
YALSA Best Books for Young Adults, 2007; School Library Journal Best Books, 2006.

Eugenides, still known as a Thief of Eddis, faces palace intrigue and assassins as he strives to prove himself both to the people of Attolia and to his new bride, their queen.

Fans who've been waiting... for the sequel to *The Queen of Attolia* (2000) and *The Thief* (1996) can finally rejoice.... To appreciate the amazingly charismatic and beguiling character of Eugenides fully, its best to read the titles in order. —*School Library Journal*

The **queen** of Attolia. Megan Whalen Turner. Greenwillow Books, 2000 279 p. (Queen's thief, 2)
Grades: 6 7 8 9
1. Thieves; 2. Women rulers; 3. Amputation; 4. Eugenides (Fictitious character); 5. Prisoners; 6. High fantasy; 7. Fantasy fiction.
9780688174231

LC 99026916
Forsaken by the gods and left to his own devices, Eugenides, Royal Thief of Eddis, summons all his wit and wiles in an attempt to conquer the rival Queen of Attolia.

The intense read is thoroughly involving and wholly satisfying on all fronts. —*Horn Book Guide*

Sequel to: *The thief*.

★ **Return** of the thief. Megan Whalen Turner. Greenwillow Books, an imprint of HarperCollins Publishers, 2020 352 p. (Queen's thief, 6)
Grades: 9 10 11 12
1. Rulers; 2. Prophecies; 3. Imaginary wars and battles; 4. Imaginary kingdoms; 5. Attolia (Imaginary place); 6. High fantasy; 7. Fantasy fiction
9780062874474

A conclusion to the best-selling series finds high king Eugenides preparing to defend the Lesser Peninsula from an invasion by the ruthless Mede empire, an effort that is complicated by a prophecy that foretells a king's death.

Sequel to: *Thick as thieves*.

★ **Thick** as thieves: a Queen's thief novel. Megan Whalen Turner. Greenwillow Books, an imprint of HarperCollins Publishers, 2017 400 p. (Queen's thief, 5)
Grades: 7 8 9 10 11 12
1. Slaves; 2. Soldiers; 3. Kidnapping victims; 4. Rulers; 5. Imaginary kingdoms; 6. High fantasy; 7. Fantasy fiction.
9780062568243

LC 2016047028
Kamet, a secretary and slave to his Mede master, has the ambition and the means to become one of the most powerful people in the Empire. But with a whispered warning the future he envisioned is wrenched away, and he is forced onto a very different path.

This series fifth can stand alone without reading the rest of the books.... This invites an older audience, but...offer[s] more teen appeal than the political drama of earlier Queen's Thief novels. —*Kirkus*

★ The **thief**. Megan Whalen Turner. Greenwillow Books, 1996 219 p. (Queen's thief, 1)
Grades: 7 8 9 10
1. Thieves; 2. Gems; 3. Stealing; 4. Prisoners; 5. Quests; 6. High fantasy; 7. Fantasy fiction; 8. First person narratives.
9780688146276

LC 95-41040
ALA Notable Children's Book, 1997; YALSA Best Books for Young Adults, 1997; YALSA Popular Paperbacks for Young Adults, 2016; Newbery Honor Book, 1997.

Gen flaunts his ingenuity as a thief and relishes the adventure which takes him to a remote temple of the gods where he will attempt to steal a precious stone.

A tantalizing, suspenseful, exceptionally clever novel.... The author's characterization of Gen is simply superb. —*Horn Book Guide*
Sequel: *The Queen of Attolia*.

Turtschaninoff, Maria
★ **Maresi**. Maria Turtschaninoff. 2016 256 p. : Illustration; Map (Red Abbey chronicles, 1)
Grades: 8 9 10 11
1. Abbeys; 2. Revenge; 3. Sexism; 4. Novitiate; 5. Kinship-based society; 6. Historical fantasy; 7. Coming-of-age stories; 8. Translations
9781419722691; 9781782690917, hardcover, UK
Amelia Bloomer List, 2018.
Utterly satisfying and completely different from standard YA fantasy, this Finnish import seems primed to win over American readers. —*Booklist*
Original edition published by Schildts and Soderstroms, 2014

Naondel. Maria Turtschaninoff; translated by A. A. Prime. Amulet Books, 2018 384 p. (Red Abbey chronicles, 2)
Grades: 8 9 10 11
1. Abused women; 2. Women prisoners; 3. Escapes; 4. Trust in women; 5. Viziers; 6. Historical fantasy; 7. Multiple perspectives; 8. Translations
9781419725555
LC 2017011854
Amelia Bloomer List, 2019.
A prequel to the award-winning Maresi traces the story of the First Sisters and founders of the Red Abbey female utopia, describing how, at great cost, they escaped from a man with dark-magic powers and struggled to trust each other in a world of oppression and exploitation.
This is not an easy story, with its perpetual backdrop of sexual violence, but in the foreground is a fierce, slow-burning exposition of female courage and resilience. —*Horn Book Guide*
Originally published in Sweden by Berghs in 2016 under title: *Naondel : kronikor fran Roda klostret*.

Uehashi, Nahoko
★ The **beast** player. Nahoko Uehashi; illustrations by Yuta Onoda; translated from the Japanese by Cathy Hirano. Holt Books for Young Readers, 2019 344 p. (Beast player, 1)
Grades: 8 9 10 11 12
1. Human/animal communication; 2. Imaginary creatures; 3. Orphans; 4. Compassion; 5. Nature; 6. Asian-influenced fantasy; 7. Coming-of-age stories; 8. Fantasy fiction.
9781250307460, HRD, US; 9781250307477, ebook, US
ALA Notable Children's Books, 2020; Batchelder Honor Book, 2020; Michael L. Printz Honor Book, 2020.
When her mother is executed for the mysterious deaths of their kingdom's protective water serpents, a girl with an inherited ability to communicate with magical beasts finds her talent ensnaring her in life-threatening war plots.
In a refreshing change for western readers, the central issue hinges on neither individual power nor romantic love but kindness balanced against responsibility. —*Kirkus*
Kemono no souja

Moribito II: guardian of the darkness. Nahoko Uehashi; translated by Cathy Hirano; illustrated by Yuko Shimizu. Arthur A. Levine Books, 2009 245 p. : Illustration (Moribito, 2)
Grades: 6 7 8 9

1. Girl warriors; 2. Conspiracies; 3. Teenage girls; 4. Heroes and heroines; 5. Young women; 6. Japan; 7. Fantasy fiction; 8. Asian-influenced fantasy
9780545102957
LC 2008037444
ALA Notable Children's Book, 2010; USBBY Outstanding International Book, 2010; Batchelder Honor Book, 2010.
The wandering female bodyguard Balsa returns to her native country of Kanbal, where she uncovers a conspiracy to frame her mentor and herself.
Once again, Uehashi immerses readers in the culture, traditions, mythologyeven dietof the populace, creating a full, captivating world.... This growing series has something for everyone. —*Publishers Weekly*
Sequel to: *Moribito : Guardian of the Spirit*.

★ **Moribito:** Guardian of the Spirit. Nahoko Uehashi; translated by Cathy Hirano; illustrated by Yuko Shimizu. Arthur A. Levine Books, 2008 248 p; (Moribito, 1)
Grades: 6 7 8 9
1. Heroes and heroines; 2. Bodyguards; 3. Spirit possession; 4. Young women; 5. Princes; 6. Japan; 7. Fantasy fiction; 8. Asian-influenced fantasy
9780545005425
LC 2007036383
Mildred L. Batchelder Award, 2009; ALA Notable Children's Book, 2009; USBBY Outstanding International Book, 2009.
The wandering warrior Balsa is hired to protect Prince Chagum from both a mysterious monster and the prince's father, the Mikado.
This book is first in a series of ten that have garnered literary and popular success in Japan.... Balsa and Chagum's story is brought to America with a strong translation.... Readers who are fans of action manga, especially with strong female characters, will enjoy the ninja-like fighting scenes.... The exciting premise, combined with an attractive cover, should insure that this title will circulate well. —*Voice of Youth Advocates*
Sequel: *Moribito II : guardian of the darkness*.

Umminger, Alison
★ **American** girls. Alison Umminger. Flatiron Books, 2016 304 p.
Grades: 8 9 10 11
1. Runaway teenage girls; 2. Film industry and trade; 3. Sisters; 4. Teenage romance; 5. Fifteen-year-old girls; 6. Los Angeles, California; 7. Realistic fiction; 8. Coming-of-age stories
9781250075000
Amelia Bloomer List, 2017; YALSA Best Fiction for Young Adults, 2017.
Fifteen-year-old Anna runs away to Los Angeles where her half-sister takes her in, but after spending days on television and movie sets, she learns LA is not the glamorous escape she imagined.
An insightful, original take on the coming-of-age story, this novel plumbs the depths of American culture to arrive at a poignant emotional truth. —*Kirkus*

Unsworth, Tania
The **one** safe place: a novel. By Tania Unsworth. Algonquin Young Readers, 2014 224 pages
Grades: 6 7 8 9 10
1. Near future; 2. Abandoned children; 3. Dystopias; 4. Orphans; 5. Survival; 6. Science fiction.
9781616203290
LC 2013043145
In a near future world of heat, greed, and hunger, Devin earns a coveted spot in a home for abandoned children that promises unlimited food and toys and the hope of finding a new family, but Devin discovers the

home's horrific true mission when he investigates its intimidating Administrator and the zombie-like sickness that afflicts some children.

Orphaned twelve-year-old Devin is invited to live at the paradisaical Home for Childhood, but something terrifying is happening to the children there. Devin's synesthesia, which makes him interesting to the Home's sinister Administrator, may provide the key to their escape. Set in a world of post climate change desperation, Unsworth's story thoughtfully explores the theme of adults' nostalgia for childhood. —*Horn Book Guide*

Vail, Rachel

Lucky. Rachel Vail. HarperTeen, 2008 233 p. (Avery sisters trilogy, 1)
Grades: 7 8 9 10
1. Wealth; 2. Popularity; 3. Sisters; 4. Parties; 5. Children of unemployed parents; 6. Realistic fiction; 7. Teen chick lit
9780060890438

As Phoebe and her clique of privileged girlfriends get ready to graduate from eighth grade, a financial scandal threatens her family's security—as well as Phoebe's social status—but ultimately it teaches her the real meaning of friendship.

Vail's insightful characterizations of teen girls and their shifting loyalties is right on target. —*Booklist*

Unfriended. Rachel Vail. Viking, published by Penguin Group, 2014 256 p.
Grades: 6 7 8 9
1. Popularity; 2. Social media; 3. Nastiness; 4. Nastiness in girls; 5. Former friends; 6. Realistic fiction; 7. Multiple perspectives; 8. First person narratives
9780670013074

LC 2014006247

When thirteen-year-old Truly is invited to sit at the Popular Table, she finds herself caught in a web of lies and misunderstandings, made unescapable by the hyperconnected social media world.

The points of view allow the reader to be drawn into the teens' motivations and illustrate the importance of clear communication, the dangers of online bullying, and the universal struggles teens face. Mean girls, misunderstood girls, awkward boys, friendship, popularity, social misfits, all play into this book that epitomizes the roller coaster that is middle school. —*Library Media Connection*

Valente, Catherynne M.

The **boy** who lost Fairyland. Catherynne M. Valente; illustrated by Ana Juan. Feiwel & Friends, 2015 256 p. (Fairyland series (Catherynne M. Valente), 4)
Grades: 5 6 7 8
1. Trolls; 2. Changelings; 3. Parallel universes; 4. Imaginary kingdoms; 5. Winds; 6. Chicago, Illinois; 7. Fantasy fiction; 8. Gateway fantasy.
9781250023490; 9781472112811, print, UK; 9781472112828, print, UK; 9781472110428, ebook; 9781250072795, ebook, US
LC 2014042417

Stolen by the Golden Wind from Fairyland and rendered a changeling in the human world, young troll Hawthorn struggles with his troll nature before stumbling upon a way back home, where he confronts power-hungry fairies that have imposed an Endless Summer.

In this fourth book in the fantastical series, a young troll named Hawthorn is stolen away by the Golden Wind and brought to live in Chicago as a changeling. When he turns 12, he finds a way back to Fairyland, a place now much changed from the magical realm he left...While readers unfamiliar with the series can certainly jump in with this novel, most will want

to start at the beginning. A phenomenal fantasy series worthy of a spot in every library collection. —*School Library Journal*

★ The **girl** who circumnavigated Fairyland in a ship of her own making. Catherynne Valente. Feiwel and Friends, 2011 256 p. (Fairyland series (Catherynne M. Valente), 1)
Grades: 4 5 6 7 8
1. Talismans; 2. Marquis and marchionesses; 3. Quests; 4. Imaginary kingdoms; 5. Parallel universes; 6. Fantasy fiction; 7. Gateway fantasy.
9780312649616; 9781780339818, print, UK
LC 2010050895

Booklist Editors' Choice: Books for Youth, 2011; Locus Young Adult Book Award, 2012; Nebula Awards: Andre Norton Award, 2009; YALSA Best Fiction for Young Adults, 2012.

Twelve-year-old September's ordinary life in Omaha turns to adventure when a Green Wind takes her to Fairyland to retrieve a talisman the new and fickle Marquess wants from the enchanted woods.

The book's appeal is crystal clear from the outset: this is a kind of *The Wonderful Wizard of Oz* by way of *Alice's Adventures in Wonderland*, made vivid by Juan's Tenniel-inflected illustrations.... Those who thrill to lovingly wrought tales of fantasy and adventure...will be enchanted. —*Publishers Weekly*
Sequel: *The girl who fell beneath Fairyland and led the revels there.*

The **girl** who fell beneath Fairyland and led the revels there. . Feiwel & Friends 2012 256 p. (Fairyland series (Catherynne M. Valente), 2)
Grades: 4 5 6 7 8
1. Quests; 2. Voyages and travels; 3. Shadows; 4. Teenage girls; 5. Rulers; 6. Fantasy fiction; 7. Gateway fantasy.
9780312649623

After returning to Fairyland, September discovers that her stolen shadow has become the Hollow Queen, the new ruler of Fairyland Below, who is stealing the magic and shadows from Fairyland folk and refusing to give them back.
Sequel to: *The girl who circumnavigated Fairyland in a ship of her own making.*

The **girl** who soared over Fairyland and cut the moon in two. By Catherynne M. Valente; with illustrations by Ana Juan. Feiwel and Friends, 2013 248 pages : Illustration (Fairyland series (Catherynne M. Valente), 3)
Grades: 4 5 6 7 8
1. Imaginary kingdoms; 2. Adventure; 3. Yeti; 4. Teenage girls; 5. Moon; 6. Fantasy fiction; 7. Gateway fantasy.
9781250023506; 9781472110015, print, UK
LC Bl2013040330

Locus Young Adult Book Award, 2014.

Longing for a new adventure that will reunite her with Ell, the Wyverary, and Saturday, September is spirited away to the moon and charged with saving Fairyland from a moon-Yeti who wields mysterious powers.

In this third volume, following *The Girl Who Fell Beneath Fairyland and Led the Revels There*, September returns to Fairyland and finds herself on a mission to stop a vengeful yeti from destroying his Fairy abusers—and everyone else on the moon. September is now wiser and sadder, and longs for autonomy; likewise, Fairyland and its inhabitants have become darker and more adult. —*Horn Book Guide*

Valentine, Jenny

★ **Me,** the missing, and the dead. Jenny Valentine. HarperTeen, 2008 201 p;
Grades: 8 9 10 11

1. Death; 2. Teenage boys; 3. Family problems; 4. Self-discovery; 5. Fathers; 6. London, England; 7. England; 8. Mysteries; 9. Coming-of-age stories
9780060850685

LC 2007014476

YALSA Best Books for Young Adults, 2009.

When a series of chance events leaves him in possession of an urn with ashes, sixteen-year-old Londoner, Lucas Swain, becomes convinced that its occupant, Violet Park, is communicating with him, initiating a voyage of self-discovery that forces him to finally confront the events surrounding his father's sudden disappearance.

Part mystery, part magical realism, part story of personal growth, and in large part simply about a funny teenager making light of his and his family's pain, this short novel is engaging from start to finish. —*School Library Journal*

Originally published in Great Britain in 2007 under the title: *Finding Violet Park*.

Van de Ruit, John

Spud. John van de Ruit. Razorbill, 2007 352 p.
Grades: 6 7 8 9 10

1. Thirteen-year-old boys; 2. Boarding schools; 3. Schools; 4. Choirboys; 5. Families; 6. South Africa; 7. Diary novels; 8. Humorous stories; 9. Realistic fiction
9781595141705; 9780143024842

LC 2007006065

YALSA Popular Paperbacks for Young Adults, 2013.

In 1990, thirteen-year-old John "Spud" Milton, a prepubescent choirboy, keeps a diary of his first year at an elite, boys-only boarding school in South Africa, as he deals with bizarre housemates, wild crushes, embarrassingly dysfunctional parents, and much more.

This raucous autobiographical novel about a scholarship boy in an elite boys' boarding school in 1990 is mainly farce but also part coming-of-age tale. —*Booklist*

Sequel: *The Madness Continues*.

Van Draanen, Wendelin

The **running** dream. Wendelin Van Draanen. Alfred A. Knopf, 2011 256 p.
Grades: 7 8 9 10 11 12

1. Teenage girls who have had amputations; 2. Teenage girl athletes; 3. Running; 4. Prosthesis; 5. Traffic accident injuries; 6. Realistic fiction.
9780375966675

LC 2010007072

Beehive Young Adult Book Award (Utah), 2013; Golden Sower Award (Nebraska), Young Adult, 2013; Schneider Family Book Award for Teens, 2012; South Carolina Book Award, Junior Books, 2014; YALSA Best Fiction for Young Adults, 2012; YALSA Popular Paperbacks for Young Adults, 2013.

When a school bus accident leaves sixteen-year-old Jessica an amputee, she returns to school with a prosthetic limb and her track team finds a wonderful way to help rekindle her dream of running again.

It's a classic problem novel in a lot of ways.... Overall, though, this is a tremendously upbeat book.... Van Draanen's extensive research into both running and amputees pays dividends. —*Booklist*

Van Etten, David

All that glitters. David Van Etten. Alfred A. Knopf, 2008 295 p; (Likely story, 2)
Grades: 7 8 9 10

1. Sixteen-year-old girls; 2. Television — Production and direction; 3. Soap operas; 4. Interpersonal relations; 5. Children of actors and actresses; 6. Hollywood, California; 7. Realistic fiction; 8. Teen chick lit
9780375846786

LC 2007050903

Now that her soap opera is in production and everyone has ideas on how it can be improved, sixteen-year-old Mallory struggles to maintain control of her original plot and characters as the broadcast premier draws near.

With more twists, turns, and intrigue than a daytime soap, this novel is great fun. —*School Library Journal*

Likely story. David Van Etten. Knopf, 2008 230 p; (Likely story, 1)
Grades: 7 8 9 10

1. Soap operas; 2. Television — Production and direction; 3. Children of actors and actresses; 4. Interpersonal relations; 5. Mothers and daughters; 6. Hollywood, California; 7. Realistic fiction; 8. Teen chick lit
9780375946769

LC 2007022724

Sixteen-year-old Mallory, daughter of the star of a long-running but faltering soap opera, writes her own soap opera script and becomes deeply involved in the day-to-day life of a Hollywood player, while trying to hold on to some shaky personal relationships.

Strong-willed, quick-witted Mallory is a sympathetic heroine, and Van Etten engagingly weds melodrama to the more mundane, universal dramas of teenage life. —*Horn Book Guide*

Vande Velde, Vivian

★ **Being** dead: stories. Vivian Vande Velde. Harcourt, 2001 203 p;
Grades: 7 8 9 10

1. Teenagers and death; 2. Death; 3. Ghosts; 4. Dead; 5. Supernatural; 6. Horror; 7. Short stories
9780152163204

LC 12996

YALSA Best Books for Young Adults, 2002.

Seven supernatural stories, all having something to do with death.

Often humorous and sometimes evoking sympathy, this anthology will be enjoyed by lovers of mild horror as well as by those who like clever short stories. —*Voice of Youth Advocates*

The **book** of Mordred. By Vivian Vande Velde; [illustrations by Justin Gerard].. Houghton Mifflin, 2005 342 p. : Illustration
Grades: 8 9 10 11 12

1. Arthur, King; 2. Knights and knighthood; 3. Wizards; 4. Camelot (Legendary place); 5. Kidnapping; 6. Mordred (Legendary character); 7. Great Britain; 8. Medieval period (476-1492); 9. Historical fantasy; 10. Arthurian fantasy.
9780618507542

LC 2004028223

As the peaceful King Arthur reigns, the five-year-old daughter of Lady Alayna, newly widowed of the village-wizard Toland, is abducted by knights who leave their barn burning and their only servant dead.

All of the characters are well developed and have a strong presence throughout.... [This] provides an intriguing counterpoint to anyone who is interested in Arthurian legend. —*School Library Journal*

Heir apparent. Vivian Vande Velde. Harcourt, 2002 315 p; (Rasmussem Corporation, 2)
Grades: 6 7 8 9

1. Determination in teenage girls; 2. Virtual reality games; 3. Protests, demonstrations, vigils, etc; 4. Censorship; 5. Role playing games; 6. Science fiction; 7. First person narratives.

9780152045609

LC 2002002441

Black-Eyed Susan Book Award (Maryland), Grades 6-9, 2005; Sunshine State Young Reader's Award (Florida), 2006; YALSA Best Books for Young Adults, 2004.

While playing a total immersion virtual reality game of kings and intrigue, fourteen-year-old Giannine learns that demonstrators have damaged the equipment to which she is connected, and she must win the game quickly or be damaged herself.

This adventure includes a cast of intriguing characters and personalities. The feisty heroine has a funny, sarcastic sense of humor and succeeds because of her ingenuity and determination. —*School Library Journal*

VanderMeer, Jeff

★ A **peculiar** peril. Jeff VanderMeer. Farrar Straus & Giroux 2020 656 p. (Misadventures of Jonathan Lambshead, 1)
Grades: 9 10 11 12

1. Inheritance and succession; 2. Mansions; 3. Interdimensional travel; 4. Parallel universes; 5. Curiosities and wonders; 6. Gateway fantasy; 7. Fantasy fiction; 8. Multiple perspectives.
9780374308865; 9780374388355

LC 2019037060

The first book in a two-volume fantasy about a teenaged boy who inherits his grandfather's mansion and discovers three strange doors, evidence his grandfather did not die of natural causes but spectacularly unnatural ones, and clues to the family's tiesto an alternate Europe immersed in a war fought with strange tech and dark magic.

Boldly drawn characters, sublimely ridiculous worldbuilding, and a witty, prismatic narrative further distinguish the unique tale Publishers Weekly

Vanhee, Jason

Engines of the broken world. Jason Vanhee. 2013 262 pages; Grades: 8 9 10 11 12

1. End of the world; 2. Undead; 3. Shapeshifters; 4. Brothers and sisters; 5. Supernatural; 6. Horror; 7. First person narratives
9780805096293

LC 2013026768

In a rural village far distant from the dead and dying cities, twelve-year-old Merciful discovers horrible secrets and must make decisions that may save or doom her world.

Unlike most action-packed dystopias, the story's slower pace...allows readers to feel the fog encroaching on Merciful and Gospel's rustic home, and hear every scratch of their dead mother's awkward movements upon the cellar stairs. —*Booklist*

Vaughn, Carrie

Steel. Carrie Vaughn. HarperTeen, 2011 304 p.
Grades: 7 8 9 10

1. Fencers; 2. Pirate ships; 3. Time travel (Past); 4. Pirates; 5. Fencing; 6. Caribbean Area; 7. 18th century; 8. Fantasy fiction
9780061547911

Amelia Bloomer List, 2012.

When Jill, a competitive high school fencer, goes with her family on vacation to the Bahamas, she is magically transported to an early-eighteenth-century pirate ship in the middle of the ocean.

This is thoroughly enjoyable.... Through her assertive, appealing protagonist and a satisfying plot that sheds light on lesser-known aspects of pirate life, Vaughn introduces readers to an intriguing sport with an ancient pedigree. —*Kirkus*

Vawter, Vince

Copyboy. By Vince Vawter; illustrated by Alessia Trunfio. Capstone Editions, 2018 240 p. (Capstone Editions)
Grades: 7 8 9 10

1. Automobile travel; 2. Stuttering; 3. Newspaper employees; 4. Legacies; 5. Self-esteem; 6. Memphis, Tennessee; 7. New Orleans, Louisiana; 8. Historical fiction; 9. Coming-of-age stories.
9781630791056

LC 2018001840

Newspaper copyboy Victor Vollmer sets out from Memphis to spread the ashes of Mr. Spiro, his friend and mentor, at the mouth of the Mississippi River, and with the help of new friend Philomene he may meet the challenge.

Sequel to: *Paperboy*.

Venkatraman, Padma

The **bridge** home. Padma Venkatraman. Nancy Paulsen Books, 2019 208 p.
Grades: 5 6 7 8

1. Homeless children; 2. Familial love; 3. Runaways; 4. Poverty; 5. Homeless persons; 6. India; 7. Epistolary novels; 8. Realistic fiction.
9781524738112, HRD, US

LC 2018035686

ALA Notable Children's Books, 2020; Booklist Editors' Choice: Books for Youth, 2019; Golden Kite Award for Middle Grade/Young Reader Fiction, 2020; Notable Books for a Global Society, 2020.

Four determined homeless children make a life for themselves in Chennai, India.

An unforgettable tale of families lost, found, and moving ahead without leaving those they love behind. —*School Library Journal*

★ **Climbing** the stairs. Padma Venkatraman. G.P. Putnam's Sons, 2008 201p.
Grades: 6 7 8 9 10

1. Families; 2. Women's role; 3. Prejudice; 4. Brain injury; 5. Fifteen-year-old girls; 6. India; 7. British Raj (1858-1947); 8. 1940s; 9. Historical fiction.
9780399247460

LC 2007021757

Amelia Bloomer List, 2009; Booklist Editors' Choice: Books for Youth, 2008; YALSA Best Books for Young Adults, 2009.

In India, in 1941, when her father becomes brain-damaged in a non-violent protest march, fifteen-year-old Vidya and her family are forced to move in with her father's extended family and become accustomed to a totally different way of life.

Venkatraman paints an intricate and convincing backdrop of a conservative Brahmin home in a time of change.... The striking cover art...will draw readers to this vividly told story. —*Booklist*

★ A **time** to dance. Padma Venkatraman. Nancy Paulsen Books, an imprint of Penguin Group (USA) Inc, 2014 320 pages
Grades: 8 9 10 11 12

1. Dancers; 2. People who have had amputations; 3. Teenage girls with disabilities; 4. Teenage girl dancers; 5. Resilience (Personal quality); 6. India; 7. Chennai, India; 8. Novels in verse; 9. Realistic fiction
9780399257100

LC 2013024244

ALA Notable Children's Book, 2015; Booklist Editors' Choice: Books for Youth, 2014; YALSA Best Fiction for Young Adults, 2015; Notable Books for a Global Society, 2015.

In India, a girl who excels at Bharatanatyam dance refuses to give up after losing a leg in an accident.

This free-verse novel set in contemporary India stars Veda, a teenage Bharatanatyam dancer. After a tragic accident, one of Veda's legs must be amputated below the knee. Veda tries a series of customized prosthetic legs, determined to return to dancing as soon as possible. Brief lines, powerful images, and motifs of sound communicate Veda's struggle to accept her changed body. —*Horn Book Guide*

Verday, Jessica
Of monsters and madness. By Jessica Verday. Egmont USA, 2014 288 pages
Grades: 9 10 11 12
1. Children of scientists; 2. Murder; 3. Teenage romance; 4. Philadelphia, Pennsylvania; 5. 1820s; 6. 19th century; 7. Horror; 8. Gothic fiction
9781606844632; 9781606844649, ebook, US
LC 2014003140
In 1820s Philadelphia, a girl finds herself in the midst of a rash of gruesome murders in which her father and his alluring assistant might be implicated.

Vernick, Shirley Reva
The **blood** lie: a novel. By Shirley Reva Vernick. Cinco Puntos Press, 2011 224 p.
Grades: 5 6 7 8
1. Jewish teenage boys; 2. Antisemitism; 3. Prejudice; 4. Missing girls; 5. Crushes in teenage boys; 6. New York (State); 7. 1920s; 8. Historical fiction.
9781933693842
LC 2011011429
YALSA Best Fiction for Young Adults, 2012.
In 1928 in Massena, New York, Jewish sixteen-year-old Jack Pool, in love with his Christian neighbor, is accused of killling her little sister for a blood sacrifice.
Based on an actual incident in Massena in 1928, the slim novel effectively mines layers of ignorance, fear, intolerance and manipulation, and it connects the incident to Henry Ford's anti-Semitic writing and to the lynching of Jewish businessman Leo Frank in 1915. —*Kirkus*

Villasante, Alexandra
The **grief** keeper. Alexandra Villasante. G. P. Putnam's Sons, 2019 320 p.
Grades: 8 9 10 11 12
1. Undocumented immigrants; 2. Medical research; 3. Teenage girl/girl relations; 4. Grief; 5. Empathy; 6. Science fiction; 7. LGBTQIA fiction.
9780525514022
Lambda Literary Award for Children's/Young Adult, 2020.
Wanting to enjoy an amazing life in America like her favorite television characters, an undocumented 17-year-old bargains for her asylum by becoming a grief keeper to save someone else's life.
Villasante builds her novel about undocumented immigrants into a suspenseful story with credible relationships, satisfying character development, and elements of science fiction. —*Kirkus*

Vivian, Siobhan
The **list**. Siobhan Vivian. Scholastic, 2012 336 p.
Grades: 7 8 9 10 11 12
1. Beauty; 2. Ugliness; 3. Self-perception in teenage girls; 4. Self-perception; 5. Self-esteem in teenage girls; 6. Realistic fiction.
9780545169172
YALSA Best Fiction for Young Adults, 2013.

Enduring a cruel annual ritual through which an anonymous list is posted naming each grade's prettiest and ugliest girl, eight selected high school girls explore how they see themselves and each other.
Offering a well-differentiated cast of complex characters and a thoughtful focus on femininity, sisterhood, relationships, eating disorders, and what it means to be singled out, Vivian proves that beauty and ugliness aren't always a matter of appearance. —*Publishers Weekly*

Vizzini, Ned
★ **It's** kind of a funny story. By Ned Vizzini. Miramax Books/Hyperion Books For Children, 2006 448 p.
Grades: 9 10 11 12
1. Teenage boys with mental illnesses; 2. Depression; 3. Self-acceptance in teenage boys; 4. Teenage boys with depression; 5. Coping in teenage boys; 6. New York City; 7. Humorous stories; 8. Realistic fiction; 9. Books to movies
9780786851966; 9780786851973
LC 2005052670
YALSA Popular Paperbacks for Young Adults, 2017; YALSA Best Books for Young Adults, 2007.
A humorous account of a New York City teenager's battle with depression and his time spent in a psychiatric hospital.
What's terrific about the book is Craig's voiceintimate, real, funny, ironic, and one kids will come closer to hear. —*Booklist*

The **other** normals. Ned Vizzini. Balzer + Bray, 2012 400 p.
Grades: 8 9 10 11
1. Teenage boy misfits; 2. Growth (Psychology); 3. Summer camps; 4. Role playing games; 5. Kissing; 6. Urban fantasy
9780062079909
LC 2012014341
A boy is sent to camp to become a man—but ends up on a fantastical journey that will change his life forever.

Vlahos, Len
★ **Life** in a fishbowl. By Len Vlahos. Bloomsbury, 2017 336 p.
Grades: 7 8 9 10
1. Reality television programs; 2. Children of people with cancer; 3. Terminal illness; 4. Brain — Tumors; 5. Families; 6. Realistic fiction; 7. Multiple perspectives
9781681190358; 9781408870631, print, UK
LC 2016022364
Fifteen-year-old Jackie is determined to reclaim her family's privacy and dignity by ending a reality television program about her father's terminal brain tumor.
From page one, its evident that the ending will not be a happy one, but numerous laugh-out-loud moments and beautifully drawn characters make for a powerful journey that will leave a lasting imprint on readers. —*Publishers Weekly*

The **Scar** Boys: a novel. Len Vlahos. 2014 256 pages (Scar Boys, 1)
Grades: 9 10 11 12
1. People with disfigurements; 2. Burn victims; 3. Bands (Music); 4. Friendship; 5. Families; 6. New York (State); 7. 1980s; 8. Historical fiction; 9. First person narratives
9781606844397
LC 2013018265
YALSA Best Fiction for Young Adults, 2015; William C. Morris Debut Award finalist, 2015.
Written as a college admission essay, eighteen-year-old Harry Jones recounts a childhood defined by the hideous scars he hid behind, and how forming a band brought self-confidence, friendship, and his first kiss.

Harry's obsession with punk music will appeal to music lovers, while his journey to accept himself for who he is—scarred face and all—is one that will likely resonate with any teen trying to find his way in the world. —*Booklist*

Voigt, Cynthia

★ **Dicey's** song. Cynthia Voigt. Atheneum, 1982 196 p. (Tillerman family, 2)
Grades: 5 6 7 8
1. Abandoned children; 2. Grandmothers; 3. Teenage girls; 4. Tillerman family (Fictitious characters); 5. Brothers and sisters; 6. Classics; 7. Realistic fiction
9780689309441

LC 82003882
ALA Notable Children's Book, 1983; Newbery Medal, 1983.

Now that the four abandoned Tillerman children are settled in with their grandmother, Dicey must decide what she wants for her siblings and herself.

The vividness of Dicey is striking; Voigt has plumbed and probed her character inside out to fashion a memorable protagonist. —*Booklist*
Sequel to: *Homecoming*.

★ **Homecoming**. Atheneum, 1981 312 p. (Tillerman family, 1)
Grades: 6 7 8 9
1. Abandoned children; 2. Thirteen-year-old girls; 3. Survival; 4. Independence in teenage girls; 5. Tillerman family (Fictitious characters); 6. Realistic fiction; 7. Classics.
9780689308338

LC 80036723
Abandoned by their mother, four children begin to search for a home and an identity.

The characterizations of the children are original and intriguing, and there are a number of interesting minor characters encountered in their travels. —*School Library Journal*
Sequel: *Dicey's song*.

★ **Izzy,** willy-nilly. By Cynthia Voigt. Atheneum, 1986 258 p.
Grades: 7 8 9 10
1. Teenage girls who have had amputations; 2. Traffic accidents; 3. Teenagers with disabilities; 4. Girls who have had amputations; 5. Fifteen-year-old girls; 6. Coming-of-age stories.
9780689312021

LC 85022933
California Young Reader Medal, Young Adult, 1990; Virginia Readers' Choice Award for High School, 1988.

A car accident causes fifteen-year-old Izzy to lose one leg and face the need to start building a new life as an amputee.

Voigt shows unusual insight into the workings of a 15-year-old girl's mind.... Just as Voigt's perceptive empathy brings Izzy to life, other characterizations are memorable, whether of Izzy's shallow former friends or of her egocentric 10-year-old sister. *Publishers Weekly.* [review of 1986 edition]

★ A **solitary** blue. By Cynthia Voigt. Atheneum, 1983 189 p. (Tillerman family, 3)
Grades: 7 8 9 10
1. Children of divorced parents; 2. Fathers and sons; 3. Abandoned children; 4. Mother-deserted families; 5. Tillerman family (Fictitious characters); 6. Classics.
9780689310089

LC 83006007
ALA Notable Children's Book, 1984; Newbery Honor Book, 1984.

Jeff's mother, who deserted the family years before, reenters his life and widens the gap between Jeff and his father, a gap that only truth, love, and friendship can heal.

This is the most mature and sophisticated of Voigt's novels.... Beautifully knit...compelling and intelligent. —*Bulletin of the Center for Children's Books*

Volponi, Paul

Black and white. By Paul Volponi. Viking, 2005 160 p.
Grades: 7 8 9 10
1. Interracial friendship; 2. High school basketball players; 3. Criminal justice system; 4. Racism; 5. Juvenile delinquents; 6. Long Island, New York; 7. Realistic fiction; 8. Multiple perspectives; 9. First person narratives; 10. Books for reluctant readers
9780670060061

LC 2004024543
International Reading Association Children's Book Award for Young Adult Fiction, 2006; YALSA Quick Picks for Reluctant Young Adult Readers, 2006; YALSA Popular Paperbacks for Young Adults, 2008; YALSA Best Books for Young Adults, 2006.

Two star high school basketball players, one black and one white, experience the justice system differently after committing a crime together and getting caught.

These complex characters share a mutual respect and struggle with issues of loyalty, honesty, and courage. Social conflicts, basketball fervor, and tough personal choices make this title a gripping story. —*School Library Journal*

The **final** four. Paul Volponi. Viking, 2012 244 p;
Grades: 9 10 11 12
1. Basketball players; 2. College basketball; 3. African American teenage boys; 4. Basketball; 5. Personal conduct; 6. Sports fiction; 7. Basketball stories; 8. Books for reluctant readers
9780670012640

LC 2011011587
Booklist Editors' Choice: Books for Youth, 2012; YALSA Best Fiction for Young Adults, 2013; YALSA Quick Picks for Reluctant Young Adult Readers, 2013.

Four players at the Final Four of the NCAA basketball tournament struggle with the pressures of tournament play and the expectations of society at large.

★ **Homestretch**. Paul Volponi. Atheneum Books for Young Readers, 2009 160 p.
Grades: 6 7 8 9 10
1. Runaway boys; 2. Race tracks; 3. Undocumented immigrants; 4. Seventeen-year-old boys; 5. Teenage boys; 6. Arkansas; 7. Realistic fiction; 8. Coming-of-age stories.
9781416939870

LC 2008030024
Five months after losing his mother, seventeen-year-old Gas runs away from an abusive father and gets a job working at an Arkansas race track, surrounded by the illegal Mexican immigrants that he and his father blame for her death.

Volponi continues his streak of well-written novels in this simply written, coming-of-age story. —*Voice of Youth Advocates*

Hurricane song: a novel of New Orleans. Paul Volponi. Viking Juvenile, 2008 144 p.
Grades: 7 8 9 10 11 12
1. Fathers and sons; 2. Hurricanes; 3. Survival; 4. Family relationships; 5. Hurricane Katrina, 2005; 6. New Orleans, Louisiana; 7. Louisiana.
9780670061600

YALSA Popular Paperbacks for Young Adults, 2010.

A brilliant blend of reality and fiction, this novel hits every chord just right. —*Voice of Youth Advocates*

Rikers High. By Paul Volponi. Viking Childrens Books, 2010 256 p. Grades: 8 9 10 11 12

1. African American teenage boys; 2. Juvenile delinquency; 3. Teacher-student relationships; 4. Jails; 5. Teenage prisoners; 6. Rikers Island (N.Y.); 7. New York City; 8. Realistic fiction; 9. Books for reluctant readers
9780670011070

LC 2009022471

YALSA Popular Paperbacks for Young Adults, 2015; YALSA Quick Picks for Reluctant Young Adult Readers, 2011.

Arrested on a minor offense, a New York City teenager attends high school in the jail facility on Rikers Island, as he waits for his case to go to court.

The author draws authentic situations and characters from his six years of teaching at Rikers.... An absorbing portrait of life in the stir.... Rare is the reader who won't find his narrative sobering. —*Booklist*

Originally published in 2002 in slightly different form by Black Heron Press under title: *Rikers*.

Rucker Park setup. By Paul Volponi. Viking, 2007 149 p; Grades: 7 8 9 10 11 12

1. African American boys; 2. Basketball; 3. Murder; 4. Personal conduct; 5. Teenage boys; 6. Harlem, New York City; 7. Realistic fiction; 8. Basketball stories; 9. Books for reluctant readers
9780670061303

LC 2006028463

YALSA Quick Picks for Reluctant Young Adult Readers, 2008.

While playing in a crucial basketball game on the very court where his best friend was murdered, Mackey tries to come to terms with his own part in that murder and decide whether to maintain his silence or tell J.R.'s father and the police what really happened.

The author's description of playing pickup ball on one of the toughest courts in the world feels wholly authentic. The characters also feel real. —*Voice of Youth Advocates*

Vrettos, Adrienne Maria

★ **Sight**. Adrienne Maria Vrettos. Margaret K. McElderry Books, 2007 254 p;
Grades: 7 8 9 10

1. Sixteen-year-old girls; 2. Teenage girls; 3. Teenage psychics; 4. Psychics; 5. Teenagers; 6. Mysteries; 7. Books for reluctant readers
9781416906575

LC 2006035999

YALSA Quick Picks for Reluctant Young Adult Readers, 2008.

Sixteen-year-old Dylan uses her psychic abilities to help police solve crimes against children, but keeps her extracurricular activities secret from her friends at school.

Vrettos has created a creepy scenario with a taut plot and a gripping climax.... She has crafted a believable setting and characters. —*Bulletin of the Center for Children's Books*

Wagner, Laura Rose

Hold tight, don't let go. By Laura Rose Wagner. Amulet Books, 2015 240 p.
Grades: 9 10 11 12

1. Earthquakes; 2. Separated friends, relatives, etc; 3. Grief in teenage girls; 4. Grief; 5. Haiti Earthquake, Haiti, 2010; 6. Haiti; 7. Port-au-Prince, Haiti; 8. 2010s; 9. Realistic fiction.
9781419712043

LC 2014019622

YALSA Best Fiction for Young Adults, 2016.

In the aftermath of the 2010 earthquake in Haiti, Nadine goes to live with her father in Miami while her cousin Magdalie, raised as her sister, remains behind in a refugee camp, dreaming of joining Nadine but wondering if she must accept that her life and future are in Port-au-Prince.

Wagner breaks away from stereotypes of an abject Haiti, giving us complex characters who connect with and care for one another, economies that rebuild, and environments that recover. By the end, readers will be buoyed by the hopeful future the author imagines for Magdalie and for Haiti. —*Booklist*

Wakefield, Vikki

Friday never leaving. Vikki Wakefield. Simon and Schuster Books for Young Readers, 2013 256 p.
Grades: 9 10 11 12

1. Mother-separated teenage girls; 2. Homeless children; 3. Life change events; 4. Crime; 5. Mothers — Death; 6. Australia; 7. Australian fiction.
9781442486522; 9781921922701

Adelaide Festival Awards (South Australia), YA Fiction Award, 2014; Children's Book Council of Australia: Notable Australian Children's Book; CBCA Children's Book of the Year Awards Honour Book, 2013.

Friday Brown and her mother Vivienne live their lives on the road, but when Vivienne succumbs to cancer, 17-year-old Friday decides to search for the father she never knew. Her journey takes her to a slum of orphans and runaways, ruled by a charismatic leader named Arden

Australian author Wakefield spins a tense, multilayered tale about loyalty, memory and survival. —*Kirkus*

Walker, Brian F.

Black boy/white school. Brian F. Walker. HarperTeen, 2012 256 p. Grades: 9 10 11 12

1. African American teenage boys; 2. Ethnic identity; 3. Belonging; 4. Race relations; 5. Fourteen-year-old boys; 6. Maine; 7. Cleveland, Ohio; 8. Realistic fiction.
9780061914836

LC 2011016608

When fourteen-year-old Anthony "Ant" Jones from the ghetto of East Cleveland, Ohio, gets a scholarship to a prep school in Maine, he finds that he must change his image and adapt to a world that never fully accepts him, but when he goes home he discovers that he no longer truly belongs there either.

Wallace, Rich

One good punch. Rich Wallace. Alfred A. Knopf, 2007 114 p. Grades: 7 8 9 10 11 12

1. Track and field athletes; 2. Dilemmas; 3. Journalism; 4. Marijuana; 5. Friendship; 6. Pennsylvania; 7. First person narratives; 8. Realistic fiction.
9780375813528

YALSA Best Books for Young Adults, 2008.

Eigtheen-year-old Michael Kerrigan, writer of obituaries for the *Scranton Observer* and captain of the track team, is ready for the most important season of his life—until the police find four joints in his school locker, and he is faced with a choice that could change everything.

This novel's success is in creating a multidimensional male character in a format that will appeal to all readers. The moral dilemma...makes this novel ripe for ethical discussions. —*Voice of Youth Advocates*

Perpetual check. Rich Wallace. Alfred A. Knopf, 2009 112 p.

Grades: 8 9 10 11
1. Brothers; 2. Frustration; 3. Chess — Tournaments; 4. Competition; 5. Frustration in teenage boys; 6. Pennsylvania; 7. Realistic fiction; 8. Multiple perspectives
9780375840586
Frustrated with his younger, more geeky brother being the better athlete, better chess player, and the first one of the two to get a girlfriend, Zeke is determined to set the record straight when they come head-to-head in the final round of the regional chess competition.

Wallace cleverly positions Randy and Zeke for a win-win conclusion in this satisfying, engaging, and deceptively simple story. —*School Library Journal*

War and watermelon. Rich Wallace. Viking, 2011 184 p;
Grades: 6 7 8 9
1. Boy football players; 2. Brothers; 3. Fathers and sons; 4. Vietnam War, 1961-1975; 5. Woodstock Festival, 1969; 6. New Jersey; 7. 1960s; 8. Historical fiction; 9. First person narratives.
9780670011520

LC 2010041043
As the summer of 1969 turns to fall in their New Jersey town, twelve-year-old Brody plays football in his first year at junior high while his older brother's protest of the war in Vietnam causes tension with their father.

Sixties culture and events...are well integrated into the story, and humorous vignettes...help lighten the mood. —*Booklist*

★ **Wrestling** Sturbridge. Rich Wallace. Alfred A. Knopf, 1996 133 p.
Grades: 7 8 9 10
1. Teenage athletes; 2. Wrestling; 3. Frustration; 4. Frustration in teenage boys; 5. High school seniors; 6. Pennsylvania; 7. Sports fiction; 8. Realistic fiction; 9. Books for reluctant readers
9780679878032

LC 9520468
YALSA Best Books for Young Adults, 1997; YALSA Popular Paperbacks for Young Adults, 2008; YALSA Quick Picks for Reluctant Young Adult Readers, 1997.
Stuck in small town Sturbridge, Pennsylvania, where no one ever leaves, and relegated by his wrestling coach to sit on the bench while his best friend Al becomes state champion, Ben decides he can't let his last high school wrestling season slip by without challenging his friend and the future.

The wresting scenes are thrilling.... Like Ben, whose voice is so strong and clear here, Wallace weighs his words carefully, making every one count in this excellent, understated first novel. —*Booklist*

Wallach, Tommy
We all looked up. Tommy Wallach. 2015 384 pages
Grades: 9 10 11 12
1. Meteors; 2. Self-fulfillment; 3. High school seniors; 4. Self-fulfillment in teenagers; 5. Friendship; 6. Seattle, Washington; 7. Science fiction; 8. Multiple perspectives
9781481418775; 9781481418782

LC 2014004565
The lives of four high school seniors intersect weeks before a meteor is set to pass through Earth's orbit, with a 66.6% chance of striking and destroying all life on the planet.

Debut novelist Wallach increases the tension among characters throughout, ending in a shocking climax that resonates with religious symbolism. Stark scenes alternating between anarchy and police states are counterbalanced by deepening emotional ties and ethical dilemmas, creating a novel that asks far bigger questions than it answers. —*Publishers Weekly*

Wallenfels, Stephen
POD. By Stephen Wallenfels. Ace Books, 2012 292 p.
Grades: 7 8 9 10
1. Aliens; 2. Human/alien encounters; 3. Survival; 4. Fifteen-year-old boys; 5. Twelve-year-old girls; 6. Earth; 7. Science fiction; 8. Multiple perspectives
9781937007430
As alien spacecraft fill the sky and zap up any human being who dares to go outside, fifteen-year-old Josh and twelve-year-old Megs, living in different cities, describe what could be their last days on Earth.

The dire circumstances don't negate the humor, the hormones, or the humanity found in the young narrators. This is solid, straightforward sci-fi. —*Booklist*

Waller, Sharon Biggs
The **forbidden** orchid. Sharon Biggs Waller. Viking Children's Books, 2016 416 p.
Grades: 7 8 9 10 11 12
1. British in China; 2. Orchids; 3. Stowaways; 4. Teenage romance; 5. Adventure; 6. China; 7. England; 8. Victorian era (1837-1901); 9. 1860s; 10. Historical fiction
9780451474117
Historical details, including the liberal prescription of morphine and Britain's patriarchal economy, lend rich, textural background. Well-researched and filled with adventure, romance, and lots of tension this work of historical fiction has all the elements of an intriguing read. —*Kirkus*

Girls on the verge. Sharon Biggs Waller. Henry Holt and Company, 2019 320 p.
Grades: 9 10 11 12
1. Abortion; 2. Teenage pregnancy; 3. Friendship; 4. Pro-choice movement; 5. Reproductive rights; 6. Texas; 7. Realistic fiction; 8. Coming-of-age stories; 9. First person narratives.
9781250151698

LC 2018015681
Camille, seventeen, gives up her spot at a prestigious theater camp to drive from Texas to New Mexico to get an abortion, accompanied by her friends Annabelle and Bea.

A **mad,** wicked folly. Sharon Biggs Waller. Viking, published by the Penguin Group, 2014 384 pages
Grades: 8 9 10 11 12
1. Seventeen-year-old girls; 2. Gender role; 3. Teenage girls; 4. Teenage artists; 5. Nobility; 6. London, England; 7. Great Britain; 8. Edwardian era (1901-1914); 9. 1900s (Decade); 10. Historical fiction.
9780670014682

LC 2013029858
Amelia Bloomer List, 2015; YALSA Best Fiction for Young Adults, 2015.
In 1909 London, as the world of debutante balls and high society obligations closes in around her, seventeen-year-old Victoria must figure out just how much is she willing to sacrifice to pursue her dream of becoming an artist.

Victoria's dream of becoming an artist leads her naively into scandals, tempts her into a convenient marriage, and drives her to join the Women's Social and Political Union. Persistence eventually triumphs, and friendships, love, and art lessons are her rewards. Sound historical research provides the backbone for this warm novel about the development of women's opportunities in Edwardian London. —*Horn Book Guide*
Includes bibliographical references.

Walrath, Dana
★ **Like** water on stone. Dana Walrath. Delacorte Press, 2014 368 p.

Grades: 8 9 10 11 12

1. Twin brothers and sisters; 2. Armenian genocide, 1915-1923; 3. Armenians in Turkey — History; 4. Genocide; 5. Escapes; 6. Turkey; 7. 1910s; 8. Historical fiction; 9. Novels in verse
9780385743976
Notable Books for a Global Society, 2015; Middle East Book Award, Honorable Mention, 2015.

This beautiful, yet at times brutally vivid, historical verse novel will bring this horrifying, tragic period to life for astute, mature readers.... A cast of characters, and author note with historical background are thoughtfully included. —*School Library Journal*

Walsh, Alice

A **long** way from home. By Alice Walsh. Second Story Press, 2012 232 p.
Grades: 7 8 9 10

1. September 11 Terrorist Attacks, 2001; 2. Refugees; 3. Muslims; 4. Muslim teenagers; 5. Refugees, Afghan; 6. Newfoundland and Labrador; 7. Canadian fiction; 8. Multiple perspectives.
9781926920795

It is September 11, 2001. Rabia, her mother, and younger brother are on their way from Afghanistan to New York hoping to start a new life away from the brutal rule of the Taliban. On the same flight is Colin and his mother, returning home after a holiday. Rabia is worried about the future, and Colin is troubled by the prospect of his parents' impending divorce Their plane is diverted to Gander Newfoundland, where they are each taken under the wing of a Gander family and shown unexpected kindness and hope for the future.

Walsh, Jill Paton

A **parcel** of patterns. Jill Paton Walsh. Farrar Straus Giroux, 1983 136 p.
Grades: 7 8 9 10

1. Plague; 2. Eyam, England; 3. Great Britain; 4. Restoration England (1660-1688); 5. Stuart period (1603-1714); 6. Historical fiction
9780374357504

LC 83048143

Mall Percival tells how the plague came to her Derbyshire village of Eyam in the year 1665, how the villagers determined to isolate themselves to prevent further spread of the disease, and how three-fourths of them died before the end of the following year.

Walter, Jon

My name is not Friday. By Jon Walter. David Fickling Books/Scholastic Inc, 2016 368 p.
Grades: 7 8 9 10

1. Slavery; 2. African American teenage boys; 3. Separated brothers; 4. Brothers; 5. Teenage boy orphans; 6. United States; 7. American Civil War era (1861-1865); 8. Historical fiction; 9. Coming-of-age stories; 10. First person narratives
9780545855228

LC 2015035464

Samuel and his younger brother, Joshua, are free black boys living in an orphanage during the Civil War, but when Samuel takes the blame for his brother's prank, he is sent South, given a new name, and sold into slavery—and somehow he must survive both captivity and the war, to find his way back to his brother.

While readers on the young end of the age range and those unfamiliar with religious concepts may find the opening chapters somewhat confusing, Samuel's endearing, immersive narration makes the novel a fascinating and unforgettable account of a brutal and shameful chapter in America's history. A heartbreaking story about family, justice, and the resilience of the human spirit. —*Kirkus*

First published in the United Kingdom in 2015.

Walters, Eric

Broken strings. Eric Walters and Kathy Kacer. Puffin Books, 2019 288 p.
Grades: 5 6 7 8 9

1. Grandfather and granddaughter; 2. Jewish girls; 3. Music; 4. School plays; 5. September 11 Terrorist Attacks, 2001; 6. New York City; 7. 2000s (Decade); 8. Historical fiction; 9. Canadian fiction.
9780735266247

A tale that teaches both history and compassion; a great choice for middle grade readers. —*School Library Journal*

Walton, Julia

Words on bathroom walls. Julia Walton. 2017 304 p.
Grades: 7 8 9 10 11 12

1. Teenagers with schizophrenia; 2. Diary writing; 3. Schizophrenia; 4. Teenage boys; 5. Teenage boys with mental illnesses; 6. Realistic fiction; 7. Diary novels; 8. Books to movies
9780399550881; 9780399550911; 9780399550904, ebook, US
LC 2016017419
International Reading Association Children's Book Award for Young Adult Fiction, 2018; YALSA Best Fiction for Young Adults, 2018.

Adam is a recently diagnosed schizophrenic and journals to his therapist about family, friends, and first loves as he undergoes a new drug trial for the mental illness that allows him to keep his secret for only so long.

First-time author Walton creates a psychologically tense story with sympathetic characters while dispelling myths about a much-feared condition. —*Publishers Weekly*

Walton, Leslye J.

The **strange** and beautiful sorrows of Ava Lavender. Leslye Walton. 2014 320 p.
Grades: 9 10 11 12 Adult

1. Teenage girls; 2. Wings; 3. Love; 4. Immigrants; 5. Great-grandmothers; 6. Coming-of-age stories; 7. Magical realism
9780763665661; 9781406348088, print, UK
LC 2013946615
YALSA Best Fiction for Young Adults, 2015; William C. Morris Debut Award finalist, 2015.

Born with bird wings, Ava Lavender is well aware that love has long made fools of her family. When pious Nathaniel Sorrows mistakes her bird wings for angel wings, 16-year-old Ava faces the man's growing obsession, which comes to a head with the rain and feathers that fly through the air during a nighttime summer solstice celebration.

[T]here are many sorrows in Walton's debut, and most of them are Ava's through inheritance. Readers should prepare themselves for a tale where myth and reality, lust and love, the corporal and the ghostly, are interchangeable and surprising. —*Booklist*

Wang, Corrie

The **takedown**. Corrie Wang. 2017 384 pages
Grades: 7 8 9 10

1. Cyberbullying; 2. Near future; 3. Multiracial teenage girls; 4. Social media; 5. Popularity; 6. New York City; 7. Brooklyn, New York City; 8. Science fiction
9781484757420

LC 2016028339

YALSA Best Fiction for Young Adults, 2018.

When a faked sex tape goes viral, Kyla Cheng must delve into a world of hackers in an attempt to take it off the Internet and figure out who is trying to damage her reputation.

A thought-provoking, entertaining read, Wang's debut illustrates a future that is easily conceivable. —*Kirkus*

Ward, David
Beneath the mask. David Ward. Amulet Books, 2008 243 p. (Grassland trilogy, 2)
Grades: 7 8 9 10
1. Freedom; 2. Guilt; 3. Extortion; 4. Self-discovery in teenagers; 5. Guards; 6. First person narratives; 7. Coming-of-age stories; 8. Fantasy fiction
9780810970748; 9780439947718
This is an excellent continuation of a trilogy fraught with daring escapes, dangerous situations, and genuine characters. —*Voice of Youth Advocates*

Escape the mask. David Ward. Amulet Books, 2008 171 p; (Grassland trilogy, 1)
Grades: 7 8 9 10
1. Teenage kidnapping victims; 2. Forced labor; 3. Guards; 4. Masks; 5. Slavery; 6. First person narratives; 7. Coming-of-age stories; 8. Fantasy fiction
9780810994775; 9780439947565
Ward's novel bursts with action and is laden with tense scenes. His excellent descriptive writing allows the reader to visualize the action. In addition, Ward's fantasy world is so believable that the text almost reads as historical fiction. —*Voice of Youth Advocates*

Ward, Rachel
The **chaos**. Rachel Ward. Chicken House/Scholastic, 2011 352 p. (Numbers, 2)
Grades: 8 9 10 11 12
1. Teenage boy orphans; 2. Psychic ability; 3. Disasters; 4. Death; 5. Interpersonal relations; 6. London, England; 7. England; 8. Science fiction.
9780545242691; 9791022400244; 9789791022408; 9781906427306, print, UK
LC 2010018294
Like his mother, Jem, when sixteen-year-old Adam looks in people's eyes he can see the dates of their deaths and now he sees the same date, six months in the future, in nearly everyone around him in the London of 2026.

In this sequel to Numbers a fascinating premise is again worked out through gripping episodes and a lightly handled metaphysical dilemma. —*Horn Book Guide*

Infinity. Rachel Ward. Chicken House/Scholastic, 2012 256 p. (Numbers, 3)
Grades: 8 9 10 11 12
1. Psychic ability; 2. Dystopias; 3. Kidnapping; 4. Death; 5. Dating (Social customs); 6. London, England; 7. England; 8. Dystopian fiction; 9. Science fiction; 10. Multiple perspectives.
9780545350921; 9780545381918; 9781906427665, print, UK
LC 2011032709
Adam, Sarah, and Mia are living together, struggling with the fame brought about by their knowing the dates when people will die, but ever since Mia swapped her number for another, her new power makes her a target that puts them all in jeopardy.

★ **Num8ers**. Rachel Ward. Chicken House/Scholastic, 2010 336 p. (Numbers, 1)
Grades: 8 9 10 11 12

1. Foster teenagers; 2. Psychic ability; 3. Terrorism; 4. Bombings; 5. Death; 6. London, England; 7. England; 8. Science fiction.
9780545142991
LC 2008055440
YALSA Best Fiction for Young Adults, 2011; USBBY Outstanding International Book, 2011; School Library Journal Best Books, 2010.
Fifteen-year-old Jem knows when she looks at someone the exact date they will die, so she avoids relationships and tries to keep out of the way, but when she meets a boy named Spider and they plan a day out together, they become more involved than either of them had planned.

Ward's debut novel is gritty, bold, and utterly unique. Jem's isolation and pain, hidden beneath a veneer of toughness, are palpable, and the ending is a real shocker. —*School Library Journal*

Warman, Janice
The **world** beneath. Janice Warman. Candlewick Press, 2016 176 p.
Grades: 8 9 10 11
1. Apartheid; 2. Racism; 3. Anti-apartheid activists; 4. Fugitives; 5. Eleven-year-old boys; 6. South Africa; 7. 1970s; 8. Historical fiction
9780763678562; 9781406337167, print, UK
Children's Africana Book Awards Notable Book, Older Readers, 2017.
A good complement to nonfiction about apartheid South Africa, a little-explored place and period in children's literature. —*Kirkus*

Warman, Jessica
Between. Jessica Warman. Walker Books for Young Readers,, 2011 464 p.
Grades: 10 11 12
1. Drowning victims; 2. Rich teenage girls; 3. Life after death; 4. Dead; 5. Family problems; 6. Connecticut; 7. Supernatural mysteries
9780802721822; 9781405260480, print, UK
LC 2010040986
YALSA Best Fiction for Young Adults, 2012.
By weaving through her memories and watching the family and friends she left behind, eighteen-year-old Liz Valchar solves the mystery of how her life ended in the Long Island Sound.

Liz runs the gamut of strong emotion throughout this compelling backtrack of a short life punctuated by early grief, parental failings, and honest, flawed love; her journey offers insight into the effects all of these things can have on an ordinary life. —*Bulletin of the Center for Children's Books*

Wasserman, Robin
★ **Awakening**. Robin Wasserman. Scholastic, 2007 207 p. (Chasing yesterday, 1)
Grades: 6 7 8 9
1. Thirteen-year-old girls; 2. Teenage girls with amnesia; 3. People with amnesia; 4. Amnesia; 5. Nightmares; 6. Thrillers and suspense; 7. Books for reluctant readers
9780439933384
YALSA Quick Picks for Reluctant Young Adult Readers, 2008.
Thirteen-year-old J.D. struggles to understand who she is, where she came from, and why she has nightmares.

[Wasserman's] characters are well developed and believable, her plot is suspenseful, and her backgrounds...are nicely detailed. —*Voice of Youth Advocates*

The **book** of blood and shadow. By Robin Wasserman. Alfred A. Knopf, 2012 352 p.
Grades: 7 8 9

1. Secret societies; 2. Conspiracies; 3. Manuscripts; 4. Supernatural; 5. Murder; 6. Prague, Czech Republic; 7. New England; 8. Thrillers and suspense
9780375968761

LC 2011003920

YALSA Best Fiction for Young Adults, 2013; YALSA Popular Paperbacks for Young Adults, 2015.

While working on a project translating letters from sixteenth-century Prague, high school senior Nora Kane discovers her best friend murdered with her boyfriend the apparent killer and is caught up in a dangerous web of secret societies and shadowy conspirators, all searching for a mysterious ancient device purported to allow direct communication with God.

Skinned. Robin Wasserman. 2008 361 p; (Skinned trilogy (Robin Wasserman), 1)
Grades: 9 10 11 12
1. Brain — Transplantation; 2. Transplantation of organs, tissues, etc; 3. Biotechnology; 4. Seventeen-year-old girls; 5. Teenage girls; 6. Science fiction; 7. Teen chick lit
9781416936343

LC 2008015306

YALSA Popular Paperbacks for Young Adults, 2010.

To save her from dying in a horrible accident, Lia's wealthy parents transplant her brain into a mechanical body.

This is a captivating story that brings up many questions for teens, including how they fit in with their peers and what is their role in larger society. There are underlying themes as well such as suicide, free will, and what makes someone human. —*Library Media Connection*

Waters, Daniel

Generation dead. Daniel Waters. Hyperion, 2008 392 p. (Generation Dead, 1)
Grades: 7 8 9 10
1. Zombies; 2. Prejudice; 3. Supernatural; 4. Teenage romance; 5. Bullying and bullies; 6. Humorous stories; 7. Paranormal fiction
9781423109211

YALSA Popular Paperbacks for Young Adults, 2011.

When teenagers that die come back to life and are labeled "living impaired" or "differently biotic," they are integrated into the school population, but the living teens don't want them around.

This is a classic desegregation story that also skewers adult attempts to make teenagers play nice.... Motivational speakers, politically correct speech and encounter groups come in for special ridicule. New York Times Book Review.

Sequel: *Kiss of life.*

Waters, Zack C.

Blood moon rider. Zack C. Waters. Pineapple Press, 2006 126 p;
Grades: 5 6 7 8
1. Fathers — Death; 2. Orphans; 3. Grandfathers; 4. Grandfather and grandson; 5. Heroes and heroines; 6. Florida; 7. United States; 8. Second World War era (1939-1945); 9. Historical fiction.
9781561643509

LC 2005030749

After his father's death in World War II, fourteen-year-old Harley Wallace tries to join the Marines but is, instead, sent to live with his grandfather in Peru Landing, Florida, where he soon joins a covert effort to stop Nazis from destroying a secret airbase on Tampa Bay.

A colorful cast of characters and a nod to teenage romance help make this a good choice for middle school boys. —*School Library Journal*

Watkins, Steve

Great Falls. Steve Watkins. Candlewick Press, 2016 245 p.
Grades: 8 9 10 11
1. Post-traumatic stress disorder; 2. Brothers; 3. Veterans; 4. Canoeing; 5. Seventeen-year-old boys; 6. Virginia; 7. Realistic fiction
9780763671556

YALSA Quick Picks for Reluctant Young Adult Readers, 2017.

Watkins (*Juvie*) delivers a powerful, emotionally raw tale, heartbreaking in its portrayal of damaged veterans, the price some pay to serve, and the toll it takes on their friends and family. It's also a raw coming-of-age journey for Shane as he struggles with his own feelings, especially toward 'the Colonel,' the brothers emotionally abusive, micromanaging, ex-military stepfather. —*Publishers Weekly*

Juvie. Steve Watkins. Candlewick Press, 2013 311 p.
Grades: 9 10 11 12
1. Juvenile corrections; 2. Sisters; 3. Self-sacrifice; 4. Resentfulness; 5. Teenage girls; 6. Virginia; 7. Realistic fiction; 8. First person narratives; 9. Books for reluctant readers
9780763655099; 9781406358629, print, UK

YALSA Quick Picks for Reluctant Young Adult Readers, 2015; YALSA Quick Picks for Reluctant Young Adult Readers: Top Ten, 2015.

When seventeen-year-old Sadie and her sister, Carla, are caught participating (unintentionally) in a drug deal, Sadie takes the blame to protect her family; her punishment is a six-month sentence in a juvenile corrections facility. The novel is bleak and brutal—which, of course, is the point—making Sadie's loyalty to Carla and resolve to survive all the more powerful. —*Horn Book Guide*

Watson, Cristy

Benched. Cristy Watson. Orca Book Publishers, 2011 106 p.
Grades: 7 8 9 10 11 12
1. Gangs; 2. Bereavement in teenagers; 3. Stealing; 4. Brothers — Death; 5. Grief; 6. First person narratives; 7. Canadian fiction; 8. High interest-low vocabulary books
9781554694099; 9781554694082; 9781554694105

Cody and his friends are pressured into stealing a park bench, without realizing the serious consequences of their actions.

This Orca Currents title packs in a lot of issues for one small paperback, but reluctant readers, especially, will be hooked as the tension builds, and the realistic story, which avoids a slick resolution, will spark discussion. —*Booklist*

High interest story designed for reluctant readers or those reading below grade level.

Watson, Renee

★ **Piecing** me together. By Renee Watson. Bloomsbury, 2017 320 p.
Grades: 7 8 9 10 11 12
1. African American teenage girls; 2. Mentoring; 3. Private schools; 4. Schools; 5. Social classes; 6. Portland, Oregon; 7. Oregon; 8. Realistic fiction; 9. African American fiction
9781681191058

ALA Notable Children's Books, 2018; Amelia Bloomer List, 2018; Coretta Scott King Award, Author Category, 2018; Josette Frank Award, 2018; School Library Journal Best Books, 2017; YALSA Best Fiction for Young Adults, 2018; Jane Addams Children's Honor Book for Older Children, 2018; Newbery Honor Book, 2018.

A timely, nuanced, and unforgettable story about the power of art, community, and friendship. —*Kirkus*

This side of home. By Renee Watson. Bloomsbury, 2015 336 p.
Grades: 9 10 11 12

1. Neighborhoods; 2. African American teenage girls; 3. Urban renewal; 4. Twin sisters; 5. Best friends; 6. Portland, Oregon; 7. Realistic fiction; 8. Coming-of-age stories; 9. African American fiction

9781599906683; 9781619632134, ebook, US

LC 2014013743

Twins Nikki and Maya Younger always agreed on most things, but as they head into their senior year they react differently to the gentrification of their Portland, Oregon, neighborhood and the new—white—family that moves in after their best friend and her mother are evicted.

Readers may be surprised to find this multicultural story set in Portland, Oregon, but that just adds to its distinctive appeal. Here's hoping Watson's teen debut will be followed by many more. —*Kirkus*

Watch us rise. By Renee Watson and Ellen Hagan. Bloomsbury, 2019 368 p.

Grades: 7 8 9 10 11 12

1. Women's rights; 2. Student organizations; 3. Best friends; 4. Feminists; 5. Bloggers; 6. New York City; 7. Coming-of-age stories; 8. First person narratives; 9. Multiple perspectives

9781547600083; 9781526600868; 9781547600090, ebook, US

LC 2018045153

School Library Journal Best Books, 2019.

Jasmine and Chelsea are best friends on a mission. Sick of the way that young women are treated at their 'progressive' New York City high school, they decide to start a Women's Right's Club. One problem—no one shows up. That won't stop them though! SALS

Told from the viewpoints of Chelsea and Jasmine, this thought-provoking novel explores ideas of body-shaming, racial stereotypes, and gender inequality. —*School Library Journal*

Watts, Irene N.

★ **No** moon. Irene N. Watts. Tundra Books, 2010 234 p;

Grades: 6 7 8 9

1. Survival (after airplane accidents, shipwrecks, etc.); 2. Shipwrecks; 3. Nannies; 4. Social classes; 5. Voyages and travels; 6. Great Britain; 7. 1910s; 8. Historical fiction; 9. First person narratives; 10. Canadian fiction.

9780887769719

LC Bl2010010100

Nursemaid Louisa Gardener still blames herself for the drowning of her two-year-old brother almost ten years earlier, and so she dreads having to accompany the family she works for as they travel to New York on the *Titanic*.

Watts provides a fascinating account of what the great unsinkable ship was like. The catastrophe is rendered in a heartbreakingly graceful style.... [This is a] uniquely engaging and satisfying coming-of-age historical adventure. —*Booklist*

Weaver, Will

Defect. Will Weaver. Farrar, Straus and Giroux, 2007 208 p.

Grades: 7 8 9 10 11 12

1. Teenage boys; 2. Birth defects; 3. Self-acceptance; 4. Secrets; 5. Misfits (Persons); 6. Minnesota; 7. Fantasy fiction.

9780374317256

LC 2006049152

Minnesota Book Award for Young Adult Books, 2008.

After spending most of his life in Minnesota foster homes hiding a bizarre physical abnormality, fifteen-year-old David is offered a chance at normalcy, but must decide if giving up what makes him special is the right thing to do.

The author skillfully interweaves the improbable with twenty-first-century realities in this provocative novel of the ultimate cost of being so, so different. —*Voice of Youth Advocates*

Memory boy: a novel. By Will Weaver. Harper Collins Publishers, 2001 152 p.

Grades: 9 10 11 12

1. Sixteen-year-old boys; 2. Survival (after disaster); 3. Families; 4. Ecology; 5. Teenage boys; 6. Minnesota; 7. Apocalyptic fiction

9780060288112; 9780060288129

LC 32049

Sixteen-year-old Miles and his family must flee their Minneapolis home and begin a new life in the wilderness after a chain of cataclysmic volcanic explosions creates dangerous conditions in their city.

Sequel: *The survivors*.

Saturday night dirt. Will Weaver. Farrar, Straus and Giroux, 2008 163 p. : Illustration (Motor series, 1)

Grades: 8 9 10 11

1. Automobile racing; 2. Teenagers; 3. Small town life; 4. Automobile racing drivers; 5. Stock car drivers; 6. Minnesota; 7. Sports fiction; 8. Realistic fiction; 9. Books for reluctant readers

9780374350604

LC 2007006988

YALSA Quick Picks for Reluctant Young Adult Readers, 2009.

In a small town in northern Minnesota, the much-anticipated Saturday night dirt-track race at the old-fashioned, barely viable, Headwaters Speedway becomes, in many ways, an important life-changing event for all the participants on and off the track.

Weaver presents compelling character studies.... Young racing fans...will find much that rings true here. —*Booklist*

Webber, Katherine

The **heartbeats** of Wing Jones. Katherine Webber. Delacorte Press, 2017 336 p.

Grades: 7 8 9 10 11 12

1. Multiracial teenage girls; 2. Brothers and sisters; 3. Emotional problems; 4. Running; 5. Fatal traffic accidents; 6. Atlanta, Georgia; 7. Georgia; 8. 1990s; 9. Historical fiction; 10. Coming-of-age stories; 11. First person narratives

9780399555022; 9781406369090

LC 2016005580

Half-Chinese, half-black Wing Jones has always worshiped her older brother, but when he kills two people in a car accident and barely survives himself, Wing's only solace is running.

Written in Wing's believable first-person voice, the novel conveys the teen's perspective of the changing world around her as the plot moves quickly along. Recommend this to fans of Jandy Nelson's and Stephanie Perkins's books. —*School Library Journal*

Wees, Alyssa

The **waking** forest. Alyssa Wees. Delacorte Press, 2019 304 p.

Grades: 8 9 10 11 12

1. Dreams; 2. Witches; 3. Forests; 4. Visions; 5. Wishing and wishes; 6. Fantasy fiction; 7. Gothic fiction.

9780525581161

LC 2018022935

When the lives of a girl, who has terrifying visions, and a witch, who grants wishes to children in the woods, collide in the most unexpected of ways, a dark, magical truth threatens to doom them both.

Dreams and stories—their power to escape reality and to restore it—are in the bones of this masterfully woven fantasy debut. And at its heart? The power of revolution in the face of coldly violent injustice. —*Kirkus*

Wegelius, Jakob

★ The **murderer's** ape. Jakob Wegelius; translated from the Swedish by Peter Graves. Delacorte Press, 2017 608 p.
Grades: 7 8 9 10
1. Innocence (Law); 2. Gorillas; 3. Adventure; 4. Friendship; 5. Human-animal relationships; 6. Historical mysteries; 7. Stories told by animals; 8. Illustrated books
9781101931752; 9781782691617, print, UK; 9781782692027, trade paperback; 9781782691754, Paperback, UK
LC 2016010508
ALA Notable Children's Books, 2018; Booklist Editors' Choice: Books for Youth, 2017; Mildred L. Batchelder Award, 2018; USBBY Outstanding International Book, 2018; YALSA Best Fiction for Young Adults, 2018.

When her best friend, the sailor Henry Koskela, is falsely accused of murder, a gorilla named Sally Jones visits the run-down docks of Lisbon, embarks on a dizzying journey across the seven seas, and calls on the Maharaja of Bhapur's magnificent court—all in an attempt to clear Henry's name.

While the sheer length and thoughtful pace of Sally Jones journey might discourage some, those who persevere will have a richly imagined and thoroughly unique adventure in store. —*Booklist*

Translated from the Swedish.

Weil, Cynthia

I'm glad I did. Cynthia Weil. Soho Teen, 2015 272 p.
Grades: 8 9 10 11 12
1. Songwriters; 2. Music industry and trade; 3. Popular music; 4. Internship programs; 5. African Americans; 6. New York City; 7. 1960s; 8. Historical mysteries; 9. Coming-of-age stories.
9781616953560; 9781616953577, ebook, US
LC 2014025047
In 1963 sixteen-year-old JJ Green, a songwriter interning at New York City's famous Brill Building, finds herself a writing partner In Luke Silver, a boy who seems to connect instantly with her music, and they start cutting their first demo with Dulcie Brown, a legend who has fallen on hard times, with a secret past.

Grammy-winning songwriter Weil makes an impressive YA debut with this period novel set against the rapidly changing music industry of the early 1960s...[s]howing both the bright and the dark sides of the music business, Weil crafts an enticing tale of a sheltered teenagers induction into a world where ambitions and morals are repeatedly tested. —*Publishers Weekly*

Wein, Elizabeth

★ **Black** dove, white raven. Elizabeth Wein. 2015 368 pages
Grades: 8 9 10 11 12
1. Pilots; 2. Race relations; 3. Italo-Ethiopian War, 1935-1936; 4. Americans in Ethiopia; 5. Brothers and sisters; 6. Ethiopia; 7. 1930s; 8. Historical fiction
9781423183105; 9780385681889
LC 2014044446
Children's Africana Book Awards, Older Readers, 2016.

Rhoda who is white and Delia who is black are stunt pilots who perform daring acrobatics. Both women dream of living in a world free of racial discrimination. When Delia is killed in a tragic accident, Rhoda is determined to make that dream come true. She leaves the United States for Ethiopia with her daughter, Em, and Delia's son, Teo and all three fall in love with the beautiful, peaceful country. But peace is soon shattered with the threat of war with Italy, and Em and Teo are drawn into the conflict.

The intellectual, psychological, and emotional substance of this story is formidable, and Wein makes it all approachable and engaging. —*Horn Book Guide*

★ **Code** name Verity. Elizabeth Wein. Hyperion Books, 2012 343 p. (Code name Verity, 1)
Grades: 9 10 11 12
1. Women pilots; 2. Friendship; 3. World War II; 4. Courage in young women; 5. Torture; 6. Great Britain; 7. France; 8. Second World War era (1939-1945); 9. Historical fiction; 10. War stories.
9781423152194, hardback, US; 9781423152880, paperback, US; 9780385676540, hardback, Canada; 9781405258210, paperback, UK; 9781405278423, paperback, UK
LC 2011024857
Amelia Bloomer List, 2013; Booklist Editors' Choice: Books for Youth, 2012; Edgar Allan Poe Award for Best Young Adult, 2013; Notable Books for a Global Society, 2013; School Library Journal Best Books, 2012; USBBY Outstanding International Book, 2013; YALSA Best Fiction for Young Adults, 2013; YALSA Popular Paperbacks for Young Adults, 2014; Michael L. Printz Honor Book, 2013.

After crash-landing in France in 1943 and being captured by Nazis, a female wireless operator for the British (who goes by Queenie, Eva, Verity, and various other aliases) reveals bits of code in exchange for reprieve from torture...and to postpone her execution.

Wein balances the horrors of war against genuine heroics, delivering a well-researched and expertly crafted adventure. —*Publishers Weekly*
Companion book to: *Rose under fire*; Prequel: *The pearl thief.*

★ The **Enigma** game. Elizabeth Wein. Hyperion, 2020 448 p.
Grades: 7 8 9 10 11 12
1. Teenagers and war; 2. Codes (Communication); 3. World War II — Cryptography; 4. Enigma machine; 5. Intrigue; 6. Scotland; 7. Second World War era (1939-1945); 8. Historical fiction; 9. War stories; 10. Thrillers and suspense.
9781368012584, HRD, US; 9781368016513, ebook, US; 9781526601650, Paperback, UK; 9780735265288, paperback, Canada
LC 2019049235
Told in multiple voices, fifteen-year-old Jamaican Louisa Adair uncovers an Enigma machine in the small Scottish village where she cares for an elderly German woman, and helps solve a puzzle that could turn the tide of World War II.

Wein again seamlessly weaves extensive research into a thriller populated by fully dimensional characters. Late in the novel, Jamie's sister, Julie, makes a cameo as a newly minted intelligence officer, a poignant reminder to readers of Code Name Verity that the war will get much worse before it ends. —*Publishers Weekly*

★ The **pearl** thief. By Elizabeth Wein. Hyperion, 2017 304 p. (Code name Verity, Prequel)
Grades: 8 9 10 11
1. Missing persons; 2. Stealing; 3. Prejudice; 4. Friendship; 5. Summer; 6. Scotland; 7. 1930s; 8. Between the Wars (1918-1939); 9. Historical mysteries.
9781484717165; 9781408866610, print, UK
LC 2016041527
Fifteen-year-old Julia Beaufort-Stuart wakes up in a hospital not knowing how she was injured, and soon befriends Euan McEwen, the Scottish Traveller boy who found her, and later, when a body is discovered, she experiences the prejudices his family has endured and tries to keep them from being framed for the crime.

A finely crafted book that brings one girl's coming-of-age story to life, especially poignant for those who already know her fate. —*Booklist*
Prequel to: *Code name Verity*.

★ **Rose** under fire. Elizabeth Wein. Hyperion, 2013 368 p. (Code name Verity, 2)
Grades: 9 10 11 12
1. Women pilots; 2. Concentration camps; 3. World War II — Prisoners and prisons, German; 4. Prisoners of war, American; 5. Women prisoners of war; 6. Second World War era (1939-1945); 7. Historical fiction; 8. War stories; 9. Diary novels.
9781423183099; 9780385679534; 9781405265119; 9781405278416, print, UK

LC 2013010337
Josette Frank Award, 2014; School Library Journal Best Books, 2013; Schneider Family Book Award for Teens, 2014; USBBY Outstanding International Book, 2014; YALSA Best Fiction for Young Adults, 2014; YALSA Best Fiction for Young Adults: Top Ten, 2014.
Rose Justice is an American pilot with Britain's Air Transport Auxiliary during the Second World War. On her way back from a routine flight she is captured by the Germans and sent to Ravensbrück, a notorious concentration camp, where she meets an unforgettable group of women, and vows to tell her fellow prisoners' stories to the world.
Wein excels at weaving research seamlessly into narrative and has crafted another indelible story about friendship borne out of unimaginable adversity. —*Publishers Weekly*
Companion book to: *Code name Verity*.

Weis, Margaret
Mistress of dragons. Margaret Weis. Tor, 2003 381 p; (Dragonvarld trilogy, 1)
Grades: 11 12 Adult
1. Dragons; 2. Shapeshifters; 3. Humans; 4. Magic; 5. Secret societies; 6. Epic fantasy.
9780765304681

LC 2003042618
Here is a world where men and dragons coexist amid political intrigue and dark magic. The uneasy balance of power between the two is on the verge of coming undone, threatening to unleash waves of distruction that will pit humans against humans as well as dragons against men for the domination of the world.
Full of intrigue, magic, and violence, this first book of Dragonvarlda projected trilogy chronicling the battle to preserve the uneasy relationship between dragons and humanslaunches the project powerfully. Weis has brilliantly conceived a world viable for both dragons and humans. —*Booklist*
Sequel: *The dragon's son*.

Weissman, Elissa Brent
The **length** of a string. Elissa Brent Weissman. 2018 384 p.
Grades: 5 6 7 8
1. African American girls; 2. Adoption; 3. Identity (Psychology); 4. Jewish girls; 5. Twelve-year-old girls; 6. Baltimore, Maryland; 7. Realistic fiction; 8. First-person narratives
9780735229471; 9780735229495, ebook, US

LC 2017043498
Twelve-year-old Imani, the only black girl in Hebrew school, is preparing for her bat mitzvah and hoping to find her birthparents when she discovers the history of adoption in her own family through her great-grandma Anna's Holocaust-era diary.

Wells, Dan
Bluescreen: a Mirador novel. Dan Wells. Balzer & Bray, 2016 352 p. (Mirador, 1)
Grades: 7 8 9 10
1. Virtual reality; 2. Near future; 3. Drugs; 4. Hackers; 5. Hispanic Americans; 6. Los Angeles, California; 7. 21st century; 8. Science fiction; 9. Cyber-thrillers; 10. Science fiction thrillers.
9780062347879
Wells thrilling tale makes great use of its setting, and its diverse cast of characters is well suited for the futuristic L.A. demographic. Though it might hold special appeal for gamers, this is a great fit for readers who fancy noir thrillers and realistically flawed characters. —*Booklist*

Fragments. Dan Wells. Balzer + Bray, 2013 352 p. (Partials sequence, 2)
Grades: 9 10 11 12
1. Post-apocalypse; 2. Dystopias; 3. Identity (Psychology); 4. Survival; 5. Medical care; 6. Science fiction.
9780062071071

LC 2012038107
With the Help of Samm and Heron, Kira sets out on a desperate search for clues as to who she is, while Marcus and the remaining human population gear up for war with the Paritals.

Partials. Dan Wells. Balzer + Bray, 2012 470 p; (Partials sequence, 1)
Grades: 9 10 11 12
1. Post-apocalypse; 2. Sixteen-year-old girls; 3. Paramedics; 4. Dystopias; 5. Teenage girls; 6. 21st century; 7. Science fiction.
9780062071040

LC 2011042146
In a post-apocalyptic eastern seaboard ravaged by disease and war with a manmade race of people called Partials, the chance at a future rests in the hands of Kira Walker, a sixteen-year-old medic in training. —Provided by publisher.

Ruins. Dan Wells. Balzer + Bray, 2014 352 p. (Partials sequence, 3)
Grades: 9 10 11 12
1. Post-apocalypse; 2. Dystopias; 3. Identity (Psychology); 4. Survival; 5. Medical care; 6. Science fiction.
9780062071101; 9780007465248, print, UK
In the wake of one apocalypse, can humans and Partials, cloned supersoldiers, live together, or will the world end again? Kira Walker found a cure for the RM plague...Wells concludes his post-apocalyptic, action-packed trilogy with a literal bang and a lot of blood. Believable characters face tough moral choices, and though the end is tidy, the twists and treachery that get readers there are all the fun. It's enjoyable alone but best read after the first two. Science (fiction) at the end of the world done right. —*Kirkus*

Wells, Martha
All systems red. Martha Wells. Tor, 2017 144 p. (Murderbot diaries, 1)
Grades: 11 12 Adult
1. Androids; 2. Artificial intelligence; 3. Scientists; 4. High technology; 5. Robots; 6. Science fiction; 7. First person narratives; 8. Adult books for young adults.
9780765397539, paperback, US; 9781250214713, hardback, US; 9780765397522, ebook, US
Alex Award, 2018.
As a heartless killing machine, I was a terrible failure," confesses the AI narrator of this fast-paced SF adventure. After hacking its own governor module and overriding its programming, security droid "Murderbot" ends up saving lives instead of ending them—but only because letting all

the humans die would interfere with its favorite activity: binge-watching some 35,000 hours' worth of entertainment media. All Systems Red's snarky protagonist and suspenseful, action-packed plot should have readers eagerly anticipating future installments of the Murderbot Diaries.

Wells gives depth to a rousing but basically familiar action plot by turning it into the vehicle by which SecUnit engages with its own rigorously denied humanity. The creepy panopticon of SecUnits multiple interfaces allows a hybrid first-person/omniscient perspective that contextualizes its experience without ever giving center stage to the humans. —*Publishers Weekly*

Emilie & the hollow world. Martha Wells. Strange Chemistry, 2013 301 p;
Grades: 9 10 11 12
1. Runaway teenage girls; 2. Ships; 3. Father-separated teenage girls; 4. Missing persons; 5. Pirates; 6. Steampunk; 7. Fantasy fiction.
9781908844491
LC 2012277394
While trying to reach her cousin in the big city, Emilie stows away on a ship bound for the interior of the planet, where she befriends Lady Marlende, who is searching for her missing father, and makes challenging decisions to return them to the surface alive.
Sequel: *Emilie & the sky world.*

Wells, Rebecca Kim
Shatter the sky. Rebecca Kim Wells. 2019 304 p. (Shatter the sky, 1)
Grades: 8 9 10 11 12
1. Rescues; 2. Kidnapping; 3. Teenage girl/girl relations; 4. Dragons; 5. Secrets; 6. Fantasy fiction
9781534437906; 9781534437913
LC 2018046224
Maren, desperate to save her kidnapped girlfriend, plans to steal one of the emporer's dragons and storm the Aurati stronghold, but her success depends on becoming an apprentice to the emporor's mysterious dragon trainer, which proves to be a dangerous venture.
A girl seeks the help of a dragon to save her heartmate. Debut author Wells' beautiful prose and compelling protagonist will leave readers eager for the sequel. —*Kirkus*
Sequel: *Storm the earth.*

Wells, Robison E.
Variant. Robison Wells. HarperTeen, 2011 356 p. (Variant (Robison Wells), 1)
Grades: 7 8 9 10
1. Foster teenagers; 2. Survival; 3. Boarding schools; 4. Schools; 5. Interpersonal relations; 6. New Mexico; 7. Science fiction; 8. First person narratives; 9. Books for reluctant readers
9780062026088
LC 2010042661
Sunshine State Young Reader's Award (Florida), 2015; YALSA Quick Picks for Reluctant Young Adult Readers, 2012.
When Benson Fisher is accepted into Maxfield Academy, he's relieved to escape from the foster care system and excited to make a fresh start. But soon after the doors of the boarding school lock behind him, Benson realizes that he's made a huge mistake. Students at Maxfield are trapped, under constant surveillance, and at war with each other—and the punishment for rule-breakers is death.
Hard to put down from the very first page, this fast-paced novel with Stepford overtones answers only some of the questions it poses, holding some of the most tantalizing open for the next installment in a series that is anything but ordinary. —*Kirkus*
Sequel: *Feedback*

Wells, Rosemary
Red moon at Sharpsburg. Rosemary Wells. Viking, 2007 240 p.
Grades: 6 7 8 9 10
1. Teenage girls; 2. War; 3. Thirteen-year-old girls; 4. Neighbors; 5. Scientists; 6. United States; 7. 1860s
9780670036387
ALA Notable Children's Book, 2008; Booklist Editors' Choice: Books for Youth, 2007; School Library Journal Best Books, 2007.
Finding courage she never thought she had, a young Southern girl musters the strength and wit to survive the ravages of the Civil War and keep her family together through it all.
This powerful novel is unflinching in its depiction of war and the devastation it causes, yet shows the resilience and hope that can follow such a tragedy. India is a memorable, thoroughly believable character. —*School Library Journal*

Wen, Abigail Hing
Loveboat, Taipei. Abigail Hing Wen. HarperTeen, 2020 432 p.
Grades: 9 10 11 12
1. Chinese American teenage girls; 2. Summer camps; 3. Self-discovery; 4. Love triangles; 5. Teenage romance; 6. Taipei; 7. Taiwan; 8. Coming-of-age stories; 9. Teen chick lit; 10. Realistic fiction.
9780062957276
Ever Wong's summer takes an unexpected turn: gone is Chien Tan, the strict educational program in Taiwan that Ever was expecting. In its place, she finds Loveboat: a summer-long free-for-all where hookups abound, adults turn a blind eye, snake-blood sake flows abundantly, and the nightlife runs nonstop.
Between hookups, glamour photo shoots, and camp classes, Wen addresses a number of hot-button issues for many Asian Americans, the foremost being the struggle to reconcile immigrant parents' expectations with personal aspirations. —*Kirkus*

Wendig, Chuck
Under the Empyrean sky. Chuck Wendig. Skyscape/Amazon Publishing, 2013 354 p. (Heartland trilogy (Chuck Wendig), 1)
Grades: 7 8 9 10
1. Post-apocalypse; 2. Dystopias; 3. Agriculture; 4. Resistance to government; 5. End of the world; 6. Dystopian fiction; 7. Science fiction.
9781477817209
Cael McAvoy, living in the corn-overrun Heartland below extravagant sky flotillas, grows tired of scavenging and living in the Empyrean Empire's shadow and vows to do something to change his lot in life.
This strong first installment rises above the usual dystopian fare thanks to Wendig's knack for disturbing imagery and scorching prose. —*Publishers Weekly*

Werlin, Nancy
★ **Double** helix. Nancy Werlin. Dial Books, 2004 252 p;
Grades: 7 8 9 10
1. Genetic engineering; 2. Bioethics; 3. People with Huntington's disease; 4. Huntington's disease; 5. Eighteen-year-old men; 6. Thrillers and suspense
9780803726062
LC 2003012269
Booklist Editors' Choice: Books for Youth, 2004; YALSA Best Books for Young Adults, 2005; School Library Journal Best Books, 2004.
Eighteen-year-old Eli discovers a shocking secret about his life and his family while working for a Nobel Prize-winning scientist whose specialty is genetic engineering.

Werlin clearly and dramatically raises fundamental bioethical issues for teens to ponder. She also creates a riveting story with sharply etched characters and complex relationships that will stick with readers long after the book is closed. —*School Library Journal*

★ **Extraordinary**. By Nancy Werlin. Dial Books for Young Readers, 2010 256 p. (Impossible series)
Grades: 8 9 10 11 12
1. Fairies; 2. Promises; 3. Self-esteem in teenage girls; 4. Self-esteem; 5. Secrets; 6. Fantasy fiction.
9780803733725

LC 2010002086
Phoebe, a member of the wealthy Rothschilds family, befriends Mallory, an awkward new girl in school, and the two become as close as sisters, but Phoebe does not know that Mallory is a faerie, sent to the human world to trap the ordinary human girl into fulfilling a promise made by her ancestor Mayer to the queen of the faeries.

The carefully nuanced, often sensual prose delivers a highly effective narrative. Characterizations are arresting and complex. —*School Library Journal*

Characters from *Extraordinary* are featured in *Unthinkable*.

Impossible: a novel. Nancy Werlin. Dial Books, 2008 384 p. (Impossible series, 1)
Grades: 7 8 9 10
1. Pregnant teenagers; 2. Curses; 3. Riddles; 4. Magic; 5. Elves; 6. Fantasy fiction.
9780803730021

LC 2008006633
Booklist Editors' Choice: Books for Youth, 2008; School Library Journal Best Books, 2008; YALSA Best Books for Young Adults, 2009; YALSA Popular Paperbacks for Young Adults, 2010.

When seventeen-year-old Lucy discovers her family is under an ancient curse by an evil Elfin Knight, she realizes to break the curse she must perform three impossible tasks before her daughter is born in order to save them both.

Werlin earns high marks for the tale's graceful interplay between wild magic and contemporary reality. —*Booklist*

Sequel: *Unthinkable*.

★ The **killer's** cousin. Nancy Werlin. Delacorte Press, 1998 229 p.
Grades: 7 8 9 10
1. Guilt in teenage boys; 2. Emotional problems of girls; 3. Secrets; 4. Dysfunctional families; 5. Seventeen-year-old boys; 6. Massachusetts; 7. Cambridge, Massachusetts; 8. Psychological suspense; 9. Books for reluctant readers
9780385325608

LC 98012950
Black-Eyed Susan Book Award (Maryland), High School, 2001; Garden State Teen Book Award (New Jersey), Fiction (Grades 9-12), 2001; Edgar Allan Poe Award for Best Young Adult Mystery Novel, 1999; YALSA Quick Picks for Reluctant Young Adult Readers, 1999; Booklist Editors' Choice: Books for Youth, 1998; YALSA Popular Paperbacks for Young Adults, 2011; YALSA Best Books for Young Adults, 1999.

After being acquitted of murder, seventeen-year-old David goes to stay with relatives in Cambridge, Massachusetts, where he finds himself forced to face his past as he learns more about his strange young cousin Lily.

Teens will find this tautly plotted thriller, rich in complex, finely drawn characters, an absolute page-turner. —*Booklist*

★ The **rules** of survival. Nancy Werlin. Dial Books, 2006 272 p.
Grades: 8 9 10 11 12

1. Child abuse; 2. Mothers with mental illnesses; 3. Fear in children; 4. Seventeen-year-old boys; 5. Teenage boys; 6. Thrillers and suspense; 7. Realistic fiction; 8. Books for reluctant readers
9780803730014

LC 2006001675
School Library Journal Best Books, 2006; YALSA Best Books for Young Adults, 2007; YALSA Quick Picks for Reluctant Young Adult Readers, 2007; YALSA Popular Paperbacks for Young Adults, 2010; National Book Award for Young People's Literature finalist, 2006.

Seventeen-year-old Matthew recounts his attempts, starting at a young age, to free himself and his sisters from the grip of their emotionally and physically abusive mother.

The author tackles the topic of child abuse with grace and insight.... Teens will empathize with these siblings and the secrets they keep in this psychological horror story. —*School Library Journal*

West, Hannah
The **bitterwine** oath. By Hannah West. Penguin Distribution Childrens 2020 320 p.
Grades: 9 10 11 12
1. Curses; 2. Female friendship; 3. Supernatural; 4. Change; 5. Second chances; 6. Texas; 7. Gothic fiction; 8. Teen chick lit
9780823445479

LC 2019055102
Can eighteen-year-old Natalie and her great-great-grandmother's magical sisterhood end the cycle of violence in Natalie's small Texas town?

This fun, chilling, and sincere gothic novel keeps its head—and its heart. —*Publishers Weekly*

West, Kasie
Pivot point. Kasie West. HarperTeen, 2013 320 p.
Grades: 7 8 9 10
1. Children of divorced parents; 2. Options, alternatives, choices; 3. Teenage romance; 4. Decision-making; 5. Murder; 6. Paranormal romances
9780062117373

LC 2012019089
YALSA Best Fiction for Young Adults, 2014.

A girl with the power to search alternate futures lives out six weeks of two different lives in alternating chapters. Both futures hold the potential for love and loss, and ultimately she is forced to choose which fate she is willing to live through.

Both love interests are developed well, and readers will be able to see Addie with either. The worldbuilding isn't as on point—the Compound raises logistical questions that are glossed over for the sake of the plot's strong pace. Minor missteps are easy to forgive given the underlying suspense of multiple mysteries. West's debut showcases riveting storytelling. —*Kirkus*

Sequel: *Split second*.

Split second. Kasie West. HarperTeen, an imprint of HarperCollinsPublishers, 2014 320 p.
Grades: 7 8 9 10
1. Memory; 2. Psychic ability; 3. Options, alternatives, choices; 4. Teenage romance; 5. High schools; 6. Paranormal romances; 7. Multiple perspectives
9780062117380

In this follow-up to *Pivot Point* (HarperCollins, 2013), Addie leaves the Compound after a bad breakup. As a Searcher, Addie can see two possible futures, and she finds it hard to believe this is the one she chose, the one in which she is betrayed by her best friend and her boyfriend... In this fast-paced fantasy, the plot is slow to begin but takes off after the first few chapters. Recommended for readers who love dystopian stories with a bit of romance. —*School Library Journal*

Sequel: *Pivot point.*

Westerfeld, Scott

Afterworlds. By Scott Westerfeld. 2014 608 pages
Grades: 9 10 11 12

1. Authors; 2. East Indian Americans; 3. Near-death experience; 4. Writing; 5. Life after death; 6. New York City; 7. Realistic fiction; 8. Paranormal romances; 9. Coming-of-age stories.
9781481422345; 9780143572046, print, Australia
LC 2014006852
Rainbow List, 2015; YALSA Best Fiction for Young Adults, 2015.

In alternating chapters, eighteen-year-old Darcy Patel navigates the New York City publishing world and Lizzie, the heroine of Darcy's novel, slips into the "Afterworld" to survive a terrorist attack and becomes a spirit guide, as both face many challenges and both fall in love.

Readers who pay attention will see how Darcy's learning curve plays out and how she incorporates and transmutes her real-world experiences into her novel. Watching Darcy's story play off Darcy's novel will fascinate readers as well as writers. —*Kirkus*

Behemoth. Written by Scott Westerfeld; illustrated by Keith Thompson. Simon Pulse, 2010 496 p. (Leviathan trilogy, 2)
Grades: 7 8 9 10

1. Princes; 2. Teenagers and war; 3. Genetically engineered animals; 4. Warships; 5. Genetic engineering; 6. 1910s; 7. Steampunk; 8. Alternative histories; 9. Science fiction.
9781416971757; 9781847386779, print, UK; 9781847386755, print, UK
Children's Book Council of Australia: Notable Australian Children's Book.

Continues the story of Austrian Prince Alek who, in an alternate 1914 Europe, eludes the Germans by traveling in the Leviathan to Constantinople, where he faces a whole new kind of genetically-engineered warships.

This exciting and inventive tale of military conflict and wildly reimagined history should captivate a wide range of readers. Thompson's evocative and detailed spot art (as well as the luridly gorgeous endpapers) only sweetens the deal. —*Publishers Weekly*

Extras. Scott Westerfeld. Simon & Schuster, 2007 417 p. (Uglies, 4)
Grades: 7 8 9 10

1. Teenage rebels; 2. Fame; 3. Dystopias; 4. Beauty; 5. Image; 6. Dystopian fiction; 7. Science fiction.
9781416951179; 9781471116407, UK; 9781847389220, print, UK
LC 2007928439
New York Times Notable Children's Book, 2007.

Aya is an extra (face rank stuck in the mid-400,000s) in a city run on a reputation economy. If Aya can win fame as a kicker, reporting with her trusty hovercam on a story that captures the city's imagination, her face rank will soar.... Westerfeld shows he has a finger on the pulse of our reputation economy, alchemizing the cult of celebrity, advertising's constant competition for consumer attention. —*Horn Book Guide*

Companion to the Uglies series.

Goliath. Written by Scott Westerfeld; illustrated by Keith Thompson. Simon Pulse, 2011 432 p. (Leviathan trilogy, 3)
Grades: 7 8 9 10

1. Princes; 2. Teenagers and war; 3. World War I; 4. Warships; 5. Genetically engineered animals; 6. 1910s; 7. Steampunk; 8. Alternative histories; 9. Science fiction
9781416971771; 9781847386786, print, UK
Children's Book Council of Australia: Notable Australian Children's Book.

Alek and Deryn are on the last leg of their round-the-world quest to end World War I, reclaim Alek's throne as prince of Austria, and finally fall in love.

The alternative-history steampunk extravaganza that began with *Leviathan* (2009) ends with this third volume, and it does not disappoint. Westerfeld propels the story to a satisfying close.... Once again, Thompson's evocative art enlivens the narrative. —*Booklist*

★ **Leviathan.** By Scott Westerfeld; illustrated by Keith Thompson. Simon Pulse, 2009 440 p. (Leviathan trilogy, 1)
Grades: 7 8 9 10

1. Princes; 2. Teenagers and war; 3. Genetic engineering; 4. Conspiracies; 5. Genetically engineered animals; 6. 1910s; 7. Steampunk; 8. Alternative histories; 9. Science fiction
9781416971733; 9780143206088, Australia; 9781847386748, print, UK
LC 2009000881
Goodreads Choice Award, 2009; Locus Young Adult Book Award, 2010; Westchester Fiction Award, 2010; ALA Notable Children's Book, 2010; YALSA Popular Paperbacks for Young Adults, 2011; YALSA Best Books for Young Adults, 2010; School Library Journal Best Books, 2009.

In an alternate 1914 Europe, fifteen-year-old Austrian Prince Alek, on the run from the Clanker Powers who are attempting to take over the globe using mechanical machinery, forms an uneasy alliance with Deryn who, disguised as a boy to join the British Air Service, is learning to fly genetically-engineered beasts.

The protagonists' stories are equally gripping and keep the story moving, and Thompson's detail-rich panels bring Westerfeld's unusual creations to life. —*Publishers Weekly*

★ **Peeps:** a novel. By Scott Westerfeld. Razorbill, 2005 312 p.
Grades: 9 10 11 12

1. Vampires; 2. Parasites; 3. Sexually transmitted diseases; 4. College students; 5. Nineteen-year-old men; 6. New York City; 7. Science fiction; 8. Horror; 9. First person narratives.
9781595140319
LC 2005008151
School Library Journal Best Books, 2005; YALSA Best Books for Young Adults, 2006.

Cal Thompson is a carrier of a parasite that causes vampirism, and must hunt down all of the girlfriends he has unknowingly infected.

This innovative and original vampire story, full of engaging characters and just enough horror without any gore, will appeal to a wide audience. —*School Library Journal*

Sequel: *The last days*

★ **Pretties.** Scott Westerfeld. Simon Pulse, 2005 370 p. (Uglies, 2)
Grades: 7 8 9 10

1. Self-perception in teenage girls; 2. Dystopias; 3. Transformations, Personal; 4. Plastic surgery; 5. Beauty; 6. Dystopian fiction; 7. Science fiction.
9780689865398; 9780857079145, UK; 9781471184895, Paperback, UK
LC 2004118120
Riveting and compulsively readable, this action-packed sequel does not disappoint. —*Booklist*

Specials. Scott Westerfeld. Simon Pulse, 2006 372 p. (Uglies, 3)
Grades: 7 8 9 10

1. Teenage nonconformists; 2. Brainwashing; 3. Dystopias; 4. Image; 5. Teenage boy/girl relations; 6. Dystopian fiction; 7. Science fiction.
9780689865404; 9780857079152, UK; 9781847389084, print, UK
LC 2005933890

Readers who enjoyed *Uglies* and *Pretties*...will not want to miss *Specials*.... Westerfeld's themes include vanity, environmental conservation, Utopian idealism, fascism, violence, and love. —*School Library Journal*

★ **Uglies**. Scott Westerfeld. Simon Pulse, 2005 448 p. (Uglies, 1)
Grades: 7 8 9 10
1. Moles (Spies); 2. Plastic surgery; 3. Dystopias; 4. Rebels; 5. Image; 6. Dystopian fiction; 7. Science fiction.
9780689865381; 9781471144929, print, UK; 9780857079138, UK; 9781471181443, Paperback, UK; 9781847389060, print, UK
LC 2004106866
Abraham Lincoln Illinois High School Book Award, 2007; Eliot Rosewater Indiana High School Book Award (Rosie Award), 2007; Garden State Teen Book Award (New Jersey), Fiction (Grades 6-8), 2008; Golden Duck Awards, Hal Clement Award for Young Adult; Virginia Readers' Choice Award for High School, 2008; YALSA Popular Paperbacks for Young Adults, 2016; YALSA Best Books for Young Adults, 2006; School Library Journal Best Books, 2005.

Just before their sixteenth birthdays, when they will be transformed into beauties whose only job is to have a great time, Tally's best friend runs away and Tally must find her and turn her in, or never become pretty at all.

Fifteen-year-old Tally's eerily harmonious, postapocalyptic society gives extreme makeovers to teens on their sixteenth birthdays.... When a top-secret agency threatens to leave Tally ugly forever unless she spies on runaway teens, she agrees to infiltrate the Smoke, a shadowy colony of refugees from the tyranny of physical perfection. —*Booklist*

Zeroes. 2015 400 p. (Zeroes, 1)
Grades: 8 9 10 11
1. Teenage superheroes; 2. Misfits (Persons); 3. Rescues; 4. Superheroes; 5. Teenagers; 6. California; 7. Superhero stories; 8. Science fiction; 9. Multiple perspectives
9781481443364; 9781471124891, print, UK; 9781471124907, ebook; 9781925266955, print, Australia; 9781760528317, Paperback, Australia; 9781481443388, ebook, US
LC 2015001667
Told from separate viewpoints, teens Scam, Crash, Flicker, Anonymous, Bellwether, and Kelsie, all born in the year 2000 and living in Cambria, California, have superhuman abilities that give them interesting but not heroic lives until they must work as a community to respond to a high stakes crisis.

A powerful tale with an emotional rawness that will resonate with readers. —*Booklist*

Weston, Carol
Speed of life. Carol Weston. Sourcebooks Jabberwocky, 2017 352 p.
Grades: 7 8 9 10
1. Grief; 2. Children and single parent dating; 3. First loves; 4. Multiracial teenage girls; 5. Advice columnists; 6. New York City; 7. Realistic fiction
9781492654490
YALSA Best Fiction for Young Adults, 2018.

In this book, by Carol Weston, "Sofi a lost her mother eight months ago, and her friends were 100% there for her. Now it's a new year and they're ready for Sofi a to move on. Problem is, Sofi a can't bounce back, can't recharge like a cellphone. She decides to write Dear Kate, an advice columnist for *Fifteen Magazine*, and is surprised to receive a fast reply. Soon the two are exchanging emails, and Sofi a opens up and spills all." —Publisher's note

Westrick, Anne
Brotherhood. Anne Westrick. Viking Juvenile, 2013 368 p.

Grades: 5 6 7 8 9
1. Race relations; 2. Loyalty; 3. Prejudice; 4. Dyslexia; 5. Schools; 6. Virginia; 7. Richmond, Virginia; 8. 1860s; 9. Historical fiction.
9780670014392
LC 2013008272
Jefferson Cup Award for Older Readers, 2014; YALSA Best Fiction for Young Adults, 2014.

The year is 1867, and the South has lost the Civil War. Those on the lowest rungs, like Shad's family, fear that the freed slaves will take the few jobs available. In this climate of despair and fear, a group has formed. Today we know it as the KKK.

Wexler, Django
Ship of smoke and steel. Django Wexler. Tor Teen, 2019 368 p. (Wells of Sorcery, 1)
Grades: 9 10 11 12
1. Ghosts; 2. Ship captains; 3. Teenage girls; 4. Ocean travel; 5. Voyages and travels; 6. High fantasy; 7. Fantasy fiction; 8. First person narratives
9780765397249; 9780765397263, ebook, US
LC 2018044553
Isoka, an eighteen-year-old ward boss in the great port city, Kahnzoka, is sent on an impossible mission to steal Soliton, a legendary ghost ship, or her sister will be killed.

In his YA debut, Wexler (*Fall of the Readers*) delivers an atmospheric adventure that expertly mixes visceral action sequences, a compelling mystery, a diverse cast, and vividly described settings. —*Publishers Weekly*
A Tom Doherty Associates Book.

Weymouth, Laura E.
The **light** between worlds. Laura E. Weymouth. HarperTeen, an imprint of HarperCollins Publishers, 2018 368 p.
Grades: 8 9 10 11 12
1. Sisters; 2. Missing women; 3. Parallel universes; 4. Home (Concept); 5. Healing — Psychological aspects; 6. London, England; 7. Second World War era (1939-1945); 8. 1950s; 9. Historical fantasy; 10. Gateway fantasy; 11. Multiple perspectives
9780062696878; 9780062696885; 9781911490036, Paperback, UK
Six years ago, when sisters Evelyn and Philippa Hapwell cowered from air strikes in a London bomb shelter, they were swept away to a strange and beautiful kingdom called the Woodlands, where they lived for years in a forest out of myth and legend. When they returned to their lives in post-WWII England, no time had passed and nothing had changed—except themselves. Now Evelyn is desperate to return, while Philippa just wants to move on. But when Ev goes missing, Philippa must confront the depth of her sister's despair and the painful truths they've been running from.

Weyn, Suzanne
Distant waves: a novel of the Titanic. Suzanne Weyn. Scholastic Press, 2009 330 p;
Grades: 8 9 10 11
1. Tesla, Nikola; 2. Time travel; 3. Spiritualists; 4. Sisters; 5. Disasters; 6. Mothers and daughters; 7. New York (State); 8. London, England; 9. 1910s; 10. Science fiction
9780545085724
LC 2008040708
In the early twentieth century, five sisters and their widowed mother, a famed spiritualist, travel from New York to London, and as the *Titanic* conveys them and their acquaintances, journalist W.T. Stead, scientist

Nikola Tesla, and industrialist John Jacob Astor, home, Tesla's inventions will either doom or save them all.

The interplay of science, spirituality, history and romance will satisfy. —*Publishers Weekly*

Empty. Suzanne Weyn. Scholastic Press, 2010 183 p;
Grades: 7 8 9 10
1. Oil supply; 2. Near future; 3. Abandoned teenagers; 4. Renewable energy sources; 5. Social change; 6. Science fiction.
9780545172783

LC 2010016743

When, just ten years in the future, oil supplies run out and global warming leads to devastating storms, senior high school classmates Tom, Niki, Gwen, Hector, and Brock realize that the world as they know it is ending and lead the way to a more environmentally-friendly society.

The realistic and thought-provoking scenario is packaged into a speedy read, and given the popularity of dystopian fiction, it should find an audience. —*Booklist*

Recruited. Suzanne Weyn. Darby Creek, 2011 104 p; (Surviving Southside)
Grades: 7 8 9 10
1. High school football players; 2. African American teenage boys; 3. Student athletes — Recruiting; 4. Ethics; 5. Football; 6. Urban fiction; 7. High interest-low vocabulary books
9780761361671

LC 2010023662

Kadeem Jones is a star quarterback for Southside High. He is thrilled when college scouts seek him out. His visit to Teller College is amazing, but then NCAA officials accuse Teller's staff of illegally recruiting top talent. Will Kadeem decide to help their investigation, even though it means the end of the good times' What will it do to his chances of playing college football?

Kadeem is ecstatic when scouts shower him with gifts, dinners, and parties and he realizes that his dream of playing college football may be coming true. His happiness quickly turns to dread, though, as he learns that the incentives offered to him are violations of recruitment policy.... [This] well-written [story reinforces] the importance of family, friends, values, and thoughtful decision-making.... [An] excellent [purchase, this book] will attract and engage reluctant readers. —*School Library Journal*

Summary adapted from p. [4] of cover; High interest story designed for reluctant readers or those reading below grade level.

Reincarnation. Suzanne Weyn. Scholastic Press, 2008 416 p.
Grades: 7 8 9 10
1. Reincarnation; 2. Space and time; 3. Men/women relations; 4. Love; 5. Fantasy fiction
9780545013239

LC 2007008743

When a young couple dies in prehistoric times, their love—and link to various green stones—endures through the ages as they are reborn into new bodies and somehow find a way to connect.

Readers with a romantic bent will be drawn to this story, which pushes the notion of eternal love to its limits: two spirits find each other again and again, at different moments in history. —*Publishers Weekly*

Whaley, John Corey
Highly illogical behavior. John Corey Whaley. 2016 256 pages
Grades: 9 10 11 12
1. Teenage boys with mental illnesses; 2. Gay teenagers; 3. Agoraphobia; 4. Panic attacks; 5. Friendship; 6. Realistic fiction; 7. Multiple perspectives
9780525428183

LC 2015025530

School Library Journal Best Books, 2016; YALSA Best Fiction for Young Adults, 2017; YALSA Quick Picks for Reluctant Young Adult Readers, 2017; Rainbow List, 2017.

Agoraphobic sixteen-year-old Solomon has not left his house in three years, but Lisa is determined to change that—and to write a scholarship-winning essay based on the results.

What looks like a typical friendship story is blended with issues of trust, vulnerability, and identity. Solomon's agoraphobia is not the only thing that defines him, which speaks to the larger message about those living with mental illness. Each character has an authentic voice and temperament that feel realistic, and the alternating narratives capture the perspective of the bright, witty, and decidedly quirky protagonists. The spare writing makes this a taut, tender, and appealing read. —*School Library Journal*

Noggin. John Corey Whaley. 2014 340 pages
Grades: 9 10 11 12
1. Self-awareness in teenagers; 2. Identity (Psychology); 3. Former girlfriends; 4. Closeted gay teenagers; 5. Interpersonal relations; 6. Missouri; 7. Science fiction; 8. First person narratives.
9781442458727; 9781442458734

LC 2013020137

Westchester Fiction Award, 2015; YALSA Best Fiction for Young Adults, 2015; YALSA Best Fiction for Young Adults: Top Ten, 2015; National Book Award for Young People's Literature finalist, 2014.

After dying at age sixteen, Travis Coates' head was removed and frozen for five years before being attached to another body, and now the old Travis and the new must find a way to coexist while figuring out changes in his relationships.

Whaley's sophomore effort eschews the complicated narrative structure of *Where Things Come Back* for a more straightforward one; and the premise isn't the most original, with variations ranging from Peter Dickinson's classic *Eva* (rev. 7/89) to Mary Pearson's recent Jenna Fox trilogy. But readers will find it easy to become invested in Travis's second coming-of age—brimming with humor, pathos, and angst—and root for him to make peace with his new life. —*Horn Book Guide*

★ **Where** things come back. John Corey Whaley. Atheneum Books for Young Readers, 2011 240 p.
Grades: 9 10 11 12
1. Extinct birds; 2. Missing teenage boys; 3. Christian missionaries; 4. Woodpeckers; 5. Drugs — Overdose; 6. Arkansas; 7. Realistic fiction.
9781442413337; 9781442413344; 9781471125331, print, UK

LC 2010024836

Michael L. Printz Award, 2012; William C. Morris YA Debut Award, 2012; YALSA Best Fiction for Young Adults, 2012.

Seventeen-year-old Cullen's summer in Lily, Arkansas, is marked by his cousin's death by overdose, an alleged spotting of a woodpecker thought to be extinct, failed romances, and his younger brother's sudden disappearance.

The realistic characters and fascinating mix of mundane with life changing and tragic events create a memorable story most young adult readers will connect to. —*Library Media Connection*

Wheeler, Thomas
Cursed. Written by Thomas Wheeler; illustrated by Frank Miller. Simon & Schuster 2019 416 p.
Grades: 9 10 11 12
1. Arthur; 2. Druids and druidism; 3. Swords; 4. Mercenaries; 5. Quests; 6. Lady of the Lake; 7. Arthurian fantasy; 8. Fantasy fiction; 9. Illustrated books.
9781534425330; 9781534477339; 9780241376621, Paperback, UK

This collaboration by beloved comics-creator Miller and Empire series creator/producer Wheeler will be getting an extra promotional push from Netflix on top of royal treatment from the publisher. —*Booklist*

Whelan, Gloria

All my noble dreams and then what happens. Gloria Whelan. Simon & Schuster Books for Young Readers, 2013 224 p.
Grades: 6 7 8 9 10
1. Windsor, Edward, Duke of, 1894-1972; 2. Children of military personnel; 3. British in India; 4. National liberation movements; 5. Families; 6. Teenage girls; 7. India; 8. London, England; 9. British Raj (1858-1947); 10. 1920s; 11. Historical fiction; 12. First person narratives
9781442449763

LC 2012018599

As Rosalind continues to straddle the proper English world of her family and the culture of 1920s India where they live, her support of Gandhi and his followers in opposing British rule grows and she considers trying to carry the rebels' message to Edward, Prince of Wales, during his visit.

A Paula Wiseman Book.

Chu Ju's house. By Gloria Whelan. Harper Collins, 2004 240 p.
Grades: 5 6 7 8
1. Independence in teenage girls; 2. Runaways; 3. Gender role; 4. Fourteen year-old girls; 5. Teenage girls; 6. China
9780060507244; 9780060507251

LC 2003006979

Amelia Bloomer List, 2005.

In order to save her baby sister, fourteen-year-old Chu Ju leaves her rural home in modern China and earns food and shelter by working on a sampan, tending silk worms, and planting rice seedlings, while wondering if she will ever see her family again.

Whelan tells a compelling adventure story, filled with rich cultural detail, about a smart, likable teenage girl who overcomes society's gender restrictions. —*Booklist*

Includes glossary.

★ **Homeless** bird. Gloria Whelan. Harper Collins, 2000 216 p.
Grades: 6 7 8 9 10
1. Homeless teenagers; 2. Abandoned teenagers; 3. Self-sufficiency; 4. Independence in teenage girls; 5. Thirteen-year-old girls; 6. India; 7. Coming-of-age stories.
9780060284541

LC 9933241

ALA Notable Children's Book, 2001; Booklist Editors' Choice: Books for Youth, 2000; National Book Award for Young People's Literature, 2000; School Library Journal Best Books, 2000; YALSA Best Books for Young Adults, 2001.

Kali discovers that the husband her parents have chosen for her is sickly.

This beautifully told, inspiring story takes readers on a fascinating journey through modern India and the universal intricacies of a young woman's heart. —*Booklist*

Small acts of amazing courage. Gloria Whelan. Simon & Schuster Books for Young Readers, 2011 160 p.
Grades: 6 7 8 9 10
1. Independence in teenage girls; 2. Children of military personnel; 3. Independence (Personal quality); 4. Aunts; 5. British in India; 6. India; 7. London, England; 8. British Raj (1858-1947); 9. 1910s; 10. Historical fiction.
9781442409316

LC 2010013164

Amelia Bloomer List, 2012.

In 1919, independent-minded fifteen-year-old Rosalind lives in India with her English parents, and when they fear she has fallen in with some rebellious types who believe in Indian self-government, she is sent "home" to London, where she has never been before and where her older brother died, to stay with her two aunts.

Whelan balances the facts with distinctive, sometimes comical characterizations and vibrant, original sensory descriptions.... Whelan's vibrant, episodic story explores the tension between doing what's right, rather than what's expected, and the infinite complexities of colonialism. —*Booklist*

A Paula Wiseman Book.

Whipple, Natalie

House of ivy and sorrow. Natalie Whipple. HarperTeen, an imprint of HarperCollinsPublishers, 2014 352 p.
Grades: 8 9 10 11 12
1. Witches; 2. Curses; 3. Black magic; 4. Witchcraft; 5. Grandmothers; 6. Iowa; 7. Urban fantasy
9780062120182

Josephine, 17, lives with her grandmother in a house under the interstate where it's rumored that an old witch can make someone love you if you're willing to give her your pinkie finger. Jo knows that the rumors are true, because her grandmother is that witch...This is a fast-paced fantasy, with just the right amount of romance and realism. Readers will relate to Jo's relationships with her family, crush, and two best friends. Despite the current glut of supernatural and urban fantasy, this tale will stand out. —*School Library Journal*

Whitaker, Alecia

The **queen** of Kentucky. By Alecia Whitaker. Little, Brown, 2011 384 p.
Grades: 7 8 9 10
1. Rural teenagers; 2. Popularity; 3. Crushes in teenage girls; 4. Children of alcoholic fathers; 5. Farm life; 6. Kentucky; 7. Realistic fiction; 8. Coming-of-age stories; 9. First person narratives.
9780316125062

LC 2010045840

Fourteen-year-old Ricki Jo, a Kentucky farm girl, learns that popularity is not all she hoped it would be when the huge changes she makes in her personality and style seem to do more to drive away old friends than to win new ones.

This is familiar territory, but Whitaker's setting is fresh, and readers from rural areas will recognize the class differences.... Ericka's first-person voice is sassy and quite believable as she tries to figure out who she is and who everybody else is, too. —*Booklist*

Whitcomb, Laura

★ A **certain** slant of light. By Laura Whitcomb. Graphia, 2005 282 p;
Grades: 9 10 11 12
1. Spirit possession; 2. Immortality; 3. First loves; 4. Young women; 5. Teenage boys; 6. Fantasy fiction; 7. First person narratives; 8. Ghost stories.
9780618585328

LC 2004027208

YALSA Popular Paperbacks for Young Adults, 2009; YALSA Best Books for Young Adults, 2006.

Although Helen died 130 years ago, her spirit is still bound to the earthly plane—and she has "cleaved" to one human host after another, watching the world around her but not really participating in it. Currently, Helen observes the world through the body of a high school English teacher, and one day, she is startled to realize that one of the teacher's students can see her within the host!

The author creatively pulls together a dramatic and compelling plot that cleverly grants rebellious teen romance a timeless grandeur. —*Bulletin of the Center for Children's Books*

Under the light: a novel. By Laura Whitcomb. Houghton Mifflin, Houghton Mifflin Harcourt, 2013 256 p.
Grades: 9 10 11 12
1. Ghosts; 2. Spirit possession; 3. Romantic love; 4. Life after death; 5. Memories; 6. Paranormal fiction
9780547367545
LC 2012033303
Helen needed a body to be with her beloved and Jenny needed to escape from hers before her spirit was broken. It was wicked, borrowing it, but love drives even the gentlest soul to desperate acts.
Companion book to: *A certain slant of light*.

White, Amy Brecount
Forget-her-nots. Amy Brecount White. Harpercollins Childrens Books, 2010 384 p.
Grades: 7 8 9 10
1. Grief in teenage girls; 2. Mothers — Death; 3. Flowers; 4. Teenage girls; 5. Flower arrangement.
9780061672989
A delicate sense of magical possibility and reverence for the natural world help elevate White's story from a typical prep-school drama into something more memorable. —*Publishers Weekly*

White, Andrea
Surviving Antarctica: reality TV 2083. Andrea White. Eos, 2005 327 p;
Grades: 7 8 9 10
1. Scott, Robert Falcon; 2. Fourteen-year-olds; 3. Teenagers; 4. Explorers; 5. Cold; 6. Voyages and travels; 7. Antarctica; 8. 21st century
9780060554545; 9780060554552
LC 2004006249
In the year 2083, five fourteen-year-olds who were deprived by chance of the opportunity to continue their educations reenact Scott's 1910-1913 expedition to the South Pole as contestants on a reality television show, secretly aided by a Department of Entertainment employee.
A real page-turner, this novel will give readers pause as they ponder the ethics of teens risking their lives in adult-contrived situations for the entertainment of the masses. —*Booklist*
Includes bibliographical references (p. 325).

Window boy. Andrea White. Bright Sky Press, 2008 255 p;
Grades: 6 7 8 9
1. Churchill, Winston, 1874-1965; 2. Cerebral palsy; 3. Imaginary playmates; 4. Nurses; 5. People with disabilities — Education; 6. First day of school; 7. 1960s; 8. Historical fiction
9781933979144
LC 2008000492
After his mother finally convinces the principal of Greenfield Junior High to admit him, twelve-year-old Sam arrives for his first day of school, along with his imaginary friend Winston Churchill, who encourages him to persevere with his cerebral palsy.
Strong character development is combined with an accurate representation of the lack of educational opportunities for those who were physically and mentally disabled pre-IDEA. —*School Library Journal*

White, Ellen Emerson
Long may she reign. Ellen Emerson White. Feiwel and Friends, 2007 708 p; (President's daughter series, 4)
Grades: 6 7 8 9 10
1. Children of presidents; 2. Post-traumatic stress disorder; 3. Women college students; 4. Forgiveness; 5. United States
9780312367671
LC 2007032635
Meg Powers, daughter of the president of the United States, is recovering from a brutal kidnapping, and in an effort to deal with her horrific experience and her anger at her mother—the president—for not negotiating for her release, Meg decides to go away for her second semester of college, where she encounters even more challenges.
The hip dialogue will hook teens.... Beneath its chick-lit veneer, this book is a thought-provoking read. —*Voice of Youth Advocates*

The **president's** daughter. Ellen Emerson White. Feiwel & Friends, 2008 304 p; (President's daughter series, 1)
Grades: 7 8 9 10
1. Children of presidents; 2. Sixteen year old girls; 3. Life change events; 4. Daughters; 5. United States
9780312374884; 9781930709249
Besides offering a solid look at the political system, this [book] has very strong characterizations. —*Booklist*
Book one in the President's Daughter series

White House autumn. Ellen Emerson White. Feiwel & Friends, 2008 343 p; (President's daughter series, 2)
Grades: 7 8 9 10
1. Seventeen year old girls; 2. Mass media; 3. Attempted assassination; 4. High school seniors; 5. Teenage girls; 6. United States; 7. Washington, D.C.
9780312374891; 9781930709256
The President's teenage daughter is a victim of kidnapping by terrorists.
Apart from its novelistic merits, the book prompts thought on the burdens of public office, the need for character in the elect and their families. —*Publishers Weekly*
Book Two in the The President's Daughter series.

White, Kiersten
And I darken. Kiersten White. 2016 496 pages (Conquerors saga (Kiersten White), 1)
Grades: 9 10 11 12
1. Princesses; 2. Hostages; 3. Brothers and sisters; 4. Gender role; 5. Teenage girls; 6. Turkey; 7. Transylvania, Romania; 8. 15th century; 9. Historical fiction.
9780553522310; 9780553522327; 9780552573740, print, UK
LC 2015020681
Rainbow List, 2017.
In this first book in a trilogy a girl child is born to Vlad Dracula, in Transylvania, in 1435—at first rejected by her father and always ignored by her mother, she will grow up to be Lada Dragwlya, a vicious and brutal princess, destined to rule and destroy her enemies.

The **dark** descent of Elizabeth Frankenstein. Kiersten White. 2018 304 p.
Grades: 9 10 11 12
1. Adopted teenage girls; 2. Scientists; 3. Characters and characteristics in literature; 4. Teenage girls; 5. Adoptive families; 6. Gothic fiction; 7. Classics-inspired fiction; 8. Historical fiction
9780525577973; 9780525577942
LC 2017037621

Bram Stoker Awards, Best Young Adult Novel, 2018; YALSA Best Fiction for Young Adults, 2019.

The events of Mary Shelley's *Frankenstein* unfold from the perspective of Elizabeth Lavenza, who is adopted as a child by the Frankensteins as a companion for their volatile son Victor.

Endlessly. Kiersten White. HarperTeen, 2012 400 p. (Paranormalcy trilogy, 3)
Grades: 8 9 10 11 12
1. Fairies; 2. Prophecies; 3. Resourcefulness in teenage girls; 4. Resourcefulness; 5. Gates; 6. Virginia; 7. Urban fantasy; 8. Paranormal romances.
9780061985881; 9780007390175, print, UK
LC 2011042117
Sixteen-year-old Evie is forced to face the truth about her supernatural past when a deadly faerie battle threatens the future of the entire paranormal world.

The **Guinevere** deception. Kiersten White. Delacorte Press, 2019 352 p. (Camelot rising (Kiersten White), 1)
Grades: 7 8 9 10 11 12
1. Arthur; 2. Knights and knighthood; 3. Women wizards; 4. Changelings; 5. Impostors; 6. Magic; 7. Arthurian fantasy; 8. Fantasy fiction; 9. Fairy tale and folklore-inspired fiction
9780525581673; 9780525581680
Deadly jousts, duplicitous knights, and forbidden romances are nothing compared to the greatest threat of all: the girl with the long black hair, riding on horseback through the dark woods toward Arthur. Because when your whole existence is a lie, how can you trust even yourself?

More diverse than many Camelot representations, this is a retelling designed for a modern audience more interested in people than battles and more intrigued by identity and affection than honor and questing. —*Kirkus*

Illusions of fate. Kiersten White. HarperTeen, an imprint of HarperCollinsPublishers, 2014 288 pages
Grades: 9 10 11 12
1. Boarding schools; 2. Social classes; 3. Misfits (Persons); 4. Schools; 5. Magic; 6. Fantasy fiction; 7. First person narratives
9780062135896
LC 2014010021
An outcast since moving from her island home of Melei to the dreary country of Albion, Jessamin meets the gorgeous, enigmatic Finn who introduces her to the secret world of Albion's nobility—a world of power, money, status, and magic—but Finn has a powerful enemy who only Jessamin can stop.

★ **Now** I rise. Kiersten White. 2017 480 pages (Conquerors saga (Kiersten White), 2)
Grades: 10 11 12
1. Princesses; 2. Espionage; 3. Sieges; 4. Rulers; 5. Brothers and sisters; 6. Transylvania, Romania; 7. Turkey; 8. 15th century; 9. Historical fiction; 10. Multiple perspectives
9780553522358; 9780553522365
LC 2016038757
A sequel to the best-selling *And I Darken* finds a vengeful Lada striking out at anyone who stands in her way and finding herself unexpectedly rejected by her skillful brother, Radu, who reluctantly works as a spy for a power-hungry Mehmed.

In this sequel to *And I Darken*, White continues to weave a dramatic tapestry of espionage, passion, and conquest. —*School Library Journal*

Paranormalcy. Kiersten White. HarperTeen, 2010 335 p; (Paranormalcy trilogy, 1)
Grades: 7 8 9 10 11 12
1. Prophecies; 2. Fairies; 3. Shapeshifters; 4. Supernatural; 5. Identity (Psychology); 6. Urban fantasy; 7. Paranormal romances.
9780061985843
LC 9780061985843 (trade bdg.)
Evie, the only known human with the ability to see through supernatural "glamours," works for the International Paranormal Containment Agency (IPCA) tracking down dangerous creatures. (Really, she finds the work dull and would rather be shopping, watching TV, or at the very least at home painting her weapons pink.) But when a mysterious shape-shifter invades the IPCA and brings news of a string of paranormal murders, things start to heat up.

White shows the technique and polish of a pro in this absorbing romance, which comes closer than most to hitting the Buffy mark.... The action is fast; fun and fear are in abundance; and Lend's father is actually a cool grownup. —*Publishers Weekly*

Supernaturally. Kiersten White. HarperTeen, 2011 320 p. (Paranormalcy trilogy, 2)
Grades: 7 8 9 10
1. Fairies; 2. Vampires; 3. Prophecies; 4. Shapeshifters; 5. Supernatural; 6. Urban fantasy; 7. Paranormal romances.
9780061985867
LC 2010040426
Sixteen-year-old Evie thinks she has left the International Paranormal Containment Agency, and her own paranormal activities, behind her when she is recruited to help at the Agency, where she discovers more about the dark faerie prophecy that threatens her future.

Evie's voice is the best part of the story, as she balances her supernatural abilities against typical teen concerns and obsessions. —*Kirkus*

Whitley, David
The **children** of the lost. David Whitley. Roaring Brook Press, 2011 320 p. (Agora trilogy, 2)
Grades: 7 8 9 10
1. Dystopias; 2. Exile (Punishment); 3. City-states; 4. Villages; 5. Dreams; 6. Dystopian fiction; 7. Fantasy fiction.
9781596436145
LC 2010028112
Banished from Agora, the ancient city-state where absolutely everything must be bartered, Mark and Lily are happy to find the apparently perfect land of Giseth except that the inhabitants seem fearful, something strange lurks in the surrounding forest, and a mysterious woman keeps appearing in their dreams urging them to find the children of the lost.

This explores tantalizing new territory and solidifies the Agora Trilogy as one of the more literary ambitious and complex fantasies going. —*Booklist*

The **midnight** charter. David Whitley. Roaring Brook Press, 2009 240 p. (Agora trilogy, 1)
Grades: 7 8 9 10
1. Elitism; 2. Child slaves; 3. Free enterprise; 4. Dystopias; 5. City-states; 6. Dystopian fiction; 7. Fantasy fiction.
9781596433816
Deft world-building and crafty plotting combine for a zinger of an ending that will leave readers poised for book two. Surprisingly sophisticated upper-middle-grade fare, with enough meat to satisfy older readers as well. —*Kirkus*

Whitman, Emily
Wildwing. Emily Whitman. Greenwillow Books, 2010 359 p;
Grades: 7 8 9 10
1. Teenage girl household employees; 2. Time travel (Past); 3. Social classes; 4. Mistaken identity; 5. Falconers; 6. Great Britain; 7.

Medieval period (476-1492); 8. 13th century; 9. Fantasy fiction; 10. First person narratives.
9780061724527

LC 2009044189

Leslie Bradshaw Award for Young Adult Literature (Oregon), 2012.

In 1913 London, fifteen-year-old Addy is a lowly servant, but when she gets inside an elevator car in her employer's study, she is suddenly transported to a castle in 1240 and discovers that she is mistaken for the lord's intended bride.

Whitman populates both of her worlds with vivid, believable characters.... This historical novel with a time-travel twist of sci-fi will find an avid readership. —*School Library Journal*

Whitney, Daisy

The **Mockingbirds**. Daisy Whitney. Little, Brown, 2010 352 p. (The Mockingbirds, 1)
Grades: 10 11 12
1. Teenage rape victims; 2. Date rape; 3. Secret societies; 4. Justice; 5. Sisters; 6. Realistic fiction; 7. First person narratives.
9780316090537

LC 2009051257

Amelia Bloomer List, 2012; YALSA Popular Paperbacks for Young Adults, 2013; YALSA Best Fiction for Young Adults, 2011.

When Alex, a junior at an elite preparatory school, realizes that she may have been the victim of date rape, she confides in her roommates and sister who convince her to seek help from a secret society, the Mockingbirds.

Authentic and illuminating, this strong...[title] explores vital teen topics of sex and violence; crime and punishment; ineffectual authority; and the immeasurable, healing influence of friendship and love. —*Booklist*

When you were here. By Daisy Whitney. Little, Brown and Company, 2013 272 p.
Grades: 7 8 9 10
1. Grief in teenage boys; 2. Children of people with cancer; 3. Mothers and sons; 4. Loss (Psychology); 5. Breaking up (Interpersonal relations); 6. Tokyo, Japan; 7. Los Angeles, California; 8. Realistic fiction; 9. Coming-of-age stories.
9780316209748

LC 2012031409

When his mother dies three weeks before his high school graduation, Danny goes to Tokyo, where his mother had been going for cancer treatments, to learn about the city his mother loved and, with the help of his friends, come to terms with her death.

Danny's mother has recently died from cancer, his father died years ago, his estranged sister lives in China, and he and Holland, the love of his life, have broken up. A trip to Japan is enlightening and helps him handle a shocking secret he learns about Holland. The extent of Danny's problems stretches credulity, but readers will be caught up in the drama. —*Horn Book Guide*

Whitney, Kim Ablon

The **perfect** distance: a novel. Kim Ablon Whitney. Alfred A. Knopf, 2005 246 p;
Grades: 9 10 11 12
1. Mexican American women; 2. Mexican American teenage girls; 3. Teenage girls — Personal conduct; 4. Teenage girls — Interpersonal relations; 5. Teenage girls and horses; 6. Coming-of-age stories
9780375832437; 9780375932434

LC 2005040726

While competing in the three junior national equitation championships, seventeen-year-old Francie Martinez learns to believe in herself and makes some decisions about the type of person she wants to be.

The author inhabits Francie's character wholly and convincingly and gets the universals of serious competition just right—any athlete will recognize the imperious, unfeeling coach; the snotty front-runner; and the unparalleled thrill of hitting the zone. —*Booklist*

Whyman, Matt

Goldstrike: a thriller. Matt Whyman. Atheneum Books for Young Readers, 2010 272 p.
Grades: 7 8 9 10
1. Fugitives; 2. Hackers; 3. Resourcefulness in teenage boys; 4. Bounty hunters; 5. Teenage fugitives; 6. London, England; 7. Thrillers and suspense
9781416995104

LC 2009017830

After escaping Camp Twilight, eighteen-year-old Carl Hobbes and Beth, his girlfriend, begin a new life in London, England, where he attempts to program Sphynx Cargo's highly intelligent supercomputer to help protect them from the CIA and assassins.

The action sequences are believable and often realistically brutal, and the climactic battle is intense and entertaining. —*Publishers Weekly*

Sequel to: *Icecore.*

Icecore: a Carl Hobbes thriller. Matt Whyman. Atheneum Books for Young Readers, 2007 307 p;
Grades: 7 8 9 10
1. Hackers; 2. Prisoners; 3. Torture; 4. Military bases; 5. Seventeen-year-old boys; 6. Arctic regions; 7. Fort Knox, Kentucky; 8. Adventure stories; 9. Thrillers and suspense
9781416949077

LC 2007002674

Seventeen-year-old Englishman Carl Hobbes meant no harm when he hacked into Fort Knox's security system, but at Camp Twilight in the Arctic Circle, known as the Guantanamo Bay of the north, he is tortured to reveal information about a conspiracy of which he was never a part.

Powered by a fast-paced narrative, this exploration of numerous timely themes...gives the eminently readable adventure a degree of depth. —*Publishers Weekly*

Sequel: *Goldstrike.*

Wiggins, Bethany

Cured. By Bethany Wiggins. Bloomsbury/Walker, 2014 336 pages
Grades: 7 8 9 10 11 12
1. Post-apocalypse; 2. Twin brothers and sisters; 3. Dystopias; 4. Survival; 5. Voyages and travels; 6. Science fiction.
9780802734204; 9780802734211, ebook, US

LC 2013024935

Now cured, Fiona Tarsis and her twin, Jonah, set out to find their mother with the help of Bowen and former neighbor Jacqui, planning to spread the cure along the way, but raiders will do anything to stop them and new ally Kevin may have ties to those raiders.

Jacqui lives as Jack in a dangerous zombie-ish dystopia caused by a vaccine's unforeseen effects. Searching for her missing older brother, Jacqui joins forces with Fiona Tarsis (Stung), who has the cure for the rabid vaccine recipients, but they are sidetracked by raiders. Mysterious romance and eleventh-hour reveals do not rescue this sequel from its meandering plot and clunky gender politics. —*Horn Book Guide*

Sequel to: *Stung.*

Stung. Bethany Wiggins. Walker & Co, 2013 294 p.
Grades: 7 8 9 10 11 12

1. Post-apocalypse; 2. Survival (after epidemics); 3. Dystopias; 4. Seventeen-year-old girls; 5. Vaccines; 6. Apocalyptic fiction; 7. Science fiction.
9780802734181

LC 2012027183

Golden Sower Award (Nebraska), Young Adult, 2016; Sunshine State Young Reader's Award (Florida), 2016.

When a vaccine to save endangered bees causes their sting to turn children into ferocious killer beasts, the uninfected build a wall to keep the beasts out, but Fiona wakes up on the wrong side of the wall.

Wiggins...muses on the dangers of science and medicine and deftly maps out the chain of events that has led to catastrophe, creating a violent world vastly different from ours but still recognizable. With a stirring conclusion and space for a sequel, it's an altogether captivating story. —*Kirkus*

Sequel: *Cured.*

Wild, Kate

Fight game. Kate Wild. Chicken House / Scholastic, 2007 279 p.
Grades: 7 8 9 10

1. Fifteen-year-old boys; 2. Teenage boys; 3. Teenagers; 4. Romanies; 5. Frameups; 6. England; 7. Thrillers and suspense
9780439871754; 9781905294237, print, UK

Intriguing supporting characters pepper Wild's debut novel and bolster an already strong portagonist.... Wild's story pulsates with raw energy. —*Voice of Youth Advocates*

Wiles, Deborah

★ **Kent** State. Deborah Wiles. Scholastic Press, 2020 144 p.
Grades: 7 8 9 10 11 12

1. Kent State shootings, May 4, 1970; 2. College students — Political activity; 3. Vietnam War, 1961-1975 — Protest movements; 4. Student movements — History; 5. Ohio; 6. 1970s; 7. Historical fiction; 8. Novels in verse; 9. Multiple perspectives
9781338356281, hardback, US; 9781338356304, ebook, US

LC 2019047100

Told from different points of view—protesters, students, National Guardsmen, and "townies—recounts the story of what happened at Kent State in May 1970, when four college students were killed by National Guardsmen, and a student protest was turned into a bloody battlefield.

The tangle of voices is stunningly realized, making this not only a thought-provoking private read but also an stellar candidate for group performance. —*Bulletin of the Center for Children's Books*

Includes a note by the author describing the sources for this story.

Wilkinson, Lili

Pink. Lili Wilkinson. HarperTeen, 2011 310 p.
Grades: 7 8 9 10 11 12

1. Lesbian teenagers; 2. Popularity; 3. Identity (Psychology); 4. Self-discovery in teenage girls; 5. Self-discovery; 6. Australia; 7. Realistic fiction; 8. Australian fiction; 9. LGBTQIA fiction; 10. Books for reluctant readers
9780061926532

Amelia Bloomer List, 2012; Rainbow List, 2012; YALSA Popular Paperbacks for Young Adults, 2013; YALSA Quick Picks for Reluctant Young Adult Readers, 2012; Stonewall Children's & Young Adult Literature Honor Book, 2012.

The novel is in turn laugh-out-loud funny, endearing, and heartbreaking as Ava repeatedly steps into teenage social land mines with unexpected results. Because Wilkinson doesn't rely on stereotypes, the characters are well-developed, and interactions between them feel genuine. —*Voice of Youth Advocates*

Willey, Margaret

Beetle boy. By Margaret Willey. Carolrhoda Lab, 2014 208 p.
Grades: 8 9 10 11

1. Eighteen-year-old men; 2. Psychic trauma in men; 3. Memories; 4. Teenage boy/girl relations; 5. Beetles.
9781467726399

LC 2013036853

Terrible memories resurface when Charlie's girlfriend asks questions about his childhood.

Willey takes readers along on Charlie's painful journey back to physical and emotional health via a meandering timeline of flashbacks, dreams and wrenching conversations, skillfully weaving together the bits and pieces of his life. Innovative use of type brings an immediacy to Charlie's struggles as he slowly looks the truth—and his brother— squarely in the face. —*Kirkus*

Williams, Alex

The **deep** freeze of Bartholomew Tullock. Alex Williams. Philomel Books; 2008 304 p.
Grades: 6 7 8 9

1. Snow; 2. Electric fans; 3. Inventions; 4. Inventors; 5. Weather; 6. Adventure stories
9780399251856

LC 2008002663

In a land of never-ending snow, Rufus Breeze and his mother must protect the family home from being seized by tyrant Bartholomew Tullock, while sister Madeline and her father, an inventor of fans that are now useless, join forces with a ne'er-do-well adventurer and his blue-haired terrier, hoping to make some money.

This offers originality of setting, a full complement of truly heinous villains, insurmountable dangers cleverly surmounted, ingenious contraptions, and plucky, appealing underdogs.... William handles his material with fizz and verve. —*Bulletin of the Center for Children's Books*

Published in Great Britain as: *The Storm Maker*, by Macmillan

Williams, Alicia

★ **Genesis** begins again. Alicia D. Williams. Atheneum, 2019 336 p.
Grades: 5 6 7 8

1. African Americans; 2. Self-esteem; 3. Racism; 4. Family problems; 5. Human skin color; 6. Realistic fiction; 7. African American fiction.
9781481465809, HRD, US; 9781481465823, ebook, US

LC 2018030079

ALA Notable Children's Books, 2020; John Steptoe Award for New Talent, Author Category, 2020; School Library Journal Best Books, 2019; Kirkus Prize for Young Readers' Literature finalist, 2019; Newbery Honor Book, 2020; William C. Morris Debut Award finalist, 2020.

Thirteen-year-old Genesis tries again and again to lighten her black skin, thinking it is the root of her family's troubles, before discovering reasons to love herself as is.

With its relatable and sympathetic protagonist, complex setting, and exceptional emotional range, this title is easy to recommend. —*Publishers Weekly*

A Caitlyn Dlouhy Book.

Williams, Carol Lynch

The **chosen** one. Carol Lynch Williams. St. Martin's Griffin, 2009 288 p.
Grades: 7 8 9 10

1. Cults; 2. Polygamy; 3. Arranged marriage; 4. Families; 5. Thirteen-year-old girls; 6. Coming-of-age stories; 7. Realistic fiction; 8. Books for reluctant readers

9780312555115

LC 2009004800
YALSA Popular Paperbacks for Young Adults, 2012; Amelia Bloomer List, 2010; YALSA Quick Picks for Reluctant Young Adult Readers, 2010; YALSA Best Books for Young Adults, 2010.

In a polygamous cult in the desert, Kyra, not yet fourteen, sees being chosen to be the seventh wife of her uncle as just punishment for having read books and kissed a boy, in violation of Prophet Childs' teachings, and is torn between facing her fate and running away from all that she knows and loves.

This book is a highly emotional, terrifying read. It is not measured or objective. Physical abuse, fear, and even murder are constants. It is a girl-in-peril story, and as such, it is impossible to put down and holds tremendous teen appeal. —*Voice of Youth Advocates*

Glimpse. Carol Lynch Williams. Simon & Schuster Books for Young Readers, 2010 496 p.
Grades: 7 8 9 10
1. Children of prostitutes; 2. Psychic trauma; 3. Suicidal behavior; 4. Psychic trauma in teenage girls; 5. Sisters; 6. Florida; 7. Realistic fiction; 8. Novels in verse; 9. First person narratives; 10. Books for reluctant readers
9781416997306

LC 2009041147
YALSA Quick Picks for Reluctant Young Adult Readers, 2011; YALSA Best Fiction for Young Adults, 2011.

Living with their mother who earns money as a prostitute, two sisters take care of each other and when the older one attempts suicide, the younger one tries to uncover the reason.

Williams leans hard on her free-verse line breaks for drama...and it works. A page-turner for Ellen Hopkins fans. —*Kirkus*

A Paula Wiseman book.

Miles from ordinary: a novel. Carol Lynch Williams. St. Martin's Press, 2011 197 p.
Grades: 7 8 9 10
1. Children of people with mental illnesses; 2. Missing women; 3. Coping in teenage girls; 4. Mothers and daughters; 5. Mental illness; 6. Realistic fiction.
9780312555122

LC 2010040324
YALSA Best Fiction for Young Adults, 2012.

As her mother's mental illness spins terrifyingly out of control, thirteen-year-old Lacey must face the truth of what life with her mother means for both of them.

The author has crafted both a riveting, unusual suspense tale and an absolutely convincing character in Lacey. The book truly is miles from ordinary, in the very best way. Outstanding. —*Kirkus*

Waiting. Carol Lynch Williams. Simon and Schuster Books for Young Readers, 2012 288 p.
Grades: 9 10 11 12
1. Grief in teenage girls; 2. Survivors of suicide victims; 3. Coping; 4. Grief; 5. Love triangles; 6. Realistic fiction; 7. Novels in verse; 8. First person narratives; 9. Books for reluctant readers
9781442443532

LC 2011043898
YALSA Quick Picks for Reluctant Young Adult Readers, 2013.

As the tragic death of her older brother devastates the family, teen-aged London struggles to find redemption and finds herself torn between her brother's best friend and a handsome new boy in town.

A Paula Wiseman book.

Williams, Ismee
Water in May. Ismee Williams. 2017 309 p.
Grades: 7 8 9 10 11 12
1. Pregnant teenagers; 2. Hispanic Americans; 3. Heart — Diseases; 4. Decision-making; 5. Teenage pregnancy; 6. Realistic fiction
9781419725395

LC 2017008518
Pregnant at fifteen, Mari Pujols believes the baby will supply the family love she yearns for but when she learns the fetus has a heart defect, her friends, sometimes boyfriend, and doctor are there for her.

Debut author Williams creates an unforgettable young character who will make readers reconsider their assumptions about teen moms, in particular Latina teen moms. —*Kirkus*

Williams, Kathryn
Pizza, love, and other stuff that made me famous. Kathryn Williams. Henry Holt, 2012 240 p.
Grades: 7 8 9 10
1. Teenage cooks; 2. Reality television programs; 3. Love triangles; 4. Cooking; 5. Television — Production and direction; 6. Teen chick lit; 7. Realistic fiction.
9780805092851

LC 2011034053
Although sixteen-year-old Sophie has grown up working in her family's Mediterranean restaurant in Washington, D.C, she is not prepared to compete on the new reality show, *Teen Test Kitchen*, when her best friend Alex convinces her to audition. Includes recipes.

Christy Ottaviano books.

Williams, Katie
Absent. By Katie Williams. Chronicle Books, 2013 288 p.
Grades: 9 10 11 12
1. Teenage girl ghosts; 2. Spirit possession; 3. High school students; 4. Suicide; 5. Ghosts; 6. Ghost stories.
9780811871501

LC 2012033600
Seventeen-year-old Paige Wheeler died in a fall off the high school roof and now her spirit seems bound to the school grounds, along with Brooke and Evan, two other teen ghosts who died there—but maybe if she can solve the mystery of her apparent suicide they will all be able to move on.

The mystery is solid, but it is complicated; funny Paige herself sets the story apart. —*Booklist*

The **space** between trees. By Katie Williams. Chronicle Books, 2010 256 p.
Grades: 8 9 10 11 12
1. Growing up; 2. Dishonesty; 3. Murder; 4. Secrets; 5. High schools; 6. Coming-of-age stories; 7. Mysteries
9780811871754

LC 2009048561
YALSA Popular Paperbacks for Young Adults, 2015.

When the body of a classmate is discovered in the woods, sixteen-year-old Evie's lies wind up involving her with the girl's best friend, trying to track down the killer.

Evie's raw honesty and the choices she makes make for difficult reading, but also a darkly beautiful, emotionally honest story of personal growth. —*Publishers Weekly*

Williams, Lori Aurelia
★ **When** Kambia Elaine flew in from Neptune. Lori Aurelia Williams. Simon & Schuster, 2000 246 p.

Grades: 7 8 9 10

1. African American girls; 2. Sexually abused teenage girls; 3. Poor African Americans; 4. Neighbors; 5. Girls — Friendship; 6. Houston, Texas; 7. Texas; 8. Realistic fiction; 9. First person narratives; 10. African American fiction
9780689824685

LC 99-65154

YALSA Best Books for Young Adults, 2001.

Shayla, an aspiring writer growing up in a poor section of Houston, can't figure out the new girl next door, Kambia Elaine, who tells fantastic stories. She slowly realizes that Kambia Elaine needs help, but Shayla doesn't know where to find it.

This is a strong and disturbing novel, told in beautiful language. Teens will find it engrossing. —*School Library Journal*

Sequel: *Shayla's double brown baby blues.*

Williams, Michael
Diamond boy. Michael Williams. Little, Brown and Company, 2014 400 p.
Grades: 7 8 9 10

1. Diamond mines and mining; 2. Corruption; 3. Blended families; 4. Shona (African people); 5. Survival; 6. Zimbabwe.
9780316320696

Written in diary format, the story brings the reader into the mind and soul of a young refugee suffering in a hell created by the greed and violence of powerful adults. More than simply a good read, Diamond Boy is a multilayered, teachable novel with a variety of approaches and is highly recommended for middle and high school collections. —*Voice of Youth Advocates*

★ **Now** is the time for running. Michael Williams. Little, Brown, 2011 240 p.
Grades: 6 7 8 9 10

1. Refugees; 2. Brothers and sisters of children with disabilities; 3. Soccer; 4. Brothers; 5. People with developmental disabilities; 6. Zimbabwe; 7. Realistic fiction.
9780316077903; 9780316077880

LC 2010043460

YALSA Best Fiction for Young Adults, 2012; Notable Books for a Global Society, 2012; YALSA Popular Paperbacks for Young Adults, 2017.

When soldiers attack a small village in Zimbabwe, Deo goes on the run with Innocent, his older, mentally disabled brother, carrying little but a leather soccer ball filled with money, and after facing prejudice, poverty, and tragedy, it is in soccer that Deo finds renewed hope.

There is plenty of material to captivate readers: fast-paced soccer matches every bit as tough as the players; the determination of Deo and his fellow refugees to survive unthinkably harsh conditions; and raw depictions of violence.... But it's the tender relationship between Deo and Innocent, along with some heartbreaking twists of fate, that will endure in readers' minds. —*Publishers Weekly*

Williams, Sean
Impossible music. Sean Williams. 2019 320 p.
Grades: 9 10 11 12

1. Teenage musicians; 2. Teenagers who are deaf; 3. Adjustment (Psychology); 4. Life change events; 5. People who have had strokes; 6. Coming-of-age stories; 7. First person narratives; 8. Realistic fiction.
9780544816206; 9781760637156, Paperback, Australia; 9781328630063, ebook, US

LC 2018051216

Devastated by a stroke that causes him to lose his hearing, a teen musician resists transition therapy before a tough new friend challenges him to create a new music form that helps him better understand his relationship to the hearing world.—

A thought-provoking examination of what music is and means through a well-researched portrayal of sudden hearing loss. —*School Library Journal*

Twinmaker. Sean Williams. HarperTeen, an imprint of HarperCollinsPublishers, 2013 491 p. (Twinmaker novels, 1)
Grades: 9 10 11 12

1. Conspiracies; 2. Technology; 3. Best friends; 4. Space and time; 5. Love triangles; 6. Science fiction; 7. Australian fiction.
9780062203212; 9781743315866

When her best friend Libby misuses instant transportation technology to alter her appearance, seventeen-year-old Clair is drawn into a shadowy world of conspiracies and cover-ups as she attempts to save Libby from the hidden consequences of her actions.

Williams marries accessibly explored moral ramifications of future technologies—a hallmark of mature science fiction—with a strong, capable teen heroine and heart-pounding action (just flip past the romance). —*Kirkus*

Williams, Suzanne
Bull rider. Suzanne Williams. Margaret K. McElderry Books, 2009 256 p.
Grades: 7 8 9 10

1. Iraq War veterans; 2. Bull riding; 3. Brothers; 4. Fourteen-year-old boys; 5. Skateboards and skateboarding; 6. Realistic fiction; 7. First person narratives
9781416961307

LC 2007052518

Western Heritage Award for Outstanding Juvenile Book, 2010.

When his older brother, a bull-riding champion, returns from the Iraq War partially paralyzed, fourteen-year-old Cam takes a break from skateboarding to enter a bull-riding contest, in hopes of winning the $15,000 prize and motivating his depressed brother to continue with his rehabilitation.

The mix of wild macho action with family anguish and tenderness will grab teens.... [This is a] powerful contemporary story of family, community, and work. —*Booklist*

Williams-Garcia, Rita
★ **Jumped**. Rita Williams-Garcia. HarperTeen, 2009 169 p.
Grades: 8 9 10 11 12

1. Urban teenagers; 2. Anger in teenage girls; 3. Violence in schools; 4. Dilemmas; 5. Bullying and bullies; 6. Realistic fiction; 7. First person narratives; 8. African American fiction
9780060760915; 9780060760939, US: pbk.

LC 2008022381

Booklist Editors' Choice: Books for Youth, 2009; YALSA Best Books for Young Adults, 2010; National Book Award for Young People's Literature finalist, 2009.

The lives of Leticia, Dominique, and Trina are irrevocably intertwined through the course of one day in an urban high school after Leticia overhears Dominique's plans to beat up Trina and must decide whether or not to get involved.

In alternating chapters narrated by Leticia, Trina, and Dominique, Williams-Garcia has given her characters strong, individual voices that ring true to teenage speech, and she lets them make their choices without judgment or moralizing. —*School Library Journal*

Amistad.

★ **Like** sisters on the homefront. Rita Williams-Garcia. Lodestar Books, 1995 165 p.
Grades: 7 8 9 10
1. Teenage mothers; 2. African American teenage girls; 3. Christian teenage girls; 4. Families; 5. Cousins; 6. Georgia; 7. Realistic fiction; 8. African American fiction; 9. Books for reluctant readers
9780525674658
LC 95003690 /AC
Booklist Editors' Choice: Books for Youth, 1995; YALSA Best Books for Young Adults, 1996; YALSA Quick Picks for Reluctant Young Adult Readers, 1996; School Library Journal Best Books, 1995; Coretta Scott King Honor Book for Authors, 1996.

Troubled fourteen-year-old Gayle is sent down South to live with her uncle and aunt, where her life begins to change as she experiences the healing power of the family.

Beautifully written, the text captures the cadence and rhythm of New York street talk and the dilemma of being poor, black, and uneducated. This is a gritty, realistic, well-told story. —*School Library Journal*

Williamson, Victoria
The **fox** girl and the white gazelle. Victoria Williamson. Kelpies, 2018 272 p.
Grades: 5 6 7 8 9
1. Refugees, Syrian; 2. Girl runners; 3. Animal rescue; 4. Bullying and bullies; 5. Foxes; 6. Realistic fiction; 7. Multiple perspectives; 8. First person narratives
9781782504900, Paperback, UK; 9781544426112
USBBY Outstanding International Books, 2019.

An unlikely friendship between twelve-year-old refugee Reema and her bullying neighbor Caylin forms after they find an injured fox.

Wilson, Diane L.
Black storm comin'. Diane Lee Wilson. Margaret K. McElderry Books, 2005 304 p.
Grades: 7 8 9 10
1. Twelve-year-old boys; 2. Multiracial children; 3. Multiracial boys; 4. Pony Express; 5. Slavery; 6. The West (United States); 7. United States; 8. Historical fiction.
9780689871375
LC 2004009438
Spur Award for Juvenile Fiction, 2006; Booklist Editors' Choice: Books for Youth, 2005.

Twelve-year-old Colton, son of a black mother and a white father, takes a job with the Pony Express in 1860 after his father abandons the family on their California-bound wagon train, and risks his life to deliver an important letter that may affect the growing conflict between the North and South.

Wilson masterfully creates a multidimensional character in Colton.... Readers will absorb greater lessons as they become engrossed in the excitement, beauty, and terror of Colton's journey to California and manhood. —*Booklist*

★ **Firehorse**. Diane Lee Wilson. Margaret K. McElderry Books, 2006 336 p.
Grades: 7 8 9 10
1. Fifteen-year-old girls; 2. Teenage girls; 3. Girls and horses; 4. Teenage girls and horses; 5. Veterinary medicine; 6. Boston, Massachusetts; 7. 19th century; 8. Historical fiction.
9781416915515
LC 2005030785
Amelia Bloomer List, 2007.

Spirited fifteen-year-old horse lover Rachel Selby determines to become a veterinarian, despite the opposition of her rigid father, her proper mother, and the norms of Boston in 1872, while that city faces a serial arsonist and an epidemic spreading through its firehorse population.

Wilson paces the story well, with tension building.... The novel's finest achievement, though, is the convincing depiction of family dynamics in an era when men ruled the household and and women, who had few opportunities, folded their dreams and put them away with the linens they embroidered. —*Booklist*

Wilson, John
Ghost moon. John Wilson. Orca Book Publishers, 2011 171 p. (Desert legends trilogy, 2)
Grades: 6 7 8 9
1. Outlaws; 2. Gunfights; 3. Murder; 4. Violence; 5. Sixteen-year-old boys; 6. New Mexico; 7. 1870s; 8. Westerns; 9. Canadian fiction.
9781554698790

The year is 1878, and young Jim is not yet ready to return to Canada. Instead he heads up to New Mexico in hopes of finding work and building a life. On the way he meets Bill Bonney (later to be known as Billy the Kid), who takes him to a ranch south of the town of Lincoln, where they both find work as cowboys. Little does Jim know that he is about to get caught up in a vicious battle for the lucrative army contracts with nearby Fort Stanton.

A young wanderer lands in the middle of New Mexico's Lincoln County War.... 16-year-old James Doolen falls in with Bill Bonney (not yet known as Billy the Kid) a charming but decidedly mercurial teenager who hares off on a vicious killing spree after their new boss, John Tunstall, is murdered by a rival merchant's gang of hired gunmen.... Action fans will thrill to the gunplay and other dangers. James' conflicting feelings about his archetypically dangerous friend...introduce thought provoking elements. A tale of the Old West with a sturdy historical base and nary a dull moment. —*Kirkus*

Victorio's war. John Wilson. Orca Book Pub, 2012 157 p. (Desert legends trilogy, 3)
Grades: 6 7 8 9
1. Outlaws; 2. Gunfights; 3. Sixteen-year-old boys; 4. Doolen, James (Fictitious character); 5. Teenage boys; 6. New Mexico; 7. 1870s; 8. Westerns; 9. Canadian fiction.
9781554698820

Wilson, Kip
White Rose. By Kip Wilson. Houghton Mifflin Harcourt, 2019 368 p.
Grades: 7 8 9 10 11 12
1. Scholl, Sophie, 1921-1943; 2. Resistance to govern- ment; 3. Courage in women; 4. Nazism; 5. White Rose (Anti-Nazi group); 6. Anti-Nazi movement; 7. Germany; 8. Second World War era (1939-1945); 9. Biographical fiction; 10. Novels in verse; 11. Historical fiction.
9781328594433
LC 2018026607
School Library Journal Best Books, 2019.

Tells the story of Sophie Scholl, a young German college student who challenges the Nazi regime during World War II as part of the White Rose, a non-violent resistance group.

Real events made deeply personal in an intense, bone-chilling reading experience. —*Kirkus*
Includes bibliographical references.

Wilson, Martin
★ **What** they always tell us. Martin Wilson. Delacorte Press, 2008 293 p.

Grades: 9 10 11 12
1. Brothers; 2. Gay teenagers; 3. Coming out (Sexual or gender identity); 4. Teenage boys — Family relationships; 5. Suicide; 6. Alabama; 7. Tuscaloosa, Alabama; 8. Coming-of-age stories; 9. Realistic fiction; 10. Multiple perspectives
9780385735070
Rainbow List, 2009.

After being distant from each other for years, popular senior James and his outcast younger brother Alex finally find a way to bond through the encouragement of a new friend, Alex's sudden passion for running, and a newfound mutual respect.

This novel does an excellent job of showing the tension with which siblings deal on a daily basis. He also does a great job of exploring controversial issues, such as suicide and homosexuality.... Public and school libraries should seriously consider adding this book to their shelves. —*Voice of Youth Advocates*

Wilson, Nathan D.
★ The **dragon's** tooth. N.D. Wilson. Random House, 2011 485 p. (Ashtown burials, 1)
Grades: 5 6 7 8
1. Parent-separated children; 2. Secret societies; 3. Apprentices; 4. Parallel universes; 5. Magic; 6. Fantasy fiction.
9780375864391

After a mysterious, violent incident that results in the kidnapping of their older brother, Cyrus and Antigone Smith discover that they're now part of the Order of Brendan, a secret society for explorers. The siblings head to the Order's headquarters in Ashtown in search of answers, but instead they encounter immortal enemies, mythological creatures, magical artifacts, and shocking family secrets.

This fast-paced fantasy quickly draws readers in to its alternate reality.... Allusions to mythology and complex character development...make Wilson's first in a proposed series a gem. —*Booklist*

Winfrey, Kerry
Things Jolie needs to do before she bites it. Kerry Winfrey. Feiwel & Friends 2018 256 p.
Grades: 8 9 10 11
1. Surgery; 2. Teenage girls; 3. Fear in teenage girls; 4. Fear of death; 5. Teenage boy/girl relations; 6. Realistic fiction
9781250119544

Anticipating surgery for a lifelong dental condition that has caused pain and unpopularity, Jolie is alarmed by a worst-case-scenario reality show and decides she wants to live life to the fullest just in case the surgery does not go as expected.

Winters, Cat
★ In the shadow of blackbirds. Cat Winters. Amulet Books, 2013 304 p.
Grades: 8 9 10 11 12
1. Spiritualism; 2. Influenza Epidemic, 1918-1919; 3. World War I; 4. Ghosts; 5. Sixteen-year-old girls; 6. San Diego, California; 7. First World War era (1914-1918); 8. 1910s; 9. Historical fiction; 10. Ghost stories.
9781419705304
LC 2012039262
School Library Journal Best Books, 2013; Westchester Fiction Award, 2014; YALSA Best Fiction for Young Adults, 2014; YALSA Popular Paperbacks for Young Adults, 2015; William C. Morris Debut Award finalist, 2014.

In San Diego in 1918, as deadly influenza and World War I take their toll, sixteen-year-old Mary Shelley Black watches desperate mourners flock to seances and spirit photographers for comfort and, despite her scientific leanings, must consider if ghosts are real when her first love, killed in battle, returns.

Winters strikes just the right balance between history and ghost story .... Vintage photographs contribute to the authenticity of the atmospheric and nicely paced storytelling. —*Kirkus*

Odd & true. By Cat Winters. 2017 368 p.
Grades: 8 9 10 11 12
1. Sisters — Family relationships; 2. Demon slayers; 3. Missing persons investigation; 4. Girls with poliomyelitis; 5. Poliomyelitis; 6. 1900s(Decade); 7. Historical fantasy.
9781419723100; 9781419735080
LC 2017009966
Booklist Editors' Choice: Books for Youth, 2017; YALSA Best Fiction for Young Adults, 2018.

Told from separate viewpoints, Odette returns in 1909 after a two-year absence, promising to rescue her disabled sister, Tru, from the monsters they were taught to believe in.

Winters has woven an intricate and innovative pattern of structure, genre, and history that cannot fail to capture readers' imaginations. —*Kirkus*

★ The **steep** and thorny way. By Cat Winters. 2016 352 pages
Grades: 8 9 10 11 12
1. Multiracial teenage girls; 2. Prejudice; 3. Murder; 4. Uncles; 5. Fathers — Death; 6. Oregon; 7. 1920s; 8. Historical fiction; 9. Shakespeare-inspired fiction
9781419719158
LC 2015022705
Jefferson Cup Award for Older Readers, 2017; Rainbow List, 2017; YALSA Best Fiction for Young Adults, 2017.

A sixteen-year-old biracial girl in rural Oregon in the 1920s searches for the truth about her father's death while avoiding trouble from the Ku Klux Klan in this YA historical novel inspired by Shakespeare's 'Hamlet'.

A fast-paced read with multiple twists, the novel delivers a history lesson wrapped inside a murder mystery and ghost story. Winters deftly captures the many injustices faced by marginalized people in the years following World War I as well as a glimmer of hope for the better America to come. A riveting story of survival, determination, love, and friendship. —*Kirkus*

Winters, Julian
How to be Remy Cameron. Julian Winters. Duet, 2019 304 p.
Grades: 8 9 10 11 12
1. Gay teenagers; 2. African American teenage boys; 3. Identity (Psychology); 4. Interpersonal relations; 5. Self-discovery; 6. Georgia; 7. Coming-of-age stories; 8. LGBTQIA fiction; 9. African American fiction.
9781945053801

Everyone on campus knows Remy Cameron. He's the out-and-proud, super-likable guy who friends, faculty, and fellow students alike admire for his cheerful confidence. The only person who isn't entirely sure about Remy Cameron is Remy himself. Under pressure to write an A+ essay defining who he is and who he wants to be, Remy embarks on an emotional journey toward reconciling the outward labels people attach to him with the real Remy Cameron within.

The racial and sexual diversity that pervades this novel feels refreshingly authentic, and Remy's struggles with being black, adopted, and gay demonstrate the author's skill as a storyteller and his res pect for the weight of the issues at play. —*Kirkus*

Wiseman, Eva

Puppet. Eva Wiseman. Tundra Books, 2008 243 p.

Grades: 7 8 9 10 11 12

1. Blood libel; 2. Jews — Persecutions; 3. Trials (Murder); 4. Murder investigation; 5. Household employees; 6. Hungary; 7. 1880s; 8. 19th century; 9. Historical fiction; 10. Canadian fiction.

9780887768286; 9781770492967

Canadian Jewish Book Award; Manitoba Writing and Publishing Awards, McNally Robinson Book for Young People Awards: Older category, 2010.

A fictionalized account of the last blood libel trial in Hungary in 1882 is told through the eyes of Julie, a friend of the murdered servant girl Esther and a servant at the jail where Morris Scharf, the accused, is imprisoned.

Times are hard in Julie Vamosi's Hungarian village in the late nineteenth-century, and the townspeople...blame the Jews. After Julie's best friend, Esther, ...disappears, the rumor spreads that the Jews cut her throat and drained her blood to drink with their Passover matzos.... Based on the records of a trial in 1883, this searing novel dramatizes virulent anti-Semitism from the viewpoint of a Christian child.... The climax is electrifying. —*Booklist*

Wiseman, Rosalind

Boys, girls, and other hazardous materials. Rosalind Wiseman. G.P. Putnam's Sons, 2010 282 p;

Grades: 8 9 10 11 12

1. Social acceptance in teenagers; 2. Crushes in teenage girls; 3. Hazing; 4. Bullying and bullies; 5. Social acceptance; 6. Realistic fiction; 7. First person narratives.

9780399247965

LC 2009018446

YALSA Popular Paperbacks for Young Adults, 2012.

Transferring to a new high school, freshman Charlotte "Charlie" Healey faces tough choices as she tries to shed her "mean girl" image.

Wiseman succeeds in delivering realistic, likable characters whose challenges and mistakes are all too relatable. —*Bulletin of the Center for Children's Books*

Withers, Pam

First descent. Pam Withers. Tundra Books, 2011 272 p.

Grades: 7 8 9 10

1. Kayaking; 2. Grandfather and grandson; 3. Seventeen-year-old boys; 4. Rivers; 5. Indigenous peoples; 6. Colombia; 7. Multiple perspectives; 8. Coming-of-age stories; 9. Canadian fiction.

9781770492578; 9781770494121

Rex is excited when he is given the opportunity to go kayaking on the El Furiso River in southwest Colombia. When he is there, he and an indígena named Myriam Calambás become caught up in the clash between paramilitaries and guerrillas.

Withers flings the reader from one perilous adventure to another. —*Booklist*

Wittlinger, Ellen

Hard love. Ellen Wittlinger. Simon & Schuster Books for Young Readers, 1999 224 p.

Grades: 7 8 9 10

1. Loneliness in teenage boys; 2. Zines; 3. Emotions in teenage boys; 4. Loneliness; 5. Writing; 6. Realistic fiction; 7. Books for reluctant readers

9780689821349

LC 98006668

Booklist Editors' Choice: Books for Youth, 1999; Lambda Literary Award for Young Adult/Children, 1999; Thumbs Up! Award (Michigan), 2000; YALSA Best Books for Young Adults, 2000; YALSA Quick Picks for Reluctant Young Adult Readers, 2000; School Library Journal Best Books, 1999; Michael L. Printz Honor Book, 2000.

After starting to publish a zine in which he writes his secret feelings about his lonely life and his parents' divorce, sixteen-year-old John meets an unusual girl and begins to develop a healthier personality.

John, cynical yet vulnerable, thinks he's immune to emotion until he meets bright, brittle Marisol, the author of his favorite zine. He falls in love, but Marisol, a lesbian, just wants to be friends. A love story of a different sortfunny, poignant, and thoughtful. —*Booklist*

Sequel: *Love & lies.*

Love & lies: Marisol's story. Ellen Wittlinger. Simon & Schuster Books for Young Readers, 2008 245 p.

Grades: 7 8 9 10

1. Lesbian teenagers; 2. Teacher-student relationships; 3. Self-discovery in women; 4. Fiction writing; 5. Lesbians; 6. Cambridge, Massachusetts; 7. Massachusetts; 8. Realistic fiction; 9. LGBTQIA fiction; 10. First person narratives.

9781416916239

LC 2007018330

Rainbow List, 2009.

When Marisol, a self-confident eighteen-year-old lesbian, moves to Cambridge, Massachusetts to work and try to write a novel, she falls under the spell of her beautiful but deceitful writing teacher, while also befriending a shy, vulnerable girl from Indiana.

The emotional morass of Marisol's life...is complex and realistic; it will draw in both fans of the earlier novel...and realistic-fiction readers seeking a love story with depth. —*Bulletin of the Center for Children's Books*

Sequel to: *Hard love.*

★ **Parrotfish**. Ellen Wittlinger. Simon & Schuster Books for Young Readers, 2007 304 p.

Grades: 7 8 9 10

1. Identity (Psychology); 2. Social acceptance; 3. Transgender teenagers; 4. Transgender teenage boys; 5. Teenagers; 6. LGBTQIA fiction; 7. Coming-of-age stories; 8. Realistic fiction.

9781416916222

LC 2006009689

Rainbow List, 2008; YALSA Popular Paperbacks for Young Adults, 2012.

Grady, a transgendered high school student, yearns for acceptance by his classmates and family as he struggles to adjust to his new identity as a male.

The author demonstrates well the complexity faced by transgendered people and makes the teen's frustration with having to fit into a category fully apparent. —*Publishers Weekly*

★ **Sandpiper**. Ellen Wittlinger. Simon & Schuster Books for Young Readers, 2005 240 p.

Grades: 9 10 11 12

1. Teenage misfits; 2. Threat (Psychology); 3. Oral sex; 4. Anger in teenage girls; 5. Anger; 6. Massachusetts; 7. Realistic fiction; 8. First person narratives.

9780689868023

LC 2004007576

YALSA Best Books for Young Adults, 2006.

When The Walker, a mysterious boy who walks constantly, intervenes in an argument between Sandpiper and a boy she used to see, their lives become entwined in ways that change them both.

While heavy on message and mature in subject matter, the novel is notable for the bold look it takes at relationships and at the myth that oral sex is not really sex. —*School Library Journal*

Wizner, Jake

Spanking Shakespeare. Jake Wizner. Random House Children's Books, 2007 287 p.
Grades: 8 9 10
1. High school seniors; 2. Seventeen-year-old boys; 3. Teenage boys; 4. Teenagers; 5. Brothers; 6. Novels-within-novels; 7. First person narratives; 8. Humorous stories.
9780375840852; 9780375940859; 9780375840869

LC 2006027035

YALSA Popular Paperbacks for Young Adults, 2014; YALSA Best Books for Young Adults, 2008.

Shakespeare Shapiro navigates a senior year fraught with feelings of insecurity while writing the memoir of his embarrassing life, worrying about his younger brother being cooler than he is, and having no prospects of ever getting a girlfriend.

Raw, sexual, cynical, and honest, this book belongs on Library shelves and gift lists. —*Voice of Youth Advocates*

Wolf, Allan

New found land: Lewis and Clark's voyage of discovery : a novel. By Allan Wolf. Candlewick Press, 2004 500 p.
Grades: 7 8 9 10
1. Clark, William, 1770-1838; 2. Explorers — History; 3. Exploration; 4. Presidents; 5. Seaman (Dog); 6. Newfoundland dogs; 7. The West (United States); 8. United States; 9. 19th century; 10. American Westward Expansion (1803-1899); 11. First person narratives; 12. Adventure stories; 13. Historical fiction.
9780763621131

LC 2003065254

YALSA Best Books for Young Adults, 2005; School Library Journal Best Books, 2004.

The letters and thoughts of Thomas Jefferson, members of the Corps of Discovery, their guide Sacagawea, and Captain Lewis's Newfoundland dog, all tell of the historic exploratory expedition to seek a water route to the Pacific Ocean.

This is an extraordinary, engrossing book that would appeal most to serious readers, but it should definitely be added to any collection. —*School Library Journal*

The **watch** that ends the night: voices from the Titanic. Allan Wolf. Candlewick Press, 2011 480 p.
Grades: 7 8 9 10
1. Shipwrecks; 2. Social classes; 3. Millionaires; 4. Socialites; 5. 1910s; 6. Historical fiction; 7. Novels in verse; 8. Multiple perspectives
9780763637033

LC 2010040150

Booklist Editors' Choice: Books for Youth, 2011; Claudia Lewis Award, 2012; YALSA Best Fiction for Young Adults, 2012.

Recreates the 1912 sinking of the Titanic as observed by millionaire John Jacob Astor, a beautiful young Lebanese refugee finding first love, "Unsinkable" Molly Brown, Captain Smith, and others including the iceberg itself.

A lyrical, monumental work of fact and imagination that reads like an oral history revved up by the drama of the event. —*Kirkus*
Includes bibliographical references.

Who killed Christopher Goodman?: based on a true crime. Allan Wolf. Candlewick Press, 2017 269 p.

Grades: 8 9 10 11 12
1. Guilt; 2. Small towns; 3. Murder investigation; 4. Murder; 5. Teenage murder victims; 6. Virginia; 7. 1970s; 8. Historical mysteries; 9. Multiple perspectives
9780763656133

Booklist Editors' Choice: Books for Youth, 2017.

Everybody likes Chris Goodman, but when he is found dead, no one understands how something like this could happen.

Wolf, Jennifer Shaw

Breaking beautiful. Jennifer Shaw Wolf. Walker, 2012 368 p.
Grades: 9 10 11 12
1. Fatal traffic accidents; 2. Dating violence; 3. Twin brothers and sisters; 4. Memory; 5. Dating (Social customs); 6. Mysteries; 7. Realistic fiction.
9780802723529

LC 2011010944

Allie is overwhelmed when her boyfriend, Trip, dies in a car accident, leaving her scarred and unable to recall what happened that night, but she feels she must uncover the truth, even if it could hurt the people who tried to save her from Trip's abuse.

Wolff, Virginia Euwer

★ **Make** lemonade. Virginia Euwer Wolff. H. Holt, 1993 200 p. (Make lemonade trilogy, 1)
Grades: 8 9 10 11 12
1. Inner city teenage girls; 2. Single teenage mothers; 3. Babysitters; 4. Poor families; 5. Inner city; 6. Realistic fiction; 7. Novels in verse; 8. First person narratives.
9780805022285

LC 92041182

Golden Kite Award for Fiction, 1993; Josette Frank Award, 1993; Leslie Bradshaw Award for Young Readers (Oregon), 1994; Thumbs Up! Award (Michigan), 1994; ALA Notable Children's Book, 1994.

In order to earn money for college, fourteen-year-old LaVaughn babysits for a teenage mother of two. Written in 66 chapters, with text lines that break at natural speaking phrases.

Fourteen-year-old LaVaughn accepts the job of babysitting Jolly's two small children but quickly realizes that the young woman, a seventeen-year-old single mother, needs as much help and nurturing as her two neglected children. The four become something akin to a temporary family, and through their relationship each makes progress toward a better life. Sixty-six brief chapters, with words arranged on the page like poetry, perfectly echo the patterns of teenage speech. —*Horn Book Guide*

The **Mozart** season. Virginia Euwer Wolff. Holt, 1991 249 p.
Grades: 6 7 8 9
1. Jewish American girls; 2. Girl violinists; 3. Music — Competitions; 4. Self-discovery in girls; 5. Self-discovery; 6. Portland, Oregon; 7. Oregon; 8. Realistic fiction; 9. Pacific Northwest fiction
9780805015713

LC 90023635

Phoenix Award, 2011; ALA Notable Children's Book, 1992.

Allegra Leah Shapiro spends her twelfth summer practicing a Mozart concerto of a violin competition and finding many significant connections in her world.

With a clear, fresh voice that never falters, Wolff gives readers a delightful heroine, a fully realized setting, and a slowly building tension that reaches a stunning climax. —*School Library Journal*

★ **Probably** still Nick Swansen. Virginia Euwer Wolff. H. Holt, 1988 144 p.
Grades: 7 8 9 10

1. Teenagers with learning disabilities; 2. Coping in teenage boys; 3. Self-acceptance in teenage boys; 4. Sisters — Death; 5. Teenage boy/girl relations; 6. Portland, Oregon; 7. Realistic fiction; 8. Pacific Northwest fiction
9780805007015

LC 88013175

International Reading Association Children's Book Award for Older Readers, 1989.

Sixteen-year-old learning-disabled Nick struggles to endure a life in which the other kids make fun of him, he has to take special classes, his date for the prom makes an excuse not to go with him, and he is haunted by the memory of his older sister who drowned while he was watching.

It is a poignant, gentle, utterly believable narrative. —*Booklist*

True believer. Virginia Euwer Wolff. Atheneum Books for Young Readers, 2001 264 p. (Make lemonade trilogy, 2)
Grades: 8 9 10 11 12
1. Inner city teenage girls; 2. Crushes in teenage girls; 3. Inner city; 4. Single-parent families; 5. Poor families; 6. Realistic fiction; 7. Novels in verse; 8. Pacific Northwest fiction
9780689828270

LC 32792

ALA Notable Children's Book, 2002; Booklist Editors' Choice: Books for Youth, 2001; Golden Kite Award for Fiction, 2001; Leslie Bradshaw Award for Young Readers (Oregon), 2001; National Book Award for Young People's Literature, 2001; School Library Journal Best Books, 2001; YALSA Best Books for Young Adults, 2002; Michael L. Printz Honor Book, 2002.

Living in the inner city amidst guns and poverty, fifteen-year-old LaVaughn learns from old and new friends, and inspiring mentors, that life is what you make it—an occasion to rise to.

LaVaughn tells her own story in heart-stopping stream-of-consciousness that reveals her convincing naivet and her blazing determination, intelligence, and growth.... Transcendent, raw, and fiercely optimistic, the novel answers some of its own questions about overcoming adversity. —*Booklist*

Wolitzer, Meg
Belzhar. Meg Wolitzer. Dutton Juvenile, 2014 272 p.
Grades: 9 10 11 12
1. Teenage girls; 2. Diary writing; 3. Parallel universes; 4. Death; 5. Fifteen-year-old girls; 6. Vermont; 7. Magical realism
9780525423058; 9780142426296

LC 2014010747

Westchester Fiction Award, 2015; YALSA Popular Paperbacks for Young Adults, 2017.

Jam Gallahue, fifteen, unable to cope with the loss of her boyfriend Reeve, is sent to a therapeutic boarding school in Vermont, where a journal-writing assignment for an exclusive, mysterious English class transports her to the magical realm of Belzhar, where she and Reeve can be together.

When Jam suffers a terrible trauma and feels isolated by grief, her parents send her to the Wooden Barn, a boarding school for highly intelligent, emotionally fragile teens. Once there she is enrolled in a class with only five specially selected students where they exclusively read Sylvia Plath...While the conclusion is a touch heavy-handed, older teen readers, especially rabid Plath fans, will relish Wolitzer's deeply respectful treatment of Jam's realistic emotional struggle. —*Booklist*

Wood, Fiona
Cloudwish. Fiona Wood. Pan Macmillan, 2015 288 p.
Grades: 7 8 9 10

1. Teenage girls; 2. Change; 3. Teenage boy/girl relations; 4. Adolescence; 5. Wishing and wishes; 6. Melbourne, Victoria; 7. Australian fiction
9781743533123, paperback, Australia; 9780316242127, hardcover, Australia

Children's Book of the Year Award for Older Readers (Children's Book Council of Australia), 2016; Children's Book Council of Australia: Notable Australian Children's Book, 2016.

Its an inspiring story with a sympathetic heroine, who will especially appeal to those who feel pressured to follow paths they dont want to travel. —*Publishers Weekly*

Wood, Maggie L.
Captured. Maggie L. Wood. Lobster Press, 2011 284 p. (Divided realms, 1)
Grades: 6 7 8 9
1. Princesses; 2. Chess; 3. Fairies; 4. Fifteen-year-old girls; 5. Grandmothers; 6. Fantasy fiction; 7. Canadian fiction.
9781770800717; 9781894549295

Listening to her grandmother's stories of a magical kingdom called Mistolear, fourteen-year-old Willow suddenly finds herself transported there and is shocked to learn it really exists and that she is a princess.

Willow was brought up believing she was just a normal girl with a grandmother that had a penchant for telling fantastic stories about another realm where she was a princess and magic and fairies were everyday occurrences.... Or, at least that is what Willow thought until the day her Nana died and she was transported to the home she never knew to save a family she never knew she had.... Wood's characters must think outside the game to save their world. Sometimes it takes an outsider to see things that those on the inside cannot. This is a wonderful bookwell written and likely to fly off the shelves while fantasy is still the hot genre. —*Voice of Youth Advocates*

Wood, Maryrose
Nightshade. By Maryrose Wood; based on a concept by the Duchess of Northumberland. Balzer + Bray, 2011 288 p. (Poison diaries trilogy, 2)
Grades: 8 9 10
1. Poisons; 2. Lost love; 3. Pharmacists; 4. Humans and plants; 5. Medicinal plants; 6. England; 7. Northumberland, England; 8. Georgian era (1714-1837); 9. 18th century; 10. Historical fantasy; 11. First person narratives.
9780061802423

Promising Weed's continued pursuit (and, hopefully, reviving the intriguing issue of Mr. Luxton's poisoning), part three's sure to levy as much page-turning enthrallment as its predecessors. —*Kirkus*

The **poison** diaries. By Maryrose Wood; based on a concept by the Duchess of Northumberland. Balzer + Bray, 2010 278 p. (Poison diaries trilogy, 1)
Grades: 8 9 10 11
1. Gardens; 2. Poisons; 3. Pharmacists; 4. Humans and plants; 5. Medicinal plants; 6. England; 7. Northumberland, England; 8. Georgian era (1714-1837); 9. 18th century; 10. Historical fantasy; 11. First person narratives.
9780061802362; 9780007354436, print, UK

LC 2009054427

In late eighteenth-century Northumberland, England, sixteen-year-old Jessamine Luxton and the mysterious Weed uncover the horrible secrets of poisons growing in Thomas Luxton's apothecary garden.

This intriguing fantasy has many tendrils to wrap around teen hearts.... The haunting ending will leave readers wanting to talk about the themes of cruelty, honesty, and loyalty. —*Booklist*

Woodfolk, Ashley

When you were everything. Ashley Woodfolk. Delacorte Press, 2020 400 p.
Grades: 9 10 11 12

1. Former friends; 2. Best friends; 3. Separation (Psychology); 4. Female friendship; 5. Teenage girls; 6. New York City; 7. Realistic fiction; 8. Coming-of-age stories; 9. First person narratives
9781524715939; 9781524715915

When her best friendship with Layla implodes beyond repair, Cleo pursues other relationships before she is assigned to tutor her former friend and forced to come to terms with her choices.

Family life, romance, and Shakespeare complicate and thicken this plot, giving reprieve from the intensity of Cleo's friendship struggles. There is a pleasantly mature ending here though, offering a perspective on friendship drama often missing in YA. —*Booklist*

Wooding, Chris

The **haunting** of Alaizabel Cray. Chris Wooding. Orchard Books, 2004 292 p.
Grades: 7 8 9 10

1. Demons; 2. Demonic possession; 3. Good and evil; 4. Supernatural; 5. Serial murderers; 6. London, England; 7. Great Britain; 8. Fantasy fiction; 9. Horror; 10. Gothic fiction
9780439546560; 9780439598514; 9781407136073, print, UK
LC 2003069108
Nestle Children's Book Prize for Nine to Eleven Year Olds, 2001; School Library Journal Best Books, 2004; YALSA Best Books for Young Adults, 2005.

As Thaniel, a wych-hunter, and Cathaline, his friend and mentor, try to rid the alleys of London's Old Quarter of the terrible creatures that infest them, their lives become entwined with that of a woman who may be either mad or possessed.

Eerie and exhilarating.... [The author] fuses together his best story-telling skills... to create a fabulously horrific and ultimately timeless underworld. —*School Library Journal*

★ **Malice**. Chris Wooding; illustrated by Dan Chernett. Scholastic Press, 2009 384 p. (Malice (Chris Wooding), 1)
Grades: 6 7 8 9 10

1. Comic books, strips, etc; 2. Good and evil; 3. Imagination; 4. Teenagers; 5. Parallel universes; 6. London, England; 7. Fantasy fiction; 8. Horror; 9. Gateway fantasy.
9780545160438
YALSA Popular Paperbacks for Young Adults, 2011.

Having read all about the sinister world in which the villainous Tall Jake resides, fans Luke, Seth, and Kady learn more about it than they ever wanted when they are suddenly pulled into the pages of their comic book and come face-to-face with Tall Jake himself!

This nail-biter will keep readers glued to the story until the very last page is turned.... Seth and Kady are strong and exciting characters. —*School Library Journal*
Sequel: *Havoc.*

Retribution Falls. Chris Wooding. Gollancz, 2009 380 p. (Tales of the Ketty Jay, 1)
Grades: 11 12 Adult

1. Spaceship captains; 2. Pirates; 3. Chases; 4. Thieves; 5. Rogues; 6. Steampunk; 7. Swashbuckling tales; 8. Fantasy fiction; 9. Adult books for young adults.
9780575085145, hbk, UK; 9780575085152, pbk, UK; 9781780620565, paperback, UK; 9780575085169, paperback, UK; 9780345522511, paperback, US
School Library Journal Best Books: Best Adult Books 4 Teens, 2011.

Darian Frey is the roguish captain of the Ketty Jay, and leader of a small and highly dysfunctional band of layabouts. They smuggle contraband, rob airships and generally make a nuisance of themselves, all the while avoiding the Coalition Navy frigates. So when Frey suddenly finds himself public enemy number one, with both the Coalition Navy and hired bounty hunters after him, he has to do something. Fast. To prove his innocence he'll have to catch the real culprit, surviving gunfights and facing down liars and lovers, Dukes and daemons along the way.

Silver. Chris Wooding. Scholastic Press, 2014 320 p.
Grades: 7 8 9 10 11 12

1. Boarding school students; 2. Beetles; 3. Survival; 4. Boarding schools; 5. Schools; 6. England; 7. Horror
9780545603928

When strange insects assault a remote boarding school in England, the kids try to save the day in this tense page-turner...Skillfully managed subplots keep the pages flying. It looks like the end of the world is nigh.... It's just all kinds of white-knuckle fun. —*Kirkus*

Velocity. Chris Wooding. Scholastic Press, 2017 336 p.
Grades: 7 8 9 10

1. Automobile racing; 2. Post-apocalypse; 3. Competition; 4. Automobile mechanics; 5. Best friends; 6. Australia; 7. Science fiction; 8. Apocalyptic fiction; 9. Books for reluctant readers
9780545944946; 9781407124292, print, UK

Dynamic as a pair because of respective strengths that make them a formidable drag racing team, best friends Cassica and Shiara set their sights on winning the year's biggest, most dangerous race only to find their efforts challenged by fundamental personal differences.

An action-packed, wild ride with unexpected twists and turns and characters readers care aboutcall it a dystopia with heart. —*Kirkus*
First published in the United Kingdom in 2015 by Scholastic Children's Books

Woodson, Jacqueline

★ **After** Tupac and D Foster. Jacqueline Woodson. G.P. Putnam's Sons, 2008 160 p.
Grades: 7 8 9 10

1. Shakur, Tupac, 1971-1996; 2. African American teenage girls; 3. Street life; 4. Independence in teenage girls; 5. Best friends; 6. Mother-deserted children; 7. Queens, New York City; 8. 1990s; 9. Coming-of-age stories; 10. Realistic fiction; 11. African American fiction
9780399246548
LC 2007023725
ALA Notable Children's Book, 2009; Josette Frank Award, 2009; Rainbow List, 2009; YALSA Best Books for Young Adults, 2009; Newbery Honor Book, 2009.

In the New York City borough of Queens in 1996, three girls bond over their shared love of Tupac Shakur's music, as together they try to make sense of the unpredictable world in which they live.

The subtlety and depth with which the author conveys the girls' relationships lend this novel exceptional vividness and staying power. —*Publishers Weekly*

Behind you. Jacqueline Woodson. G.P. Putnam's Sons, 2004 128 p.
Grades: 7 8 9 10

1. Death; 2. Grief; 3. African American teenage boys — Death; 4. Teenage girls; 5. Teenage boys — Death; 6. New York City; 7. Realistic fiction; 8. African American fiction; 9. Books for reluctant readers
9780399239885
LC 2003023179

YALSA Quick Picks for Reluctant Young Adult Readers, 2005; YALSA Best Books for Young Adults, 2005.

After fifteen-year-old Jeremiah is mistakenly shot by police, the people who love him struggle to cope with their loss as they recall his life and death, unaware that 'Miah is watching over them.

Woodson writes with impressive poetry about race, love, death, and what grief feels likethe things that snap the heart and her characters' open strength and wary optimism will resonate with many teens. —*Booklist*
Sequel to: *If You Come Softly.*

Beneath a meth moon. Jacqueline Woodson. Nancy Paulsen Books, 2012 181 p.
Grades: 9 10 11 12
1. Teenage girl drug abusers; 2. Cheerleaders; 3. Grief in teenage girls; 4. Grief; 5. Drug abuse; 6. Iowa; 7. Mississippi; 8. Realistic fiction; 9. African American fiction; 10. Books for reluctant readers
9780399252501
YALSA Best Fiction for Young Adults, 2013; YALSA Quick Picks for Reluctant Young Adult Readers, 2013.

After losing her mother and grandmother during Hurricane Katrina, Laurel moves to another town and becomes a methamphetamine addict.

★ **From** the notebooks of Melanin Sun. Jacqueline Woodson. Scholastic, 1995 141 p.
Grades: 7 8 9 10
1. Thirteen-year-old boys; 2. Children of LGBTQIA parents; 3. African American teenage boys; 4. African American mother and son; 5. Lesbian mothers; 6. Brooklyn, New York City; 7. Realistic fiction; 8. African American fiction
9780590458801
LC 93034158 /AC
Lambda Literary Award for Young Adult/Children Winners, 1995; YALSA Best Books for Young Adults, 1996; Coretta Scott King Honor Book for Authors, 1996.

Thirteen-year-old Melanin Sun's comfortable, quiet life is shattered when his mother reveals she has fallen in love with a woman.

Offering no easy answers, Woodson teaches the reader that love can lead to acceptance of all manner of differences. —*Publishers Weekly*

★ **If** you come softly. G. P. Putnam's Sons, 1998 181 p.
Grades: 7 8 9 10
1. Prep school students; 2. Interracial romance; 3. Racism; 4. Teenage romance; 5. African American teenage boys; 6. Manhattan, New York City; 7. New York City; 8. Love stories; 9. Realistic fiction; 10. African American fiction
9780399231124
Black-Eyed Susan Book Award (Maryland), High School, 2002; Virginia Readers' Choice Award for High School, 2001; YALSA Best Books for Young Adults, 1999.

The gentle and melancholy tone of this book makes it ideal for thoughtful readers and fans of romance. —*Voice of Youth Advocates*
Sequel: *Behind You.*

Lena. Delacorte Press, 1999 115 p.
Grades: 6 7 8 9
1. Thirteen-year-old girls; 2. Runaway girls; 3. Sisters; 4. Family and child abuse; 5. African American fiction
9780385323086
LC 98024317
Thirteen-year-old Lena and her younger sister Dion mourn the death of their mother as they hitchhike from Ohio to Kentucky while running away from their abusive father.

Soulful, wise and sometimes wrenching, this taut story never loses its grip on the reader. —*Publishers Weekly*

Miracle's boys. Jacqueline Woodson. G. P. Putnam's Sons, 2000 133 p.
Grades: 9 10 11 12
1. African American families; 2. Secrets; 3. Poor people; 4. Twelve-year-old boys; 5. Mothers — Death; 6. Realistic fiction; 7. African American fiction
9780399231131
LC 99040050
Coretta Scott King Award, Author Category, 2001; Los Angeles Times Book Prize for Young Adult Fiction, 2000; YALSA Popular Paperbacks for Young Adults, 2008; YALSA Best Books for Young Adults, 2001.

Twelve-year-old Lafayette's close relationship with his older brother Charlie changes after Charlie is released from a detention home and blames Lafayette for the death of their mother.

The fast-paced narrative is physically immediate, and the dialogue is alive with anger and heartbreak. —*Booklist*

Woolston, Blythe
★ **Black** helicopters. Blythe Woolston. Candlewick Press, 2013 176 p.
Grades: 9 10 11 12
1. Fifteen-year-old girls; 2. Resistance to government; 3. Terrorism; 4. Bombs; 5. Teenage girls; 6. Montana; 7. Coming-of-age stories.
9780763661465
LC 2012942619
YALSA Best Fiction for Young Adults, 2014.

Surviving in an underground den for more than a decade after her people are attacked by the forces of a hostile government, fifteen-year-old Valkyrie and her older brother emerge in a near-future Montana and struggle to acclimate to a world filled with fear and violence.

Catch & release. Blythe Woolston. Lerner Publishing Group, 2012 216 p.
Grades: 9 10 11 12
1. Teenagers with disabilities; 2. Automobile travel; 3. Bonding (Interpersonal relations); 4. Eighteen-year-old women; 5. Teenage boys; 6. Realistic fiction; 7. First person narratives.
9780761377559
Eighteen-year-old Polly and impulsive, seventeen-year-old Odd survive a deadly outbreak of flesh-eating bacteria, but resulting wounds have destroyed their plans for the future and with little but their unlikely friendship and a shared affection for trout fishing, they set out on a road trip through the West.

This is not a romance, but a tale of two people thrown together after their world has been turned upside down. Each is unique, vividly complicated and true. Engaging writing and characters lift this above the typical cliched story of disabled teens. Heartbreakingly honest. —*Kirkus*

★ The **freak** observer. By Blythe Woolston. Carolrhoda Lab, 2010 202 p.
Grades: 8 9 10 11 12
1. Post-traumatic stress disorder; 2. Emotional problems of teenage girls; 3. Grief in teenage girls; 4. Grief; 5. Nightmares; 6. Montana; 7. Realistic fiction.
9780761362128
LC 2010000989
William C. Morris YA Debut Award, 2011.

Suffering from a crippling case of post-traumatic stress disorder, sixteen-year-old Loa Lindgren tries to use her problem solving skills, sharpened in physics and computer programming, to cure herself.

Woolston's talent for dialogue and her unique approach to scenes make what sounds standard about this story feel fresh and vital.... A strong...[novel] about learning to see yourself apart from the reflection you cast off others. —*Booklist*

★ **MARTians**. Blythe Woolston. Candlewick Press, 2015 224 p.
Grades: 9 10 11 12
1. Near future; 2. Dystopias; 3. Teenage employees; 4. Consumerism; 5. Retail stores; 6. Dystopian fiction; 7. Science fiction; 8. First person narratives
9780763677565; 9781406341393, print, UK

Imagination shines through the bleak but poetic prose, love and kindness prove hearty, and once again, life proves that roses not only do, but always will, grow in concrete. Dystopian aficionados, budding social pundits, and readers who enjoy quirky characters, settings, and challenges will find a lot to love here. —*Voice of Youth Advocates*

Woon, Yvonne
Life eternal: a Dead beautiful novel. Yvonne Woon. Hyperion, 2012 400 p. (Dead beautiful novels, 2)
Grades: 9 10 11 12
1. Boarding schools; 2. Supernatural; 3. Undead; 4. Soul mates; 5. Schools; 6. Montreal, Quebec; 7. Canada; 8. Paranormal romances.
9781423119579; 9781423137627
LC 2011018257

Seventeen-year-old Renée Winters must transfer to a Montréal school exclusively for those training to kill the Undead, while unraveling a long-buried secret that may be the key to saving Dante Berlin, her Undead soulmate.

Wray, John
★ **Lowboy:** a novel. John Wray. Farrar Straus and Giroux, 2009 272 p.
Grades: 11 12 Adult
1. Sixteen-year-old boys; 2. People with paranoid schizophrenia; 3. Missing persons investigation; 4. Climate change; 5. City life; 6. New York City; 7. Psychological fiction; 8. Multiple perspectives; 9. Adult books for young adults.
9780374194161; 9781847671523, print, UK
LC 2008017921

Possessing paranoid schizophrenic beliefs that he can save the planet from climate change by cooling down his own overheated body, sixteen-year-old New York youth Will Heller pursues a terrifying and delusional odyssey through the city's tunnels and backalleys.

This is a brilliant and gutsy performance but a cryptic one. It expresses its meanings in hallucinated events that seem to vibrate on the page. At certain moments the book feels like a runaway subway car; you want it to slow down for you. —*The Buffalo News*

Wrede, Patricia C.
The **Far** West. Patricia C. Wrede. Scholastic Press, 2012 378 p. (Frontier magic, 3)
Grades: 7 8 9 10 11 12
1. Twin brothers and sisters; 2. Frontier and pioneer life; 3. Expeditions; 4. Floods; 5. Bad luck; 6. Historical fantasy
9780545033442

When the unlucky magical twin Eff joins an expedition to map the Far West, she endures a long prairie winter and encounters with previously unknown creatures before realizing the importance of ending a magical flood.

Sorcery and Cecelia, or, The enchanted chocolate pot: being the correspondence of two young ladies of quality regarding variousmagical scandals in London and the country. Patricia C. Wrede and Caroline Stevermer. Harcourt, 2003 316 p; (Cecelia and Kate novels, 1)

Grades: 7 8 9 10
1. Cousins; 2. Wizards; 3. Best friends; 4. Supernatural; 5. Magic; 6. London, England; 7. England; 8. 1810s; 9. Historical fantasy; 10. Epistolary novels.
9780152046156
LC 2002038706

YALSA Best Books for Young Adults, 2004.

In an alternative 1817 England where magic is commonplace, cousins Cecelia (who lives in the country) and Kate (who lives in London) keep in touch by writing letters about their exploits—which take a sinister turn when the young women are confronted by evil wizards and Kate is almost poisoned.

This is a fun story that quickly draws in the reader. —*Voice of Youth Advocates*

The **thirteenth** child. Patricia C. Wrede. Scholastic Press, 2009 344 p; (Frontier magic, 1)
Grades: 7 8 9 10 11 12
1. Magic; 2. Frontier and pioneer life; 3. Brothers and sisters; 4. Memories; 5. Universities and colleges; 6. Coming-of-age stories; 7. Historical fantasy
9780545033428
LC 2008034048

Eighteen-year-old Eff must finally get over believing she is bad luck and accept that her special training in Aphrikan magic, and being the twin of the seventh son of a seventh son, give her extraordinary power to combat magical creatures that threaten settlements on the western frontier.

Wrede creates a rich world where steam dragons seem as normal as bears, and a sympathetic character in Eff. —*Publishers Weekly*

Wright, Barbara
★ **Crow**. Barbara Wright. Random House, 2012 320 p.
Grades: 4 5 6 7
1. Riots; 2. African American boys; 3. Racism; 4. Families; 5. Race relations; 6. Wilmington, North Carolina; 7. 1890s; 8. 19th century; 9. Historical fiction; 10. First person narratives.
9780375969287
LC 2011014892

In 1898, Moses Thomas's summer vacation does not go exactly as planned as he contends with family problems and the ever-changing alliances among his friends at the same time as he is exposed to the escalating tension between the African-American and white communities of Wilmington, North Carolina.

An intensely moving, first-person narrative of a disturbing historical footnote told from the perspective of a very likable, credible young hero. —*Kirkus*

Wright, Bil
Putting makeup on the fat boy. Bil Wright. Simon & Schuster Books for Young Readers, 2011 208 p.
Grades: 7 8 9 10 11 12
1. Makeup artists; 2. Hispanic American teenage boys; 3. Gay teenagers; 4. Dating violence; 5. Crushes in boys; 6. New York City; 7. Realistic fiction; 8. LGBTQIA fiction; 9. African American fiction
9781416939962, HRD, US
LC 2010032450

Lambda Literary Award for Young Adult/Children, 2011; Rainbow List, 2012; Stonewall Book Award for Children's and Young Adult Literature, 2012; YALSA Popular Paperbacks for Young Adults, 2013.

Sixteen-year-old Carlos Duarte is on the verge of realizing his dream of becoming a famous make-up artist, but first he must face his jealous boss at a Macy's cosmetics counter, his sister's abusive boyfriend, and his crush on a punk-rocker classmate.

Obviously, there's a whole lot going on in Wright's novel, but it's handled deftly and, for the most part, believably. Best of all, Carlos is not completely defined by his homosexuality. —*Booklist*

When the black girl sings. Bil Wright. Simon & Schuster Books for Young Readers, 2008 266 p;
Grades: 6 7 8 9 10
1. African Americans; 2. African American girls; 3. Fourteen-year-olds; 4. Fourteen-year-old girls; 5. Teenagers; 6. Connecticut; 7. African American fiction
9781416939955
LC 2006030837

Adopted by white parents and sent to an exclusive Connecticut girls' school where she is the only black student, fourteen-year-old Lahni Schuler feels like an outcast, particularly when her parents separate, but after attending a local church where she hears gospel music for the first time, she finds her voice.

Readers will enjoy the distinctive characters, lively dialogue, and palette of adolescent and racial insecurities in this contemporary, upbeat story. —*School Library Journal*

Wulffson, Don L.

Soldier X. Don L. Wulffson. Viking, 2000 Viii, 226 p;
Grades: 7 8 9 10
1. World War II; 2. Military campaigns; 3. Teenage soldiers; 4. Sixteen-year-old boys; 5. Soviet Union; 6. Germany
9780670888634
LC 9904918

In 1943 sixteen-year-old Erik experiences the horrors of war when he is drafted into the German army and sent to fight on the Russian front.

Erik's first-person narrative records battlefield sequences with an unflinchingand occasionally numbing brutality, in a story notable for its unusual perspective. —*Horn Book Guide*

Based on a true story.

Wunder, Wendy

★ The **museum** of intangible things. Wendy Wunder. Razorbill, 2014 304 pages
Grades: 8 9 10 11 12
1. Children of alcoholics; 2. Bipolar disorder; 3. Cross-country automobile trips; 4. Best friends; 5. Friendship; 6. New Jersey; 7. Realistic fiction
9781595145147
LC 2013030169

Best friends Hannah and Zoe, seventeen, leave their down-and-out New Jersey town and drive west chasing storms, making new friends, and seeking the intangibles—audacity, insouciance, happiness—that their lives have lacked.

As Hannah and best friend Zoe (diagnosed bipolar) embark on a cross-country road trip, Zoe gives Hannah intangible lessons (e.g, Hannah learns insouciance when they overnight in an IKEA). When Zoe's irrationality gets scary, Hannah learns betrayal and, later, forgiveness. With each lesson, Hannah becomes more confident, building her own distinct identity. Meanwhile, Zoe is a complex character— intelligent, loyal, and funny. —*Horn Book Guide*

The **probability** of miracles. Wendy Wunder. Razorbill, 2011 360 p.
Grades: 8 9 10 11 12
1. Teenage girls with cancer; 2. Teenagers with terminal illnesses; 3. Miracles; 4. Children of divorced parents; 5. Moving to a new state; 6. Maine; 7. Realistic fiction.

9781595143686

Faced with death, one teen discovers life in this bittersweet debut.... Cynical and loner Campbell Cooper (an Italian-Samoan-American) gave up on magic after her parents divorced, her father died and she developed neuroblastoma.... Having exhausted Western medicine, her single mother suggests spending the summer after Cam's graduation in Promise, Maine, a hidden town...known to have mysterious healing powers.... Exploring both sides of Cam's heritage, the story unfolds through narration as beautiful as the sun's daily everlasting gobstopper descent behind the lighthouse. Irreverent humor, quirky small-town charm and surprises along the way help readers brace themselves for the tearjerker ending. —*Kirkus*

Wyatt, Melissa

Funny how things change. Melissa Wyatt. Farrar Straus Giroux, 2009 208 p.
Grades: 9 10 11 12
1. Rural life; 2. Options, alternatives, choices; 3. Small town life; 4. Mountains; 5. Interpersonal relations; 6. West Virginia; 7. Realistic fiction
9780374302337
LC 2008016190

YALSA Best Books for Young Adults, 2010.

Remy, a talented, seventeen-year-old auto mechanic, questions his decision to join his girlfriend when she starts college in Pennsylvania after a visiting artist helps him to realize what his family's home in a dying West Virginia mountain town means to him.

Laconic but full of heart, smart, thoughtful and proudly working-class, Remy makes a fresh and immensely appealing hero. —*Kirkus*

Wynne-Jones, Tim

★ **Blink** & Caution. By Tim Wynne-Jones. Candlewick Press, 2011 352 p.
Grades: 9 10 11 12
1. Runaway teenagers; 2. Witnesses; 3. Hoaxes; 4. Crime; 5. Kidnapping; 6. Toronto, Ontario; 7. Canada; 8. Realistic fiction; 9. Multiple perspectives; 10. Canadian fiction.
9780763639839; 9780763656973; 9781406337419, print, UK
LC 2010013563

Arthur Ellis Award for Best Juvenile Mystery, 2012; Boston Globe-Horn Book Award for Fiction and Poetry, 2011; YALSA Best Fiction for Young Adults, 2012; Westchester Fiction Award, 2011; School Library Journal Best Books, 2011.

Two teenagers who are living on the streets and barely getting by become involved in a complicated criminal plot, and make an unexpected connection with each other.

The short, punchy sentences Wynne-Jones fires like buckshot; the joy, fear, and doubt that punctuate the teens' every action. This is gritty, sure, but more than that, it's smart, and earns every drop of its hopeful finish. —*Booklist*

★ The **emperor** of any place. Tim Wynne-Jones. Candlewick Press, 2015 336 p.
Grades: 9 10 11 12
1. Grandfather and grandson; 2. Family secrets; 3. Castaways; 4. Sixteen-year-old boys; 5. Self-esteem; 6. Fantasy fiction.
9780763669737

Booklist Editors' Choice: Books for Youth, 2015; School Library Journal Best Books, 2015; YALSA Best Fiction for Young Adults, 2016.

Fifteen days after his father passes away, Evan enters his father's home office only to find a mysterious letter, regarding a book about a Japanese soldier on a small Pacific island during the Second World War, that leads to the discover of some family secrets that had been buried for decades.

Without spelling out the metaphoric significance of the story within the story, Wynne-Jones provides enough hints for readers to make connections and examine the lines between war and peace, as well as hate and love. —*Publishers Weekly*

The **uninvited**. Tim Wynne-Jones. Candlewick Press, 2009 354 p.
Grades: 10 11 12
1. College students; 2. Stalkers; 3. Vacation homes; 4. Brothers and sisters; 5. Musicians; 6. Canada; 7. Thrillers and suspense; 8. Canadian fiction.
9780763639846

LC 2009007520
YALSA Best Books for Young Adults, 2010; OLA Best Bets, 2009.

After a disturbing freshman year at New York University, Mimi is happy to get away to her father's remote Canadian cottage only to discover a stranger living there who has never heard of her or her father and who is convinced that Mimi is responsible for leaving sinister tokens around the property.

This suspenseful and deftly crafted family drama will appeal to older teens who are exploring their options beyond high school. —*Voice of Youth Advocates*

Yancey, Richard
★ The **5th** wave. Rick Yancey. G.P. Putnam's Sons, 2013 592 p. (5th wave, 1)
Grades: 9 10 11 12
1. Survival; 2. Brothers and sisters; 3. Teenagers; 4. Science fiction; 5. Apocalyptic fiction; 6. Multiple perspectives; 7. Books for reluctant readers
9780399162411; 9780141366470, print, Australia; 9780141345833, print, UK

LC 2012047622
Gateway Readers Award (Missouri), 2016; Green Mountain Book Award (Vermont), 2015; Iowa High School Book Award, 2016; Keystone to Reading Book Award (Pennsylvania), High School level, 2015; Sequoyah Book Awards (Oklahoma), High School Books, 2016; South Carolina Book Award, Young Adult Books, 2016; Westchester Fiction Award, 2014; YALSA Quick Picks for Reluctant Young Adult Readers, 2014; YALSA Best Fiction for Young Adults, 2014; YALSA Popular Paperbacks for Young Adults, 2016; Young Reader's Choice Award (Pacific Northwest), Intermediate, 2016.

Cassie Sullivan, the survivor of an alien invasion, must rescue her young brother from the enemy with help from a boy who may be one of them.

Yancey makes a dramatic 180 from the intellectual horror of his Monstrumologist books to open a gripping SF trilogy about an Earth decimated by an alien invasion. The author fully embraces the genre, while resisting its more sensational tendencies... It's a book that targets a broad commercial audience, and Yancey's aim is every bit as good as Cassie's. —*Publishers Weekly*
The 5th Wave was adapted into a 2016 movie of the same name.

The **curse** of the Wendigo. Rick Yancey. Simon & Schuster Books for Young Readers, 2010 448 p. (Monstrumologist, 2)
Grades: 9 10 11 12
1. Monsters; 2. Scientists; 3. Truth; 4. Supernatural; 5. Rescues; 6. New York City; 7. 1880s; 8. Horror; 9. Diary novels
9781416984504; 9781481425490
Booklist Editors' Choice: Books for Youth, 2010; YALSA Best Fiction for Young Adults, 2011.

This book is as fast-paced, elegant, and, yes, gruesome as its predecessor.... The development of the relationship between hapless Will and

the demanding monstrumologist is the most rewarding aspect of the story. —*Publishers Weekly*
Also known as: *The terror beneath*.

The **extraordinary** adventures of Alfred Kropp. By Rick Yancey. Bloomsbury, 2005 339 p; (Alfred Kropp adventures, 1)
Grades: 7 8 9 10
1. Teenage boy orphans; 2. Teenage boy misfits; 3. Magic swords; 4. Uncles; 5. Excalibur (Sword); 6. Tennessee; 7. Fantasy fiction.
9781582346939

LC 2005013044
YALSA Popular Paperbacks for Young Adults, 2009.

Through a series of dangerous and violent misadventures, teenage loser Alfred Kropp rescues King Arthur's legendary sword Excalibur from the forces of evil.

True to its action-adventure genre, the story is lighthearted, entertaining, occasionally half-witted, but by and large fun. —*School Library Journal*

The **final** descent. Rick Yancey. Simon & Schuster Books for Young Readers, 2013 448 p. (Monstrumologist, 4)
Grades: 9 10 11 12
1. Apprentices; 2. Monsters; 3. Loyalty; 4. Supernatural; 5. Scientists; 6. 19th century; 7. Horror; 8. Diary novels
9781442451537; 9781442451551, ebook, US

LC 2013015811
Booklist Editors' Choice: Books for Youth, 2013.

When Dr. Warthrop begins to doubt fourteen-year-old Will Henry's loyalty, he sets him against one of the most horrific creatures in the Monstrumarium, unaware that Will's life and his own fate will lie in the balance.

This fourth and final volume of the series (a blend of gothic horror, cryptozoology, and Sherlockiana) features apprentice Will Henry in the throes of adolescent rebellion as he seeks to escape the jealous, domineering monstrumologist Warthrop and wrest the affection of Lilly Bates away from a rival suitor. Yancey has taken some considerable risks here, ones that should thrill his ardent fans. —*Horn Book Guide*

The **infinite** sea. Rick Yancey. G. P. Putnam's Sons, 2014 480 p. (5th wave, 2)
Grades: 9 10 11 12
1. Survival; 2. Brothers and sisters; 3. Teenagers; 4. Science fiction; 5. Apocalyptic fiction; 6. Multiple perspectives.
9780399162428; 9780141345871, print, UK
Booklist Editors' Choice: Books for Youth, 2014.

Yancey's prose remains unimpeachable every paragraph is laden with setting, theme, and emotion and he uses it toward a series of horrifying set pieces, including a surgery scene that will have your pages sopping with sweat. —*Booklist*

The **last** star: the final book of the 5th wave. G.P. Putnam's Sons Books for Young Readers,, 2016 352 p. (5th wave, 3)
Grades: 9 10 11 12
1. Betrayal; 2. Survival; 3. Teenagers; 4. Science fiction; 5. Apocalyptic fiction; 6. Multiple perspectives.
9780399162435; 9780141345949

As the true agenda of the Others is revealed, Cassie, Ringer, Zombie, and the rest of the humans realize they've been betrayed and must decide what's worth saving in what appear to be Earth's final days.

★ The **monstrumologist**. Rick Yancey. Simon & Schuster Books for Young Readers, 2009 434 p. (Monstrumologist, 1)
Grades: 9 10 11 12

1. Boy apprentices; 2. Monsters; 3. Supernatural; 4. Scientists; 5. Boy orphans; 6. New England; 7. 1880s; 8. Horror; 9. Diary novels; 10. First person narratives.
9781416984481; 9781481425445

LC 2009004562

Booklist Editors' Choice: Books for Youth, 2009; YALSA Popular Paperbacks for Young Adults, 2017; YALSA Best Books for Young Adults, 2010; Michael L. Printz Honor Book, 2010.

In 1888 New England, monster-hunting doctor Pellinore Warthrop and his apprentice Will Henry encounter an Anthropophagus—a headless, supposedly extinct monster that has teeth in its belly and feeds on humans—and the two of them must track and kill an entire pod of the beasts. Alternately flowery and dripping with gore, the writing is lush and compelling; it will transport you to the Victorian age...and scare your trousers off.

As the action moves from the dissecting table to the cemetery to an asylum to underground catacombs, Yancey keeps the shocks frequent and shrouded in a splattery miasma of blood, bone, pus, and maggots.... Yancey's prose is stentorian and wordy, but it weaves a world that possesses a Lovecraftian logic and hints at its own deeply satisfying mythos.... Snap to! is Warthrop's continued demand of Will, but readers will need no such needling. —*Booklist*

Yang, Dori Jones

Daughter of Xanadu. Dori Jones Yang. Delacorte Press, 2011 352 p.
Grades: 7 8 9 10 11 12
1. Kublai Khan; 2. Mongols; 3. Teenage girl soldiers; 4. Explorers; 5. Gender role; 6. Interpersonal attraction; 7. China; 8. 13th century; 9. Historical fiction; 10. First person narratives.
9780385739238

LC 2009053652

Amelia Bloomer List, 2012.

Emmajin, the sixteen-year-old eldest granddaughter of Khublai Khan, becomes a warrior and falls in love with explorer Marco Polo in thirteenth-century China.

Daughter of Xanadu offers rich descriptions and vivid depictions of fictional characters and historical figures, making them charming and believable. A colorful and compelling read. —*School Library Journal*

Yang, Kelly

Parachutes. Kelly Yang. Katherine Tegen Books, 2020 496 p.
Grades: 9 10 11 12
1. Chinese in the United States; 2. Inequality; 3. Sex crimes; 4. Wealth; 5. Parent-separated teenagers; 6. Los, Angeles, California; 7. Realistic fiction; 8. Multiple perspectives
9780062941084, hardback, US

LC 2019951312

A teen from a privileged Asian family navigates culture shock, unexpected freedom, and a new relationship while attending school in California and renting a room from the family of an Ivy League hopeful whose debate coach has undermined her plans.

Yang writes astutely about the destabilizing combination of family expectations, copious wealth, and absence of adult supervision for Claire and her fellow parachutes, who lead a seemingly heady but ultimately emotionally precarious existence. She's also sharply perceptive about the class and race complexities of a community that contains rich Asian visitors and American-born Asians, great wealth and straitened circumstances. —*Bulletin of the Center for Children's Books*

Yansky, Brian

Alien invasion and other inconveniences. Brian Yansky. Candlewick Press, 2010 240 p.

Grades: 9 10 11 12
1. Teenage slaves; 2. Aliens (Non-humanoid); 3. Telepathy; 4. Escapes; 5. Friendship; 6. Austin, Texas; 7. Science fiction; 8. First person narratives.
9780763643843

LC 2009049103

When a race of aliens quickly takes over the earth, leaving most people dead, high-schooler Jesse finds himself a slave to an inept alien leader—a situation that brightens as Jesse develops telepathic powers and attracts the attention of two beautiful girls.

The story is action-packed, provocative, profound, and wickedly funny. Yansky takes on questions philosophical, ecological, religious, moral, and social, and the satire is right on target. —*Horn Book Guide*

Sequel: *Homicidal aliens and other disappointments*.

Yee, F. C.

★ The **epic** crush of Genie Lo: a novel. By F.C. Yee. 2017 320 pages (Genie Lo novels, 1)
Grades: 7 8 9 10
1. Chinese American teenage girls; 2. Reincarnation; 3. Demons; 4. Overachievers; 5. Teenage boy/girl relations; 6. Urban fantasy; 7. Mythological fiction; 8. First person narratives
9781419725487

LC 2017018271

The struggle to get into a top-tier college consumes sixteen-year-old Genie's every waking thought. But when she discovers she's a celestial spirit who's powerful enough to bash through the gates of heaven with her fists, her perfectionist existence is shattered.

Hard-driving, hyperachieving Chinese-American sophomore Genie Lo may have to put her take-no-prisoners rush to the Ivy Leagues aside so she can save the world, or at least the local region of California currently under attack by Chinese demons.... Loads of action, a touch of comedy, a bit of well-controlled lust, and even some serious discussion of Eastern philosophy should leave readers eager for a return performance. —*Bulletin of the Center for Children's Books*

The **iron** will of Genie Lo. By F. C. Yee. Amulet Books, 2020 304 p. (Genie Lo novels, 2)
Grades: 7 8 9 10
1. Chinese American teenage girls; 2. Parallel universes; 3. Gods and goddesses; 4. Demons; 5. Demon slayers; 6. Urban fantasy; 7. Mythological fiction; 8. First person narratives.
9781419731457, HRD, US; 9781683353812, (ebook), US

LC 2019035133

When Genie Lo learns of a cosmos-threatening force while the Jade Emperor is absent, she leads a party of quarrelsome Chinese gods through multiple planes of reality on a quest that will require sacrifice, not strength.

The politics of the gods, criticism of Silicon Valley VC funding, college parties, and the uncertainty of the future on this plane of existence (plus all the others) are all explored with Genie's hilarious and biting voice especially when she's at her most vulnerable. —*School Library Journal*

Yee, Lisa

Warp speed. By Lisa Yee. Arthur A. Levine Books, 2011 320 p.
Grades: 5 6 7 8
1. Boy misfits; 2. Bullying and bullies; 3. Popularity; 4. Running; 5. Track and field; 6. California; 7. Realistic fiction.
9780545122764
YALSA Best Fiction for Young Adults, 2012.

Yee's combination of humor and sympathy works a charm here, giving Marley a life of his own and a chance at success in this solid addition to her prismatic look at middle school. —*Kirkus*

Yee, Paul
Learning to fly. Paul Yee. Orca Book Publishers, 2008 112 p.
Grades: 7 8 9 10
1. Popularity; 2. Friendship; 3. Teenage immigrants; 4. Immigrant families; 5. Belonging; 6. Canadian fiction; 7. High interest-low vocabulary books; 8. Realistic fiction
9781551439532

Jason Chen, 17, wants to leave his small town in Canada and return to China.... His white high-school teachers do not know how smart he is, and his classmates jeer at him. Driven to join the crowd of potheads, he bonds especially with his Native American classmate, Charles (Chief). Narrated in Jason's wry, first-person, present-tense narrative, Yee's slim novel packs in a lot.... The clipped dialogue perfectly echoes the contemporary scene, the harsh prejudice felt by the new immigrant and the Native American, and their gripping friendship story. —*Booklist*

High interest story designed for reluctant readers or those reading below grade level.

Yelchin, Eugene
Spy runner. Eugene Yelchin. Henry Holt & Co, 2019 352 p.
Grades: 5 6 7 8 9
1. Suspicion; 2. Anti-Communism; 3. Children of military personnel; 4. Investigations; 5. Twelve-year-old boys; 6. 1950s; 7. Thrillers and suspense; 8. Spy fiction; 9. Historical fiction.
9781250120816; 9781250120823

A Cold War noir mystery by the Newbery Honor-winning author of *Breaking Stalin's Nose* finds a 12-year-old boy targeting a Russian boarder in his home with suspicion in his determination to learn the fate of his father, who went missing in action during World War II.

Well-plotted and -paced, Yelchin's thriller will be a favorite among readers who have an interest in history and intrigue. —*Publishers Weekly*
Illustrated by the author.

Yep, Laurence
★ **Dragon's** gate. Laurence Yep. Harper Collins, 1993 273 p. (Golden mountain chronicles, 3)
Grades: 6 7 8 9
1. Railroads; 2. Immigrants, Chinese; 3. Railroad workers; 4. Immigrant workers; 5. Chinese Americans; 6. Sierra Nevada Mountains; 7. 19th century; 8. American Westward Expansion (1803-1899); 9. Historical fiction.
9780060229719; 9780060229726

LC 92043649 /AC
ALA Notable Children's Book, 1994; Newbery Honor Book, 1994.

When he accidentally kills a Manchu, a fifteen-year-old Chinese boy is sent to America to join his father, an uncle, and other Chinese working to build a tunnel for the transcontinental railroad through the Sierra Nevada mountains in 1867. Sequel to: *"Mountain light."*

Yep has succeeded in realizing the primary characters and the irrepressibly dramatic story.... The carefully researched details will move students to thought and discussion. —*Bulletin of the Center for Children's Books*
Includes bibliographical references.

★ **Dragonwings**. Laurence Yep. Harper & Row, 1975 248 p. (Golden mountain chronicles, 5)
Grades: 6 7 8 9

1. Fathers and sons; 2. Immigrants, Chinese; 3. Prejudice; 4. Aviation; 5. Airplanes; 6. San Francisco, California; 7. Chinatown, San Francisco, California; 8. 1900s (Decade); 9. Historical fiction.
9780060267377

LC 74002625
International Reading Association Children's Book Award for Older Readers, 1976; Phoenix Award, 1995; Newbery Honor Book, 1976.

In the early twentieth century a young Chinese boy joins his father in San Francisco and helps him realize his dream of making a flying machine.

Yolen, Jane
★ **Briar** Rose. Jane Yolen. Tor Books, 1992 190 p; (Fairy tales: a series of fantasy novels retelling classic tales, 6)
Grades: 8 9 10 11 12 Adult
1. Jewish American women; 2. Storytelling; 3. Holocaust survivors; 4. Grandmothers; 5. Grandmother and granddaughter; 6. Poland; 7. Contemporary fantasy; 8. Fantasy fiction; 9. Adaptations, retellings, and spin-offs
9780312851354

LC 92025456
Mythopoeic Award for Adult Literature, 1993; YALSA Popular Paperbacks for Young Adults, 2016.

Takes the fairy tale of *Briar Rose, the Sleeping Beauty*, and tells it anew-set this time against the terrifying backdrop of the Holocaust.

Yolen takes the story of *Briar Rose* (commonly known as *Sleeping Beauty*) and links it to the Holocaust.... Rebecca Berlin, a young woman who has grown up hearing her grandmother Gemma tell an unusual and frightening version of the Sleeping Beauty legend, realizes when Gemma dies that the fairy tale offers one of the very few clues she has to her grandmother's past.... By interpolating Gemma's vivid and imaginative story into the larger narrative, Yolen has created an engrossing novel. —*Publishers Weekly*
Includes bibliographical references (p. [187]-190).

Curse of the thirteenth fey: the true tale of Sleeping Beauty. Jane Yolen. Philomel Books, 2012 256 p.
Grades: 6 7 8 9 10
1. Fairies; 2. Curses; 3. Imprisonment; 4. Magic; 5. Elves; 6. Fairy tale and folklore-inspired fiction; 7. Fantasy fiction.
9780399256646

Accident-prone, thirteen-year-old Gorse, the youngest fairy in her family, falls into a trap while on her way to the palace to bless the newborn princess, Talia, but arrives in time to give a gift which, although seemingly horrific, may prove to be a real blessing in this take-off on the classic tale of Sleeping Beauty.

Dragon's blood: a fantasy. By Jane Yolen. Harcourt Brace, 1996 Xi, 292 p. : Table (Pit dragon chronicles, 1)
Grades: 6 7 8 9
1. Animal fighting; 2. Teenage slaves; 3. Dragons; 4. Teenage boys; 5. Boys and dragons; 6. Coming-of-age stories; 7. Fantasy fiction.
9780152051266

LC 9522853
Jakkin, a bond boy who works as a Keeper in a dragon nursery on the planet Austar IV, secretly trains a fighting pit dragon of his own in hopes of winning his freedom.

An original and engrossing fantasy. —*Horn Book Guide*
Magic carpet books.

Mapping the bones. Jane Yolen. 2018 432 p.
Grades: 6 7 8 9
1. Twins; 2. Jews; 3. Escapes; 4. Ghettoes, Jewish; 5. Concentration camps; 6. Poland; 7. 1940s; 8. Historical fiction

9780399257780; 9780399546679

LC 2016059474

Golden Kite Award for Fiction, 2019.

In Poland in the 1940s, twins Chaim and Gittel rely on each other to endure life in a ghetto, escape through forests, and the horrors of a concentration camp.

Using the framework of the *Hansel and Gretel* story, Yolen does a superb job of dramatizing the horrors of WWII and the Holocaust, bringing vivid fear and suspense to her captivating story. It makes for altogether memorable and essential reading. —*Booklist*

Pay the piper. Jane Yolen and Adam Stemple. Starscape, 2005 176 p. (Rock 'n' roll fairy tales, 1)
Grades: 6 7 8 9

1. Fairies; 2. Missing children; 3. Rock music; 4. Fourteen-year-old girls; 5. Teenage girls; 6. Fantasy fiction; 7. Fairy tale and folklore-inspired fiction
9780765311580

LC 2004060118

Locus Young Adult Book Award, 2006.

When Callie interviews the band, Brass Rat, for her school newspaper, her feelings are ambivalent, but when all the children of Northampton begin to disappear on Halloween, she knows where the dangerous search must begin.

The authors have produced a rollicking good riff on the Pied Piper.... The authors keep the action moving.... An entertaining as well as meaty read. —*Booklist*

A Tom Doherty Associates book.

The **queen's** own fool: a novel of Mary Queen of Scots. By Jane Yolen and Robert J. Harris. Philomel Books, 2000 390 p. (Stuart quartet, 1)
Grades: 7 8 9 10

1. Mary, Queen of Scots, 1542-1587; 2. Fools and jesters; 3. Women rulers; 4. Nobility; 5. Scotland; 6. Medieval period (476-1492); 7. Scottish Stewart period (1371-1603); 8. Historical fiction.
9780399233807

LC 99055070

YALSA Best Books for Young Adults, 2001.

When twelve-year-old Nicola leaves Troupe Brufort and serves as the fool for Mary, Queen of Scots, she experiences the political and religious upheavals in both France and Scotland.

The authors have woven fiction and historical fact into a seamless tapestry. —*Horn Book Guide*

Yoon, David

★ **Super** fake love song. David Yoon. G. P. Putnam's Sons, 2020 368 p.
Grades: 9 10 11 12

1. Teenage misfits; 2. Mistaken identity; 3. Dishonesty; 4. Korean Americans; 5. Rock musicians; 6. Southern California; 7. Romantic comedies
9781984812230

School Library Journal Best Books, 2020.

When new-girl Cirrus mistakes self-described nerd Sunny Dae as the lead in a rock band, Sunny rolls with it forming a fake band with his friends, but as the lies continue he risks losing both Cirrus and his friends.

A clever, hilarious, and empathetic look at diverse teens exploring authenticity, identities, and code-switching. —*Kirkus*

Yoon, Nicola

★ **Everything,** everything. Nicola Yoon; illustrations by David Yoon. Delacorte Press, 2015 240 p.

Grades: 10 11 12

1. Multiracial teenage girls; 2. Allergy; 3. Children of alcoholic fathers; 4. Friendship; 5. Neighbors; 6. Contemporary romances; 7. Books to movies; 8. Books for reluctant readers
9780553496642; 9780552574235, print, UK; 9780552576482, print, UK; 9780553496666, ebook, US

LC 2015002950

Black-Eyed Susan Book Award (Maryland), High School, 2017; Buckeye Teen Book Award (Ohio), Grades 9-12, 2017; Eliot Rosewater Indiana High School Book Award (Rosie Award), 2018; Garden State Teen Book Award (New Jersey), Fiction (Grades 9-12), 2018; Gateway Readers Award (Missouri), 2018; Golden Archer Awards (Wisconsin): Senior, 2018; Iowa High School Book Award, 2018; Isinglass Teen Read Award (New Hampshire), 2017. ; Pennsylvania Young Reader's Choice Awards, Young Adult, 2017; Rhode Island Teen Book Award, 2017; School Library Journal Best Books, 2015; Soaring Eagle Book Award (Wyoming), 2017; South Carolina Book Award, Young Adult Books, 2018; Westchester Fiction Award, 2016; YALSA Best Fiction for Young Adults, 2016; YALSA Quick Picks for Reluctant Young Adult Readers, 2016; YALSA Quick Picks for Reluctant Young Adult Readers: Top Ten, 2016.

A girl confined to her house by rare and profound allergies falls hopelessly in love with her new neighbor, in a story told through vignettes, diary entries, texts, charts, lists and illustrations.

This heartwarming story transcends the ordinary by exploring the hopes, dreams, and inherent risks of love in all of its forms. —*Kirkus*
Title adapted into a film by the same name in 2017.

★ The **sun** is also a star. Nicola Yoon. Delacorte Press, 2016 384 p.
Grades: 8 9 10 11 12

1. Undocumented immigrants; 2. Deportation; 3. Asian American teenage boys; 4. Korean American teenage boys; 5. Teenage romance; 6. New York City; 7. Brooklyn, New York City; 8. Realistic fiction; 9. Multiple perspectives; 10. First person narratives
9780553496680, hardback, US; 9780553496697, library binding, US; 9780552577564, Paperback, UK

Black-Eyed Susan Book Award (Maryland), High School, 2018; Booklist Editors' Choice: Books for Youth, 2016; Iowa High School Book Award, 2019; John Steptoe Award for New Talent, Author Category, 2017; Kentucky Bluegrass Award for Grades 9-12, 2018; Pennsylvania Young Reader's Choice Awards, Young Adult, 2018; South Carolina Book Award, Young Adult Books, 2019; YALSA Best Fiction for Young Adults, 2017; Michael L. Printz Honor Book, 2017; Walter Honor Book, 2017.

Natasha, whose family is hours away from being deported, and Daniel, a first generation Korean American who strives to live up to his parents' expectations, unexpectedly fall in love and must determine which path they will choose in order to be together.

With appeal to cynics and romantics alike, this profound exploration of life and love tempers harsh realities with the beauty of hope in a way that is both deeply moving and satisfying. —*Kirkus*

Young, Moira

Blood red road. Moira Young. Margaret K. McElderry Books, 2011 464 p. (Dustlands trilogy, 1)
Grades: 6 7 8 9 10

1. Twin brothers and sisters; 2. Martial arts; 3. Orphans; 4. Kidnapping; 5. Brothers and sisters; 6. Science fiction; 7. Canadian fiction.
9781442429987; 9780385671835; 9780385671859; 9781407181141, print, UK

BC Book Prizes, Sheila A. Egoff Children's Literature Prize, 2012; Costa Children's Book Award, 2011; Stellar Awards (British

Columbia), 2013; Westchester Fiction Award, 2013; YALSA Best Fiction for Young Adults, 2012; YALSA Popular Paperbacks for Young Adults, 2016.

In a distant future, eighteen-year-old Lugh is kidnapped, and while his twin sister Saba and nine-year-old Emmi are trailing him across bleak Sandsea they are captured, too, and taken to brutal Hopetown, where Saba is forced to be a cage fighter until new friends help plan an escape.

Readers will...be riveted by the book's fast-paced mix of action and romance. It's a natural for *Hunger Games* fans. —*Publishers Weekly*

Youngdahl, Shana
As many nows as I can get. Shana Youngdahl. Dial Books, 2019 432 p.
Grades: 9 10 11 12
1. Cross-country automobile trips; 2. College students; 3. First loves; 4. Young women; 5. Former boyfriends; 6. Psychological fiction; 7. Love stories; 8. First person narratives.
9780525553854

A cerebral romance told in vibrantly detailed, nonlinear chapters follows the experiences of a grounded overachiever who falls in love with an electric-charged boy, triggering unanticipated consequences.

Grief, addiction, first loves, and traveling an unplanned road are among the many themes explored in this debut novel. After growing up in an insular town in Colorado, graduating senior Scarlett has big ambitions. Though she dabbles with alcohol and drugs, her intelligence, drive, and propensity for physics pave her way into college after college. —*Kirkus*

Yovanoff, Brenna
Fiendish. Brenna Yovanoff. Razorbill, 2014 352 pages
Grades: 9 10 11 12
1. Small towns; 2. Prejudice; 3. Magic; 4. Supernatural; 5. Teenage romance; 6. Fantasy fiction.
9781595146380
LC 2013047610

Clementine DeVore, seventeen, is determined to learn what happened ten years ago that led to her magical imprisonment and problems in her town, but a dangerous attraction to Fisher, the boy who freed her, town politics, and the terrifying Hollow get in the way.

When Clementine, in a magical coma for years, is awakened, eerie things (grotesquely mutated animals, animated plants, uncanny weather) begin to happen. Clementine must sift through the mysteries of her childhood to figure out what's causing the wild magic. Yovanoff's world-building is sophisticated and precise. Powerful, haunting prose brings to life a world overflowing with wild magic, seething prejudice, and base fear. —*Horn Book Guide*

★ **Places** no one knows. Brenna Yovanoff. 2016 384 pages
Grades: 9 10 11 12
1. Dreams; 2. Teenage romance; 3. Overachievers; 4. Sleep; 5. Slackers; 6. Magical realism; 7. Multiple perspectives; 8. First person narratives
9780553522631; 9780553522648
LC 2015015299

Waverly Camdenmar, an overachiever in every way, seems perfect, yet perfection is exhausting. She has not slept in days and then one night she falls asleep and walks into someone else's life. She dream visits a boy she could never be with and is forced to decide what matters most to her.

There are two Waverly Camdenmars. One is the Waverly everyone sees: smart, driven, untouchable. The other is the Waverly who runs at night until her feet bleed, who spends hours meticulously analyzing her fellow students so she knows how to behave, and who, one night, dreams herself into the bedroom of Marshall Holt, a thoughtful slacker-stoner with a troubled home life who shouldnt even be on her radar. As her night-

time wanderings continue and their connection grows, Waverly must decide if he is something she wants in her waking life as well.... This is a tightly woven, luminously written novel that captures the uncertain nature of high school and the difficult path of self-discovery. —*Booklist*

★ The **replacement**. By Brenna Yovanoff. Razorbill, 2010 343 p.
Grades: 9 10 11 12
1. Changelings; 2. Monsters; 3. Death; 4. Supernatural; 5. Families; 6. Fantasy fiction.
9781595143372
YALSA Best Fiction for Young Adults, 2011.

Mackie Doyle is a Replacement, left in the crib of a human baby sixteen years before, and when creatures under the hill decide that they want him back, he must decide where he really belongs and what he really wants.

Yovanoff's spare but haunting prose creates an atmosphere shrouded in gloom and secrecy so that readers, like Mackie, must attempt to make sense of a situation ruled by chaos and fear. The ethical complications of the town's deal with the creatures of Mayhem are clearly presented but never overwrought, while Mackie's problematic relationship to the townspeople as both an outsider and a savior is poignantly explored. —*Bulletin of the Center for Children's Books*

Zadoff, Allen
★ **Boy** Nobody: a novel. By Allen Zadoff. Little, Brown, 2013 352 p. (Unknown assassin, 1)
Grades: 9 10 11 12
1. Assassins; 2. Teenage boy orphans; 3. Crushes in teenage boys; 4. Teenage assassins; 5. High schools; 6. Thrillers and suspense; 7. Books for reluctant readers
9780316199681; 9780316199674
LC 2012029484
Kentucky Bluegrass Award for Grades 9-12, 2015; YALSA Quick Picks for Reluctant Young Adult Readers, 2014.

He can't remember his past or his name. Trained by the mysterious Program to be an undercover assassin, all he cares about is the mission. For this particular mission, his name is Ben, and his target is the mayor of New York. But when Ben meets the mayor's gorgeous daughter Sam, he suddenly finds himself questioning the Program and his own identity.

I am the mission: a novel. By Allen Zadoff. 2014 432 pages (Unknown assassin, 2)
Grades: 9 10 11 12
1. Assassins; 2. Brainwashing; 3. Loyalty; 4. Terrorism; 5. Teenage boys; 6. Thrillers and suspense
9780316199698; 9780316255028, ebook, US
LC 2013024561

Teen assassin Boy Nobody is sent on a mission to assassinate the head of a domestic terrorism cell, but his mission turns up more questions about his job than answers.

Zadoff has crafted another highly suspenseful, compulsively readable futuristic thriller with an agreeably intricate plot and a sympathetic—though often cold-blooded—protagonist. —*Booklist*

Zail, Suzy
Playing for the commandant. Suzy Zail. Candlewick Press, 2014 245 p.
Grades: 7 8 9 10 11 12
1. Holocaust (1933-1945); 2. Pianists; 3. Concentration camp inmates; 4. Interpersonal attraction; 5. Jewish families; 6. 1940s; 7. Historical fiction; 8. Australian fiction.
9780763664039
USBBY Outstanding International Book, 2015.

Zail's story is as gut-wrenching as any Holocaust tale... The haunting, matter-of-fact tone of Hanna's story will likely resonate with teens learning about the Holocaust. —*Booklist*

Zambrano, Mario Alberto
Loteria: a novel. Mario Alberto Zambrano. Harper, 2013 Vi, 272 p. : Color illustration
Grades: 9 10 11 12 Adult
1. Dysfunctional families; 2. Eleven-year-old girls; 3. Psychic trauma; 4. Memories; 5. Mexican American girls; 6. Coming-of-age stories; 7. First person narratives; 8. Adult books for young adults.
9780062268549
School Library Journal Best Books: Best Adult Books 4 Teens, 2013.

Using the a deck of Loteria cards as her muse, 11-year-old Luz Castillo, a ward of the state who has retreated into silence, finds each shuffle sparking a random memory that, pieced together, brings into focus the joy and pain of her life and the events that led to her present situation.

An intriguing debut and an elegiac, miniature entry in the literature of Latin American diaspora. —*Publishers Weekly*

Zappia, Francesca
★ **Eliza** and her monsters. Francesca Zappia. Greenwillow Books, an imprint of HarperCollins Publishers, 2017 385 p.
Grades: 9 10 11 12
1. Comic strip writers; 2. Fans (Persons); 3. Teenage authors; 4. Teenage girl misfits; 5. Friendship; 6. Indiana; 7. Realistic fiction; 8. First person narratives
9780062290137
YALSA Best Fiction for Young Adults, 2018.

When the anonymous teen creator of a wildly popular webcomic is tempted by a school newcomer to pursue real-world relationships, everything she has worked so hard to build crumbles in the wake of their highly publicized romance.

A wrenching depiction of depression and anxiety, respectful to fandom, online-only friendships, and the benefits and dangers of internet fame. —*Kirkus*

Zarr, Sara
Gem & Dixie. Sara Zarr. Harpercollins Childrens Books, 2017 288 p.
Grades: 8 9 10 11 12
1. Sisters; 2. Dysfunctional families; 3. Family relationships; 4. Children of drug abusers; 5. Interpersonal relations; 6. Realistic fiction.
9780062434593

Forging a deep, complex relationship with the sister who cares for her when their dysfunctional mother and absent father cannot, Gem organizes a short trip to avoid their father when he returns unexpectedly.

A thoughtful work that will resonate with Zarr's many fans and those who appreciate contemplative, character-driven novels. —*School Library Journal*

★ **How** to save a life. Sara Zarr. Little, Brown, 2011 352 p.
Grades: 6 7 8 9 10 11 12
1. Adoption; 2. Pregnant teenagers; 3. Grief in teenage girls; 4. Grief; 5. Fathers — Death; 6. Colorado; 7. Denver, Colorado; 8. Realistic fiction; 9. Multiple perspectives
9780316036061; 9781474958677, Paperback, UK
LC 2010045832
YALSA Best Fiction for Young Adults, 2012; School Library Journal Best Books, 2011.

Told from their own viewpoints, seventeen-year-old Jill, in grief over the loss of her father, and Mandy, nearly nineteen, are thrown together when Jill's mother agrees to adopt Mandy's unborn child but nothing turns out as they had anticipated.

★ The **Lucy** variations. Sara Zarr. Little, Brown, 2013 304 p;
Grades: 7 8 9 10 11 12
1. Teenage girl pianists; 2. Self-fulfillment in teenage girls; 3. Piano teachers; 4. Child prodigies; 5. Pianists; 6. San Francisco, California; 7. Realistic fiction
9780316205016; 9780316205009, paperback, US; 9780316232005, ebook, US; 9781409562689, paperback, UK
LC 2012029852
YALSA Best Fiction for Young Adults, 2014.

Sixteen-year-old San Franciscan Lucy Beck-Moreau once had a promising future as a concert pianist. Her chance at a career has passed, and she decides to help her ten-year-old piano prodigy brother, Gus, map out his own future, even as she explores why she enjoyed piano in the first place.

The third-person narration focuses entirely on Lucy but allows readers enough distance to help them understand her behavior in ways Lucy cannot. Occasional flashbacks fill out the back story. The combination of sympathetic main character and unusual social and cultural world makes this satisfying coming-of-age story stand out. —*Kirkus*

★ **Once** was lost: a novel. By Sara Zarr. Little, Brown, 2009 224 p.
Grades: 7 8 9 10
1. Teenage children of alcoholics; 2. Self-perception in teenage girls; 3. Belief and doubt; 4. Kidnapping; 5. Faith; 6. Realistic fiction; 7. Christian fiction.
9780316036047
LC 2009025187
YALSA Best Books for Young Adults, 2010.

As the tragedy of a missing girl enfolds in her small town, fifteen-year-old Samara, who feels emotionally abandoned by her parents, begins to question her faith.

This multilayered exploration of the intersection of the spiritual life and imperfect people features suspense and packs an emotional wallop. —*School Library Journal*

Roomies. Sara Zarr and Tara Altebrando. 2013 288 p.
Grades: 9 10 11 12
1. Email; 2. Roommates; 3. Friendship; 4. Leaving home; 5. High school graduates; 6. New Jersey; 7. California; 8. Realistic fiction; 9. Epistolary novels; 10. Books for reluctant readers
9780316217491; 9781444780178, print, UK
LC 2012048431
YALSA Quick Picks for Reluctant Young Adult Readers, 2015.

While living very different lives on opposite coasts, seventeen-year-old Elizabeth and eighteen-year-old Lauren become acquainted by email the summer before they begin rooming together as freshmen at UC-Berkeley.

Jersey girl Elizabeth (EB) and San Franciscan Lauren, soon to be college roommates, correspond throughout the summer; chapters with alternating perspectives unwrap each girl's backstory, personality, and coming-to-terms with changes looming on the horizon. The premise will have mass appeal with teens who fantasize about their post-high-school futures, and the authors succeed in presenting two distinct and relatable narrative voices. —*Horn Book Guide*

Story of a girl: a novel. By Sara Zarr. Little, Brown, 2007 208 p.
Grades: 10 11 12
1. Self-esteem in teenage girls; 2. Forgiveness; 3. Errors; 4. Sixteen-year-old girls; 5. Teenage girls; 6. California; 7. Realistic fiction; 8. Books for reluctant readers
9780316014533
LC 2005028467

YALSA Popular Paperbacks for Young Adults, 2012; YALSA Quick Picks for Reluctant Young Adult Readers, 2008; YALSA Best Books for Young Adults, 2008; National Book Award for Young People's Literature finalist, 2007.

In the three years since her father caught her in the back seat of a car with an older boy, sixteen-year-old Deanna's life at home and school has been a nightmare, but while dreaming of escaping with her brother and his family, she discovers the power of forgiveness.

This highly recommended novel will find a niche with older, more mature readers because of frank references to sex and some x-rated language. —*Voice of Youth Advocates*

★ **Sweethearts:** a novel. By Sara Zarr. Little, Brown and Co, 2008 217 p;
Grades: 8 9 10 11 12
1. Self-acceptance in teenage girls; 2. Child abuse victims; 3. Change (Psychology); 4. Teenage girls with eating disorders; 5. Eating disorders; 6. Utah; 7. Coming-of-age stories; 8. Realistic fiction
9780316014557
LC 2007041099
YALSA Best Books for Young Adults, 2009.

After losing her soul mate, Cameron, when they were nine, Jennifer, now seventeen, transformed herself from the unpopular fat girl into the beautiful and popular Jenna, but Cameron's unexpected return dredges up memories that cause both social and emotional turmoil.

Zarr's writing is remarkable.... She conveys great delicacy of feeling and shades of meaning, and the realistic, moving ending will inspire excellent discussion. —*Booklist*

Zeises, Lara M.
The **sweet** life of Stella Madison. Lara Zeises. Delacorte Press, 2009 240 p.
Grades: 9 10 11 12
1. Family problems; 2. Food; 3. Teenage journalists; 4. Interpersonal relations; 5. Seventeen-year-old girls; 6. Realistic fiction.
9780385731461
LC 2008032024
YALSA Popular Paperbacks for Young Adults, 2011.

Seventeen-year-old Stella struggles with the separation of her renowned chef parents, writing a food column for the local paper even though she is a junk food addict, and having a boyfriend but being attracted to another.

The author has created a refreshing protagonist sure to captivate readers, who will enjoy following along as she learns about romance through food, and vice versa. —*School Library Journal*

Zenatti, Valerie
A **bottle** in the Gaza Sea. Valerie Zenatti; translated by Adriana Hunter. Bloomsbury U.S.A. Children's Books : 2008 149 p;
Grades: 7 8 9 10 11 12
1. Toleration; 2. Interethnic conflict; 3. Interethnic friendship; 4. Interethnic friendship; 5. Arab-Israeli conflict; 6. Israel; 7. Gaza Strip; 8. Epistolary novels; 9. Realistic fiction.
9781599902005
LC 2007042361
Sydney Taylor Book Award for Teen Readers, 2009; Middle East Book Award, Honorable Mention, 2009.

Seventeen-year-old Tal Levine of Jerusalem, despondent over the ongoing Arab-Israeli conflict, puts her hopes for peace in a bottle and asks her brother, a military nurse in the Gaza Strip, to toss it into the sea, leading ultimately to friendship and understanding between her and an "enemy."

Zenatti uses short, riveting chapters,...to pack a punch with readers reluctant to voracious. The overall effect is one of a haunting relationship that will help teens understand both sides of the Israeli-Palestinian conflict. —*Kirkus*

Zentner, Jeff
★ **Goodbye** days. Jeff Zentner. Crown Books for Young Readers, 2017 416 p.
Grades: 8 9 10 11 12
1. Guilt; 2. Teenagers and death; 3. Loss (Psychology); 4. Grief; 5. Guilt in teenage boys; 6. Tennessee; 7. Realistic fiction; 8. First person narratives
9780553524062; 9780553524086, ebook, US
LC 2016008248
Keystone to Reading Book Award (Pennsylvania), High School level, 2019; YALSA Best Fiction for Young Adults, 2018.

Looks at a teen's life after the death of his best friend and how he navigates through the guilt and pain by celebrating their lives—and ultimately learning to forgive himself.

A fine cautionary tale and journey toward wisdom, poignant and realistic. —*Kirkus*

★ **Rayne** & Delilah's Midnite Matinee. Jeff Zentner. Crown, 2019 400 p.
Grades: 9 10 11 12
1. Best friends; 2. Change; 3. Teenagers — Career aspirations; 4. Television — Production and direction; 5. Friendship; 6. Multiple perspectives; 7. Realistic fiction.
9781524720216; 9781524720209; 9780735263048, print, Canada; 9781783447992, Paperback, UK; 9781524720223, ebook, US
LC 2018049011
Told in two voices, Josie and Delia struggle with growing up and growing apart as they face tough decisions about their post-high school futures and the fate of their weekly cable television show.

Written in alternating perspectives, Zentner's quick-witted, charming characters tackle real-life issues with snappy dialogue and engaging levity. —*Publishers Weekly*

★ The **serpent** king: a novel. Jeff Zentner. Crown Books for Young Readers, 2016 372 pages;
Grades: 9 10 11 12
1. Rural teenagers; 2. Self-fulfillment in teenagers; 3. Teenage musicians; 4. Self-fulfillment; 5. Children of clergy; 6. Tennessee; 7. Realistic fiction; 8. Multiple perspectives
9780553524024; 9780553524031; 9780553524048
LC 2014044883
Great Lakes Great Books Award (Michigan), Grades 9-12, 2017; International Reading Association Children's Book Award for Young Adult Fiction, 2017; Thumbs Up! Award (Michigan), 2017; Westchester Fiction Award, 2017; William C. Morris YA Debut Award, 2017; YALSA Best Fiction for Young Adults, 2017; YALSA Quick Picks for Reluctant Young Adult Readers, 2017.

The son of a Pentecostal preacher faces his personal demons as he and his two outcast friends try to make it through their senior year of high school in rural Forrestville, Tennessee without letting the small-town culture destroy their creative spirits and sense of self.

Characters, incidents, dialogue, the poverty of the rural South, enduring friendship, a desperate clinging to strange faiths, fear of the unknown, and an awareness of the courage it takes to survive, let alone thrive, are among this fine novel's strengths. Zentner writes with understanding and grace—a new voice to savor. —*Kirkus*

Zephaniah, Benjamin
    Face. Zephaniah Benjamin. Bloomsbury; 2002 207 p.
Grades: 7 8 9 10
    1. Teenage boys with disfigurements; 2. People with disfigurements; 3. Traffic accidents; 4. Prejudice; 5. Teenage boys; 6. England
9781582347745
                             LC 2002022758
    A teenage boy's face is disfigured in an automobile accident, and he must learn to deal with the changes in his life.
    This book will not only be enjoyed by teen readers for its entertaining story, but also for its statement about prejudice. —*Voice of Youth Advocates*

Zettel, Sarah
    Bad luck girl. Sarah Zettel. Random House, 2014 368 p. (American fairy trilogy, 3)
Grades: 7 8 9 10
    1. Fairies; 2. Prophecies; 3. Magic; 4. Teenage girls; 5. LeRoux, Callie (Fictitious character); 6. Chicago, Illinois; 7. 1930s; 8. Historical fantasy
9780375869402
    A conclusion to the trilogy that began with *Dust Girl* and *Golden Girl* finds Callie caught up in the war between the fairies of the Midnight Throne and the Sunlit Kingdoms before discovering a race of half-fairy misfits who need her help.
    Half-fairy, half-human Callie (*Golden Girl; Dust Girl*) has reunited with her family, thus starting a war between the two fairy kingdoms. Fleeing Los Angeles for Chicago, Callie realizes that to end the war she must stand and fight. Zettel brings the street life, locales, and culture of jazz-age Chicago into the imagery of her fantasy, packing the story with incident and adventure. —*Horn Book Guide*

    Dust girl. Sarah Zettel. Random House, 2012 336 p. (American fairy trilogy, 1)
Grades: 6 7 8 9
    1. Fairies; 2. Parent-separated teenage girls; 3. Storms; 4. Magic; 5. Teenage girls; 6. Kansas; 7. Dust Bowl (South Central United States); 8. 1930s; 9. Historical fantasy; 10. First person narratives
9780375969386
                             LC 2011043310
YALSA Best Fiction for Young Adults, 2013.
    Mixed-race Callie LeRoux has always passed for white in her Depression-era Kansas town. But after her mother disappears in a huge dust storm, Callie meets a stranger who reveals that Callie's father (whom she's never met) is not only a black man, but a fairy—and that Callie may be instrumental in a burgeoning war between the courts of the fae. Callie faces magical dangers at every turn in this story packed with atmospheric period details, intriguing characters, action, and suspense.

    A **most** dangerous deception: being a true, accurate, and complete account of the scandalous and wholly remarkable adventures of Margaret Preston Fitzroy, counterfeit lady, accused thief, and confidential agent at the court of his majesty, King G. Sarah Zettel. Harcourt, Houghton Mifflin Harcourt, 2013 320 p. (Palace of spies, 1)
Grades: 8 9 10
    1. Spies; 2. Teenage girl orphans; 3. Artists; 4. Courts and courtiers; 5. Teenage romance; 6. London, England; 7. Great Britain; 8. 18th century; 9. Georgian era (1714-1837); 10. Historical mysteries
9780544074118
    In eighteenth-century London, destitute orphan Peggy Fitzroy agrees to impersonate the recently deceased spy Lady Francesca as maid of honor to Princess Caroline. With a war of succession, jilted love, and religious turmoil in the mix, Peggy must navigate intrigue and shady liaisons to uncover the truth behind her predecessor's death. The feisty narrator and

lush period details will garner fans for this new series. —*Horn Book Guide*

Zevin, Gabrielle
    ★ **All** these things I've done. Gabrielle Zevin. Farrar Straus Giroux, 2011 368p. (Birthright (Gabrielle Zevin), 1)
Grades: 8 9 10 11 12
    1. Dystopias; 2. Organized crime; 3. Near future; 4. Rationing; 5. Crime; 6. New York City; 7. 2080s; 8. Science fiction.
9780374302108
                             LC 2010035873
    In a dystopian future where chocolate and caffeine are contraband, teenage cellphone use is illegal, and water and paper are carefully rationed, sixteen-year-old Anya Balanchine finds herself thrust unwillingly into the spotlight as heir apparent to an important New York City crime family.
    Offering the excitement of a crime drama and the allure of forbidden romance, this introduction to a reluctant Godfather-in-the making will pique the interest of dystopia-hungry readers. —*Publishers Weekly*

    Elsewhere. Gabrielle Zevin. Farrar, Straus and Giroux, 2005 288 p.
Grades: 7 8 9 10
    1. Fifteen-year-old girls; 2. Dead; 3. Life after death; 4. Teenage girls; 5. Teenagers — Growth (Psychology)
9780374320911
                             LC 2004056279
Nutmeg Children's Book Award, Teen category, 2009; ALA Notable Children's Book, 2006; Booklist Editors' Choice: Books for Youth, 2005; YALSA Popular Paperbacks for Young Adults, 2009; School Library Journal Best Books, 2005.
    After fifteen-year-old Liz Hall is hit by a taxi and killed, she finds herself in a place that is both like and unlike Earth, where she must adjust to her new status and figure out how to "live."
    Zevin's third-person narrative calmly, but surely guides readers through the bumpy landscape of strongly delineated characters dealing with the most difficult issue that faces all of us. A quiet book that provides much to think about and discuss. —*School Library Journal*

    ★ **Memoirs** of a teenage amnesiac. Gabrielle Zevin. Farrar, Straus, and Giroux, 2007 288 p.
Grades: 7 8 9 10
    1. Amnesia; 2. Identity (Psychology); 3. Accidents; 4. Teenage girls with amnesia; 5. People with amnesia; 6. Realistic fiction; 7. Books to movies
9780374349462
Blue Hen Book Award (Delaware) for Teen Books, 2009; YALSA Popular Paperbacks for Young Adults, 2015; YALSA Best Books for Young Adults, 2008.
    This is a sensitive, joyful novel.... Pulled by the the heart-bruising love story, readers will pause to contemplate irresistible questions. —*Booklist*

Zhang, Amy
    Falling into place. By Amy Zhang. Greenwillow Books, 2014 304 pages
Grades: 9 10 11 12
    1. Suicide; 2. Teenage girls in comas; 3. Imaginary companions; 4. Hospital patients; 5. Children of widows; 6. Realistic fiction; 7. Teenagers' writings.
9780062295040
                             LC 2014018247
    One cold fall day, high school junior Liz Emerson steers her car into a tree. This haunting and heartbreaking story is told by a surprising and un-

expected narrator and unfolds in nonlinear flashbacks even as Liz's friends, foes, and family gather at the hospital and Liz clings to life.

Although the subject matter is heavy and there are a few easily brushed-off awkward moments, the breezy yet powerful and exceptionally perceptive writing style, multifaceted characters, surprisingly hopeful ending, and pertinent contemporary themes frame an engrossing, thought-provoking story that will be snapped up by readers. —*School Library Journal*

Zhang, Kat
Once we were. Kat Zhang. HarperTeen, an imprint of HarperCollinsPublishers, 2013 342 p. (Hybrid chronicles, 2)
Grades: 8 9 10 11 12
1. Dystopias; 2. Resistance to government; 3. Identity (Psychology); 4. Soul; 5. Ethics; 6. Dystopian fiction; 7. Science fiction.
9780062114907
Zhang has a unique challenge: she must give each character two distinct personalities, which she skillfully manages. While this book lacks some of the freshness of *What's Left of Me* (HarperCollins, 2012), simply by virtue of being a sequel, the lovely, atmospheric storytelling is still very much present. Zhang has envisioned a complex, unique world and deftly brings it to life. —*School Library Journal*

What's left of me. Kat Zhang. Harper, 2012 336 p. (Hybrid chronicles, 1)
Grades: 8 9 10 11 12
1. Dystopias; 2. Soul; 3. Identity (Psychology); 4. Ethics; 5. Sisters; 6. Dystopian fiction; 7. Science fiction.
9780062114877
                                                LC Bl2012021631
Addie and Eva are two sisters born into the same body, and although Eva's soul was supposed to fade away, she still lingers beside Addie's dominant soul, until they meet someone who can change everything for the pair.

Zindel, Paul
★ The **pigman**: a novel. Paul Zindel. Dell, 1970 159 p.
Grades: 7 8 9 10
1. High school sophomores; 2. Social isolation; 3. Teenagers and seniors; 4. Intergenerational friendship; 5. Friends — Death; 6. Coming-of-age stories; 7. Classics.
9780030547034; 9780060268282
                                                LC 68010784
A teenage boy and girl, high school sophomores from unhappy homes, tell of their bizarre relationship with an old man.
Sequel: *The pigman's legacy.*

Zink, Michelle
Prophecy of the sisters. By Michelle Zink. Little, Brown, 2009 343 p. (Prophecy of the sisters trilogy, 1)
Grades: 7 8 9 10
1. Twin sisters; 2. Prophecies; 3. Supernatural; 4. Teenage girl orphans; 5. Good and evil; 6. New York (State); 7. 1890s; 8. 19th century; 9. Historical fantasy; 10. Gothic fiction; 11. First person narratives.
9780316027427
                                                LC 2008045290
Soon after their father dies under mysterious circumstances, orphaned twin sisters Lia and Alice Milthorpe discover that an ancient prophecy has pitted them against one another in a mystical battle between good and evil. One of them will save the world—if she can prevent the other from bringing about its end. But which one is which? Set in a small town in upstate New York in the 19th century and written with a distinct Victorian air, this haunting novel features richly drawn characters, psychological nuances, spells, fallen angels, and murder most foul.

This arresting story takes readers to other planes of existence. —*Booklist*
Sequel: *Guardian of the gate.*

Zinn, Bridget
Poison. Bridget Zinn. Disney*Hyperion, 2013 288 p.
Grades: 7 8 9 10 11 12
1. Teenage fugitives; 2. Poisons; 3. Visions; 4. Magic; 5. Princesses; 6. High fantasy; 7. Fantasy fiction.
9781423139935
                                                LC 2012008693
When sixteen-year-old Kyra, a potions master, tries to save her kingdom by murdering the princess, who is also her best friend, the poisoned dart misses its mark and Kyra becomes a fugitive, pursued by the King's army and her ex-boyfriend Hal.

Zoboi, Ibi Aanu
★ **American** Street. Ibi Zoboi. Balzer + Bray, 2017 336 p.
Grades: 9 10 11 12
1. Immigration and emigration; 2. Street life; 3. First loves; 4. Haitian Americans; 5. Girl immigrants; 6. Detroit, Michigan; 7. Coming-of-age stories; 8. Magical realism.
9780062473042
Americas Book Award for Children's and Young Adult Literature, 2018; Booklist Editors' Choice: Books for Youth, 2017; School Library Journal Best Books, 2017; YALSA Best Fiction for Young Adults, 2018; National Book Award for Young People's Literature finalist, 2017.
Separated from her detained mother after moving from Haiti to America, Fabiola struggles to navigate the home of her loud cousins and a new school on Detroit's gritty west side, where a surprising romance and a dangerous proposition challenge her ideas about freedom.
Mixing gritty street life with the tenderness of first love, Haitian Vodou, and family bonds, the book is at once chilling, evocative, and reaffirming. —*Publishers Weekly*

★ **Pride**. Ibi Zoboi. Balzer+Bray, 2018 304 p.
Grades: 8 9 10 11 12
1. Gentrification of cities; 2. Multiracial teenage girls; 3. First loves; 4. Neighborhoods; 5. Dysfunctional families; 6. Brooklyn, New York City; 7. New York City; 8. Classics-inspired fiction; 9. Contemporary romances.
9780062564047
School Library Journal Best Books, 2018; YALSA Best Fiction for Young Adults, 2019.
In a timely update of Jane Austen's *Pride and Prejudice*, critically acclaimed author Ibi Zoboi skillfully balances cultural identity, class, and gentrification against the heady magic of first love in her vibrant reimagining of this beloved classic.
This lively, innovative *Pride and Prejudice* retelling starring a fully rounded Afro-Latinx character hits the familiar notes of Austen's Bennet sisters while inventively modernizing the original's commentary about social class. —*Horn Book Guide*

★ **Punching** the air. Written by Ibi Zoboi with Yusef Salaam; illustrations by Oman T. Pasha. Balzer + Bray, an imprint of HarperCollinsPublishers, 2020 400 p.
Grades: 9 10 11 12
1. African American teenage boys; 2. Institutional racism; 3. Injustice; 4. Racism in law enforcement; 5. Racism in the criminal

justice system; 6. African American fiction; 7. Realistic fiction; 8. Novels in verse
9780062996480
School Library Journal Best Books, 2020; Walter Award, Teen, 2020.

The award-winning author of *American Street* and the prison reform activist of the Exonerated Five trace the story of a young artist and poet whose prospects at a diverse art school are threatened by a racially biased system and a tragic altercation in a gentrifying neighborhood.

The writing allows many readers to see their internal voices affirmed as it uplifts street slang, Muslim faith, and hip-hop cadences, showcasing poetry's power in language rarely seen in YA literature. The physical forms of the first-person poems add depth to the text, providing a necessary calling-in to issues central to the national discourse in reimagining our relationship to police and prisons. —*Kirkus*

Zorn, Claire
Protected. Claire Zorn. 2017 354 p.
Grades: 9 10 11 12
1. Bullying and bullies; 2. Loss (Psychology); 3. Fatal traffic accidents; 4. Sisters — Death; 5. Families; 6. Realistic fiction; 7. Australian fiction.
9781492652137; 9780702250194, Australia
Children's Book of the Year Award for Older Readers (Children's Book Council of Australia), 2015; Children's Book Council of Australia: Notable Australian Children's Book; Prime Minister's Literary Awards: Young Adult Fiction, 2015; Victorian Premier's Literary Awards, Prize for Young Adult Fiction, 2015; Western Australian Premier's Book Awards, Young Adult category, 2016.

Though the book tackles important issues, it reaches far beyond these flash points into a fully developed exploration of the aftermath of tragedy through strong characterization and genuine emotional appeal. —*Kirkus*

Zuckerman, Linda
A **taste** for rabbit. Linda Zuckerman. Arthur A. Levine Books, 2007 310 p;
Grades: 7 8 9 10
1. Rabbits; 2. Resistance to government; 3. Missing persons; 4. Brothers; 5. Foxes; 6. Fantasy fiction.
9780439869775; 9780439869782
LC 2007007787
Leslie Bradshaw Award for Young Adult Literature (Oregon), 2008.

Quentin, a rabbit who lives in a walled compound run by a militaristic government, must join forces with Harry, a fox, to stop the sinister disappearances of outspoken and rebellious rabbit citizens.

The blend of adventure, mystery and morality in this heroic tale of honor and friendship will appeal to middle-school fantasy fans. —*Publishers Weekly*

Zusak, Markus
★ The **book** thief. By Markus Zusak. Alfred A. Knopf, 2006 552 p.
Grades: 8 9 10 11 12
1. Death (Personification); 2. Girl orphans; 3. Book thefts; 4. World War II — Jews; 5. Righteous Gentiles in the Holocaust; 6. Germany; 7. Second World War era (1939-1945); 8. Historical fiction; 9. Australian fiction; 10. Books to movies
9780375831003, hardback, US; 9780375931000, library, US; 9780375842207,paperback, US; 9780385754729, paperback, US; 9780399556524, library, US; 9781101934180,hardback, US; 9788826060743, ebook, US; 9780307433848, ebook,
LC 2005008942
Association of Jewish Libraries Teen Book Award, 2007; Booklist Editors' Choice: Books for Youth, 2006; Book Sense Book of the Year for Children's Literature, 2007; Garden State Teen Book Award (New Jersey), Fiction (Grades 9-12), 2009; Kathleen Mitchell Award for Young Writers, 2006; National Jewish Book Award, 2006; School Library Journal Best Books, 2006; Sydney Taylor Book Award for Teen Readers, 2007; USBBY Outstanding International Book, 2007; YALSA Best Books for Young Adults, 2007; YALSA Popular Paperbacks for Young Adults, 2015; YALSA Popular Paperbacks for Young Adults, 2009; Michael L. Printz Honor Book, 2007.

Trying to make sense of the horrors of World War II, Death relates the story of Liesel—a young German girl whose book-stealing and story-telling talents help sustain her family and the Jewish man they are hiding, as well as their neighbors.

This hefty volume is an achievementa challenging book in both length and subject, and best suited to sophisticated older readers. —*Publishers Weekly*

Bridge of Clay. Markus Zusak. 2018 544 p.
Grades: 10 11 12
1. Brothers; 2. Loss (Psychology); 3. Family secrets; 4. Secrets; 5. Abandoned children; 6. Family sagas; 7. Realistic fiction; 8. Australian fiction.
9780375845598, Hardback; 9781743534816, Hardback, Australia; 9781760559922, Paperback, Australia; 9781984830166; 9781984830159; 9780375594595; 9780857525956, Hardback,UK; 9780375945595; 9781760781620, Paperback
LC 2018013864
Librarians' Choice (Australia), 2018.

Upon their father's return, the five Dunbar boys, who have raised themselves since their mother's death, begin to learn family secrets, including that of fourth brother Clay, who will build a bridge for complex reasons, including his own redemption.
Published in Australia by Picador Australia (2018).

★ **I** am the messenger. By Markus Zusak. Knopf, 2005 357 p.
Grades: 9 10 11 12
1. Taxicab drivers; 2. Self-esteem in teenage boys; 3. Purpose in life; 4. Nineteen-year-old men; 5. Young men; 6. Australia; 7. Mysteries; 8. Realistic fiction; 9. Australian fiction
9780375830990; 9780375930997; 9781909531369, print, UK
LC 2003027388
Children's Book of the Year Award for Older Readers (Children's Book Council of Australia), 2003; NSW Premier's Literary Awards, Ethel Turner Prize for Young People's Literature, 2003; USBBY Outstanding International Book, 2006; YALSA Popular Paperbacks for Young Adults, 2012; YALSA Best Books for Young Adults, 2006; Michael L. Printz Honor Book, 2006.

After capturing a bank robber, nineteen-year-old cab driver Ed Kennedy begins receiving mysterious messages that direct him to addresses where people need help, and he begins getting over his lifelong feeling of worthlessness.

Zusak's characters, styling, and conversations are believably unpretentious, well conceived, and appropriately raw. Together, these key elements fuse into an enigmatically dark, almost film-noir atmosphere where unknowingly lost Ed Kennedy stumbles onto a mystery—or series of mysteries—that could very well make or break his life. —*School Library Journal*

AUTHOR INDEX

AUTHOR INDEX

TITLE INDEX

M

SUBJECT INDEX

AFRICAN AMERICAN GANGS

AFRICAN AMERICAN GIRLS

AFRICAN AMERICAN MEN

AFRICAN AMERICAN MOTHER AND SON

AFRICAN AMERICAN SHARECROPPERS

AFRICAN AMERICAN STUDENTS

AFRICAN AMERICAN TEENAGE BOYS

COMMUNISM

COMMUNITIES

COMMUNITY LIFE

COMMUNITY SERVICE (PUNISHMENT)

COMPASSION

COMPETITION

COMPETITION IN BOYS

COMPETITION IN TEENAGE BOYS

COMPULSIVE BEHAVIOR

COMPULSIVE EATING

COMPUTER CRIMES

COMPUTER GAMES

COMPUTER PROGRAMS

COMPUTER VIRUSES

FAIRY GODMOTHERS

FAIRY TALE AND FOLKLORE-INSPIRED FICTION

FAITH

FAITH (CHRISTIANITY)

FAITH IN WOMEN

FALCONERS

FALCONRY

FALLOUT SHELTERS

FALSE IMPRISONMENT

FAME

SUBJECT INDEX

FRONTIER AND PIONEER LIFE

FRUSTRATION

FRUSTRATION IN TEENAGE BOYS

FUGITIVE SLAVES

FUGITIVES

FUNERAL HOMES

GRIEF IN FAMILIES

GRIEF IN TEENAGE BOYS

GRIEF IN TEENAGE GIRLS

GRIEF IN TEENAGERS

GRIEF IN WOMEN

GRIM REAPER (SYMBOLIC CHARACTER)

GRIMM, JACOB

GRIZZLY BEAR

GROUP HOMES

SUBJECT INDEX

HIGH INTEREST-LOW VOCABULARY BOOKS

HIGH SCHOOL BASKETBALL PLAYERS

HIGH SCHOOL DROPOUTS

HIGH SCHOOL FOOTBALL

HIGH SCHOOL FOOTBALL PLAYERS

HIGH SCHOOL FRESHMEN

HIGH SCHOOL GIRLS

HIGH SCHOOL GRADUATES

HIGH SCHOOL JUNIORS

HIGH SCHOOL SENIORS

HIGH SCHOOL SOPHOMORES

HISTORICAL MYSTERIES

SUBJECT INDEX

SUBJECT INDEX

MAGIC (OCCULTISM)

Friend, Natasha. How we roll, 94
Howe, Katherine. Conversion, 123
Hubbard, Jenny. And we stay, 124
Konigsberg, Bill. Honestly Ben, 143
Konigsberg, Bill. Openly straight, 143
Lo, Malinda. A line in the dark, 157
Lockhart, E. We were liars, 158
McManus, Karen M. The cousins, 181
Poblocki, Dan. The haunting of Gabriel Ashe, 224
Savage, Kim. Beautiful broken girls, 249
Thompson, Holly. The language inside, 285
Wittlinger, Ellen. Sandpiper, 319

MATCHMAKING
Condie, Allyson Braithwaite. Matched, 60

MATE SELECTION
Condie, Allyson Braithwaite. Matched, 60

MATHEMATICS
Monaghan, Annabel. A girl named Digit, 192

MAYAN GIRLS
Pellegrino, Marge. Journey of dreams, 219

MECHANICS
Meyer, Marissa. Cress, 187
Meyer, Marissa. Scarlet, 188

MEDIA FANDOM
Giles, L. R. Spin, 100
Lundin, Britta. Ship it, 162

MEDICAL CARE
Powers, J. L. This thing called the future: a novel, 227
Wells, Dan. Fragments, 304
Wells, Dan. Ruins, 304

MEDICAL ETHICS
Pearson, Mary. Fox forever, 218

MEDICAL GENETICS
Avery, Lara. The memory book, 16

MEDICAL RESEARCH
Villasante, Alexandra. The grief keeper, 295

MEDICINAL PLANTS
Wood, Maryrose. Nightshade, 321
Wood, Maryrose. The poison diaries, 321

MEDICINE SHOWS
Milford, Kate. The Boneshaker, 190

MEDIEVAL PERIOD (476-1492)
Avi. Crispin: the cross of lead, 16
Berry, Julie. The passion of Dolssa, 29
Coats, J. Anderson. The wicked and the just, 57
Vande Velde, Vivian. The book of Mordred, 293
Whitman, Emily. Wildwing, 312

MEDIUMS
Henry, April. The lonely dead, 117

MEHNDI (BODY PAINTING)
Jaigirdar, Adiba. The henna wars, 128

MELBOURNE, VICTORIA
Abdel-Fattah, Randa. Does my head look big in this?, 1
Crowley, Cath. Words in deep blue, 65
Howell, Simmone. Girl defective, 123
Wood, Fiona. Cloudwish, 321

MEMORIES
Barzak, Christopher. Wonders of the invisible world, 23
Cormier, Robert. I am the cheese, 63
Lowry, Lois. The giver, 159
Whitcomb, Laura. Under the light: a novel, 311
Willey, Margaret. Beetle boy, 314
Wrede, Patricia C. The thirteenth child, 324
Zambrano, Mario Alberto. Loteria: a novel, 331

MEMORY
Altebrando, Tara. The Leaving, 9
Avery, Lara. The memory book, 16
Belleza, Rhoda. Empress of a thousand skies, 27
Black, Holly. The white cat, 31
Cameron, Sharon. The Forgetting, 46
Cameron, Sharon. The Knowing, 46
Cypess, Leah. Mistwood, 66
Ellsworth, Loretta. Unforgettable, 83
Frick, Kit. I killed Zoe Spanos, 93
Kristoff, Jay. Dev1at3, 145
Kristoff, Jay. Lifel1k3, 145
Mazer, Harry. Somebody please tell me who I am, 173
McCormick, Patricia. Purple heart, 176
McGarry, Katie. Pushing the limits, 178
Nayeri, Daniel. Everything sad is untrue: a true story, 201
Novic, Sara. Girl at war, 207
Patrick, Cat. Forgotten: a novel, 215
Pratchett, Terry. I shall wear midnight, 227
Richards, Natalie D. Six months later, 235
Rush, Jennifer. Altered, 244
Silvera, Adam. More happy than not, 260
Stolarz, Laurie Faria. Jane Anonymous, 273
Terry, Teri. Fractured, 283
Terry, Teri. Slated, 283
West, Kasie. Split second, 306
Wolf, Jennifer Shaw. Breaking beautiful, 320

MEMPHIS, TENNESSEE
McStay, Moriah. Everything that makes you, 183
Vawter, Vince. Copyboy, 294

MEN RECLUSES
Hobbs, Will. Wild man island, 121

MEN WHO ARE MUTE
Hamilton, Steve. The lock artist, 110

SUBJECT INDEX

SUBJECT INDEX

SUBJECT INDEX

SUBJECT INDEX

SUBJECT INDEX

REALITY

REALITY TELEVISION PROGRAMS

REBELS

RECIPES

SUBJECT INDEX

Smith, Andrew. Winger, 265

RULERS
Bannen, Megan. The bird and the blade, 18
Bardugo, Leigh. King of scars, 18
Bashardoust, Melissa. Girls made of snow and glass, 23
Black, Holly. The wicked king, 31
Black, Holly. The queen of nothing, 31
Capetta, Amy Rose. Once & future, 46
Capetta, Amy Rose. Sword in the stars, 46
Cashore, Kristin. Graceling, 50
Castor, H. M. VIII, 50
Cokal, Susann. The kingdom of little wounds, 58
Cypess, Leah. Mistwood, 66
Elliott, David. Bull, 82
Hamilton, Alwyn. Hero at the fall, 110
Hamilton, Alwyn. Traitor to the throne, 110
Hand, Cynthia. My Lady Jane, 111
Holland, Sara. Everless, 121
Mae, Natalie. The kinder poison, 167
Marr, Melissa. Wicked lovely, 170
Meyer, Marissa. Heartless, 187
Miller, Sarah Elizabeth. The lost crown, 190
Morris, Gerald. The legend of the king, 195
Neumeier, Rachel. The keeper of the mist, 203
Rinaldi, Ann. The redheaded princess, 236
Ritter, William. The dire king, 236
Thomas, Rhiannon. Long may she reign, 285
Thomas, Sherry. The burning sky, 285
Turner, Megan Whalen. A conspiracy of kings, 290
Turner, Megan Whalen. Return of the thief, 290
Turner, Megan Whalen. The king of Attolia, 290
Valente, Catherynne M. The girl who fell beneath Fairyland and led the revels there, 292
White, Kiersten. Now I rise, 312

RULES
Alsaid, Adi. Never always sometimes, 8
Chayil, Eishes. Hush, 53
Patterson, James. Middle school: the worst years of my life, 215

RUMOR
Braxton-Smith, Ananda. Merrow, 37

RUNAWAY BOYS
Gleitzman, Morris. Once, 102
Volponi, Paul. Homestretch, 296

RUNAWAY GIRLS
Barnaby, Hannah Rodgers. Wonder show, 20
Farmer, Nancy. A girl named Disaster, 86
Woodson, Jacqueline. Lena, 323

RUNAWAY TEENAGE BOYS
Alonzo, Sandra. Riding invisible: an adventure journal, 8
Doctorow, Cory. Pirate cinema, 75
Fontes, Justine. Benito runs, 91
Skovron, Jon. Man made Boy, 262

RUNAWAY TEENAGE GIRLS
Amateau, Gigi. A certain strain of peculiar, 9
Arnold, David. Mosquitoland, 13
Blair, Jamie M. Leap of Faith, 32
Grey, Melissa. The girl at midnight, 107
Hopkins, Ellen. Smoke, 122
Keplinger, Kody. Run, 136
Lee, Stacey. Under a painted sky, 152
McKay, Sharon E. Thunder over Kandahar, 179
Umminger, Alison. American girls, 291
Wells, Martha. Emilie & the hollow world, 305

RUNAWAY TEENAGERS
Burgess, Melvin. Smack, 43
McCarry, Sarah. Dirty wings, 175
Shusterman, Neal. Unwind, 259
Wynne-Jones, Tim. Blink & Caution, 325

RUNAWAYS
Anderson, Laurie Halse. Ashes, 10
Arcos, Carrie. Out of reach, 13
Barratt, Mark. Joe Rat, 21
Crossan, Sarah. Being Toffee, 64
Eshbaugh, Julie. Obsidian and stars, 84
Hartman, Rachel. Tess of the road, 114
Herbach, Geoff. Nothing special, 118
McNally, Janet. The looking glass, 182
Roux, Madeleine. House of furies, 240
Rush, Jennifer. Altered, 244
Venkatraman, Padma. The bridge home, 294

RUNNERS
Deuker, Carl. Runner, 73

RUNNING
Van Draanen, Wendelin. The running dream, 293
Webber, Katherine. The heartbeats of Wing Jones, 302
Yee, Lisa. Warp speed, 327

RUNNING RACES
Mae, Natalie. The kinder poison, 167

RURAL BOYS
Moriarty, Jaclyn. The cracks in the Kingdom, 194

RURAL LIFE
Bauer, Joan. Squashed, 24
Holt, Kimberly Willis. Part of me: stories of a Louisiana family, 122
Wyatt, Melissa. Funny how things change, 325

RURAL TEENAGERS
Delsol, Wendy. Stork, 70
McGinnis, Mindy. The female of the species, 178
Murdock, Catherine Gilbert. Dairy queen: a novel, 198
Whitaker, Alecia. The queen of Kentucky, 310
Zentner, Jeff. The serpent king: a novel, 332

RUSSIA
Maguire, Gregory. Egg & spoon, 167

SCIENCE FICTION CLASSICS

SCIENCE FICTION FANDOM

SUBJECT INDEX

SINGLE MOTHERS
Simmons, Kristen. Article 5, 261
Thornburgh, Blair. Ordinary girls, 286

SINGLE TEENAGE FATHERS
Bechard, Margaret. Hanging on to Max, 26

SINGLE TEENAGE MOTHERS
Wolff, Virginia Euwer. Make lemonade, 320

SINGLE-PARENT FAMILIES
Anderson, Laurie Halse. The impossible knife of memory, 10
Arnold, Elana K. Infandous, 14
Herrick, Steven. By the river, 118
Lange, Erin Jade. Dead ends, 149
Medina, Meg. Burn baby burn, 183
Patrick, Cat. The originals, 215
Pearsall, Shelley. All shook up, 218
Tubb, Kristin O'Donnell. Selling hope, 289
Wolff, Virginia Euwer. True believer, 321

SINO-JAPANESE CONFLICT, 1937-1945
DeWoskin, Rachel. Someday we will fly, 74

SIRENS (MYTHOLOGY)
Morrow, Bethany C. A song below water, 196

SISTERS
Anderson, Laurie Halse. Chains, 10
Anderson, Natalie C. City of saints & thieves, 12
Bauman, Beth Ann. Rosie and Skate, 24
Bernard, Romily. Find me, 28
Busby, Cylin. The stranger game, 43
Caletti, Deb. The six rules of maybe, 45
Clayton, Dhonielle. The Belles, 56
Clayton, Dhonielle. The everlasting rose, 56
Cypess, Leah. Nightspell, 66
Davies, Jacqueline. Lost, 68
Dessen, Sarah. Lock and key: a novel, 72
Devlin, Calla. Tell me some-thing real, 74
Elliott, Laura. Hamilton and Peggy!: a revolutionary friendship, 82
Friedman, Aimee. The year my sister got lucky, 94
Frost, Helen. The braid, 95
Gardner, Faith. The second life of Ava Rivers, 97
Graudin, Ryan. The walled city, 105
Hardinge, Frances. Cuckoo song, 112
Hardinge, Frances. The lost conspiracy, 112
Hopkins, Ellen. Smoke, 122
Katsoulis, Gregory Scott. Access restricted, 134
Kephart, Beth. Dangerous neighbors, 135
Martin, Maggie Ann. To be honest, 171
Mazer, Norma Fox. The missing girl, 174
McCauley, Kyrie. If these wings could fly, 175
McLemore, Anna-Marie. Blanca & Roja, 180
McNally, Janet. Girls in the moon, 182
McNally, Janet. The looking glass, 182
Miller, Sarah Elizabeth. The lost crown, 190
Nix, Garth. Frogkisser!, 205

Oliver, Lauren. Vanishing girls, 211
Onyebuchi, Tochi. War girls, 211
Patrick, Cat. The originals, 215
Perkins, Mitali. Secret keeper, 220
Schrefer, Eliot. The deadly sister, 250
Sheinmel, Courtney. The survival list, 256
Sones, Sonya. Stop pretending: what happened when my big sister went crazy, 268
Suma, Nova Ren. Imaginary girls, 278
Thor, Annika. A faraway island, 286
Thor, Annika. Deep sea, 286
Thornburgh, Blair. Ordinary girls, 286
Tucholke, April Genevieve. Seven endless forests, 290
Umminger, Alison. American girls, 291
Vail, Rachel. Lucky, 292
Watkins, Steve. Juvie, 301
Weymouth, Laura E. The light between worlds, 308
Weyn, Suzanne. Distant waves: a novel of the Titanic, 308
Whitney, Daisy. The Mockingbirds, 313
Williams, Carol Lynch. Glimpse, 315
Woodson, Jacqueline. Lena, 323
Zarr, Sara. Gem & Dixie, 331

SISTERS — DEATH
Arcos, Carrie. There will come a time, 13
Bayerl, Katie. A psalm for lost girls, 25
Bowman, Akemi Dawn. Summer bird blue, 36
Foxlee, Karen. The anatomy of wings, 92
Jones, Adam Garnet. Fire song, 131
Sanchez, Erika L. I am not your perfect Mexican daughter, 248
Wolff, Virginia Euwer. Probably still Nick Swansen, 320
Zorn, Claire. Protected, 335

SISTERS — FAMILY RELATIONSHIPS
Winters, Cat. Odd & true, 318

SIXTEEN-YEAR-OLD BOYS
Avasthi, Swati. Split, 15
Booth, Coe. Bronxwood, 35
Bruchac, Joseph. Code Talker, 40
Caine, Rachel. Ink and bone, 44
Conaghan, Brian. When Mr. Dog bites, 60
Draper, Sharon M. The battle of Jericho, 78
Flinn, Alex. Breathing underwater, 90
Goslee, S. J. How not to ask a boy to prom, 103
Green, John. Looking for Alaska, 106
Johnson, Angela. The first part last, 129
McGhee, Alison. What I leave behind, 178
Mussi, Sarah. The door of no return, 198
Nicholson, William. Seeker, 204
Powell, Randy. Three clams and an oyster, 226
Sonnenblick, Jordan. Notes from the midnight driver, 268
Weaver, Will. Memory boy: a novel, 302
Wilson, John. Ghost moon, 317
Wray, John. Lowboy: a novel, 324
Wulffson, Don L. Soldier X, 325
Wynne-Jones, Tim. The emperor of any place, 325

SUBJECT INDEX

SUFFRAGISTS
Bolden, Tonya. Saving Savannah, 35

SUICIDAL BEHAVIOR
Drake, Julia. The last true poets of the sea, 78
Robinson, Gary. Standing strong, 237
Stork, Francisco X. The memory of light, 275
Williams, Carol Lynch. Glimpse, 315

SUICIDE
Asher, Jay. Thirteen reasons why: a novel, 14
Chapman, Erica M. Teach me to forget, 52
Davis, Lane. I swear, 69
Forman, Gayle. I was here, 92
Foxlee, Karen. The anatomy of wings, 92
Hubbard, Jennifer R. Try not to breathe, 124
Kephart, Beth. Dangerous neighbors, 135
Littman, Sarah. Backlash, 156
Maciel, Amanda. Tease, 166
Niven, Jennifer. All the bright places, 205
Norton, Preston. Neanderthal opens the door to the universe, 207
Pan, Emily X. R. The astonishing color of after, 213
Savage, Kim. Beautiful broken girls, 249
Sheinmel, Courtney. The survival list, 256
Summers, Courtney. Fall for anything, 278
Thompson, Holly. Orchards, 285
Williams, Katie. Absent, 315
Wilson, Martin. What they always tell us, 317
Zhang, Amy. Falling into place, 333

SUICIDE VICTIMS
Asher, Jay. Thirteen reasons why: a novel, 14

SULLIVAN, ANNIE
Miller, Sarah Elizabeth. Miss Spitfire: reaching Helen Keller, 191

SUMMER
Archer, E. Geek: fantasy novel, 13
Dessen, Sarah. That summer, 73
Fitzpatrick, Huntley. What I thought was true, 88
Griffin, Paul. Adrift, 107
Karim, Sheba. That thing we call a heart, 133
Menon, Sandhya. 10 things I hate about Pinky, 185
Meriano, Anna. This is how we fly, 185
Renn, Diana. Tokyo heist, 233
Runyon, Brent. Surface tension: a novel in four summers, 244
Trigiani, Adriana. Viola in the spotlight, 288
Wein, Elizabeth. The pearl thief, 303

SUMMER CAMPS
Combs, Sarah. Breakfast served anytime, 60
Friesen, Gayle. The Isabel factor, 95
Vizzini, Ned. The other normals, 295

SUMMER EMPLOYMENT
Buckley-Archer, Linda. The many lives of John Stone, 42
Goo, Maurene. The way you make me feel, 102
Lynch, Chris. The Big Game of Everything, 163
Strohmeyer, Sarah. How Zoe made her dreams (mostly) come true, 276

SUMMER RESORTS
Doktorski, Jennifer Salvato. The summer after you and me, 76

SUMMER ROMANCE
Dessen, Sarah. Once and for all: a novel, 72
Han, Jenny. The summer I turned pretty, 111
Ockler, Sarah. The book of broken hearts, 209
Reed, Jaime. Living violet: the Cambion chronicles, 231

SUMMER SCHOOLS
Barakiva, Michael. One man guy, 18

SUPERHERO STORIES
Bardugo, Leigh. Wonder Woman: Warbringer, 19
Bond, Gwenda. Fallout, 35,145
Daniels, April. Dreadnought, 67
Klune, TJ. The Extraordinaries, 141
Lee, C. B. Not your sidekick, 151
Lee, Mackenzi. Loki: where mischief lies, 152
Lu, Marie. Batman: Nightwalker, 160
Maas, Sarah J. Catwoman: Soulstealer, 163
Meyer, Marissa. Renegades, 188
Reynolds, Jason. Miles Morales, 235
Sanderson, Brandon. Steelheart, 249
Stohl, Margaret. Forever red, 273
Westerfeld, Scott. Zeroes, 308

SUPERHEROES
Daniels, April. Dreadnought, 67
Klune, TJ. The Extraordinaries, 141
Lee, C. B. Not your sidekick, 151
Lu, Marie. Batman: Nightwalker, 160
Maas, Sarah J. Catwoman: Soulstealer, 163
Meyer, Marissa. Renegades, 188
Westerfeld, Scott. Zeroes, 308

SUPERHEROINES
Bardugo, Leigh. Wonder Woman: Warbringer, 19
Stohl, Margaret. Forever red, 273

SUPERHUMAN ABILITIES
Aveyard, Victoria. Red queen, 16
Carson, Rae. Like a river glorious, 48
Carson, Rae. Walk on Earth a stranger, 49
Chapman, Elsie. Caster, 52
Corthron, Kara Lee. Daughters of Jubilation, 63
Coulthurst, Audrey. Of fire and stars, 63
Egan, Catherine. Julia defiant, 81
Lancaster, Mike A. The future we left behind, 148
McEntire, Myra. Hourglass, 177
Roth, Veronica. Carve the mark, 239
Roth, Veronica. The fates divide, 240
Soria, Destiny. Iron cast, 268

SUPERMAN (FICTITIOUS CHARACTER)
Bond, Gwenda. Fallout, 35,145

SUPERMARKETS
Buzo, Laura. Love and other perishable items, 43

SUBJECT INDEX

TEENAGE BOYS

SUBJECT INDEX

Williams, Michael. Now is the time for running, 316

ZINES
Mathieu, Jennifer. Moxie, 172
Prinz, Yvonne. The vinyl princess, 228
Wittlinger, Ellen. Hard love, 319

ZOMBIES
Aguirre, Ann. Enclave, 3
Ashby, Amanda. Zombie queen of Newbury High, 14
Ford, Michael Thomas. Z, 91
Higson, Charles. The enemy, 119
Higson, Charles. The dead, 119
Ireland, Justina. Deathless divide, 126
Ireland, Justina. Dread nation, 126
Kagawa, Julie. The immortal rules, 132
Kagawa, Julie. The eternity cure, 132
Kagawa, Julie. The forever song, 132

Maberry, Jonathan. Rot & Ruin, 164
Martin, T. Michael. The end games, 171
Older, Daniel Jose. Shadowshaper, 210
Perez, Marlene. Dead is a battlefield, 220
Ritter, William. The dire king, 236
Ryan, Carrie. The Forest of Hands and Teeth, 246
Ryan, Carrie. The dead-tossed waves, 246
Ryan, Carrie. The dark and hollow places, 246
Schrieve, Hal. Out of Salem, 251
Summers, Courtney. This is not a test, 278
Waters, Daniel. Generation dead, 301

ZOOS
Morpurgo, Michael. An elephant in the garden, 194

ZULU (AFRICAN PEOPLE)
Powers, J. L. This thing called the future: a novel, 227

PRINTZ AWARD WINNERS

The American Library Association's (ALA) Young Adult Library Services Association (YALSA) established this award in 2000 to recognize literary excellence in young adult literature. Each year, one title is granted the Printz Award, and up to four honor books are recognized. Please note the following list contains only award winners within the scope of YOUNG ADULT FICTION CORE COLLECTION and does not include nonfiction and/or graphic novel winners of this award.

Author	Title	Year Granted
Myers, Walter Dean	*Monster*	2000
Almond, David	*Kit's Wilderness*	2001
Na, An	*A Step From Heaven*	2002
Chambers, Aidan	*Postcards from No Man's Land*	2003
Johnson, Angela	*The First Part Last*	2004
Rosoff, Meg	*How I Live Now*	2005
Green, John	*Looking for Alaska*	2006
Yang, Gene	*American Born Chinese*	2007
McCaughrean, Geraldine	*The White Darkness*	2008
Marchetta, Melina	*Jellicoe Road*	2009
Bray, Libba	*Going Bovine*	2010
Bacigalupi, Paolo	*Ship Breaker*	2011
Whaley, John Corey	*Where Things Come Back*	2012
Lake, Nick	*In Darkness*	2013
Sedgwick, Marcus	*Midwinterblood*	2014
Nelson, Jandy	*I'll Give You the Sun*	2015
Ruby, Laura	*Bone Gap*	2016
Lewis, John	*March*	2017
LaCour, Nina	*We Are Okay*	2018
Acevedo, Elizabeth	*The Poet X*	2019
King, A.S.	*Dig*	2020
Nayeri, Daniel	*Everything Sad Is Untrue (a true story)*	2021

MORRIS AWARD WINNERS

The William C. Morris YA Debut Award is awarded to the debut work of a young adult author. It recognizes the work's overall excellence and the appeal of the work to a wide range of teen readers. Please note the following list contains only award winners within the scope of YOUNG ADULT FICTION CORE COLLECTION and does not include nonfiction and/or graphic novel winners of this award.

Author	Title	Year Granted
Bunce, Elizabeth C.	*A Curse Dark As Gold*	2009
Madigan, L. K.	*Flash Burnout*	2010
Woolston, Blythe	*The Freak Observer*	2011
Whaley, John Corey	*Where Things Come Back*	2012
Hartman, Rachel	*Seraphina*	2013
Kuehn, Stephanie	*Charm & Strange*	2014
Quintero, Isabel	*Gabi. A Girl in Pieces*	2015
Albertalli, Becky	*Simon vs. the Homo Sapiens Agenda*	2016
Zentner, Jeff	*The Serpent King*	2017
Tomas, Angie	*The Hate U Give*	2018
Khorram, Adib	*Darius the Great is Not Okay*	2019
Philippe, Ben	*The Field Guide to the North American Teenager*	2020
McCauley, Kyrie	*If These Wings Could Fly*	2021